Praise for the Reformation Commentary on Scripture

"Protestant reformers were fundamentally exegetes as much as theologians, yet (except for figures like Luther and Calvin) their commentaries and sermons have been neglected because these writings are not available in modern editions or languages. That makes this new series of Reformation Commentary on Scripture most welcome as a way to provide access to some of the wealth of biblical exposition of the sixteenth and seventeenth centuries. The editor's introduction explains the nature of the sources and the selection process; the intended audience of modern pastors and students of the Bible has led to a focus on theological and practical comments. Although it will be of use to students of the Reformation, this series is far from being an esoteric study of largely forgotten voices; this collection of reforming comments, comprehending every verse and provided with topical headings, will serve contemporary pastors and preachers very well."

Elsie Anne McKee, *Archibald Alexander Professor of Reformation Studies and the History of Worship, Princeton Theological Seminary*

"This series provides an excellent introduction to the history of biblical exegesis in the Reformation period. The introductions are accurate, clear and informative, and the passages intelligently chosen to give the reader a good idea of methods deployed and issues at stake. It puts precritical exegesis in its context and so presents it in its correct light. Highly recommended as reference book, course book and general reading for students and all interested lay and clerical readers."

Irena Backus, *Professeure Ordinaire, Institut d'histoire de la Réformation, Université de Genève*

"The Reformation Commentary on Scripture is a major publishing event—for those with historical interest in the founding convictions of Protestantism, but even more for those who care about understanding the Bible. As with IVP Academic's earlier Ancient Christian Commentary on Scripture, this effort brings flesh and blood to 'the communion of saints' by letting believers of our day look over the shoulders of giants from the past. By connecting the past with the present, and by doing so with the Bible at the center, the editors of this series perform a great service for the church. The series deserves the widest possible support."

Mark A. Noll, *Francis A. McAnaney Professor of History, University of Notre Dame*

"For those who preach and teach Scripture in the church, the Reformation Commentary on Scripture is a significant publishing event. Pastors and other church leaders will find delightful surprises, challenging enigmas and edifying insights in this series, as many Reformational voices are newly translated into English. The lively conversation in these pages can ignite today's pastoral imagination for fresh and faithful expositions of Scripture."

J. Todd Billings, *Gordon H. Girod Research Professor of Reformed Theology, Western Theological Seminary*

"The reformers discerned rightly what the church desperately needed in the sixteenth century—the bold proclamation of the Word based on careful study of the sacred Scriptures. We need not only to hear that same call again for our own day but also to learn from the Reformation how to do it. This commentary series is a godsend!"

Richard J. Mouw, *President Emeritus, Fuller Theological Seminary*

"Like the Ancient Christian Commentary on Scripture, the Reformation Commentary on Scripture does a masterful job of offering excellent selections from well-known and not-so-well-known exegetes. The editor's introductory survey is, by itself, worth the price of the book. It is easy to forget that there were more hands, hearts and minds involved in the Reformation than Luther and Calvin. Furthermore, encounters even with these figures are often limited to familiar quotes on familiar topics. However, the Reformation Commentary helps us to recognize the breadth and depth of exegetical interests and skill that fueled and continue to fuel faithful meditation on God's Word. I heartily recommend this series as a tremendous resource not only for ministry but for personal edification."

Michael S. Horton, *J. G. Machen Professor of Systematic Theology and Apologetics,*
Westminster Seminary, California

"The Reformation was ignited by a fresh reading of Scripture. In this series of commentaries, we contemporary interpreters are allowed to feel some of the excitement, surprise and wonder of our spiritual forebears. Luther, Calvin and their fellow revolutionaries were masterful interpreters of the Word. Now, in this remarkable series, some of our very best Reformation scholars open up the riches of the Reformation's reading of the Scripture."

William H. Willimon, *Professor of the Practice of Christian Ministry, Duke Divinity School*

"The Reformation Scripture principle set the entirety of Christian life and thought under the governance of the divine Word, and pressed the church to renew its exegetical labors. This series promises to place before the contemporary church the fruit of those labors, and so to exemplify life under the Word."

John Webster, *Professor of Divinity, University of St. Andrews*

"Since Gerhard Ebeling's pioneering work on Luther's exegesis seventy years ago, the history of biblical interpretation has occupied many Reformation scholars and become a vital part of study of the period. The Reformation Commentary on Scripture provides fresh materials for students of Reformation-era biblical interpretation and for twenty-first-century preachers to mine the rich stores of insights from leading reformers of the sixteenth century into both the text of Scripture itself and its application in sixteenth-century contexts. This series will strengthen our understanding of the period of the Reformation and enable us to apply its insights to our own days and its challenges to the church."

Robert Kolb, *Professor Emeritus, Concordia Theological Seminary*

"The multivolume Ancient Christian Commentary on Scripture is a valuable resource for those who wish to know how the Fathers interpreted a passage of Scripture but who lack the time or the opportunity to search through the many individual works. This new Reformation Commentary on Scripture will do the same for the reformers and is to be warmly welcomed. It will provide much easier access to the exegetical treasures of the Reformation and will hopefully encourage readers to go back to some of the original works themselves."

Anthony N. S. Lane, *Professor of Historical Theology and Director of Research, London School of Theology*

"This volume of the RCS project is an invaluable source for pastors and the historically/biblically interested that provides unparalleled access not only to commentaries of the leading Protestant reformers but also to a host of nowadays unknown commentaters on Galatians and Ephesians. The RCS is sure to enhance and enliven contemporary exegesis. With its wide scope, the collection will enrich our understanding of the variety of Reformation thought and biblical exegesis."

Sigrun Haude, *Associate Professor of Reformation and Early Modern European History, University of Cincinnati*

"The Reformation Commentary on Scripture series promises to be an 'open sesame' to the biblical exegesis, exposition and application of the Bible that was the hallmark of the Reformation. While comparisons can be odious, the difference between Reformation commentary and exposition and much that both preceded and followed it is laid bare in these pages: whereas others write about the Bible from the outside, Reformation exposition carries with it the atmosphere of men who spoke and wrote from inside the Bible, experiencing the power of biblical teaching even as they expounded it. . . . This grand project sets before scholars, pastors, teachers, students and growing Christians an experience that can only be likened to stumbling into a group Bible study only to discover that your fellow participants include some of the most significant Christians of the Reformation and post-Reformation (for that matter, of any) era. Here the Word of God is explained in a variety of accents: German, Swiss, French, Dutch, English, Scottish and more. Each one vibrates with a thrilling sense of the living nature of God's Word and its power to transform individuals, churches and even whole communities. Here is a series to anticipate, enjoy and treasure."

Sinclair Ferguson, *Senior Minister, First Presbyterian Church, Columbia, South Carolina*

"I strongly endorse the Reformation Commentary on Scripture. Introducing how the Bible was interpreted during the age of the Reformation, these volumes will not only renew contemporary preaching, but they will also help us understand more fully how reading and meditating on Scripture can, in fact, change our lives!"

Lois Malcolm, *Associate Professor of Systematic Theology, Luther Seminary*

"Discerning the true significance of movements in theology requires acquaintance with their biblical exegesis. This is supremely so with the Reformation, which was essentially a biblical revival. The Reformation Commentary on Scripture will fill a yawning gap, just as the Ancient Christian Commentary did before it, and the first volume gets the series off to a fine start, whetting the appetite for more. Most heartily do I welcome and commend this long overdue project."

J. I. Packer, *Retired Board of Governors Professor of Theology, Regent College*

"There is no telling the benefits to emerge from the publication of this magnificent Reformation Commentary on Scripture series! Now exegetical and theological treasures from Reformation era commentators will be at our fingertips, providing new insights from old sources to give light for the present and future. This series is a gift to scholars and to the church; a wonderful resource to enhance our study of the written Word of God for generations to come!"

Donald K. McKim, *Executive Editor of Theology and Reference, Westminster John Knox Press*

"Why was this not done before? The publication of the Reformation Commentary on Scripture should be greeted with enthusiasm by every believing Christian—but especially by those who will preach and teach the Word of God. This commentary series brings the very best of the Reformation heritage to the task of exegesis and exposition, and each volume in this series represents a veritable feast that takes us back to the sixteenth century to enrich the preaching and teaching of God's Word in our own time."

R. Albert Mohler Jr., *President, The Southern Baptist Theological Seminary*

"Today more than ever, the Christian past is the church's future. InterVarsity Press has already brought the voice of the ancients to our ears. Now, in the Reformation Commentary on Scripture, we hear a timely word from the first Protestants as well."

Bryan Litfin, *Professor of Theology, Moody Bible Institute*

"I am delighted to see the Reformation Commentary on Scripture. The editors of this series have done us all a service by gleaning from these rich fields of biblical reflection. May God use this new life for these old words to give him glory and to build his church."

Mark Dever, *Senior Pastor, Capitol Hill Baptist Church, and President of 9Marks.org Ministries*

"Monumental and magisterial, the Reformation Commentary on Scripture, edited by Timothy George, is a remarkably bold and visionary undertaking. Bringing together a wealth of resources, these volumes will provide historians, theologians, biblical scholars, pastors and students with a fresh look at the exegetical insights of those who shaped and influenced the sixteenth-century Reformation. With this marvelous publication, InterVarsity Press has reached yet another plateau of excellence. We pray that this superb series will be used of God to strengthen both church and academy."

David S. Dockery, *President, Trinity International University*

"Detached from her roots, the church cannot reach the world as God intends. While every generation must steward the scriptural insights God grants it, only arrogance or ignorance causes leaders to ignore the contributions of those faithful leaders before us. The Reformation Commentary on Scripture roots our thought in great insights of faithful leaders of the Reformation to further biblical preaching and teaching in this generation."

Bryan Chapell, *chancellor and professor of practical theology, Covenant Theological Seminary*

"After reading several volumes of the Reformation Commentary on Scripture, I exclaimed, 'Hey, this is just what the doctor ordered—I mean Doctor Martinus Lutherus!' The church of today bearing his name needs a strong dose of the medicine this doctor prescribed for the ailing church of the sixteenth century. The reforming fire of Christ-centered preaching that Luther ignited is the only hope to reclaim the impact of the gospel to keep the Reformation going, not for its own sake but to further the renewal of the worldwide church of Christ today. This series of commentaries will equip preachers to step into their pulpits with confidence in the same living Word that inspired the witness of Luther and Calvin and many other lesser-known Reformers."

Carl E. Braaten, *cofounder of the Center for Catholic and Evangelical Theology*

REFORMATION COMMENTARY ON SCRIPTURE

OLD TESTAMENT
V

1–2 SAMUEL, 1–2 KINGS,
1–2 CHRONICLES

EDITED BY
DEREK COOPER AND MARTIN J. LOHRMANN

GENERAL EDITOR
TIMOTHY GEORGE

ASSOCIATE GENERAL EDITOR
SCOTT M. MANETSCH

IVP Academic

An imprint of InterVarsity Press
Downers Grove, Illinois

InterVarsity Press
P.O. Box 1400, Downers Grove, IL 60515-1426
www.ivpress.com
email@ivpress.com

InterVarsity Press® is the book-publishing division of InterVarsity Christian Fellowship/USA®, a movement of students and faculty active on campus at hundreds of universities, colleges and schools of nursing in the United States of America, and a member movement of the International Fellowship of Evangelical Students. For information about local and regional activities, visit intervarsity.org.

Excerpts from The Complete Works of Menno Simons, *edited by J. C. Wenger, translated by Leonard Verduin, are copyright © 1956, 1984 by Herald Press, Harrisonburg, VA. Used by permission.*

Excerpts from John Calvin, Institutes of the Christian Religion (1559), *edited by John T. McNeill, translated by Ford Lewis Battles, Library of Christian Classics 20-21, are copyright © Westminster Press, Philadelphia, 1960. Used by permission.*

Excerpts from Early Anabaptist Spirituality: Selected Writings, *edited by Daniel Liechty, The Classics of Western Spirituality, are copyright © Paulist Press, New York, 1994. Used by permission.*

Excerpts from James Arminius, The Works of James Arminius, *translated by James Nichols and William Nichols, 3 vols., are copyright © Baker Publishing Group, Grand Rapids, 1996. Used by permission.*

Excerpts from John Calvin, Sermons on Second Samuel: Chapters 1-13, *translated by Douglas Kelly, are copyright © Banner of Truth Trust, Edinburgh, 1992. Used by permission.*

Excerpts from Philipp Melanchthon, Melanchthon on Christian Doctrine: Loci Communes 1555, *translated by Clyde Manschreck, are copyright © Oxford University Press, New York, 1965. Used by permission.*

This publication contains The Holy Bible, English Standard Version®, copyright © 2001 by Crossway, a publishing ministry of Good News Publishers. The ESV® text appearing in this publication is reproduced and published by cooperation between Good News Publishers and InterVarsity Press and by permission of Good News Publishers. Unauthorized reproduction of this publication is prohibited.

The Holy Bible, English Standard Version (ESV) is adapted from the Revised Standard Version of the Bible, copyright Division of Christian Education of the National Council of the Churches of Christ in the U.S.A. All rights reserved.

English Standard Version®, ESV® and ESV® logo are tradmarks of Good News Publishers located in Wheaton, Illinois. Used by permission.

Design: Cindy Kiple
Images: Wooden cross: iStockphoto
      The Protestant Church in Lyon: The Protestant Church in Lyon, called "The Paradise" at Bibliotheque Publique et Universitaire, Geneva, Switzerland, Erich Lessing/Art Resource, NY.

ISBN 978-0-8308-2955-2 (print)
ISBN 978-0-8308-9978-4 (digital)

Printed in the United States of America ♾

 As a member of the Green Press Initiative, InterVarsity Press is committed to protecting the environment and to the responsible use of natural resources. To learn more, visit greenpressinitiative.org.

Library of Congress Cataloging-in-Publication Data
Names: Cooper, Derek, 1978- editor.
Title: 1-2 Samuel, 1-2 Kings, 1-2 Chronicles / edited by Derek Cooper and
   Martin J. Lohrmann ; general editor, Timothy George ; associate general
   editor Scott M. Manetsch.
Description: Downers Grove : InterVarsity Press, 2016. | Series: Reformation
   commentary on Scripture. Old Testament ; 5 | Includes bibliographical
   references and index.
Identifiers: LCCN 2015051168 (print) | LCCN 2016001473 (ebook) | ISBN
   9780830829552 (hardcover : alk. paper) | ISBN 9780830899784 (eBook)
Subjects: LCSH: Bible. Samuel--Commentaries. | Bible. Kings--Commentaries. |
   Bible. Chroniclesl--Commentaries.
Classification: LCC BS1325.53 .A13 2016 (print) | LCC BS1325.53 (ebook) | DDC
   222/.07--dc23
LC record available at http://lccn.loc.gov/2015051168

| P | 26 | 25 | 24 | 23 | 22 | 21 | 20 | 19 | 18 | 17 | 16 | 15 | 14 | 13 | 12 | 11 | 10 | 9 | 8 | 7 | 6 | 5 | 4 | 3 | 2 | 1 |
| Y | 39 | 38 | 37 | 36 | 35 | 34 | 33 | 32 | 31 | 30 | 29 | 28 | 27 | 26 | 25 | 24 | 23 | 22 | 21 | 20 | 19 | 18 | 17 | 16 |

To Timothy J. Wengert, our teacher

Reformation Commentary on Scripture
Project Staff

Project Editor
David W. McNutt

---

*Managing Editor and
Production Manager*
Benjamin M. McCoy

Copyeditor
Jeffrey A. Reimer

Assistant Project Editor
Todd R. Hains

Editorial and Research Assistants
David J. Hooper
Ethan McCarthy

Assistants to the General Editors
Le-Ann Little
Jason Odom

Design
Cindy Kiple

Design Assistant
Beth McGill

Content Production
Richard M. Chung
Maureen G. Tobey
Daniel van Loon
Jeanna L. Wiggins

Proofreader
Travis Ables

Print Coordinator
Jim Erhart

InterVarsity Press

Publisher
Robert A. Fryling

Associate Publisher, Editorial
Cindy Bunch

Editorial Director, Academic
Daniel G. Reid

Production Director
Anne Gerth

CONTENTS

ACKNOWLEDGMENTS / PAGE XIII

ABBREVIATIONS / PAGE XV

A GUIDE TO USING THIS COMMENTARY / PAGE XIX

GENERAL INTRODUCTION / PAGE XXI

INTRODUCTION TO 1–2 SAMUEL, 1–2 KINGS, 1–2 CHRONICLES / PAGE XLV

COMMENTARY ON 1 SAMUEL / PAGE 1

COMMENTARY ON 2 SAMUEL / PAGE 139

COMMENTARY ON 1 KINGS / PAGE 261

COMMENTARY ON 2 KINGS / PAGE 390

COMMENTARY ON 1 CHRONICLES / PAGE 519

COMMENTARY ON 2 CHRONICLES / PAGE 585

MAP OF EUROPE AT THE TIME OF THE REFORMATION / PAGE 674

TIMELINE OF THE REFORMATION / PAGE 675

BIOGRAPHICAL SKETCHES OF REFORMATION-ERA FIGURES AND WORKS / PAGE 686

Bibliography / PAGE 729

Author and Writings Index / PAGE 735

Subject Index / PAGE 737

Scripture Index / PAGE 741

ACKNOWLEDGMENTS

As the saying goes, "The teacher is always the primary learner." This has been especially true as we have made our way through these books of the Bible and through these many writers of the Reformation. Our learning from this project will undoubtedly continue to bear personal and professional fruit in us for years to come. We hope that readers' engagement with this volume will likewise lead to new insights and a renewed love of and appreciation for God's Word.

We are grateful to InterVarsity Press for the opportunity to contribute to this great series, the Reformation Commentary on Scripture. We would especially like to express our gratitude to Timothy George, Scott Manetsch, Joel Scandrett, Michael Gibson, Brannon Ellis, David McNutt, Frank James, David Lamb, Todd Hains and David Hooper.

We are also immensely thankful to our families for their love and support over the several years, busy weeks, early mornings and long nights a project like this requires. To Barb, Gabriela, Eli and Mia Cooper; Carrie, Hilde, Jonah and Theodore Lohrmann: we thank God for you as companions in faith and in life.

Finally, we wish to dedicate this volume to the Rev. Dr. Timothy J. Wengert, who served as *Doktorvater* for both of us in our studies at The Lutheran Theological Seminary at Philadelphia. Through his outstanding teaching and guidance, Dr. Wengert has shown us how good scholarship and firm faith can go hand in hand with service to the church and the wider society. We dedicate this book to him with deep admiration, appreciation and thanks.

With all the faithful, we give thanks to God in the words of David: "The LORD is my rock and my fortress and my deliverer, my God, my rock, in whom I take refuge" (2 Sam 22:2-3).

Derek Cooper
Martin J. Lohrmann

ABBREVIATIONS

ACCS   Ancient Christian Commentary on Scripture. 29 vols. Edited by Thomas C. Oden. Downers Grove, IL: InterVarsity Press, 1998–2009.

ANF   The Ante-Nicene Fathers. 10 vols. Edited by Alexander Roberts and James Donaldson. Buffalo, NY: Christian Literature, 1885–1896. Accessible online at ccel.org.

BoC   *The Book of Concord: The Confessions of the Evangelical Lutheran Church.* Edited by Robert Kolb and Timothy J. Wengert. Translated by Charles Arand et al. Minneapolis: Fortress, 2000.

BNP   *Brill's New Pauly: Encyclopedia of the Ancient World.* Edited by Hubert Cancik and Helmuth Schneider. 20 vols. Leiden: Brill, 2002–2011.

BSLK   *Die Bekenntnisschriften der evangelisch-lutherischen Kirche.* 12th ed. Göttingen: Vandenhoeck & Ruprecht, 1998.

CHB   *Cambridge History of the Bible.* 3 vols. Cambridge: Cambridge University Press, 1963–1970.

CNTC   *Calvin's New Testament Commentaries.* 12 vols. Edited by D. W. Torrance and T. F. Torrance. Grand Rapids: Eerdmans, 1959–1972.

CO   *Ioannis Calvini Opera quae supersunt omnia.* 59 vols. Corpus Reformatorum 29–88. Edited by G. Baum, E. Cunitz and E. Reuss. Brunswick and Berlin: C. A. Schwetschke, 1863–1900. Digital copy online at archive-ouverte.unige.ch/unige:650.

Creeds Philip Schaff. *The Creeds of Christendom: With a Critical History and Notes.* 3 vols. New York: Harper & Row, 1877. Reprint, Grand Rapids: Baker, 1977. Digital copy online at ccel.org.

CRR   Classics of the Radical Reformation. 12 vols. Waterloo, ON, and Scottdale, PA: Herald Press, 1973–2010.

CTS   Calvin Translation Society edition of Calvin's commentaries. 46 vols. Edinburgh, 1843–1855. Several reprints, but variously bound; volume numbers (when cited) are relative to specific commentaries and not to the entire set. Available online at ccel.org.

DMBI *Dictionary of Major Biblical Interpreters.* Edited by Donald K. McKim. Downers Grove, IL: IVP Academic, 2007.

DNB   *Dictionary of National Biography.* Edited by Leslie Stephen and Sidney Lee. 63 vols. London: Smith, Elder, 1885–1900.

EEBO   Early English Books Online. Subscription database, eebo.chadwyck.com.

LCC   Library of Christian Classics. 26 vols. Edited by John Baillie et al. Philadelphia: Westminster, 1953–1966.

LW   *Luther's Works* [*American edition*]. 82 vols. planned. St. Louis: Concordia; Philadelphia: Fortress, 1955–1986; 2009–.

MO   *Philippi Melanthonis Opera quae supersunt omnia*. 28 vols. Corpus Reformatorum 1–28. Edited by C. G. Bretschneider. Halle: C. A. Schwetschke, 1834–1860. Digital copies online at archive.org and books.google.com.

NDB   *Neue Deutsche Biographie*. 28 vols. projected. Berlin: Duncker & Humblot, 1953–. Accessible online at www.deutsche-biographie.de.

NPNF   *A Select Library of the Nicene and Post-Nicene Fathers of the Christian Church*. 28 vols. in two series, denoted as NPNF and NPNF². Edited by Philip Schaff et al. Buffalo, NY: Christian Literature, 1887–1894. Several reprints; also accessible online at ccel.org.

OER   *Oxford Encyclopedia of the Reformation*. 4 vols. Edited by Hans J. Hillerbrand. New York: Oxford University Press, 1996.

PL   Patrologia cursus completus. Series Latina. 221 vols. Edited by J.-P. Migne. Paris: Migne, 1844–1864. Digital copy online at books.google.com.

QGT   *Quellen zur Geschichte der Täufer*. 18 vols. Leipzig: M. Heinsius; Gütersloh: Gerd Mohn, 1930–. The first two volumes are under the series title Quellen zur Geschichte der Wiedertäufer.

r, v   Some early books are numbered not by page but by folio (leaf). Front and back sides (pages) of a numbered folio are indicated by *recto* (r) and *verso* (v), respectively.

RCS   Reformation Commentary on Scripture. 28 vols. projected. Edited by Timothy George and Scott M. Manetsch. Downers Grove, IL: IVP Academic, 2011–.

TO   *Alphonsi Tostati Opera Omnia*. 27 vols. Venice: Balleoniana, 1728. Digital copy online at books.google.com.

WA   *D. Martin Luthers Werke, Kritische Gesamtausgabe: [Schriften]*. 73 vols. Weimar: Hermann Böhlaus Nachfolger, 1883–2009. Digital copy online at archive.org.

WADB   *D. Martin Luthers Werke, Kritische Gesamtausgabe: Deutsche Bibel*. 12 vols. Weimar: Böhlaus Nachfolger, 1906–1961. Partial digital copy online at archive.org.

WATR   *D. Martin Luthers Werke, Kritische Gesamtausgabe: Tischreden*. 6 vols. Weimar: Hermann Böhlaus Nachfolger, 1912–1921. Digital copy online at archive.org.

ZSW   *Huldreich Zwinglis Sämtliche Werke*. 14 vols. Corpus Reformatorum 88–101. Edited by E. Egli et al. Berlin: C. A. Schwetschke, 1905–1959. Reprint Zurich: Theologischer Verlag Zurich, 1983. Digital copy online at irg.uzh.ch.

BIBLE TRANSLATIONS

ESV	English Standard Version
KJV	King James Version
LXX	Septuagint
NRSV	New Reivsed Standard Version
Vg	Vulgate

A GUIDE TO USING THIS COMMENTARY

Several features have been incorporated into the design of this commentary. The following comments are intended to assist readers in making full use of this volume.

Pericopes of Scripture

The scriptural text has been divided into pericopes, or passages, usually several verses in length. Each of these pericopes is given a heading, which appears at the beginning of the pericope. For example, the first pericope in this commentary is 1 Samuel 1:1-28 "The Birth and Dedication of Samuel." This heading is followed by the Scripture passage quoted in the English Standard Version (ESV). The Scripture passage is provided for the convenience of readers, but it is also in keeping with Reformation-era commentaries, which often followed the patristic and medieval commentary tradition, in which the citations of the reformers were arranged according to the text of Scripture.

Overviews

Following each pericope of text is an overview of the Reformation authors' comments on that pericope. The format of this overview varies among the volumes of this series, depending on the requirements of the specific book(s) of Scripture. The function of the overview is to identify succinctly the key exegetical, theological and pastoral concerns of the Reformation writers arising from the pericope, providing the reader with an orientation to Reformation-era approaches and emphases. It tracks a reasonably cohesive thread of argument among reformers' comments, even though they are derived from diverse sources and generations. Thus, the summaries do not proceed chronologically or by verse sequence. Rather, they seek to rehearse the overall course of the reformers' comments on that pericope.

We do not assume that the commentators themselves anticipated or expressed a formally received cohesive argument but rather that the various arguments tend to flow in a plausible, recognizable pattern. Modern readers can thus glimpse aspects of continuity in the flow of diverse exegetical traditions representing various generations and geographical locations.

Topical Headings

An abundance of varied Reformation-era comment is available for each pericope. For this reason we have broken the pericopes into two levels. First is the verse with its topical heading.

The reformers' comments are then focused on aspects of each verse, with topical headings summarizing the essence of the individual comment by evoking a key phrase, metaphor or idea. This feature provides a bridge by which modern readers can enter into the heart of the Reformation-era comment.

Identifying the Reformation Authors, Texts and Events

Following the topical heading of each section of comment, the name of the Reformation commentator is given. An English translation (where needed) of the reformer's comment is then provided. This is immediately followed by the title of the original work rendered in English.

Readers who wish to pursue a deeper investigation of the reformers' works cited in this commentary will find full bibliographic detail for each Reformation title provided in the bibliography at the back of the volume. Information on English translations (where available) and standard original-language editions and critical editions of the works cited is found in the bibliography. The Biographical Sketches section provides brief overviews of the life and work of each commentator, and each confession or collaborative work, appearing in the present volume (as well as in any previous volumes). Finally, a Timeline of the Reformation offers broader context for people, places and events relevant to the commentators and their works.

Footnotes and Back Matter

To aid the reader in exploring the background and texts in further detail, this commentary utilizes footnotes. The use and content of footnotes may vary among the volumes in this series. Where footnotes appear, a footnote number directs the reader to a note at the bottom of the page, where one will find annotations (clarifications or biblical cross references), information on English translations (where available) or standard original-language editions of the work cited.

Where original-language texts have remained untranslated into English, we provide new translations. Where there is any serious ambiguity or textual problem in the selection, we have tried to reflect the best available textual tradition. Wherever current English translations are already well rendered, they are utilized, but where necessary they are stylistically updated. A single asterisk (*) indicates that a previous English translation has been updated to modern English or amended for easier reading. We have standardized spellings and made grammatical variables uniform so that our English references will not reflect the linguistic oddities of the older English translations. For ease of reading we have in some cases removed superfluous conjunctions.

GENERAL INTRODUCTION

The Reformation Commentary on Scripture (RCS) is a twenty-eight-volume series of exegetical comment covering the entire Bible and gathered from the writings of sixteenth-century preachers, scholars and reformers. The RCS is intended as a sequel to the highly acclaimed Ancient Christian Commentary on Scripture (ACCS), and as such its overall concept, method, format and audience are similar to the earlier series. Both series are committed to the renewal of the church through careful study and meditative reflection on the Old and New Testaments, the charter documents of Christianity, read in the context of the worshiping, believing community of faith across the centuries. However, the patristic and Reformation eras are separated by nearly a millennium, and the challenges of reading Scripture with the reformers require special attention to their context, resources and assumptions. The purpose of this general introduction is to present an overview of the context and process of biblical interpretation in the age of the Reformation.

Goals

The Reformation Commentary on Scripture seeks to introduce its readers to the depth and richness of exegetical ferment that defined the Reformation era. The RCS has four goals: the enrichment of contemporary biblical interpretation through exposure to Reformation-era biblical exegesis; the renewal of contemporary preaching through exposure to the biblical insights of the Reformation writers; a deeper understanding of the Reformation itself and the breadth of perspectives represented within it; and a recovery of the profound integration of the life of faith and the life of the mind that should characterize Christian scholarship. Each of these goals requires a brief comment.

   Renewing contemporary biblical interpretation. During the past half-century, biblical hermeneutics has become a major growth industry in the academic world. One of the consequences of the historical-critical hegemony of biblical studies has been the privileging of contemporary philosophies and ideologies at the expense of a commitment to the Christian church as the primary reading community within which and for which biblical exegesis is done. Reading Scripture with the church fathers and the reformers is a corrective to all such imperialism of the present. One of the greatest skills required for a fruitful interpretation of the Bible is the ability to listen. We rightly emphasize the importance of listening to the voices of contextual theologies today, but in doing so we often marginalize or ignore another crucial context—the community of believing Christians through the centuries. The serious study of Scripture requires more than the latest

Bible translation in one hand and the latest commentary (or niche study Bible) in the other. John L. Thompson has called on Christians today to practice the art of "reading the Bible with the dead."[1] The RCS presents carefully selected comments from the extant commentaries of the Reformation as an encouragement to more in-depth study of this important epoch in the history of biblical interpretation.

Strengthening contemporary preaching. The Protestant reformers identified the public preaching of the Word of God as an indispensible means of grace and a sure sign of the true church. Through the words of the preacher, the living voice of the gospel (*viva vox evangelii*) is heard. Luther famously said that the church is not a "pen house" but a "mouth house."[2] The Reformation in Switzerland began when Huldrych Zwingli entered the pulpit of the Grossmünster in Zurich on January 1, 1519, and began to preach a series of expositional sermons chapter by chapter from the Gospel of Matthew. In the following years he extended this homiletical approach to other books of the Old and New Testaments. Calvin followed a similar pattern in Geneva. Many of the commentaries represented in this series were either originally presented as sermons or were written to support the regular preaching ministry of local church pastors. Luther said that the preacher should be a *bonus textualis*—a good one with a text—well-versed in the Scriptures. Preachers in the Reformation traditions preached not only about the Bible but also from it, and this required more than a passing acquaintance with its contents. Those who have been charged with the office of preaching in the church today can find wisdom and insight—and fresh perspectives—in the sermons of the Reformation and the biblical commentaries read and studied by preachers of the sixteenth century.

Deepening understanding of the Reformation. Some scholars of the sixteenth century prefer to speak of the period they study in the plural, the European Reformations, to indicate that many diverse impulses for reform were at work in this turbulent age of transition from medieval to modern times.[3] While this point is well taken, the RCS follows the time-honored tradition of using *Reformation* in the singular form to indicate not only a major moment in the history of Christianity in the West but also, as Hans J. Hillerbrand has put it, "an essential cohesiveness in the heterogeneous pursuits of religious reform in the sixteenth century."[4] At the same time, in developing guidelines to assist the volume editors in making judicious selections from the vast amount of commentary material available in this period, we have stressed the multifaceted character of the Reformation across many confessions, theological orientations and political settings.

Advancing Christian scholarship. By assembling and disseminating numerous voices from such a signal period as the Reformation, the RCS aims to make a significant contribution to the ever-growing stream of Christian scholarship. The post-Enlightenment split between the study

---

[1] John L. Thompson, *Reading the Bible with the Dead* (Grand Rapids: Eerdmans, 2007).
[2] WA 10,2:48.
[3] See Carter Lindberg, *The European Reformations*, 2nd ed. (Malden, MA: Wiley-Blackwell, 2010).
[4] Hans J. Hillerbrand, *The Division of Christendom* (Louisville, KY: Westminster John Knox, 2007), x. Hillerbrand has also edited the standard reference work in Reformation studies, *OER*. See also Diarmaid MacCulloch, *The Reformation* (New York: Viking, 2003), and Patrick Collinson, *The Reformation: A History* (New York: Random House, 2004).

of the Bible as an academic discipline and the reading of the Bible as spiritual nurture was foreign to the reformers. For them the study of the Bible was transformative at the most basic level of the human person: *coram deo*.

The reformers all repudiated the idea that the Bible could be studied and understood with dispassionate objectivity, as a cold artifact from antiquity. Luther's famous Reformation breakthrough triggered by his laborious study of the Psalms and Paul's letter to the Romans is well known, but the experience of Cambridge scholar Thomas Bilney was perhaps more typical. When Erasmus's critical edition of the Greek New Testament was published in 1516, it was accompanied by a new translation in elegant Latin. Attracted by the classical beauty of Erasmus's Latin, Bilney came across this statement in 1 Timothy 1:15: "Christ Jesus came into the world to save sinners." In the Greek this sentence is described as *pistos ho logos*, which the Vulgate had rendered *fidelis sermo*, "a faithful saying." Erasmus chose a different word for the Greek *pistos*—*certus*, "sure, certain." When Bilney grasped the meaning of this word applied to the announcement of salvation in Christ, he tells us that "Immediately, I felt a marvellous comfort and quietness, insomuch as 'my bruised bones leaped for joy.'"[5]

Luther described the way the Bible was meant to function in the minds and hearts of believers when he reproached himself and others for studying the nativity narrative with such cool unconcern:

> I hate myself because when I see Christ laid in the manger or in the lap of his mother and hear the angels sing, my heart does not leap into flame. With what good reason should we all despise ourselves that we remain so cold when this word is spoken to us, over which everyone should dance and leap and burn for joy! We act as though it were a frigid historical fact that does not smite our hearts, as if someone were merely relating that the sultan has a crown of gold.[6]

It was a core conviction of the Reformation that the careful study and meditative listening to the Scriptures, what the monks called *lectio divina*, could yield transformative results for *all* of life. The value of such a rich commentary, therefore, lies not only in the impressive volume of Reformation-era voices that are presented throughout the course of the series but in the many particular fields for which their respective lives and ministries are relevant. The Reformation is consequential for historical studies, both church as well as secular history. Biblical and theological studies, to say nothing of pastoral and spiritual studies, also stand to benefit and progress immensely from renewed engagement today, as mediated through the RCS, with the reformers of yesteryear.

Perspectives

In setting forth the perspectives and parameters of the RCS, the following considerations have proved helpful.

---

[5]John Foxe, *The Acts and Monuments of John Foxe: A New and Complete Edition*, 8 vols., ed. Stephen Reed Cattley (London: R. B. Seeley & W. Burnside, 1837), 4:635; quoting Ps 51:8; cited in A. G. Dickens, *The English Reformation*, 2nd ed. (University Park, PA: The Pennsylvannia State University Press, 1991), 102.
[6]WA 49:176-77, quoted in Roland Bainton, "The Bible in the Reformation," in *CHB*, 3:23.

Chronology. When did the Reformation begin, and how long did it last? In some traditional accounts, the answer was clear: the Reformation began with the posting of Luther's Ninety-five Theses at Wittenberg in 1517 and ended with the death of Calvin in Geneva in 1564. Apart from reducing the Reformation to a largely German event with a side trip to Switzerland, this perspective fails to do justice to the important events that led up to Luther's break with Rome and its many reverberations throughout Europe and beyond. In choosing commentary selections for the RCS, we have adopted the concept of the long sixteenth century, say, from the late 1400s to the mid-seventeenth century. Thus we have included commentary selections from early or pre-Reformation writers such as John Colet and Jacques Lefèvre d'Étaples to seventeenth-century figures such as Henry Ainsworth and Johann Gerhard.

Confession. The RCS concentrates primarily, though not exclusively, on the exegetical writings of the Protestant reformers. While the ACCS provided a compendium of key consensual exegetes of the early Christian centuries, the Catholic/Protestant confessional divide in the sixteenth century tested the very idea of consensus, especially with reference to ecclesiology and soteriology. While many able and worthy exegetes faithful to the Roman Catholic Church were active during this period, this project has chosen to include primarily those figures that represent perspectives within the Protestant Reformation. For this reason we have not included comments on the apocryphal or deuterocanonical writings.

We recognize that "Protestant" and "Catholic" as contradistinctive labels are anachronistic terms for the early decades of the sixteenth century before the hardening of confessional identities surrounding the Council of Trent (1545–1563). Protestant figures such as Philipp Melanchthon, Johannes Oecolampadius and John Calvin were all products of the revival of sacred letters known as biblical humanism. They shared an approach to biblical interpretation that owed much to Desiderius Erasmus and other scholars who remained loyal to the Church of Rome. Careful comparative studies of Protestant and Catholic exegesis in the sixteenth century have shown surprising areas of agreement when the focus was the study of a particular biblical text rather than the standard confessional debates.

At the same time, exegetical differences among the various Protestant groups could become strident and church-dividing. The most famous example of this is the interpretive impasse between Luther and Zwingli over the meaning of "This is my body" (Mt 26:26) in the words of institution. Their disagreement at the Colloquy of Marburg in 1529 had important christological and pastoral implications, as well as social and political consequences. Luther refused fellowship with Zwingli and his party at the end of the colloquy; in no small measure this bitter division led to the separate trajectories pursued by Lutheran and Reformed Protestantism to this day. In Elizabethan England, Puritans and Anglicans agreed that "Holy Scripture containeth all things necessary to salvation: so that whatsoever is not read therein, nor may be proved thereby, is not to be required of any man" (article 6 of the Thirty-Nine Articles of Religion), yet on the basis of their differing interpretations of the Bible they fought bitterly over the structures of the church, the clothing of the clergy and the ways of worship. On the matter of infant baptism, Catholics and

Protestants alike agreed on its propriety, though there were various theories as to how a practice not mentioned in the Bible could be justified biblically. The Anabaptists were outliers on this subject. They rejected infant baptism altogether. They appealed to the example of the baptism of Jesus and to his final words as recorded in the Gospel of Matthew (Mt 28:19-20): "Go therefore, and make disciples of all nations, baptizing them in the name of the Father, and of the Son, and of the Holy Spirit, teaching them to observe all that I have commanded you." New Testament Christians, they argued, are to follow not only the commands of Jesus in the Great Commission, but also the exact order in which they were given: evangelize, baptize, catechize.

These and many other differences of interpretation among the various Protestant groups are reflected in their many sermons, commentaries and public disputations. In the RCS, the volume editors' introduction to each volume is intended to help the reader understand the nature and significance of doctrinal conversations and disputes that resulted in particular, and frequently clashing, interpretations. Footnotes throughout the text will be provided to explain obscure references, unusual expressions and other matters that require special comment. Volume editors have chosen comments on the Bible across a wide range of sixteenth-century confessions and schools of interpretation: biblical humanists, Lutheran, Reformed, Anglican, Puritan and Anabaptist. We have not pursued passages from post-Tridentine Catholic authors or from radical spiritualists and antitrinitarian writers, though sufficient material is available from these sources to justify another series.

Format. The design of the RCS is intended to offer reader-friendly access to these classic texts. The availability of digital resources has given access to a huge residual database of sixteenth-century exegetical comment hitherto available only in major research universities and rare book collections. The RCS has benefited greatly from online databases such as Alexander Street Press's Digital Library of Classical Protestant Texts (DLCPT) as well as freely accessible databases like the Post-Reformation Digital Library (prdl.org). Through the help of RCS editorial advisor Herman Selderhuis, we have also had access to the special Reformation collections of the Johannes a Lasco Bibliothek in Emden, Germany. In addition, modern critical editions and translations of Reformation sources have been published over the past generation. Original translations of Reformation sources are given unless an acceptable translation already exists.

Each volume in the RCS will include an introduction by the volume editor placing that portion of the canon within the historical context of the Protestant Reformation and presenting a summary of the theological themes, interpretive issues and reception of the particular book(s). The commentary itself consists of particular pericopes identified by a pericope heading; the biblical text in the English Standard Version (ESV), with significant textual variants registered in the footnotes; an overview of the pericope in which principal exegetical and theological concerns of the Reformation writers are succinctly noted; and excerpts from the Reformation writers identified by name according to the conventions of the *Oxford Encyclopedia of the Reformation*. Each volume will also include a bibliography of sources cited, as well as an appendix of authors and source works.

The Reformation era was a time of verbal as well as physical violence, and this fact has presented a challenge for this project. Without unduly sanitizing the texts, where they contain anti-Semitic, sexist or inordinately polemical rhetoric, we have not felt obliged to parade such comments either. We have noted the abridgement of texts with ellipses and an explanatory footnote. While this procedure would not be valid in the critical edition of such a text, we have deemed it appropriate in a series whose primary purpose is pastoral and devotional. When translating *homo* or similar terms that refer to the human race as a whole or to individual persons without reference to gender, we have used alternative English expressions to the word *man* (or derivative constructions that formerly were used generically to signify humanity at large), whenever such substitutions can be made without producing an awkward or artificial construction.

As is true in the ACCS, we have made a special effort where possible to include the voices of women, though we acknowledge the difficulty of doing so for the early modern period when for a variety of social and cultural reasons few theological and biblical works were published by women. However, recent scholarship has focused on a number of female leaders whose literary remains show us how they understood and interpreted the Bible. Women who made significant contributions to the Reformation include Marguerite d'Angoulême, sister of King Francis I, who supported French reformist evangelicals including Calvin and who published a religious poem influenced by Luther's theology, *The Mirror of the Sinful Soul*; Argula von Grumbach, a Bavarian noblewoman who defended the teachings of Luther and Melanchthon before the theologians of the University of Ingolstadt; Katharina Schütz Zell, the wife of a former priest, Matthias Zell, and a remarkable reformer in her own right—she conducted funerals, compiled hymnbooks, defended the downtrodden and published a defense of clerical marriage as well as composing works of consolation on divine comfort and pleas for the toleration of Anabaptists and Catholics alike; and Anne Askew, a Protestant martyr put to death in 1546 after demonstrating remarkable biblical prowess in her examinations by church officials. Other echoes of faithful women in the age of the Reformation are found in their letters, translations, poems, hymns, court depositions and martyr records.

Lay culture, learned culture. In recent decades, much attention has been given to what is called "reforming from below," that is, the expressions of religious beliefs and churchly life that characterized the popular culture of the majority of the population in the era of the Reformation. Social historians have taught us to examine the diverse pieties of townspeople and city folk, of rural religion and village life, the emergence of lay theologies and the experiences of women in the religious tumults of Reformation Europe.[7] Formal commentaries by their nature are artifacts of learned culture. Almost all of them were written in Latin, the lingua franca of learned discourse well past the age of the Reformation. Biblical commentaries were certainly not the primary means by which the Protestant Reformation spread so rapidly across wide sectors of sixteenth-century society. Small pamphlets and broadsheets, later called *Flugschriften* ("flying writings"), with their graphic woodcuts and cartoon-like depictions of Reformation personalities and events, became the means of choice for mass communication in the early age of printing. Sermons and works of

---

[7]See Peter Matheson, ed., *Reformation Christianity* (Minneapolis: Fortress, 2007).

devotion were also printed with appealing visual aids. Luther's early writings were often accompanied by drawings and sketches from Lucas Cranach and other artists. This was done "above all for the sake of children and simple folk," as Luther put it, "who are more easily moved by pictures and images to recall divine history than through mere words or doctrines."[8]

We should be cautious, however, in drawing too sharp a distinction between learned and lay culture in this period. The phenomenon of preaching was a kind of verbal bridge between scholars at their desks and the thousands of illiterate or semiliterate listeners whose views were shaped by the results of Reformation exegesis. According to contemporary witness, more than one thousand people were crowding into Geneva to hear Calvin expound the Scriptures every day.[9] An example of how learned theological works by Reformation scholars were received across divisions of class and social status comes from Lazare Drilhon, an apothecary of Toulon. He was accused of heresy in May 1545 when a cache of prohibited books was found hidden in his garden shed. In addition to devotional works, the French New Testament and a copy of Calvin's Genevan liturgy, there was found a series of biblical commentaries, translated from the Latin into French: Martin Bucer's on Matthew, François Lambert's on the Apocalypse and one by Oecolampadius on 1 John.[10] Biblical exegesis in the sixteenth century was not limited to the kind of full-length commentaries found in Drilhon's shed. Citations from the Bible and expositions of its meaning permeate the extant literature of sermons, letters, court depositions, doctrinal treatises, records of public disputations and even last wills and testaments. While most of the selections in the RCS will be drawn from formal commentary literature, other sources of biblical reflection will also be considered.

Historical Context

The medieval legacy. On October 18, 1512, the degree *Doctor in Biblia* was conferred on Martin Luther, and he began his career as a professor in the University of Wittenberg. As is well known, Luther was also a monk who had taken solemn vows in the Augustinian Order of Hermits at Erfurt. These two settings—the university and the monastery—both deeply rooted in the Middle Ages, form the background not only for Luther's personal vocation as a reformer but also for the history of the biblical commentary in the age of the Reformation. Since the time of the Venerable Bede (d. 735), sometimes called "the last of the Fathers," serious study of the Bible had taken place primarily in the context of cloistered monasteries. The Rule of St. Benedict brought together *lectio* and *meditatio*, the knowledge of letters and the life of prayer. The liturgy was the medium through which the daily reading of the Bible, especially the Psalms, and the sayings of the church fathers came together in the spiritual formation of the monks.[11] Essential to this understanding

---

[8]Martin Luther, "Personal Prayer Book," LW 43:42-43* (WA 10,2:458); quoted in R. W. Scribner, *For the Sake of Simple Folk: Popular Propaganda for the German Reformation* (Cambridge: Cambridge University Press, 1981), xi.

[9]Letter of De Beaulieu to Guillaume Farel (1561) in *Theodor Beza nach handschriftlichen und anderen gleichzeitigen Quellen*, ed. J. W. Baum (Leipzig: Weidmann, 1851), 2:92.

[10]Francis Higman, "A Heretic's Library: The Drilhon Inventory" (1545), in Francis Higman, *Lire et Découvrir: la circulation des idées au temps de la Réforme* (Geneva: Droz, 1998), 65-85.

[11]See the classic study by Jean Leclercq, *The Love of Learning and the Desire for God* (New York: Fordham University Press, 1961).

was a belief in the unity of the people of God throughout time as well as space, and an awareness that life in this world was a preparation for the beatific vision in the next.

The source of theology was the study of the sacred page *(sacra pagina)*; its object was the accumulation of knowledge not for its own sake but for the obtaining of eternal life. For these monks, the Bible had God for its author, salvation for its end and unadulterated truth for its matter, though they would not have expressed it in such an Aristotelian way. The medieval method of interpreting the Bible owed much to Augustine's *On Christian Doctrine*. In addition to setting forth a series of rules (drawn from an earlier work by Tyconius), Augustine stressed the importance of distinguishing the literal and spiritual or allegorical senses of Scripture. While the literal sense was not disparaged, the allegorical was valued because it enabled the believer to obtain spiritual benefit from the obscure places in the Bible, especially in the Old Testament. For Augustine, as for the monks who followed him, the goal of scriptural exegesis was freighted with eschatological meaning; its purpose was to induce faith, hope and love and so to advance in one's pilgrimage toward that city with foundations (see Heb 11:10).

Building on the work of Augustine and other church fathers going back to Origen, medieval exegetes came to understand Scripture as possessed of four possible meanings, the famous *quadriga*. The literal meaning was retained, of course, but the spiritual meaning was now subdivided into three senses: the allegorical, the moral and the anagogical. Medieval exegetes often referred to the four meanings of Scripture in a popular rhyme:

> The letter shows us what God and our fathers did;
> The allegory shows us where our faith is hid;
> The moral meaning gives us rules of daily life;
> The anagogy shows us where we end our strife.[12]

In this schema, the three spiritual meanings of the text correspond to the three theological virtues: faith (allegory), hope (anagogy) and love (the moral meaning). It should be noted that this way of approaching the Bible assumed a high doctrine of scriptural inspiration: the multiple meanings inherent in the text had been placed there by the Holy Spirit for the benefit of the people of God. The biblical justification for this method went back to the apostle Paul, who had used the words *allegory* and *type* when applying Old Testament events to believers in Christ (Gal 4:21-31; 1 Cor 10:1-11). The problem with this approach was knowing how to relate each of the four senses to one another and how to prevent Scripture from becoming a nose of wax turned this way and that by various interpreters. As G. R. Evans explains, "Any interpretation which could be put upon the text and was in keeping with the faith and edifying, had the warrant of God himself, for no human reader had the ingenuity to find more than God had put there."[13]

With the rise of the universities in the eleventh century, theology and the study of Scripture moved from the cloister into the classroom. Scripture and the Fathers were still important, but they came to function more as footnotes to the theological questions debated in the schools and

---

[12]Robert M. Grant, *A Short History of the Interpretation of the Bible* (New York: Macmillan, 1963), 119. A translation of the well-known Latin quatrain: *Littera gesta docet/Quid credas allegoria/Moralis quid agas/Quo tendas anagogia.*

[13]G. R. Evans, *The Language and Logic of the Bible: The Road to Reformation* (Cambridge: Cambridge University Press, 1985), 42.

brought together in an impressive systematic way in works such as Peter Lombard's *Books of Sentences* (the standard theology textbook of the Middle Ages) and the great scholastic *summae* of the thirteenth century. Indispensible to the study of the Bible in the later Middle Ages was the *Glossa ordinaria*, a collection of exegetical opinions by the church fathers and other commentators. Heiko Oberman summarized the transition from devotion to dialectic this way: "When, due to the scientific revolution of the twelfth century, Scripture became the *object* of study rather than the *subject* through which God speaks to the student, the difference between the two modes of speaking was investigated in terms of the texts themselves rather than in their relation to the recipients."[14] It was possible, of course, to be both a scholastic theologian and a master of the spiritual life. Meister Eckhart, for example, wrote commentaries on the Old Testament in Latin and works of mystical theology in German, reflecting what had come to be seen as a division of labor between the two.

An increasing focus on the text of Scripture led to a revival of interest in its literal sense. The two key figures in this development were Thomas Aquinas (d. 1274) and Nicholas of Lyra (d. 1340). Thomas is best remembered for his *Summa Theologiae*, but he was also a prolific commentator on the Bible. Thomas did not abandon the multiple senses of Scripture but declared that all the senses were founded on one—the literal—and this sense eclipsed allegory as the basis of sacred doctrine. Nicholas of Lyra was a Franciscan scholar who made use of the Hebrew text of the Old Testament and quoted liberally from works of Jewish scholars, especially the learned French rabbi Salomon Rashi (d. 1105). After Aquinas, Lyra was the strongest defender of the literal, historical meaning of Scripture as the primary basis of theological disputation. His *Postilla*, as his notes were called—the abbreviated form of *post illa verba textus*, meaning "after these words from Scripture"—were widely circulated in the late Middle Ages and became the first biblical commentary to be printed in the fifteenth century. More than any other commentator from the period of high scholasticism, Lyra and his work were greatly valued by the early reformers. According to an old Latin pun, *Nisi Lyra lyrasset, Lutherus non saltasset,* "If Lyra had not played his lyre, Luther would not have danced."[15] While Luther was never an uncritical disciple of any teacher, he did praise Lyra as a good Hebraist and quoted him more than one hundred times in his lectures on Genesis, where he declared, "I prefer him to almost all other interpreters of Scripture."[16]

Sacred philology. The sixteenth century has been called a golden age of biblical interpretation, and it is a fact that the age of the Reformation witnessed an explosion of commentary writing unparalleled in the history of the Christian church. Kenneth Hagen has cataloged forty-five commentaries on Hebrews between 1516 (Erasmus) and 1598 (Beza).[17] During the sixteenth century, more than seventy new commentaries on Romans were published, five of them by Melanchthon alone, and nearly one hundred commentaries on the Bible's prayer book, the Psalms.[18] There were

---

[14]Heiko Oberman, *Forerunners of the Reformation* (Philadelphia: Fortress, 1966), 284.

[15]Nicholas of Lyra, *The Postilla of Nicolas of Lyra on the Song of Songs,* trans. and ed. James George Kiecker (Milwaukee: Marquette University Press, 1998), 19.

[16]LW 2:164 (WA 42:377).

[17]Kenneth Hagen, *Hebrews Commenting from Erasmus to Bèze, 1516–1598* (Tübingen: Mohr, 1981).

[18]R. Gerald Hobbs, "Biblical Commentaries," *OER* 1:167-71. See in general David C. Steinmetz, ed., *The Bible in the Sixteenth Century* (Durham: Duke University Press, 1990).

two developments in the fifteenth century that presaged this development and without which it could not have taken place: the invention of printing and the rediscovery of a vast store of ancient learning hitherto unknown or unavailable to scholars in the West.

It is now commonplace to say that what the computer has become in our generation, the printing press was to the world of Erasmus, Luther and other leaders of the Reformation. Johannes Gutenberg, a goldsmith by trade, developed a metal alloy suitable for type and a machine that would allow printed characters to be cast with relative ease, placed in even lines of composition and then manipulated again and again, making possible the mass production of an unbelievable number of texts. In 1455, the Gutenberg Bible, the masterpiece of the typographical revolution, was published at Mainz in double columns in gothic type. Forty-seven copies of the beautiful Gutenberg Bible are still extant, each consisting of more than one thousand colorfully illuminated and impeccably printed pages. What began at Gutenberg's print shop in Mainz on the Rhine River soon spread, like McDonald's or Starbucks in our day, into every nook and cranny of the known world. Printing presses sprang up in Rome (1464), Venice (1469), Paris (1470), the Netherlands (1471), Switzerland (1472), Spain (1474), England (1476), Sweden (1483) and Constantinople (1490). By 1500, these and other presses across Europe had published some twenty-seven thousand titles, most of them in Latin. Erasmus once compared himself with an obscure preacher whose sermons were heard by only a few people in one or two churches while his books were read in every country in the world. Erasmus was not known for his humility, but in this case he was simply telling the truth.[19]

The Italian humanist Lorenzo Valla (d. 1457) died in the early dawn of the age of printing, but his critical and philological studies would be taken up by others who believed that genuine reform in church and society could come about only by returning to the wellsprings of ancient learning and wisdom—*ad fontes*, "back to the sources!" Valla is best remembered for undermining a major claim made by defenders of the papacy when he proved by philological research that the so-called Donation of Constantine, which had bolstered papal assertions of temporal sovereignty, was a forgery. But it was Valla's *Collatio Novi Testamenti* of 1444 that would have such a great effect on the renewal of biblical studies in the next century. Erasmus discovered the manuscript of this work while rummaging through an old library in Belgium and published it at Paris in 1505. In the preface to his edition of Valla, Erasmus gave the rationale that would guide his own labors in textual criticism. Just as Jerome had translated the Latin Vulgate from older versions and copies of the Scriptures in his day, so now Jerome's own text must be subjected to careful scrutiny and correction. Erasmus would be *Hieronymus redivivus*, a new Jerome come back to life to advance the cause of sacred philology. The restoration of the Scriptures and the writings of the church fathers would usher in what Erasmus believed would be a golden age of peace and learning. In 1516, the Basel publisher Froben brought out Erasmus's *Novum Instrumentum*, the first published edition of the Greek New Testament. Erasmus's Greek New Testament would go through five editions in his lifetime, each one with new emendations to the text and a growing section of annotations that expanded to include not only

---

[19]E. Harris Harbison, *The Christian Scholar in the Age of the Reformation* (New York: Charles Scribner's Sons, 1956), 80.

technical notes about the text but also theological comment. The influence of Erasmus's Greek New Testament was enormous. It formed the basis for Robert Estienne's *Novum Testamentum Graece* of 1550, which in turn was used to establish the Greek *Textus Receptus* for a number of late Reformation translations including the King James Version of 1611.

For all his expertise in Greek, Erasmus was a poor student of Hebrew and only published commentaries on several of the psalms. However, the renaissance of Hebrew letters was part of the wider program of biblical humanism as reflected in the establishment of trilingual colleges devoted to the study of Hebrew, Greek and Latin (the three languages written on the *titulus* of Jesus' cross [Jn 19:20]) at Alcalá in Spain, Wittenberg in Germany, Louvain in Belgium and Paris in France. While it is true that some medieval commentators, especially Nicholas of Lyra, had been informed by the study of Hebrew and rabbinics in their biblical work, it was the publication of Johannes Reuchlin's *De rudimentis hebraicis* (1506), a combined grammar and dictionary, that led to the recovery of *veritas Hebraica*, as Jerome had referred to the true voice of the Hebrew Scriptures. The pursuit of Hebrew studies was carried forward in the Reformation by two great scholars, Konrad Pellikan and Sebastian Münster. Pellikan was a former Franciscan friar who embraced the Protestant cause and played a major role in the Zurich reformation. He had published a Hebrew grammar even prior to Reuchlin and produced a commentary on nearly the entire Bible that appeared in seven volumes between 1532 and 1539. Münster was Pellikan's student and taught Hebrew at the University of Heidelberg before taking up a similar position in Basel. Like his mentor, Münster was a great collector of Hebraica and published a series of excellent grammars, dictionaries and rabbinic texts. Münster did for the Hebrew Old Testament what Erasmus had done for the Greek New Testament. His *Hebraica Biblia* offered a fresh Latin translation of the Old Testament with annotations from medieval rabbinic exegesis.

Luther first learned Hebrew with Reuchlin's grammar in hand but took advantage of other published resources, such as the four-volume Hebrew Bible published at Venice by Daniel Bomberg in 1516 to 1517. He also gathered his own circle of Hebrew experts, his *sanhedrin* he called it, who helped him with his German translation of the Old Testament. We do not know where William Tyndale learned Hebrew, though perhaps it was in Worms, where there was a thriving rabbinical school during his stay there. In any event, he had sufficiently mastered the language to bring out a freshly translated Pentateuch that was published at Antwerp in 1530. By the time the English separatist scholar Henry Ainsworth published his prolix commentaries on the Pentateuch in 1616, the knowledge of Hebrew, as well as Greek, was taken for granted by every serious scholar of the Bible. In the preface to his commentary on Genesis, Ainsworth explained that "the literal sense of Moses's Hebrew (which is the tongue wherein he wrote the law), is the ground of all interpretation, and that language hath figures and properties of speech, different from ours: These therefore in the first place are to be opened that the natural meaning of the Scripture, being known, the mysteries of godliness therein implied, may be better discerned."[20]

---

[20]Henry Ainsworth, *Annotations upon the First Book of Moses Called Genesis* (Amsterdam, 1616), preface (unpaginated).

The restoration of the biblical text in the original languages made possible the revival of scriptural exposition reflected in the floodtide of sermon literature and commentary work. Of even more far-reaching import was the steady stream of vernacular Bibles in the sixteenth century. In the introduction to his 1516 edition of the New Testament, Erasmus had expressed his desire that the Scriptures be translated into all languages so that "the lowliest women" could read the Gospels and the Pauline epistles and "the farmer sing some portion of them at the plow, the weaver hum some parts of them to the movement of his shuttle, the traveler lighten the weariness of the journey with stories of this kind."[21] Like Erasmus, Tyndale wanted the Bible to be available in the language of the common people. He once said to a learned divine that if God spared his life he would cause the boy who drives the plow to know more of the Scriptures than he did![22] The project of allowing the Bible to speak in the language of the mother in the house, the children in the street and the cheesemonger in the marketplace was met with stiff opposition by certain Catholic polemicists such as Johann Eck, Luther's antagonist at the Leipzig Debate of 1519. In his *Enchiridion* (1525), Eck derided the "inky theologians" whose translations paraded the Bible before "the untutored crowd" and subjected it to the judgment of "laymen and crazy old women."[23] In fact, some fourteen German Bibles had already been published prior to Luther's September Testament of 1522, which he translated from Erasmus's Greek New Testament in less than three months' time while sequestered in the Wartburg. Luther's German New Testament became the first bestseller in the world, appearing in forty-three distinct editions between 1522 and 1525 with upward of one hundred thousand copies issued in these three years. It is estimated that 5 percent of the German population may have been literate at this time, but this rate increased as the century wore on due in no small part to the unmitigated success of vernacular Bibles.[24]

Luther's German Bible (inclusive of the Old Testament from 1534) was the most successful venture of its kind, but it was not alone in the field. Hans Denck and Ludwig Hätzer, leaders in the early Anabaptist movement, translated the prophetic books of the Old Testament from Hebrew into German in 1527. This work influenced the Swiss-German Bible of 1531 published by Leo Jud and other pastors in Zurich. Tyndale's influence on the English language rivaled that of Luther on German. At a time when English was regarded as "that obscure and remote dialect of German spoken in an off-shore island," Tyndale, with his remarkable linguistic ability (he was fluent in eight languages), "made a language for England," as his modern editor David Daniell has put it.[25] Tyndale was imprisoned and executed near Brussels in 1536, but the influence of his biblical work

[21]John C. Olin, *Christian Humanism and the Reformation* (New York: Fordham University Press, 1987), 101.

[22]This famous statement of Tyndale was quoted by John Foxe in his *Acts and Monuments of Matters Happening in the Church* (London, 1563). See Henry Wansbrough, "Tyndale," in *The Bible in the Renaissance*, ed. Richard Griffith (Aldershot, UK: Ashgate, 2001), 124.

[23]John Eck, *Enchiridion of Commonplaces*, trans. Ford Lewis Battles (Grand Rapids: Baker, 1979), 47-49.

[24]The effect of printing on the spread of the Reformation has been much debated. See the classic study by Elizabeth L. Eisenstein, *The Printing Press as an Agent of Change* (Cambridge: Cambridge University Press, 1979). More recent studies include Mark U. Edwards Jr., *Printing, Propaganda and Martin Luther* (Minneapolis: Fortress, 1994), and Andrew Pettegree and Matthew Hall, "The Reformation and the Book: A Reconsideration," *Historical Journal* 47 (2004): 1-24.

[25]David Daniell, *William Tyndale: A Biography* (New Haven: Yale University Press, 1994), 3.

among the common people of England was already being felt. There is no reason to doubt the authenticity of John Foxe's recollection of how Tyndale's New Testament was received in England during the 1520s and 1530s:

> The fervent zeal of those Christian days seemed much superior to these our days and times; as manifestly may appear by their sitting up all night in reading and hearing; also by their expenses and charges in buying of books in English, of whom some gave five marks, some more, some less, for a book: some gave a load of hay for a few chapters of St. James, or of St. Paul in English.[26]

Calvin helped to revise and contributed three prefaces to the French Bible translated by his cousin Pierre Robert Olivétan and originally published at Neuchâtel in 1535. Clément Marot and Beza provided a fresh translation of the Psalms with each psalm rendered in poetic form and accompanied by monophonic musical settings for congregational singing. The Bay Psalter, the first book printed in America, was an English adaptation of this work. Geneva also provided the provenance of the most influential Italian Bible published by Giovanni Diodati in 1607. The flowering of biblical humanism in vernacular Bibles resulted in new translations in all of the major language groups of Europe: Spanish (1569), Portuguese (1681), Dutch (New Testament, 1523; Old Testament, 1527), Danish (1550), Czech (1579–1593/94), Hungarian (New Testament, 1541; complete Bible, 1590), Polish (1563), Swedish (1541) and even Arabic (1591).[27]

Patterns of Reformation

Once the text of the Bible had been placed in the hands of the people, in cheap and easily available editions, what further need was there of published expositions such as commentaries? Given the Protestant doctrine of the priesthood of all believers, was there any longer a need for learned clergy and their bookish religion? Some radical reformers thought not. Sebastian Franck searched for the true church of the Spirit "scattered among the heathen and the weeds" but could not find it in any of the institutional structures of his time. *Veritas non potest scribi, aut exprimi,* he said, "truth can neither be spoken nor written."[28] Kaspar von Schwenckfeld so emphasized religious inwardness that he suspended external observance of the Lord's Supper and downplayed the readable, audible Scriptures in favor of the Word within. This trajectory would lead to the rise of the Quakers in the next century, but it was pursued neither by the mainline reformers nor by most of the Anabaptists. Article 7 of the Augsburg Confession (1530) declared the one holy Christian church to be "the assembly of all believers among whom the Gospel is purely preached and the holy sacraments are administered according to the Gospel."[29]

Historians of the nineteenth century referred to the material and formal principles of the Reformation. In this construal, the matter at stake was the meaning of the Christian gospel: the

---

[26]Foxe, *Acts and Monuments*, 4:218.

[27]On vernacular translations of the Bible, see *CHB* 3:94-140 and Jaroslav Pelikan, *The Reformation of the Bible/The Bible of the Reformation* (New Haven: Yale University Press, 1996), 41-62.

[28]Sebastian Franck, *280 Paradoxes or Wondrous Sayings*, trans. E. J. Furcha (Lewiston, NY: Edwin Mellen Press, 1986), 10, 212.

[29]BoC 42 (BSLK 61).

liberating insight that helpless sinners are graciously justified by the gift of faith alone, apart from any works or merits of their own, entirely on the basis of Christ's atoning work on the cross. For Luther especially, justification by faith alone became the criterion by which all other doctrines and practices of the church were to be judged. The cross proves everything, he said at the Heidelberg disputation in 1518. The distinction between law and gospel thus became the primary hermeneutical key that unlocked the true meaning of Scripture.

The formal principle of the Reformation, *sola Scriptura*, was closely bound up with proper distinctions between Scripture and tradition. "Scripture alone," said Luther, "is the true lord and master of all writings and doctrine on earth. If that is not granted, what is Scripture good for? The more we reject it, the more we become satisfied with human books and human teachers."[30] On the basis of this principle, the reformers challenged the structures and institutions of the medieval Catholic Church. Even a simple layperson, they asserted, armed with Scripture should be believed above a pope or a council without it. But, however boldly asserted, the doctrine of the primacy of Scripture did not absolve the reformers from dealing with a host of hermeneutical issues that became matters of contention both between Rome and the Reformation and within each of these two communities: the extent of the biblical canon, the validity of critical study of the Bible, the perspicuity of Scripture and its relation to preaching, and the retention of devotional and liturgical practices such as holy days, incense, the burning of candles, the sprinkling of holy water, church art and musical instruments. Zwingli, the Puritans and the radicals dismissed such things as a rubbish heap of ceremonials that amounted to nothing but tomfoolery, while Lutherans and Anglicans retained most of them as consonant with Scripture and valuable aids to worship.

It is important to note that while the mainline reformers differed among themselves on many matters, overwhelmingly they saw themselves as part of the ongoing Catholic tradition, indeed as the legitimate bearers of it. This was seen in numerous ways including their sense of continuity with the church of the preceding centuries; their embrace of the ecumenical orthodoxy of the early church; and their desire to read the Bible in dialogue with the exegetical tradition of the church.

In their biblical commentaries, the reformers of the sixteenth century revealed a close familiarity with the preceding exegetical tradition, and they used it respectfully as well as critically in their own expositions of the sacred text. For them, *sola Scriptura* was not *nuda Scriptura*. Rather, the Scriptures were seen as the book given to the church, gathered and guided by the Holy Spirit. In his restatement of the Vincentian canon, Calvin defined the church as "a society of all the saints, a society which, spread over the whole world, and existing in all ages, and bound together by the one doctrine and the one spirit of Christ, cultivates and observes unity of faith and brotherly concord. With this church we deny that we have any disagreement. Nay, rather, as we revere her as our mother, so we desire to remain in her bosom." Defined thus, the church has a real, albeit relative and circumscribed, authority since, as Calvin admits, "We cannot fly without wings."[31] While the reformers could not agree with the Council of Trent (though some recent Catholic

---

[30]LW 32:11-12* (WA 7:317).
[31]John C. Olin, ed., *John Calvin and Jacopo Sadoleto: A Reformation Debate* (New York: Harper Torchbooks, 1966), 61-62, 77.

theologians have challenged this interpretation) that Scripture and tradition were two separate and equal sources of divine revelation, they did believe in the coinherence of Scripture and tradition. This conviction shaped the way they read and interpreted the Bible.[32]

Schools of Exegesis

The reformers were passionate about biblical exegesis, but they showed little concern for hermeneutics as a separate field of inquiry. Niels Hemmingsen, a Lutheran theologian in Denmark, did write a treatise, *De methodis* (1555), in which he offered a philosophical and theological framework for the interpretation of Scripture. This was followed by the *Clavis Scripturae Sacrae* (1567) of Matthias Flacius Illyricus, which contains some fifty rules for studying the Bible drawn from Scripture itself.[33] However, hermeneutics as we know it came of age only in the Enlightenment and should not be backloaded into the Reformation. It is also true that the word *commentary* did not mean in the sixteenth century what it means for us today. Erasmus provided both annotations and paraphrases on the New Testament, the former a series of critical notes on the text but also containing points of doctrinal substance, the latter a theological overview and brief exposition. Most of Calvin's commentaries began as sermons or lectures presented in the course of his pastoral ministry. In the dedication to his 1519 study of Galatians, Luther declared that his work was "not so much a commentary as a testimony of my faith in Christ."[34] The exegetical work of the reformers was embodied in a wide variety of forms and genres, and the RCS has worked with this broader concept in setting the guidelines for this compendium.

The Protestant reformers shared in common a number of key interpretive principles such as the priority of the grammatical-historical sense of Scripture and the christological centeredness of the entire Bible, but they also developed a number of distinct approaches and schools of exegesis.[35] For the purposes of the RCS, we note the following key figures and families of interpretation in this period.

Biblical humanism. The key figure is Erasmus, whose importance is hard to exaggerate for Catholic and Protestant exegetes alike. His annotated Greek New Testament and fresh Latin translation challenged the hegemony of the Vulgate tradition and was doubtless a factor in the decision of the Council of Trent to establish the Vulgate edition as authentic and normative. Erasmus believed that the wide distribution of the Scriptures would contribute to personal spiritual renewal and the reform of society. In 1547, the English translation of Erasmus's *Paraphrases* was ordered to be placed in every parish church in England. John Colet first encouraged Erasmus

---

[32]See Timothy George, "An Evangelical Reflection on Scripture and Tradition," *Pro Ecclesia* 9 (2000): 184-207.

[33]See Kenneth G. Hagen, "'De Exegetica Methodo': Niels Hemmingsen's *De Methodis* (1555)," in *The Bible in the Sixteenth Century*, ed. David C. Steinmetz (Durham: Duke University Press, 1990), 181-96.

[34]LW 27:159 (WA 2:449). See Kenneth Hagen, "What Did the Term *Commentarius* Mean to Sixteenth-Century Theologians?" in *Théorie et pratique de l'exégèse*, eds., Irena Backus and Francis M. Higman (Geneva: Droz, 1990), 13-38.

[35]I follow here the sketch of Irena Backus, "Biblical Hermeneutics and Exegesis," *OER* 1:152-58. In this work, Backus confines herself to Continental developments, whereas we have noted the exegetical contribution of the English Reformation as well. For more comprehensive listings of sixteenth-century commentators, see Gerald Bray, *Biblical Interpretation* (Downers Grove, IL: InterVarsity Press, 1996), 165-212; and Richard A. Muller, "Biblical Interpretation in the Sixteenth and Seventeenth Centuries," *DMBI* 22-44.

to learn Greek, though he never took up the language himself. Colet's lectures on Paul's epistles at Oxford are reflected in his commentaries on Romans and 1 Corinthians.

Jacques Lefèvre d'Étaples has been called the "French Erasmus" because of his great learning and support for early reform movements in his native land. He published a major edition of the Psalter, as well as commentaries on the Pauline Epistles (1512), the Gospels (1522) and the General Epistles (1527). Guillaume Farel, the early reformer of Geneva, was a disciple of Lefèvre, and the young Calvin also came within his sphere of influence.

Among pre-Tridentine Catholic reformers, special attention should be given to Thomas de Vio, better known as Cajetan. He is best remembered for confronting Martin Luther on behalf of the pope in 1518, but his biblical commentaries (on nearly every book of the Bible) are virtually free of polemic. Like Erasmus, he dared to criticize the Vulgate on linguistic grounds. His commentary on Romans supported the doctrine of justification by grace applied by faith based on the "alien righteousness" of God in Christ. Jared Wicks sums up Cajetan's significance in this way: "Cajetan's combination of passion for pristine biblical meaning with his fully developed theological horizon of understanding indicates, in an intriguing manner, something of the breadth of possibilities open to Roman Catholics before a more restrictive settlement came to exercise its hold on many Catholic interpreters in the wake of the Council of Trent."[36] Girolamo Seripando, like Cajetan, was a cardinal in the Catholic Church, though he belonged to the Augustinian rather than the Dominican order. He was an outstanding classical scholar and published commentaries on Romans and Galatians. Also important is Jacopo Sadoleto, another cardinal, best known for his 1539 letter to the people of Geneva beseeching them to return to the church of Rome, to which Calvin replied with a manifesto of his own. Sadoleto published a commentary on Romans in 1535. Bucer once commended Sadoleto's teaching on justification as approximating that of the reformers, while others saw him tilting away from the Augustinian tradition toward Pelagianism.[37]

Luther and the Wittenberg School. It was in the name of the Word of God, and specifically as a doctor of Scripture, that Luther challenged the church of his day and inaugurated the Reformation. Though Luther renounced his monastic vows, he never lost that sense of intimacy with *sacra pagina* he first acquired as a young monk. Luther provided three rules for reading the Bible: prayer, meditation and struggle *(tentatio)*. His exegetical output was enormous. In the American edition of Luther's works, thirty out of the fifty-five volumes are devoted to his biblical studies, and additional translations are planned. Many of his commentaries originated as sermons or lecture notes presented to his students at the university and to his parishioners at Wittenberg's parish church of St. Mary. Luther referred to Galatians as his bride: "The Epistle to the Galatians is my dear epistle. I have betrothed myself to it. It is my Käthe von Bora."[38] He considered his 1535 commentary on Galatians his greatest exegetical work, although his massive commentary on

---

[36]Jared Wicks, "Tommaso de Vio Cajetan (1469-1534)," *DMBI* 283-87, here 286.

[37]See the discussion by Bernard Roussel, "Martin Bucer et Jacques Sadolet: la concorde possible," *Bulletin de la Société de l'histoire de protestantisme français* (1976): 525-50, and T. H. L. Parker, *Commentaries on the Epistle to the Romans, 1532–1542* (Edinburgh: T&T Clark, 1986), 25-34.

[38]WATR 1:69 no. 146; cf. LW 54:20 no. 146. I have followed Rörer's variant on Dietrich's notes.

Genesis (eight volumes in LW), which he worked on for ten years (1535–1545), must be considered his crowning work. Luther's principles of biblical interpretation are found in his *Open Letter on Translating* and in the prefaces he wrote to all the books of the Bible.

Philipp Melanchthon was brought to Wittenberg to teach Greek in 1518 and proved to be an able associate to Luther in the reform of the church. A set of his lecture notes on Romans was published without his knowledge in 1522. This was revised and expanded many times until his large commentary of 1556. Melanchthon also commented on other New Testament books including Matthew, John, Galatians and the Petrine epistles, as well as Proverbs, Daniel and Ecclesiastes. Though he was well trained in the humanist disciplines, Melanchthon devoted little attention to critical and textual matters in his commentaries. Rather, he followed the primary argument of the biblical writer and gathered from this exposition a series of doctrinal topics for special consideration. This method lay behind Melanchthon's *Loci communes* (1521), the first Protestant theology textbook to be published. Another Wittenberger was Johannes Bugenhagen of Pomerania, a prolific commentator on both the Old and New Testaments. His commentary on the Psalms (1524), translated into German by Bucer, applied Luther's teaching on justification to the Psalter. He also wrote a commentary on Job and annotations on many of the books in the Bible. The Lutheran exegetical tradition was shaped by many other scholar-reformers including Andreas Osiander, Johannes Brenz, Caspar Cruciger, Erasmus Sarcerius, Georg Maior, Jacob Andreae, Nikolaus Selnecker and Johann Gerhard.

The Strasbourg-Basel tradition. Bucer, the son of a shoemaker in Alsace, became the leader of the Reformation in Strasbourg. A former Dominican, he was early on influenced by Erasmus and continued to share his passion for Christian unity. Bucer was the most ecumenical of the Protestant reformers seeking rapprochement with Catholics on justification and an armistice between Luther and Zwingli in their strife over the Lord's Supper. Bucer also had a decisive influence on Calvin, though the latter characterized his biblical commentaries as longwinded and repetitious.[39] In his exegetical work, Bucer made ample use of patristic and medieval sources, though he criticized the abuse and overuse of allegory as "the most blatant insult to the Holy Spirit."[40] He declared that the purpose of his commentaries was "to help inexperienced brethren [perhaps like the apothecary Drilhon, who owned a French translation of Bucer's *Commentary on Matthew*] to understand each of the words and actions of Christ, and in their proper order as far as possible, and to retain an explanation of them in their natural meaning, so that they will not distort God's Word through age-old aberrations or by inept interpretation, but rather with a faithful comprehension of everything as written by the Spirit of God, they may expound to all the churches in their firm upbuilding in faith and love."[41] In addition to writing commentaries on all four Gospels, Bucer published commentaries on Judges, the Psalms, Zephaniah, Romans and Ephesians. In the early years of the

---

[39]CNTC 8:3 (CO 10:404).

[40]*DMBI* 249; P. Scherding and F. Wendel, eds., "Un Traité d'exégèse pratique de Bucer," *Revue d'histoire et de philosophie religieuses* 26 (1946): 32-75, here 56.

[41]Martin Bucer, *Enarrationes perpetuae in sacra quatuor evangelia*, 2nd. ed. (Strasbourg: Georg Ulrich Andlanus, 1530), 10r; quoted in D. F. Wright, "Martin Bucer," *DMBI* 290.

Reformation, there was a great deal of back and forth between Strasbourg and Basel, and both were centers of a lively publishing trade. Wolfgang Capito, Bucer's associate at Strasbourg, was a notable Hebraist and composed commentaries on Hosea (1529) and Habakkuk (1527).

At Basel, the great Sebastian Münster defended the use of Jewish sources in the Christian study of the Old Testament and published, in addition to his famous Hebrew grammar, an annotated version of the Gospel of Matthew translated from Greek into Hebrew. Oecolampadius, Basel's chief reformer, had been a proofreader in Froben's publishing house and worked with Erasmus on his Greek New Testament and his critical edition of Jerome. From 1523 he was both a preacher and professor of Holy Scripture at Basel. He defended Zwingli's eucharistic theology at the Colloquy of Marburg and published commentaries on 1 John (1524), Romans (1525) and Haggai–Malachi (1525). Oecolampadius was succeeded by Simon Grynaeus, a classical scholar who taught Greek and supported Bucer's efforts to bring Lutherans and Zwinglians together. More in line with Erasmus was Sebastian Castellio, who came to Basel after his expulsion from Geneva in 1545. He is best remembered for questioning the canonicity of the Song of Songs and for his annotations and French translation of the Bible.

The Zurich group. Biblical exegesis in Zurich was centered on the distinctive institution of the *Prophezei*, which began on June 19, 1525. On five days a week, at seven o'clock in the morning, all of the ministers and theological students in Zurich gathered into the choir of the Grossmünster to engage in a period of intense exegesis and interpretation of Scripture. After Zwingli had opened the meeting with prayer, the text of the day was read in Latin, Greek and Hebrew, followed by appropriate textual or exegetical comments. One of the ministers then delivered a sermon on the passage in German that was heard by many of Zurich's citizens who stopped by the cathedral on their way to work. This institute for advanced biblical studies had an enormous influence as a model for Reformed academies and seminaries throughout Europe. It was also the seedbed for sermon series in Zurich's churches and the extensive exegetical publications of Zwingli, Leo Jud, Konrad Pellikan, Heinrich Bullinger, Oswald Myconius and Rudolf Gwalther. Zwingli had memorized in Greek all of the Pauline epistles, and this bore fruit in his powerful expository preaching and biblical exegesis. He took seriously the role of grammar, rhetoric and historical research in explaining the biblical text. For example, he disagreed with Bucer on the value of the Septuagint, regarding it as a trustworthy witness to a proto-Hebrew version earlier than the Masoretic text.

Zwingli's work was carried forward by his successor Bullinger, one of the most formidable scholars and networkers among the reformers. He composed commentaries on Daniel (1565), the Gospels (1542–1546), the Epistles (1537), Acts (1533) and Revelation (1557). He collaborated with Calvin to produce the *Consensus Tigurinus* (1549), a Reformed accord on the nature of the Lord's Supper, and produced a series of fifty sermons on Christian doctrine, known as *Decades*, which became required reading in Elizabethan England. As the *Antistes* ("overseer") of the Zurich church for forty-four years, Bullinger faced opposition from nascent Anabaptism on the one hand and resurgent Catholicism on the other. The need for a well-trained clergy and scholarly resources, including Scripture commentaries, arose from the fact that the Bible was "difficult or obscure to the unlearned, unskillful, unexercised, and malicious or corrupted wills." While for-swearing papal claims to infallibility, Bullinger and other leaders of the magisterial Reformation saw the need for a kind of Protestant magisterium as a check against the tendency to read the Bible in "such sense as everyone shall be persuaded in himself to be most convenient."[42]

Two other commentators can be treated in connection with the Zurich group, though each of them had a wide-ranging ministry across the Reformation fronts. A former Benedictine monk, Wolfgang Musculus, embraced the Reformation in the 1520s and served briefly as the secretary to Bucer in Strasbourg. He shared Bucer's desire for Protestant unity and served for seventeen years (1531–1548) as a pastor and reformer in Augsburg. After a brief time in Zurich, where he came under the influence of Bullinger, Musculus was called to Bern, where he taught the Scriptures and published commentaries on the Psalms, the Decalogue, Genesis, Romans, Isaiah, 1 and 2 Corinthians, Galatians and Ephesians, Philippians, Colossians, 1 and 2 Thessalonians, and 1 Timothy. Drawing on his exegetical writings, Musculus also produced a compendium of Protestant theology that was translated into English in 1563 as *Commonplaces of Christian Religion.*

Peter Martyr Vermigli was a Florentine-born scholar and Augustinian friar who embraced the Reformation and fled to Switzerland in 1542. Over the next twenty years, he would gain an international reputation as a prolific scholar and leading theologian within the Reformed community. He lectured on the Old Testament at Strasbourg, was made regius professor at Oxford, corresponded with the Italian refugee church in Geneva and spent the last years of his life as professor of Hebrew at Zurich. Vermigli published commentaries on 1 Corinthians, Romans and Judges during his lifetime. His biblical lectures on Genesis, Lamentations, 1 and 2 Samuel, and 1 and 2 Kings were published posthumously. The most influential of his writings was the *Loci communes* (*Commonplaces*), a theological compendium drawn from his exegetical writings.

The Genevan reformers. What Zwingli and Bullinger were to Zurich, Calvin and Beza were to Geneva. Calvin has been called "the father of modern biblical scholarship," and his exegetical work is without parallel in the Reformation. Because of the success of his *Institutes of the Christian Religion* Calvin has sometimes been thought of as a man of one book, but he always intended the *Institutes*, which went through eight editions in Latin and five in French during his lifetime, to serve as a guide to the study of the Bible, to show the reader "what he ought especially to seek in Scripture and to what end he ought to relate its contents." Jacob Arminius, who modified several principles of Calvin's theology, recommended his commentaries next to the Bible, for, as he said, Calvin "is incomparable in the interpretation of Scripture."[43] Drawing on his superb knowledge of Greek and Hebrew and his thorough training in humanist rhetoric, Calvin produced commentaries on all of the New Testament books except 2 and 3 John and Revelation. Calvin's Old Testament commentaries originated as sermon and lecture series and include Genesis, Psalms, Hosea, Isaiah,

---

[42]Euan Cameron, *The European Reformation* (Oxford: Oxford University Press, 1991), 120.

[43]Letter to Sebastian Egbert (May 3, 1607), in *Praestantium ac eruditorum virorum epistolae ecclesiasticae et theologicae varii argumenti,* ed. Christiaan Hartsoeker (Amsterdam: Henricus Dendrinus, 1660), 236-37. Quoted in A. M. Hunter, *The Teaching of Calvin* (London: James Clarke, 1950), 20.

minor prophets, Daniel, Jeremiah and Lamentations, a harmony of the last four books of Moses, Ezekiel 1–20, and Joshua. Calvin sought for brevity and clarity in all of his exegetical work. He emphasized the illumination of the Holy Spirit as essential to a proper understanding of the text. Calvin underscored the continuity between the two Testaments (one covenant in two dispensations) and sought to apply the plain or natural sense of the text to the church of his day. In the preface to his own influential commentary on Romans, Karl Barth described how Calvin worked to recover the mind of Paul and make the apostle's message relevant to his day:

> How energetically Calvin goes to work, first scientifically establishing the text ("what stands there?"), then following along the footsteps of its thought; that is to say, he conducts a discussion with it until the wall between the first and the sixteenth centuries becomes transparent, and until there in the first century Paul speaks and here the man of the sixteenth century hears, until indeed the conversation between document and reader becomes concentrated upon the substance (which must be the same now as then).[44]

Beza was elected moderator of Geneva's Company of Pastors after Calvin's death in 1564 and guided the Genevan Reformation over the next four decades. His annotated Latin translation of the Greek New Testament (1556) and his further revisions of the Greek text established his reputation as the leading textual critic of the sixteenth century after Erasmus. Beza completed the translation of Marot's metrical Psalter, which became a centerpiece of Huguenot piety and Reformed church life. Though known for his polemical writings on grace, free will and predestination, Beza's work is marked by a strong pastoral orientation and concern for a Scripture-based spirituality.

Robert Estienne (Stephanus) was a printer-scholar who had served the royal household in Paris. After his conversion to Protestantism, in 1550 he moved to Geneva, where he published a series of notable editions and translations of the Bible. He also produced sermons and commentaries on Job, Ecclesiastes, the Song of Songs, Romans and Hebrews, as well as dictionaries, concordances and a thesaurus of biblical terms. He also published the first editions of the Bible with chapters divided into verses, an innovation that quickly became universally accepted.

The British Reformation. Commentary writing in England and Scotland lagged behind the continental Reformation for several reasons. In 1500, there were only three publishing houses in England compared with more than two hundred on the Continent. A 1408 statute against publishing or reading the Bible in English, stemming from the days of Lollardy, stifled the free flow of ideas, as was seen in the fate of Tyndale. Moreover, the nature of the English Reformation from Henry through Elizabeth provided little stability for the flourishing of biblical scholarship. In the sixteenth century, many "hot-gospel" Protestants in England were edified by the English translations of commentaries and theological writings by the Continental reformers. The influence of Calvin and Beza was felt especially in the Geneva Bible with its "Protestant glosses" of theological notes and references.

---

[44]Karl Barth, *Die Römerbrief* (Zurich: TVZ, 1940), 11, translated by T. H. L. Parker as the epigraph to *Calvin's New Testament Commentaries*, 2nd ed. (Louisville, KY: Westminster John Knox, 1993).

During the later Elizabethan and Stuart church, however, the indigenous English commentary came into its own. Both Anglicans and Puritans contributed to this outpouring of biblical studies. The sermons of Lancelot Andrewes and John Donne are replete with exegetical insights based on a close study of the Greek and Hebrew texts. Among the Reformed authors in England, none was more influential than William Perkins, the greatest of the early Puritan theologians, who published commentaries on Galatians, Jude, Revelation and the Sermon on the Mount (Mt 5–7). John Cotton, one of his students, wrote commentaries on the Song of Songs, Ecclesiastes and Revelation before departing for New England in 1633. The separatist pastor Henry Ainsworth was an outstanding scholar of Hebrew and wrote major commentaries on the Pentateuch, the Psalms and the Song of Songs. In Scotland, Robert Rollock, the first principal of Edinburgh University (1585), wrote numerous commentaries including those on the Psalms, Ephesians, Daniel, Romans, 1 and 2 Thessalonians, John, Colossians and Hebrews. Joseph Mede and Thomas Brightman were leading authorities on Revelation and contributed to the apocalyptic thought of the seventeenth century. Mention should also be made of Archbishop James Ussher, whose *Annals of the Old Testament* was published in 1650. Ussher developed a keen interest in biblical chronology and calculated that the creation of the world had taken place on October 26, 4004 B.C. As late as 1945, the Scofield Reference Bible still retained this date next to Genesis 1:1, but later editions omitted it because of the lack of evidence on which to fix such dates.[45]

Anabaptism. Irena Backus has noted that there was no school of "dissident" exegesis during the Reformation, and the reasons are not hard to find. The radical Reformation was an ill-defined movement that existed on the margins of official church life in the sixteenth century. The denial of infant baptism and the refusal to swear an oath marked radicals as a seditious element in society, and they were persecuted by Protestants and Catholics alike. However, in the RCS we have made an attempt to include some voices of the radical Reformation, especially among the Anabaptists. While the Anabaptists published few commentaries in the sixteenth century, they were avid readers and quoters of the Bible. Numerous exegetical gems can be found in their letters, treatises, martyr acts (especially *The Martyrs' Mirror*), hymns and histories. They placed a strong emphasis on the memorizing of Scripture and quoted liberally from vernacular translations of the Bible. George H. Williams has noted that "many an Anabaptist theological tract was really a beautiful mosaic of Scripture texts."[46] In general, most Anabaptists accepted the apocryphal books as canonical, contrasted outer word and inner spirit with relative degrees of strictness and saw the New Testament as normative for church life and social ethics (witness their pacifism, nonswearing, emphasis on believers' baptism and congregational discipline).

We have noted the Old Testament translation of Ludwig Hätzer, who became an antitrinitarian, and Hans Denck that they published at Worms in 1527. Denck also wrote a notable commentary on Micah. Conrad Grebel belonged to a Greek reading circle in Zurich and came to his Anabaptist convictions while poring over the text of Erasmus's New Testament. The only Anabaptist

---

[45]*The New Scofield Reference Bible* (New York: Oxford University Press, 1967), vi.
[46]George H. Williams, *The Radical Reformation*, 3rd ed. (Kirksville, MO: Sixteenth Century Journal Publishers, 1992), 1247.

leader with university credentials was Balthasar Hubmaier, who was made a doctor of theology (Ingolstadt, 1512) in the same year as Luther. His reflections on the Bible are found in his numerous writings, which include the first catechism of the Reformation (1526), a two-part treatise on the freedom of the will and a major work (*On the Sword*) setting forth positive attitudes toward the role of government and the Christian's place in society. Melchior Hoffman was an apocalyptic seer who wrote commentaries on Romans, Revelation and Daniel 12. He predicted that Christ would return in 1533. More temperate was Pilgram Marpeck, a mining engineer who embraced Anabaptism and traveled widely throughout Switzerland and south Germany, from Strasbourg to Augsburg. His "Admonition of 1542" is the longest published defense of Anabaptist views on baptism and the Lord's Supper. He also wrote many letters that functioned as theological tracts for the congregations he had founded dealing with topics such as the fruits of repentance, the lowliness of Christ and the unity of the church. Menno Simons, a former Catholic priest, became the most outstanding leader of the Dutch Anabaptist movement. His masterpiece was the *Foundation of Christian Doctrine* published in 1540. His other writings include *Meditation on the Twenty-fifth Psalm* (1537); *A Personal Exegesis of Psalm Twenty-five* modeled on the style of Augustine's *Confessions*; *Confession of the Triune God* (1550), directed against Adam Pastor, a former disciple of Menno who came to doubt the divinity of Christ; *Meditations and Prayers for Mealtime* (1557); and the *Cross of the Saints* (1554), an exhortation to faithfulness in the face of persecution. Like many other Anabaptists, Menno emphasized the centrality of discipleship (*Nachfolge*) as a deliberate repudiation of the old life and a radical commitment to follow Jesus as Lord.

Reading Scripture with the Reformers

In 1947, Gerhard Ebeling set forth his thesis that the history of the Christian church is the history of the interpretation of Scripture. Since that time, the place of the Bible in the story of the church has been investigated from many angles. A better understanding of the history of exegesis has been aided by new critical editions and scholarly discussions of the primary sources. The *Cambridge History of the Bible*, published in three volumes (1963–1970), remains a standard reference work in the field. The ACCS built on, and itself contributed to, the recovery of patristic biblical wisdom of both East and West. Beryl Smalley's *The Study of the Bible in the Middle Ages* (1940) and Henri de Lubac's *Medieval Exegesis: The Four Senses of Scripture* (1959) are essential reading for understanding the monastic and scholastic settings of commentary work between Augustine and Luther. The Reformation took place during what has been called "le grand siècle de la Bible."[47] Aided by the tools of Renaissance humanism and the dynamic impetus of Reformation theology (including permutations and reactions against it), the sixteenth century produced an unprecedented number of commentaries on every book in the Bible. Drawing from this vast storehouse of exegetical treasures, the RCS allows us to read Scripture along with the reformers. In doing so, it serves as a practical homiletic and devotional guide to some of the greatest masters of biblical interpretation in the history of the church.

---

[47]J-R. Aarmogathe, ed., *Bible de tous les temps*, 8 vols.; vol. 6, *Le grand siècle de la Bible* (Paris: Beauchesne, 1989).

The RCS gladly acknowledges its affinity with and dependence on recent scholarly investigations of Reformation-era exegesis. Between 1976 and 1990, three international colloquia on the history of biblical exegesis in the sixteenth century took place in Geneva and in Durham, North Carolina.[48] Among those participating in these three gatherings were a number of scholars who have produced groundbreaking works in the study of biblical interpretation in the Reformation. These include Elsie McKee, Irena Backus, Kenneth Hagen, Scott H. Hendrix, Richard A. Muller, Guy Bedouelle, Gerald Hobbs, John B. Payne, Bernard Roussel, Pierre Fraenkel and David C. Steinmetz. Among other scholars whose works are indispensable for the study of this field are Heinrich Bornkamm, Jaroslav Pelikan, Heiko A. Oberman, James S. Preus, T. H. L. Parker, David F. Wright, Tony Lane, John L. Thompson, Frank A. James and Timothy J. Wengert.[49] Among these scholars no one has had a greater influence on the study of Reformation exegesis than David C. Steinmetz. A student of Oberman, he has emphasized the importance of understanding the Reformation in medieval perspective. In addition to important studies on Luther and Staupitz, he has pioneered the method of comparative exegesis showing both continuity and discontinuity between major Reformation figures and the preceding exegetical traditions (see his *Luther in Context* and *Calvin in Context*). From his base at Duke University, he has spawned what might be called a Steinmetz school, a cadre of students and scholars whose work on the Bible in the Reformation era continues to shape the field. Steinmetz serves on the RCS Board of Editorial Advisors, and a number of our volume editors have pursued doctoral studies under his supervision.

In 1980, Steinmetz published "The Superiority of Pre-critical Exegesis," a seminal essay that not only placed Reformation exegesis in the context of the preceding fifteen centuries of the church's study of the Bible but also challenged certain assumptions underlying the hegemony of historical-critical exegesis of the post-Enlightenment academy.[50] Steinmetz helps us to approach the reformers and other precritical interpreters of the Bible on their own terms as faithful witnesses to the church's apostolic tradition. For them, a specific book or pericope had to be understood within the scope of the consensus of the canon. Thus the reformers, no less than the Fathers and the schoolmen, interpreted the hymn of the Johannine prologue about the preexistent Christ in consonance with the creation narrative of Genesis 1. In the same way, Psalm 22, Isaiah 53 and Daniel 7 are seen as part of an overarching storyline that finds ultimate fulfillment in Jesus Christ. Reading the Bible with the resources of the new learning, the reformers challenged the exegetical conclusions of their medieval predecessors at many points. However, unlike Alexander

---

[48]Olivier Fatio and Pierre Fraenkel, eds., *Histoire de l'exégèse au XVIe siècle: texts du colloque international tenu à Genève en 1976* (Geneva: Droz, 1978); David C. Steinmetz, ed., *The Bible in the Sixteenth Century* [Second International Colloquy on the History of Biblical Exegesis in the Sixteenth Century] (Durham: Duke University Press, 1990); Irena Backus and Francis M. Higman, eds., *Théorie et pratique de l'exégèse. Actes du troisième colloque international sur l'histoire de l'exégèse biblique au XVIe siècle, Genève, 31 aôut-2 septembre 1988* (Geneva: Droz, 1990); see also Guy Bedouelle and Bernard Roussel, eds., *Bible de tous les temps*, 8 vols.; vol. 5, *Le temps des Réformes et la Bible* (Paris: Beauchesne, 1989).

[49]For bibliographical references and evaluation of these and other contributors to the scholarly study of Reformation-era exegesis, see Richard A. Muller, "Biblical Interpretation in the Era of the Reformation: The View From the Middle Ages," in *Biblical Interpretation in the Era of the Reformation: Essays Presented to David C. Steinmetz in Honor of His Sixtieth Birthday*, ed. Richard A. Muller and John L. Thompson (Grand Rapids: Eerdmans, 1996), 3-22.

[50]David C. Steinmetz, "The Superiority of Pre-Critical Exegesis," *Theology Today* 37 (1980): 27-38.

Campbell in the nineteenth century, their aim was not to "open the New Testament as if mortal man had never seen it before."[51] Rather, they wanted to do their biblical work as part of an interpretive conversation within the family of the people of God. In the reformers' emphatic turn to the literal sense, which prompted their many blasts against the unrestrained use of allegory, their work was an extension of a similar impulse made by Thomas Aquinas and Nicholas of Lyra.

This is not to discount the radically new insights gained by the reformers in their dynamic engagement with the text of Scripture; nor should we dismiss in a reactionary way the light shed on the meaning of the Bible by the scholarly accomplishments of the past two centuries. However, it is to acknowledge that the church's exegetical tradition is an indispensible aid for the proper interpretation of Scripture. And this means, as Richard Muller has said, that "while it is often appropriate to recognize that traditionary readings of the text are erroneous on the grounds offered by the historical-critical method, we ought also to recognize that the conclusions offered by historical-critical exegesis may themselves be quite erroneous on the grounds provided by the exegesis of the patristic, medieval, and reformation periods."[52] The RCS wishes to commend the exegetical work of the Reformation era as a program of retrieval for the sake of renewal—spiritual réssourcement for believers committed to the life of faith today.

George Herbert was an English pastor and poet who reaped the benefits of the renewal of biblical studies in the age of the Reformation. He referred to the Scriptures as a book of infinite sweetness, "a mass of strange delights," a book with secrets to make the life of anyone good. In describing the various means pastors require to be fully furnished in the work of their calling, Herbert provided a rationale for the history of exegesis and for the Reformation Commentary on Scripture:

> The fourth means are commenters and Fathers, who have handled the places controverted, which the parson by no means refuseth. As he doth not so study others as to neglect the grace of God in himself and what the Holy Spirit teacheth him, so doth he assure himself that God in all ages hath had his servants to whom he hath revealed his Truth, as well as to him; and that as one country doth not bear all things that there may be a commerce, so neither hath God opened or will open all to one, that there may be a traffic in knowledge between the servants of God for the planting both of love and humility. Wherefore he hath one comment[ary] at least upon every book of Scripture, and ploughing with this, and his own meditations, he enters into the secrets of God treasured in the holy Scripture.[53]

Timothy George
General Editor

---

[51]Alexander Campbell, *Memoirs of Alexander Campbell*, ed. Robert Richardson (Cincinnati: Standard Publishing Company, 1872), 97.
[52]Richard A. Muller and John L. Thompson, "The Significance of Precritical Exegesis: Retrospect and Prospect," in *Biblical Interpretation in the Era of the Reformation: Essays Presented to David C. Steinmetz in Honor of His Sixtieth Birthday*, ed. Richard A. Muller and John L. Thompson (Grand Rapids: Eerdmans, 1996), 342.
[53]George Herbert, *The Complete English Poems* (London: Penguin, 1991), 205.

INTRODUCTION TO 1-2 SAMUEL, 1-2 KINGS, 1-2 CHRONICLES

Samuel, Kings and Chronicles: Enduring Value and Depth

The six books studied in this volume contain some of the greatest characters and moments of Scripture. Here are prophets like Samuel, Nathan, Elijah and Elisha, inspiring saints like Hannah and Jonathan, and infamous villains like Ahab and Jezebel. These books describe the lives and works of the kings of Israel and Judah, especially the first three: Saul, David and Solomon. Here, too, are the timeless stories of David and Goliath, Solomon's wisdom and Elijah's chariots of fire. Beyond such a "greatest hits" list are even more gems, including Abigail and Nabal, the witch of En-dor, the steadfast prophet Micaiah, the prophetess Huldah and righteous kings like Jehoshaphat, Hezekiah and Josiah. The biblical books of 1–2 Samuel, 1–2 Kings and 1–2 Chronicles are indeed spiritual and literary treasures.

Jesus of Nazareth and the writers of the New Testament also knew these books well. Each of the Synoptic Gospels (Mt 12:1-8; Mk 2:23-28; Lk 6:1-5) includes Jesus telling the story of David and his army eating the bread of the Presence in 1 Samuel 21. In the Gospel of Luke (Lk 4:16-30), Jesus scandalously invokes Elijah's miraculous deeds for the widow of Zarephath in 1 Kings 17 and Elisha's healing of Naaman in 2 Kings 5 to foreshadow Jesus' mission to the Gentiles. And both the Gospels of Matthew (Mt 23:33-36) and of Luke (Lk 11:49-51) mention 2 Chronicles 24, where, according to Jesus' comments in the Gospels, the priest Zechariah was "murdered between the sanctuary and the altar" as a holy and unjustly persecuted martyr. Such references only begin to plumb the depths of the New Testament writers' frequent discussion of the kingdom of Israel, its naming of Jesus as the "Son of David" and its many other allusions to the kings and prophets of Israel. Further, the importance of these books for the New Testament becomes exceedingly clear when we recall that Jesus identified his crucified and risen body with the holy temple promised to David and first built by Solomon. The histories and theologies of each of the books in this volume deeply informed the theology and witness of the New Testament and the early church.

In terms of literary style and theological content, 1–2 Samuel, 1–2 Kings and 1–2 Chronicles are enduring and endearing because they present complex people, themes and events. While cherished images like David the shepherd boy, Solomon the wise ruler or Elijah the righteous prophet capture the popular imagination, there are deeper struggles and questions lingering below the surface. In addition to being a humble shepherd boy, David was also a shrewd and cunning leader from the beginning, with a reign that revealed deep character flaws, including his adultery with Bathsheba, the murder of noble Uriah and a civil war against his cherished son Absalom. In the next generation, Solomon—despite his proverbial wisdom—could not overcome idolatry and the misuse of power, so that the kingdom quickly fell apart under his successors. And though Elijah is one of the great holy men of the Bible, he was also—as the epistle of James says—"a man with a nature like ours" (Jas 5:17), intimately familiar with fear, disappointment and despair. Irony, tragedy, humor and pathos fill the narratives of these six books and invite readers into deep reflection on the many ups and downs of sharing a personal and communal life with God.

Reformation Interpretations of Biblical History

Commentators of the Reformation era were well aware of these complexities. Readers of this volume will be struck by our commentators' close attention to detail and nuance. From the beginning of the sixteenth century onward, Christian scholars in Europe had access to critical editions of the Hebrew Scriptures and to quality grammatical aids.[1] They also knew the historical-critical reality that Samuel and Kings provide the narrative peak and denouement of what is called the Former Prophets in the Jewish tradition (later referred to by modern critical scholars as the "Deuteronomistic History"), that cycle of books based on Deuteronomy that includes Joshua, Judges, Samuel and Kings.[2] The internal continuity of 1–2 Samuel and 1–2 Kings was also clear in the fact that they were named together as the four books of Kings in the Greek Septuagint, a tradition the influential Latin Vulgate continued.

Although 1–2 Chronicles relate many of the same stories as 1–2 Samuel and 1–2 Kings, sixteenth- and seventeenth-century interpreters recognized that the Chronicler's narratives share a literary heritage with Ezra and Nehemiah rather than with the Former Prophets. Reformation-era scholars, therefore, knew very well that some of the same biblical stories had been told in two intentionally different ways. Additionally, although the sixteenth century became a watershed epoch in the history of biblical interpretation, reforming exegetes did not forget or neglect commentaries and other interpretive aids from earlier times. Readers of this volume will therefore discover that our commentators not only referred to Scripture but also to interpreters from across the centuries, including early church writers and medieval Christian and Jewish scholars, to advance their understanding of the text. Through their own attention to detail and their use of existing resources, scholars of the Reformation era were able to study, interpret and apply the teachings found in Samuel, Kings and Chronicles with a high level of sophistication and self-awareness.

---

[1]See Stephen G. Burnett, "The Strange Career of the *Biblia Rabbinica* among Christian Hebraists, 1517–1620," in *Shaping the Bible in the Reformation: Books, Scholars and Their Readers in the Sixteenth Century*, ed. Bruce Gordon and Matthew McLean (Leiden: Brill, 2012), 63-84.

[2]In the Hebrew Scriptures, 1–2 Samuel and 1–2 Kings stand within the prophetic books (*Nevi'im*) and 1–2 Chronicles belong to the Writings (*Ketuvim*). Samuel, Kings and Chronicles were each written as one book in the Hebrew and later divided into two books each when translated into the Greek (Septuagint).

Respect for the Bible as holy and Spirit-breathed Scripture did not prevent Reformation interpreters from careful and critical textual study. On the contrary, reverence for the Word of God pushed them to think seriously about biblical texts, especially when it came to more challenging passages. They did this in a number of ways, beginning with close grammatical and historical study. For instance, the second-generation Lutheran theologian Lucas Osiander recognizes inconsistencies between Samuel, Kings and Chronicles about names and places, but he does not view these as a theological problem. Instead, Osiander asserts that the Chronicler served the church by doing the best work possible with the best available, but ultimately inaccurate sources.[3] Martin Luther puts it more bluntly:

> The author of the books of Kings goes a hundred thousand steps beyond the author of the books of Chronicles. For he has described the most important and special events, passing over rocky and unimportant matters. If at any place Kings varies from Chronicles, I trust the author of Kings more than the author of Chronicles. And so I agree with neither what Jerome nor Nicholas of Lyra says—that Kings provokes many questions, unlike Chronicles. Kings is to be greatly preferred.[4]

John Calvin, when confronted with hard passages about God's actions or emotions, developed a concept of accommodation to emphasize that the cultural complexities inherent to Scripture's way of speaking must be understood in the broader context of the divine message of grace. Relevant for this volume, Calvin raises this point in his *Institutes* when considering the issue of God's repentance, a question especially present in the rise and fall of King Saul.[5] On the question of biblical authority and hard textual questions, the Wittenberg Reformer Johannes Bugenhagen in his 1550 commentary on Jonah quotes Augustine of Hippo.

> For Augustine wrote most blessedly to St. Jerome something that they even have in their papal decrees, distinction 9: He says, "I have learned to yield this respect and honor [of authority] only to the canonical books of Scripture: of these alone do I most firmly believe that the authors were completely free from error. And if in these writings I am perplexed by anything which appears to me opposed to truth, I do not hesitate to suppose that either the manuscript is faulty, or the translator has not caught the meaning of what was said, or I myself have failed to understand it."[6]

Though they were without many of the historical-critical tools of today's scholarship, Reformation-era interpreters were by no means naive about the complexities of biblical texts. Instead, for the sake of good preaching and teaching, they used the best sources, grammatical aids, scriptural commentaries and logical skills possible to derive clear interpretations. This task often meant gathering smaller individual points of teaching (*loci*) within a passage in order to discern the broader meaning (*scopus*) of a chapter or book. Philipp Melanchthon employs this "*loci* method" in his *Loci*

---

[3] See Osiander's comments on 1 Chron 3, p. 532.
[4] WATR 1:364-65, no. 765.
[5] As in Calvin's discussion of God's "repentance," LCC 20:227 (CO 2:165-66); *Institutes* 1.17.13.
[6] Johannes Bugenhagen, *Ionas Propheta expositus* (Wittenberg: Veit Kreutzer,1550), V8r; quoted from Martin Lohrmann, *Bugenhagen's Jonah: Biblical Interpretation as Public Theology* (Minneapolis: Lutheran University Press, 2012), 184-85; citing one of Augustine's letters to Jerome, NPNF 1:350 (PL 33:277).

communes rerum theologicarum (1521), a work in which he let these smaller touchstones (*loci communes*) lead him through the main points that Paul conveys in the letter to the Romans.

The famous Reformation slogan *sola Scriptura* expresses that desire to go deep into the truths and wonders of the Christian faith through the careful study of Scripture. Contemporary readers should be aware that in the sixteenth and seventeenth centuries, *sola Scriptura* was not used as an excuse to put an end to critical thinking; indeed, such an approach would have been dismissed as unbiblical and unpersuasive by theologians of all confessional backgrounds. While some theologians were more confident of human reason's ability to come to edifying scriptural conclusions than others, nevertheless they all engaged Scripture with the idea that the good use of reason and critical thinking was essential to good biblical interpretation. Therefore, trusting in the triune God of Scripture and following the rule of faith in their various contexts, interpreters sought to gain wisdom and edification even in the Bible's most mysterious passages by applying their hearts and their minds to spiritual truth.[7]

Diverse Confessional Perspectives

While the commentators collected here each sought to be faithful to the "Spirit that gives life" in their work, their diversity of perspectives is immediately apparent. Thus an exciting aspect of this volume is the chance to study why various commentators chose to comment on the themes and *loci* that they did. Although the goal of all writers was to share good biblical teaching with their audiences, they often did this in different ways. For instance: was David the ideal prophet, priest and king whose model should be the guide and norm for all godly leaders? Or was he a man of blood, war and sin, whose greatest example for later generations are his moments of humble faith, sincere repentance and servant leadership? Interpreters colored David's successes and failures differently, depending on the theological points they viewed as most important in the biblical text itself. Some upheld David as the godly ruler par excellence, while others viewed him in his best and worst moments as a great example of *simul iustus et peccator* ("simultaneously righteous and sinner"). In either case, interpreters aimed to be faithful to Scripture and persuasive to their audiences.

For this reason, readers should be aware that this volume is not a collection of answers. Instead, it is more like an invitation to listen to theological and exegetical conversations from the Reformation era. Sometimes these conversations included the (relatively) confessionally neutral discussion of grammatical points and relevant cross-references to other parts of the Bible. Some of the conversations readers will overhear in this volume, however, took place amid the more heated debates of the period. If such conversations never happened in person, they often found written expression. For instance, the Augsburg Confession invoked David as a good example to follow as a godly king but not as a source of holy mediation or intercession, a position based

---

[7]On the rule of faith, what it is and how it is practiced, see further RCS OT 7:xlvi-lii; Kathryn Greene-McCreight, "Literal Sense" and "Rule of Faith," in *Dictionary for Theological Interpretation of the Bible*, ed. Kevin J. Vanhoozer (Grand Rapids: Baker Academic, 2005), 455-56, 703-4; Mark Sheridan, *Language for God in Patristic Tradition: Wrestling with Biblical Anthropomorphism* (Downers Grove, IL: IVP Academic, 2015), 217-36.

on Scripture's descriptions of David as a man who sinned and required forgiveness.[8] In another example, when addressing antinomian reformers who wanted to abrogate the authority of the Hebrew Scriptures, the Anglican Thirty-Nine Articles reaffirmed the Old Testament writings as divinely inspired works whose moral commandments ought to remain binding.[9] Working in this theological context, English commentators therefore often emphasized the lasting moral and spiritual wisdom to be found in these biblical histories. As a third example of how these books influenced public discourse, John Calvin and his followers were involved in written controversies with Lutherans about how best to interpret David and the "messianic psalms."[10] Although Calvin tended to prefer a more historical or moral reading of these psalms and the Lutherans tended to argue for a more christological interpretation, all parties sought to offer interpretations that were faithful to the text itself and to its spiritual meaning that gives life (2 Cor 3:6). This volume, therefore, offers a fascinating look into the relationship between biblical interpretation and the development of church doctrine, practice and polity. While all interpreters aimed for faithfulness to the text, their respective encounters with the text led to different—biblically grounded!—insights, which bore different fruits.

These general confessional differences quickly become evident in the comments on Samuel, Kings and Chronicles. Reformed and Puritan writers commented much more on matters of discipline and holy living than Lutheran writers, who saw justification by faith and the theology of the cross almost everywhere they looked in these historical books of the Old Testament.[11] For their part, Anabaptist writers brought their interests in knowing and experiencing spiritual truth to their exegesis. Discerning readers, therefore, will certainly find instances of various streams of Protestantism, each of which imports their theological preferences into their exegesis. This fact does not reduce interpreters to mere representatives of their confessional traditions or accuse them of hand-picking their biblical theology; on the contrary, it reveals the large extent to which confessional diversity was itself rooted in a variety of encounters with Scripture and came from many different ways of reading the same holy texts.

Using This Resource

Recognizing that this volume offers a plurality of perspectives rather than a collection of "right answers" is critical to using this resource well. Whether in sermons, commentaries, devotional

---

[8]BoC 58.

[9]*Creeds* 3:491-92.

[10]See further G. Sujin Pak, *The Judaizing Calvin: Sixteenth-Century Debates over the Messianic Psalms* (Oxford: Oxford University Press, 2010).

[11]Because human reason and expectations through sin have inverted God's works and words, theologians of the cross assert that, rooted in the death, resurrection and ascension of God's Son, we must turn things right side up. "Theologians of glory call evil good and good evil; theologians of the cross call things what they really are" (Heidelberg Disputation, 1518; WA 1:354; LW 31:45). Human beings are inclined to think that by their efforts they can progress toward perfection and relationship with God. Theologians of the cross, however, know that progress in perfection and relationship with God are impossible apart from union with the crucified and resurrected Lord. See further Robert Kolb, "Luther on the Theology of the Cross," *Lutheran Quarterly* 16, no. 1 (2002): 443-66; Timothy J. Wengert, "'Peace, Peace . . . Cross, Cross': Reflections on How Martin Luther Relates the Theology of the Cross to Suffering," *Theology Today* 59, no. 2 (2002): 190-205.

books or theological tracts, Reformation-era authors wrote in order to clarify their audience's understanding of Scripture and to help people apply it to their lives as beneficially as possible. Many of these authors, of course, were either implicitly or expressly writing to refute competing interpretations. And yet here we have scandalously set them side by side as equals, without judgment. We especially hope that readers will avoid the temptation of using this volume as an updated type of *Glossa ordinaria*, that is, as a collection of diverse sources that somehow presents a unified and internally coherent interpretation of 1–2 Samuel, 1–2 Kings and 1–2 Chronicles.[12]

Beyond this caveat, however, great benefits abound in this volume. First, many of the insights and interpretations presented are incredibly perceptive, instructive and relevant for contemporary study, preaching and teaching. Second, readers will gain a deeper appreciation for the various theological streams of the Reformation era by paying attention to the way they interpreted Scripture. Third, in a manner that resonates with the Reformation slogan *ad fontes* ("back to the sources"), this project invites readers to enjoy direct study of the Scriptures themselves, the "pure, clear fountain of Israel."[13]

Far more interesting and edifying than looking for "right answers," therefore, is this volume's invitation to read the Bible with a wide range of church reformers. In such an environment, readers will have a chance to learn what these interpreters found inspiring and instructive about the people of Israel and their kings. Readers will also get to compare differing perspectives from biblical history about matters like church and state, with insights coming both from those who knew a magisterial Reformation (as in the Lutheran, Reformed and Anglican experiences) and from those who were on the margins of political authority (as was true of Anabaptists and English Dissenters). Readers will also get a chance to consider for themselves the relative advantages of emphasizing moral purity in these texts (as did the Puritans) or the *simul iustus et peccator* paradox of the Lutherans.

Most of all, readers will enjoy reflecting with these commentators on the central question of what it means to belong to the people of God. The insights may be different—perhaps even in opposition to each other—but they can certainly enrich contemporary understandings of the Scriptures for the sake of faithful Christian study and witness today. Here readers are surrounded by a cloud of witnesses who each testify to the enduring value of Samuel, Kings and Chronicles for piety, proclamation and practice today.

A Structural Overview of This Volume

Of the six biblical books studied in this volume, 1–2 Samuel received the most attention from Reformation writers. Why? These are the two books that most fully describe the life of King David, a central figure for the entire Bible. Although Reformation-era commentators greatly criticized David for his moral failures, they also lauded him as the greatest of kings. David personally embodies

---

[12]On the complex medieval use of the *Glossa ordinaria*, see Richard A. Muller, *Post-Reformation Reformed Dogmatics: The Rise and Development of Reformed Orthodoxy, ca. 1520 to ca. 1725*, 4 vols., 2nd ed. (Grand Rapids: Baker Academic, 2003), esp. 2:31-37.

[13]BoC 527.

the promises made to Abraham, the teachings given to Moses, the inheritance given to the people of Israel and the promise of a redeemer. His story provides the heart and climax of the Former Prophets. The dramatic narratives about David's life enjoy additional spiritual depth through their relationship with the Psalms, many of which were "about," "for" or "by" David, according to the Hebrew headings.[14] Finally, David takes an exalted place for Christian interpreters as both the forefather of Jesus Christ and as a type of Christ himself. That is, through the Holy Spirit at work in David's faith and leadership, the stories and psalms connected to David become stories and psalms of the eternal Christ at work in the history of God's chosen people. Because of David's immense importance for the Christian church, many writers of the Reformation era embraced these books, either in whole or in part, producing an abundance of riches reflected in these pages.

In contrast, those who published works on Kings and Chronicles, particularly Chronicles, were most often commenting on them as part of larger studies on the entire Bible, the Old Testament or the so-called historical books. This has presented the editorial challenge of not having the same range of sources available for 1–2 Kings and 1–2 Chronicles as for 1–2 Samuel. This potential problem brings the corresponding blessing that readers get the chance to know a few interpreters better. For this reason, this volume's work on 1–2 Kings is also a treasure, as we have been able to highlight writers whose works are not widely known or available in English.

While they are interesting and valuable in their own right or when paired with Ezra–Nehemiah, the books of 1–2 Chronicles repeat many of the same narratives found in Samuel and Kings. Indeed, the title most commonly used by Reformation-era writers for Chronicles was *Paralipomenon*, a Greek word from antiquity that means "the things left over" or "of things passed over."[15] With such a long history of being overlooked or overshadowed, it is not surprising that fewer early modern interpreters wrote commentaries on these two books. For those who did venture into writing commentaries on 1–2 Chronicles, their sparse comments often conformed to the nature of the text itself, which at times employs lists and genealogies rather than narrative writing.

Still, we have secured comments for each pericope in 1–2 Chronicles, with some sections containing vigorous and detailed discussions due to the theological richness evoked by the passage at hand. For readers who would like to explore these sections in more depth, we have followed the example of the fifth volume in the Ancient Christian Commentary on Scripture, referring readers of 1–2 Chronicles to parallel passages in 1–2 Samuel and 1–2 Kings.

Introduction to the Commentators

The two theological giants of the sixteenth century, Martin Luther and John Calvin, appear with some regularity in this volume. Though Luther translated the entire Bible and lectured on many of its books, he did not publish commentaries on any of the historical books of the Old Testa-

---

[14]See further RCS OT 7:31.

[15]Although 1 and 2 Chronicles were originally written as one book in Hebrew (like Samuel and Kings), they were divided into "Things Left Over A" and "Things Left Over B" in the Septuagint, that is, *Paralipomenon A* and *Paralipomenon B*. See Sebastian Münster's comment, p. 519.

ment. Nevertheless, because of his voluminous knowledge of Scripture and his exegetical practice of "interpreting Scripture with Scripture," we have culled many excerpts from other writings. Calvin, however, preached on 1 Samuel (1561–1562) and 2 Samuel 1–13 (1562–1563). Although some of these sermons have been ably translated into English, they may be largely unfamiliar to readers. For this reason, we have proudly featured Calvin's sermons on 2 Samuel in this volume.

Similarly, Philipp Melanchthon—the great "teacher of Germany" and a prolific exegete—appears here primarily through excerpts from various editions of his *Loci communes*. Instead of leaning on Luther, Calvin and Melanchthon for this volume, we have embraced the goal set by this series of drawing extensively from the writings of reformers whose works have been much less studied or are not as widely available in English.

Among Lutheran reformers, we have included many comments from Luther's pastor and colleague Johannes Bugenhagen, as well as Lucas Osiander and Viktorin Strigel. In their comments on Samuel, Kings and Chronicles, Lutherans consistently emphasized the primacy of faith as the saving relationship between God and human beings. Through this trusting relationship of faith, God gives the righteousness of Jesus Christ to sinners who contribute nothing but themselves and their trust, a faith planted by the Holy Spirit.[16] Here Christian discipleship is not merely a matter of imitating the saints in righteousness or good works but (like David) of returning to God daily in repentance and faith, confession and thanksgiving. With the theology of the cross as a model, Lutheran interpreters could view the fall of Israel and Jerusalem not only as signs of God's judgment against sin but also as the way God would bring a more complete victory through the promised Messiah.

Alongside Lutheranism, the Continental Reformed tradition stands as perhaps the most intellectually robust stream of early Protestantism. Indeed, the majority of comments in this volume come from capable and learned Reformed commentators, particularly Konrad Pellikan and Johannes Piscator. Pellikan taught biblical languages in Zurich and wrote the first Hebrew grammar in Europe. While he regularly cribs others' work—for example, Martin Bucer's Psalms commentary, Desiderius Erasmus's New Testament paraphrases and Johannes Oecolampadius's Hebrews commentary—he does not appear to do so for his coverage of Samuel, Kings and Chronicles. Piscator compiled Latin commentaries on every book in the Bible. These commentaries contain three parts: first a "logical analysis" of each chapter in the spirit of the popular Ramist school of thought (based on the teachings of the Huguenot Peter Ramus); then linguistic annotations on specific words used in each verse; and finally ethical and theological observations that highlighted the moral qualities of the people and actions discussed in each verse. The wide influence of Pellikan and Piscator as Hebraists makes them valuable contributors to this volume.

This volume also includes select excerpts from marginal commentary on the Geneva Bible as well as several different books of annotations: Giovanni Diodati's *Annotationes in Biblia*, the *Dutch Annotations* and the *English Annotations*. Often overlooked in scholarship of the period, they provide a great contrast to individual commentaries, because they reflect joint ventures sanc-

---

[16]BoC 355.

---

tioned by local churches or regions for teaching and instruction.[17] Popular readers of the Bible as well as clergy used these resources as an aid to interpretation, especially "upon all the hard places" of Scripture.[18] These works typically offer brief remarks on linguistic, theological or historical features of the text.

Among the English reformers, we have featured two prominently: Andrew Willet and John Mayer. An Anglican priest, Willet had read widely of the Christian tradition before him and incorporated the comments of many previous interpreters into his own writing. His commentaries on 1–2 Samuel follow the *loci* method and cover a wide range of theological, linguistic, historical and ethical matters. While serving as a pastor, Mayer wrote a commentary on every book of the Bible. Like Willet, he made ample use of previous historians and interpreters such as Josephus, Augustine, Chrysostom, Calvin and Peter Martyr Vermigli. He intertwined his commentaries on 1–2 Kings and 1–2 Chronicles as a historical harmony.

With respect to Radical and Anabaptist writers, none of them published commentaries on any of the books included in this volume. Indeed, commentaries by Anabaptists—especially on the Old Testament—are a rarity given their focus on the New Testament, not to mention the persecution and life-threatening situations many of their most learned theologians endured. Despite this lack of a full-length commentary on Samuel, Kings or Chronicles, it is clear that the Anabaptists cared deeply for these books. In this volume well-known Radicals, such as Menno Simons, Hans Denck, Balthasar Hubmaier and Dirk Philips, explore themes related to David and to God's promise of an everlasting posterity.

The overwhelming majority of comments in this volume intentionally come from Protestant theologians and pastors. However, we also included comments from pre-Tridentine Catholics, particularly Alonso Tostado and Cardinal Cajetan. Tostado, the learned bishop of Ávila, sought and enacted reform in the Catholic Church in Spain. His commentaries employed the *quaestio* method, in which he commented on each chapter by means of dozens of theological and moral questions.[19] Cajetan, an equally scholarly churchman, wrote commentaries on each of the books of the Bible, except Song of Songs and Revelation. He especially focused on linguistic and grammatical matters.

Finally, although official commentaries serve as the foundation of each of the books in this volume, we have incorporated many comments from sixteenth- and seventeenth-century publications that remain outside of the genre of commentary. Some of the authors of these works are generally well known, including writers like the English Reformer William Tyndale, the Swiss reformer Heinrich Bullinger, the Dutch theologian Jacobus Arminius and the Anglican bishop Lancelot Andrewes. But others, such as the French jurist Lambert Daneau and the English clergyman Thomas Adams, remain more obscure. In this regard, intermittent comments from both

---

[17]The victors at the Synod of Dordrecht commissioned the *Dutch Annotations*; the Westminster Assembly, the *English Annotations*. Rather than reflecting an original work, the *Dutch Annotations* and *English Annotations* repurpose commentary from well-known figures such as Calvin, Beza and Diodati.

[18]Lloyd E. Berry, ed., *The Geneva Bible: A Facsimile of the 1560 Edition* (Peabody, MA: Hendrickson, 2007), 12.

[19]Because Tostado lived several generations before reformers like Luther, we have not included as many of his incredibly insightful comments as we otherwise would have.

renowned and less recognized reformers appear throughout this volume. Indeed, they complement well the more sustained interpretation from those who wrote biblical commentaries on these historical books.

❖   ❖   ❖

In 1532, Luther wrote a glowing preface for a new commentary on 1 Samuel.[20] He commends this resource as a model for answering the thorny question, What does history, particularly this ancient history, have to do with us today? Or, put differently, why should we read this history?

> [Justus Menius] has referred everything back to the fount and source, teaching that the faith of the saints toward God is the preeminent thing in the histories. . . . You will see that these histories are being reborn and renovated through the use of faith, as if through a baptism of their own, and that they live for us in our own age—or, rather, forever—and, with their magnificent and most glorious examples of faith they serve usefully for instruction, for argument, for teaching, for consolation, indeed, for everything for which, as Paul writes, the word of faith is powerful. For what is the sacred history but a visible word or a work of faith that teaches us by event and deed what the Scriptures elsewhere transmit in word and speech?[21]

We need these stories, so we know that we are not alone in our suffering and doubting, in our rejoicing and believing. By the example and in the company of others we are stirred up and strengthened in our faith in God's promises. Others have been there before, are there now and will be there in the future. Believers, separated by space and time, are united in Christ by his Spirit. And together they are instructed, corrected and consoled in Scripture.

Derek Cooper
Martin J. Lohrmann

---

[20]Justus Menius, *In Samuelis Librum Priorem enarratio* (Wittenberg: Johannes Lufft, 1532).
[21]LW 60:9 (WA 30,3:539-40); citing 2 Tim 3:16-17. Luther praised Menius's volume as "an example of how to handle [the sacred histories] skillfully according to the analogy of faith" (LW 60:10; WA 30,3:540; citing Rom 12:6).

COMMENTARY ON 1 SAMUEL

OVERVIEW: The reformers regard Samuel not only as a prophet but also as the last of the judges of Israel, thereby serving as a bridge between the era of the judges and that of the kings. According to these interpreters, the first part of 1 Samuel focuses on the desire of the Israelites to secure a king like the surrounding nations. Due to their lack of trust in God, the first king of Israel was a tyrant, while the second king, David, serves as a figure of the Messiah.

Prolegomena: What This Book Is About

THE FOUR BOOKS OF KINGS, THAT IS, SAMUEL AND KINGS. SEBASTIAN MÜNSTER: The four books of Kings are only two books in Hebrew, namely the book of Samuel and the book of Kings. Both of these books the Latin translators have divided into two books. We too will follow these translators, except that the first and second books we will call First and Second Samuel; the third and fourth books we will name First and Second Kings. THE TEMPLE OF THE LORD: 1 SAMUEL 1.[1]

BOOK OF PROPHETS. LUCAS OSIANDER: The first book of Samuel, as it is called, teaches not only that the majority of this book was written by Samuel, as can be observed from 1 Chronicles 29, but also the deeds of this same prophet. For this Samuel was the last judge or governor of the people of Israel. Until that time the judges had ruled; afterward the Israelites asked

to receive a king. For this reason, because the kings are described in the later parts of this book, we also call this book the First Book of Kings. . . . In Matthew 12, Jesus cites this book about David and the bread of the Presence. And Paul recounted the history of these books in Acts 13. The second book speaks especially clearly of Christ when it tells the promises to David. Many examples of divine sovereignty over against the impious are displayed, as are converse examples of the goodness of God's mercy to the pious. From these examples we should learn to fear God, to trust in him with our whole heart and to love him from our soul. ANNOTATIONS ON 1 SAMUEL.[2]

SAMUEL DID NOT WRITE THE WHOLE BOOK. CARDINAL CAJETAN: The title of both this book and the one that follows is Samuel, from the teachers of the Jews, who is initially discussed in this book. The book is believed to have been written by Samuel in the first part; however, it is clear that Samuel himself did not write about the events after his death. COMMENTARY ON 1 SAMUEL.[3]

TEMPLATE FOR GOD'S PEOPLE. GENEVA BIBLE: According to Deuteronomy 17:14, God ordained that when the Israelites should reside in the land of Canaan, he would appoint them a king. Consequently, this first book of Samuel narrates the state of this people under their first

[1]Münster, *Miqdaš YHWH*, 514.

[2]Osiander, *Liber Iosue*, 271-72; citing 1 Chron 29:29-30; Mt 12:3-4.

[3]Cajetan, *Opera Omnia in Sacrae Scripturae Expositionem*, 2:75.

king, King Saul. However, contrary to God's timing, the people were not content with the current government God had erected, and so demanded a king so that the Israelites might be like the other nations, which the Israelites believed to be safer since they had a king. The Israelites did not ask for a king so that they could better serve God under a godly person who represented Jesus Christ, the true deliverer. Therefore God gave them a tyrant and a hypocrite to rule over them so they might learn that a human king is not sufficient to defend them. Rather, only a ruler who was empowered and helped by God could do so. Therefore, God punished the ingratitude of his people, and he sent them continual wars both at home and abroad. And because Saul, who was not truly worthy of the office of king, did not acknowledge God's mercy toward him but rather disposed of the Word of God and was not zealous for God's glory, he was put down by the voice of God. In his place, David, the true figure of the Messiah, was placed on the throne. Indeed, David's patience, modesty, constancy, persecution by open enemies, false friends and lying flatterers are left to the church, and to every member of the body of Christ, as a template for their vocations as God's people. ARGUMENT OF 1 SAMUEL.[4]

---

[4]*Geneva Bible* (1560), 121r*.

1:1-28 THE BIRTH AND DEDICATION OF SAMUEL

¹There was a certain man of Ramathaim-zophim of the hill country of Ephraim whose name was Elkanah the son of Jeroham, son of Elihu, son of Tohu, son of Zuph, an Ephrathite. ²He had two wives. The name of the one was Hannah, and the name of the other, Peninnah. And Peninnah had children, but Hannah had no children.

³Now this man used to go up year by year from his city to worship and to sacrifice to the Lord of hosts at Shiloh, where the two sons of Eli, Hophni and Phinehas, were priests of the Lord. ⁴On the day when Elkanah sacrificed, he would give portions to Peninnah his wife and to all her sons and daughters. ⁵But to Hannah he gave a double portion, because he loved her, though the Lord had closed her womb.ᵃ ⁶And her rival used to provoke her grievously to irritate her, because the Lord had closed her womb. ⁷So it went on year by year. As often as she went up to the house of the Lord, she used to provoke her. Therefore Hannah wept and would not eat. ⁸And Elkanah, her husband, said to her, "Hannah, why do you weep? And why do you not eat? And why is your heart sad? Am I not more to you than ten sons?"

⁹After they had eaten and drunk in Shiloh, Hannah rose. Now Eli the priest was sitting on the seat beside the doorpost of the temple of the Lord. ¹⁰She was deeply distressed and prayed to the Lord and wept bitterly. ¹¹And she vowed a vow and said, "O Lord of hosts, if you will indeed look on the affliction of your servant and remember me and not forget your servant, but will give to your servant a son, then I will give him to the Lord all the days of his life, and no razor shall touch his head."

¹²As she continued praying before the Lord, Eli observed her mouth. ¹³Hannah was speaking in her heart; only her lips moved, and her voice was not heard. Therefore Eli took her to be a drunken woman. ¹⁴And Eli said to her, "How long will you go on being drunk? Put your wine away from you." ¹⁵But Hannah answered, "No, my lord, I am a woman troubled in spirit. I have drunk neither wine nor strong drink, but I have been pouring out my soul before the Lord. ¹⁶Do not regard your servant as a worthless woman, for all along I have been speaking out of my great anxiety and vexation." ¹⁷Then Eli answered, "Go in peace, and the God of Israel grant your petition that you have made to him." ¹⁸And she said, "Let your servant find favor in your eyes." Then the woman went her way and ate, and her face was no longer sad.

¹⁹They rose early in the morning and worshiped before the Lord; then they went back to their house at Ramah. And Elkanah knew Hannah his wife, and the Lord remembered her. ²⁰And in due time Hannah conceived and bore a son, and she called his name Samuel, for she said, "I have asked for him from the Lord."ᵇ

²¹The man Elkanah and all his house went up to offer to the Lord the yearly sacrifice and to pay his vow. ²²But Hannah did not go up, for she said to her husband, "As soon as the child is weaned, I will bring him, so that he may appear in the presence of the Lord and dwell there forever." ²³Elkanah her husband said to her, "Do what seems best to you; wait until you have weaned him; only, may the Lord establish his word." So the woman remained and nursed her son until she weaned him. ²⁴And when she had weaned him, she took him up with her, along with a three-year-old bull,ᶜ an ephahᵈ of flour, and a skin of wine, and she brought him to the house of the Lord at Shiloh. And the child was young. ²⁵Then they slaughtered the bull, and they brought the child to Eli. ²⁶And she said, "Oh, my lord! As you live, my lord, I am the woman who was standing here in your presence, praying to the Lord. ²⁷For this child I prayed, and the Lord has granted me my petition that I made to him. ²⁸Therefore I have lent him to the Lord. As long as he lives, he is lent to the Lord."

And he worshiped the Lord there.

---

a Syriac; the meaning of the Hebrew is uncertain. Septuagint *And, although he loved Hannah, he would give Hannah only one portion, because the Lord had closed her womb*   b *Samuel* sounds like the Hebrew for *heard of God*   c Dead Sea Scroll, Septuagint, Syriac; Masoretic Text *three bulls*   d An *ephah* was about 3/5 bushel or 22 liters

OVERVIEW: The reformers concentrate on Elkanah's polygamy, a sensitive topic for some of the commentators on account of their association with rulers who sometimes aspired to having more than one wife. Both Bucer and Melanchthon, for instance, attended the marriage of Philip of Hesse (1504–1567) to a second wife in 1540, and Luther's role in the bigamous union incited controversy.[1] Bugenhagen interprets Elkanah's marriage to two women as a spiritual mystery indicating two responses to faith: hypocrisy and belief. Other interpreters criticize the cultural practice of polygamy among biblical patriarchs. Elkanah, however, is recognized as a just man who worships God faithfully. More importantly, Hannah is regarded as the ideal woman who trusted in God despite hardship. Her sincere prayer for a child is answered by God, but the reformers, opposed to the vows of parents who dedicated their children as oblates in medieval monasteries, argue that Hannah's entrusting of little Samuel to Eli is not a perpetual vow.

1:1-2 Polygamy

ELKANAH'S TWO WIVES. JOHANNES BUGENHAGEN: The mystery of these two wives is the same as Hagar and Sarah, about whom you read in Genesis and in the epistle to the Galatians. Furthermore, see how thoroughly this point is made in all of Scripture. These two women contrast our native hypocrisy and our faith, hypocrites and believers.

---

[1]On Philip's bigamy, see Heiko A. Oberman, *Luther: Man Between God and the Devil*, trans. Eileen Walliser-Schwarzbart (New Haven, CT: Yale University Press, 2006), 284-89; Martin Brecht, *Martin Luther*, trans. James L. Schaaf (Minneapolis: Fortress, 1993), 3:205-15; see further William Walker Rockwell, *Die Doppelehe des Landgrafen Philipp von Hessen* (Marburg: N. G. Elwert'sche Verlagsbuchhandlung, 1904); Hastings Eells, *The Attitude of Martin Bucer Toward the Bigamy of Philip of Hesse* (New Haven, CT: Yale University Press, 1924). On legal definitions of illicit marriages in the sixteenth century, see Marjorie Elizabeth Plummer, "'The Much Married Michael Kraemer': Evangelical Clergy and Bigamy in Ernestine Saxony, 1522–1542," in *Ideas and Cultural Margins in Early Modern Germany: Essays in Honor of H. C. Erik Midelfort*, ed. Marjorie Elizabeth Plummer and Robin Barnes (Farnham, UK: Ashgate, 2009), 99-115.

Peninnah respected marriage, was not guilty of a bad reputation and ascended to the holy place, as was seen before God and before people. God is viewed as approving of this holy goodness when he gives her the honor of rewards, that is, children. Hannah, whose womb is closed, seems to be cast down. This is certainly a curse, just as the earth is cursed when planted seeds do not bear fruit. And yet a person cannot judge rightly about this case. For not only Peninnah but also the good man Eli was wrong when he mistook sadness and affliction for drunkenness. Hypocritical opinions have their wisdom, piety and righteousness not only when they concern others but also concerning oneself. These ideas abound in everyone and multiply in people: "God has given abundantly," as if merits had been accepted. These carry the certainty of the Pharisee's decree when he judged, "I am not like other people. Surely God does not love others! No, God hates all those who fall to the depths!"

Through bad fruits such as these, God's disciples can see this and know that these are the ones whom Scripture calls "men of blood," that is, they want evil for others. While they are proud of their works and gifts to God, they cannot help but hate others. They have no compassion for anyone with sin. They scorn not only sin but also the cross where God was placed. And they think further that their scorn is a curse from the same God whom they themselves do not receive, as if God himself works against the faithful. This is the greatest pious temptation for their own pitiful selves.

This is why Hannah was scorned: God had closed her womb. As it says in the psalm: "many are saying of my soul, there is no salvation for him in God." And again, "God has forsaken him; pursue and seize him, for there is none to deliver him." But by believing that it is proper to condescend, to impose the cross and daily to scatter the benefits of God while ascending into glory through the cross, then through glory these blind ones descend into death (even as the faith of the righteous blessedly ascends). And so their blasphemy never ends. "But many who are first will be last, and the last first," and the greater shall serve the lesser: "I have loved

Jacob but Esau I have hated. I have laid waste his hill country and left his heritage to jackals of the desert." Hannah declares all of this in her song of chapter 2. COMMENTARY ON 1 SAMUEL.[2]

POLYGAMY TOLERATED BUT NOT APPROVED. JOHANNES PISCATOR: We have an example of polygamy in this holy man Elkanah, the father of Samuel. This raises the question of whether polygamy is allowed. If it is allowed, it appears to be approved here, given that many of the holy men in the Old Testament were polygamous: Abraham, Jacob, David, etc. For their polygamy never seem to be reproved or condemned. But, in fact, polygamy was not allowed. That's because the whole notion of polygamy fights against the institution of marriage given by God, which was created and established for our first parents between a man and a woman. According to Genesis 2, Adam proclaimed that the man and woman shall unite and "become one flesh." This is affirmed in Matthew 19:4-6. Let me respond to this question from a different angle. As for whether polygamy is allowed, it is important to note that the life of holy people is not a rule for us exactly, because holy people had their warts just like we do. But ultimately we are to imitate them in the acts they do that we recognize as conforming to the divine law. As for the other matter, although the polygamy carried about by the holy patriarchs before the law was not condemned, it is prohibited after the law was given, in accordance with Leviticus: "And you shall not take a woman as a rival wife to her sister, uncovering her nakedness while her sister is still alive." Therefore, although God tolerated the polygamy of holy men, God did not approve it. COMMENTARY ON 1 SAMUEL.[3]

TROUBLE WITH POLYGAMY. ANDREW WILLET: This presence of polygamy under the law in marrying two or more wives was not simply lawful or dispensed with, which is the opinion of many. . . . Such an interpretation cannot be, for our Savior says concerning this matter: "from the beginning it was not so." So also the Prophet Malachi: "Did he not make them one, with a portion of the Spirit in their union? And what was the one God seeking? Godly offspring." Therefore, the best interpretation is that polygamy was a human infirmity in the patriarchs in which they took for themselves two or more wives. And such marriages were not without great inconveniencies. There was continual competition between them, as between Sarah and Hagar, Leah and Rachel and here between these two wives of Elkanah.

The first polygamist in the Bible was Lamech, of the cursed seed of Cain. Yet because at this time the temporal promises of the Jewish nation depended upon their carnal generation, it pleased God to wink at this infirmity and to tolerate it in the patriarchs. God did so until the Messiah came, when the church of God should no longer be tied to the people of the Jews, but spiritual children should be begotten unto God from all nations, even among the Gentiles. HARMONY ON 1 SAMUEL.[4]

1:3-8 Elkanah Goes to Worship Year After Year

GOING UP TO SHILOH. JOHANNES BUGENHAGEN: And Elkanah went up according to the law of Deuteronomy 16. The Lord's tabernacle had been in Shiloh since the time of Joshua, as is said in Joshua. Doubtlessly the ark was there too, for it had been moved under Eli's authority, as you will see. The Lord speaks of Shiloh in Jeremiah: "Do not trust in the external worship of God even as God has commanded, unless faith is there, because trusting in anything as holy is most assuredly not allowed." COMMENTARY ON 1 SAMUEL.[5]

---

[2]Bugenhagen, *In Regum duos ultimos libros*, 184-85; citing Gen 16:1-6; 21:8-21; Gal 4:21-31; Lk 18:9-14; Ps 3:1-2; 71:11; Mt 19:30; Gen 25:23; Mal 1:2-3.
[3]Piscator, *Commentarii in omnes libros Veteris Testamenti*, 2:115; citing Gen 2:24; Lev 18:18.
[4]Willet, *Harmony on 1 Samuel*, 2*; citing Mt 19:8; Mal 2:15.
[5]Bugenhagen, *In Samuelem prophetam*, 185; citing Josh 18:1; Jer 7:12-14.

Holy Worship. Lucas Osiander: Elkanah went up to the Lord's tabernacle in order to worship God and to sacrifice to the Lord of hosts—as he is called, because all creatures serve him as if they were his soldiers. At that time the Lord of hosts had his holy tabernacle in Shiloh. For under the law the fathers strengthened their faith through sacrifices, which foreshadowed Christ's death. And it is fitting for us to gather frequently and diligently to hear the Word of God and to strengthen our faith through the enjoyment of the Lord's Supper. Annotations on 1 Samuel.[6]

Recognizing the Mediator. Viktorin Strigel: Every year Elkanah took his family to Shiloh, where there was then a tabernacle, to hear the teaching concerning the law and the Messiah. And he prayed and gave thanks for all spiritual and material blessings. For it is explicitly said that he worshiped and gave sacrifices, so that it would be indicated that he does not placate God through ceremonies, unless first the foundation has been considered, that is, the Mediator has been recognized. Through the Mediator the remission of sins, reconciliation with God and the beginnings of moral obedience are received. Commentary on 1 Samuel.[7]

The Feast and Eli's Line. Giovanni Diodati: Here Elkanah went to the feast of the Passover with all his family [just like Jesus did with his family] in Luke 2:41. It is very likely that Elkanah observed the law so faithfully that he attended the feasts on all three solemn festivals in accordance with Exodus 23:17. There is no mention made of this Eli anywhere else. However, it appears based on 2 Samuel 8:17 and 1 Chronicles 24:3-4 that he was one of Ithamar's posterity, who was Aaron's younger brother. It also appears that for some unknown reason there had been an interruption in the succession of the priesthood in Eleazar, the firstborn in his line, who was afterward reestablished in the line of Zadok. Annotations on 1 Samuel.[8]

Hannah's Portion and Prayer. Johannes Bugenhagen: Elkanah gave Hannah "one part" because she was alone, not having children to whom more parts could be given. She had not taken the food; it had not pleased her to eat, so she ate little even though it says below, "after they had all eaten and drunk." Then it says, "She was deeply distressed." Here is the cross, even while hypocrites reign secure as if near to God. Also, one does not fight against enemies here, for the heaviest troubles that need to be fought are known to be those on the inside. But prayers are multiplied before God. Commentary on 1 Samuel.[9]

Hannah's Example of Faith and Love. Viktorin Strigel: Hannah is truly a mirror on which all pious and honest women should reflect. She does not harbor hatred or rage against God in the midst of her troubles. She is obedient to God, recognizing and deploring her peculiar sin and weakness, even as she asks God for help, knowing that barrenness and fertility are not accidents but both are the work of God. And what did her husband Elkanah do? He tolerated the foolish Peninnah and most gently consoled Hannah with his words: "Why do you weep? And why do you not eat? Am I not more to you than many sons?" It is as if he said, "Peninnah has the shell but you have the kernel. For as she has the fruit of my body, so you rest in my heart. You sweetly surround this better part and you do not need to desire more than this." Commentary on 1 Samuel.[10]

Pleasure Divided from Pain. Daniel Dyke: It is noted that Elkanah loved Hannah more than his other wife, promising no doubt a greater matter of comfort to himself in her than in the other. But what followed? He loved her, says the prophet, and

---

[6]Osiander, *Liber Iosue*, 273.
[7]Strigel, *Libri Samuelis, Regum et Paralipomenon*, 1; citing Lk 2:41.
[8]Diodati, *Pious Annotations*, 163*; referring to 2 Sam 15:27; 1 Kings 2:27, 35.
[9]Bugenhagen, *In Samuelem prophetam*, 185.
[10]Strigel, *Libri Samuelis, Regum et Paralipomenon*, 1-2.

the Lord made her barren. Mark the connection of his loving her and God's making her barren. So shall it be in all such earthly creatures, where we cleave inordinately and falsely promise joy to ourselves in their use. God in his just judgment shall make these barren, so that they shall not yield us a quarter of that comfort or benefit that we expected. The rich fool promised himself a little heaven in his riches: "Soul, you have ample goods laid up for many years; relax, eat, drink, be merry. . . ." But, alas, how soon did God give him unease? "Fool, this night your soul is required of you, and the things you have prepared, whose will they be?" Here is the reason for this deceit: We look only at the apparent and outward good of those things we desire or expect. In other words, we extract the sweet from the sour and the pleasure from the pain. But when we get what we want, we feel more of the sour than of the sweet. And hence it comes to pass that nothing pleases us so well in the expectation itself. Indeed, almost nothing that pleasures us when hoped for gives us more displeasure once acquired. THE MYSTERY OF SELF-DECEIVING.[11]

1:9-11 *Hannah's Vow and Prayer*

HANNAH'S VOW. JOHANNES BUGENHAGEN: Here Hannah has nothing in her power, nothing in her free will, no presumptive claims, rather everything relating to the vow is committed to God; all things here are entirely in the hands of God. "If you give me a son, I will give him to you. If you do not give, I can give nothing to you. If you do not desire to give, you will not give. If you do desire it, you give it. And the one entrusted to me, I will give to you, so that he might minister in the tabernacle and serve the priests. Then if something else should be pleasing in your sight, I will have made sure that he does not remain in his ministry, for I do not presume to determine your calling through this vow. He will be yours. You will do as it has pleased you. A vow against your will is impious. If you give this and he is presented to you, you will make sure

that the child whom you give has the mind to obey me in this. You will grant this to pious parents, so that the son does my will according to God. Yes indeed, this one whom God gives me will at the same time recognize the calling of God and honor the commandment about parents. If through later impiety the child comes to condemn God's calling and parental orders, nevertheless I will be responsible to the vow for the child in my keeping while he is under my care. I truly vow nothing here that brings danger to the child's conscience. So if he grasps it, it is already done alone as a free person who can change, which is very important. For I am making a vow to you, not against you." COMMENTARY ON 1 SAMUEL.[12]

HEART LIKE A FLOWER. EDWARD REYNOLDS: A godly heart is . . . like a flower. For flowers shut when the sun sets and the night comes, but open again when the sun returns and shines on them. If God withdraws his favor and sends a night of affliction, they shut up themselves as well as their thoughts in silence. But if he shines again and sheds abroad the light and sense of his love on them, then their heart and mouth are wide open toward heaven, in lifting up praises to God. Hannah prayed silently, so long as she was in bitterness of soul and of a sorrowful spirit. But as soon as God answered her prayers and filled her heart with joy in him, her mouth immediately opened into a song of thanksgiving. SEVEN SERMONS ON FOURTEENTH CHAPTER OF HOSEA.[13]

PRAYER AS A KEY. LANCELOT ANDREWES: Prayer may be compared to a key. An example is when Elisha opened the heavens by prayer when they were shut up. . . . Likewise, when God shuts up the wombs of women . . . so that they become barren, prayer is the key that opens them. By this key was the womb of Hannah opened so that she brought forth Samuel. COLLECTION OF LECTURES.[14]

---

[11]Dyke, *The Mystery of Self-Deceiving*, 253-54*.

[12]Bugenhagen, *In Samuelem prophetam*, 186-88.
[13]Reynolds, *Works*, 3:254*.
[14]Andrewes, *A Collection of Lectures*, 567*.

Spiritual Children. Lancelot Andrewes: Children whom God gives to parents upon a plentiful contrition and repentance usually prove to be excellent in all spiritual graces. The first example of this is Seth, who is not only the foundation of the church but of all humankind. . . . It also appeared in Hannah, who having bewailed her own case in the bitterness of her soul, received from the Lord a blessed seed who came to be called Samuel. He is the one who restored religion and settled the state of the kingdom. Collection of Lectures.[15]

1:12-20 *Eli's Response to Hannah*

Comfort from Eli. Johannes Bugenhagen: Hannah received the word of consolation from the mouth of Eli as if from the mouth of God. Doubtless, if you prayed an invocation to God and a holy man responded, would you not be consoled by a sure word through this one as if from the Lord? Thus we believe that in former times God consoled the saints through holy people, and only rarely through special revelation. For this reason, Hannah was not more sorrowful. This is the nature of God's consolation after the cross and hell. Commentary on 1 Samuel.[16]

Eli's Ministry. Viktorin Strigel: The priest Eli might be considered as a primary example of a faithful ministry, because he did not seek pleasure, useless leisure or sloth. Instead, "Sparta is your country, make the most of it."[17] He was offered all the work of his office and he took it. For that reason he sat in the forecourt of the temple, so that he might bring wanderers or erring people back, fortify the inexperienced, strengthen the weak, shed light on dark and intricate questions and loosen the

bonds of those hopelessly wrapped up in doubts. Therefore, by this example of Eli, let us learn to avoid thoughtless judgments, which will require repentance. As the old saying says: "He who judges quickly shall soon repent." Commentary on 1 Samuel.[18]

No Drinking Allowed. Johann Arndt: People were not to drink wine or strong drink when they went into the tabernacle. . . . This signifies that if a man wishes to go into the eternal tabernacle of God, that is, to eternal life, he must give up the pleasure and lusts of the flesh of this world and everything by which the flesh conquers the spirit, so that the flesh will not be stronger than the spirit and conquer it. The love of this world, pleasure and pride is a strong sweet wine by which the soul and the spirit are conquered. True Christianity.[19]

The Talk of Fools. John Dod: Those who are too conceited of themselves and of their own wits are here to be sharply reproved. These are the types who will brag and boast that they are not so simple, but they know well enough how to serve God and how to do the duties that pertain to them in their families. Although they have not lived in the world for long and are just recently married, yet they know sufficiently without teaching what belongs to the duty of a husband, of a father, of a master and of all other things a Christian man should know. By saying such things, these foolish men consider little what they speak against themselves and how far they discover their own nakedness. Hereby they make it apparent that they have in them no Christianity at all. For let's ask ourselves this: Are they wiser than all the prophets and righteous people who lived in ancient times? They saw and acknowledged their great lack of the understanding of holy things. . . . How foully was Eli overtaken through ignorance in censuring and condemning good Hannah for drunkenness when she was pouring out her soul

---

[15]Andrewes, *A Collection of Lectures*, 488*.
[16]Bugenhagen, *In Samuelem prophetam*, 188.
[17]A line from Euripides' play *Telephus* §739, where Agamemnon commands Menelaus, "You inherited Sparta—govern her!" See Euripides, *Fragments: Oedipus-Chyrsippus; Other Fragments*, ed. and trans. Christopher Collard and Martin Cropp (Cambridge, MA: Harvard University Press, 2008), 210-11; cf. RCS NT 11:66.

[18]Strigel, *Libri Samuelis, Regum et Paralipomenon*, 2.
[19]Arndt, *True Christianity*, 113.

before the Lord because she moved her lips only? Although she uttered no words in his hearing, she spoke in her heart to God. And the like might be said of many indiscreet speeches and actions of the disciples of Christ before the resurrection, and till they had received the Spirit of understanding in a more plentiful measure. THE THIRD SERMON OF THE LORD'S SUPPER.[20]

1:21-28 Hannah Prepares and Delivers Samuel to the Lord

VOWS CAN BE REVOKED. MARTIN LUTHER: Samuel, whose mother dedicated him to God, did not always observe the vow, but, as Samuel clearly indicated, become a ruler, traveled around the country, served the people and did not always remain in the temple as had been vowed. On the contrary, Samuel later lived in Ramah, and his example is a powerful argument against eternally binding monastic vows. AN ANSWER TO SEVERAL QUESTIONS ON MONASTIC VOWS.[21]

SAMUEL IS LENT TO THE LORD. JOHANNES BUGENHAGEN: This vow is not a perpetual vow, as it says, "As long as he lives, he is lent to the LORD." For because he was a Levite from Kohath, he has been given not by his mother's vow but the law of God in Numbers 4 to minister from his thirtieth year to his fiftieth, at which time the law restores his freedom. This background also explains why Samuel will be described later as being in Ramah in possession of his father's house and a judge in Israel for many years. COMMENTARY ON 1 SAMUEL.[22]

SAMUEL'S SACRIFICE AS A TYPE OF CHRIST'S. LANCELOT ANDREWES: Oblations were of two sorts according to Numbers 28:4, a "morning lamb" and an "evening lamb." The presentation of Christ in the temple by his parents was the morning lamb; and the offering up of himself as a sacrifice in his passion was the evening lamb. In his oblation he was the author and beginning of our faith; in his passion, he was the finisher and accomplishment of our faith. For the application of this Scripture—that it may not seem strange but lawful and warrantable both by Scripture and by practice of Christ's church—we are to know that it is lawful and usual to compare things spiritual . . . with things natural. COLLECTION OF LECTURES.[23]

TEMPORAL VERSUS SPIRITUAL PRAYERS. ANDREW WILLET: Some question whether it is lawful to pray for temporal and indifferent things, as here Hannah prays for a child and obtains one. . . . Temporal things are only to be prayed for in general, as we pray for them under the name of bread in the Lord's Prayer. However, it appears by the examples of holy people in the Scripture that it is lawful to pray for temporal things, as Abraham prayed for Ishmael and Moses prayed for victory against Amalek. But there are two conditions required for temporal prayers: first, that we should pray for them transitorily, that is, not with as great a fervency and desire as for spiritual things; and second, that we must demonstrate how they will be used for God's glory. But we must not think that we are heard for the merit of our prayer. God hears us in mercy, though prayer is appointed as the way and the means by which we walk. It is not the cause of granting our requests. HARMONY ON 1 SAMUEL.[24]

PERPETUAL NAZIRITE. LANCELOT ANDREWES: If we ask why Hannah . . . gives something to God, the reason is because God has been offended by humankind and therefore must be appeased; and nothing more serves to appease wrath than a gift. . . . But if we will appease by a gift there must be an equality; we may not offer a thing under the value of the thing that was taken away. That is the reason why all the sacrifices of the law could not appease God. . . . The value of our obedience to God is such as cannot appease and satisfy his majesty, having

[20]Dod, *Ten Sermons*, 76*.
[21]LW 46:148.
[22]Bugenhagen, *In Samuelem prophetam*, 188; citing 1 Chron 6:16; 1 Sam 8:1-4.

[23]Andrewes, *A Collection of Lectures*, 565*.
[24]Willet, *Harmony on 1 Samuel*, 7*.

been offended. . . . But if we can offer to God a thing of equal price to the obedience that we owe to God, then no doubt God will be appeased, especially if we offer a thing of a higher rate. . . . To offer Samuel as a Nazirite was not enough, for that

continues but for certain days. . . . But Hannah gives her son to the Lord all his life, that is, forever. Collection of Lectures.[25]

---

[25]Andrewes, *A Collection of Lectures*, 569*.

2:1-10 THE PRAYER OF HANNAH

¹And Hannah prayed and said,

"My heart exults in the LORD;
 my horn is exalted in the LORD.
My mouth derides my enemies,
 because I rejoice in your salvation.

²"There is none holy like the LORD:
 for there is none besides you;
 there is no rock like our God.
³Talk no more so very proudly,
 let not arrogance come from your mouth;
for the LORD is a God of knowledge,
 and by him actions are weighed.
⁴The bows of the mighty are broken,
 but the feeble bind on strength.
⁵Those who were full have hired themselves out
 for bread,
 but those who were hungry have ceased to
 hunger.
The barren has borne seven,

but she who has many children is forlorn.
⁶The LORD kills and brings to life;
 he brings down to Sheol and raises up.
⁷The LORD makes poor and makes rich;
 he brings low and he exalts.
⁸He raises up the poor from the dust;
 he lifts the needy from the ash heap
to make them sit with princes
 and inherit a seat of honor.
For the pillars of the earth are the LORD's,
 and on them he has set the world.

⁹"He will guard the feet of his faithful ones,
 but the wicked shall be cut off in darkness,
 for not by might shall a man prevail.
¹⁰The adversaries of the LORD shall be broken
 to pieces;
 against them he will thunder in heaven.
The LORD will judge the ends of the earth;
 he will give strength to his king
 and exalt the horn of his anointed."

OVERVIEW: Hannah's prayer, according to the reformers, signifies much more than mere praise of God for the gift of a child. It foretells the reign of Christ, and also provides the basis for Mary's prayer in Luke 1:46-55.[1] The commentators regard this as one of chief passages where the messianic king, Jesus Christ, is predicted in the Old Testament. The reformers, intent on safeguarding the sovereignty of God, dwell on Hannah's words that the Lord both takes and restores life, which Strigel interprets as true conversion to God. The story of a barren yet faithful woman who ends up with a baby boy is a common one in the Bible, but the commentators see more spiritual significance in the story than first meets the eye.

2:1-5 Overview of Hannah's Prayer

HANNAH SINGS OF GOD'S GLORY. JOHANNES BUGENHAGEN: From her experience, Hannah, full of the Spirit, sings against the glory of human hypocrisy and sings about God's glory, through which God graciously makes the barren fruitful. This means that Gentiles and sinners acquire grace. This divine grace and glory has been declared and entered the world through the reign of Christ, whose strength God exalts against all of the world's powers, knowledge, righteousness and especially all human hypocrisy. COMMENTARY ON 1 SAMUEL.[2]

HANNAH'S FAITHFUL AND PROPHETIC PRAYER. VIKTORIN STRIGEL: Hannah conforms to the

---

[1]Cf. Ps 34; RCS OT 7:270.

[2]Bagenhagen, *In Samuelem prophetam*, 189.

pattern given in James: "Is anyone among you suffering? Let him pray. Is anyone cheerful? Let him sing praise." Just as she brought prayers and vows to God earlier, she then celebrated the goodness and mercy of God with the sweetest song. But Hannah's song is so admirably worthy not only because it praises the source of the gift but also because it foretells the reign of Christ, which lasts even to the end of the earth. Further, she teaches faith in God alone to be such that one can be killed and made alive, taken down to hell and brought back. COMMENTARY ON 1 SAMUEL.[3]

GIVING ALL. THOMAS ADAMS: God gave Samuel to Hannah, Hannah gave Samuel back again to God. In a similar way, return part of your riches to God, who gave all to you in the first place. COMMENTARY ON 2 PETER.[4]

PRAYER OF ALL CREATURES. LANCELOT ANDREWES: The want of so great a blessing as is the bearing of a child moved Hannah to break forth into this desire of prayer. Yet it is most certain that the Virgin Mary needed a Savior—for which she also confessed that her spirit rejoiced—more so than Hannah needed a son. And as Mary's need was greater, so her prayer was stronger than Hannah's prayer. For Hannah prayed alone; but as for Mary's prayer, it was accompanied with the desire and prayer of all creatures. COLLECTION OF LECTURES.[5]

2:6-9 Killing and Bringing to Life

TAKING AND GIVING LIFE. HANS DENCK: The righteousness of God is God himself. Sin is what raises itself up against God; it is in truth nothing. The righteousness works through the Word that was from the beginning and is subsequently divided in two, law and gospel, on account of the twofold office that Christ as king of righteousness exercises,

namely, to destroy the unbelievers and to bring to life the believers. Now, all believers were once unbelievers. Consequently, in becoming believers, they thus first had to die in order that they might thereafter no longer live for themselves, as unbelievers do, but for God through Christ that their walk might indeed no longer be on earth but in heaven, as Paul says. David also verifies this where he says: The Lord leads down into hell and up again. All this I believe (Lord, crush my unbelief) in truth, awaiting now whoever wishes to deny and overthrow it. NUREMBERG CONFESSION.[6]

LAW VERSUS GOSPEL. JOHANN GERHARD: God kills and makes alive, and he leads down to hell and brings back again. Specifically, God kills by contrition that he may make alive by consolation. And God leads down to hell by the hammer of the law that he may bring back from hell by the comfort of the gospel. THE CONQUEST OF TEMPTATIONS.[7]

TRUE REPENTANCE INVOLVES DYING AND RISING. VIKTORIN STRIGEL: Hannah's song describes true repentance, or conversion to God, in which there are two moves: dying and being made alive. Dying points to the heart's recognizing God's wrath against sin with true fear and suffering. Scripture describes this suffering: "Like a lion he breaks all my bones." In these sufferings, which come from awareness of God's wrath, there is mortification of the flesh, or of the old and corrupt nature. This suffering may be greater or smaller in various people, but contrition is necessary in all conversions, as it says in 2 Corinthians: "You were grieved into repenting . . . for godly grief produces a repentance that leads to salvation." COMMENTARY ON 1 SAMUEL.[8]

STUDYING AT GOD'S SCHOOL. MARTIN LUTHER: I have often seen excellent men horribly vexed by terrors, afflictions and the severest persecutions, so

[3]Strigel, *Libri Samuelis, Regum et Paralipomenon*, 5; citing Jas 5:13.
[4]Adams, *Commentary upon 2 Peter*, 46.
[5]Andrewes, *A Collection of Lectures*, 567*; citing Lk 1:47.
[6]Denck, *Spiritual Legacy*, 61*.
[7]Gerhard, *Conquest of Temptations*, 17*.
[8]Strigel, *Libri Samuelis, Regum et Paralipomenon*, 6-7; citing Is 38:13; 2 Cor 7:9-10.

much so that they nearly experienced despair of heart. But these things must be learned so that we may be able to comfort such men and interpret the temptations as the special manner by which God is accustomed to wrestle with us in the form of a destroyer and that we may exhort them firmly to retain the promise, or lamp and spark, of the Word in the hope that the rescue will certainly follow. For God leads down to hell and brings back. Now you see his back parts, and God seems to be shunning you, but sometime later you will see his front parts and his face. This is what it means for him to love those whom he chastises. This love must be learned from experience, nor should chastisement be avoided and shunned. The story is told of a peasant who, when he heard this consolation from his pastor, that the afflictions and troubles by which God afflicts us are signs of his love, replied: "Ah, how I would like him to love others and not me!" LECTURES ON GENESIS.[9]

ALL IS GOD'S OWN. DAVID CLARKSON: God has the right to dispose of all as he wills, and does actually dispose of any things and persons as he thinks is good. He has *jus praesenter disponendi*, "the right of present disposal," which is properly dominion or property. He gives possession and ejects, puts in and throws out, lifts up and casts down, whom and when he will. . . . Why does God thus dispose of all? Because all is his own. SERMON ON 1 CHRONICLES 29:11.[10]

2:10 God Blessed His Church

ANOTHER PREDICTION ABOUT THE MESSIAH. CARDINAL CAJETAN: According to the Hebrew, the passage states: "He will give strength to his king; he will raise the horn of his Messiah." Before this time, however, no king had been instituted in Israel. Therefore, this passage speaks about the messianic king, for God gave him strength and elevated his power. In fact, in Hebrew the word

Messiah means "anointed," while in Greek the word is translated as *Christ*. Now, it is evident that Christ will come at the time of judgment in strength and in great stature. And for this reason it is manifest that he will be a person who judges the ends of the earth according to the prophecy from the book of Job. And this is the fourth passage in which the Messiah is clearly predicted: first, during the time of Abraham; second, during the time of Jacob; third, during the time of Moses; and fourth, during the time of Samuel. Later the Messiah is predicted in the book of Job. COMMENTARY ON 1 SAMUEL.[11]

DAVID, THE CHOSEN ONE. JOHN CALVIN: Before a king had been established over the people, Hannah, the mother of Samuel, describing the happiness of the godly, already says in her song: "God will give strength to his king and exalt the horn of his Messiah." By these words she means that God will bless his church. To this corresponds the prophecy that is added a little later: "The priest whom I shall raise up . . . will walk in the presence of my Christ." And there is no doubt that our heavenly Father willed that we perceive in David and his descendants the living image of Christ. Accordingly David, wishing to urge the pious fear of God, commands them to "kiss the Son." To this corresponds the saying of the Gospel: "He who does not honor the Son does not honor the Father." Therefore, although the kingdom collapsed because of the revolt of the ten tribes, yet the covenant God made with David and his successors had to stand, just as he spoke through the prophets: "I will not tear away all the kingdom . . . for the sake of David my servant and for the sake of Jerusalem, which I have chosen . . . but to your son one tribe will remain." This same promise is repeated a second and a third time. It is expressly stated: "I will . . . afflict David's descendants, but not eternally." Sometime later it is said: "For the sake of David his servant, God gave him a lamp in Jerusalem, to

[9]LW 6:151-52*.
[10]Clarkson, *The Practical Works of David Clarkson*, 1:388.
[11]Cajetan, *Opera Omnia in Sacrae Scripturae Expositionem*, 2:79.

raise himself up a son and to protect Jerusalem." Then, although affairs verged on ruin, it was again said: "The Lord was unwilling to destroy Judah, for the sake of David his servant, since he promised to give a lamp to him and to his sons forever." To sum up: While all others were passed over, David alone was chosen as the one in whom God's pleasure should rest. INSTITUTES 2.6.2.[12]

[12]LCC 20:343-44 (CO 2:249); citing 1 Sam 2:10; 2:35; Ps 2:12; Jn 5:23; 1 Kings 11:34, 39; 15:4; 2 Kings 8:19.

2:11-36 REJECTION OF ELI'S WICKED SONS AND HIS HOUSEHOLD

[11]Then Elkanah went home to Ramah. And the boy[a] was ministering to the Lord in the presence of Eli the priest.

[12]Now the sons of Eli were worthless men. They did not know the Lord. [13]The custom of the priests with the people was that when any man offered sacrifice, the priest's servant would come, while the meat was boiling, with a three-pronged fork in his hand, [14]and he would thrust it into the pan or kettle or cauldron or pot. All that the fork brought up the priest would take for himself. This is what they did at Shiloh to all the Israelites who came there. [15]Moreover, before the fat was burned, the priest's servant would come and say to the man who was sacrificing, "Give meat for the priest to roast, for he will not accept boiled meat from you but only raw." [16]And if the man said to him, "Let them burn the fat first, and then take as much as you wish," he would say, "No, you must give it now, and if not, I will take it by force." [17]Thus the sin of the young men was very great in the sight of the Lord, for the men treated the offering of the Lord with contempt.

[18]Samuel was ministering before the Lord, a boy clothed with a linen ephod. [19]And his mother used to make for him a little robe and take it to him each year when she went up with her husband to offer the yearly sacrifice. [20]Then Eli would bless Elkanah and his wife, and say, "May the Lord give you children by this woman for the petition she asked of the Lord." So then they would return to their home. [21]Indeed the Lord visited Hannah, and she conceived and bore three sons and two daughters. And the boy Samuel grew in the presence of the Lord.

[22]Now Eli was very old, and he kept hearing all that his sons were doing to all Israel, and how they lay with the women who were serving at the entrance to the tent of meeting. [23]And he said to them, "Why do you do such things? For I hear of your evil dealings from all these people. [24]No, my sons; it is no good report that I hear the people of the Lord spreading abroad. [25]If someone sins against a man, God will mediate for him, but if someone sins against the Lord, who can intercede for him?" But they would not listen to the voice of their father, for it was the will of the Lord to put them to death.

[26]Now the boy Samuel continued to grow both in stature and in favor with the Lord and also with man.

[27]And there came a man of God to Eli and said to him, "Thus says the Lord, 'Did I indeed reveal myself to the house of your father when they were in Egypt subject to the house of Pharaoh? [28]Did I choose him out of all the tribes of Israel to be my priest, to go up to my altar, to burn incense, to wear an ephod before me? I gave to the house of your father all my offerings by fire from the people of Israel. [29]Why then do you scorn[b] my sacrifices and my offerings that I commanded for my dwelling, and honor your sons above me by fattening yourselves on the choicest parts of every offering of my people Israel?' [30]Therefore the Lord, the God of Israel, declares: 'I promised that your house and the house of your father should go in and out before me forever,' but now the Lord declares: 'Far be it from me, for those who honor me I will honor, and those who despise me shall be lightly esteemed. [31]Behold, the days are coming when I will cut off your strength and the strength of your father's house, so that there will not be an old man in your house. [32]Then in distress you will look with envious eye on all the prosperity that shall be bestowed on Israel, and there shall not be an old man in your house forever. [33]The only one of you whom I shall not cut off from my altar shall be spared to weep his[c] eyes out to grieve his heart, and all the descendants[d] of your house shall die by the sword of men.[e] [34]And this that shall come upon your two sons, Hophni and Phinehas, shall be the sign to you: both of them shall die on the same day. [35]And I will raise up for myself a faithful priest, who shall do according to what is in my heart and in my mind. And I will build him a sure house, and he shall go in and out before my

anointed forever. ³⁶And everyone who is left in your house shall come to implore him for a piece of silver or a loaf of bread and shall say, "Please put me in one of the priests' places, that I may eat a morsel of bread."'"

a Hebrew *na'ar* can be rendered *boy* (2:11, 18, 21, 26; 3:1, 8), *servant* (2:13, 15), or *young man* (2:17), depending on the context   b Hebrew *kick at*   c Septuagint; Hebrew *your*; twice in this verse   d Hebrew *increase*   e Septuagint; Hebrew *die as men*

OVERVIEW: According to the interpreters, leadership of God's people is a great responsibility, not to be taken lightly. Melanchthon exhorts us not to discredit the gospel by our bad behavior. The reformers believe that leaders, particularly members of the clergy, are to display exemplary lives in accordance with good doctrine. When God's people see poor behavior in their leaders, they are drawn to imitate their bad example rather than seek the higher road to goodness and righteousness. Eli's sons are evil leaders juxtaposed with Samuel's godly leadership. Moreover, the reformers criticize Eli for being too lenient toward his sons, and the commentators use this passage to encourage parents to follow the wisdom of Proverbs by disciplining their children. When Eli tries to admonish his sons' behavior, however, it is too late. According to the interpreters, Eli is unable to intercede with God on his sons' behalf, and God rightly condemns his sons for their wicked behavior. Despite the free actions of Eli's sons, the removal of Eli's lineage from the priesthood is part of God's sovereign plan, which prompts an explanation of the difference between conditional and unconditional promises.

2:11-17 *The Differences Between Godly and Ungodly Leaders*

INTEGRITY AMONG MINISTERS. PHILIPP MELANCHTHON: We, who confess the gospel, are especially to consider how severely God is angered if we give the gospel an evil name. For such sin God cast aside the high priest Eli and his sons, as the text says, 1 Samuel 2:17, "Thus the sin of the young men was very great in the sight of the Lord; for they treated the offering of the Lord with contempt." As God was angry with those who gave reason for speaking of the sacrifice, you should not give reason for, or support, blasphemy or contempt of the gospel. We must, therefore, be careful in doctrine and customs, so that we do not incur the anger of God with offensive doctrine or injurious examples. THEOLOGICAL COMMONPLACES (1555).[1]

SAMUEL'S STEADFASTNESS CONTRASTS WITH ELI'S SONS. VIKTORIN STRIGEL: Samuel possessed great and amazing virtue, because he did not imitate the depraved example of Eli's sons. For he very much shows examples of self-governance in both parts of valor. For they are especially strong who have close friendships at home and who attend closely to God. Therefore, when Samuel did not follow the impious and otherwise wicked sons of Eli, then his incorruptibility can rightly be described as Pyrrhus spoke of Fabricius (as stated in Eutropius's history). Such is Samuel, who was as hard to separate from honesty as Saul was quick. For he was always true to himself, unchanging in all matters. COMMENTARY ON 1 SAMUEL.[2]

THE ROLE OF A CHURCH LEADER. HEINRICH BULLINGER: Let us consider how pastors are to lead the church of Christ and exemplify a holy life. The Lord said to his disciples in the Gospel: "You are the light of the world. A city on a hill cannot be hidden. Neither do people light a lamp and put it under a bowl. Instead they put it on its stand, and it gives light to everyone in the house. In the same way, let your light shine before men, that they may see your good deeds and praise your Father in

---

[1]*Melanchthon on Christian Doctrine*, 322.
[2]Strigel, *Libri Samuelis, Regum et Paralipomenon*, 9. Strigel here refers to a history of Rome written by the fourth-century Christian historian Eutropius. In meetings with the Sicilian commander Pyrrhus, the Roman consul Gaius Fabricius became famous for his incorruptibility and honesty.

heaven." As such, pastors are to give light to their churches by means of a holy life and not just by means of doctrine. After seeing that the pastor's life agrees with sound doctrine, the people of the church will be moved toward innocence of life. For the most part, an example of a holy and good person may be found in the study of the virtues; on the contrary, Scripture testifies in many ways how the corrupt sons of Eli, the chief leaders of religion, served as an example to corrupt the people. For Scripture says, "This sin of the young men was very great in the Lord's sight, for they were treating the Lord's offering with contempt." For it is apparent that people begin to doubt the whole doctrine when they see the corrupt life of the ministers of the church. The people cry out, "If the pastor truly believed the things he teaches us, he would not lead such an immoral life." In this way, the teachers are said to have overthrown in their evil life what they had constructed in their unsound doctrine. DECADES 5.4.[3]

THE MANY OFFENSES OF ELI'S SONS. ANDREW WILLET: The sin Eli's sons committed against the offerings of the Lord was not of one sort but many. First, they were guilty of theft and robbery. For whereas only the breast and right shoulder belonged to the priest of the peace offerings, they took more and were not content with the ordinary portion brought up by their utensils. Second, they also committed sacrilege. For whereas the Lord was to be served first and the fat burned first, they exacted their fee and more, even before the Lord had gotten his due. Third, they did this with contemptuous hostility and violence, not staying to receive it at the offerer's hand, but being their own carvers. Fourth, they were also guilty of the sin of wantonness. They took the flesh while it was yet raw, so that they might dress it to the priest's liking. In short, the sin of the young men was very great: in respect to themselves . . . who, being priests, should have given a good example to others; in

regard to God, against whom they were presumptuous; and in respect to the great hurt and inconvenience that arose from this, they caused the people to abhor the sacrifices of the Lord. HARMONY ON 1 SAMUEL.[4]

2:18-21 Samuel and His Ephod

THE EPHOD LINEN. JOHANNES BUGENHAGEN: This was the ephod garment of the Levites, spoken of in Exodus 28, which covered over the priests' lower body. But when it was put on Samuel, it signified his public ministry and his Levitical priesthood in the tabernacle. COMMENTARY ON 1 SAMUEL.[5]

DIFFERENT KINDS OF EPHODS. ANDREW WILLET: There were two kinds of ephods belonging to the service of the tabernacle, one peculiar to the high priest wrought with gold and blue silk; and another of linen only, which was common to all the Levites and priests. . . . Of this sort was Samuel's ephod. Yet there was also a third kind of ephod, which was a civil garment of white linen used in the time of celebration and joy. Such is the type of ephod David put on when he danced before the ark and about which the Preacher said, "Let your garments be always white." HARMONY ON 1 SAMUEL.[6]

2:22-26 The Sins of the Sons

SCATTERING THE WOLVES. MARTIN BUCER: Let us be admonished by those horrible punishments that were suffered by the priest Eli . . . and the whole people of Israel on account of their wicked indulgence and misguided compassion toward those against whom they should have treated severely—by God's command, who alone is truly compassionate and merciful. We should not imagine that anyone—contrary to God's teaching

---

[3]Bullinger, *Sermonum decades quinque*, 391-92; citing Mt 5:13-16; 1 Sam 2:17.

[4]Willet, *Harmony on 1 Samuel*, 9-10*; citing Lev 7:31.
[5]Bugenhagen, *In Samuelem prophetam*, 190.
[6]Willet, *Harmony on 1 Samuel*, 10*; citing 2 Sam 6:14; Eccles 9:8.

and to the church of God's ruin—will be shown leniency or pardoned at all. Christian leniency and mercy must be shown to *Christ's* sheep—by which they should be protected from wolves—not to wolves, so that they can scatter and destroy the sheep. REIGN OF CHRIST.[7]

PARENTAL RESPONSIBILITY. PHILIPP MELANCHTHON: Also we need to teach parents their responsibility to instill in their children the fear of God, to teach and let them learn the Word of God. Thus we read in the Proverbs of Solomon: "For folly is bound up in the heart of a child, but the rod of discipline drives it far from him." So Paul in Ephesians 6 says: "Fathers, do not provoke your children to anger, but bring them up in the discipline and instruction of the Lord." Such is the example of Eli who according to 1 Samuel 2 was punished by God and deprived of his priestly office because he had not taken seriously the rearing of this children. Never have youth been more insolent than today—we see how little they obey, how little they respect their parents. On this account, undoubtedly, the world is full of plagues, war, rebellion and other evils. INSTRUCTIONS BY THE VISITORS OF PARISH PASTORS: ON TRUE CHRISTIAN PRAYER.[8]

GOD WILL PUNISH ELI'S CORRUPT SONS. JOHANNES BUGENHAGEN: A priest holds the office of mediation between God and people, to teach the people God's Word and to make sacrifices. These all stumble wherever the Word of God is despised. For what good does it do to add piety to impiety? In the same way, these priests stretched what was written in the Lord's law about the portions given to priests and the sacrifices of the law concerning the fat burned to the Lord as written in Leviticus. They did not come back to their senses when

admonished by the people but rather used violence against those who questioned them. When their father rightly admonished them, they despised his great forbearance and earned God's judgment, as it is written, "It was the will of the LORD to put them to death." This is an example of how human doctrines gather people against God's Word while the glory of wealth and worldly opinions of justice are sought instead. Here are erring spirits, which little by little possess what they want by violent means. COMMENTARY ON 1 SAMUEL.[9]

SCANDALOUS SACRIFICE. ROBERT SANDERSON: In judging the cases of scandal, we are not so much to look at the event, what that is or may be, as we are at the cause from where it comes. . . . The first is when a person does something before another person that is in itself evil, unlawful and sinful. In which case, neither the intention of the one who does it nor the event, as to him who sees it done, is of any consideration. It does not matter whether the doer had an intention to draw the other into sin or not. Nor does it matter whether the other was induced to commit sin or not. The fact that the action itself is evil, and done before others, is sufficient to render the doer guilty of having given scandal, though he had neither any intention himself so to do, nor was any person actually scandalized by it. This is because whatsoever is in itself and in its own nature evil is also of itself, and in its own nature, scandalous, and of evil example. Thus did Hophni and Phinehas, the sons of Eli, give scandal by their wretched profaneness and greediness about the sacrifices of the Lord as well as their vile and shameless abusing of the women. THE CASE DETERMINED.[10]

MULTIPLYING SIN. THOMAS ADAMS: The sin of the clergy is like a sickness, which rising from the stomach into the head, drops down upon the lungs . . . until all the members of the body languish into corruption. Eli's lewd sons acted intolerably when they sinned in the tabernacle.

---

[7]Bucer, *De Regno Christi*, 92*.
[8]LW 40:281; citing Prov 22:15; Eph 6:4; 1 Sam 2:30. The title page credits no author, though the seals of Luther and Melanchthon are present. Melanchthon wrote this document in conversation with Luther and Bugenhagen for the Saxon Parish Visitations (1526–1528).

[9]Bugenhagen, *In Samuelem prophetam*, 189-90.
[10]Sanderson, *Works*, 5:84-85*.

Although their sacrifices could do away the sins of others, no sacrifice could do away their own sin. Although many a soul was the cleaner for the blood of those beasts they shed, their own souls were the fouler by it. By one and the same service, they atoned for the people's offenses and multiplied their own. THE TEMPLE.[11]

WHY WE MUST READ THE SCRIPTURES. JOHN JEWEL: Are you a father? Do you have children? Read the Scriptures and they will teach you. If you have sons, instruct them. Eli the prophet, by sparing his wanton children, cast away himself and his children: They were killed, the ark of God was taken and old Eli fell down and broke his neck. OF THE HOLY SCRIPTURES.[12]

2:27-36 The Lord Rejects Eli's Household

THERE CAME A MAN OF GOD. JOHANNES BUGENHAGEN: Another prophet was sent by God. As Eli's own words show, he was not ignorant of his sin of releasing his ungodly sons into the priesthood and letting this matter become a disgrace. Here the law or judgment of God is revealed clearly to him, which confounds his conscience. Love for his sons keeps him from coming to his senses, even though the priesthood should not be a private honor. But he heard the judgment of God again from Samuel when he said, "It is the LORD. Let him do what seems good to him." COMMENTARY ON I SAMUEL.[13]

ELI'S THREE ERRORS. VIKTORIN STRIGEL: The prophet's remembrance of the earlier blessings given to the Levites is followed by the most egregious accusations, in which three of Eli the priest's crimes are brought up. The first is profaning the sacrifice. The second is being fawning and overindulgent to his children. The third is avarice. COMMENTARY ON I SAMUEL.[14]

BUT IT SHOULD NOT BE SO. ANDREW WILLET: Here arises a great doubt, given we know that God's promises are most certain and that his decree is immutable. How, then, does the Lord make a promise and then go back on it? The answer is that some of God's promises are absolute without any condition, as was the promise of the Messiah. However, others of God's promises are given to us conditionally, especially the temporal promises made to the Israelites. These conditional promises, such as the priesthood being promised to the family of Eli, depended on the condition of their obedience. So now, life everlasting is promised to those who have faith and believe. But will some say: Does God's election, therefore, depend on our works or belief? Not in any way. For God, as he has promised the reward—so also, to those whom he purposes to make heirs of his promise—he has likewise ordained the means to give them faith (and all other graces) to apprehend and lay hold of the promises. God's promises, then, are only effectual to those who, by a lively faith, apprehend them. The rest, which by their disobedience fall off from God's promises, do not work any alteration in the purpose of God, who has foreseen both their disobedience and that his promises did not belong to them. HARMONY ON I SAMUEL.[15]

---

[11]Adams, *The Temple*, 15-16*.
[12]Jewell, *Writings*, 59*.
[13]Bugenhagen, *In Samuelem prophetam*, 191; citing I Sam 3:18.

[14]Strigel, *Libri Samuelis, Regum et Paralipomenon*, 10-11.
[15]Willet, *Harmony on 1 Samuel*, 16*.

3:1–4:1A SAMUEL'S CALLING

[1]Now the boy Samuel was ministering to the Lord in the presence of Eli. And the word of the Lord was rare in those days; there was no frequent vision.

[2]At that time Eli, whose eyesight had begun to grow dim so that he could not see, was lying down in his own place. [3]The lamp of God had not yet gone out, and Samuel was lying down in the temple of the Lord, where the ark of God was.

[4]Then the Lord called Samuel, and he said, "Here I am!" [5]and ran to Eli and said, "Here I am, for you called me." But he said, "I did not call; lie down again." So he went and lay down.

[6]And the Lord called again, "Samuel!" and Samuel arose and went to Eli and said, "Here I am, for you called me." But he said, "I did not call, my son; lie down again." [7]Now Samuel did not yet know the Lord, and the word of the Lord had not yet been revealed to him.

[8]And the Lord called Samuel again the third time. And he arose and went to Eli and said, "Here I am, for you called me." Then Eli perceived that the Lord was calling the boy. [9]Therefore Eli said to Samuel, "Go, lie down, and if he calls you, you shall say, 'Speak, Lord, for your servant hears.'" So Samuel went and lay down in his place.

[10]And the Lord came and stood, calling as at other times, "Samuel! Samuel!" And Samuel said, "Speak, for your servant hears." [11]Then the Lord said to Samuel, "Behold, I am about to do a thing in Israel at which the two ears of everyone who hears it will tingle. [12]On that day I will fulfill against Eli all that I have spoken concerning his house, from beginning to end. [13]And I declare to him that I am about to punish his house forever, for the iniquity that he knew, because his sons were blaspheming God,[a] and he did not restrain them. [14]Therefore I swear to the house of Eli that the iniquity of Eli's house shall not be atoned for by sacrifice or offering forever."

[15]Samuel lay until morning; then he opened the doors of the house of the Lord. And Samuel was afraid to tell the vision to Eli. [16]But Eli called Samuel and said, "Samuel, my son." And he said, "Here I am." [17]And Eli said, "What was it that he told you? Do not hide it from me. May God do so to you and more also if you hide anything from me of all that he told you." [18]So Samuel told him everything and hid nothing from him. And he said, "It is the Lord. Let him do what seems good to him."

[19]And Samuel grew, and the Lord was with him and let none of his words fall to the ground. [20]And all Israel from Dan to Beersheba knew that Samuel was established as a prophet of the Lord. [21]And the Lord appeared again at Shiloh, for the Lord revealed himself to Samuel at Shiloh by the word of the Lord.

4 And the word of Samuel came to all Israel.

a Or blaspheming for themselves

Overview: There was a general sense among Reformation interpreters that in their day God was dismantling the church of old on account of its faithlessness and breathing new life into the church—not very different from the way God was ending Eli's line and starting afresh with Samuel. Due to the godlessness on the part of Israelite leadership, God sends a spiritual famine in accordance with Scripture. As the last of the judges, Samuel is a true prophet of God, who begins to restore the Israelites to proper worship of God. Although Samuel does not initially understand God's voice, God chooses him to lead God's people into the truth. His first assignment is to deliver a divine word to his teacher Eli. The reformers commend Eli's humility to Christian believers.

Like Eli, Christians must always affirm and patiently accept the word of the Lord, regardless of the immediate pain it causes us or the difficulty that ensues. For the commentators, the beauty of this passage is that God gives partial revelation to Samuel and partial revelation to Eli, reminding us of Paul's analogy of the church as one body with many members.

Called by God Alone. Viktorin Strigel: This particular chapter recounts the direct calling of Samuel to prophetic service. Samuel was not called by people or through the agency of people but by God. And Samuel was called in this way so that he could be an expounder of the law and a witness of the Messiah, who would govern the political realm. Commentary on 1 Samuel.[1]

3:1 The Scarcity of God's Word in Those Days

Eli Establishes Samuel as a Prophet. Lucas Osiander: Prophets and divine revelations were rare then. At that time the godlessness of the priests and the people was very great. As the Lord said in Amos: "I will send a famine on the land— not a famine of bread, nor a thirst for water, but for hearing the words of the Lord." Because God's people then deserved punishment, a prophet was raised up, namely Samuel. For when God punishes his people's sins, he first sends someone to invite and call them to repentance, saying, "Come to your senses and escape punishment." Already, therefore, Samuel is called to the office of prophet. . . . [He then replied to God's call, saying]: "I am humbly ready to receive the word that you will tell me." And so Eli, who was denied prophetic visions, nevertheless established Samuel in how he prepared him to hear the divine oracle. Annotations on 1 Samuel.[2]

Neglected Word. Viktorin Strigel: At this time there were not many preachers or pastors. It was as if sacred Scripture was covered in mold or dust. The study of Scripture was neglected when Samuel came along, who roused and illuminated the study of it again. And just as the supreme good of any church is the preservation of the true doctrine of God, so the worst thing that can happen to a church is to have a famine, not of bread, but of the Word of God. Whenever the Word is lost or obscured, a horrible darkness concerning the benefits of Christ, concerning true prayer and concerning faith must inevitably follow. Therefore we give thanks to God because his Word desires to dwell among us abundantly with all wisdom. Commentary on 1 Samuel.[3]

There Was No Manifest Vision. Andrew Willet: God, for the sin of his people, brought a famine on them—"not a famine of bread, or a thirst for water"—just as he threatened by his prophet Amos: "They shall wander from sea to sea, and from north to east; they shall run to and fro, to seek the word of the Lord, but they shall not find it." Although there might be some private and particular visions and revelations—as to Manoah in Judges 13—yet the public office of prophets was ceased and intermittent. For this is not to be understood of the written word—for they had the books of Moses—but of the word of prophecy. And if there were any such visions, they were dark, hidden and obscure. As the Septuagint reads, there was no "distinct vision," that is, opened, unfolded and applied. Christ Jesus the Word of God, by whom the Lord spoke to Samuel in 1 Samuel 3:21 and to David in 2 Samuel 7:21, sparingly revealed and manifested himself to his servants the prophets. Harmony of 1 Samuel.[4]

3:2-18 God's Revelation

The Same Lord Empowering Everyone. Johannes Brenz: God provided the revelation in this way so Eli could recognize that what was first

---

[1]Strigel, *Libri Samuelis, Regum et Paralipomenon*, 12.
[2]Osiander, *Liber Iosue*, 292, 294; citing Amos 8:11.
[3]Strigel, *Libri Samuelis, Regum et Paralipomenon*, 13.
[4]Willet, *Harmony on 1 Samuel*, 19-20*; citing Amos 8:11-12.

revealed to Samuel through a dream was truly divine. Thus after Eli heard Samuel describe the revelation, he was convinced by his own testimony that this was no mere dream but a certain pronouncement from the Lord. In this way Eli might recognize and be frightened by his own true unworthiness before the Lord, and thereby be revived. This passage shows us the wonderful plan of God that one person is not given all gifts but rather that individuals are given individual gifts. To Samuel was given the gift of hearing the voice of God, though he was not given the gift of recognizing it as God's voice without being taught to know it by Eli. To Eli it was given that he might recognize the voice of God through his intellect, though it was not given him to hear the Lord himself. As Paul says, "Now there are varieties of gifts, but the same Spirit; and there are varieties of service, but the same Lord; and there are varieties of activities, but it is the same God who empowers them all in everyone." Sermons on Samuel.[5]

Listening Like Samuel. Johann Arndt: The
Lord says, "Hear my voice and open unto me." In a house in which there is the noise of this world, no sweet music can be heard. In a like manner, God cannot be heard in a worldly heart, for it is not opened toward God and does not let him in. Therefore such an earthly heart cannot taste the heavenly manna. When the tumult of this world is still in the heart, God comes and knocks and allows himself to be heard. Then you can say with the prophet Samuel: "Speak, Lord, for your servant hears." True Christianity.[6]

How Samuel Did Not Know the Lord.
Andrew Willet: Some read: "This is what Samuel did before he knew the Lord." However, the passage is better interpreted as: "Samuel did not yet know the Lord," as the Hebrew here signifies both *not yet* and *before that*. At any rate, the first interpretation is more proper here, which

makes the sense full without any other addition. But in the other reading something must be supplied. Now there is a twofold knowledge of God: ordinary and extraordinary. One is common to all servants of God, the other only to the prophets when the will of God is revealed concerning things to come: Samuel was not without the ordinary knowledge of God before, but the latter he had no experience of until now. As the next words shows, "The word of the Lord had not yet been revealed to him," which the Jews interpret as prophecy. Therefore Eli gave him instruction and informed him that it was the Lord who spoke to him. Harmony on 1 Samuel.[7]

Samuel Preaches Repentance to Eli.
Viktorin Strigel: We can see how merciful and long-suffering our heavenly father is when we consider that Eli the priest was told to repent by two prophets. For in the previous chapter Eli heard the most fervent advice of the unnamed prophet. Now he is invited to repentance by the ministry of the prophet Samuel. But then consider Samuel's great sorrow upon seeing his master and teacher's unhappy end. Commentary on 1 Samuel.[8]

What Seems Good to God. Lancelot
Andrewes: We must bear quietly the punishment laid on us, for out of affliction the godly gather a matter of thanks for having all taken from them. . . . The godly praise God for the cup of affliction as well as for the cup of salvation, and are as thankful to God for the benefits the Lord bestows on them by means of affliction against their will as for those that come to them by their will and good liking. And this is the perfection we are to strive toward. But if we do not at all reckon them as benefits, nevertheless we must say with Eli, "It is the Lord; let him do what seems good to him." Collection of Lectures.[9]

Eli Confesses His Sins. Lucas Osiander:
When Eli responded, "It is the Lord. Let him do

---

[5] Brenz, *Opera*, 2:270; citing 1 Cor 12:4-6.
[6] Arndt, *True Christianity*, 160; citing 1 Sam 3:10.
[7] Willet, *Harmony on 1 Samuel*, 21; citing 1 Sam 3:7.
[8] Strigel, *Libri Samuelis, Regum et Paralipomenon*, 14.
[9] Andrewes, *A Collection of Lectures*, 445*.

what seems good to him," it was as if he were saying, "I recognize my sin and the righteous wrath of the Lord. And I understand that I and my posterity are no longer allowed to continue the sacrifices or serve as mediators as a punishment for our sins. I will bear this patiently, content in this one thing: that I know the Lord God seriously desires repentance and not that we are cast into eternal damnation." Therefore, even if we are not able to escape from such physical punishment, we still should not doubt the mercy of God, which leads to eternal life. Instead, we should subject ourselves to the will of God with continual, humble and patient supplications. ANNOTATIONS ON I SAMUEL.[10]

NOT ETERNAL CONDEMNATION. THOMAS JACKSON: Now when Samuel had delivered this fearful and reproving sentence to Eli, the latter replied no more than this: "It is the Lord. Let him do what seems him good to him." Had this message been delivered by that "man of God" who brought the former prophecy of doom to this good old man, Eli—though he was a weak judge—he probably would have happily ignored it, for such did he do when the man of God spoke to him. At the least, he would have called the messenger's prophecy into question. But because this latter and more terrible doom was delivered to him by a child—who was far removed from secular cunning and sophisms of corrupt priests or Levites, who could not even distinguish the voice of the Lord from the voice of his teacher until he was instructed by him and who depended on Eli completely as his foster father—his message was to Eli more authentic. In other words, Samuel's message, both in its content and in its presentation, was freer from all suspicion of imposture.

Eli's response is of the same alloy of Job's reply to the sad news his servants brought to him. "The LORD," says Job, "gave and has taken away; blessed be the name of the LORD." Such is how he spoke after he had seen himself and his family utterly

undone for worldly substance, deprived of all earthly contentment. Eli knew that this sentence against him was denounced as by oath. It was as certain and impossible to be reversed as if it had already happened. For this reason, I believe, the old man, Eli, did consider a more submissive answer to Samuel than he had vouchsafed to the man of God who was sent to him on the same errand. The humility and modesty of his answer persuades me that the fearful sentence denounced against him extended no further than to the irreversible deposition of him and his family from the legal or temporary priesthood to the poor and humble estate where his posterity after the disaster of his two sons were to live here on the earth. Nor have I any warrant from God's Word to say, and Christian charity forbids me to think, that either Eli himself, his two lewd sons or his posterity were absolutely or irreversibly decreed from this time forward to everlasting damnation. A TREATISE OF THE SON OF GOD TO HIS EVERLASTING PRIESTHOOD.[11]

3:19-4:1a *Samuel's Calling to the Lord*

THE WORD OF GOD REESTABLISHED UNDER SAMUEL. JOHANNES BUGENHAGEN: This describes the Lord's first revelation to the young Samuel. It came at a time when the Lord had ceased to appear in Shiloh, for the reasons clearly explained in chapter two. Here you see an example of this: "You have hidden these things from the wise and understanding and revealed them to little children." So Samuel grew before God and the people, for he had the word of God and became known by all of Israel as a faithful prophet. COMMENTARY ON I SAMUEL.[12]

SAMUEL'S CALLING. ANDREW WILLET: Three things are expressed whereby the excellence of Samuel's gifts and the prerogative of his calling appear. First, the certainty of his predictions and prophecies all came to pass and none were spoken

---

[10]Osiander, *Liber Iosue*, 296; citing 3:18.

[11]Jackson, *Works*, 996*; citing 1 Sam 2:27; Job 1:21.
[12]Bugenhagen, *In Samuelem prophetam*, 193; citing Mt 11:25.

in vain. Samuel did not need any signs or miracles for the demonstrations of his calling, as the effect and accomplishment of his prophecies were a sufficient evidence. Second, Samuel was faithful, without any partiality or accepting of persons, in delivering the word of God to Israel—just as Moses is said to have been faithful in the Lord's house. Finally, after the Lord had begun in this way to reveal himself to Samuel, God continued to do so, and he added further to reveal to Samuel his will and to appear to him. Samuel therefore was an honorable prophet, because in him the word of prophesying revived out of its previous decay. And therefore Scripture says, "No Passover like it had been kept in Israel since the days of Samuel the prophet," since he restored the religion that had been greatly corrupted. Harmony on 1 Samuel.[13]

---

[13]Willet, *Harmony on 1 Samuel*, 24-25*; citing Num 12:3; 2 Chron 35:18.

4:1B–7:2 THE ARK CAPTURED AND RETURNED

[1] Now Israel went out to battle against the Philistines. They encamped at Ebenezer, and the Philistines encamped at Aphek. [2] The Philistines drew up in line against Israel, and when the battle spread, Israel was defeated before the Philistines, who killed about four thousand men on the field of battle. [3] And when the people came to the camp, the elders of Israel said, "Why has the LORD defeated us today before the Philistines? Let us bring the ark of the covenant of the LORD here from Shiloh, that it[a] may come among us and save us from the power of our enemies." [4] So the people sent to Shiloh and brought from there the ark of the covenant of the LORD of hosts, who is enthroned on the cherubim. And the two sons of Eli, Hophni and Phinehas, were there with the ark of the covenant of God.

[5] As soon as the ark of the covenant of the LORD came into the camp, all Israel gave a mighty shout, so that the earth resounded. [6] And when the Philistines heard the noise of the shouting, they said, "What does this great shouting in the camp of the Hebrews mean?" And when they learned that the ark of the LORD had come to the camp, [7] the Philistines were afraid, for they said, "A god has come into the camp." And they said, "Woe to us! For nothing like this has happened before. [8] Woe to us! Who can deliver us from the power of these mighty gods? These are the gods who struck the Egyptians with every sort of plague in the wilderness. [9] Take courage, and be men, O Philistines, lest you become slaves to the Hebrews as they have been to you; be men and fight."

[10] So the Philistines fought, and Israel was defeated, and they fled, every man to his home. And there was a very great slaughter, for thirty thousand foot soldiers of Israel fell. [11] And the ark of God was captured, and the two sons of Eli, Hophni and Phinehas, died.

[12] A man of Benjamin ran from the battle line and came to Shiloh the same day, with his clothes torn and with dirt on his head. [13] When he arrived, Eli was sitting on his seat by the road watching, for his heart trembled for the ark of God. And when the

man came into the city and told the news, all the city cried out. [14] When Eli heard the sound of the outcry, he said, "What is this uproar?" Then the man hurried and came and told Eli. [15] Now Eli was ninety-eight years old and his eyes were set so that he could not see. [16] And the man said to Eli, "I am he who has come from the battle; I fled from the battle today." And he said, "How did it go, my son?" [17] He who brought the news answered and said, "Israel has fled before the Philistines, and there has also been a great defeat among the people. Your two sons also, Hophni and Phinehas, are dead, and the ark of God has been captured." [18] As soon as he mentioned the ark of God, Eli fell over backward from his seat by the side of the gate, and his neck was broken and he died, for the man was old and heavy. He had judged Israel forty years.

[19] Now his daughter-in-law, the wife of Phinehas, was pregnant, about to give birth. And when she heard the news that the ark of God was captured, and that her father-in-law and her husband were dead, she bowed and gave birth, for her pains came upon her. [20] And about the time of her death the women attending her said to her, "Do not be afraid, for you have borne a son." But she did not answer or pay attention. [21] And she named the child Ichabod, saying, "The glory has departed[b] from Israel!" because the ark of God had been captured and because of her father-in-law and her husband. [22] And she said, "The glory has departed from Israel, for the ark of God has been captured."

5 When the Philistines captured the ark of God, they brought it from Ebenezer to Ashdod. [2] Then the Philistines took the ark of God and brought it into the house of Dagon and set it up beside Dagon. [3] And when the people of Ashdod rose early the next day, behold, Dagon had fallen face downward on the ground before the ark of the LORD. So they took Dagon and put him back in his place. [4] But when they rose early on the next morning, behold, Dagon had fallen face downward on the ground before the

ark of the Lord, and the head of Dagon and both his hands were lying cut off on the threshold. Only the trunk of Dagon was left to him. ⁵This is why the priests of Dagon and all who enter the house of Dagon do not tread on the threshold of Dagon in Ashdod to this day.

⁶The hand of the Lord was heavy against the people of Ashdod, and he terrified and afflicted them with tumors, both Ashdod and its territory. ⁷And when the men of Ashdod saw how things were, they said, "The ark of the God of Israel must not remain with us, for his hand is hard against us and against Dagon our god." ⁸So they sent and gathered together all the lords of the Philistines and said, "What shall we do with the ark of the God of Israel?" They answered, "Let the ark of the God of Israel be brought around to Gath." So they brought the ark of the God of Israel there. ⁹But after they had brought it around, the hand of the Lord was against the city, causing a very great panic, and he afflicted the men of the city, both young and old, so that tumors broke out on them. ¹⁰So they sent the ark of God to Ekron. But as soon as the ark of God came to Ekron, the people of Ekron cried out, "They have brought around to us the ark of the God of Israel to kill us and our people." ¹¹They sent therefore and gathered together all the lords of the Philistines and said, "Send away the ark of the God of Israel, and let it return to its own place, that it may not kill us and our people." For there was a deathly panic throughout the whole city. The hand of God was very heavy there. ¹²The men who did not die were struck with tumors, and the cry of the city went up to heaven.

6 The ark of the Lord was in the country of the Philistines seven months. ²And the Philistines called for the priests and the diviners and said, "What shall we do with the ark of the Lord? Tell us with what we shall send it to its place." ³They said, "If you send away the ark of the God of Israel, do not send it empty, but by all means return him a guilt offering. Then you will be healed, and it will be known to you why his hand does not turn away from you." ⁴And they said, "What is the guilt offering that we shall return to him?" They answered, "Five golden tumors and five golden mice,

according to the number of the lords of the Philistines, for the same plague was on all of you and on your lords. ⁵So you must make images of your tumors and images of your mice that ravage the land, and give glory to the God of Israel. Perhaps he will lighten his hand from off you and your gods and your land. ⁶Why should you harden your hearts as the Egyptians and Pharaoh hardened their hearts? After he had dealt severely with them, did they not send the people away, and they departed? ⁷Now then, take and prepare a new cart and two milk cows on which there has never come a yoke, and yoke the cows to the cart, but take their calves home, away from them. ⁸And take the ark of the Lord and place it on the cart and put in a box at its side the figures of gold, which you are returning to him as a guilt offering. Then send it off and let it go its way ⁹and watch. If it goes up on the way to its own land, to Beth-shemesh, then it is he who has done us this great harm, but if not, then we shall know that it is not his hand that struck us; it happened to us by coincidence."

¹⁰The men did so, and took two milk cows and yoked them to the cart and shut up their calves at home. ¹¹And they put the ark of the Lord on the cart and the box with the golden mice and the images of their tumors. ¹²And the cows went straight in the direction of Beth-shemesh along one highway, lowing as they went. They turned neither to the right nor to the left, and the lords of the Philistines went after them as far as the border of Beth-shemesh. ¹³Now the people of Beth-shemesh were reaping their wheat harvest in the valley. And when they lifted up their eyes and saw the ark, they rejoiced to see it. ¹⁴The cart came into the field of Joshua of Beth-shemesh and stopped there. A great stone was there. And they split up the wood of the cart and offered the cows as a burnt offering to the Lord. ¹⁵And the Levites took down the ark of the Lord and the box that was beside it, in which were the golden figures, and set them upon the great stone. And the men of Beth-shemesh offered burnt offerings and sacrificed sacrifices on that day to the Lord. ¹⁶And when the five lords of the Philistines saw it, they returned that day to Ekron.

¹⁷These are the golden tumors that the Philistines returned as a guilt offering to the LORD: one for Ashdod, one for Gaza, one for Ashkelon, one for Gath, one for Ekron, ¹⁸and the golden mice, according to the number of all the cities of the Philistines belonging to the five lords, both fortified cities and unwalled villages. The great stone beside which they set down the ark of the LORD is a witness to this day in the field of Joshua of Beth-shemesh.

¹⁹And he struck some of the men of Beth-shemesh, because they looked upon the ark of the LORD. He struck seventy men of them,^c and the people mourned because the LORD had struck the people with a great

blow. ²⁰Then the men of Beth-shemesh said, "Who is able to stand before the LORD, this holy God? And to whom shall he go up away from us?" ²¹So they sent messengers to the inhabitants of Kiriath-jearim, saying, "The Philistines have returned the ark of the LORD. Come down and take it up to you."

7 And the men of Kiriath-jearim came and took up the ark of the LORD and brought it to the house of Abinadab on the hill. And they consecrated his son Eleazar to have charge of the ark of the LORD. ²From the day that the ark was lodged at Kiriath-jearim, a long time passed, some twenty years, and all the house of Israel lamented after the LORD.

a Or *he*   **b** Or *gone into exile*; also verse 22   **c** Most Hebrew manuscripts *struck of the people seventy men, fifty thousand men*

OVERVIEW: According to the commentators, God uses the war between the Israelites and the Philistines to take the lives of Eli and his sons as punishment for their sins. The interpreters are also agreed that taking the ark of the covenant to the battlefield is a foolish act with dire consequences. Nevertheless, when the Philistines place the Israelite ark, which signifies the presence of Yahweh, alongside their god Dagon, the Lord God guards his sanctity despite the godlessness of the Israelites. In fact, God punishes the Philistines, who ironically display more reverence toward the ark than the Israelites had, sending it back to Bethshemesh with materials for guilt offerings and burnt offerings. Although the men of Bethshemesh should have known better, the interpreters explain, they violate the law of God by opening the ark and not handling it lawfully. God, therefore, rightly takes the lives of the guilty men. In this same passage, God takes the lives of Hophni, Phinehas, Eli and Phinehas's wife. Although it is a harsh concept for many of us today, the commentators take to heart Hannah's earlier song that "the LORD kills . . . ; he brings down to Sheol" (1 Sam 2:6). The interpreters do not distinguish here between God's role in the taking of human life and the giving of it.

4:1b-11 The Priests Accompany the Ark into Battle

FIGHTING BATTLES WITHOUT GOD'S WORD.
JOHANNES BUGENHAGEN: Whoever goes to war without the word of God and trusts in his own strength will fall, because victory is the Lord's. The self-appointed masters Hophni and Phinehas show that they did not have this word of God. You will not remain standing against "the Philistines," whether that means people of God or enemies of the faith, unless the spiritual word guards your heart. For there are some among us who have the word of God (like the Israelites), who then produce great speeches of human knowledge, pointing to the Scriptures and arguing against adversaries, saying that it is good to destroy whomever and to strive to win on the holy day, as if conducting worship would be a lie and hypocrisy, as if the sacraments were just another kind of communion, as if they were not a righteous work to share with all and that Scripture says so. However that may be, they do not know that faith happens in the heart. They do not know that the gospel is not letter but spirit, not doctrine but life. And while they themselves trust that the sacraments show only an external salvation (however otherwise beautiful), they crumble in the face of

their adversaries. This is what it means that the Israelites hoped for salvation from the ark, which was a sacrament according to the word of God. It had the propitiator who is Christ and the two cherubim, which are the two testaments of propitiation gazing on each other. But without the word of God, that is, without faith in their hearts, the ark was nothing but that death which they shamefully brought on themselves. Commentary on 1 Samuel.[1]

Blaming God for Defeat. Viktorin Strigel: Just as Brutus exclaimed before meeting his end, "O Jupiter, the cause of all evils!" so the people of Israel disputed the reason for their loss in the battlefield. And just as Brutus was rightly punished for his monstrous scheming, first when he drove Caesar out of Cyprus and then when he killed him in the Senate out of ingratitude, so the people of Israel were rightly punished by God for their disobedience and ingratitude. Therefore, in our times of calamity, we ought to praise God's righteousness and cry out with David, "Against you, you only, have I sinned and done what is evil in your sight." And "You are righteous, O Lord, and your judgment is righteous." Commentary on 1 Samuel.[2]

4:12-22 Death and Life

Eli's Death. Andrew Willet: The principal cause of Eli's death was the justice of God in punishing, by this temporal judgment, Eli's negligence in not correcting his sons. For, as he did not bow the necks of his sons to the yoke, so his neck, now bowed and broken, served as a just recompense. The subordinate cause of Eli's death was the lamentable report of so many calamities, which all fell out together—Israel fleeing, his sons' deaths and the ark's capture, for which he grieved most of all. The messenger made no pause at all but uttered all his heavy news at once, as if it were on purpose to oppress and overload Eli with grief. However, if the messenger had taken time to tell the story by degrees, Eli's grief might have been allayed. Finally, the instrumental cause of Eli's death was his falling from his feet, which was not a low stool but a high throne, which was proper for a high priest and chief judge. So he fell high and, since he was also very old—almost one hundred years old—his body was fat and round, and he was not nimble enough to shift himself. What's more, he was very dim-sighted and so could not see which way to help himself as he fell. Harmony on 1 Samuel.[3]

An Eli in Every Age. John Robinson: It is dangerous in the course of religion and godliness to fall forward by errors, preposterous zeal or another misguidance; yet not so much so as to fall backward by an unfaithful heart. The former may break his face thereby and lose his comfort in a great measure both with God and with people. But the latter is in danger utterly to break the neck of his conscience, as old Eli broke his neck bodily by falling backward from his seat and died. Are there not many Eli's in all ages? Essays.[4]

The Birth of Ichabod. Lucas Osiander: The attending woman said to the wife of Phinehas, "Do not fear, get your soul back together, for you have borne a son. Recover your soul in hope, because when other mothers have given birth to their children they are often overwhelmed with great joy." Truly, the new mother was by no means cheered up, because she did not respond to hearing the consolation of the child's birth and she did not direct her mind to it, or in Hebrew, "she did not apply her heart to it." That is, she did not sense any recovery. She named the newborn child Ichabod, saying, "Glory (that is, our glory, all glory, and the majesty of the people of Israel) has departed." Annotations on 1 Samuel.[5]

---

[1]Bugenhagen, *In Samuelem prophetam*, 195-96.
[2]Strigel, *Libri Samuelis, Regum et Paralipomenon*, 16; citing Ps 51:4; Ps 119:37 (translated from the Latin).
[3]Willet, *Harmony on 1 Samuel*, 28*.
[4]Robinson, *Works*, 1:27*.
[5]Osiander, *Liber Iosue*, 302-3; citing Jn 16:21.

THE DEATH OF PHINEHAS'S WIFE. ANDREW
WILLET: Phinehas's wife grieved more for the loss
of the ark than in rejoicing that she had gained a
son. She gave up the ghost based on her zeal and
love of religion, which was absent in her husband.
In fact, she did not even take into account the
death of her husband and father-in-law, but was
highly concerned about the capture of the ark and
how its glory was lost. She therefore named her
son Ichabod, which consists of two words: the first
signifying "woe" or "where" . . . and the second,
"glory." The name Ichabod, then, means "Where is
the glory?," or "No glory." Josephus thinks that she
gave birth before her time, and that Ichabod was
born at seven months. However, that is not likely,
because the child lived. Nonetheless, here Samuel's
prophecy is fulfilled—that there would not be an
old man left of Eli's house. This translating of the
glory of God to the Philistines prefigured the
offering of grace to the Gentiles and the removing
of the glory of religion from the Jews. HARMONY
ON 1 SAMUEL.[6]

5:1-12 *The Lord Versus Dagon*

TRUSTING IN FALSE GODS. JOHANNES BUGEN-
HAGEN: Just as the Israelites impiously trusted in
the ark, despising the truly sacramental word of
God, so the Gentiles impiously betrayed God too.
They presumed to rule over God, standing the ark
next to their god Dagon. But they were the ones
who were themselves undone by God's Scriptures
and sacraments. They were terribly ignorant of
God, not having even a crumb of the Spirit, which
a disciple of Christ shows by his or her fruits. For
these others stand next to their god, that is, next to
their trust in works, traditions and human
inventions, which they want to establish in this way,
as if they already had God's testimony for their
impieties and idolatries. But this is against the first
commandment: "You shall have no other gods
before me." COMMENTARY ON 1 SAMUEL.[7]

**GOD'S POWER ROUSED AGAINST ENEMIES
AND IDOLS.** VIKTORIN STRIGEL: While the
triumphing, blasphemous enemies rise against the
church and yell taunts against the God of Israel,
God was then thought to be asleep or buried in his
cups. But then he was roused, so that the Philistines were brought together to confess the thing
itself, the infinite separation between the true and
living God and the false and fabricated god known
as Dagon. And so God is announced in his glory
even without our prayers, even though Samuel and
other pious people in Israel were doubtlessly
making vows like this one: "Therefore arise, O Lord
God, and sanctify your name, which they desecrate.
Strengthen in us your kingdom, which they would
destroy. Let your will be done, which they would
suppress. Grant that your name not be trampled
on because of our sin by those who do not seek to
punish our sin but who desire only to destroy in us
the knowledge of thy holy Word, of your name and
of your work, so that they might dethrone you and
rob you of a people that proclaims and confesses
you and trusts in you. Amen." COMMENTARY ON
1 SAMUEL.[8]

GOD IS NOT MOCKED. LUCAS OSIANDER: The
Philistines set the ark beside Dagon, evidently as if
in triumph about taking captive the God of Israel,
whose captured ark was taken into their idol's
temple like spoils of war. For it was the custom to
be arrogant in such victories, especially when
enemies conquered God's people. Then the true
God and his religion was mocked. But God did not
let a day go by without avenging their insults
against him. Then "Dagon had fallen face downward on the ground before the ark of the LORD," as
if adoring the ark in veneration. For when an act of
true religion is seen, then God begins to bring a
great number people to himself. Quite sensibly,
then, from this miracle the Philistines recognized
the Israelite religion as truth and their idol Dagon

---

[6]Willet, *Harmony on 1 Samuel*, 30*.
[7]Bugenhagen, *In Samuelem prophetam*, 197-98; citing Ex 20:3.

[8]Strigel, *Libri Samuelis, Regum et Paralipomenon*, 19-20; citing a
prayer attributed to Martin Luther against the Turks and other
enemies in LW 43:233.

as vanity. But with blinded minds, they did not totally comprehend it. Annotations on 1 Samuel.[9]

The Philistine God Is Merely a Fish. Cardinal Cajetan: Consider, prudent reader, that here for the second time Dagon fell on its face on the ground before the ark of the covenant, and that its head and hands were cut off on the threshold. And so understand that this text does not say that Dagon's trunk remained in its place . . . but it says that nothing remained in the idol's place except *dāg*, that is, the form of a fish—for the Hebrews, Dagon sounds like "fish." And they say that this idol was an image of a man mixed with a fish, so that its head and hands were human, but the rest of its body was of a fish. And this fits very well with the letter of the Hebrew, which clearly states: only Dagon remained left over. For with its human members severed off, only a fish remained, prostrate before the ark of God. Commentary on 1 Samuel.[10]

Unfit Companions. Charles Drelincourt: Just as the Lord's ark and Dagon cannot dwell together under one roof, so the love of God and the love of the world can never subsist together. Therefore St. John advises us, "Do not love the world or the things in the world. If anyone loves the world, the love of the Father is not in him." Christian Defense Against the Fears of Death.[11]

6:1-12 *The Philistines*

No Peace of Conscience Without God. Viktorin Strigel: Whenever humans and reason dominate, the word of God is removed from their midst and from any collective glory. Then the true priesthood falls and is extinguished, the cause of which is the wrath of God. But the victors never have peace in the consciences after

this. For wherever the word of God is corrupted, pestilence and destruction are driven on consciences, just as the ark did to the Philistines. At length they had to confess their own shamefulness, that they had adulterated God's word, the ark. So they got themselves together in order to return it unblemished. This is what the golden rings and mice signify: they are arcane signs for the pains of conscience, which are ultimately revealed through the word of God. As Paul says, "They will not get very far, for their folly will be plain to all." Commentary on 1 Samuel.[12]

The Reverence of the Philistines. Andrew Willet: The Philistines were punished for their gross rudeness in profaning the ark and for consecrating it as one of their chief spoils to their idol, thereby making the great God inferior to their abominable invention. This breach of the natural and moral law did not escape unpunished. However, as for the ceremonial law—which prohibited the Israelites from coming near the ark or gazing on it—it was given only to the Israelites and so the heathen were ignorant of it. In this we see that the Lord requires a stricter obedience at the hands of his own people than of uninformed foreigners. What's more, the Lord accepts this kind of reverence, which the Philistines out of their simple knowledge yielded to the ark—not allowing it to go empty but bestowing on it jewels of gold. They also used choice cows that were never before hitched to the yoke in addition to providing a new cart, which befits the holiness of the ark. The Philistines thereby expressed their reverence for the ark in this regard, by actually following the prescript of Moses' law. Harmony on 1 Samuel.[13]

Human Advice. Giovanni Diodati: This first part of the Philistines' answer is naturally grounded on the ordinary means of appeasing God's wrath by offerings. . . . It was likely consid-

---

[9]Osiander, *Liber Iosue*, 303-4.
[10]Cajetan, *Opera Omnia in Sacrae Scripturae Expositionem*, 2:84.
[11]Drelincourt, *Christian's Defense Against the Fears of Death*, 170*; citing 1 Jn 2:15.
[12]Strigel, *Libri Samuelis, Regum et Paralipomenon*, 18. This passage by Strigel is an extended citation of Luther, source unknown; citing 2 Tim 3:9.
[13]Willet, *Harmony on 1 Samuel*, 38*.

ered a trespass-offering, for it was a kind of trespass—though committed through ignorance—by which it was believed that God would be appeased and that the people would know that his wrath had been the cause of the people's evils. . . . At the same time, the specification of the offerings—which is really absurd and ridiculous to think the Deity wants, for instance, images of mice—seems to be suggested by the devil in contempt of God. Who would accept this as a memorial that he had overcome his enemies by such poor and contemptible means—unless even in those days it was customary to consecrate a resemblance of those parts of the body in which they were healed, or of the annoyances which they were freed from, to that Deity which they were devoted to or from which they acknowledged the said deliverance? But because God's law decreed nothing of the sort, it was truly an idolatrous superstition. ANNOTATIONS ON 1 SAMUEL.[14]

6:13-18 The Israelites

GOD ALONE BROUGHT THE ARK BACK TO ISRAEL. VIKTORIN STRIGEL: God restored the ark of Israel by sending illustrious miracles, so that he might show that his church is gathered and protected not by human decisions or strength but by divine power. Yet though they had not set this miracle in motion, the Israelites with their meager human counsels would still move away from the form of government that God had instituted, as it says in chapter eight below. COMMENTARY ON 1 SAMUEL.[15]

CONTINUANCE OF THE ARK. ANDREW WILLET: Here we may see the miserable state of Israel at this time—that they were deprived of that visible sign of God's presence among them, namely, the ark, where the two tables of commandments dwelled. During this time they seemed to be forlorn and forsaken of God. Indeed, such times may sometimes fall out in the church of God: For

a time, the Lord may allow sinners to be deprived of the true use of God's Word and the sacraments. The Philistines held the ark for awhile—thinking that in time plagues would lessen. Afterward they purposed to keep the ark in enslavement and captivity still. At this time the ark sojourned among the Philistines without any profit to them at all. In the same way, a long time passed among the unrighteous Gentiles before truth was revealed to them, as the apostle says, since the time had not yet come for the Jews to be utterly dispossessed of the ark. But now we see that the ark of the gospel has been transferred to the believing Gentiles, and it has continued among them for hundreds of years, working in them faith and obedience to the truth. HARMONY ON 1 SAMUEL.[16]

6:19–7:2 God's Judgment for Looking at the Ark

UNHOLY CURIOSITY. JOHANNES BUGENHAGEN: We have spoken above about looking at the ark out of curiosity. The law prohibits this under the penalty of death: no one should look at the ark, no one should come close to it and no one should look at it in the holy of holies. This is your death and you will be unable to avoid meeting it. You will be blinded by this inaccessible light, where you will have wanted to measure what is from God by your reason and wisdom. God reveals them to be small and foolish, whoever lets go of God in favor of their own works and judgment. For he hides this from the wise and the intelligent, as it says in Romans, "Oh, the depth of the riches and wisdom and knowledge of God!" and in Ecclesiasticus, "Seek not the things that are too high for you." See this example of people's conventional wisdom, how they push down the divine things that are seen as troublesome. They ask for kindness, but do not know even if they might be counted among the people of God. COMMENTARY ON 1 SAMUEL.[17]

---

[14]Diodati, *Pious Annotations*, 166*.
[15]Strigel, *Libri Samuelis, Regum et Paralipomenon*, 22.

[16]Willet, *Harmony on 1 Samuel*, 34-35*.
[17]Bugenhagen, *In Samuelem prophetam*, 201-2; citing Rom 11:33; Sir 3:22.

Causal but Not Casual. Lancelot Andrewes: The sickness and mortality of people is causal and not casual. For nothing is more contrary to judgment than chance or fortune. Just as a sparrow cannot fall on the ground without God's providence—such is God's care for them. . . . It is a senseless thing to think that sickness can befall a person by chance. Therefore the Philistines, being plagued by God, would boldly test whether that disease came of God's hand or by chance. . . . But the very name *plague* signifies "judgment," which shows that it is no casual thing. Collection of Lectures.[18]

Smiting Bethshemesh. Andrew Willet: The Bethshemites were offensive in several ways. First, they did not receive the ark with great reverence and devotion when they saw it coming. Instead, they entertained it, as apparently they thought best, with shouting and signs of joy, as was common during the time of harvest. Second, they sacrificed female cows, namely, the two cows that drew the cart. However, according to the law, only bulls were to be offered. (Some also think that the Bethshemites themselves offered sacrifice rather than consulting with priests or the prophet Samuel. But that is not likely. . . .) Finally, the main reason why the Lord killed the Bethshemites was because "they looked on the ark of the Lord," which was contrary to Numbers 5:20. . . . Josephus thinks that they also handled it irreverently with their hands. However, the fact that they looked on the ark without being priests was sufficient reason to procure God's judgment. It is, of course, possible that the priests may have offended God by not approaching and drawing near with sufficient reverence. Nonetheless, it seems that by the number of them that were killed, most of them were of the common sort rather than priests. Harmony on 1 Samuel.[19]

Unusual Circumstance. Giovanni Diodati: Kiriath-jearim was not a city that belonged to the priests as Bethshemesh was. As such, it was unlawful for anyone other than priests to touch the ark. It is therefore to be imagined that all this was done by the ministry of some priests who were sent for from some other place—unless there was some great toleration from God in such an extraordinary case as this was. Annotation on 1 Samuel.[20]

---

[18]Andrewes, *A Collection of Lectures*, 653*.

[19]Willet, *Harmony on 1 Samuel*, 39-40*.
[20]Diodati, *Pious Annotations*, 166*.

7:3–8:22 SAMUEL JUDGES WHILE
ISRAEL DEMANDS A KING

³And Samuel said to all the house of Israel, "If you are returning to the Lord with all your heart, then put away the foreign gods and the Ashtaroth from among you and direct your heart to the Lord and serve him only, and he will deliver you out of the hand of the Philistines." ⁴So the people of Israel put away the Baals and the Ashtaroth, and they served the Lord only.

⁵Then Samuel said, "Gather all Israel at Mizpah, and I will pray to the Lord for you." ⁶So they gathered at Mizpah and drew water and poured it out before the Lord and fasted on that day and said there, "We have sinned against the Lord." And Samuel judged the people of Israel at Mizpah. ⁷Now when the Philistines heard that the people of Israel had gathered at Mizpah, the lords of the Philistines went up against Israel. And when the people of Israel heard of it, they were afraid of the Philistines. ⁸And the people of Israel said to Samuel, "Do not cease to cry out to the Lord our God for us, that he may save us from the hand of the Philistines." ⁹So Samuel took a nursing lamb and offered it as a whole burnt offering to the Lord. And Samuel cried out to the Lord for Israel, and the Lord answered him. ¹⁰As Samuel was offering up the burnt offering, the Philistines drew near to attack Israel. But the Lord thundered with a mighty sound that day against the Philistines and threw them into confusion, and they were defeated before Israel. ¹¹And the men of Israel went out from Mizpah and pursued the Philistines and struck them, as far as below Beth-car.

¹²Then Samuel took a stone and set it up between Mizpah and Shenᵃ and called its name Ebenezer;ᵇ for he said, "Till now the Lord has helped us." ¹³So the Philistines were subdued and did not again enter the territory of Israel. And the hand of the Lord was against the Philistines all the days of Samuel. ¹⁴The cities that the Philistines had taken from Israel were restored to Israel, from Ekron to Gath, and Israel delivered their territory from the hand of the Philistines.

There was peace also between Israel and the Amorites.

¹⁵Samuel judged Israel all the days of his life. ¹⁶And he went on a circuit year by year to Bethel, Gilgal, and Mizpah. And he judged Israel in all these places. ¹⁷Then he would return to Ramah, for his home was there, and there also he judged Israel. And he built there an altar to the Lord.

8When Samuel became old, he made his sons judges over Israel. ²The name of his firstborn son was Joel, and the name of his second, Abijah; they were judges in Beersheba. ³Yet his sons did not walk in his ways but turned aside after gain. They took bribes and perverted justice.

⁴Then all the elders of Israel gathered together and came to Samuel at Ramah ⁵and said to him, "Behold, you are old and your sons do not walk in your ways. Now appoint for us a king to judge us like all the nations." ⁶But the thing displeased Samuel when they said, "Give us a king to judge us." And Samuel prayed to the Lord. ⁷And the Lord said to Samuel, "Obey the voice of the people in all that they say to you, for they have not rejected you, but they have rejected me from being king over them. ⁸According to all the deeds that they have done, from the day I brought them up out of Egypt even to this day, forsaking me and serving other gods, so they are also doing to you. ⁹Now then, obey their voice; only you shall solemnly warn them and show them the ways of the king who shall reign over them."

¹⁰So Samuel told all the words of the Lord to the people who were asking for a king from him. ¹¹He said, "These will be the ways of the king who will reign over you: he will take your sons and appoint them to his chariots and to be his horsemen and to run before his chariots. ¹²And he will appoint for himself commanders of thousands and commanders of fifties, and some to plow his ground and to reap his harvest, and to make his implements of war and the equipment of his chariots. ¹³He will take your daughters to be perfumers and cooks and bakers. ¹⁴He will take the best of your

fields and vineyards and olive orchards and give them to his servants. ¹⁵He will take the tenth of your grain and of your vineyards and give it to his officers and to his servants. ¹⁶He will take your male servants and female servants and the best of your young men^c and your donkeys, and put them to his work. ¹⁷He will take the tenth of your flocks, and you shall be his slaves. ¹⁸And in that day you will cry out because of your king, whom you have chosen for yourselves, but the LORD will not answer you in that day."

¹⁹But the people refused to obey the voice of Samuel. And they said, "No! But there shall be a king over us, ²⁰that we also may be like all the nations, and that our king may judge us and go out before us and fight our battles." ²¹And when Samuel had heard all the words of the people, he repeated them in the ears of the LORD. ²²And the LORD said to Samuel, "Obey their voice and make them a king." Samuel then said to the men of Israel, "Go every man to his city."

a Hebrew; Septuagint, Syriac *Jeshanah*   b *Ebenezer* means *stone of help*   c Septuagint *cattle*

OVERVIEW: In these two chapters, we witness the transition from judgeship to kingship in Israel. The reformers regard Samuel as a true prophet of God who leads the Israelites toward repentance and restores them to proper worship of God. In particular, the Lutheran interpreters note the concept of conversion in the leadership of Samuel. Because of Samuel's godly leadership, the Israelites defeat the Philistines since faith proves the best of all weapons. Despite this victory, the reformers recognize the impiety of the Israelites for wanting a king like the rest of the nations rather than trusting in God as their king. The commentators interpret this desire as undue trust in worldly things such as power and comfort, while also seeing God's hand in providing an earthly king whose descendants will lead to the King of kings, Jesus Christ. Some of the commentators, astute readers of the Old Testament and of the interpretive tradition before them, draw a parallel between this passage, about the role of a king, and the duties of a king set out in Deuteronomy 17.

7:3-17 *Victory by Humility*

RETURNING TO GOD'S WORD AND TO FAITH. JOHANNES BUGENHAGEN: Under Samuel, the people truly turn back to God, are liberated by God, receive peace and triumph over their enemies, because in Samuel they have the word of God. "Since we have been justified by faith, we have peace,"

and we put the kingdom of Satan and antichrist under foot. "Therefore," as Christ says, "pray earnestly to the Lord of the harvest to send out laborers into his harvest." For the wrath of God comes with the removal of God's word, as in Isaiah 3:8 and Amos 8:11. COMMENTARY ON 1 SAMUEL.[1]

CONTRITION, FAITH AND THE NEW OBEDIENCE. VIKTORIN STRIGEL: This chapter shows extraordinary examples of true conversion to God, which is grasped through contrition, faith and the new obedience. The signs of contrition are true confession of sin, tears and fasting. The fruits of faith are prayers of invocation and the rejection of idols, for "how shall they call on him unless they believe?" After this conversion follows the clearest victory, which freed the people of Israel from a sad servitude. For no one can have strength of weapons without true repentance and invocation. How else can we be free from the many fighting Turks and other enemies of the church? Not by weapons alone, but also by crying out to God for conversion. That is our help in tribulation, for human salvation is vanity. COMMENTARY ON 1 SAMUEL.[2]

MEANINGFUL OFFERINGS. LANCELOT ANDREWES: As Samuel not only prayed to God for the

---

[1]Bugenhagen, *In Samuelem prophetam*, 204-5; citing Rom 5:11; Mt 9:38; Ps 62:8; Jas 5:15.
[2]Strigel, *Libri Samuelis, Regum et Paralipomenon*, 23; citing the Augsburg Confession, especially articles 6, 12 and 20; Rom 10:14.

people but also sacrificed a suckling lamb and offered it up to God for them . . . so Christ, our intercessor to God, not only prayed but also made an offering on our behalf. He made an offering in the morning when he was presented to God his Father to yield obedience to the law; and he made an offering in the evening when he died. Not only was Christ the ear and firstfruit of the corn, but he also became the vine in his death by shedding his blood. And he not only prayed but also gave meaning to our prayers. In this way, not only did he make an offering for us, but he also gives meaning to our offerings. COLLECTION OF LECTURES.[3]

ERECTING A STONE. LUCAS OSIANDER: Samuel took a stone and called the name of the place Ebenezer, that is, a stone of help. This stone was erected as a sure testimony and memorial to divine goodness and power, which helped the people subdue their enemies. So Samuel said, "Till now the LORD has helped us against the Philistines," that is, let us preserve the memory of such great kindness with grateful souls and pass it on to those who come after us. We therefore truly erect such an image of God whenever we preach and sing the same glory, both privately and publicly. ANNOTATIONS ON 1 SAMUEL.[4]

GREATNESS OF THE VICTORY. ANDREW WILLET: Three things set forth and commend the greatness of this victory. First, the people were unprepared and unarmed since they gathered together in common prayer and supplication, while their enemies came on them hastily and all of a sudden. Second, they used no carnal weapons or outward defense. Instead, Samuel only offered a sacrifice and prayed for them. Finally, God humbled the Philistines from heaven. The earth trembled under them, and they fell. The thunder astonished them and the lightning blasted them. This victory is like that which God gave to Barak and Deborah against Sisera (Judg 5) and that

which God gave to Joshua when the Lord cast down stones on his enemies (Josh 10:10-11). HARMONY ON 1 SAMUEL.[5]

8:1-9 *Asking for a King*

THE PEOPLE'S REQUEST. JOHANNES BUGENHAGEN: Recognizing the occasion provided by the sins of Samuel's sons, the people impiously asked for a king who might defend them according to the customs of the Gentiles. They did not look to God, who had thus far been a king to them and fought for them, as Moses had said, "The LORD will fight for you, and you have only to be silent." God did this for them through the judges Moses, Aaron, Joshua, Eleazar and other successors described in the book of Judges. Through them the people were saved from their enemies until the time of Eli, when God served the people without regard to Eli's impiety and the people's idolatry. Then the rejected sons of Eli gave way to the greater Samuel. So it was already a great impiety to ask Samuel for a king while he was still living and not to expect that a judge would be given as usual to replace his impious sons, just as Samuel had been given to them instead of Eli's sons. This is clearly a rejection of God and trusting in humans, in whom there is no salvation, as it says in the Psalms. COMMENTARY ON 1 SAMUEL.[6]

DISTRUST AND AUDACITY. VIKTORIN STRIGEL: Someone might ask how the people sinned in asking for a new form of government, when it seems wise to have deliberated on fixed leadership. Here is my simple reply. Two great sins are most severely punished, distrust and the audacity to set up new political forms according to human ideas rather than divine ones. For God wants to gather, protect and serve the church through the son, who is the head of the church. They do not need human protection, and God wants them to expect divine assistance, just

---

[3]Andrewes, *A Collection of Lectures*, 571*.
[4]Osiander, *Liber Iosue*, 315-16.

[5]Willet, *Harmony on 1 Samuel*, 46*.
[6]Bugenhagen, *In Samuelem prophetam*, 205-6; citing Ex 14:14; Ps 60:11; 146:3.

as they expected deliverance from Egypt after more than eighty years. The elders rejected this faith, thinking of human assistance. The other trespass is the audacity to constitute a new political form without God's establishment. For God does not want the teaching, worship or laws that have been handed down to change. God does not want to change the political forms, because such changes also shake the laws and doctrines and because legal restraints often make kings feel ill. Many also bend religion to serve their own desires, as when the kings of Samaria established new forms of worship during their reigns. COMMENTARY ON 1 SAMUEL.[7]

NEW MEDIATOR. LANCELOT ANDREWES: Now, there is great disagreement between God and humankind by reason of sin, which has made a separation. And therefore we are to inquire who shall be the mediator between the two. It is certain Samuel, while he lived, stood between God and the people as a mediator to appease God by sacrifice. But his role as mediator has come to an end. Therefore we must look for a more perfect Mediator—such a one as Samuel himself needed. Now, the Mediator who stands between God and us is not Samuel the priest—but Christ. COLLECTION OF LECTURES.[8]

DID THE PEOPLE CAST OFF THE LORD'S GOVERNMENT? ANDREW WILLET: It is not quite true to say that the government under kings is a shaking off of the Lord's yoke. For the Lord is with kings and he rules his people through them: They are the ordinance of God. Wisdom says, "By me kings reign." Indeed, the Lord blessed the governments of David, Jehoshaphat, Hezekiah and Josiah. Yet the people . . . rejected the Lord's government because they disliked the form of administration the Lord had set on them. They desired change and innovation without any direction from God. But it will be further questioned: Did God also reign together with bad kings? Yes. Even the

authority of wicked kings is of God, which they abuse to tyranny. And for their evil and abuse of the government they shall give account to God. But although the people are evil who govern, yet the authority they possess is lawful and good. For even under tyrants there are many good things, such as the enacting of political laws, the administration of justice and the punishment of lawbreakers. HARMONY ON 1 SAMUEL.[9]

OBEYING AUTHORITIES, OBEYING GOD. JOHN DAVENANT: Work and its reward are related. Therefore, equity demands that for whom the work is done, from him the reward should be expected. It will seem scarcely credible that those who discharged the basest offices among people here on earth should be said on that very account to serve Christ himself, who sits in the heavens most glorious and by no means needing human service. But the reason is manifest . . . , namely, that whatever duties are performed by people according to the direction and at the command of Christ, and on account of the appointment and for the glory of Christ, they are judged to be offered and rendered to Christ himself. For "he serves God who for the sake of God serves people," as Jerome has rightly observed. . . . Christ himself shows this: "As you have done it to the least of these, you have done it to me; As you did not do it to one of the least of these, you did not do it to me."

Jesus speaks in this place about almsgiving, as far as they are done or denied to people. But it ought to be extended to all the works of obedience commanded by God. For when these are rendered to people they are rendered to God, who commanded them to be done; when denied to people, they are deemed as denied to God himself. And this is right. For if the one who is commanded by God to obey people refuses to yield to human authority, this person would—if he had the power—also shake off the divine government.

There are three corollaries to this. First, no service is dishonorable in which people conduct

---

[7]Strigel, *Libri Samuelis, Regum et Paralipomenon*, 27.
[8]Andrewes, *A Collection of Lectures*, 570*.

[9]Willet, *Harmony on 1 Samuel*, 51-52*; citing Prov 8:15.

themselves well and faithfully: For such people and actions serve Christ himself, which is the height of dignity and honor. Second, no honor or authority screens a wicked person from dishonor and disgrace: For they who are of that character serve the devil, which is the abyss of infamy and misery. Third, those who, being placed under the rule of others, are unwilling to serve are rebels not only against people but also against God and Christ. Hence that reproof of God himself against the Israelites wishing to shake off the government of Samuel: "They have not rejected you, but they have rejected me." EXPOSITION OF COLOSSIANS.[10]

8:10-22 *The King's Duties*

NO DIVINE SANCTION TO ABUSE AUTHORITY. PHILIPP MELANCHTHON: Because there are some God-fearing rulers, this doctrine about property is emphasized so they may remember that the goods of the subjects are not to be appropriated by the master unless the common necessity of the country requires this. But some will quote the passage from 1 Samuel 8:11, "These will be the ways of the king who will reign over you; he will take your sons, your best fields...." These words do not empower the sovereign power to do anything more than to requisition things for the common protection of the land. THEOLOGICAL COMMONPLACES (1555).[11]

THE RULE OF KINGS. JOHANNES BUGENHAGEN: It is not that this legal system before God will necessarily be as Samuel describes, because the law says of a king, "His heart may not be lifted up above his brothers." Rather, it will not be otherwise but that the people will want to have a king

according to the customs of the Gentiles. When the Lord truly gives assent to a king, he gives assent to that which kingly majesty requires before the world, how the king's heart shall be directed according to Deuteronomy 17. As long as they all give their assent to this good, then the monarchy will have turned back to God through Christ. COMMENTARY ON 1 SAMUEL.[12]

KINGS, TAXES AND JUSTICE. VIKTORIN STRIGEL: Here some say that this describes a tyrant, not a king, and that it does not speak of a condition of servitude sanctioned by God. But the text calls this the rule of kings and speaks of the tax burden caused by their establishment. It does not authorize the power to establish severe servitude against divine law, because Deuteronomy 17 commands that a king shall study the law and follow it in all governance. This differentiation between dominion according to the holy law punishes Ahab, who wanted to elevate himself when he stole away Naboth's vineyard against his will. Therefore such a great threat from Samuel about taxes was perceptive; that is, kings will raise themselves up greatly by way of private means, with as much legitimate tax as is fitting. This is just, because the benefit of defending the community clearly pertains to the individual, even as individuals need to unite with others. Romans 13 teaches that it is right to pay taxes. Therefore return what is determined, as the Baptist says, "Do not extort money from anyone by threats or by false accusation, and be content with your wages." Do not be endlessly greedy, or invoke taxes as a pretext for all kinds of plundering. This is the true and simple meaning of Samuel to the assembly. COMMENTARY ON 1 SAMUEL.[13]

---

[10]Davenant, *Exposition of Colossians*, 2:207-8*; citing Mt 25:40, 45; 1 Sam 8:7.
[11]*Melanchthon on Christian Doctrine*, 338-39.

[12]Bugenhagen, *In Samuelem prophetam*, 207; citing Deut 17:20.
[13]Strigel, *Libri Samuelis, Regum et Paralipomenon*, 27-28; citing Rom 13:6-7; Lk 3:14.

9:1–10:27 SAUL CHOSEN AS KING

[1]There was a man of Benjamin whose name was Kish, the son of Abiel, son of Zeror, son of Becorath, son of Aphiah, a Benjaminite, a man of wealth. [2]And he had a son whose name was Saul, a handsome young man. There was not a man among the people of Israel more handsome than he. From his shoulders upward he was taller than any of the people.

[3]Now the donkeys of Kish, Saul's father, were lost. So Kish said to Saul his son, "Take one of the young men with you, and arise, go and look for the donkeys." [4]And he passed through the hill country of Ephraim and passed through the land of Shalishah, but they did not find them. And they passed through the land of Shaalim, but they were not there. Then they passed through the land of Benjamin, but did not find them.

[5]When they came to the land of Zuph, Saul said to his servant[a] who was with him, "Come, let us go back, lest my father cease to care about the donkeys and become anxious about us." [6]But he said to him, "Behold, there is a man of God in this city, and he is a man who is held in honor; all that he says comes true. So now let us go there. Perhaps he can tell us the way we should go." [7]Then Saul said to his servant, "But if we go, what can we bring the man? For the bread in our sacks is gone, and there is no present to bring to the man of God. What do we have?" [8]The servant answered Saul again, "Here, I have with me a quarter of a shekel[b] of silver, and I will give it to the man of God to tell us our way." [9](Formerly in Israel, when a man went to inquire of God, he said, "Come, let us go to the seer," for today's "prophet" was formerly called a seer.) [10]And Saul said to his servant, "Well said; come, let us go." So they went to the city where the man of God was.

[11]As they went up the hill to the city, they met young women coming out to draw water and said to them, "Is the seer here?" [12]They answered, "He is; behold, he is just ahead of you. Hurry. He has come just now to the city, because the people have a sacrifice today on the high place. [13]As soon as you enter the city you will find him, before he goes up to the high place to eat. For the people will not eat till he comes, since he must bless the sacrifice; afterward those who are invited will eat. Now go up, for you will meet him immediately." [14]So they went up to the city. As they were entering the city, they saw Samuel coming out toward them on his way up to the high place.

[15]Now the day before Saul came, the LORD had revealed to Samuel: [16]"Tomorrow about this time I will send to you a man from the land of Benjamin, and you shall anoint him to be prince[c] over my people Israel. He shall save my people from the hand of the Philistines. For I have seen[d] my people, because their cry has come to me." [17]When Samuel saw Saul, the LORD told him, "Here is the man of whom I spoke to you! He it is who shall restrain my people." [18]Then Saul approached Samuel in the gate and said, "Tell me where is the house of the seer?" [19]Samuel answered Saul, "I am the seer. Go up before me to the high place, for today you shall eat with me, and in the morning I will let you go and will tell you all that is on your mind. [20]As for your donkeys that were lost three days ago, do not set your mind on them, for they have been found. And for whom is all that is desirable in Israel? Is it not for you and for all your father's house?" [21]Saul answered, "Am I not a Benjaminite, from the least of the tribes of Israel? And is not my clan the humblest of all the clans of the tribe of Benjamin? Why then have you spoken to me in this way?"

[22]Then Samuel took Saul and his young man and brought them into the hall and gave them a place at the head of those who had been invited, who were about thirty persons. [23]And Samuel said to the cook, "Bring the portion I gave you, of which I said to you, 'Put it aside.'" [24]So the cook took up the leg and what was on it and set them before Saul. And Samuel said, "See, what was kept is set before you. Eat, because it was kept for you until the hour appointed, that you might eat with the guests."[e]

So Saul ate with Samuel that day. [25]And when they came down from the high place into the city, a bed was spread for Saul[f] on the roof, and he lay down to sleep. [26]Then at the break of dawn[g] Samuel called to Saul on the roof, "Up, that I may send you on your way." So Saul arose, and both he and Samuel went out into the street.

[27]As they were going down to the outskirts of the city, Samuel said to Saul, "Tell the servant to pass on before us, and when he has passed on, stop here yourself for a while, that I may make known to you the word of God."

10Then Samuel took a flask of oil and poured it on his head and kissed him and said, "Has not the LORD anointed you to be prince[h] over his people Israel? And you shall reign over the people of the LORD and you will save them from the hand of their surrounding enemies. And this shall be the sign to you that the LORD has anointed you to be prince[i] over his heritage. [2]When you depart from me today, you will meet two men by Rachel's tomb in the territory of Benjamin at Zelzah, and they will say to you, 'The donkeys that you went to seek are found, and now your father has ceased to care about the donkeys and is anxious about you, saying, "What shall I do about my son?"' [3]Then you shall go on from there farther and come to the oak of Tabor. Three men going up to God at Bethel will meet you there, one carrying three young goats, another carrying three loaves of bread, and another carrying a skin of wine. [4]And they will greet you and give you two loaves of bread, which you shall accept from their hand. [5]After that you shall come to Gibeath-elohim,[j] where there is a garrison of the Philistines. And there, as soon as you come to the city, you will meet a group of prophets coming down from the high place with harp, tambourine, flute, and lyre before them, prophesying. [6]Then the Spirit of the LORD will rush upon you, and you will prophesy with them and be turned into another man. [7]Now when these signs meet you, do what your hand finds to do, for God is with you. [8]Then go down before me to Gilgal. And behold, I am coming down to you to offer burnt offerings and to sacrifice peace offerings. Seven days you shall wait, until I come to you and show you what you shall do."

[9]When he turned his back to leave Samuel, God gave him another heart. And all these signs came to pass that day. [10]When they came to Gibeah,[k] behold, a group of prophets met him, and the Spirit of God rushed upon him, and he prophesied among them. [11]And when all who knew him previously saw how he prophesied with the prophets, the people said to one another, "What has come over the son of Kish? Is Saul also among the prophets?" [12]And a man of the place answered, "And who is their father?" Therefore it became a proverb, "Is Saul also among the prophets?" [13]When he had finished prophesying, he came to the high place.

[14]Saul's uncle said to him and to his servant, "Where did you go?" And he said, "To seek the donkeys. And when we saw they were not to be found, we went to Samuel." [15]And Saul's uncle said, "Please tell me what Samuel said to you." [16]And Saul said to his uncle, "He told us plainly that the donkeys had been found." But about the matter of the kingdom, of which Samuel had spoken, he did not tell him anything.

[17]Now Samuel called the people together to the LORD at Mizpah. [18]And he said to the people of Israel, "Thus says the LORD, the God of Israel, 'I brought up Israel out of Egypt, and I delivered you from the hand of the Egyptians and from the hand of all the kingdoms that were oppressing you.' [19]But today you have rejected your God, who saves you from all your calamities and your distresses, and you have said to him, 'Set a king over us.' Now therefore present yourselves before the LORD by your tribes and by your thousands."

[20]Then Samuel brought all the tribes of Israel near, and the tribe of Benjamin was taken by lot. [21]He brought the tribe of Benjamin near by its clans, and the clan of the Matrites was taken by lot;[l] and Saul the son of Kish was taken by lot. But when they sought him, he could not be found. [22]So they inquired again of the LORD, "Is there a man still to come?" and the LORD said, "Behold, he has hidden himself among the baggage." [23]Then they ran and took him from there. And when he stood among the people, he was taller than any of the people from his shoulders upward. [24]And Samuel said to all the people, "Do you see him whom the LORD has chosen? There is none like him among all the people." And all the people shouted, "Long live the king!"

²⁵Then Samuel told the people the rights and duties of the kingship, and he wrote them in a book and laid it up before the LORD. Then Samuel sent all the people away, each one to his home. ²⁶Saul also went to his home at Gibeah, and with him went men of valor whose hearts God had touched. ²⁷But some worthless fellows said, "How can this man save us?" And they despised him and brought him no present. But he held his peace.

a Hebrew *young man*; also verses 7, 8, 10, 27   b A *shekel* was about 2/5 ounce or 11 grams   c Or *leader*   d Septuagint adds *the affliction of*   e Hebrew *appointed, saying, 'I have invited the people'*   f Septuagint; Hebrew *and he spoke with Saul*   g Septuagint; Hebrew *And they arose early and at the break of dawn*   h Or *leader*   i Septuagint; Hebrew lacks *over his people Israel? And you shall…. to be prince*   j *Gibeath-elohim* means *the hill of God*   k *Gibeah* means *the hill*   l Septuagint adds *finally he brought the family of the Matrites near, man by man*

OVERVIEW: For the commentators here, both human and divine forces are at work in the choosing of Israel's first king, Saul. God chooses the person he wants to rule the Israelites by orchestrating several seemingly unrelated events. Indeed, the reformers recognize God's providence in Saul's life in the very manner he is selected king through the circumstance of his father's straying donkeys. At the same time, the reformers note Saul's humble beginnings from the smallest tribe of Israel, Benjamin, and they cite his lack of confidence and leadership. Saul's anointing by Samuel, however, temporarily invigorates him. As the commentators explain, anointings in the Old Testament impart supernatural gifts, and Saul becomes a new man who is regarded as a prophet on account of his changed behavior and new leadership gifts. Despite Saul's reluctance to be Israel's king, God's plan cannot be thwarted.

9:1-20 God's Providence in Saul's Life

BENJAMIN'S WEAKNESS AND SAUL'S GREAT STATURE. LUCAS OSIANDER: This ninth chapter now tells how Saul will rise up and where he had his beginnings. His ancestor Aphiah was of the tribe of Benjamin. On the diminishment of that tribe at that time when the king of Israel was chosen from it, see Judges 21. For we are reminded that God chooses what is low and despised and lifts them up on high. But Saul's father Kish was valiant and strong; he was a brave hero. His son was called Saul, excellent and good; that is, he was an extraordinary character, even commended with

a gifted soul. No man in Israel was his better. That is, he had no equal or comparison in terms of his body and his majestic form, because "from his shoulders upward he was taller than any of the people." For although the soul's strength is preferable to physical form, nevertheless his extraordinary height was a gift of God and was accompanied by a certain honor from the people. ANNOTATIONS ON 1 SAMUEL.[1]

GOD'S PROMISES HAPPEN OVER TIME. VIKTORIN STRIGEL: The beginning recites Saul's genealogy, so that the reader knows from which tribe the people of Israel's first king was chosen. For although kingship had been promised to the tribe of Judah in Genesis 49 and Deuteronomy 33, yet God did not choose a king according to that first counsel from the tribe of Judah but from the tribe of Benjamin. Thus is grasped the rule of all promises to the flesh: they cannot be seized by our plans without divine calling, just as Abraham was promised land, even though he never possessed it. And the ancestors in Egypt knew they had been promised the land of Canaan, but they did not occupy it either; still they awaited the call. Even so, it was promised that David would be king, but he could not take it during Saul's lifetime. COMMENTARY ON 1 SAMUEL.[2]

DONE BY PROVIDENCE. HULDRYCH ZWINGLI: The straying donkeys, in search of which Saul had

---

[1]Osiander, *Liber Iosue*, 323.
[2]Strigel, *Libri Samuelis, Regum et Paralipomenon*, 29; citing Gen 49:8-10; Deut 33:7.

left his father's house, show clearly enough that they went astray at the ordination of God, since the son sought donkeys and found a kingdom that he had not sought, and the father got not only the donkeys he was concerned about but also a king for a son, which he had never anticipated.... In this we see that everywhere the things we *say* occur by accident are done and regulated by providence. On the Providence of God.[3]

Arranged by God. Johannes Bugenhagen: In this story you see that things like luck, prudence, industry and study are human causes. With God there is providence. For what great fortune could have seen that Saul would be anointed king when he was looking for donkeys and then rushing to consult a seer, so that through these things God would call and anoint him? Therefore all the spontaneous things we do like this or somehow feel compelled to do get put in motion or pushed along by God. Whether it is for God's mercy or judgment, these things are not active in themselves as we want or determine them to be. In the end, they have been arranged by God in ways we have not known or could not have known. Commentary on 1 Samuel.[4]

9:21-27 Saul's Refusal and Samuel's Teaching

Samuel Teaches Saul Servant Leadership. Viktorin Strigel: In this conversation with Saul, Samuel undoubtedly greatly admonished the future king about the office of pious governance, which is no different from being a good parent. See how he exhorts him to follow the law of all government, as Deuteronomy 17 most gravely teaches. For kingly authorities have been established from heaven, so that they defend laws, peace, and discipline and well preserve responsible public human society. This is just as Paul says in Romans 13: The magistrate is "God's servant for your good." Daniel also gave this direction to the king of the

Chaldeans: "Break off your sins by practicing righteousness, and your iniquities by showing mercy to the oppressed." To this end, princes surely need to know and consider that dominion should not resemble piracy, as it finally does among all those who inflict harm on others. In short, Samuel encouraged the future king to think about how his kingship came directly from God for the benefit of all humankind. Commentary on 1 Samuel.[5]

Of Saul's Refusal of the Kingdom. Andrew Willet: Saul excuses himself by three arguments. First, his tribe was the smallest in Israel, since it had not yet recovered from the loss and slaughter it had received in the battle with Israel in Judges 20. Second, his father's house was of small account in the tribe. And third, he himself was the least in his father's house. In fact, some think Saul was stalling and that he was full of hypocrisy, attributes that later manifested themselves during his reign as king. But I rather agree with those who think that Saul modestly refused the kingdom at this time and that he really tried to excuse himself from the honor of being king. This is clear from Saul's different responses to Samuel, such as, "Why ... have you spoken to me in this way?" Although it is clear that Saul later played the hypocrite, yet here he had another heart and he spoke from simplicity and humility. Harmony on 1 Samuel.[6]

10:1 The Anointing

God's Royal Priesthood. Johannes Bugenhagen: The godly anointing used among the people of Israel looked toward Christ's anointing, the anointing of the Lord, as it says in Isaiah, "The Spirit of the Lord God is upon me, because the Lord has anointed me." And in the psalm, "You have loved righteousness and hated wickedness. Therefore God, your God, has anointed you with the oil of gladness beyond your companions." For

---

[3]Zwingli, *Latin Works*, 2:214 (ZSW 6,3:203-4).
[4]Bugenhagen, *In Samuelem prophetam*, 209.
[5]Strigel, *Libri Samuelis, Regum et Paralipomenon*, 31-32; citing Rom 13:4; Dan 4:27.
[6]Willet, *Harmony on 1 Samuel*, 58*.

Christ is the priest and king who puts an end to priesthood and royal dignity in Israel, for he is the true and eternal reality of all those figures who had come before. And through this one, all Christians are Christ's: that is, priests and kings just as Abraham, Isaac and Jacob had been, of whom the psalm speaks, "Touch not my anointed ones, do my prophets no harm!" In that way, God's external institution is not a human invention but has signified a spiritual and internal anointing. For this reason, what the gospel has publicly proclaimed in the world is not the work God instituted for a time being. This does not permit us to act or speak in this way: "God instituted this and wanted it to signify thus; so therefore whatever similar things we have instituted deserve the same significance." For ours is a time of ungodliness, and we make human and divine signs equal, without any word of God. But 1 John 2 speaks of Christian anointing, how they are those who have had the oil of righteousness, just like Abraham, Isaac and Jacob. The psalm says, "the oil of gladness," which is the Holy Spirit in your heart. But this impious argument is made against us: "The thing you admire is not in the words themselves. Those whom God commanded to anoint priests or kings were themselves anointed to be priests or kings before God. Therefore those whom we anoint as priests or kings without God's command are truly ordained priests or kings before God." Who told this to you, that from your hearts you have decided that God will definitely accept your word on this, whether it is true or false? The Lord commanded this anointing and Samuel said, "The LORD has anointed you." COMMENTARY ON 1 SAMUEL.[7]

GROUNDED ON THE HOLY SPIRIT. GIOVANNI DIODATI: Ordinary ceremonies of anointing of the Old Testament were grounded on the communication of the gifts of the Holy Spirit and were figured by the oil. Now it is not said that it was anything other than the ordinary oil used by a priest,

whereas it is likely that the horn of oil by which David was anointed was afterward kept in the tabernacle. Afterward other kings, when occasion served, were anointed with the same oil, as is the case in 1 Kings 1:39. ANNOTATIONS ON 1 SAMUEL.[8]

THE GIFTS OF THE HOLY SPIRIT. ANDREW WILLET: This anointing in the Old Testament signified the gifts of the Holy Spirit that were necessary for those who would rule. This was a type and figure of the spiritual anointing of the Messiah—to be our Priest, Prophet and King. However, this ceremony was not necessary to continue in the New Testament. The Jews think Saul was not anointed in the same way that David and Solomon were anointed. They believe that David's and Solomon's anointing oil came from the tabernacle, but that Saul's did not. And they also believe that the oil poured over David and Solomon came from a horn, while the oil poured over Saul came from a vial—the same way Jehu was anointed. This type of anointing, coming as it did from a brittle vessel like a vial—regardless of whether it was made of glass or of earth—signified the unstableness and short continuance of Saul's and Jehu's two kingdoms. By contrast, the oil coming from a horn indicated the firm and durable state of the kingdoms of David and Solomon. HARMONY ON 1 SAMUEL.[9]

10:2-9 A Sign, the Spirit and a Command

FAITH BEFORE WORKS. MARTIN LUTHER: Here Samuel does not set forth one single work, but he sends a man, changed by the Spirit, as into a forest of works. Because he has become another man, therefore, other works follow. Our opponents do not understand this theology, but turn it upside down. They prescribe and teach that people should do works until they are changed and become different. But a man or person must first be changed. . . . Afterward, everything will be made

---

[7]Bugenhagen, *In Samuelem prophetam*, 210-11; citing Is 61:11; Ps 45:6-6; Ps 105:15.

[8]Diodati, *Pious Annotations*, 168*.
[9]Willet, *Harmony on 1 Samuel*, 59-60*.

right. . . . Everything now pleases God because the person pleases God, not for their own sake but for the sake of the sacrifice of Christ and the mercy which faith grasps. COMMENTS ON PSALM 51.[10]

SIGNS AND SACRAMENTS FROM GOD. JO-HANNES BUGENHAGEN: Samuel said, "And this shall be the sign to you." This reality was new and hardly believable to Saul. Therefore it was confirmed by many foretold signs from God, so that he would believe the word of God. In the same way the external sacraments are confirmed to us. COMMENTARY ON 1 SAMUEL.[11]

HOW THE SPIRIT OF GOD CAME ON SAUL. ANDREW WILLET: The spirit of God is taken here as (1) the gift of prophesying, (2) the ability to achieve and prosper in an undertaking or (3) the gift of sanctification. Saul was endued with the spirit of God in the first two ways. First, he received a temporary gift of prophesying that confirmed him in his calling, just as the seventy elders prophesied temporarily in Numbers 11:25. Second, he was also furnished with gifts fit for that calling, as courage and generosity were necessary for the office of a king. However, as for the third sense, he was far off from true inward sanctification, as his latter actions demonstrated. He became another man in these two respects: first, because he should now show himself a prophet—singing divine songs and hymns among the prophets as though he had from his youth been trained up among them. And, second, that he should now put on a princely mind and meditate on matters belonging to the kingdom—whereas he was before but conversant only with his cattle. Yet this was but a civil kind of change in him. There was no inward renewal; nor did he become a regenerated man who was born of the Spirit. HARMONY ON 1 SAMUEL.[12]

LEAVING CERTAINTY FOR UNCERTAINTY. DANIEL DYKE: [One of the many manifestations of] deceit is when we are occupied in thinking of some good thing to come to make us neglect our present duty. Here we should remember that saying of Samuel to Saul, " . . . Do what your hand finds to do, for God is with you." It is a folly to leave certainties for uncertainties. If you will lay hold of the present occasion, you may do so. But as for that which is to come, you are wholly uncertain. You do not know whether there will ever be any occasion of good for you to lay hold of or not. THE MYSTERY OF SELF-DECEIVING.[13]

10:10-16 Saul Among the Prophets

"IS SAUL ALSO AMONG THE PROPHETS?" JOHANNES BUGENHAGEN: This proverb, that Saul is among the prophets, means that many can be made suitable, even those who do not seemingly belong: *Nos poma natamus.* To condemn the gifts of God because of a person's outward appearance is truly the foolishness of human wisdom. Christ addressed this when he said, "No prophet is acceptable in his hometown." This point condemns anyone who makes the mistake of marveling about another person, just as they so greatly seized on the son of Kish when they said, "Who is their father?" as if he needed to be from the prophets. So it is shown that prophets are not made by parents or from the flesh but by the gift of God, who gives it to anyone he desires, including those not accustomed to titles great or small or respectable. This is not a work of the flesh but of the will of God. COMMENTARY ON 1 SAMUEL.[14]

WHO IS THEIR FATHER? ANDREW WILLET: Many marveled at this sudden change in Saul, whom they had known to be a valiant and courageous man before—but no prophet. . . . Nevertheless, we should not marvel that Saul prophesies, even though he does not have a prophet for a father. For the gift of prophecy is not hereditary. True prophets are not

---

[10]LW 12:401.
[11]Bugenhagen, *In Samuelem prophetam,* 211.
[12]Willet, *Harmony on 1 Samuel,* 62-63*.

[13]Dyke, *The Mystery of Self-Deceiving,* 278*; citing 1 Sam 10:7.
[14]Bugenhagen, *In Samuelem prophetam,* 213; citing a Latin proverb literally meaning: "We apples float," which refers to strangers becoming friends through shared misfortunes; and citing Lk 4:24.

such because their fathers were prophets. Rather, it is the Spirit of God who is their father. The Spirit of God is their instructor. Prophets are not so much taught by people as taught by the spirit of God, who works freely and who accepts no person's worth. For the Spirit of God can raise up prophets even from among the most wretched and abject of people. HARMONY ON 1 SAMUEL.[15]

10:17-24 The Selection and Hiding of Saul

CASTING LOTS AND TRUSTING GOD. JOHANNES BUGENHAGEN: Proverbs says, "The lot is cast into the lap, but its every decision is from the LORD." It is not necessary to ask whether casting lots may be allowed. It is allowed if you will have faithfully and modestly gathered together to cast lots from God, committing prayers to God for safekeeping in all things, so that this sign shows you the important thing it wants to show. You read that the apostles did exactly this in Acts 1. This is not tempting God but seeking God's own will in matters in which you do not know everything that should be done, especially what is right to do for the glory of God and the salvation of your neighbors. The fear of God does this for those who do not at all dare to trust human advice. It is rightly translated "casting lots" in Latin, because in Hebrew it shows an external sign by which God indicates whom he has chosen. But why did Samuel do this? I reply: He did not do this for himself but for the people, so that the people know who had been chosen to be king by God, so as to prevent what had been done earlier with Aaron and the priests in Numbers 16. Therefore among ministers of the Word it is most important to know that which should be taught in order to be an apostle of God; otherwise, how will you believe? COMMENTARY ON 1 SAMUEL.[16]

HIDING THE BAGGAGE WITHIN. DANIEL DYKE: There are not so many, nor so cunning, devices for the hiding of natural infirmities of the body—such

as the crookedness of the legs or back or the lack of a tooth or an eye—as there are for the unnatural deformities of the soul. But once their desires are granted, they show themselves. Then the waters, which were previously stopped and damned up, run over and rage furiously.... And this is surely like it was when Saul hid himself in the baggage when he was to be chosen king. In the same way, the wicked—when they look either by election or other means to get this or that—they very soon hide in themselves their filthy stuff and baggage within. THE MYSTERY OF SELF-DECEIVING.[17]

HIDING DOES NOT FOIL PROVIDENCE. THOMAS ADAMS: Saul is appointed to the kingdom of Israel by God and anointed by the prophet Samuel; yet still he must be designated by lot. Was this to leave behind certainty and put it to chance? No, for of all the tribes in Israel, Benjamin is taken; of all the families of Benjamin, Matri is taken; of all the kindred of Matri, the house of Kish is taken; of all the house of Kish, Saul is chosen to be king. Saul had hidden himself, but he could not hope that his being hidden should foil the purpose of God. He who designed his name among the thousands of Israel (he might well think) could easily find Saul in a tent, and bring him forth to honor. COMMENTARY ON 2 PETER.[18]

10:25-27 The Good and the Bad

ONLY THE HOLY SPIRIT WORKS FAITH. JOHANNES BUGENHAGEN: The text speaks of "those whose hearts God had touched." This is the nature of God's word and activity, that it is not received or accepted unless God's Spirit touches the heart. You see this in 1 Esdras 1, which speaks of the return from the Babylonian Captivity.... Those who had previously sinned by asking for a king now most grievously sin again by despising the one whom God had chosen with clear signs. They did not look to God's will but to human

---

[15]Willet, *Harmony on 1 Samuel*, 63-64*.
[16]Bugenhagen, *In Samuelem prophetam*, 214-15; citing Prov 16:33.

[17]Dyke, *The Mystery of Self-Deceiving*, 18-19*.
[18]Adams, *Commentary upon 2 Peter*, 1221.

appearances, just as the flesh always does. It has nothing to do with the spirit of faith but with trying to have all kinds of things without wisdom or righteousness. Commentary on 1 Samuel.[19]

The Human Heart Is Not Able to Rest in God Alone. Viktorin Strigel: Samuel finds fault with the ungrateful people, and he exposes their audacity and mistrust. For the God who so far had defended the church by the power of his hand, preserved and freed it was also repeatedly able to carry them without human assistance by his help and deliverance. But so great is the mistrust of the human heart that it is not able to rest in God alone. Therefore all people seek help from visible sources while they can. Then when these sources lead to ruin, they shatter many souls and do not permit any consolation. This shows the anguish of confiding only in visible things instead of God. It is permitted to use things ordained by God, as David used them for his army. But faith in things without

faith in God scorns the divine voice, "Cursed is the man who trusts in man and makes flesh his strength, whose heart turns away from the Lord." Commentary on 1 Samuel.[20]

Victory by Leniency. Andrew Willet: These "worthless fellows" were men of Belial, that is, men without a yoke who refused to submit themselves to Saul's government. They thought that because he was of low parentage and of no power, he was not a likely man to save the people. Therefore they did not come to show their respects to the king, nor bring him presents as others did. For by such gifts of acknowledgment, subjects express their loyal affection to the magistrate. But Saul held his peace and winked at this fault to avoid sedition and to win them by leniency. Harmony on 1 Samuel.[21]

[20]Strigel, *Libri Samuelis, Regum et Paralipomenon*, 34; citing Jer 17:5. From "Therefore all people" to the end of the paragraph, Strigel is quoting Melanchthon's *Loci communes Theologici*; see further Philipp Melanchthon, *Melanchthons Werke in Auswahl [Studienausgabe]*, 7 vols., ed. Robert Stupperich (Gütersloh: C. Bertelsmann, 1951–1975), 2,2:639-40. [21]Willet, *Harmony on 1 Samuel*, 67*.

[19]Bugenhagen, *In Samuelem prophetam*, 215-16; citing 1 Esdr 1:50-58.

11:1-15 BATTLE AGAINST THE AMMONITES

¹*Then Nahash the Ammonite went up and besieged Jabesh-gilead, and all the men of Jabesh said to Nahash, "Make a treaty with us, and we will serve you."* ²*But Nahash the Ammonite said to them, "On this condition I will make a treaty with you, that I gouge out all your right eyes, and thus bring disgrace on all Israel."* ³*The elders of Jabesh said to him, "Give us seven days' respite that we may send messengers through all the territory of Israel. Then, if there is no one to save us, we will give ourselves up to you."* ⁴*When the messengers came to Gibeah of Saul, they reported the matter in the ears of the people, and all the people wept aloud.*

⁵*Now, behold, Saul was coming from the field behind the oxen. And Saul said, "What is wrong with the people, that they are weeping?" So they told him the news of the men of Jabesh.* ⁶*And the Spirit of God rushed upon Saul when he heard these words, and his anger was greatly kindled.* ⁷*He took a yoke of oxen and cut them in pieces and sent them throughout all the territory of Israel by the hand of the messengers, saying, "Whoever does not come out after Saul and Samuel, so shall it be done to his oxen!" Then the dread of the* Lord *fell upon the people, and they came out as one man.* ⁸*When he mustered them at Bezek, the people of Israel were three hundred thousand, and the men of Judah thirty thousand.* ⁹*And they said to the messengers who had come, "Thus shall you say to the men of Jabesh-gilead: 'Tomorrow, by the time the sun is hot, you shall have salvation.'"* When the messengers came and told the men of Jabesh, they were glad. ¹⁰*Therefore the men of Jabesh said, "Tomorrow we will give ourselves up to you, and you may do to us whatever seems good to you."* ¹¹*And the next day Saul put the people in three companies. And they came into the midst of the camp in the morning watch and struck down the Ammonites until the heat of the day. And those who survived were scattered, so that no two of them were left together.*

¹²*Then the people said to Samuel, "Who is it that said, 'Shall Saul reign over us?' Bring the men, that we may put them to death."* ¹³*But Saul said, "Not a man shall be put to death this day, for today the* Lord *has worked salvation in Israel."* ¹⁴*Then Samuel said to the people, "Come, let us go to Gilgal and there renew the kingdom."* ¹⁵*So all the people went to Gilgal, and there they made Saul king before the* Lord *in Gilgal. There they sacrificed peace offerings before the* Lord, *and there Saul and all the men of Israel rejoiced greatly.*

OVERVIEW: The reformers recognize this passage as narrating Saul's first assignment as king of Israel. Several commentators dwell on issues related to authority and governance. For example, Luther interprets this passage in light of the Peasants' Revolt of 1524–1525, juxtaposing the divinely sanctioned leadership of Saul with that of renegade theologian Thomas Müntzer, who played an active role in the German revolt. Luther raises, but does not answer, a larger question related to authority: How do we determine legitimate leadership? Other commentators emphasize that the Holy Spirit empowers Saul to gain victory over the Ammonites, though they disagree on the personal and spiritual motives of Saul when it comes to his actions surrounding the battle. While some of the reformers comment positively on Saul's refusal to kill those Israelites opposed to his leadership, others are tempted to interpret all of Saul's actions in light of his overall failure as a godly king. As the story of Saul unfolds, however, the commentators become increasingly critical of his character and leadership, finding little to salvage from his reign as king of Israel.

11:1-11 *Saul's New Rule*

The Honor of Agriculture. Lucas Osiander: Even though he had been chosen as king, still he was not ashamed to continue farming, just like the old Romans formerly were not ashamed of rural matters. Some of them were called from the plow to the office of dictator.[1] Agriculture is an honest way of life—the least shameful way of life for a free person. Annotations on 1 Samuel.[2]

Reading the Bible Carefully. Martin Luther: I have often warned that much good sense is needed when passing judgment on the works of the saints. When the Spirit had come on Saul, he cut oxen to pieces and threatened that the same thing would happen to the sheep of those who would not follow him and Samuel to war. Success followed the impulse, which was both heroic and from the Holy Spirit. After Thomas Müntzer had aroused the peasants to take up arms, he was also sure of victory in what seemed to him a just cause. But he perished, and rightly so; for his actions came from his own spirit, not from the Spirit of God. Nor could he get any support from the examples of the Old Testament saints, the examples on which he was nevertheless relying. Lectures on Genesis.[3]

Beneficial Authority Is a Gift of God. Viktorin Strigel: Authority should not be matched up to our efforts. It is rather an exceptional and singular gift of God, as when the young Alexander the Great was followed by a large army such that no other leader will be followed in the same way. Similarly, Julius Caesar was such an authority that he could make a fleeing army stand put. Thus in this place the Lord bedecks the new king with authority, inclining the souls of the people to him. For it is a mistake to make an unwilling hound go hunting. But having been put under a clear, guiding and auspicious sequence of events about their government, the people can endure great things. Therefore whoever wants to enter into matters of government should ask God for wisdom beyond what the eye sees and the ear hears, as Solomon did.

Three benefits accompanied the state of being a king. First, any kind of pious king delighted in doing good for the preservation of doctrine, just as David, Solomon, Jehoshaphat, Hezekiah and Josiah cherished the study of doctrine and true worship. Second, through the king's victories God gave illustrious testimony of his presence among the people, making himself visible, giving witness to doctrine and the church, and sending prophets to the kings. The third benefit about the kingly station was that he did whatever was good for the strengthening of the state. These benefits were great and singular works of God to those who acknowledged them, just as Scripture says, "Unless the Lord watches over the city, the watchman stays awake in vain." And so that these highest goods relate to our states, let us pray most ardently for this and—wherever it is given—acknowledge this to be the work of God, celebrate God as the gracious author and custodian of this and remain diligent for him. Commentary on 1 Samuel.[4]

What Spirit of God Came to Saul? Andrew Willet: It is best to understand this passage as indicating that the spirit of fortitude came on Saul. This is similar to the way the spirit of God came on Sampson in Judges 14:5, when he tore apart the lion. It was, then, a heroic spirit that he received: the spirit of strength and courage. . . . It was not the spirit of sanctification or regeneration. By this it is evident that a person, even in civil actions, has need of the direction of God's Spirit to bring him or her to a good end. This is as before: "Saul also went to his home at Gibeah, and with

---

[1]Cincinnatus (519–430 bc), for example; the Roman Senate would appoint a dictator for a set term during times of crisis or emergency.
[2]Osiander, *Primus et Secundus Samuelis*, 336.
[3]LW 2:30-31.

[4]Strigel, *Libri Samuelis, Regum et Paralipomenon*, 36-37; citing Ps 127:1.

him went men of valor whose hearts God had touched." People do not have any free will of themselves in moral actions to do that which is good and pleasing in the sight of God, unless such a person is drawn and guided by the Spirit of God. Harmony on 1 Samuel.[5]

Waiting for Public Installation. Dutch Annotations: Even though Saul was privately anointed king over Israel by Samuel and he accepted the greatest part of the position, he did not as yet begin to execute that office in public. Instead, he lived a retired life until he was publicly installed by all the people. . . . Then the Spirit of the Lord came on him; that is, then God immediately, by the power of his Spirit, gave Saul the gifts of strength and courage to oppose the Ammonites. . . . And he took a couple of oxen, and hewed them in pieces. . . . He did this so that the Israelites would see the pieces of the oxen and remember what damage would befall them if they refused to follow Saul in this expedition. Annotations on 1 Samuel.[6]

11:12-15 Saul's Appearance of Grandeur

Forgiveness for the Sake of Public Tranquility. Viktorin Strigel: Saul's dissimilation is praiseworthy, as he had not yet been confirmed as king. Rather, he is long and greatly honored for this moderation in victory, which he achieved as an unjustly forgotten person. Whoever thus conquers his soul at the height of its power over all things is comparable to one who finds the greatest way of life. It is like when David returned to Jerusalem after the war of sedition in 2 Samuel 19 and he swore that no one would be destroyed. These examples remind us that we should forgive anyone their most bitter wrongs and pardon private offenses for the sake of public tranquility. Commentary on 1 Samuel.[7]

Evil Deeds Beget Evil Deeds. Thomas Adams: Saul was pious and began his reign with God, but the end of his reign was bloody. The further he went, the worse he was till even the night before he died, he consulted with a witch and ended his reign with the devil. Commentary on 2 Peter.[8]

Superficially Infused. Andrew Willet: Saul here shows his piety, humanity and wisdom. He shows the first by not seeking private revenge, and the second by bearing with the people's scruples and doubtfulness, since they had not yet received him as their king. Saul demonstrates his wisdom by seeking to win them with leniency. Such qualities are also seen in David (2 Sam 19:25) in pardoning Shimei and granting him his life. Saul gives this reason: "For today the Lord has worked salvation in Israel." Saul would not have the joy of that day obscured and polluted with the shedding of blood. For, as God had shown the people mercy in sending them such a joyful deliverance, so he thought it fit that a similar mercy should be showed to others. Rabbi Ben Gerson thinks that Saul did not pardon these men but only delayed their punishment. But that is not likely. For until now Saul had proved himself to be an innocent man and a good prince. But afterward Saul forgot his own rule when he tried to kill Jonathon for unknowingly breaking Saul's rash vow. . . . This mutability in Saul and his changeable nature—in falling from clemency to cruelty, from piety to profanity, from being a good governor to becoming a tyrant—shows that these virtues were not thoroughly grounded in him but were only superficially infused. Harmony on 1 Samuel.[9]

---

[5]Willet, *Harmony on 1 Samuel*, 69-70*; citing 1 Sam 10:26.
[6]Haak, trans., *Dutch Annotations*, n.p.
[7]Strigel, *Libri Samuelis, Regum et Paralipomenon*, 37.
[8]Adams, *Commentary upon 2 Peter*, 1308.
[9]Willet, *Harmony on 1 Samuel*, 73-74*.

12:1-25 SAMUEL GIVES A FAREWELL ADDRESS

¹And Samuel said to all Israel, "Behold, I have obeyed your voice in all that you have said to me and have made a king over you. ²And now, behold, the king walks before you, and I am old and gray; and behold, my sons are with you. I have walked before you from my youth until this day. ³Here I am; testify against me before the Lord and before his anointed. Whose ox have I taken? Or whose donkey have I taken? Or whom have I defrauded? Whom have I oppressed? Or from whose hand have I taken a bribe to blind my eyes with it? Testify against me[a] and I will restore it to you." ⁴They said, "You have not defrauded us or oppressed us or taken anything from any man's hand." ⁵And he said to them, "The Lord is witness against you, and his anointed is witness this day, that you have not found anything in my hand." And they said, "He is witness."

⁶And Samuel said to the people, "The Lord is witness,[b] who appointed Moses and Aaron and brought your fathers up out of the land of Egypt. ⁷Now therefore stand still that I may plead with you before the Lord concerning all the righteous deeds of the Lord that he performed for you and for your fathers. ⁸When Jacob went into Egypt, and the Egyptians oppressed them,[c] then your fathers cried out to the Lord and the Lord sent Moses and Aaron, who brought your fathers out of Egypt and made them dwell in this place. ⁹But they forgot the Lord their God. And he sold them into the hand of Sisera, commander of the army of Hazor,[d] and into the hand of the Philistines, and into the hand of the king of Moab. And they fought against them. ¹⁰And they cried out to the Lord and said, 'We have sinned, because we have forsaken the Lord and have served the Baals and the Ashtaroth. But now deliver us out of the hand of our enemies, that we may serve you.' ¹¹And the Lord sent Jerubbaal and Barak[e] and Jephthah and Samuel and delivered you out of the hand of your enemies on every side, and you lived in safety. ¹²And when you saw that Nahash the king of the Ammonites came against you, you said to me, 'No, but a king shall reign over us,' when the Lord your God was your king. ¹³And now behold the king whom you have chosen, for whom you have asked; behold, the Lord has set a king over you. ¹⁴If you will fear the Lord and serve him and obey his voice and not rebel against the commandment of the Lord, and if both you and the king who reigns over you will follow the Lord your God, it will be well. ¹⁵But if you will not obey the voice of the Lord, but rebel against the commandment of the Lord, then the hand of the Lord will be against you and your king.[f] ¹⁶Now therefore stand still and see this great thing that the Lord will do before your eyes. ¹⁷Is it not wheat harvest today? I will call upon the Lord, that he may send thunder and rain. And you shall know and see that your wickedness is great, which you have done in the sight of the Lord, in asking for yourselves a king." ¹⁸So Samuel called upon the Lord, and the Lord sent thunder and rain that day, and all the people greatly feared the Lord and Samuel.

¹⁹And all the people said to Samuel, "Pray for your servants to the Lord your God, that we may not die, for we have added to all our sins this evil, to ask for ourselves a king." ²⁰And Samuel said to the people, "Do not be afraid; you have done all this evil. Yet do not turn aside from following the Lord, but serve the Lord with all your heart. ²¹And do not turn aside after empty things that cannot profit or deliver, for they are empty. ²²For the Lord will not forsake his people, for his great name's sake, because it has pleased the Lord to make you a people for himself. ²³Moreover, as for me, far be it from me that I should sin against the Lord by ceasing to pray for you, and I will instruct you in the good and the right way. ²⁴Only fear the Lord and serve him faithfully with all your heart. For consider what great things he has done for you. ²⁵But if you still do wickedly, you shall be swept away, both you and your king."

a Septuagint; Hebrew lacks *Testify against me*   b Septuagint; Hebrew lacks *is witness*   c Septuagint; Hebrew lacks *and the Egyptians oppressed them*   d Septuagint *the army of Jabin king of Hazor*   e Septuagint, Syriac; Hebrew *Bedan*   f Septuagint; Hebrew *fathers*

Overview: The interpreters here recognize the godly leadership of Samuel over the people of Israel but see different themes within that larger unity. In terms of the speech Samuel gives, some regard it as a sermon that aims to bring about conversion, while other commentators focus on issues related to integrity or the duties of government officials. The reformers interpret the violent weather that accompanied Samuel's speech as divine proof of God's displeasure at the people's request for a king. Like the biblical authors themselves, the reformers readily adduce God's finger in physical occurrences such as weather. Samuel is not only a judge of the people but also their priest and mediator; the reformers emphasize the burden he carries as the people's priest to pray for the people.

12:1-15 One's Clear Conscience and Good Leadership

Samuel Conquers Hardened Hearts.
Johannes Bugenhagen: Because the people were often reminded by God's Word that they had sinned by asking for a king and by not wanting to acknowledge sins, Samuel confronted their sins with this biting address about God's clearly extensive works; he does by retelling the whole story in only a few words. . . . By telling this history, Samuel declares that God had ruled the people to this point and that the people had confidently lived under God. The prophets had already promised this grace to all who believe in Christ, so that they might have confidence in spirit. That means they might have an untroubled conscience before God and have the peace of God in their hearts through the one reigning there, as in Jeremiah 23 and Isaiah 32. . . . Samuel showed how for so long God had been a king and continuously raised up good leaders in those days. He did this so that the people would acknowledge what they had done. And by a clear miracle of God, Samuel conquered their hardened hearts. He led them to confess the sin, and they judged his wisdom to be real, useful, necessary and salutary. Commentary on 1 Samuel.[1]

The Glorious Testimony of a Good Conscience. Viktorin Strigel: The approval of a good conscience and the testimony of others to the honest fact of that judgment are truly glorious things. But much is meant by the true approval of our consciences. For when the conscience judges truly, it recognizes its infirmities, fears God and also faithfully obeys God's call. It then carries the one who is called not by personal striving but by recognizing oneself as being supported by God. Samuel glories in this, that he has the true testimony of conscience. He knows that he did not steal leadership but obeyed the call. He did not mix up personal gain with the happy burden of having authority from God. This glory, that is, this good testimony of the conscience, is rightly desired, because God wants us to live with a good conscience. Commentary on 1 Samuel.[2]

Samuel and Moses' Example. Johannes Aepinus: These two godly men, Moses and Samuel, teach us by their example that magistrates ought not to take or receive any manner of gifts from people who stand before them in judgment. Their example also teaches us that magistrates are bound to obey the precepts and commandments of God without any manner of denial or grudge. Exposition on Psalm 15.[3]

Who Samuel Meant for His Anointed. Andrew Willet: Some think that under the type of Saul the anointed king, Samuel understands the Messiah, the anointed of God, whom the Lord had appointed to be judge of the world and before whom we must give account of all our doings. But it is evident that Samuel means something different. Verse 5 states, "His anointed is witness this day." Samuel's use of "this day" refers to Saul, in whose hearing he made this statement. In the same sense, David later calls Saul the Lord's anointed (1 Sam 24:10). Now Samuel makes special mention of Saul in two regards. First, in respect of himself,

---

[1]Bugenhagen, *In Samuelem prophetam*, 218; citing Jer 23:6; Is 32:1.

[2]Strigel, *Libri Samuelis, Regum et Paralipomenon*, 38.
[3]Aepinus, *Fruitful Exposition upon Psalm 15*, 151*.

he provides Saul a pattern on how to govern the people uprightly and justly without oppression. Second, in respect of the people, that they might see what difference there was (as they latter discovered) between the upright government that they had enjoyed under their judges, and the hard service they would feel under some of their kings—as Samuel had foretold them before. Finally, Samuel also means to preserve his own name, which is lawful to preserve, lest in time the people wrongly accuse him and speak ill of him after he is gone. Harmony on 1 Samuel.[4]

12:16-18 God and Thunder

The Lord Sent Thunder and Rain. Viktorin Strigel: This thunder and rain is like the terrifying crashes that accompanied the giving of the law on Mount Sinai. Thus the gathering, where Samuel was exhorting the people to repent, was confirmed and sealed by a divine sign. For the gathering of repentant people in the church is not an empty sound, but a sound that strikes the heart with a sense of God's wrath and prepares it to accept the seed of the gospel. Commentary on 1 Samuel.[5]

Why Samuel Called for Thunder. Andrew Willet: Here the Lord showed his power. And the people saw their foolishness in not being content with having such a mighty God for their protector who could fight for them with thunder and rain against their enemies, as he did for Israel against the host of Pharaoh and against the Philistines. And besides, it appeared that they had little reason to be wary of Samuel's government, who by prayer could fetch down rain and thunder from heaven. In these two signs the Lord showed his mercy and judgment: The rain is, for the most part, a sign of his mercy, while the thunder and lightning are signs of his judgment. And as the rain mitigates the heat and the raging of the lightning . . . so the Lord's

judgments are tempered with mercy. Harmony on 1 Samuel.[6]

12:19-25 Samuel as Priest and Intercessor

The Duties of a Priest. Martin Luther: The duty of a priest is twofold: in the first place, to turn to God and pray for himself and for his people; in the second place, to turn from God to people by means of doctrine and the Word. Thus Samuel states in 1 Samuel 12:23: "Far be it from me not to pray for you and not to lead you to the good and the right way." He acknowledges that this is essential to his office. Lectures on Genesis.[7]

Gospel Follows Confession. Johannes Bugenhagen: "Do not be afraid." The law was proclaimed up to this point. Here now the gospel follows the recognition of sin. Now the triumphant Samuel does not cease to pray or instruct those who are in the office of priest. This is for "his great name's sake." God does not bless us on account of our merits or demerits, but on account of two things Scripture insists upon: mercy and truth. Commentary on 1 Samuel.[8]

Praying for the Church. Viktorin Strigel: The office of priest contains two main roles. The first is to teach. The second is to pray for the church. Samuel shows himself to have been most faithful in each of the two. In the same way, all pious people are priests, whether—according to their calling—they are teaching in the temple, in a school or in their homes. And they pray for the church, which is not only a place of speaking or Scriptures but a place where many great prayers are boldly offered. Commentary on 1 Samuel.[9]

Continual Prayer. John Davenant: Persistence in prayer is commanded in Scripture: "We ought always to pray and not to lose heart,"

---

[4]Willet, *Harmony on 1 Samuel*, 78-79*.
[5]Strigel, *Libri Samuelis, Regum et Paralipomenon*, 40.
[6]Willet, *Harmony on 1 Samuel*, 81-82*.
[7]LW 2:19.
[8]Bugenhagen, *In Samuelem prophetam*, 220.
[9]Strigel, *Libri Samuelis, Regum et Paralipomenon*, 41.

"pray without ceasing" and "The prayer of a righteous person has great power as it is working." But it may be said: How is it possible that Paul should never cease from prayer, when the weakness of human nature will not sustain continual praying? Indeed, some who have feigned to be part of the church have made constant prayer the pretext of indolence and sluggishness, and are reckoned among heretics in Theodoret and Augustine. I answer: We are said not to cease from prayer or not to leave off praying for anything when we have a fixed desire of that thing in our heart. As Augustine says regarding Psalm 37: "Your desire is your prayer; if there is a continual desire, there is continual prayer." Second, we are said not to faint, or not to cease from praying, when we exercise it in its proper time and place. For it is idleness in a person, and he ceases from his work when he does not perform what he can and ought to do. In either respect, therefore, Paul said truly, "We have not ceased to pray for you." For there was both a perpetual desire in his mind (at least as to the habit) of promoting their good; and that also, as much as in him lay, he did promote by his prayers as often as opportunity of praying offered itself to him. Observe, then, not only is the duty of the pastor to teach his flock and to commend them to God in public prayers, but also in his private prayer he ought never to be unmindful of the people committed to his care. Thus Samuel was actuated toward the people of God, "Moreover, as for me, far be it from me that I should sin against the Lord by ceasing to pray for you." EXPOSITION OF COLOSSIANS.[10]

PRAYING WITHOUT CEASING. JOHN DOD: God commands us to pray one for another. Now if those who are not connected to us in any way are to be recommended to God in our prayers, how much more so those whom God has more specially united to us either by nature or by duty and service! Indeed, Christ Jesus directly commands us to pray for our enemies. And if that is a bound duty, how much more is it to pray for our friends, especially if they also are God's friends? For by our prayers they may be helped a great deal and endangered without them. The prophet Samuel understood that this was a duty when he accounted the neglect of it to be a sin against God. . . . For when the people were frightened and humbled, both by the words of Samuel and by the miraculous work of God in sending extraordinary thunder and rain in the time of the wheat harvest, they came to Samuel saying: "Pray for your servants to the Lord your God, that we might not die." And his answer was, " . . . as for me, far be it from me that I should sin against the Lord by ceasing to pray for you." THE FOURTH SERMON ON THE LORD'S SUPPER.[11]

[10]Davenant, *Exposition of Colossians*, 1:113*; citing Lk 18:1; 1 Thess 5:17; Jas 5:16; Col 1:9; 1 Sam 12:23.
[11]Dod, *Ten Sermons*, 114-15; citing Jas 5:16; Mt 5:44; 1 Sam 12:19, 23.

13:1–14:52 SAUL GOES TO BATTLE AGAINST THE PHILISTINES

¹Saul lived for one year and then became king, and when he had reigned for two years over Israel,ᵃ ²Saul chose three thousand men of Israel. Two thousand were with Saul in Michmash and the hill country of Bethel, and a thousand were with Jonathan in Gibeah of Benjamin. The rest of the people he sent home, every man to his tent. ³Jonathan defeated the garrison of the Philistines that was at Geba, and the Philistines heard of it. And Saul blew the trumpet throughout all the land, saying, "Let the Hebrews hear." ⁴And all Israel heard it said that Saul had defeated the garrison of the Philistines, and also that Israel had become a stench to the Philistines. And the people were called out to join Saul at Gilgal.

⁵And the Philistines mustered to fight with Israel, thirty thousand chariots and six thousand horsemen and troops like the sand on the seashore in multitude. They came up and encamped in Michmash, to the east of Beth-aven. ⁶When the men of Israel saw that they were in trouble (for the people were hard pressed), the people hid themselves in caves and in holes and in rocks and in tombs and in cisterns, ⁷and some Hebrews crossed the fords of the Jordan to the land of Gad and Gilead. Saul was still at Gilgal, and all the people followed him trembling.

⁸He waited seven days, the time appointed by Samuel. But Samuel did not come to Gilgal, and the people were scattering from him. ⁹So Saul said, "Bring the burnt offering here to me, and the peace offerings." And he offered the burnt offering. ¹⁰As soon as he had finished offering the burnt offering, behold, Samuel came. And Saul went out to meet him and greet him. ¹¹Samuel said, "What have you done?" And Saul said, "When I saw that the people were scattering from me, and that you did not come within the days appointed, and that the Philistines had mustered at Michmash, ¹²I said, 'Now the Philistines will come down against me at Gilgal, and I have not sought the favor of the Lord.' So I forced myself, and offered the burnt offering." ¹³And Samuel said to Saul, "You have done

foolishly. You have not kept the command of the Lord your God, with which he commanded you. For then the Lord would have established your kingdom over Israel forever. ¹⁴But now your kingdom shall not continue. The Lord has sought out a man after his own heart, and the Lord has commanded him to be princeᵇ over his people, because you have not kept what the Lord commanded you." ¹⁵And Samuel arose and went up from Gilgal. The rest of the people went up after Saul to meet the army; they went up from Gilgalᶜ to Gibeah of Benjamin.

And Saul numbered the people who were present with him, about six hundred men. ¹⁶And Saul and Jonathan his son and the people who were present with them stayed in Geba of Benjamin, but the Philistines encamped in Michmash. ¹⁷And raiders came out of the camp of the Philistines in three companies. One company turned toward Ophrah, to the land of Shual; ¹⁸another company turned toward Beth-horon; and another company turned toward the border that looks down on the Valley of Zeboim toward the wilderness.

¹⁹Now there was no blacksmith to be found throughout all the land of Israel, for the Philistines said, "Lest the Hebrews make themselves swords or spears." ²⁰But every one of the Israelites went down to the Philistines to sharpen his plowshare, his mattock, his axe, or his sickle,ᵈ ²¹and the charge was two-thirds of a shekelᵉ for the plowshares and for the mattocks, and a third of a shekelᶠ for sharpening the axes and for setting the goads.ᵍ ²²So on the day of the battle there was neither sword nor spear found in the hand of any of the people with Saul and Jonathan, but Saul and Jonathan his son had them. ²³And the garrison of the Philistines went out to the pass of Michmash.

14 One day Jonathan the son of Saul said to the young man who carried his armor, "Come, let us go over to the Philistine garrison on the other side." But he did not tell his father. ²Saul was staying in the outskirts of Gibeah in the pomegranate caveʰ at Migron. The people who were with him were about six hundred men, [3]including Ahijah the son of Ahitub, Ichabod's brother, son of Phinehas, son of Eli, the priest of the LORD in Shiloh, wearing an ephod. And the people did not know that Jonathan had gone. [4]Within the passes, by which Jonathan sought to go over to the Philistine garrison, there was a rocky crag on the one side and a rocky crag on the other side. The name of the one was Bozez, and the name of the other Seneh. [5]The one crag rose on the north in front of Michmash, and the other on the south in front of Geba.

[6]Jonathan said to the young man who carried his armor, "Come, let us go over to the garrison of these uncircumcised. It may be that the LORD will work for us, for nothing can hinder the LORD from saving by many or by few." [7]And his armor-bearer said to him, "Do all that is in your heart. Do as you wish.[i] Behold, I am with you heart and soul." [8]Then Jonathan said, "Behold, we will cross over to the men, and we will show ourselves to them. [9]If they say to us, 'Wait until we come to you,' then we will stand still in our place, and we will not go up to them. [10]But if they say, 'Come up to us,' then we will go up, for the LORD has given them into our hand. And this shall be the sign to us." [11]So both of them showed themselves to the garrison of the Philistines. And the Philistines said, "Look, Hebrews are coming out of the holes where they have hidden themselves." [12]And the men of the garrison hailed Jonathan and his armor-bearer and said, "Come up to us, and we will show you a thing." And Jonathan said to his armor-bearer, "Come up after me, for the LORD has given them into the hand of Israel." [13]Then Jonathan climbed up on his hands and feet, and his armor-bearer after him. And they fell before Jonathan, and his armor-bearer killed them after him. [14]And that first strike, which Jonathan and his armor-bearer made, killed about twenty men within as it were half a furrow's length in an acre[j] of land. [15]And there was a panic in the camp, in the field, and among all the people. The garrison and even the raiders trembled, the earth quaked, and it became a very great panic.[k]

[16]And the watchmen of Saul in Gibeah of Benjamin looked, and behold, the multitude was dispersing here and there.[l] [17]Then Saul said to the people who were with him, "Count and see who has gone from us." And when

they had counted, behold, Jonathan and his armor-bearer were not there. [18]So Saul said to Ahijah, "Bring the ark of God here." For the ark of God went at that time with the people[m] of Israel. [19]Now while Saul was talking to the priest, the tumult in the camp of the Philistines increased more and more. So Saul said to the priest, "Withdraw your hand." [20]Then Saul and all the people who were with him rallied and went into the battle. And behold, every Philistine's sword was against his fellow, and there was very great confusion. [21]Now the Hebrews who had been with the Philistines before that time and who had gone up with them into the camp, even they also turned to be with the Israelites who were with Saul and Jonathan. [22]Likewise, when all the men of Israel who had hidden themselves in the hill country of Ephraim heard that the Philistines were fleeing, they too followed hard after them in the battle. [23]So the LORD saved Israel that day. And the battle passed beyond Beth-aven.

[24]And the men of Israel had been hard pressed that day, so Saul had laid an oath on the people, saying, "Cursed be the man who eats food until it is evening and I am avenged on my enemies." So none of the people had tasted food. [25]Now when all the people[n] came to the forest, behold, there was honey on the ground. [26]And when the people entered the forest, behold, the honey was dropping, but no one put his hand to his mouth, for the people feared the oath. [27]But Jonathan had not heard his father charge the people with the oath, so he put out the tip of the staff that was in his hand and dipped it in the honeycomb and put his hand to his mouth, and his eyes became bright. [28]Then one of the people said, "Your father strictly charged the people with an oath, saying, 'Cursed be the man who eats food this day.'" And the people were faint. [29]Then Jonathan said, "My father has troubled the land. See how my eyes have become bright because I tasted a little of this honey. [30]How much better if the people had eaten freely today of the spoil of their enemies that they found. For now the defeat among the Philistines has not been great."

[31]They struck down the Philistines that day from Michmash to Aijalon. And the people were very faint. [32]The people pounced on the spoil and took sheep and oxen and calves and slaughtered them on the ground.

And the people ate them with the blood. ³³ Then they told Saul, "Behold, the people are sinning against the LORD by eating with the blood." And he said, "You have dealt treacherously; roll a great stone to me here."^o ³⁴ And Saul said, "Disperse yourselves among the people and say to them, 'Let every man bring his ox or his sheep and slaughter them here and eat, and do not sin against the LORD by eating with the blood.'" So every one of the people brought his ox with him that night and they slaughtered them there. ³⁵ And Saul built an altar to the LORD; it was the first altar that he built to the LORD.

³⁶ Then Saul said, "Let us go down after the Philistines by night and plunder them until the morning light; let us not leave a man of them." And they said, "Do whatever seems good to you." But the priest said, "Let us draw near to God here." ³⁷ And Saul inquired of God, "Shall I go down after the Philistines? Will you give them into the hand of Israel?" But he did not answer him that day. ³⁸ And Saul said, "Come here, all you leaders of the people, and know and see how this sin has arisen today. ³⁹ For as the LORD lives who saves Israel, though it be in Jonathan my son, he shall surely die." But there was not a man among all the people who answered him. ⁴⁰ Then he said to all Israel, "You shall be on one side, and I and Jonathan my son will be on the other side." And the people said to Saul, "Do what seems good to you." ⁴¹ Therefore Saul said, "O LORD God of Israel, why have you not answered your servant this day? If this guilt is in me or in Jonathan my son, O LORD, God of Israel, give Urim. But if this guilt is in your people Israel, give Thummim."^p And Jonathan and Saul were taken, but the people escaped. ⁴² Then Saul said, "Cast the lot between me and my son Jonathan." And Jonathan was taken.

⁴³ Then Saul said to Jonathan, "Tell me what you have done." And Jonathan told him, "I tasted a little honey with the tip of the staff that was in my hand. Here I am; I will die." ⁴⁴ And Saul said, "God do so to me and more also; you shall surely die, Jonathan." ⁴⁵ Then the people said to Saul, "Shall Jonathan die, who has worked this great salvation in Israel? Far from it! As the LORD lives, there shall not one hair of his head fall to the ground, for he has worked with God this day." So the people ransomed Jonathan, so that he did not die. ⁴⁶ Then Saul went up from pursuing the Philistines, and the Philistines went to their own place.

⁴⁷ When Saul had taken the kingship over Israel, he fought against all his enemies on every side, against Moab, against the Ammonites, against Edom, against the kings of Zobah, and against the Philistines. Wherever he turned he routed them. ⁴⁸ And he did valiantly and struck the Amalekites and delivered Israel out of the hands of those who plundered them.

⁴⁹ Now the sons of Saul were Jonathan, Ishvi, and Malchi-shua. And the names of his two daughters were these: the name of the firstborn was Merab, and the name of the younger Michal. ⁵⁰ And the name of Saul's wife was Ahinoam the daughter of Ahimaaz. And the name of the commander of his army was Abner the son of Ner, Saul's uncle. ⁵¹ Kish was the father of Saul, and Ner the father of Abner was the son of Abiel.

⁵² There was hard fighting against the Philistines all the days of Saul. And when Saul saw any strong man, or any valiant man, he attached him to himself.

---

a Hebrew *Saul was one year old when he became king, and he reigned two years over Israel* (see 1 Samuel 10:6); some Greek manuscripts give Saul's age when he began to reign as thirty years   **b** Or *leader*   **c** Septuagint; Hebrew lacks *The rest of the people… from Gilgal*   **d** Septuagint; Hebrew *plowshare*   **e** Hebrew *was a pim*   **f** A shekel was about 2/5 ounce or 11 grams   **g** The meaning of the Hebrew verse is uncertain   **h** Or *under the pomegranate* [tree]   **i** Septuagint *Do all that your mind inclines to*   **j** Hebrew *a yoke*   **k** Or *became a panic from God*   **l** Septuagint; Hebrew *they went here and there*   **m** Hebrew; Septuagint *"Bring the ephod." For at that time he wore the ephod before the people*   **n** Hebrew *land*   **o** Septuagint; Hebrew *this day*   **p** Vulgate and Septuagint; Hebrew *Therefore Saul said to the LORD, the God of Israel, "Give Thummim."*

OVERVIEW: The reformers see the beginnings of Saul's eventual downfall in this section of the biblical narrative. They do not agree, however, as to the exact cause, and they offer various reasons why Saul does not prove to be a godly king. While most commentators focus on Saul's shortcomings, some also apply lessons from his life to our own, exhorting us to become people who are sincere and without hypocrisy. Jonathan, however, is the real hero in this section. The reformers recognize the juxtaposition the biblical authors make between Jonathan and Saul. Sensitive to the misuse of vows before and during their time period in the Catholic Church, the reformers interpret Jonathan's breaking of Saul's vow as more an example of a rash decision on Saul's part than a faulty action on Jonathan's.

13:1-7 The Beginning of Saul's Kingdom

THE CHARACTER NOT THE CHRONOLOGY OF SAUL'S REIGN. CARDINAL CAJETAN: According to the Hebrew the words are: "Saul, a one-year-old son, in his reign."[1] That is, according to the image of a one-year-old son Saul ruled innocently. Accordingly it describes the character of his reign and says nothing about the beginning of his reign.

"And for two years he reigned over Israel." Immediately the question concerning the truth of these words occurs. For it is evident that Saul waged so many wars, which are narrated below, thus witnessing to the fact that his reign included many more years. And the apostle Paul in Acts 13 clearly says that Saul reigned forty years. Although Josephus, at the end of book six of the *Antiquities*, says that Saul reigned twenty years—eighteen while Samuel was alive and two after Samuel's death. The solution is that in this passage the years of Saul's reign are not calculated absolutely, but, as it was said before, the years are calculated by the character of his reign. COMMENTARY ON 1 SAMUEL.[2]

SAUL IS A SUPREME EXAMPLE OF SELF-DECEPTION. JOHANNES BUGENHAGEN: Thus far we have seen the gifts of God in Saul, and no one would have any reason to suspect any evil of him. But a person's heart is deep and inscrutable, even to himself. Real and unavoidable afflictions reveal this.

Therefore what follows reveals Saul's hypocrisy and impiety. He looks after himself, not trusting in God and becoming a person of blood against his neighbors. All who do this are hypocrites, imposing human judgments under the form of holiness to suit the occasion. We can see this all the way to Saul's death. He is someone who rules and administers without faith. He has gifts from God but misuses them, which is to say, he does not have faith in God and does not fear God. You will not find anything in Saul's story that smacks of faith in God. One sees nothing but sheer mistrust, thoughtlessness, hypocrisy, and ambition, even though the king should be the best in all things. You will not easily find another example that uncovers the hypocrisy of the human heart. COMMENTARY ON 1 SAMUEL.[3]

REIGN OF TYRANNY. DANIEL DYKE: What a humble man was Saul before he was king, and in the first beginning of the kingdom! But afterward, being confirmed in his kingdom, what a tyrant did he prove to be? Therefore, it is said that Saul reigned but two years, because after the two first years, though he held the government still in his hands, his deceitful heart was discovered, and he no longer reigned but tyrannized. THE MYSTERY OF SELF-DECEIVING.[4]

13:8-23 Saul's Unlawful Sacrifice

SAUL'S TEMPTATION. JOHANNES BUGENHAGEN: Saul's temptation is described. The people were scattering, and Saul did not expect Samuel to arrive. Mistrust disguised as necessity compelled Saul to sacrifice, against the word of God. Hypocrisy does not believe the word of God but takes refuge in works and despairs. And then even the attempt to placate God is itself a way of dishonoring God, as you will see in chapter 15. Anyone who fears the seeming necessity of the moment more than they fear the Lord always acts foolishly. Such

---

[1]Heb *Ben-šānâ šāʾûl bĕmālkô.*
[2]Cajetan, *Opera Omnia in Sacrae Scripturae Expositionem,* 2:96; citing Acts 13:21.
[3]Bugenhagen, *In Samuelem prophetam,* 221.
[4]Dyke, *The Mystery of Self-Deceiving,* 334-35*.

are all the works and even worship of those who do not receive the word of God, "for whatever does not proceed from faith is sin." For this reason, God rejects Saul because Saul had rejected God. But Saul does not see this judgment in the world, for he reigned among the people for forty years, as Paul says. COMMENTARY ON 1 SAMUEL.[5]

SAUL'S REIGN SERVES AS A WARNING. HEINRICH BULLINGER: Saul, the first king of Israel, was very fortunate and victorious as long as he followed the word of God in all things. However, once he gave place to his own good intentions, being rejected by God, he heard Samuel essentially announce to him: "You have refused and rejected the word of the Lord; therefore, the Lord has also rejected you from being king over Israel." I will not explain here the amount of evil he was involved in from that time. For, as he himself was horribly agitated by an evil spirit, so he did not cease to agitate and torment his kingdom until he had brought them all into great danger when he and his soldiers were crudely taken down by the pagan nations, leaving behind an eternal and shameful legacy. DECADES 3.1.[6]

WHERE SAUL OFFENDED. ANDREW WILLET: Some think Saul's sin at this time was distrust in God's help and assistance, because the people fell away from him—as though the Lord could not save as well with few as with many. It is similar to the plight of Moses when he was not allowed to go into the land of Canaan because he doubted God's power and did not believe him when he struck the rock. But there was another special sin with which Samuel charged Saul, namely, that he had broken the commandment of God. Or it may be thought that Saul had an evil opinion of Samuel—that Samuel failed in his promise and that he forgot the time he had appointed for Saul. . . . Some think Saul broke Samuel's charge in that he did not stay

for him a full seven days, but in the beginning of the seventh day he offered sacrifice. For as soon as he had made an end of sacrificing, Samuel came. But it seems that this was not the greatest matter: For whereas Saul exonerated himself by claiming that Samuel had not come at the day set, Samuel answered nothing and only charged him with the breach of God's commandment. Therefore there were two parts of Samuel's charges: first, that he should wait for Samuel for seven days; second, that he should attempt nothing before Samuel came: "Seven days you shall wait, until I come to you and show you what you shall do." Saul offended more in the second than in the first. That is, he presumed of himself, without direction from the prophet Samuel, to command sacrifice to be offered—thinking that God would be pleased with the external act of sacrificing, which apparently was not made in faith or obedience. HARMONY ON 1 SAMUEL.[7]

TAKING BEFORE PUNISHING. LANCELOT ANDREWES: Just as when Saul had lost his spirit the kingdom did not last long without him, so if our talents are once taken away, we may perceive that God will lay a punishment on our persons. If we fall from our first love . . . and do not use our talents to God's glory, we may justly fear our persons. But as God first commanded Lot to go out of Sodom before he destroyed the city itself, so God will first take away the talent so that it will not perish; and afterward the person will be punished. COLLECTION OF LECTURES.[8]

MAN OF SINCERITY. DANIEL DYKE: The special hatred and antipathy that is in God against deceitfulness should be a strong motive for us to show sincerity. There can be no union between God and the hypocrites in regard to the great dissimilitude of disposition. God is single; he is not double. We are to be as David, a person according to God's heart. The hypocrite is crooked, and God is straight. And how will you connect these

---

[5]Bugenhagen, *In Samuelem prophetam*, 222-23; citing Acts 13:21; Rom 14:23.
[6]Bullinger, *Sermonum decades quinque*, 220.

[7]Willet, *Harmony on 1 Samuel*, 95-96*; citing 1 Sam 10:8.
[8]Andrewes, *A Collection of Lectures*, 561*; citing Rev 2:4.

together, and make something straight and crooked? How can there be friendship between those who are every way of contrary dispositions? But where there is likeness of manners, there easily will be hearts that are glued and riveted together. The Mystery of Self-Deceiving.[9]

Cold Religion. John Calvin: Saul took the priest with him when he went to battle. . . . Although there was an outward appearance of religion, it was very coldly and grudgingly performed. We must realize that it takes far more than making a formal profession and merely declaring that we are God's people and want to serve him. When we hear what was pronounced by the Spirit of God, it should encourage us to seek him voluntarily, and not in such a cold manner. If someone had asked all the people in the time of Saul, "Do you not want to seek God?" each one would have replied, "Yes, this is my intention." But so what? God disdained their talk, and declared that they were despising and rejecting him, and in fact denying him. Why? Because they had no zeal and no pure and true affection for him. Let us therefore be careful not to seek God halfway. On the contrary, let us earnestly seek his face, driving ourselves forward as we realize that he is the mainspring of our whole life, on whom we must concentrate all our thoughts and study in order to be pleasing to him. Sermons on 2 Samuel.[10]

Fickle Faith. Johannes Bugenhagen: Seeing the Philistines routed, the rest of the Hebrews went to join up with the army. This is a sign of those people who come to the gospel while it is in full bloom but who leave under the cross. It is a sign of those who believe for a time but then fall away in the time of trial. Commentary on 1 Samuel.[11]

Glorious Victories. Charles Drelincourt: And just as the servant of Jonathan, who

was Saul's son, dispatched and killed those whom his master had cast down, in the same way we need only pursue the glorious victories of the son of the King of kings, or rather, we need only gather up the pleasant fruits of his conquests. For this prince of life that has overcome death for us offers to overcome it also in us with the weapons with which he arms us. In short, to speak properly, there can be no death for those who are incorporated in Jesus Christ by a true and lively faith. For the one who lives and believes in him shall never die; and the one who believes in him, though he were dead, yet he shall live. Christian Defense Against the Fears of Death.[12]

Of Jonathan's Creeping up the Hill. Andrew Willet: Some believe that where it is said that Jonathan went up on his hands and feet, the meaning is that he went up with all his strength. However, this passage merely shows the manner of his climbing up: Because the place was steep, he was said to creep up it on all fours and to take hold with his hands and feet. He went up the hill with much patience rather than in haste. For he could not make great haste when going up so steep a rock. But it is further to be considered [that Jonathan and his armor-bearer climbed right up the Philistine garrison in plain sight]. This rare adventure and hard enterprise shows that God was with them and that he assisted them far beyond their own strength. Foreign histories highly commend Alexander's taking of Aornos when he sent up his soldiers onto those steep rocks on their hands and feet. But more worthy is the memory of Jonathan who, with much less power than Alexander had, succeeded in a harder work and achieved a greater victory—since he had such confidence in his God, who intended nothing but victory from and praise for him. Harmony on 1 Samuel.[13]

---

[9]Dyke, *The Mystery of Self-Deceiving*, 383*.

[10]Calvin, *Sermons on Second Samuel*, 1:230-31.

[11]Bugenhagen, *In Samuelem prophetam*, 225.

[12]Drelincourt, *Christian's Defense Against the Fears of Death*, 289*.

[13]Willet, *Harmony on 1 Samuel*, 103-4*; citing Alexander the Great's siege in Aornos (current Swat, Pakistan), which took place in the winter of 326 BC.

14:1-52 Saul's Offense

SAUL IS LIKE JEPHTHAH. JOHANNES BUGENHA-
GEN: Here you see hypocrisy even among those
who reign and judge and who otherwise are
supposed to be near to God and seek nothing but
God's glory. As proof, you have this example of a
rash vow or oath, which was just like that of
Jephthah. I wonder what good this vow was
supposed to do, not only in itself but also inasmuch as it endangered all the people? Jonathan, full
of faith, wondered the same thing when he
reproved his father's actions, saying, "My father has
troubled the land," etc. Because of this rashness,
God immediately reproved Saul for this vow to
strike down even his own innocent and holy child,
in order to show that it was just as impious and
destructive as that of rash Jephthah, who did not
know that he was so painfully obligating himself to
the Lord to sacrifice his daughter. The people were
right to identify as an injustice the king's rash vow
to condemn the innocent. The same is true of all of
our rash vows made without faith and in hypocrisy,
when we (if such a thing were possible) offer our
own souls to the devil in the name of God's glory.
COMMENTARY ON 1 SAMUEL.[14]

CONCERNING OATHS. ANDREW WILLET:
Jonathan is not to be considered the special
offender at whom God should here shoot, as God,
on a similar occasion, brought Achan's sin to light
(Judg 7). So neither is he to be altogether excused:
For although it is a sin to make a rash oath and
vow to begin with, it is also a fault to break such a
rash oath. Yet it is a greater sin to keep it with
greater inconvenience and hurt. And ignorance,
though it qualifies the offense, does not altogether
justify it. Ignorance excuses from so great a fault,
but not from the entire fault. As the Preacher says,

"It is better that you should not vow than that you
should vow and not pay."

We must therefore consent that Jonathan was
somewhat faulty in breaking the oath, though
ignorantly, because the lots fell out justly. Yet Saul
was faultier in making it in the first place. For the
Lord does not by this lot show who was most at
fault, but only who it was that had broken the
oath—which was the thing Saul earnestly requested.
But though Jonathan was somewhat touched in this
action, as his own heart misgives him—which the
disposing of the lots and his own confession
reveal—yet it was not God's principal intention to
uncover the offense of Jonathan as it was to lay open
Saul's hypocrisy, which damaged his own son,
troubled the soldiers and hindered the victory. Yet it
was also by this means that God would humble
Jonathan, lest he become too puffed up with the joy
of his victory. Finally, it must be considered that, as
God by lot brought Jonathan to light and so into
this danger, yet God also provided a means whereby
Jonathan should escape it, namely, by the mediation
of the people. HARMONY ON 1 SAMUEL.[15]

INNOCENT AND FAULTLESS. THE ENGLISH
ANNOTATIONS: Jonathan really and truly was
innocent and faultless, but not in Saul's sense. But
why is Jonathan taken by lot since he was innocent? First, some think that God acted in this way
to show how severe he is in allowing any show of
disobedience to princes. Second, to make children
fear and avoid even the rash and causeless curses of
parents, which out of God's secret judgment are
sometimes inflicted. Third, to punish Saul's rash
oath by bringing his dearest son into extreme
danger. And finally, to discover Saul's great
hypocrisy, who scrupulously kept a rash and
wicked oath but was not reluctant to kill his
innocent son. ANNOTATIONS ON 1 SAMUEL.[16]

---

[14]Bugenhagen, *In Samuelem prophetam*, 225-26; citing Judg
11:29-40.

[15]Willet, *Harmony on 1 Samuel*, 111-12*; citing Eccl 5:5.
[16]Downame, ed., *Annotations* (1645), EE1r*.

15:1-35 THE REJECTION OF SAUL BY THE LORD

[1]And Samuel said to Saul, "The LORD sent me to anoint you king over his people Israel; now therefore listen to the words of the LORD. [2]Thus says the LORD of hosts, 'I have noted what Amalek did to Israel in opposing them on the way when they came up out of Egypt. [3]Now go and strike Amalek and devote to destruction[a] all that they have. Do not spare them, but kill both man and woman, child and infant, ox and sheep, camel and donkey.'"

[4]So Saul summoned the people and numbered them in Telaim, two hundred thousand men on foot, and ten thousand men of Judah. [5]And Saul came to the city of Amalek and lay in wait in the valley. [6]Then Saul said to the Kenites, "Go, depart; go down from among the Amalekites, lest I destroy you with them. For you showed kindness to all the people of Israel when they came up out of Egypt." So the Kenites departed from among the Amalekites. [7]And Saul defeated the Amalekites from Havilah as far as Shur, which is east of Egypt. [8]And he took Agag the king of the Amalekites alive and devoted to destruction all the people with the edge of the sword. [9]But Saul and the people spared Agag and the best of the sheep and of the oxen and of the fattened calves[b] and the lambs, and all that was good, and would not utterly destroy them. All that was despised and worthless they devoted to destruction.

[10]The word of the LORD came to Samuel: [11]"I regret[c] that I have made Saul king, for he has turned back from following me and has not performed my commandments." And Samuel was angry, and he cried to the LORD all night. [12]And Samuel rose early to meet Saul in the morning. And it was told Samuel, "Saul came to Carmel, and behold, he set up a monument for himself and turned and passed on and went down to Gilgal." [13]And Samuel came to Saul, and Saul said to him, "Blessed be you to the LORD. I have performed the commandment of the LORD." [14]And Samuel said, "What then is this bleating of the sheep in my ears and the lowing of the oxen that I hear?" [15]Saul said, "They have brought them from the Amalekites, for the people

spared the best of the sheep and of the oxen to sacrifice to the LORD your God, and the rest we have devoted to destruction." [16]Then Samuel said to Saul, "Stop! I will tell you what the LORD said to me this night." And he said to him, "Speak."

[17]And Samuel said, "Though you are little in your own eyes, are you not the head of the tribes of Israel? The LORD anointed you king over Israel. [18]And the LORD sent you on a mission and said, 'Go, devote to destruction the sinners, the Amalekites, and fight against them until they are consumed.' [19]Why then did you not obey the voice of the LORD? Why did you pounce on the spoil and do what was evil in the sight of the LORD?" [20]And Saul said to Samuel, "I have obeyed the voice of the LORD. I have gone on the mission on which the LORD sent me. I have brought Agag the king of Amalek, and I have devoted the Amalekites to destruction. [21]But the people took of the spoil, sheep and oxen, the best of the things devoted to destruction, to sacrifice to the LORD your God in Gilgal." [22]And Samuel said,

"Has the LORD as great delight in burnt
    offerings and sacrifices,
  as in obeying the voice of the LORD?
Behold, to obey is better than sacrifice,
  and to listen than the fat of rams.
[23]For rebellion is as the sin of divination,
  and presumption is as iniquity and idolatry.
Because you have rejected the word of the LORD,
  he has also rejected you from being king."

[24]Saul said to Samuel, "I have sinned, for I have transgressed the commandment of the LORD and your words, because I feared the people and obeyed their voice. [25]Now therefore, please pardon my sin and return with me that I may bow before the LORD." [26]And Samuel said to Saul, "I will not return with you. For you have rejected the word of the LORD, and the LORD has rejected you from being king over Israel." [27]As Samuel turned to go away, Saul seized the skirt of his robe, and it tore. [28]And Samuel said to him, "The LORD has torn the kingdom of Israel from you

this day and has given it to a neighbor of yours, who is better than you. ²⁹*And also the Glory of Israel will not lie or have regret, for he is not a man, that he should have regret."* ³⁰*Then he said, "I have sinned; yet honor me now before the elders of my people and before Israel, and return with me, that I may bow before the* LORD *your God."* ³¹*So Samuel turned back after Saul, and Saul bowed before the* LORD.

³²*Then Samuel said, "Bring here to me Agag the king of the Amalekites." And Agag came to him*

cheerfully.^d *Agag said, "Surely the bitterness of death is past."* ³³*And Samuel said, "As your sword has made women childless, so shall your mother be childless among women." And Samuel hacked Agag to pieces before the* LORD *in Gilgal.*

³⁴*Then Samuel went to Ramah, and Saul went up to his house in Gibeah of Saul.* ³⁵*And Samuel did not see Saul again until the day of his death, but Samuel grieved over Saul. And the* LORD *regretted that he had made Saul king over Israel.*

a That is, set apart (devote) as an offering to the Lord (for destruction); also verses 8, 9, 15, 18, 20, 21   **b** The meaning of the Hebrew term is uncertain   **c** See also verses 29, 35   **d** Or *haltingly* (compare Septuagint); the Hebrew is uncertain

---

OVERVIEW: Focusing on Samuel's rebuke of Saul, the reformers remind us that human reason can easily deceive us. Even though Saul thought he was acting mercifully toward Agag, the interpreters understand his actions differently. Divine obedience, they assert, takes precedence over everything else. Drawing a point of application from Saul's lack of obedience, some of the reformers warn readers about the dangerous consequences of not mortifying the flesh, that is, of not constantly pruning the evil that lies hidden within all of us. They also applaud the pastoral spirit of Samuel toward Saul despite the latter's wickedness. Finally, the commentators take great pains to clarify what it means for God to repent or regret an action.

15:1-8 Saul's Feigned Obedience

SAUL'S WOULD-BE MERCY. MENNO SIMONS: How little the Word of the Lord is regarded which says, "You shall not do after that which is right in your own eyes, but observe whatsoever I command you." Did not the Father testify from heaven and declare, "This is my beloved Son in whom I am well pleased; listen to him?" Does not the whole Scripture direct us to Christ? Are we not baptized in his name that we should hear his voice, and be obedient to his Word? Do you not boast to be the apostolic church? Why then do you go from Christ and antichrist and from the apostolic doctrine and

practice to that of the learned ones? Observe how severely and frequently God has punished human inventions they considered holy transactions and religion! ... Saul had mercy on Agag, the king of the Amalekites, and prompted by his invention he spared the best and fattest sheep and oxen to sacrifice to the Lord, contrary to the word of the prophet. That act of would-be mercy and illustrious zeal was punished as a sin of witchcraft and idolatry because he acted according to his own invention and not according to the word of the prophet. He was reproved by the prophet, smitten with pestilence, and his kingdom was taken from him and given to a more faithful man. FOUNDATION OF CHRISTIAN DOCTRINE.[1]

REJECTING BLIND REASON AND GOOD INTENTIONS. JOHANNES BUGENHAGEN: Saul's otherwise most generous-looking actions reveal his impiety. It is nothing but blind human reason, which sees nothing here but piety and is therefore deceived by the appearance of holiness. According to God's Word, Saul struck down the impious and led his people to victory through God, whom he appeared to serve as king among the people. If, as everyone knew, he was going to use the cattle piously for sacrifice and for worshiping God, then what can be condemned about this? Who would not commend

---

[1]Simons, *Complete Writings*, 127.

him as a great king in the sight of the people and pious in the sight of God? But this has been written so that we learn not to follow blind reason but truly fear God's judgment, so that we do not forsake God's Word on account of our good intentions and our contrived worship of God. Commentary on 1 Samuel.[2]

More Merciful Than God. John Calvin: Saul committed his first transgression when God sent him to destroy the Amalekites. . . . He was not supposed to spare anything, yet he preserved the king in order to show him off. . . . He was not content merely with sparing the people but . . . also wanted the keep the cattle—either out of avarice or ambition, or for some other reason. He had been told that if he had disobeyed God's command, evil would rebound on him, and that condemnation would fall on his head. . . . Then he was shown by the prophet Samuel that obedience is better than all the sacrifices in the world; and to obey God's voice is far better than the fat of sheep. . . . Here, then, was Saul's sin. He wished to be more merciful than God. Sermons on 2 Samuel.[3]

15:9 Killing Sin

Turning Against All Sin. Edward Reynolds: This, then, we must first and principally remember—to set ourselves against all sin. In confession, we are not to lie; in supplication, we are not to stop; in conversion, we are not to forget anyone. Never give up so long as any remains. . . . When people kill snakes or vipers, they do not stop striking them until certain they are dead. Sin, like the thief on the cross when it is fast nailed and kept from its old tyranny, will, as much as it can, revile and spit out venom on Christ. Therefore do not give in; break its legs; crucify it clean through till it is quite dead. None can pray or turn to God in truth or hope to be delivered from judgment in mercy so long as he holds fast any known sin. Can

any person look to receive benefit by the blood of Christ who hugs the enemy that shed it? Is it not treason to knowingly harbor and entertain a traitor? Whoever loves and holds fast to sin lies to God in every prayer that he makes. This proves and humbles us for our hypocrisy and halving with God in our conversions from sin and confessions of it. We are willing to pray for the pardon of them all; we would have none hurt us. But when it comes to parting and taking all away, this we cannot get away. Some are fat and delicate golden sins. We must not spare these, as Saul did Agag. Seven Sermons on the Fourteenth Chapter of Hosea.[4]

Killing Secret Desires. Johann Arndt: Saul cast Agag . . . into prison, although according to God's commandment he was to have killed him. In the same way, many people secretly conceal their desires that they should kill. It is not enough that you hide away your lusts; you must kill them or you will be cast out of the kingdom as Saul was, that is, out of eternal life." True Christianity.[5]

Destroying Our Flesh. Daniel Dyke: Though your feelings, desires and motions are good, and do not always come from devilish illusion—but from the spirit of God—they are not sufficient. It is good and well that you have spiritually surpassed those who do not know what these kinds of feelings mean. It is good that you are not treading on thorny or stony ground but are nearer to the good ground. But so what? Because you have come thus far in the way, will you go no further? Do you therefore think yourself well enough? No, as our Savior said to the young man, so I say to you: "One thing you still lack": There lies in you some leaven of hypocrisy that must be purged out; some root of bitterness that must be weeded up; some thorn of covetousness, pride and vainglory that must be cut down. . . . You have many wonderful graces, and they make you to shine as a wonderful and beautiful temple of the Holy Spirit. Only one thing is lacking: There is

---

[2]Bugenhagen, *In Samuelem prophetam*, 227.
[3]Calvin, *Sermons on Second Samuel*, 1:111-12.

[4]Reynolds, *Works*, 3:192.
[5]Arndt, *True Christianity*, 71.

some error in the foundation. It is sandy, and you must dig a little deeper. You need to get a little more humility of spirit and truth and purity of heart; or else, when a storm comes, all your other labor about the building will be lost. I am the more earnest in this exhortation because of those fearful shipwrecks that many ships, richly laden with many precious jewels of grace, have suffered in all ages on this rock of an evil and unrenewed heart. Take heed of it, then, as the very bane and poison of all grace, and so the only cause of those many deceits of temporary believers. Enter, therefore, into those dark parts of your heart, take the light of the world in the one hand and the sword of the spirit in the other: and whatever Agagite or Amalekite that light discovers, kill, spare none, with Saul, make havoc of all a universal destruction. Save only one thing: yourself. The Mystery of Self-Deceiving.[6]

Level and Random Shots. Edward Reynolds: The natural conscience shoots only by aim and level against some sins and spares the rest, as Saul in the slaughter of the Amalekites. But the spiritual conscience shoots by level against not only particular notorious sins but collectively as well, against the whole army of sin. And it is by this means that our lusts are wounded and weakened, which it did not distinctly observe in itself by complaining to God against the body of sin by watching over the course and frame of the heart by acquainting itself out of the Word with the armor and devices of Satan. The opposition, then, between the natural conscience and sin is like the opposition between fire and hardness in some subjects, while the conflict between the spiritual conscience and sin is like the opposition between fire and coldness. Put metal into the fire and the heat will dissolve and melt it: but put a brick into the fire and it will neither melt nor soften. . . . However, if you put either one or the other into the fire, the coldness of it will be removed. The Sinfulness of Sin.[7]

15:10-11 *The Lord's Repentance*

Saul Not a Christian. John Knox: Where God says, "I regret that I have made Saul king," he does not mean that Saul at any time was a member of Christ's body; he means only that he was a temporal officer, promoted of God and yet most disobedient to his commandment. Therefore God would provide another to occupy his office. And where God says, "I regret," we must understand him to speak after the manner of mortals, accommodating himself to our understanding. God did not repent, because his majesty knew the disobedience and rebellion of the wicked king beforehand. And so . . . God the Father cannot regret that he has engrafted us as members of Christ's body. Otherwise God would regret the honor of his own Son and thereby his own good work in us. Letters.[8]

How the Lord Is Said to Repent. Andrew Willet: God is properly not said to repent as a person repents (1 Sam 15:29). And although the passage says that God repented, this is a literary phrase spoken in a way that humans can understand. From our perspective, God is said to repent when anything goes contrary to his temporal election. That is, God is said to repent not in respect of his counsel—which is constant and immutable, even in things that are mutable—but in respect of the thing that is altered and changed, which God himself decreed should be changed. As Augustine says, "The repentance of God is an unchangeable course of changeable things." This is the case here. God did not change in regard to Saul, for God had decreed that the kingdom should not continue in his posterity. Rather, it was Saul who changed in forgetting his duty and obedience toward God. So God's decree concerning Saul was unchangeable: He foresaw that Saul would fall away and decreed the change of the kingdom. But though Saul was changeable—and the kingdom did change—God's decree remained unchangeable. Here repentance is joined with grief. By this is signified the Lord's grief,

---

[6]Dyke, *The Mystery of Self-Deceiving*, 133-35*; citing Lk 18:22.
[7]Reynolds, *Works*, 1:283.

[8]Knox, *Practical Works*, 313-14*.

as it were, for Saul, for Saul's disobedience made himself unworthy of the kingdom. Indeed, human beings often change. For as they are mutable creatures, so they have changeable minds. What's more, things occur otherwise than what people sometimes think. But God is of an immutable nature. His foreknowledge cannot be frustrated or deceived. Nor can anything occur other than what he has decreed. Harmony on 1 Samuel.[9]

God's Accommodation to Humankind. John Knox: The Spirit of God must accommodate and submit himself oftentimes to our weakness and speak to us who, by corruption, are made ignorant and vulgar, so that we may understand what he works by his incomprehensible wisdom and inscrutable providence. For instance, there is no such thing as our God having a mouth to speak vocal words as the first sense appears in David's statement: "O Lord, rebuke me not in your anger." Indeed, many other places of Scripture attribute to God not only such body parts as human beings possess but also such affections and unstable passions that nevertheless are not in God, who always in himself remains stable, constant, holy and just. And of that sort is that manner of speech, "I regret that I have made Saul king." That is to say, "My justice is compelled to reject and throw down the rebellious king from that estate and dignity in which I have placed him; and so I shall *appear* to repent of my former work." The Scripture attributes to God such conditions, qualities and affections as his majesty *appears* to show in his works on his creatures. As when he plagues the world, Scripture says, "God did it in his anger." When he delivers those who have long suffered trouble, the Scripture states, "God stretched out his hand" or "God lifted up his eyes, his face or countenance." Yet no such thing can be in the Godhead. And therefore . . . do not think that God is changeable and repents or regrets, although it appears thus; for the Scripture speaks this way to instruct our weakness. For before God appointed Saul to be king, his majesty

knew his disobedience and how he was to be subjected. Nor did Saul please God in Jesus his Son, but Saul was always reprobate and never embraced the promise of remission of sins and reconciliation in such promises, although the Lord did promote him to worldly dignity. However, this is no sure sign of God's everlasting love and favor, given that the ungodly are oftentimes placed alongside the godly. Letters.[10]

15:12-21 Saul's Pride in Saving Part of the Spoil

Love of Self. Johann Gerhard: Sacrifice was an acceptable work to God in the Old Testament. Nevertheless, God was not pleased that Saul set apart the spoils of the Amalekites to offer sacrifice to God. Why? Because this did not proceed from the love of God. For if Saul had truly loved God, he would not have held in contempt the commandment of God to burn the spoils. Rather than loving God, Saul loved himself and his own devotion. Sacred Meditations.[11]

Of Saul's Excuse and Defense. Andrew Willet: Saul's hypocrisy is discovered. He boasts that he had fulfilled God's commandment, whereas he had really transgressed it. This is the manner of hypocrites: They say they have fulfilled the commandment of the Lord when in reality they have not. Saul excuses himself by laying the fault on the people and putting it away from himself. He cloaks and colors his covetousness with a pretense of zeal and religion, as though he had spared the best things for sacrifice. He afterward justifies his sin, as though he had for all this done well and obeyed the voice of God. Ultimately he does make a semblance of sorrow and repentance, but it was far from true submission. Saul does this on a vain ostentation, only desiring that Samuel would honor him before the people. Harmony on 1 Samuel.[12]

---

[9]Willet, *Harmony on 1 Samuel*, 124*.

[10]Knox, *Practical Works*, 314-15*.
[11]Gerhard, *Gerhardi Meditationes Sacrae*, 137-38.
[12]Willet, *Harmony on 1 Samuel*, 125-26*.

15:22 *God Desires Obedience*

Nothing Without God's Word. William Tyndale: Do nothing without God's word. And to his word add nothing, nor pull anything from it. . . . Serve God in the Spirit, and serve your neighbor with all outward service. Serve God as he has appointed you, and not with your good intent and good zeal. Remember that Saul was cast away of God forever for his good intent. God requires obedience to his word, and he abhors all good intents and good zeal that are without God's word, for they are nothing else than plain idolatry and the worshiping of false gods. Doctrinal Treatises and Introductions to Other Portions of Holy Scriptures.[13]

Don't Ask Why. Martin Luther: Therefore let no one add this detestable and fatal little word *why* to God's commands. But when the command is certain, let us obey at once without any argument, and let us conclude that God is wiser than we are. He who argues about why God gives a particular command actually doubts that God is wise, just and good. What sin can be more hideous and more intolerable to God? Therefore we must believe—this is part of our duty—and not argue, for these matters are too lofty for us to be able to argue about them. Lectures on Genesis.[14]

15:23 *Idolatry Is Divination*

On True Obedience. Martin Luther: At this point there arises an opportunity to discuss obedience, which is extolled to such an extent in the monasteries that no monk has been too unlearned not to leave some writing about it. And in his decretals the pope puts greater stress on obedience to his laws than on anything else. As a result, the statement of Samuel has been heard from every pulpit: "To obey is better than sacrifice. Rebellion is as a sin of divination." To this true

statement they appended the inference: "Hence no kind of life is better than that of the monks." Surely a fine conclusion, which, as used to be said in the schools, has the force of the argument from the staff to the corner. . . . True obedience is not to do what you yourself choose or what you impose on yourself, but what the Lord has commanded you through his Word. Lectures on Genesis.[15]

Sin of Divination. Giovanni Diodati: Idolatry is a sin against God's majesty. It's not the case that all sins are equal or alike. The meaning of the passage is that idolatry is a sin against God, which is also repugnant and contrary to his will, to the truth and to the glory of his nature and essence. In fact, magic arts and idolatry are alike, and therefore deserve the same punishment that is due to all sin: namely, death. At the same time there are degrees of severity to God's justice. Annotations on 1 Samuel.[16]

Rebellion Is the Sin of Witchcraft. Andrew Willet: In order to amplify Saul's sin, Samuel compares it with two great transgressions: soothsaying and divining by magical predictions and committing idolatry. Samuel touches on two kinds of idolatry: the first one being inward in the superstition of the mind, which signifies a lie or a falsehood. The Septuagint refers to this as injustice or unrighteousness, but it is properly applied to false worship. The other kind of idolatry is the outward adoration of idols, here called *teraphim*. Some think a comparison is made here not of the sins but of the punishment: that rebellion deserves capital punishment as much as either idolatry or soothsaying. But the prophet speaks directly of the sin itself, as before of the virtue of obedience: "to obey is better than sacrifice." Samuel must be understood not to speak of transgressions—either of ignorance or infirmity—but of the sin of obstinacy, contumacy and rebellion. Such are the sins of those who know the

---

[13]Tyndale, *Doctrinal Treatises*, 330.
[14]LW 2:172.

[15]LW 2:270.
[16]Diodati, *Pious Annotations*, 171.*

will of God but willfully resist it. For this proceeds from the same cause, namely, infidelity—which is the corollary sin of witchcraft and idolatry. The one who does not fear to break God's commandments does not acknowledge the Lord to be God. Further, such people actually make themselves wiser than God, as though they could discover a better way than the Lord had prescribed. HARMONY ON 1 SAMUEL.[17]

15:24-26 The Difference Between Saul and David's Repentance

SAME WORDS BUT DIFFERENT HEARTS.
MARTIN LUTHER: David's word to Nathan (2 Sam 12:13), "I have sinned," must be understood altogether differently from the word of Saul, who likewise said to Samuel: "I have sinned." It is indeed the same word, the same voice and face of compunction or repentance, but the hearts are very different. LECTURES ON GENESIS.[18]

SMELLING OF PRIDE. LANCELOT ANDREWES: To cover and conceal sin is a double sin; and not to confess it plainly is partly pride and presumption, or else servile fear and despair. The sinners fear, lest they should have to confess all to God. This assumes that God has no goodness or mercy, and that it is not enough to forgive them. Or else these sinners conceal their sins out of pride, presuming that God cannot see and find out that which they do and hide from the eyes of people. . . . In short, pride makes people ashamed to confess their sins, or else so to confess that one may see a plain difference between the confession of a proud sinner and a poor, humble sinner; the difference between the confession of the good and faithful, and confession of evil and unfaithful. This is the difference between Saul's and David's confessions. Saul's confession smells of pride. . . . "I have sinned," he says, "yet honor me." That is, he would so confess his sin that he might keep his credit and

have his reputation, and not to lose one jot of either. COLLECTION OF LECTURES.[19]

FAILURE TO ACKNOWLEDGE SIN. ANDREW WILLET: There was great difference between Saul's repentance here and David's, who forthwith confesses: "I have sinned." David, as soon as his sin was shown to him, confessed it. But Saul is hardly brought to acknowledge his sin. Indeed, he is an example of slow and late repentance. He does not make a simple and plain confession, but minces and extenuates his sin, because he feared the people, and so at their instigation did as he did. It is very hard for hypocrites to be brought to make a true confession of their sin. Instead, they prefer to lay the fault on others. Saul only confesses his sin out of the fear of losing the kingdom rather than for the grief that he had offended God: For till such time as Samuel had said that the Lord had rejected and cast him off, Saul would not confess himself as guilty. HARMONY ON 1 SAMUEL.[20]

15:27-29 The Kingdom Torn

NO DOUBT ABOUT GOD'S CONSTANCY. JOHN CALVIN: We should have said enough concerning God's providence to achieve the perfect instruction and comfort of believers (for nothing whatsoever can be sufficient to satisfy the curiosity of vain people, nor ought we want to satisfy it) if certain passages did not stand in the way. These seem to suggest, contrary to the above exposition, that the plan of God does not stand firm and sure, but is subject to change in response to the disposition of things below. . . . Hence many contend that God has not determined the affairs of humans by an eternal decree, but that, according to each person's deserts or according as he deems fair and just, he decreed this or that each year, each day and each hour. Concerning repentance, we ought so to hold that it is no more chargeable against God than is ignorance, or error, or powerlessness. For if no one

---

[17]Willet, *Harmony on 1 Samuel*, 126*.
[18]LW 6:43.

[19]Andrewes, *A Collection of Lectures*, 311*.
[20]Willet, *Harmony on 1 Samuel*, 127-28*; citing 2 Sam 12:13.

willingly and wittingly puts themselves under the necessity of repentance, we shall not attribute repentance to God without saying that he is ignorant of what is going to happen, or cannot escape it, or hastily and rashly rushes into a decision of which he immediately has to repent. But this is far removed from the intention of the Holy Spirit, who in the very reference to repentance says that God is not moved by compunction because he is not a man so that he can repent. And we must note that in the same chapter both are so joined together that the comparison well harmonizes the apparent disagreement. When God repents of having made Saul king, the change of mind is to be taken figuratively. A little later it is added: "The strength of Israel will not lie, nor be turned aside by repentance; for he is not a man, that he may repent." By these words openly and unfiguratively God's unchangeableness is declared. Therefore it is certain that God's ordinance in the managing of human affairs is both everlasting and above all repentance. And lest there be doubt as to his constancy, even his adversaries are compelled to render testimony to this. Institutes 1.17.12.[21]

How the Kingdom Is Torn from Saul. Andrew Willet: By this present occasion of tearing the piece of Samuel's garment, Samuel confirms God's former sentence in the rejection of Saul. It's not that he was immediately deposed, for he continued being king until his dying day. Rather, he was deprived of the right of the kingdom, which was given to David. Accordingly, although the kingdom was not immediately taken from his own person, it was taken from his posterity and succession. And this is how we can insinuate the violent death of Saul, who should by force be pulled from the kingdom and taken from it. And whereas David is said to be better than Saul, it is not understood of any difference in their nature—for we are all by nature the children of wrath. Nor is their difference so much in respect of outward works, which—in some of them—David offended

more than Saul. But this difference is to be taken, first, in respect of God, of whom David was better accepted and more favored and his sins pardoned; and, second, in respect of David, who had a more obedient heart wrought in him by grace to do the will of God and to seek and set forth God's glory. However, Saul's heart was not like this, but was rather averse and estranged from God. Harmony on 1 Samuel.[22]

Not Using God's Things. Thomas Adams: When God threatened . . . Saul, he did not intend for there to be no more kings or turn back the kingdom to the former state of judges: no, only the kingdom would lose Saul, but Israel would not lose the kingdom. It is a clear testimony in nature that things dedicated to God should not be used by people. The Temple.[23]

15:30-33 Saul Seeks Honor Before the People

Panting After Air. Lancelot Andrewes: Mark it when you will: There is no animal so ambitious, no chameleon that so pants after air, as does the hypocrite after popular praise. For it he fasts, and so hungry and thirsty is he after it that you shall even hear him beg for it. "Honor me now before the elders of my people," says one of them—it is Saul. On Repentance and Fasting: Sermon 6.[24]

Why Samuel Returned with Saul. Andrew Willet: Initially Samuel refused to return with Saul, lest he give the appearance of approving Saul's sins. Accordingly, Samuel did not simply deny Saul but said, in effect, that he would not go with him yet or at that time. As Christ said, "You go up to the feast. I am not going up to this feast, for my time has not yet fully come"; and yet afterward, Jesus went. Some think that because Saul only required Samuel to honor him in a civil

---

[21]LCC 20:225-26 (CO 2:164-65); citing 1 Sam 15:29.

[22]Willet, *Harmony on 1 Samuel*, 128-29*.
[23]Adams, *The Temple*, 12.
[24]Andrewes, *Ninety-Six Sermons*, 1:411*.

ceremony in the presence of the people, Samuel did not refuse. But seeing that Saul worshiped God—with Samuel being present—it is probable that Samuel also worshiped God with Saul, as Josephus well observes. But though Samuel vouchsafed his presence to Saul in prayer, he did not pray for the restoring of the kingdom to Saul or for the reversing of God's sentence. Had Samuel done so, he would have prayed against the will of God. However, Samuel only assisted Saul in his prophetic office according to the will of God. One reason also of Samuel's returning might be to see just execution done on Agag the king of Amalek, whom Samuel hewed in pieces before the Lord. This reverent and respective behavior of Samuel toward Saul demonstrates that ministers of God should yield outward honor even to evil magistrates. HARMONY ON 1 SAMUEL.[25]

15:34-35 Samuel Mourns over Saul

MOURNING FOR A TIME. DUTCH ANNOTATIONS: Samuel saw Saul no more. Or, alternatively interpreted, Samuel visited Saul no more to instruct him concerning the government of the kingdom or to ask counsel of God for him. At the same time, Samuel did see Saul unawares at Naioth in Rama . . . and in other places until the day of his death. But these later encounters are not reckoned as proper seeing, thus implying that Samuel never visited Saul again after this time. Nevertheless, Samuel did mourn for Saul. Samuel did so not for the rest of his life but so long until he was forbidden by God to mourn. Thereafter he was commanded by God to anoint David king over Israel. ANNOTATIONS ON 1 SAMUEL.[26]

MINISTERING AFFECTIONATELY. HENRY AIRAY: Great and godly affection . . . ought to be in the pastor toward his people. In fact the pastor's affection ought to be so great that it should grieve him and even cause him to shed tears to see the enemies of the truth trouble his people or to see his people drawn into any sin or error by anyone or anything. For this is how we testify to our affection for the church of God—if we are grieved to see Satan assault God's people or attempt to prevail against them. For so we see how Samuel mourned for Saul when he had provoked the Lord to anger by means of his disobedience against him. LECTURES ON PHILIPPIANS.[27]

WHY SAMUEL MOURNED FOR SAUL. ANDREW WILLET: Though he mourned, Samuel did not so much mourn for Saul as he did for the fact that Saul had been rejected and deposed from the kingdom. For Samuel knew that the sentence of God was irrevocable, and that it was not good to be discontented with the Lord's will. Yet Samuel lamented the hardness of Saul's impenitent heart, seeing that Saul continued in his sin without any remorse—as was evident in the persecution of David. What's more, Samuel also foresaw the misery in which Saul was likely to fall—relative to the loss not only of the kingdom but of his life as well. Indeed, though Samuel knew that God's rejection of Saul from the kingdom could not be reversed, yet he grieved and tried to entreat the Lord for the forgiveness of Saul's sin. Here Samuel shows his tender and loving affection, in addition his complete lack of envy: he felt sorry for the misery of Saul, even though Saul had succeeded him in the government. HARMONY ON 1 SAMUEL.[28]

---

[25]Willet, *Harmony on 1 Samuel*, 129-30*.
[26]Haak, trans., *Dutch Annotations*, np.
[27]Airay, *Lectures on Philippians*, 296*.
[28]Willet, *Harmony on 1 Samuel*, 132-33*.

16:1-23 DAVID IS ANOINTED AND ENTERS SAUL'S SERVICE

¹The LORD said to Samuel, "How long will you grieve over Saul, since I have rejected him from being king over Israel? Fill your horn with oil, and go. I will send you to Jesse the Bethlehemite, for I have provided for myself a king among his sons." ²And Samuel said, "How can I go? If Saul hears it, he will kill me." And the LORD said, "Take a heifer with you and say, 'I have come to sacrifice to the LORD.' ³And invite Jesse to the sacrifice, and I will show you what you shall do. And you shall anoint for me him whom I declare to you." ⁴Samuel did what the LORD commanded and came to Bethlehem. The elders of the city came to meet him trembling and said, "Do you come peaceably?" ⁵And he said, "Peaceably; I have come to sacrifice to the LORD. Consecrate yourselves, and come with me to the sacrifice." And he consecrated Jesse and his sons and invited them to the sacrifice.

⁶When they came, he looked on Eliab and thought, "Surely the LORD's anointed is before him." ⁷But the LORD said to Samuel, "Do not look on his appearance or on the height of his stature, because I have rejected him. For the LORD sees not as man sees: man looks on the outward appearance, but the LORD looks on the heart." ⁸Then Jesse called Abinadab and made him pass before Samuel. And he said, "Neither has the LORD chosen this one." ⁹Then Jesse made Shammah pass by. And he said, "Neither has the LORD chosen this one." ¹⁰And Jesse made seven of his sons pass before Samuel. And Samuel said to Jesse, "The LORD has not chosen these." ¹¹Then Samuel said to Jesse, "Are all your sons here?" And he said, "There remains yet the youngest,ᵃ but behold, he is keeping the sheep." And Samuel said to Jesse, "Send and get him, for we will not

sit down till he comes here." ¹²And he sent and brought him in. Now he was ruddy and had beautiful eyes and was handsome. And the LORD said, "Arise, anoint him, for this is he." ¹³Then Samuel took the horn of oil and anointed him in the midst of his brothers. And the Spirit of the LORD rushed upon David from that day forward. And Samuel rose up and went to Ramah.

¹⁴Now the Spirit of the LORD departed from Saul, and a harmful spirit from the LORD tormented him. ¹⁵And Saul's servants said to him, "Behold now, a harmful spirit from God is tormenting you. ¹⁶Let our lord now command your servants who are before you to seek out a man who is skillful in playing the lyre, and when the harmful spirit from God is upon you, he will play it, and you will be well." ¹⁷So Saul said to his servants, "Provide for me a man who can play well and bring him to me." ¹⁸One of the young men answered, "Behold, I have seen a son of Jesse the Bethlehemite, who is skillful in playing, a man of valor, a man of war, prudent in speech, and a man of good presence, and the LORD is with him." ¹⁹Therefore Saul sent messengers to Jesse and said, "Send me David your son, who is with the sheep." ²⁰And Jesse took a donkey laden with bread and a skin of wine and a young goat and sent them by David his son to Saul. ²¹And David came to Saul and entered his service. And Saul loved him greatly, and he became his armor-bearer. ²²And Saul sent to Jesse, saying, "Let David remain in my service, for he has found favor in my sight." ²³And whenever the harmful spirit from God was upon Saul, David took the lyre and played it with his hand. So Saul was refreshed and was well, and the harmful spirit departed from him.

a Or smallest

OVERVIEW: God cannot lie. So when God commands Samuel to conceal a truth, the reformers clarify how to interpret this passage. They also humanize the prophet Samuel—they do not confuse saintliness with sinlessness. The interpreters use the occasion of Samuel's confusion about which of Jesse's sons to anoint to reflect on the differences between the outward and the inward, the ungodly and the godly. Indeed, they ponder the well-known passage that "the Lord sees not as man sees." This truth is not always convenient for God's people—for example, despite his royal anointing, David endures years of persecution before undisputedly claiming the throne of Israel. The reformers also dwell on the spirit that tormented Saul, struggling to understand the relationship between the devil and God when it comes to working in the life of unbelievers, and how David's delightful music was able to expel the evil spirit inflicting Saul.

16:1-5 Samuel Questions God

Samuel Was a Sinner Like Us. Johannes Bugenhagen: Samuel said, "How can I go? If Saul hears it, he will kill me." You see that Samuel was a sinner the same as us. It is impossible to have this kind of fear without sin, without letting go of what God commands. So this fear is a great impurity when it comes near you. Faith swallows this sin so that it is not imputed to us. I freely offer this example from the holy ones. Otherwise what consolation could I have from their miracles? Commentary on 1 Samuel.[1]

Whether Samuel Lied. Andrew Willet: Three things excuse, or rather, justify Samuel's act here. First, he is excused because the author of this command was God, who does not command sin to be performed. Nor is God the author of any evil. Samuel, therefore, being bid to say what he did by the Lord, would not even have sinned had he killed someone—given that it was the Lord who commanded him to do so. Second, it is the *end* that always has to be considered. It is unlawful to lie or evade, for instance, if it is done in malice or in order hurt someone. But this evasion here by Samuel brought no such inconvenience with it. None received any hurt by it. Finally, the *manner* of this

action makes Samuel's excuse lawful: For he told no untruth, but only concealed part of the truth. Although he sacrificed, that was not the chief or only purpose of his coming. In this way, to conceal a great or weighty affair, and to reveal nothing at all, is providence—not hypocrisy. In the same way, the prophet Jeremiah—upon being asked by the princes what communication he had with King Zedekiah—only told them that he had entreated him to not return to Jonathan's house to die there. But concerning the rest of the conversation, he did not utter anything. Harmony on 1 Samuel.[2]

16:6-9 Appearances Can Deceive

The Lord Looks on the Heart. Johannes Bugenhagen: Samuel looked on Eliab. In this example to us, the Lord commands Samuel not to judge Eliab by appearances, since indeed they were all already falling because of Saul. If they have to follow their eyes, they will be deceived, whether they are hypocrites or even good kinds of saints. I know this from 1 John regarding the "desires of the eyes." But in the psalm, the Lord promises us his eyes: "I will instruct you and teach you in the way you should go; I will counsel you with my eye upon you." The boy is given the kingdom, which neither his father or brothers or Samuel himself recognize. The kingdom of God is not seen by observation. The Lord knows who belongs to him, and all of Isaiah 53 shows that Christ is not known by people because of the form of the cross. But hypocrites follow Eliab because of his stature, speaking hatefully about David, "Why have you come down?" Commentary on 1 Samuel.[3]

Prefiguring of Jesus' Baptism by John. Thomas Jackson: Although John the Baptist no more knew our Savior by face from other men than Samuel did the sons of Jesse—one of which he was appointed to anoint as king in Saul's place

---

[1]Bugenhagen, *In Samuelem prophetam*, 233.

[2]Willet, *Harmony on 1 Samuel*, 134-35*.
[3]Bugenhagen, *In Samuelem prophetam*, 233-34; citing 1 Jn 2:16; Ps 32:8; 1 Sam 17:28.

over Israel—yet when our Savior came to be baptized, he knew him to be the Messiah by some divine instinct or revelation as Samuel knew David (whose face he had never seen before) to be the man whom God had appointed him to anoint.... For it is evident ... that although Samuel knew none of Jesse's sons by face, yet he had received a distinct revelation from God.... "Do not look on his appearance or on the height of his stature, because I have rejected him." But when David was brought before him, the Lord said, "Arise, anoint him, for this is he." Samuel had no visible sign given from God by which to know the man whom he was to anoint from among his brothers; rather, he was merely to rely on the revelation or instruction that God had promised to give him in the very act or situation. God said, "invite Jesse to the sacrifice, and I will show you what you shall do. And you shall anoint for me him whom I declare to you." Christ's Answer to John's Question.[4]

Of Samuel's Error. Andrew Willet: Samuel, in saying that the Lord's anointed was before him, meant he believed that Eliab was chosen and approved of God to be anointed king. It is as if a person casts his eye on that which he loves and turns his eyes away from that which he hates. But here Samuel speaks unadvisedly of himself, without God's warrant, as Nathan did to David when he encouraged him to build God a house (2 Sam 7:3). Samuel looked to the outward stature, lineaments and proportion of Eliab's body, which indeed are attractive qualities in magistrates and governors, but the inward parts and gifts of the mind are more to be respected. These are the things on which the Lord looks. God does not look to the outward person. What's more, Samuel already had experience of a king in the outward comeliness and stature of the body who exceeded all others. Indeed, none in Israel compared with Saul. Yet God was not pleased with Saul, nor were the inwards parts of his mind answerable to the outward ones any more than were Eliab's—as may

appear by his unkind and discourteous conversation toward David. Harmony on 1 Samuel.[5]

Inside Versus Outside. Thomas Adams: Jesse could find nothing in David worthy of honor in relation to his brothers, but God found something in him that honored David before them all. David's father thought him fit to keep sheep, and his brothers fit to rule over people. God thought David fit to rule, and for his brothers to serve.... Here was all the difference.... Jesse saw things based on the outside, God by the inside: Jesse saw the composition of the body, God saw the disposition of the mind. The Holy Choice.[6]

16:10 Jesse's Other Sons

God's Kindness. John Fisher: Jesse, the father of David, had seven sons. David was the youngest of them all, the least in appearance, the least established, and he kept his father's sheep. Nevertheless, the goodness of Almighty God not only elected and chose him, but all his brothers were rejected and set aside. Then God commanded Samuel, the bishop and prophet, to anoint him king of Israel. Was not this a great kindness that Almighty God showed to such a, so to speak, vile person who was used to the habit of keeping beasts? God, out of his goodness, called David from so vile an office and set him by his commandment as king and head of all his people. Commentary on the Seven Penitential Psalms.[7]

Of the Number of Jesse's Sons. Andrew Willet: Josephus thinks Jesse only had seven sons—six in addition to David—and that David was the seventh. Josephus names all seven sons according to the names set down in 1 Chronicles 2:13-15, which are these: Eliab, also called Elihu, Abinadab ..., Shimea, also called Shammah, Nethanel, Raddai, whom Josephus calls Rael, and

---

[4]Jackson, *Works*, 563*.

[5]Willet, *Harmony on 1 Samuel*, 135-36*.
[6]Adams, *Five Sermons*, 61.
[7]Fisher, *Commentary on the Seven Penitential Psalms*, 3*.

Ozem.... These six are said to be Jesse's sons, and David the seventh. However, in this present passage six sons were brought before Samuel before David came. And it is stated explicitly that Jesse had eight sons. To reconcile this discrepancy, we may conjecture that the "eighth son" was one of the elder brother's sons. Most likely it was Jonadab, son of Shimea, about whom mention is made in 2 Samuel 13:3, for in the Hebrew the word "nephew" is also translated as "son." HARMONY ON I SAMUEL.[8]

UNDIVIDED HEART. EDWARD REYNOLDS: Samuel said to Jesse "Are all your children here? If any remain, we will not sit down till he comes here." We must be the same way in our confessions and renunciation of sin. Christ asks us, "Are any still here? If any are remaining, I will not take possession till they are cast out." ... God's law, as well as humankind's, disallows inmates in the same house; he will not endure a divided heart; he is heir of all things; there lies no writ of partition in his inheritance; his title is so good that he will never yield to a composition; he will have all the heart or none. SEVEN SERMONS ON THE FOURTEENTH CHAPTER OF HOSEA.[9]

16:11-13 *David's Anointing*

WHETHER DAVID WAS ANOINTED. ANDREW WILLET: Some think David was not anointed. Accordingly, when it is said in the text that Samuel "anointed him in the midst of his brothers," these commentators interpret this passage in this way: Samuel merely anointed one of the brothers, in this case, the youngest of all the brothers.... It is also to be gathered out of this passage that all the brothers sat down together at the feast. As Samuel said after Jesse informed the prophet that David was not yet present at the meal: "Send and get him, for we will not sit down till he comes here." Josephus thinks Samuel, having placed David next to

him at the table, whispered in his ear that God had appointed him to be king, and only then poured the anointed oil on him. However, seeing that he was anointed "in the midst of his brothers," so that David's brothers perceived what the prophet intended, to what end should Samuel have concealed the words? And I should also mention that the people of Israel, when they later anointed David king, repeated the words Samuel had used at David's first anointing: "You shall be shepherd of my people Israel, and you shall be prince over Israel." It is likely that these words were not whispered in David's ear, for how then should they come to the notice of all Israel? Therefore some think it more probable that Samuel both spoke to David in the audience of his brothers and anointed him in their sight. Yet David's brothers did not greatly regard David's anointing, nor think the prophet did it seriously. On the contrary, they condemned it, as appears from Eliab's unkind reception of David in the camp after this (1 Sam 17:28). This mirrors Joseph's brothers disregard of his dreams—only Jacob taking them to heart—and the Pharisee's and Jewish leaders' refusal to acknowledge Christ—of whom David was a type—as their Messiah and King.

Now, then, whereas some think David was not anointed in front of his brothers before they sat down and some think he was anointed in their presence but they did not realize the significance, I take a middle position. Though his brothers saw him being anointed in their presence, they understood nothing concerning the kingdom. For if they had understood this, then Eliab would not have spoken to David so insolently afterward. However, when they heard David sing prophetic psalms, they might have thought he was anointed to be a prophet. Yet there is no evidence that David was unaware of the significance of his anointing in relation to the kingdom, for the word of promise was annexed to the outward sign of his anointing. Those words Samuel spoke to David were afterward published by Samuel or David himself. And if all David's brothers had been acquainted with this secret, it could not have been kept from Saul,

---

[8]Willet, *Harmony on 1 Samuel*, 136*; citing 1 Chron 27:18; 1 Sam 17:13.
[9]Reynolds, *Works*, 3:194; citing 1 Sam 16:11.

who just like his brother Eliab was envious of David. HARMONY ON 1 SAMUEL.[10]

ANOINTED BUT NOT ENTHRONED. GENEVA BIBLE: Though David was now anointed king by the prophet, God would exercise him in many ways before he had the command of his kingdom. ANNOTATIONS ON 1 SAMUEL.[11]

SUFFERING BEFORE GLORY. MARTIN LUTHER: David, after being anointed to be king, lives in exile for ten years, is a servant of servants and is king only in name and in accordance with the empty words he heard from Samuel. Yet he holds out, and he perseveres in faith and expectation, until the outcome corresponds in richest abundance to the promise. This is the constant course of the church at all times, namely, that promises are made and that then those who believe the promises are treated in such a way that they are compelled to wait for things that are invisible, to believe what they do not see and to hope for what does not appear. He who does not do this is not a Christian. For Christ himself entered into his glory only by first descending into hell. When he is about to reign, he is crucified. When he is to be glorified, he is spit on. For he must suffer first and then at length be glorified. LECTURES ON GENESIS.[12]

AN ALLEGORY ON THE TWO KINGS. JOHANNES BUGENHAGEN: The people of God are described by two kingdoms, that of Saul and that of David. One is a kingdom of hypocrisy; the other, a kingdom of the elect. The one group blossoms and is judged to be wise, powerful and righteous until the cross comes. But the other group is led through the cross and death into glory and life. In the meantime, however, you see nothing in them other than contempt, folly, sin and condemnation. They see nothing good in themselves whatsoever either, just as you see in many psalms. This is the hidden way of God in the flesh, which has been revealed to

little children. It is said of Saul's reign in the last chapter of Isaiah, "Before she was in labor, she gave birth." That is not of God. But David's reign is of God, which is from eternity in Christ. At first, David truly represents Christ, our head. Ever after, he represents all who are in Christ. COMMENTARY ON 1 SAMUEL.[13]

OF THE SPIRIT OF GOD THAT CAME ON DAVID. ANDREW WILLET: By the spirit we understand the excellent graces and gifts of the spirit with which David was now endued and made fit for the kingdom—Saul being deprived, since he was rejected from the kingdom. An example of the gift of the Spirit was fortitude and magnanimity, through which David did not fear to fight with a lion and a bear. David was also given a gift of prophecy, through which he began to craft and sing divine psalms and hymns to the praise of God. The blessing of God was with David, and his spirit assisted him through which he did all things happily, providentially and prosperously. . . . Besides, the spirit of God came in a further degree on David than it had on Saul, for it framed David's heart to obedience to the will of God and it wrought in him true sanctification, which Saul did not have since he only received the Spirit for a certain time to perform temporary heroic acts. HARMONY ON 1 SAMUEL.[14]

16:14a *God's Spirit Departs from Saul*

TEMPORARY SPIRIT. JOHANNES BUGENHAGEN: It says that "the Spirit departed from Saul." I ask: what is this? Has not enough of Saul's impiety been described above? Why is this the first time that it is written that the Spirit of the Lord departed from him? I answer: Thus is the Spirit of the Lord to sinners who have fallen away from God. It argues against the unbelief of their conscience, just as Christ says: the Spirit "will

---

[10]Willet, *Harmony on 1 Samuel*, 138-39*; citing 2 Sam 5:2.
[11]*Geneva Bible* (1560), 128r*.
[12]LW 5:202.

[13]Bugenhagen, *In Samuelem prophetam*, 232-33; citing Is 66:7; Mt 11:25.
[14]Willet, *Harmony on 1 Samuel*, 139-40*.

convict the world concerning sin and righteousness and judgment: concerning sin, because they do not believe in him." But it withdraws at that time when those who are despairing surrender to a depraved mind, when a chiding spirit can no longer strengthen them. They are despisers, and they rush into wicked deeds. This is what the Lord said in Genesis: "My Spirit shall not abide in humans forever." Therefore, before this time Saul could be conscious of his sins; after this, he despises everything and wants to establish himself as king, even when he sees the kingdom going to David, as you will see below. You can be sure that this is the highest impiety, to want to fight openly against God. Commentary on 1 Samuel.[15]

God Can Revoke His Gifts. Hans Denck: Now, since God does not will sin but still knows that it happens, we should not in this case trouble ourselves about him. God will not become desperate in himself, as we do. His foreknowledge, which is unknown to us, will surely accord with his will (of which even the perverse know something) apart from our inquisitiveness. But thus the clever must become fools who yearn to know God's mysteriousness and to despise the acknowledged intention of his commandments.

You say: We do not need foreknowledge, as you say, except for a consolation to all the elect that they may know that all their help and salvation lie in the hand of God and that no power is so mighty that it will or could wrest it from him. Response: This consolation you can give no one and also none can take from you, for he who has committed himself to the chastisement of the Father and who has tasted partially the sweetness of the bitter cross, to him the Father reveals himself through his Spirit in defiance before all his enemies, but, nonetheless, he must fear God and despise no one. For those whom God has received in faith he can and will reject again if he does not remain in faith, since he did not even spare the angels because they were so secure

that they thereby developed satisfaction in themselves and forgot God. Therefore also Paul, the elect instrument of God, says now in vain: Let him who stands take heed lest he fall! If God gave his Spirit to Saul the king and took it again, and if it is nevertheless true that he never regrets his gifts, what should be wrong if he were to take from us the talent he gave us so that we have nothing—that is, would the one for whom grace means nothing nevertheless remain true and just? Speak out, whoever will, is it not a misuse of foreknowledge to want to be certain of the Lord's reward (God help us!) regardless of how well we serve him? Whether God Is the Cause of Evil.[16]

16:14b-15 A Harmful Spirit Sent from the Lord

All God's Doing. John Calvin: I confess indeed that it is often by means of Satan's intervention that God acts in the wicked, but in such a way that Satan performs his part by God's impulsion and advances as far as he is allowed. An evil spirit troubles Saul; but it is said to have come from God, that we may know that Saul's madness proceeds from God's just vengeance. . . . To sum up, since God's will is said to be the cause of all things, I have made his providence the determinative principle for all human plans and works, not only in order to display its force in the elect, who are ruled by the Holy Spirit, but also to compel the reprobate to obedience. Institutes 1.18.2.[17]

Evil Spirits Sent by God Alone. George Gifford: I hold it no small folly for any person to think that the Lord does not now scourge his children, at least some of them, for their good, by the devil. There is no doubt that the devil has power given him to afflict, uses all the craft he can and will seem to be sent by a witch. The devil will make it appear that he is not sent from God but from the anger of a poor woman. And now,

---

[15]Bugenhagen, *In Samuelem prophetam*, 234-35; citing Jn 16:8-9; Gen 6:3.

[16]Denck, *Spiritual Legacy*, 104-7; citing 1 Cor 10:22.
[17]LCC 20:233 (CO 2:169-70).

touching the wicked, who provoke God by their wicked sins and unbelief, may we not read in the Scriptures that an evil spirit was sent from God to King Saul, which haunted and vexed him? Was this spirit sent by a witch? . . . As I said before, here is the deep craft of Satan: that he will appear to be sent by witches whereas, in truth, God sent him, seeing none can send him but God. A DIALOGUE CONCERNING WITCHES AND WITCHCRAFT.[18]

WORKING BY EMISSION AND PERMISSION. ANDREW WILLET: Satan's service and ministry is not absolutely accepted and pleasing to God. Further, there is a double work to be considered in the evil ministering spirits. For either they are ministers of outward punishments only—as in vexing and afflicting the body in which case they work by *emission*, that is, sending from God; or they also urge on and tempt to evil, in which case they work only by the *permission* or sufferance of God. Satan assaulted Saul in both of these ways, for both his body was vexed and his mind was tempted. HARMONY ON 1 SAMUEL.[19]

16:16-23 David's Music Soothes Saul's Bad Spirit

RESTRAINING SAUL'S EVIL SPIRIT. MARTIN LUTHER: David . . . often banished the evil spirit of Saul or restrained and subdued it with his lyre. . . . For the evil spirit is ill at ease wherever God's Word is sung or preached in true faith. He is a spirit of gloom and cannot abide where he finds a spiritually happy heart, that is, where the heart rejoices in God and in his Word. TREATISE ON THE LAST WORDS OF DAVID.[20]

THE GODLY ARE LIKE DAVID'S HARP. THOMAS ADAMS: One good person can do much good for many. They not only act as chains to the hands of God by holding them back from judgment, but they

are also a happy prevention of sin. They keep God from being angry; and when God is angry, they calm God. Godly people are like David's harp; they chase away evil spirits from people's company. . . . For in his presence . . . insolence grows ashamed, course jokes appear foolish, drunkards become sober, blasphemers have their lips sealed up and the mouth of all wickedness is stopped. This good comes by the good. THE SPIRITUAL NAVIGATOR.[21]

MUSIC, THE JOY ON THE EARTH. MARTIN LUTHER:

Of all the joys upon this earth
None has for men a greater worth
Than what I give with my ringing
And with voices sweetly singing.
There cannot be an evil mood
Where there are singing fellows good,
There is no envy, hate nor ire,
Gone are through me all sorrows dire;
Greed, care and lonely heaviness
No more do they the heart oppress.
Each man can in his mirth be free
Since such a joy no sin can be.
But God in me more pleasure finds
Than in all joys of earthly minds.
Through my bright power the devil shirks
His sinful, murderous, evil works.
Of this King David's deeds do tell
Who pacified King Saul so well
By sweetly playing on the lyre
And thus escaped his murderous ire.

A PREFACE FOR ALL GOOD HYMNALS.[22]

THE REMEDY OF DAVID'S HARP. CHARLES DRELINCOURT: Take pleasure to meditate often on God's wonderful works and sing forth his praises. The spiritual songs inspired by the Holy Spirit commonly appease all the evil motions of our mind and they also produce in us a holy joy and celestial peace. Just like when Saul was tormented with a

---

[18]Clifford, *Dialogue Concerning Witches*, 34*.
[19]Willet, *Harmony on 1 Samuel*, 140-41*.
[20]LW 15:274.

[21]Adams, *Black Devil*, 21.
[22]LW 53:319-20.

wicked spirit, David was appointed with his harp to play before him and by that means quieted his troubled mind. Likewise, when hatred, anger, revenge, covetousness, ambition, lust or any other of the unruly passions—which are like evil spirits—disturb and torture our souls within us, we must seek a remedy from David's harp and sing to the Lord in spiritual songs and hymns. CHRISTIAN DEFENSE AGAINST THE FEARS OF DEATH.[23]

GOOD MUSIC DRIVES OUT BAD HABITS.
THOMAS ADAMS: A gambler will hold so long as his money lasts, an adulterer so long as his loins last, but a drunkard so long as his lungs and life last. A philosopher, once finding himself in the company of drunkards where a musician ruled the disorderly gathering, charged the musician to change his music into a better tune. By doing so he brought the drunkards to sobriety; and casting away their drinks, they were ashamed of all they had done. But our drunkards have not the patience to hear such music. Saul was vexed with an evil spirit, but David's harp expelled him. O that we knew that instrument or lesson, which could work such a reformation! We would double and triple that note, which might bring about such a cure. COMMENTARY ON 2 PETER.[24]

PLAYING MUSIC WITH DAVID. JOHANNES BUGENHAGEN: The art of instrumental music back then was delightful in itself, just as it is now. But unlike we who rejoice in dirty songs, they only sang to God about praise and mercy, composing psalms and hymns that the devil could not bear and in which faith was played and sung. This was no

doubt true of David's songs too. Therefore, as often as you sing from a spirit of instruction to the Lord, you understand how to play the harp with David, especially when those songs restore the senses from the snare of the devil through God's Word. But, as in David's case, it is also important that the Lord is sought. Otherwise, "We played the flute for you, and you did not dance; we sang a dirge, and you did not weep." COMMENTARY ON 1 SAMUEL.[25]

MUSIC AND MADNESS. GIOVANNI DIODATI: The musician was only sought for when Saul had fits of rage or melancholy, for he had some respites and spaces between these fits. . . . It's not that musical sounds or any other corporal and sensible means have any power over the devil, who is only let loose, it should be noted, by God's permission. The situation was this: With the supernatural madness or rage, there was a bodily defect in the mind and an exasperation of the spirits, which are the organs of diabolical operation in such cases. And music, by reducing the spirits of human beings for a time to some sweet concordance and harmony, makes the corporal or bodily instrument less subject to the devil's operation. That is, unless this sound was accompanied with some divine word or subject whose power and respect repressed and quelled the devil's action for the present. It's also possible that some motion of God's Spirit was awakened in Saul at times by prophetic music, as when he later prophesied. . . . Or finally, it's possible that God of his free will determined to cooperate with David's playing of music to lead Saul to need David to remain in the king's court. ANNOTATIONS ON 1 SAMUEL.[26]

---

[23]Drelincourt, *Christian's Defense Against the Fears of Death*, 170*.
[24]Adams, *Commentary upon 2 Peter*, 135.

[25]Bugenhagen, *In Samuelem prophetam*, 235; citing Lk 7:32.
[26]Diodati, *Pious Annotations*, 172.*

17:1-58 DAVID AND GOLIATH

¹Now the Philistines gathered their armies for battle. And they were gathered at Socoh, which belongs to Judah, and encamped between Socoh and Azekah, in Ephes-dammim. ²And Saul and the men of Israel were gathered, and encamped in the Valley of Elah, and drew up in line of battle against the Philistines. ³And the Philistines stood on the mountain on the one side, and Israel stood on the mountain on the other side, with a valley between them. ⁴And there came out from the camp of the Philistines a champion named Goliath of Gath, whose height was six^a cubits^b and a span. ⁵He had a helmet of bronze on his head, and he was armed with a coat of mail, and the weight of the coat was five thousand shekels^c of bronze. ⁶And he had bronze armor on his legs, and a javelin of bronze slung between his shoulders. ⁷The shaft of his spear was like a weaver's beam, and his spear's head weighed six hundred shekels of iron. And his shield-bearer went before him. ⁸He stood and shouted to the ranks of Israel, "Why have you come out to draw up for battle? Am I not a Philistine, and are you not servants of Saul? Choose a man for yourselves, and let him come down to me. ⁹If he is able to fight with me and kill me, then we will be your servants. But if I prevail against him and kill him, then you shall be our servants and serve us." ¹⁰And the Philistine said, "I defy the ranks of Israel this day. Give me a man, that we may fight together." ¹¹When Saul and all Israel heard these words of the Philistine, they were dismayed and greatly afraid.

¹²Now David was the son of an Ephrathite of Bethlehem in Judah, named Jesse, who had eight sons. In the days of Saul the man was already old and advanced in years.^{d} ¹³The three oldest sons of Jesse had followed Saul to the battle. And the names of his three sons who went to the battle were Eliab the firstborn, and next to him Abinadab, and the third Shammah. ¹⁴David was the youngest. The three eldest followed Saul, ¹⁵but David went back and forth from Saul to feed his father's sheep at Bethlehem. ¹⁶For forty days the Philistine came forward and took his stand, morning and evening.

¹⁷And Jesse said to David his son, "Take for your brothers an ephah^e of this parched grain, and these ten loaves, and carry them quickly to the camp to your brothers. ¹⁸Also take these ten cheeses to the commander of their thousand. See if your brothers are well, and bring some token from them."

¹⁹Now Saul and they and all the men of Israel were in the Valley of Elah, fighting with the Philistines. ²⁰And David rose early in the morning and left the sheep with a keeper and took the provisions and went, as Jesse had commanded him. And he came to the encampment as the host was going out to the battle line, shouting the war cry. ²¹And Israel and the Philistines drew up for battle, army against army. ²²And David left the things in charge of the keeper of the baggage and ran to the ranks and went and greeted his brothers. ²³As he talked with them, behold, the champion, the Philistine of Gath, Goliath by name, came up out of the ranks of the Philistines and spoke the same words as before. And David heard him.

²⁴All the men of Israel, when they saw the man, fled from him and were much afraid. ²⁵And the men of Israel said, "Have you seen this man who has come up? Surely he has come up to defy Israel. And the king will enrich the man who kills him with great riches and will give him his daughter and make his father's house free in Israel." ²⁶And David said to the men who stood by him, "What shall be done for the man who kills this Philistine and takes away the reproach from Israel? For who is this uncircumcised Philistine, that he should defy the armies of the living God?" ²⁷And the people answered him in the same way, "So shall it be done to the man who kills him."

²⁸Now Eliab his eldest brother heard when he spoke to the men. And Eliab's anger was kindled against David, and he said, "Why have you come down? And with whom have you left those few sheep in the wilderness? I know your presumption and the evil of your heart, for you have come down to see the battle." ²⁹And David said, "What have I done now? Was it not but a word?" ³⁰And he turned away from

him toward another, and spoke in the same way, and the people answered him again as before.

³¹When the words that David spoke were heard, they repeated them before Saul, and he sent for him. ³²And David said to Saul, "Let no man's heart fail because of him. Your servant will go and fight with this Philistine." ³³And Saul said to David, "You are not able to go against this Philistine to fight with him, for you are but a youth, and he has been a man of war from his youth." ³⁴But David said to Saul, "Your servant used to keep sheep for his father. And when there came a lion, or a bear, and took a lamb from the flock, ³⁵I went after him and struck him and delivered it out of his mouth. And if he arose against me, I caught him by his beard and struck him and killed him. ³⁶Your servant has struck down both lions and bears, and this uncircumcised Philistine shall be like one of them, for he has defied the armies of the living God." ³⁷And David said, "The LORD who delivered me from the paw of the lion and from the paw of the bear will deliver me from the hand of this Philistine." And Saul said to David, "Go, and the LORD be with you!"

³⁸Then Saul clothed David with his armor. He put a helmet of bronze on his head and clothed him with a coat of mail, ³⁹and David strapped his sword over his armor. And he tried in vain to go, for he had not tested them. Then David said to Saul, "I cannot go with these, for I have not tested them." So David put them off. ⁴⁰Then he took his staff in his hand and chose five smooth stones from the brook and put them in his shepherd's pouch. His sling was in his hand, and he approached the Philistine.

⁴¹And the Philistine moved forward and came near to David, with his shield-bearer in front of him. ⁴²And when the Philistine looked and saw David, he disdained him, for he was but a youth, ruddy and handsome in appearance. ⁴³And the Philistine said to David, "Am I a dog, that you come to me with sticks?" And the Philistine cursed David by his gods. ⁴⁴The Philistine said to David, "Come to me, and I will give your flesh to the birds of the air and to the beasts of the field." ⁴⁵Then David said to the Philistine, "You come to me with a sword and with a spear and with a javelin,

but I come to you in the name of the LORD of hosts, the God of the armies of Israel, whom you have defied. ⁴⁶This day the LORD will deliver you into my hand, and I will strike you down and cut off your head. And I will give the dead bodies of the host of the Philistines this day to the birds of the air and to the wild beasts of the earth, that all the earth may know that there is a God in Israel, ⁴⁷and that all this assembly may know that the LORD saves not with sword and spear. For the battle is the LORD's, and he will give you into our hand."

⁴⁸When the Philistine arose and came and drew near to meet David, David ran quickly toward the battle line to meet the Philistine. ⁴⁹And David put his hand in his bag and took out a stone and slung it and struck the Philistine on his forehead. The stone sank into his forehead, and he fell on his face to the ground.

⁵⁰So David prevailed over the Philistine with a sling and with a stone, and struck the Philistine and killed him. There was no sword in the hand of David. ⁵¹Then David ran and stood over the Philistine and took his sword and drew it out of its sheath and killed him and cut off his head with it. When the Philistines saw that their champion was dead, they fled. ⁵²And the men of Israel and Judah rose with a shout and pursued the Philistines as far as Gath^f and the gates of Ekron, so that the wounded Philistines fell on the way from Shaaraim as far as Gath and Ekron. ⁵³And the people of Israel came back from chasing the Philistines, and they plundered their camp. ⁵⁴And David took the head of the Philistine and brought it to Jerusalem, but he put his armor in his tent.

⁵⁵As soon as Saul saw David go out against the Philistine, he said to Abner, the commander of the army, "Abner, whose son is this youth?" And Abner said, "As your soul lives, O king, I do not know." ⁵⁶And the king said, "Inquire whose son the boy is." ⁵⁷And as soon as David returned from the striking down of the Philistine, Abner took him, and brought him before Saul with the head of the Philistine in his hand. ⁵⁸And Saul said to him, "Whose son are you, young man?" And David answered, "I am the son of your servant Jesse the Bethlehemite."

a Hebrew; Septuagint, Dead Sea Scroll and Josephus *four*   b A *cubit* was about 18 inches or 45 centimeters   c A *shekel* was about 2/5 ounce or 11 grams   d Septuagint, Syriac; Hebrew *advanced among men*   e An *ephah* was about 3/5 bushel or 22 liters   f Septuagint; Hebrew *Gai*

OVERVIEW: For some of the reformers, the famous battle between David and Goliath serves as an allegory, which symbolizes the battle of Christ against Satan and that of belief against disbelief. Due to his strong faith in God, David, often regarded by the reformers as a type of Christ, proves victorious over a visibly more terrifying foe. Unarmed but for a few stones, David overpowers the giant Goliath by God's providence. Fighting in the name of the Lord against the giant, David cannot lose the battle, inciting these interpreters to apply the battle between the humble David and the arrogant Goliath to our spiritual lives.

AN ALLEGORY ON DAVID AND GOLIATH.
JOHANNES BUGENHAGEN: Goliath, lord of the Philistines, is the ruler of the world. Saul is a shepherd without faith. David is Christ and anyone who has a firm spirit in Christ. The Israelites are the common people, as yet unsure about the gospel, which goes forth from Christ and the good shepherd, that is, the inspired preacher of the gospel who stands above all enemies. Saul is in the habit of delaying, which makes all Israel fear the one Philistine. For this is what the kingdom of hypocrisy is like against Satan. God's righteousness cannot endure this, for this is not the spirit of victory. But David alone (that is, Christ) saves the people. For this reason, it is among the most esteemed stories you will ever read in human history. Here you see David's marvelous faith and zeal for his people against the blasphemy of their enemies, as he blazed—carried by the Spirit—for the glory of God. These are Christ's benefits, presented to us so that from the beginning of his anointing David might show through God what the kingdom itself will produce through Christ, David's son. This is also the result of all faith fighting against Satan's cunning and against worldly wisdom and power. These are not the weapons of the flesh but the armor of God. COMMENTARY ON 1 SAMUEL.[1]

THE PERENNIAL DUEL. VIKTORIN STRIGEL: The story of the duel between David and Goliath provides an eminent and wonderful example of faith. For David, full of faith and hope, requests and awaits the help of God. David undertakes this dangerous task, which God guides for the fortune and advantage of the church. This story reminds us of the victory of Christ and the church. This story admonishes us [to keep in mind] the victory of Christ and the church. For Christ repels the devil, opposing him with the word and prayer, just as the church, through the Word of God and through prayer, repels the same enemy and his heretical and tyrannical instruments. COMMENTARY ON 1 SAMUEL.[2]

17:1-11 *The Giant Goliath Frightens the Israelites*

DIABOLICAL GOLIATH. LUCAS OSIANDER: Goliath's tremendous size suggests that he might have come from the huge race of the giants, or Anakim, of whom some remained in the city of Gath (around Gaza and Ashdod) as recorded in Joshua 11. . . . From the weight of his armor, we can imagine what a monster of a man this Goliath was. This Goliath signifies the devil, who is terrifying and powerful and whose strength surpasses that of humans. ANNOTATIONS ON 1 SAMUEL.[3]

PROTECTION FROM THE VILE AND POWERFUL CREATURE. VIKTORIN STRIGEL: This splendid description of Goliath and his armor illustrates the faith of David. Even though he was an unadorned and unarmed novice, David nevertheless dared to go against an experienced and noble enemy in hand-to-hand combat. Meanwhile, the stature and weaponry of this dreaded and monstrous giant brought fear on Saul and the whole of Israel. Now, Goliath is a picture of the devil, whose power is described in the following words from Job 41: "He counts iron as straw, and bronze as rotten wood. On earth he has no equal, a creature without fear."

---

[1] Bugenhagen, *In Samuelem prophetam*, 236-37; citing 2 Cor 10:4; Eph 6:11.

[2] Strigel, *Libri Samuelis, Regum et Paralipomenon*, 59.
[3] Osiander, *Liber Iosue*, 380; citing Deut 2:21; 9:2; Josh 11:21-23.

To which defense should we seek refuge so that we are protected from this very powerful spirit? God strengthens us and is our refuge and defense! Commentary on 1 Samuel.[4]

Parallel Fear and Faith. Johannes Brenz: The more Goliath's ferocity grew, the more the timidity and cowardice of the Israelites increased. The more abject the Israelites' fear became, the more Goliath's fearsome majesty increased, until the people's souls fell to their feet and they became the most shameful sort of deserters. Those who notice this relationship between Goliath's increasing ferocity and the Israelites increasing fearfulness will notice the parallel way in which the Lord gloriously restored David, who had been despised and turned away by the people. For we should learn that in the same way as God would exalt the one person David by his grace, so would God allow Saul and all his people who first scorned David to fall into a disgraceful ruin. Sermons on Samuel.[5]

17:12-30 David Cares for God's Flock

Over the Course of Forty Days. Andrew Willet: God ordained that forty days should be spent this way, thereby serving as the occasion through which David was sent to the camp to visit his brothers. This is the means by which the Lord appointed the conquest of Goliath. Likewise, the more the Israelites were in fear and the greater their perplexity, the more famous their victory and deliverance was, which they did not expect. This further evidences the great change and alteration that took place in Saul, namely, how the Spirit of God had forsaken him. From a valiant and courageous man with a heroic spirit, he grew to be a despicable coward. Whereas before in one day he had killed almost forty thousand of the Philistines, now, over the course of forty days, he was afraid to fight just one man. Harmony on 1 Samuel.[6]

Obeying His Father. Lucas Osiander: David had been anointed king by Samuel in the previous chapter. Even so, he was not carrying himself around as if he were king. Instead, he was humbly obeying his father and providing for his absent brothers. For though Christ (the true David) was in the form of God, he emptied himself for our sake, taking the form of a servant and obeying the Father, even to death on a cross. And though he was sent first to his brothers (the Jewish people), it became known that he had in fact come to free all of humankind from Satan's tyranny. Therefore children ought to imitate David's obedience and remember that he rose to glory and dignity through obedience. Annotations on 1 Samuel.[7]

God Makes an Example of David. Johannes Brenz: When Goliath insulted the armies of Israel, there were many pious men in the army. However, they did not sin by not engaging Goliath in single combat because God had inspired for them to do so by means of a spiritual gift. Only David received this gift because God wanted to make him illustrious. Commentary on Genesis.[8]

Of the Rewards. Andrew Willet: It is fit and proper that, as in the case with David, rewards should be given to those who offer their service in the defense of the commonwealth. For although we do not deserve an everlasting reward from the hands of God, yet a temporary reward may be deserved from the hands of people. And such rewards may be respected and aimed for, though chiefly the glory of God and the good of his church ought to move everyone to perform his duty. Now the rewards that Saul gave to David were three: (1) to join him in affinity in making him his son-in-law; (2) in endowing him with riches and enlarging his house—as in setting it free from taxes and other impositions—and (3) in advancing David to the state of nobility. But here Saul's inconstancy

[4]Strigel, *Libri Samuelis, Regum et Paralipomenon*, 60; citing Job 41:27, 33.
[5]Brenz, *Opera*, 2:608.
[6]Willet, *Harmony on 1 Samuel*, 150*.

[7]Osiander, *Liber Iosue*, 383; citing Phil 2:6-7.
[8]Brenz, *Opera*, 1:143.

and fickleness appeared: he was liberal in promising but slow in performing, which was evident in his unkind attitude toward David afterward. HARMONY ON 1 SAMUEL.[9]

WHETHER DAVID WAS OVERLY AMBITIOUS.

ANDREW WILLET: David was not incited or stirred up by the hope of any kind of reward. . . . Rather, David was incited by the honor of God and the love of the people of God. Therefore, when David says: "What shall be done for the man who kills this Philistine and takes away the reproach from Israel?" he says in effect: "Who cares about receiving a promise? The indignity of the insult to the people of God, and the reproach they bear at the hand of this Philistine, is sufficient to provoke any man to action." David offers two reasons for his decision. The first was taken from the person of the Philistine, who was an uncircumcised foreigner. The other was taken from one of the Israelites, who served the living God. In short, the Philistine's insult was not to be endured. In this way, it was the honor of God and the reproach of the people of God that moved David to act. It was not the consideration of the reward. No, David was not won with these promises. In fact, when David appeared before Saul, he made no mention of any reward nor did he require any provision or promise from the king. HARMONY ON 1 SAMUEL.[10]

WHEN THE SHEPHERD IS AWAY, THE WOLVES WILL SLAY. ANDREW WILLET: The care and

charge David had of his flock (being morally applied) shows what duty is required of the spiritual pastor toward his people. It also shows what causes of absence are allowable and when the shepherd ought not to be absent. Pastors ought not to be absent from their charges for long. And when their necessary occasions of being absent are completed, they are bound in conscience to return to their places. That these reasons are grounded on the Word of God and agreeable to the continual

practice of the church of Christ we may demonstrate as follows.

First, there is a great danger that accrues and grows to the pastors themselves if any of those souls that are committed to their charge perish in their absence through their negligence. As the prophet Ezekiel says, "If I say to the wicked, 'O wicked one, you shall surely die,' and you do not speak to warn the wicked to turn from his way, that wicked person shall die in his iniquity, but his blood I will require at your hand."

I do wonder how negligent pastors, when they read this passage, can pass it over without trembling—seeing what danger they incur in omitting to admonish the people committed to them. As Jerome well says, "The loss of the flock is the shame of the shepherd." In fact, such loss even leads to the shepherd's everlasting shame and confusion—without God's great mercy.

Second, the absence and negligence of the pastor proceeds from lack of love toward the flock. The one who does not love the flock does not love the one who owns the flock. Therefore our Savior says to Peter after he asked if he loved him, "Feed my sheep." Therefore Pope Damasus I warns that anyone who is negligent in feeding the Lord's flock, despite clear commendation, is found not to love the chief shepherd. And how can the one who does not love Christ be assured of Christ's love toward him?

Third, let the inconveniences be considered that grow when pastors are absent. To begin with, the people will soon fall away from zeal to coldness and from virtue to vice. Where good seed is not sown, thistles and weeds will spring up instead. The apostle found this to be true by experience in the church of the Galatians when he was absent from them. As he says, "It is always good to be made much of for a good purpose, and not only when I am present with you, my little children, for whom I am again in the anguish of childbirth until Christ is formed in you! I wish I could be present with you now and change my tone, for I am perplexed about you." It seems that while the apostle was present, the Galatians were very enthusiastic and zealous, but in his absence their

---

[9]Willet, *Harmony on 1 Samuel*, 152-53*.
[10]Willet, *Harmony on 1 Samuel*, 153*.

zeal and first love abated. Therefore the apostle Paul wished he was among them, so that he might change and apply his voice to admonition or exhortation, as each person's case required. This is the same thing Ambrose feared. Being on some necessary occasion absent from his church, he wrote: "I was mindful of you, fearing, lest in my absence any might fall through negligence and succumb to the ways of Satan." And Augustine complains that while he was absent from Hippo, the citizens lost a certain godly custom among them of clothing and coating the poor. Therefore it is evident that good things will soon be discontinued and grow out of use where the pastor is not present to call on the people.

Fourth, the more diligent the spiritual adversary is to harm the flock, the more vigilant the pastor should be to watch over it. Now the devil, as Saint Peter says, "prowls around like a roaring lion, seeking someone to devour." And the wolf is most likely to invade the flock when the pastor is not near at hand to defend them. Therefore Saint Paul says, "I know that after my departure fierce wolves will come in among you, not sparing the flock." So Ambrose says well that the wolves watch for the pastor's absence, because while the pastors are present they cannot invade the sheep of Christ.

Fifth, how necessary the presence and residence of pastors and ministers in their churches is appears by the excellence and price of that object where their cure and charge lies. For indeed, they are watchmen not of people's bodies, but of their souls; and they must give account for them. If a steward, a dispenser of temporal things, must be faithful, as Jacob watched his flock by day and night and whatever perished he made it good (Gen 31:39), how much more careful, circumspect and vigilant ought the dispenser of spiritual things be? The imperial laws have provided that advocates should stay out of the cities and places where they practiced. They should not busy themselves with other people's affairs but attend to their own calling and charge. If those who merely fight for people's bodies and their goods give such diligent attendance, how much more so is the same requisite for

those who are charged with people's souls? But nowadays it is counted so ordinary and easy a thing to be the pastor of souls that a person will require more diligence at his servant's hands about his cattle than many will perform in the feeding of souls! God, in his good time, opens the eyes of some so they may see the great danger in which they, by their negligence and carelessness, cast themselves. God also makes them aware, so they may feel the heavy weight of the burden of souls.

Finally, not to heap up more arguments in so evident a matter, but pastors give great offense when they are absent unnecessarily. It is as if they were seeking to feed on their church rather than feeding their church. As the prophet Ezekiel complains of such idle shepherds, "You eat the fat, you clothe yourselves with the wool, you slaughter the fat ones, but you do not feed the sheep." Saint Paul says to the Corinthians, "I seek not what is yours but you." But those who do not care for Christ's flock evidently proclaim that they do not seek them, but theirs. Of this kind of scandal and offense Augustine had experience in his people of Hippo. Of his flock he writes, "The people of Hippo, whose servant the Lord has made me, are so altogether weak that a little trouble is able to make them very sick: I found them at my return dangerously scandalized with my absence." If the people took offense at Augustine's necessary absence—for we know that such a holy man would not be absent without just cause—how much more grievous is the offense given by a pastor's unnecessary absence? Harmony of 1 Samuel.[11]

David's Eldest Brother. Andrew Willet: Some think Eliab was speaking sternly to David out of the love and protection of an older brother for a younger one. Yet by means of the rough words he used and the untrue surmises he made, it is evident that Eliab spoke out of envy. Indeed, he spoke with great indignation. And this might be

---

[11]Willet, *Harmony on 1 Samuel*, 155-57*; citing Ezek 33:8; Jerome, *Epistle* 54, to Furia; Jn 21:17; Gal 4:18-20; Ambrose, *Sermon* 28; 1 Pet 5:8; Acts 20:29; Heb 13:17; Ezek 34:3; 2 Cor 12:14; Augustine, *Epistle* 7.

the reason why Eliab envied David, namely, because David was advanced to the king's service and court, while Eliab, the firstborn brother, was neglected. It was for this reason that Eliab blamed David when he should have commended him—for by leaving his flock, David was merely obeying his father's command to visit his brothers. In fact, Eliab took it on himself to judge David's heart and affection, reckoning David's goodness to pride and malice, whereas such virtues actually came forth from the Spirit of God in him. In this way David was envied by his brothers to serve as a type of Christ, who was rejected by his brothers the Jews. HARMONY ON 1 SAMUEL.[12]

17:31-37 David Prepares for Battle

SERVING UNDER A PRINCE. EDWARD REYNOLDS: Nothing makes a person more fearful of wars than the dangers and hazards that accompany them. But if a person can serve under such a prince whose employments are not only honorable but also safe; if he, who is able and faithful to make good his promise to us that none of the strategies or forces of the enemy will hurt us, but that they shall fly before us while we resist them; who would not volunteer in such services as are not liable to the casualties and vicissitudes, which usually attend other wars, where he might fight with safety, and come off with honor? David had experience of God's power in delivering him from the lion and the bear. He was well assured that God, who was careful of sheep, would be more caring to his people Israel. This gave him greater willingness to encounter Goliath, whose assurance was only in himself and not in God. THE SINFULNESS OF SIN.[13]

CIRCUMCISION OF THE HEART. ANDREW WILLET: As David holds the Philistine to be without defense—since he is uncircumcised—so he encourages himself because he was circumcised and so within God's covenant. But David does not look

to mere circumcision. Instead, he looks at it in relation to the covenant. Otherwise there were many who were bodily circumcised who did not belong to the covenant and many bodily uncircumcised who were the servants of God. (This appears, for instance, in the book of Job.) As circumcision, then, was a mark and outward recognition of God's people, so baptism is now. As David's circumcision defended him from Goliath, so baptism now shields us from Satan—but not merely the washing of the flesh, but as it is a seal of the covenant of grace in Christ. HARMONY ON 1 SAMUEL.[14]

NO FEAR. HENRY AIRAY: We read that David—after having experienced God's help in his deliverance out of the paw of the lion and out of the paw of the bear—did not fear to encounter Goliath, but assured himself that "the Lord who delivered him out of the paw of the lion and the paw of the bear will deliver him from the hand of this Philistine." In the same way, the children of God—after having felt the love of God in Christ Jesus in their souls and the testimony of the Spirit witnessing to their spirits that they are the sons of God—should not fear to encounter sin or Satan, but should assure themselves that nothing is able to separate them from the love of God in Christ Jesus. LECTURES ON PHILIPPIANS.[15]

17:38-40 Saul Outfits David but David Finds His Own Weapon

WHY DAVID PUT OFF SAUL'S ARMOR. ANDREW WILLET: David would have used the armor if it had been helpful for him. But perceiving that they would rather be an impediment to him than a help, he laid them aside. This also brought about God's providence, in the sense that God would not have David use any external defense, so that the glory of the victory might only be given to God. Furthermore, as there was a difference between the spirits of David and of Saul in the way in which they were

---

[12]Willet, *Harmony on 1 Samuel*, 153-54*.
[13]Reynolds, *Works*, 1:293*.

[14]Willet, *Harmony on 1 Samuel*, 174-175*.
[15]Airay, *Lectures on Philippians*, 26-27.

led, so also their armor was different. Saul trusted in his helmet and breastplate, but David put his confidence in God. In this way David was a figure of Christ, who conquered Satan not by outward pomp and worldly power but by spiritual weapons. HARMONY ON 1 SAMUEL.[16]

OF DAVID'S WEAPONS. ANDREW WILLET: David takes only his sling and certain smooth stones, for by such means the Lord brings to pass mighty things. Indeed, so that the glory and power of God might more fully be made manifest in the blessing of so simple a means—just as Moses brought waters out of the rock with his rod, Elisha healed the waters with salt and Christ cured the blind with spittle—David used this simple weapons because Israelites were formerly forbidden by the Philistines to use any iron weapons. David takes more than one stone—five all together—so that if at the first throw he fails, he might cast the others as needed. The typical application of these five stones to the five books of Moses, in which Satan is vanquished, is somewhat far-fetched, and therefore I will not stand on it. HARMONY ON 1 SAMUEL.[17]

LEAVING ROOM FOR THE CAPTAIN. EDWARD REYNOLDS: When David went forth against Goliath, he did not grapple with him by his own strength, but with his sling and his stone overthrew him at a distance. It is not good to let Satan come too close to the soul, to let in his temptation, or to enter into any private and intimate combat with him. This was only for our captain to do who, we know, entered into the field with him as being certain of his own strength. But our only way to prevail against him is to take faith as a sling and Christ as a stone. THE SINFULNESS OF SIN.[18]

WALKING IN GOD'S WAYS. JOHANNES BRENZ: David approached Goliath, walking in the calling of God. Therefore God established his portion against Goliath. Why, if you wished, God would

establish your portion *if* you walked by faith. COMMENTARY ON ROMANS.[19]

17:41-58 *Fighting in the Name of the Lord*

OVERCOMING DEATH. CHARLES DRELINCOURT: When David showed himself with a purpose to fight with Goliath, he spoke to this dreadful Philistine in this manner: "I come to you in the name of the Lord of hosts, the God of the armies of Israel." But you, Christian souls, when you are encountering death, you may say to it, "Not only do I come to you in the name of he who commands legions of angels and all the armies of immortal spirits, but I also come to you clothed with his armor, strengthened by his Holy Spirit and assisted by him in person." For Jesus Christ, who has overcome death *for us*, intends to overcome death *by us*. We are the living stones that he has chosen of his wonderful grace and mercy to bring down that proud insulting enemy, who causes all creatures to tremble and cover their faces with shame and confusion. CHRISTIAN DEFENSE AGAINST THE FEARS OF DEATH.[20]

THE GOSPEL OF DAVID'S VICTORY. WILLIAM TYNDALE: When David had killed Goliath the giant, glad tidings came to the Israelites that their fearful and cruel enemy was dead and that they were delivered out of all danger. For this gladness, they sang, danced and were joyful. In like manner, the good news or "gospel" of God is joyful tidings; and, as some say, it is a good hearing proclaimed by the apostles throughout all the world of Christ as the real heir of David. It is good news of how he has fought with sin, death and the devil and overcome them. The result of this is that all people who were in bondage to sin, wounded with death and overcome of the devil are— without their own merits or deserving—freed, justified, restored to life and saved. They are brought to liberty and

---

[16]Willet, *Harmony on 1 Samuel*, 177*.
[17]Willet, *Harmony on 1 Samuel*, 178*.
[18]Reynolds, *Works*, 1:110-11.

[19]Brenz, *Opera*, 7:652.
[20]Drelincourt, *Christian's Defense Against the Fears of Death*, 313*; citing 1 Sam 17:45.

reconciled to the favor of God and set at one with him again. These are tidings to as many as believe, laud, praise and thank God; and who are glad, sing and dance for joy. DOCTRINAL TREATISES AND INTRODUCTIONS TO OTHER PORTIONS OF HOLY SCRIPTURES.[21]

ALL CHRISTIANS ARE STRONG. MARTIN LUTHER: For though David was insignificant in person and weak compared with others, he nevertheless became a greater hero than Goliath and slew him. Therefore, because Christians all have the same Christ and his Spirit, every one of them, when they are most insignificant and weak, can do as much as the very strongest. For they shall, all of them, conquer sin, death and the world. They all gain the same victory, however different they may be. For there is one Spirit and one Christ in all of them, who protects them and helps them. To the world they may therefore appear to be nothing but falling and all be heroes and victors in that world. LECTURES ON ZECHARIAH.[22]

LITTLE PERSON, BIG RESULTS. JOHN FISHER: No man among all the great multitude of Israelites had the audacity or boldness to make battle with this monstrous creature, this Philistine, save only this little person David. It was Almighty God who gave him so great a boldness, although he was but little in appearance and stature. Nevertheless, he in no way feared to fight and make battle with this great and mighty giant. COMMENTARY ON THE SEVEN PENITENTIAL PSALMS.[23]

THE LOVE OF GOD. EDWARD REYNOLDS: Our very actions are wrought in us and carried to their end by the power of Christ, who has enough mercy, wisdom and strength to rescue us from the power of hell and death and from the danger of our own sick and proud hearts. To see a person—half a mile from his enemy—draw a sword to encounter him or take up a stone to hit him would be a ridiculous spectacle. For what could he do with such weapons by his own strength at such a distance? But if he mounted a cannon and pointed his target against the enemy, we would not wonder at this even though the distance would be great between them because the effect of it proceeds from the force of the materials and instruments he uses, namely, the powder, the bullet, the fire and the cannon. It seemed absurd in the eyes of the enemy for little David—with a shepherd's bag and a sling—to go against an armed giant like Goliath. This produced in the giant's proud heart much disdain and offense. But when we hear David mention the name of God, in the strength and confidence where he came against so proud an enemy, this makes us conclude that weak David was strong enough to battle against great Goliath. It was not our own strength but the love of God that is the foundation of our triumph over all enemies. SEVEN SERMONS ON FOURTEENTH CHAPTER OF HOSEA.[24]

---

[21]Tyndale, *Doctrinal Treatises*, 8-9*.
[22]LW 20:327.
[23]Fisher, *Commentary on the Seven Penitential Psalms*, 4*.
[24]Reynolds, *Works*, 3:383*.

18:1-30 DAVID CONTINUES TO PREVAIL

¹As soon as he had finished speaking to Saul, the soul of Jonathan was knit to the soul of David, and Jonathan loved him as his own soul. ²And Saul took him that day and would not let him return to his father's house. ³Then Jonathan made a covenant with David, because he loved him as his own soul. ⁴And Jonathan stripped himself of the robe that was on him and gave it to David, and his armor, and even his sword and his bow and his belt. ⁵And David went out and was successful wherever Saul sent him, so that Saul set him over the men of war. And this was good in the sight of all the people and also in the sight of Saul's servants.

⁶As they were coming home, when David returned from striking down the Philistine, the women came out of all the cities of Israel, singing and dancing, to meet King Saul, with tambourines, with songs of joy, and with musical instruments.ᵃ ⁷And the women sang to one another as they celebrated,

"Saul has struck down his thousands,
    and David his ten thousands."

⁸And Saul was very angry, and this saying displeased him. He said, "They have ascribed to David ten thousands, and to me they have ascribed thousands, and what more can he have but the kingdom?" ⁹And Saul eyed David from that day on.

¹⁰The next day a harmful spirit from God rushed upon Saul, and he raved within his house while David was playing the lyre, as he did day by day. Saul had his spear in his hand. ¹¹And Saul hurled the spear, for he thought, "I will pin David to the wall." But David evaded him twice.

¹²Saul was afraid of David because the LORD was with him but had departed from Saul. ¹³So Saul removed him from his presence and made him a commander of a thousand. And he went out and came in before the people. ¹⁴And David had success in all his undertakings, for the LORD was with him. ¹⁵And when Saul saw that he had great success, he stood in fearful awe of him. ¹⁶But all Israel and Judah loved David, for he went out and came in before them.

¹⁷Then Saul said to David, "Here is my elder daughter Merab. I will give her to you for a wife. Only be valiant for me and fight the LORD's battles." For Saul thought, "Let not my hand be against him, but let the hand of the Philistines be against him." ¹⁸And David said to Saul, "Who am I, and who are my relatives, my father's clan in Israel, that I should be son-in-law to the king?" ¹⁹But at the time when Merab, Saul's daughter, should have been given to David, she was given to Adriel the Meholathite for a wife.

²⁰Now Saul's daughter Michal loved David. And they told Saul, and the thing pleased him. ²¹Saul thought, "Let me give her to him, that she may be a snare for him and that the hand of the Philistines may be against him." Therefore Saul said to David a second time,ᵇ "You shall now be my son-in-law." ²²And Saul commanded his servants, "Speak to David in private and say, 'Behold, the king has delight in you, and all his servants love you. Now then become the king's son-in-law.'" ²³And Saul's servants spoke those words in the ears of David. And David said, "Does it seem to you a little thing to become the king's son-in-law, since I am a poor man and have no reputation?" ²⁴And the servants of Saul told him, "Thus and so did David speak." ²⁵Then Saul said, "Thus shall you say to David, 'The king desires no bride-price except a hundred foreskins of the Philistines, that he may be avenged of the king's enemies.'" Now Saul thought to make David fall by the hand of the Philistines. ²⁶And when his servants told David these words, it pleased David well to be the king's son-in-law. Before the time had expired, ²⁷David arose and went, along with his men, and killed two hundred of the Philistines. And David brought their foreskins, which were given in full number to the king, that he might become the king's son-in-law. And Saul gave him his daughter Michal for a wife. ²⁸But when Saul saw and knew that the LORD was with David, and that Michal, Saul's daughter, loved him, ²⁹Saul was even more afraid of David. So Saul was David's enemy continually.

³⁰Then the commanders of the Philistines came out to battle, and as often as they came out David had more success than all the servants of Saul, so that his name was highly esteemed.

a Or *triangles*, or *three-stringed instruments* b Hebrew *by two*

Overview: The reformers consistently view David as a messianic figure whose righteousness incites criticism and attacks from the unrighteous. In this case, Saul serves as the instrument of attack on account of his jealous and ungodly motives. Saul's behavior toward David is malicious and, according to some of the commentators, demonic. Saul slyly offers his daughter to David, according to the interpreters, as a snare (and later marries her to another man). David's friendship with Jonathan, by contrast, is the paradigm of godly and virtuous friendship, the likes of which set the ideal for relationships on earth.

18:1-5 David and Jonathan's Friendship

The Difference Between Jonathan and Saul. Johannes Bugenhagen: We see the faith of David, which is necessary when following the cross and when faith gets tested. His victory over Goliath is itself the occasion of persecutions, for Saul could not bear someone else to be liked more. We see from this that the saints bear punishment just as sinners do, but not on account of sins but on account of righteousness. For what honor would not have been worthy of David for such a holy deed? But it happens just as Christ says in the psalm, "In return for my love they accuse me, but I give myself to prayer. So they reward me evil for good, and hatred for my love." Scripture truly describes the difference between Jonathan and Saul with respect to David. Jonathan's character was shown earlier in his love of virtue and piety, according to these words, "Those who fear you will see me and rejoice, because I have hoped in your word." But it is impossible for the ungodly to do anything but hate and persecute the godly. But Jonathan is not afraid of losing glory and majesty, even though his father's kingdom would have

belonged to him, because he does not look on his own concerns but those of God. But it would be with him like it is with us when some look kindly on us, while others despise or hate us. The one group is more hidden and appears weaker before the world than the majority and the powerful who are able to be secure. Still, God cares for us, so that we see God's work in every desperate situation, believing in God's mercy and protecting hand even in the midst of death and hell, and not (as Paul says in 2 Cor 1) trusting in ourselves. Commentary on 1 Samuel.[1]

True Friendship. Lambert Daneau: The ground and foundation of true Christian friendship is the admiration of virtue or of some special gift of God that resides in another—the praise or use of which respects either God himself or a person. This moved Jonathan to knit himself in most firm friendship with David, whom for his valiant heart and noble courage in vanquishing proud Goliath he highly esteemed, honored and entirely loved. Such persons—as either some singular gift of true godliness or some special praise of some moral virtue (whether justice, fortitude, liberality, etc.)—excel others, and are therefore worthily invested with the title of deserved commendation, whom we thoroughly love, entirely reverence and heartily favor. And this latter is the secret or the next cause that we commonly use to respect and to regard. But the former of the two is that which is occasioned, bred and brought forth by a secret instinct of the Spirit from God: namely, the mutual knitting together of minds and a like inclination and conformity of wills. For all true and holy friendship has its ground from God, in whom it is firmly established

---

[1]Bugenhagen, *In Samuelem prophetam*, 241-242; citing Ps 109:4; 119:74.

and by whom alone it continues sure, steadfast and permanent. True and Christian Friendship.[2]

Religion and Friendship. Henry Airay: Sincerity in religion and true fear of the Lord are the best bands of Christian friendship. We read in secular stories of some individuals who were renowned for their rare friendships. But what are these but shadows in respect to the Christian body? What friendship of theirs came ever near that of Jonathan and David? . . . Indeed, generally where religion and fear of the Lord knits the knot, there the friendship is most sure and the duties thereof are best performed. If, therefore, you will have such a friend . . . when need requires it . . . join yourself to someone who is religious and who fears the Lord; and let your love be in the Lord and for the Lord. For what is the cause that friendship is so rare, and why is there such slackness in all sorts of people to help one another and to comfort one another in any time of need? Surely this is the reason: because our love is only a cold love, grounded on this or that worldly respect, instead of our love for one another being in the Lord and for the Lord. Lectures on Philippians.[3]

Keeping One's Promise. Lambert Daneau: It is written of Jonathan that he gave to David as a pledge, bond or pawn of their newly begotten friendship not only the solemn citing of the name of God but also other visible gifts and outward testimonies—namely, his robe, girdle, sword, bow and such other garments and furniture he had at that time. For such hearty courtesies make people not only the more mindful but also the more religious in the keeping and observing of their promises and covenants. True and Christian Friendship.[4]

Disarming Death. Charles Drelincourt: Just as our Savior has once overcome death for us,

he continues to subdue it in and by us. He does us not let us encounter our enemies alone, nor leave us in our agonies. In a day of battle a wise and provident general has an eye to every place and encourages his soldiers by his action and with his voice when he perceives they are at blows with the enemy: some he loads with praises, others with promises. By that means he encourages those who act bravely and rescue the weak and feeble, and those who are overwhelmed he furnishes with fresh supplies. This is the same way our Lord and Savior Jesus Christ, the great Lord of hosts, who sits above in the heavens in triumph and beholds all our combats and encounters, deals with us. When he perceives that we are too weak, in order that we might not be overcome by our dreadful enemies he furnishes us with his Holy Spirit, and his own armor, as Jonathan did David, when he delivered to him his cloak, his bow, his belt and his sword. Besides, this merciful Savior disarms death of its most hurtful weapons and takes away all its arrows and darts. Christian Defense Against the Fears of Death.[5]

18:6-16 *Saul's Jealousy of David*

Rules for Dancing. Martin Bucer: Because human nature has that feebleness by which it cannot always concentrate on grave and serious things but demands other rest besides sleep, there must also be provision made for certain rest from work and useful studies and a certain recreation of the strength of the spirit and of the body in play and games. This is especially the case when grave and serious things have been satisfied in wise moderation and prudence, insomuch that the kind of game is prescribed and exhibited for adults and youth in such a way that they do not have to fear any lessening of morals or delight in wicked idleness, and in a way that there can also be gained a certain strengthening of health as well as some addition in the cultivation of the mind. . . . These

---

[2]Daneau, *True and Christian Friendship*, A3r-v*.

[3]Airay, *Lectures on Philippians*, 198*.

[4]Daneau, *True and Christian Friendship*, A8r*.

[5]Drelincourt, *Christian's Defense Against the Fears of Death*, 32*.

games should come from musical and gymnastic art. From this music should come poems and songs that present nothing futile, nothing inappropriate to the Christian profession and nothing obscene and wicked, but only sounds that set forth the praises of God and of his servants from all his works and judgments as these are set forth in holy Scripture.... To these may be added dances, but the dances of godly girls should be separate from the dances of young men, which may be danced to pure, wholesome and holy songs, with chaste and modest motion that befits those who profess godliness.... Such was the dance of holy girls who celebrated a song of victory for David and Saul when they returned from the killing of the Philistines. REIGN OF CHRIST.[6]

SAUL'S SIN AGAINST THE HOLY SPIRIT.
JOHANNES BUGENHAGEN: As you know, we do not carelessly regard the words of Scripture to be the simple legends they seem to be. For this chapter clearly shows us Saul's envy, which is the sin against the Holy Spirit. Scripture insists more than once that Saul knew the Lord had departed from him to be with David, along with all the counsel and favor that went with him, so that Saul has fallen. He is clearly fighting against knowledge of the truth, and therefore against God, as you see shortly. This is not a mistake or ignorance; rather it is pure folly and desperate ungodliness. COMMENTARY ON 1 SAMUEL.[7]

VINDICTIVENESS IS A GREAT ANGER. PHILIPP MELANCHTHON: Vindictiveness is a great anger, stemming from pride, one's own wantonness to overwhelm or to blot out others without the orderly office of authority; such pride is often great, even though the perpetrator has no reason, as Cain, for imagining that God honors only the other and wishes to do nothing for him. This is very common, and all rational beings can understand that this vice is repugnant to many divine commandments.

Pride, through which anger is kindled like a fire in the heart, is against the first commandment. Saul wishes to drive David out of the way in order that he alone may have authority. This unrighteous anger, this jealousy and hate and thirst for blood are against the commandment, "You shall not kill." THEOLOGICAL COMMONPLACES (1555).[8]

ADVANTAGES OF ADVERSITY. ROGER HUTCHINSON: Our nature is such that prosperity depraves us. Prosperity brings many people to destruction and fills them with pride and covetousness; it makes them negligent, dissolute, forgetful and unthankful.... Therefore the wise person admonishes..."When you have refreshed yourself and are full of food and drink and other things, then take heed to yourself; you stand on a slippery ground." Adversity, on the other hand, makes us lowly, gentle, diligent, circumspect and pitied. It garnishes us with all flowers of virtue and expels all sin. David, as long as he was in trouble and vexation under Saul, was in favor with God and famous among the people; but after he reigned and governed Israel prosperously, did he not fall into sin? ... The devil is crafty. Those he cannot supplant by adversity he overthrows with prosperity. TWO SERMONS OF OPPRESSION, AFFLICTION AND PATIENCE.[9]

DAVID'S TRIUMPH. JOHANNES BRENZ: Saul knew that David would succeed him as king. And so, considering himself to be in great danger, he planned to kill David. But all of his spirited attempts were in vain. And another event eventually showed this. For Joseph became the leader of his older brothers at the right time. And David became king, not as a normal family member of Saul's. For Saul sinned to such an extent that not even David could preserve his family since it would all soon fall. But to David's credit, the line of Saul was not damned. For although God removed a gift from someone and conferred it on another, he did

---

[6]Bucer, *De Regno Christi*, 207-8.
[7]Bugenhagen, *In Samuelem prophetam*, 242.

[8]*Melanchthon on Christian Doctrine*, 134; citing Ex 20:13.
[9]Hutchinson, *Two Sermons*, 308*.

not do it here for this reason, so that it would affect him inconveniently, but he would take counsel to his advantage by removal. COMMENTARY ON ROMANS.[10]

LEERING EYE. LANCELOT ANDREWES: There are two ways to convey sin to us: by the ear and by the eye. And there are two ways to discover sin: by the mouth and by the eye. This is because the eye is a way both in the conveyance and discovery of the sin.... When Saul saw how David was esteemed, it is there said that he "eyed David from that day on," as if he looked asquint, in that he looked on David with a leering eye. This is because he envied and hated David. COLLECTION OF LECTURES.[11]

LACK OF TRUE OBEDIENCE. DANIEL DYKE: Note that constancy accompanies true obedience. For instance, the Scripture says that when we walk in the commandments of the Lord, we walk in peace. Conversely, the wicked are said to be involved in covetousness in that they constantly follow it as the thief does his trade. However, the "temporary" wicked person does not walk in these ways as does the honest traveler in the broad highway.... His obedience is like the true Christian's disobedience, which is not settled and constant but is only for a time. The good Christian quickly remembers himself and returns to his course of godliness when, through a temporary lapse, he has begun to stray. In the same way, the "temporary" Christian quickly returns to his intermittent wickedness even though he occasionally stumbles on piety. His obedience is a moody and passionate obedience; it is soon forgotten. It is like Saul's affection for David. When the evil spirit came on Saul, the piety about which he before seemed to make much of departed along with the spear in his hand. He did not, nor could he, cleave to the Lord with a full purpose of heart as the true believer can. THE MYSTERY OF SELF-DECEIVING.[12]

18:17-30 *Saul Offers Michal to David as a Wife at a Price*

ON HYPOCRISY. MARTIN LUTHER: King Saul did not like David and would have liked to kill him; but since he wanted to be holy, he decided not to kill him himself, but to send him among the Philistines to be killed there, so that his hand would remain innocent. Look at this beautiful Pharisaic holiness! It can purify itself and stay pious as long as it does not kill with its own hand, though its heart may be crammed full of anger, hate and envy, of hidden and evil schemes of murder, and though its tongue may be loaded with curses and blasphemies. THE SERMON ON THE MOUNT.[13]

SAUL'S DECEITFUL PLAN. JOHANNES BUGENHAGEN: Saul said to David, "Behold, my daughter." This is an example of the greatest men being seen as hypocrites. They see themselves as good men. They handle themselves in such a way as to excuse their sins. They say to us, "It is not lawful for us to put anyone to death" and they did not enter Pilate's quarters so that they would not be defiled and could eat the Passover. Scripture calls them men of blood, of deceit, of lies and of works of iniquity, as in Psalms 5, 58, 140 and Isaiah 59, etc. This reveals Saul's hypocrisy, which continues to the end of the chapter. COMMENTARY ON 1 SAMUEL.[14]

GOD'S THREE-KNOT CHAIN. LANCELOT ANDREWES: With people it oftentimes happens that saying is without doing. That is, too often people promise and say much, but do nothing; and many times we see a person's doing to be without completing.... Saul said he would give Michal to David, but he did not do it. However, it is not so with God; for he is not "yes" in saying, and "no" in doing and performing. Rather, as certain as he says a thing, so surely it is done—for his word is truth, and his deeds declare it.... If God begins a good work, he will surely finish it thoroughly.... If he is the beginner

---

[10]Brenz, *Opera*, 7:708.
[11]Andrewes, *A Collection of Lectures*, 270-71*.
[12]Dyke, *The Mystery of Self-Deceiving*, 118-19*.

[13]LW 21:74.
[14]Bugenhagen, *In Samuelem prophetam*, 244; citing Jn 18:28-32.

and author of anything, he will also perfect it. . . .
This is the first consideration when it comes to God:
that these three things—saying, doing and perfect-
ing—are inseparable in him, joined and linked
together as a chain, where all proceed after the other
and all follow the first. COLLECTION OF LECTURES.[15]

HIDDEN AGENDA. THOMAS ADAMS: David had
grown so gracious with the people that the king
could not harm him. Therefore he lured him into
the jaws of death by no less a price than his eldest
daughter. What could be spoken more honorably,
more graciously? A king could not offer a more
noble gift than his own daughter nor desire a more
gracious reward than to fight the Lord's battles.
What a saint, what a friend was Saul! Yet he never
meant so much mischief to David and so much
unfaithfulness to God as in this offer! A good man
is never safe from the false-hearted: For when they
make the fairest weather, that's when the greatest
danger is. Whatever the appearance was, Saul meant
nothing to David but death. Yet this falsehood did
discover itself, for Merab was not given to David but
to Adriel. Seeing that all these dangers could not
bring about what Saul desired, he himself would not
bring about what he promised. Yet still he would be
a friend and he had another daughter for David;
even though she was younger, she was the more
affectionate one. She was as sick in love as her father
was of hate toward David. Saul was glad of this, as
his daughter could never live to do him better service.
If she could betray David, David would have his
goodwill to marry her. Thus this false-hearted king
sacrificed his own child to his envy, hoping that her
honest and sincere love would betray her worthy
and innocent husband. There is a story of an
emperor in Turkey who married his own daughter
to a man on the one day and then after a night's
pleasure sent for his head the next morning. Are
there none who care not to cast away a daughter on
their friend for their own ends? Such is the rage of
desperate malice; rather than not ruin those they
hate, they will do it through the means of their own
children. "Faithful are the wounds of a friend, but
the kisses of an enemy are deceitful." . . . We pray,
from the hands of all our enemies, and (of all our
enemies) from the hands of our deceitful friends,
good Lord deliver us. COMMENTARY ON 2 PETER.[16]

GIFTLESS GIFT. DANIEL DYKE: The devil
sometimes gives the truth. In fact, he sometimes
sets a snare to catch the truth. He does so as Saul,
a good student in Satan's school, did for David in
giving him Michal as a wife. "I will give him her,"
Saul reasons, "so that she may be a snare to him
and so that the hand of the Philistines may be
upon him." What a splendid show of favor and
goodwill! Yet David was so ravished by the offer,
thinking about his lowness of birth, that he was
honored with the prospect of so great a marriage.
But it is but bait—a phony poison is covering up
the hook. . . . It is just as the proverb says: Saul's
gift to David was a "giftless gift." It was bread in one
hand and a stone in the other. THE MYSTERY OF
SELF-DECEIVING.[17]

THE BENEFIT OF AN ENEMY. EDWARD REYN-
OLDS: We may not deny but that a person may
have gain by an enemy, as poison to some creatures affords nourishment. . . . They say the
sweetest roses are the ones that grow near garlic.
In the same way, the nearness of an enemy makes a
good person even better. . . . When Saul, David's
enemy, eyed and persecuted him, this made him
walk more circumspectly, pray more and trust in
God more: He thought, "I will guard my ways,
that I may not sin with my tongue; I will guard
my mouth with a muzzle, so long as the wicked
are in my presence." . . . A malicious enemy that
watches for our halting will make us look the
better to our ways. SEVEN SERMONS ON THE
FOURTEENTH CHAPTER OF HOSEA.[18]

---

[15]Andrewes, *A Collection of Lectures*, 44*.

[16]Adams, *Commentary upon 2 Peter*, 892*; citing Prov 27:6.
[17]Dyke, *The Mystery of Self-Deceiving*, 14*.
[18]Reynolds, *Works*, 3:466*; citing Ps 39:1.

19:1–20:42 SAUL MAKES AN ATTEMPT
ON DAVID'S LIFE

¹And Saul spoke to Jonathan his son and to all his servants, that they should kill David. But Jonathan, Saul's son, delighted much in David. ²And Jonathan told David, "Saul my father seeks to kill you. Therefore be on your guard in the morning. Stay in a secret place and hide yourself. ³And I will go out and stand beside my father in the field where you are, and I will speak to my father about you. And if I learn anything I will tell you." ⁴And Jonathan spoke well of David to Saul his father and said to him, "Let not the king sin against his servant David, because he has not sinned against you, and because his deeds have brought good to you. ⁵For he took his life in his hand and he struck down the Philistine, and the LORD worked a great salvation for all Israel. You saw it, and rejoiced. Why then will you sin against innocent blood by killing David without cause?" ⁶And Saul listened to the voice of Jonathan. Saul swore, "As the LORD lives, he shall not be put to death." ⁷And Jonathan called David, and Jonathan reported to him all these things. And Jonathan brought David to Saul, and he was in his presence as before.

⁸And there was war again. And David went out and fought with the Philistines and struck them with a great blow, so that they fled before him. ⁹Then a harmful spirit from the LORD came upon Saul, as he sat in his house with his spear in his hand. And David was playing the lyre. ¹⁰And Saul sought to pin David to the wall with the spear, but he eluded Saul, so that he struck the spear into the wall. And David fled and escaped that night.

¹¹Saul sent messengers to David's house to watch him, that he might kill him in the morning. But Michal, David's wife, told him, "If you do not escape with your life tonight, tomorrow you will be killed." ¹²So Michal let David down through the window, and he fled away and escaped. ¹³Michal took an image*a* and laid it on the bed and put a pillow of goats' hair at its head and covered it with the clothes. ¹⁴And when Saul sent messengers to take David, she said,

"He is sick." ¹⁵Then Saul sent the messengers to see David, saying, "Bring him up to me in the bed, that I may kill him." ¹⁶And when the messengers came in, behold, the image was in the bed, with the pillow of goats' hair at its head. ¹⁷Saul said to Michal, "Why have you deceived me thus and let my enemy go, so that he has escaped?" And Michal answered Saul, "He said to me, 'Let me go. Why should I kill you?'"

¹⁸Now David fled and escaped, and he came to Samuel at Ramah and told him all that Saul had done to him. And he and Samuel went and lived at Naioth. ¹⁹And it was told Saul, "Behold, David is at Naioth in Ramah." ²⁰Then Saul sent messengers to take David, and when they saw the company of the prophets prophesying, and Samuel standing as head over them, the Spirit of God came upon the messengers of Saul, and they also prophesied. ²¹When it was told Saul, he sent other messengers, and they also prophesied. And Saul sent messengers again the third time, and they also prophesied. ²²Then he himself went to Ramah and came to the great well that is in Secu. And he asked, "Where are Samuel and David?" And one said, "Behold, they are at Naioth in Ramah." ²³And he went there to Naioth in Ramah. And the Spirit of God came upon him also, and as he went he prophesied until he came to Naioth in Ramah. ²⁴And he too stripped off his clothes, and he too prophesied before Samuel and lay naked all that day and all that night. Thus it is said, "Is Saul also among the prophets?"

20 Then David fled from Naioth in Ramah and came and said before Jonathan, "What have I done? What is my guilt? And what is my sin before your father, that he seeks my life?" ²And he said to him, "Far from it! You shall not die. Behold, my father does nothing either great or small without disclosing it to me. And why should my father hide this from me? It is not so." ³But David vowed again, saying, "Your father knows well that I have found favor in your eyes, and he thinks, 'Do not let Jonathan know this, lest he be grieved.' But truly, as the Lord lives and as your soul lives, there is but a step between me and death." ⁴Then Jonathan said to David, "Whatever you say, I will do for you." ⁵David said to Jonathan, "Behold, tomorrow is the new moon, and I should not fail to sit at table with the king. But let me go, that I may hide myself in the field till the third day at evening. ⁶If your father misses me at all, then say, 'David earnestly asked leave of me to run to Bethlehem his city, for there is a yearly sacrifice there for all the clan.' ⁷If he says, 'Good!' it will be well with your servant, but if he is angry, then know that harm is determined by him. ⁸Therefore deal kindly with your servant, for you have brought your servant into a covenant of the Lord with you. But if there is guilt in me, kill me yourself, for why should you bring me to your father?" ⁹And Jonathan said, "Far be it from you! If I knew that it was determined by my father that harm should come to you, would I not tell you?" ¹⁰Then David said to Jonathan, "Who will tell me if your father answers you roughly?" ¹¹And Jonathan said to David, "Come, let us go out into the field." So they both went out into the field.

¹²And Jonathan said to David, "The Lord, the God of Israel, be witness!ᵇ When I have sounded out my father, about this time tomorrow, or the third day, behold, if he is well disposed toward David, shall I not then send and disclose it to you? ¹³But should it please my father to do you harm, the Lord do so to Jonathan and more also if I do not disclose it to you and send you away, that you may go in safety. May the Lord be with you, as he has been with my father. ¹⁴If I am still alive, show me the steadfast love of the Lord, that I may not die; ¹⁵and do not cut offᶜ your steadfast love from my house forever, when the Lord cuts off every one of the enemies of David from the face of the earth." ¹⁶And Jonathan made a covenant with the house of David, saying, "Mayᵈ the Lord take vengeance on David's enemies." ¹⁷And Jonathan made David swear again by his love for him, for he loved him as he loved his own soul.

¹⁸Then Jonathan said to him, "Tomorrow is the new moon, and you will be missed, because your seat will be empty. ¹⁹On the third day go down quickly to the place where you hid yourself when the matter was in hand, and remain beside the stone heap.ᵉ ²⁰And I will shoot

three arrows to the side of it, as though I shot at a mark. ²¹And behold, I will send the boy, saying, 'Go, find the arrows.' If I say to the boy, 'Look, the arrows are on this side of you, take them,' then you are to come, for, as the Lord lives, it is safe for you and there is no danger. ²²But if I say to the youth, 'Look, the arrows are beyond you,' then go, for the Lord has sent you away. ²³And as for the matter of which you and I have spoken, behold, the Lord is between you and me forever."

²⁴So David hid himself in the field. And when the new moon came, the king sat down to eat food. ²⁵The king sat on his seat, as at other times, on the seat by the wall. Jonathan sat opposite,ᶠ and Abner sat by Saul's side, but David's place was empty. ²⁶Yet Saul did not say anything that day, for he thought, "Something has happened to him. He is not clean; surely he is not clean." ²⁷But on the second day, the day after the new moon, David's place was empty. And Saul said to Jonathan his son, "Why has not the son of Jesse come to the meal, either yesterday or today?" ²⁸Jonathan answered Saul, "David earnestly asked leave of me to go to Bethlehem. ²⁹He said, 'Let me go, for our clan holds a sacrifice in the city, and my brother has commanded me to be there. So now, if I have found favor in your eyes, let me get away and see my brothers.' For this reason he has not come to the king's table."

³⁰Then Saul's anger was kindled against Jonathan, and he said to him, "You son of a perverse, rebellious woman, do I not know that you have chosen the son of Jesse to your own shame, and to the shame of your mother's nakedness? ³¹For as long as the son of Jesse lives on the earth, neither you nor your kingdom shall be established. Therefore send and bring him to me, for he shall surely die." ³²Then Jonathan answered Saul his father, "Why should he be put to death? What has he done?" ³³But Saul hurled his spear at him to strike him. So Jonathan knew that his father was determined to put David to death. ³⁴And Jonathan rose from the table in fierce anger and ate no food the second day of the month, for he was grieved for David, because his father had disgraced him.

³⁵In the morning Jonathan went out into the field to the appointment with David, and with him a little boy. ³⁶And he said to his boy, "Run and find the arrows that I shoot." As the boy ran, he shot an arrow beyond him.

³⁷And when the boy came to the place of the arrow that Jonathan had shot, Jonathan called after the boy and said, "Is not the arrow beyond you?" ³⁸And Jonathan called after the boy, "Hurry! Be quick! Do not stay!" So Jonathan's boy gathered up the arrows and came to his master. ³⁹But the boy knew nothing. Only Jonathan and David knew the matter. ⁴⁰And Jonathan gave his weapons to his boy and said to him, "Go and carry them to the city." ⁴¹And as soon as the boy had gone, David rose from beside the stone heapᵍ and fell on his face to the ground and bowed three times. And they kissed one another and wept with one another, David weeping the most. ⁴²Then Jonathan said to David, "Go in peace, because we have sworn both of us in the name of the LORD, saying, 'The LORD shall be between me and you, and between my offspring and your offspring, forever.'" And he rose and departed, and Jonathan went into the city.ᵇ

a Or *a household god* b Hebrew lacks *be witness* c Or *but if I die, do not cut off* d Septuagint *earth,* ¹⁶*let not the name of Jonathan be cut off from the house of David. And may* e Septuagint; Hebrew *the stone Ezel* f Compare Septuagint; Hebrew *stood up* g Septuagint; Hebrew *from beside the south* h This sentence is 21:1 in Hebrew

---

OVERVIEW: The interpreters here find comfort in David's protection from Saul. For example, Knox deduces that God protects the godly from evil snares. Some regard Jonathan as driven by God's Spirit and Saul as driven by an evil spirit. The reformers weigh Michal's actions—did she lie to her father Saul? Luther uses this instance to cite Augustine's threefold definition of lies. The combined actions of Saul's children Michal and Jonathan, both of whom come to the aid and support of David over against Saul, are indications of God's providence and goodness.

SAUL IS DRIVEN BY A HIDDEN HATRED.
JOHANNES BUGENHAGEN: These chapters set before our eyes the fact that the Spirit of God drove Jonathan and an evil spirit drove Saul. The one loves and defends the innocent and godly; the other hates and persecutes it. This hatred fills him with such rage that his son Jonathan is not spared from it. No wonder, when he rages and is indignant against the divine judgment that God begins to prefer David, as we clearly saw in chapter 18. This state of being lives most horribly in the hearts of the ungodly, so that they are not able to see it hidden in themselves. But immediately and clearly through the revealed Spirit, the godly sense to come to pray, acknowledging that they do not follow God's will in all things and saying, "your will be done." COMMENTARY ON 1 SAMUEL.[1]

19:1-7 Saul Announces His Plan to Kill David

SAUL'S FALSE WORDS. JOHANNES BUGENHAGEN: By speaking the truth, Jonathan convinces Saul, who then swears falsely to God that he will not kill David, even though he cannot bear his hatred for him. By this you see how a person does not have free will. Some people are driven by evil spirits like Saul; others are led by the Spirit of God, like the godly in Romans 8. And this Spirit, even at those times when we cannot see, is given occasions to reveal itself. For the blessed one is like a good tree that yields fruit in its season, as Psalm 1 says. Similarly, the ungodly receive occasions to yield the fruits of their unbelief. You have this example in Saul, who—despite having made his oath—seeks to kill David, after David had fought bravely and saved the people's life. Thus blindness and impiety lead to hatred. This sign is a figure for those who persecute the gospel, that is, the kingdom of Christ the true David. . . . Saul hoped that the Philistines would do away with David, just as Satan once led Christ to the cross. But this only made David's glory increase, as he is cleansed wherever he goes, being driven by God, who delivers him even in death and leads him to the kingdom through the cross, against the will of Satan. You see this in those hypocrites who say with Saul, "I will not lay my hand on him." COMMENTARY ON 1 SAMUEL.[2]

---

[1]Bugenhagen, *In Samuelem prophetam*, 247; citing Mt 6:10.

[2]Bugenhagen, *In Samuelem prophetam*, 244-45.

God's Deliverance. John Knox: The notion that God delivers his chosen from their enemies is not written for David only, but for all those who shall suffer tribulation, until the end of the world. For I, John Knox—let this be said to the acclaim and praise of God alone—in anguish of mind and vehement tribulation and affliction, called on the Lord when not only the ungodly but even my faithful brothers (even my own self, that is, my natural understanding) judged my case to be irremediable. And yet, in my greatest calamity, and when my pains were most cruel, God's eternal wisdom willed that my hands should be a writer, far contrary to the judgment of carnal reason, which his mercy has proved true, blessed be his holy name. And therefore I dare to be bold in the truth of God's Word to promise that—notwithstanding the vehemence of trouble, the long continuance of it, the despair of all people and the fearfulness, danger, pain and anguish of our own hearts—yet if we call constantly to God, even beyond all human expectation, he shall deliver. Treatise on Prayer.[3]

Forgiving and Forgetting. Thomas Becon: King David was unjustly persecuted by Saul, and his life very narrowly sought. Yet the Spirit of God was so strong in David that he did not only not seek to avenge himself but also forgave his enemy Saul and never did or sought out any evil against him. Even when Saul was in his clutches he not only did not kill him but also did not even touch him. A New Catechism.[4]

19:8-17 *Michal's Ruse*

On Lying. Martin Luther: Augustine says there are three kinds of lies. It is a harmful lie when a falsehood is spoken out of a desire to deceive one's neighbor for the purpose of injuring them, their property, their reputation or their very life. And this is worst when lies and false doctrines are spread under the name of God. God forbids this in the eighth commandment when he says: "You shall not bear false witness." The second kind is the obliging lie, that is, a lie of love or compassion, as when the government happened to be searching for a thief to punish him and I knew where he was yet said that I did not know. In that case I am lying, not to harm, but to help my neighbor. Or if I saw that someone had designs on the chastity of a virgin or matron, and I pretended not to know her, then I would be lying to help, and out of respect for, the girl. Thus Michal is lying to her father when she says that David went way away, but she is doing this to help David. Accordingly, where it can be done without harm to the government or to parents, one may protect and defend those whom they are seeking or are asking about. Lectures on Genesis.[5]

Righteous Deceptions. Johannes Bugenhagen: Whether through Jonathan or through Michal, God's providence keeps David unharmed wherever he goes. You ask: Is it allowed to deceive enemies in word or deed, both of which you see here? I reply: the law allows interest to be taken from Gentiles. Snares may be set for enemies to fall on, as they are even set by God sometimes. You see this in history, that it is allowed for the godly to do this against enemies but not allowed for others. You see many examples in the Scriptures, where the saints deceive the ungodly for the well-being of themselves and others. Commentary on 1 Samuel.[6]

Two Bodies Cannot Be in the Same Place Simultaneously. Lambert Daneau: Do you not remember . . . what Michal, David's wife, did and what device she practiced when she concealed the sight of her husband from her father Saul and his servants, who sought to slay him? Have you not read that which is written in this section, how she by craft and colorable means placed an image in place of David's body—but not by any devilish art nor after the manner of sorcerers? She laid pillows

---

[3]Knox, *Practical Works*, 40*.
[4]Becon, *Catechism*, 179*.

[5]LW 5:40; citing Ex 20:16.
[6]Bugenhagen, *In Samuelem prophetam*, 245-46; citing Deut 23:20.

under his head, trimming him with garments so finely and cunningly that Saul's servants clearly thought David was there, as they beheld David's counterfeit so lively set forth before their eyes. So likewise Satan, to the intent he may keep from us the absence of his adherents, in place of their true body—which is away—places there a false body when we chance to inquire. Whereby it comes to pass that many supposed that sorcerers are not bodily present at their secret assemblies, which they themselves contend that they were at, and because they perceive and find false and counterfeit bodies— instead of their own bodies—laid in their rooms and beds by Satan. But surely those who judge so are very much confused. DIALOGUE OF WITCHES.[7]

ON GOD'S PROVIDENCE. HEINRICH BULLINGER: The prophet and king David said clearly: "But I trust in you, O Lord; I say, 'You are my God.' My times are in your hands." Nevertheless, even he, who was one who totally joined himself to divine providence, carefully considered how he could diligently and industriously elude the deception of his father-in-law Saul. Nor did he despise the help and machinations of his beloved wife Michal. He did not reply to her: "All has occurred through the providence of God; therefore, there will be no need for scheming. God, who is all powerful, is able to rescue me from the hands of our father's soldiers or to save me in another miraculous way. Let us be in peace and allow God to do something for us." Rather, David understood that providence proceeds in a certain order through means of other things, so that it was his task to apply himself, in the fear of the Lord, to his own protection. DECADES 4.4.[8]

PERSISTENT IDOLATRY. MARTIN LUTHER: The statue Michal placed in the bed in place of David, I think, was an image that had been preserved somewhere from among the relics of superstition and idolatry. Among us, too, many statues are left that are preserved in one place in memory of the

old idolatry, in another place as exhibits and objects of amusement for children, not worship. In David's time such idols lay hidden away in the corners of buildings. Now when Michal had nothing else at hand, she quickly pulled out the statue and put it in David's place. Undoubtedly there remained even at that time many vestiges of superstitions and idolatries from the kingdom and religion of the Jebusites as well as shouts of protest that could not be completely dispelled. Of this the worried complaints of many of the psalms testify, in which David with great grief prays and fights against idolatry. LECTURES ON GENESIS.[9]

CHRISTOLOGICAL UNDERTONES. NIKOLAUS SELNECKER: Such histories about David's cross-bearing, suffering and deliverance are figures and images that signify the Lord Christ and his church—how, as several scribes point out excellently, Michal therefore placed an image in David's place in bed and a goatskin at the head of the bed, so that the true David signifies Christ and the true sacrifice. THE WHOLE PSALTER.[10]

19:18-24 *The Spirit of God Co-opts Saul and His Attendants*

ON PROPHECY: WHAT IT IS AND WHO DOES IT. HIERONYMUS WELLER VON MOLSDORF: In this passage the word "to prophesy" means . . . to hear, interpret and discuss the Word of God. But because the passage seems to prompt a discussion, let us speak about prophecy. Prophecy is threefold. First, there is what we otherwise call "the gift of interpretation," when we interpret the prophetic and apostolic writings, and rightly instruct, strengthen and exhort consciences in the Word of God. This prophecy holds the highest rank, for it preserves the ministry of the gospel (1 Cor 12). Second is the prediction of things to come. When Joseph in Egypt interpreted Pharaoh's dream—that was this kind of prophecy. Also, when Daniel

---

[7]Daneau, *Dialogue of Witches*, G8v-H1r*.
[8]Bullinger, *Sermonum decades quinque*, 279; citing Ps 31:14-15.

[9]LW 6:33* (WA 44:24).
[10]Selnecker, *Der gantze Psalter*, 2:45r.

expounded Nebuchadnezzar's dream as well as the image in his other dream. Also, when the prophets foretold the fall of kingdoms, the destruction of cities and the defeat of nations. These two particular kinds of prophecy are confirmed in Scripture. The third kind of prophecy is astrology, when either from the observation and orbit of the stars or by the inspiration of some particular angel they foretell wars, seditions, plagues and similar calamities. However, these divinations that happen from the observation of the stars are ambiguous and uncertain. Those that happen by the inspiration of angels are certain, and the events correspond to them.

"The Spirit of God also came upon them." That is, they too began to hear, cherish and meditate on the Word of God. For the same thing happened to them that happened to the servants of the Pharisees who were sent to arrest Christ (John 7). For in the same way that by hearing Christ's preaching, those servants changed their minds and converted, so also the attendants of Saul as soon as they began to hear Samuel's preaching, they immediately changed their mind about dragging David off for punishment, and instead they reverently cherished and contemplated the Word of God. For to prophesy in Scripture not only means to interpret the Word but also to hear and contemplate it, to glorify the name of God and give thanks to God. For "the Spirit of the Lord came upon them," that is, the Holy Spirit touched their hearts by hearing the Word. This idea stands firm in Isaiah 55: "My Word does not return to me void, but effects whatever I will, and it will succeed in the matter for which I sent it." We should gather this here from their example, who, even though they did not want to learn, because of the holy preaching they heard they were nevertheless converted.

"And again Saul sent a third group of messengers." Saul was not at all moved by this miracle: that the previous attendants whom he sent to seize David had been converted by hearing Samuel's preaching. Instead he proceeds to send a third group. Thus hardened enemies of the gospel are not moved by any miracles, so that they come to their senses. . . .

"The Spirit of God came over him also, and as he walked, he prophesied until he came to Naioth in Ramah." That is, the Holy Spirit stirred Saul up too, so that he prophesied. This agrees with Matthew 7, as well as the examples of Balaam, Caiaphas and Judas the traitor—sometimes even the impious are given the gift of prophecy from God. For there is absolutely no doubt that Judas, just like the other apostles, was able to prophesy; that is, he was able to teach the gospel and to perform miracles. But this is the difference between people like Judas and true prophets: true prophets teach the pure and unadulterated Word of God, and they reflect the true and genuine meaning of the Scripture. Accordingly those like Judas persevere in sound doctrine, but "they do not walk in step with the truth of the gospel." However, they eventually introduce distortions to the Word of God—even as they teach the Word of God, pure and unadulterated, against their own will, or as they seem to be true teachers. Nevertheless, afterward they abandon sound doctrine and conspire with the enemies of true doctrine. ANNOTATIONS ON 1 SAMUEL.[11]

20:1-23 *A Covenant Between Jonathan and David*

THE SAINTS' EXAMPLES, GOOD AND BAD, ARE FOR OUR CONSOLATION AND INSTRUCTION. JUSTUS MENIUS: It cannot happen, whenever the human mind begins to waver concerning the truth of God's promises, that it could entrust itself to any other protection no matter how great, firm and safe it may be. Accordingly, David begins to doubt even most faithful Jonathan's friendship, loyalty and help. Truly nothing is safe enough, no indeed, nothing is not suspect for a conscience hesitating in faith. Now these words reveal David's mistrustful mind, when he says, "If there is any iniquity in me, kill me yourself, and bring me to your father."

---

[11]Weller, *Samuelis liber primus*, 156-57; citing Gen 40; Dan 4:1-37; 2:1-49; Jn 7:32-36, 45-52; Is 55:11; Mt 7:21-23; Num 24:1-25; Jn 11:49-52; Gal 2:14.

There are two reasons why Scripture records the saints' weakness and sin. Indeed the first is for our consolation, certainly, so that it might rouse our faith, lest we despair at the sight of our sin or some other weakness. Imagining that in the flesh the saints lived without sin, full of faith, full of the Spirit and full of righteousness, as if in complete and constant perfection, we focus on how plainly hopeless such perfection is; we will never be able to achieve it. Second, lest we slip into self-assured security and, unwisely abandoning all fear of God, we impiously place trust in our self-righteousness and hypocrisy, and we judge ourselves to be perfect, even in what we have not yet begun rightly. For who will dare to boast of their perfection when they see David's weak faith and elsewhere that he falls into such stupid and shameful deeds? And not only when we regard this one man but also so great a host of God's saints? So then, let us consider the saints' weakness and sin, so that, firm in faith, even when we fall through our weakness, we would always fear, trust and pray to God; so that when we stand firm, God would guard us through his grace, not desert us, and when we fall, through his mercy he would lift us up and sustain us. Commentary on 1 Samuel 20.[12]

Friend over Father. Lambert Daneau: When a person is faithfully professed in a league of sincere and true friendship, he prefers and more esteems his friend than he does any other person. He bears toward him a far greater affection and zeal than to all other people, for Jonathan did seem to prefer his dear friend David before his own natural father. This type of friendship is not displeasing to God, nor does it willfully transgress his holy will and commandment. For Jonathan revealed and opened his father's secret counsel to David and discovered by devices what his father's purpose, sayings and meanings were toward him. Indeed, Jonathan was not at all afraid to reveal and disclose to David the shameful thoughts of his father, King Saul. True and Christian Friendship.[13]

20:24-31 Jonathan's Excuse and Saul's Response

Lying for a Friend. Lambert Daneau: It is not lawful to lie for the sake of a friend, thereby to help his cause or to bring him out of a difficult situation. However, sometimes and in some cases it is not forbidden us to cause to evade a matter for a friend, or to give an impression and countenance some things as though they were true, which in deed are not so. I am referring to such things whereby God is neither dishonored nor our neighbor damned. True and Christian Friendship.[14]

Of Jonathan's Excuse. Andrew Willet: Because Jonathan charitably intended to do good to David and to do no harm to anyone in excusing David in this manner, he is freed from any great imputation of untruth. And besides, the sum and substance of the excuse—that there was a yearly feast at Bethlehem for David's family—was likely true. It is also likely that David really asked leave to go there. Yet it seems that Jonathan added other details, namely, that David's brother had commanded him to go there. However, David did not make mention of his brother sending for him; nor did he ask Jonathan to say so. On the contrary, David merely asked permission to go to Bethlehem. Josephus mentions that Jonathan's addition to David's words show duplicity to some degree. However, Jonathan was not accustomed to making such excuses, and he therefore speaks somewhat uncertainly and timorously. Harmony on 1 Samuel.[15]

Exasperating One's Children. John Davenant: Children are provoked if parents endeavor to load them with impious and unjust commands. It was impious of Saul when he commanded Jonathan to seize and bring David his friend, guiltless of any crime, that he might be put

---

[12]Menius, In Samuelis Librum Priorem enarratio, 56r-v.
[13]Daneau, True and Christian Friendship, B6v-B7r*.

[14]Daneau, True and Christian Friendship, B8v*.
[15]Willet, Harmony on 1 Samuel, 222*.

to death. Hence we read that Jonathan was inflamed with grief and anger. . . . It pertains to this provocation as well, when parents being seized with anger rashly revile and wound their children when they do not deserve it, with contemptuous and unbecoming language. For such scorn has a certain sting, which it is very difficult for even prudent persons to endure. Saul also provoked his son Jonathan with this kind of injury where he breaks forth in these words, "You son of a perverse and rebellious woman! Don't I know that you have sided with the son of Jesse to your own shame and to the shame of the mother who bore you?" What could be said to be more bitter to provoke a son than that in order to reproach him he even reviles his own wife as a common prostitute? EXPOSITION OF COLOSSIANS.[16]

20:32-42 *Jonathan's Goodness Versus His Father's Evil*

SAUL'S MADNESS OVER DAVID. MENNO SIMONS: Saul regarded neither the piety nor the kindness, the fidelity nor the good deeds of David toward him and all Israel, nor the grace, the works and the will of God. He became so insane and drunken in his wrath and envy that the enemies and betrayers of David . . . were highly regarded and honored by him. But the peacemakers and those who advised for good, such as his own son Jonathan, were hated by him and considered suspect. In short, David had to take to his heels . . . until Saul was vanquished on Mount Gilboa by the Philistines, and there through utter despair and gloom he plunged the sword, which he had drawn against the righteous and the innocent, into his own heart, taking his own life. CROSS OF THE SAINTS.[17]

JONATHAN AS A GOOD SON. HEINRICH BULLINGER: Jonathan the son of Saul is a very godly and pious example for us. His father's fury against

David as well as his father's injuries against himself caused him great pain and anguish. Nevertheless he prudently tolerated and concealed it until he could speak of it to him at the appropriate time and place. He never helped his father in his wicked ways. Instead he always clung to righteous and good things, he deplored his father's stubbornness, and he did not resist him in boldness when he was dealt with violently but simply fled. Through all this, nevertheless, he loved his father and prayed for his health, in all ways showing himself to be a son who shows great respect. This is truly the duty of a godly son. DECADES 2.5.[18]

JONATHAN'S HUMILITY. PHILIPP MELANCHTHON: Jonathan is humble; he knows that he is too weak for the kingdom; he knows that blissful rule is God's work alone, and he has fear of God in the knowledge of his sins and unworthiness. He remains in his calling; he does not wish to make himself king; he does not wish to push David aside; he relies on God, who helps and gives him success in his station. Later he is obedient to God, even though God removes him entirely away. THEOLOGICAL COMMONPLACES (1555).[19]

LOVE AS THE FOUNDATION. EDWARD REYNOLDS: The love of the church is the foundation of all our prayers and endeavors for the prosperity of the church. A person will not very hastily seek the good of those whom he does not love. Therefore when Christ requires that we should love our enemies, he adds as a fruit of it that we should pray for them. Love made Jonathan intercede with his father for David even when he knew his displeasure against him. How much more will it move us to intercede with God for his beloved people, the spouse of his own Son? SEVEN SERMONS ON FOURTEENTH CHAPTER OF HOSEA.[20]

SAUL IS DRIVEN BY A HIDDEN HATRED. JOHANNES BUGENHAGEN: Again this chapter sets

---

[16]Davenant, *Exposition of Colossians*, 2:191*.
[17]Simons, *Complete Writings*, 590.
[18]Bullinger, *Sermonum decades quinque*, 132.
[19]*Melanchthon on Christian Doctrine*, 90.
[20]Reynolds, *Works*, 3:444*.

before our eyes the fact that the Spirit of God drove Jonathan and an evil spirit drove Saul. The one loves and defends the innocent and godly; the other hates and persecutes it. This hatred fills him with such rage that his son Jonathan is not spared from it. No wonder, when he rages and is indignant against the divine judgment that God begins to prefer David, as we clearly saw in chapter 18. This state of being lives most horribly in the hearts of the ungodly, so that they are not able to see it hidden in themselves. But immediately and clearly through the revealed spirit, the godly sense to come to pray, acknowledging that they do not follow God's will in all things and saying, "your will be done." Commentary on 1 Samuel.[21]

Increasing Friendship. Lambert Daneau: Friendship requires the company, the sight and the familiar conversation of friends together among themselves. Therefore it is only among those who are either daily conversant with another or have previously spent much time together. For familiar conversation and frequent keeping in company increases (as the proverb says) this friendship, and sews people together in this indissoluble agreement of minds. No friendship has so much love and affection that there cannot possibly be any greater increase, or to which nothing can be either added or put into it. It requires therefore a mutual meeting and familiar conversation, because it is by this that our goodwill, liking and affection is increased, strengthened and made greater. It was this sort of friendship David and Jonathan shared, not only at the first occasion of their friendship . . . when they spoke in Saul's house, but also as it continued to increase and grow. For . . . this frequent meeting and being together feeds (as it were) this new-kindled fire or flame or ardent affection, which burns alike in the breasts of either party. True and Christian Friendship.[22]

---

[21]Bugenhagen, *In Samuelem prophetam*, 247; citing Mt 6:10.

[22]Daneau, *True and Christian Friendship*, A5r-v*; citing 1 Sam 18:1.

21:1–22:23 DAVID FLEES

¹ᵃ Then David came to Nob to Ahimelech the priest. And Ahimelech came to meet David trembling and said to him, "Why are you alone, and no one with you?" ²And David said to Ahimelech the priest, "The king has charged me with a matter and said to me, 'Let no one know anything of the matter about which I send you, and with which I have charged you.' I have made an appointment with the young men for such and such a place. ³Now then, what do you have on hand? Give me five loaves of bread, or whatever is here." ⁴And the priest answered David, "I have no common bread on hand, but there is holy bread—if the young men have kept themselves from women." ⁵And David answered the priest, "Truly women have been kept from us as always when I go on an expedition. The vessels of the young men are holy even when it is an ordinary journey. How much more today will their vessels be holy?" ⁶So the priest gave him the holy bread, for there was no bread there but the bread of the Presence, which is removed from before the LORD, to be replaced by hot bread on the day it is taken away.

⁷Now a certain man of the servants of Saul was there that day, detained before the LORD. His name was Doeg the Edomite, the chief of Saul's herdsmen.

⁸Then David said to Ahimelech, "Then have you not here a spear or a sword at hand? For I have brought neither my sword nor my weapons with me, because the king's business required haste." ⁹And the priest said, "The sword of Goliath the Philistine, whom you struck down in the Valley of Elah, behold, it is here wrapped in a cloth behind the ephod. If you will take that, take it, for there is none but that here." And David said, "There is none like that; give it to me."

¹⁰And David rose and fled that day from Saul and went to Achish the king of Gath. ¹¹And the servants of Achish said to him, "Is not this David the king of the land? Did they not sing to one another of him in dances,

'Saul has struck down his thousands,
  and David his ten thousands'?"

¹²And David took these words to heart and was much afraid of Achish the king of Gath. ¹³So he changed his behavior before them and pretended to be insane in their hands and made marks on the doors of the gate and let his spittle run down his beard. ¹⁴Then Achish said to his servants, "Behold, you see the man is mad. Why then have you brought him to me? ¹⁵Do I lack madmen, that you have brought this fellow to behave as a madman in my presence? Shall this fellow come into my house?"

22 David departed from there and escaped to the cave of Adullam. And when his brothers and all his father's house heard it, they went down there to him. ²And everyone who was in distress, and everyone who was in debt, and everyone who was bitter in soul,ᵇ gathered to him. And he became commander over them. And there were with him about four hundred men.

³And David went from there to Mizpeh of Moab. And he said to the king of Moab, "Please let my father and my mother stayᶜ with you, till I know what God will do for me." ⁴And he left them with the king of Moab, and they stayed with him all the time that David was in the stronghold. ⁵Then the prophet Gad said to David, "Do not remain in the stronghold; depart, and go into the land of Judah." So David departed and went into the forest of Hereth.

⁶Now Saul heard that David was discovered, and the men who were with him. Saul was sitting at Gibeah under the tamarisk tree on the height with his spear in his hand, and all his servants were standing about him. ⁷And Saul said to his servants who stood about him, "Hear now, people of Benjamin; will the son of Jesse give every one of you fields and vineyards, will he make you all commanders of thousands and commanders of hundreds, ⁸that all of you have conspired against me? No one discloses to me when my son makes a covenant with the son of Jesse. None of you is sorry for me or discloses to me that my son has stirred up my servant against me, to lie in wait, as at this day." ⁹Then answered Doeg the Edomite, who stood by the servants of Saul, "I saw the son of Jesse coming to Nob, to

Ahimelech the son of Ahitub, ¹⁰and he inquired of the Lord for him and gave him provisions and gave him the sword of Goliath the Philistine."

¹¹Then the king sent to summon Ahimelech the priest, the son of Ahitub, and all his father's house, the priests who were at Nob, and all of them came to the king. ¹²And Saul said, "Hear now, son of Ahitub." And he answered, "Here I am, my lord." ¹³And Saul said to him, "Why have you conspired against me, you and the son of Jesse, in that you have given him bread and a sword and have inquired of God for him, so that he has risen against me, to lie in wait, as at this day?" ¹⁴Then Ahimelech answered the king, "And who among all your servants is so faithful as David, who is the king's son-in-law, and captain overᵈ your bodyguard, and honored in your house? ¹⁵Is today the first time that I have inquired of God for him? No! Let not the king impute anything to his servant or to all the house of my father, for your servant has known nothing of all this, much or little." ¹⁶And the king said, "You shall surely die, Ahimelech, you and all your father's house." ¹⁷And the king said

to the guard who stood about him, "Turn and kill the priests of the Lord, because their hand also is with David, and they knew that he fled and did not disclose it to me." But the servants of the king would not put out their hand to strike the priests of the Lord. ¹⁸Then the king said to Doeg, "You turn and strike the priests." And Doeg the Edomite turned and struck down the priests, and he killed on that day eighty-five persons who wore the linen ephod. ¹⁹And Nob, the city of the priests, he put to the sword; both man and woman, child and infant, ox, donkey and sheep, he put to the sword.

²⁰But one of the sons of Ahimelech the son of Ahitub, named Abiathar, escaped and fled after David. ²¹And Abiathar told David that Saul had killed the priests of the Lord. ²²And David said to Abiathar, "I knew on that day, when Doeg the Edomite was there, that he would surely tell Saul. I have occasioned the death of all the persons of your father's house. ²³Stay with me; do not be afraid, for he who seeks my life seeks your life. With me you shall be in safekeeping."

a Ch 21:2 in Hebrew   b Or *discontented*   c Syriac, Vulgate; Hebrew *go out*   d Septuagint, Targum; Hebrew *and has turned aside to*

Overview: The reformers concentrate on the story about David's army eating the holy bread, which was reserved only for priests. Does this signify that David was destined to be a great priestly king? Do the holy loaves foreshadow the holy Eucharist representing Christ's body? The reformers interpret the passage within the context of Jesus' larger message of love taking precedence over stringent interpretations of the law (Mt 12:1-8; Mk 2:23-28; Lk 6:1-5). Some cite this incident as an example of David's freedom through faith, a concept that would only gradually be revealed during the time of Christ. David's hardships and persecutions allowed these commentators to continue to interpret David's life messianically. They also suggest that perhaps God used Saul to tame David and make him fit for kingship. At the same time, Saul's scandalous treatment of the priests and inhabitants of Nob leads these

commentators to consider him not only unfit for ruling but also irreversibly evil.

21:1-6 Common People Eating What Is Holy

Holy Vessels. Johannes Bugenhagen: Here you elegantly read about matters that pertained to the sanctification of the outward person, which were not in conflict with godly desires. The Lord imposes a similar law about not going near a woman in Exodus 19. And Paul judges it good to abstain from marital relations for a time in order to grow in prayer, but only with mutual consent. Therefore it was a practice to keep the bodies of servants holy and clean by keeping away from women. Yes, truly, we say nothing against any uncleanness, whether nocturnal emissions or other unclean contact according to the law, but on the same day it will have been passed over, for the law speaks of common or regular daily impurities, which will be gone by evening. There is no danger here if there is no other hindrance than external impurity. Paul spoke of this use of vessels, "For this is the will of God, your sanctification: that you abstain from sexual immorality; that each one of you know how to control his own body in holiness and honor." For in the Hebrew tradition, a vessel stands for all kinds of instruments, as in Ezekiel: ". . . each with his destroying weapon in his hand." Our bodies are our instruments, with which we act. And the saints are said to be God's instruments, through whom God's Spirit itself is working, just as Christ called Paul "a chosen instrument of mine."

This is a sign, as Christ interpreted it in Matthew 12 and Mark 2, as Moses wanted to be heard in Deuteronomy 18. Christ sees David and this priest and lets it happen under the umbrella of legal cleanliness: "To the pure, all things are pure," and "everything created by God is good," and "all things are yours, whether Paul or Apollos or Cephas or the world or life or death or the present or the future— all are yours, and you are Christ's, and Christ is God's." As Psalm 8 says, "You have given him dominion over all the works of your hands. . . . O Lord, our Lord, how majestic is your name in all the earth."

If, therefore, David was allowed to use this freedom through faith, not yet revealed by the light of the gospel and at a time when this was still prohibited by God's law, then how much more are we turned away from the decrees and elements of this world? For it has been revealed that the kingdom of God is not of this world. Necessity and love oversee the divine law, just as Christ interpreted. We most stupidly mangle this use when we set up and bind ourselves to human laws and the doctrines of demons. Commentary on 1 Samuel.[1]

Of the Holy Bread. Andrew Willet: The law here is set down in Leviticus 24:5-9, concerning the matter of how the bread should be made, of the type of flour used, how much should be in every loaf, how many loaves should be baked in all, where they should be placed, how long they should continue from sabbath to sabbath and in what manner they should be presented, namely, with incense. The Jews used four kinds of breads. The first was common bread; the second was the bread the people used in the sacred feasts; the third was the kind of bread the priests ate with their families; and the fourth was the most holy bread, which was lawful only for the priests to eat within the tabernacle. The holy bread was called the "show-bread" because it was always in the presence of God, which was a type of the true bread Christ Jesus who came down from heaven. The holy bread also shadowed forth the Eucharist of the New Testament, which is celebrated with bread. And there was the same signification of their sacraments with ours, except that ours are clearer and more manifest as a memorial of Christ already exhibited, whereas theirs foreshadowed him as the one who was to come. Harmony on 1 Samuel.[2]

Love Is the Only Excuse. Hieronymus Weller von Molsdorf: Even though it was not lawful for anyone to eat the sacred bread, which we usually call the bread of the Presence, nevertheless David demands it be given to him, and Ahimelech does not hesitate to submit to David's demand. And Christ in Matthew 12 defends this event and shows that the entirety of the ceremonial law should yield to love. Now what was said concerning the ceremonial law should also be said about ecclesiastical rites, namely, that in matters of need or demand we faithfully and righteously act in love, if by disregard of ecclesiastical ceremonies or rites we take care of our neighbors in need or look out for them. Outside of this case it is not lawful for the pious to disregard ecclesiastical ceremonies. So then, how much more lawful is it to disregard those ceremonies and rites that draw consciences into a trap, or that produce scandals or cause rebellions and strengthen the raging of our opponents—that

---

[1]Bugenhagen, *In Samuelem prophetam*, 251-52; citing Ex 19:15; 1 Cor 7:5; 1 Thess 4:3-4; Ezek 9:1; Mt 12:1-8; Mk 2:23-28; Deut 18:19; Ps 8:6-9; Acts 9:15; Tit 1:15; 1 Tim 4:4; 1 Cor 3:21-23.

[2]Willet, *Harmony on 1 Samuel*, 227-28*.

is, those which seem to be instituted to please enemies of the gospel, so that their wrath is placated. ANNOTATIONS ON 1 SAMUEL.[3]

LOVE TRUMPS CUSTOMS. HANS DENCK: Baptism, which is the sign of the covenant, should be given and not denied to any of those who by God's power have been invited to it through knowledge of genuine love and who desire this love and agree to be its followers. However, they are not to be compelled to stay in this love by any other person within the covenant unless love itself compels them. This is as it is written in the Psalter: "Your people will be there willingly."

However, disregarding the customs of the law is a freedom permitted by love; it is not a command-ment. For although it occasionally happened that even the holy patriarchs had to break these com-mands but without harm to themselves, no one can say therefore that anything other than love excused them. For this reason Jesus, who is genuine love, was silent and did not command or forbid any of these, as if he wanted to demonstrate that someone may come to this love without any of these customs. . . . Thus love permits her friends to be exempt from customs. CONCERNING TRUE LOVE.[4]

21:7-9 David Retakes Goliath's Sword

WHETHER DAVID SINNED IN TAKING GOLI-ATH'S SWORD. ANDREW WILLET: Some think David sinned by taking Goliath's old sword, which had been consecrated to God as a monument of great victory against the Philistine, and then converting it back to profane use. This action also brought the priest into danger. Now, it is acknowl-edged that it was David's oversight, in the presence of Doeg, whom he suspected of evil, to ask for and receive these things from the priest. . . . And beside, it might have placed David in danger among the Philistines, when they saw Goliath's sword. Yet, simply in using the sword—no other sword was

available—David is excused by his necessity, like before in taking the showbread. For just as the Jews gave the Babylonians vessels of silver and gold to redeem their peace and were not reproved by the prophets, so David is excused for using the vessel of the sword for profane use. And who doubts but that the church may and ought, where there is no other remedy, sell the church vessels in order to help the poor. Besides, David took this sword to remind him of God's former deliverance, so that he might by the sight of it be stirred up to wait on him still. And further, it is not unlikely that David later restored this monument again after he became king. By this example of David it is gathered . . . that it is lawful for the servants of God, where their cause is good, to wear armor and use weapons. HARMONY ON 1 SAMUEL.[5]

REMEMBERING EXPERIENCES. JOHN ARROW-SMITH: Reflect on former experiences and let them be encouragements from time to time. The psalmist did so when he said, "I consider the days of old, the years long ago." "Then I said, 'I will appeal to this: to the years of the right hand of the Most High. I will remember the deeds of the Lord; yes, I will remember your wonders of old." Some inquire why David—when he asked for a sword and Ahimelech told him there was none at hand but that of Goliath—called for it, and said, "There is none like that." It is probable that David might have found swords of better metal or just as good; perhaps he even found some more fit for his strength. Yet he prefers this above all because of his experience, for God had formerly blessed him in the use of that sword. CHAIN OF PRINCIPLES.[6]

21:10-15 Fools for the Lord

DAVID'S FOOLISHNESS: AN ALLEGORY ON THE CROSS. JOHANNES BUGENHAGEN: Christ and Christians appear to be insane before the powers of earth and the wisdom of the flesh. As Isaiah 53 says,

---

[3]Weller, *Samuelis liber primus*, 171; citing Mt 12:1-8.
[4]Denck, *Spiritual Legacy*, 190-92; citing Ps 110:3.
[5]Willet, *Harmony on 1 Samuel*, 236-37*.
[6]Arrowsmith, *Armilla Catechetica*, 357-58; citing Ps 77:5, 10-11.

they are worthy who have been despised and rejected. For nothing is seen except the cross and foolishness. And it shall be that the faithful themselves see nothing but their sins and how Christ bore them for us. Truly, in the meantime, Satan's blindness and the world's foolishness do not recognize the wisdom of his victory. COMMENTARY ON 1 SAMUEL.[7]

GOD PROVIDES COUNSEL IN TIMES OF NEED. JOHANNES BUGENHAGEN: Jonathan loved David, all Israel loved David, and so he lost favor with Saul and thought it better to flee to his enemies than to stay among friends. For who could hate David more than the people of Gath, from whom Goliath had come? You see from this that David acted from necessity. There is nothing easy described in David's persecutions. As the following story will show, things are more clearly seen among enemy Gentiles than among the Israelites, whom the Lord often saved by intervening himself. We have spoken of such complications above. It is truly foolish when we dispute such things as whether or not the saints have sinned. The saints have sinned when they acted according to their own counsel, not seeking or requiring us to imitate them. We do not need to make their actions into a law. This applies to David, and something else applies to you through God. So therefore one course of action may appear to him, and maybe something else might arise if you had occasion today to evade prison and be delivered from your enemies without detriment to your salvation or without causing scandal to the gospel, which often comes during persecution. David's liberation certainly did not come from his trickery but from God, who gave the counsel about trickery to the one whom he wanted to liberate. This is abundantly declared in the Hebrew heading of Psalm 34, where it shows that this story clearly teaches to trust God in all needs of body and mind. COMMENTARY ON 1 SAMUEL.[8]

GOD'S MERCIES. DAVID DICKSON: Sometimes people in fear for their lives fly from one danger and fall into one that is worse, as David did when he fled into an unhallowed place among God's enemies. For fear of Saul, he falls into the hands of Achish. However, God pities the infirmity of his children, and sometimes gives success to weak and unwise decisions. This is seen here, as David "pretended to be insane" to escape. God can and does dispose of people's hearts as he has a mind to work by them: For he moved the heart of Achish to take no notice of David other than to regard him as an unstable man. EXPLICATION OF THE FIRST FIFTY PSALMS.[9]

22:1-5 David at the Cave of Adullam

MADE TO SERVE. WILLIAM TYNDALE: God promised David a kingdom, but immediately stirred up King Saul against him to persecute him, to hunt him as hunters do hares with greyhounds and to ferret him out of every hole. And God did this for the space of many years to tame David, to make him meek, to kill his lusts, to make him feel other people's infirmities, to make him merciful and to make him understand that he was made king to minister and serve his brothers. In short, he was persecuted so that he should not think his subjects were made to minister to his lusts, or that it was lawful for him to take away from them life and goods at his pleasure. DOCTRINAL TREATISES AND INTRODUCTIONS TO OTHER PORTIONS OF HOLY SCRIPTURES.[10]

GOOD BRINGS GOOD OUT OF BAD. JOHANNES BRENZ: David loved God and had God as his friend. Therefore, when he was forced to flee from Saul he ascended in his exile almost by degree to the majesty of king. . . . Christ, the son of God, loved God, and had him as his friend. Therefore, when he was afflicted at the crucifixion and died, he attained great glory through the cross and his death.

---

[7]Bugenhagen, *In Samuelem prophetam*, 253-54.
[8]Bugenhagen, *In Samuelem prophetam*, 253; citing Ps 34's heading.
[9]Dickson, *First Fifty Psalms*, 200*; citing 1 Sam 21:13.
[10]Tyndale, *Doctrinal Treatises*, 136*.

"But," you say, "I am neither Jacob nor Joseph nor David nor Christ. Therefore, none of these examples apply to me." We rightly admit that we are not Christ ourselves; but we know that Christ came in our place so that all adverse things that come our way, even by way of our enemies, are used by God for our good. COMMENTARY ON GENESIS.[11]

SAUL AND THE HOUSE OF ELI. JOHANNES BUGENHAGEN: Look with astonishment at the plans of God. The Lord had spoken against the house of Eli in the second chapter, which Saul fulfilled here through his most grave and manifest sin. For he not only sought the death of the Lord's anointed king but also—because of David—did not spare the priesthood, which had been ordained and instituted by God. COMMENTARY ON 1 SAMUEL.[12]

22:6-17 Saul's Murderous Rage Against the Priests at Nob

WE MUST DISOBEY UNJUST RULERS. PHILIPP MELANCHTHON: Here an unalterable rule applies: "We should obey God rather than men." For this reason, if an authority commands us to act against God, we should not obey, but should act like the three men in Babylon who refused to worship the idols or countenance idolatry, even though King Nebuchadnezzar had proclaimed a frightful command regarding it. As the worthy soldiers connected with the tyranny of Saul would not murder the innocent priest Ahimelech, the other priests, and their pious wives and children, even though Saul had commanded them to do it, so are we to act now. If the great lords command us to keep untrue doctrine and idolatry, we should not obey such commands. We should not assist in the murdering of the innocent or of Christians on account of their confession of the gospel, as many of the learned do by remaining silent because of fear. Such murder, along with

such hypocrisy, will receive the terrible punishment of which Christ speaks in Matthew 23:35, "That on you may come all the righteous bloodshed on earth, from the blood of innocent Abel on . . . ," for the Son of God will judge, and will hurl all the godless into eternal punishment. THEOLOGICAL COMMONPLACES (1555).[13]

DO NOT DEFEND A TYRANT. JOHANNES BUGENHAGEN: This chapter shows all of David's descendants not to defend the kingdom of Saul for David's sake, because of his striking down of the priests of the Lord. Who could fully describe this tyrant's insanity? Neither God nor humans owe respect when a soul gets enslaved by a godless malady that is visible to all who look for it. For the best men do not act to suit an occasion; instead, they are known by their demeanor. At the same time, all who want to stand forever go to ruin. And yet wherever these atrocities are judged, some have tried to defend the good aspects of King Saul, especially those that are shown by his speech. For he was pursuing David, whom everyone favored, which made everyone guilty of conspiracy against the king. "Thus iniquity has betrayed itself." And so a just and righteous confessor bears not only persecutions and hatred, but everyone wishes the persecutor well, according to the verse, "If you were of the world, the world would love you as its own." COMMENTARY ON 1 SAMUEL.[14]

SAUL AS ANTICHRIST. ANDREW WILLET: Saul's speech to his servants is full of dissimulation and hypocrisy. Here he shows, first, his cruelty by charging his servants with negligence and unfaithfulness toward him because they were not more eager to pursue David, even though they were more removed from David and closer to Saul. Thus the wicked dislike all those who do not run together with them step by step, as Saint Peter says: "The sinful Gentiles are surprised when you

---

[11]Brenz, *Opera*, 1:269.
[12]Bugenhagen, *In Samuelem prophetam*, 256.

[13]*Melanchthon on Christian Doctrine*, 334; citing Acts 5:29; Dan 3:1-30.
[14]Bugenhagen, *In Samuelem prophetam*, 254-55; citing Ps 27:12; Jn 15:19.

do not join them in the same flood of debauchery, and they malign you." Harmony on 1 Samuel.[15]

22:18-23 Doeg Murders for Saul

The Ungodly Edomite. Johannes Bugenhagen: This ungodly Edomite, looking for honor and seeking the favor of his lord, betrays innocent people. He is a figure of all who only think about their own advancement and opportunity; they thereby help to trample on God's truth and those who profess it. The heading of Psalm 52 shows this, where the impious ones—like Saul—are scolded, because they love and hope in their own ideas and things. But the righteous ones are like David, saying, "But I am like a green olive tree in the house of God. I trust in the steadfast love of God forever and ever." Commentary on 1 Samuel.[16]

The People Pleaser. Robert Sanderson: Sometimes we apply ourselves to the wills of others with an eye to our own benefit or satisfaction in some other carnal or worldly respect. This is our fleshliness, and the fault is in the heart. This sin is one of the worst kinds, and therefore in the first place to be avoided. It is the worst and most unconscionable people who often transgress this way. They do this for a variety of reasons: for fear of a frown or worse displeasure; to curry favor with those they may have use of in hope either of raising themselves to some advancement or of raising to themselves some advantage; or for some other like respects. As they do this, they become officious instruments to others for the accomplishing of their lusts in such services as are evidently, even to their own apprehensions, sinful and wicked. So Doeg did King Saul service in shedding the blood of eighty-five innocent priests. To the People.[17]

---

[15]Willet, *Harmony on 1 Samuel*, 247*; citing 1 Pet 4:4.
[16]Bugenhagen, *In Samuelem prophetam*, 257; citing Ps 52's heading and Ps 52:8.

---

[17]Sanderson, *Works*, 3:286-87*.

23:1–24:22 DAVID SAVES KEILAH AND SPARES SAUL

¹Now they told David, "Behold, the Philistines are fighting against Keilah and are robbing the threshing floors." ²Therefore David inquired of the Lord, "Shall I go and attack these Philistines?" And the Lord said to David, "Go and attack the Philistines and save Keilah." ³But David's men said to him, "Behold, we are afraid here in Judah; how much more then if we go to Keilah against the armies of the Philistines?" ⁴Then David inquired of the Lord again. And the Lord answered him, "Arise, go down to Keilah, for I will give the Philistines into your hand." ⁵And David and his men went to Keilah and fought with the Philistines and brought away their livestock and struck them with a great blow. So David saved the inhabitants of Keilah.

⁶When Abiathar the son of Ahimelech had fled to David to Keilah, he had come down with an ephod in his hand. ⁷Now it was told Saul that David had come to Keilah. And Saul said, "God has given him into my hand, for he has shut himself in by entering a town that has gates and bars." ⁸And Saul summoned all the people to war, to go down to Keilah, to besiege David and his men. ⁹David knew that Saul was plotting harm against him. And he said to Abiathar the priest, "Bring the ephod here." ¹⁰Then David said, "O Lord, the God of Israel, your servant has surely heard that Saul seeks to come to Keilah, to destroy the city on my account. ¹¹Will the men of Keilah surrender me into his hand? Will Saul come down, as your servant has heard? O Lord, the God of Israel, please tell your servant." And the Lord said, "He will come down." ¹²Then David said, "Will the men of Keilah surrender me and my men into the hand of Saul?" And the Lord said, "They will surrender you." ¹³Then David and his men, who were about six hundred, arose and departed from Keilah, and they went wherever they could go. When Saul was told that David had escaped from Keilah, he gave up the expedition. ¹⁴And David remained in the strongholds in the wilderness, in the hill country of the wilderness of Ziph. And Saul sought him every day, but God did not give him into his hand.

¹⁵David saw that Saul had come out to seek his life. David was in the wilderness of Ziph at Horesh. ¹⁶And Jonathan, Saul's son, rose and went to David at Horesh, and strengthened his hand in God. ¹⁷And he said to him, "Do not fear, for the hand of Saul my father shall not find you. You shall be king over Israel, and I shall be next to you. Saul my father also knows this." ¹⁸And the two of them made a covenant before the Lord. David remained at Horesh, and Jonathan went home.

¹⁹Then the Ziphites went up to Saul at Gibeah, saying, "Is not David hiding among us in the strongholds at Horesh, on the hill of Hachilah, which is south of Jeshimon? ²⁰Now come down, O king, according to all your heart's desire to come down, and our part shall be to surrender him into the king's hand." ²¹And Saul said, "May you be blessed by the Lord, for you have had compassion on me. ²²Go, make yet more sure. Know and see the place where his foot is, and who has seen him there, for it is told me that he is very cunning. ²³See therefore and take note of all the lurking places where he hides, and come back to me with sure information. Then I will go with you. And if he is in the land, I will search him out among all the thousands of Judah." ²⁴And they arose and went to Ziph ahead of Saul.

Now David and his men were in the wilderness of Maon, in the Arabah to the south of Jeshimon. ²⁵And Saul and his men went to seek him. And David was told, so he went down to the rock and lived in the wilderness of Maon. And when Saul heard that, he pursued after David in the wilderness of Maon. ²⁶Saul went on one side of the mountain, and David and his men on the other side of the mountain. And David was hurrying to get away from Saul. As Saul and his men were closing in on David and his men to capture them, ²⁷a messenger came to Saul, saying, "Hurry and come, for the Philistines have made a raid against the land." ²⁸So Saul returned from pursuing after David and went against the Philistines. Therefore that place was called the Rock of Escape.ᵃ ²⁹ᵇAnd David went up from there and lived in the strongholds of Engedi.

24 ^c When Saul returned from following the Philistines, he was told, "Behold, David is in the wilderness of Engedi." ²Then Saul took three thousand chosen men out of all Israel and went to seek David and his men in front of the Wildgoats' Rocks. ³And he came to the sheepfolds by the way, where there was a cave, and Saul went in to relieve himself.^d Now David and his men were sitting in the innermost parts of the cave. ⁴And the men of David said to him, "Here is the day of which the Lord said to you, 'Behold, I will give your enemy into your hand, and you shall do to him as it shall seem good to you.'" Then David arose and stealthily cut off a corner of Saul's robe. ⁵And afterward David's heart struck him, because he had cut off a corner of Saul's robe. ⁶He said to his men, "The Lord forbid that I should do this thing to my lord, the Lord's anointed, to put out my hand against him, seeing he is the Lord's anointed." ⁷So David persuaded his men with these words and did not permit them to attack Saul. And Saul rose up and left the cave and went on his way.

⁸Afterward David also arose and went out of the cave, and called after Saul, "My lord the king!" And when Saul looked behind him, David bowed with his face to the earth and paid homage. ⁹And David said to Saul, "Why do you listen to the words of men who say, 'Behold, David seeks your harm'? ¹⁰Behold, this day your eyes have seen how the Lord gave you today into my hand in the cave. And some told me to kill you, but I spared you.^e I said, 'I will not put out my hand against my lord, for he is the Lord's anointed.' ¹¹See, my father, see the corner of your robe in my hand. For by the fact that I cut off the corner of your robe and did not kill you, you may know and see that there is no wrong or treason in my hands. I have not sinned against you, though you hunt my life to take it. ¹²May the Lord judge between me and you, may the Lord avenge me against you, but my hand shall not be against you. ¹³As the proverb of the ancients says, 'Out of the wicked comes wickedness.' But my hand shall not be against you. ¹⁴After whom has the king of Israel come out? After whom do you pursue? After a dead dog! After a flea! ¹⁵May the Lord therefore be judge and give sentence between me and you, and see to it and plead my cause and deliver me from your hand."

¹⁶As soon as David had finished speaking these words to Saul, Saul said, "Is this your voice, my son David?" And Saul lifted up his voice and wept. ¹⁷He said to David, "You are more righteous than I, for you have repaid me good, whereas I have repaid you evil. ¹⁸And you have declared this day how you have dealt well with me, in that you did not kill me when the Lord put me into your hands. ¹⁹For if a man finds his enemy, will he let him go away safe? So may the Lord reward you with good for what you have done to me this day. ²⁰And now, behold, I know that you shall surely be king, and that the kingdom of Israel shall be established in your hand. ²¹Swear to me therefore by the Lord that you will not cut off my offspring after me, and that you will not destroy my name out of my father's house." ²²And David swore this to Saul. Then Saul went home, but David and his men went up to the stronghold.

a Or *Rock of Divisions*   b Ch 24:1 in Hebrew   c Ch 24:2 in Hebrew   d Hebrew *cover his feet*   e Septuagint, Syriac, Targum; Hebrew *it* [my eye] *spared you*

Overview: The Lord's favor rests with David, as he proves victorious in battle, prudent in character and respectful of the king's authority. Bugenhagen, committed to interpreting the Bible through the lens of law and gospel, cites this story as another example of God humbling David through the law so that he could receive God's grace. The interpreters also reflect on David's deference to King Saul.

Although Saul is eager to kill David in the face of all the good he has done for him, David refuses to lay even a finger on Saul out of respect for his position as king. The reformers believe David would have sinned had he made an attempt on Saul's life. Saul's momentary remorse, however, does not trick the reformers into changing their negative assessment of the king.

23:1-14 *Keilah and Possible Contingencies*

God's Knowledge. Jacobus Arminius: I am thoroughly persuaded that God's knowledge is eternal, immutable and infinite, and that it extends to all things . . . which he himself does with or without mediation, and which he permits to be done by others. But the mode in which he knows future contingencies, and especially those that appertain to the free will of creatures, and which he has decreed to permit, but not to do of himself—this I do not comprehend, not even in that measure in which I think it is understood by others of greater skill than myself. I know there are some who say that all things are present to God from eternity; and that the mode in which God knows future contingencies certainly and infallibly is this: that those contingencies coexist with God in the Now of eternity, and so are in him indivisible and in the infinite Now of eternity, which embraces all time. If that is so, it is not difficult to know in what way God knows future contingencies certainly and infallibly. For contingencies are not opposed to the certainty of knowledge, except as they are future, but not as they are present. But that reasoning does not exhaust all the difficulties that may arise in the consideration of these matters. For God knows, also, those things that may happen, but never do happen, and consequently do not coexist with God in the Now of eternity, which would happen unless they be stopped. Friendly Discussion Concerning Predestination.[1]

David's Lonely Escape. Johannes Bugenhagen: Who does not see that this revelation from God about David's being surrendered to Saul should be understood with the clear condition: "unless you flee." It is like Jonah's "Yet forty days, and Nineveh shall be overthrown!" that is, implicitly, "unless you repent." Here you see that David was not troubled about those people whom he had protected, just as we learn from Jeremiah 17:5 not to trust in humans. God did not want David to

have that kind of trust. For now you have a well-fortified city, the citizens are indebted to you, all of Israel is favorably disposed to you because you have repelled the Philistines, and the king will not be able or permitted to hurt you. But God wanted David to despair of everyone and everything, being forsaken and exposed by his own forces, so that he would hope in God alone. Commentary on 1 Samuel.[2]

Deceitfulness of the Heart. Daniel Dyke: One form of deceit is when in temptation our hearts betray us like Judas's did into the devil's hands. If a person is very close to you so that we trust him, should we not consider him a deceitful person if—when walking about and we are accosted by an enemy or a criminal—he runs away from you? How much more so if this friend should conspire with the enemy and take part in the violence against you? . . . But this is exactly how the half-hearted men of Keilah would have done with David. As David mistrusted them, so we should our deceitful hearts. We do not need to ask the question, as David did of the men of Keilah, "Will they deliver us?" We must assure ourselves that they certainly will. The Mystery of Self-Deceiving.[3]

23:15-29 *Jonathan Renews His Covenant with David*

Jonathan Renews His Vow for the Sake of the Truth. Johannes Bugenhagen: Now Jonathan keeps and renews his faithful vow with David, so that—touched by the Spirit of God—he prophesied and comforted David. For all that, he did not come in order to be the second greatest himself, because the vow pertains not only to Jonathan and David but also to their descendants, as chapter 20 says. Then he most gravely condemns his father before God when he says, "Saul my father also knows this." For he could not hide anymore from Saul now that the Lord had anointed David

[1]Arminius, *Works*, 3:66*.

[2]Bugenhagen, *In Samuelem prophetam*, 260; citing Jon 3:4.
[3]Dyke, *The Mystery of Self-Deceiving*, 289*.

in Bethlehem through the prophet Samuel and now that Saul came to know the Lord had departed from him to be with David. On this point Scripture cannot keep silence, for it shows this hypocrisy fighting against conscience in order to fight against God, for it wants to be seen before people as fighting against the one who lies in wait for the king and disturbs the kingdom. In the same way, those who now want to suppress the gospel give the pretext that all things are being disturbed. Commentary on 1 Samuel.[4]

True Friendship Lasts. Lambert Daneau: Friendship does not cease or utterly perish even when absent because it grows on just and reasonable causes. As we may see in David and Jonathan, the whole friendship continued and lasted despite the one being absent from the other, for such deep-rooted goodwill and such ardent affection cannot be easily quenched. Therefore friendship—being strongly and surely grounded between persons present—continues still between them when they are absent. And the further they are separated, the greater is the longing desire of one for the other and the more vehemently their inflamed hearts increase. True and Christian Friendship.[5]

24:1-5 David Spares Saul's Life

David's Conscience. Johannes Bugenhagen: When David's heart sunk, it shows the working of his conscience. Scripture writes this in order to show the fear of God in David, who—even though he was able to—did not want to act against Saul, one who was duly installed by God, just as it says in Romans 13 about submitting to God by submitting to authorities. At the same time, however, David perceives that God has departed from Saul, who will perish when God wants it. Commentary on 1 Samuel.[6]

The Heart of the Matter. Thomas Adams: Saul would kill David but could not. David could kill Saul but would not. Commentary on 2 Peter.[7]

David Overcomes His Flesh. Johannes Brenz: David was a truly pious man and did not take advantage of Saul, who was the greatest of his enemies, even when he was offered up to him in the cave. Naturally, David's flesh suggested: "Take him, David. You now have your enemy in your hands. Kill him and you will have not only the king but also the kingdom!" But David not only crucified his fleshly thoughts but also mastered his earthly desires. Commentary on Galatians.[8]

24:6-15 Honoring the Lord's Anointed One

Unlawful. William Tyndale: Why did David not kill Saul given that he was so wicked, not only in persecuting David but also in disobeying God's commandments? And not only that, but he had also murdered eighty-five of God's priests wrongfully? Truly, because it was not lawful. For if David would have done it, he would have sinned against God. This is because God makes the king in every realm judge over all, and over him there is no judge. The one who judges the king judges God; and the one who lays hands on the king lays hands on God. And the one who resists the king resists God and damns God's laws and ordinances. If the subject sins, he or she must be brought to the king's judgment. But if the king sins, he must be reserved to the judgment, wrath and vengeance of God. And as it is to resist the king, so is it to resist his officer, who is set or sent to execute the king's commandment. Doctrinal Treatises and Introductions to Other Portions of Holy Scriptures.[9]

David Extends Grace. John Calvin: When we become indignant against someone, we very

---

[4]Bugenhagen, *In Samuelem prophetam*, 261; citing 1 Sam 20:42.
[5]Daneau, *True and Christian Friendship*, A5v*.
[6]Bugenhagen, *In Samuelem prophetam*, 264.

[7]Adams, *Commentary upon 2 Peter*, 47*.
[8]Brenz, *Opera*, 7:901.
[9]Tyndale, *Doctrinal Treatises*, 177*.

often fail to take account of all the favors God has given to the one whom we hate, as though those favors were beneath contempt. Even when we must hate and detest a person's evil side, we must not be so carried away with the violence of our feelings that we are utterly unable to accept the good, for then we have lost our perception and discernment. On the contrary, we must honor the Lord for everything that comes from him. This is what we are to remember from David. David certainly knew that Saul was a desperate man. Nonetheless, God had chosen him to reign over his people, and had anointed him for that purpose. What is more, David knew that he would offend the Lord, and would commit a sacrilege if he ignored this grace God had put in Saul. SERMONS ON 2 SAMUEL.[10]

INVIOLABLE MAJESTY. JOHN CALVIN: We owe this attitude of reverence and therefore piety toward all our rulers in the highest degree, whatever they may be like. I therefore the more often repeat this: that we should learn not to examine the men themselves, but take it as enough that they bear, by the Lord's will, a character on which he has imprinted and engraved an inviolable majesty. But (you will say) rulers owe responsibilities in turn to their subjects. This I have already admitted. But if you conclude from this that service ought to be rendered only to just governors, you are reasoning foolishly. INSTITUTES 4.20.29.[11]

DAVID'S RESPECT FOR GOD'S MESSIAH. JEREMIAS BASTINGIUS: In the Old Testament prophets, priests and kings were anointed by the commandment and ordinance of God. . . . Such ceremonies served as a seal of their calling that God would teach and govern his people by them, whereupon they were called "the Christ" or "the Anointed" of the Lord; as in the psalm: "Do not touch my anointed ones; do my prophets no harm." So David calls Saul "the Lord's anointed," and for this reason would not hurt him even though he

could. AN EXPOSITION ON THE CATECHISM OF THE LOW COUNTRIES..[12]

CONQUERING BY FORBEARANCE. JOHN DAVENANT: The one who forbears conquers the very malice of his enemy. For when two competitors are in contention and conflict, the one who draws the other into similarity with itself conquers; and the one who is drawn and changed by the other is conquered. Therefore, as we say water is overcome by fire when it becomes warm; and on the contrary to have overcome it if, retaining its own cold, it can subdue the fire. So we say a Christian is overcome by a wicked person as often as he, by the provocation of attack, is drawn into similar fury; on the contrary, we may pronounce him to have conquered when he retains his own disposition and, by bearing with the violence of the other, changes and mollifies his ferocity. We see a beautiful example of this here where David, by forbearing and refraining from revenge, so mollifies and changes Saul from breathing blood and slaughter that he melts into tears and entreaties, confesses his fault and is compelled to acknowledge and extol David's innocence and meekness. Who does not here see the malice of Saul overcome, and the patience of David triumphant? EXPOSITION OF COLOSSIANS.[13]

24:16-22 David's Determining Whether Saul Was Sincere

HEARTS AS CRAFTY AS A FOX. DANIEL DYKE: If a person had a reputation of being a common deceiver, we would never take his word for anything. However, if we had to deal with him for business, we would be sure to have everything done according to the law and with proper documentation. Indeed, we are to be wise and wary in matters of this life. Yet our hearts are far more cunning and deceitful than the craftiest fox. Do not be so simple as to believe every sigh, every wish and word, every motion and every inclination of your heart. Yet we

---

[10]Calvin, *Sermons on Second Samuel*, 1:6.
[11]LCC 21:1516 (CO 2:1115).

[12]Bastingius, *An Exposition upon the Catechism*, 39*; citing Ps 105:15.
[13]Davenant, *Exposition of Colossians*, 2:110-11*; citing Prov 16:32.

too often allow our hearts to have sway over our lives. We think that when we feel some inordinate affection for something, we believe that we will prove victorious and that sin will never prevail against us. Saul, though seemingly moved by David's apology, acknowledged both David's innocence and his own injustice. In fact, it was in tears and kind words that he said, "Is this your voice, my son David?" He added, "I will no more do you harm." Yet for all Saul said, David did not trust Saul at all. For what heed is to be taken to a false and fickle-hearted man's words like Saul's? Because our hearts are as fickle and unstable in their affections toward the Lord as Saul's were toward David, we must not slavishly trust our hearts. The Mystery of Self-Deceiving.[14]

Saul's Brief Moment of Repentance. Johannes Bugenhagen: Now Saul wastes no time, being certain that he will capture David, but is handed over by God into David's hands instead. Then he is reluctantly summoned. He tearfully acknowledges the hand of God, David's innocence and his own iniquity against both of them. That is because he is used to judging David's faith falsely, even though David had often protected him, as you see again in chapter 26. For a sudden brief stupor comes over him when he hears that he was in the hands of David, whom he knows will reign after him. He weeps, he confesses, he makes a vow. But the word he proclaims is the repentance of a hypocrite, as we have often said before. Commentary on 1 Samuel.[15]

Acknowledging David's Righteousness. Edward Reynolds: When Saul, out of the force of natural ingenuity, saw the evidence of David's integrity—who refused to kill Saul even when the Lord had delivered him into his hands—he relented for the time and wept. He acknowledged David's righteousness above his own and spoke in all earnestness. The Sinfulness of Sin.[16]

Tears of Remorse. Andrew Willet: Some think these tears of Saul and this kind of confession of his fault were done in hypocrisy, which Saul counterfeited out of deference to others, who would have thought Saul to be too hardhearted if he would not have been mollified by David's submission. It was also hoped that because of this David would be persuaded to return to the court.... But it seems by Saul's accusation of himself, his acknowledgment that David should be king and his instance in making David swear to him that Saul was truly touched. For, although the wicked have no true feeling of their sins, they may sometimes be moved in conscience even if it does not continue long. Indeed, Pharaoh confessed to Moses that he had sinned, and Judas also knew that he had sinned by betraying the innocent blood: for by the instinct of nature, the conscience in some degree both excuses and accuses, as the apostle shows in Romans 2:14-15. As David's music had before diverse times allayed Saul's malady, so now his divine voice worked some remorse in Saul. Harmony on 1 Samuel.[17]

---

[14]Dyke, *The Mystery of Self-Deceiving*, 361-62*; citing 1 Sam 24:16.
[15]Bugenhagen, *In Samuelem prophetam*, 262.

[16]Reynolds, *Works*, 1:284-85*.
[17]Willet, *Harmony on 1 Samuel*, 268*.

25:1-44 NABAL, ABIGAIL AND DAVID

[1]Now Samuel died. And all Israel assembled and mourned for him, and they buried him in his house at Ramah.

Then David rose and went down to the wilderness of Paran. [2]And there was a man in Maon whose business was in Carmel. The man was very rich; he had three thousand sheep and a thousand goats. He was shearing his sheep in Carmel. [3]Now the name of the man was Nabal, and the name of his wife Abigail. The woman was discerning and beautiful, but the man was harsh and badly behaved; he was a Calebite. [4]David heard in the wilderness that Nabal was shearing his sheep. [5]So David sent ten young men. And David said to the young men, "Go up to Carmel, and go to Nabal and greet him in my name. [6]And thus you shall greet him: 'Peace be to you, and peace be to your house, and peace be to all that you have. [7]I hear that you have shearers. Now your shepherds have been with us, and we did them no harm, and they missed nothing all the time they were in Carmel. [8]Ask your young men, and they will tell you. Therefore let my young men find favor in your eyes, for we come on a feast day. Please give whatever you have at hand to your servants and to your son David.'"

[9]When David's young men came, they said all this to Nabal in the name of David, and then they waited. [10]And Nabal answered David's servants, "Who is David? Who is the son of Jesse? There are many servants these days who are breaking away from their masters. [11]Shall I take my bread and my water and my meat that I have killed for my shearers and give it to men who come from I do not know where?" [12]So David's young men turned away and came back and told him all this. [13]And David said to his men, "Every man strap on his sword!" And every man of them strapped on his sword. David also strapped on his sword. And about four hundred men went up after David, while two hundred remained with the baggage.

[14]But one of the young men told Abigail, Nabal's wife, "Behold, David sent messengers out of the wilderness to greet our master, and he railed at them.

[15]Yet the men were very good to us, and we suffered no harm, and we did not miss anything when we were in the fields, as long as we went with them. [16]They were a wall to us both by night and by day, all the while we were with them keeping the sheep. [17]Now therefore know this and consider what you should do, for harm is determined against our master and against all his house, and he is such a worthless man that one cannot speak to him."

[18]Then Abigail made haste and took two hundred loaves and two skins of wine and five sheep already prepared and five seahs[a] of parched grain and a hundred clusters of raisins and two hundred cakes of figs, and laid them on donkeys. [19]And she said to her young men, "Go on before me; behold, I come after you." But she did not tell her husband Nabal. [20]And as she rode on the donkey and came down under cover of the mountain, behold, David and his men came down toward her, and she met them. [21]Now David had said, "Surely in vain have I guarded all that this fellow has in the wilderness, so that nothing was missed of all that belonged to him, and he has returned me evil for good. [22]God do so to the enemies of David[b] and more also, if by morning I leave so much as one male of all who belong to him."

[23]When Abigail saw David, she hurried and got down from the donkey and fell before David on her face and bowed to the ground. [24]She fell at his feet and said, "On me alone, my lord, be the guilt. Please let your servant speak in your ears, and hear the words of your servant. [25]Let not my lord regard this worthless fellow, Nabal, for as his name is, so is he. Nabal[c] is his name, and folly is with him. But I your servant did not see the young men of my lord, whom you sent. [26]Now then, my lord, as the LORD lives, and as your soul lives, because the LORD has restrained you from bloodguilt and from saving with your own hand, now then let your enemies and those who seek to do evil to my lord be as Nabal. [27]And now let this present that your servant has brought to my lord be given to the young men who follow my lord. [28]Please forgive the

trespass of your servant. For the LORD will certainly make my lord a sure house, because my lord is fighting the battles of the LORD, and evil shall not be found in you so long as you live. ²⁹If men rise up to pursue you and to seek your life, the life of my lord shall be bound in the bundle of the living in the care of the LORD your God. And the lives of your enemies he shall sling out as from the hollow of a sling. ³⁰And when the LORD has done to my lord according to all the good that he has spoken concerning you and has appointed you prince[d] over Israel, ³¹my lord shall have no cause of grief or pangs of conscience for having shed blood without cause or for my lord working salvation himself. And when the LORD has dealt well with my lord, then remember your servant."

³²And David said to Abigail, "Blessed be the LORD, the God of Israel, who sent you this day to meet me! ³³Blessed be your discretion, and blessed be you, who have kept me this day from bloodguilt and from working salvation with my own hand! ³⁴For as surely as the LORD, the God of Israel, lives, who has restrained me from hurting you, unless you had hurried and come to meet me, truly by morning there had not been left to Nabal so much as one male." ³⁵Then David received from her hand what she had brought him. And he said to her, "Go up in peace to your house. See, I have obeyed your voice, and I have granted your petition."

³⁶And Abigail came to Nabal, and behold, he was holding a feast in his house, like the feast of a king. And Nabal's heart was merry within him, for he was very drunk. So she told him nothing at all until the morning light. ³⁷In the morning, when the wine had gone out of Nabal, his wife told him these things, and his heart died within him, and he became as a stone. ³⁸And about ten days later the LORD struck Nabal, and he died.

³⁹When David heard that Nabal was dead, he said, "Blessed be the LORD who has avenged the insult I received at the hand of Nabal, and has kept back his servant from wrongdoing. The LORD has returned the evil of Nabal on his own head." Then David sent and spoke to Abigail, to take her as his wife. ⁴⁰When the servants of David came to Abigail at Carmel, they said to her, "David has sent us to you to take you to him as his wife." ⁴¹And she rose and bowed with her face to the ground and said, "Behold, your handmaid is a servant to wash the feet of the servants of my lord." ⁴²And Abigail hurried and rose and mounted a donkey, and her five young women attended her. She followed the messengers of David and became his wife.

⁴³David also took Ahinoam of Jezreel, and both of them became his wives. ⁴⁴Saul had given Michal his daughter, David's wife, to Palti the son of Laish, who was of Gallim.

a A *seah* was about 7 quarts or 7.3 liters   b Septuagint *to David*   c *Nabal* means *fool*   d Or *leader*

OVERVIEW: The reformers remark that on account of his godly leadership, Samuel, Israel's last judge, is buried properly in Ramah. The story of foolish Nabal leads these interpreters to apply the lessons from Nabal's dealings with David to our own lives: we should prefer others over ourselves, show thankfulness and not waste our time casting pearls before swine. But the story about Nabal also warns us of the excesses of anger. Despite the patience David bears when wronged by others, these interpreters believe that David acts too rashly when he vows to harm Nabal for being rude and refusing to acknowledge social norms.

DAVID AVOIDS SHEDDING BLOOD. JOHANNES BUGENHAGEN: In this story of David against Nabal, let us first say that David could have used the law of the sword to fight impiety and blasphemy because he was a king ordained by God over Nabal, who was a big man in and around Judah and a descendant of the excellent man Caleb. But while we thus excuse David's situation, we fall into danger of speaking against Scripture, which says that David sought protection from human zeal. In this matter, he could have had a good conscience, for this impious man deserved to die and be slain; he could have made a vow against

Nabal through the God of Israel. But see the words of Abigail. See David's words of thanksgiving that he had been kept from shedding blood. Accordingly, you also will see this to be as clear as day. David sought relief from the unlawfulness being introduced to him, which Scripture prohibits. And, as a person, it would certainly be a sin to fall on him without consulting the Lord (as he usually did) instead of deciding about the righteousness of the matter based on what the Lord wants. For God establishes nothing more than this desire even in the saints, that we unite God's word and will to our good intentions (as they call them). For indeed, it appears as if David's cause is just, so that even his vow in verse 22 looks to him as something about to be accomplished, striking down the impious and blasphemous one, as if it were not against God's law but in accordance with law and right. His conscience was certainly good. But while conscience is at its highest, it is impiously not being guided by the Word of God. This is indeed just as Paul says, he who was converted to a good conscience before God as his ancestors were (2 Tim 1), from having been a blasphemer and persecutor of the church (1 Tim 1). Therefore David gives thanks to God, who turned him away from his plans through Abigail. COMMENTARY ON 1 SAMUEL.[1]

ABIGAIL AS ALLEGORY OF THE CHURCH.
ANDREW WILLET: Nabal is described by his place of dwelling in Maon, though he kept his cattle in Carmel, where his business lay. According to Joshua 15:55, Maon, Ziph and Carmel were not far from each other. Carmel generally signifies any place tilled or planted. It was the proper name of two places, one in Issachar, where Baal's priests were killed, and another in Judah, where this story takes place. Moreover, Nabal is set forth by his name, which means "fool." By his riches and qualities, he was churlish and evil-conditioned. Indeed, riches, where God's grace is not bestowed, make people proud and insolent. By his kindred, Nabal was of the posterity of Caleb. However, good men do not

always have good issue. Parents may leave to their children riches and possessions, but they cannot bequeath them wisdom, understanding and piety; for these attributes only proceed from God. And if there might be a certain descent of these spiritual graces, as of temporal ones, they would be thought to be natural. As for Abigail, whose name is interpreted as "the joy of the father," she was a virtuous woman who was unequally matched with a wicked husband. Ambrose makes this allegory concerning her: Abigail signifies the church, which first served under a foolish and unwise husband, the philosophers and other vain men among the heathen. But afterward she was joined in marriage to Christ, just as Abigail became David's wife. But this figure does not hold water on every point. For Abigail was a beautiful and wise woman before she was married to David, while the church of God was deformed and without any spiritual attractiveness or beauty until she was espoused to Christ. HARMONY ON 1 SAMUEL.[2]

25:1 The Death of Samuel

ISRAEL'S LAST JUDGE. JOHANNES BUGENHAGEN: You might wonder that Saul did not manifestly threaten Samuel with evil, for Samuel himself said, "If Saul hears it, he will kill me." But it is clear that he was afraid of the people, with whom this admirable prophet had lived from his youth until he was a holy judge in Israel, so that even the king was afraid of Samuel, as the story above in chapter 15 declared. The same is true in chapter 28 below, where in anguish Saul wanted to raise him up from death himself, which he wanted not out of any sense of sorrow but because of his own failure. . . . Here dies the last judge of Israel, the one who established the kingdom. COMMENTARY ON 1 SAMUEL.[3]

BURIAL WITH REVERENCE. ANDREW WILLET: The people had great cause to mourn for Samuel, the Lord's prophet. He was an upright man. In

[1]Bugenhagen, *In Samuelem prophetam*, 265-66.

[2]Willet, *Harmony on 1 Samuel*, 272-73*.
[3]Bugenhagen, *In Samuelem prophetam*, 264-65; citing 1 Sam 16:2.

fact, at this time two calamities happened together: first, the death of Samuel, so great a prophet, and the exile of David. And second, not long after Samuel's death, the Philistines prevailed against Saul after he and his three sons died in battle. It is not likely that Saul publicly mourned for Samuel as Samuel had done for Saul. And he did not wait long after Samuel's death before pursuing David. Therefore David took this opportunity to escape to the utmost parts of the land, while others were busy with the burial of Samuel. There was a very great assembly of all Israel to honor Samuel's funeral, for the bodies of the saints are to be interred in a dignified way. They are to be brought to the ground with honorable solemnity according to their defects while they lived. . . . Indeed, the bodies of Christians should not be neglected and cast away as unclean. This is how the heathens act, who have no regard for the immortality of the soul. Accordingly, they make a small account of the dead. In fact, the pagan emperors of Rome let the bodies of Christians lie unburied. However, the bodies of Christians, in hope of the resurrection and as temples of the Holy Spirit, should be commended and committed to Christian burial with reverence. Harmony on 1 Samuel.[4]

25:2-12 Foolish Nabal

Riches and Blessings Are Wasted on Fools. Johannes Bugenhagen: Proverbs says, "What good does it do a fool to have riches when he cannot buy wisdom?" Here you have an example. It is all for the worst whenever power and riches fall on foolish people, that is, among those ignorant of God's Word. How much do you really value the cross carried by this wise, God-fearing woman Abigail? What impious company, which congregates in any and every place where you read of a good woman in Scripture! But God later makes her the queen and holiest wife of David, for God often leads the elect through hell

and back again, and the impious are preserved until the day of evil. Moreover, hypocrites say yes presumptively to God's love as long as the better gifts of God are visible: power, riches, eloquence, worldly wisdom, expertise in the law, righteousness of the flesh, a robust body and appearance, and so on. We use these examples to oppose the notion that Nabal was great or wealthy or that he deserved to be given the greatest wife, for there is nothing greater in this life than that. Commentary on 1 Samuel.[5]

Tending to Christ's Sheep. Thomas Adams: Nabal thinks only of his sheep and does not have any concern for David. If the truth were known, there are many Nabals today who love their own sheep better than Christ's sheep. The White Devil.[6]

Being Thankful Unlike Nabal. John Davenant: We ought to be thankful to God because without gratitude there can be no spiritual blessings within us. For since every spiritual blessing depends on a certain perpetual influx of divine grace, ingratitude is that infernal bar that interrupts the flow and the course of divine goodness. Therefore we ought to be thankful, lest we should be deprived of all our gifts.

But gratitude toward people is also required so that peace may be kept inviolate, because troubles and enmities sometimes arise from kindnesses not duly repaid or from injuries inflicted. We perceive this in the example of Nabal, who by his ingratitude so exasperated the mind of David that unless the prudence and humanity of Abigail had relieved him, that ungrateful man and his whole family would have been ruined.

There are two instructions we may gather from this: First, if we would have God remain kind to us, we ought to show ourselves thankful to him and grateful for the benefits conferred on us. Second,

---

[4]Willet, *Harmony on 1 Samuel*, 270-71*.

[5]Bugenhagen, *In Samuelem prophetam*, 268; citing Prov 17:16 (following the Latin); Prov 18:22.
[6]Adams, *White Devil*, 21*.

the best proof we can give of our gratitude is that we obey the divine will. . . . Those benefited by kindnesses are bound by the divine command (if occasion offers) to return thanks to their benefactors not in mere words, but in reality. EXPOSITION ON COLOSSIANS.[7]

25:13-35 David's Rashness

BY GOD'S PERMISSION. JACOBUS ARMINIUS: God permitted David to resolve in his mind to destroy with the sword Nabal and all his domestics, and to go instantly to him; but he did not permit him to shed innocent blood, and to save himself by his own hand. DISPUTATION 10: ON THE RIGHTEOUSNESS AND EFFICACY OF GOD'S PROVIDENCE CONCERNING EVIL[8]

DAVID'S HASTY AND SUDDEN RAGE. ANDREW WILLET: It may seem strange that David, who patiently bore both the wrongs Saul perpetrated against him as well as the ravings of Shimei later on when he was king, could not at this time hold himself back from Nabal's insult. On the contrary, he quickly armed himself to take revenge. His first reason for doing so was due to the ingratitude of Nabal, who returned to him "evil for good," as David says in verse 21. The other reason was due to the indignity and contempt with which Nabal spoke to David's servants. Here it is clear that people can endure greater violence offered to their bodies than contempt and reproaches to their good name. HARMONY ON 1 SAMUEL.[9]

ON DAVID'S LIE. BENEDICT ARETIUS: David swore he would kill Nabal, but afterward he did not do so. We respond: He rashly swore, but he later more wisely changed his mind. In the thought was sin but in his change of heart is praise. Therefore, there is no profit for the one who lies. COMMON PLACES OF THE CHRISTIAN RELIGION.[10]

25:36-38 Not Reasoning with a Drunken Person

TAKING THE WISE COURSE. LANCELOT ANDREWES: That course Abigail took . . . is the course God uses, that is, in the spirit of discretion to deal with people when the fit of rage of sin is past and when their blood is cold. For there is no meddling with a person in their drunken fit or in their fury of heat and rage, because their judgment and senses are then taken away. COLLECTION OF LECTURES.[11]

WAITING TILL THE WINE'S GONE OUT. JOHN ARROWSMITH: You may see a drunk person reeling to and fro, today entertaining this odd conceit, tomorrow that . . . and unstable in all his ways. In fact, the drunk may be vomiting and casting out scornful reproaches on all who are of a contrary judgment. . . . You may perceive them full of slander, as drunkards commonly used to be, prating and venting their own apprehensions everywhere. . . . "One drunkard," our proverb says, "is forty men strong." Whoever attempts to reason with them will easily find them as incapable of conviction as Nabal was of Abigail's narration till his wine was gone out of him. CHAIN OF PRINCIPLES.[12]

25:39-44 David's Polygamy

EXAMPLE FOR ADMONISHING, NOT IMITATING. JOHANNES PISCATOR: This admission of polygamy in the holy figure of David is not given as an example to follow. Rather, it's given as a way to admonish the weaknesses of the saints. COMMENTARY ON 1 SAMUEL.[13]

POLYGAMY AMONG CAVE WANDERING. CARDINAL CAJETAN: See how great the Jewish inclination toward procreation was! The zeal of the Jews was so great for producing children that they

[7]Davenant, Exposition of Colossians, 2:128-29*; citing Col 3:15.
[8]Arminius, Works, 1:506-7*.
[9]Willet, Harmony on 1 Samuel, 274-75*.
[10]Aretius, Loci communes, 585.

[11]Andrewes, A Collection of Lectures, 294-95*.
[12]Arrowsmith, Armilla Catechetica, 84*.
[13]Piscator, Commentarii in omnes libros Veteris Testamenti, 2:177.

managed to multiply wives while also wandering through caves. COMMENTARY ON 1 SAMUEL.[14]

MULTIPLE WIVES AND SINGULAR FAITH.

KONRAD PELLIKAN: David was allowed to have multiple wives, just as other saints similarly were welcomed amid great sins. Nevertheless, he knew that such temptations of the flesh were quite unbearable. We are not allowed to take many wives, as the saints were before us, without it causing trouble. Solomon did not handle having many wives well, nor did David, as we have seen. The Lord had advised them well, yet did not count their actions as a grave sin, as it would have been among others. On the contrary, Saul had few wives and yet displeased God; David had many and pleased the Lord. Wives did not cause this, rather faith. COMMENTARY ON 1 SAMUEL.[15]

MANY WIVES ARE PERMISSIBLE. ANDREW

WILLET: Because the law is given in Deuteronomy 17:17 that the king shall not multiply many wives lest his heart turn away, there is great doubt whether David did not offend against that law. That's because this passage explicitly mentions that David had three wives (and many more afterward). Some answer that as in the same place the king is forbidden to have many horses, yet Solomon—before his fall, while his wisdom remained with him—had forty thousand stalls of horses, meaning that as it was lawful for the king to have a number of horses for the maintenance of the state, as long as they were necessary and not excessive. They were not to be kept only for ostentation and pleasure. According to such an interpretation, therefore, the king would be permitted to have two, three or more wives, so long as they were not multiplied out of measure. Such was Solomon's sin and not David's. But some do not find this interpretation satisfying. For although Solomon had hundreds more wives than David, David still had more than one wife; in fact, he had six. Nor

does the comparison hold between the number of horses and wives: For one wife may suffice, where many thousands of horses are not sufficient for the state and service of a king. Some therefore think that the issue is not about having many wives but about not multiplying them such as would turn the king's heart away from God. Again, in such a circumstance, Solomon's wives did turn his heart away from God while David's wives did not. But this answer is not sufficient either. That's because this law is meant for all the kings of Israel, just as much as it is for all others. For anyone who has multiple wives will be put in peril, though some by God's grace are kept from that danger.

Therefore the occasion of the danger is to be shunned completely, for no one knows their own strength. The same law is prescribed, namely, that they should not take the daughters of the foreign nations to their sons lest they make them "whore after their gods." Yet was it simply forbidden to marry them even though no idolatry ensued? For example, although the people confessed that they had trespassed against God by taking foreign wives of the people of the land in Ezra 10:2, no mention is made that by them they fell into idolatry. Accordingly, some think the king was forbidden to violently take away other men's wives, as they did before the flood. Such would have been David's great offense by taking Uriah's wife. If this was the meaning, however, then Solomon would not have transgressed against this law by taking many wives, for it does not appear that any of his queens and concubines were another's wife. Nor yet can it be thought that such a holy man as David would transgress such a manifest law. Therefore, though it was a general infirmity in those days not only in kings but also in their people to have many wives . . . yet the meaning of this law does not appear to simply forbid many wives. This is apparent by the verse which indicates that the Lord gave power and liberty to David to take his master's wives: "And I gave you your master's house and your master's wives into your arms and gave you the house of Israel and of Judah. And if this were too little, I would add to you as much more." The Lord would

---

[14]Cajetan, *Opera Omnia in Sacrae Scripturae Expositionem,* 2:122.
[15]Pellikan, *Commentaria Bibliorum,* 1:99v-100r.

not have gone against his own law. Therefore, in this passage, it is not the *thing* that is forbidden, but the *manner*. In other words, the king was not to take many wives to give himself to lust and pleasure, and so neglect the office and duty of the kingdom. And just as the king was forbidden to multiply horses, gold and silver, so he was restrained from multiplying wives. But it was lawful in and of itself for the king to have many horses, silver and gold, as Solomon had. However, he was not to trust in them. To conclude, it was permitted in those times to have many wives. Yet the kings were not to use their wives for lust and concupiscence, but for procreation. The kings were not to be addicted to them. HARMONY ON 1 SAMUEL.[16]

---

[16]Willet, *Harmony on 1 Samuel*, 284-85*; citing Ex 34:16; 2 Sam 12:8.

26:1–27:12 DAVID SPARES SAUL AGAIN AND THEN FLEES

¹Then the Ziphites came to Saul at Gibeah, saying, "Is not David hiding himself on the hill of Hachilah, which is on the east of Jeshimon?" ²So Saul arose and went down to the wilderness of Ziph with three thousand chosen men of Israel to seek David in the wilderness of Ziph. ³And Saul encamped on the hill of Hachilah, which is beside the road on the east of Jeshimon. But David remained in the wilderness. When he saw that Saul came after him into the wilderness, ⁴David sent out spies and learned that Saul had indeed come. ⁵Then David rose and came to the place where Saul had encamped. And David saw the place where Saul lay, with Abner the son of Ner, the commander of his army. Saul was lying within the encampment, while the army was encamped around him.

⁶Then David said to Ahimelech the Hittite, and to Joab's brother Abishai the son of Zeruiah, "Who will go down with me into the camp to Saul?" And Abishai said, "I will go down with you." ⁷So David and Abishai went to the army by night. And there lay Saul sleeping within the encampment, with his spear stuck in the ground at his head, and Abner and the army lay around him. ⁸Then Abishai said to David, "God has given your enemy into your hand this day. Now please let me pin him to the earth with one stroke of the spear, and I will not strike him twice." ⁹But David said to Abishai, "Do not destroy him, for who can put out his hand against the LORD's anointed and be guiltless?" ¹⁰And David said, "As the LORD lives, the LORD will strike him, or his day will come to die, or he will go down into battle and perish. ¹¹The LORD forbid that I should put out my hand against the LORD's anointed. But take now the spear that is at his head and the jar of water, and let us go." ¹²So David took the spear and the jar of water from Saul's head, and they went away. No man saw it or knew it, nor did any awake, for they were all asleep, because a deep sleep from the LORD had fallen upon them.

¹³Then David went over to the other side and stood far off on the top of the hill, with a great space between them. ¹⁴And David called to the army, and to Abner the son of Ner, saying, "Will you not answer, Abner?" Then Abner answered, "Who are you who calls to the king?" ¹⁵And David said to Abner, "Are you not a man? Who is like you in Israel? Why then have you not kept watch over your lord the king? For one of the people came in to destroy the king your lord. ¹⁶This thing that you have done is not good. As the LORD lives, you deserve to die, because you have not kept watch over your lord, the LORD's anointed. And now see where the king's spear is and the jar of water that was at his head."

¹⁷Saul recognized David's voice and said, "Is this your voice, my son David?" And David said, "It is my voice, my lord, O king." ¹⁸And he said, "Why does my lord pursue after his servant? For what have I done? What evil is on my hands? ¹⁹Now therefore let my lord the king hear the words of his servant. If it is the LORD who has stirred you up against me, may he accept an offering, but if it is men, may they be cursed before the LORD, for they have driven me out this day that I should have no share in the heritage of the LORD, saying, 'Go, serve other gods.' ²⁰Now therefore, let not my blood fall to the earth away from the presence of the LORD, for the king of Israel has come out to seek a single flea like one who hunts a partridge in the mountains."

²¹Then Saul said, "I have sinned. Return, my son David, for I will no more do you harm, because my life was precious in your eyes this day. Behold, I have acted foolishly, and have made a great mistake." ²²And David answered and said, "Here is the spear, O king! Let one of the young men come over and take it. ²³The LORD rewards every man for his righteousness and his faithfulness, for the LORD gave you into my hand today, and I would not put out my hand against the LORD's anointed. ²⁴Behold, as your life was precious this day in my sight, so may my life be precious in the sight of the LORD, and may he deliver me out of all tribulation." ²⁵Then Saul said to David,

"Blessed be you, my son David! You will do many things and will succeed in them." So David went his way, and Saul returned to his place.

27 *Then David said in his heart, "Now I shall perish one day by the hand of Saul. There is nothing better for me than that I should escape to the land of the Philistines. Then Saul will despair of seeking me any longer within the borders of Israel, and I shall escape out of his hand." ²So David arose and went over, he and the six hundred men who were with him, to Achish the son of Maoch, king of Gath. ³And David lived with Achish at Gath, he and his men, every man with his household, and David with his two wives, Ahinoam of Jezreel, and Abigail of Carmel, Nabal's widow. ⁴And when it was told Saul that David had fled to Gath, he no longer sought him.*

⁵Then David said to Achish, "If I have found favor in your eyes, let a place be given me in one of the country towns, that I may dwell there. For why should your servant dwell in the royal city with you?" ⁶So that day Achish gave him Ziklag. Therefore Ziklag has belonged to the kings of Judah to this day. ⁷And the number of the days that David lived in the country of the Philistines was a year and four months.

⁸Now David and his men went up and made raids against the Geshurites, the Girzites, and the Amalekites, for these were the inhabitants of the land from of old, as far as Shur, to the land of Egypt. ⁹And David would strike the land and would leave neither man nor woman alive, but would take away the sheep, the oxen, the donkeys, the camels, and the garments, and come back to Achish. ¹⁰When Achish asked, "Where have you made a raid today?" David would say, "Against the Negeb of Judah," or, "Against the Negeb of the Jerahmeelites," or, "Against the Negeb of the Kenites." ¹¹And David would leave neither man nor woman alive to bring news to Gath, thinking, "lest they should tell about us and say, 'So David has done.'" Such was his custom all the while he lived in the country of the Philistines. ¹²And Achish trusted David, thinking, "He has made himself an utter stench to his people Israel; therefore he shall always be my servant."

OVERVIEW: The theme of David as a messianic figure and Saul as an evil oppressor continues in these two chapters. One of the Anabaptist commentators, likely drawing on his own experience as a persecuted minority, draws direct connections between David and Christ's persecutions. In addition, David's deception of Achish, though used to protect the Judeans, is not to be an example for believers—the works and words of God, not human beings, are.

26:1-5 The Hunt Continues

DAVID'S PERSECUTED THEN ENTHRONED HEIR. DIRK PHILIPS: Christ also was persecuted by unbelieving and godless people and often had to escape from Judea and hide himself in the wilderness. But after this he received his kingdom and was established and inaugurated by God his Father as the mighty king on Mount Zion. God gave him the throne of David to rule in the house of Jacob for eternity, a kingdom without end. ENCHIRIDION: CONCERNING SPIRITUAL RESTITUTION.[1]

NO REST FOR THE WICKED. THOMAS ADAMS: The wicked cannot sleep until they have done mischief. Saul would not give over the chase of David, but hunts him savagely through every wilderness. The very desert is held too good a refuge for innocence; the hills and rocks are searched in an angry jealousy. The very wild goats of the mountains were not allowed to be companions for the one who had no other fault but his virtue. Still David's success is Saul's vexation. Where will that person rest who seeks rest in sin? They cannot find rest in this life, for they walk in circles, grind in the devil's mill. Will they rest hereafter? No, then they will eat of their own grist, and labor in torment. Only there is some difference in the manner of their working, and of the time; here with pleasure, there with horror: for a while here, there forever. Still

---

[1]Liechty, ed., *Early Anabaptist Spirituality*, 236; cf. CRR 6:337.

these obstinate seducers who are obsessed with mischief go on, from strength in sin, to strength of sinning, till every one appears before their master in hell. Commentary on 2 Peter.[2]

How the Lord Stirs Up. Andrew Willet:

God stirs no one up nor tempts the person to evil, just as he himself is not tempted of any evil. Yet the Lord may be said here to stir Saul up to the action of pursuing of David in three kinds of ways. First, God acts instrumentally. He justly uses here the ministry of the evil spirits, which were the instruments and ministers of God in stirring up Saul. God justly sent them on Saul to do his will. Second, God, acting efficiently, may be said to stir up the magistrate to act justly. But here Saul acted unjustly. Finally, the Lord occasionally stirs up when the wicked take occasion by God's mercies on others to fret and show their malice. Such is how Pharaoh hated the people of God because he saw that they increased plentifully. And so Saul was David's enemy because the Lord had caused him to be anointed as king. Harmony on 1 Samuel.[3]

26:6-25 David's Great Restraint

Wickedness by Another. William Tyndale: If any person might have avenged himself on his superior, it would have justifiably been David's actions done on King Saul, who so wrongfully persecuted David. And he did this for no other cause than that God had anointed David king and promised him the kingdom. Yet when God had delivered Saul into the hands of David, he could not do what he may have wanted to do with him. . . . As the old proverb says, "Out of the wicked shall wickedness proceed, but my hand will not be on you," meaning that God always punishes one who is wicked by another. Doctrinal Treatises and Introductions to Other Portions of Holy Scriptures.[4]

On Being a Good Subject. Heinrich Bullinger: We learn partly through the example of David and partly through the teachings of Jeremiah and the apostles in what way subjects are to be influenced by their hard and cruel princes or tyrants. David was not ignorant of the type of person Saul was—an ungodly and cruel bandit; as such, he fled from him. But when the occasion arose for him once or twice to take him down, David did not kill Saul but spared the tyrant and honored him as if he were his own father. Decades 2.6.[5]

Practice in Afflictions. Johannes Bugenhagen: As always, here goes Saul, except now with even more impiety since David overlooked his sins and false oaths above in chapter 24. Indeed, David does not turn away from his innocence this time either, as he still does not want to strike down the king until the Lord strikes him down. He trusts God's vindication, perhaps having learned in the previous chapter that it might be harmful to follow our whims. And it clearly happens again as it did in chapter 4 that David has been well versed to this point in having a strong faith in his soul, so that by his own will he and his companions go down into Saul's camp. For he has been protected so often that he knows himself to be in God's care and that he cannot perish in Saul's impiety. Only practice in afflictions can produce such faith in us. For God exalts through faith for faith, so that we might grow to full maturity. Moreover, this story has it that the wisdom of the flesh is mocked and the Spirit cares for the one to whom it has been given. A deep sleep from the Lord had come over David's enemies. In this miracle, we see how much God cared for David, who entrusted himself to God with the highest faithfulness. Commentary on 1 Samuel.[6]

---

[5]Bullinger, *Sermonum decades quinque*, 154.
[6]Bugenhagen, *In Samuelem prophetam*, 271-72. Bugenhagen refers to *exercita tentationibus* (practice in afflictions), which is a typical way for Lutherans to speak of experiencing and learning the theology of the cross.

---

[2]Adams, *Commentary upon 2 Peter*, 907*.
[3]Willet, *Harmony on 1 Samuel*, 297*.
[4]Tyndale, *Doctrinal Treatises*, 176*.

CONFIDENT PRAYER WHILE BEING HUNTED.
JOHN KNOX: What is necessary to be followed in prayer is a sure hope to obtain what we ask for. For nothing more offends God than when we ask doubtfully whether he will grant our petitions. For in so doing we doubt if God is true and if he is mighty and good. Such, says James, obtain nothing, and therefore Jesus Christ commands that we firmly believe in order to obtain whatever we ask for. For all things are possible to the one who believes. And therefore, in our prayers, desperation is always to be expelled. I do not mean that any person in extremity of trouble can be without present pain and without a greater fear of trouble to follow. Rather, trouble and fear are the very spurs to prayer. For when a person, encircled with vehement calamities and vexed with continual anxiety—having, by human help, no hope of deliverance, with an oppressed and punished heart, fearing also greater punishment to follow from the deep pit of tribulation—calls to God for comfort and support, such prayer ascends to God's presence, and does not return in vain.

This is seen, for instance, in Saul's vehement persecution of David, as the latter was hunted and chased from every hole, fearing that one day or other he should fall into the hands of his persecutors. After that he complained that no place of rest was left to him, vehemently praying, "O LORD my God, in you do I take refuge; save me from all my pursuers and deliver me, lest like a lion they tear my soul apart, rending it in pieces, with none to deliver. O LORD my God, if I have done this, if there is wrong in my hands, if I have repaid my friend with evil or plundered my enemy without cause, let the enemy pursue my soul and overtake it, and let him trample my life to the ground and lay my glory in the dust." In the midst of these anguishes, the goodness of God sustained David, so that the present tribulation was tolerable. And the infallible promises of God so assured him of deliverance that fear was partly mitigated and gone, as plainly appears to those who diligently observe the process of his prayer. TREATISE ON PRAYER.[7]

DAVID'S GOOD EXAMPLE. THOMAS BECON: It is good to follow the example of David, who showed such honor and reverence to King Saul, both a wicked ruler and his mortal enemy, that he would not once hurt him, nor yet suffer any other to do it, although he had sufficient opportunity . . . and occasion at diverse times to have slain him, if he had been minded. A NEW CATECHISM.[8]

INNOCENCE BEFORE GOD. DAVID DICKSON: Though innocence cannot exempt a person from being unjustly slandered, yet it will furnish him with a good conscience and much boldness in the specific things before God. . . . The more a person renders good for evil, the more confidence he will have when he comes to God. For innocence served David for this good use, namely, that he delivered Saul—who was his enemy for no good reason. . . . The one who is conscious of doing or intending injury to his neighbor will have his own conscience against him, and in that case will be forced to justify God's righteousness against himself. EXPLICATION OF THE FIRST FIFTY PSALMS.[9]

27:1-12 David Flees to the Philistines

THE ENEMY OF YOUR ENEMY. JOHANNES BUGENHAGEN: Here David in his anguish is driven away, deciding he will be better off among enemies than among his own people. And he flees to the one he was with before, Achish in Gath of the Philistines, the enemy of Israel. David receives the city of Ziklag from him to live in as a prince. But why does he flee to the one before whom he was so afraid that he pretended to be out of his mind? I reply: By this time it had become known that the life of this prince who had dispatched Goliath was being sought by the king of Israel. For this reason, the king of the Philistines was not afraid of any traps but warmly accepted this great man as a Philistine, of whom it might be expected that he would do great evil against Saul. COMMENTARY ON 1 SAMUEL.[10]

---

[7]Knox, *Practical Works*, 38-39*; citing Ps 37:1-5.

[8]Becon, *Catechism*, 89-90.
[9]Dickson, *First Fifty Psalms*, 34*.
[10]Bugenhagen, *In Samuelem prophetam*, 273.

David's Unbelief and Belief. Justus Menius: Here David's weakened faith is described. He feared that he would eventually fall into Saul's hands; therefore he departed from the borders of Israel into the land of the Philistines. Now, as by this David's faith had been weakened in part, so that he fled Saul; so also, again, in a different way his faith was strengthened in part, so that he dared to entrust himself to a most hostile people. For if you would consider what a wicked reputation he had earned for himself among the Philistines—because he killed Goliath and, in addition, he cut down two hundred of them and cut off their foreskin—you would easily recognize that there was nothing more dangerous than to dwell in this race's country. Yes, although David was in the midst of an impious people, nevertheless he did not at the same time abandon faith, no indeed, he did nothing apart from faith. Commentary on 1 Samuel 27.[11]

David's Answers to King Achish. Johannes Bugenhagen: The king asked, "Where have you made a raid today?" David's words were true, but through them he nevertheless deceived the king, who thought that David was bringing evil to the Judeans as an enemy. For the king greatly desired that David might sacrifice himself against the nations, and so he did not condemn those things, even though he did not know what was being plundered. Thus David deceived the king without being condemned by the king in order to defend himself and protect his own, which God was allowing to him to do. We spoke of this fraud earlier, that one may not make a rule of deception based on this. For it is the well-practiced hypocritical wisdom of the flesh that makes a law out of the works of the saints, as if the saints were not able to sin. We should follow the Word of God, not the works of the saints, unless we even want to imitate David in committing adultery and murder. Commentary on 1 Samuel.[12]

---

[11]Menius, *In Samuelis Librum Priorem enarratio*, 70v-71r.

[12]Bugenhagen, *In Samuelem prophetam*, 274; citing 2 Sam 11.

28:1-25 SAUL AND THE MEDIUM AT EN-DOR

[1]In those days the Philistines gathered their forces for war, to fight against Israel. And Achish said to David, "Understand that you and your men are to go out with me in the army." [2]David said to Achish, "Very well, you shall know what your servant can do." And Achish said to David, "Very well, I will make you my bodyguard for life."

[3]Now Samuel had died, and all Israel had mourned for him and buried him in Ramah, his own city. And Saul had put the mediums and the necromancers out of the land. [4]The Philistines assembled and came and encamped at Shunem. And Saul gathered all Israel, and they encamped at Gilboa. [5]When Saul saw the army of the Philistines, he was afraid, and his heart trembled greatly. [6]And when Saul inquired of the LORD, the LORD did not answer him, either by dreams, or by Urim, or by prophets. [7]Then Saul said to his servants, "Seek out for me a woman who is a medium, that I may go to her and inquire of her." And his servants said to him, "Behold, there is a medium at En-dor."

[8]So Saul disguised himself and put on other garments and went, he and two men with him. And they came to the woman by night. And he said, "Divine for me by a spirit and bring up for me whomever I shall name to you." [9]The woman said to him, "Surely you know what Saul has done, how he has cut off the mediums and the necromancers from the land. Why then are you laying a trap for my life to bring about my death?" [10]But Saul swore to her by the LORD, "As the LORD lives, no punishment shall come upon you for this thing." [11]Then the woman said, "Whom shall I bring up for you?" He said, "Bring up Samuel for me." [12]When the woman saw Samuel, she cried out with a loud voice. And the woman said to Saul, "Why have you deceived me? You are Saul." [13]The king said to her, "Do not be afraid. What do you see?" And the woman said to Saul, "I see a god coming up out of the earth." [14]He said to her, "What is his appearance?" And she said, "An old man is coming up, and he is wrapped in a robe." And Saul knew that it was Samuel, and he bowed with his face to the ground and paid homage.

[15]Then Samuel said to Saul, "Why have you disturbed me by bringing me up?" Saul answered, "I am in great distress, for the Philistines are warring against me, and God has turned away from me and answers me no more, either by prophets or by dreams. Therefore I have summoned you to tell me what I shall do." [16]And Samuel said, "Why then do you ask me, since the LORD has turned from you and become your enemy? [17]The LORD has done to you as he spoke by me, for the LORD has torn the kingdom out of your hand and given it to your neighbor, David. [18]Because you did not obey the voice of the LORD and did not carry out his fierce wrath against Amalek, therefore the LORD has done this thing to you this day. [19]Moreover, the LORD will give Israel also with you into the hand of the Philistines, and tomorrow you and your sons shall be with me. The LORD will give the army of Israel also into the hand of the Philistines."

[20]Then Saul fell at once full length on the ground, filled with fear because of the words of Samuel. And there was no strength in him, for he had eaten nothing all day and all night. [21]And the woman came to Saul, and when she saw that he was terrified, she said to him, "Behold, your servant has obeyed you. I have taken my life in my hand and have listened to what you have said to me. [22]Now therefore, you also obey your servant. Let me set a morsel of bread before you; and eat, that you may have strength when you go on your way." [23]He refused and said, "I will not eat." But his servants, together with the woman, urged him, and he listened to their words. So he arose from the earth and sat on the bed. [24]Now the woman had a fattened calf in the house, and she quickly killed it, and she took flour and kneaded it and baked unleavened bread of it, [25]and she put it before Saul and his servants, and they ate. Then they rose and went away that night.

OVERVIEW: The scene between Saul and the witch at En-dor elicits more commentary from the interpreters than perhaps any other passage in First or Second Samuel. Indeed, this passage provides a rich diversity of interpretation from all the major confessions of the Reformation era. All agree that seeking out a witch is a desperate and depraved act. There are three principal interpretive options when it comes to identifying the spirit the witch calls forth: it is Samuel in person, an illusion or a demon (perhaps even Satan himself). The reformers carefully examine the words of the spirit—that Saul and his sons would die tomorrow on the battlefield. That this prophecy came to pass complicates the issue of identifying exactly what or who the spirit is.

IN DISTRESS AND TEMPTATION, SAUL TURNS TO IDOLATRY. JOHANNES BUGENHAGEN: First, Samuel's death was described in chapter 25, so that you know what follows about his rising to be a demonic illusion. Next, it is shown what kind of righteous and pious king this desperate hypocrite pretended to be after Samuel's death, sweeping away the magicians—soothsayers and mediums—as if following the law of Leviticus 20, Deuteronomy 18 and Isaiah 8. For hypocrites insist upon forcing the works of the law upon the people, while neglecting and despising faith in God. Therefore it is written of Saul in 1 Chronicles, "Saul died for his breach of faith. He broke faith with the LORD in that he did not keep the command of the LORD, and also consulted a medium, seeking guidance. He did not seek guidance from the LORD. Therefore the LORD put him to death and turned the kingdom over to David the son of Jesse."

What good did it do Saul to have a name among men that soothsayers would not be suffered, as he had heard from Samuel earlier: "Rebellion is as the sin of divination, and presumption is as iniquity and idolatry." All the righteous ones are idolaters when they cast off the Word of God, etc. Further, this story reveals Saul's hypocrisy, for he sought in distress that which he had publicly condemned. Hypocrisy boasts of being beyond temptation

through the works of the law and of being seen in worship of God, but then it despairs in times of real temptation, because it never had true faith in God. Thus it says, "When Saul saw the army of the Philistines, he was afraid, and his heart trembled greatly." COMMENTARY ON 1 SAMUEL.[1]

28:1-10 *Saul's Desperate Act*

SAUL'S WICKED ACT. JOHN CALVIN: Saul was to the very end a rebel against God; he despised him like someone who is incorrigible. Not only did he persecute the innocent, but wishing to reverse the decree of God, he committed a most wicked act. He went like a wretched magician or enchanter to ask counsel of a witch. . . . That was the most desperate act of all. SERMONS ON 2 SAMUEL.[2]

IMPATIENCE LEADS TO SIN. PHILIPP MELANCHTHON: All those who allow the devil to embitter them with impatience, who give way to the flesh and who mumble and become angry against God allow faith and obedience to God to depart (which is frightful). Impatient, angry, embittered hearts think that God does not pay attention to them, that there is no point in praying, or in waiting and expecting comfort and help. In truly great temptations the heart will impatiently grasp at blasphemy, despondency and human comfort and assistance, against God's commandment, just as King Saul sought out the witch. Such frightfully heavy sins against the first table of the Decalogue come from impatience. A little patience, however, often produces much good. THEOLOGICAL COMMONPLACES (1555).[3]

APPEALING TO GOD TOO LATE. THOMAS ADAMS: The more hold a person takes of the world, the more they lose hold of the Lord. Covetous people cleave to the world so long as they can; but when that staff breaks, then they turn to the Lord. Extremity of distress will send the most profane to

---

[1]Bugenhagen, *In Samuelem prophetam*, 275-76; citing Lev 20:6; Deut 18:10-11; Is 8:19-21; 1 Chron 10:13-14; 1 Sam 15:23.
[2]Calvin, *Sermons on Second Samuel*, 1:38.
[3]*Melanchthon on Christian Doctrine*, 293.

God: as the drowning person stretches out their hand to that lifejacket, which they condemned while safe on shore. So Saul retired himself to "inquire of the Lord, but the Lord did not answer him." It is an unreasonable inequality to hope to find God at our command, when we would not be at his: to look that he should regard our voice in trouble, when we would not regard his voice in peace. Let your conversation be without covetousness. Why? Because God has said, "I will never leave you nor forsake you." We credit the promise of a wealthy and trusty friend: yet a person may lie, a person may die and a person may be unable to help themselves. God is too constant to be changed, too powerful to be crossed, too wise to be deceived. "I will never leave you": not in a year, not in age, not in sickness, not in death. Those who believe this cannot be covetous. The wealth you keep is not your own, but God's. Commentary on 2 Peter.[4]

The Devil in God's Place. George Gifford: No doubt many refuse to hear the voice of God and be instructed by him. They despise his word, and therefore they are given up to listen to devils. All those who have sought out the work of the devil and have now come to see their offense ought to show repentance for this, but not as for a light sin. It is no small abomination to go for help to the devil. It is to set him in God's place and to honor him as God. It rises from infidelity to and distrust of help from God. We may see this in the example of King Saul who, finding neither answer nor comfort from God, whom he had so wickedly disobeyed, went to a witch. The heathen man said, "If I cannot entreat the gods, I will drown among the devils." A Dialogue Concerning Witches and Witchcraft.[5]

Truth Ministered by the Devil. Thomas Jackson: Saul, who had followed the customs of other nations and not the prescripts of God's Word, "asked of the Lord, but the Lord did not

answer him, either by dreams, or by Urim, or by prophets." His sins had made a separation between him and the God of Israel, who for this cause would not allow his presence to his priests or prophets—who came as mediators between God and Saul—to be manifested. Much less would vouchsafe his Spirit to priests and prophets who were carnally minded themselves. . . . Yet it cannot be denied that the pagans were oftentimes, by God's permission, truly spoken to through the means of dreams and oracles—though ultimately ministered by the devil—of events that should come to pass. But such resolutions were rarely for their good. For example, when Saul inquired after a witch . . . when God had cast him off, she did in fact procure Saul a true prediction of his fearful end. The Eternal Truth of Scriptures.[6]

28:11-14 Is It Samuel, an Overactive Imagination, a Demon or the Devil?

From Saul's Perspective. Martin Luther: The Scriptures do not expressly state whether it was really Samuel; they only call him Samuel. This proves that the Scriptures put the matter as it was in the heart of Saul, who did not know but that it was Samuel; and the spirit skillfully spoke all the words of Samuel and added more to them. The Holy Spirit, however, intends that we should be warned and armed by this commandment . . . so that we might know that whatever happens contrary to it does not proceed from a good spirit or from the children of a good spirit. The Misuse of the Mass.[7]

On How People Live and Die Once. Heinrich Bullinger: Some people oppose Samuel's appearance taken here from holy Scripture, which they contend to prove that souls return again after death and teach people about speculative matters. We answer briefly that this figure who seemed to be the prophet was called Samuel by a

---

[4]Adams, *Commentary upon 2 Peter*, 924*; citing 1 Sam 28:6; Josh 1:5.
[5]Clifford, *Dialogue Concerning Witches*, 53*.
[6]Jackson, *Works*, 33-34*.
[7]LW 36:196; citing Deut 18:9-14.

trope, but in fact it was not Samuel. In truth, it was a ghost—a delusion and illusion of Satan—for magic is strictly prohibited in the law of the Lord. Therefore blessed spirits do not submit to such prohibited things and unspeakable arts, which when they were still united with their flesh fought against and abhorred all of their ways. As for damned spirits, they do involve themselves in this. Now, who would believe their oracles? But Samuel predicts that which, they say, happened the next day. And then what? This was not difficult for the demon, given that the true and living Samuel had predicted many things a little while before. . . . Tertullian says in his book *On the Soul*: "God forbid that we should believe that any soul, much less that of a prophet, could be called forth by a demon, since we are taught that 'Satan disguises himself as an angel of light'—much less into a man of light—even asserting himself as God and presenting wonderful signs to overthrow, if possible, even the elect." St. Augustine is of the same opinion about this appearance in his book *To Simplician* 2.3 and others. By these passages I hope that it is abundantly proved that souls of people separated from bodies do not wander or appear in these regions after death. For they remain until judgment in the destination appointed for them by the declaration of God. They are neither sent by the Lord nor are they able to enter into people; neither can they give warning of either present or future things. From this it follows that the appearances of souls, revelations and oracles are mere delusions of Satan, instituted contrary to the sincerity and purity of true religion. DECADES 4.10.[8]

SAUL DECEIVED BY A DEMON. JOHANNES BUGENHAGEN: I wonder how could it have been possible to have this damnable power over death unless Satan had taken the appearance of Samuel? Since the law reveals that the ungodly consult the dead, as in Deuteronomy 18 and Isaiah 8, who does not see that this was a diabolical illusion? Scripture

does not write that this was truly Samuel but that Saul and the woman believed it was him. In its simplicity here, Scripture does not withdraw the prohibition not to seek truth by means of the dead. Such images are truly not the dead but demons who are wrongly believed to have been raised up among the living. Moreover, it is no wonder that the devil reports and predicts accurately. For he sees what is already everywhere: for no one hid the fact that David would soon reign or that Saul would soon perish. For against the Philistine forces, Saul himself saw no defense, neither from people, nor from God, whom Saul was already fighting through his adversaries, nor from David, who alone God might use to save, because David was not there. Therefore the devil could easily make certain conjectures as prophecy, especially because he is eager to cause and inspire failure. God allowed all these things to be spoken truly by Satan, so that all those who have refused to love the truth might be more fully confirmed in their errors, as it says in 2 Thessalonians 2. And in Deuteronomy 13 the law prohibits believing those who come forth to prophesy, offering signs so that we defect to a foreign god, for it says that "the Lord your God is testing you, to know whether you love the Lord your God with all your heart and with all your soul." COMMENTARY ON 1 SAMUEL.[9]

SAMUEL'S BODY BUT THE DEVIL'S SPIRIT. HEINRICH BULLINGER: Devils are spiritual substances. But no one, I think, is able to say exactly in what way they assume bodies or how they appear to human beings. Indeed, the story of Samuel being brought up by a witch shows clearly that devils put on bodies and shapes that are different from their own. It was not Samuel who was brought up from the dead; rather, the chief architect of lies—the devil—deceived King Saul by pretending to be Samuel. For Paul testifies that "Satan disguises himself as an angel of light." Other stories testify that the devil is an extraordinary

---

[8]Bullinger, *Sermonum decades quinque*, 341-42; citing Tertullian, *On the Soul* 57; 2 Cor 11:14; Mt 24:24. [9]Bugenhagen, *In Samuelem prophetam*, 276-77; citing Deut 18:11; Is 8:19; 2 Thess 2:9-12; Deut 13:1-5.

deceiver who assumes various forms and shapes. DECADES 4.9.[10]

COUNTERFEIT SAMUEL. ANDREW WILLET: It seems by Saul's question to the soothsayer that he did not at first see the apparition. In fact, the rabbis think Saul only heard the voice, and that only the woman both saw and heard. But Saul's servants neither heard nor saw. Now, the woman was in another room, since witches back then did not like to be seen when they worked their magic. And it is likely that afterward Saul was admitted to see the apparition. This is indicated by both the reverence he showed to it, in bowing himself, and by the communication he had with the apparition of Samuel. It may be gathered also by the text that the woman did not hear the communication. For it is said that she entered or "came to Saul," implying that she had gone forth beforehand. Presumably, after raising the spirit she left Saul alone in the bedchamber, as it expressed in verse 23. Now, where the woman said, "I saw a god coming up out of the earth," some believe she indicated an excellent person who was ascending. But it is likely that these gods were certain attractive, satanic apparitions (as Satan can transform himself into an angel of light). Thus Samuel appears wrapped about with a mantle, which was the custom of magistrates and prophets to wear to distinguish them from the common sort. Josephus thinks it was a priestly garment. But Samuel was no priest, though he was of the tribe of Levi. The witch recognized him as Samuel, having so learned of the devil who told her who it was. And this counterfeit Samuel yielded to Saul. HARMONY OF 1 SAMUEL.[11]

THE DEVIL APPEARS. LAMBERT DANEAU: First, I agree with you that Satan can appear to people in the shape of a person. In fact, if we should say this cannot be done, then we must deny the meeting and talking together of Christ with the devil, about which the Scripture makes mention in Matthew 4,

where it is written how Satan appeared visibly and in the shape of a man to Christ. Second, I will easily grant you that sorcerers can learn no good thing of Satan, but only such counsels and precepts as proceed from a vile and mischievous disposition, such as to revenge himself, to deceive strangers, to slay people at unawares and to do all these things secretly, none knowing about it or witnessing it. DIALOGUE OF WITCHES.[12]

28:15-25 Concerning the Accuracy of "Samuel's" Prophecy

JUDGMENT LEFT FOR GOD ALONE. ANDREW WILLET: Some interpret this phrase—"tomorrow you and your sons shall be with me"—as though the devil, counterfeiting Samuel's person, said that Saul would be with Samuel, that is, in the state of grace and in the favor of God, but that Satan here lied to him. However, as the rest of these words to Saul fell out to be true—that Saul would be delivered into the hands of the Philistines—so it is likely that the rest also should be true. Indeed, the event happened just as it was spoken. Both Saul and his sons were killed the next day. David Kimchi, along with other rabbis, thinks this is to be understood of the happy estate, where Saul should be. And that here nothing was uttered but truth. For these rabbis hold that Saul, dying for his country and not giving over the defense of Israel to pagans, died in the favor of God. Indeed, Josephus commends Saul as a worthy man who died for his country. But this resolution in Saul to die for his country was only a civil virtue. It was far from piety. Rather, it was like the fortitude of the heathen among the Romans who died for their country. And it was more a matter of God's justice that forced him into this battle rather than his own will and resolution to defend his country. Besides, seeing that Saul killed himself and so died without repentance and ending his days in despair, how could he die in the favor and grace of God? But we will not hastily pronounce a verdict on his everlast-

---

[10]Bullinger, *Sermonum decades quinque*, 327; citing 2 Cor 11:14.
[11]Willet, *Harmony on 1 Samuel*, 313-14*; citing 1 Sam 28:21.

[12]Daneau, *Dialogue of Witches*, G1r-v*; citing Mt 4:1-11.

ing reprobation, though he was rejected from the kingdom. For that, we leave him to the judgment of the Lord. HARMONY OF 1 SAMUEL.[13]

HIDING BEHIND WORDS. FRANCOIS PERRAULT: We read here that the devil, speaking to King Saul under the figure of Samuel, makes himself into an ambiguous form, saying to him, "and tomorrow you and your sons shall be with me," which is to say, you all will die, but he speaks confidently and deceptively, using this word *tomorrow*, which signifies not only the day immediately following but also the time to come indefinitely and at large, as in that passage speaking of the Eternal One: "When your sons will inquire of you tomorrow, saying, 'What is this here?'" This word *tomorrow* means hereafter and of the time to come. In this same sense must be understood that which our Lord Jesus Christ says in Saint Matthew, "Do not be anxious about tomorrow." And in order to make it evident that Saul would not die the next day, or the day following the conference that he had with the devil under the figure of Samuel, but only a year or so afterward, it is necessary to diligently examine the story. But the devil will consider that it certainly appeared by the state and disposition of events that that which he was saying must happen, and nevertheless not being assured he limits nothing certainly, thus hiding in the ambiguity of this word *tomorrow*, wanting to always preserve an avenue door behind for escape. It is thus that he has nearly always deceived the pagans by the ambiguity of his oracles, and not only has he spoken strongly among the pagans, but also he has deceived many Christians by this means, as we have an infinity of examples in the histories. DEMONOLOGY.[14]

EVEN THE DEVIL CAN SPEAK TRULY. THOMAS ADAMS: It is pleasing to the wisdom of God to express himself even by the tongues of faulty instruments. In fact, Satan himself sometimes receives notice from God of his future actions that

otherwise that evil Spirit could neither foretell nor foresee. Such, in all likelihood, was his information concerning the end of Saul: ". . . tomorrow you and your sons shall be with me." How could Satan tell this? Did the devil become a prophet? No. But as he was once a good angel, so he can still act what he was. Even lewd men may be good preachers when Satan himself plays the prophet. What prophet could speak better words than this foul spirit in Samuel's mantle? "Why do you consult me, now that the Lord has turned away from you and become your enemy?" Samuel himself while he was alive could not have spoken more gravely, more severely, more divinely, than this hellish counterfeit. Good words are no rule to distinguish a prophet from a devil. This kind of knowledge is both rare and common: rare, in that it is seldom given to any; common, in that it is indifferently given to the good and bad. Prophecy does not always presuppose sanctification. Many have had visions from God who will never enjoy the vision of God. COMMENTARY ON 2 PETER.[15]

THE DEVIL AT PLAY. DANIEL DYKE: The devil played with Saul by taking it on himself to foretell future events in the hands of God: "tomorrow you and your sons shall be with me," that is, they shall die. Now how did the devil come to reveal God's counsel? How is he able to determine with certainty the end of any person's days given that they are numbered by God alone? However, if you look carefully, you will notice that the devil does not define Saul's death in certain terms, but speaks darkly and deceitfully. For "tomorrow" does not only signify the day immediately following, but it also signifies the time to come indefinitely and at large. For instance, our Savior said, "Therefore do not be anxious about tomorrow"; that is, Jesus refers to the hereafter in the time to come. Moreover, the poet Horace said, "Do not seek what shall be tomorrow, for I care about only what is today. For who knows tomorrow?" In fact, Saul did not die the next day after this appearance—as the

---

[13]Willet, *Harmony on 1 Samuel*, 315*.
[14]Perrault, *Demonologie*, 91-92; citing Ex 13:4; Mt 6:34.
[15]Adams, *Commentary upon 2 Peter*, 1536-37*; citing 1 Sam 28:19, 16.

more diligent reader of the whole context of that history will detect. It was only that Satan discerned the likelihood of it, and ventured so to speak as if the next day Saul should have died. However, because he was not sure of it, the devil tempered his speech with the ambiguity of the word *tomorrow*, so that his reputation might be preserved. THE MYSTERY OF SELF-DECEIVING.[16]

---

[16]Dyke, *The Mystery of Self-Deceiving*, 23-24*; citing 1 Sam 28:19; Mt 6:34.

29:1–31:13 THE PHILISTINES REJECT
DAVID AND SAUL DIES

[1]Now the Philistines had gathered all their forces at Aphek. And the Israelites were encamped by the spring that is in Jezreel. [2]As the lords of the Philistines were passing on by hundreds and by thousands, and David and his men were passing on in the rear with Achish, [3]the commanders of the Philistines said, "What are these Hebrews doing here?" And Achish said to the commanders of the Philistines, "Is this not David, the servant of Saul, king of Israel, who has been with me now for days and years, and since he deserted to me I have found no fault in him to this day." [4]But the commanders of the Philistines were angry with him. And the commanders of the Philistines said to him, "Send the man back, that he may return to the place to which you have assigned him. He shall not go down with us to battle, lest in the battle he become an adversary to us. For how could this fellow reconcile himself to his lord? Would it not be with the heads of the men here? [5]Is not this David, of whom they sing to one another in dances,

'Saul has struck down his thousands,
and David his ten thousands'?"

[6]Then Achish called David and said to him, "As the Lord lives, you have been honest, and to me it seems right that you should march out and in with me in the campaign. For I have found nothing wrong in you from the day of your coming to me to this day. Nevertheless, the lords do not approve of you. [7]So go back now; and go peaceably, that you may not displease the lords of the Philistines." [8]And David said to Achish, "But what have I done? What have you found in your servant from the day I entered your service until now, that I may not go and fight against the enemies of my lord the king?" [9]And Achish answered David and said, "I know that you are as blameless in my sight as an angel of God. Nevertheless, the commanders of the Philistines have said, 'He shall not go up with us to the battle.' [10]Now then rise early in the morning with the servants of your lord who came with you, and start early in the morning, and depart as soon as you have light." [11]So David set out with his men early in the morning to return to the land of the Philistines. But the Philistines went up to Jezreel.

30 Now when David and his men came to Ziklag on the third day, the Amalekites had made a raid against the Negeb and against Ziklag. They had overcome Ziklag and burned it with fire [2]and taken captive the women and all[a] who were in it, both small and great. They killed no one, but carried them off and went their way. [3]And when David and his men came to the city, they found it burned with fire, and their wives and sons and daughters taken captive. [4]Then David and the people who were with him raised their voices and wept until they had no more strength to weep. [5]David's two wives also had been taken captive, Ahinoam of Jezreel and Abigail the widow of Nabal of Carmel. [6]And David was greatly distressed, for the people spoke of stoning him, because all the people were bitter in soul,[b] each for his sons and daughters. But David strengthened himself in the Lord his God.

[7]And David said to Abiathar the priest, the son of Ahimelech, "Bring me the ephod." So Abiathar brought the ephod to David. [8]And David inquired of the Lord, "Shall I pursue after this band? Shall I overtake them?" He answered him, "Pursue, for you shall surely overtake and shall surely rescue." [9]So David set out, and the six hundred men who were with him, and they came to the brook Besor, where those who were left behind stayed. [10]But David pursued, he and four hundred men. Two hundred stayed behind, who were too exhausted to cross the brook Besor.

[11]They found an Egyptian in the open country and brought him to David. And they gave him bread and he ate. They gave him water to drink, [12]and they gave him a piece of a cake of figs and two clusters of raisins. And when he had eaten, his spirit revived, for he had not eaten bread or drunk water for three days and three nights. [13]And David said to him, "To whom do you belong? And where are you from?" He said, "I am a

young man of Egypt, servant to an Amalekite, and my master left me behind because I fell sick three days ago. [14]We had made a raid against the Negeb of the Cherethites and against that which belongs to Judah and against the Negeb of Caleb, and we burned Ziklag with fire." [15]And David said to him, "Will you take me down to this band?" And he said, "Swear to me by God that you will not kill me or deliver me into the hands of my master, and I will take you down to this band."

[16]And when he had taken him down, behold, they were spread abroad over all the land, eating and drinking and dancing, because of all the great spoil they had taken from the land of the Philistines and from the land of Judah. [17]And David struck them down from twilight until the evening of the next day, and not a man of them escaped, except four hundred young men, who mounted camels and fled. [18]David recovered all that the Amalekites had taken, and David rescued his two wives. [19]Nothing was missing, whether small or great, sons or daughters, spoil or anything that had been taken. David brought back all. [20]David also captured all the flocks and herds, and the people drove the livestock before him,[c] and said, "This is David's spoil."

[21]Then David came to the two hundred men who had been too exhausted to follow David, and who had been left at the brook Besor. And they went out to meet David and to meet the people who were with him. And when David came near to the people he greeted them. [22]Then all the wicked and worthless fellows among the men who had gone with David said, "Because they did not go with us, we will not give them any of the spoil that we have recovered, except that each man may lead away his wife and children, and depart." [23]But David said, "You shall not do so, my brothers, with what the LORD has given us. He has preserved us and given into our hand the band that came against us. [24]Who would listen to you in this matter? For as his share is who goes down into the battle, so shall his share be who stays by the baggage. They shall share alike." [25]And he made it a statute and a rule for Israel from that day forward to this day.

[26]When David came to Ziklag, he sent part of the spoil to his friends, the elders of Judah, saying, "Here is a present for you from the spoil of the enemies of the LORD." [27]It was for those in Bethel, in Ramoth of the Negeb, in Jattir, [28]in Aroer, in Siphmoth, in Eshtemoa, [29]in Racal, in the cities of the Jerahmeelites, in the cities of the Kenites, [30]in Hormah, in Bor-ashan, in Athach, [31]in Hebron, for all the places where David and his men had roamed.

31 Now the Philistines were fighting against Israel, and the men of Israel fled before the Philistines and fell slain on Mount Gilboa. [2]And the Philistines overtook Saul and his sons, and the Philistines struck down Jonathan and Abinadab and Malchi-shua, the sons of Saul. [3]The battle pressed hard against Saul, and the archers found him, and he was badly wounded by the archers. [4]Then Saul said to his armor-bearer, "Draw your sword, and thrust me through with it, lest these uncircumcised come and thrust me through, and mistreat me." But his armor-bearer would not, for he feared greatly. Therefore Saul took his own sword and fell upon it. [5]And when his armor-bearer saw that Saul was dead, he also fell upon his sword and died with him. [6]Thus Saul died, and his three sons, and his armor-bearer, and all his men, on the same day together. [7]And when the men of Israel who were on the other side of the valley and those beyond the Jordan saw that the men of Israel had fled and that Saul and his sons were dead, they abandoned their cities and fled. And the Philistines came and lived in them.

[8]The next day, when the Philistines came to strip the slain, they found Saul and his three sons fallen on Mount Gilboa. [9]So they cut off his head and stripped off his armor and sent messengers throughout the land of the Philistines, to carry the good news to the house of their idols and to the people. [10]They put his armor in the temple of Ashtaroth, and they fastened his body to the wall of Beth-shan. [11]But when the inhabitants of Jabesh-gilead heard what the Philistines had done to Saul, [12]all the valiant men arose and went all night and took the body of Saul and the bodies of his sons from the wall of Beth-shan, and they came to Jabesh and burned them there. [13]And they took their bones and buried them under the tamarisk tree in Jabesh and fasted seven days.

a Septuagint; Hebrew lacks *and all*   b Compare 22:2   c The meaning of the Hebrew clause is uncertain

Overview: David's predicament about whether he should (or would be allowed to) fight with the Philistines against his fellow Israelites causes these interpreters to wonder about his motives. Was David waiting for the Lord to act? Would he have fought against Israel? Or would he have turned deceptively against the Philistines? At the same time, the reformers praise David's shrewd leadership after Ziklag is captured and burned. Saul, by contrast, meets a lonely death on account of his poor leadership decisions.

29:1-11 *Rejection of David*

Living by God's Word in Troubled Times. Johannes Bugenhagen: David is seen to have had some doubts. It is as if he were thinking, "The children of Israel are my people, yet I have sworn faithfulness to the king of the Philistines. At the same time, God wants to punish the impious children of Israel. God does not want to give his faithful servant over to God's enemies, but I should also not make my faith into more than the will of God (just as they now do with their monastic vows). I understand neither the one option nor the other. But I know this: I can follow neither side with a good conscience. Therefore I wait for the will of God in whatever I am called to do, for God will not push me away in this time of need, nor will God cause me to do what is against his will. Either way the people will have passed judgment over me." Faith in humans comes to nothing when faith in God requires something else. God presents the second table of the law so that we should excel in keeping faith, promises, oaths and the like with each other, but not at the expense of the first table. In fact, no oaths or vows are superior to the first table of the law, unless you want to stand before the devil rather than God. For your own thoughtlessness does not need to be so great that you do injury to divine truth. God is truth, you are given to lying, and you ought to be humble before God, who will cause you to fall by the vows and oaths on which it is impossible to stand without going against God's Word. Therefore God liberates David here and gathers the advice of the Philistines about sending him back. For in this case, if you let God work, then God will give counsel, so that you will be liberated without a bad conscience. In the same way, God liberates those who had been devoted to human traditions, so that they can conscientiously violate those vows through the Word of God, which has been taught from God. This is like the time when David did not have anything against his conscience in chapter 25 above, but rather gave thanks to God that he did not proceed with his oath. On this subject, however, there are those today who without the Word of God (and therefore in bad conscience) heedlessly attack everything, doing so in the name of gospel freedom. This is the freedom of the flesh and a great scandal to the gospel. This is not, I say, the same thing I have just been describing. Commentary on 1 Samuel.[1]

Fencing in the Heart. Daniel Dyke: When the Philistines were going out to war against the Israelites, they dared not allow David to go with them. They were jealous of him because of the love he bore to his own country. Therefore they put him out of the military. How happy would our spiritual war with Satan be if we could as easily rid ourselves of our deceitful hearts as they did themselves of David! Without doubt we have far greater cause to suspect our hearts than they did of David. The acquaintance of the flesh with Satan—and Satan's interest in the flesh—is greater than the Israelites' acquaintance of David. Besides that, the Philistines never had any experience of David's deceitfulness and unfaithfulness as we have had of our flesh. Therefore I wish we could rid ourselves entirely of this treacherous and perfidious flesh! But since it sticks so close to us, and we cannot possibly remove it from ourselves, we must always have an eye over it just as we would over an untrustworthy and pilfering servant who—if not closely observed—would steal from us. For certainly such is the deceitfulness of our hearts that if we took our eyes off of them they would throw off the yoke of the

---

[1]Bugenhagen, *In Samuelem prophetam*, 278-80.

Lord and make a run for it! Therefore we must keep our hearts as closely monitored as the jailor does his prisoner. The Mystery of Self-Deceiving.[2]

Did David Lie? Andrew Willet: Some think David had no intention at all to fight against Israel. Rather, he would have only defended the king's person, who said he would make David keeper of his head for ever. But this does not agree with David's own words. David seemed to be discontented because he was sent back and not allowed to fight against the enemies of the king. It seems therefore that he was fully in support of the Philistine king and that he was willing to go and fight against Israel. Others think that the Philistines' war against Saul at this time was just, because this was the way the Lord intended to punish Saul's wickedness. And besides, the kingdom rightly belonged to David, and therefore he was merely seeking what was his own. But neither of these makes the war just. For regardless of how God intended to judge Saul here, the Philistines went to battle against the people of God in a malicious way. And though David was the anointed king, that is, the apparent heir of the kingdom, he had no such commandment to invade the kingdom of Israel. Instead, he was to wait his time. Some are of the opinion that David would have turned his force against Achish in the battle had he been allowed to fight. Yet in such a case David, rather than supporting the Philistine king, would have disrespected Achish, with whom he had found such kind hospitality. Therefore the best solution to this question is that David very astutely neither directly promised his help, as Josephus believed, nor directly affirmed it. Instead he waited on God for his direction. He prayed to God fervently in his heart that some impediment might occur so that he would not be forced to fight against the Israelites, and especially against his dear and beloved friend Jonathan. Harmony on 1 Samuel.[3]

Faith Among the Gentiles. Johannes Bugenhagen: Because the Gentile king Achish swears by God and later invokes God's angels, it is clear to see that an awareness of the true God had remained in the land from the time of the patriarchs, even though the false worship of God reigned there. Canaan—the son of Ham the son of Noah—first possessed the land, as you see illustrated later in the journeys of Abraham, Isaac and Jacob in Genesis. Many of them surely preached and taught the fear of God, as when Abraham, for instance, found Melchizedek that priest of God Most High in the land of Salem, among others. In Genesis 20 you also see how Abimelech, the king of the Palestinians in Gerar, had a holy conscience. But even though ideas about God survived to posterity, nothing remained of godliness except false worship where the preaching of God's Word had ceased. Commentary on 1 Samuel.[4]

30:1-20 David Overcomes Adversity

Always Expecting Trials. John Calvin: We must learn from the example given to us here. David had recovered his wives. After that, he won a great quantity of spoil from his enemies, and everyone who was in his company made themselves rich in one day. Well, two days had been spent in this business. But the third day brought them news of the defeat of the people of Israel (2 Sam 1:2). Thus when God has given us cause to rejoice—whether for a day or a month—let us learn to accept any trial with which he chooses to test us. . . . For we need to be continually tried, because our senses are too attached to this world; and we wish to make our own paradise on earth as though there were no blessedness greater than that! That is why God subjects us to so many changes, and causes us to be cast from one side to the other. Sermons on 2 Samuel.[5]

---

[2]Dyke, *The Mystery of Self-Deceiving*, 358*.
[3]Willet, *Harmony on 1 Samuel*, 307*.

[4]Bugenhagen, *In Samuelem prophetam*, 280.
[5]Calvin, *Sermons on Second Samuel*, 1:3-4.

Persecuted and Weeping. Andrew Willet: David was a figure of our Savior Christ, who was hated by his own people. Moses, that faithful servant of God, was also a figure of Christ. Thus it pleased the Lord to test David's patience; and now, being as it were plunged in the depth of sorrow, it was a sign to him that his deliverance was near at hand. David excessively wept together with the rest of the men for their present loss, since their wives and children had been carried away. But David further wept because he knew the Lord was chastising him for his sin. David's grievous weeping and lamenting serves as an example to us and, as such, confutes the opinion of the Stoics that a wise person is one who shows no passion, affection or ever changes his countenance. Harmony of 1 Samuel.[6]

30:21-31 The Men's Selfishness and David's Generosity

Equal Sharing of Goods. Peter Walpot: Humanity will hold a great sabbath. Yes, they will have a continual sabbath and will lead a most holy life on earth, when they rid their nature of two words—"mine" and "yours." These words have been and are today the cause of many wars. From where comes war and bloodshed, quarreling and fighting, envy and hatred, disunity and disruption, if not from private possessions and greed? For whoever deals in mine and yours, that is, with possessions, becomes a friend of avarice. . . . When the evil men of Belial said that the one hundred who remained behind during the raid on Ziklag should not share in the booty won there, David said, "Do not be like that, brothers, with what God has given us. Who will agree with you on this? The share of those who went shall be the share of those who remained behind. It should be divided equally." And since that time to this day that has been the custom and law in Israel. . . . How much more should this be the custom and law among the children of the New Testament?

What God has given us should be divided equally. True Yieldedness.[7]

David's Shrewd Generosity. Andrew Willet: David had found hospitality among some in his tribe, where he was able to hide himself while Saul pursued him. Therefore David showed his thankfulness by sending them presents. Besides, these people were his kindred and brothers, and it was therefore reasonable for David to first show his kindness to them. Moreover, these cities of Judah also had been robbed and spoiled by the Amalekites, as the Egyptian told David in verse 14. And because the Amalekites had robbed on the coast of Judah, David thought it reasonable that some restitution should be made to them for their losses. Additionally, it is by this means that David prepared their hearts and ingratiated himself into their affections, who afterward faithfully took part with David against the house of Saul. Harmony on 1 Samuel.[8]

31:1-13 Saul and His Sons Die

Saul Dies in His Unbelief. Johannes Bugenhagen: It is written in the Psalms: "Precious in the sight of the Lord is the death of his saints." This is no less true for the righteous Jonathan, who died fighting for the Lord's inheritance. For "the righteous, though they die early, will be at rest," as you read of the deaths of the righteous whom the world has judged to be contemptible and evil. But against others, it says in the psalm, "The death of the wicked is very evil." You read that here as it applies to Saul, who did not hope in the God of Israel and instead consulted the soothsayer, as it says in 1 Chronicles. Therefore, when pressed on by enemies while desperately leading in battle, Saul perished like the apostle Judas, who also perished as one who had earlier been greatly blessed by God. In the end, Saul was a blasphemer of the God of Israel among both the Gentiles and those who exalt God in the holy places. This is how

---

[6]Willet, *Harmony on 1 Samuel*, 334*.

[7]Liechty, ed., *Early Anabaptist Spirituality*, 139-41; citing Is 66.
[8]Willet, *Harmony on 1 Samuel*, 341*.

hypocrites meet their end, as it says in all of Job: "Do you not know this from of old, since humans were placed on earth, that the exulting of the wicked is short, and the joy of the godless but for a moment?" They reign gloriously and appear to be wise, righteous and the saviors of others, but their end reveals them to be in disgrace and blasphemy of God. This point relates to what Christ says of salt that has lost its flavor and what Paul wrote to the Romans: "The name of God is blasphemed among the Gentiles because of you." Then and now, God unmasks our hypocrites, who are covered in the most Christian skins before God begins to judge them by his word and expel them from the kingdom, as he turned the kingdom to David, that is, to Christ the son of David through faith in the holy gospel. COMMENTARY ON 1 SAMUEL.[9]

THE DEATH OF SAUL'S SONS. ANDREW WILLET: Here only three of Saul's sons are mentioned to have died in this battle. Ish-bosheth was not present, either because he was not a warrior or because he was left at home to be overseer of the families. All three of these sons died together with their father. None of them bore his father's punishment or suffered for his sin. They had sins of their own. Indeed, God's judgments worked in such a way that they coincided with the punish-ment of their father. This was so that evil parents might be warned that their wickedness may bring God's judgment on themselves and their posterity. But concerning Jonathan, because he was a good man his lamentable end deserves more compassion. It must be considered this way: Because Jonathan was a good man, regardless of how he ended his days he could not die in evil. God no doubt turned this temporal death of Jonathan to his everlasting glory. In fact God might have foreseen that if Jonathan had remained alive, his heart may have changed toward David. Therefore the Lord took him away. In this way God's judgments, though secret and hidden to us, are most just. HARMONY ON 1 SAMUEL.[10]

SAUL'S MULTIPLE DEATHS. JOHN CALVIN: Saul had to beg someone who was his enemy to kill him, since he was unable to do so himself (2 Sam 1:9). Saul, in desperation, had thrown himself on his sword in order to kill himself, but then he was not able to achieve it by himself and, as I have said, he had to beg his enemies to help him to do so. Since he had wickedly persecuted David, who was chosen and elected by God to succeed him, there was a very good reason why he should not simply die one death, but that he should actually die two or three times, as it were. SERMONS ON 2 SAMUEL.[11]

---

[9]Bugenhagen, *In Samuelem prophetam*, 283-84; citing Ps 116:15; Wis 4:7; Ps 34:21 (Vg); 1 Chron 10:13; Job 20:4-5; Rom 2:24.

[10]Willet, *Harmony on 1 Samuel*, 342-43*.
[11]Calvin, *Sermons on Second Samuel*, 1:11.

COMMENTARY ON 2 SAMUEL

OVERVIEW: While this book encompasses the lives of Saul, Samuel and David, the reformers emphasize the role of David in the story of 2 Samuel, particularly as he serves as a type of Christ. These commentators praise David for his obedience to God and for being the vessel through whom Christ would come, but they also acknowledge David's sinful behavior and, thus, his occasional denial of the work of the Spirit in his life.

Prolegomena: *What This Book Is About*

OCCASIONS OF THE PSALMS. PETER MARTYR VERMIGLI: The first book of Samuel encompassed the things of Saul, the acts and sayings of Samuel and the beginning of David's reign. For David was inaugurated as king by Samuel secretly and separately, whereupon he conquered Goliath and began making incursions against the Philistines. How long Saul reigned is not able to be gathered in this story. Josephus said that Saul reigned for eighteen years while Samuel was living and then for twenty years after Samuel's death. In total, then, this would make Saul's reign to have lasted thirty-eight years. Nevertheless, Paul said in Acts 13 that Saul reigned for forty years. So it appears that Josephus is lacking two years in his calculation; but that's not too much. For often the year is diminished and out of order when numbering on behalf of the whole reign. But we know that David was inaugurated secretly by Samuel before he was designated as king publicly before all the people. Nevertheless, he had the full legal right to rule before he concluded the skirmish the Jabeshites had with the Philistines. Truly in this book and in the one before David's kingdom is discussed; and these books offer many occasions of the psalms without which I am scarcely able to understand them. COMMENTARY ON 2 SAMUEL.[1]

THE SPIRIT'S PRESERVATION OF THE KINGDOM. GIOVANNI DIODATI: The history of this book sets down the incomparable blessing through which David's life and reign were crowned and rewarded while he governed himself in this laudable manner by glorious victories and conquests, in peace, in security and in wealth. David had obedience, love and perfect respect from his people. His household was fruitful, prosperous and tranquil. He also enjoyed goodwill and respect from foreign nations and princes. But from another perspective, this history sets down how David deviated into fostering irregular desires, violence, dishonesty, ambition and pride. Such are the vices that ordinarily accompany absolute power. These actions thus brought about God's heavy hand, which included tragic occurrences and confusions. Such things happened in David's own family, in public revolts and in practices against his person. In turn, divisions, factions, civil wars, plagues and other scourges occurred in his kingdom.

In the end, however, the Holy Spirit, by which David was sealed, never utterly abandoned him to

---

[1]Vermigli, *In duos libros Samuelis*, 181.

unbridled liberty. Rather, by the ministry of his Word, the Spirit continually recalled David to humble and sincere confessions, genuine regrets and a deep repentance and loyal conversion. This was followed by an exemplary patience and humility in bearing God's punishments for his offenses. As a result, God tempered his severity against David. God received him again into grace and peace, and for his love of him had mercy on his people. God converted all these evil actions into a greater rest, glory and happiness. All of this was done by virtue of God's free will, for God chose David as a sacred type of Christ and progenitor according to the flesh. This was done so that God would give a sign and pledge of the eternity and blessedness of Christ's kingdom in the subsistence and prosperity of David's kingdom and posterity. ANNOTATIONS ON 2 SAMUEL.[2]

KINGDOM LIKE A MUSTARD SEED. ANDREW WILLET: As the former book contains the histories of such things that were done under Samuel and Saul, so this book sets forth the acts of David. In particular, three things are dealt with in this book. The first includes the beginning, increase and flourishing of David's reign, and then the many troubles, treasons and oppositions against his kingdom. It also includes the story of David's fall and his rising again and reconciliation with God. The second part includes a notable difference between the reign of Saul and of David. For Saul's kingdom began with great glory and renown but ended in shame. Conversely, David's kingdom had but small beginnings yet increased more and more. The final part demonstrates how David was a lively type of Christ who found many enemies in the world that sought to suppress his kingdom from its infancy. But his dominion prevailed, and from a corner of the earth it has overtaken the world. HARMONY ON 2 SAMUEL.[3]

---

[2]Diodati, *Pious Annotations*, 179-80*.

[3]Willet, *Harmony on 2 Samuel*, 1*.

1:1-27 DAVID MOURNS THE DEATHS OF SAUL AND JONATHAN

¹*After the death of Saul, when David had returned from striking down the Amalekites, David remained two days in Ziklag.* ²*And on the third day, behold, a man came from Saul's camp, with his clothes torn and dirt on his head. And when he came to David, he fell to the ground and paid homage.* ³*David said to him, "Where do you come from?" And he said to him, "I have escaped from the camp of Israel."* ⁴*And David said to him, "How did it go? Tell me." And he answered, "The people fled from the battle, and also many of the people have fallen and are dead, and Saul and his son Jonathan are also dead."* ⁵*Then David said to the young man who told him, "How do you know that Saul and his son Jonathan are dead?"* ⁶*And the young man who told him said, "By chance I happened to be on Mount Gilboa, and there was Saul leaning on his spear, and behold, the chariots and the horsemen were close upon him.* ⁷*And when he looked behind him, he saw me, and called to me. And I answered, 'Here I am.'* ⁸*And he said to me, 'Who are you?' I answered him, 'I am an Amalekite.'* ⁹*And he said to me, 'Stand beside me and kill me, for anguish has seized me, and yet my life still lingers.'* ¹⁰*So I stood beside him and killed him, because I was sure that he could not live after he had fallen. And I took the crown that was on his head and the armlet that was on his arm, and I have brought them here to my lord."*

¹¹*Then David took hold of his clothes and tore them, and so did all the men who were with him.* ¹²*And they mourned and wept and fasted until evening for Saul and for Jonathan his son and for the people of the* Lord *and for the house of Israel, because they had fallen by the sword.* ¹³*And David said to the young man who told him, "Where do you come from?" And he answered, "I am the son of a sojourner, an Amalekite."* ¹⁴*David said to him, "How is it you were not afraid to put out your hand to destroy the* Lord's *anointed?"* ¹⁵*Then David called one of the young men and said, "Go, execute him." And he struck him down* so that he died. ¹⁶*And David said to him, "Your blood be on your head, for your own mouth has testified against you, saying, 'I have killed the* Lord's *anointed.'"*

¹⁷*And David lamented with this lamentation over Saul and Jonathan his son,* ¹⁸*and he said it*ᵃ *should be taught to the people of Judah; behold, it is written in the Book of Jashar.*ᵇ *He said:*

¹⁹*"Your glory, O Israel, is slain on your high*
    places!
  How the mighty have fallen!
²⁰*Tell it not in Gath,*
    publish it not in the streets of Ashkelon,
  lest the daughters of the Philistines rejoice,
    lest the daughters of the uncircumcised exult.

²¹*"You mountains of Gilboa,*
    let there be no dew or rain upon you,
    *nor fields of offerings!*ᶜ
  For there the shield of the mighty was defiled,
    the shield of Saul, not anointed with oil.

²²*"From the blood of the slain,*
    from the fat of the mighty,
  the bow of Jonathan turned not back,
    and the sword of Saul returned not empty.

²³*"Saul and Jonathan, beloved and lovely!*
    In life and in death they were not divided;
  they were swifter than eagles;
    they were stronger than lions.

²⁴*"You daughters of Israel, weep over Saul,*
    who clothed you luxuriously in scarlet,
    who put ornaments of gold on your apparel.

²⁵*"How the mighty have fallen*
    in the midst of the battle!

"Jonathan lies slain on your high places.
  ²⁶*I am distressed for you, my brother*
        Jonathan;
  very pleasant have you been to me;

> your love to me was extraordinary,
>   surpassing the love of women.

>   [27]"How the mighty have fallen,
>   and the weapons of war perished!"

a Septuagint; Hebrew *the Bow*, which may be the name of the lament's tune   b Or *of the upright*   c Septuagint *firstfruits*

OVERVIEW: David experiences a range of feelings upon the death of Saul and Jonathan. While these deaths in battle open the way for David to assume the kingship without any further rivalry, Saul had been David's respected sovereign and Jonathan his dear friend. As Calvin points out, the blessed end of exile quickly leads to new challenges for the returned leader, including a case requiring immediate judgment. In contrast to the pacifism of Anabaptists, some commentators notice that the Hebrew title for David's lament—"the song of the bow"—appears to support the rightful use of arms.

1:1-10 *The Amalekite's Tale*

DAVID'S LOVE FOR THE CHURCH. JOHN CALVIN: There was only one way for David to be able to relax his guard, and that was for him to know that Saul was dead. For it was while Saul was alive that David had first been banished from the land of Israel. After that, his life was in continual peril, so he lived in a nation where he was not welcome. He was suspect there and from one day to the next could be sought out and accused if anyone wished to catch him and his people. He was thus in a miserable and perplexing situation and would be a fugitive until God removed Saul from the world. Yet when this did happen, David began mourning, and the death of Saul was harder for him to bear than his own death. This was not because of Saul himself, but because of the consequences. For the people of God were so disastrously defeated that it seemed as though the worship of God would be abolished. It is quite certain that the well-being of the church was more precious to David than his own life. So when it seemed that God wished to give him relief, it was then in fact that he became even more distressed. Thus we can see how God exercised him

in all sorts of conditions, which provides an example for us. SERMONS ON 2 SAMUEL.[1]

TRYING TO WIN DAVID'S FAVOR. JOHN MAYER: After David's return from the slaughter of the Amalekites to Ziklag, a man came to him and brought him news of Saul's death. The man said that he had killed Saul at his own request once it became clear that Saul's case was hopeless. But here the man was lying. This appears by that which was said before at the end of 1 Samuel, which more accurately described Saul's death. The man told this story to David because he thought by doing so he could win favor with David. COMMENTARY ON 2 SAMUEL.[2]

THE YOUNG AMALEKITE LIES. JOHN CALVIN: Now the young man's story seemed very likely, and it was confirmed when he presented Saul's crown and bracelets to David. These insignia proved that Saul was dead, but they did not prove that the young man had killed him. Indeed, it is more likely that he lied, that he was boasting of something that was not true. This is how we take the words of David: "Your blood be upon you, in that you have testified that you have killed the anointed of the Lord" (2 Sam 1:16). David would not have chosen to express it like this if he had not perceived that his boasting was false. That is why David said that his blood would be on his own head. SERMONS ON 2 SAMUEL.[3]

WAS IT JUST TO PUT THE AMALEKITE TO DEATH? ANDREW WILLET: If this young man spoke the truth and gave an accurate account, he was justly killed. This is both out of respect for Saul who, as the Lord's anointed, should not have had

---

[1]Calvin, *Sermons on Second Samuel*, 1:1.
[2]Mayer, *Many Commentaries in One*, 356*.
[3]Calvin, *Sermons on Second Samuel*, 1:4.

any hand laid on him and out for respect of himself, a proselyte converted to the faith of Israel. We must also consider David's role, who was not the lawful magistrate. Second, even if this was a fabricated story he told, his condemnation was just, for he was judged by his own mouth. And in accordance with the imperial laws, a false testimony must be punished with the penalty of retaliation or equality. Third, it will be objected that one shouldn't die without the testimony of two or three witnesses. However, this is to be understood where there is no confession. But the voluntary confession of the party may suffice without further witness, as Joshua caused Achan to be stoned upon his own confession. Finally, we consider whether the confession was voluntary or forced and extorted by torment. For in this case the imperial laws provide clemency. But the confession of the Amalekite was voluntary. HARMONY ON 2 SAMUEL.[4]

1:11-16 David and His Men Mourn

BEING PATIENT WHEN AFFLICTED. JOHN CALVIN: Let us remember David's grief over Saul's death when the Lord multiplies our sadness. For we may be expecting him to reassure us. Indeed, he may give us the opportunity to feel his grace, and yet at the same time we may have the opposite experience of being angered and frustrated. Since this has already happened to David, we will by no means find it a new experience. So when God does not put an end to our distress and anxieties, we will not complain at all. In fact, when he withdraws one perplexity from us, he sends something else on us from which we were desperately fleeing! Thus our faith and our patience have to be tried in various conditions. Let us humble ourselves and submit ourselves to what God knows to be just and expedient. Above all, let us benefit from the example of David, so that we will not be dismayed when we experience what God was doing in him. SERMONS ON 2 SAMUEL.[5]

DAVID FORESHADOWS CHRIST'S COMMAND TO LOVE OUR ENEMIES. JOHN MAYER: There was great reason for David's being sorrowful for his dear friend Jonathan and for the people of God, but how he could truly be sorrowful for Saul does not so easily appear. For much good came of Saul's destruction. First, an end was put to tyranny under which the commonwealth had suffered. Second, David was rid of his deadly enemy who always fought against his life. And, third, the expected time now came of fulfilling the promise made to David concerning the prophecy of taking the kingdom from Saul. Yet it is not to be thought that David feigned this great sorrow, even for Saul. For although Saul hated David, David still loved Saul just as Christ bids us to love our enemies. What's more, as David's king and father-in-law, he could not but be greatly grieved at the news of Saul's death. COMMENTARY ON 2 SAMUEL.[6]

WHY DAVID MOURNED FOR SAUL AND JONATHAN. ANDREW WILLET: David and his whole band wept and mourned together after hearing of the lamentable death of Saul and of his sons. Afterward David himself continued to mourn as he uttered the song of lamentation. David mourned for Jonathan as a friend and because he was a good man. Although Saul was no friend to David, David still mourned for him because he was a valiant defender of the Israelites against their enemies. David, in fact, had spared Saul twice and refused to lay his hands on him, lamenting how he came to this miserable death. David benefited from the death of Saul since it ended Saul's cruel hatred and persecution of him. What's more, Saul's death brought about God's promise to David. And even though Saul's death was the result of his own poor decisions, David still lamented the king's death. Whereas David gave thanks to God for having vindicated his rebuke against Nabal, here he does not rejoice for Saul's overthrow because the situation was different. God was not dishonored. For although the kingdom suffered no loss by the

---

[4]Willet, *Harmony on 2 Samuel*, 4*.
[5]Calvin, *Sermons on Second Samuel*, 1:2.

[6]Mayer, *Many Commentaries in One*, 357*.

death of Nabal, it did with Saul's death. HARMONY OF 2 SAMUEL.[7]

1:17-27 David's Lament

DAVID'S ENCOURAGEMENT TO ISRAEL. JOHN CALVIN: David had composed this lamentation so that it would be spread all over the land. It was especially to encourage the children of Judah to practice shooting with the bow and to engage in military exercises so as not to lose courage after such a terrible defeat. The point is that this lamentation was linked with David's exhortation to the people always to be valiant. SERMONS ON 2 SAMUEL.[8]

JUSTIFICATION FOR THE BEARING OF ARMS. ANDREW WILLET: By this example of David, who in the midst of his mourning did not forget what was necessary for the good of the commonwealth, we are taught not to be overcome with grief and pensiveness, forgetting our duty and neglecting the means. Jacob said to his sons when they were ready to be famished for failure to help themselves, "Why do you look at one another?" And when Moses cried to God while the Egyptians pursued them, not knowing which way to turn himself, the Lord said to him, "Why do you cry to me? Tell the people of Israel to go forward." Since David taught his people the use of the bow, it is evident that there is a lawful use of armor and weapons, and that the servants of God may defend themselves against their enemies. This is contrary to the preposterous opinion of the Anabaptists, who deny the Christian all use of weapons. HARMONY ON 2 SAMUEL.[9]

SORROW FOR A FRIEND. LAMBERT DANEAU: In discussing the bounds and ends of true and Christian friendship, there are two special points to be decided on that are commonly brought into question. The first concerns the time: how long

friendship ought to remain and be continued. The second concerns the manner and how it ought to be observed, retained and kept: that is to say, what, how far and how much one friend is to perform and to do for another.

Concerning the first, which is of the time, let this stand for a definitive and resolute answer: it ought to be endless and to continue between them perpetually, even so long as they both shall live in this world.

And yet many times without any fault of theirs, by some casual error and mishap, it may so fall out that there may be good cause, either utterly to renounce and break off, or at least to withdraw and relent, friendship. For what if one of the friends should deny his faith and . . . become a faithless unbeliever. . . . Certainly in this case all friendship is to be utterly forsaken and all amity (if after sundry exhortations and admonitions the unbeliever still persists in his obstinate wrongdoing) must be quickly renounced. This should be done even though it causes the friend many times to suspend his determination and to linger some while in hope of amendment and repentance. For, even so likewise, at the death of a real friend (although we truly believe and rest assured that his soul is received into everlasting bliss) yet we have sorrow and lament— and sometimes very much so—as we may see in David. TRUE AND CHRISTIAN FRIENDSHIP.[10]

BETTER THAN A WOMAN'S LOVE. JOHN MAYER: The rest of David's lamentation is made for Jonathan, whose love toward David passed the love of women. This can be understood in one of two ways: passively, it refers to the love by which women are beloved of men, which is most fervent; actively, it refers to the love by which women love men as they are inclined to do by nature, which is oftentimes exceedingly great. COMMENTARY ON 2 SAMUEL.[11]

---

[7]Willet, *Harmony on 2 Samuel*, 4*.
[8]Calvin, *Sermons on Second Samuel*, 1:19.
[9]Willet, *Harmony on 2 Samuel*, 4-5*; citing Gen 42:1; Ex 14:15.

[10]Daneau, *True and Christian Friendship*, C2v-C3r*.
[11]Mayer, *Many Commentaries in One*, 361*.

2:1-32 DAVID GETS CLOSER TO KINGSHIP

[1]*After this David inquired of the Lord, "Shall I go up into any of the cities of Judah?" And the Lord said to him, "Go up." David said, "To which shall I go up?" And he said, "To Hebron."* [2]*So David went up there, and his two wives also, Ahinoam of Jezreel and Abigail the widow of Nabal of Carmel.* [3]*And David brought up his men who were with him, everyone with his household, and they lived in the towns of Hebron.* [4]*And the men of Judah came, and there they anointed David king over the house of Judah.*

When they told David, "It was the men of Jabesh-gilead who buried Saul," [5]*David sent messengers to the men of Jabesh-gilead and said to them, "May you be blessed by the Lord, because you showed this loyalty to Saul your lord and buried him.* [6]*Now may the Lord show steadfast love and faithfulness to you. And I will do good to you because you have done this thing.* [7]*Now therefore let your hands be strong, and be valiant, for Saul your lord is dead, and the house of Judah has anointed me king over them."*

[8]*But Abner the son of Ner, commander of Saul's army, took Ish-bosheth the son of Saul and brought him over to Mahanaim,* [9]*and he made him king over Gilead and the Ashurites and Jezreel and Ephraim and Benjamin and all Israel.* [10]*Ish-bosheth, Saul's son, was forty years old when he began to reign over Israel, and he reigned two years. But the house of Judah followed David.* [11]*And the time that David was king in Hebron over the house of Judah was seven years and six months.*

[12]*Abner the son of Ner, and the servants of Ish-bosheth the son of Saul, went out from Mahanaim to Gibeon.* [13]*And Joab the son of Zeruiah and the servants of David went out and met them at the pool of Gibeon. And they sat down, the one on the one side of the pool, and the other on the other side of the pool.* [14]*And Abner said to Joab, "Let the young men arise and compete before us." And Joab said, "Let them arise."* [15]*Then they arose and passed over by number, twelve for Benjamin and Ish-bosheth the son of Saul, and twelve of the servants of David.* [16]*And each caught his opponent by the head and thrust his sword in his opponent's side, so they fell down together. Therefore that place was called Helkath-hazzurim,[a] which is at Gibeon.* [17]*And the battle was very fierce that day. And Abner and the men of Israel were beaten before the servants of David.*

[18]*And the three sons of Zeruiah were there, Joab, Abishai, and Asahel. Now Asahel was as swift of foot as a wild gazelle.* [19]*And Asahel pursued Abner, and as he went, he turned neither to the right hand nor to the left from following Abner.* [20]*Then Abner looked behind him and said, "Is it you, Asahel?" And he answered, "It is I."* [21]*Abner said to him, "Turn aside to your right hand or to your left, and seize one of the young men and take his spoil." But Asahel would not turn aside from following him.* [22]*And Abner said again to Asahel, "Turn aside from following me. Why should I strike you to the ground? How then could I lift up my face to your brother Joab?"* [23]*But he refused to turn aside. Therefore Abner struck him in the stomach with the butt of his spear, so that the spear came out at his back. And he fell there and died where he was. And all who came to the place where Asahel had fallen and died, stood still.*

[24]*But Joab and Abishai pursued Abner. And as the sun was going down they came to the hill of Ammah, which lies before Giah on the way to the wilderness of Gibeon.* [25]*And the people of Benjamin gathered themselves together behind Abner and became one group and took their stand on the top of a hill.* [26]*Then Abner called to Joab, "Shall the sword devour forever? Do you not know that the end will be bitter? How long will it be before you tell your people to turn from the pursuit of their brothers?"* [27]*And Joab said, "As God lives, if you had not spoken, surely the men would not have given up the pursuit of their brothers until the morning."* [28]*So Joab blew the trumpet, and all the men stopped and pursued Israel no more, nor did they fight anymore.*

[29]*And Abner and his men went all that night through the Arabah. They crossed the Jordan, and marching the whole morning, they came to Mahanaim.*

³⁰*Joab returned from the pursuit of Abner. And when he had gathered all the people together, there were missing from David's servants nineteen men besides Asahel. ³¹But the servants of David had struck down* of Benjamin 360 of Abner's men. ³²*And they took up Asahel and buried him in the tomb of his father, which was at Bethlehem. And Joab and his men marched all night, and the day broke upon them at Hebron.*

a *Helkath-hazzurim* means *the field of sword-edges*

OVERVIEW: For the reformers, that David seeks and obeys the guidance of the Lord witnesses to the value of prayer and spiritual discernment. The commandment to honor father and mother undergirds David's praise of the Jebusites for burying Saul. Sensitive to contemporary debates about baptism, magisterial reformers interpret David's second anointing at Hebron as an outward affirmation of his earlier call to lead, not as a second baptism. In similarly pointed comments against Anabaptists, many interpreters highlight David's just use of military force in this chapter. However, as a more cautionary tale, Asahel's trust in his own strength and his determination to pursue Abner leads to an untimely death.

2:1-3 David Seeks the Lord

GUIDED BY GOD'S WORD. JOHN CALVIN: Now it is stated that "David took counsel of God" . . . and received the reply that he could go up to the country of Judah. God even told him the precise town: Hebron. Here we must note that David did not enter battle without good preparation. He would undertake absolutely no enterprise unless he was continually guided by the will of God. It had to be proved to him that it was the right way. We have already seen this several times, but it is a doctrine that cannot too often be repeated. That is why it is mentioned so often in holy Scripture. Let us by no means think it a waste of time for us to study most carefully how David plodded on in such humility, how he never moved a finger, so to speak, or lifted a foot to go one way or the other, unless God guided him with the infallible testimony of his Word. SERMONS ON 2 SAMUEL.[1]

CERTAIN YET UNCERTAIN. PETER MARTYR VERMIGLI: David was certain of the former promise of God that he would be king; but he was uncertain about when or at which place this would occur. Therefore David consulted God of the place and the time in which he should take the auspices of the kingdom. . . . Actually, David already had the right to be king by law after Saul's death; nevertheless he was not willing to take possession of the kingdom without the clear command of God. COMMENTARY ON 2 SAMUEL.[2]

DAVID'S INQUIRY ABOUT WHICH CITY OF JUDAH. KONRAD PELLIKAN: Although David knew for sure that he had been elected by God as king, he did not know the time in which the kingdom would be extended to him. And he did not rashly seize the kingdom after Saul's death as though it were a debt owed him, but everything depended on the Lord, without whose will and command David presumed nothing. . . . After hearing about the king's death, David consulted the Lord by means of the priest whether he should go up to one of the cities of Judah. Now Judah was the tribe long before designated as the tribe of rule and kingship after Jacob's death. Nevertheless, David did not inquire whether the kingdom deserved to come to him; for he waited patiently on the calling of God and did not seek the kingdom. But he asked whether he would be allowed to depart to one of the cities of Judah. That is because Ziklag, although it technically belonged to the territory of Judah, was too much in the extremities of the tribe and David really only held that territory by the gift and benefit of Achish [the king of the Philistines]. Therefore,

---

[1]Calvin, *Sermons on Second Samuel*, 1:48.

[2]Vermigli, *In duos libros Samuelis*, 185.

after inquiring of which city in Judah he should go, David heard "Hebron," and so he entered the city with his wives and family. COMMENTARY ON 2 SAMUEL.[3]

2:4 David's Second Anointing

ONE BAPTISM, TWO ANOINTINGS. JOHN CALVIN: Now a question may be raised here: how could the men of Judah dare anoint David, given that this would efface the original anointing, or declare it insufficient? And how could David allow it? For when Samuel came to him, David knew that he was the organ and instrument of the hand of God (1 Sam 16:1-13). Though David had received that anointing, he then seems not to be content with it, and despises the authority of God and of his prophet by receiving this new anointing by the people. We must note that that anointing was not like baptism, for we are baptized only once, and if we return for a second baptism, this is in effect wishing to negate the true baptism, which was ordained by God. But anointing was different. For when Samuel came to David, it was to assure him that God had chosen and kept him. So when the people anointed David, they were not implying that what Samuel did was ineffective, or that it was not powerful enough to accomplish anything. Rather, it is as though they were replying "Amen," and ratifying what had been done. We should understand, therefore, that David is not elected king here by the desire of men, but that he received approbation because God authorized it, and thus people agree with it. SERMONS ON 2 SAMUEL.[4]

THE SECOND OF THREE ANOINTINGS. JOHANNES BUGENHAGEN: David was anointed king three times. First, Samuel anointed him by God's command to be God's chosen king. Second, he was anointed by Judah. Third, he was anointed by all Israel, when they all declared him to be their king. This external anointing by people has signified nothing new, other than public acclamation. COMMENTARY ON 2 SAMUEL.[5]

GOD'S PROMISES ARE SURE BUT SLOW. PETER MARTYR VERMIGLI: The end of Saul's reign is the beginning of David's.... David was first inaugurated as king secretly and separately by Samuel. Then two confirmations followed this. The first confirmation occurred so that David would be received in some part of the land of Judah, which was the tribe from which he came; the second confirmation then occurred before the entire kingdom. In this way we see that God does not fulfill his promises immediately, but gradually.... For instance, God initially gives Abraham a promise in the form of a seed, then as the land of Canaan, and finally as Christ, through whom he blesses the whole world. But none of these things came about quickly. First it was given to the sons of Isaac, who had two sons: Jacob and Esau. And Jacob had twelve sons, who became patriarchs who went down to Egypt. After three hundred years the people there had increased, were led out of Egypt by Moses and then were brought together by Joshua into the land of Canaan. And then after this were added all of the judges. Then Samuel and Saul strengthened the people. But David fulfilled the promise of the kingdom, and although it was interrupted and there were gaps in successive reigns, it endured in a certain way until the time of Christ. In this way, although God certainly keeps his promises, he sometimes delays in fulfilling them. COMMENTARY ON 2 SAMUEL.[6]

A SECOND ANOINTING TO GIVE CONFIRMATION. ANDREW WILLET: This anointing was done for David's further confirmation, namely, that by this second anointing he might be strengthened in the absolute expectation of the kingdom. For it is in our weakness that we need to be continually supported. For the first anointing by Samuel revealed that God had elected him. The second

[3]Pellikan, *Commentaria Bibliorum*, 2:106r.
[4]Calvin, *Sermons on Second Samuel*, 1:55-56.
[5]Bugenhagen, *In Samuelem prophetam*, 292; citing 2 Sam 5.
[6]Vermigli, *In duos libros Samuelis*, 181-82.

anointing by the men of Judah showed their consent and approbation. David was a type of Christ. And the spiritual anointing of our Messiah was often testified and declared to the church for our further confirmation by predictions from the old prophets, Jesus' baptism by John the Baptist, God's own voice from heaven at Jesus' baptism and many other signs and miracles. HARMONY ON 2 SAMUEL.[7]

2:5-7 David's Blessing of the Jabeshites

HONORING ONE'S "PARENTS." PETER MARTYR VERMIGLI: "May you be blessed by Jehovah," that is, he was saying: "Truly you are to be praised, for your action of honoring Saul's body was right because it agreed with the Word of God." For God commands that we honor our parents. And the magistrate is the common parent of the kingdom. Paul says to the Ephesians that this is the first command "with a promise" attached to it. For God willed that this promise be clearly shown so that we, Paul says, live long in the land. But, you might say, Paul also said that honoring God was a higher command, and it appears that fleeing idolatry is attached to that promise. For instance, it says, "I will the visit iniquity of the fathers on the children and the children's children, to the third and the fourth generation." But he also promises the opposite—that he himself wishes to extend mercy to a thousand generations. But this promise is general. For it is not given what that future mercy will be, though it is certain that this mercy will be specific to long life. COMMENTARY ON 2 SAMUEL.[8]

A KINGDOM THAT BEGINS WITH GENEROSITY. ANDREW WILLET: Some think the men of Jabesh Gilead were expressing disapproval of David by means of their loyalty to his professed enemy. But it seems that David himself had made inquiries about the bodies of Saul and his sons. He wanted to give them an honorable burial. And for that he gave

thankful commendation to the men of Jabesh Gilead for what they had done. When David commended this dutiful regard to them, he demonstrated that he was very unlike the examples of the pagan captains and commanders Sylla, Marius, Antonius and Octavius, who sought revenge on those who had taken part against them. David wished that God would show mercy and truth to the men of Jabesh Gilead. God's mercy and goodness is seen as a promising reward for our faithful service, including his truth and fidelity in performing it. There is, therefore, no revenge at God's hands, but he crowns and rewards in mercy the faithfulness of his servants. David also promised to pay back the kindness that the men showed to their master. Their loving affection toward their king deserved a man's reward. David, succeeding in the kingdom, decided it was his job to see such good subjects compensated. They didn't deserve God's hand, but they may deserve a good turn or blessing from a man's hand. And so David begins his kingdom with princely generosity and charity, which wins the hearts of subjects. These subjects are in God's stead here on earth, and represent and imitate that great king in mercy and bounty. David also demonstrated that he was a good king. He was appointed to punish the wicked and to praise and reward those who did good. Just as when he put to death the Amalekite for confessing he had killed Saul, so now he promised rewards to the Jabeshites for their kindness toward him. HARMONY ON 2 SAMUEL.[9]

2:8-32 Fighting Between Joab and Abner

NOT A SPORT. LANCELOT ANDREWES: If peace is a blessing, and a chief of God's blessings, we may reduce from this what war is. We may do no worse than to say it is "the rod of God's anger" in Isaiah, God's "iron" teeth in Amos and "the hammer of the whole earth" in Jeremiah—whereby God dashes two nations together. One of them must fall in pieces; both are the worse for it. War is no matter of sport. Indeed I see Abner esteem it as a sport: "Let's have

[7]Willet, *Harmony on 2 Samuel*, 9*.
[8]Vermigli, *In duos libros Samuelis*, 186; citing Eph 6:2; Ex 34:7.
[9]Willet, *Harmony on 2 Samuel*, 9-10*.

some of the young men get up," he says to Joab, "and fight hand to hand in front of us." But I see the same Abner before the end of the same chapter weary of his sport and treating with Joab for an end of it. "Must the sword devour forever?" he says. "Don't you realize that this will end in bitterness?" So it may begin as a sport; but it will "end in bitterness" if it holds long. COLLECTION OF LECTURES.[10]

AFFIRMATION OF THE JUST WAR THEORY. ANDREW WILLET: Joab, by David's authority, fought against Abner and his men. He obtained victory over them and destroyed Abner and his 360 men. We see, therefore, that it is lawful for Christians on certain occasions to enter battle. This is apparent from Scripture. First, when the soldiers came to John the Baptist, he did not ask them to renounce their calling. He only said, "Do not extort money from anyone by threats or by false accusation, and be content with your wages." He would only have them keep limitations within boundaries. Second, Cornelius the centurion in Acts 10 pleased God in his calling as a soldier. His prayers were heard, and his alms were accepted before God. Third, God gave many laws to his people about war. In Deuteronomy 20:6-7, it is prescribed who should be exempted from battle and in what manner they should behave themselves. But if it had been unlawful at all to make war, it would have been altogether prohibited and restrained instead of only certain orders and rules that were commended. Fourth, war is also ascribed to God: "The Lord will have war with Amalek." In yet another passage, David is said to be "fighting the battles of the Lord." Yet God is not the author of evil. HARMONY ON 2 SAMUEL.[11]

NOT BY STRENGTH ALONE. JOHN CALVIN: The first detail we must notice concerning the death of Asahel is that he was "swift in running." This is intended to show that those who have some strong point always presume on it more than they should. That is what caused the death of Asahel. He trusted too much in his own agility. He pushed himself in running, and he thought it was great to have pursued and caught up with his enemy. He gave no thought to their encounter, and felt that he was valiant enough to fight Abner. He thought that he had done enough by merely stopping him, but was foolishly deceiving himself. Let us learn, therefore, from this example, that when God gives us some strength, we are to be so temperate that we will in no way abuse it. SERMONS ON 2 SAMUEL.[12]

SWIFT AS A HORSE. ANDREW WILLET: Asahel was a brother to Joab and Abishai. All were in this battle and numbered among David's worthies. Asahel is said to be swift as a deer, like Saul and Jonathan, who are said to be swifter than eagles. Josephus wrote that he was so swift that he not only contended with men but even contended with a horse in running. We see in Ecclesiastes that "The race is not to the swift, nor the battle to the strong. . . ." Asahel's swiftness, which he trusted too much, was the cause of his ruin. It teaches us not to be too confident in our strength or in any other gift, whether inward or outward. Josiah, a good prince, trusted his own strength and went against Pharaoh. But he should not have done so, for he was killed in battle. Cicero's eloquence was the cause of his confusion. And finally, Milo, renowned for his strength, tried to bend an oak with his arms and was caught in the cleft; the tree then returned to its place and Milo was left to be a prey to the wild beasts. HARMONY ON 2 SAMUEL.[13]

---

[10]Andrewes, *A Collection of Lectures*, 330-31*; citing Is 10:5; Am 1:3; Jer 50:23.

[11]Willet, *Harmony on 2 Samuel*, 14*; citing Lk 3:14; Ex 17:16; 1 Sam 25:28.

[12]Calvin, *Sermons on Second Samuel*, 1:77-78.

[13]Willet, *Harmony on 2 Samuel*, 13*; citing Eccl 9:11.

3:1–4:12 THE END OF DAVID'S OPPOSITION

¹There was a long war between the house of Saul and the house of David. And David grew stronger and stronger, while the house of Saul became weaker and weaker.

²And sons were born to David at Hebron: his firstborn was Amnon, of Ahinoam of Jezreel; ³and his second, Chileab, of Abigail the widow of Nabal of Carmel; and the third, Absalom the son of Maacah the daughter of Talmai king of Geshur; ⁴and the fourth, Adonijah the son of Haggith; and the fifth, Shephatiah the son of Abital; ⁵and the sixth, Ithream, of Eglah, David's wife. These were born to David in Hebron.

⁶While there was war between the house of Saul and the house of David, Abner was making himself strong in the house of Saul. ⁷Now Saul had a concubine whose name was Rizpah, the daughter of Aiah. And Ish-bosheth said to Abner, "Why have you gone in to my father's concubine?" ⁸Then Abner was very angry over the words of Ish-bosheth and said, "Am I a dog's head of Judah? To this day I keep showing steadfast love to the house of Saul your father, to his brothers, and to his friends, and have not given you into the hand of David. And yet you charge me today with a fault concerning a woman. ⁹God do so to Abner and more also, if I do not accomplish for David what the LORD has sworn to him, ¹⁰to transfer the kingdom from the house of Saul and set up the throne of David over Israel and over Judah, from Dan to Beersheba." ¹¹And Ish-bosheth could not answer Abner another word, because he feared him.

¹²And Abner sent messengers to David on his behalf,ᵃ saying, "To whom does the land belong? Make your covenant with me, and behold, my hand shall be with you to bring over all Israel to you." ¹³And he said, "Good; I will make a covenant with you. But one thing I require of you; that is, you shall not see my face unless you first bring Michal, Saul's daughter, when you come to see my face." ¹⁴Then David sent messengers to Ish-bosheth, Saul's son, saying, "Give me my wife Michal, for whom I paid the bridal price of a hundred foreskins of the Philis-

tines." ¹⁵And Ish-bosheth sent and took her from her husband Paltiel the son of Laish. ¹⁶But her husband went with her, weeping after her all the way to Bahurim. Then Abner said to him, "Go, return." And he returned.

¹⁷And Abner conferred with the elders of Israel, saying, "For some time past you have been seeking David as king over you. ¹⁸Now then bring it about, for the LORD has promised David, saying, 'By the hand of my servant David I will save my people Israel from the hand of the Philistines, and from the hand of all their enemies.'" ¹⁹Abner also spoke to Benjamin. And then Abner went to tell David at Hebron all that Israel and the whole house of Benjamin thought good to do.

²⁰When Abner came with twenty men to David at Hebron, David made a feast for Abner and the men who were with him. ²¹And Abner said to David, "I will arise and go and will gather all Israel to my lord the king, that they may make a covenant with you, and that you may reign over all that your heart desires." So David sent Abner away, and he went in peace.

²²Just then the servants of David arrived with Joab from a raid, bringing much spoil with them. But Abner was not with David at Hebron, for he had sent him away, and he had gone in peace. ²³When Joab and all the army that was with him came, it was told Joab, "Abner the son of Ner came to the king, and he has let him go, and he has gone in peace." ²⁴Then Joab went to the king and said, "What have you done? Behold, Abner came to you. Why is it that you have sent him away, so that he is gone? ²⁵You know that Abner the son of Ner came to deceive you and to know your going out and your coming in, and to know all that you are doing."

²⁶When Joab came out from David's presence, he sent messengers after Abner, and they brought him back from the cistern of Sirah. But David did not know about it. ²⁷And when Abner returned to Hebron, Joab took him aside into the midst of the gate

to speak with him privately, and there he struck him in the stomach, so that he died, for the blood of Asahel his brother. ²⁸Afterward, when David heard of it, he said, "I and my kingdom are forever guiltless before the Lord for the blood of Abner the son of Ner. ²⁹May it fall upon the head of Joab and upon all his father's house, and may the house of Joab never be without one who has a discharge or who is leprous or who holds a spindle or who falls by the sword or who lacks bread!" ³⁰So Joab and Abishai his brother killed Abner, because he had put their brother Asahel to death in the battle at Gibeon.

³¹Then David said to Joab and to all the people who were with him, "Tear your clothes and put on sackcloth and mourn before Abner." And King David followed the bier. ³²They buried Abner at Hebron. And the king lifted up his voice and wept at the grave of Abner, and all the people wept. ³³And the king lamented for Abner, saying,

> "Should Abner die as a fool dies?
> ³⁴Your hands were not bound;
>   your feet were not fettered;
> as one falls before the wicked
>   you have fallen."

And all the people wept again over him. ³⁵Then all the people came to persuade David to eat bread while it was yet day. But David swore, saying, "God do so to me and more also, if I taste bread or anything else till the sun goes down!" ³⁶And all the people took notice of it, and it pleased them, as everything that the king did pleased all the people. ³⁷So all the people and all Israel understood that day that it had not been the king's will to put to death Abner the son of Ner. ³⁸And the king said to his servants, "Do you not know that a prince and a great man has fallen this day in Israel? ³⁹And I was gentle today, though anointed king. These men, the sons of Zeruiah, are more severe than I. The Lord repay the evildoer according to his wickedness!"

4 When Ish-bosheth, Saul's son, heard that Abner had died at Hebron, his courage failed, and all Israel was dismayed. ²Now Saul's son had two men who were captains of raiding bands; the name of the one was Baanah, and the name of the other Rechab, sons of Rimmon a man of Benjamin from Beeroth (for Beeroth also is counted part of Benjamin; ³the Beerothites fled to Gittaim and have been sojourners there to this day).

⁴Jonathan, the son of Saul, had a son who was crippled in his feet. He was five years old when the news about Saul and Jonathan came from Jezreel, and his nurse took him up and fled, and as she fled in her haste, he fell and became lame. And his name was Mephibosheth.

⁵Now the sons of Rimmon the Beerothite, Rechab and Baanah, set out, and about the heat of the day they came to the house of Ish-bosheth as he was taking his noonday rest. ⁶And they came into the midst of the house as if to get wheat, and they stabbed him in the stomach. Then Rechab and Baanah his brother escaped.ᵇ ⁷When they came into the house, as he lay on his bed in his bedroom, they struck him and put him to death and beheaded him. They took his head and went by the way of the Arabah all night, ⁸and brought the head of Ish-bosheth to David at Hebron. And they said to the king, "Here is the head of Ish-bosheth, the son of Saul, your enemy, who sought your life. The Lord has avenged my lord the king this day on Saul and on his offspring." ⁹But David answered Rechab and Baanah his brother, the sons of Rimmon the Beerothite, "As the Lord lives, who has redeemed my life out of every adversity, ¹⁰when one told me, 'Behold, Saul is dead,' and thought he was bringing good news, I seized him and killed him at Ziklag, which was the reward I gave him for his news. ¹¹How much more, when wicked men have killed a righteous man in his own house on his bed, shall I not now require his blood at your hand and destroy you from the earth?" ¹²And David commanded his young men, and they killed them and cut off their hands and feet and hanged them beside the pool at Hebron. But they took the head of Ish-bosheth and buried it in the tomb of Abner at Hebron.

---

a Or where he was; Septuagint at Hebron   b Septuagint And behold, the doorkeeper of the house had been cleaning wheat, but she grew drowsy and slept. So Rechab and Baanah his brother slipped in

OVERVIEW: The reformers focus on the complicated nature of human relationships in the following texts. David's relationship with his wives and his children (who are introduced here) are well-known sources of trouble. Joab's murder of Abner results in the strange situation of David mourning an enemy commander and requiring his general Joab to attend Abner's burial. Though David defers in punishing Joab, he swiftly judges against Ish-bosheth's killers; as in the cases of Saul, Jonathan and Abner, David makes sure that his rival receives an honorable burial. Most of all, commentators emphasize that David works with God's favor, leading to his increase and the decrease of all who work against God's purposes.

3:1 Contrast Between Kingdoms

DAVID ALWAYS INCREASES. PETER MARTYR VERMIGLI: One statement in the beginning of this chapter can be stated to represent the whole section: The house of David always increased, while the house of Saul continuously decreased. The increasing of David's house is demonstrated by means of his many ascensions: first, by means of his growing progeny, which he began in Hebron; then by means of the treaty he struck with Abner, through which all of the Israelites inclined toward him; then by means of the restitution of his wife Michal; and finally by means of the death of Abner. This struggle was long-lasting, but David increased because he depended on faith and patience. But Ish-bosheth diminished day by day because he retained a kingdom that was opposed to God's Word. COMMENTARY ON 2 SAMUEL.[1]

DAVID RULES WITH GOD'S FAVOR. JOHANNES BUGENHAGEN: The beginning of this chapter could hardly describe a more elegant contrast between the fortunes awaiting Saul's reign and David's reign, that is, the difference between hypocrisy and truth. There was a battle in which one side was stronger and the other was weaker.

But gradually the one side increased because of God and the other failed. Moreover, the story describes how Abner, the leader of Ish-bosheth's military, after having grown angry with his lord the king, wanted to lead all Israel to David's command, for everyone acknowledged belonging to him. David rejoiced that the entire kingdom came to him without bloodshed and attributed this to the Lord's will and providence. Just as it is written in the psalm, "The Lord casts away the counsel of the princes," who are of the flesh, while the Lord wanted David to become king of all the people in such a way that no one could revoke their acceptance of him. COMMENTARY ON 2 SAMUEL.[2]

3:2-5 David's Children

DAVID'S DOUBLE SIN. JOHN CALVIN: Although David's virtue is lauded here, on the other hand we are shown that he did not keep God in mind in all his conduct.... For it is stated that he abandoned and forgot his true position most seriously, in that he had several wives—although he was not ignorant of the law of God. Since he already had one wife, it was as though his marriage was violated and broken by this plurality of women. For as was shown earlier, God did not create two women for one man, but a man must be the husband of one wife only. Here is the sentence God pronounced on the matter: "It is not good for a man to be alone, let us make a helper suitable for him" (Gen 2:18). He does not say, "Let us make him two or three women," but simply one. Thus it is a direct overturning of the ordinance of God and the institution of marriage when a man takes several wives. Moreover, David committed a double sin, for in addition to the common law, which speaks to everyone, it is stated particularly that the king should not take several wives (Deut 17:17). Now that prohibition is even stricter on kings, because kings tend to allow themselves more license, either when they are flattered or when no one dares to contradict them. Hence they may think they are

---

[1]Vermigli, *In duos libros Samuelis*, 195.

[2]Bugenhagen, *In Samuelem prophetam*, 294; citing Ps 33:10 (Vg).

not bound by the rules that control the common herd. That is why God pronounced this law. . . . Indeed, the point is not that he merely took two or three women, for he already had two when he began reigning in Hebron—Abigail the Carmelite and Ahinoam the Jezreelitess. . . . It is also stated above that he took a daughter of Talmai, king of Geshur. . . . It is likely that he did this in order to make an alliance and strengthen himself. He did not do it out of intemperance, but saw that he needed to gain friends. But be that as it may, he is still not to be excused for it. For if he was not excused for one iniquity, how could he be excused for increasing iniquities, especially since the law is expressly laid down for kings? He deserved, therefore, the chastisement of God. Hence, there is not the least excuse for David—no matter what circumstances one may allege. Indeed, after the third wife he takes the fourth, and fifth, and even the sixth—and finally he wants Michal back. SERMONS ON 2 SAMUEL.[3]

THE INTRODUCTION OF DAVID'S SONS. JO-HANNES BUGENHAGEN: These additions to the family are important. We should never truly trust in the flesh, for David's sons imposed a large cross on him. Amnon raped his sister, for which Absalom killed him. Then Absalom drove his father out of the kingdom. And without his father's knowledge, Adonijah wanted to occupy the throne. COMMENTARY ON 2 SAMUEL.[4]

THE NEED TO PRAY FOR ONE'S CHILDREN. ANDREW WILLET: God's providence extended to David while he was in exile. He had no children, but now being settled in his kingdom he had sons born to him. With six wives he had only six sons. This may be observed that the marriage of many wives was not blessed with fruitfulness: Solomon had seven hundred wives and three hundred concubines, yet only one son: Rehoboam. It seemed as though nature itself opposed such

marriages since they were contrary to the first institution in the creation. David had small comfort by these children. His eldest son Amnon committed incest and was killed by Absalom. Absalom rebelled against his father. Adonijah was put to death by Solomon. Therefore good men may be cursed in their children, so parents to whom God sends children must pray to God to make them good children. HARMONY ON 2 SAMUEL.[5]

3:6-30 Joab Murders Abner

ABNER AND JOAB. JOHANNES BUGENHAGEN: Already given occasion to turn his favor toward David because of his anger, Abner condemned himself before God in many settings by saying, "The Lord has sworn to David" and "The Lord has promised David, saying, 'By the hand of hand of my servant David I will save my people Israel from the hand of the Philistines, and from the hand of their enemies.'" If Abner knew these things, why did he take part in establishing another king according to blood, and for whose defense blood was shed? Moreover, why would Abner, who if allowed would have perpetually served the king against David, change his mind, unless the king were getting in the way of his desires? Therefore, he perished, but not before this great leader in Israel had come to his senses. He was much better and more righteous than the predatory Joab, by whom he was killed. For Joab, there was always a reason to fight, as you see in David's words in 1 Kings 2 and in Solomon's similar words. There it was given to Joab to know that because he avenged his brother's death with such hatred, Abner was always seen as the worthier leader by David. COMMENTARY ON 2 SAMUEL.[6]

JOAB'S EXPLOITS. JACOBUS ARMINIUS: Joab performed many distinguished deeds, which were prescribed by God, in fighting bravely against the

---

[3]Calvin, *Sermons on Second Samuel*, 1:93.
[4]Bugenhagen, *In Samuelem prophetam*, 295.

[5]Willet, *Harmony on 2 Samuel*, 14*.
[6]Bugenhagen, *In Samuelem prophetam*, 295; citing 1 Kings 2:31-32; 2:5.

enemies of the people of God on behalf of Israel, that it might be well with God's people. But God did not incline Joab's mind to do this as he ought. It is apparent that Joab sought his own glory in those deeds from the fact that he, by wicked treachery, destroyed human beings equal to himself in bravery and generalship, in order that he alone would be held in honor. An Examination of the Treatise of William Perkins Concerning Predestination.[7]

A Divine Blessing in Disguise. Andrew Willet: The causes that moved Joab to kill Abner were twofold: his hatred for the murder of his brother Asahel and his envy of Abner, who could have grown too great in the king's favor and so obscure him. The latter was the greater motive, which afterward caused him to kill Amasa. Yet he pretended it was the other reason, namely, the death of his brother, as the end of the verse shows. In the end Joab killed Abner in the same place where he previously killed Asahel. Joab committed that which was unworthy of himself and his master the king. Because of this he justly suffered afterward under Solomon. Nevertheless, the judgment of God justly fell on Abner, who was a wicked and bloody man. The Lord turned it to good for David in removing a newly reconciled enemy, who would hardly have proved faithful. Harmony on 2 Samuel.[8]

3:31-37 Mourning for Abner

Why David Made Joab Mourn for Abner. Andrew Willet: Joab might have thought about rejoicing and being glad that Abner was overthrown. Accordingly, it seems very strange that he would want to celebrate Abner's funeral. Some think David forced him to attend the funeral and made him play the hypocrite. But it was right and necessary that Joab—being a chief man under David—should not be lacking in this. David

therefore required him to do what was right. If Joab acted falsely, it was his own fault. For this reason it is good for civil leaders to want their subjects to come under the influence of religion. And if their subjects do not present themselves with true devotion, the offense rests with themselves and not in the one who commanded them. . . . David sought to fulfill this same duty to Joab as part of a punishment. . . . And this might be a way to bring Joab to acknowledge his sin, seeing the great lamentation that was made for Abner, whom he had killed. Harmony on 2 Samuel.[9]

David Forgets His Dignity. John Mayer: David said to Joab and to all the people, "Tear your clothes and put on sackcloth and mourn before Abner." It is strange . . . that David should command Joab to do this. Does he want Joab to feign sorrow when he is really happy that Abner is dead? The reason why David caused Joab to come and mourn was to honor the death of Abner, not only publicly with other captains and tribunes, but also so that Joab, who was the chief of all military commanders, would be brought to repentance by mourning. David thought that by weeping and being sorrowful with others, Joab might thereby be afflicted with sorrow and shame, since he was the primary actor of so great a mischief that moved so many, including the king himself. In fact, King David followed the casket to honor Abner. This is something a king never did, for regardless who is carried forth to burial, the king never goes after him in any country. This therefore showed how greatly David was affected by Abner's death. By forgetting his kingly dignity, he vowed to give him his honor. Commentary on 2 Samuel.[10]

3:38-39 These Sons of Zeruiah

Unflattering Phrase. Edward Kellett: Zeruiah, the mother of the three famous brothers Joab, Abishai and Asahel, was perhaps married to

---

[7] Arminius, *Works*, 3:436-37*.
[8] Willet, *Harmony on 2 Samuel*, 19*.
[9] Willet, *Harmony on 2 Samuel*, 21*.
[10] Mayer, *Many Commentaries in One*, 370-71*.

some base and ignoble man before David came to his greatness. Or she herself was an extraordinarily domineering woman, active in state and scheming and furthering the plots of her children, though she crossed her brother David. As a result, as I understand it, she is named not so much in honor as in dislike, "These men, the sons of Zeruiah, are more severe than I." Or another interpretive option is to understand the father of Joab and his brothers as having committed such a sin or sins that the remembrance of him was odious and might resemble Judas Iscariot, who deserved that "his name be blotted out in the second generation." MISCELLANIES OF DIVINITY.[11]

DAVID'S WEAKNESS AGAINST THE SONS OF ZERUIAH. JOHN MAYER: All the people understood that David was innocent and had no hand in Abner's death. Nevertheless David further cleared himself by saying, "Do you not know that a prince and a great man has fallen this day in Israel?" He said this to show how much he esteemed Abner and to prove that he was far from consenting to his destruction. And if any man should have objected and inquired why he did not punish the murderers, he added, "I am gentle today. . . . These men, the sons of Zeruiah, are more severe than I." This is as if David had said, "I am in my kingdom like a tender plant easily plucked up. If I were to provoke the sons of Zeruiah, as Ish-bosheth did Abner, they may soon draw all the people from me as Abner did from him."

But this was a great weakness in David to be so apprehensive in executing justice, especially since he had a promise from God of the kingdom that he could depend on against all conspirators. But there are many things alleged by some to exonerate David. First, they allege that David only deferred Joab's punishment, for he later ordered Solomon to put him to death, just as God himself often defers to punish the wicked. Second, for David to have punished Joab at that moment would have caused the commonwealth to greatly

weaken, which a prudent king ought to protect against. For when Honorius the emperor had cut off his general, Flavius Stilicho, it is said that he cut off his own hands. And indeed, Honorius never did any worthy act after this event. Third, the law of putting murderers to death does not bind one to do so at all times; instead the most astute decision must be made. Fourth, David was a figure of Christ, who was gentle toward the foulest sinners. And last, these interpreters allege, it is possible that by delaying to punish Joab, David was guided by the Spirit of God, as in many other things. COMMENTARY ON 2 SAMUEL.[12]

THE REASON WHY DAVID DELAYED PUNISHING JOAB. ANDREW WILLET: David prudently delayed in punishing Joab. He did so not because Joab was his kinsman and had been faithful to him in the time of his affliction, or because he deserved it and could not spare his service. David did so because the sons of Zeruiah were too hard and strong for him. And it seemed, in the history of Absalom, that Joab had more influence over his soldiers and military than David did. Therefore a wise person must consider what might be done and what ought to be done. David was not taking Joab's sin lightly, but thoughtfully charged his son to see justice executed. But here David prudently deferred the punishment only, which could not at present be undertaken without great risk. At other times, when it was in his power, he did not delay to do justice. This happened with the Amalekite who said he had killed Saul, and it also happened with those two who killed Ish-bosheth. A similar example is found with Jacob, who when his two sons Simeon and Levi had committed that shameful murder of the Shechemites, didn't proceed against them even though there was a magistrate in his own family. Instead he deferred justice till his death (Gen 49:5). For both his children were stubborn and unruly. They were too strong for him; and besides, there was no time to make a stir in his

---

[11]Kellett, *Miscellanies*, 41; citing 2 Sam 3:39; Ps 109:13.

[12]Mayer, *Many Commentaries in One*, 371-72*.

own family since they were surrounded by their enemies. HARMONY ON 2 SAMUEL.[13]

4:1-8 Ish-bosheth Murdered

THREE REASONS WHY THE ASSASSINS ENTERED AT THIS TIME. ALONSO TOSTADO: Someone will ask why these two men entered to kill Ish-bosheth at midday. I respond that these two men had been seeking an opportunity to kill Ish-bosheth, and therefore they selected midday because they thought such a time would be most accommodating for doing so. There are three reasons for this. First, at midday no one would see them in the village and be able to recognize them since it was then at the heat of the day—and in that land it was so hot that no one remained in the street but in their homes at such a time of day. These men feared to be recognized since they were already in the service of King Ish-bosheth and they had fled from their assignment; and because they thought they would not be seen at such a time, they entered the palace. The second reason these two men entered at midday was because all of the servants of the king were also in their homes, so they themselves were absent from the palace. They were away for the same reason the king was indisposed, for at this time of day all of the king's attendants were also taking a rest and therefore no one remained in the palace. In short, then, there were no impediments: Nobody remained in the palace, nobody entered and no servants were around threshing grain, etc. The third reason these two men chose this time of day was because they wanted to go to the king at such an occasion when it would be most easy to kill him, and such was the case when he himself was sleeping on his couch. And because they themselves knew the king would be resting on his couch, they chose to enter at this specific time to kill him. COMMENTARY ON 2 SAMUEL.[14]

ISH-BOSHETH'S DEATH. JOHN CALVIN: Now the custom of those times was different from ours today, for the ancients in this Eastern country were not accustomed to dining at midday, which was when they slept. For they got up with the sun in the summer, and stayed awake in winter until the sun had risen, so that they took part of their sleep in the middle of the day. And thus it is stated that Ish-bosheth, being on his couch, had his throat cut by these two brigands Rechab and Baanah—who nevertheless were his captains. Well, we have here reason to contemplate the judgments of God. Even though it was a despicable act, that those who were officers of the king should come and cut off his head, still it was a just ordinance of God, inasmuch as Ish-bosheth was reigning contrary to his will. And why is it that his subjects had been faithful to him, seeing that they did not want to submit to David, who was God's lieutenant and deputy? He knew that God had put David on the royal throne—indeed, as his lieutenant and officer—but Ish-bosheth desired to receive the perpetual inheritance of the crown, under the excuse that Saul his father had reigned. But God did not want it to be this way. SERMONS ON 2 SAMUEL.[15]

4:9-12 Judgment for Rechab and Baanah

ISH-BOSHETH AND HIS MURDERERS ARE ALL PUNISHED. JOHANNES BUGENHAGEN: They see nothing who cannot perceive that God has set all things in motion. These words doubtlessly apply to the fall of Saul's house. To fear David so much was fitting. But look! The head of the king, the last of Saul's sons, was brought to him. And Mephibosheth, Saul's grandson, was injured and lame. The king passed away under God's judgment, because he wanted to reign in opposition to the word of the Lord, of which he was not ignorant. These two leaders of Ish-bosheth's army also perished in judgment, because they impiously (to their own detriment) wanted to obtain the favor of pious David. According to God's will, the king was

---

[13]Willet, *Harmony on 2 Samuel*, 22-23*.
[14]TO 13:26.

[15]Calvin, *Sermons on Second Samuel*, 1:149.

murdered and God handed over the murderers into David's judgment. For judgment belonging to anyone other than David would be impious. David knew the kingdom to be his, but he could not yet hope for tranquility or that it would come to him without war. Thus while David kept his peace, God attended to everything, so that David would not only be king but Abner and these two other leaders of Ish-bosheth's army would also perish. So even in Christ's kingdom now, we ought not to hope that the adversaries of the gospel come to ruin in order that the gospel's elect might somehow come to reign. COMMENTARY ON 2 SAMUEL.[16]

DAVID JUDGES THE TRAITORS. ANDREW WILLET: David desired to be avenged of Rechab and Baanah more so than of the Amalekite who said he killed Saul. Both Rechab and Baanah were servants to Ish-bosheth and of the same tribe, whereas the Amalekite was a stranger and not of Israel. Also the one who was killed was a righteous person. Those who conspired against him, he deserved well of them, but not so with Saul and the Amalekites, whom he had destroyed. Saul had already received a wound from which he would not recover, but Ish-bosheth was asleep and in good health. The one was killed in the field; the other, in his own house. Additionally David was then but a private man when he commanded the Amalekite to be killed, but now he was anointed king in Hebron. Therefore in all these three respects, there were legitimate reasons why he should put these two men to death instead of the other. HARMONY ON 2 SAMUEL.[17]

JUST END, UNJUST MEANS. JOHN MAYER: Now although Ish-bosheth deserved to die and God secretly wrought to take him out of the way by means of his providence—so that David might no longer be hindered from the kingdom—this does not excuse the wickedness of these two men who killed him treacherously, partly hoping to receive a great reward at the hands of David.

Therefore David dealt with them according to their just deserts by putting them to death. They nevertheless came to David with a most plausible oration, namely, that "the Lord [had] avenged my lord the king this day on Saul and on his offspring," thus making God a party in their murder. However, these men were not interested in fulfilling God's will at all or in doing any good to David. Instead, they were only interested in their own welfare. . . . David, clean contrary to the expectation of these two men, told them most seriously how he had put to death one who brought tidings to him in Ziklag of Saul's death, even though that young man thought he would be rewarded for his labor. In the same way, David gave judgment against these two men, who were much more worthy of death than the Amalekite. . . . And just as they cut off the head of Ish-bosheth, so David caused their hands, which committed that murder, to be cut off, and for their feet, which carried them to the murder, to be hanged over the pool in Hebron. David thus displayed them as a spectacle for all people to see, so that everyone else would fear ever committing such wickedness. COMMENTARY ON 2 SAMUEL.[18]

---

[16]Bugenhagen, *In Samuelem prophetam*, 297-98.
[17]Willet, *Harmony on 2 Samuel*, 25*.
[18]Mayer, *Many Commentaries in One*, 372-73*.

5:1-25 THE ANOINTING OF
DAVID AS KING OF ISRAEL

[1] Then all the tribes of Israel came to David at Hebron and said, "Behold, we are your bone and flesh. [2] In times past, when Saul was king over us, it was you who led out and brought in Israel. And the LORD said to you, 'You shall be shepherd of my people Israel, and you shall be prince[a] over Israel.'" [3] So all the elders of Israel came to the king at Hebron, and King David made a covenant with them at Hebron before the LORD, and they anointed David king over Israel. [4] David was thirty years old when he began to reign, and he reigned forty years. [5] At Hebron he reigned over Judah seven years and six months, and at Jerusalem he reigned over all Israel and Judah thirty-three years.[b]

[6] And the king and his men went to Jerusalem against the Jebusites, the inhabitants of the land, who said to David, "You will not come in here, but the blind and the lame will ward you off"—thinking, "David cannot come in here." [7] Nevertheless, David took the stronghold of Zion, that is, the city of David. [8] And David said on that day, "Whoever would strike the Jebusites, let him get up the water shaft to attack 'the lame and the blind,' who are hated by David's soul." Therefore it is said, "The blind and the lame shall not come into the house." [9] And David lived in the stronghold and called it the city of David. And David built the city all around from the Millo inward. [10] And David became greater and greater, for the LORD, the God of hosts, was with him.

[11] And Hiram king of Tyre sent messengers to David, and cedar trees, also carpenters and masons who built David a house. [12] And David knew that the LORD had established him king over Israel, and that he had exalted his kingdom for the sake of his people Israel.

[13] And David took more concubines and wives from Jerusalem, after he came from Hebron, and more sons and daughters were born to David. [14] And these are the names of those who were born to him in Jerusalem: Shammua, Shobab, Nathan, Solomon, [15] Ibhar, Elishua, Nepheg, Japhia, [16] Elishama, Eliada, and Eliphelet.

[17] When the Philistines heard that David had been anointed king over Israel, all the Philistines went up to search for David. But David heard of it and went down to the stronghold. [18] Now the Philistines had come and spread out in the Valley of Rephaim. [19] And David inquired of the LORD, "Shall I go up against the Philistines? Will you give them into my hand?" And the LORD said to David, "Go up, for I will certainly give the Philistines into your hand." [20] And David came to Baal-perazim, and David defeated them there. And he said, "The LORD has broken through my enemies before me like a breaking flood." Therefore the name of that place is called Baal-perazim.[c] [21] And the Philistines left their idols there, and David and his men carried them away.

[22] And the Philistines came up yet again and spread out in the Valley of Rephaim. [23] And when David inquired of the LORD, he said, "You shall not go up; go around to their rear, and come against them opposite the balsam trees. [24] And when you hear the sound of marching in the tops of the balsam trees, then rouse yourself, for then the LORD has gone out before you to strike down the army of the Philistines." [25] And David did as the LORD commanded him, and struck down the Philistines from Geba to Gezer.

a Or leader   b Dead Sea Scroll lacks verses 4–5   c Baal-perazim means lord of bursting through

---

OVERVIEW: After long years of exile and waiting, David's perseverance is rewarded with a growing kingdom, which, for Lutheran commentators, signifies a theology of the cross and the endurance of the saints. The good shepherd metaphor also appears in this chapter, resonating with other biblical images of leadership from the Prophets, Psalms and Gospels. As in the previous section, commentators debate the morality of David's having many wives and concubines: these relationships are interpreted variously as signs of God's blessing, contrasting symbols of faithfulness (wives) and hypocrisy (concubines) within the church, and David's unfaithful attempt to secure a large family for himself through his own efforts. Regardless, commentators view David's growing kingdom as foreshadowing the kingdom of God in Christ, which would also come from humble origins and rest on God's good provision.

5:1 *All the Tribes Affirm David as Their Own Flesh and Blood*

DAVID'S SONS SOLOMON AND NATHAN. JOHANNES BUGENHAGEN: The fact that David had more children is relevant to the peace and multiplication of the kingdom. We have read above that Saul's descendants came to ruin, including Saul's daughter, David's wife Michal, who (according to the next chapter) had no children. That said, two of the names of these sons stand out above the others: Solomon, through whom the kingdom descended, whose line fell away, leaving leaders from Nathan to oversee the people. Christ the Lord came from Nathan's line, as you see in Luke. But it is ridiculous that the prophet Nathan, whom you will see later, should be the one thought to have been named by Luke, as if he were somehow adopted by David. For Scripture clearly says that Christ was born of David's seed according to the flesh. COMMENTARY ON 2 SAMUEL.[1]

HOW ALL THE TRIBES CAME TO DAVID. ANDREW WILLET: The whole multitude of Israel did not come but only the elders and highest names, messengers and ambassadors from all the tribes. They give three reasons and persuasions, which moved them to support David as their king. First, he was of their bones and flesh, as they were

appointed by the law to make a king from among their people (Deut 17:15). Second, they had experience of his strength in the days of Saul, when he led the people in and out. Third, the Lord elected him. Just as the law required that they should make him their king whom the Lord would choose, so they did. The Lord said to him by Samuel when he anointed him, "You will feed my people," and the sign did not go without the word. HARMONY ON 2 SAMUEL.[2]

5:2 *David as Shepherd*

LASTING WORDS. PETER MARTYR VERMIGLI: These words "You shall be shepherd of my people Israel . . ." were first said by Samuel, and it is also possible that other prophets said them. Later these words became more credible and they were not forgotten. For God spoke through Jacob that kingship would come from the tribe of Judah. COMMENTARY ON 2 SAMUEL.[3]

A SHEPHERD FOR THE PEOPLE. JOHANNES BUGENHAGEN: To be a shepherd of the people is a beautiful metaphor. Rulers rarely recognize that they owe this to their people, as clearly expressed in the Psalm, "He chose David his servant and took him from the sheepfolds; from following the nursing ewes he brought him to shepherd Jacob his people, Israel his inheritance. With upright heart he shepherded them and guided them with his skillful hand." This took place not only before the face of the Lord, as if invoking the Lord who tests the hearts, but also in the outward worship of God, so that whatever was done externally could also be said to have been done "before the Lord," as was often done in the books of Moses. That this was a holy place of sacrifice is shown later in chapter 15, when the impious Absalom sacrificed there. In earlier times, Abraham built an altar there too, as you read in Genesis 13. COMMENTARY ON 2 SAMUEL.[4]

---

[1]Bugenhagen, *In Samuelem prophetam*, 304-5; citing Lk 3:31.

[2]Willet, *Harmony on 2 Samuel*, 25*; citing Deut 17:15.
[3]Vermigli, *In duos libros Samuelis*, 206.
[4]Bugenhagen, *In Samuelem prophetam*, 300-301; citing Ps 78:20-22; Gen 13:18.

The Good Shepherd. John Calvin: The office of a good king is expressed to us in this reign of David; namely, that he must care for his subjects as a shepherd for his flock. Now two things are required of a shepherd. The first is that he provide his animals with good pasture, and then that he keep them safe from all thieves and wolves and trouble. Now that (I say) is what princes must do. If they think they will render an account to God for the charge that is committed to them, they must see to it that their subjects live in peace and that they are maintained; and then, in the second place, that they defend them against all troubles. Sermons on 2 Samuel.[5]

5:3-5 David's Patience

David's Vindication After Many Trials. Johannes Bugenhagen: Even though David already ruled over Israel by the word of the Lord, God arranged it that he was chosen not only by God but by the people as well, as the psalm says, "Blessed be the Lord, my rock . . . who subdues peoples under me," and "Oh grant us help against the foe, for vain is the salvation of man! With God we shall do valiantly; it is he who will tread down our foes." Therefore, expelling the Jebusites, he took possession of Jerusalem and the stronghold of Zion, built a house, was blessed with children and royal descendants, and withstood the Philistines, trampling them in the mud. And so finally the king reigns, even though up to this point so many of his deeds seem to have been abandoned by God. In this way, God spreads his truth abroad and tests our faith, not at the time of our choosing but in God's own time. Commentary on 2 Samuel.[6]

Adversity in the Morning, Prosperity in the Evening. Johann Gerhard: David spent ten years in exile but forty in his kingdom. Here is prefigured the brevity of our suffering and the glory of eternity to follow. It is but a point of time when the saints are exercised by the cross; but the mercies by which they are comforted are forever. And therefore adversity in the morning is followed by prosperity in the evening. Sacred Meditations.[7]

Waiting with David. Henry Airay: If your sorrows come thick on you, know that nothing will befall you but that which pertains to the children of God. Wait for the Lord to act, be strong and he will comfort your heart. Oh, but you have waited long and yet find no ease. What! Longer than David waited for the kingdom of Israel even though he was anointed king over Israel by Samuel? After he was anointed by Samuel, he waited in great affliction, persecution and peril for many years before he reigned over Judah. And after that he waited seven and a half years before he reigned over Israel. Lectures on Philippians.[8]

5:6-12 David's Prosperity

God Is Especially with the Godly. Peter Martyr Vermigli: David increased because the Lord was with him. Such is the only foundation, the root of all good things. For our happiness does not arise from anything else other than from the one God. . . . For this reason, David increased and enlarged by means of all this abundance of God's presence, since God was with him. Now although God is indeed everywhere, it can nevertheless be reasonably said that God is particularly and specially present with those who are godly. Commentary on 2 Samuel.[9]

Day by Day. John Calvin: Here we must note, in the first place, that inasmuch as the kingdom of David was a type of our Lord Jesus Christ, which is the state of the church, it was not enough that God, in one swoop, should establish the kingdom of his Son. Rather, he had to cause it to grow and

[5]Calvin, *Sermons on Second Samuel*, 1:177.
[6]Bugenhagen, *In Samuelem prophetam*, 299-300; citing Ps 144:1-2; 108:12-13.
[7]Gerhard, *Gerhardi Meditationes Sacrae*, 188-89.
[8]Airay, *Lectures on Philippians*, 257-58*.
[9]Vermigli, *In duos libros Samuelis*, 217.

multiply day by day, which is quite necessary. For when God had given some sign of advancing his church and making it fruitful, it seems that all has been won, and that only laughter awaits us—and we, like foolish people, despise this grace which is so necessary. It is the same as if we no longer had the least need of God, and were carrying in our pocket everything we could wish. It says that God must build his church, give it foundations and direct it (see Eph 2:20). On the other hand, he must maintain it, and not only that, but he must make it grow and increase. For the reign of our Lord Jesus Christ will never be perfect in this world. Far from it. First, there will always be afflictions and contradictions, and second, there will be much hypocrisy and internal enemies, who under the pretense of making a profession of faith will only cause scandals to keep our Lord Jesus Christ from reigning. Even the faithful will be full of many weaknesses and imperfections. Hence it means nothing for the reign of Jesus Christ to be set up once in our midst unless it is maintained. For because we are so fragile without his help, all will fall down like water if not fortified from on high. SERMONS ON 2 SAMUEL.[10]

5:13-16 *David's Many Wives and Concubines*

DAVID'S WISE AND LAWFUL POLYGAMY.
ALONSO TOSTADO: Someone will ask why David took so many wives, and whether he sinned in doing so. For he took six wives previously in Hebron, and from these wives it should have sufficed to have had enough offspring. As such, it would appear that David only took more wives as an enticement of the flesh, in which case it would follow that David sinned. I respond that David took many wives for a couple of reasons. The first reason is out of his desire to have many offspring for the purpose of maintaining proper religion and for the multiplication of the people of God. For sometimes it happens that from only one wife, or only a few, it is not possible to have many children;

yet it is possible to do so from many wives. Therefore for this cause it appears to be a lawful need unless the law prohibits it. The second reason is that David took many wives in order create an alliance for himself with the great men of his kingdom. For David desired to rule strongly, and that would not be possible unless he aligned himself at the beginning of his reign. This is how he received many of his wives, namely, by marrying the daughters of important men by means of alliances. In other words, David took many wives because he sought many alliances.

As for the second question, some will say that David sinned by taking so many wives since Deuteronomy 17 prohibits the marrying of many women. And because David certainly took many wives, it might appear that he sinned. But I respond that he did not sin. For God gave David many wives as if a gift, as appears later in the twelfth chapter of this book: "I gave you your master's house and your master's wives into your arms and gave you the house of Israel and of Judah." And because God does not give evil gifts, it is clear that David did not sin in taking many wives. COMMENTARY ON 2 SAMUEL.[11]

A HEAP OF WIVES DOES NOT EQUAL MANY CHILDREN. JOHN CALVIN: It is true that God did not fail to bless David in giving him offspring.... Even if he had not had such a number of wives, he would not have failed to have children. We have seen above that the children he had in Hebron were not so numerous that he could not have had them by one wife. Each of his wives had only one child (2 Sam 3:2-5), and one wife could have had twelve—indeed, even up to twenty-five. When it says that David had six wives and six children in Hebron, although it was a sign of the grace of God, still it was also a mark and sign of shame in that now he had a veritable "heap" of wives, and yet did not have a comparable number of children! This is sufficient to show that the grace of God was not fully reflected in his experience. Therefore, when

[10]Calvin, *Sermons on Second Samuel*, 193-94.

[11]TO 13:31; citing Deut 17:17; 2 Sam 12:8.

we see it, let us realize, on the one hand, that God chose to put up with David's polygamy—but also, on the other hand, that he did not allow him enough to cause him to rejoice too much, as would have been the case if he had had greater number of offspring. SERMONS ON 2 SAMUEL.[12]

TEMPORARY TOLERANCE OF POLYGAMY. JOHN MAYER: David's concubines were his wives also, but they were called by another name to show that they were secondary wives and not the principal ones. Back then it was tolerated to take wives and concubines for a mystical meaning. For example, David's wives signified the churches of Jews and Gentiles joined by faith in Christ.... His concubines, by contrast, signified the sects of heretics in these churches. And the more children that were born to David, the more that were converted to the faith.... But now, however, it is not tolerable to have multiple wives. COMMENTARY ON 2 SAMUEL.[13]

BORN IN SIN. MARTIN BORRHAUS: The teaching of having such a multitude of wives is not prohibited by God in the old covenant. "But," you say, "what are we to make of that law of Moses that warns against a king having many wives?" It forbids many wives inasmuch as the king is led to have his heart turned away from God in lust. But the limit of wives is not a human judgment but one by the Holy Spirit. Nevertheless, I do not totally absolve David from all sin. For the man was not innocent of sin, as he confessed: "In sin did my mother conceive me." COMMENTARY ON 2 SAMUEL.[14]

5:17-25 David Defeats the Philistines

GOD'S MOTHERING OF THE ANCIENTS. JOHN CALVIN: We must notice that however strong David felt against the Philistines, still he did not trust in his own strength, but turned to God and asked him if he should go against them.... We

should apply this example to our own situation, for though we do not have the special revelation that was given at that time, God still declares that he always has available the Spirit of wisdom to guide us, and by it calls us to himself. Thus when we do not know which way to turn and are in real perplexity, we must come straight to him, and pray to him to hear us and show us what is expedient for us. Even if today this particular benefit of God making himself known by revelation and through the prophets is no longer in the church, our condition is none the worse for that. Instead, we have some compensation . . . so that we ought not to be envious of the ancient fathers for how God assisted them. For although a hen leads her chicks when they are little, one must not be surprised when their mother no longer covers them, and no longer hides them beneath her wings after they become able to provide for themselves. It is the same with children whom you get up and put to bed! When they have become adults, it would be unnatural if they still wanted to be treated in the same way! Hence, the reason our Lord gave special revelations to the ancient fathers was to strengthen their weakness, for they were like little children. SERMONS ON 2 SAMUEL.[15]

A MONUMENT TO CELEBRATE THE VICTORY. ANDREW WILLET: Now the time had come when the Philistines should receive just punishment for so disrespectfully behaving themselves when Saul and Jonathan were killed. And God was pleased, in his wise providence, that they should first provoke David to battle. He didn't begin with them, lest he seemed unthankful seeing he had found harbor and entertainment among them in the days of Saul. The Philistines set up camp in the valley of Rephaim, which was not far from Jerusalem and belonged to the tribe of Judah. Some take it to be the same place that is called Baal-perazim, but it seems to be two different places. The Philistine host was so large with the Phoenicians and other nations assisting them, as Josephus said, that the one part was in the

---

[12]Calvin, *Sermons on Second Samuel*, 1:206.
[13]Mayer, *Many Commentaries in One*, 378*; citing 1 Chron 14:3.
[14]Borrhaus, *Mystica Messiae*, 480; citing Deut 17:17; Ps 51:5.

[15]Calvin, *Sermons on Second Samuel*, 1:217-18.

valley and the other reached to Baal-perazim. They were two places . . . for the Philistines went up from the valley to Rephaim to Baal-perazim. David, before the battle, consulted with God by the priest with the Urim and Thummim. He then went to the fort (which is likely to have been the tower of Zion). However, it is not the case that David put his trust in the fort to defend him; it was rather so he could consult with God. After the battle was finished and the victory obtained, to show his thankfulness to God David left a monument of the victory by giving the name Baal-perazim to the place, which meant "the land of division." It was this way because David broke in on them, like water in a great overflowing wave, as he said himself. HARMONY ON 2 SAMUEL.[16]

---

[16]Willet, *Harmony on 2 Samuel*, 28-29*.

6:1-23 THE ARK RETURNED TO JERUSALEM

[1]David again gathered all the chosen men of Israel, thirty thousand. [2]And David arose and went with all the people who were with him from Baale-judah to bring up from there the ark of God, which is called by the name of the LORD of hosts who sits enthroned on the cherubim. [3]And they carried the ark of God on a new cart and brought it out of the house of Abinadab, which was on the hill. And Uzzah and Ahio,[a] the sons of Abinadab, were driving the new cart,[b] [4]with the ark of God, and Ahio went before the ark.

[5]And David and all the house of Israel were celebrating before the LORD, with songs[c] and lyres and harps and tambourines and castanets and cymbals. [6]And when they came to the threshing floor of Nacon, Uzzah put out his hand to the ark of God and took hold of it, for the oxen stumbled. [7]And the anger of the LORD was kindled against Uzzah, and God struck him down there because of his error, and he died there beside the ark of God. [8]And David was angry because the LORD had broken out against Uzzah. And that place is called Perez-uzzah[d] to this day. [9]And David was afraid of the LORD that day, and he said, "How can the ark of the LORD come to me?" [10]So David was not willing to take the ark of the LORD into the city of David. But David took it aside to the house of Obed-edom the Gittite. [11]And the ark of the LORD remained in the house of Obed-edom the Gittite three months, and the LORD blessed Obed-edom and all his household.

[12]And it was told King David, "The LORD has blessed the household of Obed-edom and all that belongs to him, because of the ark of God." So David went and brought up the ark of God from the house of Obed-edom to the city of David with rejoicing. [13]And when those who bore the ark of the LORD had gone six steps, he sacrificed an ox and a fattened animal. [14]And David danced before the LORD with all his might. And David was wearing a linen ephod. [15]So David and all the house of Israel brought up the ark of the LORD with shouting and with the sound of the horn.

[16]As the ark of the LORD came into the city of David, Michal the daughter of Saul looked out of the window and saw King David leaping and dancing before the LORD, and she despised him in her heart. [17]And they brought in the ark of the LORD and set it in its place, inside the tent that David had pitched for it. And David offered burnt offerings and peace offerings before the LORD. [18]And when David had finished offering the burnt offerings and the peace offerings, he blessed the people in the name of the LORD of hosts [19]and distributed among all the people, the whole multitude of Israel, both men and women, a cake of bread, a portion of meat,[e] and a cake of raisins to each one. Then all the people departed, each to his house.

[20]And David returned to bless his household. But Michal the daughter of Saul came out to meet David and said, "How the king of Israel honored himself today, uncovering himself today before the eyes of his servants' female servants, as one of the vulgar fellows shamelessly uncovers himself!" [21]And David said to Michal, "It was before the LORD, who chose me above your father and above all his house, to appoint me as prince[f] over Israel, the people of the LORD—and I will celebrate before the LORD. [22]I will make myself yet more contemptible than this, and I will be abased in your[g] eyes. But by the female servants of whom you have spoken, by them I shall be held in honor." [23]And Michal the daughter of Saul had no child to the day of her death.

a Or *and his brother*; also verse 4   b Compare Septuagint; Hebrew *the new cart, and brought it out of the house of Abinadab, which was on the hill*   c Septuagint, 1 Chronicles 13:8; Hebrew *fir trees*   d *Perez-uzzah* means *the breaking out against Uzzah*   e Vulgate; the meaning of the Hebrew term is uncertain   f Or *leader*   g Septuagint; Hebrew *my*

OVERVIEW: The ark of the covenant inspired many reformers to consider what it means to live in the presence of God and to worship accordingly. In addition, Uzzah's death and David's corresponding anger at God present a challenge to interpreters: was this death the work of a just or unjust God? Was David's anger appropriate to the situation, or did it reveal a failure on his part? The commentators interpret the dancing and music that accompanies the ark's entrance into Jerusalem differently. Reformed theologians like Calvin and Bullinger discuss what kind of music is appropriate in Christian worship; Lutherans like Bugenhagen and Arndt understand David's dance as an affirmation that God's foolishness is wiser than human wisdom; Martin Bucer ponders the cultural difference between ancient peoples and his more reserved contemporaries. Finally, the exchange between David and Michal highlights the continued removal of divine blessing from the house of Saul.

6:1 The Number of and Reason for So Many Soldiers

SCRIPTURAL DISCREPANCY. JOHN CALVIN: David assembled thirty thousand men, as we read here. . . . Apparently we have a discrepancy here from the other passage, where we read that he assembled all Israel from Egypt to the other end of the land, which reached to the Euphrates (1 Chron 13:5). If he had literally assembled all Israel, the number would have been infinite. But the Scripture is simply using everyday language. When one gathers people together from all over a country, one can say that the whole country is assembled. But there it is speaking of his deliberations with his captains and officers (1 Chron 13:1). Here it simply says that they gathered everyone together. SERMONS ON 2 SAMUEL.[1]

PLANS TO BRING BACK THE ARK. ANDREW WILLET: In Chronicles a number is not expressed stating how many were gathered together, but here they are said to be thirty thousand. Neither is here described the boundaries or the limits of the land, or how far and from where they were called. It is said that David gathered them together from Sychar of Egypt to the entering of Hamath, which is from the south boundaries of the land to the north. The causes of this great assembly were many. First, that with solemn display and due devotion they might bring the ark. Second, so David might have soldiers ready at hand if the enemy should attempt to disturb them. Third, becoming a moderate and godly prince, David would have the consent of the states and the people. . . . Fourth, Rupertus compares the bringing of the ark to a type of Christ, whereby the ark represented a figure of the solemn preaching and proclamation of the resurrection of Christ by the apostles through the world. Fifth, the ark was brought to Jerusalem to show that David's first thoughts and counsel, after he was established and settled in his kingdom, was to seek after God and to reform religion. But in Saul's time they did not seek the ark of God, for Saul was troubled and concerned about the succession of the kingdom and the pursuing of David instead of consulting with God at the ark. Rather than consulting God, he instead went to witches, which ended in his ruin. HARMONY ON 2 SAMUEL.[2]

6:2-4 The Ark

DAVID'S DESIRE FOR AND TRANSPORTATION OF THE ARK. ALONSO TOSTADO: Someone may ask why David wanted to bring the ark of the Lord from Kiriath-jearim to Jerusalem, and whether he sinned by doing so. As for the first question, David was very devoted to the worship of God in the beginning of his kingdom. He himself even wanted to build a temple for the Lord since no one had done so previously and God had not lived in a house even since the days God led the Israelites out of Egypt. On the contrary, God had always lived in tents. But David's desire to build a temple for the Lord was something new, and he desired for the ark to live in more honor than it had

---

[1] Calvin, *Sermons on Second Samuel*, 1:229.

[2] Willet, *Harmony on 2 Samuel*, 30*.

been when it was in the house of Abinadab. For in Jerusalem the ark could be held in more honor since David would construct a home for it, and he wanted the ark to rest in Jerusalem while he built a permanent dwelling place for it. As for the second question, concerning whether David sinned in bringing the ark to Jerusalem, I respond that David did not sin. For although the ark should have been in the holy of holies in the tabernacle, God nevertheless disposed it to be residing elsewhere for the time being. For it had been outside of the tabernacle in Kiriath-jearim ever since the death of Eli the high priest; but eventually it would reside in the newly constructed temple that Solomon would build. COMMENTARY ON 2 SAMUEL.[3]

THE ARK IS THE CHURCH. JOHANNES BUGEN-HAGEN: The ark was significant for the godliness of the Davidic kingdom, especially after it had suffered neglect under Saul. At this point, after having been taken back from the Philistines, it had been in the house of Abinadab. This ark was very holy to the Jews; it was in itself the holy of holies. It signified Christ and the church, in which we hope in God's promises. For the ark is the church, in which are hidden the two tables of the law, namely, the Spirit of life in our hearts through faith, over which is Christ who made atonement, who was given a golden crown, signifying the kingdom. The two cherubim—poised to fly—are the two testaments, whose preaching ought to fly around the world. They stand atoned to each other, kindly facing one another, because they harmoniously preach the one Christ. God watches over it, for Christ is the head of the church and "the head of Christ is God." God is all in all; "in Christ God was reconciling the world to himself." Now, David held this office, so that the ark's entrance into Jerusalem and the stronghold of Zion might signify the entrance of the church. For from Christ comes the introduction of the gospel into the church, through which all are received and taken possession of, as we have said elsewhere. COMMENTARY ON 2 SAMUEL.[4]

GOD DWELLING IN THE SACRAMENTS. JOHN CALVIN: Now let us apply this to ourselves. . . . When we have access to the preached Word, God speaks in a common and ordinary fashion to us. It is an illustration of his condescension. Hence the preaching of the gospel is like God descending to earth in order to seek us. We must not abuse this simplicity of the Word of God by disdaining it. Rather, we must receive it all the more, recognizing that he indeed deigns to transfigure himself, so to speak, that we might approach him. He is not content with giving us his Word, but he adds baptism to confirm it. When we are baptized—though only a little water is used—it stands for crucifying our old person, for renewing our souls and for being united with the angels. Baptism is performed to ensure that we inherit the eternal kingdom, to make us enjoy adoption, by which we are companions and siblings of the angels— but can a little water do that? The point, of course, is that since God has come down to us (in this symbol), we must go up to him (in faith). . . . Similarly, today in the waters of baptism, it is the same as if the blood of our Lord Jesus Christ poured down from heaven to water our souls and cleanse them from their uncleanness. When we have the bread and wine in the Lord's Supper, it is the same as if Jesus Christ were coming down from heaven and making himself our food, so that we could be filled with him. We must not, therefore, take these signs as visible things and figures that are to feed our spiritual senses, but are to realize that God joins his virtue and truth to them, so that the thing and the effect are joined to the figure. We must not put asunder what God has joined together. That, in sum, is what we must keep in mind from the statement that the ark of God has the name: the name of the God of hosts, dwelling between the cherubim. SERMONS ON 2 SAMUEL.[5]

---

[3]TO 13:26.
[4]Bugenhagen, *In Samuelem prophetam*, 305-6; citing Rom 3:25; 1 Cor 11:3; 2 Cor 5:19.

[5]Calvin, *Sermons on Second Samuel*, 1:235-36.

6:5 Music in Worship

No Musical Instruments in Church. John Calvin: It would be nothing but mimicry if we followed David today in singing with cymbals, flutes, tambourines and psalteries. In fact, some Christians were seriously deceived in their desire to worship God with their pompous inclusion of organs, trumpets, oboes and similar instruments. That has only served to amuse the people in their vanity, and to turn them away from the true institution that God had ordained. We must, at the same time, be aware of all the privileges we have in common with the fathers who have lived under the law and, on the other hand, be aware of all the things wherein they are separated from us. All those things we have in common with them are lasting, and must be maintained until the end of the world. But we are not to keep observing these things that were only for the time of the law, unless we want to make a confused mixture that confounds heaven and earth. In a word, the musical instruments were in the same class as sacrifices, candelabra, lamps and similar things. . . .

As I have said, we must notice that what God had instituted for the time of symbols (before the coming of our Lord Jesus Christ) must be put aside and not enforced today. It is true that God ought to be heartily praised, both by musical instruments and by mouth. But it is another matter when we conduct the worship of God in church. If we want to sing praises in the name of God, we would do much better to have psalms instead of common dissolute songs. We sing in order to give him thanks—and not in order to produce a solemn ceremony as a meritorious work that we do for God. Those who take this approach are reverting to a sort of Jewishism, as if they wanted to mingle the law and the gospel, and thus bury our Lord Jesus Christ. When we are told that David sang with a musical instrument, let us carefully remember that we are not to make a rule of it. Rather, we are to recognize today that we must sing the praises of God in simplicity, since the shadows of the law are past, and since in our Lord Jesus Christ we have the truth and embodiment of all these things that were given

to the ancient fathers in the time of their ignorance or smallness of faith. They did not have such revelation as we have today in the gospel. Sermons on 2 Samuel.[6]

Singing as a Shadow Now Fulfilled. Heinrich Bullinger: I now need to say something about singing in church. . . . Now, let nobody assume that that prayers sung with a human voice are more pleasing to God than those that are plainly recited. For God is neither prevailed on by the sweetness of a person's voice nor offended by a hoarse recitation of a prayer. This is because prayer is commended for the purpose of faith and godliness of mind, not for any outward show. Rather, these outward things are made use of in order to stir us up, even though they have little effect unless the Spirit of the Lord kindles our hearts. And nobody is able to deny that the custom of singing is very ancient. . . . Nor is anyone able to deny, I think, that the toilsome kind of music that David brought into the temple of God was counted among the ceremonies and that it was also eliminated together with the temple and the ceremonies. Decades 5.5.[7]

The Mind and Heart Singing Together. Andrew Willet: The purpose of these instruments was to stir the minds of the hearers to the praise of God, for otherwise God is not delighted with sounds. And so music now has a commendable and proper use in the church of God if we use it to God's praise and glory. This is how the mind and heart sing together with the voice. Harmony on 2 Samuel.[8]

6:6-8 Uzzah and the Ark

Poor Uzzah. John Calvin: We have here a strange story, that a man attempting to honor God, burning with a good and holy devotion, was

---

[6]Calvin, *Sermons on Second Samuel*, 1:241-42.
[7]Bullinger, *Sermonum decades quinque*, 401-2.
[8]Willet, *Harmony on 2 Samuel*, 32-33*; citing Eph 5:19.

punished like a criminal. Now this certainly offends our feelings. . . . For if we could have been the judge, Uzzah would certainly have been swiftly absolved. Why? Because he who does something with a good motive (says the proverb) cannot be considered bad. The intention of Uzzah was good, as far as one can judge, for it would seem that he was moved by a virtuous zeal that deserved a reward, rather than chastisement. Nevertheless, after men have squawked all they want to, they still remain confused, and God always closes their mouths, for he clearly knows how to justify himself when he pleases (Ps 51:4). Let us remember, therefore, what it says here—namely, that God justly punished Uzzah, inasmuch as it was his responsibility to discern between good and evil. God's will is the sole standard of all perfection, and we cannot comprehend the reason for his admirable works because of our crudeness. The very angels of paradise are confused in looking at the glory of God, and have their faces hidden. . . . What shall it be with us who are only poor vessels of clay? Now that is the attitude with which we must begin to read this story, in which God so gravely punished Uzzah. SERMONS ON 2 SAMUEL.[9]

DAVID'S UNLAWFUL USE OF THE ARK. HEINRICH BULLINGER: Did not David himself bring the ark of the Lord of hosts to Jerusalem with great devotion and much joyful melody? However, because he did not transport it in a lawful manner on the shoulders of the priests, great sorrow arose at once instead of much joy. This shows that it is not enough to make use of the sacraments and ordinances of God—unless they are used in a lawful way. DECADES 5.1.[10]

OBEDIENCE REQUIRED. OSMUND LAKE: God is served well only by obedience, and obedience looks only to the Word. And the Word gives warrant that the thing we do is lawful to serve God. And generally for your good intent, remember that obedience must have these two bounds: that it looks to a good end and that it draws to that end by good means. Otherwise it will prove to be sin. And the means to bring good service to God can in no way be good unless they are marshaled by faith. A PROBE THEOLOGICAL.[11]

GOD'S SCANDALOUS WAYS. THOMAS BRIGHTMAN: Just as the word and worship of God is a great scandal, so also are the works of God. This is because humankind is not able to understand the reason for them (for God does not give a reason, as the book of Job explains); as such, a person presumes to measure them by the line of his crooked judgment, and is offended when God's works do not correspond to his judgment. Thus David was offended at the work of God in killing Uzzah. THE DANGER OF SCANDAL AND OFFENSES.[12]

DAVID GRIEVED AGAINST GOD'S WILL. JOHANNES BUGENHAGEN: When Uzzah died, David suffered in his conscience. He even got angry against God's sentence of death and considered his own unworthiness. This also happens in Christ's church, where those who think they have been abandoned by God become angry. Already in this story there were times when David had truly decided not to be in accord with God's Word, earlier times when he had not listened, either. Therefore, wherever we want to introduce the gospel, we really ought to call on God so that all things are done according to God's Word and will, rather than trust in our own wisdom or virtue. COMMENTARY ON 2 SAMUEL.[13]

UZZAH GOES BEYOND HIS VOCATION. JOHN CALVIN: Unlike Uzzah, let us note that we must undertake nothing outside of our vocation. For what may seem to be virtue to us will be considered vice before God if we go beyond our limits. Why? Because our vocation is to prove the obedience that we render to him. We call vocation the duty to

---

[9]Calvin, *Sermons on Second Samuel*, 1:244-46.
[10]Bullinger, *Sermonum decades quinque*, 359.
[11]Lake, *Probe Theologicall*, 31*.
[12]Brightman, *The Post-Human Offspring*, 30.
[13]Bugenhagen, *In Samuelem prophetam*, 308.

which God binds us. It is that which belongs to the office of someone in the condition and degree to which God has called them. This word *vocation* signifies calling. Well, this calling means that people do not thrust themselves forward, and that everyone does not take their own portion and share. Rather, when God says to one: "Do this" and to another: "Do this," that is how each one should walk and follow him. Therefore, when we desire that God should call us, it is a sign that we must not go further than is legitimate for us. But he who does go beyond his limits is acting just as though he wanted to overrule God in the matter, and wanted to have the fruit of God's grace as defined by his own thoughts! Well, we are not to act in this way.

In the example of Uzzah, we are instructed not to attempt to go beyond the demands of our own office, nor beyond the condition or degree to which we are called by God. It is as if a private citizen wanted to take the office of magistrate or if, quite indiscriminately, he wanted to take authority—as if someone wanted to rule the house of his neighbor and of this one and that one. Such things would be utterly preposterous! If someone argues: "It is done in good faith and with good intentions"—yes, but it is not for us to put ourselves forward in such a way. Therefore such presumption and recklessness are displeasing to God, particularly when we prefer to do that which is not our business, so that everyone takes over what is by no means given to him. In sum, let us be modest enough to pay attention to that to which God calls us, which he strictly requires from us and which belongs to our office. Let everyone openly devote himself to it, so that we will not go beyond our boundaries like wild horses. SERMONS ON 2 SAMUEL.[14]

6:9-10 *David Fears God*

MISPLACED FEAR. JOHN CALVIN: It says that David "feared" . . . to have the ark of God brought to his house or to the city of David. He was a prophet

of God and an excellent one, but now was acting like a small child. He was utterly shocked and afraid of falling into the same peril as Uzzah, which . . . should serve as an example for us to be all the more dedicated to the service of God. David certainly should have been as affected as the others, to think that the ark of God had not been honored as it should. Therefore he ought to have thought of what God had commanded in the law. In the same way, let us determine to submit to God's law, and not to go beyond our bounds. Now that is what David should have remembered, and if his fear had been in line with Scripture, it would have been good and holy. But he drew a false conclusion from a good principle. For he feared God, and then was seized by anger, and he finally concluded that the ark did not have to come to him. SERMONS ON 2 SAMUEL.[15]

WHY DAVID WAS NOT PLEASED. ANDREW WILLET: The original words are, "David was angry." Some understand that David was not angry with the Lord, for God could not be accused of injustice here, and it was far from David to lay such accusation on God. Rather, it is believed that David was angry with the negligence of the priests and of his own oversight, in such an apparent transgression of the law. But the text gives this reason instead: Because the Lord killed Uzzah, David showed that this was the cause of his grief. Therefore the meaning is that it displeased David, or David was moved and troubled, similar to when the Lord had cast off Saul and Samuel was moved to cry to the Lord all night (1 Sam 15:11). As David was moved and troubled, so it is said that David feared the Lord that day. Both of these show that David set the same punishment on the Philistines that was on the Bethshemites for their irreverent behavior toward the ark. David feared the same punishment himself, and therefore he did not dare to go further with the ark. This made David more careful afterward, to attempt nothing beside the doctrine of the law. HARMONY ON 2 SAMUEL.[16]

---

[14]Calvin, *Sermons on Second Samuel*, 1:246-47.

[15]Calvin, *Sermons on Second Samuel*, 1:247.
[16]Willet, *Harmony on 2 Samuel*, 34*.

6:11-13 *The Ark's Blessings*

ENVIOUS OF THE ARK'S BLESSINGS. JOHN CALVIN: David repented for having placed the ark of God elsewhere than in his city.... Nevertheless David's understanding was not totally and immediately converted, for he was still confused about several important matters. He really based his action simply on the prosperity of Obed-edom, as if he envied him, and wanted to bring back the ark to himself, and derive profit from it. Why did he not rather think of the promises God had given him? It is true to say that the examples of the grace of God that we have before our eyes ought to strengthen our trust. But we must look higher, namely, to the promises of God. For we must not only focus our attention on what we see; God must speak, and we must hear him. So here was another fault in David's change of mind. He really should have said: "Since God is always consistent with himself, I shall trust in his promises. Now he has declared what is required in his worship, and so I shall bring back the ark in accordance with his instructions and put it in a convenient place for all the people, so that none can make the excuse that it is inaccessible." But he drew back from such appropriate action until he actually saw the fruit of this promise, which he found hard to believe. Thus, when he saw that the house of Obed-edom prospered, he concluded: "I must have the ark." SERMONS ON 2 SAMUEL.[17]

WHY DAVID MOVED THE ARK. ANDREW WILLET: God had blessed the house of Obed-edom and all that he had because of the presence of the ark, which he used with great reverence. No such thing is expressed of Abinadab, in whose house the ark resided many years either because it is omitted in Scripture—as many things of fact are—or because the ark was not afforded the same reverence as Obed-edom. This was a great alteration and change, that whereas the Lord punished before, he now blessed. However, this change was not in God, who is immutable and always the same.

Rather, the change was in those who carried themselves differently toward the Lord's ark: Uzzah was punished for his lack of reverence, while Obed-edom was rewarded for his obedience. HARMONY ON 2 SAMUEL.[18]

6:14-15 *Dancing Before the Lord*

DAVID'S STRANGE ACT OF DANCE. JOHN CALVIN: But now it says that David leaped before the ark "with all his might" (2 Sam 6:14), which is to say that he danced. Well, we may find this very strange indeed, but let us note in the first place that God permitted his people to have many things in common with the pagans. Now it was customary for the pagans to dance and leap while worshiping their idols. God guided his people in that matter, indeed, so that they would not give themselves to wicked superstitions, nor say: "We lack this; we must have it like the others." Although dancing before the ark may not seem to be an action that we would really approve, nevertheless God could have granted such permission to his people.... Therefore, when we are told that David danced before the ark, let us note that it was in order that he and all the faithful at that time, instead of rejoicing in dissolute and lascivious dances, might exercise themselves in the praises of God and place all their joy in that. Be that as it may, it was done in accordance with the times, which we must always remember. SERMONS ON 2 SAMUEL.[19]

DAVID DANCED. JOHANNES BUGENHAGEN: This dancing was the work of God and the Spirit of God rejoicing in David's heart. Certainly in the eyes of the world it looked foolish for the king to do this, as are all truly good works of genuine saints. They are seen to be foolish. It is far from the good, which is held by the greatest hypocrites, whose works—even the really good ones—are quite ungodly. For this reason Saul's daughter Michal (along with all those who have nothing of

---

[17]Calvin, *Sermons on Second Samuel*, 1:259.

[18]Willet, *Harmony on 2 Samuel*, 39*.
[19]Calvin, *Sermons on Second Samuel*, 1:267.

the Spirit) condemns David's actions with her rationality, wise judgment of the flesh, great pride and audacity. And the Spirit worked thus in David, that he did not see their impiety, which called him a disgrace, shameless and a buffoon. The king's boldness was astonishing, but that is the spirit in which hypocrites and the wisdom of the flesh receives it. For they certainly think that they deliberate or act rightly, so that they in their wisdom consign us to our foolishness. This is the kind of person for whom Christ's crucifixion is foolishness. In the same way, those who accept Christ's blessing receive abuse, just as David came into his own house, standing and asking for blessings and benefits for his family and wives after he had blessed the people. And so the lovely Michal received a curse instead of a blessing, because she did not want to be blessed by that kind of person. COMMENTARY ON 2 SAMUEL.[20]

MOVED BY THE SPIRIT. MARTIN BUCER: It is clear that a strong sense of divine blessings moved David, though he was a king, to transport the ark of the Lord, which he danced before. He was a Palestinian, I confess, from a people that is more emotional and unrestrained than our European people. REIGN OF CHRIST.[21]

EXPRESSIONS OF JOY. EDWARD REYNOLDS: Joy is, of all affections, the most communicative: It leaps out into the eyes, the feet and the tongue. It does not remain in one's heart; rather, it bursts forth into the hearts of many others. Such is how David expressed his joy, namely, by dancing before the ark. SEVEN SERMONS ON FOURTEENTH CHAPTER OF HOSEA.[22]

6:16-23 David and Michal

TRAMP FOR THE LORD. JOHN CALVIN: Now it says Michal reproached him for "having acted like a tramp." The word implies someone vile, as they say: a good-for-nothing. She compares him (I say) to a tramp, since he stripped himself before the ark of God. Now he was not alone, but it seemed to her that he should not put himself in the rank of the common people but retain his royal gravity. She put the worst possible construction on David's self-abasement, and claimed that he had made himself like a tramp. This showed how deeply infected her heart was with pride because of her royal blood. How often we see this in those who have some noble ancestry. Even though God has abased them and removed every opportunity to be proud of themselves, yet they never fail to flatter themselves with that pride rooted in them by nature. We see many of them who cannot bow their neck, even when God has conquered them, but always remain haughty, even when they have their heads nearly cracked and broken! SERMONS ON 2 SAMUEL.[23]

CONTEMPTIBLE AND ABASED. LANCELOT ANDREWES: It is well known that when a great and high person falls into low estate, they care not so much for being low as much as appearing such. Do not reveal this and you do them a pleasure. It is worse for them to be found out than it is to be what they. It is naturally given us to hide our abasement as much as we can. Our misery must be kept as a secret, and that secret must not be revealed in any way. . . . This was Michal's grief— that David should have been humble in heart before God and his ark, while Michal was born in highness. Her grief was that David made this manifest by uncovering himself and wearing an ephod. In this way she thought he mightily disgraced them, as he became "contemptible . . . and . . . abased" in the eyes of his servants. This is why she took so ill—not so much in being made low as for her lowness being revealed. ON THE NATIVITY: SERMON 3.[24]

---

[20]Bugenhagen, *In Samuelem prophetam*, 309-10.
[21]Bucer, *De Regno Christi*, 207.
[22]Reynolds, *Works*, 3:404*.

[23]Calvin, *Sermons on Second Samuel*, 1:280-81; citing 2 Sam 6:20.
[24]Andrewes, *Ninety-Six Sermons*, 1:39-40*.

The Condescension of Love. Edward
Reynolds: Another effect of love is condescension
to things below us, that we may please or profit
those whom we love. It teaches a person to deny
their own judgment and to do that which one who
looks on might happily esteem weakness or
indecency, out of a fervent desire to express
affection to the thing beloved. Thus David's great
love to the ark of God's presence propelled him to
leap, dance and perform many other expressions of
joy, which Michal, out of pride, despised in her
heart. Treatise on the Passions and Facul-
ties of the Soul.[25]

On Becoming Nothing. Johann Arndt: If
you wish to demonstrate in your deeds that God
alone is everything, you must become nothing in
your heart . . . You must be as David when Michal
despised him and he danced before the seat of
grace and said: "I will make myself yet more
contemptible than this before the Lord." . . . The
one who wishes to be something is the material out
of which God makes nothing. . . . However, those
who wish to be nothing and consider themselves as
nothing are the material out of which God makes
something. True Christianity.[26]

Saul's Daughter. Andrew Willet: Michal is
rightly called "the daughter of Saul" in this passage,
for she clearly replicated the quality of her father.
He was a hypocrite, conceited and sought only the
praise of people. By contrast, David referred to

God's glory. Apparently Michal had forgotten how
her father Saul had behaved himself in a similar
manner when "he too stripped off all his clothes"
among the prophets and prophesied naked all day
and all night. Harmony on 2 Samuel.[27]

The End of Saul's Line. John Calvin: God
condemned the pride of Michal when he rendered
her sterile for the rest of her life. It is true that
some . . . make a gloss on the text here. Where it
says that "from the day of her trespass, she had no
children" . . . they claim that she had some, but that
they were born dead, inasmuch as they could not
gain the crown! Now that is a mockery, for it is
understood that she was made sterile. If she had
had children, if she had had a son, he would have
had to be king. It is true that the decree God had
pronounced ought to have been inviolable. Yet
according to the general judgment of humans, the
children who were descended from the family of
Saul would have been preferred. Well, God made
her sterile, and it was to show that he wanted to
cut off her family, and that he wanted the royal
dignity to be transferred. We have to remember
from these words what is fairly common in
Scripture: that is, that to have descendants is a
blessing of God, a sign of his grace and favor. Also
on the contrary, when it pleases him for men to
have no offspring, it shows that he is humbling
them to that degree, and that he wants them to
realize that they are not worthy to have this favor
of being called fathers. Sermons on 2 Samuel.[28]

---

[25]Reynolds, *Works*, 6: 317*.
[26]Arndt, *True Christianity*, 99.

[27]Willet, *Harmony on 2 Samuel*, 37-38*; citing 1 Sam 19:24.
[28]Calvin, *Sermons on Second Samuel*, 1:293.

7:1-29 GOD MAKES A COVENANT WITH DAVID

[1]Now when the king lived in his house and the LORD had given him rest from all his surrounding enemies, [2]the king said to Nathan the prophet, "See now, I dwell in a house of cedar, but the ark of God dwells in a tent." [3]And Nathan said to the king, "Go, do all that is in your heart, for the LORD is with you."

[4]But that same night the word of the LORD came to Nathan, [5]"Go and tell my servant David, 'Thus says the LORD: Would you build me a house to dwell in? [6]I have not lived in a house since the day I brought up the people of Israel from Egypt to this day, but I have been moving about in a tent for my dwelling. [7]In all places where I have moved with all the people of Israel, did I speak a word with any of the judges[a] of Israel, whom I commanded to shepherd my people Israel, saying, "Why have you not built me a house of cedar?"' [8]Now, therefore, thus you shall say to my servant David, 'Thus says the LORD of hosts, I took you from the pasture, from following the sheep, that you should be prince[b] over my people Israel. [9]And I have been with you wherever you went and have cut off all your enemies from before you. And I will make for you a great name, like the name of the great ones of the earth. [10]And I will appoint a place for my people Israel and will plant them, so that they may dwell in their own place and be disturbed no more. And violent men shall afflict them no more, as formerly, [11]from the time that I appointed judges over my people Israel. And I will give you rest from all your enemies. Moreover, the LORD declares to you that the LORD will make you a house. [12]When your days are fulfilled and you lie down with your fathers, I will raise up your offspring after you, who shall come from your body, and I will establish his kingdom. [13]He shall build a house for my name, and I will establish the throne of his kingdom forever. [14]I will be to him a father, and he shall be to me a son. When he commits iniquity, I will discipline him with the rod of men, with the stripes of the sons of men, [15]but my steadfast love will not depart from him, as I took it from Saul, whom I put away from before you. [16]And your house and your kingdom shall be made sure forever before me.[c] Your throne shall be established forever.'" [17]In accordance with all these words, and in accordance with all this vision, Nathan spoke to David.

[18]Then King David went in and sat before the LORD and said, "Who am I, O LORD God, and what is my house, that you have brought me thus far? [19]And yet this was a small thing in your eyes, O LORD God. You have spoken also of your servant's house for a great while to come, and this is instruction for mankind, O LORD God! [20]And what more can David say to you? For you know your servant, O LORD God! [21]Because of your promise, and according to your own heart, you have brought about all this greatness, to make your servant know it. [22]Therefore you are great, O LORD God. For there is none like you, and there is no God besides you, according to all that we have heard with our ears. [23]And who is like your people Israel, the one nation on earth whom God went to redeem to be his people, making himself a name and doing for them[d] great and awesome things by driving out[e] before your people, whom you redeemed for yourself from Egypt, a nation and its gods? [24]And you established for yourself your people Israel to be your people forever. And you, O LORD, became their God. [25]And now, O LORD God, confirm forever the word that you have spoken concerning your servant and concerning his house, and do as you have spoken. [26]And your name will be magnified forever, saying, 'The LORD of hosts is God over Israel,' and the house of your servant David will be established before you. [27]For you, O LORD of hosts, the God of Israel, have made this revelation to your servant, saying, 'I will build you a house.' Therefore your servant has found courage to pray this prayer to you. [28]And now, O LORD God, you are God, and your words are true, and you have promised this good thing to your servant. [29]Now therefore may it please you to bless

the house of your servant, so that it may continue forever before you. For you, O LORD God, have

spoken, and with your blessing shall the house of your servant be blessed forever."

a Compare 1 Chronicles 17:6; Hebrew *tribes*   b Or *leader*   c Septuagint; Hebrew *you*   d With a few Targums, Vulgate, Syriac; Hebrew *you*   e Septuagint (compare 1 Chronicles 17:21); Hebrew *for your land*

OVERVIEW: Discussing David's desire to build a house for God, Reformation-era interpreters wonder about the mistake Nathan and David make in their judgment about this important project. Their questions include the following: Did David and Nathan incorrectly interpret previous words of God about the ark's abiding place (see Ex 12:25; Deut 12:10-11)? Did these holy leaders properly listen for God's will? Was this a case of the Lord dramatically revealing that his ways are different from human ways? Commentators also consider the Lord's promise to build a house for David, asking whether this promise refers primarily to Solomon, to Christ or to both. Their responses provide insight into the reformers' respective views of literal and spiritual interpretations of the Bible, as well as how they understand the difference between the earthly kingdom of the Davidic monarchy and the spiritual kingdom of Christ. Finally, in light of the prayer of thanksgiving that David offers after receiving these promises from God, these reformers take the occasion to discuss what prayer is and what it does.

7:1-2 David's Attempt to Make God a House

WHY DAVID WANTED TO BUILD A TEMPLE. ALONSO TOSTADO: Someone will ask why David wished to build a temple for the Lord. I respond that there are two reasons. The first is because David had always wished to build a temple for the Lord but because the threat of war was always present, he was not able to. But now that the Lord had given him rest from his enemies, he was therefore able to build it. Similarly, the second reason is that because Deuteronomy 12 says that when Israel has rest from her enemies and is no longer living in fear that the Lord would select a

place where burnt offerings and sacrifices can be made. And now that Israel was given rest during the time of David unlike in former times, David therefore believed that he was more capable of constructing the sanctuary than those before him. In this way David was motivated by the simple fact that he had peace, and God had given him rest from all of his enemies. COMMENTARY ON 2 SAMUEL.[1]

DAVID'S GOOD BUT MISTAKEN INTENTIONS. JOHANNES BUGENHAGEN: "See now," said David. This is a human way of thinking: "I dwell in a house of cedar, but the ark of God dwells in a tent, and God deserves a better dwelling place than people." The heart, meanwhile, meditates like this: "I am seeking my own good, which is unworthy because it makes me unable to seek out what is of God, for I have built myself a house of cedar." But our thoughts are nothing to God unless they have God's word. And so you see from David and Nathan that our good intentions are nothing when we do not have the word of God going before us, as it says, "Your word is a lamp to my feet and a light to my path." COMMENTARY ON 2 SAMUEL.[2]

WHY DAVID MADE GOD A HOUSE. ANDREW WILLET: David knew well enough that God didn't dwell in houses made with hands, nor could any temple be made to comprehend his majesty. Yet the ark was a visible symbol of God's presence, and so he thought that the reverent entertainment gave God honor, along with other good thoughts and purposes from the Spirit of God. David's only oversight was that he ran before the Lord's commandment. David learns this worthy lesson, that people should not be addicted to setting forth their own pomp or

---

[1]TO 13:40-41; citing Deut 12:10-12.
[2]Bugenhagen, *In Samuelem prophetam*, 311-12; citing Ps 119:105.

garnishing their own houses, as the Jews did, merely because they dwelled in field houses and made the house of God waste away. David, by taking the advice of Nathan the prophet, didn't rely on his own counsel as if he were a wise and holy man. By doing so, he became an example to princes and magistrates to consult and advise with wise and religious people. HARMONY ON 2 SAMUEL.[3]

7:3 Nathan Speaks Out of Turn

A PROPHET'S LACK OF FORESIGHT. JOHN CALVIN: Nathan replied to David: "Go, and do all that you think, for God is with you." . . . Here the prophet Nathan is much more to blame than David, for since David came to him seeking counsel, he should not have been so very hasty. Rather, he should have prayed for God for revelation. Anyway, he gave a response he had to take back later. We see here how God has always deliberately distributed the gifts of his Spirit in limited measure to those whom he has truly established as teaching doctors in his church. It is true that what he wanted to do he revealed to his prophets. . . . But that is not to say that the prophets had perfect knowledge about everything, for this passage refers to what is appropriate for the edification of the church. . . . Nathan did not keep himself in proper bounds. For it is said that the prophets should never undertake to pronounce a word that was not spoken to them. SERMONS ON 2 SAMUEL.[4]

NATHAN WAS DECEIVED WHEN HE APPROVED DAVID. ANDREW WILLET: Nathan was deceived because he saw that God was with David, and believed that he couldn't be deceived. He reasoned, as they say in school, that God was with him at this time, since some things were blessed and therefore assumed that he was with him in all things. This teaches us that we should not ascribe too much to the worthiness or dignity of any, as though they could not make mistakes, as here

Nathan seemed to think of David. HARMONY ON 2 SAMUEL.[5]

7:4-11 The Lord Will Make David a House

DAVID'S HASTE. JOHN CALVIN: We have here an act of David that was highly praiseworthy, and yet it was utterly condemned by God. This is to show that all our devotion must be properly directed and that we are being thoughtless and presumptuous when we fail to recognize what is right, but instead imagine in our head that things are a certain way. It is true that David's basic motive was good and holy—that is, to build a temple for God. For however much "he dwells not in a house made by human hands" (Acts 17:24), still he wanted to be worshiped in this manner during the time of the figures of the law. But David was too hasty in not waiting for God to order him to do this, and so he took on himself more than was appropriate for him. And yet it was not that he failed to handle himself with modesty, or that he failed to leave himself open to submitting to God. For he did not call in his counselors so that he could tell them: "Here is what I have concluded—it must be carried out!" The pride of earthly kings is such that they want people to agree with them, and they want all that they have said to come into effect. Well, David did not proceed to act so presumptuously. Rather, he called Nathan, the prophet. Indeed, although God had given him the spirit of prophecy to teach others, he still submitted himself to seek out the will of God. Nevertheless, he was still at fault, because in addition to addressing the prophet, he ought to have waited patiently for a fuller revelation to be given him. SERMONS ON 2 SAMUEL.[6]

GOD ESTABLISHES DAVID'S HOUSE. JOHANNES BUGENHAGEN: The Lord said, "I took you from the pasture." This is a reminder of the blessings David received in faith. That is, God says, "I accept nothing from humans. I am very far above humans.

---

[3]Willet, *Harmony on 2 Samuel*, 39*.
[4]Calvin, *Sermons on Second Samuel*, 1:298-99.
[5]Willet, *Harmony on 2 Samuel*, 34*.
[6]Calvin, *Sermons on Second Samuel*, 1:295-96.

It was I who raised you up, who gave you a sure and peaceful place among my people, and who built a house for you, not you for me. Therefore I will increase and strengthen your family's kingdom." Before this it had always been uncertain where the people would make sacrifice, but now the Lord promised the fixed place, which had been mentioned in Exodus 12.

But how can it be granted that the great men who were promised this received what they had been expecting, when the people were carried away over time, as if by a net? The kingdom was confirmed under David, and there were forty years of peace under Solomon, but was that really any longer than the peace that existed under the judge Ehud? For everything fell apart under Solomon, who himself turned to folly. For the promises of God were not thought to have been fulfilled in themselves. For the temple was often profaned, and it was destroyed by the Babylonians, and then finally by the Romans, so that not a stone remained on stone. So it was not apparent that God's promises had been fulfilled through this house.

In the flesh, therefore, the kingdom of David and Solomon and the building of the temple were outward signs and visible shadows of that which was promised. This has been fulfilled in the kingdom of Christ, who established the heavenly Jerusalem, a spiritual temple, and the church of God, in which is peace forever, according to God and our consciences. He has been confirmed as eternal king and son of God, with all things belonging in him. Whoever sins certainly does not belong to him, for he is himself the righteousness and wisdom of God, as it clearly says in Psalm 89; even as a beloved son he makes atonement through afflictions, the cross and persecutions. But God's mercy is not taken from him; neither is his eternal kingdom. What a consolation, that Christ's kingdom, which has not been tainted by sin or corruption, reconciles the father and the son and does not count sins. COMMENTARY ON 2 SAMUEL.[7]

7:12-17 *Nathan's Prophecy of David's Descendant(s)*

CHRIST ALONE. MARTIN LUTHER: We do not deny that word for word this text can be understood as referring both to Solomon and to Christ. Nevertheless, as one can gather from the text itself, then from the prophets, who repeat the same text so often and proclaim it with the greatest diligence, especially in the Psalms, it can be abundantly shown that it has been stated as well as understood concerning Christ alone. LECTURES ON HEBREWS.[8]

DAVID'S TWO HEIRS: SOLOMON AND CHRIST. DIRK PHILIPS: As was the case with the church of the apostles and is clearly shown in Scripture, the apostles apply the promises of Solomon to Christ. What God promised to David, that the fruit of his loins would sit on the throne, was literally fulfilled. Solomon replaced his father as king over Israel, as is clearly shown in Scripture and as Solomon himself witnessed. But spiritually this is to be understood as the true Solomon, Jesus Christ. His throne will remain in eternity and he is the King of his community, over the whole of spiritual Israel. ENCHIRIDION: CONCERNING SPIRITUAL RESTITUTION.[9]

WHETHER THIS PROMISE REFERS TO SOLOMON OR TO CHRIST. ALONSO TOSTADO: Someone will ask in what way this passage is to be literally interpreted, that is, whether this passage refers totally to Christ, totally to Solomon or to a mixture of the two. The *Glossa ordinaria* and Augustine in the *City of God* posit that this promise refers totally to Christ and not at all to Solomon. And that before this time David's temporal reign was spoken about; but here God introduces the spiritual reign of Christ. And here the reign of Christ related to David in this way, namely, that Christ is from the seed of David. COMMENTARY ON 2 SAMUEL.[10]

---

[7]Bugenhagen, *In Samuelem prophetam*, 312-13; citing Ex 12:25.

[8]LW 29:114.
[9]Liechty, ed., *Early Anabaptist Spirituality*, 236; cf. CRR 6:337.
[10]TO 13:43.

THE SPIRIT AND THE LETTER. MENNO SIMONS: That this is spoken of Solomon literally he himself testifies in plain words (1 Kings 3:6; 8:20). Solomon, without doubt, represented in figure Christ Jesus, as in his glory, wisdom, building of the temple, etc. You see, very dear sirs, we should not take the letter for the spirit, and the sprit for the letter. But that the promise according to the Spirit had reference to Christ is incontrovertible; for this the holy prophets of God plainly show (especially Is 9:6; Jer 23:5; 33:15). BRIEF AND CLEAR CONFESSION.[11]

NATHAN'S PROPHECY OF CHRIST, NOT SOLOMON. HEINRICH BULLINGER: It is certain that Scripture draws the lineal descent of Christ very diligently from the loins of Abraham to Jacob, from Jacob to Judah and from Judah to David. And to David are renewed the promises about the incarnation of the Son of God. For Nathan says to David: "When your days are over and you rest with your fathers, I will raise up your offspring to succeed you, who will come from your own body, and I will establish his kingdom. He is the one who will build a house for my Name, and I will establish the throne of his kingdom forever." Now there is no reason why this should be interpreted as referring to Solomon. For he was born when his father David was alive, and his kingdom quickly fell to pieces. But David speaks about a son who would be born to David after his death. "When you rest with your fathers," he says, "I will raise up your offspring to succeed you." And what manner this may be, he declares very clearly by saying, "it will come from your own body." For we read in the Psalms: "From the fruit of your body I will establish your throne." DECADES 4.6.[12]

DAVID'S KNOWLEDGE OF THE MESSIAH. JACOBUS ARMINIUS: What man ever received more promises concerning the Messiah than David, or who has prophesied more largely about him? Yet anyone may with some show of reason entertain doubts as to whether David really understood that the Messiah would be a spiritual and heavenly Monarch; for when he seems to be pouring out his whole soul before the Lord, he did not suffer a single word to escape that might indicate the bent of his understanding to this point. APOLOGY: ARTICLE 11.[13]

DEALING CLEANLY WITH SCRIPTURE. MARTIN LUTHER: One must deal cleanly with the Scriptures. From the very beginning the word has come to us in various ways. It is not enough simply to look and see whether God has said it; rather we must look and see to whom it has been spoken, whether it fits us. That makes all the difference between night and day. God said to David, "Out of you shall come the king," etc. But this does not pertain to me, nor has it been spoken to me. He can indeed speak to me if he chooses to do so. You must keep your eye on the word that applies to you, that is, spoken to you. The word in Scripture is of two kinds: the first does not pertain or apply to me, the other kind does. And on that word which does pertain to me I can boldly trust and rely, as on a strong rock. But if it does not pertain to me, then I should stand still. HOW CHRISTIANS SHOULD REGARD MOSES.[14]

JESUS IN A PAINTING. JOHN CALVIN: This passage cannot be understood of Solomon, nor of all those who succeeded David as far as the temporal kingdom is concerned. Yet at that time, God did begin fulfilling this promise that is mentioned here. We must therefore harmonize the two things. That is, that God was considering Solomon and the situation concerning the country of Judea when he said there would be a king who would reign, and yet he wanted to bring David further, that is, to expect the Redeemer of the world. And that is why this king, who was given as a type of our Lord Jesus Christ, had to be ruined, so that he finally fell away very shamefully, so that indeed not a trace would remain of him. That (I

---

[11]Simons, *Complete Writings*, 436*.
[12]Bullinger, *Sermonum decades quinque*, 299; citing 2 Sam 7:12-13; Ps 132:11.

[13]Arminius, *Works*, 1:314*.
[14]LW 35:170.

say) was necessary. For otherwise, we would have stopped short too quickly, since humans always seek their happiness here below. For although God lifts up our heads and holds us up, as it were, by force to make us consider the eternal kingdom, we continue to be poor beasts with our snouts stuck down in a decaying pasture! Since humans cannot aspire to the heavenly kingdom of God, it was necessary for the type of the kingdom of our Lord Jesus Christ to be removed, in order to draw upward those whose hearts are here below. Nevertheless there had to be some figure in the absence of our Lord Jesus Christ, that is, in the time before he was made manifest. For if the Jews had not had some previous taste of this promise, they would have been unable to draw the definite conclusion that they should hope for the coming of the Redeemer to receive full salvation. Thus they had to have some sign and testimony before their eyes. However, God had to warn them that it was not their goal, and that they must look beyond it.

Now here is how the two matters fit together. David was, therefore, truly the son of God in that he was a type of our Lord Jesus Christ. The same thing is said here of Solomon and of all those who succeeded in his kingdom. In this sense, they were more perfect and more excellent than the angels of paradise. . . . However, if we have our view solely fixed on David, we will not discover what he really represents. For the text presupposes that he who is named here is alone and set apart from the ranks of all other mortals, which will not be found true of David. Therefore, it is our Lord Jesus Christ who must be represented here, as though in a painting or a mirror. SERMONS ON 2 SAMUEL.[15]

ONE SURE MEANING. MARTIN LUTHER: It is Nicholas of Lyra's explanation that the statement . . . ("he will be my son, and I shall be his father") deals, in its less important meaning, with Solomon, the son of David; but he says that it must be understood as referring principally to Christ. Lyra thinks this fundamental principle helps students

acquire the ability to extricate themselves from other obscure passages; but I am of the opposite opinion and maintain that to follow this fundamental principle in the church is neither safe nor profitable. You must always strive to arrive at one sure and simple meaning of an account; and if you change it or depart from it, you should realize that you have departed from Scripture and, in addition, are following an uncertain and doubtful interpretation. LECTURES ON GENESIS.[16]

TWO SENSES. JOHN BALL: In this Davidic covenant . . . the internal efficacy and outward administration is to be distinguished. Part of the promise is absolutely promised; the other part of the promise is conditional upon the actions of those who received the promise. If the conditions were met, God would have made good the promises; but because some of the promises were not accomplished, we know that God did not allow them to take effect on account of human disobedience.

In the first sense, God promised a son to David who should sit on his throne and build a house to the Lord God of Israel. God promised also to establish David's throne forever. But this did not take effect in Solomon, but in Christ—who came of the loins of David and in whose hand the spiritual kingdom was established forever: "I will raise up your offspring after you, who shall come from your body, and I will establish his kingdom." If you seek for bodily succession in the stock of David, it failed together with the kingdom. But this eternity is to be found in Christ, who built a kingdom that shall never fade. He built a heavenly and spiritual kingdom that shall not cease before things that are in heaven perish and vanish away, which is never. In other words, the kingdom is not earthy or bodily, which is subject to change and alteration. In this sense, David says, "This was all his salvation and all his desire, although he did not allow it to bud, that is, he rested in this alone." That is, David believed God would effect and make good his promise: not for righteousness of his

---

[15]Calvin, *Sermons on Second Samuel*, 1:339-40.

[16]LW 3:27.

descendants (for David's house was not as it ought to have been, since it did not keep covenant with God), but for God's great namesake.

In the second sense, many things were promised that never took effect. And yet God is faithful and true even though the condition was broken. To the spiritual house of David, so to speak, was promised pardon of sin, adoption, comfort, joy and a heavenly inheritance. All this was made good, for God freely called them by his Spirit and by his power kept them by faith to salvation. Though the house of David lost the kingdom and government in Israel, God preserved his posterity until Christ came, in whom the throne of David was established forever. For this was absolutely promised. But the temporal glory of David's house and the peace of Israel were changed, because they changed the ordinances, neglected the charge and broke God's commandments. COVENANT OF GRACE.[17]

7:18-29 The Prayer of David

GOD'S ELECTION OF DAVID. JOHN CALVIN: When it says: "You have known your servant," this can be understood to refer to the grace of election, that is, that God had chosen David before the world was created. It is true that afterward David would add: even as God has done all things according to his eternal counsel. However, there is no doubt here that he wanted to say: "Well, Lord, although I am a poor creature here, and my mind is totally confused and I do not know what to say; still you know me. Behold, here am I, guide me as you see fit." Thus this is a passage that offers us good doctrine, when we see that even when we have many weaknesses, still they do not exclude us from God. But on the contrary, we are not to lose courage and grow weary. We are to resign everything to him, and be assured that he will not fail to accept us, even though we are ashamed of ourselves and do not want him to cast his eye on us. SERMONS ON 2 SAMUEL.[18]

HEIR AND HERITAGE. LANCELOT ANDREWES: God promised to David through Nathan that his kingdom should be established forever, though David said, "Who am, O Lord God, and what is my house, that you have brought me thus far?" Though David's people were small, God nevertheless multiplied them and gave continuance to his seed. Now, there are two parts of propagation. The one is to have an heir, the other to have a heritage. Both are here given to David. COLLECTION OF LECTURES.[19]

PROOF OF THE BLESSED TRINITY. ANDREW WILLET: The word "gods," here being plural, is understood with the opinion of those who think there are many gods, according to the saying of Saint Paul, ". . . as indeed there are many 'gods' and many 'lords.' . . ." But there is mention here of the redemption of Israel from Egypt, so it must refer to the true God. Rabbi David Kimchi thought that David spoke about God in the plural as a way to attribute honor to him. But the custom of using plural for singular in order to give more honor and dignity was not used in those days. If that had been the reason, why would David afterward in his prayer use the singular number speaking to God? Some think that "gods" refers to Moses and Aaron, who went to redeem the people. Magistrates and governors are sometimes referred to in Scripture as "gods," but here it is evident that the prophet spoke of God himself: "And who is like your people Israel, the one nation on earth whom God went to redeem to be his people. . . ." The best interpretation is that the word "gods" refers to God as the blessed Trinity: the Father, the Son and the Holy Spirit. Here the word is put in the plural number, "the gods." . . . The plurality of persons is a demonstration and proof of the blessed Trinity, whom in the unity of essence he is said before to be but one. And there is none like him. HARMONY ON 2 SAMUEL.[20]

[17] Ball, *A Treatise on the Covenant of Grace*, 152-53*. [18]Calvin, *Sermons on Second Samuel*, 1:364. [19]Andrewes, *A Collection of Lectures*, 100*. [20]Willet, *Harmony on 2 Samuel*, 45*; citing 1 Cor 8:5.

The Purpose of Prayer. John Calvin: Let us carefully note these words, where it says: "Lord, since it is thus, let the house therefore of your servant be established for ever." ... God had declared he would do this. David was relying on this promise so as to rest on it. And why, then, does he add this prayer? It seems that it would be superfluous. But on the contrary, these are inseparable things, as I have said: the prayer itself and the desire we have to pray for God to accomplish it all and make us feel it in reality. When, therefore, we pray to God, it is not that we are doubting whether he is already inclined to do us good; or whether he watches out to support us in all our necessities; or whether he knows them well; or that when he has spoken, he does not want to carry out his Word. Rather, the fact is that our faith ought to be exercised, and that God, in offering us his mercy and grace, invites us to have the boldness to call on him (Eph 2:18). Without this, he cannot give us free access. Sermons on 2 Samuel.[21]

---

[21]Calvin, *Sermons on Second Samuel*, 1:387.

8:1–10:19 THE WARS OF DAVID

[1]After this David defeated the Philistines and subdued them, and David took Metheg-ammah out of the hand of the Philistines.

[2]And he defeated Moab and he measured them with a line, making them lie down on the ground. Two lines he measured to be put to death, and one full line to be spared. And the Moabites became servants to David and brought tribute.

[3]David also defeated Hadadezer the son of Rehob, king of Zobah, as he went to restore his power at the river Euphrates. [4]And David took from him 1,700 horsemen, and 20,000 foot soldiers. And David hamstrung all the chariot horses but left enough for 100 chariots. [5]And when the Syrians of Damascus came to help Hadadezer king of Zobah, David struck down 22,000 men of the Syrians. [6]Then David put garrisons in Aram of Damascus, and the Syrians became servants to David and brought tribute. And the LORD gave victory to David wherever he went. [7]And David took the shields of gold that were carried by the servants of Hadadezer and brought them to Jerusalem. [8]And from Betah and from Berothai, cities of Hadadezer, King David took very much bronze.

[9]When Toi king of Hamath heard that David had defeated the whole army of Hadadezer, [10]Toi sent his son Joram to King David, to ask about his health and to bless him because he had fought against Hadadezer and defeated him, for Hadadezer had often been at war with Toi. And Joram brought with him articles of silver, of gold, and of bronze. [11]These also King David dedicated to the LORD, together with the silver and gold that he dedicated from all the nations he subdued, [12]from Edom, Moab, the Ammonites, the Philistines, Amalek, and from the spoil of Hadadezer the son of Rehob, king of Zobah.

[13]And David made a name for himself when he returned from striking down 18,000 Edomites in the Valley of Salt. [14]Then he put garrisons in Edom; throughout all Edom he put garrisons, and all the Edomites became David's servants. And the LORD gave victory to David wherever he went.

[15]So David reigned over all Israel. And David administered justice and equity to all his people. [16]Joab the son of Zeruiah was over the army, and Jehoshaphat the son of Ahilud was recorder, [17]and Zadok the son of Ahitub and Ahimelech the son of Abiathar were priests, and Seraiah was secretary, [18]and Benaiah the son of Jehoiada was over[a] the Cherethites and the Pelethites, and David's sons were priests.

9 And David said, "Is there still anyone left of the house of Saul, that I may show him kindness for Jonathan's sake?" [2]Now there was a servant of the house of Saul whose name was Ziba, and they called him to David. And the king said to him, "Are you Ziba?" And he said, "I am your servant." [3]And the king said, "Is there not still someone of the house of Saul, that I may show the kindness of God to him?" Ziba said to the king, "There is still a son of Jonathan; he is crippled in his feet." [4]The king said to him, "Where is he?" And Ziba said to the king, "He is in the house of Machir the son of Ammiel, at Lo-debar." [5]Then King David sent and brought him from the house of Machir the son of Ammiel, at Lo-debar. [6]And Mephibosheth the son of Jonathan, son of Saul, came to David and fell on his face and paid homage. And David said, "Mephibosheth!" And he answered, "Behold, I am your servant." [7]And David said to him, "Do not fear, for I will show you kindness for the sake of your father Jonathan, and I will restore to you all the land of Saul your father, and you shall eat at my table always." [8]And he paid homage and said, "What is your servant, that you should show regard for a dead dog such as I?"

[9]Then the king called Ziba, Saul's servant, and said to him, "All that belonged to Saul and to all his house I have given to your master's grandson. [10]And you and your sons and your servants shall till the land for him and shall bring in the produce, that your master's grandson may have bread to eat. But Mephibosheth your master's grandson shall always eat at my table." Now Ziba had fifteen sons and twenty servants. [11]Then Ziba said to the king,

"According to all that my lord the king commands his servant, so will your servant do." So Mephibosheth ate at David's[b] table, like one of the king's sons. ¹²And Mephibosheth had a young son, whose name was Mica. And all who lived in Ziba's house became Mephibosheth's servants. ¹³So Mephibosheth lived in Jerusalem, for he ate always at the king's table. Now he was lame in both his feet.

10After this the king of the Ammonites died, and Hanun his son reigned in his place. ²And David said, "I will deal loyally[c] with Hanun the son of Nahash, as his father dealt loyally with me." So David sent by his servants to console him concerning his father. And David's servants came into the land of the Ammonites. ³But the princes of the Ammonites said to Hanun their lord, "Do you think, because David has sent comforters to you, that he is honoring your father? Has not David sent his servants to you to search the city and to spy it out and to overthrow it?" ⁴So Hanun took David's servants and shaved off half the beard of each and cut off their garments in the middle, at their hips, and sent them away. ⁵When it was told David, he sent to meet them, for the men were greatly ashamed. And the king said, "Remain at Jericho until your beards have grown and then return."

⁶When the Ammonites saw that they had become a stench to David, the Ammonites sent and hired the Syrians of Beth-rehob, and the Syrians of Zobah, 20,000 foot soldiers, and the king of Maacah with 1,000 men, and the men of Tob, 12,000 men. ⁷And when David heard of it, he sent Joab and all the host of the mighty men. ⁸And the Ammonites came out and drew up in battle array at the entrance of the gate, and the Syrians of Zobah and of Rehob and the men of Tob

and Maacah were by themselves in the open country.

⁹When Joab saw that the battle was set against him both in front and in the rear, he chose some of the best men of Israel and arrayed them against the Syrians. ¹⁰The rest of his men he put in the charge of Abishai his brother, and he arrayed them against the Ammonites. ¹¹And he said, "If the Syrians are too strong for me, then you shall help me, but if the Ammonites are too strong for you, then I will come and help you. ¹²Be of good courage, and let us be courageous for our people, and for the cities of our God, and may the Lord do what seems good to him." ¹³So Joab and the people who were with him drew near to battle against the Syrians, and they fled before him. ¹⁴And when the Ammonites saw that the Syrians fled, they likewise fled before Abishai and entered the city. Then Joab returned from fighting against the Ammonites and came to Jerusalem.

¹⁵But when the Syrians saw that they had been defeated by Israel, they gathered themselves together. ¹⁶And Hadadezer sent and brought out the Syrians who were beyond the Euphrates.[d] They came to Helam, with Shobach the commander of the army of Hadadezer at their head. ¹⁷And when it was told David, he gathered all Israel together and crossed the Jordan and came to Helam. The Syrians arrayed themselves against David and fought with him. ¹⁸And the Syrians fled before Israel, and David killed of the Syrians the men of 700 chariots, and 40,000 horsemen, and wounded Shobach the commander of their army, so that he died there. ¹⁹And when all the kings who were servants of Hadadezer saw that they had been defeated by Israel, they made peace with Israel and became subject to them. So the Syrians were afraid to save the Ammonites anymore.

a Compare 20:23, 1 Chronicles 18:17, Syriac, Targum, Vulgate; Hebrew lacks *was over*   b Septuagint; Hebrew *my*   c Or *kindly*; twice in this verse   d Hebrew *the River*

OVERVIEW: Here the reformers consider David's expanding kingdom in terms of both the increased land promised to the people of Israel and the spread of the spiritual kingdom of God. David's mercy to Jonathan's son Mephibosheth stands as a contrast to both Saul's treatment of David and David's harsher treatment of other surrounding peoples like the Moabites, Ammonites and Syrians. Regarding the ethical implications of these wars, these interpreters pay attention to cultural standards of how ambassadors ought to be treated. Following Augustine and Thomas Aquinas (who both built on Cicero's foundation), Calvin condenses classical definitions of just war theory into defending the faith and protecting the people.[1] Finally, these commentators offer interpretations of the enigmatic phrase that "David's sons were priests" (2 Sam 8:18), shedding light on how they approach challenging texts. They consider the meaning of the word *priest* in light of its other Old Testament usages to conclude that the meaning here describes that the sons were raised to be important public examples of piety but not sacerdotal priests.

8:1-17 *David's Various Battles*

MERCY FOR A TIME. JOHN CALVIN: Here one could ask why David treated the Moabites so cruelly. For whatever the case, it certainly seems that they should have regarded their origin. They were descendants of Lot, the nephew of Abraham, and even God had taken this relationship into consideration, so that the Moabites were exempted as by privilege. How is it, therefore, that David thus went out of bounds? Well, in the first place we have to note that the mercy God gave to the Moabites was only for a time, and was to render them all the more inexcusable. If they had had a drop of sense, they would have thought: "Now here is the God of Israel who was worshiped by Lot, our father, who was nourished and taught in the house of Abraham. Well, we now see how he employs his infinite virtue." This should have reunited them with Israel so they could be members of the church. But far from taking this into consideration, they hardened themselves and puffed themselves up against the children of Israel, just as Moses fully explains. And then they never ceased to keep causing as many injuries as they could to this poor people. Hence the temporary grace that God had bestowed on them served for their greater condemnation. For if God had given them a sign of his goodness, they could, like the others, have behaved in ignorance against the people. Or if the children of Israel had unsheathed their swords against them, they could have had reason to act villainously. And when a war begins, the enemy is not easily appeased. That could have excused them in some sense. But they were convinced that the children of Israel were abstaining from hurting them and were holding themselves back; not because they were not the strongest, but because they were forbidden to attempt anything. Since, therefore, our Lord gave them so many occasions to moderate themselves and yet they grew worse and inflamed themselves in all cruelty, it was quite fair for them to be punished in good measure, once for all, and for their arrogance to be broken. Now that is why, therefore, the stringency David exercised against the Moabites ought not to be considered cruelty, but to be the just judgment of God, since they had abused his long patience and had mocked him. SERMONS ON 2 SAMUEL.[2]

EXPANDING THE EARTHLY AND HEAVENLY KINGDOMS. JOHANNES BUGENHAGEN: Having accepted the promises of an eternal kingdom, the earthly kingdom gets confirmed in the subjection of the Philistines, Moabites, Edomites, Ammonites, Syrians and others all the way to the Euphrates. Up to this point, the Jews had been vexed with many evils on earth because of God's promises. But now the impious people who thought they were seeing the illusions of God might now see them as God's promises. Seeing God's promises in all things is a work of strong faith, because things can take on such divergent appearances. Thus through King David and then Solomon the promised borders described in Numbers 34 could come about and the truth of God's word could be seen by all. But then the people lost it, a sign that the

---

[1]Traditional just war theory expands protecting the people into such practical factors as civilian casualties, proportional responses and the legitimate possibility of a lasting peace. On just war theory, see further J. Daryl Charles, *Between Pacifism and Jihad: Just War and Christian Tradition* (Downers Grove, IL: IVP Academic, 2005); Nigel Biggar, *In Defence of War* (Oxford: Oxford University Press, 2013).

[2]Calvin, *Sermons on Second Samuel*, 1:405-6.

Lord only gives his promises to those who believe. These things clearly signify how Christ's kingdom would be expanded to the Gentiles, just as he began to reign through his gospel in Judea and then expanded its edges to the ends of the earth, as its says in Luke 24, Acts 1, and Psalm 19 and 71. COMMENTARY ON 2 SAMUEL.[3]

DAVID MAKES MOAB A TRIBUTARY. ANDREW WILLET: The Hebrews think that David, when he was pursued by Saul, left his father and mother with the King of Moab, who had them put to death. David's killing of Moab, therefore, would be interpreted as him taking revenge on him. But there is no evidence to support such things in Scripture, and therefore small credit is to be given to such uncertain narrations. The Israelites were indeed commanded not to meddle with the Moabite country, nor to provoke them to battle. First, they were friends to Israel, although by now they had done many wrongs. They had broken and violated that brotherly right and amity that should have been between them. Second, the Moabites had hired Balaam to curse Israel, and did not give them any bread or water. They were forbidden to make any peace with them. In the time of the judges, the Moabites oppressed Israel when the Lord stirred up Ehud, who killed Eglon king of the Moabites. Therefore David had a justified reason to go to war with them. Third, although David had received some kindness at the hands of Moab in the days of Saul, either that king was now dead or David was no longer in that friendship to spare that whole wicked nation against God's commandment. That commandment was given to the Israelites because the subduing of them was reserved for David's time. Though David killed two parts of the inhabitants, he did not do it to take possession of their country or distribute their lands, but only to make them a tributary. HARMONY ON 2 SAMUEL.[4]

8:18 Whether David's Sons Were Priests

DAVID'S HONORABLE MEN. ALONSO TOSTADO: Someone will ask in what way David's sons were considered "priests." For priests came only from the tribe of Levi and from the progeny of Aaron. If anyone else were to assume ministry as a priest beyond this tribe and progeny, he would die, as Numbers 3 and Numbers 18 demonstrate. But the sons of David were clearly from the tribe of Judah, out of which tribe there were never any priests. In fact the apostle writes in Hebrews 7 that Christ was not able to be a priest according to the Mosaic law, because he was from the tribe of Judah. The passage says: "For the one of whom these things are spoken belonged to another tribe, from which no one has ever served at the altar. For it is evident that our Lord was descended from Judah, and in connection with that tribe Moses said nothing about priests." Therefore, if a person of another tribe were to attempt to perform a priestly function in the presence of God, he would die. Or, as in the case of King Uzziah, who desired thus to offer sacrifice to God, he was immediately made a leper and continued to remain one until his death, as mentioned in 2 Chronicles 26:18-21. Therefore David's sons were not priests, nor did they ever do ministry as priests. Nonetheless they were called "priests," which also meant a powerful or distinguished person; for priest in this sense meant prince or honorable man. And such is what David's son were, namely, honorable men among the people. COMMENTARY ON 2 SAMUEL.[5]

READING OBSCURE PASSAGES. JOHN CALVIN: This passage says that the "sons of David were priests." This expression is commonly used in Scripture. At first glance, it could almost seem that David was instructing his children in the worship of God so that they could be in the priesthood. That is why some think David had his sons educated by the doctors of the law as their disciples, so that they could later be in charge of the church. . . . When we

---

[3]Bugenhagen, *In Samuelem prophetam,* 317.
[4]Willet, *Harmony on 2 Samuel,* 48-49*.

[5]TO 13:55; citing Heb 7:13-14.

have an obscure passage like this one, our only action should be to clarify it by comparison with another passage of Scripture. Thus we compare the obscure statement in 2 Samuel 8 with 1 Chronicles 18:17, which says that "the children of David were preeminent." So this word in the latter passage certainly cannot mean priest. Indeed, David would have committed sacrilege if he had wanted to introduce his sons into the priesthood. We know what happened to Uzziah for merely wishing to attempt to offer the incense to God (2 Chron 26:16-17). "He was not content with being king," but also wanted to usurp the priesthood, and so he was stricken with leprosy, and was separated in shame from the people. Uzziah certainly wanted to stand apart from the common rank of men, but this was far more than he bargained for—to be cut off as an unclean creature. This proves that David could not have made his sons priests. SERMONS ON 2 SAMUEL.[6]

IMPORTANCE OF STRONG LEADERSHIP.
ANDREW WILLET: The Latin Vulgate translates the Hebrew word *kohanim* as *sacerdotes*, or "priests." But it is not likely that David's sons—since they were of the tribe of Judah—took on themselves the priesthood, which only belonged to Levi. For the kingdom was invested in Judah and the priesthood in Levi. Those who attempted to confound these offices were not successful. Uzziah the king was stricken with leprosy because he attempted to burn incense, which only the priests could do. And the Maccabees—since they were Levites—usurped the kingdom and procured much woe for themselves and to the entire nation. Some think they were scholars of the priests and were brought up under them; therefore they were called priests just as the students of the schools of the prophets were called prophets. But the schools of the prophets later became prophets, as Elisha after Elijah; but these men never were priests. Other interpreters think that David's sons are better understood to have been princes or chief rulers, for *kohen* signifies a chief or principal man

bearing sacred or civil public office. So they were called the "chief officials" in 1 Chronicles 18:17. Finally, the advancing of David's sons so soon turned afterward to hurt David. For by this Absalom aspired to the kingdom, and Adonijah schemed against Solomon. Yet David did the part of a prudent prince to acquaint his children with the affairs of state. Here are reckoned up the chief officers of David, both in the civil and the ecclesiastical state, showing that a kingdom cannot exist without good officers and governors of both kinds. HARMONY ON 2 SAMUEL.[7]

9:1-13 David Shows Kindness to Saul's House

AN AMBIVALENT ACT. JOHN CALVIN: The deed of David recounted here is surely worthy of being praised as a great virtue. And yet, it was not without an element of vice, so that on the one hand David was worthy of praise for what he did, but on the other hand he was not without blame. The fact that he remembered the house of Saul shows that he had forgotten all vengeance—which is a very rare thing to do, especially if we consider the terribly cruel persecutions that have been spoken of before. David therefore could have been a mortal enemy of the whole race of Saul, and the fact that now he was inclined to kindness is a very rare virtue, which one scarcely ever finds among humankind. But the fact that he waited so long and did not carry out the oath made with Jonathan shows that he forgot it, as though prosperity had intoxicated him. SERMONS ON 2 SAMUEL.[8]

CARING FOR MEPHIBOSHETH FOR GOD'S SAKE. JOHANNES BUGENHAGEN: This chapter is woven among the stories of David's victories so that you can see he was true to his promise and vow to Jonathan that he would be a support to Jonathan's house. Even as Saul violated his promises and vows of faith, so it is said that David preserved them. For if Saul had shown no previous

---

[6]Calvin, *Sermons on Second Samuel*, 1:425.

[7]Willet, *Harmony on 2 Samuel*, 53-54*.
[8]Calvin, *Sermons on Second Samuel*, 1:430.

faith in God, it is no wonder that he would not have excelled in faithfulness to his neighbors. A new fruit needed to grow from that old root. Therefore David then called on the mercy of God, so that he might give benefits to his neighbor for God's sake. For you know that if you do not do so, then you are going against God. So David told Mephibosheth, "Do not fear." He comforted Mephibosheth to say that he did not need to fear evil intentions against him because of Saul. COMMENTARY ON 2 SAMUEL.[9]

OBLIGATION TO A DECEASED FRIEND. LAMBERT DANEAU: Thus did the friendship between Jonathan and David reach and extend to the children of Jonathan. Although this may seem to be done by pact and covenant, which the two made when they first met, doubtless this is included in the wish and desire of all friends: that the fruit of their mutual friendship and love should also extend and be received on their children. Every godly and faithful man has special respect to provide for this, not only for himself but also for his children and those who depend on him. Therefore both the wife and the children of the deceased friend are to be tenderly loved, and all other things besides that belong to him—and all this through an inward affection of hearty goodwill born to the late owner, and by the law and duty of perfect friendship. Nevertheless this should not be in such measure and proportion of the friend who is deceased, but according to the exceeding great love and vehement zeal of the two men's late friendship . . . as the memory of his deceased friend lives still in the breast of him who remains alive, and sends forth many sparks of his unfeigned love—wherever he beholds and is brought unto godly remembrance of his deceased friend by his true and lively images, which are his children left behind. TRUE AND CHRISTIAN FRIENDSHIP.[10]

PATIENT FORBEARANCE. ROGER HUTCHINSON: True and Christian patience is not conceited or void of faith. It is connected with humility and powdered and salted with obedience to all God's commandments. It is garnished with hope of the life to come, with modesty, soberness, gravity, wisdom and love not only of our friends and lovers but also of our slanderers, backbiters, mockers, scorners, oppressors, robbers and even our most cruel enemies. Who was a crueler enemy than King Saul was to David? Saul sought his death continually, chased and pursued him from post to pillar, from place to place; yet look at what patience David forbore him! In his lifetime he obeyed him, gave him honorable and valiant service in his wars, spared and delivered him from death many times when he might have killed him and have been king after him; and after his death, then being in possession of the kingdom, he did not destroy his enemies' blood, nor did he seek vengeance. On the contrary he chiefly declared how much he loved his enemies while he lived. Saul had but one son alive named Mephibosheth, and he was lame. David took him home to his palace, endued him with great lands and honored him so much for his father's sake that he neither dined nor supped without Mephibosheth. David delighted much in his company, and he did not entertain the notion that his table was contaminated with the presence of a lame man. Therefore God favored and prospered David. Such love and patience must be in us. We may not inflame and revile, curse and threaten. We must love and embrace our oppressors; and not only them but also their children, as David did Mephibosheth. TWO SERMONS OF OPPRESSION, AFFLICTION AND PATIENCE.[11]

10:1-5 David's Kindness and Hanun's Disrespectful Response

THE DANGERS OF DISTRUST. JOHN CALVIN: Now if Hanun had killed the ambassadors from David, he would not have committed a greater outrage, and without doubt this action was contrary to universal common law. For from time immemo-

---

[9]Bugenhagen, *In Samuelem prophetam*, 319-20.
[10]Daneau, *True and Christian Friendship*, C4v-C5r*.

[11]Hutchinson, *Two Sermons*, 322*.

rial, people have considered ambassadors to be sacred and privileged, even in time of war. If anyone is sent as an ambassador with a message that displeases the enemy, people still protect their right to return, for an ambassador is like a passport. And in fact, an ambassador ought to be favored because they tend to maintain peace among humankind, or to remove troubles that have already started. That is why God impresses on all people, by nature, the rule and law that ambassadors ought to be sacred. Now here we see, above all, what distrust is. That is why it is not good for us to be consumed by a distrustful spirit—like many people who, thinking they are wise, consider everything doubtful and accept nothing without suspicion. We see some who are so wicked that they actually cultivate this distrustful attitude out of ambition and vanity. . . . What is the outcome? Their attitude causes wars and quarrels. Well, when we are consumed by this sort of distrust, it is certain that we will start fires to which there will be neither end nor measure, and we will not be able to put them out once they have been started. SERMONS ON 2 SAMUEL.[12]

DAVID AND NAHASH. JOHANNES BUGENHAGEN: This is the same Nahash against whom Saul fought, with the Lord's help, in 1 Samuel 11. We do not read in this history that Nahash earned David's gratitude during his exile, although you might understand it based on other things written about what David endured. That seems to be the case here. Just as he would not forget Jonathan, David wanted to give credit even to the Gentiles. But the Ammonites lost this hidden judgment of God through David when they turned a friend into a divine foe. By the will of God, they dragged many other people into this too, just as the Philistines—from whom David had received good things—perished after they attacked Israel and King David in chapter 5 above. This had already happened to the Ammonites in chapter 8 too. COMMENTARY ON 2 SAMUEL.[13]

GENERATIONAL KINDNESS. MARTIN BORRHAUS: The biblical story does not explain what kindness the king of the Ammonites must have shown David. Some interpreters think David and his people may have been exiled for a time in Ammon and the king there kindly showed hospitality to David's displaced people. David wished to extend his gratitude to Hanun for such kindness, just as he wished to show Mephibosheth kindness in memory of his father Jonathan. For such is the way grateful people are prepared to act: They extend a similar love to the children of the love they had for their parents while alive. COMMENTARY ON 2 SAMUEL.[14]

NOT DESPISING MINISTERS. JOHN DAVENANT: A minister of Christ is a minister of the Supreme King of heaven, earth and hell. Not even angels disdain to minister to and serve this Lord. But a minister in what (for this also adds much to the dignity of the ministry)? Not in any base or abject business, but in the dispensation of the most precious treasure, namely, gospel grace. Among the ministers of kings, the treasurer is accounted one of the most honorable: how much honor therefore should people attach to those through whom the treasure of the grace of the Gospel is dispensed to people?

. . . From this title, which is given to preachers of the word, it may be deduced that, since they are the ministers of Christ, they may not be despised or injured with impunity by any person. David avenged the injury done to his ambassadors by the Ammonites, who shaved the Israelites' beards and cut off their garments. How much more shall Christ avenge his ambassadors and ministers if anything is done against them injuriously or contemptuously by Ammonites among us? EXPOSITION OF COLOSSIANS.[15]

10:6-19 David and Joab Engage in Battle

JUSTIFICATION FOR A JUST WAR. JOHN CALVIN: There are two bases for a just war among human-

---

[12]Calvin, *Sermons on Second Samuel*, 1:451.
[13]Bugenhagen, *In Samuelem prophetam*, 320-21.
[14]Borrhaus, *Mystica Messiae*, 500.
[15]Davenant, *Exposition of Colossians*, 1:104*.

kind, which are: for the honor and worship of God and for the safety of all the people. Here are the two considerations that all those who rule and whom God has chosen to bear his sword should have: first, that the honor of God be maintained and religion kept in its purity, and second, that the people be maintained in peace. Those who are seated on the tribunal of justice and have superiority are ordained as officers of God for the protection of his subjects. However, they must not forget the main thing—namely, that God is to have his sovereign empire and all people are to give homage to him. That is how wars can be legitimate, namely, if the honor of God is procured and if the rulers have regard for the peace and welfare of the people.

Now it could certainly be the case that a war is undertaken with a just cause, and yet the one directing the war actually offends, because they are only using the honor of God as a pretext for their war-making. We see many people who argue for a good cause and, indeed, seem to be motivated by nothing but zeal. Yet when we look at their motives more closely, we discover that under the pretext of the honor of God and the public good, they are actually seeking an occasion to enrich themselves. For instance, in these troubled times, how many are there who are fighting under the very shadow of the banner of Jesus Christ, making profession of the gospel, and yet in actuality are addicted to pillaging and plundering, and sing of nothing but their wealth and grab money wherever they can get their hands on it? Why? Now if it really is only a matter of marching and doing their duty, and of procuring the honor and service of God without any profit in it, very soon their zeal will become as cold as ice! But if it is simply a question of gathering into the treasury and banks, suddenly they become the greatest zealots in the world. So zeal is not the only thing that counts, but we must also have pure motives in order to honor God.

Well, when we are fully determined to worship God and to maintain the common peace and welfare, then we will be able to practice effectively what Joab says here, namely, to strengthen ourselves and have an invincible constancy (2 Sam 10:12). For a good cause that is right will always make us brave. It is true that the wicked will be brave enough in their audacity—and too much so. But if a good conscience is leading us to walk honestly before God, to do what he approves, and to serve the common good of the people, it is certain that it will strengthen us much more than if we had all the weapons in the world on our side and the men in hand to defeat a great number of our enemies. Let us carefully note, therefore, that in the first place we should have the foundation of a good conscience, so that we attempt nothing that is not part of our calling and in God's good will. Thus we will not gnaw our bridle with our teeth, nor carelessly roam somewhere that is questionable, but be determined to stay within the will of God. Sermons on 2 Samuel.[16]

Following One's Calling. Martin Luther: We must be guided according to our calling, not according to that which we may think is predestined and about which we are in the dark and know nothing for certain. We have to put this idea out of our minds and hearts and allow the future to be a hidden secret. We have to do what we know we ought to do according to God's Word and the light he has given us. That which God has decreed will come to pass without our doing. Appeal for Prayer Against the Turks.[17]

False Security. John Calvin: We are warned that when God has helped us once, it does not mean we can remain in perpetual repose! What is said here about a people must be applied to each one personally. When God has extended his hand to us in order to help us in need—although there was no defeated army involved, but rather, in one way or another, he has shown that he cares for our salvation—still let us not believe that we are relieved forever. Let us not foolishly think that from here on it is only a question of our rejoicing and winning triumphs—for that kind of thinking will deceive us.

---

[16]Calvin, *Sermons on Second Samuel*, 1:461-62.
[17]LW 43:236.

When people promise themselves this and that, one must not be surprised if they do not get what they wanted. Why? Because when we boast to ourselves about reaching some goal by our wisdom, since we have invented some method in our head, we will be cast down and frustrated in our attempt, and rightly so. Now that is how we must think of ourselves, so that we are prepared to return to battle anew when God once delivers us from this or that conflict. Let us realize that it is only a delay, so that we might have the leisure to refresh ourselves, so to speak, and take courage to enable us always to march on forward. Here again is what we have to observe concerning the statement here, that the Syrians[18] fled. SERMONS ON 2 SAMUEL.[19]

---

[18]Arameans.
[19]Calvin, *Sermons on Second Samuel*, 1:469-470.

11:1-27 DAVID AND BATHSHEBA

[1]In the spring of the year, the time when kings go out to battle, David sent Joab, and his servants with him, and all Israel. And they ravaged the Ammonites and besieged Rabbah. But David remained at Jerusalem.

[2]It happened, late one afternoon, when David arose from his couch and was walking on the roof of the king's house, that he saw from the roof a woman bathing; and the woman was very beautiful. [3]And David sent and inquired about the woman. And one said, "Is not this Bathsheba, the daughter of Eliam, the wife of Uriah the Hittite?" [4]So David sent messengers and took her, and she came to him, and he lay with her. (Now she had been purifying herself from her uncleanness.) Then she returned to her house. [5]And the woman conceived, and she sent and told David, "I am pregnant."

[6]So David sent word to Joab, "Send me Uriah the Hittite." And Joab sent Uriah to David. [7]When Uriah came to him, David asked how Joab was doing and how the people were doing and how the war was going. [8]Then David said to Uriah, "Go down to your house and wash your feet." And Uriah went out of the king's house, and there followed him a present from the king. [9]But Uriah slept at the door of the king's house with all the servants of his lord, and did not go down to his house. [10]When they told David, "Uriah did not go down to his house," David said to Uriah, "Have you not come from a journey? Why did you not go down to your house?" [11]Uriah said to David, "The ark and Israel and Judah dwell in booths, and my lord Joab and the servants of my lord are camping in the open field. Shall I then go to my house, to eat and to drink and to lie with my wife? As you live, and as your soul lives, I will not do this thing." [12]Then David said to Uriah, "Remain here today also, and tomorrow I will send you back." So Uriah remained in Jerusalem that day and the next. [13]And David invited him, and he ate in his presence and drank, so that he made him drunk. And in the evening he went out to lie on his couch with the servants of his lord, but he did not go down to his house.

[14]In the morning David wrote a letter to Joab and sent it by the hand of Uriah. [15]In the letter he wrote, "Set Uriah in the forefront of the hardest fighting, and then draw back from him, that he may be struck down, and die." [16]And as Joab was besieging the city, he assigned Uriah to the place where he knew there were valiant men. [17]And the men of the city came out and fought with Joab, and some of the servants of David among the people fell. Uriah the Hittite also died. [18]Then Joab sent and told David all the news about the fighting. [19]And he instructed the messenger, "When you have finished telling all the news about the fighting to the king, [20]then, if the king's anger rises, and if he says to you, 'Why did you go so near the city to fight? Did you not know that they would shoot from the wall? [21]Who killed Abimelech the son of Jerubbesheth? Did not a woman cast an upper millstone on him from the wall, so that he died at Thebez? Why did you go so near the wall?' then you shall say, 'Your servant Uriah the Hittite is dead also.'"

[22]So the messenger went and came and told David all that Joab had sent him to tell. [23]The messenger said to David, "The men gained an advantage over us and came out against us in the field, but we drove them back to the entrance of the gate. [24]Then the archers shot at your servants from the wall. Some of the king's servants are dead, and your servant Uriah the Hittite is dead also." [25]David said to the messenger, "Thus shall you say to Joab, 'Do not let this matter displease you, for the sword devours now one and now another. Strengthen your attack against the city and overthrow it.' And encourage him."

[26]When the wife of Uriah heard that Uriah her husband was dead, she lamented over her husband. [27]And when the mourning was over, David sent and brought her to his house, and she became his wife and bore him a son. But the thing that David had done displeased the LORD.

OVERVIEW: The interpreters identify many moral faults and lessons in this chapter. In David's bad behavior, the reformers identify vices including idleness, lusting with the eyes and the body, adultery, self-deception, hypocrisy, drunkenness, serving as an accomplice to sin, plotting against the innocent, forgetting the Lord and spurning the Holy Spirit. On this last point, the reformers note that the Holy Spirit returns to David through his confession to Nathan. With respect to Bathsheba, some commentators blame her for intentionally or unintentionally giving occasion for David to sin; others hold her innocent of any misdeed. Calvin chides her for not being more modest or careful, though he does not blame her for David's actions. Arcangela Tarabotti provides an important female voice in this conversation, as she upbraids men for their hypocrisy and quickness to blame the victims of male lust and inappropriate behavior. Additionally, the reformers raise questions of why God might allow such sins and suffering, noting that David's sins in this chapter sow the seeds of much of the conflict yet to come in 2 Samuel. Still, David's sin is his own and is not excused by appeals to God's will or providence.

IF DAVID REALLY IS SO GODLY, WHY DID HE EXPERIENCE SO MUCH TROUBLE? MARTIN LUTHER: A psalm was read at dinner: "Save your people, O Lord." . . . It was asked how then did it happen that David—the king who by divine ordination had replaced another king—had had so many offenses and scourges? As also his psalms indicate, which are full of complaints—he must not have had many good days! Luther answered, "He was disturbed by impious teachers, saw a rebellious people and suffered many rebellions. That taught him well how to pray. Without temptation he was quite free and ready to sin, as he betrays in the murder of Uriah and his adultery. O, dear Lord God! That you let such great people fall! This David had six wives. . . . Beside these six David had two concubines. But he still became an adulterer! Indeed we all desire to rule. But when we come into control, it's toil and labor. May our

Lord God help us, so that those who have begun the contest would finish well!" TABLE TALK.[1]

11:1-2a *David Does Not Go to War but Is Idle*

TRACES OF SIN. PETER MARTYR VERMIGLI: In order for us to see the traces of David's engagement in the shameful acts that follow, let us observe the place and time of his circumstances. He was sleeping securely in the middle of the day in his room. This is proof of a person's ease and idleness. Ish-bosheth, thus, while he was sleeping in the middle of the day, was killed. Although David, while he was engrossed in the same idleness, did not come to utter ruin like Ish-bosheth. For if David had been earnestly thinking about the law, about the blessings of God and the way in which he showered affection on him, about the present war that was being waged and about the danger of his kingdom, he never would have fallen on such shameful actions. Such is what it is like to be idle. COMMENTARY ON 2 SAMUEL.[2]

VICTORIOUS ABROAD, DEFEATED AT HOME. JOHN MAYER: The springtime was the most apt time for the soldiers to fight abroad in the fields, since the air was more temperate, the days were longer and the time of the year was most fit for action for about five or six months altogether. This year is generally thought to have been the forty-ninth of David's age and the nineteenth of his reign. He had not yet taken revenge on the Ammonites, and the former year was so far spent in warring against the Syrians. . . . Therefore this year he chose to stay at home while his men went to battle. On this occasion, he by chance saw fair Bathsheba washing herself from the battlements of his house, where he walked in the evening. Burning in lust toward her once he saw her bathing, David sent for her and lay with her. He should have, as Konrad Pellikan says, gone forth to battle with his men

---

[1]WATR 4:241-42, no. 4344.
[2]Vermigli, *In duos libros Samuelis*, 233r.

rather than resting idly at home. For it is the part of the king not to live in pleasure and idleness, but in times of war to go before their subjects and encourage them. But because David refused to do so and instead remained idly at home, he was assaulted and shamefully defeated at home, even though he had always been so victorious abroad. COMMENTARY ON 2 SAMUEL.[3]

A LONG VACATION. ROBERT SANDERSON: Whereas the devil's greatest business is to tempt other people, the idle person's only business is to tempt the devil. Experience of all histories and times shows us what advantages the devil has won on otherwise godly and hard-working people, as on David, . . . only by watching the opportunity of their idle hours and plying them with suggestions of attractive lusts at such times as they had given themselves but some little break more from their ordinary activities. How will the devil not, then, lead captive at his pleasure those whose whole lives are nothing else but a long vacation and who care nothing but to take up space? TO THE PEOPLE.[4]

TRIAL IN PROSPERITY, NOT IN ADVERSITY. DANIEL DYKE: Trial comes in the midst of prosperity. It is not outdone by adversity. . . . There are many whom affliction has not detected, though peace and prosperity have affected them. Some of those in Queen Mary's days, who kept their garments of faith and good conscience on for all the shaking of the boisterous winds that raged most fiercely at that time, yet afterward—by the flattering rays of that sweet sunshine that followed—were enticed to unbutton themselves and throw off their coats or, at least, to wear them more loosely. How chaste David was in his afflictions! If a hundred Bathshebas had then met him in the wilderness, he would not have been moved at all. But afterward, when he was at rest in his kingdom, how easily he fell! In this way, that which those women formerly sang of Saul and David by way of

joy and congratulations—"Saul has struck down his thousands, and David his ten thousands"—may we truly sing of David's trials by way of mourning and lamentation: "Adversity has struck down its thousands, and prosperity its ten thousands." THE MYSTERY OF SELF-DECEIVING.[5]

WEALTH AND COMFORT PRODUCE FAITHLESSNESS. THOMAS BECON: The stories of the Bible show plainly that, so long as the people of Israel . . . were assaulted with the temptation of adversity and were kept low and were nurtured under the cross, they called on God and walked in the obedience of his holy Word. But when they had peace and quietness, health and wealth, riches and abundance of all things, then they ran in search of strange gods, fell to reveling, to dancing, to adultery, to idleness, to oppression of the poor and most wickedly lived without the fear of God in all carnal security and fleshly quietness. . . . David, so long as he was under the cross, walked in the ways of the Lord. But . . . once he came into prosperity—which enabled him to live in wealth, in idleness and without care—he immediately forgot God and became both an adulterer and a murderer. A NEW CATECHISM.[6]

11:2b *Bathsheba Bathes on a Roof*

BATHSHEBA SINS BY WASHING HERSELF PUBLICLY. ALONSO TOSTADO: Someone will ask whether Bathsheba sinned by washing herself while the king was able to see her. Some say that it would appear that to wash one's entire body like this would be a sign of idleness as well as an enticement, and therefore a sin. I respond that this question includes two parts—whether Bathsheba sinned because she washed her body and whether she sinned by washing herself in such a place where she could be seen. As for the first question . . . Bathsheba washed herself for the sake of legal cleanliness. For women were unclean according to the law during times of menstruation or during the

---

[3]Mayer, *Many Commentaries in One*, 402*.
[4]Sanderson, *Works*, 3:98*.

[5]Dyke, *The Mystery of Self-Deceiving*, 332-33*; citing 1 Sam 18:7.
[6]Becon, *Catechism*, 187.

flow of blood. And when women suffered from menstruation, whatever time of the month it was, as happens regularly to all women, they were to be separated for seven days and were considered ritually impure. Then at the end of her impurity she was to wash her clothes, herself and her bed and she would be clean again, as Leviticus 15 explains. And it is likely that Bathsheba had just finished her menstruation and was now washing herself; and as such, she did not sin by washing herself. On the contrary, not to wash at this time would have opposed to the law. . . .

As for the second question—whether Bathsheba sinned because she washed herself in such a place where she could be seen by the king—either she washed herself there to be seen by the king or someone else, or not. If it is the former, Bathsheba committed a mortal sin since she desired to entice another person toward lust. But here it does not appear to be sufficiently believable. And if someone will say that Bathsheba did not seek to be seen, I respond that she still acted too incautiously, because she made herself naked as if it were a public place. For the terraces of homes at that time were completely open and visible since they did not have walls around them. . . . Therefore Bathsheba was able to be seen from anywhere on a higher terrace, and she was seen from the king's terrace. In this way Bathsheba was too incautious, for from David's terrace he was able to see her nude. . . . As a result, I say that Bathsheba did sin because she behaved too incautiously, making herself bare in such a place where many could be scandalized. But as for whether she committed a mortal sin or not, that is more difficult and has to do with whether she was negligent or whether she had inadvertently done this. COMMENTARY ON 2 SAMUEL.[7]

ACCIDENTAL HORROR. HULDRYCH ZWINGLI: Bathsheba seems to have gone accidently to bathe and David to have been an accidental spectator of this, but when we hear the tragic end of the story, aren't we seized with wondering horror? David had violated the wife of his most faithful champion and, having inflamed rather than satisfied his lust, formed the wicked design of destroying the innocent husband who had no thought of vengeance, and of thus being able to satisfy his desire for the woman to his heart's content. ON THE PROVIDENCE OF GOD.[8]

REMAINING ON GUARD. JOHN CALVIN: David "gazes on this woman whom he sees bathing." We do not know whether it was by necessity or otherwise. For the manner of bathing then was fairly general, and if one condemns Bathsheba for bathing, what will it be with Susannah, of whom we read the same? We must not, therefore, invent vices in order to condemn someone else. But let us weigh what is good or bad in the scales of God, and not of our own fantasy. Now in regard to Bathsheba, she is not to be condemned because she bathed. But she should have exercised discretion, so as not to be seen. For a chaste and upright woman will not show herself in such a way as to allure men, nor be like a net of the devil to "start a fire." Bathsheba, therefore, was immodest in that regard. This can certainly happen to those who are otherwise on their guard, as we read of Isaac, who would never have thought that the king of the Philistines had observed him with Rebecca. Nevertheless, when he was privately with his wife, the king looked at him. Hence, we see that the most modest and temperate can often be surprised. Again, this ought to instruct us to remain on our guard. For if those who do not undress, and neither act nor look immodestly, sometimes fall by being off their guard, what will it be with those who act licentiously? Now that is what we have to note about this point. SERMONS ON 2 SAMUEL.[9]

DO NOT BLAME THE VICTIM! ARCANGELA TARABOTTI: Why on earth publish lying fictions just when you dedicate yourselves to assaulting the

---

[7]TO 13:101-2; citing Lev 15:19-30.

[8]Zwingli, *Latin Works*, 2:218 (ZSW 6,3:210-11).
[9]Calvin, *Sermons on Second Samuel*, 1:481-82; citing Sus 1:15; Gen 26:8.

fortress of chastity as Cupid's disciples? You preach a sheltered life for women, digging up evidence from the tale of Bathsheba: while bathing in an open place she made even King David lie—that holy prophet whose heart was in tune with God's. Ask yourselves, witless ones, who was the true cause of her fall, and then deny it if you can. It was nothing else but the king's lust. Uriah's wife was at home, minding her own affairs bathing—whether for enjoyment or necessity, it matters little—but David eyed her too. Her beauty inflamed him, and his eyes were the gateway to his heart; by various ruses he obtained the satisfaction his sensuality demanded. What blame can one possibly attribute to that innocent woman, overwhelmed by the splendor of the king's majesty? She is more worthy of pardon than the royal harp player: she allowed herself to be overcome by a force from on high, as it were; he succumbed to the pull of flesh doomed soon to rot and darts from two eyes that pierce only those wanting to be wounded. PATERNAL TYRANNY.[10]

11:3-5 David Engrossed in Sin

FROM BAD TO WORSE. MENNO SIMONS: It is evident that abominable, carnal sins, such as fornication, adultery and the like, generally arise from sheer blindness of heart, are committed premeditatedly and intentionally, and are of unclean, inflamed passions and carnal lusts, even though the beginning comes by surprise. Of this we have a good example in David, for although he was a man after God's own heart, and by the power of his faith slew the fierce giant Goliath, whom all Israel dreaded, and rescued the lamb from the jaws of lions and bears, he was so captivated in his flesh by the sight of his eyes that it made him a great and terrible sinner. For as soon as he gave in, sin was born in him, and his heart, which before that time was a temple of the Holy Spirit, was made so blind and foolish that he without hesitation went from one deadly sin and wickedness to another. INSTRUCTION ON EXCOMMUNICATION.[11]

DAVID THE MONSTER. JOHN CALVIN: Now here is a story that should make our hair stand straight up on end whenever we think of it—that a servant of God as excellent as David should fall into such a serious and enormous sin that he could be judged as the most morally lax and promiscuous person in the world. For it would be extremely difficult to find anyone anywhere among the tyrants, or among those who have been the most desperate of all, committing such an excessive crime as David, who thus put himself in the class of monster! For here was David, who was the king and consequently ought to have been the soul of the law in order to give it force. He should have maintained control so that each person could enjoy their own possessions. He should have been the protector of chastity in order to preserve marriages. He should have maintained the life of his subjects. He should have prevented anyone from committing any violence or extortion. SERMONS ON 2 SAMUEL.[12]

ENTICED TO SIN. JOHANNES BRENZ: David, when he saw Bathsheba, the wife of Uriah, from the terrace of his home, was not only enticed to adultery but was also repelling the Holy Spirit by another calling, and he yielded to the affections of his flesh. And although the Spirit was departing from him, David had not yet contaminated himself from another wife, but neither had he looked after his own marriage at the same time. Nevertheless, at this time David was in the flesh and his spirit only revived again when the prophet Nathan later rebuked him. APOLOGY OF WITTENBERG CONFESSION.[13]

MORE BITTERNESS IN SIN THAN HONEY. DANIEL DYKE: Sin deceives us as it tickles our affections and sets our desires afloat by presenting to us the mere and pure pleasure of sin. For whether the pleasure of sin is completely painful or only partially so, our hearts cunningly hide and conceal it. The flesh, by vehemence of temptation, raises such clouds that the light of our understand-

---

[10]Tarabotti, *Paternal Tyranny*, 115.
[11]Simons, *Complete Writings*, 982.
[12]Calvin, *Sermons on Second Samuel*, 1:476.
[13]Brenz, *Opera*, 8:303.

ing is taken away. Just like David in his adultery, the flesh so possessed him with the enjoyment of the present pleasurable delight of his sin that he could not think of the shame, the grief, the wounds of conscience, the broken spirit and those sharp corrections that were to follow. Thus the devil dealt with our Savior when he showed him the world and all the glory in it. But there was also much grief as well as glory in the world. Yet the devil showed him none of that. But there is far more gall and bitterness in sin than there is honey and sweetness. Yet our deceitful hearts will not let us take any notice of it. . . . Sin may well bring with it a flattering pleasure in the beginning, but it always closes with bitter remorse in the end. THE MYS-TERY OF SELF-DECEIVING.[14]

ON PUTTING TO DEATH THE FLESH. JOHN DAVENANT: The general exhortation to mortify our earthly bodies—which comes from Scripture: "Put to death therefore what is earthly in you"—leads us to deduce some corollaries. First, the one who does not labor to mortify the flesh has not risen with Christ. For from the virtue of the death and resurrection of Christ, which he communicated to us, there always follows a desire of mortification and holiness. Therefore those who delight in the flesh are not mortified, but are dead in sin. Second, a true desire of external mortification cannot exert itself in people corrupted by sin, unless they have within them the effective principle of internal mortification—the grace, I mean, of the Spirit of regeneration. Therefore the external exercises that are sometimes wrought by the wicked and bear the resemblance of mortification are not the genuine effects of internal mortification, but are rather false appearances. From the act commanded, "Put to death," we infer, third, that the regenerate themselves never attain such perfect mortification in this life, but that they must always strive to mortify themselves more and more. Finally, if the regenerate relax in this desire to put to death their flesh, that which happened to holy David may happen to

everyone—that he is carried away by the impetuosity of his lusts and, for a time, may be a wretched slave to sin, over which he had before triumphed gloriously. EXPOSITION OF COLOSSIANS.[15]

KINDLING GOD'S GRACE. JOHN CALVIN: This text warns us that when we feel tempted and inclined to some vice, we must immediately control ourselves and keep Satan from entering any further to take possession of us. Let us therefore be careful not to kindle an evil fire, but rather let us listen to the admonition of St. Paul to Timothy: "Kindle the grace of God" (2 Tim 1:6). He used this picture, which means: to make the favors he has received prevail. He calls that "to kindle the fire." Why? Because when God plants in us some little drop of his grace, if we are too lazy and negligent to make it prevail, it is just as if we were totally extinguishing this drop of purity. We must therefore put it into operation. It is like a fire that is ready to go out being rekindled, so that it may once more burst into flame and keep burning. Indeed, this is sufficiently often referred to in the Scriptures—that to extinguish the grace of God is like putting out the fire. But when we possess one single spark of the grace of God, we must immediately be filled with a true zeal and ardor so that this fire will not go out. Let us be careful, therefore, not to put it out by our carelessness, but let us protect it by prayers and petitions, and also seek to kindle it. That is, when we have some evil thought, let us not nourish it until our heart is finally set on fire, so that we go on to carry it out as well as merely thinking it. Nor let us encourage ourselves in a perverse desire and mix it in with another vicious thought that we already have. So this is what we must consider when we see that David inquired who this woman was. SERMONS ON 2 SAMUEL.[16]

11:6-13 David's Ploys with Uriah

DAVID'S WICKED WAYS. MENNO SIMONS: David never once, it seems, thought of the Lord

---

[14]Dyke, *The Mystery of Self-Deceiving*, 198-99, 201.

[15]Davenant, *Exposition of Colossians*, 2:36*; citing Col 3:5.
[16]Calvin, *Sermons on Second Samuel*, 1:482-83.

who called him to such distinguished honor and had endowed him with such a precious Spirit. For when it was told him of Bathsheba that she was with child by him he sought with trickery to hide his horrid deed. He had Uriah called in from the field and pretended he wished to consult him in relation to the war, and admonished him twice that he should go into his house. Why can be easily surmised. Afterward he invited him to a feast, as though he were very fond of him, so that he might make him drunk and so send him to his wife and cover his own shame. But when he failed in all this, he gave this truly noble man an ungodly, treacherous letter, that Joab should place him in such a point where the battle was the most severe, and then leave him alone so that he might be slain. Behold, this one wicked act engendered another in David, because he consented to the lusts of the eyes, and gave place to conceived sin. Yes, he was blinded to such a degree in his inflamed flesh, and was so intimate with sin, that according to the rigor of the law, had he not himself wielded the scepter, he would have been doubly guilty of the ban of death; first, because he was an adulterer; and second, because he was guilty of innocent blood. INSTRUCTION ON EXCOMMUNICATION.[17]

GOD ATTEMPTS TO AWAKEN DAVID'S CONSCIENCE.

JOHN CALVIN: Now here was David, who thought he had found a good plan when he called Uriah, to make him sleep with his wife; but David was frustrated in his expectation. And who caused this? God, who was pursuing him. It is true that it was for his salvation. Now there are some illnesses in which sleep brings death. In those cases, the physician will annoy the poor patient terribly by pulling his nose and ears and pushing him on every side. Then the patient will be very angry and distressed over this, for he wants nothing but sleep. But to let him sleep ... would be to lose him. So it is with sinners who just try to flatter themselves and to put their conscience to sleep. For if God awakens them, not allowing them to be like

animals, they become angry about it, even though it is for their own good.

Since God had procured the salvation of David, he wanted his shame to be known by everyone, and this was why he did not permit Uriah to go to sleep with his wife, and thus provide David's adultery with a cloak or covering. The same thing can happen to us, which is why David's experience should serve as an instructive example. We see by experience that those who seek to disguise or bury their evil deeds simply wear a hypocritical face. They double the evil, and thus make themselves all the more ridiculous by thinking that they have invented this or that in order to provide such hiding places where they will not be perceived by anyone. God, on the contrary, causes their actions to be even better known and to be held in greater mockery and shame than if, at first sight, they had frankly confessed their first transgression. SERMONS ON 2 SAMUEL.[18]

DAVID'S ATTEMPTED CONCEALMENT.

HENRY AINSWORTH: Because Bathsheba was pregnant with his child, David first sought to cover his sin by having Uriah sent home to sleep with his wife, so that it would appear that Uriah was the father. After David's plan failed, he sent Uriah back with a private letter for Joab, which called for Uriah's death. After Uriah was killed, David married Uriah's wife Bathsheba to try to conceal his sin.... Although David concealed his sin from the public, he could not conceal his sin from God. ANNOTATIONS ON PSALMS.[19]

SOBER DAVID WORSE THAN DRUNKEN URIAH.

THOMAS ADAMS: Many have lost their lives because they would not get drunk; noble Uriah was made drunk, yet could not save his life. King David had impregnated his wife, and his plan was to shelter it with the name of her husband. Uriah had protested against feasting at home, against luxurious delights. He could not be won with

[17]Simons, *Complete Writings*, 982.

[18]Calvin, *Sermons on Second Samuel*, 1:492-493.
[19]Ainsworth, *Annotations on the Psalms*, 117.

words; therefore, the courtiers must now try him with wine. . . . I do not think Uriah intended any excess but only to obey the king. But wine is a mocker; it goes plausibly in, but who can imagine how it will work? It steals in like a lamb, but then rages like a lion. The one who imbibes that traitor will complain of a surprise before too long. In the end even good Uriah is made drunk; the holiest soul may be overtaken. . . . Uriah was made drunk so that he might desire his own wife; many husbands are so drenched that other men may have access to their wives. What was the issue? The plan fails. Grace is stronger than wine, the fury of the grape cannot carry Uriah to his own bed. . . . David meant by procuring the sin of another to hide his own; but he could not hide it. We have often heard that those who sought to overthrow others were soon overtaken themselves. Whose is the chief offense? Uriah's drunkenness is more David's sin than his own: sober David is worse than drunken Uriah. Woe to him who gives his neighbor a drink to discover his shame; in fact he shall discover his own shame. The one who gives a person wine to deceive them is first drunk in soul before they can bring about the other's bodily drunkenness. . . . David's worthy men were honored for their deeds of arms, not for their great drinking. The one who makes a person drunk to deceive him, to turn another into a beast, makes himself a devil. To deceive someone under the guise of friendship is the most despicable villainy. Feasting implies friendship, and friendship admits of no deceit. . . . Nothing is easier than this deceit, nothing more unpardonable. . . . Uriah must be set in the forefront of the battle; honor is pretended to him, murder is meant. He was a valiant soldier, and before he had the title of David's worthy, he dearly earned it. COMMENTARY ON 2 PETER.[20]

ON DRUNKENNESS. JOHN CALVIN: We see how the tongue of Uriah was governed by the secret counsel of God, so that he taught David in such a way that he received greater condemnation. As I said,

these words were like so many blows with the fist and with darts to break and pierce his heart. But did it lead him to repentance? Indeed no. Rather he continued wanting to seek avenues of escape: "He made Uriah remain another day, and the next day he called him to the banquet and made him drunk. . . ." Uriah was not literally drunk, but this word *drunk* is used figuratively in Scripture to describe all banquets where people have drunk more than usual, although they have eaten soberly. . . . Now this does not mean that we are to let down our guard, for we see that when people allow themselves to drink more than nourishment requires, drunkenness eventually gets the best of them. A person must surely restrain themselves. But that is not to say that when they are at a banquet, they cannot rejoice in such a way that they will drink a few more glasses of wine than usual, without bothering either their body or mind.

Now it would seem, at first sight, that this would serve to give us license to drink beyond measure, but it is the contrary. Actually, we must be aware of all those things that are legitimate for us. For "everything that is done without faith," says St. Paul, "is always sin" (Rom 14:23). Therefore, when we do not know whether God has permitted something, we dare not budge a finger, lest our conscience becomes seared as with a hot iron. Consequently, we would not know whether to eat a piece of bread, until we had the kind of certitude that St. Paul requires in this passage. That is, we must know that God has given us permission to do it, and that it is according to his good will. Hence a person should not dare drink a drop of wine unless they know they are receiving it from the hand of God. Therefore, when one rejoices, granted that it is with true moderation and without excess, it is a legitimate thing. So this is what should be understood when it says that Uriah became "drunk."

It is true that David intended to make Uriah drink until he was too merry, as they say, and that hence he would go and sleep with his wife. But what was the drunkenness of Uriah really like? He stayed away from his wife, as he had the previous night. If he had been literally drunk, it is certain that he would not have done that, and would not

---

[20]Adams, *Commentary upon 2 Peter*, 890-91*.

have been able to abstain from going to his wife. Therefore, when he was content to be at the king's door and soberly to maintain his chastity, it was a sign that when he came away from the table, his mind was not confused. Now that is a good type of drunkenness—that is, a man should be permitted to relax and to rejoice, under the condition that he is always disposed to honor God and to apply himself to carry out his duty. For we must keep these two considerations in mind when we drink and eat: that is, to keep from hurting either our body or mind, so that we may always be free to employ ourselves in the service of God and in whatever way he calls us. SERMONS ON 2 SAMUEL.[21]

11:14-27 David Has Uriah Killed and God Is Displeased

ON SILENCE AND SIN. MARTIN LUTHER: For one who keeps silent (that is, who does not confess), their bones quickly grow old, that is, their powers in which they formerly stood in good things are always reduced more and more by sins. For sin that is not washed away by repentance soon draws to another sin by its own weight, as is clear in the case of David. First he committed adultery, then he made Uriah drunk and finally he had him killed. SCHOLIA ON PSALM 32:2.[22]

DAVID'S PIMPS CONCEAL CORRUPTION. JOHN CALVIN: David's sin instructs us . . . not to let down our guard when we begin to do evil. For the devil will surely know how to make us plunge deeper and deeper until we are completely swallowed up. As I say, let us be fearful and not even think of covering one evil with another, and hardening ourselves. When we are guilty before God, let us be prepared to admit it before others, rather than to abandon ourselves to our sin, as David did.

Nevertheless, we see how God blinded him. For Joab must have known his villainy. It is true that David certainly wanted to color what he was doing,

and without a doubt he pretended that Uriah fully merited being treated in this way, for he did not explain to Joab the reason why he wanted him to die. But he was to presume that Uriah had behaved badly and that the king had found him disloyal, because people always judge another's decision according to that person's level of authority. But be that as it may, this was not sufficient to hide David's corruption. Hence God permitted him to be found guilty, by one person after another. He became indebted to his domestic servants when he made them his pimps. Thus the story had already become public knowledge. But for the present, David took refuge in Joab. SERMONS ON 2 SAMUEL.[23]

DEATH BY LETTER. DANIEL DYKE: When the truth of obedience and power of godliness is lacking, surely there is small difference between an Israelite and an Ishmaelite, a circumcised Hebrew and an uncircumcised Philistine, a baptized Englishman and an unwashed Turk. Neither is the barren fig tree in God's orchard in any better case than is the bramble in the wilderness. . . . This therefore will be but a pathetic plea before God: "We have gone to church, frequented prayers, heard the sermons." Indeed, even the plea of preaching sermons will not be admitted. When you bring to God the sermons you have head, you bring Uriah's letter, on which are written your own death and damnation. For God will judge and condemn you so much more severely and soberly by comparison to how much you should have repented. Therefore all the earth should be cursed, because having been watered with the dew of heaven, it brings forth nothing but brambles and briars. THE MYSTERY OF SELF-DECEIVING.[24]

HIGH PRESUMPTUOUS SIN. ROBERT SANDERSON: David was not such a stranger in the law of God as not to know that the willful murder of an innocent party, such as was the case with Uriah, was a most loud crying sin. As such, it is clear that

---

[21]Calvin, *Sermons on Second Samuel*, 1:500-502.
[22]LW 10:147* (WA 3:175).

[23]Calvin, *Sermons on Second Samuel*, 1:505-6.
[24]Dyke, *The Mystery of Self-Deceiving*, 62-63*.

this was not merely a sin of ignorance. Neither yet was it properly a sin of infirmity, and so capable of that extenuating circumstance of being done in the heart of lust (although that extenuation will not be allowed to pass for an excuse . . .). But having time and leisure enough to imagine himself what he was about, he did it in cool blood, and with a good deal of deliberation, plotting and contriving this way and that way to perfect his design. David was resolved, whatever should become of it, to have it done. And as such, this sin of David's was therefore a high presumptuous sin. SEVENTEEN SERMONS.[25]

HEAVEN AS REWARD FOR EARTH'S INJUSTICE. JOHN CALVIN: One might find it strange that God permitted Uriah to die like this, given that he was innocent. For we have seen the reverence he manifested in the service of God, and that the ark was so precious to him that he was even conscientious about entering his house to rest or take his ease while the ark of God was in the field. Why, then, did God not help him in time of need? Where were the promises by which God testified that he would never forsake his own; that their blood would be precious to him; that even a hair of their head would not fall, and that they were numbered by him; that he would guide their steps, and that he would cause them to be guided by his angels; and that they would be fortified with a double rampart; that he would be their strength and their shield; that he would hold them dear as the apple of his eye; and everything else that it is possible to say? It seems . . . that these promises failed for Uriah. . . .

But from this we can gather the exact opposite: the faithful have no stopping place in this world as their final goal. Otherwise one would have to conclude that God is an idol or a phantom. When we accept the principle that God is the Judge of the world, and that we must all pass before his bar and render account of our works; when we thoroughly accept this truth, the death of Uriah, as well as that of Abel and the like, will serve to confirm our belief in eternal life. Indeed, there must be a better life

than this one, for otherwise we would have to say that God was asleep in the heavens when Uriah was put to death, and when Abel was killed. Hence we see that this death, instead of horrifying us, is useful to us, because it is like a mirror that represents eternal life before our eyes. Although it could have caused unbelievers who hastily judge the works of God to quit his service, those who use it as an excuse to reject God's service are motivated by nothing but their own presumption. SERMONS ON 2 SAMUEL.[26]

ALL ARE LIARS. EDWARD REYNOLDS: "All humankind are liars": As soon as a person is left to themselves, they become a miserable spectacle of weakness and mutability. . . . Who could have thought that David, a man after God's own heart, with one miscarrying glance of his eye should have plunged into such a gulf of sin and misery as he fell into? That so spiritual and heavenly a soul should be so suddenly overcome with so sensual a temptation? That so merciful and righteous a man should so greatly wrong a faithful servant as he did Uriah, and then make the innocent blood of him whom he wronged a mantle to palliate and to cover the wrong, and make use of his fidelity to convey the letters and instructions for his own ruin? SEVEN SERMONS ON THE FOURTEENTH CHAPTER OF HOSEA.[27]

ASHES FOR A TIME. HENRY AIRAY: It may be asked whether it can be that those who are God's children in the Lord should always continue in the Lord? Here is my answer: Those of God's children who are grafted in the true olive tree may, for a season, seem like withered branches; and the graces of God's Spirit may decay in them and lie smothered so that they appear no more than the fire under the ashes or embers. This is how we may see David in this season of his life. Even after having committed murder and adultery, he walked on a long time without ever being touched with any

---

[25]Sanderson, *Works*, 1:92-93*.

[26]Calvin, *Sermons on Second Samuel*, 1:507-8; citing Ps 37:28; 72:14; Heb 12:24; Mt 10:30; Ps 91:11; 28:7; Deut 32:10; Ps 17:8. [27]Reynolds, *Works*, 3:378*; citing Ps 116:11.

remorse for his grievous sins. Indeed, it seemed as if he were a withered branch. . . . Nevertheless David could not ultimately fall from grace, for as Paul says, "He who began a good work in you will bring it to completion at the day of Jesus Christ." LECTURES ON PHILIPPIANS.[28]

---

[28] Airay, *Lectures on Philippians*, 322*; citing Phil 1:6.

12:1-31 DAVID REBUKED AND PUNISHED

¹And the Lord sent Nathan to David. He came to him and said to him, "There were two men in a certain city, the one rich and the other poor. ²The rich man had very many flocks and herds, ³but the poor man had nothing but one little ewe lamb, which he had bought. And he brought it up, and it grew up with him and with his children. It used to eat of his morsel and drink from his cup and lie in his arms,ᵃ and it was like a daughter to him. ⁴Now there came a traveler to the rich man, and he was unwilling to take one of his own flock or herd to prepare for the guest who had come to him, but he took the poor man's lamb and prepared it for the man who had come to him." ⁵Then David's anger was greatly kindled against the man, and he said to Nathan, "As the Lord lives, the man who has done this deserves to die, ⁶and he shall restore the lamb fourfold, because he did this thing, and because he had no pity."

⁷Nathan said to David, "You are the man! Thus says the Lord, the God of Israel, 'I anointed you king over Israel, and I delivered you out of the hand of Saul. ⁸And I gave you your master's house and your master's wives into your arms and gave you the house of Israel and of Judah. And if this were too little, I would add to you as much more. ⁹Why have you despised the word of the Lord, to do what is evil in his sight? You have struck down Uriah the Hittite with the sword and have taken his wife to be your wife and have killed him with the sword of the Ammonites. ¹⁰Now therefore the sword shall never depart from your house, because you have despised me and have taken the wife of Uriah the Hittite to be your wife.' ¹¹Thus says the Lord, 'Behold, I will raise up evil against you out of your own house. And I will take your wives before your eyes and give them to your neighbor, and he shall lie with your wives in the sight of this sun. ¹²For you did it secretly, but I will do this thing before all Israel and before the sun.'" ¹³David said to Nathan, "I have sinned against the Lord." And Nathan said to David, "The Lord also has put away your sin; you shall not die. ¹⁴Neverthe-

less, because by this deed you have utterly scorned the Lord,ᵇ the child who is born to you shall die." ¹⁵Then Nathan went to his house.

And the Lord afflicted the child that Uriah's wife bore to David, and he became sick. ¹⁶David therefore sought God on behalf of the child. And David fasted and went in and lay all night on the ground. ¹⁷And the elders of his house stood beside him, to raise him from the ground, but he would not, nor did he eat food with them. ¹⁸On the seventh day the child died. And the servants of David were afraid to tell him that the child was dead, for they said, "Behold, while the child was yet alive, we spoke to him, and he did not listen to us. How then can we say to him the child is dead? He may do himself some harm." ¹⁹But when David saw that his servants were whispering together, David understood that the child was dead. And David said to his servants, "Is the child dead?" They said, "He is dead." ²⁰Then David arose from the earth and washed and anointed himself and changed his clothes. And he went into the house of the Lord and worshiped. He then went to his own house. And when he asked, they set food before him, and he ate. ²¹Then his servants said to him, "What is this thing that you have done? You fasted and wept for the child while he was alive; but when the child died, you arose and ate food." ²²He said, "While the child was still alive, I fasted and wept, for I said, 'Who knows whether the Lord will be gracious to me, that the child may live?' ²³But now he is dead. Why should I fast? Can I bring him back again? I shall go to him, but he will not return to me."

²⁴Then David comforted his wife, Bathsheba, and went in to her and lay with her, and she bore a son, and he called his name Solomon. And the Lord loved him ²⁵and sent a message by Nathan the prophet. So he called his name Jedidiah,ᶜ because of the Lord.

²⁶Now Joab fought against Rabbah of the Ammonites and took the royal city. ²⁷And Joab sent messengers to David and said, "I have fought against Rabbah; moreover, I have taken the city of waters.

²⁸Now then gather the rest of the people together and encamp against the city and take it, lest I take the city and it be called by my name." ²⁹So David gathered all the people together and went to Rabbah and fought against it and took it. ³⁰And he took the crown of their king from his head. The weight of it was a talent^d of gold, and in it was a precious stone, and it was placed on David's head. And he brought out the spoil of the city, a very great amount. ³¹And he brought out the people who were in it and set them to labor with saws and iron picks and iron axes and made them toil at^e the brick kilns. And thus he did to all the cities of the Ammonites. Then David and all the people returned to Jerusalem.

a Hebrew *bosom;* also verse 8   b Masoretic Text *the enemies of the* LORD; Dead Sea Scroll *the word of the* LORD   c *Jedidiah* means *beloved of the* LORD   d A *talent* was about 75 pounds or 34 kilograms   e Hebrew *pass through*

OVERVIEW: Reformation-era writers discuss the themes of repentance, judgment and forgiveness that arise in Nathan's righteous rebuke of David in this chapter. Luther and Melanchthon, for instance, point to the great liberation that comes through the confession of sin and holy words of forgiveness; this is a good example of how confession and absolution retained near sacramental status in the Lutheran tradition. Other commentators address the challenging relationship between God's righteous punishment of sin and the death of David and Bathsheba's first child together. Continuing a prominent theme of medieval Christianity, the reformers disagree whether there is a distinction between the spiritual guilt of sin and the earthly punishment of sin. More pastorally, many of these same theologians reflect tenderly on the grief that comes with the death of a child. Finally, the reformers consider the birth of Solomon, whose two names (Solomon and Jedidiah) respectively mean "peace" and "beloved of the Lord."

12:1-4 Nathan Tells a Story

ACCEPTING GOD'S DISCIPLINE. JOHN CALVIN: Nathan . . . had the door open, as it were, when David, at first hearing, declared that this man was not to be tolerated (2 Sam 12:5). It is true that he was not thinking of himself, for hypocrisy was still holding him in this ignorance, as we have seen. But still he showed us a good principle. Nathan went further when he saw that David was already disposed to receive the correction. For it was a sign that he was already making himself meek when he judged in favor of equity and uprightness, and when he even had such zeal that he did not want the evil to be tolerated, but wanted to rebuke it with his royal authority. Now that is one thing.

Nevertheless, we should note that if God treats us sharply at the first encounter before making us feel his mercy, we should not find it strange, but subject ourselves willingly to it. It is true that we certainly like him to begin gently, and indeed we would like him to bow down before us in order to please us. Indeed, we would like to strike him in the face, as if he were a common lodger in our house. Now this impudence will come out in nearly everyone when God does not restore them as they would like. Let us learn, therefore, when God comes to us in such force, to bow our heads and recognize that we need chastisement. SERMONS ON 2 SAMUEL.[1]

FOURFOLD PAYMENT ACCORDING TO THE LAW. THE ENGLISH ANNOTATIONS: The scope of this parable was to awaken David out of his deep sleep of security and sin by causing him unknowingly to pass an impartial sentence against himself, in the person of another, so that he might be brought to a genuine repentance . . . according to the law in Exodus 22:1. And this penalty was inflicted on David. In line with the law for killing Uriah, David lost four sons: the infant, Amnon, Absalom and Adonijah. ANNOTATIONS ON 2 SAMUEL.[2]

[1]Calvin, *Sermons on Second Samuel,* 1:530-31.
[2]Downame, ed., *Annotations* (1645), FF4v*; citing Ex 22:1.

A Friendly Rebuke Goes a Long Way. John Dod: As humans, we are so full of self-love that others may easily discern more evil in us than we can see in ourselves. And these of all others are the best and most faithful of friends. These are the ones who will mercifully and wisely—though sharply and roundly—tell us of our faults as Nathan dealt with David when his heart had been a long time hardened by lying in unrepented sin. This private admonition of his, as we may observe, was a more effectual means for his rousing out of that dead slumber than any or all of the public ordinances of God—including the sacrifices of the law and sermons of the prophets—which all that while he had heard or attended to. And sometimes it is found by experience yet still that a wholesome, sound and wise reproof of a minister of God or of some Christian friend in private—when it is thoroughly set up and effectually applied—is able to do (through God's blessing) what many holy and excellent sermons could not effect and bring to pass. The Second Sermon of the Lord's Supper.[3]

David's Lengthy Residence in Sin. Andrew Willet: It is evident that David lived in sin for about ten months. The child that was conceived in adultery was born after this admonition of the prophet. Nathan was sent for after a long time, not as some think, by watching for the best opportunity. When a person is upset, it is best to wait until all of the emotions are calmed, for the more one is grounded by continual sin, the stronger they are brought to repentance. Neither is it that David in the meantime was otherwise admonished and put in mind of his sin by reading Scripture, and by remembering Uriah's words to him. For it appeared by David's answer to Nathan, when he gave sentence against himself, that David was not yet awakened from his sin. But it pleased God to defer the prophet's coming to him since, due to the weakness and impotency of our nature, it is never able to rise independently to repentance. And God manifests his love toward his elect by not allowing

them to rest in their sin, but always calling them home in time. Harmony of 2 Samuel.[4]

12:5-12 Nathan Delivers God's Judgment to David

Application Versus Explication. Thomas Adams: The prophets found that actual application pierced more than verbal explication. Nathan, for instance, brought David's heart to a humble confession. He drew the proposition from David's own lips: ". . . the man who has done this deserves to die." And then Nathan struck while the iron was hot by inferring the conclusion: "You are the man!" The Sinner's Passing-Bell.[5]

David, Not Bathsheba, Is Punished. Arcangela Tarabotti: God's reproof of adulterous King David is ample testimony that men deserve greater punishment than women in violating the marriage bed. He said nothing to Bathsheba, who fell on being tempted by the king. Your lying insulting tongues never cease preaching that the source and origin of all fornication and adultery is woman. As they are supposedly cunning and shrewd in hiding their desires, they inveigle people to their dooms with charms and flattery—at least, this is how your evil minds would have it. Many of you are enemies of our sex, and still you know how to go to extremes, without opposition, or any woman's part, in a way that deserves the most burning outbursts of God's anger, since only heaven's fire is a fitting scourge for them. Paternal Tyranny.[6]

Ramifications of David's Adultery. Heinrich Bullinger: In truth there are some smooth fellows, if you please, that seem to make adultery into a sport. They believe that David's adultery is made on their side, and that our Lord was favorable to the adulteress who was taken away for the act of adultery. Why don't these people

---

[3]Dod, *Ten Sermons*, 56*.

[4]Willet, *Harmony on 2 Samuel*, 65-66*.
[5]Adams, *Devil's Banquet*, 215*; citing 2 Sam 12:5, 7.
[6]Tarabotti, *Paternal Tyranny*, 112*.

consider how severely David was punished for this same offense? The calamitous house of David was soon polluted by filthy incest. For Amnon raped his sister Tamar by force. And David's house was crudely defamed by murder, as Absalom murdered his brother Amnon while he was at a banquet. That same Absalom corrupted and defiled his father David's wives—and in the open—putting aside all sense of shame. He drove his father from the kingdom and hastened to shorten his days. David acknowledges that all these calamities were fair punishments for his crimes of adultery and murder. DECADES 2.10.[7]

CALAMITY FALLS. DAVID DICKSON: How great calamity may befall the best of God's children— and that from those persons from whom they could least expect to be troubled. For David was deserted by his own subjects and chased from his palace and royal state by his own son, Absalom. Although the Lord does not follow the sins of his children with vindictive justice, yet by the sharp rods of fatherly correction he can make his own children, and all the beholders of their scandalous sins, see how bitter a thing it is to provoke him to wrath, as David had done. Even when sin has drawn on judgment, God must be dealt with for relief, no less than if it had sent for trial only—as David does in the case of the correcting and purging of the pollution of his family by the insurrection of his son against him. EXPLICATION OF THE FIRST FIFTY PSALMS.[8]

DOUBLE AFFLICTION. ROBERT SANDERSON: God himself, when he graciously pardoned a high presumptuous sin as he did David's great sin in the matter of Uriah, commonly lays forth some lasting affliction on the offender . . . , who, after sealing his pardon for that sin by Nathan, scarcely ever had a quiet day all his life long. The reason for this seems to be double. It is partly for admonition to others that none presume to provoke God in like manner lest

they suffer for it also in like manner. And it is partly for the good of the offender, that they may by the suffering be brought to the deeper sense of their error, and be repeatedly reminded of it, lest they should too soon forget it. THE CASES DETERMINED.[9]

GOD'S CLOUD. HUGH BINNING: Look on the very end and purpose of God's hiding himself and withdrawing. It is this, that we may come and "seek him early." When God is angry, mercy and compassion balances it, for anger is sent out to bring in wanderers. God's anger is not capricious but is resolute, deliberate and walks on good grounds. This is seen in the case of David, where in his prosperity he did not miss God. When all things went according to his plan, then he let God go where he wanted to; therefore, the Lord in mercy must hide his own heart with a frowning countenance and cover himself with a cloud, that David may be troubled and so return to God. HEART-HUMILIATION: SERMON 18.[10]

NEVER LACKING WOE. ROBERT SANDERSON: What a world of mischief and misery did David create for himself by that one presumptuous act in the matter of Uriah, almost all the days of his life from then on! The prophet Nathan, at the very same time when he delivered him God's royal and gracious pardon for it . . . , "The Lord also has put away your sin," yet he still read him the bitter consequences of it. . . . And just as Nathan foretold him, it fell out with him accordingly. His daughter was defiled by her brother Amnon; that brother slain by another brother Absalom; a strong conspiracy raised against him by his own son Absalom; his concubines openly defiled by the same son; himself afflicted with the untimely and uncomfortable death of that son, who was his darling; and reviled and cursed to his face by a base and unworthy companion Shimei. And besides all these things, there were many other affronts, troubles and vexations continually. David had few

---

[7]Bullinger, *Sermonum decades quinque*, 206-7; citing Jn 7:53–8:11.
[8]Dickson, *First Fifty Psalms*, 15*.
[9]Sanderson, *Works*, 5:70*.
[10]Binning, *Works*, 463*; citing Hos 5:15.

quiet hours all his life long, and even on his deathbed his life was not a little disquieted with the rumble of his two sons Solomon and Adonijah, almost up in arms about the succession. We used to say, "The willful person never lacks woe." And truly, David felt by sad experience what woe his willfulness wrought him. SEVENTEEN SERMONS.[11]

CORRECTION BUT NOT PUNISHMENT. HENRY AIRAY: We see that the Lord's judgments are executed on the unfaithful and wicked . . . but his children are not punished, and yet they escape not free; for we see David, for his adultery and murder, what judgments followed. . . . His own concubines were defiled by his sons, he was almost driven from his kingdom and one slew another. In fact, after his death, his posterity did not cease to shed blood, as in the beginning of Solomon's reign. Yet this is not a punishment; for a punishment is death, which is only to the wicked, but to God's children he gives a correction. LECTURES ON PHILIPPIANS.[12]

12:13a David Repents

GOD'S FORGIVENESS DEPENDENT ON DAVID'S REPENTANCE. MARTIN LUTHER: Now if David had excused or praised himself, as Saul did, and had wanted to cover his sin and not to be regarded as a sinner but as righteous and inno-cent, he would have perished forever. Therefore God is helpful. If we could use original sin properly, and if anyone had fallen and turned immediately to the spiritual use, then God is bountiful with his grace and forgiveness. There-fore let us learn to use evils and sins for our good, in order that we may experience how merciful and kind the Lord is. If you have fallen and can say from the heart: "I have sinned," then he too can say: "I have forgiven." On the other hand, if you defend and conceal your sin, he will say that he cannot forgive it. LECTURES ON GENESIS.[13]

OUR REPENTANCE BEFORE GOD. MENNO SIMONS: Lord, Lord! With the holy David I pray to you, do not punish me in your anger and do not chastise me in your indignation. For I know that my wounds are many, infected and stinking. My sins weigh on me like a heavy weight, and there is no peace in my bones. As the beloved David did, I humble myself before you from the depths of my heart. Beloved Lord! You are a great and terrible God! I have sinned, done injustice before you. I have been godless and fallen away from you. I have not walked according to your commandments and laws. I have scorned your grace and cast away your holy Word. I have crucified your beloved Son, grieved your Holy Spirit and done injustice in all of my works. Lord, I am frightened by the measure of my sins, for I know of no evil I have not done. As Cain, I have been greedy. As Sodom, I have been proud and impure. As the Pharaoh, I have been hardhearted. As Korah, I have been rebellious. As Shimri, I have been lecherous. As Saul, I have been disobedient. As Jeroboam, I have worshiped idols. As Joab, I have been a hypocrite. As Nebuchadnezzar, I have been arrogant. As Balaam, I have been envious. As Nabal, I have been a drunkard. As Sennacherib, I have been a braggart. As Rabshakeh, I have been a blasphemer. As Herod, I have been bloodthirsty. As Ananias, I have been a liar. I can say with King Manasseh, my sins are more numerous than the sands of the sea and the stars in the heavens. They haunt me day and night, and nothing good dwells in my flesh. What I seek and bring forth is all unrighteousness and sin. I do not do that which I will, but that which I do not want to do. Miserable man that I am, I do not know where to turn. In myself I find nothing but failings, impure desires and a vat of sinfulness. If I go to my neighbor, they have nothing that can help me, neither herb nor dressing. Your Word alone can heal all things. As Paul said, the reward for sin is death, but your grace is eternal life. I seek and desire this grace, for it alone is the medicine that can heal my sick soul. . . . David sought this grace when he had put the innocent Uriah to death and slept with Bathsheba. His sickness was great when he saw his evil deed and he said, "I have sinned against the Lord." . . . From

---

[11]Sanderson, *Works*, 1:99-100*; citing 2 Sam 12:13.
[12]Airay, *Lectures on Philippians*, 48*.
[13]LW 7:274.

that moment on, the word of the prophet was full of grace to his ears, "Your sins have been taken away." His heart was at peace and he praised your name. Your mercies were proclaimed far and wide, and he praised your grace above all of your works. Lord! Beloved Lord! I am a miserable sinner, suffering from the same sickness. I need the same medicine. Do not close to me the pharmacy of your mercifulness. I seek no comfort but from you alone. Lord, help me for your holy name's sake, so that I may give you thanks and praise eternally. Wash away all of my sins and be merciful toward my misdeeds, for they are many. MEDITATION ON PSALM 25.[14]

GOD'S PROVISION FOR THE ELECT. JOHN CALVIN: It will often . . . happen that, for a period, the elect can seem devoid of the Spirit, and you would think that the Spirit given to them has been totally quenched, for they no longer seem to know what religion is, or feel the fear of God. But in a single moment, God can make them feel their offenses, clearly showing that they have been asleep, so to speak, and not dead at all. Thus if they have been insensible, it is because the grace of God has been stifled by their ingratitude. Be that as it may, still this life is never totally dead within us. We see evidence of this in David when he so suddenly recognized himself for what he was and, not turning away in the least, honestly and openly declared that the prophet Nathan had every right to accuse him. SERMONS ON 2 SAMUEL.[15]

EVANGELICAL PROMISE IN NATHAN'S LITERAL WORDS. PHILIPP MELANCHTHON: We recalled before how David was undone by the voice of the prophet Nathan. And he certainly would have perished if he had not at once heard the gospel: "The Lord also has put away your sin; you shall not die." Some think that only allegories are to be looked for in the narratives of the Old Testament, but here you see how much you can learn from this one example

of David when you consider only the literal meaning. In fact this alone is to be considered, for by it the Spirit of God has richly shown us the works both of his wrath and of his mercy. What more evangelical expression can be conceived of than this: "The Lord has put away your sin"? Is not this the sum of the gospel or of the preaching of the New Testament: sin has been taken away? You may add to these examples many stories from the Gospels. Luke tells of the sinful woman who washes the feet of the Lord; he consoles her with these words: "Your sins are forgiven." And what is better known than the story in Luke of the prodigal son, who confesses his sin? How lovingly his father receives, embraces and kisses him! In the Gospel of Luke Peter, stunned by the miracle and, what is more, struck in his own heart, exclaims: "Depart from me, for I am a sinful man, O Lord." Christ consoles and restores him by saying: "Do not be afraid," etc. From these examples I believe it can be understood what the difference is between law and gospel, and what the power of the gospel is as well as that of the law. The law terrifies; the gospel consoles. The law is the voice of wrath and death; the gospel is the voice of peace and life, and to sum up, "the voice of the bridegroom and the voice of the bride," as the prophet says. THEOLOGICAL COMMONPLACES (1521).[16]

CONTRITE HEART. LANCELOT ANDREWES: David . . . not only confesses plainly against himself saying to Nathan, "I have sinned," but also makes a psalm of it and sets this preface to it, or caused it to be set before it: "A psalm of David, when the prophet Nathan went to him, after he had gone into Bathsheba." He does this as if he should not stick to shame himself in this world, so that he might be without blame in the world to come. And indeed it is a perfect sign of a humble and good mind when one can say from his heart: "Let me bear the shame and punishment of my sin as a fatherly correction in this life. Only, O Lord, pardon and forgive me that I may escape your wrath and judgment in the life to come." The one who can be

---

[14]Liechty, ed., *Early Anabaptist Spirituality*, 256-57; cf. Simons, *Complete Writings*, 72-73.
[15]Calvin, *Sermons on Second Samuel*, 1:554.

[16]LCC 19:84-85; citing Lk 7:48, 5:8, 10; Jer 7:34.

content to do this is one of a good humble and contrite heart. COLLECTION OF LECTURES.[17]

12:13b-15 The Lord Puts Away David's Sins but Takes the Child's Life

GOD'S JUDGMENT OF THE SON. JOHN CALVIN: The judgment of God must be carried out in the person of his own son. Now here was a little child, who had just been born. Must he be punished for the sin of his father? How can the passage be true which shows that the child will not bear the iniquity of the father and that the father will not suffer for the child (Ezek 18:20)? It seems that God is contradicting himself. Now let us note that when the prophet Ezekiel says that the son will not bear the iniquity of the father, he meant to put limits on the poisoned thinking that existed among those people. For the Jews had this proverb: "Our fathers have eaten sour grapes, and our teeth are set on edge" (Ezek 18:2). That is to say, our fathers have offended, and we are punished for it. Thus they were accusing God of being cruel. So, speaking to them, he says that the son will not bear the iniquity of the father, for God will be quite able to deal with all people individually. Thus, while it may be that a one-year-old child will not be found guilty, as far as we can tell, nevertheless, from the womb of our mothers we are nothing but filth (Ps 51:5) . . . and . . . we have nothing but corruption within ourselves. We must therefore be "children of wrath," as Scripture calls us (Eph 2:3); that is to say, heirs of eternal damnation.

In fact, why is it that little children are baptized, unless they are guilty before God? If this were not the case, it would be like a game! Has this little child offended God? There is no evident reason for anyone to condemn them. But what we have here is a "child of wrath," as I have already said. So what is it that saves them? The pure grace of God. Now it is true that God does indeed save the little children of his faithful people without baptism. But the sign is still to show us and provide proof that little children are cursed by God until he has received

them in mercy, and according to his promise, which says: I will be your children's God (Gen 17:7).

We see, therefore, that when the little child of David was punished, it was certainly right, for God holds all creatures in his hand to do with them what seems good to him. Consequently the child did not suffer an unjust judgment—but also we must return to the root cause, which we have already explained, that it was to humble David more deeply, and draw him to true repentance. . . .

To conclude the matter, let us notice carefully what is mentioned here; that is, when David's child died, the result was that David felt how much God detested the sin that he had committed. For offspring are a sign of the blessing of God on humankind, and when he makes them fathers, it is like communicating to them the title that belongs to him alone (Eph 3:14-15). So also, when he removes children, he is certainly afflicting the fathers. In this way God wanted to cause David to feel his evil, for what he had already felt was not enough. For even if we remembered this lesson every day and humbled ourselves before God, and even if we really exerted ourselves to do so, we would still not go as far as we could. SERMONS ON 2 SAMUEL.[18]

ONE STANDARD FOR GOD AND ANOTHER FOR HUMANS. HULDRYCH ZWINGLI: What God does, he does freely, uninfluenced by any evil emotion. Therefore it is without sin. David's adultery, so far as concerning whether God was the author of it, is no more a sin to God than when a bull covers and impregnates a whole herd. And even when God kills a person by the hand of a robber or of an unjust judge, God sins no more than when he kills a wolf by means of another wolf or an elephant by means of a dragon. For all things are God's, and he has no wrong feeling toward anything. Therefore God is not under the law, because the one who cannot be influenced by any evil emotions has no need of law. However, humankind does sin. Humans have need of a law because they yield to emotions, and when they transgress the law they become liable to punishment.

---

[17]Andrewes, *A Collection of Lectures*, 312*; citing Ps 51:1.

[18]Calvin, *Sermons on Second Samuel*, 1:577-79.

Hence the same deed that is done at the instigation and direction of God brings honor to God, while it is a crime and sin to humankind. Therefore it is right that the guilty are punished, whether in this life by the judge or in the next life by the King of kings and Lord of lords. For they have sinned against the law, not as principals, but as accessory instruments, which God can use as he will more freely than the father of a family may drink water or pour it out on the ground. And although God impels people to some deed that is wicked to the instrument that performs it, it is not wicked to God. For God's movements are free. Nor does God do wrong to the instrument, since all things are God's more than any artisan's tools are their own, and to these a person does no wrong if they turn a file into a hammer or a hammer into a file. God instigates the robber, therefore, to kill even the innocent and those unprepared for death. For the hairs of our heads are numbered in God's sight. How much more are our souls! ON THE PROVIDENCE OF GOD.[19]

INSTRUCTIONS ON EXCOMMUNICATION.
MENNO SIMONS: For since we are not to punish the ugly, carnal transgressors with fire, stoning or sword, as Israel did of old, but only by excommunication, as is well known to all who are taught of God, therefore it behooves us to consign those with their wicked deeds to the place to which the Scriptures consign them, namely, into the death and wrath of God, even as holy Nathan did to the bloodguilty and adulterous David. When they then by such a dread and severe sentence pronounced on them, by and according to the Scriptures, by the means of the ban in true love, and they by the grace of God come under conviction, and are with David provoked to true repentance, so that we may see by all their words, works and conduct that the gracious Father has again received them in faith, and endowed them with his Spirit, and has taken away their sins, then, and not until then (understand well what I say), we have the same word of promise whereby we may

comfort them again and proclaim to them the grace of the Lord, namely, "The Lord also has put away your sin, you shall not die. Your sins are forgiven, go in peace," and similar words of comfort. For that a truly penitent person should be left uncomforted by God or humans is impossible. Oh, reflect on what has been said. INSTRUCTION ON EXCOMMUNICATION.[20]

REMOVING GUILT BUT NOT PUNISHMENT.
JOHANNES AEPINUS: From these and other similar testimonies of Scripture we see that God's mercy forgives the guilt of sin but not the penalty, though God's mercy mitigates it. We have such an example from the life of David, for he acknowledged his sin and the prophet Nathan said to him: "The Lord . . . has put away your sin; you shall not die." Nevertheless, after announcing the forgiveness of sin, God imposed horrendous punishments on the house of David on account of his great sin. ON PURGATORY.[21]

12:16-23 The Death of David and Bathsheba's Child

SIN FORGIVEN BUT PENALTIES FOLLOW.
ANDREW WILLET: Some Christians, on this example, base an assertion that while sin is remitted, the punishment may still remain. They make this the grounds for the pains experienced in Purgatory, where those whose sins are pardoned still merit some torment. According to God's Word, there is no warrant for this doctrine. Where God forgives sins, he does not remember them and they will not be mentioned. As the prophet says: "None of the transgressions that he has committed shall be remembered against him; for the righteousness that he has done he shall live." But if sin's punishment remains, there is therefore a remembrance of the sin. Now, although punishment does not remain, penalties do. And those penalties that remain are for the example of others and for the further admonition of the parties themselves. They

---

[19]Zwingli, *Latin Works*, 2:182* (ZSW 6,3:154-54).

[20]Simons, *Complete Writings*, 983.
[21]Aepinus, *Liber de Purgatorio*, 5r.

are the chastisements, not of an angry God but of a loving God. HARMONY OF 2 SAMUEL.[22]

A BAD IMAGE. JOHN DAVENANT: To walk in wisdom is to do all things cautiously and circumspectly, as people are wont to do when they perceive that they are beset on every side with difficulties and dangers, for danger is the whetstone of wisdom. Believers in those days lived in the midst of heathens ruling over Christians themselves, and serving idols and demons. There was need therefore of remarkable and precise wisdom, so to keep the middle course between Scylla and Charybdis, as neither to confirm the pagans themselves in their idolatries and impiety, nor seem to oppose government and lawful power.... [Believers must also] look well not to cast any spot of disgrace on that God whom they worship, and the religion they profess, by living badly. For it is presumed that servants conform themselves to the disposition of their masters. Hence the pagans, as soon as they saw wickedness committed by Christians, spoke against the God himself whom they worshiped, and imputed the wickedness of private people to our religion. This was likewise charged to the adultery of David by the prophet, "By doing this you have made the enemies of the Lord to blaspheme." EXPOSITION OF COLOSSIANS.[23]

DAVID PRAYS FOR HIS CHILD. JOHANNES BUGENHAGEN: Because the Lord lifted the grave sentence of death from him, David had the smallest hope that this other cross would also be lifted if he prayed, as this might not have been a final sentence, just as is written of Nineveh. COMMENTARY ON 2 SAMUEL.[24]

SIGN OF ELECTION. HULDRYCH ZWINGLI: Since neither Esau could have died in infancy because the Lord had arranged differently in his case, nor the little son of David whom he begot in faithless and wicked adultery could have lived, because the

Lord had determined to kill him, it is evident that when the infant children of the faithful die, it is a sign of their election and summons to the glory of the blessed. For they are taken away that wickedness may not stain their souls, that is, that they might not by a wicked life betray their rejection to the world, as they would do if they had been rejected. ON THE PROVIDENCE OF GOD.[25]

SIN OF THE PARENTS, NOT THE CHILD. HENRY AIRAY: Some think that children who are unbaptized are damned. But that cannot be because there was no such thing to be feared of those who died before circumcision, being the eighth day. For we see the Lord commanded that circumcision should not be before the eighth day, to the end that the children should be strong to abide the great pain of the wounds. Now if as many children died as should be condemned, the Lord would have provided poorly for his people, that for a small temporary commodity would deprive them of everlasting life.... Before David's son died, he fasted and lay on the ground. After he heard he was dead, he rose up and washed his face. He showed himself comfortable and professed that he would "go to him." From this it is evident that he was persuaded he was in peace, whereas we see that he mourned for his son Absalom, whom he loved as dearly, because he feared his condemnation since he had lived and died wickedly. So, if the children are unbaptized, it is not theirs but their parents' sin. LECTURES ON PHILIPPIANS.[26]

HOPE FOR GRIEVING PARENTS. CHARLES DRELINCOURT: God blesses us with children. Let us understand that we are reminded by them of our mortality, they come to take our room and to succeed in our estate. Does God take away to his rest those of whom we are most fond? Let this notify us that God intends to cut off all the lower roots that tie us to this earth, to unloose our hearts and affections, that we may offer them up to him alone instead of spending our lives in tears, indulging our foolish humors in

---

[22]Willet, *Harmony on 2 Samuel*, 68-69*; citing Ezek 18:22.
[23]Davenant, *Exposition of Colossians*, 2:251*; citing 2 Sam 12:14.
[24]Bugenhagen, *In Samuelem prophetam*, 326; citing Jon 3.

[25]Zwingli, *Latin Works*, 2:206 (ZSW 6,3:190).
[26]Airay, *Lectures on Philippians*, 36*; citing 2 Sam 12:23.

needless displeasures. Let us comfort ourselves with this consideration—by this means a part of us enters into heaven, and the other part will follow in time. Let us say with David, "We shall go to them, they will not return to us." CHRISTIAN DEFENSE AGAINST THE FEARS OF DEATH.[27]

12:24-31 Solomon Is Born

HOW DAVID COMFORTS BATHSHEBA. ANDREW WILLET: Bathsheba was mourning, not only for the death of the child but also because of the sin she had committed with David. David did his part to comfort her. The Hebrews think that Bathsheba refused to stay with David, lest that child die as the former did. Therefore David told her that this child was born to the kingdom, and that the Messiah would come from him. She then required David to swear to her that the child should be king. It is certain that David made this promise for this matter, as is confirmed later: "And the king swore, saying: 'As the Lord lives, who has redeemed my soul out of every adversity, as I swore to you by the Lord, the God of Israel, saying, "Solomon your son shall reign after me, and he shall sit on my throne in my place," even so will I do this day.'" But it is uncertain whether David made this promise at the time immediately after David and Bathsheba's first son died. Bathsheba's name signified "the daughter of an oath," but she was called this before the oath was made to her by David. The special comfort David ministered to her was in declaring to her how God had forgiven their sin. It should also be noted that she was called "Uriah's wife" at the birth of the first child conceived in adultery. But after the Lord forgave their sin and ratified the marriage, she is called "David's wife." HARMONY ON 2 SAMUEL.[28]

SOLOMON'S TWO NAMES. MARTIN BORRHAUS: David's son has two names. The first name, Solomon, meant peace. And with Solomon as king, the Israelites flourished. The other name, Jedidiah, referred to love. For God embraced the boy and initiated this name. Each of these earthly names comes together and is overshadowed by the heavenly Messiah. For, if you are considering peace, we read from the prophet Isaiah: "For a child is born to us . . . and his name shall be called . . . Prince of Peace." And from the apostles, all of the blood of the world would be pacified through him. And if you are looking for the love of God, this testimony of Scripture stands out: "This is my beloved Son." COMMENTARY ON 2 SAMUEL.[29]

THE IMPORTANCE OF SOLOMON'S NAME. ANDREW WILLET: Here David is said to call his name Solomon. However, in 1 Chronicles 22:9 it is said the Lord gave him that name. David gave the name by direction from God, specifically by the hand of his prophet Nathan, who was sent by the Lord and called Solomon by another name: Jedidiah, that is, "beloved of the Lord." Some think David committed the child to Nathan, trusting his education to the prophet. But it is evident in the title of Proverbs 31 that Solomon, in his infancy and childhood, was brought up under his mother Bathsheba, for he was too young to be committed to any other. And here it is observed that the Lord used Nathan's ministry again: Earlier he had sent a heavy message to David; now he brought him good news. . . . And in that Solomon is called Jedidiah, "beloved of the Lord," it may be an argument of his eternal salvation: that he was not a reprobate or castaway, but was renewed again after his fall by repentance. These two names, Solomon and Jedidiah, signify the one peace that Israel enjoyed under Solomon's reign as well as the love of God toward Solomon. God gave Solomon more love than he gave him peace. God did this for the sake of Christ, in whom Solomon was acceptable to God; and of whom he was a lively type, both in respect of the spiritual peace of Christ's kingdom, and he was indeed the only beloved son of God. HARMONY OF 2 SAMUEL.[30]

---

[27]Drelincourt, *Christian's Defense Against the Fears of Death*, 57*.
[28]Willet, *Harmony on 2 Samuel*, 77*; citing 1 Kings 1:29-30.

[29]Borrhaus, *Mystica Messiae*, 513-14; citing Is 9:7; Mt 3:17.
[30]Willet, *Harmony on 2 Samuel*, 77*.

13:1–14:33 ABSALOM'S BANISHMENT AND REINSTATEMENT

¹Now Absalom, David's son, had a beautiful sister, whose name was Tamar. And after a time Amnon, David's son, loved her. ²And Amnon was so tormented that he made himself ill because of his sister Tamar, for she was a virgin, and it seemed impossible to Amnon to do anything to her. ³But Amnon had a friend, whose name was Jonadab, the son of Shimeah, David's brother. And Jonadab was a very crafty man. ⁴And he said to him, "O son of the king, why are you so haggard morning after morning? Will you not tell me?" Amnon said to him, "I love Tamar, my brother Absalom's sister." ⁵Jonadab said to him, "Lie down on your bed and pretend to be ill. And when your father comes to see you, say to him, 'Let my sister Tamar come and give me bread to eat, and prepare the food in my sight, that I may see it and eat it from her hand.'" ⁶So Amnon lay down and pretended to be ill. And when the king came to see him, Amnon said to the king, "Please let my sister Tamar come and make a couple of cakes in my sight, that I may eat from her hand."

⁷Then David sent home to Tamar, saying, "Go to your brother Amnon's house and prepare food for him." ⁸So Tamar went to her brother Amnon's house, where he was lying down. And she took dough and kneaded it and made cakes in his sight and baked the cakes. ⁹And she took the pan and emptied it out before him, but he refused to eat. And Amnon said, "Send out everyone from me." So everyone went out from him. ¹⁰Then Amnon said to Tamar, "Bring the food into the chamber, that I may eat from your hand." And Tamar took the cakes she had made and brought them into the chamber to Amnon her brother. ¹¹But when she brought them near him to eat, he took hold of her and said to her, "Come, lie with me, my sister." ¹²She answered him, "No, my brother, do not violate^a me, for such a thing is not done in Israel; do not do this outrageous thing. ¹³As for me, where could I carry my shame? And as for you, you would be as one of the outrageous fools in Israel. Now therefore, please speak to the king, for he will not withhold me from you." ¹⁴But he would not listen to her, and being stronger than she, he violated her and lay with her.

¹⁵Then Amnon hated her with very great hatred, so that the hatred with which he hated her was greater than the love with which he had loved her. And Amnon said to her, "Get up! Go!" ¹⁶But she said to him, "No, my brother, for this wrong in sending me away is greater than the other that you did to me."^b But he would not listen to her. ¹⁷He called the young man who served him and said, "Put this woman out of my presence and bolt the door after her." ¹⁸Now she was wearing a long robe^c with sleeves, for thus were the virgin daughters of the king dressed. So his servant put her out and bolted the door after her. ¹⁹And Tamar put ashes on her head and tore the long robe that she wore. And she laid her hand on her head and went away, crying aloud as she went.

²⁰And her brother Absalom said to her, "Has Amnon your brother been with you? Now hold your peace, my sister. He is your brother; do not take this to heart." So Tamar lived, a desolate woman, in her brother Absalom's house. ²¹When King David heard of all these things, he was very angry.^d ²²But Absalom spoke to Amnon neither good nor bad, for Absalom hated Amnon, because he had violated his sister Tamar.

²³After two full years Absalom had sheepshearers at Baal-hazor, which is near Ephraim, and Absalom invited all the king's sons. ²⁴And Absalom came to the king and said, "Behold, your servant has sheepshearers. Please let the king and his servants go with your servant." ²⁵But the king said to Absalom, "No, my son, let us not all go, lest we be burdensome to you." He pressed him, but he would not go but gave him his blessing. ²⁶Then Absalom said, "If not, please let my brother Amnon go with us." And the king said to him, "Why should he go with you?" ²⁷But Absalom pressed him until he let Amnon and all the king's sons go with him. ²⁸Then Absalom commanded his servants, "Mark when Amnon's heart is merry with wine, and

when I say to you, 'Strike Amnon,' then kill him. Do not fear; have I not commanded you? Be courageous and be valiant." ²⁹So the servants of Absalom did to Amnon as Absalom had commanded. Then all the king's sons arose, and each mounted his mule and fled.

³⁰While they were on the way, news came to David, "Absalom has struck down all the king's sons, and not one of them is left." ³¹Then the king arose and tore his garments and lay on the earth. And all his servants who were standing by tore their garments. ³²But Jonadab the son of Shimeah, David's brother, said, "Let not my lord suppose that they have killed all the young men, the king's sons, for Amnon alone is dead. For by the command of Absalom this has been determined from the day he violated his sister Tamar. ³³Now therefore let not my lord the king so take it to heart as to suppose that all the king's sons are dead, for Amnon alone is dead."

³⁴But Absalom fled. And the young man who kept the watch lifted up his eyes and looked, and behold, many people were coming from the road behind him*e* by the side of the mountain. ³⁵And Jonadab said to the king, "Behold, the king's sons have come; as your servant said, so it has come about." ³⁶And as soon as he had finished speaking, behold, the king's sons came and lifted up their voice and wept. And the king also and all his servants wept very bitterly.

³⁷But Absalom fled and went to Talmai the son of Ammihud, king of Geshur. And David mourned for his son day after day. ³⁸So Absalom fled and went to Geshur, and was there three years. ³⁹And the spirit of the king*f* longed to go out*g* to Absalom, because he was comforted about Amnon, since he was dead.

14 Now Joab the son of Zeruiah knew that the king's heart went out to Absalom. ²And Joab sent to Tekoa and brought from there a wise woman and said to her, "Pretend to be a mourner and put on mourning garments. Do not anoint yourself with oil, but behave like a woman who has been mourning many days for the dead. ³Go to the king and speak thus to him." So Joab put the words in her mouth.

⁴When the woman of Tekoa came to the king, she fell on her face to the ground and paid homage and said, "Save me, O king." ⁵And the king said to her, "What is your trouble?" She answered, "Alas, I am a widow; my husband is dead. ⁶And your servant had two sons, and they quarreled with one another in the field. There was no one to separate them, and one struck the other and killed him. ⁷And now the whole clan has risen against your servant, and they say, 'Give up the man who struck his brother, that we may put him to death for the life of his brother whom he killed.' And so they would destroy the heir also. Thus they would quench my coal that is left and leave to my husband neither name nor remnant on the face of the earth."

⁸Then the king said to the woman, "Go to your house, and I will give orders concerning you." ⁹And the woman of Tekoa said to the king, "On me be the guilt, my lord the king, and on my father's house; let the king and his throne be guiltless." ¹⁰The king said, "If anyone says anything to you, bring him to me, and he shall never touch you again." ¹¹Then she said, "Please let the king invoke the LORD your God, that the avenger of blood kill no more, and my son be not destroyed." He said, "As the LORD lives, not one hair of your son shall fall to the ground."

¹²Then the woman said, "Please let your servant speak a word to my lord the king." He said, "Speak." ¹³And the woman said, "Why then have you planned such a thing against the people of God? For in giving this decision the king convicts himself, inasmuch as the king does not bring his banished one home again. ¹⁴We must all die; we are like water spilled on the ground, which cannot be gathered up again. But God will not take away life, and he devises means so that the banished one will not remain an outcast. ¹⁵Now I have come to say this to my lord the king because the people have made me afraid, and your servant thought, 'I will speak to the king; it may be that the king will perform the request of his servant. ¹⁶For the king will hear and deliver his servant from the hand of the man who would destroy me and my son together from the heritage of God.' ¹⁷And your servant thought, 'The word of my lord the king will set me at rest,' for my lord the king is like the angel of God to discern good and evil. The LORD your God be with you!"

¹⁸Then the king answered the woman, "Do not hide from me anything I ask you." And the woman said, "Let my lord the king speak." ¹⁹The king said, "Is the hand of Joab with you in all this?" The woman

answered and said, "As surely as you live, my lord the king, one cannot turn to the right hand or to the left from anything that my lord the king has said. It was your servant Joab who commanded me; it was he who put all these words in the mouth of your servant. ²⁰In order to change the course of things your servant Joab did this. But my lord has wisdom like the wisdom of the angel of God to know all things that are on the earth."

²¹Then the king said to Joab, "Behold now, I grant this; go, bring back the young man Absalom." ²²And Joab fell on his face to the ground and paid homage and blessed the king. And Joab said, "Today your servant knows that I have found favor in your sight, my lord the king, in that the king has granted the request of his servant." ²³So Joab arose and went to Geshur and brought Absalom to Jerusalem. ²⁴And the king said, "Let him dwell apart in his own house; he is not to come into my presence." So Absalom lived apart in his own house and did not come into the king's presence.

²⁵Now in all Israel there was no one so much to be praised for his handsome appearance as Absalom. From the sole of his foot to the crown of his head there was no blemish in him. ²⁶And when he cut the hair of his head (for at the end of every year he used to cut it;

when it was heavy on him, he cut it), he weighed the hair of his head, two hundred shekels^h by the king's weight. ²⁷There were born to Absalom three sons, and one daughter whose name was Tamar. She was a beautiful woman.

²⁸So Absalom lived two full years in Jerusalem, without coming into the king's presence. ²⁹Then Absalom sent for Joab, to send him to the king, but Joab would not come to him. And he sent a second time, but Joab would not come. ³⁰Then he said to his servants, "See, Joab's field is next to mine, and he has barley there; go and set it on fire." So Absalom's servants set the field on fire.ⁱ ³¹Then Joab arose and went to Absalom at his house and said to him, "Why have your servants set my field on fire?" ³²Absalom answered Joab, "Behold, I sent word to you, 'Come here, that I may send you to the king, to ask, "Why have I come from Geshur? It would be better for me to be there still." Now therefore let me go into the presence of the king, and if there is guilt in me, let him put me to death.'" ³³Then Joab went to the king and told him, and he summoned Absalom. So he came to the king and bowed himself on his face to the ground before the king, and the king kissed Absalom.

a Or *humiliate*; also verses 14, 22, 32   b Compare Septuagint, Vulgate; the meaning of the Hebrew is uncertain   c Or *a robe of many colors* (compare Genesis 37:3); also verse 19   d Dead Sea Scroll, Septuagint add *But he would not punish his son Amnon, because he loved him, since he was his firstborn*   e Septuagint *the Horonaim Road*   f Dead Sea Scroll, Septuagint; Hebrew *David*   g Compare Vulgate *ceased to go out*   h A shekel was about 2/5 ounce or 11 grams   i Septuagint, Dead Sea Scroll add *So Joab's servants came to him with their clothes torn, and they said to him, "The servants of Absalom have set your field on fire."*

OVERVIEW: Many tragedies follow David's sin in chapter 11, and yet some of the commentators commend people to have faith in the midst of such troubles, for the Lord remains with David despite his unworthiness. This reading interprets the complex stories that surround David's family as examples of the struggles Christians continuously face in this fallen world. Other commentators, however, evaluate these stories in terms of clear moral imperatives, successes and failures. The interpreters consider the many internal thoughts, motives and feelings that surrounded Amnon's rape and then rejection of

his sister Tamar. They disagree whether David was justified or negligent in his failure to condemn Amnon, referring to rabbinical and earlier Christian interpretations as they present their views. The reformers also consider the effects of good and bad advice, ranging from Jonadab's evil scheming with Amnon to the woman of Tekoa's careful work with Joab to restore Absalom to the king's good graces. Warning their readers not to be fooled by looks, some commentators point out that Absalom's outward handsomeness does not reflect any corresponding inner beauty, wisdom or faith.

13:1-2 The Consequences of David's Sin Begin to Unfold

HARDSHIPS CHALLENGE FAITH. JOHANNES BUGENHAGEN: From this point until chapter 19, we see evil raised up from within David's own house, just as the prophet Nathan had foretold. Amnon raped his sister and was then killed by his brother Absalom. Then this one who had been dealt with graciously cast out his father the king, violating his father's concubines and dying in a terrible way. Thus the word of God about David's cross proved true. Nevertheless, even in these deepest afflictions of sin, he was protected and stood firm in the promises of God, as it says, "for those who love God all things work together for good." For David here, faith in the promise of an eternal reign was shaken beyond measure. He was attacked by his sins from all sides, attacked by his offspring, his iniquities before God and his lowliness in the eyes of the people. Cast out from his kingdom, he said, "if [God] says, 'I have no pleasure in you,' behold, here I am, let him do to me what seems good to him." Where now is the promise of an eternal kingdom? Why not follow the rebellions of Israel described in chapter 20? The earthly warfare of the kingdom of David and Christ is thus full of afflictions and dangers to faith, which is why Christ exhorts us to stay awake. For all the sins we commit and the afflictions that attack us from the inside and from the outside lead to this one thing: they lead us away from faith in God's promises. For this reason we pray that we not enter into temptation. For no one will stand firm, except those who despair of their own strength and continuously call on the power of God. Therefore you have this remembrance of David's life, which was without a doubt written for our sakes. COMMENTARY ON 2 SAMUEL.[1]

THE PUNISHMENT FOR DAVID. ANDREW WILLET: Nathan had told David of two grievous crosses: that the sword should not depart from his house and that his own concubines should be defiled by another. This was because he had committed two grievous sins of murder and adultery, so God's justice, which does not sleep, began now to show itself. Three great calamities follow one after another: the rape of Tamar by Amnon and his slaughter by Absalom, the defiling of David's concubines by Absalom and his unnatural rebellion against his father. In this first punishment, David is repaid by the law of retribution: since he killed Uriah, having first committed adultery with his wife and betrayed him into his enemy's hand. And so his daughter is ravished and his son Amnon is killed, in the same manner by the treachery of his brother. Thus in David's family, who worshiped God, those foul enormities broke forth, showing that the church of God is not perfect here on earth, but many offenses may be raised even among the people of God. HARMONY ON 2 SAMUEL.[2]

13:3-14 Jonadab's Evil Counsel and Amnon's Evil Act

THE GOAL OF THE LAW. JOHN CALVIN: This passage warns us to fight against all such temptations. If we begin thinking about something that could cause us to consider the moral consequences of our actions, do we profit from it? In what way? When we are tempted to fornication, and God sends us a good thought, how will we use it? We can say the same thing about theft, and every other vice. Let us bear in mind that "this is accursed," and conclude: "If I do this, am I an abomination to God?" For this is the goal to which the law leads us, to flee evil and to pursue good. If that thought enters our memory, we should immediately make a shield out of the will of God (Eph 6), and arm ourselves with prayer in order to break down the cursed temptation, which is doing its uttermost to drag us down. SERMONS ON 2 SAMUEL.[3]

---

[1]Bugenhagen, *In Samuelem prophetam*, 328-29; citing 2 Sam 12:11; Rom 8:28; 2 Sam 15:26.

[2]Willet, *Harmony on 2 Samuel*, 79*.
[3]Calvin, *Sermons on Second Samuel*, 1:623.

Two Characteristics of Wise People.

ANDREW WILLET: Jonadab is called Amnon's friend, but he was his enemy, for a true friend will not give dishonest counsel or do anything dishonest for his friend. Jonadab is also called a wise and prudent man, but his was a carnal, not spiritual, wisdom. Such wise people, as the prophet speaks about, are wise to do evil; but to do well, they have no knowledge. For in wise counsel two things must be considered: that both the end of a person's counsel is good and that the means to it are also honest and lawful. But Jonadab's counsel failed in both ways. Such flattering counselors abound in the court of princes, who are ready for their own advancement to serve the whims of great people, and by their crafty heads they devise how to entertain their desires. HARMONY ON 2 SAMUEL.[4]

13:15-19 Amnon's Love Turns into Hate

PANGS OF PASSION. JOHN ROBINSON: As in a tempestuous sea, the waves are sometimes lifted up and the depths are sometimes revealed, so in an unmortified and passionate heart, one unlawful and inordinate passion often breaks forth inordinately over more sensible emotions. Such was Amnon's inordinate love for his sister Tamar, and then later his excessive hatred of her. In this way some prodigals become extremely covetous; those who are credulous become suspicious; and those who are usually content become sad without measure. The cause of all these things is a person's lack of guidance from their reason and conscience. Instead they are carried headlong by pangs of passion and driven by the devil. ESSAYS.[5]

Deceived by Affections. DANIEL DYKE: Up to this point we have spoken of that deceitfulness of the heart which is jointly in the mind and affections. It remains now for us to speak of that deceitfulness of the affections by themselves. First, we shall speak of their deceit in general and, second,

of some special affections. The deceit of the affections in general manifests itself in two things. First, in that they are of so variable and mutable a disposition that the face of the heavens is not so diverse, nor the sea or weather so inconstant nor the chameleon so unchangeable. There is nothing so unstable or so uncertain; not only changed this day from yesterday; but this hour, indeed, this moment from the former.... Who would have thought, for instance, that Amnon's hot affection for his sister could ever have been cooled? Yet for all that presently after his lust was satisfied, his hatred of her exceeded his former love. THE MYSTERY OF SELF-DECEIVING.[6]

Why Amnon Hated Tamar. JOHN MAYER:

That Amnon hated Tamar exceedingly appears strange and contrary to the common manner. For after having enjoyed the person whom he so much desired, how is it possible now for his most ardent love to be turned into extreme hatred? For Shechem, after raping Dinah in Shechem, only fell more in love with Dinah and desired to marry her. And this happened to many others as well.... The rabbis give the following reason: that, in sleeping with her by force, Amnon hurt himself, especially given that she later spoke so directly to him. Cardinal Cajetan argues that, now that his desire was satisfied, he experienced a turning of his feelings and therefore of his affections for her. But Peter Martyr Vermigli offers the best explanation. He argues that Amnon was pricked in conscience and ashamed of his horrible sin. Therefore he grew to hate the one with whom he had committed something so horrible. COMMENTARY ON 2 SAMUEL.[7]

13:20-22 David Is Angry but Does Nothing

David Excused from Punishing His Children. CARDINAL CAJETAN: According to the Hebrew text, David was "very angry" when he

---

[4]Willet, Harmony on 2 Samuel, 80-81*.
[5]Robinson, Works, 1:219*.

[6]Dyke, The Mystery of Self-Deceiving, 292.
[7]Mayer, Many Commentaries in One, 415*.

heard this news of Amnon and Tamar. But it is not written what he said or what he did. And so it may be asked whether David should be accused of committing a sin of omission, for Amnon suppressed a virgin by force and committed incest with his sister, the daughter of his father. Both of these crimes were deserving of punishment in the law of Moses. But the solution is that the case of Amnon was not brought to trial by law, nor was there any real evidence of the accused crime being committed. It's true that Tamar tore her clothes while crying and was in mourning, but these events were not made public, though we read that Absalom learned of the act from questioning Tamar and Amnon of course was aware. However, no witnesses were brought forward. In this way the case was not brought to the king or to the judges. David was excused from punishing his son Amnon through the judiciary as well as his daughter Tamar, who also could have been accused of death since she did not cry out when she was taken by force. COMMENTARY ON 2 SAMUEL.[8]

DAVID FEELS THE GUILT OF AMNON'S SIN. KONRAD PELLIKAN: David was not willing to afflict the spirit of his son Amnon because he loved him as his firstborn. For he was expecting the judgment of the Lord, as was promised in the chapter before; and he did not believe that he was able to hinder it. David did not only grieve over the evil actions, but much more so, he understood himself to be the one who imputed the evil. For although his son deserved punishment, David deserved it much more so. And so David did not judge the sin of his son Amnon, since he himself had committed a similar sin and was responsible for it. Therefore there was nothing that David could do other than wait anxiously for the hand of the Lord and humbly embrace it, and attempt to pacify God's clemency by prayers. COMMENTARY ON 2 SAMUEL.[9]

DAVID'S OVERINDULGENCE OF HIS SON. JOHN MAYER: Some wonder whether David ought to have done more than simply be angry or grieved for what happened to his children. Some interpreters say that he should have judged Amnon according to the law since he was the supreme judge in the land of Israel. They argue that David should have judged and brought to execution the offense committed against God's laws, according to which Amnon would have been put to death. This is because he committed double crimes against God's laws: both for committing incest with his sister and for raping someone. Yet it was David's overindulgent affection for his son Amnon that made him unwilling to grieve Amnon more by speaking or doing anything against him. Nicholas of Lyra, however, was of the opinion that David later corrected his son in private as only a father can. COMMENTARY ON 2 SAMUEL.[10]

13:23-39 Absalom Murders Amnon and Flees

UNFIT FOR THE TASK. JOHN CALVIN: Since David was king and it was God who had made him sit on the seat of justice, and handed him the sword, he ought to have punished evildoers justly, and not have spared his son. Yes, he was perplexed over it. But what of that? This was not carrying out the duty to which he was called, nor performing his office as he should have done. Hence, when a person is in a position of justice, let them try—insofar as they are able—to reprimand crimes and scandals, and let them know that it is not enough simply to be angry about them. It is, of course, true that there is some virtue in merely detesting evil. For instance, a father who is displeased with the evil his children commit is not as wicked as one who readily accepts their wrongdoing. But even so, the courage of a man who is obliged to uphold justice must not (I say) melt away, so that when he has made some semblance of having repaid the evildoer he thinks he has done enough. Now this, in summary, is what we have to remember.

---

[8]Cajetan, *Opera Omnia in Sacrae Scripturae Expositionem*, 2:152; citing 2 Sam 13:21. For the various laws concerning rape, see Deut 22:23-29.

[9]Pellikan, *Commentaria Bibliorum*, 2:120v.

[10]Mayer, *Many Commentaries in One*, 416*.

In fact, what follows this story shows that David was chastised as he deserved for not punishing Amnon. If David had done his duty, he could have prevented the horrendous homicide that took place; the wrath of Absalom would have been appeased. If he had seen Amnon condemned—in prison for life, or suffering some other punishment—even though he was still wicked, Absalom's vengeance would in fact have been put to death. If our enemies are afflicted, however, it may be that we forget the injuries that once irritated us because we are ashamed of "fighting against a dead dog," as they say. Now here was David, who could have appeased his son if he had carried out his duty. But when he did not perform his office, and left evil punished, it was the same as putting the noose around Absalom's neck, as if to say: "Avenge yourself; since I am the king and want to enjoy myself, I shall be lazy and let you do it." That is how he caused the murder Absalom committed, and roused the wrath of God against himself for not having punished his son. SERMONS ON 2 SAMUEL.[11]

WHY GOD LET DAVID'S FAMILY GET ATTACKED.
ANDREW WILLET: It is true that the Lord said to David by his prophet Nathan that the Lord forgave his sin and he would not die. Yet some chastisement still remained, which was not as a punishment but as a medicine. And for the following reasons the Lord allows afflictions on his children, even after the remission of their sin. First, that he may have some way to admonish us of our misery. Second, that we may still have reason to call on God and to run to him in our afflictions and needs. Third, that the members of Christ may be transformed to the head. "... Provided we suffer with him in order that we also be glorified with him." Paul said, "Now I rejoice in my sufferings for your sake, and in my flesh I am filling up what is lacking in Christ's afflictions for the sake of his body, that is, the church." Not that anything is lacking from the personal sufferings of Christ, but because Christ suffered with his members, they are called the afflictions of Christ. Fourth, we must pay attention to the error of the

Roman Catholics, who think that the servants of God satisfy their sins by their afflictions. But seeing that nothing horrible happened to God's children, which is not deserved by their sin, they cannot satisfy. They must leave that work to the one who was without sin and therefore did not deserve to suffer in himself what was laid on him for our sins. HARMONY ON 2 SAMUEL.[12]

A KING'S DISGRACE. JOHN CALVIN: There is no doubt that David recognized in Amnon's murder the conclusion of the sentence that Nathan had pronounced to him: "Blood will not depart from your house" (2 Sam 12:10). He saw therefore that God was punishing him in this for the murder he had committed against Uriah, and that this deed proceeded from that one. Therefore, when David mourned, it was not only for the wicked deed Absalom had committed; it was not that he was deprived of his son, but because he knew that his sin was the root of the evil that had happened. It was exactly as though God were holding him there on a scaffold, to disgrace him before the whole world, and were sounding the trumpet to engrave his condemnation permanently in our memory, by bringing before our eyes this second murder that had been committed. Indeed, all the people could have openly said: "How did it happen that one of the king's sons should have killed another like this? Oh, of course—the father was a murderer himself. God told him that he would be his Judge, and so here now is the execution of that judgment." So this is how David's confusion was renewed before the whole world. SERMONS ON 2 SAMUEL.[13]

14:1-24 The Woman's Parable by Means of Joab

JOAB'S SHREWDNESS. JOHANNES BUGENHAGEN: Here you see how the children of this world "are more shrewd in dealing with their own generation than the sons of light." The shrewd counselor Joab

---

[11]Calvin, Sermons on Second Samuel, 1:642.
[12]Willet, Harmony on 2 Samuel, 83*; citing Rom 8:17; Col 1:24.
[13]Calvin, Sermons on Second Samuel, 1:655.

gave advice for Absalom about his father. He wanted good for Absalom, wanted to advise David in this matter and at the same time wanted to gain the thanks of both of them when the father and son reunited. The following narrative reveals that this is indeed what David had wanted, especially after Absalom had been run through with a spear while suspended by his hair. This truly yielded bad advice, as generally happens with all impious advice. For they do not, as Scripture says, ask the mouth of the Lord. And, from the heart, they do not entrust their cause to God. Nevertheless, by following this plan that seemed good to them, they accomplished what the hand and counsel of the Lord decreed, not what they themselves intended. COMMENTARY ON 2 SAMUEL.[14]

UNTRUE THINGS FOR A TRUE PURPOSE.
ANDREW WILLET: The woman's parable consisted of two parts: the proposition of the parable, verse 12, then the outcome of it to Absalom, verses 12 to 21. There are three reasons the woman used to persuade compassion: It was an honest thing that was desired, it was profitable and it was easy to be done. First, it was honest both by the law of nature, where humans defend themselves, and the intolerance of wrong by force and might, as her son did to defend himself from his brother's wrong. Second, it was honest by the written law, which appointed cities of refuge for involuntary offenders. Finally, it was a profitable thing to her house that her son should live; otherwise she would not live if both her sons were taken away. It was an easy matter for the king to determine, who was an angel of God, that is, of great dexterity in hearing both good and bad. Additionally, the woman spoke about many different things in her parable, which were not true in the case of Amnon and Absalom. One of these supposed sons did not intend another's death; rather, it happened in the heat of the moment. But Absalom had intentionally pursued Amnon's death long

before. One of these invaded another, but Amnon did not assault Absalom. There were no witnesses present; here all the king's sons were assembled together. The cities of refuge were not appointed for willful murders, such as Absalom's was. She pretended that if her other son died, all hope of posterity should be cut off unless Absalom should never return since the king had more sons. So she intentionally told her story with some untrue things, so that the king should realize her true purpose. HARMONY ON 2 SAMUEL.[15]

EYES OF AN ANGEL. DANIEL DYKE: As our heart is deceitful, so also are our eyes in seeing and in judging the deceitfulness of our hearts—so much so that they cannot see when it is most clear. In fact our eyes cannot give any infallible or definitive sentence concerning anyone's heart, but only by discernment from God. But in this conjectural knowledge the angels excel for the simple reason that their eyes pierce deeper than ours. They can see both the inward and outer parts of our bodies, though in the outward they are able to see far more than we. Hence David, for his wisdom in finding out secrets, is compared to an angel of God by the woman of Tekoa. THE MYSTERY OF SELF-DECEIVING.[16]

JOAB AS MEDIATOR. THOMAS ADAMS: We are God's enemies due to our corrupt nature and his perfect justice, and there is no reconciliation but through the blood of Christ's everlasting covenant. He reconciles us to God like Joab reconciled Absalom to David by the woman of Tekoa. THE CITY OF PEACE.[17]

14:25-27 *Absalom's Great Features*

ABSALOM'S HAIR. JOHANNES BUGENHAGEN: Scripture likes to describe such things as Absalom's handsomeness in order to reveal the ubiquity of human hypocrisy to us. There was nothing the

---

[14]Bugenhagen, *In Samuelem prophetam*, 331-32; citing Josh 9:14; Lk 16:8; Acts 4:28.

[15]Willet, *Harmony on 2 Samuel*, 88*.
[16]Dyke, *The Mystery of Self-Deceiving*, 401*.
[17]Adams, *Eirenopolis*, 177-78*.

people would have found blameworthy about Absalom, who—like Saul and Joab—would similarly cover up his impiety, as the following narrative reveals. If I may say so, the wonderful beauty of his hair (which is the most flimsy and vain part of a person and certainly not a very deep part) is described so that you see most clearly how hypocrisy glories in empty and vain things. It is not only good for nothing, but it also destroys the soul, as you read below that, suspended by his hair, Absalom's glory and vanity became confusion and death. For what good is this glory of beauty, which seemed to have counted for so much? Wouldn't it have been better to be bald? Therefore let us use a proverb: "Absalom's hair" is what we should call whatever glory and holy appearance we might see in the flesh and in which people put their trust. This differs from what you read about Samson, for his hair gave him strength that the world could not see because it came from God, whose power is hidden in the weakness of the saints. COMMENTARY ON 2 SAMUEL.[18]

BEAUTY IS NO VIRTUE. ANDREW WILLET: It is mentioned here of Absalom's beauty to show his pride, which grew insolent and ambitious in respect of his beauty and savor. It grew so insolent, in fact, that he soon aspired to the crown. But beauty is no virtue, yet it is a commendable gift of nature, especially if it be accompanied with these two things: humanity and chastity. Joseph was a beautiful person who excelled in both of these. He was courteous toward his brothers and faithful to his ministry. But both of these virtues were lacking in Absalom. HARMONY ON 2 SAMUEL.[19]

14:28-33 *Absalom Gets Impatient*

WHEN GOD BURNS OUR FIELDS. ROBERT SANDERSON: Absalom had a mind to speak with Joab, but Joab had no mind to speak with him. Absalom sent for him, one messenger after another; but still Joab did not come. And so he sent him some of his people to burn his cornfields, and that fetched him! Then he came running in all haste, to know what the matter was. In the same way, God sends messenger after messenger for us, one sermon after another to bring us in. We show little regard for it, but sit it out and will not come in until he burns our cornfields or does us some displeasure. And that will only bring us to him sometimes. SEVENTEEN SERMONS.[20]

LOVING LIKE GOD. EDWARD REYNOLDS: A man may be angry with his wife, children or friend even though he dearly loves them. And God is said to be angry with his people in a similar way when the effects of displeasure are discovered in them. Now upon our repentance and conversion, God promises not only to love us freely but also to clear up his countenance toward us. He promises to make us, by the removal of judgment, to see and know the fruits of his free love and bounty to us. When David called Absalom home from banishment, this was the result of love. But when he said, "He is not to come into my presence," this was the continuation of anger. But at last, when he admitted him into his presence and kissed him, that anger was turned away from him. SEVEN SERMONS ON FOURTEENTH CHAPTER OF HOSEA.[21]

---

[18]Bugenhagen, *In Samuelem prophetam*, 333-34; citing Judg 16:17; 2 Cor 12:9.
[19]Willet, *Harmony on 2 Samuel*, 91*.

[20]Sanderson, *Works*, 1:268*.
[21]Reynolds, *Works*, 3:296-97*; citing 2 Sam 14:33.

15:1–16:14 ABSALOM'S
CONSPIRACY AND DAVID'S FLIGHT

¹After this Absalom got himself a chariot and horses, and fifty men to run before him. ²And Absalom used to rise early and stand beside the way of the gate. And when any man had a dispute to come before the king for judgment, Absalom would call to him and say, "From what city are you?" And when he said, "Your servant is of such and such a tribe in Israel," ³Absalom would say to him, "See, your claims are good and right, but there is no man designated by the king to hear you." ⁴Then Absalom would say, "Oh that I were judge in the land! Then every man with a dispute or cause might come to me, and I would give him justice." ⁵And whenever a man came near to pay homage to him, he would put out his hand and take hold of him and kiss him. ⁶Thus Absalom did to all of Israel who came to the king for judgment. So Absalom stole the hearts of the men of Israel.

⁷And at the end of four^a years Absalom said to the king, "Please let me go and pay my vow, which I have vowed to the LORD, in Hebron. ⁸For your servant vowed a vow while I lived at Geshur in Aram, saying, 'If the LORD will indeed bring me back to Jerusalem, then I will offer worship to^b the LORD.'" ⁹The king said to him, "Go in peace." So he arose and went to Hebron. ¹⁰But Absalom sent secret messengers throughout all the tribes of Israel, saying, "As soon as you hear the sound of the trumpet, then say, 'Absalom is king at Hebron!'" ¹¹With Absalom went two hundred men from Jerusalem who were invited guests, and they went in their innocence and knew nothing. ¹²And while Absalom was offering the sacrifices, he sent for^c Ahithophel the Gilonite, David's counselor, from his city Giloh. And the conspiracy grew strong, and the people with Absalom kept increasing.

¹³And a messenger came to David, saying, "The hearts of the men of Israel have gone after Absalom." ¹⁴Then David said to all his servants who were with him at Jerusalem, "Arise, and let us flee, or else there will be no escape for us from Absalom. Go quickly, lest he overtake us quickly and bring down ruin on us

and strike the city with the edge of the sword." ¹⁵And the king's servants said to the king, "Behold, your servants are ready to do whatever my lord the king decides." ¹⁶So the king went out, and all his household after him. And the king left ten concubines to keep the house. ¹⁷And the king went out, and all the people after him. And they halted at the last house.

¹⁸And all his servants passed by him, and all the Cherethites, and all the Pelethites, and all the six hundred Gittites who had followed him from Gath, passed on before the king. ¹⁹Then the king said to Ittai the Gittite, "Why do you also go with us? Go back and stay with the king, for you are a foreigner and also an exile from your home. ²⁰You came only yesterday, and shall I today make you wander about with us, since I go I know not where? Go back and take your brothers with you, and may the LORD show^d steadfast love and faithfulness to you." ²¹But Ittai answered the king, "As the LORD lives, and as my lord the king lives, wherever my lord the king shall be, whether for death or for life, there also will your servant be." ²²And David said to Ittai, "Go then, pass on." So Ittai the Gittite passed on with all his men and all the little ones who were with him. ²³And all the land wept aloud as all the people passed by, and the king crossed the brook Kidron, and all the people passed on toward the wilderness.

²⁴And Abiathar came up, and behold, Zadok came also with all the Levites, bearing the ark of the covenant of God. And they set down the ark of God until the people had all passed out of the city. ²⁵Then the king said to Zadok, "Carry the ark of God back into the city. If I find favor in the eyes of the LORD, he will bring me back and let me see both it and his dwelling place. ²⁶But if he says, 'I have no pleasure in you,' behold, here I am, let him do to me what seems good to him." ²⁷The king also said to Zadok the priest, "Are you not a seer? Go back^e to the city in peace, with your two sons, Ahimaaz your son, and Jonathan the son of Abiathar. ²⁸See, I will wait at the fords of the

wilderness until word comes from you to inform me." ²⁹So Zadok and Abiathar carried the ark of God back to Jerusalem, and they remained there.

³⁰But David went up the ascent of the Mount of Olives, weeping as he went, barefoot and with his head covered. And all the people who were with him covered their heads, and they went up, weeping as they went. ³¹And it was told David, "Ahithophel is among the conspirators with Absalom." And David said, "O LORD, please turn the counsel of Ahithophel into foolishness."

³²While David was coming to the summit, where God was worshiped, behold, Hushai the Archite came to meet him with his coat torn and dirt on his head. ³³David said to him, "If you go on with me, you will be a burden to me. ³⁴But if you return to the city and say to Absalom, 'I will be your servant, O king; as I have been your father's servant in time past, so now I will be your servant,' then you will defeat for me the counsel of Ahithophel. ³⁵Are not Zadok and Abiathar the priests with you there? So whatever you hear from the king's house, tell it to Zadok and Abiathar the priests. ³⁶Behold, their two sons are with them there, Ahimaaz, Zadok's son, and Jonathan, Abiathar's son, and by them you shall send to me everything you hear." ³⁷So Hushai, David's friend, came into the city, just as Absalom was entering Jerusalem.

16 When David had passed a little beyond the summit, Ziba the servant of Mephibosheth met him, with a couple of donkeys saddled, bearing two hundred loaves of bread, a hundred bunches of raisins, a hundred of summer fruits, and a skin of wine. ²And the king said to Ziba, "Why have you brought these?" Ziba answered, "The donkeys are for the king's household to ride on, the bread and summer fruit for the young men to eat, and the wine for those who faint in the wilderness to drink." ³And the king said, "And where is your master's son?" Ziba said to the king, "Behold, he remains in Jerusalem, for he said, 'Today the house of Israel will give me back the kingdom of my father.'" ⁴Then the king said to Ziba, "Behold, all that belonged to Mephibosheth is now yours." And Ziba said, "I pay homage; let me ever find favor in your sight, my lord the king."

⁵When King David came to Bahurim, there came out a man of the family of the house of Saul, whose name was Shimei, the son of Gera, and as he came he cursed continually. ⁶And he threw stones at David and at all the servants of King David, and all the people and all the mighty men were on his right hand and on his left. ⁷And Shimei said as he cursed, "Get out, get out, you man of blood, you worthless man! ⁸The LORD has avenged on you all the blood of the house of Saul, in whose place you have reigned, and the LORD has given the kingdom into the hand of your son Absalom. See, your evil is on you, for you are a man of blood."

⁹Then Abishai the son of Zeruiah said to the king, "Why should this dead dog curse my lord the king? Let me go over and take off his head." ¹⁰But the king said, "What have I to do with you, you sons of Zeruiah? If he is cursing because the LORD has said to him, 'Curse David,' who then shall say, 'Why have you done so?'" ¹¹And David said to Abishai and to all his servants, "Behold, my own son seeks my life; how much more now may this Benjaminite! Leave him alone, and let him curse, for the LORD has told him to. ¹²It may be that the LORD will look on the wrong done to me,ᶠ and that the LORD will repay me with good for his cursing today." ¹³So David and his men went on the road, while Shimei went along on the hillside opposite him and cursed as he went and threw stones at him and flung dust. ¹⁴And the king, and all the people who were with him, arrived weary at the Jordan.ᵍ And there he refreshed himself.

---

a Septuagint, Syriac; Hebrew *forty*   b Or *will serve*   c Or *sent*   d Septuagint; Hebrew lacks *may the LORD show*   e Septuagint *The king also said to Zadok the priest, "Look, go back*   f Septuagint, Vulgate *will look upon my affliction*   g Septuagint; Hebrew lacks *at the Jordan*

OVERVIEW: The commentators here warn readers to avoid the internal sins that accompanied Absalom's vain rise to power and to beware of those like Absalom and Ahithophel who appear or sound good on the outside. These exegetes reflect on the importance of people honoring their station in life and avoiding sedition even when the cause seems righteous, because so many unintended consequences inevitably arise. In contrast to Absalom's ambition, the reformers observe David's trust in the Lord in this time of disgrace. They identify David's suffering as participation in the theology of the cross.

15:1-4 Absalom Thinks He Would Be a Better King Than David

Manifest Folly. Martin Luther: Stupid and arrogant people do not understand what an important thing it is to serve God's ordinance and empires. For they neither dream the well-known statement in the comedy: "I should have been a king," or when they realize that they have been born kings and princes, they at the same time also arrogate to themselves wisdom and sufficient strength to rule. Ruling over others is surely not a matter of human wisdom or prudence. It is manifest folly and madness on the part of godless people when they seek civil authority and force themselves into it. In the end they even destroy this authority, unless God happens to have compassionate regard for the common interest and presents an Alexander or some similar hero. Lectures on Genesis.[1]

Accepting the Role God Has Given. Edward Reynolds: If the heart was in the head or the liver in the shoulder, if there was any unnatural separation of the vital parts in our bodies, the body could not grow but would perish. Similarly, the way for the church to prosper and flourish is for every member to keep in their own rank and order, to remember their own measure, to act in their own sphere and to manage their particular condition and relationships with spiritual wisdom and humility. In this way, the eye is to do the work of an eye, the hand of a hand, etc. But such is not how Absalom thought: "Oh that I were judge in the land! . . . I would give

[every man] justice." But consider what role God has assigned to you, and in this role live out the gospel. Seven Sermons on Fourteenth Chapter of Hosea.[2]

If I Were a Rich Man. Daniel Dyke: It is our usual deceit that we secretly promise to the Lord the doing of this or that, only *after* our present state is changed. "Oh," we say, "if I were thus and thus, I would do such and such!" "If I were a king," says Absalom, "I would see justice done to every person." Are we so naive as to think that he would have been as good a king as his words suggested? Assuredly no one would have been more tyrannical! "If I were a rich man," he says, "how fair and free-hearted would I be!" For his sake, God actually let Absalom have his wish, but Absalom did not let God have his promise. God gave riches to him, but he did not give generosity back. The Mystery of Self-Deceiving.[3]

15:5-12 Absalom Steals the Hearts of the People

On Rebelling Against Authorities. Heinrich Bullinger: It sometimes occurs that governmental leaders think it good to promote religion, advance public justice, defend the law and favor honesty. Nevertheless, they are still troubled by their vices, which are great indeed. However, it is not right therefore for the people to condemn them and deject them completely. David had his sins, although he was otherwise a good king. His act of adultery particularly damaged his people and kingdom. Nonetheless, Absalom sinned even more gravely, who wished to remove his father from power. In the same way regarding other leaders, there is no small number of vices that move or ought to move godly people to sedition, so long as justice is preserved and good laws and public peace are defended. Decades 2.5.[4]

---

[1] LW 7:144; citing Terence, *Phormio* 1.2.20.

[2] Reynolds, *Works*, 3:350-51*; citing 2 Sam 15:4.
[3] Dyke, *The Mystery of Self-Deceiving*, 259*.
[4] Bullinger, *Sermonum decades quinque*, 136.

The Ignorance and the Wisdom of the Flesh. Johannes Bugenhagen: Using the craftiness of the flesh and his hypocrisy, Absalom seduced the hearts of the simple. They were ignorant of the evil being conducted under the appearance of good, and so they encouraged it as if it were something righteous while never suspecting evil. At the same time, Ahithophel was a discerning man according to the wisdom of the flesh, so that under his council you—or even David himself— might not see anything to fear. Commentary on 2 Samuel.[5]

Absalom as Adam. Johann Arndt: The fall occurred first in the human heart and thereafter was revealed and made clear in the eating of the apple. It is also to be noted in various ways in the fall and sin of Absalom.... He was also (1) the son of a king, (2) a most beautiful man in whom there was no fault from head to toe and (3) a son dearly beloved by his father.... Absalom was not satisfied to remain with this glory, but he wished to be king himself, and he took for himself the royal honor. When he so decided this in his heart, he became his father's mortal enemy and sought after his life. Adam too was (1) God's son, (2) the most beautiful among the creatures; there was no flaw in him in body or soul, and he was (3) God's beloved child. Nor was he satisfied to remain in this glory but wished to be God himself and therefore became an enemy of God, and if it were possible he would have killed God. True Christianity.[6]

One Heart, Many Sins. Thomas Adams: There is room enough in one heart for many sins.... Absalom had treason, ambition, pride, incest and ingratitude for his heart's stuffing.... The heart is so small a piece of flesh that it would scarcely be able to feed a tiny bird her breakfast; yet behold how sizeable and roomy it is to give space to seven devils! The Black Devil.[7]

The Importance of Self Denial. Edward Reynolds: There is no greater argument of an unsound repentance than indulgent thoughts and reserved delight and complacency in sin. The devil will diligently observe and hastily catch a glance of this nature ... and make use of it to do us mischief. David would have been free from some of his greatest troubles if he had not relented toward Absalom and allowed him home from banishment. He no sooner kissed Absalom than Absalom courted and kissed the people to steal their hearts away from David. As there are, in points of faith, fundamental articles, so there are, in points of practice, fundamental duties. And among these duties none are more primary and essential to true Christianity than self-denial. And this is one special part and branch of self-denial: to keep ourselves from our own iniquity and to say to our most costly and darling lusts, "Get away ... idols, go away! I would rather be fatherless than rely on such helpers." Seven Sermons on Fourteenth Chapter of Hosea.[8]

15:13-37 David Flees and Trusts in the Lord

Reasons for Calamity. Heinrich Bullinger: Now, let the faithful believer consider the reasons for which David is afflicted with calamities. Either he is persecuted by people for his desire to pursue justice and right religion, or he suffers on account of his sins and offenses. Let the one who suffers persecution on account of justice give joy and thanks to God. For just as the apostles rejoiced for being persecuted, so should these individuals rejoice and give thanks for being found worthy to suffer for the name of Christ.... However, if anyone experiences the punishment of God for their own sins, let them recognize that God's just judgment has fallen on him. Let him humble himself under the Lord's powerful hand, confess his sins to God, meekly ask pardon for them and suffer the consequences their sins fully deserve. Let them follow the example ... of David.... For

---

[5]Bugenhagen, *In Samuelem prophetam*, 336-37; citing Ps 33:10; 2 Sam 7:11-17; 12:11.
[6]Arndt, *True Christianity*, 33.
[7]Adams, *Black Devil*, 70*.

[8]Reynolds, *Works*, 3:277-78*.

David, after he was forced to flee and go into exile, said to the priest who was carrying the ark: "Carry the ark of God back into the city. If I find favor in the eyes of the Lord, he will bring me back and let me see both it and his dwelling place. But if he says, 'I have no pleasure in you,' behold, here I am, let him do to me what seems good to him." Indeed, it is much better to be punished in this world and afterward live forever than to live here without afflictions, and in the other world to suffer everlasting pains. DECADES 3.3.[9]

FOREGOING FICKLENESS. JOHN CALVIN: When David spoke in this way, he was not like a man in despair, but on the contrary he was clearly trusting in God, although his human circumstances had been severely disturbed. Hence, no matter what our external conditions may be, let us allow him to dispose events differently from what we think should happen, and let us not be so heated in our feelings that we are angered when things happen contrary to our desires. Or let us not be lazy, and let us not lose control, as many people do when they fail to see the progress they had imagined. They know how to withdraw themselves easily and to pucker their lips, pretending they do not know what is the matter. Well, so as not to be so fickle, we must practice in every circumstance what is said here—that the Lord will do what seems good to him. Now that is the content of this passage. SERMONS ON 2 SAMUEL.[10]

THE CHURCH ALWAYS UNDER THE CROSS. JOHN KNOX: We know the church at all times to be under the cross. In asking for temporal things, and especially deliverance from trouble, let us offer to God obedience. If it shall please him in his goodness that are we not exercised from grief, let us patiently abide it. We see this in David, who when desirous to be restored to his kingdom when he was exiled by his own son, offered to God obedience,

saying, "If I find favor in the eyes of the Lord, he will bring me back and let me see both it and his dwelling place. But if he says, 'I have no pleasure in you,' behold, here I am, let him do to me what seems good to him." TREATISE ON PRAYER.[11]

GODLY AFFLICTIONS. JOHANNES BUGENHAGEN: David said, "Today the house of Israel will give me back the kingdom of my father." Here is the fullness of our death so that we give ourselves over to the hands of God. And here the kindly hand of God manages such afflictions so as to produce this feeling in us. Afterward it is not possible to lose even one hair of our head, because we have given everything to the one from whose hands no one can steal. COMMENTARY ON 2 SAMUEL.[12]

DAVID'S SPIRITUAL JOY. JOHANNES BRENZ: We have a great example of joy from David's life, who was overthrown from the kingdom by his son. Therefore David was forced to flee for a time. But David, in the midst of fleeing, retained a spiritual joy because he understood from God's promises that God would be favorable and that he would not be rejected during his exile. Christ himself was captured and affixed on a cross, and grieved over death yet retained a spiritual joy. In joy, he said to the criminal, "Today, you will be with me in Paradise." COMMENTARY ON PHILIPPIANS.[13]

16:1-4 David and Ziba

THE DECEPTIVE SERVANT. LUCAS OSIANDER: Ziba said he left because his master Mephibosheth had said, "Today the house of Israel will give me back the kingdom of my father." As if Ziba were saying to David, "Mephibosheth has forsaken you in your exile because he hopes that amid the tumult of this war, the kingdom of Israel will ultimately revert to him. For he is the son of Saul, your predecessor and the first king of Israel." Ziba meant

---

[9]Bullinger, *Sermonum decades quinque*, 93-94; citing Acts 5:41; Mt 5:10-12; 2 Sam 15:25-26.
[10]Calvin, *Sermons on Second Samuel*, 1:478-69.
[11]Knox, *Practical Works*, 51*; citing 2 Sam 15:25-26.
[12]Bugenhagen, *In Samuelem prophetam*, 338.
[13]Brenz, *Opera*, 7:971; citing Lk 23:43.

to do wickedness by this. For Mephibosheth had thought nothing like this but had himself commanded Ziba to prepare the donkeys so that Ziba might ride on and go with the king, as it clearly says later in chapter 19. But Ziba did not do that, speeding ahead instead to give gifts to the king. His master had stayed in Jerusalem, hoping (as the text later testifies) for nothing other than to convey his heartfelt sympathy in the sufferings of the exiled king. Here you see how a wicked servant of either great or low authority can devise evil against his master. Therefore it is unwise to be entirely trusting. For this servant was creating wicked accusations and betraying his master, who was really a good man. ANNOTATIONS ON 2 SAMUEL.[14]

TWO KINDS OF SIN. JACOBUS ARMINIUS: Sin is distributed into what is *contrary to conscience*, and what is *not contrary to conscience*. (1) A sin *against conscience* is one that is perpetrated through malice and deliberate purpose, laying waste the conscience, and (if committed by holy persons) grieving the Holy Spirit so much as to cause him to desist from his usual functions of leading them into the right way, and of making them glad in their consciences by his inward testimony.... (2) A sin *not against conscience* is either what is by no means such, and which is not committed through a willful and wished-for ignorance of the law; as the person who neglects to know what he is capable of knowing. Or it is what, at least, is not such in a primary degree, but is perpetrated through rashness, the cause of which is a vehement and unforeseen temptation. Of this kind was the too hasty judgment of David against Mephibosheth, produced by the grievous accusation of Ziba, at the very time when David fled. This bore a strong resemblance to a falsehood.... Yet what, when once committed, is not contrary to conscience becomes contrary to it when more frequently repeated, and when the person neglects self-correction. DISPUTATION 8: ON ACTUAL SINS.[15]

POOR IMITATION OF FRIENDSHIP. LAMBERT DANEAU: There grows yet another question about that gift of goods that David bestowed on Ziba, the servant of Mephibosheth. Even though David was afterward better informed of the truth of that matter and of Ziba's treacherous infidelity to his master, he did not wholly and entirely revoke the gift he had given him. For he gave the goods that rightly belonged to Mephibosheth (who was the son of Jonathan) to Ziba, whereas he had before—in remembrance of his friend Jonathan—appointed the same goods to his son, and had given commandment that the same should be assigned and assured to him. He did this to show himself thankful and mindful of the firm friendship between himself and Jonathan, father of the said Mephibosheth. Yet David being afterward subtly beguiled and craftily deceived by Ziba revoked his former gift made to Mephibosheth and took away from him all that he had formerly bestowed on him.

Now the question is this: whether this last act of David may be defended? . . . Certainly, in this case, I think David cannot in any way be excused. He greatly offended and sinned, and did so in more ways than one: first in respect of being a king, and second as being the protector and sworn friend of Jonathan, the father of this Mephibosheth. TRUE AND CHRISTIAN FRIENDSHIP.[16]

16:5-14 *Shimei Curses David*

SHIMEI'S CURSE. JACOBUS ARMINIUS: Let us consider Shimei, David and the act of God that may be called "the precept of cursing." Shimei was already a hater of David, of a most slanderous tongue and bitter mind, impious, and a despiser of God and the divine law, which had commanded, "You shall not curse the ruler of your people." David by his act against God and his neighbor had rendered himself deserving of that disgrace, and altogether needed to be chastened and tried by it. Moreover, he was endowed with the gift of

---

[14]Osiander, *Liber Iosue*, 567-68; citing 2 Sam 16:3.
[15]Arminius, *Works*, 1:488-89*. On medieval and early modern

understanding of conscience, see further RCS OT 7:62-63.
[16]Daneau, *True and Christian Friendship*, C5v-C6r*.

patience to endure that reproach with equanimity. The act of God was the casting out and expulsion of David from the royal city and kingdom, whence arose David's flight, the carrying of that rumor to the ears of Shimei, the arrangement that David and Shimei should meet. And so by God's act David, fleeing, and driven away by his son, was presented to Shimei—"a man of the family and house of Saul," and an enemy of David—ready to curse him. Add, if you choose, the hardening of Shimei's heart, lest, on account of the companions of David, he should be afraid to curse David, so that by this means he might satisfy his own mind and his inveterate hatred against David. Therefore that opportunity, by which David in his flight was offered to Shimei, and the hardening of Shimei's heart, divinely caused, and also the direction of the cursing tongue are acts belonging to that command of God, apart from which no other action of God can be given in that command which does not impinge on the justice of God, and make God the author of sin.

Now, if we compare all these things, we shall see that Shimei, not so much as God, was the author the malediction. Shimei alone was the author of the volition, yet it is rather to be attributed to God, as he effected what he willed, not by moving Shimei to the malediction but by procuring for Shimei the opportunity to curse David, and the confidence to use that opportunity. From this it appears most plainly that God is without blame, and Shimei is involved in the guilt. An Examination of the Treatise of William Perkins Concerning Predestination.[17]

Fighting God's Elect. Johannes Bugenhagen: See what hatred the house of Saul still held for the house of David. Having the appearance of external strength, the hypocrites could vent their inner hatred against the one whom God had elected. They burned with this hatred, even calling someone else a "man of blood," as if they

were not the ones who sought destruction rather than well-being. They did not judge this hatred to be murder, because this Shimei could not overlook anything David had done to them. In the same way, today's hypocrites of Saul's kingdom gladly remember everything, and create more troubles, if possible. I ask: How did David sin against Saul's house, except that God chose him to be king? The guilt therefore belongs to God, so that Shimei was recklessly speaking not against David but against God, thereby abandoning the kingdom of the Lord. Shimei impiously condemned based on the evidence before him and was led into error. In the same way, Job's friends impiously condemned Job's misery, while they did not see the one whom God glorified through his cross. Commentary on 2 Samuel.[18]

Humility Accepts Insult. Johann Arndt: External insult, rejection and injury you are to not only accept without anger, wrath and the desire for vengeance but think also that it is a test of your heart by which God wishes to reveal what is hidden in you, whether there is meekness and humility in you or whether there is pride and wrath. . . . If there is meekness and humility in you, you will conquer all insult with meekness. (1) Indeed, you will consider it to be a chastisement of the almighty, as David said when Shimei attacked him. . . . (2) The suffering of insult is a great part of the injury that Christ suffered and that the true members of Christ must bear. . . . (3) God is so good and faithful that he will give much more honor and grace for undeserved injury. King David held it for a certain sign that God would honor him again when he suffered injury from Shimei, and this indeed came about. . . . Therefore you have not to be concerned [with] what anyone says against you but you should rather be happy that the spirit of glory stands above those who despise and curse you. True Christianity.[19]

---

[17]Arminius, *Works*, 3:390-91*; citing Ex 22:28.
[18]Bugenhagen, *In Samuelem prophetam*, 341.
[19]Arndt, *True Christianity*, 181.

16:15–17:29 THE COUNSEL OF AHITHOPHEL AND HUSHAI

¹⁵Now Absalom and all the people, the men of Israel, came to Jerusalem, and Ahithophel with him. ¹⁶And when Hushai the Archite, David's friend, came to Absalom, Hushai said to Absalom, "Long live the king! Long live the king!" ¹⁷And Absalom said to Hushai, "Is this your loyalty to your friend? Why did you not go with your friend?" ¹⁸And Hushai said to Absalom, "No, for whom the Lord and this people and all the men of Israel have chosen, his I will be, and with him I will remain. ¹⁹And again, whom should I serve? Should it not be his son? As I have served your father, so I will serve you."

²⁰Then Absalom said to Ahithophel, "Give your counsel. What shall we do?" ²¹Ahithophel said to Absalom, "Go in to your father's concubines, whom he has left to keep the house, and all Israel will hear that you have made yourself a stench to your father, and the hands of all who are with you will be strengthened." ²²So they pitched a tent for Absalom on the roof. And Absalom went in to his father's concubines in the sight of all Israel. ²³Now in those days the counsel that Ahithophel gave was as if one consulted the word of God; so was all the counsel of Ahithophel esteemed, both by David and by Absalom.

17 Moreover, Ahithophel said to Absalom, "Let me choose twelve thousand men, and I will arise and pursue David tonight. ²I will come upon him while he is weary and discouraged and throw him into a panic, and all the people who are with him will flee. I will strike down only the king, ³and I will bring all the people back to you as a bride comes home to her husband. You seek the life of only one man,^a and all the people will be at peace." ⁴And the advice seemed right in the eyes of Absalom and all the elders of Israel.

⁵Then Absalom said, "Call Hushai the Archite also, and let us hear what he has to say." ⁶And when Hushai came to Absalom, Absalom said to him, "Thus has Ahithophel spoken; shall we do as he says? If not, you speak." ⁷Then Hushai said to Absalom,

"This time the counsel that Ahithophel has given is not good." ⁸Hushai said, "You know that your father and his men are mighty men, and that they are enraged,^b like a bear robbed of her cubs in the field. Besides, your father is expert in war; he will not spend the night with the people. ⁹Behold, even now he has hidden himself in one of the pits or in some other place. And as soon as some of the people fall^c at the first attack, whoever hears it will say, 'There has been a slaughter among the people who follow Absalom.' ¹⁰Then even the valiant man, whose heart is like the heart of a lion, will utterly melt with fear, for all Israel knows that your father is a mighty man, and that those who are with him are valiant men. ¹¹But my counsel is that all Israel be gathered to you, from Dan to Beersheba, as the sand by the sea for multitude, and that you go to battle in person. ¹²So we shall come upon him in some place where he is to be found, and we shall light upon him as the dew falls on the ground, and of him and all the men with him not one will be left. ¹³If he withdraws into a city, then all Israel will bring ropes to that city, and we shall drag it into the valley, until not even a pebble is to be found there." ¹⁴And Absalom and all the men of Israel said, "The counsel of Hushai the Archite is better than the counsel of Ahithophel." For the Lord had ordained^d to defeat the good counsel of Ahithophel, so that the Lord might bring harm upon Absalom.

¹⁵Then Hushai said to Zadok and Abiathar the priests, "Thus and so did Ahithophel counsel Absalom and the elders of Israel, and thus and so have I counseled. ¹⁶Now therefore send quickly and tell David, 'Do not stay tonight at the fords of the wilderness, but by all means pass over, lest the king and all the people who are with him be swallowed up.'" ¹⁷Now Jonathan and Ahimaaz were waiting at En-rogel. A female servant was to go and tell them, and they were to go and tell King David, for they were not to be seen entering the city. ¹⁸But a young man saw them and told Absalom. So both of them

went away quickly and came to the house of a man at Bahurim, who had a well in his courtyard. And they went down into it. ¹⁹And the woman took and spread a covering over the well's mouth and scattered grain on it, and nothing was known of it. ²⁰When Absalom's servants came to the woman at the house, they said, "Where are Ahimaaz and Jonathan?" And the woman said to them, "They have gone over the brookᵉ of water." And when they had sought and could not find them, they returned to Jerusalem.

²¹After they had gone, the men came up out of the well, and went and told King David. They said to David, "Arise, and go quickly over the water, for thus and so has Ahithophel counseled against you." ²²Then David arose, and all the people who were with him, and they crossed the Jordan. By daybreak not one was left who had not crossed the Jordan.

²³When Ahithophel saw that his counsel was not followed, he saddled his donkey and went off home to his own city. He set his house in order and hanged himself, and he died and was buried in the tomb of his father.

²⁴Then David came to Mahanaim. And Absalom crossed the Jordan with all the men of Israel. ²⁵Now Absalom had set Amasa over the army instead of Joab. Amasa was the son of a man named Ithra the Ishmaelite,ᶠ who had married Abigal the daughter of Nahash, sister of Zeruiah, Joab's mother. ²⁶And Israel and Absalom encamped in the land of Gilead.

²⁷When David came to Mahanaim, Shobi the son of Nahash from Rabbah of the Ammonites, and Machir the son of Ammiel from Lo-debar, and Barzillai the Gileadite from Rogelim, ²⁸brought beds, basins, and earthen vessels, wheat, barley, flour, parched grain, beans and lentils,ᵍ ²⁹honey and curds and sheep and cheese from the herd, for David and the people with him to eat, for they said, "The people are hungry and weary and thirsty in the wilderness."

a Septuagint; Hebrew *back to you. Like the return of the whole is the man whom you seek*   b Hebrew *bitter of soul*   c Or *And as he falls on them*   d Hebrew *commanded*   e *The meaning of the Hebrew word is uncertain*   f Compare 1 Chronicles 2:17; Hebrew *Israelite*   g Hebrew adds *and parched grain*

OVERVIEW: These commentators wrestle with the examples of two important advisors: Hushai, who remains faithful to David by lying to Absalom, and Ahithophel, who gives crafty counsel to a faithless cause. They see Ahithophel's cleverness as a sign of the worldly wisdom that remains so alluring in this life. Across the board, the commentators underscore how thoroughly God thwarts such efforts at worldly cleverness. Because of his treachery and his self-inflicted death, some interpreters connect Ahithophel with Judas Iscariot.

16:15-19 Hushai Slyly Pledges Loyalty to Absalom

WHETHER HUSHAI WAS GUILTY OF LYING. ANDREW WILLET: There are three kinds of lies: a joking lie, an officious lie and a malicious lie. Some think the first two are lawful, and that to make a charitable lie by doing good to some and not hurting others is not unlawful. But this is not good reasoning because every lie, regardless of the pretense, is an offense since we do not speak the truth from the heart. St. Paul's rule must be observed: "not [to] do evil that good may come." HARMONY OF 2 SAMUEL.[1]

THE SIN OF LYING. LAMBERT DANEAU: We must not countenance the example and act of Hushai the Archite, nor in any way think it right and lawful to imitate those who—for that dutiful service that he would seem to do to David and for that entire and loyal friendship that he bore toward him—circumvented and entrapped another person, namely, Absalom, by craft and subtlety. For he lied and evaded the truth with Absalom, and therein he greatly sinned, although he was not only advised and admonished but also requested and earnestly entreated by David so to deal and so to do to his son, the king. TRUE AND CHRISTIAN FRIENDSHIP.[2]

---

[1]Willet, *Harmony on 2 Samuel*, 95*; citing Rom 3:8.
[2]Daneau, *True and Christian Friendship*, DIr-v*.

16:20-23 *Ahithophel Advises Absalom to Sleep with David's Concubines*

ROGUE AT HEART. MARTIN LUTHER: The godless often receive much better and nobler gifts and skills from God in secular affairs, so that they are almost indispensable at home or in the government; in fact the pious are not even pupils in comparison with them. Such a one was Ahithophel; at that time he far surpassed all the skilled and wise people in David's kingdom, so that his proposals were regarded as if God himself had proposed the things that he suggested. And yet he was an archrascal, traitor and rogue at heart, and afterward also in deed. COMMENTS ON PSALM 101.[3]

A FATHER'S DISGRACE. JOHN CALVIN: David was driven from the kingdom by his own son, who pursued him even to death. And his wives, by whom he glorified himself, had to be shut up. David had to go into a bedroom to commit adultery, but here was his own son sleeping with them. In what way? Did he hide himself? By no means! Rather, he built a platform in an eminent place, and there committed his villainy in the presence of all the people and of the sun itself. Well, this was such a detestable and enormous crime that it ought to make our hair stand on end every time we read this story! For this detestable villain was not content with separating himself from his father, but in despising him, he despised God and all his works—as if he were saying, "And what do I have to do with my father? That old man has abandoned himself to pleasure, and is he worthy of being king? Well, I want to show that it belongs to me, and that he cannot keep me from enjoying the crown. And far from my being afraid of it, in the very place where he has been honored I will put him to public disgrace and shame." All of these things are God's chastisement of David. SERMONS ON 2 SAMUEL.[4]

AHITHOPHEL'S IMPIOUS ADVICE. JOHANNES BUGENHAGEN: Ahithophel said, "Go in to your father's concubines." This was Ahithophel's advice: "This is probably not usual for Israel, for seeing your father's death is not something that Israelites do, for fathers are revered and sons would not sin against them. Yet you will be seen as desiring the kingdom so much that you would make it evident by nothing less a clear sign that you want the worst for your father. But it will not be a pleasant sign, because you should terribly violate your father's consorts whom he abandoned. Then everyone will know that you do not want him to live, since you violated his throne." This is clearly the wisdom of the flesh, where there is no regard for God or human in order to seek his own impious wants. These words of advice were accepted as if from the place of God's counsels, so that you ought not to be amazed when we today blindly accept the "teachings of demons." But God will make a fool of Ahithophel's advice about "going in" and his inauguration of a kingdom of impiety. You see no different in the reign of the Pharisees today, where Absalom reigns after having driven David out (that is, Christ with his gospel). They glorify this Absalom, son of the king, who presumes to rule in the place of David, just as today they show themselves off as Christians and sit in the seat of Christ, conspiring against God and his Christ, as it says in Psalm 2. But from afar the Lord has fulfilled his word through these impious and paltry fellows, which he first spoke to the prophet Nathan. COMMENTARY ON 2 SAMUEL.[5]

ABSALOM'S DOUBLE DEED. JACOBUS ARMINIUS: God permitted Absalom incestuously to pollute his father's wives or concubines in two ways. For it was permitted both as an act and as sin. As an act, it served for the punishment of David, who had adulterously polluted Uriah's wife. As a sin it was permitted because God willed that Absalom should by this wickedness cut himself off from all hope of reconciliation with his offended father, and in that

---

[3]LW 13:179.
[4]Calvin, *Sermons on Second Samuel*, 1:207-8.
[5]Bugenhagen, *In Samuelem prophetam*, 342-43; citing 1 Tim 4:1.

way might accelerate his own destruction, the just punishment of his rebellion against his father. An Examination of the Treatise of William Perkins Concerning Predestination.[6]

Advice Contrary to God's Word. Andrew Willet: Ahithophel gave counsel that was contrary to the Word of God. He advised Absalom to sleep with his father's concubines or wives, which was forbidden by God's law. He respected his own profit more than the glory of God. For his policy was to make Absalom odious to his father, that there might be no hope of reconciliation. He feared that if Absalom should be received to his father's favor, all the people who took his part should be ruined. This was very probable, but not necessary. For though Ruben defiled his father's bed, Jacob did not utterly cast him off from being counted among his brothers. However, he did deprive him of his birthright. David, notwithstanding this villainy, did not altogether withdraw his affection from his son, as demonstrated by his mourning for him. The Hebrews think that Ahithophel avenged his own quarrel because David had committed adultery with Bathsheba, who was Ahithophel's niece by his son Eliam, who was the son of Ahithophel, and is numbered among David's worthies. Harmony of 2 Samuel.[7]

God's Foreknowledge of Absalom's Act. John Robinson: If the thing is good, it is so by God's working it. If it is evil, it is by God's allowing it and governing the creature in working it. But you will respond that God, from eternity, certainly and infallibly foresaw Absalom's incest, because Absalom would certainly and undoubtedly practice it in time.

But I would like to know further from where this certainty and doubtlessness of Absalom's practice arose, so as it could not possibly but be, nor God be deceived in his prescience or foreknowledge? It was not of any absolute necessity of itself that Absalom should be born. Nor was it of

any absolute necessity that once he was born he should be preserved and survive to that time. Nor was it of any absolute necessity that being preserved until this time he should have natural ability and opportunity by which to practice that sin.

We must also recognize that it was not impossible for David to have taken his wives with him or for them to have fled elsewhere and hid themselves. In all these things God did not merely allow these things but rather he was a powerful worker by his providence. But suppose the being of all these things was Absalom's heart by the devil's work, and his own, fraught with lust and impiety this way. Yet Absalom was a changeable creature, having in himself freedom or liberty of will to have forborne that act at that time or to have exercised his lust on some other object. How, then, could that particular event follow unchangeably from God's changeable will? How necessarily and unavoidably, from his choice of will, which was free in itself either to that act or to another of that kind or to neither? Either, therefore, God's decree from eternity—and so his work in time—must be acknowledged for the disposing and ordering of all events unavoidably, or his knowledge should be denied in foreseeing them infallibly. Defense of the Doctrine Propounded by the Synod of Dordrecht.[8]

17:1-14 *Battle of the Advisors*

God the Great Thwarter. Martin Luther: Ahithophel advised Absalom to concentrate on one man, namely, David. He offered to pursue David with twelve thousand men and deliver him into Absalom's hands. This was sage advice. But God sends Hushai into their counsels; he changes their minds and confuses them, saying: "Do not do this, Absalom. I advise you to gather all Israel, for your father is an expert in war; otherwise you are lost." This is the way of our God. Hushai's advice was downright ridiculous, but through him God defeated the wise and clever counsel of Ahithophel.

---

[6]Arminius, *Works*, 3:433-34*.
[7]Willet, *Harmony on 2 Samuel*, 103*.

[8]Robinson, *Works*, 1:279-80*.

God is a master at this. . . . Thus God can thwart and confuse the plans of a whole country, yes, of the entire world, through one person and one man. And if no one is available, then God acts alone. He takes the hearts and the thoughts of people, changes them and obstructs their plans. SERMONS ON THE GOSPEL OF ST. JOHN.[9]

AHITHOPHEL'S AMBITION. ANDREW WILLET: Counsel in and of itself is a sacred thing. It is commended in Scripture, and it is of necessary use in all affairs. But it is especially useful in battle, which must be waged in counsel. As the proverb says: "By wise guidance you can wage your war, and in abundance of counselors there is victory."

But here counsel is abused by this crafty man Ahithophel. His counsel offended God's Word in three ways: in the matter, the means and the end. For the matter, there are two things that do not fall under consultation, that which is certain and necessary and cannot be prevented, and that which is subject to chance and has no certainty at all. . . . Now, as for the first thing, the matter of Ahithophel's advice, it failed because it was not able to be accomplished. That's because God had determined that David's kingdom should be established. Second, the means in deliberation should be honest. But that which Ahithophel proposed were most dishonest. Finally, the end also was ungodly, since Ahithophel sought to overthrow the Lord's anointed. Now, as for the special cause—why Ahithophel is thus bent against David—it was because Ahithophel ambitiously aspired to honor and riches. And because he was reputed to be a wise counselor, he took it on him to be the captain and leader of Absalom's army. He did this so that he might, in every way, grow great and high in reputation with Absalom and the people. The Hebrews give another reason for his hatred against David, namely, that Bathsheba was his close relative, which I touched on earlier. HARMONY ON 2 SAMUEL.[10]

WELCOMING PROVIDENCE. CHARLES DRELINCOURT: When it pleases God to remove someone out of the world, he allows them to shut their eyes to all the light of reason and prudence and to cast themselves headlong into the most apparent danger. Just like when he designed to destroy Absalom and to cut him off, he caused him to be led away by evil counsel and to disregard the discreet and prudent advice of Ahithophel. Therefore since God has appointed or foreordained before the creation of humankind the time and manner of our deaths— at what hour, in what place and by what means whatsoever God calls away our friends or strikes at our person—it is always our duty to possess our souls with patience and not to allow the least disparaging or despairing word to proceed out of our mouths. CHRISTIAN DEFENSE AGAINST THE FEARS OF DEATH.[11]

17:15-29 The End of Ahithophel

AHITHOPHEL'S DEMISE. JOHANNES BUGENHAGEN: Because Ahithophel was an intelligent man, he started thinking things over. He said to himself, "Absalom did not listen to me, and David will be preserved against the one whom I led. Then we will be in the worst possible distress. And how might Absalom be preserved, whom I will support even though he despised my advice (which up to this point I had received from God), listening to my peer rather than to me? It will be better for me to part with life than for people to view me in contempt or in something other than wisdom and intelligence. Farewell, life! For I see that another is preferred over me." Thus perished his intelligence, which in the end actually revealed foolishness. Just as Ahithophel perished having betrayed David, so Judas also perished after having betrayed Christ. Each of them fought against David's kingdom and each ended up in a noose. They perished no less desperately than those who have declared their foolishness to the world and have conspired against Christ's gospel, which is the Pharisaical tradition of

---

[9]LW 23:301-2.
[10]Willet, *Harmony on 2 Samuel*, 104*; citing Prov 24:6.

[11]Drelincourt, *Christian's Defense Against the Fears of Death*, 85*.

advising ambition and riches. Commentary on 2 Samuel.[12]

Typological Understanding of David and Ahithophel. Thomas Jackson: Judas's treachery was expressly foreshadowed by Ahithophel's treason against David, of whom it is probable that the former complaints were literally meant. Both treasons were abominably wicked, but Ahithophel was more generous while Judas was most basely wicked. Indeed, Judas did not have any cause to perpetrate vengeance on his Master, who had never done him or any living soul wrong. On the contrary, Judas's Master went about doing good to all. He healed all who went to him for help, even those possessed with devils. But this kind of healing Judas did not seek, but rather through entertainment of greedy and covetous projects, he invited the devil to enter into his heart at that very time when the door of saving health and entrance into the kingdom of heaven was to be set open to all.

Ahithophel, on the other hand, had some pretense or provocation to avenge himself on his Master, David, by reason of the indignity done to his family and the staining of his blood by David. For David had defiled Ahithophel's near kinswoman or niece, Bathsheba. Yet Ahithophel's malice toward David's person was bitterer. For Ahithophel sought his life and resolved to wreak havoc on him in the highest degree. And he would have certainly achieved his purpose if only Absalom would have obeyed the second part of his advice [to crush David's armies immediately] as he did the first part of it. . . . Indeed, Ahithophel's first piece of advice to sleep with David's concubines greatly pleased Absalom in addition to all the elders of Israel. But after Ahithophel saw his second, and more deadly, piece of advice defeated by the contrary counsel of Hushai, he regarded himself and his very life as lost. And in deep melancholy—yet willing to set his house in order—he immediately hanged himself.

Judas, in like manner, after the chief priests and elders had taken over his plot—which was only to gain some money and to gain their favor for his grateful service, as he had no desire of blood—was also cast away by hanging himself. . . .

After David had been assuredly informed of Absalom's conspiracy against him, he forsook Jerusalem. And he, and all his train or necessary attendants, went on their bare feet with their heads covered and weeping over the Mount of Olives. And thus the Son of David, a little after he saw Judas resolved to betray him—or rather, after it pleased him to take notice of the conspiracy against him between Judas and the chief priests and elders—marched in the same direction with a lesser train, accompanied only with his disciples. However, Jesus had a fuller assurance of the disciples' deliverance from present danger than David's great train had. That's because he carried the true ark of the Lord in his breast, whose type or shadow—David being uncertain or doubtful of the event—sent back again to Jerusalem with the priests that waited on it. Yet Jesus himself went over the Kidron valley with a sadder heart than David his father had done. David and his train— though much greater and better able to resist the violence of the pursuer than Jesus' train was— marched further in that night when they fled from Absalom than the Mount of Olives. The Son of David took up his station in a garden, near the Mount of Olives. And there he expected the encounter of the arch-Ahithophel, Satan, who had vanquished the first Adam in a garden, and who was now attended with a greater host of infernal associates than Ahithophel required of Absalom for his attack on David and his train at about the same place, or not far beyond it. The Humiliation of the Son of God.[13]

---

[12]Bugenhagen, *In Samuelem prophetam*, 344-45.   [13]Jackson, *Works*, 874-75.

18:1–19:8A THE DEATH OF ABSALOM

[1]Then David mustered the men who were with him and set over them commanders of thousands and commanders of hundreds. [2]And David sent out the army, one third under the command of Joab, one third under the command of Abishai the son of Zeruiah, Joab's brother, and one third under the command of Ittai the Gittite. And the king said to the men, "I myself will also go out with you." [3]But the men said, "You shall not go out. For if we flee, they will not care about us. If half of us die, they will not care about us. But you are worth ten thousand of us. Therefore it is better that you send us help from the city." [4]The king said to them, "Whatever seems best to you I will do." So the king stood at the side of the gate, while all the army marched out by hundreds and by thousands. [5]And the king ordered Joab and Abishai and Ittai, "Deal gently for my sake with the young man Absalom." And all the people heard when the king gave orders to all the commanders about Absalom.

[6]So the army went out into the field against Israel, and the battle was fought in the forest of Ephraim. [7]And the men of Israel were defeated there by the servants of David, and the loss there was great on that day, twenty thousand men. [8]The battle spread over the face of all the country, and the forest devoured more people that day than the sword.

[9]And Absalom happened to meet the servants of David. Absalom was riding on his mule, and the mule went under the thick branches of a great oak,[a] and his head caught fast in the oak, and he was suspended between heaven and earth, while the mule that was under him went on. [10]And a certain man saw it and told Joab, "Behold, I saw Absalom hanging in an oak." [11]Joab said to the man who told him, "What, you saw him! Why then did you not strike him there to the ground? I would have been glad to give you ten pieces of silver and a belt." [12]But the man said to Joab, "Even if I felt in my hand the weight of a thousand pieces of silver, I would not reach out my hand against the king's son, for in our hearing the king commanded you and Abishai and Ittai, 'For my sake protect the young man Absalom.' [13]On the other hand, if I had dealt treacherously against his life[b] (and there is nothing hidden from the king), then you yourself would have stood aloof." [14]Joab said, "I will not waste time like this with you." And he took three javelins in his hand and thrust them into the heart of Absalom while he was still alive in the oak. [15]And ten young men, Joab's armor-bearers, surrounded Absalom and struck him and killed him.

[16]Then Joab blew the trumpet, and the troops came back from pursuing Israel, for Joab restrained them. [17]And they took Absalom and threw him into a great pit in the forest and raised over him a very great heap of stones. And all Israel fled every one to his own home. [18]Now Absalom in his lifetime had taken and set up for himself the pillar that is in the King's Valley, for he said, "I have no son to keep my name in remembrance." He called the pillar after his own name, and it is called Absalom's monument[c] to this day.

[19]Then Ahimaaz the son of Zadok said, "Let me run and carry news to the king that the LORD has delivered him from the hand of his enemies." [20]And Joab said to him, "You are not to carry news today. You may carry news another day, but today you shall carry no news, because the king's son is dead." [21]Then Joab said to the Cushite, "Go, tell the king what you have seen." The Cushite bowed before Joab, and ran. [22]Then Ahimaaz the son of Zadok said again to Joab, "Come what may, let me also run after the Cushite." And Joab said, "Why will you run, my son, seeing that you will have no reward for the news?" [23]"Come what may," he said, "I will run." So he said to him, "Run." Then Ahimaaz ran by the way of the plain, and outran the Cushite.

[24]Now David was sitting between the two gates, and the watchman went up to the roof of the gate by the wall, and when he lifted up his eyes and looked, he saw a man running alone. [25]The watchman called out and told the king. And the king said, "If he is alone, there is news in his mouth." And he drew nearer and nearer. [26]The watchman saw another man running. And the watchman called to the gate and

said, "See, another man running alone!" The king
said, "He also brings news." [27] The watchman said, "I
think the running of the first is like the running of
Ahimaaz the son of Zadok." And the king said, "He
is a good man and comes with good news."

[28] Then Ahimaaz cried out to the king, "All is well."
And he bowed before the king with his face to the
earth and said, "Blessed be the LORD your God, who
has delivered up the men who raised their hand
against my lord the king." [29] And the king said, "Is it
well with the young man Absalom?" Ahimaaz
answered, "When Joab sent the king's servant, your
servant, I saw a great commotion, but I do not know
what it was." [30] And the king said, "Turn aside and
stand here." So he turned aside and stood still.

[31] And behold, the Cushite came, and the Cushite
said, "Good news for my lord the king! For the LORD
has delivered you this day from the hand of all who
rose up against you." [32] The king said to the Cushite,
"Is it well with the young man Absalom?" And the
Cushite answered, "May the enemies of my lord the
king and all who rise up against you for evil be like
that young man." [33] [d] And the king was deeply moved
and went up to the chamber over the gate and wept.
And as he went, he said, "O my son Absalom, my son,
my son Absalom! Would I had died instead of you, O
Absalom, my son, my son!"

19 It was told Joab, "Behold, the king is weeping
and mourning for Absalom." [2] So the victory
that day was turned into mourning for all the people,
for the people heard that day, "The king is grieving for
his son." [3] And the people stole into the city that day as
people steal in who are ashamed when they flee in
battle. [4] The king covered his face, and the king cried
with a loud voice, "O my son Absalom, O Absalom,
my son, my son!" [5] Then Joab came into the house to
the king and said, "You have today covered with
shame the faces of all your servants, who have this
day saved your life and the lives of your sons and your
daughters and the lives of your wives and your
concubines, [6] because you love those who hate you and
hate those who love you. For you have made it clear
today that commanders and servants are nothing to
you, for today I know that if Absalom were alive and
all of us were dead today, then you would be pleased.
[7] Now therefore arise, go out and speak kindly to your
servants, for I swear by the LORD, if you do not go,
not a man will stay with you this night, and this will
be worse for you than all the evil that has come upon
you from your youth until now." [8] Then the king arose
and took his seat in the gate. And the people were all
told, "Behold, the king is sitting in the gate." And all
the people came before the king.

a Or *terebinth*; also verses 10, 14   b Or *at the risk of my life*   c Or *Absalom's hand*   d Ch 19:1 in Hebrew

---

OVERVIEW: The commentators in this section
differ in how they view David's plea that Absalom
be spared: some see here a sign of David forgiving
as he had been forgiven, leaving room for Absalom
to truly repent; others find an allegory on the power
of self-deceit, in which people love their sins and
refuse to face them honestly; others understand
David's immense and intense desire to spare
Absalom as a strong and mature response, rooted in
God's Word. Regarding the manner of Absalom's
death, Absalom being suspended in the branches of
a tree reminds some that the soul exists suspended
between spirit and flesh; others observe the irony of
Absalom being undone by what he prized most: his

beautiful hair. Commentators cautiously agreed
with Joab's rebuke of David, though they note that
his motives were not pure and his words too
extreme. Melanchthon's poem "Epigram for
Absalom," composed in the context of the Schmalkald War, identifies David's grief as a final lasting
injury that Absalom inflicts on his father.

18:1-5 David Commands His Leaders to Spare His Son

DAVID'S CONSTANCY OF CHARACTER. VIKTO-
RIN STRIGEL: David suffered an immense amount
of terrible sorrow from his conscience, the wrath of

God, exile, disgrace, splitting of the kingdom, scandal, the crime of his son against him. Nevertheless he preserved his constancy of character. First, he raised up consolation in the hearts of many, when he showed them that God was placated by admonishing them to employ the grace befitting an officer of God. For he did not succumb to his sorrow, but instead asked for and expected aid for Absalom, proposing a peaceful settlement. He wanted to present a good example of a heart called back from the greatest sadness and desperation. Second, he took his place by the gate as the master who had preserved his domain. Though his soul was heavy with sorrow, still he did not demand the death of his enemy—as Hercules had done—nor did he avoid a clash with him—as Bellerophon did. Instead, he carried out the war with great care, managed his advisors and counseled them to use great prudence concerning those whom he thought would be useful to himself and others in the future. Therefore to have such good intentions in the face of everything David experienced is a great example for building faith in one's soul when things go terribly wrong. BOOK OF 2 SAMUEL.[1]

PRAYING FOR ONE'S ENEMIES. ANDREW WILLET: David commanded the captains to spare Absalom. That's because David's own conscience told him that he was raised up as an instrument of God's judgment on him for his sin. He was afraid that if Absalom was cut off in the midst of his rebellion, he would surely die. Therefore he desired that he might have a time of repentance given him. David, in sparing his enemy and praying for the one who persecuted him, was a type of Christ, who prayed for his enemies. HARMONY ON 2 SAMUEL.[2]

PRICKING OUR DARLING SINS. DANIEL DYKE: We are here reminded of David when he sent his subjects against Absalom, yet willed them to pay special attention to not hurting him. But when our deceitful hearts attempt to urge us to show this favor to our Absalom—that is, to our darling sins—we should no more regard them than Joab did David's charge concerning Absalom. Rather, with stomach and courage, we are to run them through with the two-edged sword of the Spirit. This is different from the way we usually attack our darling sins: We prefer to give them merely a little pinch, as a prick with a pin. THE MYSTERY OF SELF-DECEIVING.[3]

18:6-18 Absalom Trapped in a Tree When Joab Kills Him

HANGING BETWEEN SPIRIT AND FLESH. BALTHASAR HUBMAIER: The soul stands between the spirit and the flesh. It is as Adam, who stood between God, who told him not to eat of the tree of knowledge of good and evil, and his Eve, who told him to eat of that tree. The soul is again free and may follow either the spirit or the flesh. If it follows the flesh it becomes as the flesh. But if it is obedient to the spirit, it becomes as the spirit. But the soul should be warned not to remain too long at that tree of human decision. It should decide which to follow, the flesh or the spirit. For it must not become as Absalom, who hung between heaven and earth. Otherwise it may be stabbed by that slave of sin, the flesh, receiving three wounds of will, word and deed. . . . Therefore, through the sent Word, the soul is again made healthy and truly free from the fall. It may then choose to will and do the good. Much is expected of it, for it can command the flesh, tame and master it, so that, contrary to the nature of the flesh, it must go into the fire along with the spirit and soul for Christ's name. And although there remains in us, unworthy servants that we are, a measure of imperfection, weakness and defect both of commission and omission, this is not on account of the soul, but rather on account of that evil and useless instrument, the flesh. CONCERNING THE FREEDOM OF THE WILL.[4]

---

[1] Strigel, *Libri Samuelis, Regum et Paralipomenon*, 175; citing Hercules and Bellerophon, heroic warriors from the *Iliad*.
[2] Willet, *Harmony on 2 Samuel*, 110*.

[3] Dyke, *The Mystery of Self-Deceiving*, 146*.
[4] Liechty, ed., *Early Anabaptist Spirituality*, 33*; cf. CRR 5:440-41.

Absalom Hangs by a Hair. Andrew Willet: Absalom was punished for what he most delighted in and in what he had the most pride. He was hanged by the hair of his head, which he nourished and kept long in order to glory in it. God's justice takes place when it punishes a person for their sins. In this passage even nature itself conspires to take vengeance on this wicked man, for even the oak that holds on above and the mule walking away under him work together to punish Absalom's wickedness. The oak had boughs winding and wrapping one within another, like a bramble or a bush. Absalom was caught by the hair in the oak, as the ram had been by its horns in the bush in Genesis 22:13. In this passage the same word is used to refer to this entanglement. Absalom hanged between heaven and earth, as accursed by God. For this kind of death was accursed by the law of God. The same shameful death came to Ahithophel for his similar sin of rebellion and disobedience. In the same way, Judas afterward, whom Ahithophel resembled in many ways, hanged himself after he had betrayed Christ. Harmony on 2 Samuel.[5]

Guarding the Affections. Charles Drelincourt: When Absalom was hanged by the hair of his head in a tree of the forest, Joab took three darts and struck him through the heart. In the same way, when our affections are too much entangled with the world and with the expectation of earthly contentment, it is then that they are miserably exposed to all the darts and violent attempts of death. Christian Defense Against the Fears of Death.[6]

18:19-33 David's Grief over Absalom's Death

An Epigram for Absalom. Philipp Melanchthon:

> Unworthy son, you unjustly seized your
>   parent's scepter,
> O youth, bitter plague of your father.

> A fitting punishment shadowed your deeds
>   as you wandered astray
> With their leafy boughs, the foliage has
>   enfolded you.
> Whirring from his mighty arm, Joab's spear
>   dripped,
> Stained by the blood of your pierced breast.
> The punishment of your crimes having been
>   struck, your father surrenders;
> Go now and ambush your father's goods.

Book of 2 Samuel.[7]

David Sees His Sins. Viktorin Strigel: David did not rejoice in his winning the civil war but compared these tragic events to the predictions of the prophet Nathan. He acknowledged the cause as being his own many sins and scandals that followed his lapses. He says, "Because of my sins, the wrath of God has allowed sedition to stir, even among my son. Sedition followed my defiled union with Bathsheba, and because of the sedition came many deaths throughout the kingdom and many other evil deeds that were brought with this internal discord, oppressing countless souls with the eternal wrath of God." On account of scandal, many saints have died of grief. And on account of the contagion of sedition, many saints have cast off the Holy Spirit, oppressed by the eternal wrath of God. No doubt some of David's wives were crushed by grief. When David considers all this mass of evil, he knew himself to be a plague on the church of God, a vessel of wrath and maybe even forsaken by God. Nevertheless, in these sorrows, he was comforted by this voice: "In your offspring shall all the nations of the earth be blessed." David included himself in this universal promise, and he stood certain of God's will to teach us that we are accepted in God's promises and are welcomed back when we accept them. It is better to be taught these things as an exercise of faith than as idle speculation. Book of 2 Samuel.[8]

---

[5]Willet, *Harmony on 2 Samuel*, 110-11*.
[6]Drelincourt, *Christian's Defense Against the Fears of Death*, 44*.
[7]MO 10:594-95; also cited in Strigel, *Libri Samuelis, Regum et Paralipomenon*, 176.
[8]Strigel, *Libri Samuelis, Regum et Paralipomenon*, 177-78; citing Gen 22:18.

DAVID'S LAMENT. LUCAS OSIANDER: "O Absalom, my son, my son!" This was the repeated lament of a greatly sorrowing soul, supplemented with many tears. For David not only grieved because of a parent's love for his son but was also greatly vexed in his soul by the violent manner of his death, which David had feared; namely, that his son would depart this life without repentance in eternal anguish. For that reason, he wished that he himself would have died (for he knew that he would have a pious death) so that he might ransom a long life for his son. For the death of a man of sin is the worst. Those who die as such will rightly suffer afflictions, so that they are in danger of perishing forever. There is no doubt that David's sacrifice and prayers for the dead son would have been heard if he had believed that the requests of the living are of use to the dead, but we read nothing of this in the canonical books of holy Scripture. ANNOTATIONS ON 2 SAMUEL.[9]

WHY WOULD DAVID FORFEIT HIS LIFE FOR ABSALOM? HIERONYMUS WELLER VON MOLSDORF: Nicholas of Lyra sweats vigorously to explain this question: why would David wish to die for his son Absalom? But the answer is easy. David was certain that even if he were suddenly overcome by death, nevertheless he would not perish apart from the grace of God. Because he had been correctly fortified by the Word of God, and he always walked in the fear of God, and he meditated in the law of the Lord day and night. Such people, whatever kind of death they are overcome by, will not perish. "Whether we live or we die, we are the Lord's." Again: "Precious in the sight of the Lord is the death of his saints." Romans again, "I am certain that neither death nor life will be able to separate us from the love of God which is in Christ Jesus our Lord." Every day, every hour and every minute the saints prepare themselves for death. And so death will never be able to overcome them unexpectedly. They conduct their lives in continual repentance. In contrast, the impious conduct their lives in the most self-assured manner, and they promise themselves a very long life. ANNOTATIONS ON 2 SAMUEL.[10]

THE NEED FOR JOY IN THE LORD. HENRY AIRAY: If death seizes a son or daughter, or anyone dear to us, we break out into outcries with David . . . saying, "O my son Absalom! My son, my son Absalom! Would I have died instead of you, O Absalom, my son, my son!" But though Joab tried, he could not comfort David. . . . And so it is when people do not put their comfort in God. Whatever befalls them in this life destroys them. If this or that thwarts them, by and by they are cast down. And why? It's because they have not learned how to rejoice in the Lord at all times. It is therefore very needful, you see, that we rejoice in the Lord always. This is for two reasons. First, the rejoicing we have in the Lord allows us to stand against whatever opposes us; and second, it is a lack of rejoicing in the Lord that makes us fall and be overcome whenever storms arise and troubles assault us. LECTURES ON PHILIPPIANS.[11]

19:1-8a Joab Rebukes David

JOAB'S HALF-TRUTH. LUCAS OSIANDER: Joab rebuked David, saying, "If your handsome little son were alive and we all traded places with him, it seems like you would be pleased." These words were partly true and partly a wrongful accusation. For David loved some of his enemies, according to the commandment of God: "Love those who hate you." But then Joab added a threat: "Now therefore arise, go out and speak in public, giving thanks to those who worked so strenuously and zealously for you in this war . . . otherwise everyone will leave you and look for someone else to be their king." ANNOTATIONS ON 2 SAMUEL.[12]

JOAB'S HARSH REBUKE TO DAVID. ANDREW WILLET: Joab certainly forgets his rank here as he

---

[9]Osiander, *Liber Iosue*, 588; citing Lk 6:27.

[10]Weller, *Samuelis liber secundus*, 324-25; citing Rom 14:8; Ps 116:15; Rom 8:38-39.

[11]Airay, *Lectures on Philippians*, 336*; citing 2 Sam 18:33.

[12]Osiander, *Liber Iosue*, 589-90; citing Mt 5:44.

speaks so boldly and irreverently to the king. Joab also charged David with untruth: For although it was apparent that David loved his enemies, David did not hate his friends. And in this way, Joab upbraids David for his former severities shown to those who killed his enemies, for instance, as when David put to death the Amalekite for killing Saul and Rechab and Baanah for killing Ish-bosheth. Joab essentially says, "After doing all these things, now you hypocritically hate me for killing Abner before and Absalom now?" It is true that we are to love our enemies to a certain degree, namely, to pray for them and to wish their repentance. Nevertheless, we are not to so love them that the glory of God and the safety of his people have lesser importance. Therefore Joab wisely admonished the king, though he did so more sharply than he ought to have. HARMONY ON 2 SAMUEL.[13]

---

[13]Willet, *Harmony on 2 Samuel*, 113*.

19:8B–22:51 DAVID'S CHALLENGES
UPON RETURNING TO JERUSALEM

⁸*Then the king arose and took his seat in the gate. And the people were all told, "Behold, the king is sitting in the gate." And all the people came before the king.*

Now Israel had fled every man to his own home. ⁹*And all the people were arguing throughout all the tribes of Israel, saying, "The king delivered us from the hand of our enemies and saved us from the hand of the Philistines, and now he has fled out of the land from Absalom.* ¹⁰*But Absalom, whom we anointed over us, is dead in battle. Now therefore why do you say nothing about bringing the king back?"*

¹¹*And King David sent this message to Zadok and Abiathar the priests: "Say to the elders of Judah, 'Why should you be the last to bring the king back to his house, when the word of all Israel has come to the king?ª* ¹²*You are my brothers; you are my bone and my flesh. Why then should you be the last to bring back the king?'* ¹³*And say to Amasa, 'Are you not my bone and my flesh? God do so to me and more also, if you are not commander of my army from now on in place of Joab.'"* ¹⁴*And he swayed the heart of all the men of Judah as one man, so that they sent word to the king, "Return, both you and all your servants."* ¹⁵*So the king came back to the Jordan, and Judah came to Gilgal to meet the king and to bring the king over the Jordan.*

¹⁶*And Shimei the son of Gera, the Benjaminite, from Bahurim, hurried to come down with the men of Judah to meet King David.* ¹⁷*And with him were a thousand men from Benjamin. And Ziba the servant of the house of Saul, with his fifteen sons and his twenty servants, rushed down to the Jordan before the king,* ¹⁸*and they crossed the ford to bring over the king's household and to do his pleasure. And Shimei the son of Gera fell down before the king, as he was about to cross the Jordan,* ¹⁹*and said to the king, "Let not my lord hold me guilty or remember how your servant did wrong on the day my lord the king left Jerusalem. Do not let the king take it to heart.* ²⁰*For your servant knows that I have sinned. Therefore, behold, I have come this day, the first of all the house of Joseph to*

come down to meet my lord the king." ²¹*Abishai the son of Zeruiah answered, "Shall not Shimei be put to death for this, because he cursed the* LORD's *anointed?"* ²²*But David said, "What have I to do with you, you sons of Zeruiah, that you should this day be as an adversary to me? Shall anyone be put to death in Israel this day? For do I not know that I am this day king over Israel?"* ²³*And the king said to Shimei, "You shall not die." And the king gave him his oath.*

²⁴*And Mephibosheth the son of Saul came down to meet the king. He had neither taken care of his feet nor trimmed his beard nor washed his clothes, from the day the king departed until the day he came back in safety.* ²⁵*And when he came to Jerusalem to meet the king, the king said to him, "Why did you not go with me, Mephibosheth?"* ²⁶*He answered, "My lord, O king, my servant deceived me, for your servant said to him, 'I will saddle a donkey for myself,ᵇ that I may ride on it and go with the king.' For your servant is lame.* ²⁷*He has slandered your servant to my lord the king. But my lord the king is like the angel of God; do therefore what seems good to you.* ²⁸*For all my father's house were but men doomed to death before my lord the king, but you set your servant among those who eat at your table. What further right have I, then, to cry to the king?"* ²⁹*And the king said to him, "Why speak any more of your affairs? I have decided: you and Ziba shall divide the land."* ³⁰*And Mephibosheth said to the king, "Oh, let him take it all, since my lord the king has come safely home."*

³¹*Now Barzillai the Gileadite had come down from Rogelim, and he went on with the king to the Jordan, to escort him over the Jordan.* ³²*Barzillai was a very aged man, eighty years old. He had provided the king with food while he stayed at Mahanaim, for he was a very wealthy man.* ³³*And the king said to Barzillai, "Come over with me, and I will provide for you with me in Jerusalem."* ³⁴*But Barzillai said to the king, "How many years have I still to live, that I should go up with the king to Jerusalem?* ³⁵*I am this day eighty years old. Can I*

discern what is pleasant and what is not? Can your servant taste what he eats or what he drinks? Can I still listen to the voice of singing men and singing women? Why then should your servant be an added burden to my lord the king? ³⁶Your servant will go a little way over the Jordan with the king. Why should the king repay me with such a reward? ³⁷Please let your servant return, that I may die in my own city near the grave of my father and my mother. But here is your servant Chimham. Let him go over with my lord the king, and do for him whatever seems good to you." ³⁸And the king answered, "Chimham shall go over with me, and I will do for him whatever seems good to you, and all that you desire of me I will do for you." ³⁹Then all the people went over the Jordan, and the king went over. And the king kissed Barzillai and blessed him, and he returned to his own home. ⁴⁰The king went on to Gilgal, and Chimham went on with him. All the people of Judah, and also half the people of Israel, brought the king on his way.

⁴¹Then all the men of Israel came to the king and said to the king, "Why have our brothers the men of Judah stolen you away and brought the king and his household over the Jordan, and all David's men with him?" ⁴²All the men of Judah answered the men of Israel, "Because the king is our close relative. Why then are you angry over this matter? Have we eaten at all at the king's expense? Or has he given us any gift?" ⁴³And the men of Israel answered the men of Judah, "We have ten shares in the king, and in David also we have more than you. Why then did you despise us? Were we not the first to speak of bringing back our king?" But the words of the men of Judah were fiercer than the words of the men of Israel.

20 Now there happened to be there a worthless man, whose name was Sheba, the son of Bichri, a Benjaminite. And he blew the trumpet and said,

"We have no portion in David,
and we have no inheritance in the son of Jesse;
every man to his tents, O Israel!"

²So all the men of Israel withdrew from David and followed Sheba the son of Bichri. But the men of Judah followed their king steadfastly from the Jordan to Jerusalem.

³And David came to his house at Jerusalem. And the king took the ten concubines whom he had left to care for the house and put them in a house under guard and provided for them, but did not go in to them. So they were shut up until the day of their death, living as if in widowhood.

⁴Then the king said to Amasa, "Call the men of Judah together to me within three days, and be here yourself." ⁵So Amasa went to summon Judah, but he delayed beyond the set time that had been appointed him. ⁶And David said to Abishai, "Now Sheba the son of Bichri will do us more harm than Absalom. Take your lord's servants and pursue him, lest he get himself to fortified cities and escape from us."ᶜ ⁷And there went out after him Joab's men and the Cherethites and the Pelethites, and all the mighty men. They went out from Jerusalem to pursue Sheba the son of Bichri. ⁸When they were at the great stone that is in Gibeon, Amasa came to meet them. Now Joab was wearing a soldier's garment, and over it was a belt with a sword in its sheath fastened on his thigh, and as he went forward it fell out. ⁹And Joab said to Amasa, "Is it well with you, my brother?" And Joab took Amasa by the beard with his right hand to kiss him. ¹⁰But Amasa did not observe the sword that was in Joab's hand. So Joab struck him with it in the stomach and spilled his entrails to the ground without striking a second blow, and he died.

Then Joab and Abishai his brother pursued Sheba the son of Bichri. ¹¹And one of Joab's young men took his stand by Amasa and said, "Whoever favors Joab, and whoever is for David, let him follow Joab." ¹²And Amasa lay wallowing in his blood in the highway. And anyone who came by, seeing him, stopped. And when the man saw that all the people stopped, he carried Amasa out of the highway into the field and threw a garment over him. ¹³When he was taken out of the highway, all the people went on after Joab to pursue Sheba the son of Bichri.

¹⁴And Sheba passed through all the tribes of Israel to Abel of Beth-maacah,ᵈ and all the Bichritesᵉ assembled and followed him in. ¹⁵And all the men who were with Joab came and besieged him in Abel of Beth-maacah. They cast up a mound against the city, and it stood against the rampart, and they were battering the wall to throw it down. ¹⁶Then a wise

woman called from the city, "Listen! Listen! Tell Joab, 'Come here, that I may speak to you.'" [17] And he came near her, and the woman said, "Are you Joab?" He answered, "I am." Then she said to him, "Listen to the words of your servant." And he answered, "I am listening." [18] Then she said, "They used to say in former times, 'Let them but ask counsel at Abel,' and so they settled a matter. [19] I am one of those who are peaceable and faithful in Israel. You seek to destroy a city that is a mother in Israel. Why will you swallow up the heritage of the LORD?" [20] Joab answered, "Far be it from me, far be it, that I should swallow up or destroy! [21] That is not true. But a man of the hill country of Ephraim, called Sheba the son of Bichri, has lifted up his hand against King David. Give up him alone, and I will withdraw from the city." And the woman said to Joab, "Behold, his head shall be thrown to you over the wall." [22] Then the woman went to all the people in her wisdom. And they cut off the head of Sheba the son of Bichri and threw it out to Joab. So he blew the trumpet, and they dispersed from the city, every man to his home. And Joab returned to Jerusalem to the king.

[23] Now Joab was in command of all the army of Israel; and Benaiah the son of Jehoiada was in command of the Cherethites and the Pelethites; [24] and Adoram was in charge of the forced labor; and Jehoshaphat the son of Ahilud was the recorder; [25] and Sheva was secretary; and Zadok and Abiathar were priests; [26] and Ira the Jairite was also David's priest.

21 Now there was a famine in the days of David for three years, year after year. And David sought the face of the LORD. And the LORD said, "There is bloodguilt on Saul and on his house, because he put the Gibeonites to death." [2] So the king called the Gibeonites and spoke to them. Now the Gibeonites were not of the people of Israel but of the remnant of the Amorites. Although the people of Israel had sworn to spare them, Saul had sought to strike them down in his zeal for the people of Israel and Judah. [3] And David said to the Gibeonites, "What shall I do for you? And how shall I make atonement, that you may bless the heritage of the LORD?" [4] The Gibeonites said to him, "It is not a matter of silver or gold between us and Saul or his house; neither is it for us to put any man to death in Israel." And he said,

"What do you say that I shall do for you?" [5] They said to the king, "The man who consumed us and planned to destroy us, so that we should have no place in all the territory of Israel, [6] let seven of his sons be given to us, so that we may hang them before the LORD at Gibeah of Saul, the chosen of the LORD." And the king said, "I will give them."

[7] But the king spared Mephibosheth, the son of Saul's son Jonathan, because of the oath of the LORD that was between them, between David and Jonathan the son of Saul. [8] The king took the two sons of Rizpah the daughter of Aiah, whom she bore to Saul, Armoni and Mephibosheth; and the five sons of Merab[f] the daughter of Saul, whom she bore to Adriel the son of Barzillai the Meholathite; [9] and he gave them into the hands of the Gibeonites, and they hanged them on the mountain before the LORD, and the seven of them perished together. They were put to death in the first days of harvest, at the beginning of barley harvest.

[10] Then Rizpah the daughter of Aiah took sackcloth and spread it for herself on the rock, from the beginning of harvest until rain fell upon them from the heavens. And she did not allow the birds of the air to come upon them by day, or the beasts of the field by night. [11] When David was told what Rizpah the daughter of Aiah, the concubine of Saul, had done, [12] David went and took the bones of Saul and the bones of his son Jonathan from the men of Jabesh-gilead, who had stolen them from the public square of Beth-shan, where the Philistines had hanged them, on the day the Philistines killed Saul on Gilboa. [13] And he brought up from there the bones of Saul and the bones of his son Jonathan; and they gathered the bones of those who were hanged. [14] And they buried the bones of Saul and his son Jonathan in the land of Benjamin in Zela, in the tomb of Kish his father. And they did all that the king commanded. And after that God responded to the plea for the land.

[15] There was war again between the Philistines and Israel, and David went down together with his servants, and they fought against the Philistines. And David grew weary. [16] And Ishbi-benob, one of the descendants of the giants, whose spear weighed three hundred shekels[g] of bronze, and who was armed with a new sword, thought to kill David. [17] But Abishai the

son of Zeruiah came to his aid and attacked the Philistine and killed him. Then David's men swore to him, "You shall no longer go out with us to battle, lest you quench the lamp of Israel."

¹⁸After this there was again war with the Philistines at Gob. Then Sibbecai the Hushathite struck down Saph, who was one of the descendants of the giants.¹⁹And there was again war with the Philistines at Gob, and Elhanan the son of Jaare-oregim, the Bethlehemite, struck down Goliath the Gittite, the shaft of whose spear was like a weaver's beam.ᵇ ²⁰And there was again war at Gath, where there was a man of great stature, who had six fingers on each hand, and six toes on each foot, twenty-four in number, and he also was descended from the giants. ²¹And when he taunted Israel, Jonathan the son of Shimei, David's brother, struck him down. ²²These four were descended from the giants in Gath, and they fell by the hand of David and by the hand of his servants.

22 And David spoke to the Lord the words of this song on the day when the Lord delivered him from the hand of all his enemies, and from the hand of Saul. ²He said,

"The Lord is my rock and my fortress and my
    deliverer,
  ³myⁱ God, my rock, in whom I take refuge,
my shield, and the horn of my salvation,
  my stronghold and my refuge,
  my savior; you save me from violence.
⁴I call upon the Lord, who is worthy to be
    praised,
  and I am saved from my enemies.

⁵"For the waves of death encompassed me,
  the torrents of destruction assailed me;ʲ
⁶the cords of Sheol entangled me;
  the snares of death confronted me.

⁷"In my distress I called upon the Lord;
  to my God I called.
From his temple he heard my voice,
  and my cry came to his ears.

⁸"Then the earth reeled and rocked;
  the foundations of the heavens trembled
  and quaked, because he was angry.

⁹Smoke went up from his nostrils,ᵏ
  and devouring fire from his mouth;
  glowing coals flamed forth from him.
¹⁰He bowed the heavens and came down;
  thick darkness was under his feet.
¹¹He rode on a cherub and flew;
  he was seen on the wings of the wind.
¹²He made darkness around him his canopy,
  thick clouds, a gathering of water.
¹³Out of the brightness before him
  coals of fire flamed forth.
¹⁴The Lord thundered from heaven,
  and the Most High uttered his voice.
¹⁵And he sent out arrows and scattered them;
  lightning, and routed them.
¹⁶Then the channels of the sea were seen;
  the foundations of the world were laid bare,
at the rebuke of the Lord,
  at the blast of the breath of his nostrils.

¹⁷"He sent from on high, he took me;
  he drew me out of many waters.
¹⁸He rescued me from my strong enemy,
  from those who hated me,
  for they were too mighty for me.
¹⁹They confronted me in the day of my calamity,
  but the Lord was my support.
²⁰He brought me out into a broad place;
  he rescued me, because he delighted in me.

²¹"The Lord dealt with me according to my
    righteousness;
  according to the cleanness of my hands he
    rewarded me.
²²For I have kept the ways of the Lord
  and have not wickedly departed from my
    God.
²³For all his rules were before me,
  and from his statutes I did not turn aside.
²⁴I was blameless before him,
  and I kept myself from guilt.
²⁵And the Lord has rewarded me according to
    my righteousness,
  according to my cleanness in his sight.

²⁶"With the merciful you show yourself merciful;

with the blameless man you show yourself
    blameless;
[27]with the purified you deal purely,
    and with the crooked you make yourself
      seem tortuous.
[28]You save a humble people,
    but your eyes are on the haughty to bring
      them down.
[29]For you are my lamp, O Lord,
    and my God lightens my darkness.
[30]For by you I can run against a troop,
    and by my God I can leap over a wall.
[31]This God—his way is perfect;
    the word of the Lord proves true;
    he is a shield for all those who take refuge in
      him.

[32]"For who is God, but the Lord?
    And who is a rock, except our God?
[33]This God is my strong refuge
    and has made my[l] way blameless.[m]
[34]He made my feet like the feet of a deer
    and set me secure on the heights.
[35]He trains my hands for war,
    so that my arms can bend a bow of bronze.
[36]You have given me the shield of your salvation,
    and your gentleness made me great.
[37]You gave a wide place for my steps under me,
    and my feet[n] did not slip;
[38]I pursued my enemies and destroyed them,
    and did not turn back until they were
      consumed.
[39]I consumed them; I thrust them through, so
    that they did not rise;
    they fell under my feet.

[40]For you equipped me with strength for the battle;
    you made those who rise against me sink
      under me.
[41]You made my enemies turn their backs to me,[o]
    those who hated me, and I destroyed them.
[42]They looked, but there was none to save;
    they cried to the Lord, but he did not
      answer them.
[43]I beat them fine as the dust of the earth;
    I crushed them and stamped them down
      like the mire of the streets.

[44]"You delivered me from strife with my people;[p]
    you kept me as the head of the nations;
    people whom I had not known served me.
[45]Foreigners came cringing to me;
    as soon as they heard of me, they obeyed me.
[46]Foreigners lost heart
    and came trembling[q] out of their fortresses.

[47]"The Lord lives, and blessed be my rock,
    and exalted be my God, the rock of my
      salvation,
[48]the God who gave me vengeance
    and brought down peoples under me,
[49]who brought me out from my enemies;
    you exalted me above those who rose
      against me;
    you delivered me from men of violence.
[50]"For this I will praise you, O Lord, among
    the nations,
    and sing praises to your name.
[51]Great salvation he brings[r] to his king,
    and shows steadfast love to his anointed,
    to David and his offspring forever."

---

a Septuagint; Hebrew *to the king, to his house* b Septuagint, Syriac, Vulgate *Saddle a donkey for me* c Hebrew *and snatch away our eyes* d Compare 20:15; Hebrew *and Beth-maacah* e Hebrew *Berites* f Two Hebrew manuscripts, Septuagint; most Hebrew manuscripts *Michal* g A *shekel* was about 2/5 ounce or 11 grams h Contrast 1 Chronicles 20:5, which may preserve the original reading i Septuagint (compare Psalm 18:2); Hebrew lacks *my* j Or *terrified me* k Or *in his wrath* l Or *his*; also verse 34 m Compare Psalm 18:32; Hebrew *he has blamelessly set my way free*, or *he has made my way spring up blamelessly* n Hebrew *ankles* o Or *You gave me my enemies' necks* p Septuagint *with the peoples* q Compare Psalm 18:45; Hebrew *equipped themselves* r Or *He is a tower of salvation*

OVERVIEW: The reformers examine David's actions as the restored ruler of all Israel. Having examined many of Joab's strengths and weaknesses up to this point, these commentators mostly (but not entirely) sympathize with David's demotion of this long-serving general. Less clear is their judgment of how David dealt with Ziba; Luther primarily sees the power of flattery at work here. Recalling earlier stories of Abigail and the wise woman of Tekoa, some praise the wisdom of the woman of Abel, through whom God saved a town from bloodshed. The reformers meditate on David's psalm of deliverance in chapter 22—his "swan song" as Strigel calls it—and apply its message to all the faithful. For example, Luther interprets this passage in a manner consistent with the medieval tradition, emphasizing the importance of faith and the gospel in the life of believers. Willet similarly interprets the "rock of my salvation" as Jesus Christ.

19:8b-23 *The Demotion of Joab and Promotion of Amasa*

JOAB'S RETIREMENT FROM THE MILITARY. CARDINAL CAJETAN: According to the Hebrew text, it says that "You [Amasa] will stand before me as leader of the army for all your days in place of Joab." But a question immediately arises regarding the justice of this promise. For Joab had obtained the right to be a leader of the army since he was the first person to go up into the citadel of Zion, as is written in 1 Chronicles 11. Therefore it would not seem to be right for Joab to be deprived of his leadership without just cause. Here's the solution: David indeed promised that the one who first ascended to the citadel of Zion would be a commander. However, it is never read that David had promised Joab to be head of the entire army. For there is a difference between being a leader or commander in the army and being leader of the *entire* army. Many, in fact, were leaders or commanders in the army. However, only one was the leader of the entire army, including commander over the other leaders. And therefore David was free to choose the leader of the entire army, whom he had chosen as Joab previously. This was written above in chapter 8. And this is fitting to reason. David, by his own accord, would now promise to grant the head of the army to Amasa instead of to Joab so that Amasa would not delay the restoration of the tribes of Judah to King David. I myself think that Joab supported David, so that he—now being quite old—could rest with him in Jerusalem and so that he could cease from his rule over all the kingdom and over all things relating to war now that the opportunity had been offered. COMMENTARY ON 2 SAMUEL.[1]

JOAB DEMOTED. LUCAS OSIANDER: David reflected on removing his highest officer Joab, deciding that he was entirely able to do without his contributions and to release him without injury. For although he had zealously served the king in many good ways in the past, he was nevertheless a cruel and impious man. For instance, he had treacherously slain Abner and killed Absalom against the express command of the king. Furthermore, Joab had given orders to David, which the king endured from him, as was clearly shown in the insolent way he spoke to him at the beginning of this chapter. ANNOTATIONS ON 2 SAMUEL.[2]

WHY DAVID REMOVED JOAB FROM BEING CAPTAIN. ANDREW WILLET: Some think that David had just cause for removing Joab from his rank as captain, both because he had so disrespectfully behaved himself toward David and because he had killed Absalom contrary to David's command. But neither of these was a sufficient cause, since in both cases Joab intended David's good as well as the safety of the people. Therefore the better opinion is that David here showed his human emotions, because Joab had before by his valor deserved that place. And David at once here forgot all the benefits he formerly received by Joab's service. In other words, David removed Joab for political reasons: As David did before in order to advance Abner for the same cause, so now David preferred Amasa over Joab, thinking that he would win the hearts of the people by doing so. At the same time, we must not rashly criticize David's acts,

---

[1]Cajetan, *Opera Omnia in Sacrae Scripturae Expositionem*, 2:162; citing 1 Chron 11:5-6; 2 Sam 8:16.
[2]Osiander, *Liber Iosue*, 592.

since we know that he did many other things by the instinct of God's Spirit, so it is possible that he did so here as well. HARMONY ON 2 SAMUEL.[3]

19:24-43 David's Decisions

THAT WENCH, ADULATION. MARTIN LUTHER: Whether there ever has been, or ever will be, a king or a prince who stayed undeceived by this beautiful wench Adulation, this I do not know; and I will let them look after it. But this I know very well from holy Scripture: that the highest king of all kings, David himself, did not remain immune to her. What his own son Absalom did to him with a handsome figure and fine words is obvious enough. Later Ziba tickled his ears at the right time and smeared his mouth so well that he deprived poor Mephibosheth of some properties that he had already promised him, and gave the kitten Ziba the half thereof. COMMENTS ON PSALM 101.[4]

BREACH OF FRIENDSHIP. LAMBERT DANEAU: If any person wanting to excuse David will say that because he had bound himself by an oath and had now already given the same goods to Ziba that therefore he could not lawfully call back his promise—the answer here is easily discovered. For David had previously given the very same goods to Mephibosheth, and therefore—in that division of them that he granted to be equally made between them both—does not clear himself from the conscience of his oath before God. For he swore also to Ziba that he would give him all of Mephibosheth's goods, and not just a portion of them. And yet he assigned unto him only a part, and took another part away from him. And therefore, even in this same division, David broke his oath, and therein he is manifestly guilty before God for taking his divine name in vain. To be short, there can be no excuse pretended, nor any reason (as I think) alleged, whereby David can be cleared in this case either from the spiritual fault of breach of

friendship or of his solemn oath long before sworn to Jonathan. TRUE AND CHRISTIAN FRIENDSHIP.[5]

GOD HAS NO CO-PARTNERS. DAVID CLARKSON: [God] is total owner of all. He has a full title to all and the right is wholly in him. He has no copartner nor associates. When David gave the possession between Ziba and Mephibosheth, they had a joint interest, just as Jehoshaphat and Ahaziah would have had in the navy and adventure if they had joined their ships according to the proposal. But none has a joint interest with God. [God] has a plenary title to the whole world, not a half or a divided right. SERMON ON 1 CHRONICLES 29:11.[6]

20:1-26 Sheba and the Wise Woman of Abel

THE WISE WOMAN. JOHANNES BUGENHAGEN: Just as you read of a wise woman from Tekoa in chapter 14 above, here an entire city was preserved through one wise woman. God is no respecter of persons, of those whom the world looks up to and admires. Instead, God chooses whomever he wants in order to work salvation, often those who are viewed with scorn, as it says in 1 Corinthians 1. This fits with what we saw earlier with Abigail, the wife of Nabal. The proverb she invokes comes from that locale, showing that wise people live there and have been taught by the Spirit of God and that they like many in Israel were accustomed to following its good counsel. COMMENTARY ON 2 SAMUEL.[7]

DIVINELY APPOINTED PILLARS PROTECT THE COMMUNITY. HIERONYMUS WELLER VON MOLSDORF: Now we hear what kind of death Sheba had. When he had retreated to the town of Abel, he imagined that he would be safe there. But the citizens, because they were unable to endure the siege for long, followed the counsel, wisdom and eloquence of a certain excellent woman in order to be freed from danger. They killed Sheba and threw

[3]Willet, Harmony on 2 Samuel, 113*.
[4]LW 13:206.

[5]Daneau, True and Christian Friendship, C6v-C7r*.
[6]Clarkson, Practical Works, 1:373*; citing 2 Sam 19:29; 1 Kings 22:49.
[7]Bugenhagen, In Samuelem prophetam, 351-52; citing 1 Cor 1:26-29.

his severed head over the wall to Joab, who immediately ceased the siege.

In the first place, we should learn what great disaster one criminal and impious person can cause an entire region and community. Here Sheba threw all the citizens of Abel into the greatest danger. On the contrary, however, a single person by his excellent piety and wisdom blesses and preserves many thousands of people not only by his prayers but also by his counsel. Thus Naaman the Syrian blessed Syria;[8] Joseph, Egypt; Lot, Sodom and Gomorrah—for as long as he remained there, God was unable to annihilate them, but as soon as he left that place, they were annihilated; and Luther, Germany.

Such people Scripture calls "pillars of the region" (Ps 75). "I strengthen its pillars," the Lord says. There God promises that he will preserve the pious in the midst of widespread misfortune; through the pious he is accustomed to bestow all kinds of blessings on the thankless world. Again he calls them *sōtēras*, "saviors" and "gods of the region." Thus God said to Moses: "I have made you a god to Pharaoh," that is, a savior, so that if Pharaoh would listen to you and would obey my voice, he would be saved with his people; if not, not at all—instead he will be utterly destroyed.

To every community and region God gives his people as *sōtēras* and pillars. To Egypt he gave Joseph as a pillar; to Syria, Naaman; to Samaria, Elijah and after him Elisha. But as soon as these *sōtēras* are removed from the midst of the community and region, horrible misfortunes follow, which sometimes ruin the entire community and region. As it is seen in the example of Joseph: after God freed him from human concerns, the people of Israel were overcome with the most painful slavery in Egypt. After Josiah, king of Judah, was killed, the destruction of Jerusalem soon followed. For through such people placed over the community, God delays impending punishment. Thus, while that man of God Dr. Luther lived, Germany remained peaceful; as soon as he died, that calami-

tous civil war broke out, and many other misfortunes, public and private, followed. In addition to these, terrible quarrels, *schismata* and scandals arose in the church. For Dr. Luther alone, while still alive, was that pillar and *sōtēr* of Germany, who like Atlas supported the heavens on his shoulders; that is, by his most ardent prayers he hindered the imminent punishment of sin that our ingratitude had merited, and he restrained the arms of God which threatened the destruction of Germany.

Citizens should remember that God bestows certain *sōtēra* to them, so that they should honor every kind of office in that way, and cherish them. Lest they treat such pillars and saviors abusively or they drown them in grief, and it should often happen that they aggravate the wrath of God and invite terrible punishment on themselves. ANNOTATIONS ON 2 SAMUEL.[9]

21:1-14 *The Gibeonites*

OF THE GIBEONITES. JOHANNES BUGENHAGEN: You read in Joshua 9 of the Gibeonites, who lived harmlessly among the Israelites and served them according to Joshua's decree. They are a sign of those who would come among God's people from the Gentiles. With a foolish zeal (as the text says here) Saul had recklessly wanted to destroy things, and so he sought to strike them down. It was clear that Saul was a law unto himself. But he was strong and was accustomed to looking after his own desires and ambitions. They could follow the impious law, but they could do nothing about changing it. And so you see here that God wants all of the Gibeonites to serve in faith, though they had originally gained that judgment through deceit. Here it was clear that the name of God was being blasphemed among the Gentiles. COMMENTARY ON 2 SAMUEL.[10]

THE POWER OF PRAYER. HIERONYMUS WELLER VON MOLSDORF: Both the prayers and imprecations of the saints are efficacious—a very eminent

---

[8]That is, Aram.

[9]Weller, *Samuelis liber secundus*, 342-43; citing Ps 75:3; Ex 7:1.
[10]Bugenhagen, *In Samuelem prophetam*, 353; citing Rom 2:24.

example of this is displayed here in the Gibeonites, who did not plead with the people of Israel but entreated God to consider them, oppressed and wretched, and to vindicate the injustice inflicted on them. By their groans and tears they caused God to punish the people of Israel with famine, because they would not punish Saul's descendants. Yes, as soon as Saul's descendants were executed—the Gibeonites had begun to bless the heritage of the Lord—the famine ceased. So also as soon as Abraham had begun to pray on behalf of King Abimelech, who had returned to Abraham his wife Sarah, whom he had taken away, the plague with which God had stricken Abimelech's entire family was removed. And the moment Samuel stopped praying on behalf of Saul, Saul had no success afterward. ANNOTATIONS ON 2 SAMUEL.[11]

WHY SAUL HAD FORMERLY KILLED THE GIBEONITES. ANDREW WILLET: Some think Saul killed the Gibeonites out of malice toward the priests who were killed in Nob. They were killed because the Gibeonites were servants to the tabernacle and for the cleaving of wood and drawing of water. But Saul did this out of zeal, not of malice. Some think his zeal was toward the Israelites to convey the inheritance, lands and possessions of the Gibeonites that they might have a more commodious dwelling. But this would have been from a covetous mind rather than one of zeal. Some think his zeal was here because in Joshua's times they had deceived the elders of Israel and therefore he was seeking revenge. But after such a long time, it was not likely that he would punish them for an error that Joshua and the elders of Israel had already pardoned when it was first committed and fresh in memory. It is therefore more probable that while Saul expelled sorcerers and witches out of Israel because the Gentiles and Canaanites were given to such devilish fiends, he also sought to root out the Gibeonites who were a remnant of the Canaanites from among them. He did this out of zeal and not out of malice. By this we learn that zeal, while

intended for good, is unacceptable to God if it is administered without knowledge or warrant from God's word. HARMONY ON 2 SAMUEL.[12]

21:15-22 *War with the Philistines*

INTERNAL FEARS AND EXTERNAL BATTLES. JOHANNES BUGENHAGEN: The history now recounts these wars that involved David. It describes four giants who came from a renowned race of giants, so that you see what afflictions David suffered. There were times when he was right to be afraid or when he sensed that he was near mortal danger, which the Lord sent to him. Thus he suffered internal fears and external battles from friends and strangers alike, though the Lord did not desert him. You should also not be ignorant that in Christ's kingdom it happens that he sets an ambush for all the inferior forces of the right hand and the left hand, and that he rises for eternity. COMMENTARY ON 2 SAMUEL.[13]

FALSE CONFIDENCE. JOHN MAYER: The Philistines pursued these battles out of a false sense of confidence. They based this confidence on their new champions, called giants. These so-called giants were Goliath-like warriors. No one was able to stand against them. However, four of them fell in four battles. The reason they fell is because God in his providence determined to end these wars so that the state of the kingdom might be left quiet and peaceable to Solomon. COMMENTARY ON 2 SAMUEL.[14]

22:1-51 *David's Song*

SEE ALSO PSALM 18. SEBASTIAN MÜNSTER: This passage is identical with Psalm 18, except that it differs in a few terms. THE TEMPLE OF THE LORD: 2 SAMUEL 22.[15]

---

[11]Weller, *Samuelis liber secundus*, 345; citing Gen 20; 1 Sam 15–16.

[12]Willet, *Harmony on 2 Samuel*, 122*; cf. Münster, *Miqdaš YHWH*, 617.
[13]Bugenhagen, *In Samuelem prophetam*, 354.
[14]Mayer, *Many Commentaries in One*, 454*.
[15]Münster, *Miqdaš YHWH*, 620. See also RCS OT 7:133-43.

David's Swan Song. Viktorin Strigel: The argument this psalm is making is clear partly from its title and partly from the sequence of the history. The introduction shows that David is giving thanks for defense against the power of his opponents and the treachery of his enemies, while the following history shows this to be David's swan song[16] before he is called out of this life. For just as the swan dies with a song, so David and all pious people on their migration out of this life glorify God with invocation, thanksgiving and confession. Though the psalm is spoken joyfully and easily, pious people know the various enemies David had. First he was bitterly opposed by Saul, who burned with ambition and afflicted others, including his most courageous son, who bore his tyranny. With a burning desire for vengeance, Saul not only sought to ambush David but also murdered the priests who had provided hospitality to David and all their families. . . . Then there was constant warfare with the neighboring peoples: Philistines, Syrians, Edomites, Amalekites, Ammonites and Moabites, just as Psalm 60 lists the enemies of God's people. Third, David knows the domestic wound inflicted by his son Absalom. No one could have imagined a more bitter wound, as Sophocles said, "No wound is worse than love betrayed." Finally, David experienced the treachery of Sheba and other most unruly cities, which was described in 2 Samuel 20. Therefore, who would not rightly be amazed that David could manage to govern the kingdom for forty years among such great impediments? But, as Dr. Luther was wont to say, he was a king of faith and a king of the promise; that is, faith and the Word of God conquer the devil and the world: "This is the victory that has overcome the world—our faith." Book of 2 Samuel.[17]

Historical Versus Figurative Interpretation. Andrew Willet: The psalm David sang to God after all his great deliverances is inferred in Psalm 19. But there is a difference in the words that are omitted here: "I love you, O Lord, my strength." And just as David was a type of Christ, so many things in this psalm are to be understood of Christ. Here is prophesied the passion, resurrection, ascension of Christ, his rejection by the Jews and the calling of the Gentiles. Indeed, this last point—"For this I will praise you, O Lord, among the nations"—proves the vocation of the Gentiles. But there may be a double error committed in the interpretation of this psalm. It may be either all historically applied to David or all mystically understood of Christ. Therefore what is historically set down must be historically applied to David, and what is figuratively uttered must be figuratively expounded of the Messiah. Harmony on 2 Samuel.[18]

The Horn of Salvation. Martin Luther: In Scripture the horn often denotes royal power as the chief power, or the king himself as the chief, especially the victorious and warlike power. Therefore also the church is called the horn of Christ: "His horn will be exalted in glory" (Ps 112); and "The horns of the righteous shall be exalted" (Ps 75), that is, the kingdoms and churches of Christ, "I will break all the horns of sinners." Thus Luke 1 reads: "He has raised up a horn of salvation," that is, Christ as victorious salvation, "for us in the house of his servant David." In Psalm 114 we read, "Judea was made his sanctuary, Israel his dominion" (that is, his kingdom); and in Psalm 78: "He built his sanctuary as of unicorns."[19] But the kingdom of Christ is called his horn. Accordingly, he himself

---

[16]Gk *kykneion asma.*

[17]Strigel, *Libri Samuelis, Regum et Paralipomenon,* 189; citing Sophocles *Antigone,* line 652; 1 Jn 5:4. See Sophocles, *Antigone, The Women of Trachis, Philocetus, Oedipus at Colonus,* ed. and trans. Hugh Lloyd Jones, Loeb Classical Library 21 (Cambridge, MA: Harvard University Press, 1994), 62.

[18]Willet, *Harmony on 2 Samuel,* 125*; citing Ps 18:1, 49.

[19]"That is, invincible and firm" (*glossa* on Psalm 78:69; WA 3:559). Modern editions of the Masoretic text point this word as *rāmîm* (lit. "exalted places"; "high heavens" [esv, nrsv]; "high palaces" [kjv]). Luther follows the Vg and lxx, which give the pointing as *rēmîm,* an alternate form of *rĕʾēm,* unknown horned wild animals (often translated as "wild oxen" or "buffalo"). Almost all of the reformers either translated *rĕʾēm* as *unicornes* or transliterated the lxx, resulting in *monocerotes.* Modern commentators universally reject this solution, but they are unsure as to the animal's exact identity. See further RCS OT 7:181-82.

has one horn, or one realm, as it were, because he is the Lord of only one church. For just as a horned beast . . . fights and wages war with the horns as weapons, so Christ fights and vanquishes the world and its prince through the church, which is his exceedingly strong and invincible horn. The church, on the contrary, calls Christ her horn, because it also denotes the King himself, as I have said, because Christ is the strength of his church through whom it triumphs over the world. He himself is strength and wisdom for all who believe in him. Thus the avenging God is the strength and invincible might of Christ, in which he has overcome all things. Accordingly, he says here, "the horn of my salvation," for God is the victorious might of Christ for salvation. Therefore, just as the church is Christ's, Christ is God's and, on the contrary, God is also Christ's, and Christ is the church's, so the church is the horn of Christ, Christ is the horn of God and, on the contrary, God is the horn of Christ, and Christ is the horn of the church. For here there is reciprocal power, and it is united in one. But first there is God, from whom both Christ and the church have strength and that he is a horn. God, however, is entirely of himself. Therefore in this psalm, which is altogether

anagogical, he attributes to God that he is the horn of his salvation. In a tropological sense, however, it is the faith of God, of Christ and of the church. For this is your victory, your faith. Therefore the horn denotes a warlike and victorious kingdom or king, as well as the Word of God, or the gospel. SCHOLIA ON PSALM 18:2.[20]

A HUMAN CANNOT BE THE ROCK OF THE CHURCH. ANDREW WILLET: A rock is a hard place and a sure defense from outward assaults. It is also a firm foundation to build on, so in both these respects God is David's rock. In other words, God is a faithful mass to preserve him from dangers and temptations and to give perseverance and strength. And this has a special reference to Christ, who is the rock and foundation of his church, on whom we are built by faith. Christ is for this rock and he is this rock. As verse 32 says so clearly: "And who is a rock, except our God?" It is therefore blasphemy to make Peter (or any other apostle) the rock of the church. HARMONY ON 2 SAMUEL.[21]

---

[20]LW 10:113-14* (WA 3:120); citing Ps 112:9; 75:10; Lk 1:69; Ps 114:2; 78:69; 1 Jn 5:4.
[21]Willet, *Harmony on 2 Samuel*, 126*.

23:1-39 DAVID'S LAST WORDS AND HIS MIGHTY MEN

¹Now these are the last words of David:

The oracle of David, the son of Jesse,
    the oracle of the man who was raised on
        high,
the anointed of the God of Jacob,
    the sweet psalmist of Israel:ᵃ

²"The Spirit of the LORD speaks by me;
    his word is on my tongue.
³The God of Israel has spoken;
    the Rock of Israel has said to me:
When one rules justly over men,
    ruling in the fear of God,
⁴he dawns on them like the morning light,
    like the sun shining forth on a cloudless
        morning,
    like rainᵇ that makes grass to sprout from
        the earth.

⁵"For does not my house stand so with God?
    For he has made with me an everlasting
        covenant,
    ordered in all things and secure.
For will he not cause to prosper
    all my help and my desire?
⁶But worthless menᶜ are all like thorns that are
        thrown away,
    for they cannot be taken with the hand;
⁷but the man who touches them
    arms himself with iron and the shaft of a
        spear,
    and they are utterly consumed with fire."ᵈ

⁸These are the names of the mighty men whom David had: Josheb-basshebeth a Tahchemonite; he was chief of the three.ᵉ He wielded his spearᶠ against eight hundred whom he killed at one time.

⁹And next to him among the three mighty men was Eleazar the son of Dodo, son of Ahohi. He was with David when they defied the Philistines who were gathered there for battle, and the men of Israel withdrew. ¹⁰He rose and struck down the Philistines until his hand was weary, and his hand clung to the sword. And the LORD brought about a great victory that day, and the men returned after him only to strip the slain.

¹¹And next to him was Shammah, the son of Agee the Hararite. The Philistines gathered together at Lehi, where there was a plot of ground full of lentils, and the men fled from the Philistines. ¹²But he took his stand in the midst of the plot and defended it and struck down the Philistines, and the LORD worked a great victory.

¹³And three of the thirty chief men went down and came about harvest time to David at the cave of Adullam, when a band of Philistines was encamped in the Valley of Rephaim. ¹⁴David was then in the stronghold, and the garrison of the Philistines was then at Bethlehem. ¹⁵And David said longingly, "Oh, that someone would give me water to drink from the well of Bethlehem that is by the gate!" ¹⁶Then the three mighty men broke through the camp of the Philistines and drew water out of the well of Bethlehem that was by the gate and carried and brought it to David. But he would not drink of it. He poured it out to the LORD ¹⁷and said, "Far be it from me, O LORD, that I should do this. Shall I drink the blood of the men who went at the risk of their lives?" Therefore he would not drink it. These things the three mighty men did.

¹⁸Now Abishai, the brother of Joab, the son of Zeruiah, was chief of the thirty.ᵍ And he wielded his spear against three hundred menʰ and killed them and won a name beside the three. ¹⁹He was the most renowned of the thirtyⁱ and became their commander, but he did not attain to the three.

²⁰And Benaiah the son of Jehoiada was a valiant manʲ of Kabzeel, a doer of great deeds. He struck down two arielsᵏ of Moab. He also went down and struck down a lion in a pit on a day when snow had fallen. ²¹And he struck down an Egyptian, a handsome man. The Egyptian had a spear in his hand, but Benaiah went down to him with a staff

and snatched the spear out of the Egyptian's hand and killed him with his own spear. ²²These things did Benaiah the son of Jehoiada, and won a name beside the three mighty men. ²³He was renowned among the thirty, but he did not attain to the three. And David set him over his bodyguard.

²⁴Asahel the brother of Joab was one of the thirty; Elhanan the son of Dodo of Bethlehem, ²⁵Shammah of Harod, Elika of Harod, ²⁶Helez the Paltite, Ira the son of Ikkesh of Tekoa, ²⁷Abiezer of Anathoth, Mebunnai the Hushathite, ²⁸Zalmon the Ahohite, Maharai of Netophah, ²⁹Heleb the son of Baanah of Netophah, Ittai the son of Ribai of Gibeah of the people of Benjamin, ³⁰Benaiah of Pirathon, Hiddai of the brooks of Gaash, ³¹Abi-albon the Arbathite, Azmaveth of Bahurim, ³²Eliahba the Shaalbonite, the sons of Jashen, Jonathan, ³³Shammah the Hararite, Ahiam the son of Sharar the Hararite, ³⁴Eliphelet the son of Ahasbai of Maacah, Eliam the son of Ahithophel of Gilo, ³⁵Hezro¹ of Carmel, Paarai the Arbite, ³⁶Igal the son of Nathan of Zobah, Bani the Gadite, ³⁷Zelek the Ammonite, Naharai of Beeroth, the armor-bearer of Joab the son of Zeruiah, ³⁸Ira the Ithrite, Gareb the Ithrite, ³⁹Uriah the Hittite: thirty-seven in all.

a Or *the favorite of the songs of Israel*   b Hebrew *from rain*   c Hebrew *worthlessness*   d Hebrew *consumed with fire in the sitting*   e Or *of the captains*   f Compare 1 Chronicles 11:11; the meaning of the Hebrew expression is uncertain   g Two Hebrew manuscripts, Syriac; most Hebrew manuscripts *three*   h Or *slain ones*   i Compare 1 Chronicles 11:25; Hebrew *Was he the most renowned of the three?*   j Or *the son of Ishhai*   k The meaning of the word *ariel* is unknown   l Or *Hezrai*

OVERVIEW: These commentators highlight the rich trinitarian and christological themes in David's song, noting that he speaks of Christ's eternal kingdom through the power of the Holy Spirit. While David possesses this great spiritual honor, several writers point out that he continues to know himself as the humble son of Jesse. Comments about David's mighty men focus on the holy blessing that loyal friends, servants and leaders provide to individuals and communities. The reformers differ concerning God's work in the world: some distinguish between service to the kingdom of God and valuable (but not salvific) service to the state; others more closely identify these military leaders' service to a righteous commonwealth as marks of successful spiritual battles.

23:1 David's Oracle

DAVID THE PROPHET AND POET. JOHANNES BUGENHAGEN: At the end of his life, David spoke through the Holy Spirit, as you see in the psalm you have here. Christ spoke of this, saying, "everything written about me in the Law of Moses and the Prophets and the Psalms must be fulfilled." And the disciples spoke of this, saying, "through the mouth of our father David, your servant, [you] said by the Holy Spirit. . . ." For here David praised God's merciful grace toward him and—against those who despise God—he prophesied that his kingdom would remain firm and that opponents of his kingdom would perish. COMMENTARY ON 2 SAMUEL.[1]

UNASHAMED. MARTIN LUTHER: How modestly David introduces his speech. He does not boast of his circumcision nor of his holiness nor of his kingdom, but he identifies himself simply as "the son of Jesse." He is not ashamed of his lowly descent, that he was a shepherd. TREATISE ON THE LAST WORDS OF DAVID.[2]

DAVID'S DENIAL. JOHANN ARNDT: The marks of . . . a soul that has died to the world are as follows: A person draws their will in all things to God's will, self-love is put out, fleshly desire is mortified, the

---

[1] Bugenhagen, *In Samuelem prophetam*, 355; citing Lk 24:44; Acts 4:25.
[2] LW 15:271.

pleasure of the world flees, they consider themselves as the smallest among human beings, they do not easily judge and direct their neighbor, they allow God to pass judgment and sentence, they do not lift themselves up if they wish to be praised, they are not disturbed if they are slandered, they bear all things in patience and complain about no one. An example of such a scarified will is to be found in King David.... David greatly wished to drink water from the well at Bethlehem. Three heroes traveled through enemy country to bring the king water. He poured it out before the Lord; that is, he gave up his own will because the three heroes had risked their lives for his will. In this is the true perfection of the Christian life. Perfection is not, as some think, a high, great, spiritual, heavenly joy and meditation, but it is a denial of one's own will, love, honor, a knowledge of one's nothingness, a continual completion of the will of God, a burning love for neighbor, a heart-held compassion and, in a word, a love that desires, thinks and seeks nothing other than God alone insofar as this is possible in the weakness of this life. In this is true Christian virtue, true freedom and peace in the conquering of the flesh and fleshly affections. TRUE CHRISTIANITY.[3]

23:2 *The Spirit of the Lord*

HOLY TRINITY. MARTIN LUTHER: Here David begins to talk about the exalted Holy Trinity, of the divine essence. In the first place, he mentions the Holy Spirit. To him he ascribes all that is foretold by the prophets.... And Christ himself states in Matthew 22: "If David thus calls him Lord, how is he his Son?" To be sure, without the Spirit he would neither call him that nor know in what way Christ is his Son and his Lord. The Holy Spirit, however, is not Christ the Son nor the Father. He cannot be another God. It follows cogently that there is but one God and yet three separate persons, Father, Son and Holy Spirit, from eternity to eternity. TREATISE ON THE LAST WORDS OF DAVID.[4]

THE TRINITY SPEAKING TO DAVID. ANDREW WILLET: God the Father and God the Son, who in verse 3 are called the rock of Israel, spoke to David by the Holy Spirit. Here is an evident demonstration of the Trinity: the Father, Son and Holy Spirit. This collection, although not sufficient to convince the incredulous Jews, is very comforting to we who are persuaded of this belief. So it may be concluded that the Father, Son and Holy Spirit are all one and the same substance and power because the same action is ascribed to them all, for all are said to speak to David. And here the dignity and worthiness of the Psalms is set forth, which were not written by any private motion, but instead proceeded from the Spirit of God, who spoke out of the mouth of David. Indeed, the apostle Paul said that the Spirit spoke "through the mouth of our father David." HARMONY ON 2 SAMUEL.[5]

UNFAILING COVENANT. EDWARD REYNOLDS: In times of plenty, security and peace, people go calmly on without fear or suspicion: but when storms arise, when God either hides his face or lets out his displeasure or throws people on any extremities; then there is no hope but in our anchor; no stay nor relief but in God's promises, which are settled and sure, established in heaven, and therefore never reversed or canceled in the earth. And if this faithful and sure Word had not been David's delight and comfort; if he had not, in all the changes and chances of his own life, remembered that all God's promises are made in heaven, where there is no inconstancy or repentance, he had perished in his affliction. Though David, by a prophetical spirit, foresaw that God would not make his house to grow but to become a dry and withered stock of Jesse, yet herein was the ground of all his salvation, and of all desire: the Lord had made a covenant with him, ordered in all things and sure; that he had sworn by his holiness that he would not fail David. So it was as impossible for God to be unholy as for the word of promise made to David to fall to the ground and be untrue. THE SINFULNESS OF SIN.[6]

---

[3]Arndt, *True Christianity*, 224.
[4]LW 15:276, 295; citing Mt 22:45.

[5]Willet, *Harmony on 2 Samuel*, 130-31*; citing Acts 4:25.
[6]Reynolds, *Works*, 1:313*.

23:3-7 *Dawns Like the Morning Light*

SPRINGTIME. MARTIN LUTHER: For just as the prophet David here by the season of spring typifies the blessed time of grace, which dawns on us through Messiah, his Son, so he also suggests that the season of winter indicates the opposite, namely, the time of wrath under original sin, which we inherited from Adam. In that way God symbolized sin and grace to us in his creation as a lasting reminder until the last day, when years, earth and heaven will change. Sin and grace are to be proclaimed to us daily and annually by summer and winter, if we but have ears to hear and eyes to see. In accord with such spiritual interpretation, Adam first lived in the charming season of spring, for he too was physically created in spring, in the beginning of the year. But through sin he soon called spiritual winter down on his head, which Christ, the dear Sun, again dispelled, reinstating spring. And now this is the order: he who lives in spring will never die; he who dies in winter will never live. In other words: "He who believes and is baptized will be saved; but he who does not believe will be condemned" (Mk 16:16). For the Sun, which David here foretold, sets on the latter but rises on the former. . . . But in the days of Messiah, says David, when . . . God himself will reign to justify us and to save us by grace, it will be as enchanting as the most delightful time in spring in the wake of a refreshing, warm rain, that is, following the preaching of the comforting gospel, immediately after which the Sun, Christ, rises in our hearts through true faith and devoid of Moses' clouds and thunder and lightning. Then all luxuriates, greens and blossoms, and the day is filled with joy and peace, the like of which is unknown to the rest of the year. For here winter, clouds, sin, death and all terrors are overcome, and a joyous, beautiful Easter Day is now celebrated into eternity. Behold, that is what David means when he compares his Son's, Messiah's, rule to a day in spring, when it rains early in the morning and then the sun rises in all its splendor and makes everything green and blooming and fragrant and live and merry. Ask yourself if this is not the best and happiest time of the year. TREATISE ON THE LAST WORDS OF DAVID.[7]

WELL-ORDERED AND SECURE. MARTIN LUTHER: The following two words, ʿărûkâ and šəmurâ, "well-ordered and secure," were chosen deliberately for instruction and for comfort. For if you take a glimpse at history, it will seem to you that God has forgotten his covenant and not kept it. David's house and that of his descendants lies desolate and disorganized. Yet it was not only maintained up to the time of Messiah but also kept in order and secure against all devils and all people. No one was able to overthrow or subdue it, but as promised all were obliged to leave the scepter of Judah unimpaired until the advent of Messiah.

However, after Messiah came, his kingdom, the church, when viewed externally, impresses one as more desolate and disordered. It seems that there is no more dismembered, wretched and ineffectual dominion or reign than the Christian church, Christ's kingdom. On the one hand the tyrants rend and devastate it with fire, water, sword and every type of violence; on the other hand factious spirits and heresies uproot and destroy it. Besides, false Christians do the same with their evil life. They make it seem as though there were no more disgraceful and disorderly rule on earth. And all of these work with the one aim in mind—rather, the evil spirit works through them—to annihilate Christ's rule, or at least to make it a miserable, muddled affair. In brief Christ acts as though he had forgotten about his dominion, it seems that he can be found nowhere, and neither ʿărûkâ nor šəmurâ is visible to reason. And yet it is *bakōl* ʿărûkâ and šəmurâ, all is "well-ordered and secure." And even though this is hidden from our view, he sees it who says in the Song of Songs: "My vineyard, my very own, is for myself," in Matthew 28: "Lo, I am with you always, to the close of the age," and in John 16: "Be of good cheer, I have overcome the world." At the same time we also observe that there always has been and always is a

---

[7]LW 15:348-49.

people that honors the name of Christ, that has his Word, baptism, the sacrament, the office of the keys and the Spirit against all the gates of hell. TREATISE ON THE LAST WORDS OF DAVID.[8]

23:8-39 David's Mighty Men

HEROES AGAINST HERESY. LUCAS OSIANDER: God repeatedly raises up heroes who do great things for the benefit of humankind. Some such most excellent fathers have existed in the church, boldly and blessedly opposing the fury of heretics. In political matters, such outstanding men stand firm against those who would perturb the peace of the republic. It is right to honor and give thanks to God for such men. ANNOTATIONS ON 2 SAMUEL.[9]

THE BLESSING OF GOOD LEADERS. VIKTORIN STRIGEL: Blessed is the republic where men such as these are present, whom God supported by giving them ardent passions and through whose counsel God governed and worked. As Psalm 127 says, "Blessed is the man who fills his quiver with them! He shall not be put to shame when he speaks with his enemies in the gate." He calls such a quiver a band of governors. They are not feathers but strong arrows to be brandished in the hand. BOOK OF 2 SAMUEL.[10]

TYPES OF CHRIST'S DISCIPLES. ANDREW WILLET: These worthy men who are named were very faithful to David. They served him not only in prosperity after he came to the kingdom but also before his united kingship. For instance, Abishai and Asahel were both killed by Abner, while David still reigned in Hebron. They numbered thirty-seven in all, as we see in verse 39. But these thirty-seven were divided into two ranks. There was one company of thirty where Asahel is named the first and Asahel the last, but these were of the second sort. The other seven were more valiant than these, and they were in the first rank of worthies. These worthy men who served David foreshadowed the twelve apostles and the seventy-two disciples, who were worthy and stout champions, fighting the Lord's spiritual battles under the true David and beloved of God, Christ Jesus. The names and acts of these worthy men are not suppressed but committed to memory, demonstrating that the Lord will not forget the faithful service and labor of his saints. It is also evident that it never goes better with the commonwealth than when virtue is advanced and men and women are respected according to their faithful service. But all things begin to decay when honor and promotion are carried away with flattery. HARMONY ON 2 SAMUEL.[11]

JOAB NOT ON THE LIST. LUCAS OSIANDER: These excellent heroes acquired eternal glory for themselves, their family and their country. They justly took up arms for the defense of true religion and the republic, not sparing their own blood or lives. For true nobility does not consist in titles or appearances but rather in true piety, honesty, virtue and greatness of soul. But one might wonder why David's captain Joab, who successfully led many battles, is not numbered among these lauded heroes. He darkened all of his virtuous deeds with two murders, when he wickedly and treacherously killed first Abner and then Amasa, both of whom were excellent men. For even those things that are done by good people are darkened and forgotten because of shame. Therefore innocence ought to be desired above all else. ANNOTATIONS ON 2 SAMUEL.[12]

---

[8]LW 15:349-50; citing Song 8:12; Mt 28:20; Jn 16:33.
[9]Osiander, *Liber Iosue*, 632.
[10]Strigel, *Libri Samuelis, Regum et Paralipomenon*, 197; citing Ps 127:5.
[11]Willet, *Harmony on 2 Samuel*, 133*.
[12]Osiander, *Liber Iosue*, 637.

24:1-25 THE CENSUS AND THE THRESHING FLOOR

[1]Again the anger of the LORD was kindled against Israel, and he incited David against them, saying, "Go, number Israel and Judah." [2]So the king said to Joab, the commander of the army,[a] who was with him, "Go through all the tribes of Israel, from Dan to Beersheba, and number the people, that I may know the number of the people." [3]But Joab said to the king, "May the LORD your God add to the people a hundred times as many as they are, while the eyes of my lord the king still see it, but why does my lord the king delight in this thing?" [4]But the king's word prevailed against Joab and the commanders of the army. So Joab and the commanders of the army went out from the presence of the king to number the people of Israel. [5]They crossed the Jordan and began from Aroer,[b] and from the city that is in the middle of the valley, toward Gad and on to Jazer. [6]Then they came to Gilead, and to Kadesh in the land of the Hittites;[c] and they came to Dan, and from Dan[d] they went around to Sidon, [7]and came to the fortress of Tyre and to all the cities of the Hivites and Canaanites; and they went out to the Negeb of Judah at Beersheba. [8]So when they had gone through all the land, they came to Jerusalem at the end of nine months and twenty days. [9]And Joab gave the sum of the numbering of the people to the king: in Israel there were 800,000 valiant men who drew the sword, and the men of Judah were 500,000.

[10]But David's heart struck him after he had numbered the people. And David said to the LORD, "I have sinned greatly in what I have done. But now, O LORD, please take away the iniquity of your servant, for I have done very foolishly." [11]And when David arose in the morning, the word of the LORD came to the prophet Gad, David's seer, saying, [12]"Go and say to David, 'Thus says the LORD, Three things I offer[e] you. Choose one of them, that I may do it to you.'" [13]So Gad came to David and told him, and said to him, "Shall three[f] years of famine come to you in your land? Or will you flee three months before your foes while they pursue you? Or shall there be three days' pesti-lence in your land? Now consider, and decide what answer I shall return to him who sent me." [14]Then David said to Gad, "I am in great distress. Let us fall into the hand of the LORD, for his mercy is great; but let me not fall into the hand of man."

[15]So the LORD sent a pestilence on Israel from the morning until the appointed time. And there died of the people from Dan to Beersheba 70,000 men. [16]And when the angel stretched out his hand toward Jerusalem to destroy it, the LORD relented from the calamity and said to the angel who was working destruction among the people, "It is enough; now stay your hand." And the angel of the LORD was by the threshing floor of Araunah the Jebusite. [17]Then David spoke to the LORD when he saw the angel who was striking the people, and said, "Behold, I have sinned, and I have done wickedly. But these sheep, what have they done? Please let your hand be against me and against my father's house."

[18]And Gad came that day to David and said to him, "Go up, raise an altar to the LORD on the threshing floor of Araunah the Jebusite." [19]So David went up at Gad's word, as the LORD commanded. [20]And when Araunah looked down, he saw the king and his servants coming on toward him. And Araunah went out and paid homage to the king with his face to the ground. [21]And Araunah said, "Why has my lord the king come to his servant?" David said, "To buy the threshing floor from you, in order to build an altar to the LORD, that the plague may be averted from the people." [22]Then Araunah said to David, "Let my lord the king take and offer up what seems good to him. Here are the oxen for the burnt offering and the threshing sledges and the yokes of the oxen for the wood. [23]All this, O king, Araunah gives to the king." And Araunah said to the king, "May the LORD your God accept you." [24]But the king said to Araunah, "No, but I will buy it from you for a price. I will not offer burnt offerings to the LORD my God that cost me nothing." So David bought the threshing floor and the oxen for fifty shekels[g] of silver.

²⁵*And David built there an altar to the LORD and offered burnt offerings and peace offerings. So the* | LORD *responded to the plea for the land, and the plague was averted from Israel.*

a Septuagint *to Joab and the commanders of the army*   b Septuagint; Hebrew *encamped in Aroer*   c Septuagint; Hebrew *to the land of Tahtim-hodshi*   d Septuagint; Hebrew *they came to Dan-jaan and*   e Or *hold over*   f Compare 1 Chronicles 21:12, Septuagint; Hebrew *seven*   g A *shekel* was about 2/5 ounce or 11 grams

---

OVERVIEW: The reformers wrestle with the complex theological issues that arise through David's census and God's punishment. They discuss how and why sin is present in a saint like David; they consider what it means that the Lord might incite harm against the people; and they observe David's willingness to suffer as a sign of his repentance and of his compassion for the people. Following Hebrews 13, some commentators interpret the construction of an altar christologically. Concluding their comments on 2 Samuel, some reformers reemphasize the relationship between the temporal establishment of David's kingdom and the spiritual reality of Christ's eternal kingdom.

24:1-9 *The Census*

GODLINESS OR MANLINESS. ANDREAS BODENSTEIN VON KARLSTADT: Saul enumerated his people and God did not show disfavor. . . . But when David enumerated his people, it was a sin unto death. . . . David undertook to number his people and understood in the end only that he had acted foolishly and sinfully. . . . I do not know the reason, especially since David recognized his folly and sin only when God struck his heart, but I fancy and guess that David forgot his great modesty and sought instead to gain victory and power with a great horde and with a multitude of people, as is the case now with all commanders and soldiers. They number their people and assess the usefulness of their armor and of everything else. And when they have plenty of people, and a variety of military equipment, and a good advantage, they hope to maintain their advantage. But when they have few people and weak weapons and defenses, they soon give up their manliness. Their heart drops, I don't know where, and

they totally forget . . . that they ought to fear God alone. WILL OF GOD.[1]

POWERFUL YET IMPERFECT. MARTIN LUTHER: David was a holy king, and he ruled by divine aid and favor. . . . Yet he was responsible for many injustices. . . . To state the matter briefly, it is impossible for people in power not to sin; neither are they able to administer justice to everyone. The reason is that the magnitude of affairs and Satan's artfulness exceed their strength. COMMENTS ON PSALM 45.[2]

PEOPLE CAN EASILY ERR. PHILIPP MELANCHTHON: Jeremiah reminds us to recognize our weakness in judgment and in deed. People can easily err, and many very exalted persons have erred frightfully in judgment, as David did in taking a census of the people, and as Josiah, Pericles, Demosthenes, Pompey, Brutus and others have done. Moreover, even if we do not err, we may still lack good fortune if God does not help us. For this reason, as previously stated, in all our undertakings we should carefully consider these three things: First, whether we are following God's command, and not undertaking some unnecessary thing because of our own forwardness. Second, whether we are obeying God's command in our calling, and not neglecting the work of our calling, for Scripture says, "Each one is to labor in his calling." Third, whether in our hearts we are crying to God for help, and trusting him, waiting for final deliverance, and asking that we not depart from him in sorrow and misfortune. THEOLOGICAL COMMONPLACES (1555).[3]

---

[1]CRR 8:222-23.
[2]LW 12:236.
[3]*Melanchthon on Christian Doctrine*, 64; citing 1 Cor 7:20, 24.

Not Afraid to Speak as the Scripture Does. Andrew Willet: Now it's certain that Satan principally tempted David here to commit evil. But in this place the nominative case is rather to be sought in the words going before them. But seeing that Scripture elsewhere ascribes as much to God as in Isaiah: "The Lord has mingled within her a spirit of confusion." The same prophet says: "O Lord, why do you make us wander from your ways and harden our heart." We need not be afraid to speak as the Scripture does, namely, that the Lord stirred up Shimei to curse David. As David said to his men: "Leave [Shimei] alone, and let him curse, for the Lord has told him to." Therefore, in a similar way, God is said to have moved David. That is, God permitted and allowed Satan to put it into David's heart to number the people. God was the moving cause in the sense that God did not give to David at this time the direction of his Spirit. The general virtue and power of moving is from God, but the evilness of the action is of ourselves. God used this fall and slip of David to turn it to another end. In this way God's justice showed itself in punishing his people. And it was an occasion of greater good. By this means the place was pointed out where afterward the temple was built. Harmony on 2 Samuel.[4]

Coworkers with Satan. Edward Reynolds: It is said that Satan provoked David to number the people, and yet David's heart smote himself and did not charge Satan with the sin. That's because it was the lust of his own heart that let in and gave way to Satan's temptation. If there were the same mind in us as in Christ, that Satan could find no more in us to mingle his temptations than he did in him, they would be equally without success. But this is Satan's greatest advantage, that he heats our evil nature to help him and hold intelligence with him. And therefore we must rise as high as that in our humiliations for sin, for such will keep us always humble. That's because our sinful flesh will always be stirring in us. And it will make us

thoroughly humble because by it sin is made altogether our own when we attribute it not to casualties or accidental miscarriages but to our own nature. The Sinfulness of Sin.[5]

Joab Tries to Dissuade the King From Counting the People. Andrew Willet: By Joab's actions we see that he believed it was God who would increase the number of people. Joab recognized that David should acknowledge the blessings he had, and not to take on himself God's job, as if by him the people could be increased by numbering them. And secretly he insinuated that David should give serious attention to the matter, lest by this action the numbers of the people might diminish rather than multiply and increase by God. He further insinuated that there was no end of numbering the people, for they all professed to be David's servants as explained in 1 Chronicles 21:3. Therefore, to that end, they did not need to be numbered. Further, he foretold that this would be a great sin in Israel; and that God, being offended, would punish his people. It is not that they were numbered without that leave appointed by Moses, for Moses himself did not always leave that sum when he numbered the people. But Joab's heart knew this proceeded from pride and carnal confidence, which the Lord would punish. But regardless of these reasons assumed by Joab and the rest of the princes and captains, David's word prevailed, for the Lord had determined on this occasion to bring a plague on Israel. Harmony of 2 Samuel.[6]

24:10-17 *The Lord Judges David*

Blame on the People. Martin Luther: And the very best of kings, his own beloved David, who had no peer among temporal rulers before, beside or after him, filled as he was with the fear and the wisdom of God, and directing his whole rule not after his own reason but according to God's command alone, nevertheless stumbled more than once.

---

[4]Willet, *Harmony on 2 Samuel*, 139*; citing 1 Chron 21:1; Is 19:14; 63:17; 2 Sam 16:11.
[5]Reynolds, *Works*, 1:191*.
[6]Willet, *Harmony on 2 Samuel*, 140*.

Therefore the Scripture, unable to blame his reign and yet finding it necessary to narrate the calamity that befell the people on his account, put the blame not on David but on the people. It says that God's anger was kindled against them so that he let the saintly David be moved by the devil to number the people; on account of this, seventy thousand of them were destroyed by pestilence. All these things were foreordained by God in order to terrify those in authority, to keep them in fear and to admonish them of their peril. THE SERMON ON THE MOUNT.[7]

GOD'S POWER. HULDRYCH ZWINGLI: We poor human beings desire to be continuously strutting about, which is very distasteful to God, as we can see ... when David took a census of the children of Israel in order to see how powerful he was, doubtlessly ascribing all credit for the might of the nation to himself. Therefore God became angry and offered David the choice of three plagues, one of which he must select as punishment for having counted the people. David selected the bubonic plague, so that he himself might be stricken. Note that when David wished to brag and count his force, he showed that he desired to know the extent of that power which was not his, but God's. For this David was severely punished, so that he might remember the words of Moses ... : "How should one chase a thousand, and two put ten thousand to flight, except their Rock had sold them, and the Lord had shut them up?" WARNING AGAINST CONTROL OF FOREIGN LANDS.[8]

PREFERABLE PUNISHMENTS. LUCAS OSIANDER: David preferred that God punish him directly rather than that it come through the cruelty of enemies. For though such punishments are imposed on us by others, they also come from God; thus they lead to no other end than that prescribed by God himself. Those punishments that come from God and not from the actions of other people are seen to contain a certain amount

of mercy. Therefore they inspire less impatience in us and do not give room to the desire for vengeance. ANNOTATIONS ON 2 SAMUEL.[9]

SPARE THE CREATURES. CHARLES DRELINCOURT: Because of our rebellion and our treason against God, he has punished the world for our sakes and has made it sensible of his wrath. But now that our peace is made, or rather now that God has made peace by the blood of his son, we may justly expect that he will remove all signs of his displeasure and revenge. Concerning this matter, I remember what David said to God when he saw the angel destroy Jerusalem. "I have sinned, and I have done wickedly. But these sheep, what have they done?" In the same way, every believer may say to God: "I have sinned, Lord, I have acted wickedly. But these inanimate creatures, what have they done? *Our* sins have defiled the earth. And all that may be objected to heaven is to have yielded light and assistance to us rebels. Since, therefore, you have blotted out our sins and pardoned our rebellions, spare these harmless creatures, which are only being punished for our sakes." CHRISTIAN DEFENSE AGAINST THE FEARS OF DEATH.[10]

GODLY SORROW. DANIEL DYKE: To feel oneself a sinner and to be touched with the sense of our misery is not always repentance. . . . Godly sorrow fears the sin more than the punishment. It is to make the repenting sinner to be of the mind that they do not care about what outward punishment they endure. Rather, they more feel the guilt of their sin and the need for it to be washed out of their conscience. In this way they look toward the loving countenance of God in Christ. We can see the voice of godly sorrow in the case of David: "But now, O Lord, please take away the iniquity of your servant." It is the trespass he wanted to be taken away. But as for the punishment, let his own words afterward witness when he speaks in this way to

---

[7] LW 21:356-57.
[8] Zwingli, *Latin Works*, 1:136-37* (ZSW 1:172); citing Deut 32:30.

[9] Osiander, *Liber Iosue*, 642; citing Heb 10:31.
[10] Drelincourt, *Christian's Defense Against the Fears of Death*, 476*; citing 2 Sam 24:17.

God: "Behold, I have sinned . . . But these sheep, what have they done? Please let your hand be against me." THE MYSTERY OF SELF-DECEIVING.[11]

CHOOSE ANOTHER ACTIVITY. LANCELOT ANDREWES: War is God's rod, God's fearful rod. It is so fearful that King David, though a warrior when he was younger, preferred the plague before it, and desired either of the other two options. Since war, therefore, is God's rod, choose some other activity. COLLECTION OF LECTURES.[12]

DAVID CHOSE THE EASIER PUNISHMENT. ANDREW WILLET: The apostle said to the Hebrews, "It is a terrifying thing to fall into the hands of the living God." Yet David thought it would be better to fall into the hands of God than of people. But it must be considered that the apostle spoke about sins where the Lord is provoked, as of despising the Spirit of grace and counting the blood of the Testament as an unholy thing. For such things, indeed, to fall into the hands of God is a grievous thing. But here David spoke of the temporal punishments inflicted by the Lord, which are easier and more profitable than those that are executed by people. David also spoke of the purity the Lord imposed from a fatherly affection, and seeking the amendment of his children in love. But the apostle spoke of the punishments that are inflicted by the Lord as an angry judge. HARMONY OF 2 SAMUEL.[13]

DAVID PLEADS FOR HIS PEOPLE. LUCAS OSIANDER: David prayed, "If you want to punish all of my sin, punish it in me and my family and turn your wrath from my citizens." Through these words, David did not mean to accuse God of injustice. Instead David acknowledged his sin and that he had done such a thing, even as he recognized it to be a particular penalty that this public calamity would occur because of his private sins. He wanted the punishment to be diverted to himself so that his subjects might escape harm. For pious people under the cross are truly humble, for they admit their unworthiness and accuse themselves greatly in all things. ANNOTATIONS ON 2 SAMUEL.[14]

24:18-25 David Builds an Altar

IN SEARCH OF GLORY. JOHANNES BUGENHAGEN: Scripture always condemns and views as nothing those who serve the flesh and do not serve or fear God. Because the Israelites often acted impiously under Saul and under Absalom, not recognizing sin and acting without fear, they were gathered together and even stricken so that they might see their iniquity. And in order for God to do this, God took away the good and gave David an evil spirit, so that he might gravely sin, causing the people to perish. For the more serious the sin, the more the wrath of God flows down. So you should not wonder if the Lord pours evil over a people through evil leaders, for contempt of God and neglect for the holy gospel may come even under the best king. Therefore we always ask God not to leave us so that we do not perish in the security of flesh. This kingdom of David's (that is, Christ's kingdom) is not only attacked by flesh and blood but also by Satan and is driven to despair by sin. Death and hell strive to swallow us up and are even reluctantly glorified at the gates of hell. This is all described to you so that you never hope for security in the flesh or according to the flesh. May the preachers of the gospel see this example, through which Christ lifts up David's kingdom. For they are the ones of his who—like David—increase the people of God through the gospel despite many persecutions and the hatred of others. But where they see an increase in numbers they begin to be pleased and seek glory according to the flesh. There God leaves them, so that some may start to fear after many have been slain in unfaithfulness and others are cut down by plagues. David sought glory by numbering the people, and this plague hurt a great number of them. But as for the rest, you have this example of the judgment and

[11]Dyke, *The Mystery of Self-Deceiving*, 91-92*; citing 2 Sam 24:10, 17.
[12]Andrewes, *A Collection of Lectures*, 331*.
[13]Willet, *Harmony on 2 Samuel*, 143*; citing Heb 10:31.
[14]Osiander, *Liber Iosue*, 644.

mercy of God: judgment in how the people, not David, were attacked; mercy in how Jerusalem was spared, the plague ceased among the people and David was forgiven. Commentary on 2 Samuel.[15]

God's Eternal Plan. Lancelot Andrewes: God has revealed from all times that the gate of faith should be opened to the Gentiles to enter into the flock of Christ . . . in order to signify that Christ should save both Jews and Gentiles. Thus the matching of Jews with Gentiles demonstrates the affinity that should grow between the two churches. This was shown by the fact that . . . the first temple that was built came from the ground of a Gentile named Araunah. Collection of Lectures.[16]

Why It Was Lawful for David to Build His Altar There. Andrew Willet: David did not build this of himself, for the angel told David where to build the altar. So it is likely that when the holy people of God sacrificed in the high places, they did it with God's guidance even though it was not always expressed. The tabernacle was at Gibeon at this time, where most of the priests gave their attendance. Yet there were also many, the primary ones of which were Zadok and Abiathar, who remained with the ark in Jerusalem. And there was another reason why David could not go to Gibeon: He was afraid the sword of the angel might strike with some infirmity. So he was in great fear because of this present danger. This altar built was a type of the true altar, Christ Jesus, who was to suffer in Jerusalem. In this way, the apostle called Christ the "altar" in Hebrews. That place did not serve to prove that there ought to be any material altars in the church. But some interpreters explained that they had no authority to eat any food but Christ at that altar. Therefore he does not mean by that altar. The following words must be weighed: They have no authority to eat what is served in the tabernacle. But those who are under the gospel eat of this altar. Harmony on 2 Samuel.[17]

Conclusion to the Books of Samuel. Johannes Bugenhagen: Thus you have these two books, which tell how the kingdom of Israel began and how the true kingdom of David and his descendants was established for eternity in Jesus Christ our Lord. Commentary on 2 Samuel.[18]

---

[15]Bugenhagen, *In Samuelem prophetam*, 357-58.
[16]Andrewes, *A Collection of Lectures*, 557*.
[17]Willet, *Harmony on 2 Samuel*, 146*; citing Heb 13:10.
[18]Bugenhagen, *In Samuelem prophetam*, 361.

COMMENTARY ON 1 KINGS

OVERVIEW: Commentators here identify themes such as the people's continuing struggle to follow the Lord, God's enduring mercy to Israel and Judah, and the harmful effects of sin among God's people. They highlight important kings featured in this book like Solomon, Ahab and Jehoshaphat, as well as key biblical moments like the construction of the temple and the division of the kingdom. Commenting more broadly, some locate this book within the larger narrative of the rise of David's kingdom, its fall into unfaithfulness and ruin, and God's promise to redeem the people from captivity. However, all our commentators recognize that 1 Kings is a book that ultimately points to Christ, the true King of kings.

Prolegomena: What This Book Is About

FAR BETTER THAN CHRONICLES. MARTIN LUTHER: The author of the books of Kings goes a hundred thousand steps beyond the author of the books of Chronicles. For he has described the most important and special events, passing over rocky and unimportant matters. If at any place Kings varies from Chronicles, I trust the author of Kings more than the author of Chronicles. And so I agree with neither what Jerome nor Nicholas of Lyra say—that Kings provokes many questions, unlike Chronicles. Kings is to be greatly preferred. TABLE TALK.[1]

FROM DAVID TO THE BABYLONIAN CAPTIVITY. JOHANNES BUGENHAGEN: In the time after David, Solomon's glory is described here. Under him, the building of a temple for worship of God was not a vulgar thing, for God fulfilled the wisdom of Solomon's words and hopes. But when he defected to impiety, God's judgment divided the kingdom. Then two tribes, Benjamin and Judah (the ones that remained of David's descendants), became the kingdom of Judea, while the other ten tribes constituted the kingdom of Israel. After this the kingdom of Israel labored perpetually in idolatry and unfaithfulness and, having forsaken God, was carried off to Assyria and never brought back. They received no benefit from the rebukes and prophecies of many outstanding prophets, except that they received even greater guilt from God's judgment for having despised the prophets and the word of God. Nor was it any better in the kingdom of Judah, even though worship according to God's law endured there for some time and was repeatedly restored. Those who were accused were not only the pious ones who loved the law and holy prophets but also kings, even though a few still held to the worship of the true God. They assented to such a great mass of impiety that God gave them into the hands of the Chaldeans, which was then called the Babylonian captivity. This is how the books of Kings end. Truly, after seventy years of this, the king of Persia returned the Judeans to their own land after God touched his

---

[1]WATR 1:364-65, no. 765.

heart. You read this in Ezra, not only so that the words of the prophet Jeremiah would be seen to be true but also so that the time and place that had been foretold of Christ would be fulfilled, who came from the tribe of Judah and who sits on the throne of his father David, reigning over the house of Jacob in eternity, whose kingdom shall have no end. COMMENTARY ON 1 KINGS.[2]

ACTS OF THE KINGS. JOHANNES PISCATOR: The first book of Kings contains the acts of the first five kings of Judah: Solomon, Rehoboam, Abijah, Asa and Jehoshaphat. It also contains the acts of the first kings of Israel: Jeroboam, Nadab, Baasha, Elah, Zimri, Tibni, Omri and Ahab. Those things concerning Solomon are narrated in the first eleven chapters. And those things concerning the other kings are as follows: Rehoboam and Jeroboam in the twelfth to the fourteenth chapters. Abijah, Asa, Nadab, Baasha, Zimri, Tibni and Omri are in the fifteenth and sixteenth chapters. And Ahab's story is told from the sixteenth to the twenty-second chapter, where Jehoshaphat is picked up until the end of the book.

The principal parts of the story of this book are the following: the building of the temple, the judgment of Solomon, the division of the kingdom, the idolatry of the golden calf, the battle of Elijah against the prophets of Baal and the killing of Naboth. COMMENTARY ON 1 KINGS.[3]

THE VARIETIES AND CHANGE OF THINGS. GENEVA BIBLE: Because the children of God should look for no continual rest and quietness in this world, the Holy Spirit sets before one's eyes in this book the varieties and change of things, which came to the people of Israel from the death of David, of Solomon and of the rest of the kings even to the death of Ahab. This book declares how kingdoms will only flourish if they are preserved by God's protection. In other words, God protects his people when his word is set forth, virtue is esteemed, vice is punished and harmony is maintained. Otherwise the kingdom will fall into corruption and division, as appears at the dividing of the kingdom under Rehoboam and Jeroboam. For formerly the kingdom was all one people. But God's just judgment made a division of the two kingdoms, where Judah and Benjamin chose to stay close to Rehoboam, while the other ten tribes held with Jeroboam. The king of Judah had his throne in Jerusalem, and the king of Israel had his throne in Samaria after it was built by Omri, Ahab's father.

And because our Savior was to come from the stock of David according to the flesh, the genealogies of the kings of Judah are detailed—from Solomon to Jehoram, the son of Jehoshaphat, who reigned over Judah in Jerusalem just as Ahab did over Israel in Samaria. ARGUMENT OF 1 KINGS.[4]

---

[2]Bugenhagen, *In Regum duos ultimos libros*, 3-4; citing Ezra 1.
[3]Piscator, *Commentarii in omnes libros Veteris Testamenti*, 2:251.
[4]*Geneva Bible* (1560), 148r*.

1:1-53 THE FIGHT FOR SUCCESSION BEGINS

¹*Now King David was old and advanced in years. And although they covered him with clothes, he could not get warm.* ²*Therefore his servants said to him, "Let a young woman be sought for my lord the king, and let her wait on the king and be in his service. Let her lie in your arms,ᵃ that my lord the king may be warm."* ³*So they sought for a beautiful young woman throughout all the territory of Israel, and found Abishag the Shunammite, and brought her to the king.* ⁴*The young woman was very beautiful, and she was of service to the king and attended to him, but the king knew her not.*

⁵*Now Adonijah the son of Haggith exalted himself, saying, "I will be king." And he prepared for himself chariots and horsemen, and fifty men to run before him.* ⁶*His father had never at any time displeased him by asking, "Why have you done thus and so?" He was also a very handsome man, and he was born next after Absalom.* ⁷*He conferred with Joab the son of Zeruiah and with Abiathar the priest. And they followed Adonijah and helped him.* ⁸*But Zadok the priest and Benaiah the son of Jehoiada and Nathan the prophet and Shimei and Rei and David's mighty men were not with Adonijah.*

⁹*Adonijah sacrificed sheep, oxen, and fattened cattle by the Serpent's Stone, which is beside En-rogel, and he invited all his brothers, the king's sons, and all the royal officials of Judah,* ¹⁰*but he did not invite Nathan the prophet or Benaiah or the mighty men or Solomon his brother.*

¹¹*Then Nathan said to Bathsheba the mother of Solomon, "Have you not heard that Adonijah the son of Haggith has become king and David our lord does not know it?* ¹²*Now therefore come, let me give you advice, that you may save your own life and the life of your son Solomon.* ¹³*Go in at once to King David, and say to him, 'Did you not, my lord the king, swear to your servant, saying, "Solomon your son shall reign after me, and he shall sit on my throne"? Why then is Adonijah king?'* ¹⁴*Then while you are still speaking with the king, I also will come in after you and confirmᵇ your words."*

¹⁵*So Bathsheba went to the king in his chamber (now the king was very old, and Abishag the Shunammite was attending to the king).* ¹⁶*Bathsheba bowed and paid homage to the king, and the king said, "What do you desire?"* ¹⁷*She said to him, "My lord, you swore to your servant by the LORD your God, saying, 'Solomon your son shall reign after me, and he shall sit on my throne.'* ¹⁸*And now, behold, Adonijah is king, although you, my lord the king, do not know it.* ¹⁹*He has sacrificed oxen, fattened cattle, and sheep in abundance, and has invited all the sons of the king, Abiathar the priest, and Joab the commander of the army, but Solomon your servant he has not invited.* ²⁰*And now, my lord the king, the eyes of all Israel are on you, to tell them who shall sit on the throne of my lord the king after him.* ²¹*Otherwise it will come to pass, when my lord the king sleeps with his fathers, that I and my son Solomon will be counted offenders."*

²²*While she was still speaking with the king, Nathan the prophet came in.* ²³*And they told the king, "Here is Nathan the prophet." And when he came in before the king, he bowed before the king, with his face to the ground.* ²⁴*And Nathan said, "My lord the king, have you said, 'Adonijah shall reign after me, and he shall sit on my throne'?* ²⁵*For he has gone down this day and has sacrificed oxen, fattened cattle, and sheep in abundance, and has invited all the king's sons, the commandersᶜ of the army, and Abiathar the priest. And behold, they are eating and drinking before him, and saying, 'Long live King Adonijah!'* ²⁶*But me, your servant, and Zadok the priest, and Benaiah the son of Jehoiada, and your servant Solomon he has not invited.* ²⁷*Has this thing been brought about by my lord the king and you have not told your servants who should sit on the throne of my lord the king after him?"*

²⁸*Then King David answered, "Call Bathsheba to me." So she came into the king's presence and stood before the king.* ²⁹*And the king swore, saying, "As the LORD lives, who has redeemed my soul out of every adversity,* ³⁰*as I swore to you by the LORD, the God of Israel, saying, 'Solomon your son shall reign after me,*

and he shall sit on my throne in my place,' even so will I do this day." ³¹Then Bathsheba bowed with her face to the ground and paid homage to the king and said, "May my lord King David live forever!"

³²King David said, "Call to me Zadok the priest, Nathan the prophet, and Benaiah the son of Jehoiada." So they came before the king. ³³And the king said to them, "Take with you the servants of your lord and have Solomon my son ride on my own mule, and bring him down to Gihon. ³⁴And let Zadok the priest and Nathan the prophet there anoint him king over Israel. Then blow the trumpet and say, 'Long live King Solomon!' ³⁵You shall then come up after him, and he shall come and sit on my throne, for he shall be king in my place. And I have appointed him to be ruler over Israel and over Judah." ³⁶And Benaiah the son of Jehoiada answered the king, "Amen! May the LORD, the God of my lord the king, say so. ³⁷As the LORD has been with my lord the king, even so may he be with Solomon, and make his throne greater than the throne of my lord King David."

³⁸So Zadok the priest, Nathan the prophet, and Benaiah the son of Jehoiada, and the Cherethites and the Pelethites went down and had Solomon ride on King David's mule and brought him to Gihon. ³⁹There Zadok the priest took the horn of oil from the tent and anointed Solomon. Then they blew the trumpet, and all the people said, "Long live King Solomon!" ⁴⁰And all the people went up after him, playing on pipes, and rejoicing with great joy, so that the earth was split by their noise.

⁴¹Adonijah and all the guests who were with him heard it as they finished feasting. And when Joab heard the sound of the trumpet, he said, "What does this uproar in the city mean?" ⁴²While he was still

speaking, behold, Jonathan the son of Abiathar the priest came. And Adonijah said, "Come in, for you are a worthy man and bring good news." ⁴³Jonathan answered Adonijah, "No, for our lord King David has made Solomon king, ⁴⁴and the king has sent with him Zadok the priest, Nathan the prophet, and Benaiah the son of Jehoiada, and the Cherethites and the Pelethites. And they had him ride on the king's mule. ⁴⁵And Zadok the priest and Nathan the prophet have anointed him king at Gihon, and they have gone up from there rejoicing, so that the city is in an uproar. This is the noise that you have heard. ⁴⁶Solomon sits on the royal throne. ⁴⁷Moreover, the king's servants came to congratulate our lord King David, saying, 'May your God make the name of Solomon more famous than yours, and make his throne greater than your throne.' And the king bowed himself on the bed. ⁴⁸And the king also said, 'Blessed be the LORD, the God of Israel, who has granted someoneᵈ to sit on my throne this day, my own eyes seeing it.'"

⁴⁹Then all the guests of Adonijah trembled and rose, and each went his own way. ⁵⁰And Adonijah feared Solomon. So he arose and went and took hold of the horns of the altar. ⁵¹Then it was told Solomon, "Behold, Adonijah fears King Solomon, for behold, he has laid hold of the horns of the altar, saying, 'Let King Solomon swear to me first that he will not put his servant to death with the sword.'" ⁵²And Solomon said, "If he will show himself a worthy man, not one of his hairs shall fall to the earth, but if wickedness is found in him, he shall die." ⁵³So King Solomon sent, and they brought him down from the altar. And he came and paid homage to King Solomon, and Solomon said to him, "Go to your house."

a Or *in your bosom* b Or *expand on* c Hebrew; Septuagint *Joab the commander* d Septuagint *one of my offspring*

OVERVIEW: Commentators in this section examine the medical, legal and moral issues surrounding the aging David's inability to get warm. Jerome, repulsed by the absurdity that only a girl's embrace could warm David, allegorically interpreted Abishag as wisdom. The reformers affirm the historicity of David's

marriage to Abishag, and then give an allegorical interpretation of their own: David did not rely on but had fleshly wisdom. Commentators further discuss Adonijah's proud plan to receive the kingship as a sign of worldly striving against the will of God; they point out that Solomon's rise provides another example of how God casts down the mighty and lifts up the lowly. Finally, here the reformers identify Solomon—the son of David—as a forerunner to the coming Christ.

1:1 *David Is Cold*

David's Afflictions Catch Up with Him. Johannes Bugenhagen: David "could not get warm." Some are amazed at this inability to get warm, though it is written that he had lived about seventy years in 2 Samuel 5. They seek natural causes for why this may have happened, without considering the horrendous afflictions that he had experienced through his entire life, during which it is recorded that not once did he say what he so often wrote in the Psalms: "My bones are troubled. My soul also is greatly troubled." For the things that happened to him, described at the end of the previous book, should encourage us to pass over this or let this alone be enough. For it is no surprise if the old flesh should fail after it had been vexed by all the afflictions of death and hell, as the story above relates. They do not want this vexation in the bones (or they want to minimize it) whenever they sense that the hand of God has frightened the conscience or made us anxious about death. The Psalms speak correctly of this. Commentary on 1 Kings.[1]

David's Cold Blood. Peter Martyr Vermigli: David was thirty years old when he began reigning as king, and he reigned in total for forty years. According to Psalm 90, seventy years is the just end of a human life. As the psalm says: "The years of our life are seventy, or even by reason of strength eighty; yet their span is but toil and trouble; they are soon gone, and we fly away." The king became cold and could not warm himself. And although his body was cold, nevertheless his vigor, wisdom and spirit were strong. As Virgil's *Georgics* says: "But if the cold blood around my heart prevents me from attaining those parts of nature. . . ." Commentary on 1 Kings.[2]

Always Cold and Never Warm. John Mayer: David's coldness was based on three things. First, it was due to his great pains taken in his youth and the hardship he endured in body. I am referring to when he fled from Saul and lived for a while in one place and then in another for ten years altogether, where he endured the scars of many wars. Second, the coldness was due to the trouble of his mind, since it was often in straits and very perplexed over his children's wickedness. Third, it was due to his many sicknesses, as we may gather from many of his psalms. Each of these causes led David to be always cold and never warmed.

But although David was cold in body, his understanding continued onward, as appeared by his wise ordering of everything about the temple, including the speeches he made to his son Solomon and to his princes before his death. Commentary on 1 Kings.[3]

1:2-4 *Abishag*

A Young Companion. Martin Luther: David married a young maid, Abishag the Shunammite, to warm him, because none of his other wives dared to approach him after they had been violated by Absalom. Treatise on the Last Words of David.[4]

In What Way David Did Not "Know" Abishag. Alonso Tostado: It may be asked why it is said that David did not "know" Abishag. For it was not required that it be put here; for if it benefited something to excuse David it would have been useful to say so, just as it was concerning the Blessed Virgin. For it is said that she was Joseph's wife and because many thought that Christ was born from the seed of Joseph, the Gospels added that Joseph took her as her wife "but knew her not until she had given birth to a son." But this was not the case with David. For, whether or not he had sex

---

[1]Bugenhagen, *In Regum duos ultimos libros*, 5-6; citing Ps 6:2-3.
[2]Martyr, *In duos libros Samuelis*, 1; citing Ps 90:10; *Georgics* 2.
[3]Mayer, *Many Commentaries in One*, 1*.
[4]LW 15:271 (WA 54:31); citing 2 Sam 16:2.

with Abishag, he could not have sinned because she was his wife and his concubine. And David could not have sinned having sex with her, since David was given a dispensation to have many wives as I explained in 2 Samuel 3:2-5.

Now, I respond that it is stated that David did not have intercourse with Abishag for two reasons. The first was to signal the status of Abishag, namely, that she remained a virgin after the king's death. That's because when Abishag slept together with David and kept him warm, it appears difficult that she moved the old man to warmth and not to pleasure as well, as Jerome says. Also, because they were able to have intercourse at that time, therefore it is plausibly reckoned that Abishag was sexually approached by David. So, in order to signal David's integrity, the prophets testify that David did not have intercourse with her. The other reason why this passage says that David did not have intercourse with Abishag has to do with Adonijah, for it will be mentioned in the next chapter that he asked for Abishag to be his wife. However, if David had had sexual intercourse with Abishag, such an intention of marriage between Adonijah and Abishag would have been completely illegal. But Solomon did not reject Adonijah's request in and of itself, but only because Adonijah aspired to the kingship by marrying Abishag. And had David truly had intercourse with Abishag, Adonijah would have been ashamed to have asked to marry her.

In sum, I say that Abishag had not had intercourse with David all the way up to his death, and that is why Adonijah was not ashamed to petition Solomon to take her as his wife. This is why Scripture says that "the king knew her not." COMMENTARY ON 1 KINGS.[5]

ABISHAG, JEROME, THE LETTER AND THE SPIRIT. JOHANNES BUGENHAGEN: When it says that Abishag was a Shunammite, you should accept this. First, David received her help of physical aid. This ought to be granted and not made to appear as if he were condemned for this

inclination in his soul. For everyone wanted to do a good service for such a man. You are dreaming if you will not allow this, that he was given this Shunammite wife. For it was not conducted as a secret thing, because—as it says—they searched to the ends of Israel for her. I ask, ought this not have been lawful for the old king and a prophet full of the Spirit of God? This is what David's impious son Adonijah believed when he later asked for Abishag to be his wife without his father's knowledge. Moreover, it is shameful what Jerome said about this history: "It is not," he says, "as it appears to you. If following the letter kills, is this a fiction or an Athenian play?"[6] But does it honor the holy Scriptures in truth to say that they certainly do not mean what was written but that they require another modification? Does it honor the Scriptures to modify what you don't know in order to say that your modification and your dreams are the "spirit that gives life" and that you read clearly what is the letter that kills? How might this letter kill me, when it does not kill the story of David's adultery and murder? How then shall we learn to understand Paul's words "The letter kills, but the Spirit gives life"? Therefore, if you should prefer an allegory to this history, then it is the end of this story's integrity. It is true history that the warm and most beautiful virgin Abishag, of substantial flesh and blood, was sleeping with David but he did not know her. The following allegory may be accepted: if they are pious like David, the old know the wisdom of the flesh but they do not depend on it. If meanness is meant against the good Abishag, which is wrongly called the wisdom of the flesh and an abomination to God, then you are accepting the flesh and worldly things, which is not what the aged or the "spiritual" people among humans or the Scriptures call knowledge. This knowledge is how we know and discern the things that happen, so that you know when you sin, when you are disobedient and when you are fleeing. When they have been tested, spiritual people recognize these things, teach them to others and give similarly

---

[5]TO 14:5; citing Mt 1:25.

[6]See ACCS OT 5:2-3 (NPNF² 6:89-90).

good advice. At the same time, they neither confide in such things nor teach such confidence to others. That is what it means to have Abishag but not to know her. COMMENTARY ON 1 KINGS.[7]

WARM COMFORT AFTER THE DISMISSAL OF DAVID'S FORMER CONCUBINES. JOHN MAYER: Because David's servants saw that no clothes could heat David, they proposed another way to warm him, namely, for a young virgin to be brought to him to lie down with him. And so Abishag, a fair virgin, was brought to him and she ministered to him. These servants of David's are regarded to be his physicians, who sought to keep the king warm in response to the king's habitual coldness. Some question whether this entire matter was lawful. But it is answered that there is little doubt that David took Abishag as his wife, since he had formerly put away all his concubines after they had been defiled by Absalom. Moreover, David's wives, such as Bathsheba, were probably too old to attend to David's coldness by lying with him. Nevertheless, Jerome thinks that it is absurd to interpret this literally. He therefore interprets it altogether allegorically, that is, of wisdom—which David had in his old age—and the heart of zeal warming him. COMMENTARY ON 1 KINGS.[8]

1:5-10 *How Adonijah Gains Firstborn Status*

WHETHER ADONIJAH WAS THE RECIPIENT OF PRIMOGENITURE. ALONSO TOSTADO: It may be asked whether Adonijah was the recipient of primogeniture (and therefore the heir of the kingdom) in regard to all of David's sons now living. I respond that Adonijah was the fourth-born of David's sons, as we read about in 2 Samuel 3:2-5. Two of the first four sons, Amnon and Absalom, had died earlier, as explained in 2 Samuel.

Mention is made of a middle son named Chileab, but his whereabouts are dubious and it's best to assume that he died. That's because no one dared to raise up against Adonijah when he sought the kingdom and when he was crowned at his feast. . . . Similarly, when powerful David was still living, the men of Judah and also his brothers joined with Adonijah at the celebratory feast where he was crowned, as we read about. For this reason it seems clear that Adonijah was the recipient of primogeniture and thus the heir of the kingdom. For the chapter says that Adonijah was born next after Absalom, and so after Absalom's death Adonijah would have been next in line. This was the reason why Absalom had previously acquired horses and chariots, since none of David's sons were older than he was and therefore could compete with him for the kingship. In the same way, we read that Adonijah called for a feast so that all of his brothers, the king's sons, would join with him at his coronation. And if a brother was older than Adonijah, everyone would not have gone to crown him. COMMENTARY ON 1 KINGS.[9]

ADONIJAH DID NOT HAVE GOD'S WORD OR CALL. JOHANNES BUGENHAGEN: Six sons were born to David in Hebron. Amnon and Absalom had died, and nothing is recorded of Chileab, so that Adonijah was now the greatest among the surviving brothers. The rest of David's sons, including Solomon, were born later in Jerusalem. Adonijah put his faith in this, that no one ought to be king after David's death but him. This is clear in chapter 2 below when he said, "You know that the kingdom was mine," etc. Without a command, without a call, without the word of God Adonijah wanted to occupy the kingship, as if it were owed him by right. He put his trust in this: that he was born first; that he was loved by his father; that he marched with glorious chariots and horsemen; and that Joab the commander of the army, Abiathar the priest and all his brothers and David's sons besides Solomon were under this impression too. This was

---

[7]Bugenhagen, *In Regum duos ultimos libros*, 6-7; citing 2 Cor 3:6. Bugenhagen quoted the opening lines of the *Glossa ordinaria's* Commentary on 1 Kings. (*Liber Regum Tertius*), which begin with comments from Jerome about the implausibility of the literal meaning of this story.
[8]Mayer, *Many Commentaries in One*, 2*.

[9]TO 14:7.

the impious feeling as long as the strength of the flesh was secure, trusting in its own cause and not fearing God. COMMENTARY ON 1 KINGS.[10]

A GOOD HEART IS BETTER THAN A GOOD APPEARANCE. PETER MARTYR VERMIGLI:
Adonijah was now the oldest son of David. For Amnon, the firstborn, had been killed by his brother Absalom, and Absalom had died in battle. David's other older sons like Chileab, who is called David in 1 Chronicles 3:1, must have been deceased. And in this way it is believed that Adonijah was now the oldest surviving son of David. Adonijah's external appearance was marveled at by the common people. . . . He was thus praised in the same way Saul and Absalom were. But David, who was also good-looking, was commended and elected of God for his heart. And we certainly learn this saying in Proverbs, that it is deceptive and vain to praise beauty in itself; rather we are to praise a woman's beauty inasmuch as she fears God. And if this is said of a woman, how much more so is it appropriate for a man. COMMENTARY ON 1 KINGS.[11]

LIKE OLDER BROTHER, LIKE YOUNG BROTHER.
JOHN MAYER: Adonijah trod in the very footsteps of Absalom, and accordingly was soon cut off, as he was well known for his ambition. The thing that put him onto this ambition was his father's indulgence who, it is said, never reproved him. What also gave him ambition was his priority in age, for he was now the eldest son living. He was next in age to Absalom, and also just as beautiful as he was. When Eli was indulgent with his sons, the Lord dealt more severely with them. But their wickedness was indeed greater, since they put God's service into contempt. But it was doubtless a sin in David to wink at his sons' wickedness, for he could not have been ignorant of Adonijah's ambitious proceedings. Some, however, think that David was unaware, as this passage suggests. But

although David did not know of this particular proceeding, it does not mean that David was unaware of Adonijah's preparations of chariots and horsemen. For although he did not go inquire, it is most probable that some close to David told him of it. . . . But as soon as he heard of Adonijah trying to usurp the kingdom, David opposed him. It is answered by Peter Martyr Vermigli and others that David should have called him in question about this, especially seeing that Absalom had made the same preparations before rebelling against him. COMMENTARY ON 1 KINGS.[12]

1:11-27 How Solomon Becomes King

WHEN DAVID PROMISED BATHSHEBA THAT SOLOMON WOULD BE KING. ALONSO TOSTADO:
It may be asked when David promised Bathsheba that Solomon would reign as king after him. Rabbi David Kimchi and other Jews respond that this happened after the death of the first son whom David sired by Bethsheba. For when David went to comfort Bathsheba after their son's death, Bathsheba did not permit David to enter, saying she feared that all of their sons would die just as their first son did. But David said to her that not only would none of their sons die in the same way, but one of them would become the king after David's death, and so he swore to and promised Bathsheba that this would come to pass. Another story goes that Bathsheba did not allow David to sleep with her after the death of their firstborn because she said that all of their children together would be considered illegitimate and born in sin and they would be contemptible. So she therefore refused to let David see her since she did not want to give birth to contemptible children. But then David said to her that not only would none of their children be contemptible but also that one of their sons would one day become king after David, and he then he swore to her this.

But I say that there is a better explanation. For David would not venture to determine which of

---

[10]Bugenhagen, *In Regum duos ultimos libros*, 7-8; citing 2 Sam 3; 1 Kings 2:15.
[11]Martyr, *In duos libros Samuelis*, 3.

[12]Mayer, *Many Commentaries in One*, 2*.

his sons would succeed him unless he knew that it was pleasing to God. Therefore this is how it happened. In the past, David heard from Nathan the prophet that the next son to be born to him would succeed him (and already all of his other wives had had sons and he did not believe that he was to have more, nor did he after the prophecy). And Bathsheba had two sons, but God showed his favor to Solomon and gave him a special name, as we read about in 2 Samuel: "Then David comforted his wife, Bathsheba, and went in to her and lay with her, and she bore a son, and he called his name Solomon. And the Lord loved him and sent a message by Nathan the prophet. So he called his name Jedidiah, because of the Lord." And this is when David clearly knew that Solomon was the one about whom God spoke, and therefore he swore to Bathsheba that Solomon would succeed him as king. COMMENTARY ON 1 KINGS.[13]

A PROPHET AND A WOMAN DETERMINE WHO IS KING. JOHN MAYER: Here follows the means by which God overthrew all the preparations of ambitious Adonijah and advanced Solomon quickly to the kingdom, which David had promised him. It was not by the means of power. Rather it was by means of Nathan, a prophet, and Bathsheba, a woman and a weak instrument whom Adonijah's company doubtlessly condemned, considering her to be no better than an adulterer. Moreover, Adonijah's company probably regarded Solomon, for whom Bathsheba and the prophet stood, no better than a bastard who was unworthy to reign. But such people knew well enough that they were merely kicking against the pricks in seeking to frustrate God's determination. It appears that they were not ignorant of God's determination, for Adonijah's company invited all of David's sons except Solomon, against whom he competed for the kingdom. . . . In this way we note how God confounds the wise and accomplishes his own will by weak means. COMMENTARY ON 1 KINGS.[14]

1:28-40 *Solomon Crowned*

GOD PUT AN END TO HUMAN PLANS. JOHANNES BUGENHAGEN: God wanted someone to be king but not the one who appeared to be king by human acclamation. Without a divine revelation, Nathan advocated for Solomon, sending the wife first to the king. Then he spoke to David, saying, "Have you not told me, your servant, who should sit on the throne of my lord the king after him?" In this difficult matter, you see that God does not delay in effecting this result through Nathan and Bathsheba. Human reason attributes this to human industry. But piety says, "God wanted this, God gave the occasion and God put a stop to Adonijah's plans." COMMENTARY ON 1 KINGS.[15]

JOYOUS ANOINTING. HENRY AIRAY: When Solomon was anointed king over Israel in succession to David his father, it is said that "all the people went up after him, playing flutes and rejoicing with great joy, so that the earth was split by their noise." So the people of Israel thus rejoiced at the crowning of Solomon. Shall not we much more rejoice as Christ Jesus is placed in heaven at the right hand of his Father, and has the everlasting scepter of his kingdom put in his hand? LECTURES ON PHILIPPIANS.[16]

SYMBOLIC LOCATION OF SOLOMON'S ANOINTING. JOHN MAYER: The place where Solomon was brought to be anointed was Gihon, which was the same place . . . as Shiloh. Solomon was taken to Shiloh because it was the place where waters ran continually. This place was meant to show the perpetuity of Solomon's kingdom, just as the waters there ran perpetually. And he was to be anointed by both the priest and the prophet, as Samuel had before anointed Saul and David, to show the grace of the Spirit with which the king must be imbued. Also, by being anointed by a

---

[13]TO 14:11; citing 2 Sam 12:24-25.
[14]Mayer, *Many Commentaries in One*, 3*.

[15]Bugenhagen, *In Regum duos ultimos libros*, 9-10. The ESV has a plural rather than a singular in 1:27: "have you not told your servants. . . ."
[16]Airay, *Lectures on Philippians*, 128*; citing Ps 105:15.

priest and a prophet it was meant to signify that Solomon should be subject and ready to hearken to the priest's and prophet's instructions, since they would be able to inform him of God's will. Finally, David ordered that Solomon mount his own mule and to be guarded by his servants in order to show that this anointing was done on David's authority. COMMENTARY ON 1 KINGS.[17]

1:41-53 Solomon Extends Mercy to Adonijah

THE HORNS OF THE ALTAR. JOHANNES BUGEN-HAGEN: Nowhere in the law does it say that there would be safety for someone who flees to the altar of the Lord if he has sinned against the law in such a way as to be condemned to death. For whom does the Lord condemn to be slain according to the law and then later defend from the Lord at the altar of the Lord? And so Solomon pronounced a death sentence against Adonijah, if he should be deemed guilty of even a small offense. In the next chapter, Joab was killed at the altar when Solomon commanded it. Yet the people still had some fear of where the worship of God took place, so that they would not hear of arresting or killing a criminal there. The words of the law reveal that this way of thinking about and venerating this place came from their own reasoning, for Exodus 21 says, "if a man willfully attacks another to kill him by cunning, you shall take him from my altar, that he may die." This way of thinking is why Athaliah was taken to be killed outside of the temple in 2 Kings 11. Therefore the place where we gather to hear the word of God and receive the Lord's sacraments is not the same as other human places. Still, we ought not grant this place's holiness, for God does not grant it. But this is just what people demand when they want to bind our consciences to the principles of this world. On the origins of the horns of the altar, see Exodus 27. COMMENTARY ON 1 KINGS.[18]

ADONIJAH BOWS TO SOLOMON LIKE WE DO TO CHRIST. JOHN MAYER: "Let King Solomon swear to me today," that is, pardon what has happened before today, that he will not kill me. The new king was easily entreated, since he was willing to begin his reign with the showing of mercy. Solomon promised that not a hair of Adonijah's hair should fall to the ground, that is, that he should not have the least hurt for his former ambition so long as he refrained from all ambitious courses from this day forward. And thus Adonijah was brought from the altar not by force but by persuasion. Adonijah went and paid homage to Solomon, the older brother bowing to the younger, just as Joseph's older brothers did him. And in the same way, we all submit to the greatest in the world, Christ, who was at first neglected and condemned as Solomon had been, who typified Christ. COMMENTARY ON 1 KINGS.[19]

MERCY THEN WISDOM. JOHANNES PISCATOR: An example of mercy is set forth by Solomon, for when his brother Adonijah implores him for mercy, he easily forgives him. But an example of wisdom is also set forth in Solomon, for when his brother is guilty of the same crime and tries to ask for pardon, Solomon has him killed. COMMENTARY ON 1 KINGS.[20]

---

[17]Mayer, *Many Commentaries in One*, 3-4*.

[18]Bugenhagen, *In Regum duos ultimos libros*, 11-12; citing Ex 21:14; 2 Kings 11:15.
[19]Mayer, *Many Commentaries in One*, 5*.
[20]Piscator, *Commentarii in omnes libros Veteris Testamenti*, 2:254.

2:1-46 THE BEGINNING OF SOLOMON'S REIGN

¹*When David's time to die drew near, he commanded Solomon his son, saying,* ²*"I am about to go the way of all the earth. Be strong, and show yourself a man,* ³*and keep the charge of the LORD your God, walking in his ways and keeping his statutes, his commandments, his rules, and his testimonies, as it is written in the Law of Moses, that you may prosper in all that you do and wherever you turn,* ⁴*that the LORD may establish his word that he spoke concerning me, saying, 'If your sons pay close attention to their way, to walk before me in faithfulness with all their heart and with all their soul, you shall not lack^a a man on the throne of Israel.'*

³*"Moreover, you also know what Joab the son of Zeruiah did to me, how he dealt with the two commanders of the armies of Israel, Abner the son of Ner, and Amasa the son of Jether, whom he killed, avenging^b in time of peace for blood that had been shed in war, and putting the blood of war^c on the belt around his^d waist and on the sandals on his feet.* ⁶*Act therefore according to your wisdom, but do not let his gray head go down to Sheol in peace.* ⁷*But deal loyally with the sons of Barzillai the Gileadite, and let them be among those who eat at your table, for with such loyalty^e they met me when I fled from Absalom your brother.* ⁸*And there is also with you Shimei the son of Gera, the Benjaminite from Bahurim, who cursed me with a grievous curse on the day when I went to Mahanaim. But when he came down to meet me at the Jordan, I swore to him by the LORD, saying, 'I will not put you to death with the sword.'* ⁹*Now therefore do not hold him guiltless, for you are a wise man. You will know what you ought to do to him, and you shall bring his gray head down with blood to Sheol."*

¹⁰*Then David slept with his fathers and was buried in the city of David.* ¹¹*And the time that David reigned over Israel was forty years. He reigned seven years in Hebron and thirty-three years in Jerusalem.* ¹²*So Solomon sat on the throne of David his father, and his kingdom was firmly established.*

¹³*Then Adonijah the son of Haggith came to Bathsheba the mother of Solomon. And she said, "Do you come peacefully?" He said, "Peacefully."* ¹⁴*Then he said, "I have something to say to you." She said, "Speak."* ¹⁵*He said, "You know that the kingdom was mine, and that all Israel fully expected me to reign. However, the kingdom has turned about and become my brother's, for it was his from the LORD.* ¹⁶*And now I have one request to make of you; do not refuse me." She said to him, "Speak."* ¹⁷*And he said, "Please ask King Solomon—he will not refuse you—to give me Abishag the Shunammite as my wife."* ¹⁸*Bathsheba said, "Very well; I will speak for you to the king."*

¹⁹*So Bathsheba went to King Solomon to speak to him on behalf of Adonijah. And the king rose to meet her and bowed down to her. Then he sat on his throne and had a seat brought for the king's mother, and she sat on his right.* ²⁰*Then she said, "I have one small request to make of you; do not refuse me." And the king said to her, "Make your request, my mother, for I will not refuse you."* ²¹*She said, "Let Abishag the Shunammite be given to Adonijah your brother as his wife."* ²²*King Solomon answered his mother, "And why do you ask Abishag the Shunammite for Adonijah? Ask for him the kingdom also, for he is my older brother, and on his side are Abiathar^f the priest and Joab the son of Zeruiah."* ²³*Then King Solomon swore by the LORD, saying, "God do so to me and more also if this word does not cost Adonijah his life!* ²⁴*Now therefore as the LORD lives, who has established me and placed me on the throne of David my father, and who has made me a house, as he promised, Adonijah shall be put to death today."* ²⁵*So King Solomon sent Benaiah the son of Jehoiada, and he struck him down, and he died.*

²⁶*And to Abiathar the priest the king said, "Go to Anathoth, to your estate, for you deserve death. But I will not at this time put you to death, because you carried the ark of the LORD God before David my father, and because you shared in all my father's affliction."* ²⁷*So Solomon expelled Abiathar from being*

priest to the Lord, thus fulfilling the word of the Lord that he had spoken concerning the house of Eli in Shiloh.

²⁸When the news came to Joab—for Joab had supported Adonijah although he had not supported Absalom—Joab fled to the tent of the Lord and caught hold of the horns of the altar. ²⁹And when it was told King Solomon, "Joab has fled to the tent of the Lord, and behold, he is beside the altar," Solomon sent Benaiah the son of Jehoiada, saying, "Go, strike him down." ³⁰So Benaiah came to the tent of the Lord and said to him, "The king commands, 'Come out.'" But he said, "No, I will die here." Then Benaiah brought the king word again, saying, "Thus said Joab, and thus he answered me." ³¹The king replied to him, "Do as he has said, strike him down and bury him, and thus take away from me and from my father's house the guilt for the blood that Joab shed without cause. ³²The Lord will bring back his bloody deeds on his own head, because, without the knowledge of my father David, he attacked and killed with the sword two men more righteous and better than himself, Abner the son of Ner, commander of the army of Israel, and Amasa the son of Jether, commander of the army of Judah. ³³So shall their blood come back on the head of Joab and on the head of his descendants forever. But for David and for his descendants and for his house and for his throne there shall be peace from the Lord forevermore." ³⁴Then Benaiah the son of Jehoiada went up and struck him down and put him to death. And he was buried in his own house in the wilderness. ³⁵The king put Benaiah the son of Jehoiada over the army in place of Joab, and the king put Zadok the priest in the place of Abiathar.

³⁶Then the king sent and summoned Shimei and said to him, "Build yourself a house in Jerusalem and dwell there, and do not go out from there to any place whatever. ³⁷For on the day you go out and cross the brook Kidron, know for certain that you shall die. Your blood shall be on your own head." ³⁸And Shimei said to the king, "What you say is good; as my lord the king has said, so will your servant do." So Shimei lived in Jerusalem many days.

³⁹But it happened at the end of three years that two of Shimei's servants ran away to Achish, son of Maacah, king of Gath. And when it was told Shimei, "Behold, your servants are in Gath," ⁴⁰Shimei arose and saddled a donkey and went to Gath to Achish to seek his servants. Shimei went and brought his servants from Gath. ⁴¹And when Solomon was told that Shimei had gone from Jerusalem to Gath and returned, ⁴²the king sent and summoned Shimei and said to him, "Did I not make you swear by the Lord and solemnly warn you, saying, 'Know for certain that on the day you go out and go to any place whatever, you shall die'? And you said to me, 'What you say is good; I will obey.' ⁴³Why then have you not kept your oath to the Lord and the commandment with which I commanded you?" ⁴⁴The king also said to Shimei, "You know in your own heart all the harm that you did to David my father. So the Lord will bring back your harm on your own head. ⁴⁵But King Solomon shall be blessed, and the throne of David shall be established before the Lord forever." ⁴⁶Then the king commanded Benaiah the son of Jehoiada, and he went out and struck him down, and he died.

So the kingdom was established in the hand of Solomon.

a Hebrew *there shall not be cut off for you*   b Septuagint; Hebrew *placing*   c Septuagint *innocent blood*   d Septuagint *my*; twice in this verse   e Or *steadfast love*   f Septuagint, Syriac, Vulgate; Hebrew *and for him and for Abiathar*

OVERVIEW: The occasion of David's death invites the reformers to reflect on mortality, eternal life, faithfulness and what it means to leave a legacy; in doing so they often refer to other parts of the Bible. The commentators continue their refrain that David is a forerunner of the Messiah. They also recognize that Adonijah seeks to marry Abishag as a way to reignite his candidacy for the kingship. But Solomon immediately sees through this plan. The commentators do not question Solomon, the rightful king and heir to David, when he orders the deaths of Adonijah, Joab and Shimei.

2:1-9 *David Instructs Solomon*

WHY DAVID DELAYED GIVING HIS PRECEPTS TO SOLOMON. ALONSO TOSTADO: It may be asked why David delayed in giving his precepts to Solomon until the time of his death. I respond that David delayed because that was the custom. . . . For at death was the time when the fathers in the Old Testament admonished their sons to stay faithful. For instance, on his deathbed Jacob declared to his sons in Genesis 49 what was to happen in the future. In the same way, Moses blessed the Israelites in his old age, and he recounted all the laws to the people in Deuteronomy. And then after reciting the laws and composing a song for the Israelites, he ascended Mount Pisgah and died. For these men knew that their words achieved a greater efficacy when they were united with death. And so David gave his warnings to Solomon as he approached death. COMMENTARY ON 1 KINGS.[1]

BELIEF IN THE AFTERLIFE. MARTIN LUTHER: Therefore the fathers concluded . . . that another life remains and that the saints do not perish like cattle but are gathered to the people in the land of the living. And this is the reason why they are buried by their sons with such respect and honor—which it is not customary to do in the case of beasts—doubtless because of the certain expectation of another life. Accordingly this serves to comfort us, lest we, like others, who have no hope (1 Thess 4:13), be frightened by or shudder at death. For in Christ death is not bitter, as it is for the ungodly, but it is a change of this wretched and unhappy life into a life that is quiet and blessed. This statement should convince us fully that we do not pass from a pleasant life into a life that is unhappy, but that we pass from afflictions into tranquility. For since the fathers had this comfort from these passages long before Christ, how much more reasonable it is for us to guard and preserve the same comfort! We have it in far greater abundance. LECTURES ON GENESIS.[2]

DON'T TRUST YOUR OWN REASON. JOHANNES BUGENHAGEN: David tells Solomon to be strong. You see the same thing in Joshua 1. The leader should be fearless in spirit through God so that, fearing only him, the leader who rightly accepts God also pleases God. Otherwise what will they do during deprivations and afflictions if they start to fear people and are not able to sit with God in their conscience? As it says in the Psalm, "God has taken his place in the divine council; in the midst of the gods he holds judgment." Then David says, "keep the charge of the Lord your God," etc. That is, "seek first the kingdom of God and his righteousness." This was certainly a necessary admonition, for—as the following history relates—how often would the entire kingdom be led by ungodly princes, go against this command and be dragged to hell all together. David then adds, "as it is written in the Law of Moses." He wanted Solomon to read Deuteronomy, especially what is commanded to kings in Deuteronomy 17, a command Joshua first accepted in Joshua 1. He concludes by saying, "So that you may understand all that you do." Here he notes that Solomon does not know what to do— how to avoid sin or commit sin, how to please God or displease God—unless he is taught from the Word of God and follows what God commands, thereby giving a good example, just as Christ said in John 8, "If you abide in my word, you are truly my disciples, and you will know the truth, and the truth will set you free." But if you trust yourself to your own stinking reason, you will err in all things. COMMENTARY ON 1 KINGS.[3]

CONTEXT FOR DAVID'S COMMANDS TO SOLOMON. JOHN MAYER: Here is set forth the death of David and his exhortation made to his son Solomon before his death. But before David's death and after Solomon's coronation, there are many other memorable passages recorded in 1 Chronicles that are lacking here. Therefore passages from 1 Chronicles 22 etc. should be

---

[1]TO 14:16.
[2]LW 4:310-11.

[3]Bugenhagen, *In Regum duos ultimos libros*, 12-13; citing Josh 1:6, 9; Ps 82:1; Mt 6:33; Deut 17:18-20; Josh 1:7-8; Jn 8:31-32.

annexed to this passage. Specifically, it should be noted that David provided workmen and materials for the house of God. As stated in 1 Chronicles, "Here shall be the house of the Lord God and here the altar of burnt offering for Israel." To whom does David say this? It is doubtless that David is speaking to his princes and elders of the people, who are assembled together after Solomon's inauguration as king. They are assembled so that they might take notice of Solomon's succession to his father in the kingdom and for them to be obedient to him, although this is not expressly stated. COMMENTARY ON 1 KINGS.[4]

THE GOOD SEED CONTINUES. CHARLES DRELINCOURT: When King David had ended his mortal race, God took him into his rest. It seemed at first that the loss of so good a prince could not be repaired. But God caused Solomon to sit on his father's throne and made him the wisest and the happiest ruler in the world. David only removed God's ark, but Solomon built for God a stately and magnificent temple. David was a type of the encounters and victories of the Son of God, but Solomon represented his glorious triumphs and that eternal peace with which he will bless his chosen in the kingdom of heaven. CHRISTIAN DEFENSE AGAINST THE FEARS OF DEATH.[5]

2:10-12 David's Death and Burial

MAGNIFICENTLY BURIED. JOHN MAYER: The place of David's burial is said to be in his own city, not Bethlehem, as some have thought, but Zion. For that is where the kings, his successors, should afterward be buried also. Josephus said that his son Solomon buried him magnificently in Jerusalem, and that into his sepulcher were put very great riches. For out of it 1,300 years later John Hyrcanus took three thousand talents to give to Antiochus Epiphanes to remove his siege. And after that Herod took much money out of another cell. And in his

itinerary Benjamin, a Jew, tells of two workmen who spied a den when digging up the stones of an old wall. Once they entered it, they saw a palace with pillars of marble and a table of silver before it, with a scepter and crown of gold on it. But when they attempted to go into that palace, they were struck with a whirlwind as if dead. And having lain so until night, they were revived again and then heard a voice saying, "Arise and go out of this place." Therefore that hole was, by the command of the patriarch, stopped up again. None dared to enter it anymore. COMMENTARY ON 1 KINGS.[6]

DAVID WAS A FIGURE OF CHRIST IN TEN WAYS. JOHN MAYER: Such was the end of David, who was a figure of Christ in the following ten ways: (1) David was from the tribe of Judah and the city of Bethlehem. (2) David was held in favor, as Christ was also held highly "in favor with God and man." (3) David chased away the evil spirit from Saul, and killed a lion and a bear; similarly, Christ cast out devils and destroyed their power. (4) David lived obscurely, just as Christ did for three years. (5) David killed Goliath not by force of arms but with a sling. (6) David's brothers envied him and Saul sought to kill him. (7) David had given a dowry of two hundred foreskins for Michal, but she was later taken away; in the same way, Christ did not have a spouse with the Jewish church but only of the Gentile church. (8) David was anointed three times as king, just as Christ had a threefold right to reign: first, as God; second, as David's successor in his line; and, third, because as God and man all power was given to him. (9) David ordered the priests and Levites, just as Christ ordered the apostles. (10) David prepared materials for the temple. COMMENTARY ON 1 KINGS.[7]

2:13-25 Adonijah's Plan to Marry Abishag Backfires

SOLOMON BREAKS ONE PROMISE TO KEEP ANOTHER. JOHANNES BUGENHAGEN: Adonijah

---

[4]Mayer, *Many Commentaries in One*, 6*; citing 1 Chron 22:1.
[5]Drelincourt, *Christian's Defense Against the Fears of Death*, 195*.

[6]Mayer, *Many Commentaries in One*, 14*.
[7]Mayer, *Many Commentaries in One*, 14*; citing Lk 2:52.

lost his life through the righteous judgment of God when he asked Solomon to wed the woman who had been his father's wife, whom his father had not known. This ruse further reveals that Solomon was chosen by God, which is how he saw this poorly hidden plan. For he said to his mother, "Ask for him the kingdom also!" This again shows that the saints reject their promises and vows where they conflict with the Word of God. For Solomon had promised his mother, "Make your request, my mother, for I will not refuse you." He did not say, "It is commanded that I must reject your wish" and kill the one for whom his mother petitioned. But he would not do anything, either from his mother or his father, that went against the divine law. Moreover, this event does not affirm what some foolishly say: that in this place Bathsheba is Mary the mother of Christ, the true Solomon, who denies nothing when she intercedes for us. I certainly do not want her interceding for me if it means I will be killed! COMMENTARY ON 1 KINGS.[8]

UNWISE REQUEST. JOHN MAYER: Here is shown on what occasion Adonijah, the competitor of the kingdom, was cut off. . . . Adonijah, as expositors generally think, requested to marry Abishag through the counsel of Joab and Abiathar, who would soon be removed. Because Abishag had been David's wife, Adonijah's request was both contrary to the law of God . . . and it was not lawful for anyone in the commonwealth to marry her unless he himself was king. Therefore Adonijah, in seeking this, sought to come as near to the kingdom as he could. And having the chief captain Joab and the chief priest Abiathar on his side, Adonijah was not without hope to attain Abishag by this means. At least, his ambitious mind was fed with such a conceit. Solomon saw all this in his wisdom, but his mother did not. But when Solomon spoke, she perceived this and most probably was content to have her request denied. . . . And therefore it was just for Solomon to put Adonijah to death, since

it was plain that his former ambition was still with him. COMMENTARY ON 1 KINGS.[9]

DIVINE PERCEPTION. GIOVANNI DIODATI: By divine inspiration Solomon perceived to what end Adonijah's request went, namely, to trouble and contend with him for the kingdom. Adonijah sought to gain the goodwill of influential court members, with whom Abishag was very gracious. Besides, it was one of the successor's rights to have the deceased king's concubines. What's more, it was a grievous sin for Adonijah to desire his father's concubine. Once Adonijah had received Abishag as a wife, he would have attempted to completely take over the kingdom, even against God's express command. ANNOTATIONS ON 1 KINGS.[10]

2:26-35 The Death of Joab

GOD'S VENGEANCE ON WICKED JOAB. JOHANNES PISCATOR: In the supplication of Joab, an example of God's vengeance on murderers and treacherous people is set forth. For although Joab was not able to be punished on account of power by David, nevertheless he was dragged forth by God to supplication under Solomon since his power had now diminished under the greater power of Solomon. We also see the example of Solomon's severity in killing Joab. In fact Solomon gave the order for Joab to be killed at a sacred place upon refusing to leave it. COMMENTARY ON 1 KINGS.[11]

JUST ORDER OF JOAB'S DEATH. JOHN MAYER: Solomon's command to Benaiah is here set forth by anticipation. For Joab first refused to come out of the altar, so Solomon ordered Benaiah to kill him there. Nicholas of Lyra said that Rabbi Solomon yielded this reason for why Benaiah did not kill him at first: Because Joab had said to Benaiah that when he had killed Abner, David cursed him to suffer, saying: "May it fall upon the head of Joab and upon

---

[8]Bugenhagen, *In Regum duos ultimos libros*, 15.

[9]Mayer, *Many Commentaries in One*, 14*.
[10]Diodati, *Pious Annotations*, 3*.
[11]Piscator, *Commentarii in omnes libros Veteris Testamenti*, 2:258.

all his father's house, and may the house of Joab never be without one who has a discharge or who is leprous or who holds a spindle or who falls by the sword or who lacks bread!" Therefore Joab said that if Benaiah now punished him with death, it would be unjust unless Solomon would take these curses on himself and his posterity. Then Benaiah returned this answer to the king, Solomon took these curses upon himself and Benaiah returned to kill Joab. . . . And it is understood that these curses were passed on, for Uzziah had leprosy, Asa held a spindle, and Hezekiah, when besieged, lacked bread. But this interpretation is so vain that it is not even worth mentioning. For these kings were punished for other faults. What's more, Joab deserved to die for killing Amasa and Abner, and it cannot be imagined that Solomon would take these curses on himself. Finally, David had given Solomon a charge to kill Joab. Therefore it is not to be doubted but that this was a just order, seeing that the command came from such a holy king. COMMENTARY ON 1 KINGS.[12]

2:36-46 *The Death of Shimei*

IN SOLOMON'S WISDOM, SHIMEI CONDEMNS HIMSELF. JOHANNES BUGENHAGEN: If you push the issue and say that David did wrong by commanding Solomon to kill Shimei after he had made an oath to God concerning him, I reply that (if I remember correctly) we talked about oaths and vows in the first book during the story of David and Nabal, when David clearly broke his vows when they seemed to stand against God's law. Since then, David had restored the blessings of God to the kingdom. He publicly considered Shimei's supplications and his begging for forgiveness from his guilt. At that time, David vowed that he would not have him killed. He had said that

blood would not be spilled when the salvation of all Israel had just come to pass through God. He kept his vow in its time, for there are no examples of this king ever using God's name in vain. But then it is seen that David had a troubled conscience on account of this vow to one whom he already knew deserved to die, for Shimei had blasphemed the king and God against the law. He knew that the death had a better status in the law of God than his vow. Yet he was not like those who are ignorant of this freedom and think they can act against their vows. "You shall not bear false witness." We need not only carry this out before God but also before all people. David committed this matter to Solomon's wisdom. So Solomon pressured the one who deserved death according to the law, but not in a burdensome way that would transgress the judgment of God. Shimei then received the reward of his iniquities, when Solomon said to him, "So the Lord will bring back your harm on your own head." Therefore, this is how one ought to confess before God: Lord God, I have vowed something, but because your law and your word require something else, let everyone be a liar "so that you may be justified in your words and blameless in your judgment." COMMENTARY ON 1 KINGS.[13]

DAVID'S PLEA FOR VENGEANCE. JEREMIAS BASTINGIUS: Although David knew Shimei was sent by God to curse him and to rail on him when he fled from the face of Absalom (2 Sam 16:5-13), yet in his last speech to his son and successor, King Solomon, he does not excuse him. Much less will those who wickedly . . . oppress their neighbor be without fault before God or escape his punishment. AN EXPOSITION ON THE CATECHISM OF THE LOW COUNTRIES.[14]

---

[12]Mayer, *Many Commentaries in One*, 16*; citing 2 Sam 3:29.

[13]Bugenhagen, *In Regum duos ultimos libros*, 14-15; citing 2 Sam 19:23; Ex 20:16; Deut 5:20; Ps 51:4; Ps 116:11 (Vg).
[14]Bastingius, *An Exposition upon the Catechism*, 385*.

3:1-28 SOLOMON'S WISDOM

¹Solomon made a marriage alliance with Pharaoh king of Egypt. He took Pharaoh's daughter and brought her into the city of David until he had finished building his own house and the house of the LORD and the wall around Jerusalem. ²The people were sacrificing at the high places, however, because no house had yet been built for the name of the LORD.

³Solomon loved the LORD, walking in the statutes of David his father, only he sacrificed and made offerings at the high places. ⁴And the king went to Gibeon to sacrifice there, for that was the great high place. Solomon used to offer a thousand burnt offerings on that altar. ⁵At Gibeon the LORD appeared to Solomon in a dream by night, and God said, "Ask what I shall give you." ⁶And Solomon said, "You have shown great and steadfast love to your servant David my father, because he walked before you in faithfulness, in righteousness, and in uprightness of heart toward you. And you have kept for him this great and steadfast love and have given him a son to sit on his throne this day. ⁷And now, O LORD my God, you have made your servant king in place of David my father, although I am but a little child. I do not know how to go out or come in. ⁸And your servant is in the midst of your people whom you have chosen, a great people, too many to be numbered or counted for multitude. ⁹Give your servant therefore an understanding mind to govern your people, that I may discern between good and evil, for who is able to govern this your great people?"

¹⁰It pleased the LORD that Solomon had asked this. ¹¹And God said to him, "Because you have asked this, and have not asked for yourself long life or riches or the life of your enemies, but have asked for yourself understanding to discern what is right, ¹²behold, I now do according to your word. Behold, I give you a wise and discerning mind, so that none like you has been before you and none like you shall arise after you. ¹³I give you also what you have not asked, both riches and honor, so that no other king shall compare with you, all your days. ¹⁴And if you

will walk in my ways, keeping my statutes and my commandments, as your father David walked, then I will lengthen your days."

¹⁵And Solomon awoke, and behold, it was a dream. Then he came to Jerusalem and stood before the ark of the covenant of the LORD, and offered up burnt offerings and peace offerings, and made a feast for all his servants.

¹⁶Then two prostitutes came to the king and stood before him. ¹⁷The one woman said, "Oh, my lord, this woman and I live in the same house, and I gave birth to a child while she was in the house. ¹⁸Then on the third day after I gave birth, this woman also gave birth. And we were alone. There was no one else with us in the house; only we two were in the house. ¹⁹And this woman's son died in the night, because she lay on him. ²⁰And she arose at midnight and took my son from beside me, while your servant slept, and laid him at her breast, and laid her dead son at my breast. ²¹When I rose in the morning to nurse my child, behold, he was dead. But when I looked at him closely in the morning, behold, he was not the child that I had borne." ²²But the other woman said, "No, the living child is mine, and the dead child is yours." The first said, "No, the dead child is yours, and the living child is mine." Thus they spoke before the king.

²³Then the king said, "The one says, 'This is my son that is alive, and your son is dead'; and the other says, 'No; but your son is dead, and my son is the living one.'" ²⁴And the king said, "Bring me a sword." So a sword was brought before the king. ²⁵And the king said, "Divide the living child in two, and give half to the one and half to the other." ²⁶Then the woman whose son was alive said to the king, because her heart yearned for her son, "Oh, my lord, give her the living child, and by no means put him to death." But the other said, "He shall be neither mine nor yours; divide him." ²⁷Then the king answered and said, "Give the living child to the first woman, and by no means put him to death; she is his mother." ²⁸And

all Israel heard of the judgment that the king had rendered, and they stood in awe of the king, because *they perceived that the wisdom of God was in him to do justice.*

OVERVIEW: The reformers examine the tension between Solomon's marriage to Pharaoh's daughter and the laws forbidding the marriage of Jewish kings to foreigners—under the pretext that a non-Israelite spouse would seduce an Israelite from worshiping Yahweh. Solomon, like his father David, who also was not a priest, makes sacrifices to the Lord on various altars throughout Israel before the temple in Jerusalem is built. With the exception of Piscator, the commentators here do not find fault with Solomon's sacrifices in the high places, a practice God condemns in other parts of the Old Testament. On the contrary, the reformers praise Solomon's desire for discernment when God appears to him in a dream in Gibeon. God's response to Solomon's request, namely, that God would reward the young king with more wisdom than anyone before or after him, prompts some to consider whether Solomon was indeed wiser than Adam, Moses or even Christ himself. Whatever the case may be, the reformers acknowledge Solomon's great wisdom as illustrated in the story of the two prostitutes.

3:1 Solomon's Marriage to the Daughter of Pharaoh

EXCEPTIONS TO THE RULE ABOUT FOREIGN WIVES. JOHANNES BUGENHAGEN: In Exodus 34 it was prohibited for the Israelites to marry foreign women from among the Canaanites. Deuteronomy 7 extended this to include Moabites, Ammonites and others, while Deuteronomy 23 extends this exclusion from the church of God even to the tenth generation: "No one born of a forbidden union may enter the assembly." The same was not said of Edomites or Egyptians: "You shall not abhor an Edomite, for he is your brother. You shall not abhor an Egyptian, because you were a sojourner in his land." For this reason Solomon could marry the daughter of the pharaoh, though

she ought to have converted to Judaism. Otherwise the sons of Israel must abstain from all foreign women, so that their hearts may not be turned to foreign gods because of them, as you see at the end of Nehemiah. Solomon was also seduced by them in chapter 11 below, where he was accused of giving preference to the religions of those women whom he loved more than he loved God; then he acted foolishly. Therefore you should not always accuse Solomon of sin because of this beginning with Pharaoh's daughter, for here you see him described as being pious and as having been loved by God very much. For there was an exception to this law whenever there was no cause of fearing what gave rise to the law, that is, where there was no danger that a wife would lead her spouse into idolatry. Thus Boaz received Ruth the Moabite, who according to Matthew is in the line of Christ. In fact there are other places in the law that conditionally permit marrying non-Canaanite foreign women, as in Deuteronomy 21. Allegorically this may also be understood as Christ taking a wife from the Gentiles, for he came "not to call the righteous, but sinners." COMMENTARY ON 1 KINGS.[1]

MARRIAGE BETWEEN PERSONS OF DIFFERENT FAITHS. JOHANNES PISCATOR: It may be asked whether the marriage of Solomon to the daughter of the pharaoh was legal. If he led her (as it is probable that he did) to the profession and practicing of the true religion, it appears that their marriage would have been legal. For the Egyptians were not one of the people that God prohibited the Israelites from marrying. . . . Nevertheless, from this explanation of this law (that is, on account of the danger of being seduced into idolatry) . . . marriage of the Hebrews to other Gentiles was forbidden unless, of course, the nonethnic Jew had

---

[1]Bugenhagen, *In Regum duos ultimos libros*, 17-18; citing Ex 34:11-16; Deut 7:1-4; 23:2-3, 7; Neh 13:23-29; Deut 21:10-14; Mt 9:13.

beforehand taken on the religion of the Jews. There appears a unique example of this in the case of Rahab of Jericho, whom Salmon had married since she had taken on the Jewish religion, as is mentioned in Matthew 1:5. But this unique marriage between a Jew and non-Jew was on account of Rahab's excellent and unique faith in professing to the spies: "for the Lord your God, he is God in the heavens above and on the earth beneath." Yet the prohibition of a Jew marrying a non-Jew is still prohibited today. Nevertheless, if during the marriage a difference of religion appears among the couple, the faithful partner should not leave the unfaithful one. But if the unfaithful partner did leave, by this act the bond of marriage would be dissolved, to which the apostle attests in 1 Corinthians 7:13-15. COMMENTARY ON 1 KINGS.[2]

MARRIAGE FOR INSTRUCTION. JOHN MAYER: In the last verse of the former chapter it is said that the kingdom was established to Solomon after the death of Joab, Adonijah and Shimei, and the putting down of Abiathar from the high priesthood, so that no enemy now remained to the endangering of his estate. Here it is added that he sought further to establish the kingdom by contracting affinity with Pharaoh, a mighty neighbor king, by marrying his daughter. He was assured . . . by the promises of God that his kingdom should stand firm, yet human means were not to be neglected and without doubt he, being so zealously affected to the true God, did not take her but to instruct and convert her. . . . And because Salmon took Rahab the Canaanite, Boaz took Ruth and David took the daughter of the king of Geshur as a wife, Solomon determined that, if any heathen woman would turn and embrace the true religion, she might by a particular dispensation be taken as a wife. Otherwise it was to yoke an ox and a donkey together, which was unlawful. COMMENTARY ON 1 KINGS.[3]

3:2-3 Sacrificing at the High Places

THE HIGH PLACE. THE ENGLISH ANNOTATIONS: A high place used to be on a hill where fair spreading trees grew, under which worshipers erected altars for sacrifices. . . . Idolatrous Israelites superstitiously used such high places and the groves on them. . . . They did this in imitation of the heathen. At the same time, however, the true worshipers of God also used them as convenient places from the time that the ark and the tabernacle were removed from Shiloh until the temple was built. The first high place that we read of to be used by the people of God is mentioned 1 Samuel 9:12. . . . In this current passage, it is said to be the "great high place." It is named so for four reasons. First, the place was spacious and fair. Second, many people worshiped there. Third, the most important religious persons, such as chief priests and Levites, frequented it. . . . In fact even David and Solomon and their princes and courtiers used this space. Finally, the tabernacle and the altar that Moses built had been pitched there. ANNOTATIONS ON 1 KINGS.[4]

PERVERSE IMITATION OF PATRIARCHS. GIOVANNI DIODATI: In the beginning of Solomon's reign God's service was maintained in great purity in all its parts. The only exception was not having a settled place for sacrifices until the time came for a temple to be built according to God's command in Deuteronomy 12:5. Until this time, liberty was repressed and the pretenses for it were taken away. The high places were on certain little hills and rising places, which were established based on a perverse imitation of the ancient patriarchs. And although Moses' altar in those days was in Gibeon, the people assumed liberty to sacrifice elsewhere. They did this either because the place was too little and incommodious for a people so mightily increased or because they simply abused a practice that had been tolerated in extraordinary cases and for certain persons. ANNOTATIONS ON 1 KINGS.[5]

---

[2]Piscator, *Commentarii in omnes libros Veteris Testamenti*, 2:260; citing Deut 7:1, 3; Josh 2:11.
[3]Mayer, *Many Commentaries in One*, 17*.

[4]Downame, ed., *Annotations* (1645), 152*; citing 1 Kings 3:4.
[5]Diodati, *Pious Annotations*, 3*.

Imperfect Piety. Johannes Piscator: The sacrifices Solomon and the people of Israel made in the high places are examples of the imperfection of the godly in this life. For God had commanded the Israelites to destroy the high places: "You shall break down their altars and dash in pieces their pillars and chop down their Asherim and burn their carved images with fire." Commentary on 1 Kings.[6]

More Power Than Wisdom. Thomas Adams: Solomon saw he had enough power, but not enough wisdom; and he understood that a king without wisdom was equivalent to complete dishonor: a very calf made of golden earrings. . . . An ignorant ruler is like a blind pilot; who can save the vessel from ruin? The Holy Choice.[7]

3:4 Solomon at Gibeon

Waiting for the Wisdom of God Before Building the Temple. John Mayer: Nothing about the high places is said here to detract from Solomon, for he is immediately commended for his love to the Lord. And Solomon is said to have walked in all the precepts of David except his sacrificing in the high place, which is not mentioned as a fault in him. In this particular action Solomon varied from his own practice, who after he had begun in the threshing floor of Araunah never sacrificed anywhere else. For Solomon went to Gibeon, where the tabernacle and the altar of Moses were, purposely to show great devotion and honor God. And God showed how well he liked Solomon's intention because he appeared there to him. But it may seem strange that three years had now expired since the death of David, and Solomon did not yet begin to build the temple even though all things were before prepared by David. . . . To this it may be conceived that still more preparation of materials was to be made, as seen in the fifth chapter, about which so many thousands are

there said to have been employed and sent over into the country of Tyre to work there. Indeed, the levying of men, the sending of ambassadors to that king, the cutting down of cedars and fir trees, the getting of everything ready so that no knocking or hewing might be at the building as well as the transportation of the materials could not have taken up less time. What's more, because the task Solomon would undertake was so great and required extraordinary wisdom in him, Solomon happily thought himself not yet sufficient for it. Therefore he delayed until he had obtained the wisdom of God, as shown in this chapter. Commentary on 1 Kings.[8]

Mercy Trumps Judgment. Johannes Piscator: It seems strange that God would approve of the sacrifices that Solomon made in the high places at Gibeon. But that's because he had been commanded to make sacrifices in Gibeon since the holy tabernacle resided there. At the same time, God did not commend the sacrifices Solomon made in the high places. But it was out of God's mercy that he did not impute this sin to Solomon. Commentary on 1 Kings.[9]

Solomon Seeks Wisdom After Marriage. John Mayer: The thousand burnt offerings Solomon offered here were according to the practice of the Hebrews. They were either offered on several days or all at one time, but the first is most probable. Although his going to Gibeon to sacrifice is spoken of *after* his marriage to Pharaoh's daughter, some think it was before because so holy a man would not do any other act of greater consequence before he had sought wisdom from which to be directed. And in Wisdom 8 Solomon says that he sought wisdom "in [his] youth" and that he sought it from the beginning of his reign in Wisdom 9. . . . But I say that Solomon's sacrificing at Gibeon was before his marriage to Pharaoh's daughter. I can see no

---

[6]Piscator, *Commentarii in omnes libros Veteris Testamenti*, 2:260; citing Deut 7:5.
[7]Adams, *Five Sermons*, 69*.
[8]Mayer, *Many Commentaries in One*, 18*.
[9]Piscator, *Commentarii in omnes libros Veteris Testamenti*, 2:260.

reason of force to persuade me otherwise, and both the text and Josephus are for another order, placing the marriage before his sacrificing. Solomon, then, after this marriage was solemnized went to Gibeon to sacrifice that he might prosper in this estate by seeking God's blessing, and to be the better prepared for the great work of building the temple, which he thought it now time to address. COMMENTARY ON 1 KINGS.[10]

3:5-15 Solomon Asks for Discernment

SEEKING THE WISDOM OF GOD. JOHANNES BUGENHAGEN: Here you see Solomon's piety and the wisdom given to him by God. You therefore have this excellent example of what Christ said, "seek first the kingdom of God and his righteousness, and all these things will be added to you." And so it is with you in whatever you need. In your calls of distress, it is best that you ask for wisdom from God so that you will first be right with God in your heart. Then you can truly lead in such a way that you serve all those who have been put in your care. COMMENTARY ON 1 KINGS.[11]

"I AM BUT A LITTLE CHILD." LUCAS OSIANDER: Solomon prayed, "I am but a little child." By this, he was not referring to his age (for he had already married the pharaoh's daughter) but to his good sense. That is, he was saying, "I see that I do not have great abilities to govern with complete royal authority. It is as if I were a little child here. I am truly a child compared to such important things, not knowing even whether to come in or go out. I don't know how to behave correctly. I don't know where to come or go, where to begin or end." ANNOTATIONS ON 1 KINGS.[12]

SEEKING GOD'S KINGDOM FIRST. JOHANNES PISCATOR: If we first ask God for those things that look toward God's glory and salvation and then

others things for ourselves, God often throws in the good earthly things alongside those things considering the advantage of life. In fact, we are shown the truth of this example of Solomon in that it was confirmed by Christ in the Gospel of Matthew: "But seek first the kingdom of God and his righteousness, and all these things will be added to you." COMMENTARY ON 1 KINGS.[13]

THANKSGIVING AND INVOCATION GO TOGETHER. VIKTORIN STRIGEL: Solomon begins his prayer by giving thanks. For it is proper to give thanks for past blessings before asking for new blessings, as Chrysostom said: "An act of gratitude is an invitation to more of the same." In the same way, Paul connected the command to pray with thanksgiving. Then Solomon admitted himself to be unequal to the weight of governing and unable to avoid the snares of the devil and grave lapses. For this is what the true voice of Jeremiah says, "I know, O Lord, that the way of man is not in himself, that it is not in man who walks to direct his steps." "The way of man" means that a calling is not guided only by human decisions or strength, nor can it be happy without God. Therefore, God is the first cause of happy decisions and events. BOOK OF KINGS.[14]

PRAYING FOR KEEN JUDGMENT. MARTIN BUCER: The king was to write God's law and to read it all the days of his life so that he might learn to fear God his Lord, to keep his Word and the injunctions of the law, neither to raise his heart in pride above his brethren nor to deviate either to the right or to the left.... If a person, therefore, is to govern beneficially and not to be a tyrant, it is necessary that they be elected by God and from among the people of God. That is to say, they must be a true believer who have not themselves stepped forward for the office but have been called to it. The Christian official, recognizing themselves as an

[10]Mayer, *Many Commentaries in One*, 19*; citing Wis 8:2.
[11]Bugenhagen, *In Regum duos ultimos libros*, 19; citing Mt 6:33.
[12]Osiander, *Liber Iosue*, 675; citing 1 Kings 3:7.

[13]Piscator, *Commentarii in omnes libros Veteris Testamenti*, 2:260; citing Mt 6:33.
[14]Strigel, *Libri Samuelis, Regum et Paralipomenon*, 214-215; citing 1 Thess 4:16-18; Jer 10:23.

undershepherd of sheep that are not their own but God's, thinks to govern them not as it seems good to them but according to the law of God to whom the sheep belong. Consequently a civil officer should day by day govern and treat the people of God according to the divine law. In great humility and constant awe, they stand before God in order to avoid the least mistake in executing such a great commission. This Solomon observed. He asked God to give him a teachable heart before all things, so that he might judge his people and know the difference between good and evil. . . . In this prayer he confesses that he had been placed above God's people and not above a people belonging to Solomon himself . . . to judge it, to lead it to good and to keep it from evil. He also confesses that human reason does not have the power of distinguishing between evil and the true good, of judging rightly, but needs to learn such things from God. INSTRUCTION IN CHRISTIAN LOVE.[15]

WAS SOLOMON WISER THAN JESUS? JOHN MAYER: It is not Solomon's case alone to ask for this wisdom and obtain it. Rather, whoever is willing to ask for it in faith shall obtain it, as James says: "If any of you lacks wisdom, let him ask God, who gives generously to all without reproach, and it will be given him." The prayer of Solomon for wisdom is more largely set forth in Wisdom 9 and also Sirach 51. With this petition of Solomon, God was so pleased that he gave him both wisdom exceeding that of all others before and after him, and riches and honor. He also promised him long life if he continued to walk in God's commandments. But is it meant that in wisdom Solomon should excel all others? Was he wiser than Adam, Moses, the prophets, the apostles and also Christ Jesus? And did he excel all kings without exception in riches and glory, as Croesus, Xerxes, Alexander and Nebuchadnezzar?

I answer that Jesus Christ was not only man but God, and therefore he cannot come into question in this comparison. As for Adam, before

his fall he was without doubt as wise as Solomon both in natural and in divine things. The comparison, therefore, is made between Solomon and all other mere humans since the fall. In things natural, none was ever so suddenly made as wise as Solomon was in youth, for Sirach 7 says that it was given to him to know the constitution of the world and elements, the nature of beasts, trees and plants in addition to divine things. Still, the prophets and apostles excelled him in divine things. There are several things concerning this wisdom, therefore. First, as for natural and political wisdom enabling one to govern, there was none like him. Second, for all kinds of wisdom, no king was ever comparable to him, and the comparison is expressly made between him and all other kings. Last, as for riches and glory, no king of Israel was ever like him. And for other things—taking all three together: wisdom, riches and glory—there was never any who might be compared to him in any country. For although one might have a larger dominion and more riches, he would still come short of Solomon in wisdom, which is the greatest property. Whereas long life is promised to him if he kept the commandments, it seems that God foresaw his soul falling into idolatry and therefore spoke in this way. And the event answered the prediction, for Solomon died before he was very old, namely, about sixty years old. COMMENTARY ON 1 KINGS.[16]

3:16-28 Solomon's Wisdom on Display

PUBLIC HOUSES. KONRAD PELLIKAN: In this exemplary specimen of wisdom, Lord Solomon—confidently applying himself to deciding this case—showed the entire kingdom that he was being assisted by divine wisdom, so that the people were impressed and submitted to him with increased reverence. These two Hebrew women speak not simply of being prostitutes but of being fellow boarders. While it is usually not honest work among the people of God, sometimes prostitution was permitted such that there might

---

[15]Bucer, *Instruction in Christian Love*, 36.

[16]Mayer, *Many Commentaries in One*, 20*; citing Jas 1:5.

always be a modest place for male and female prostitutes to offer their services out of the public eye. The context of being fellow boarders, however, appears to be honest and not worth raising extra suspicions. It is a modest description, for such a place of dwelling could be permitted as not necessarily breaking God's law against prostitution and not requiring a marriage of necessity and honesty, which Scripture universally commends for a pure bed. COMMENTARY ON 1 KINGS.[17]

USING EVIDENCE FROM GOD'S CREATION.
JOHANNES BUGENHAGEN: This judgment declares the wisdom of God given to Solomon, just as it says at the end of the chapter. This is the wisdom without which a king or queen rules unproductively. Solomon could not have made this judgment according to the law and by hearing oral testimony, nor was it given him to know their secret hearts. Therefore he considered the work of God: God had created such a thing as maternal affection. And so he pretended, not in order to deceive but so that the false might reveal what was true to the court. Solomon's initial command to kill the infant certainly brought suffering, but it immediately revealed that no judgment could have been better or wiser. Thus when he could not use human testimony, he went to the testimony of God, whose work was tested in the form of maternal affection.

With their universal truths and speculations, what advantages have the scholastic theologians derived? Those who experiment with the things of nature are better off, for they can be more certain in discerning what is being examined. But then they will have received wisdom from God, from whom you must learn what true wisdom is. It is first being upright in God. This then gives benefit to human counsel, for everything else you call wisdom is foolishness to God and the plague of humankind, and whether it concerns spiritual or secular matters, you will learn nothing. COMMENTARY ON 1 KINGS.[18]

SILLY ADVICE AT FIRST BUT SAGACIOUS IN THE END.
JOHN MAYER: When Solomon began to suggest dividing the infant by killing him to find out the true mother, it is supposed that the courtiers standing by first derided him in their hearts as being about to act childishly. But in the end they perceived the depth of his understanding and so feared him. That is, the just reverenced him for his singular endowments, conceiving that they should have justice done them although they had to deal with subtle adversaries. And the wicked feared him, as conceiving that they could not lie hidden with a king of such sagacity, but would surely be found out and receive just punishments for their evil doings. COMMENTARY ON 1 KINGS.[19]

---

[17]Pellikan, *Commentaria Bibliorum*, 2:143r.

[18]Bugenhagen, *In Regum duos ultimos libros*, 20.
[19]Mayer, *Many Commentaries in One*, 21*.

4:1–5:18 SOLOMON'S FAME AND BUILDING PREPARATIONS

[1]King Solomon was king over all Israel, [2]and these were his high officials: Azariah the son of Zadok was the priest; [3]Elihoreph and Ahijah the sons of Shisha were secretaries; Jehoshaphat the son of Ahilud was recorder; [4]Benaiah the son of Jehoiada was in command of the army; Zadok and Abiathar were priests; [5]Azariah the son of Nathan was over the officers; Zabud the son of Nathan was priest and king's friend; [6]Ahishar was in charge of the palace; and Adoniram the son of Abda was in charge of the forced labor.

[7]Solomon had twelve officers over all Israel, who provided food for the king and his household. Each man had to make provision for one month in the year. [8]These were their names: Ben-hur, in the hill country of Ephraim; [9]Ben-deker, in Makaz, Shaalbim, Beth-shemesh, and Elonbeth-hanan; [10]Ben-hesed, in Arubboth (to him belonged Socoh and all the land of Hepher); [11]Ben-abinadab, in all Naphath-dor (he had Taphath the daughter of Solomon as his wife); [12]Baana the son of Ahilud, in Taanach, Megiddo, and all Beth-shean that is beside Zarethan below Jezreel, and from Beth-shean to Abel-meholah, as far as the other side of Jokmeam; [13]Ben-geber, in Ramoth-gilead (he had the villages of Jair the son of Manasseh, which are in Gilead, and he had the region of Argob, which is in Bashan, sixty great cities with walls and bronze bars); [14]Ahinadab the son of Iddo, in Mahanaim; [15]Ahimaaz, in Naphtali (he had taken Basemath the daughter of Solomon as his wife); [16]Baana the son of Hushai, in Asher and Bealoth; [17]Jehoshaphat the son of Paruah, in Issachar; [18]Shimei the son of Ela, in Benjamin; [19]Geber the son of Uri, in the land of Gilead, the country of Sihon king of the Amorites and of Og king of Bashan. And there was one governor who was over the land.

[20]Judah and Israel were as many as the sand by the sea. They ate and drank and were happy. [21a]Solomon ruled over all the kingdoms from the Euphrates[b] to the land of the Philistines and to the border of Egypt. They brought tribute and served Solomon all the days of his life.

[22]Solomon's provision for one day was thirty cors[c] of fine flour and sixty cors of meal, [23]ten fat oxen, and twenty pasture-fed cattle, a hundred sheep, besides deer, gazelles, roebucks, and fattened fowl. [24]For he had dominion over all the region west of the Euphrates[d] from Tiphsah to Gaza, over all the kings west of the Euphrates. And he had peace on all sides around him. [25]And Judah and Israel lived in safety, from Dan even to Beersheba, every man under his vine and under his fig tree, all the days of Solomon. [26]Solomon also had 40,000[e] stalls of horses for his chariots, and 12,000 horsemen. [27]And those officers supplied provisions for King Solomon, and for all who came to King Solomon's table, each one in his month. They let nothing be lacking. [28]Barley also and straw for the horses and swift steeds they brought to the place where it was required, each according to his duty.

[29]And God gave Solomon wisdom and understanding beyond measure, and breadth of mind like the sand on the seashore, [30]so that Solomon's wisdom surpassed the wisdom of all the people of the east and all the wisdom of Egypt. [31]For he was wiser than all other men, wiser than Ethan the Ezrahite, and Heman, Calcol, and Darda, the sons of Mahol, and his fame was in all the surrounding nations. [32]He also spoke 3,000 proverbs, and his songs were 1,005. [33]He spoke of trees, from the cedar that is in Lebanon to the hyssop that grows out of the wall. He spoke also of beasts, and of birds, and of reptiles, and of fish. [34]And people of all nations came to hear the wisdom of Solomon, and from all the kings of the earth, who had heard of his wisdom.

5[f] Now Hiram king of Tyre sent his servants to Solomon when he heard that they had anointed him king in place of his father, for Hiram always loved David. [2]And Solomon sent word to Hiram, [3]"You know that David my father could not build a house for the name of the LORD his God because of the warfare with which his enemies surrounded him, until the LORD put them under the soles of his feet.

⁴*But now the LORD my God has given me rest on every side. There is neither adversary nor misfortune. ⁵And so I intend to build a house for the name of the LORD my God, as the LORD said to David my father, 'Your son, whom I will set on your throne in your place, shall build the house for my name.' ⁶Now therefore command that cedars of Lebanon be cut for me. And my servants will join your servants, and I will pay you for your servants such wages as you set, for you know that there is no one among us who knows how to cut timber like the Sidonians."*

⁷*As soon as Hiram heard the words of Solomon, he rejoiced greatly and said, "Blessed be the LORD this day, who has given to David a wise son to be over this great people." ⁸And Hiram sent to Solomon, saying, "I have heard the message that you have sent to me. I am ready to do all you desire in the matter of cedar and cypress timber. ⁹My servants shall bring it down to the sea from Lebanon, and I will make it into rafts to go by sea to the place you direct. And I will have them broken up there, and you shall receive it. And you shall meet my wishes by providing food*

*for my household." ¹⁰So Hiram supplied Solomon with all the timber of cedar and cypress that he desired, ¹¹while Solomon gave Hiram 20,000 cors*ᵍ *of wheat as food for his household, and 20,000*ᵇ *cors of beaten oil. Solomon gave this to Hiram year by year. ¹²And the LORD gave Solomon wisdom, as he promised him. And there was peace between Hiram and Solomon, and the two of them made a treaty.*

¹³*King Solomon drafted forced labor out of all Israel, and the draft numbered 30,000 men. ¹⁴And he sent them to Lebanon, 10,000 a month in shifts. They would be a month in Lebanon and two months at home. Adoniram was in charge of the draft. ¹⁵Solomon also had 70,000 burden-bearers and 80,000 stonecutters in the hill country, ¹⁶besides Solomon's 3,300 chief officers who were over the work, who had charge of the people who carried on the work. ¹⁷At the king's command they quarried out great, costly stones in order to lay the foundation of the house with dressed stones. ¹⁸So Solomon's builders and Hiram's builders and the men of Gebal did the cutting and prepared the timber and the stone to build the house.*

a Ch 5:1 in Hebrew   **b** Hebrew *the River*   **c** A *cor* was about 6 bushels or 220 liters   **d** Hebrew *the River*; twice in this verse   **e** Hebrew; one Hebrew manuscript (see 2 Chron. 9:25 and Septuagint of 1 Kings 10:26) *4,000*   **f** Ch 5:15 in Hebrew   **g** A *cor* was about 6 bushels or 220 liters   **h** Septuagint; Hebrew *twenty*

OVERVIEW: These commentators notice how the wisdom of Solomon extends to all matters of inquiry: he is an example of religious, political and economic wisdom. The reformers see Solomon as a type of Christ who illumines the secret things of the world not only to leaders like the queen of Sheba but also to the common people. The commentators applaud Solomon for his prudent dealings with Hiram, paving the way for the construction of the temple in the following section.

4:1-19 Solomon's Officials

GOOD GOVERNMENT IS A GIFT OF GOD.
JOHANNES BUGENHAGEN: Solomon's wisdom included the prudent administration of the entire kingdom and his own household through wise governors, learned priests and skilled managers. This is described below in chapter 10 with the visit of the queen of Sheba, when she "had seen all the wisdom of Solomon," etc. They who do not have leaders or overseers who are wise through God instead have impious scoundrels, adulterers and thieves for their advisors and crude hypocrites and asses for their priests, who take too much of their allowances and portions and through whom everyone perishes. When the king rules in foolishness and impiety, then there is no rule, wealth, nourishment or peace, because true wisdom is missing. Holy wisdom and providence make it so that when all resources of the court have arrived, the subjects are not lacking but they abound in all riches. COMMENTARY ON 1 KINGS.[1]

---

[1]Bugenhagen, *In Regum duos ultimos libros*, 22; citing 1 Kings 10:4-9.

POLITICAL AND ECONOMIC WISDOM. JO-HANNES PISCATOR: In Solomon is set forth an example of both political and economic wisdom. We see his political wisdom inasmuch as he established high officials who oversaw ordinary and civil matters as well as those who oversaw sacred and godly things. We also see his economic wisdom inasmuch as he established twelve district officers who arranged for food for Solomon and his family once a month. These officers also provided for Solomon's horses, and they also took charge of equally distributing the horses' food. COMMEN-TARY ON 1 KINGS.[2]

MAGNIFICENT MINISTERS. KONRAD PELLIKAN: This passage describes the king's magnificence through the nobility of his appointed ministers and officials across the king's entire domain, namely, the twelve tribes on both sides of the Jordan. That such an arrangement endured under Solomon means that it is an example of the reign of Christ our Lord, who reigns in peace forever over the faithful of all generations around the entire world, both in this life and in the blessed age to come. COMMENTARY ON 1 KINGS.[3]

4:20-34 The Wealth and Wisdom of Solomon

TOO MANY HORSES? JOHANNES BUGENHAGEN: Solomon had "40,000 stalls of horses for his chariots and 12,000 horsemen," which seems to be against the law given in Deuteronomy 17. But who will dare to pronounce this against the one whose God-given piety and wisdom has been described? Or did God cover this sin in holiness and not impute it? I believe that Solomon did not sin, for the law does not simply prohibit having a multitude of horses but that the king not "cause the people to return to Egypt in order to acquire many horses," which Solomon did not do. COMMENTARY ON 1 KINGS[4]

FLOCKING TO THE SCHOOL OF WISDOM. JOHN MAYER: The fame of Solomon's extraordinary wisdom was soon spread abroad into all parts, and as such many who desired to learn from him came from all countries to his court. They came as if they were coming to a famous school, and kings who could not come in person sent others to learn from Solomon, so that their knowledge could be improved and so that they could be better able to govern and instruct their people.... Solomon did not hide his light under a bushel, but communicated his wisdom to all common people, teaching all those who excel in knowledge to do the same.... And concerning Solomon's antitype Christ, the people did also flock from all parts to hear and learn from him. COMMENTARY ON 1 KINGS.[5]

WISE MEN FROM THE EAST. KONRAD PELLIKAN: The Chaldeans, magi, astronomers and other investigators of the natural world are called children of the East who excelled in all beneficial and upright instruction. I consider them to be those children of the East who drank of that perfect and highest knowledge of the magi. They charted a course of lasting value for many, including Pythagoras, Empedocles, Democritus and Plato, who each spoke of going back to them for their ancient learning. The wisdom of the Egyptians you truly get to know in the secrets of the natural world and their method of instruction. Solomon was wiser than all of these, because he acknowledged, believed in, loved and was close to God, the foundation of everything. COMMENTARY ON 1 KINGS.[6]

ONLY CHIEF AND SACRED SAYINGS REMAINED. JOHN MAYER: Nicholas of Lyra observes that in all the book of Proverbs, there are 915 verses, and sometimes two verses or more make up but one proverb. Therefore, all the proverbs that Solomon spoke are not recorded. He uttered them at different times and in different places, but did not write them down. Only others wrote them down as memorable

---

[2]Piscator, *Commentarii in omnes libros Veteris Testamenti*, 2:262.
[3]Pellikan, *Commentaria Bibliorum*, 2:143v.
[4]Bugenhagen, *In Regum duos ultimos libros*, 22; citing Deut 17:16.

[5]Mayer, *Many Commentaries in One*, 25*.
[6]Pellikan, *Commentaria Bibliorum*, 2:145r.

sayings. Afterwards, the most important and the most sacred of these proverbs were gathered together, while the rest were left out. The same applies to his verses or songs. COMMENTARY ON 1 KINGS[7]

WISDOM AND FREEDOM. JOHANNES BUGENHAGEN: God gives wisdom, prudence and intelligence where he is acknowledged and where others are directed to him. God also gives latitude to people's hearts, that is, a free soul, which is a conscience led into all freedom with respect to God. A person cannot be given anything greater than this. It is rarely accepted. COMMENTARY ON 1 KINGS[8]

5:1-18 *Preparation for the Temple*

FAITHFUL GENTILES. KONRAD PELLIKAN: Hiram, king of Tyre and Sidon, had enjoyed perpetual friendship with David. After David's death an envoy was sent to renew that peace with Solomon, whom he heard had succeeded his father. We do not read that Solomon sought a treaty with Hiram using either warnings or favors but instead that the pagan king voluntarily sought out the company of Solomon. This clearly signifies that the Hebrews could accept the Gentiles' voluntary devotion to the worship of the one and only true God, in which they would remain forever. This would be true when the Israelites themselves, even with many clear and tremendous benefits, were unable to preserve such worship of the true God but turned away from the law and worship of God and slipped into idolatry for flimsy reasons. In contrast, once the Gentiles acknowledged the true God, they never went astray nor returned to the worship of idols. COMMENTARY ON 1 KINGS.[9]

BUILDING THE TEMPLE, BUILDING FAITH. JOHANNES BUGENHAGEN: Here we see the peace Solomon built up during his entire life. With God's help, David's hands had worked to this end,

so that Solomon might govern in peace and most carefully guard it. You can see this as signifying the reign of Christ in their hearts, where satanic darkness is cast out through the gospel. For what else is it to build the temple than to build the church? The apostle says, "For God's temple is holy, and you are that temple." We have been built up so that we might live "from faith for faith," "until we all attain to the unity of the faith and of the knowledge of the Son of God, to mature manhood, to the measure of the stature of the fullness of Christ." Ephesians 2 and 1 Peter 2 also speak of this "building." That the Gentiles rightly belong to this church is clear in how the rocks, precious stones, skills and labor were requested of the Gentiles, for without them the temple could not have been built. Second Chronicles 2 describes how many workers came from Judea and how many were foreigners. The Israelites who were put in charge of this project signify the remnant of Jacob who were sent to teach salvation to the Gentiles. Up to this point the tabernacle of Moses had been carried without gathering any adoration from the Gentiles, serving figuratively as a sign of the future abolition of the law through Christ. But now through the wisdom of Solomon, a temple was built up by Jews and Gentiles, which could not be carried to another place, to which Isaiah alluded when he wrote of the church in chapter 33, "Your eyes will see Jerusalem, an untroubled habitation, an immovable tent," etc. COMMENTARY ON 1 KINGS.[10]

MAKING THE MOST OF EVERY OCCASION. JOHANNES PISCATOR: In Solomon an example of wisdom is set forth in making the best of an occasion. For instance, when occasion came by means of Hiram offering his congratulations, Solomon immediately asked Hiram for help in the construction of the temple. This petition, in fact, is a type of what seems to be the vocation of the Gentiles. COMMENTARY ON 1 KINGS.[11]

[7]Mayer, *Many Commentaries in One*, 25*.
[8]Bugenhagen, *In Regum duos ultimos libros*, 24.
[9]Pellikan, *Commentaria Bibliorum*, 2:145r.
[10]Bugenhagen, *In Regum duos ultimos libros*, 25-26; citing 1 Cor 3:17; Rom 1:17; Eph 4:13; 2:19-22; 1 Pet 2:2-10; Is 33:20.
[11]Piscator, *Commentarii in omnes libros Veteris Testamenti*, 2:263.

MEN OF TYRE PREFIGURE THE GENTILES IN THE SPIRITUAL TEMPLE. JOHN MAYER: The reasons why Solomon sought Hiram for the cedars rather than any other king were several. First, there was a great friendship between them, as well as between Hiram and Solomon's father, David. Second, Hiram had sent Solomon ambassadors congratulating him. Third, the skillfulness of the men of Tyre was well known in comparison to those of other nations. Finally, it is held that God was disposed to use the people of Tyre, that is, Gentiles, to be employed in doing this work for the temple to prefigure the vocation of the Gentiles in their future in building the spiritual temple. COMMENTARY ON 1 KINGS.[12]

---

[12]Mayer, *Many Commentaries in One*, 27*.

6:1–7:51 SOLOMON BUILDS THE TEMPLE AND HIS PALACE

[1] *In the four hundred and eightieth year after the people of Israel came out of the land of Egypt, in the fourth year of Solomon's reign over Israel, in the month of Ziv, which is the second month, he began to build the house of the LORD.* [2] *The house that King Solomon built for the LORD was sixty cubits[a] long, twenty cubits wide, and thirty cubits high.* [3] *The vestibule in front of the nave of the house was twenty cubits long, equal to the width of the house, and ten cubits deep in front of the house.* [4] *And he made for the house windows with recessed frames.[b]* [5] *He also built a structure[c] against the wall of the house, running around the walls of the house, both the nave and the inner sanctuary. And he made side chambers all around.* [6] *The lowest story[d] was five cubits broad, the middle one was six cubits broad, and the third was seven cubits broad. For around the outside of the house he made offsets on the wall in order that the supporting beams should not be inserted into the walls of the house.*

[7] *When the house was built, it was with stone prepared at the quarry, so that neither hammer nor axe nor any tool of iron was heard in the house while it was being built.*

[8] *The entrance for the lowest[e] story was on the south side of the house, and one went up by stairs to the middle story, and from the middle story to the third.* [9] *So he built the house and finished it, and he made the ceiling of the house of beams and planks of cedar.* [10] *He built the structure against the whole house, five cubits high, and it was joined to the house with timbers of cedar.*

[11] *Now the word of the LORD came to Solomon,* [12] *"Concerning this house that you are building, if you will walk in my statutes and obey my rules and keep all my commandments and walk in them, then I will establish my word with you, which I spoke to David your father.* [13] *And I will dwell among the children of Israel and will not forsake my people Israel."*

[14] *So Solomon built the house and finished it.* [15] *He lined the walls of the house on the inside with boards of cedar. From the floor of the house to the walls of the ceiling, he covered them on the inside with wood, and he covered the floor of the house with boards of cypress.* [16] *He built twenty cubits of the rear of the house with boards of cedar from the floor to the walls, and he built this within as an inner sanctuary, as the Most Holy Place.* [17] *The house, that is, the nave in front of the inner sanctuary, was forty cubits long.* [18] *The cedar within the house was carved in the form of gourds and open flowers. All was cedar; no stone was seen.* [19] *The inner sanctuary he prepared in the innermost part of the house, to set there the ark of the covenant of the LORD.* [20] *The inner sanctuary[f] was twenty cubits long, twenty cubits wide, and twenty cubits high, and he overlaid it with pure gold. He also overlaid[g] an altar of cedar.* [21] *And Solomon overlaid the inside of the house with pure gold, and he drew chains of gold across, in front of the inner sanctuary, and overlaid it with gold.* [22] *And he overlaid the whole house with gold, until all the house was finished. Also the whole altar that belonged to the inner sanctuary he overlaid with gold.*

[23] *In the inner sanctuary he made two cherubim of olivewood, each ten cubits high.* [24] *Five cubits was the length of one wing of the cherub, and five cubits the length of the other wing of the cherub; it was ten cubits from the tip of one wing to the tip of the other.* [25] *The other cherub also measured ten cubits; both cherubim had the same measure and the same form.* [26] *The height of one cherub was ten cubits, and so was that of the other cherub.* [27] *He put the cherubim in the innermost part of the house. And the wings of the cherubim were spread out so that a wing of one touched the one wall, and a wing of the other cherub touched the other wall; their other wings touched each other in the middle of the house.* [28] *And he overlaid the cherubim with gold.*

[29] *Around all the walls of the house he carved engraved figures of cherubim and palm trees and open flowers, in the inner and outer rooms.* [30] *The*

floor of the house he overlaid with gold in the inner and outer rooms.

³¹For the entrance to the inner sanctuary he made doors of olivewood; the lintel and the doorposts were five-sided.ʰ ³²He covered the two doors of olivewood with carvings of cherubim, palm trees, and open flowers. He overlaid them with gold and spread gold on the cherubim and on the palm trees.

³³So also he made for the entrance to the nave doorposts of olivewood, in the form of a square, ³⁴and two doors of cypress wood. The two leaves of the one door were folding, and the two leaves of the other door were folding. ³⁵On them he carved cherubim and palm trees and open flowers, and he overlaid them with gold evenly applied on the carved work. ³⁶He built the inner court with three courses of cut stone and one course of cedar beams.

³⁷In the fourth year the foundation of the house of the LORD was laid, in the month of Ziv. ³⁸And in the eleventh year, in the month of Bul, which is the eighth month, the house was finished in all its parts, and according to all its specifications. He was seven years in building it.

7 Solomon was building his own house thirteen years, and he finished his entire house.

²He built the House of the Forest of Lebanon. Its length was a hundred cubitsⁱ and its breadth fifty cubits and its height thirty cubits, and it was built on fourʲ rows of cedar pillars, with cedar beams on the pillars. ³And it was covered with cedar above the chambers that were on the forty-five pillars, fifteen in each row. ⁴There were window frames in three rows, and window opposite window in three tiers. ⁵All the doorways and windowsᵏ had square frames, and window was opposite window in three tiers.

⁶And he made the Hall of Pillars; its length was fifty cubits, and its breadth thirty cubits. There was a porch in front with pillars, and a canopy in front of them.

⁷And he made the Hall of the Throne where he was to pronounce judgment, even the Hall of Judgment. It was finished with cedar from floor to rafters.ˡ

⁸His own house where he was to dwell, in the other court back of the hall, was of like workmanship. Solomon also made a house like this hall for Pharaoh's daughter whom he had taken in marriage.

⁹All these were made of costly stones, cut according to measure, sawed with saws, back and front, even from the foundation to the coping, and from the outside to the great court. ¹⁰The foundation was of costly stones, huge stones, stones of eight and ten cubits. ¹¹And above were costly stones, cut according to measurement, and cedar. ¹²The great court had three courses of cut stone all around, and a course of cedar beams; so had the inner court of the house of the LORD and the vestibule of the house.

¹³And King Solomon sent and brought Hiram from Tyre. ¹⁴He was the son of a widow of the tribe of Naphtali, and his father was a man of Tyre, a worker in bronze. And he was full of wisdom, understanding, and skill for making any work in bronze. He came to King Solomon and did all his work.

¹⁵He cast two pillars of bronze. Eighteen cubits was the height of one pillar, and a line of twelve cubits measured its circumference. It was hollow, and its thickness was four fingers. The second pillar was the same.ᵐ ¹⁶He also made two capitals of cast bronze to set on the tops of the pillars. The height of the one capital was five cubits, and the height of the other capital was five cubits. ¹⁷There were lattices of checker work with wreaths of chain work for the capitals on the tops of the pillars, a latticeⁿ for the one capital and a lattice for the other capital. ¹⁸Likewise he made pomegranatesᵒ in two rows around the one lattice-work to cover the capital that was on the top of the pillar, and he did the same with the other capital. ¹⁹Now the capitals that were on the tops of the pillars in the vestibule were of lily-work, four cubits. ²⁰The capitals were on the two pillars and also above the rounded projection which was beside the latticework. There were two hundred pomegranates in two rows all around, and so with the other capital. ²¹He set up the pillars at the vestibule of the temple. He set up the pillar on the south and called its name Jachin, and he set up the pillar on the north and called its name Boaz. ²²And on the tops of the pillars was lily-work. Thus the work of the pillars was finished.

²³Then he made the sea of cast metal. It was round, ten cubits from brim to brim, and five cubits high, and a line of thirty cubits measured its circumference. ²⁴Under its brim were gourds, for ten

cubits, compassing the sea all around. The gourds were in two rows, cast with it when it was cast. [25]It stood on twelve oxen, three facing north, three facing west, three facing south, and three facing east. The sea was set on them, and all their rear parts were inward. [26]Its thickness was a handbreadth,[p] and its brim was made like the brim of a cup, like the flower of a lily. It held two thousand baths.[q]

[27]He also made the ten stands of bronze. Each stand was four cubits long, four cubits wide, and three cubits high. [28]This was the construction of the stands: they had panels, and the panels were set in the frames, [29]and on the panels that were set in the frames were lions, oxen, and cherubim. On the frames, both above and below the lions and oxen, there were wreaths of beveled work. [30]Moreover, each stand had four bronze wheels and axles of bronze, and at the four corners were supports for a basin. The supports were cast with wreaths at the side of each. [31]Its opening was within a crown that projected upward one cubit. Its opening was round, as a pedestal is made, a cubit and a half deep. At its opening there were carvings, and its panels were square, not round. [32]And the four wheels were underneath the panels. The axles of the wheels were of one piece with the stands, and the height of a wheel was a cubit and a half. [33]The wheels were made like a chariot wheel; their axles, their rims, their spokes, and their hubs were all cast. [34]There were four supports at the four corners of each stand. The supports were of one piece with the stands. [35]And on the top of the stand there was a round band half a cubit high; and on the top of the stand its stays and its panels were of one piece with it. [36]And on the surfaces of its stays and on its panels, he carved cherubim, lions, and palm trees, according to the space of each, with wreaths all around. [37]After this manner he made the ten stands. All of them were cast alike, of the same measure and the same form.

[38]And he made ten basins of bronze. Each basin held forty baths, each basin measured four cubits, and there was a basin for each of the ten stands. [39]And he set the stands, five on the south side of the house, and five on the north side of the house. And he set the sea at the southeast corner of the house.

[40]Hiram also made the pots, the shovels, and the basins. So Hiram finished all the work that he did for King Solomon on the house of the Lord: [41]the two pillars, the two bowls of the capitals that were on the tops of the pillars, and the two lattice works to cover the two bowls of the capitals that were on the tops of the pillars; [42]and the four hundred pomegranates for the two latticeworks, two rows of pomegranates for each latticework, to cover the two bowls of the capitals that were on the pillars; [43]the ten stands, and the ten basins on the stands; [44]and the one sea, and the twelve oxen underneath the sea.

[45]Now the pots, the shovels, and the basins, all these vessels in the house of the Lord, which Hiram made for King Solomon, were of burnished bronze. [46]In the plain of the Jordan the king cast them, in the clay ground between Succoth and Zarethan. [47]And Solomon left all the vessels unweighed, because there were so many of them; the weight of the bronze was not ascertained.

[48]So Solomon made all the vessels that were in the house of the Lord: the golden altar, the golden table for the bread of the Presence, [49]the lampstands of pure gold, five on the south side and five on the north, before the inner sanctuary; the flowers, the lamps, and the tongs, of gold; [50]the cups, snuffers, basins, dishes for incense, and fire pans, of pure gold; and the sockets of gold, for the doors of the innermost part of the house, the Most Holy Place, and for the doors of the nave of the temple.

[51]Thus all the work that King Solomon did on the house of the Lord was finished. And Solomon brought in the things that David his father had dedicated, the silver, the gold, and the vessels, and stored them in the treasuries of the house of the Lord.

a A *cubit* was about 18 inches or 45 centimeters **b** Or *blocked lattice windows* **c** Or *platform*; also verse 10 **d** Septuagint; Hebrew *structure*, or *platform* **e** Septuagint, Targum; Hebrew *middle* **f** Vulgate; Hebrew *and before the inner sanctuary* **g** Septuagint *made* **h** The meaning of the Hebrew phrase is uncertain **i** A *cubit* was about 18 inches or 45 centimeters **j** Septuagint *three* **k** Septuagint; Hebrew *posts* **l** Syriac, Vulgate; Hebrew *floor* **m** Targum, Syriac (compare Septuagint and Jeremiah 52:21); Hebrew *fingers. And a line of twelve cubits measured the circumference of the second pillar* **n** Septuagint; Hebrew *seven*; twice in this verse **o** Two manuscripts (compare Septuagint); Hebrew *pillars* **p** A *handbreadth* was about 3 inches or 7.5 centimeters **q** A *bath* was about 6 gallons or 22 liters

Overview: The reformers remind us that the temple, as glorious as it appeared under King Solomon, prefigured Christ, our far more glorious King; it was a shadow in contrast to the reality of Christ himself. These interpreters find great spiritual significance in the smallest of details in the temple; spiritual interpretations abound. Bugenhagen describes the various furnishings in and around the temple, all of which point to the gospel in one way or another. Our commentators praise Solomon for first deciding to construct God's temple before building his own dwelling place. At the same time, some draw connections between the opulence of Solomon's construction and later Israelite idolatry with the beauty of contemporary buildings filled with people who lack spiritual fervor.

6:1 The Spiritual Meaning of the Temple

The Symbolic Temple. Dirk Philips: The consecration of the symbolic temple of Solomon in Jerusalem shows us that the community of the Lord is consecrated by God through Jesus Christ with his Holy Spirit. It is a holy temple, a house of the living God, a pillar and foundation of truth. God wills to be worshiped in spirit and in truth in this temple. Here God receives offerings. Here are the true priests and Levites, the children and descendants of the spiritual Aaron, our one high priest Jesus Christ. Here is the tabernacle of our God, the ark of the covenant, the pure and holy Word of the gospel with all of God's promises of grace concerning forgiveness of sins, reconciliation with God and of eternal life through Jesus Christ. Here is the holy mystery of the signs of sacrament, of baptism and the Lord's Supper, which were given by Christ to all believers.

We must come to this temple to celebrate spiritually to the Lord the feast of the Passover, of Pentecost and of Tabernacles. We celebrate the Passover by preaching that Jesus Christ is our Passover Lamb who was slain for us. By faith in him we are cleansed of the old yeast of ill-will and evil and become a new bread. So we spiritually eat our Passover Lamb with the unleavened bread of integrity. We meditate on our terrible captivity in Egypt, which was under Satan and the rule of darkness, and on how we were delivered from this by the mighty hand of God. The precious blood of the perfect Passover Lamb Jesus Christ is sprinkled on our conscience, protecting us from the coming of judgment of this blind world.

We celebrate the feast of Pentecost[1] by coming before God, confessing that we were once captives in Egypt under the terrible pharaoh. But God marvelously delivered us from that and chose and accepted us as the firstfruits of his creation and as heirs of his eternal kingdom in heaven. He has generously given to us the gifts of heaven and blessed us. For this we praise and thank God and offer him the fruits of justice and thanksgiving from the lips of those who confess his name. It is very important that we truly confess our ignorance, blindness and the weight of sin that weighed us down, but which is countered by the riches of the grace of God, which is poured out on us through Jesus Christ. We meditate on this and praise and thank God for the inexpressible gift of his benevolence, which we have received.

We celebrate the feast of Tabernacles by confessing that we are pilgrims in this world and have no abiding place in it. We are underway toward the Promised Land. We long for entrance into that blessed rest, the heavenly Jerusalem, the city of the living God. There Jesus Christ has prepared a palace for us. There we have a tabernacle not made by hands. It is eternal and heavenly, and we shall put it on when our earthly tabernacles are broken. That is, when we lay aside this corruptible and mortal flesh and put on a body that is incorruptible, immortal and magnified. Enchiridion: Concerning Spiritual Restitution.[2]

---

[1]Pentecost celebrated the institution of the law after the Lord delivered the Israelites out of Egypt; the reformers saw this as a foreshadowing of the "greater" Pentecost to come when Jesus sent his Spirit. See RCS NT 6:19.

[2]Liechty, ed., *Early Anabaptist Spirituality*, 236-37; cf. CRR 6:337-38.

JESUS' TEMPLE. JOHN CALVIN: Solomon . . . certainly built the temple in which God was served and worshiped. However, our Lord Jesus Christ, being the true temple, also built a house for God his Father, especially since he reconciled us to him (Eph 2:14-18). For by this means we are consecrated to the service of God in such a way that he inhabits us by his Holy Spirit. And we have this honor and this privilege, even though we are nothing but vessels of clay (2 Cor 4:7)—indeed, rotten and infected—yet God receives us and wants to have his dwelling and sanctuary not only in our souls, which are more precious to him, but also in our bodies, which are poor carcasses, as the Scripture describes them! Therefore we see how our Lord Jesus Christ built the spiritual temple in a manner much more worthy and more noble than Solomon did. There was stone and wood in that temple. It was exquisitely sumptuous. Its workmanship was very great and excellent. But here is a kind of house that is far more perfect than the building which was on the mountain of Zion. It is a temple in which so many men and women who have been converted to the faith of the gospel are like numerous stones that have been assembled so that God might dwell throughout all the earth, so that his name might be honored and worshiped by all, and so that everyone might offer him a freewill sacrifice. SERMONS ON 2 SAMUEL.[3]

CHRIST THE FOUNDATION, GOD'S WORD THE CEILING. JOHANNES BUGENHAGEN: We already know Christ the foundation, on whom stand the apostles and prophets and whoever is in harmony with them, and on which he raises a holy building to the Lord, that is, the temple which is the holy church. For this reason we will easily see what they wanted to describe here, so that we would not be ignorant what this is and what it teaches to Christians. First, the time of the construction is rightly described. Here, so that you might not be mistaken, you must start by building prayer: "In the fourth year of Solomon's reign over Israel, in

the month of Ziv, which is the second month, he began to build the house of the Lord." The first month for the Hebrews is the month of the Passover (see Exodus 12), which—since the Hebrews observe a lunar calendar—largely corresponds to our month of April, so that the second month mostly corresponds to our May, and so on. You can see a clear picture of the external temple in the illustrated translation by Dr. Martin Luther.[4] But once we know the temple of Solomon to be the church of Christ, we need to know it is built by his Word. Therefore all should truly return to the Word and to the ministry of the Word, which—since Christ is the foundation—is the ceiling or head, the protection that encloses everyone in the temple, for Christ himself is all and in all and the head of the church. For the width, length and height of the church covers the sphere of the earth, which begins with the north side of the temple, as Psalm 48 says. COMMENTARY ON 1 KINGS.[5]

THE THREE TYPES OF THE TEMPLE. JOHANNES PISCATOR: Solomon's temple contained three types. The first type is in relation to Christ's body, as appears from several passages in the New Testament. For instance, Jesus said, "Destroy this temple, and in three days I will raise it up.' . . . But he was speaking about the temple of his body." Also, Paul says: "For in [Jesus] the whole fullness of deity dwells bodily." The second type is in relation to the church, which also appears from several passages in the New Testament. For instance, Peter says: "You yourselves like living stones are being built up as a spiritual house, to be a holy priesthood, to offer spiritual sacrifices acceptable to God through Jesus Christ." The third type of the temple is in relation to each believer. This shows itself from many of Paul's words, for instance: "Or do you not know that your body is a temple of the Holy Spirit within you, whom you have from God?"

---

[3]Calvin, *Sermons on Second Samuel*, 1:328.

[4]*Das Annder teyl des alten Testaments*, trans. Martin Luther et al. (Strasbourg: Johann Knoblouch, 1524), 86v.
[5]Bugenhagen, *In Regum duos ultimos libros*, 26; citing Col 3:11; Ps 48:2 (Vg).

The explanation of the types is that, inasmuch as God inhabited Solomon's temple—accepting there the prayers of the godly—in the same way God inhabits the bodily Christ by the hypostatic union and then through the great abundance of spiritual gifts. And, truly, in the whole of the church, God inhabits each of the believers through the measure of certain spiritual gifts. Commentary on 1 Kings.[6]

The Temple's Mystical Significance. John Mayer: Mystically the temple is to be understood as the church of God. The gold signifies the governors, and the silver signifies the preachers, who are most excellent. The brass signifies lesser preachers, and the iron signifies those who protect and fight in the defense of the church. The cedars signify those who are high, that is, those who pursue the contemplative life, and the stones signify those who lead an active life, that is, those who sustain others. Commentary on 1 Kings.[7]

The Meeting Place. David Dickson: The Lord's holy temple or tabernacle represents Jesus Christ and his church. It also represents the mutual relations between God and his people. From this we learn the following: The way to refresh and strengthen faith is to look to God in Christ the Mediator, reconciling the world to himself just as he was shadowed forth in the temple of Jerusalem; and as he is still held forth in the church, in his Word and in other ordinances. . . . Christ is the meeting place, where God is constantly to be found on his mercy seat; for the Lord is in his holy temple, which speaks of the church by way of typology. Explication of the First Fifty Psalms.[8]

6:2-38 The Design and Furnishings of the Temple

The Temple Is a Type of Spiritual Person. Martin Luther: The windows are so wide on the inside and so narrow on the outside, that a person cannot peer into the temple very well. But a person can see well and wide looking out from the windows. This fits with the mystery that a spiritual person judges all things and is himself judged by no one. A spiritual person knows everything and sees well, but no one knows him. This, in my opinion, is what the text means by "The windows to the house were open and shut." To me on the inside they are open; to you on the outside they are shut. Marginal Gloss on 1 Kings 6:4 (1545).[9]

The Mystery of the Ark. Heinrich Bullinger: Now, it remains for us to touch on and examine the holy instruments used in the tabernacle or the temple. The first of these instruments was the ark of the covenant, which was so called because the two tables of the covenant were placed in it. It was also called the ark of the Lord God of hosts. On top of it were the cherubim, and by this the Lord was called by the name "the one who sits between the cherubim," since this is how he gave responses to the priests. The ark was placed in the midst of the people as a sign that God's presence was among them. Concerning the materials and forms from which the ark was constructed, I will say nothing about that here. For these things are clearly described in Exodus 25. Concerning the meaning, mystery and use of the ark, I will only say a little. As human beings, we lay up our treasures in boxes and chests. Therefore we understand that the treasures of the church were laid in the ark, including all the good things the faithful valued. But we must not seek out these things in human beings, whether Noah, Abraham, Isaac, Moses, David, Mary, Joanne, Peter or Paul. . . . Rather we must seek out him in whom "all the fullness of God was pleased to dwell." We must seek out him in whom all the treasures of God's wisdom and knowledge are hidden. This one is not seen on earth but is in the holy of holies in heaven. I am speaking of course of Jesus Christ, whose divinity is signified by the purest gold and whose humanity is signified by the

---

[6]Piscator, *Commentarii in omnes libros Veteris Testamenti*, 2:265; citing Jn 2:19, 21; 1 Pet 2:5; 1 Cor 6:19.
[7]Mayer, *Many Commentaries in One*, 7-8*.
[8]Dickson, *First Fifty Psalms*, 58*.

[9]WADB 9,1:413.

wood of Sittim, that is, a cedar tree or rather white thorns. For he assumed on himself flesh similar to our sinful nature, but of which nothing was sinful. Indeed there was in him no thorn of sin. It is out of this ark, Christ himself, that the godly bring forth all good and necessary things. For in the ark we read that there dwelled the tables of the covenant, the jar of manna and the budding rod of Aaron, just as in Christ we have heard there dwells the treasures of the church. Christ is our wisdom, law and Word from the Father. Christ is the consummation and fulfillment of the law. He is both just and our justice. In Christ is heavenly food, for he is the living bread that came from heaven, so that we may eat of him and live eternally. In Christ the priesthood budded again. And although it seemed that at his death on the cross it was cut down, at his resurrection he reclaimed the priesthood, which will be eternal. For now he is standing at the right hand of the Father, where he intercedes for us. But the ark was crowned with a coronet since Christ our Lord is a King, who frees his faithful subjects from all evil and who makes us children of God. On the ark we read that there was placed the mercy seat. This was either a covering of the ark or it served as a seat that was positioned on the ark. The apostles John and Paul interpret the mercy seat as Christ our Lord, who is the throne of grace and who "is the propitiation for our sins, and not for ours only but also for the sins of the whole world." It was out of the mercy seat that the oracles of God were given forth. For the use of the mercy seat in the sacred Scriptures was shown forth to be the place on which Moses, after entering the tabernacle, received responses from God, which he in turn spoke to the people and it is through Christ that our heavenly Father speaks and declares to us his will. It is Christ alone about whom the Father has given us to hear, "This is my beloved Son; listen to him." Two cherubim looked toward the mercy seat, where they sat in contemplation of one another. Such is the reason why St. Peter says the Savior of the world is the one on whom "angels long to look." It is through him that the good news is proclaimed. These same angels serve our Lord and assist the Lord of the universe as needed. Now, only the priests of the Lord carried the ark of the Lord. For only those who are anointed with the Holy Spirit and are endowed with the true faith receive Christ and are made participants of his gifts. Nor should we overlook what was said in 1 Samuel 4–5 about when the Israelites were killed by the Philistines and the ark was taken into captivity due to its abuse and use for something Scripture did not allow for. Through this we learn that we are not to apply the sacraments and mysteries of God in a way that is not convenient. Nor are we to apply them to any other use than that for which the Lord has instituted. For the ark was not allowed in 1 Samuel to be taken for God, even though it contained God's name. Nor was it to be used under the assumption that people should look for grace and help from it, as we read they did. Instead, the ark was given to them as witness—that God, their federal leader, was in the midst of the people so long as they kept the tables of the covenant that were kept in the ark and so long as they adhered only to God. The people were to look for all good things through Christ, which the ark prefigured. DECADES 3.5.[10]

BUILT AROUND THE WORD OF GOD. JOHANNES BUGENHAGEN: The temple had an outer walkway, which in John 10 was called the colonnade of Solomon. I believe this is where the people stood when the priest annually atoned for the temple and the holy of holies with blood, corresponding to how the temple had three stories: this one, a middle one and an upper room. For there were times when the priest was not allowed to stand in the open air because of the people's sin but rather went alone into the tabernacle to make atonement, as it says in Leviticus 16. At that hour incense was burned over all the people outside, as in Luke 1. Next was the sacred space called the "court of the Gentiles," where offerings of incense were made on a golden altar, with golden lamps and a table for bread, of which we will say more below. This place

---

[10]Bullinger, *Sermonum decades quinque*, 150-151; citing Col 1:19; 1 Jn 2:2; Mk 9:7; 1 Pet 1:12.

was open so that all of its astonishing glory could be clearly seen by the world, as you see here. Third was the holy of holies, in which they spoke the oracles. This place had no outside light, so that no one could look inside and none of the glory could be seen (even that which was only glorious), for without its other spiritual aspects it would have been a sham and hypocrisy. For here was the ark containing the tablets written by the finger of God, which are themselves a kind of container of the church. This is the Word of God, which holds the one who makes atonement, covered in a golden crown, who is Christ the king, the head and protector of the church, as was promised in Exodus 25 and Exodus 29. God has sat among the people, taught and listened. In this glorious temple, songs were sung and prayers were made, but the dark holiness was respected as the songs and prayers were heard. COMMENTARY ON 1 KINGS.[11]

THREE PARTS OF THE OUTER COURT. JOHN

MAYER: The inner court . . . was next to the temple before the porch. And beyond that eastward was another court into which came the people so that they might look into it and see the altar that stood there, along with the priests offering their sacrifices on it. The outer court was called the great court. It was so spacious that it compassed the inner court and the temple around it, having a wall thirty cubits high to which galleries were adjoined within which the people could stand and be sheltered in rainy weather and from the heat of the sun. From there they could see both what was done in the inner court and see the temple and worship toward it, for they were not able to enter the inner court. Only the priests and Levites were allowed in it to execute their office by preparing and offering their sacrifices on the altar that stood there. They washed these sacrifices in the brazen sea, which also stood there. They cut them out on tables, of which eight stood there, and they washed themselves in ten lavers that were also placed there. Both

this court and the other bore the name of the temple, and therefore when it is later said that the brazen sea and these have been placed on the sides of the temple, it is to be understood in this court.

And when Jesus is said to have taught in the temple, it was in the outer court. Of this there were three parts: first, for the men of Israel to enter who were clean; second, for the women who were also clean; and third, for the unclean and for the Gentiles, who came there to worship. And the temple stood on a mount, to which they ascended by degrees. The same is also probably true for Herod's temple, seeing that Solomon's temple was a pattern propounded in the building of it. And if it had varied from it, it would not have been accepted by the Jews, whom Herod tried to please by building such a costly building. COMMENTARY ON 1 KINGS.[12]

PILLARS AS A TYPE OF THE FAITHFUL.

JOHANNES PISCATOR: Two of these bronze pillars were a type of the faithful and particularly the first Christian martyrs. We read this from the words of Christ to the church in Philadelphia in the Apocalypse: "The one who conquers, I will make him a pillar in the temple of my God." The faithful remain firm in the faith in persisting through God's grace, and their faith conquers the world. COMMENTARY ON 1 KINGS.[13]

SYMBOLISM WITHIN THE TEMPLE. JOHANNES

BUGENHAGEN: The two cherubim that were posed as if flying are the two testaments, as it says in the Psalm, "He sends out his command to the earth; his word runs swiftly." The wings touched in the middle, because they offer mutual care and turn their faces in respect to Christ, who makes atonement. The colonnade, outer walkway and atrium signify teaching, in which the young are held and encouraged so that they might come to Christ. The middle court is death, because all people are included within the temple until that which lies within the

---

[11]Bugenhagen, *In Regum duos ultimos libros*, 29-30; citing Jn 10:23; Lk 1:8-10; Ex 25:8, 22; 29:42-46.

[12]Mayer, *Many Commentaries in One*, 33*.
[13]Piscator, *Commentarii in omnes libros Veteris Testamenti*, 2:269; citing Rev 3:12.

holy of holies is revealed. The holy of holies is the gospel and the kingdom of heaven, in which there is no light of human reason or wisdom, because God is light, as in Isaiah 60, where God's holiness is with all people, though it is not seen by the world. We truly enter here following the way of blood revealed by our high priest Christ. (See the letter to the Hebrews.) The windows of the temple are the preaching of the Word, as in "Your word is a lamp to my feet and a light to my path," and in Isaiah, "Who are these that fly like a cloud, and like doves to their windows?" For what would the glory of the temple be without these windows, that is, light? Ascending the steps to the higher and broader story means growing in the Word, so that you might rise to the maturity of the soul's breadth until you reach the ceiling, that is, Christ the head. The hewn stones "prepared at the quarry" are the true Christians of whom the church is built. Therefore no hammer was heard among these, for they do not need any other fastening or forging, for Christians do not oppose judgment nor fight with the sword, etc. The gate in the middle of the right wall is Christ: "I am the door. If anyone enters by me, he will be saved and will go in and out and find pasture," etc. The walls are living stones, as in 1 Peter 2. These are covered in a wedding garment, cedar and fir trees, wood that is not only incorruptible when dry but also odiferous, just as the bride is said to smell of the woods of the region of Lebanon in Song of Solomon 4. "For we are the aroma of Christ to God among those who are being saved and among those who are perishing." This wood is overlaid with pure gold, for nothing else is seen in this temple except the pure wisdom of the Word of God in its entire sense, because peaceful Christians do not know separation. This is signified in how they are covered with a single gold patina, even though they may appear as diverse engravings or pictures, which are the various gifts and ministries of the church (1 Cor 12 and Eph 4). These are all described in Psalm 45, "your robes are all fragrant with myrrh and aloes and cassia. . . . At your right hand stands the queen dressed in gold, surrounded by varieties . . . All glorious is the princess in her chamber, with robes interwoven with gold." Commentary on 1 Kings.[14]

The Bond of Charity. Johann Gerhard: Charity is the bond of Christian perfection, just as the members of the body are joined together by the Spirit, that is, the soul. So the true members of the body are united by the Holy Spirit in the bond of charity. In Solomon's temple everything was covered "in pure gold." In the same way, in the spiritual temple of God, let all be decorated inside and outside in charity. Let charity move your heart to compassion and your hand to contribution. Compassion is not enough unless there is also outward contribution. Neither is outward contribution enough unless there is also inward compassion. Faith accepts everything from God, and charity gives everything back to your neighbor. Sacred Meditations.[15]

Sacred Vessels Like Spiritual Gifts. Johannes Piscator: In Solomon's temple there were various vessels that were used in various ways, but nevertheless they were all sacred. Also, there were some things that were of more precious value than another—for instance, one thing was made of bronze while another was made of gold—but they were still all precious. In the same way in the church of the faithful, some of the spiritual gifts excel those of others, but all the gifts nonetheless serve God. Commentary on 1 Kings.[16]

Symbolic Features of the Temple. John Mayer: And for the conclusion about this magnificent building, it is to be understood that it was figurative, as the tabernacle set up by Moses prefigured the old church of the Jews. In the same way, this house was figurative of the church of the Gentiles, which was built long after in the days of Christ the true Solomon, on Mount Moriah in a parcel of ground belonging to Araunah, a Gentile. And it was

---

[14]Bugenhagen, *In Regum duos ultimos libros*, 30-32; citing Ps 147:15. Also citing Ps 119:105; Is 60:8; Jn 10:9; 1 Pet 2:5, Song 4:8, 11; 2 Cor 2:15; 1 Cor 12; Eph 4:4-16; Ps 45:8-9, 13, following Vg at v. 9.
[15]Gerhard, *Gerhardi Meditationes Sacrae*, 161-62.
[16]Piscator, *Commentarii in omnes libros Veteris Testamenti*, 2:269.

set up on a mountain because this church was most conspicuous, and it consisted of these parts:

First, the doors all stood eastward toward the rising of the sun so that it might shine on them. The sunlight shone first on the porch to show that the heavenly light, by which the church is enlightened, shines first to those of the primitive times who lived in the days of Christ and his apostles. It then shone to those who lived in the times immediately succeeding the ministry of those who were raised up after the apostles in the times of those grievous persecutions. And it then shone on those who lived in the days of Constantine the Great and afterward, when the church experienced peace.

Second, this house had windows that were narrow inside and wider outside. This was to show the light of teaching, which increases more and more. And all the walls, and all things about it, were covered with gold and set with precious stones and adorned with many pictures to show the many virtues that shine in the faithful.

Third, the galleries about the temple of these stories figured the many degrees of the faithful. And the door on the right side of the temple, by which they ascended into all these galleries, figured the side of Christ pierced with a spear, out of which flowed water and blood, which was a figure of both sacraments.

Fourth, the pavement of marble covered with fir set forth faith in the heart, as well as a heavenly conversation outwardly. The fir tree aptly signified this by its straight and high growth. And the plates of gold above all these signified love.

Finally, the partition between the temple and the most holy place was twenty cubits high through which none might enter save only the high priest only once a year. Yet the sum of the incense went daily through the void room above this wall into it. This showed that although no one could enter into heaven until death, their prayers, as sweet as perfume, continually entered heaven while they lived and were accepted by God. COMMENTARY ON 1 KINGS.[17]

7:1-12 Solomon Builds His Palace

BUILDING UP THE SPIRIT, THEN THE BODY.
JOHANNES BUGENHAGEN: Solomon not only built the things that pertain to God, that is, spiritual things, but he also built up those things that pertain to human life. Admired by all in all things, he gave here a sample of his wisdom and intelligence that had been given by God. First he built a house for the Lord, then he provided for everything else. This is the correct order, that we seek first the kingdom of God then turn our attention and cares to that which has been entrusted to us. This signifies that the kingdom of Christ is established not only for matters of faith but also for the wise administration of external things, so that everything might be (according to Paul) "for building you up and not for destroying you." COMMENTARY ON 1 KINGS.[18]

BUILDING HIS HOUSE. KONRAD PELLIKAN: The fourth thing Solomon built was his own house, in which (according to Hebrew custom) he would live with his family for eating, drinking, sleeping and other things. It was constructed like the other buildings, using precious wood and stones, as the text describes. Next to this house was a wide courtyard, which was between his house and the throne room. Also attached to a different part of the king's palace was the house of the queen, who was Pharaoh's daughter and Solomon's wife. COMMENTARY ON 1 KINGS.[19]

THE ROYAL PALACE. GIOVANNI DIODATI: This referred to Solomon's royal palace, which, as it is thought, had three bodies of buildings, severed from each other by great courts. One building was for the king; one was for the queen; and the third was for pleasure and for public feasts, games, pastimes, orchards, walks, gardens and groves. And in this third building was also the magazine of arms, which were of great value. The palace was

---

[17]Mayer, *Many Commentaries in One*, 33-34*.

[18]Bugenhagen, *In Regum duos ultimos libros*, 37; citing 2 Cor 10:8. [19]Pellikan, *Commentaria Bibliorum*, 2:148v.

called the house of the forest of Lebanon, whether it was by reason of the groves planted about it or by reason of the great number of cedar columns brought from Lebanon of which it consisted.

Now this building was contrived after this manner: In the middle there was a great vacant space from the very ground to the roof; it was majestically covered with a vault of timberwork and about it there were three stories of galleries or porticoes over one another. Each portico was born up by two rows of columns on each side, which made the four rows of columns or pillars. And they were put together in this way: The first row joined to the wall and bore up the beams that rested on the other row of columns, which were of the same level. ANNOTATIONS ON 1 KINGS.[20]

7:13-51 Temple Furnishings

OUTLASTING GOLDEN SPLENDORS. KONRAD PELLIKAN: What has been described here is not how Solomon built and decorated all these things according to some commandment that God had given him. He was not a steadfast person; accordingly he built all these things not according to a clear command of God but according to human inclinations. They pleased God a little, insofar as the people were drawn to the worship of God through such splendor built by Gentiles, by admiration for such great ceremonies and by the beautiful sanctuary, which had no equal in the world. But after enough time had passed and the foundations were carried off for the worship of idols, the institution of the true worship of the true God in spirit and truth across the whole world outlasted all these golden splendors. Then the hearts of the elect imbibed the spirit of piety that is worthy of honor and gives reason to serve it. COMMENTARY ON 1 KINGS.[21]

THE TWO PILLARS OF BRONZE. JOHANNES BUGENHAGEN: These two pillars were placed at the vestibule of the temple. They supported nothing. Did Solomon therefore fashion them only for great ornamentation? I do not believe so. The pillars are seen as signifying that earlier time when God used to appear before the tabernacle as a pillar of cloud. Because the people are the temple, these columns took them back to remembering when God used to lead the people as a pillar in the desert. This was the Spirit of God. It was one, but it was seen as two pillars, because it appeared one way during the day and another way at night. Therefore Solomon placed the pillar of cloud to the right to give shade during the day, and he placed the pillar of fire to the left to give light, illumination and warmth at night. This is how members of the church of God ought to interpret Isaiah 4: "Then the Lord will create over the whole site of Mount Zion and over her assemblies a cloud by day, and smoke and the shining of a flaming fire by night; for over all the glory there will be a canopy. There will be a booth for shade by day from the heat, and for a refuge and a shelter from the storm and rain." COMMENTARY ON 1 KINGS.[22]

THE NAMES OF THE PILLARS. JOHANNES BUGENHAGEN: The pillar on the right was called Jachin, which means "is established, right, perfect and blessed." For thus it leads us to where we delight in the consolation of the Spirit and are freed from temptations, so that all of us might be built up. The pillar on the left was called Boaz, that is, "strength." For the work of the Spirit in great strength is that we may persevere whenever adversity assails us, as during temptations or persecutions. COMMENTARY ON 1 KINGS.[23]

THE CAPITALS DEPICT THE FRUIT OF THE SPIRIT. JOHANNES BUGENHAGEN: The capitals at the tops of the pillars had images of fruit on the tree. These may be understood as sound doctrine,

---

[20]Diodati, *Pious Annotations*, 5*.
[21]Pellikan, *Commentaria Bibliorum*, 2:150r.

[22]Bugenhagen, *In Regum duos ultimos libros*, 40; citing Ex 13:21; Is 4:5-6. The Vulgate describes the two pillars as being placed to the "right" and to the "left" of the temple. The ESV describes them as being at the north and south of the temple respectively.
[23]Bugenhagen, *In Regum duos ultimos libros*, 40-41.

which is produced by the Spirit of God in the church for our instruction, whether one turns to the right or the left. The pillars are the Spirit, when it inwardly leads and teaches us; the capitals are then what the Spirit produces in us when we are taught by it. And the lattices all around are themselves love, in which we are mutually held and made one and experience the same good things. The pomegranates that hang on the two rows are the fruit of the Spirit and works of love (Gal 5), just as it says in the Song of Solomon, "Your shoots are an orchard of pomegranates with all choicest fruits." For love does not come from itself, but it happens among two and belongs by necessity to another. These lattices are doubled, one set on one pillar and another set on the other, and each one has two rows of pomegranates, one above and one below, so that everywhere the two rows of pomegranates are seen to be connected. Each row contains one hundred pomegranates; that is, there is a multiplication of the fruit of the Spirit and works of love (which are set up in the two rows), so that you may see that everything returns to this binary number of love. The lily (or rose) that appears over all of this signifies the external conversion of Christians: for the world wonders that we are not in the same foul distress as others (as Peter says), but it does not see the root that produces these fruits. COMMENTARY ON 1 KINGS.[24]

MYSTICAL MEANING OF TEMPLE FURNISHINGS. JOHN MAYER: The brazen sea prefigured baptism, where all the priests, that is, the elect, wash themselves and are cleansed so they may appear acceptably before God. And it is well called a sea because a natural sea, that is, the Red Sea, first prefigured baptism.... The twelve oxen, which bore up this sea, prefigured the twelve apostles, who went into all parts of the world teaching and baptizing. Three looked to the east, three to the west, three to the north and three to the south.

That oxen aptly resemble preachers is shown in 1 Corinthians, where it is said: "You shall not muzzle an ox when it treads out the grain."

The sea contained two thousand baths to show that out of the baptism prefigured here came two peoples, the Jews and the Gentiles. The ten bases bearing up the lavers, in which the sacrifices were washed and afterward put on the altar to be burned with fire, also prefigured the preachers of the Word, by whose ministry the elect are washed in baptism as priests to serve God at his altar. As they are washed as offerings by the imposition of hands, the Holy Spirit as fire came on them and made them sacrifices to God, which is when they are filled with his guilt. The accomplishment of this is most notably to be seen in the believing Samaritans, baptized by Philip, but afterward by the imposition of the hands of Peter receiving the Holy Spirit.

The four wheels that each of these bases had set forth the four Evangelists on which they ran into all parts and their answer to one another in all things the harmony between the Evangelists. The lavers set on these bases contained forty baths, said Bede, to show that all those who are truly baptized believe the faith set forth in the four Gospels and keep the commandments, because ten multiplied by four makes forty. And to show that baptism was hereby prefigured, all these vessels were made near the Jordan River, where Christ was baptized. COMMENTARY ON 1 KINGS.[25]

THE OXEN SUPPORTING THE SEA. JOHANNES BUGENHAGEN: The sea of cast metal was carried by twelve oxen, that is, by preaching to the four corners of the earth. These threshing oxen do not need an allegory, for as Paul said, they labor in the Lord's fields, leading others to bathe in the Word. The oxen's rears lay beneath the sea, because the Word covers our weaker members, bathing them in the Word too. As Paul said, "We have this treasure in jars of clay, to show that the surpassing power belongs to God and not to us." You see their feet and mouth, so that you might see how they

---

[24]Bugenhagen, *In Regum duos ultimos libros*, 41-42; citing Gal 5:22-23; Song 4:13; 1 Pet 4:4.

[25]Mayer, *Many Commentaries in One*, 37*; citing 1 Cor 9:9.

tread and hear what they preach. Entrust their weaker members to God, for you may be offended by the weakness of those who bring the Word to you and prayers to God, which they do to redeem you from your wickedness and impiety. COMMENTARY ON 1 KINGS.[26]

---

[26]Bugenhagen, *In Regum duos ultimos libros*, 42-43; citing 2 Tm 2:6; 2 Cor 4:7.

8:1-66 THE DEDICATION OF THE TEMPLE

[1]Then Solomon assembled the elders of Israel and all the heads of the tribes, the leaders of the fathers' houses of the people of Israel, before King Solomon in Jerusalem, to bring up the ark of the covenant of the LORD out of the city of David, which is Zion. [2]And all the men of Israel assembled to King Solomon at the feast in the month Ethanim, which is the seventh month. [3]And all the elders of Israel came, and the priests took up the ark. [4]And they brought up the ark of the LORD, the tent of meeting, and all the holy vessels that were in the tent; the priests and the Levites brought them up. [5]And King Solomon and all the congregation of Israel, who had assembled before him, were with him before the ark, sacrificing so many sheep and oxen that they could not be counted or numbered. [6]Then the priests brought the ark of the covenant of the LORD to its place in the inner sanctuary of the house, in the Most Holy Place, underneath the wings of the cherubim. [7]For the cherubim spread out their wings over the place of the ark, so that the cherubim overshadowed the ark and its poles. [8]And the poles were so long that the ends of the poles were seen from the Holy Place before the inner sanctuary; but they could not be seen from outside. And they are there to this day. [9]There was nothing in the ark except the two tablets of stone that Moses put there at Horeb, where the LORD made a covenant with the people of Israel, when they came out of the land of Egypt. [10]And when the priests came out of the Holy Place, a cloud filled the house of the LORD, [11]so that the priests could not stand to minister because of the cloud, for the glory of the LORD filled the house of the LORD.

[12]Then Solomon said, "The LORD[a] has said that he would dwell in thick darkness. [13]I have indeed built you an exalted house, a place for you to dwell in forever." [14]Then the king turned around and blessed all the assembly of Israel, while all the assembly of Israel stood. [15]And he said, "Blessed be the LORD, the God of Israel, who with his hand has fulfilled what he promised with his mouth to David my father, saying, [16]'Since the day that I brought my people Israel out of Egypt, I chose no city out of all the tribes of Israel in which to build a house, that my name might be there. But I chose David to be over my people Israel.' [17]Now it was in the heart of David my father to build a house for the name of the LORD, the God of Israel. [18]But the LORD said to David my father, 'Whereas it was in your heart to build a house for my name, you did well that it was in your heart. [19]Nevertheless, you shall not build the house, but your son who shall be born to you shall build the house for my name.' [20]Now the LORD has fulfilled his promise that he made. For I have risen in the place of David my father, and sit on the throne of Israel, as the LORD promised, and I have built the house for the name of the LORD, the God of Israel. [21]And there I have provided a place for the ark, in which is the covenant of the LORD that he made with our fathers, when he brought them out of the land of Egypt."

[22]Then Solomon stood before the altar of the LORD in the presence of all the assembly of Israel and spread out his hands toward heaven, [23]and said, "O LORD, God of Israel, there is no God like you, in heaven above or on earth beneath, keeping covenant and showing steadfast love to your servants who walk before you with all their heart; [24]you have kept with your servant David my father what you declared to him. You spoke with your mouth, and with your hand have fulfilled it this day. [25]Now therefore, O LORD, God of Israel, keep for your servant David my father what you have promised him, saying, 'You shall not lack a man to sit before me on the throne of Israel, if only your sons pay close attention to their way, to walk before me as you have walked before me.' [26]Now therefore, O God of Israel, let your word be confirmed, which you have spoken to your servant David my father.

[27]"But will God indeed dwell on the earth? Behold, heaven and the highest heaven cannot contain you; how much less this house that I have built! [28]Yet have regard to the prayer of your servant and to his plea, O LORD my God, listening to the cry and to the prayer that your servant prays before you this day, [29]that your eyes may be open night and day toward this house, the

place of which you have said, 'My name shall be there,' that you may listen to the prayer that your servant offers toward this place. ³⁰And listen to the plea of your servant and of your people Israel, when they pray toward this place. And listen in heaven your dwelling place, and when you hear, forgive.

³¹"If a man sins against his neighbor and is made to take an oath and comes and swears his oath before your altar in this house, ³²then hear in heaven and act and judge your servants, condemning the guilty by bringing his conduct on his own head, and vindicating the righteous by rewarding him according to his righteousness.

³³"When your people Israel are defeated before the enemy because they have sinned against you, and if they turn again to you and acknowledge your name and pray and plead with you in this house, ³⁴then hear in heaven and forgive the sin of your people Israel and bring them again to the land that you gave to their fathers.

³⁵"When heaven is shut up and there is no rain because they have sinned against you, if they pray toward this place and acknowledge your name and turn from their sin, when you afflict them, ³⁶then hear in heaven and forgive the sin of your servants, your people Israel, when you teach them the good way in which they should walk, and grant rain upon your land, which you have given to your people as an inheritance.

³⁷"If there is famine in the land, if there is pestilence or blight or mildew or locust or caterpillar, if their enemy besieges them in the land at their gates,[b] whatever plague, whatever sickness there is, ³⁸whatever prayer, whatever plea is made by any man or by all your people Israel, each knowing the affliction of his own heart and stretching out his hands toward this house, ³⁹then hear in heaven your dwelling place and forgive and act and render to each whose heart you know, according to all his ways (for you, you only, know the hearts of all the children of mankind), ⁴⁰that they may fear you all the days that they live in the land that you gave to our fathers.

⁴¹"Likewise, when a foreigner, who is not of your people Israel, comes from a far country for your name's sake ⁴²(for they shall hear of your great name

and your mighty hand, and of your outstretched arm), when he comes and prays toward this house, ⁴³hear in heaven your dwelling place and do according to all for which the foreigner calls to you, in order that all the peoples of the earth may know your name and fear you, as do your people Israel, and that they may know that this house that I have built is called by your name.

⁴⁴"If your people go out to battle against their enemy, by whatever way you shall send them, and they pray to the LORD toward the city that you have chosen and the house that I have built for your name, ⁴⁵then hear in heaven their prayer and their plea, and maintain their cause.

⁴⁶"If they sin against you—for there is no one who does not sin—and you are angry with them and give them to an enemy, so that they are carried away captive to the land of the enemy, far off or near, ⁴⁷yet if they turn their heart in the land to which they have been carried captive, and repent and plead with you in the land of their captors, saying, 'We have sinned and have acted perversely and wickedly,' ⁴⁸if they repent with all their mind and with all their heart in the land of their enemies, who carried them captive, and pray to you toward their land, which you gave to their fathers, the city that you have chosen, and the house that I have built for your name, ⁴⁹then hear in heaven your dwelling place their prayer and their plea, and maintain their cause ⁵⁰and forgive your people who have sinned against you, and all their transgressions that they have committed against you, and grant them compassion in the sight of those who carried them captive, that they may have compassion on them ⁵¹(for they are your people, and your heritage, which you brought out of Egypt, from the midst of the iron furnace). ⁵²Let your eyes be open to the plea of your servant and to the plea of your people Israel, giving ear to them whenever they call to you. ⁵³For you separated them from among all the peoples of the earth to be your heritage, as you declared through Moses your servant, when you brought our fathers out of Egypt, O LORD God."

⁵⁴Now as Solomon finished offering all this prayer and plea to the LORD, he arose from before the altar of the LORD, where he had knelt with hands outstretched

toward heaven. ⁵⁵And he stood and blessed all the assembly of Israel with a loud voice, saying, ⁵⁶"Blessed be the Lord who has given rest to his people Israel, according to all that he promised. Not one word has failed of all his good promise, which he spoke by Moses his servant. ⁵⁷The Lord our God be with us, as he was with our fathers. May he not leave us or forsake us, ⁵⁸that he may incline our hearts to him, to walk in all his ways and to keep his commandments, his statutes, and his rules, which he commanded our fathers. ⁵⁹Let these words of mine, with which I have pleaded before the Lord, be near to the Lord our God day and night, and may he maintain the cause of his servant and the cause of his people Israel, as each day requires, ⁶⁰that all the peoples of the earth may know that the Lord is God; there is no other. ⁶¹Let your heart therefore be wholly true to the Lord our God, walking in his statutes and keeping his commandments, as at this day."

⁶²Then the king, and all Israel with him, offered sacrifice before the Lord. ⁶³Solomon offered as peace offerings to the Lord 22,000 oxen and 120,000 sheep. So the king and all the people of Israel dedicated the house of the Lord. ⁶⁴The same day the king consecrated the middle of the court that was before the house of the Lord, for there he offered the burnt offering and the grain offering and the fat pieces of the peace offerings, because the bronze altar that was before the Lord was too small to receive the burnt offering and the grain offering and the fat pieces of the peace offerings.

⁶⁵So Solomon held the feast at that time, and all Israel with him, a great assembly, from Lebo-hamath to the Brook of Egypt, before the Lord our God, seven days.ᶜ ⁶⁶On the eighth day he sent the people away, and they blessed the king and went to their homes joyful and glad of heart for all the goodness that the Lord had shown to David his servant and to Israel his people.

a Septuagint *The Lord has set the sun in the heavens, but*   b Septuagint, Syriac *in any of their cities*   c Septuagint; Hebrew *seven days and seven days, fourteen days*

Overview: The dedication of the temple marks an important transition in the Old Testament from the time of the tent of meeting to the time of the temple. The commentators here recognize that Solomon oversees the dedication and blessing of the temple in Jerusalem as not only the king of Israel but also as teacher and priest. The reformers also draw attention to Solomon's prayer about foreigners coming to worship the true God in Jerusalem, foreshadowing the preaching of the gospel to all peoples after the time of Christ in the book of Acts.

is the one who makes atonement, and above the one who makes atonement is God, as was described about the ark and the cherubim. The old tabernacle became inactive after it had been led into the new temple, for the law ceases through the gospel which makes all things new. Here the priests and the Levites bring everything in; that is, they are ministers of the gospel. The people truly sacrificed countless animals; that is, they offered themselves to God as it says in Romans 12. Any other external sacrifice is hypocrisy, as is interpreted by all the prophets. Commentary on 1 Kings.[1]

8:1-13 A Permanent House of God

The Law Inscribed on the Heart. Johannes Bugenhagen: The ark was led with the old tabernacle into this new temple, where it would not be moved. This move means that Solomon (that is, Christ) leads his church into the gospel, for the ark contained that law was covered, signifying the new law inscribed on the heart. Above the law

A Home for the Covenant. Konrad Pellikan: Because of the law and the covenant of the Lord that it contained, the ark was holy and venerated. Up to this point it had not had a fixed location but was moved according to changing and uncertain circumstances and times. But after the construction of the temple, which had been spoken

---

[1]Bugenhagen, *In Regum duos ultimos libros,* 45; citing Rom 12:1.

of from eternity, it was allowed that the divine presence of the sacramental ark could be moved this last little bit. From this time on, the covenant was firmly and assuredly fixed: the kingdom of the eternal son of David would be preserved until the new covenant would be established for all ages and all peoples. COMMENTARY ON 1 KINGS.[2]

THE HISTORY OF THE TABERNACLE. THE ENGLISH ANNOTATIONS: Moses originally made the tabernacle.... As a sacred monument it was now laid up in the temple, never to be removed again as it had been in former times. For, first, in the wilderness it was carried up and down for the space of forty years. It then abode in Gilgal for fourteen years. Next it remained in Shiloh until Samuel's time. Thereafter it was in Nob until Saul destroyed that place, and it was in Gibeon all of David's life. And, finally, from there it was brought into Zion to be accompanied with the ark into the temple. ANNOTATIONS ON 1 KINGS.[3]

GOD'S HOUSE. THOMAS ADAMS: It is vain to ask what God should do with a house, given what we do in our own: what but dwell in it? Instead the real question revolves around asking in what way God dwells in his house. THE TEMPLE.[4]

8:14-53 Solomon's Speech and Prayer

DOCTOR SOLOMON. VIKTORIN STRIGEL: As we have seen elsewhere, Solomon was not only a king but also a teacher of the church [*doctor Ecclesiae*]. Just as it belonged to his kingly duties to build the temple, so now he takes up the teaching office: pronouncing blessing on the people, giving thanks and invoking God on behalf of himself and the entire assembly. In this thanksgiving he was honoring the truth of the divine promise, which was being confirmed in his presence and in the

presence of the people against the doubts that otherwise overwhelm individuals like a darkness. For ugly doubts continuously assail people, through which the devil overthrows and separates many from God, saying, "Is God really a healer of people? Is the teaching of the church really true?" Souls can be greatly tormented through such afflictions and increasing hardships, which Paul called "the flaming darts of the evil one." But with faith as a shield, such things are opposed and repelled, because faith surrounds doctrine. It truly prepares us to be healed, heard and protected by God. It affirms that we are children of God, guarded by the very present hand of God, just as God "causes his glorious arm to go at the right hand of Moses, who divided the waters before them," as it says in Isaiah 63. BOOK OF KINGS.[5]

THE POSTURE AND FORM OF PRAYER. VIKTORIN STRIGEL: As he began his prayer, Solomon lifted his eyes and his hands to heaven. This gesture signifies a remarkable and momentous movement of the heart and the soul. Although it would have been possible for him to pray silently, the text here wants to describe the posture of the one praying so that we might remember it about our teacher Solomon. We should thus be taught through the speech of others, and we should make use of such pious forms and learned compositions without superstition and without magic. First, he distinguished the God of Israel from all creatures and idols. Second, he approached God not on the basis of his own worthiness but through faith in the promise of the Mediator. Third, he named the thing he was praying about. Finally, he eloquently pronounced the final cause, that is, the reason why we and the church are bringing this matter before God in prayer. BOOK OF KINGS.[6]

GOD CANNOT BE CONTAINED. JOHANNES BUGENHAGEN: Solomon said, "Behold, heaven and

---

[2]Pellikan, *Commentaria Bibliorum*, 2:151r.

[3]Downame, ed., *Annotations* (1645), IIIr*; citing Ex 36:8; 40:2; Josh 4:20; 18:1; 1 Sam 4:4; Ps 78:60; Jer 7:12; 1 Sam 21:1; 22:19; 1 Chron 16:39; 2 Macc 2:5.

[4]Adams, *The Temple*, 7*.

[5]Strigel, *Libri Samuelis, Regum et Paralipomenon*, 230-31; citing Eph 6:16; Is 63:12.

[6]Strigel, *Libri Samuelis, Regum et Paralipomenon*, 231.

the highest heaven cannot contain you; how much less this house that I have built!" He thought little of the house in itself, even though it was honored as God's inhabitance. And if the house is nothing without God, then the same is true of all people who themselves go without God, so that you see that faith alone is what is commended to them all. Thus what Solomon offers is a prayer of faith about the house, as it says in the last chapter of Isaiah and in Deuteronomy 12. COMMENTARY ON 1 KINGS.[7]

OUR POSTURE WHEN PRAYING. JOHN MAYER: The corresponding passage in 2 Chronicles 6:13 says that Solomon set up a brazen scaffold and, from there, that he kneeled to the ground, stretched out his hand and prayed. He is said to have kneeled on both his knees. This scaffold was set up so that he might be seen and heard better by the people around him. He bowed his knees for reverence to God, as we ought also to do. We are especially to do this in our public prayers because this gesture is commended to us in the holy Scriptures, although it is not to be doubted that devout and humble prayers made in faith are accepted in whatever position of the body in which a person may give them. For instance, a person may be standing, walking, riding, lying down or sitting. And in prayer we must lift up our hands to show that we look for all our help and comfort from heaven. COMMENTARY ON 1 KINGS.[8]

WISE ADVICE. LANCELOT ANDREWES: Without keeping from sin, there is no keeping with God— out of whose keeping there is no safety. This advice is so fitting, so agreeable to reason and religion both. As it is in every way for our good, it remains for us to set ourselves to think of it and keep it. "Each one aware of the afflictions of his own heart," Solomon says, "in famine or plague," whatever sins have grieved God—everyone should make a covenant with themselves to henceforth to stand

more carefully on their guard and not go forth to sin or entertain sin as a friend. Rather, they should repute it as an enemy and keep themselves from it. ON REPENTANCE AND FASTING: SERMON 2.[9]

GOD'S IMMENSITY. JACOBUS ARMINIUS: Immensity is a preeminent mode of the essence of God, by which it is void of place according to space and limits: Being coextended space, because it belongs to simple entity, not having part and part, therefore not having part beyond part. Being also its own encircling limits, or beyond which it has no existence, because it is of infinite entity. And before all things, God alone was both the world, and place, and all things to himself; but he was alone, because there was nothing outwardly beyond, except himself. DISPUTATION 4: ON THE NATURE OF GOD.[10]

SOLOMON PRAYS FOR FOREIGNERS. HENRY AINSWORTH: When Solomon dedicated the temple, he prayed even for strangers who dwelt in far countries to come to pray in this house when they heard about God, "so that all peoples of the earth may know your name and fear you." DEFENSE OF HOLY SCRIPTURES.[11]

PRAYER FOR GENTILES. JOHN MAYER: Here is the fifth particular case of foreigners, that is, those not of the seed of Abraham, coming to the temple to pray. For a court was to be made just as much for those who were not yet clean as for those, namely, the Jews, who were already clean. And this was done to allure the Gentiles to the worship of the true God. This was not done in vain, because many went there to worship and learn the knowledge of God. Such is seen in the steward of the queen of Ethiopia in Acts 8 and in the gathering of foreigners from all the nations in Acts 2. And it is not to be doubted that this passage is prophetic of the nations flowing to the mountain of the Lord and coming up to it in Isaiah 2. Solomon prays that the Lord would hear and and grant all of the prayers of

---

[7]Bugenhagen, *In Regum duos ultimos libros*, 47-48; citing Is 66:1; Deut 12:30.
[8]Mayer, *Many Commentaries in One*, 41*.
[9]Andrewes, *Ninety-Six Sermons*, 1:333*.
[10]Arminius, *Works*, 1:440*.
[11]Ainsworth, *Defence of the Holy Scriptures*, 52*.

the strangers, which, as the rabbis note, indicates that Solomon prayed more for the Gentiles than for the Israelites. That's because to have everything granted that a person desires is a greater thing than to be dealt with according to his ways. But the rabbis say that Solomon prayed in this way for the Gentiles because they were ignorant of the laws of God. Therefore, if God should have done for them according to their ways, none of their petitions could have been granted. However, from the Israelites, who knew the law and were instructed in it, it was expected that they could pray for the foreigners. COMMENTARY ON 1 KINGS.[12]

ROTTENNESS OF THE FLESH. JOHN CALVIN: We confess that while through the intercession of Christ's righteousness God reconciles us to himself, and by free remission of sins accounts us righteous, his beneficence is at the same time joined with such a mercy that through his Holy Spirit he dwells in us, and by his power the lusts of our flesh are each day more and more mortified. We are indeed sanctified, that is, consecrated to the Lord in true purity of life, with our hearts formed to obedience to the law. The end is that out especial will may be made to serve his will and by every means to advance his glory alone. But even while by the leading of the Holy Spirit we walk in the ways of the Lord, to keep us from forgetting ourselves and becoming puffed up, traces of out imperfection remain to give us occasion for our humility. Scripture says: There is no righteous one, no one who will do good and not sin. What sort of righteousness will they obtain, then, from their works? First, I say that the best work that can be brought forward from them is still always spotted and corrupted with some impurity of the flesh, and has, so to speak, some dregs mixed with it. Let a holy servant of God, I say, choose from the whole course of life what of an especially noteworthy character he thinks he has done. Let him well turn over in his mind its several parts. Undoubtedly he will somewhere perceive that it savors of the

rottenness of flesh, since our eagerness for well-doing is never what it ought to be but our great weakness slows down our running in the race. . . . We have not a single work going forth from the saints that if it be judged in itself deserves not shame as its just reward. INSTITUTES 3.14.9.[13]

8:54-61 Solomon's Blessing of the Assembly

SOLOMON'S GOSPEL PRAYER. JOHANNES BUGENHAGEN: The dedication of the temple saw a seven-day celebration, for through the gospel we devote ourselves to God during all the time we live here on earth (which is what these seven days represent), after which we shall see God "face to face," for now we see in part and in mystery, that is, we say that you see this dimly. On top of this, nothing is more important than Solomon's thanksgiving for the promise that God had watched over them and his prayers for the Israelites and Gentiles, which was pure gospel; that is, it is the true promise of God and the forgiveness of sins. COMMENTARY ON 1 KINGS.[14]

THE HEIGHT OF PIETY. KONRAD PELLIKAN: Many ceremonies were required of the people of Israel, testing their frequent lapses into Gentile ceremonies. Therefore Solomon their king did not pray without ceremony, so that the faithful should not scorn such things if their hearts express devotion and not the mere hypocrisy that angers the Lord. Such hypocrisy and lack of fear before God's face does not impress him who regards the heart and searches the innermost parts. Accordingly Solomon bent his knee and prayed with hands outstretched to heaven. Then he rose and prayed intensely for every one of the people with a clear voice. Again he began to give thanks, diligently driving home the true promise of God, so that they might adhere to a sure faith in the Lord, always faithfully and entirely depending on God's

---

[12]Mayer, *Many Commentaries in One*, 42-43*.

[13]LCC 20:776-77 (CO 2:570); citing 1 Kings 8:46.
[14]Bugenhagen, *In Regum duos ultimos libros*, 45-46; citing 1 Cor 13:12.

grace. This is the height of piety. COMMENTARY ON
1 KINGS.[15]

8:62-66 Solomon's Sacrifices

HOW TO SACRIFICE. VIKTORIN STRIGEL: Here
the text eloquently explains how to offer a sacrifice
to God in a way that distinguishes Solomon's
sacrifice from the large-scale ritual sacrifices of the
Gentiles. . . . Solomon's sacrifice differed from those
of the Gentiles on the basis of three causes:
efficient, formal and final. For Solomon's action
was in harmony with God's command, took place
in order to light the way for faith and referred to
the proper end: to celebrate that the true God had
been revealed to the people of Israel. For the
Gentiles sacrifice without God's command,
without faith and without looking to the goal that

ought to be the real purpose of every sacrifice.
Therefore, when godly and ungodly people do the
same thing, they are not in fact the same. Instead
the causes or reasons need to be distinguished.
BOOK OF KINGS.[16]

CONSECRATED PEOPLE. KONRAD PELLIKAN:
This number of sacrifices, the largest that can be
imagined, could not have been done in one day or
in two weeks. Rather it was a succession of
offerings by the Levites in the most celebratory
amounts. In them the people could rejoice, watch
in wonder and be reconciled through such solemn
worship of God, initiated in accordance with the
law. In these sacrifices they were consecrated at the
sacrificial altar just as much as the buildings of the
Lord's house. COMMENTARY ON 1 KINGS.[17]

---

[15]Pellikan, *Commentaria Bibliorum*, 2:152v.

[16]Strigel, *Libri Samuelis, Regum et Paralipomenon*, 237.
[17]Pellikan, *Commentaria Bibliorum*, 2:152v.

9:1-28 THE ACTS OF SOLOMON

[1]As soon as Solomon had finished building the house of the LORD and the king's house and all that Solomon desired to build, [2]the LORD appeared to Solomon a second time, as he had appeared to him at Gibeon. [3]And the LORD said to him, "I have heard your prayer and your plea, which you have made before me. I have consecrated this house that you have built, by putting my name there forever. My eyes and my heart will be there for all time. [4]And as for you, if you will walk before me, as David your father walked, with integrity of heart and uprightness, doing according to all that I have commanded you, and keeping my statutes and my rules, [5]then I will establish your royal throne over Israel forever, as I promised David your father, saying, 'You shall not lack a man on the throne of Israel.' [6]But if you turn aside from following me, you or your children, and do not keep my commandments and my statutes that I have set before you, but go and serve other gods and worship them, [7]then I will cut off Israel from the land that I have given them, and the house that I have consecrated for my name I will cast out of my sight, and Israel will become a proverb and a byword among all peoples. [8]And this house will become a heap of ruins.[a] Everyone passing by it will be astonished and will hiss, and they will say, 'Why has the LORD done thus to this land and to this house?' [9]Then they will say, 'Because they abandoned the LORD their God who brought their fathers out of the land of Egypt and laid hold on other gods and worshiped them and served them. Therefore the LORD has brought all this disaster on them.'"

[10]At the end of twenty years, in which Solomon had built the two houses, the house of the LORD and the king's house, [11]and Hiram king of Tyre had supplied Solomon with cedar and cypress timber and gold, as much as he desired, King Solomon gave to Hiram twenty cities in the land of Galilee. [12]But when Hiram came from Tyre to see the cities that Solomon had given him, they did not please him. [13]Therefore he said, "What kind of cities are these that you have given me, my brother?" So they are called the land of Cabul to this day. [14]Hiram had sent to the king 120 talents[b] of gold.

[15]And this is the account of the forced labor that King Solomon drafted to build the house of the LORD and his own house and the Millo and the wall of Jerusalem and Hazor and Megiddo and Gezer [16](Pharaoh king of Egypt had gone up and captured Gezer and burned it with fire, and had killed the Canaanites who lived in the city, and had given it as dowry to his daughter, Solomon's wife; [17]so Solomon rebuilt Gezer) and Lower Beth-horon [18]and Baalath and Tamar in the wilderness, in the land of Judah,[c] [19]and all the store cities that Solomon had, and the cities for his chariots, and the cities for his horsemen, and whatever Solomon desired to build in Jerusalem, in Lebanon, and in all the land of his dominion. [20]All the people who were left of the Amorites, the Hittites, the Perizzites, the Hivites, and the Jebusites, who were not of the people of Israel— [21]their descendants who were left after them in the land, whom the people of Israel were unable to devote to destruction[d]—these Solomon drafted to be slaves, and so they are to this day. [22]But of the people of Israel Solomon made no slaves. They were the soldiers, they were his officials, his commanders, his captains, his chariot commanders and his horsemen.

[23]These were the chief officers who were over Solomon's work: 550 who had charge of the people who carried on the work.

[24]But Pharaoh's daughter went up from the city of David to her own house that Solomon had built for her. Then he built the Millo.

[25]Three times a year Solomon used to offer up burnt offerings and peace offerings on the altar that he built to the LORD, making offerings with it[e] before the LORD. So he finished the house.

[26]King Solomon built a fleet of ships at Ezion-geber, which is near Eloth on the shore of the Red Sea, in the land of Edom. [27]And Hiram sent with the fleet

his servants, seamen who were familiar with the sea, together with the servants of Solomon. ²⁸*And they* *went to Ophir and brought from there gold, 420 talents, and they brought it to King Solomon.*

a Syriac, Old Latin; Hebrew *will become high*   b A *talent* was about 75 pounds or 34 kilograms   c Hebrew lacks *of Judah*   d That is, set apart (devote) as an offering to the Lord (for destruction)   e Septuagint lacks *with it*

OVERVIEW: These commentators glory over the impressive accomplishments of Solomon, drawing out an important theological point: All of the external commandments of God are valuable inasmuch as they incite faith, but they are not ends in and of themselves. Fully aware that the eternal kingdom promised to Solomon and his Jewish descendants was conditioned on faith, the reformers explain that all divine promises in the Old Testament are ultimately fulfilled in the person of Christ. They extend this insight, encouraging Christians today not to think lightly of God's commandments but to obey them so that God's promises may come to fruition.

9:1-9 The Lord Appears to Solomon Again

THE FIRST COMMANDMENT IS FAITH. JO-HANNES BUGENHAGEN: Solomon accomplished everything, just as God had commanded David, yet you should not think that this could happen without the Word of God (as we said at the beginning of this book). Thus God accepts all that had happened, so that you may see it entirely as the will of God. This added condition (as we also said above) shows you this clear point of Scripture, namely, the will of God. The Law and all Prophets point to the fact that all those external matters—even those that God has commanded to be done, such as the temple, sacrifices, fasts, songs, festivals, altars, etc.—are never anything but damnable without the first commandment, that is, without faith. For God himself wanted to make those things to be signs and sacraments. Therefore God is only mocked by those who boast in their own worship of God. They are condemned hypocrites. For our sins offend God, who freely gave the Son. But hypocrisy tries to cheat God, whose majesty cannot be known or endured, as the Psalm says, "For [a wicked person] flatters himself in his own eyes that his iniquity cannot be found out and hated." COMMENTARY ON 1 KINGS.[1]

THE PROMISED MESSIAH. KONRAD PELLIKAN: God not only promised grace and his enduring presence to the people but he also promised Solomon personally a long-lasting and perpetual kingdom for his descendants. They would be preserved in the law of the Lord if they walked in David's way of perfect faith and devotion. If their sins made it impossible for this to be fulfilled or only imperfectly fulfilled, then they should be restored in this way: that in Christ the messiah, the true seed of David and Abraham, what was promised has been fulfilled, fulfilling the promise once and for all. COMMENTARY ON 1 KINGS.[2]

PROMISES LASTING UNTIL THE MESSIAH. JOHN MAYER: The Lord appeared to Solomon a second time. This time he appeared to him at night, just as he did the first time in Gibeon in a dream. And now God told Solomon that he had heard his prayer and had sanctified this house and put his name there forever. He also said that if he and his posterity walked in the Lord's ways, the Lord promised that his kingdom would be perpetual. But if they degenerated, God threatened to cast off Israel and this house. . . . God's sanctification of that house was his setting it apart for divine worship, as is further expressed by saying that his name would reside there and be called on. This meant that the Lord's benefits would be distributed among those who worshiped him in that place.

---

[1] Bugenhagen, *In Regum duos ultimos libros*, 49-50; citing Ps 36:2; Jer 7:5-7; Jer 7:4.
[2] Pellikan, *Commentaria Bibliorum*, 2:153r.

Where it is added, "forever," this Hebrew word is to be understood as referring to a "long period of time." This time was unknown then, as the length of legal rites and ceremonies until the coming of the Messiah, who was prefigured by this temple. For by the time of Christ, the use of the temple was ended, although the children of Israel had not yet provoked God to destroy it on account of their sins. COMMENTARY ON 1 KINGS.[3]

SAME PRINCIPLE AS TODAY. JOHANNES PISCATOR: God promises both Solomon and the people of Israel that if they would observe his commandments he would bless them, just as he would drive them out if they transgressed the commandments. This should be the same way we respond to the commandments of God, for they will always be similar. That is, we must be diligent in observing the commands of God and we must be careful to avoid transgressing those same laws. COMMENTARY ON 1 KINGS.[4]

9:10-28 Further Acts of Solomon

TWENTY VILLAGES IN GALILEE. JOHANNES BUGENHAGEN: Here is described how Hiram gave back the villages that Solomon had given him. Solomon then rebuilt them, for they had displeased Hiram. They say that in Phoenician "Cabul" means displeasure, but we cannot judge this for sure beyond what this story itself says it means. From the Hebrew, it might mean "land full of clay," which would certainly be an unfruitful land. Either because these villages were inhabited by Gentiles since Solomon's time or because they gave tribute to Hiram the king of Tyre, it was called "Galilee of the Gentiles" in Isaiah 9. COMMENTARY ON 1 KINGS.[5]

UNTHANKFULNESS. ROBERT SANDERSON: Where is there a person so constantly and equally content with his portion that he has not sometime

or other grudged at the leanness of his own, or envied at the abundance of another's lot? We deal with our God . . . as Hiram did with Solomon. "King Solomon gave to Hiram twenty cities in the land of Galilee. But when Hiram came from Tyre to see the cities that Solomon had given him, they did not please him. Therefore he said, 'What kind of cities are these that you have given me, my brother?' So they are called the land of Cabul to this day," which means "dirty." In the same way, we are witty to quibble and quarrel at God's gifts, if they are not in every respect such as we, in our vain hopes or fancies, have imagined for ourselves. We think, *this is dirty, that barren; this too solitary, that too populous; this ill-wooded, that ill-watered; a third with foul air, a fourth with bad neighbors.* This griping and complaining at our portions as well as our faulting of God's gifts, which is so frequent among us, shows only too much how unthankful our hearts are toward God. TO THE PEOPLE.[6]

FINISHING THE HOUSE. KONRAD PELLIKAN: Solomon established rites for honoring God to be diligently kept by the Levites according to the law. He ordained twenty-four groups of priest who would provide for daily offerings and for the burnt offerings and sacrifices, incense and perfumes for the feast of Passover, the feast of Weeks, the feast of Tabernacles, the New Year's festival and for the sabbath, which are described briefly in Chronicles. These occurred at the great bronze altar that stood in the priest's court in front of the gate, and the incense was lit within the bronze oracle inside the holy gilded temple. This then is what is meant where it says, "he finished his temple." COMMENTARY ON 1 KINGS.[7]

WHETHER SOLOMON JUSTIFIABLY GAVE TOWNS TO HIRAM. JOHN MAYER: Was it justifiable for Solomon to give to a heathen king any part of the Lord's inheritance appropriated to the children of Israel? For although the present king

---

[3]Mayer, *Many Commentaries in One*, 44*.
[4]Piscator, *Commentarii in omnes libros Veteris Testamenti*, 2:276.
[5]Bugenhagen, *In Regum duos ultimos libros*, 50-51; citing 2 Chron 8:2; Is 9:1.

[6]Sanderson, *Works*, 3:191*; citing 1 Kings 9:11-13.
[7]Pellikan, *Commentaria Bibliorum*, 2:154r.

was godly, his successors could be idolaters again, as he initially was (according to the testimony of Josephus) before his acquaintance with David. For by having these lands in the hands of a pagan nation there would be danger of corrupting the people of Israel who dwelt there. Some answer that Solomon did not give them to Hiram in a way that the children of Israel lost any land thereby, for Hiram gave Solomon many cities in his country according to 2 Chronicles 8. But 2 Chronicles 8 says neither that Hiram gave him an equal amount of cities or that he gave these in his own country. It only says that "Solomon rebuilt the cities that Hiram had given to him, and settled the people of Israel in them." Others think that Hiram, disliking the cities given him by Solomon, gave them back again, and so by the providence of God it fell that none of the Holy Land was alienated. But the passage quoted above makes this interpretation impossible. Some say that Solomon cannot be

justified in this any more than other holy men of old in all their actions. Others justify Solomon's act by saying that it was done as a figure of the conversion of the Gentiles and the making of the Jews and Gentiles into one people. These interpreters believe Solomon moved and acted according to the instinct of the Spirit. And some say that Solomon did not give these towns to Hiram forever; rather, for a certain number of years the profits arising out of them were required to be sent to Hiram. But seeing it is said that Solomon "had given" them to Hiram, this is but a light conjecture. It seems to me that Solomon gave Hiram these towns for his lifetime, but not for his heirs afterward. He might very well have done this out of his love to him for being such a good friend. . . . At the same time, I do not exclude the mystical meaning before spoken of, and think that it may be taken into account as well. COMMENTARY ON 1 KINGS.[8]

---

[8]Mayer, *Many Commentaries in One*, 44-45*; citing 2 Chron 8:2.

10:1-29 THE QUEEN OF SHEBA VISITS

[1]Now when the queen of Sheba heard of the fame of Solomon concerning the name of the Lord, she came to test him with hard questions. [2]She came to Jerusalem with a very great retinue, with camels bearing spices and very much gold and precious stones. And when she came to Solomon, she told him all that was on her mind. [3]And Solomon answered all her questions; there was nothing hidden from the king that he could not explain to her. [4]And when the queen of Sheba had seen all the wisdom of Solomon, the house that he had built, [5]the food of his table, the seating of his officials, and the attendance of his servants, their clothing, his cupbearers, and his burnt offerings that he offered at the house of the Lord, there was no more breath in her.

[6]And she said to the king, "The report was true that I heard in my own land of your words and of your wisdom, [7]but I did not believe the reports until I came and my own eyes had seen it. And behold, the half was not told me. Your wisdom and prosperity surpass the report that I heard. [8]Happy are your men! Happy are your servants, who continually stand before you and hear your wisdom! [9]Blessed be the Lord your God, who has delighted in you and set you on the throne of Israel! Because the Lord loved Israel forever, he has made you king, that you may execute justice and righteousness." [10]Then she gave the king 120 talents[a] of gold, and a very great quantity of spices and precious stones. Never again came such an abundance of spices as these that the queen of Sheba gave to King Solomon.

[11]Moreover, the fleet of Hiram, which brought gold from Ophir, brought from Ophir a very great amount of almug wood and precious stones. [12]And the king made of the almug wood supports for the house of the Lord and for the king's house, also lyres and harps for the singers. No such almug wood has come or been seen to this day.

[13]And King Solomon gave to the queen of Sheba all that she desired, whatever she asked besides what was given her by the bounty of King Solomon. So she turned and went back to her own land with her servants.

[14]Now the weight of gold that came to Solomon in one year was 666 talents of gold, [15]besides that which came from the explorers and from the business of the merchants, and from all the kings of the west and from the governors of the land. [16]King Solomon made 200 large shields of beaten gold; 600 shekels[b] of gold went into each shield. [17]And he made 300 shields of beaten gold; three minas[c] of gold went into each shield. And the king put them in the House of the Forest of Lebanon. [18]The king also made a great ivory throne and overlaid it with the finest gold. [19]The throne had six steps, and the throne had a round top,[d] and on each side of the seat were armrests and two lions standing beside the armrests, [20]while twelve lions stood there, one on each end of a step on the six steps. The like of it was never made in any kingdom. [21]All King Solomon's drinking vessels were of gold, and all the vessels of the House of the Forest of Lebanon were of pure gold. None were of silver; silver was not considered as anything in the days of Solomon. [22]For the king had a fleet of ships of Tarshish at sea with the fleet of Hiram. Once every three years the fleet of ships of Tarshish used to come bringing gold, silver, ivory, apes, and peacocks.[e]

[23]Thus King Solomon excelled all the kings of the earth in riches and in wisdom. [24]And the whole earth sought the presence of Solomon to hear his wisdom, which God had put into his mind. [25]Every one of them brought his present, articles of silver and gold, garments, myrrh, spices, horses, and mules, so much year by year.

[26]And Solomon gathered together chariots and horsemen. He had 1,400 chariots and 12,000 horsemen, whom he stationed in the chariot cities and with the king in Jerusalem. [27]And the king made silver as common in Jerusalem as stone, and he made cedar as plentiful as the sycamore of the Shephelah. [28]And Solomon's import of horses was from Egypt and Kue, and the king's traders received them from Kue at a price. [29]A chariot could be imported from

Egypt for 600 shekels of silver and a horse for 150, and so through the king's traders they were exported

to all the kings of the Hittites and the kings of Syria.

a A *talent* was about 75 pounds or 34 kilograms   b A *shekel* was about 2/5 ounce or 11 grams   c A *mina* was about 1 1/4 pounds or 0.6 kilogram   d Or *and at the back of the throne was a calf's head*   e Or *baboons*

OVERVIEW: The story of the queen of Sheba captures the imagination of the commentators. The location of the land of Sheba is not fully explained in the biblical text, leading some to wonder if it correlates with what the Romans called *Arabia Felix* ("fertile Arabia"). The reformers examine this story through typology, that is, how Old Testament people, events and stories foreshadow Christ and his revelation in the New Testament. For some, the exotic travels of the queen of Sheba typify the universal church that is assembled from all regions of the world. Others liken the queen of Sheba to the soul in pursuit of Christ. Naturally such typology applies even to Solomon's opulent wealth in the form of cups and shields.

10:1-13 *The Queen of Sheba*

SOLOMON'S GLOBAL FAME. JOHANNES BUGEN-HAGEN: This chapter presents the high point of Solomon's reign, where even the Gentiles proclaimed his wisdom and acknowledged the Lord with gift offerings. But no such wisdom and no such wealth come to pass at all, except as you see in the fulfilled promise of God from chapter 3 above. "Now when the queen of Sheba heard of the fame of Solomon concerning the name of the Lord, she came to test him with hard questions." That is, the queen had heard that God had given Solomon such great wisdom. In Hebrew, Sheba is the name of what we read in the histories as *Arabia Felix*, where gold and frankincense abounded. Then "there was no more breath in her." In Hebrew, that is a way of saying that she had to stop, for she went on to say what she was thinking in her heart. When she spoke of Solomon's "works," she was referring to his riches or possessions. Regarding Hiram's fleet, I believe that Ophir belonged

somehow to the region of India, according to Genesis 10, where it says that Ophir was a son of Joktan, just like Sheba. And the sons of Joktan lived "from Mesha in the direction of Sephar to the hill country in the east." In India are great and powerful elephants. That region also abounds in the other animals, which you read were later brought to Solomon from across the sea. COMMENTARY ON 1 KINGS.[1]

SOLOMON THE THEOLOGIAN. KONRAD PEL-LIKAN: God gave Solomon great wisdom, wealth and fame to the glory of the people of Israel. There is almost nothing more desirable than an illustrious kingdom. Because such things quickly pass, this teaches that nothing on earth is free from guilt or danger. Solomon's great wisdom inspired the queen of Sheba, who desired to learn the things of God from him. It seems plain that she wanted to hear of divine things from Solomon the theologian, for already the great glory of the God who created all things had spread to all the nations on account of Solomon's glory. This was a type of the church that is assembled from the nations to the worship of the one God through David's son, Christ, who brings peace. COMMENTARY ON 1 KINGS.[2]

STUDENTS OF WISDOM. JOHANNES PISCATOR: In the queen of Sheba we are given an example of the pursuit of wisdom. Indeed, she had come to hear of Solomon from a very long distance. It would be shameful of us, therefore, if we did not studiously and regularly attend sacred assemblies that are nearby to listen to the sermons coming

---

[1]Bugenhagen, *In Regum duos ultimos libros*, 52-53. *Arabia Felix* (meaning "fertile Arabia") was the region of modern Yemen on the Arabian Peninsula. On the sons of Joktan, see Gen 10:26-30. [2]Pellikan, *Commentaria Bibliorum*, 2:154r.

from the mouth of God's ministers. And if we do not, "The queen of the south will rise up at the judgment with this generation and condemn it, for she came from the ends of the earth to hear the wisdom of Solomon, and behold, something greater than Solomon is here." COMMENTARY ON 1 KINGS.[3]

THE SOUL ON A HEAVENLY JOURNEY. JOHANN GERHARD: The queen who went to Solomon is the soul traveling to the heavenly Jerusalem, to Christ. She enters with a great multitude of holy angels, with gold and precious stones of various virtues. She will marvel at the wisdom of Christ the King, the order of his ministers, that is, the angels and the saints; the food on his table, that is, the fullness of a restored eternity; the value of his clothes, that is, the glorified bodies; the beauty of his home, that is, the magnitude of his heavenly palace; and the sacrifices, that is, the multitude of divine praises. She will be turned into amazement and not be able to believe what she now sees with her eyes. SACRED MEDITATIONS.[4]

10:14-29 The Wealth of Solomon

WEAPONS OF PEACE. JOHANNES BUGENHAGEN: The Hebrew says the shields were made of "three minas" of gold each. The Latin makes this "three hundred pounds." You see how much peace abounded under this peaceful Solomon, so that he even played with instruments of war and could produce them for decoration rather than for necessity. Otherwise wouldn't he use bronze instead of gold? This is written of Christ's kingdom in Isaiah 2: "They shall beat their swords into plowshares, and their spears into pruning hooks." For in the kingdom of Christ there is not only peace of conscience but also an external peace among Christians themselves, as Romans 12 says, "Live in harmony with one another" and as Matthew 5 says, "If anyone would sue you and take

your tunic, let him have your cloak as well"; see 1 Corinthians 6 too. But these shields were taken away during the time of Solomon's son Rehoboam, and then Rehoboam made shields of bronze, as you read in chapter 14. That impious man could not rejoice in peace when he lost God's protection. COMMENTARY ON 1 KINGS.[5]

PEACE ABOUNDING. KONRAD PELLIKAN: Such peace abounded that Solomon could have weapons made out of gold instead of bronze just for the sport of it. For such golden spears and javelins would only give the appearance of being sharp spikes, while embossed shields would be almost entirely useless in war. Such weapons cast out of gold were made to be mostly beautiful and were kept under protections in times of war and ambition. COMMENTARY ON 1 KINGS.[6]

THE POWER OF MERCY. EDWARD REYNOLDS: When Solomon set forth the glory and magnificence of his kingdom, he made "200 large shields of beaten gold . . . and 300 shields of beaten gold." It is a sign of power to be able to hurt. But, above all, protection and mercy are the works of honor. For instance, princes commit their power to punishing, while they commit their ministers to perform works of justice. But princes still reserve to themselves works of clemency and the power to pardon. God himself, who is glorious in all his attributes, nevertheless singles out his goodness and protection as the primary ways to show himself glorious. For justice and power make majesty terrible, but goodness and mercy make it lovable. SEVEN SERMONS ON THE FOURTEENTH CHAPTER OF HOSEA.[7]

MAGNIFICENT TYPE OF KINGSHIP. JOHANNES PISCATOR: In Solomon's making larger golden shields, smaller golden shields, an ivory throne decorated with gold and golden cups, we are given

[3]Piscator, *Commentarii in omnes libros Veteris Testamenti*, 2:278; citing Mt 12:42.
[4]Gerhard, *Gerhardi Meditationes Sacrae*, 212-13.
[5]Bugenhagen, *In Regum duos ultimos libros*, 55-56; citing Is 2:4; Rom 12:16; Mt 5:40; 1 Cor 6:1-8; 1 Kings 14:26-27.
[6]Pellikan, *Commentaria Bibliorum*, 2:155r.
[7]Reynolds, *Works*, 3:272*.

a magnificent and splendid example of kingship. This splendor was a type of the glorious reign of Christ, as seen in Revelation 21–22. COMMENTARY ON 1 KINGS.[8]

SOLOMON'S THRONE AND THE JUDGMENT OF GOD. JOHANNES BUGENHAGEN: This throne was used for judgment and signifies the judgment of Solomon's kingdom, that is, Christ. For the Spirit was already judging through Christ and condemning everything about us, in order that we might revolt against those things that are ours and go to those things that are of God. Happy are they who are judged for the sake of their own health; others are greatly provoked by this judgment against God and have been blinded. There are twelve lions on the right and the left, so that you may see all who have this kind of judgment. These are truly prophets, apostles and everyone who is faithful,

who preaches the word and who judges all that is ours through the Word. Then, at the last judgment with Christ, we might judge all the ungodly. As it says, "Morning by morning I will destroy all the wicked in the land, cutting off all the evildoers from the city of the Lord." And according to the word of Christ—whether you experience it beforehand in the judgment of the church or whether you consider it in the future—you "will also sit on twelve thrones, judging the twelve tribes of Israel." One is truly brought up to this judgment by steps. For the judgment of God is revealed to us gradually, until we suddenly recognize the more secret sins of our hearts and we know with a sure judgment from the Spirit what has pleased God and what has not. That all the furnishings were covered in gold signifies this as being the pure ministry of the word in the church of Christ. COMMENTARY ON 1 KINGS.[9]

---

[8]Piscator, *Commentarii in omnes libros Veteris Testamenti*, 2:278.

[9]Bugenhagen, *In Regum duos ultimos libros*, 56-57; citing Ps 101:8; Mt 19:28.

11:1-43 SOLOMON'S DOWNFALL

Now King Solomon loved many foreign women, along with the daughter of Pharaoh: Moabite, Ammonite, Edomite, Sidonian, and Hittite women, [2]from the nations concerning which the LORD had said to the people of Israel, "You shall not enter into marriage with them, neither shall they with you, for surely they will turn away your heart after their gods." Solomon clung to these in love. [3]He had 700 wives, who were princesses, and 300 concubines. And his wives turned away his heart. [4]For when Solomon was old his wives turned away his heart after other gods, and his heart was not wholly true to the LORD his God, as was the heart of David his father. [5]For Solomon went after Ashtoreth the goddess of the Sidonians, and after Milcom the abomination of the Ammonites. [6]So Solomon did what was evil in the sight of the LORD and did not wholly follow the LORD, as David his father had done. [7]Then Solomon built a high place for Chemosh the abomination of Moab, and for Molech the abomination of the Ammonites, on the mountain east of Jerusalem. [8]And so he did for all his foreign wives, who made offerings and sacrificed to their gods.

[9]And the LORD was angry with Solomon, because his heart had turned away from the LORD, the God of Israel, who had appeared to him twice [10]and had commanded him concerning this thing, that he should not go after other gods. But he did not keep what the LORD commanded. [11]Therefore the LORD said to Solomon, "Since this has been your practice and you have not kept my covenant and my statutes that I have commanded you, I will surely tear the kingdom from you and will give it to your servant. [12]Yet for the sake of David your father I will not do it in your days, but I will tear it out of the hand of your son. [13]However, I will not tear away all the kingdom, but I will give one tribe to your son, for the sake of David my servant and for the sake of Jerusalem that I have chosen."

[14]And the LORD raised up an adversary against Solomon, Hadad the Edomite. He was of the royal house in Edom. [15]For when David was in Edom, and Joab the commander of the army went up to bury the slain, he struck down every male in Edom [16](for Joab and all Israel remained there six months, until he had cut off every male in Edom). [17]But Hadad fled to Egypt, together with certain Edomites of his father's servants, Hadad still being a little child. [18]They set out from Midian and came to Paran and took men with them from Paran and came to Egypt, to Pharaoh king of Egypt, who gave him a house and assigned him an allowance of food and gave him land. [19]And Hadad found great favor in the sight of Pharaoh, so that he gave him in marriage the sister of his own wife, the sister of Tahpenes the queen. [20]And the sister of Tahpenes bore him Genubath his son, whom Tahpenes weaned in Pharaoh's house. And Genubath was in Pharaoh's house among the sons of Pharaoh. [21]But when Hadad heard in Egypt that David slept with his fathers and that Joab the commander of the army was dead, Hadad said to Pharaoh, "Let me depart, that I may go to my own country." [22]But Pharaoh said to him, "What have you lacked with me that you are now seeking to go to your own country?" And he said to him, "Only let me depart."

[23]God also raised up as an adversary to him, Rezon the son of Eliada, who had fled from his master Hadadezer king of Zobah. [24]And he gathered men about him and became leader of a marauding band, after the killing by David. And they went to Damascus and lived there and made him king in Damascus. [25]He was an adversary of Israel all the days of Solomon, doing harm as Hadad did. And he loathed Israel and reigned over Syria.

[26]Jeroboam the son of Nebat, an Ephraimite of Zeredah, a servant of Solomon, whose mother's name was Zeruah, a widow, also lifted up his hand against the king. [27]And this was the reason why he lifted up his hand against the king. Solomon built the Millo, and closed up the breach of the city of David his father. [28]The man Jeroboam was very able, and when Solomon saw that the young man was industrious he gave him charge over all the forced labor of the house of Joseph. [29]And at that time, when Jeroboam went out of

Jerusalem, the prophet Ahijah the Shilonite found him on the road. Now Ahijah had dressed himself in a new garment, and the two of them were alone in the open country. ³⁰Then Ahijah laid hold of the new garment that was on him, and tore it into twelve pieces. ³¹And he said to Jeroboam, "Take for yourself ten pieces, for thus says the LORD, the God of Israel, 'Behold, I am about to tear the kingdom from the hand of Solomon and will give you ten tribes ³²(but he shall have one tribe, for the sake of my servant David and for the sake of Jerusalem, the city that I have chosen out of all the tribes of Israel), ³³because they have*ᵃ* forsaken me and worshiped Ashtoreth the goddess of the Sidonians, Chemosh the god of Moab, and Milcom the god of the Ammonites, and they have not walked in my ways, doing what is right in my sight and keeping my statutes and my rules, as David his father did. ³⁴Nevertheless, I will not take the whole kingdom out of his hand, but I will make him ruler all the days of his life, for the sake of David my servant whom I chose, who kept my commandments and my statutes. ³⁵But I will take the kingdom out of his son's hand and will give it to you,

ten tribes. ³⁶Yet to his son I will give one tribe, that David my servant may always have a lamp before me in Jerusalem, the city where I have chosen to put my name. ³⁷And I will take you, and you shall reign over all that your soul desires, and you shall be king over Israel. ³⁸And if you will listen to all that I command you, and will walk in my ways, and do what is right in my eyes by keeping my statutes and my commandments, as David my servant did, I will be with you and will build you a sure house, as I built for David, and I will give Israel to you. ³⁹And I will afflict the offspring of David because of this, but not forever.'" ⁴⁰Solomon sought therefore to kill Jeroboam. But Jeroboam arose and fled into Egypt, to Shishak king of Egypt, and was in Egypt until the death of Solomon.

⁴¹Now the rest of the acts of Solomon, and all that he did, and his wisdom, are they not written in the Book of the Acts of Solomon? ⁴²And the time that Solomon reigned in Jerusalem over all Israel was forty years. ⁴³And Solomon slept with his fathers and was buried in the city of David his father. And Rehoboam his son reigned in his place.

a Septuagint, Syriac, Vulgate *he has*; twice in this verse

OVERVIEW: Even if interpreted figuratively, the colossal number of Solomon's wives and concubines—seven hundred and three hundred respectively—grabs the attention of the commentators here. Several of them link Solomon's polygamy with the teaching of levirate marriage found in Deuteronomy 25:5-10, Deuteronomy 17 or Genesis 25 and the story of Abraham. Solomon's polygamy is related to his idolatry. The interpreters, previously favorable to Solomon, marvel at how the wisest man in the world could so easily fall into idolatry, leading them to urge their readers to take the example of Solomon to heart and to flee from sin and temptation. The sin of Solomon, from the point of view of these interpreters, cannot go unpunished, so God raises up Jeroboam to be king of Israel after Solomon dies. Even though Solomon attempts to take Jeroboam's life, God's providence cannot be thwarted by human invention.

11:1-3 Solomon's Many Women

GOD'S MERCY TO WIDOWS. MARTIN LUTHER: With respect to the law that is in Moses concerning the raising up of a brother's seed, I think our Lord God wished to provide for that sex. Most of the males perished in war and other dangers, but the females were spared such dangers and survived. Consequently our Lord God wishes to give them an advantage and made this provision for them, and if a man was unwilling to cohabit with his deceased brother's wife, he nevertheless supported her. It's from this, I think, that Solomon came to have so many wives. TABLE TALK.[1]

CHEATING ON GOD. JOHANNES BUGENHAGEN: I spoke already of these wives in chapter 3. God

---

[1]LW 54:109; citing Deut 25:5-10.

would have not passed judgment about these wives if the cause that gave rise to this prohibition were lacking, namely, if none of them had led Solomon to turn from God. For the law makes this point in this story too: it does not make accusations against even the taking of many foreign wives, unless the king defects to foreign gods through them. Deuteronomy 17 says this concerning the king, "He shall not acquire many wives for himself, lest his heart turn away." When Solomon had previously recognized the blessings of God, he was loved by God. This history alludes to his many wives as if he had not been impious concerning them. Far from it: he had not had a bad conscience before God about them. As it says in Song of Solomon 6, "There are sixty queens and eighty concubines, and virgins without number. My dove, my perfect one, is the only one." Where God or Christ speaks as a spouse, it means "they run around in sects when they have any more than me. And whoever wants to be seen as a worshiper and lover of God is one who has no sect, who has holy faith alone, and is loved by me." Just as only a mother recognizes her true son, so mother church knows those who are born of the seed of the Holy Spirit, that is, those who are conceived by the Word of God and born as a beloved son, daughter and spouse of God, as you see in Psalm 45. COMMENTARY ON 1 KINGS.[2]

WOMEN OF A MIDDLE CONDITION. THE ENGLISH ANNOTATIONS: These concubines were neither wives nor whores. Rather, they were in a kind of middle condition. They were not wives since they were not solemnly married or endowed with a dowry. Nor did any of their children have any right of inheritance. At the same time, these women were not whores since they were taken by a man to be his alone. In this way they were like wives and, in fact, were even regarded as wives by some. . . . Concubines, therefore, were a kind of wives, but in an inferior degree. It is probable, in regard to the seven hundred wives and three hundred concubines here mentioned,

that Solomon dealt with many of them as Ahasuerus did with many of the maidens that went in to him. ANNOTATIONS ON 1 KINGS.[3]

SOLOMON'S GREAT SHAME AND DISHONOR. JOHN MAYER: For the number of Solomon's women, they are said to have been seven hundred wives and three hundred concubines. Here Solomon sinned greatly, in that he multiplied his wives exceedingly, contrary to the charge given to kings in Deuteronomy 17:17, where this is forbidden. . . . It is most probable . . . that this was the occasion of his stupendous multiplying of wives: wallowing in wealth, pampering his body, living in all ease—after his work was finished and his books written—he grew in his elder years most libidinous. Whenever he saw any prince's or nobleman's daughter that pleased his eye, he desired to have his carnal pleasure of her. And because she refused to consent to his pleasure unless he would take her as his wife, he did so. Solomon did the same thing for the women of inferior rank, in making them his concubines so that he could sleep with them. And because Solomon's lust, to which he had basely given himself, was insatiable, he sent abroad for more wives in other countries and was not at all deterred from doing so even though they were women of a different religion. Although they become proselytes to the Israelite religion in order to become his wives, they soon fell into idolatry and drew him into their idolatry along with them. And thus Solomon, to his great shame and dishonor, exceeded in the multiplicity of his wives of all who ever lived before or after him. COMMENTARY ON 1 KINGS.[4]

11:4-13 Solomon's Spiral into Idolatry

ISRAEL'S DOWNFALL. JOHANNES BUGENHAGEN: We have already seen two kinds of kingdoms in the two previous books: the kingdom of hypocrisy, that is, the hidden impiety of Saul; and the kingdom of

---

[2]Bugenhagen, *In Regum duos ultimos libros*, 59-60; citing Deut 17:17; Song 6:8-9.

[3]Downame, ed., *Annotations* (1645), II3r*; citing Gen 21:10; 25:1, 6; 1 Chron 1:32; Gen 30:4; 35:22; Judg 19:1-2; Gen 22:24; 30:4; Esther 2:14.

[4]Mayer, *Many Commentaries in One*, 52*; citing Deut 17:17.

true piety of David and Solomon. From now on, though, the kingdom will be one of clear impiety until the end of these next two books, so that hardly any salutary kings were left even in Judah. This is horrible to watch: how all the leaders and their people—who should have been the people of God—gave that up by forsaking God. They despised the word of Deuteronomy, that is, the Word of God, and were given up to crude reason. Unhappy is the kingdom where ambition and lust rule instead of God's truth itself. As we will see, the holy prophets stood against such kings and popular opinions, but often in vain; for the holy prophets were cast aside and false prophets were listened to, until all would perish through the judgment of God, not only before God but also before the world. All this great impending horror began with the clearly impious reign of Solomon, who became a figure of folly and impiety even though up to this point his wisdom and piety had exceeded all people on the earth. Who will now trust in themselves, after seeing such downfall among the ungodly? Our wisdom and righteousness are nothing if the mercy of God does not preserve them. Some say that Solomon repented at the end of his life in a book he wrote, as is written in Ecclesiastes. But why then did he not put an end to the idolatrous abominations, which remained long after him until the time of the Judean king Josiah, as you read in 2 Kings 23? We ought to fear this judgment of God, especially when we do not know it. COMMENTARY ON 1 KINGS.[5]

SOLOMON'S IDOLATRY. JOHANNES AEPINUS: Solomon passed and excelled in all other things very wisely, but he was brought into the detestable vice of idolatry due to the company and conversation of his wicked wives. Because the conversation of evil people can cause great hurt, the godly should forsake and flee from them if they want to remain undefiled. Although our minds may be strong, steadfast and completely established in godliness and the knowledge of God—to the degree that we may think the company of wicked

people could not do us any manner of hurt—yet we ought not be conversant with them due to the example of Solomon. EXPOSITION ON PSALM 15.[6]

PATTERN OF HUMAN WEAKNESS. JOHN MAYER: Solomon enjoyed all worldly felicity above other kings of the earth, as has been shown. He is now set forth as a pattern of human weakness, so that we may neither dote on worldly things—which are very dangerous and prone to corrupt us—nor be confident of our standing in grace. Rather, with fear and trembling we must always work out our own salvation, seeing that Solomon—who stood steady so long—eventually fell headlong into sin in his old age. This is to teach us to flee from marrying idolaters, in whom there is so great and so irresistible danger to the wisest who ever was. COMMENTARY ON 1 KINGS.[7]

PRAYING FOR PROTECTION AGAINST TEMPTATION. JOHANNES PISCATOR: In Solomon's completely giving himself over to the idolatry of his wives not only in helping and approving it but also in providing for those partaking in it, we are given an example of the weakness of humankind in overcoming what remains in us. This is why we must pray to God that we will not be led into temptation. COMMENTARY ON 1 KINGS.[8]

THE MISSING PEACE. JOHANNES BUGENHAGEN: The person who has grace with God has peace, just as Paul always joined "grace and peace" and just as Romans 5 says, "since we have been justified by faith, we have peace with God." Therefore whoever defects from God or is without God cannot have peace any more than Cain or Judas, unless—by grace—they return to the one who is the fount of peace. "'There is no peace,' says the Lord, 'for the wicked.'" For freedom of conscience first perishes before God. Then all creatures reach a place of confusion and—where it first seemed like our righteousness was appearing— they sin. This history says that when Solomon

[6]Aepinus, *Fruitful Exposition upon Psalm 15*, 64-65*.
[7]Mayer, *Many Commentaries in One*, 52*.
[8]Piscator, *Commentarii in omnes libros Veteris Testamenti*, 2:281.

[5]Bugenhagen, *In Regum duos ultimos libros*, 58-59; citing Rom 1:26.

trusted in God, he had a superior kind of peace. But when he turned to impiety, adversaries were raised up from every side, three of whom are described here. COMMENTARY ON 1 KINGS.[9]

THE BOUND WILL. KONRAD PELLIKAN: Solomon's transgression became clear and incurred the tremendous judgment of God. For God had loved him since his infancy, mercifully speaking with him through visions two times, promising him great things and bestowing many benefits that had been foretold to his father. Nevertheless, Solomon dared to provoke the Lord, despising the warnings as much as the promises. Such wrath had somehow not turned the heart of Solomon to God, for the freedom and strength of the human will can do nothing once sin has started to work. Then the will does not receive the Word of God continuously falls into wickedness: serious sin always follows as the penalty of seemingly lighter sins. COMMENTARY ON 1 KINGS.[10]

GOD'S KINDNESS ALONGSIDE HIS TRUTHFULNESS. JOHANNES PISCATOR: We are here given an example of both God's kindness but also God's truth and truthfulness. For even though Solomon had sinned greatly, God refused to tear away the kingdom from Solomon while he lived. Similarly, God refused to tear not only the kingdom away from Solomon but even away from his ancestors, for God decided to allow one tribe to remain of his sons. And this was due to God's former promise to David that he would leave him an everlasting dynasty. COMMENTARY ON 1 KINGS.[11]

11:14-43 Adversaries of Solomon and Anointing of Jeroboam

WONDERFUL JOY OF PROVIDENCE. HULDRYCH ZWINGLI: What sort of man Jeroboam was from his early years until he divided Israel and brought in idolatry, I do not need to expound. But however wicked and reckless he was, he was yet installed, as it were, in royal power by the prophet Abijah, when he cut his cloak into twelve parts and gave ten to the future king of the ten tribes. Since, therefore, he had set up golden calves to be worshiped, why did God not only allow but also order him to seize the kingdom? God undertook this affair, with these methods, that we might see that things are done according to God's will and not according to our decisions.... Everything that is done, whether we call it accidental or premeditated and determined on, is done by the immediate providence of God, whether it has to do with inanimate things or with things endowed with life, mind and understanding—however much we, being immersed in such a deep darkness of ignorance, on account of gross sluggishness of the flesh, fail to see all this clearly. And if to any it is given to look at these things from a somewhat higher point of view, good Lord, what delight they feel, when they detect everywhere the wisdom and goodness of the Deity, so that the contemplation of the universe, beautiful as it is, is a sordid thing beside the delightfulness that meets them when they mount to God, and consider the architect of the structure of the universe! For what wondering admiration do you think enters the pious heart, when ... it considers the aforesaid Jeroboam, who was ordained by God to separate Israel into two kingdoms, and presently abandoned him whom God had installed, after he had set up golden calves to be worshiped! This thing first brought Israel and then Judah to destruction, for it was an unworthy deed to lead people away from the true God to idolatry, but it would have been an ill-considered plan on God's part to raise a person like this to the throne who was going to revolt against him, unless God had determined to use his treachery for the thing he was preparing.

When, I say, piety considers what follows, it is far from passing judgment against God that it even wonders and extols God's ways. Supreme Goodness had determined to give up the Jewish race at last and choose the nations given over to idols. That downfall, therefore, that Providence was going to bring on Israel, was paved by means of Jeroboam. For from this point Israel began to totter until she

[9]Bugenhagen, *In Regum duos ultimos libros*, 61; citing Rom 1:7, 5:1; Is 48:22.
[10]Pellikan, *Commentaria Bibliorum*, 2:156r.
[11]Piscator, *Commentarii in omnes libros Veteris Testamenti*, 2:281.

fell into the Babylonian and Roman captivities. But the people of the Gentiles, after being put in their place, triumphed in the knowledge of the Deity. When the religious heart sees this so clearly, is it not carried away with a wonderful joy?

... That God made humankind to let them fall, fills many with wonder. However, when they consider that matter more deeply and see how, when God determined to fashion humankind, God also determined to redeem them through his Son (for as soon as God began to think of fashioning them, God saw how humankind was going to fall—to speak, of course, as we must after the manner of mortals), the human beings at once understand that it was an inestimable blessing that they were so made that they could fall. Otherwise the Son of God would never have put on human nature. Thus good always follows from the works of God, even though the beginnings may not be free from some marked evil. ON THE PROVIDENCE OF GOD.[12]

JEROBOAM FLEES SOLOMON. JOHANNES BUGENHAGEN: Solomon wanted to kill Jeroboam for no other reason than that he heard Jeroboam had been chosen by God to reign over Israel. As if human effort could impede God's ordination! Thus Jeroboam fled and became his adversary. This is the impiety of Saul against David, the one whom God had chosen, as we said in first and second Samuel. COMMENTARY ON 1 KINGS.[13]

GOD'S GENERAL GOODNESS TO ALL. JOHN MAYER: The Lord spoke kindly to Jeroboam by his prophet ... even though he knew he would be a most gross idolater ... and even worse than Solomon. But the Lord did this out of his general goodness, which diffuses itself to all alike—to the good and the bad and to the just and to the unjust. Therefore, when the person proves to be bad, they will be more justly and severely punished, as we see in the case of Jeroboam and in his posterity. In fact, none of his posterity would be spared, all being cut off just as Saul was

before and many others afterward. God spoke this way to set up Jeroboam for the punishment of idolatry, so that it could be proved afterward that God was not the author of it but that this evil sprang up from his own corruption. In this way he was most violently carried away against the most effectual premonitions and promises the Lord could make to him. And from this we are to learn that we are not to charge God with our sins, as some do who say: "I am the way I am because God made me so." COMMENTARY ON 1 KINGS.[14]

THE SIGN OF THE TORN CLOAK AS ANALOGOUS TO THE LORD'S SUPPER. JOHANNES PISCATOR: The prophet Ahijah tore ten pieces of the cloak that he wore while Jeroboam watched. And by giving Jeroboam the ten pieces of cloth, he annexed the promise that God would give him the ten tribes of Solomon. We are advised of this method in regard to the sacraments. The explanation is this: A divine promise consists partly of declaration and partly of a seal. And indeed the declaration is ordained in analogy or likeness to the signs and the things signified. That is, here the tearing of the cloak into ten pieces and the distribution of it to Jeroboam represents the ten tribes. Indeed the seal is ordained in the passing on of the sign, so that here it is the passing on of the ten pieces of cloth. In the same way concerning the Lord's Supper, the promise of God of the remission of sins by the death of Christ is declared and sealed in faith. It is declared in the analogy of the sign and in the things signified to the extent the breaking of bread represents the crucifixion of the body of Christ. And in the same way, the pouring forth of the wine and the drinking of it in a cup represents the shedding of Christ's blood on the cross. Truly the promise is sealed by faith through the broken bread and the poured wine in a cup, and it is sealed in the tradition of eating and drinking. COMMENTARY ON 1 KINGS.[15]

---

[12]2:219-22 (ZSW 6,3:210-14).
[13]Bugenhagen, *In Regum duos ultimos libros*, 65.
[14]Mayer, *Many Commentaries in One*, 63*.
[15]Piscator, *Commentarii in omnes libros Veteris Testamenti*, 2:281.

12:1-33 THE KINGDOM DIVIDED

¹Rehoboam went to Shechem, for all Israel had come to Shechem to make him king. ²And as soon as Jeroboam the son of Nebat heard of it (for he was still in Egypt, where he had fled from King Solomon), then Jeroboam returned from^a Egypt. ³And they sent and called him, and Jeroboam and all the assembly of Israel came and said to Rehoboam, ⁴"Your father made our yoke heavy. Now therefore lighten the hard service of your father and his heavy yoke on us, and we will serve you." ⁵He said to them, "Go away for three days, then come again to me." So the people went away.

⁶Then King Rehoboam took counsel with the old men, who had stood before Solomon his father while he was yet alive, saying, "How do you advise me to answer this people?" ⁷And they said to him, "If you will be a servant to this people today and serve them, and speak good words to them when you answer them, then they will be your servants forever." ⁸But he abandoned the counsel that the old men gave him and took counsel with the young men who had grown up with him and stood before him. ⁹And he said to them, "What do you advise that we answer this people who have said to me, 'Lighten the yoke that your father put on us'?" ¹⁰And the young men who had grown up with him said to him, "Thus shall you speak to this people who said to you, 'Your father made our yoke heavy, but you lighten it for us,' thus shall you say to them, 'My little finger is thicker than my father's thighs. ¹¹And now, whereas my father laid on you a heavy yoke, I will add to your yoke. My father disciplined you with whips, but I will discipline you with scorpions.'"

¹²So Jeroboam and all the people came to Rehoboam the third day, as the king said, "Come to me again the third day." ¹³And the king answered the people harshly, and forsaking the counsel that the old men had given him, ¹⁴he spoke to them according to the counsel of the young men, saying, "My father made your yoke heavy, but I will add to your yoke. My father disciplined you with whips, but I will discipline you with scorpions." ¹⁵So the king did not listen to the people, for it was a turn of affairs brought about by the LORD that he might fulfill his word, which the LORD spoke by Ahijah the Shilonite to Jeroboam the son of Nebat.

¹⁶And when all Israel saw that the king did not listen to them, the people answered the king, "What portion do we have in David? We have no inheritance in the son of Jesse. To your tents, O Israel! Look now to your own house, David." So Israel went to their tents. ¹⁷But Rehoboam reigned over the people of Israel who lived in the cities of Judah. ¹⁸Then King Rehoboam sent Adoram, who was taskmaster over the forced labor, and all Israel stoned him to death with stones. And King Rehoboam hurried to mount his chariot to flee to Jerusalem. ¹⁹So Israel has been in rebellion against the house of David to this day. ²⁰And when all Israel heard that Jeroboam had returned, they sent and called him to the assembly and made him king over all Israel. There was none that followed the house of David but the tribe of Judah only.

²¹When Rehoboam came to Jerusalem, he assembled all the house of Judah and the tribe of Benjamin, 180,000 chosen warriors, to fight against the house of Israel, to restore the kingdom to Rehoboam the son of Solomon. ²²But the word of God came to Shemaiah the man of God: ²³"Say to Rehoboam the son of Solomon, king of Judah, and to all the house of Judah and Benjamin, and to the rest of the people, ²⁴'Thus says the LORD, You shall not go up or fight against your relatives the people of Israel. Every man return to his home, for this thing is from me.'" So they listened to the word of the LORD and went home again, according to the word of the LORD.

²⁵Then Jeroboam built Shechem in the hill country of Ephraim and lived there. And he went out from there and built Penuel. ²⁶And Jeroboam said in his heart, "Now the kingdom will turn back to the house of David. ²⁷If this people go up to offer sacrifices in the temple of the LORD at Jerusalem, then the heart of this people will turn again to their lord, to Rehoboam king of Judah, and they will kill me and return to Rehoboam king of Judah." ²⁸So the king took counsel

and made two calves of gold. And he said to the people, "You have gone up to Jerusalem long enough. Behold your gods, O Israel, who brought you up out of the land of Egypt." ²⁹*And he set one in Bethel, and the other he put in Dan.* ³⁰*Then this thing became a sin, for the people went as far as Dan to be before one.*ᵇ ³¹*He also made temples on high places and appointed priests from among all the people, who were not of the Levites.* ³²*And Jeroboam appointed a feast on the*

fifteenth day of the eighth month like the feast that was in Judah, and he offered sacrifices on the altar. So he did in Bethel, sacrificing to the calves that he made. And he placed in Bethel the priests of the high places that he had made. ³³*He went up to the altar that he had made in Bethel on the fifteenth day in the eighth month, in the month that he had devised from his own heart. And he instituted a feast for the people of Israel and went up to the altar to make offerings.*

a Septuagint, Vulgate (compare 2 Chronicles 10:2); Hebrew *lived in*   b Septuagint *went to the one at Bethel and to the other as far as Dan*

Overview: Rehoboam and Jeroboam now stand as rival rulers of the formerly united kingdom of Israel. According to the commentators here, Rehoboam was prudent to ask counsel concerning the people's request but foolishly ignored the better advice from the elders. Because he did not follow sound counsel, some explain, God allowed him to lose the kingdom to Jeroboam. Jeroboam's shrewd yet idolatrous decision to erect new gods for the kingdom of Israel to worship in Bethel and Dan invites strong rebuke from the commentators, who agree that his change of divine worship is the source of great sin and wickedness—and his eventual downfall.

12:1-5 The Kingdom Demands a Lighter Yoke from Rehoboam

Leniency Is Best in the Beginning. John Mayer: Rehoboam acted wisely to take counsel before giving an answer, as is advised in Sirach: "Do nothing without counsel." And Proverbs speaks about rash words being cause for condemnation. Yet in this case, since the people were already exasperated, it would have been wiser to show lenience with some gentle answer. For this is a general principle among kings: By no means show rigor in the beginning of one's reign, but try to win the people's hearts by leniency. Commentary on 1 Kings.[1]

Cunning and Disloyal People. Johannes Piscator: In the Israelites' asking Rehoboam for a lessening of their burdens, an example is given of both cunning and also injustice in refusing to obey their superiors. For they were obligated to Rehoboam as the legitimate successor of Solomon and therefore as their king and master to obey even though he would not lessen their burden. But the people only gave their obedience on the condition that he would lessen their burden. They sought this lessening of their burden as a pretext for seeking an occasion to defect from Rehoboam. For here they summoned Jeroboam from Egypt with the plan of placing him in command as their king. Commentary on 1 Kings.[2]

Fulfilled Prophecy. Edward Reynolds. There are two great principles of human actions: wisdom, which directs, and labor, which executes. Wisdom guides labor by counsel; and labor, through experience, increases wisdom. Wisdom is fruitless if it is not managed by wisdom. Some conceive that Solomon foresaw that Rehoboam would scatter many of those great works and lose much of that ample power and wealth which his father had received by his wisdom. Meditations on the Holy Sacrament.[3]

---

[1] Mayer, *Many Commentaries in One*, 65*; citing Sir 32:19.

[2] Piscator, *Commentarii in omnes libros Veteris Testamenti*, 2:283.
[3] Reynolds, *Works*, 3:76*; citing Eccles 2:19.

12:6-15 *Following the Advice of His Friends*

REHOBOAM'S STUPID WISDOM. JOHANNES BUGENHAGEN: Rehoboam thought he should heed his young advisors; Scripture soon reveals that this happened in order to fulfill God's Word. Therefore, Rehoboam in his foolishness had sought a wisdom that would undo him. For his foolishness led him to impiously think that he could stand firm apart from God. Some have grown accustomed to extolling this example to say that we should not abandon the advice of the elders for the greatly pleasing advice of the young and that we should not commit ourselves to the untested ideas of the ignorant. Additionally I hope you understand this: flatterers should not be listened to, whether they are old or young, especially not by kings who then agree to listen to such evil, which is the example of this story. For all these others are nothing but advisers, while we ought to commit the thing to God so that a thing might prosper. Otherwise we may be led astray by elders too, indeed even through wise people whom the emperor wants to consult, as is written of the Egyptians and their wisdom in Isaiah. Because Rehoboam committed everything to humans and not to God and did not consult God as his father David, God allowed this loss to happen through humans. Therefore you must not respect such things in your elders, who can be tempted away from God in such matters. COMMENTARY ON 1 KINGS.[4]

GOD WORKS THROUGH FOOLISH ADVICE. JOHN MAYER: Although there was no ground of truth in Rehoboam's friends' advice, it greatly pleased this foolish man because he thought that in saying these words he would speak more like a king who had power and command over the people. But to speak the advice of the elders, Rehoboam thought, would have been to abase himself to his subjects. . . . But the reason why Rehoboam was so cruelly bent and foolishly led was due to the hand of the Most High, who was hereby punishing Solomon in his posterity according to his word

spoken by Ahijah. The Lord did not give wisdom to Rehoboam to discern the best counsel from the worst, whereby he might have been kept from this pride and cruelty. But in God's just judgment, God stirred up Jeroboam and the people to take this occasion to revolt from Rehoboam. God did not put into the people a spirit of rebellion; rather, he permitted them to be carried on by the bitterness of their own minds. COMMENTARY ON 1 KINGS.[5]

EARNESTLY SEARCHING FOR GOD'S WORD. EDWARD REYNOLDS: Rehoboam's weakness was the following: that, by passionate and foolish counsels, he allowed his honor to be stained, his interest to be weakened and his conscience to be defiled with resolutions of violence and injustice. Now, there is no counsel like God's Word: It enlightens the eyes, makes wise the simple and is able to make a person wise for himself and also for salvation. No other counsel can do this. There is no case—even one of great intricacy and perplexity—that can stump it. There is no difficulty or no temptation so knotty and involved that it cannot resolve it. There is no condition where a person can be brought to desperation and not be brought back with it. There is no employment so dark and uncouth that it cannot rescue a person. And there is no discouragement so great that God's Word cannot offer greater encouragement. In all this it is clear that people ought to run to God's Word. For if a person has any judgment or spiritual sense, they will earnestly search God's Word. SEVEN SERMONS ON FOURTEENTH CHAPTER OF HOSEA.[6]

THE ENLARGER. LANCELOT ANDREWES: People set great titles on empty boxes. Indeed, many times the names given by wise people fall out quite the opposite than they intended. Solomon called his son Rehoboam, which means "the enlarger of people." Rehoboam enlarged his people from ten tribes to two. ON THE NATIVITY: SERMON 9.[7]

---

[4]Bugenhagen, *In Regum duos ultimos libros*, 67-68; citing Is 30:1-7.

[5]Mayer, *Many Commentaries in One*, 65-66*; citing 1 Kings 12:10-11.
[6]Reynolds, *Works*, 3:406-7*.
[7]Andrewes, *Ninety-Six Sermons*, 1:142*.

REVEALED THROUGH THE WORD. JOHANNES BUGENHAGEN: God's mercy is immense, for God does not want the people who had been punished to perish. Instead, God clearly reveals his will through the Word, so that they recognize the guilt and loss they had suffered and stop exalting in their pride, as if their own counsel and strength had achieved anything. The counsel of God would be declared as long as people were able to reprimand the foolishness of Rehoboam, who did not listen to his elders. COMMENTARY ON 1 KINGS.[8]

12:16-24 *"Israel Went to Their Tents"*

THE TRIBE OF EPHRAIM. JOHANNES BUGENHAGEN: This chapter reveals God's Word, described above, to be true concerning the kingdom's division. Here you see how great Ephraim had become, according to Jacob's prophecy in Genesis 48 and of Ephraim's physical father Joseph in Genesis 49. For this reason, the tribe of Ephraim and the sons of Joseph saw themselves as being somewhat set apart even in the time of Joshua, as all the sacrifices to God with the old tabernacle had taken place there in Shiloh, though the Psalms speak against this: "He rejected the tent of Joseph; he did not choose the tribe of Ephraim, but he chose the tribe of Judah, Mount Zion, which he loves." After this the kingdom of the ten tribes was variously named by the prophets as the kingdom of Israel and the house of Jacob (even though all the Jews came from Jacob, whose other name was Israel). Ephraim was the principal tribe, and so it was sometimes called the house of Joseph. Samaria was the capital city and Jezreel was another city of the region. The kingdom of two tribes was called the house of David or Judah or Jerusalem, but rarely Benjamin. Thus the physical blessings moved to Ephraim, but—because of that kingdom's impiety— the spiritual blessing remained in Judah, because from there was to come the Messiah, according to Jacob's prophecy. COMMENTARY ON 1 KINGS.[9]

ENMITY AND DISSENSION. JACOBUS ARMINIUS: Enmities and dissensions of the heart and affections branch out and become schisms, factions and secessions into different parties. For as love is an affection of union, so hatred is an affection of separation. Thus synagogues are erected, consecrated and thronged with people, in opposition to other synagogues, churches against churches and altars against altars, when neither party wishes to have communication with the other. This also is the reason why we frequently hear expressions, entirely similar to those that were clamorously echoed through the assembled multitude of the children of Israel when they were separating into parties—"To your tents, O Israel! For our adversaries have no portion in God, nor any inheritance in his Son Christ Jesus." For both factions equally appropriate to themselves the renowned name of "the true Israel," which they severally deny to their adversaries, in such peremptory manner as might induce one to imagine each of them exclusively endowed with a plenary power of passing judgment on the other. ORATION 5: ON RECONCILING RELIGIOUS DISSENSIONS AMONG CHRISTIANS.[10]

THE NATION DIVIDED INTO ISRAEL AND JUDAH. JOHANNES BRENZ: The holy Scriptures tell us that King Saul first received the kingdom of Israel according to divine consent. After him came David and then Solomon, a son of David. But after Solomon's death the kingdom was torn in two through the mysterious providence of God. The larger territory crowned as king one of Solomon's servants, Jeroboam son of Nebat, who set up his own worship with golden calves in Dan and Bethel once he became king. He did this so that his people could hold worship more properly away from Jerusalem. Because it was the bigger part, it was named Israel. It remained its own kingdom until King Shalmaneser of Assyria destroyed it and filled it with foreign peoples, as described in 2 Kings 17. The second, smaller, other territory (which only consisted of the two tribes of Benjamin and Judah)

---

[8]Bugenhagen, *In Regum duos ultimos libros*, 68.
[9]Bugenhagen, *In Regum duos ultimos libros*, 65-66; citing Gen 48:14-20; 49:22-26; Josh 16–17; Ps 78:67-68; Gen 49:9-12.

[10]Arminius, *Works*, 1:157-58*.

took Solomon's son Rehoboam, and he replaced his father as king in Jerusalem. His kingdom was named after the noble tribe of Judah. This is the kingdom from which came the descendants of David, until finally our Lord Christ came from that same family and established an eternal kingdom. HISTORY OF JEHOSHAPHAT.[11]

REHOBOAM AND HIS JUST DESERTS. THOMAS ADAMS: Rehoboam would make his finger heavier than his father's loins. Therefore his loins would be made lighter than his father's finger. COMMENTARY ON 2 PETER.[12]

12:25-33 Jeroboam's New Religion

JERODOAM AS A TYPE OF ANTICHRIST. DIRK PHILIPS: Because of Jeroboam, there was . . . a falling away from the kingdom of Solomon. He left behind the true worship of God and chose a false kind of worship. He erected two calves at Bethel and Dan and installed priests and Levites from among the worst of the people. He filled their hands and erected an altar for offerings. And so he led Israel into error and sin, until they were finally taken into captivity by the Assyrian kings. Likewise, because of the antichrist, there was a spiritual falling away from true doctrine in the kingdom of Christ. He left behind the true worship of God in Jerusalem and erected for himself a false worship. In a hypocritical way, he copied all that Christ taught and commanded, with all of his priests, altars, offerings, church services and pomp and his terrible defilement of the sacraments of Jesus Christ. All of this he adorned with passages from Scripture, just as if it were the true service of God, as if it were in the service of the almighty God in heaven. But it is finally nothing but terrible idolatry and blasphemy against God. For it is all so obviously contrary to the gospel of Christ, just as clearly as what was done by Jeroboam, doing what he thought was right, was contrary to the law of

Moses. Therefore God-fearing people should not go to these calves to pray. Rather, with the pious Israelites, they must shun this false worship of the spiritual Jeroboam, the antichrist. ENCHIRIDION: CONCERNING SPIRITUAL RESTITUTION.[13]

DIVINE AND HUMAN CEREMONIES. HEINRICH BULLINGER: Now either God or humankind institutes ceremonies. God, for instance, institutes one kind for the people of the Old Testament and another kind (at the first coming of Christ) for the people of the New Testament. I will speak about the ceremonies of the New Testament when I address the church and the churchly sacraments. For the present time I will discuss the ceremonies for the people of the Old Testament. They were divinely instituted actions or holy rites for the people of Israel handed over by God himself until a time of amendment. They were to represent and veil the mysteries of God . . . and also to keep the people of God in godly religion and in the company of one churchly body. Now humankind has instituted many and various ceremonies. . . . Among the Hebrews, Jeroboam, the king of Israel, to the ruin of him and his house, completely changed the divine ceremonies into his own ceremonies, that is, human and ungodly ones. Of the ceremonies instituted by humankind, there is no end to them in this later age of the world of ours. Many learned people have deplored and continue to deplore this. DECADES 3.5.[14]

A NEW RELIGION. JACOBUS ARMINIUS: In both sacred and profane history, egregious examples are recorded of princes and private persons, who, being instigated by such a desire of power as partook at once of ambition and avarice, have invented new modes of religion, and accommodated them to the capacities, the wishes and the opinions of their people. By these means they might either restrain their own subjects within the bounds of their duty, or might subdue to their way the people who were

---

[11]Brenz, *Werke: Frühschriften*, 2:132.
[12]Adams, *Commentary upon 2 Peter*, 161*.
[13]Liechty, ed., *Early Anabaptist Spirituality*, 240; cf. CRR 6:341-42.
[14]Bullinger, *Sermonum decades quinque*, 143.

under the rule of other princes. Ambition and avarice suggest to such aspiring persons the desire of inventing those modes of religious worship; while an itching for novelty, a wish to enjoy their pleasures and the obvious agreement of the new doctrine with their preconceived opinions influence the people to embrace the modish religion. With these intentions, and under the impulse of these views, Jeroboam was the first author of a change of religion in the Israelite church. He built altars in Dan and Bethel, and made golden calves, that he might prevent the people from proceeding at stated periods to Jerusalem, for the purpose of offering sacrifice, according to the command of God, and from returning to the house of David, from which they had rent themselves. ORATION 5: ON RECONCILING RELIGIOUS DISSENSIONS AMONG CHRISTIANS.[15]

SLIPPERY SLOPE. SEBASTIAN MÜNSTER: The solemnity the Jews were commanded to celebrate in the seventh month, which is Tishri, Jeroboam commanded to be celebrated in the eighth month, which is Heshvan, so that gradually he would lead the sons of Israel away from the rites of their fathers. THE TEMPLE OF THE LORD: 1 KINGS 12.[16]

REMNANTS OF A FALSE FAITH IN EGYPT. JOHN MAYER: Now Jeroboam begins to show the wickedness of his heart and what little faith he had in God, even though he had made him king and had promised to establish him in averting the danger by Rehoboam's mighty army from him. By leaving God, Rehoboam trusted in his own policy, devising a means to keep the people from Jerusalem and so from all danger of being drawn to the obedience of Rehoboam again. And this was by setting up two golden calves, one in Bethel and the other in Dan. In these places he built temples and instituted a new priesthood, and a new feast the fifteenth day of the eighth month. He offered sacrifices to these calves, as in Jerusalem by divine

institution, on the fifteenth day of the seven month. It may well be surmised that Jeroboam learned this idolatry of the golden calves from Egypt, while he lived there with Shishak the king of Egypt, whose daughter he is also said by some to have married. For the Hebrews acted the same way when they came out of Egypt. When Moses was gone from them for forty days, they compelled Aaron to make them a golden calf. COMMENTARY ON 1 KINGS.[17]

THE SCANDAL OF INTENTION. ROBERT SANDERSON: It is a scandal when a person does something before another with a direct intention and formal purpose of drawing him to commit sin. In which case neither the matter of the action nor the event is of any consideration. It makes no difference as to the sin of giving scandal whether any person is actually enticed to commit sin or not. Neither does it make any difference whether the thing done is in itself unlawful or not, so long as it had an appearance of evil and from that an aptitude to draw another to do that, by imitation, which would be wholly and intrinsically evil. The wicked intention alone, regardless of the effect or what means should be used to promote it, is sufficient to bring about the guilt of giving scandal on the doer. This was Jeroboam's sin in setting up the calves with a formal purpose and intention of instituting his own secular and ambitious ends, to corrupt the purity of religion and to draw the people to idolatrous worship. It is for this reason that he is so often stigmatized with a note of infamy—to always be attached to him while the world lasts. For he is scarcely mentioned in the Scripture without this addition, "Jeroboam, the son of Nebat, which made Israel to sin. . . ." Here is the lesson we learn: Do nothing, whether good or evil, with an intention to give scandall. THE CASES DETERMINED.[18]

JEROBOAM'S TRANSGRESSIONS. JOHANNES BUGENHAGEN: Jeroboam's first impiety was that he cast aside the promise of God, which he already

---

[15]Arminius, *Works*, 1:169*.
[16]Münster, *Miqdaš YHWH*, 660.
[17]Mayer, *Many Commentaries in One*, 68*.
[18]Sanderson, *Works*, 5:50-51*.

had from the last chapter. He trusted in his own providence and counsel, imagining that he defended himself and had gained the kingdom by himself. In a second clear impiety, he then cast aside those things of God that God had commanded in Deuteronomy. He raised up golden calves as gods, along with ways of worshiping that differed from the law. Third, he thrust this seemingly holy pretext onto future generations and hypocritically invented the adoration of these calves that had supposedly led them out of Egypt. COMMENTARY ON 1 KINGS.[19]

ILLICIT LOCATION OF THE TEMPLE. HEINRICH BULLINGER: Now, Jeroboam, with the other kings of Israel, sinned greatly when they deserted the temple to make sacrifices in the high places—in both Bethel and Dan as well as in other unpleasant places. The people of Judea, with their kings, sinned greatly either for sacrificing to God in the high places or in not cutting down those high places. For the Lord willed and designated himself to be worshiped in one place. The plain teaching of this law is taught in Deuteronomy 12, and is clearly brought forth in Leviticus 17. As the words from this chapter say. . . .

Three things are to be observed from this passage. First, it was only lawful to sacrifice in one place, namely, before the altar of burnt offerings.

Second, from this we are to note that the commandment was given so that all people would understand how to make a legitimate sacrifice to God, to whom the tabernacle belonged. Third, to make a sacrifice in a different place was against God's commandment and it was tantamount to worshiping the devil. The one who offered this illegitimate worship was to be judged as a murderer and excommunicated by the Lord God as a person who was excluded from God and God's holy consort. It is true Samuel, Elijah and certain others made sacrifices to God in other places for specific reasons, but they did so based on a dispensation from God. Therefore those who make sacrifices to God in the high places, even if to God alone, sin, first, by disobedience. For God disapproves, in fact curses, all worship done to him outside what his Word has instituted. What pleases God most is faithful obedience. Second, these individuals sin by disrupting the unity of the church. And third, they despise the mystery of Christ. That is because Christ was to be offered on Mount Golgotha; he was to be the meaning behind the Israelite's sacrifices to God, who is the only sacred type of their sacrifices. Last, the people sinned in their sacrifices by trusting in their works and by neglecting the rightful worship of God in favor of the peculiar worship they invented. DECADES 3.5.[20]

---

[19]Bugenhagen, *In Regum duos ultimos libros*, 68-69.

[20]Bullinger, *Sermonum decades quinque*, 150-51; citing Lev 17:1-10.

13:1–14:31 THE REIGNS OF JEROBOAM AND REHOBOAM

¹And behold, a man of God came out of Judah by the word of the Lord to Bethel. Jeroboam was standing by the altar to make offerings. ²And the man cried against the altar by the word of the Lord and said, "O altar, altar, thus says the Lord: 'Behold, a son shall be born to the house of David, Josiah by name, and he shall sacrifice on you the priests of the high places who make offerings on you, and human bones shall be burned on you.'" ³And he gave a sign the same day, saying, "This is the sign that the Lord has spoken: 'Behold, the altar shall be torn down, and the ashes that are on it shall be poured out.'" ⁴And when the king heard the saying of the man of God, which he cried against the altar at Bethel, Jeroboam stretched out his hand from the altar, saying, "Seize him." And his hand, which he stretched out against him, dried up, so that he could not draw it back to himself. ⁵The altar also was torn down, and the ashes poured out from the altar, according to the sign that the man of God had given by the word of the Lord. ⁶And the king said to the man of God, "Entreat now the favor of the Lord your God, and pray for me, that my hand may be restored to me." And the man of God entreated the Lord, and the king's hand was restored to him and became as it was before. ⁷And the king said to the man of God, "Come home with me, and refresh yourself, and I will give you a reward." ⁸And the man of God said to the king, "If you give me half your house, I will not go in with you. And I will not eat bread or drink water in this place, ⁹for so was it commanded me by the word of the Lord, saying, 'You shall neither eat bread nor drink water nor return by the way that you came.'" ¹⁰So he went another way and did not return by the way that he came to Bethel.

¹¹Now an old prophet lived in Bethel. And his sons*ᵃ* came and told him all that the man of God had done that day in Bethel. They also told to their father the words that he had spoken to the king. ¹²And their father said to them, "Which way did he go?" And his sons showed him the way that the man of God who came from Judah had gone. ¹³And he said to his sons, "Saddle the donkey for me." So they saddled the donkey for him and he mounted it. ¹⁴And he went after the man of God and found him sitting under an oak. And he said to him, "Are you the man of God who came from Judah?" And he said, "I am." ¹⁵Then he said to him, "Come home with me and eat bread." ¹⁶And he said, "I may not return with you, or go in with you, neither will I eat bread nor drink water with you in this place, ¹⁷for it was said to me by the word of the Lord, 'You shall neither eat bread nor drink water there, nor return by the way that you came.'" ¹⁸And he said to him, "I also am a prophet as you are, and an angel spoke to me by the word of the Lord, saying, 'Bring him back with you into your house that he may eat bread and drink water.'" But he lied to him. ¹⁹So he went back with him and ate bread in his house and drank water.

²⁰And as they sat at the table, the word of the Lord came to the prophet who had brought him back. ²¹And he cried to the man of God who came from Judah, "Thus says the Lord, 'Because you have disobeyed the word of the Lord and have not kept the command that the Lord your God commanded you, ²²but have come back and have eaten bread and drunk water in the place of which he said to you, "Eat no bread and drink no water," your body shall not come to the tomb of your fathers.'" ²³And after he had eaten bread and drunk, he saddled the donkey for the prophet whom he had brought back. ²⁴And as he went away a lion met him on the road and killed him. And his body was thrown in the road, and the donkey stood beside it; the lion also stood beside the body. ²⁵And behold, men passed by and saw the body thrown in the road and the lion standing by the body. And they came and told it in the city where the old prophet lived.

²⁶And when the prophet who had brought him back from the way heard of it, he said, "It is the man

of God who disobeyed the word of the Lord; therefore the Lord has given him to the lion, which has torn him and killed him, according to the word that the Lord spoke to him." ²⁷And he said to his sons, "Saddle the donkey for me." And they saddled it. ²⁸And he went and found his body thrown in the road, and the donkey and the lion standing beside the body. The lion had not eaten the body or torn the donkey. ²⁹And the prophet took up the body of the man of God and laid it on the donkey and brought it back to the city[b] to mourn and to bury him. ³⁰And he laid the body in his own grave. And they mourned over him, saying, "Alas, my brother!" ³¹And after he had buried him, he said to his sons, "When I die, bury me in the grave in which the man of God is buried; lay my bones beside his bones. ³²For the saying that he called out by the word of the Lord against the altar in Bethel and against all the houses of the high places that are in the cities of Samaria shall surely come to pass."

³³After this thing Jeroboam did not turn from his evil way, but made priests for the high places again from among all the people. Any who would, he ordained to be priests of the high places. ³⁴And this thing became sin to the house of Jeroboam, so as to cut it off and to destroy it from the face of the earth.

14 At that time Abijah the son of Jeroboam fell sick. ²And Jeroboam said to his wife, "Arise, and disguise yourself, that it not be known that you are the wife of Jeroboam, and go to Shiloh. Behold, Ahijah the prophet is there, who said of me that I should be king over this people. ³Take with you ten loaves, some cakes, and a jar of honey, and go to him. He will tell you what shall happen to the child."

⁴Jeroboam's wife did so. She arose and went to Shiloh and came to the house of Ahijah. Now Ahijah could not see, for his eyes were dim because of his age. ⁵And the Lord said to Ahijah, "Behold, the wife of Jeroboam is coming to inquire of you concerning her son, for he is sick. Thus and thus shall you say to her."

When she came, she pretended to be another woman. ⁶But when Ahijah heard the sound of her feet, as she came in at the door, he said, "Come in, wife of Jeroboam. Why do you pretend to be another? For I am charged with unbearable news for you. ⁷Go, tell Jeroboam, 'Thus says the Lord, the

God of Israel: "Because I exalted you from among the people and made you leader over my people Israel ⁸and tore the kingdom away from the house of David and gave it to you, and yet you have not been like my servant David, who kept my commandments and followed me with all his heart, doing only that which was right in my eyes, ⁹but you have done evil above all who were before you and have gone and made for yourself other gods and metal images, provoking me to anger, and have cast me behind your back, ¹⁰therefore behold, I will bring harm upon the house of Jeroboam and will cut off from Jeroboam every male, both bond and free in Israel, and will burn up the house of Jeroboam, as a man burns up dung until it is all gone. ¹¹Anyone belonging to Jeroboam who dies in the city the dogs shall eat, and anyone who dies in the open country the birds of the heavens shall eat, for the Lord has spoken it."'

¹²Arise therefore, go to your house. When your feet enter the city, the child shall die. ¹³And all Israel shall mourn for him and bury him, for he only of Jeroboam shall come to the grave, because in him there is found something pleasing to the Lord, the God of Israel, in the house of Jeroboam. ¹⁴Moreover, the Lord will raise up for himself a king over Israel who shall cut off the house of Jeroboam today. And henceforth, ¹⁵the Lord will strike Israel as a reed is shaken in the water, and root up Israel out of this good land that he gave to their fathers and scatter them beyond the Euphrates,[c] because they have made their Asherim, provoking the Lord to anger. ¹⁶And he will give Israel up because of the sins of Jeroboam, which he sinned and made Israel to sin."

¹⁷Then Jeroboam's wife arose and departed and came to Tirzah. And as she came to the threshold of the house, the child died. ¹⁸And all Israel buried him and mourned for him, according to the word of the Lord, which he spoke by his servant Ahijah the prophet.

¹⁹Now the rest of the acts of Jeroboam, how he warred and how he reigned, behold, they are written in the Book of the Chronicles of the Kings of Israel. ²⁰And the time that Jeroboam reigned was twenty-two years. And he slept with his fathers, and Nadab his son reigned in his place.

²¹Now Rehoboam the son of Solomon reigned in Judah. Rehoboam was forty-one years old when he began to reign, and he reigned seventeen years in Jerusalem, the city that the LORD had chosen out of all the tribes of Israel, to put his name there. His mother's name was Naamah the Ammonite. ²²And Judah did what was evil in the sight of the LORD, and they provoked him to jealousy with their sins that they committed, more than all that their fathers had done. ²³For they also built for themselves high places and pillars and Asherim on every high hill and under every green tree, ²⁴and there were also male cult prostitutes in the land. They did according to all the abominations of the nations that the LORD drove out before the people of Israel.

²⁵In the fifth year of King Rehoboam, Shishak king of Egypt came up against Jerusalem. ²⁶He took away the treasures of the house of the LORD and the treasures of the king's house. He took away everything. He also took away all the shields of gold that Solomon had made, ²⁷and King Rehoboam made in their place shields of bronze, and committed them to the hands of the officers of the guard, who kept the door of the king's house. ²⁸And as often as the king went into the house of the LORD, the guard carried them and brought them back to the guardroom.

²⁹Now the rest of the acts of Rehoboam and all that he did, are they not written in the Book of the Chronicles of the Kings of Judah? ³⁰And there was war between Rehoboam and Jeroboam continually. ³¹And Rehoboam slept with his fathers and was buried with his fathers in the city of David. His mother's name was Naamah the Ammonite. And Abijam his son reigned in his place.

a Septuagint, Syriac, Vulgate; Hebrew *son*   b Septuagint; Hebrew *he came to the city of the old prophet*   c Hebrew *the River*

OVERVIEW: The intransigence of Jeroboam in these two chapters gives the commentators further opportunity to criticize his reign as king and his religious leadership over Israel. They can hardly fathom Jeroboam's persistence in disobeying God in spite of a clear demonstration of divine disapproval. Still, some emphasize God's mercy in dealing with Jeroboam in the face of his bad decisions. For the reformers, obedience to God's Word is paramount. Therefore even though the old prophet deceives the man of God, the commentators still hold the man of God accountable for accepting the old prophet's invitation to dine with him since the invitation goes against the original commandment he receives. These interpreters also understand God's justice to be active in the death of Jeroboam's line on account of his repeated blasphemy. Nor do the reformers mince words about the evil of Rehoboam, Jeroboam's rival king.

TWO THINGS TO CONSIDER. JOHANNES BUGENHAGEN: There are two things to be considered in this chapter. The first is the impiety and blindness of Jeroboam, who remained impervious to such signs. Here you see what Christ said, "If they do not hear Moses and the Prophets, neither will they be convinced if someone should rise from the dead." This is horrible to see in light of the history of the children of Israel who perished in the desert after having seen so many miracles. The miracles certainly admonished in the same way as sacred words did. But where God is not admitted to the heart and where God is not the teacher, such things are heard in vain, as is seen in Jeroboam's vanity in this story. This is clearly said at the end of this chapter, "After this thing Jeroboam did not turn from his evil way," etc. This is also against those who say in Matthew, "If we had lived in the days of our fathers, we would not have taken part with them in shedding the blood of the prophets." That is, if we had seen those miracles and heard those words they saw and heard, we would not have followed what their free wills invented. But instead they hear from Jesus, "Fill up, then, the measure of your fathers."

Second, a holy prophet is deceived and killed. But even in receiving this sentence of death, he remains holy because he acknowledged his mistake and entrusted himself to the will of God. This is just like Moses, who accepted the sentence of his death on account of his unbelief at the waters of Meribah. This point should be greatly noted, that God wants us simply to cling to his Word. Once the Word has been accepted, we should not turn to another different word, however much it might seem to shine with holiness, even if we see some miracles, for God tests you through miracles, as Deuteronomy 13 says. And we should never be led astray by false signs, just as Paul has foretold in 2 Thessalonians 2. COMMENTARY ON 1 KINGS.[1]

THREE LESSONS FOR MINISTERS OF GOD'S WORD. JOHANNES PISCATOR: There are three things to observe here concerning the ministers of the Word of God. The first example concerns that man of God, that is, the prophet from Judah who went to Bethel. He gives a warning to the ministers of the Word of God that when necessity calls, they must not fear kings or princes who have been committed to their care. They must condemn sin and declare the punishment of God. Similarly, ministers of the Word of God must not shrink back at all from the office to which they have been commissioned. Second, this liberty usually produces a trial before the kings and princes, which is to be seized on. And finally, God, if he is seen in this way, protects protects ministers of the Word from the power of princes by punishing their persecutors—indeed, he even causes these persecutors to offer his benefits to his ministers. COMMENTARY ON 1 KINGS.[2]

13:1-10 A Man of God Rebukes Jeroboam for His Idolatry

HEARING BUT NOT HEEDING. KONRAD PELLIKAN: The king was admonished not only with the word but also with clear signs, so that he began to stop the pilgrimages of worship,

heresies of faith and ceremonies that he had established against God's law. And so the new altar was torn down, for if he had not acknowledged the miracle, the king's arm would have gone back to being useless. But even though the prophet's prayer restored the king's arm, in the end he remained in his campaign of contempt. Thus we learn that miracles performed by good people on account of evil may themselves produce nothing but testimony for condemnation where there is no faith or conversion, having been found frightening more than inspiring. Ungodly people hear the man of God but do not heed him. COMMENTARY ON 1 KINGS.[3]

A PEOPLE'S WHOSE FAITH HAD BECOME COLD. JOHN MAYER: Even though Jeroboam had fallen into such gross idolatry, the Lord, who had set him up to be king, did not leave him. Rather, he sent his prophet to him to reprove and threaten him to try to get him to humble and reform himself, if by any means he might do so. And this man of God is said to have come out of Judah since . . . none in Jeroboam's kingdom would dare oppose him in his wicked proceedings. From this we may gather how cold Israel's love for God and zeal for the truth had become. This greatly contrasts with the zeal of the Israelites during the time of Joshua, when an altar set up by the Reubenites, Gadites and the half-tribe of Manasseh was enough to get the rest to fight. Yet the godliest in those parts were all gone to Judah out of a dislike of Jeroboam's doings. COMMENTARY ON 1 KINGS.[4]

13:11-19 The Man of God's Disobedience and the Prophet's Lie

OBEYING ONLY GOD'S COMMANDMENTS. ANDREAS BODENSTEIN VON KARLSTADT: Note, when we have words of the Lord but are disobedient to the voice of God, allowing another to persuade and deceive us, we have to die. Though the persuader

---

[1]Bugenhagen, *In Regum duos ultimos libros*, 71-72; citing Lk 16:31; Mt 23:29-32; Num 20:12-13; Deut 13:1-3; 2 Thess 2:9.
[2]Piscator, *Commentarii in omnes libros Veteris Testamenti*, 2:286.
[3]Pellikan, *Commentaria Bibliorum*, 2:159r.
[4]Mayer, *Many Commentaries in One*, 72*.

or deceiver has the appearance of a prophet, an angel, a teacher, or a Christian who extends Christian benevolence and provides food and drink, if such benevolence prevents you from obeying God's commandment and Word, you must not follow him, though he be a big, strong and opulent monk or doctor. ON THE REMOVAL OF IMAGES.[5]

WHETHER THE "OLD PROPHET" WAS A TRUE OR FALSE PROPHET.

JOHN MAYER: The old prophet heard about the man of God from his sons, who may have been present at Jeroboam's sacrifice. He heard that the man of God came from Judah and gave a sign, but departed from there without eating or drinking because God had forbidden him to do so. The prophet therefore rode after him to fetch him back to his house to eat with him. He lied to him, saying that it was revealed to him that he should return to eat with him. But in this action he was dissembling....

Touching this old prophet, some hold him to have been a false prophet and a worshiper of Jeroboam's calves. These interpreters believe that he was an encourager of Jeroboam in his wickedness and that he sought to trap the man of God in stealth, so that he might destroy him. And these interpreters also hold that when he had persuaded the man of God to remain, he went to the king and convinced him that the man of God was a vain and wicked man, as later appeared by the judgment befalling him. In this line of thought the prophet told Jeroboam that there was not any cause why he should be troubled at the man of God's prophecy or sign, seeing that the altar could be made new again and used for sacrifices, and that the strength of his arm might have failed him through the weariness in standing and holding the censer of incense for so long a time....

But other interpreters believe that the prophet was a true prophet of God, but frigid and without zeal to oppose Jeroboam in his idolatry. Yet they say he was glad that one came to reprove Jeroboam, and he earnestly desired to do the man of God any

good service he could and to become acquainted with him. Therefore, not being otherwise able to bring the man of God back to his house, he faked a revelation made to him from God....

Upon the foresaid reasons, then, because in the sacred history he is called nothing other than an "old prophet," I conclude that he was not a false prophet. He did not stand for idolatry, as Josephus pretends, or for wicked wizardry, as Balaam had. Rather he was a prophet of the Lord, yet subject to be overly swayed by a good intention to show kindness to the man of God, so that he lied to him but sought again later by repentance to do away with his sin. But the prophet did show the man of God the best offices of love that he could by burying the man honorably, lamenting his death and confirming his word by being buried in the same grave with him. COMMENTARY ON 1 KINGS.[6]

13:20-34 The Lion's Strange Behavior

THE LION AND DONKEY TESTIFY.

KONRAD PELLIKAN: The judgments of God are always terrible to us, who have our ignorance punished in this life. Even the saints cry out, "Enter not into judgment with your servant, for no one living is righteous before you." But in the true saints, this death is made glorious: "Precious in the sight of the Lord is the death of his saints." This is seen in the miracle of the lion who did not devour the prophet or eat the donkey but wanted to stand by the body as a guard until the guilty prophet would come to the dead one. Thus even the lion and the donkey testified to the truth of the prophecy that was predicted against the king and the kingdom. COMMENTARY ON 1 KINGS.[7]

GOD'S GOVERNANCE OVER THE LION.

JOHANNES PISCATOR: It is a very beautiful example of the providence and governance of God that the lion God had sent to kill the prophet was so governed that it remained

---

[5]CRR 8:113.

[6]Mayer, Many Commentaries in One, 73*.
[7]Pellikan, Commentaria Bibliorum, 2:160r; citing Ps 143:2; 116:15.

peaceful by the dead body and the donkey. Indeed, it did not even try to consume either of them. COMMENTARY ON 1 KINGS.[8]

14:1-20 Abijah's Sickness, Jeroboam's Lie and Abijah's Threat

EARLY PROPHECY OF ISRAEL'S DEMISE. JOHANNES BUGENHAGEN: Through the prophet, God foretold the uprooting not only of Jeroboam's line but also of the line of Israel. This was because of the sin of idolatry, in which they invented other words of God for themselves, following them and honoring them as if they were from God. Second Kings 17 reveals how this story came to completion. As is typical of the prophets, the death of the boy at his mother's return was added to be a certain sign of all of this. But Jeroboam would still not come to his senses. He was hardened like Pharaoh, as you see here, a "vessel of wrath prepared from destruction," so that no sign and no admonitions would be believed. But we should learn the pure judgment of God. God added to Jeroboam's impiety so that he might believe the true prophet, who had prophesied about his kingdom and condemned it. COMMENTARY ON 1 KINGS.[9]

EMBARRASSED BY A BAD CONSCIENCE. KONRAD PELLIKAN: The wickedness of the superstitious and ungodly king was punished in his son and his descendants. For he had a son Abijah who got sick and died. Jeroboam had not been affected by God's miraculous warnings through the prophet of the Lord but instead advanced in evil. Alarmed by his son's illness and not fully trusting in his calves or their priests who gave him no courage for his anxiety, he sought to entreat the true God. For he was not ignorant of God but he was oppressed by a bad conscience so that he did not dare to pray to God for his son's health, considering God's grace to be a small thing. Therefore he knew he would be

embarrassed to approach the true prophet whom he had previously disregarded. So he sent his wife to ask for prayer for their son or to foretell his eventual death. Thus everyone who sets their faith in creatures and not in God alone is thrown into confusion and forced to despair. And in the end those who have preferred false helpers only understand their damnable unbelief and begin to seek the truly and only God too late. The Lord's prophet Ahijah, who lived alone at a desolate place in Shiloh, discerned the king's evil and did not try to change God's judgment because of the king's high office. For he had already said enough to Jeroboam in person when he had been chosen by God. COMMENTARY ON 1 KINGS.[10]

JEROBOAM'S FOOLISH ATTEMPT AT TRICKERY. JOHANNES PISCATOR: In Jeroboam's consultation of the prophet Ahijah regarding his son's possible death, an example of hypocrisy is set forth in two ways. First, Jeroboam consults God through the prophet even though he had despised God by insolently persevering in idolatry, which was a great perversity. Second, Jeroboam attempted to deceive the prophet who nevertheless could see through his deceit, for the death of Jeroboam's son had been revealed to the prophet beforehand. Jeroboam's attempt was simultaneously tricky and foolish. From this we learn the lesson that trickery never aids hypocrites. For God detects frauds, as this passage indicates concerning the concealing of Jeroboam's wife to Ahijah, and God makes come to pass that which individuals feared despite their deceitful attempts at aversion. In this way, it comes to pass that Ahijah gravely reprimanded Jeroboam on account of his idolatry COMMENTARY ON 1 KINGS.[11]

SEEKING GOD TOO LATE. JOHN MAYER: This wicked king . . . not being moved to repent by all the signs he had seen, now begins to be punished in his best son, Abijah, who is struck with sickness. And because Jeroboam knew that the idols he served had

---

[8]Piscator, *Commentarii in omnes libros Veteris Testamenti*, 2:286.
[9]Bugenhagen, *In Regum duos ultimos libros*, 74-75; citing Ex 7:3; Rom 9:22.

[10]Pellikan, *Commentaria Bibliorum*, 2:160r.
[11]Piscator, *Commentarii in omnes libros Veteris Testamenti*, 2:289.

no power to help him, for only the true God could, he sent his servant to Ahijah the prophet. He thought that he might receive favor from him, with whom he had earlier had an experience when this prophet foretold Jeroboam that he would reign over Israel, for he was a true prophet. But being conscious of the great idolatry that shamed him and knowing that he himself could not be seen sending someone to a true prophet, he caused his wife to disguise herself. In this way Jeroboam was greatly confounded in his time of trouble, as are all those who refuse to seek the true God. That's because they have formerly forsaken him and, having cast aside all fear, have turned to worshiping creatures. Such is the case of all the wicked: they eventually come to see the hurt that was caused by their sins, and they seek God to end their misery only too late. COMMENTARY ON 1 KINGS.[12]

14:21-31 *Shishak of Egypt Plunders Jerusalem*

GOD'S HOLY WRATH. JOHANNES BUGENHAGEN: As it says in 2 Chronicles, they lived piously for three years under Rehoboam. But then they withdrew from God no less impiously than the kingdom of Israel. Not only did they do this as their ancestors had done earlier in the wilderness and in the Promised Land during the time of the judges, but also, even worse, they imitated the abominations the Canaanites had previously made when they had been cast out of their land by God. But nothing deterred or admonished them, not even the holy place where the worship and word of God happened in Jerusalem, for the impious people deserted God and followed the impious king and his impious mother, who was an Ammonite and one of the ones who had led Rehoboam's father Solomon astray. Therefore, as they saw the wrath of God through the king of Egypt, the things that had been piously presented during Solomon's time were carried off by wicked men. For "'there is no peace,' says the Lord, 'for the wicked.'" So whenever we might see this judgment

of God, let us pray with a holy fear that God not desert us. For we can be polluted by these impieties, if God does not protect our hearts. COMMENTARY ON 1 KINGS.[13]

A FOOLISH KING FOR AN UNGRATEFUL PEOPLE. KONRAD PELLIKAN: Rehoboam, the king of Judah, took the throne when he was forty-one years old. That would be a fine age, if he had not been foolish and evil by nature. The reason given for this is that his mother was an Ammonite woman. The fact that this wretched and foolish king succeeded the exceedingly wise Solomon came from the people's ingratitude to God, for they did not deserve a better king. . . . They did not imitate their good ancestors but the ungodly ones, even surpassing their sins and evil. They followed the customs of their ancestors in building high places, altars, idols, statues and the sacred groves of the Gentiles, practicing their idolatries in the hills, mountains, forests and valleys, as if abandoning the law of the Lord that had been given. By this they provoked the Lord's great wrath. COMMENTARY ON 1 KINGS.[14]

JUDAH'S COMPETITION OF SIN WITH ISRAEL. JOHN MAYER: God had chosen Jerusalem to set up his name there. However, in spite of God, Jeroboam had set up idols there. And by this means Judah was more corrupted than during Solomon's, or in any of their forefather's, times. That's because idolatry was more generally followed after Rehoboam's time than at any time before. The great sin of Judah is not lessened by comparing it with Israel's sin under Jeroboam. Israel sinned more than Judah on account of Jeroboam's initiation of idolatry into the land and his prohibition of the people from going to Jerusalem to worship the proper way. Rehoboam did not do this, seeing that the people were still free to sacrifice according to the law. But the particular way in which Judah

---

[12]Mayer, *Many Commentaries in One*, 75-76*.

[13]Bugenhagen, *In Regum duos ultimos libros*, 76; citing 2 Chron 11:17; Is 48:22.
[14]Pellikan, *Commentaria Bibliorum*, 2:161r.

exceeded the sin of their forefathers was in the act of allowing males to prostitute themselves at their idolatrous feasts. In these abominations they acted like the heathen whom God had previously cut off. Indeed these actions are noted to be a judgment by which the heathen were given over in Romans 1, and the people of Judah committed the same sin. COMMENTARY ON 1 KINGS.[15]

---

[15]Mayer, *Many Commentaries in One*, 80-81*.

15:1–16:34 FROM THE REIGN OF ABIJAM TO AHAB

[1]Now in the eighteenth year of King Jeroboam the son of Nebat, Abijam began to reign over Judah. [2]He reigned for three years in Jerusalem. His mother's name was Maacah the daughter of Abishalom. [3]And he walked in all the sins that his father did before him, and his heart was not wholly true to the LORD his God, as the heart of David his father. [4]Nevertheless, for David's sake the LORD his God gave him a lamp in Jerusalem, setting up his son after him, and establishing Jerusalem, [5]because David did what was right in the eyes of the LORD and did not turn aside from anything that he commanded him all the days of his life, except in the matter of Uriah the Hittite. [6]Now there was war between Rehoboam and Jeroboam all the days of his life. [7]The rest of the acts of Abijam and all that he did, are they not written in the Book of the Chronicles of the Kings of Judah? And there was war between Abijam and Jeroboam. [8]And Abijam slept with his fathers, and they buried him in the city of David. And Asa his son reigned in his place.

[9]In the twentieth year of Jeroboam king of Israel, Asa began to reign over Judah, [10]and he reigned forty-one years in Jerusalem. His mother's name was Maacah the daughter of Abishalom. [11]And Asa did what was right in the eyes of the LORD, as David his father had done. [12]He put away the male cult prostitutes out of the land and removed all the idols that his fathers had made. [13]He also removed Maacah his mother from being queen mother because she had made an abominable image for Asherah. And Asa cut down her image and burned it at the brook Kidron. [14]But the high places were not taken away. Nevertheless, the heart of Asa was wholly true to the LORD all his days. [15]And he brought into the house of the LORD the sacred gifts of his father and his own sacred gifts, silver, and gold, and vessels.

[16]And there was war between Asa and Baasha king of Israel all their days. [17]Baasha king of Israel went up against Judah and built Ramah, that he might permit no one to go out or come in to Asa king of Judah. [18]Then Asa took all the silver and the gold that were left in the treasures of the house of the LORD and the treasures of the king's house and gave them into the hands of his servants. And King Asa sent them to Ben-hadad the son of Tabrimmon, the son of Hezion, king of Syria, who lived in Damascus, saying, [19]"Let there be a covenant[a] between me and you, as there was between my father and your father. Behold, I am sending to you a present of silver and gold. Go, break your covenant with Baasha king of Israel, that he may withdraw from me." [20]And Ben-hadad listened to King Asa and sent the commanders of his armies against the cities of Israel and conquered Ijon, Dan, Abel-beth-maacah, and all Chinneroth, with all the land of Naphtali. [21]And when Baasha heard of it, he stopped building Ramah, and he lived in Tirzah. [22]Then King Asa made a proclamation to all Judah, none was exempt, and they carried away the stones of Ramah and its timber, with which Baasha had been building, and with them King Asa built Geba of Benjamin and Mizpah. [23]Now the rest of all the acts of Asa, all his might, and all that he did, and the cities that he built, are they not written in the Book of the Chronicles of the Kings of Judah? But in his old age he was diseased in his feet. [24]And Asa slept with his fathers and was buried with his fathers in the city of David his father, and Jehoshaphat his son reigned in his place.

[25]Nadab the son of Jeroboam began to reign over Israel in the second year of Asa king of Judah, and he reigned over Israel two years. [26]He did what was evil in the sight of the LORD and walked in the way of his father, and in his sin which he made Israel to sin.

[27]Baasha the son of Ahijah, of the house of Issachar, conspired against him. And Baasha struck him down at Gibbethon, which belonged to the Philistines, for Nadab and all Israel were laying siege to Gibbethon. [28]So Baasha killed him in the third year of Asa king of Judah and reigned in his place. [29]And as soon as he was king, he killed all the house of Jeroboam. He left to the house of Jeroboam not one that breathed, until he had destroyed it, according to the word of the LORD that he spoke by his servant

Ahijah the Shilonite. ³⁰It was for the sins of Jeroboam that he sinned and that he made Israel to sin, and because of the anger to which he provoked the Lord, the God of Israel.

³¹Now the rest of the acts of Nadab and all that he did, are they not written in the Book of the Chronicles of the Kings of Israel? ³²And there was war between Asa and Baasha king of Israel all their days.

³³In the third year of Asa king of Judah, Baasha the son of Ahijah began to reign over all Israel at Tirzah, and he reigned twenty-four years. ³⁴He did what was evil in the sight of the Lord and walked in the way of Jeroboam and in his sin which he made Israel to sin.

16 And the word of the Lord came to Jehu the son of Hanani against Baasha, saying, ²"Since I exalted you out of the dust and made you leader over my people Israel, and you have walked in the way of Jeroboam and have made my people Israel to sin, provoking me to anger with their sins, ³behold, I will utterly sweep away Baasha and his house, and I will make your house like the house of Jeroboam the son of Nebat. ⁴Anyone belonging to Baasha who dies in the city the dogs shall eat, and anyone of his who dies in the field the birds of the heavens shall eat."

⁵Now the rest of the acts of Baasha and what he did, and his might, are they not written in the Book of the Chronicles of the Kings of Israel? ⁶And Baasha slept with his fathers and was buried at Tirzah, and Elah his son reigned in his place. ⁷Moreover, the word of the Lord came by the prophet Jehu the son of Hanani against Baasha and his house, both because of all the evil that he did in the sight of the Lord, provoking him to anger with the work of his hands, in being like the house of Jeroboam, and also because he destroyed it.

⁸In the twenty-sixth year of Asa king of Judah, Elah the son of Baasha began to reign over Israel in Tirzah, and he reigned two years. ⁹But his servant Zimri, commander of half his chariots, conspired against him. When he was at Tirzah, drinking himself drunk in the house of Arza, who was over the household in Tirzah, ¹⁰Zimri came in and struck him down and killed him, in the twenty-seventh year of Asa king of Judah, and reigned in his place.

¹¹When he began to reign, as soon as he had seated himself on his throne, he struck down all the house of Baasha. He did not leave him a single male of his relatives or his friends. ¹²Thus Zimri destroyed all the house of Baasha, according to the word of the Lord, which he spoke against Baasha by Jehu the prophet, ¹³for all the sins of Baasha and the sins of Elah his son, which they sinned and which they made Israel to sin, provoking the Lord God of Israel to anger with their idols. ¹⁴Now the rest of the acts of Elah and all that he did, are they not written in the Book of the Chronicles of the Kings of Israel?

¹⁵In the twenty-seventh year of Asa king of Judah, Zimri reigned seven days in Tirzah. Now the troops were encamped against Gibbethon, which belonged to the Philistines, ¹⁶and the troops who were encamped heard it said, "Zimri has conspired, and he has killed the king." Therefore all Israel made Omri, the commander of the army, king over Israel that day in the camp. ¹⁷So Omri went up from Gibbethon, and all Israel with him, and they besieged Tirzah. ¹⁸And when Zimri saw that the city was taken, he went into the citadel of the king's house and burned the king's house over him with fire and died, ¹⁹because of his sins that he committed, doing evil in the sight of the Lord, walking in the way of Jeroboam, and for his sin which he committed, making Israel to sin. ²⁰Now the rest of the acts of Zimri, and the conspiracy that he made, are they not written in the Book of the Chronicles of the Kings of Israel?

²¹Then the people of Israel were divided into two parts. Half of the people followed Tibni the son of Ginath, to make him king, and half followed Omri. ²²But the people who followed Omri overcame the people who followed Tibni the son of Ginath. So Tibni died, and Omri became king. ²³In the thirty-first year of Asa king of Judah, Omri began to reign over Israel, and he reigned for twelve years; six years he reigned in Tirzah. ²⁴He bought the hill of Samaria from Shemer for two talents[b] of silver, and he fortified the hill and called the name of the city that he built Samaria, after the name of Shemer, the owner of the hill.

²⁵Omri did what was evil in the sight of the Lord, and did more evil than all who were before him. ²⁶For he walked in all the way of Jeroboam the son of Nebat, and in the sins that he made Israel to sin, provoking

the Lord, the God of Israel, to anger by their idols. [27]Now the rest of the acts of Omri that he did, and the might that he showed, are they not written in the Book of the Chronicles of the Kings of Israel? [28]And Omri slept with his fathers and was buried in Samaria, and Ahab his son reigned in his place.

[29]In the thirty-eighth year of Asa king of Judah, Ahab the son of Omri began to reign over Israel, and Ahab the son of Omri reigned over Israel in Samaria twenty-two years. [30]And Ahab the son of Omri did evil in the sight of the Lord, more than all who were before him. [31]And as if it had been a light thing for

him to walk in the sins of Jeroboam the son of Nebat, he took for his wife Jezebel the daughter of Ethbaal king of the Sidonians, and went and served Baal and worshiped him. [32]He erected an altar for Baal in the house of Baal, which he built in Samaria. [33]And Ahab made an Asherah. Ahab did more to provoke the Lord, the God of Israel, to anger than all the kings of Israel who were before him. [34]In his days Hiel of Bethel built Jericho. He laid its foundation at the cost of Abiram his firstborn, and set up its gates at the cost of his youngest son Segub, according to the word of the Lord, which he spoke by Joshua the son of Nun.

a Or *treaty*; twice in this verse   b A *talent* was about 75 pounds or 34 kilograms

---

Overview: The reformers comment on the revolving door of kings of Israel and Judah in these two chapters, following the biblical text closely and affirming divine blessing or punishment over these kings based on their faithfulness or faithlessness respectively. They marvel at God's patience in allowing Abijam to reign for even three years. Asa, though praised for his faithfulness to the Lord, is also censured by these commentators for refusing to destroy shrines in the high places, intimating his partial commitment to God. Jehu's divinely given words to Baasha, "I exalted you," provokes some discussion from these commentators, who consider God's role, if any, in using evil to punish evil. All the rest of the kings included in this section are condemned by the interpreters, especially King Ahab. In line with the biblical text, the reformers cite Ahab as the worst of all kings, a persecutor of the truth and a blasphemer against the Holy Spirit.

15:1-4 Abijam Reigns in Judah

King Abijam. Johannes Bugenhagen: Insofar as he trusted in God with his people, this King Abijam was made strong against his adversaries in Israel, as you read in 2 Chronicles 13, so that you see salvation only through faith in God and not through military might or human strength. But "Oh, the depth" of God's judgment! Through him

God afflicted the Israelites. But then Abijam and the people were condemned for their own impiety, as the text says that he strayed, after not only having known but also experiencing God's favor. Commentary on 1 Kings.[1]

Absalom's Impious Grandson. Konrad Pellikan: It was an act of God's mercy that this impious Abijam, himself the son of an impious father, reigned for the brief span of three years. He was born of an impious mother, clearly the daughter of Absalom, who passed her father's hostile spirit down to her son. Commentary on 1 Kings.[2]

15:5-8 "David Did What Was Right in the Eyes of the Lord"

For David's Sake. Johannes Bugenhagen: David had done what was right. Clearly much of what had been right in him had already come from God, as David often sang in his psalms. But you say, "What about this 'merit' that I see here?" I respond that this merit came after him, for God makes us holy so that we may live and act in holiness. For if God has not made us holy, then we can neither act nor live in holiness. As Augustine says, "God crowns

---

[1]Bugenhagen, *In Regum duos ultimos libros*, 76-77; citing Rom 11:33.
[2]Pellikan, *Commentaria Bibliorum*, 2:161v, following the Vulgate's rendering of the name *Abishalom* as *Absalom*.

his own gifts in us." Or see what David himself said in 2 Samuel 7, where he considered how everything came from God's promises alone. An "except" was also added with respect to David's faithfulness, first, so that impious people in praise of David do not forget to reckon with his murder and adultery, and second, so we know that the saints, whom God loves, sin and then return to holiness by being forgiven by God, who is himself a city of refuge for sinners. COMMENTARY ON 1 KINGS.[3]

DIFFERENT KINDS OF DECEIT. DANIEL DYKE: The heart of the wicked is deceitful with a full, strong and reigning deceitfulness. The deceitfulness in the heart of the godly is weaker, for it can be discerned as evil and fought against. The heart of the wicked shows its deceitfulness in the whole course of their lives, while the heart of the godly only shows its deceitfulness in some particular actions. As it is said of David, he was upright in all things, "except in the matter of Uriah." The general current of his life was free from deceitfulness, though not that particular action. On the other hand, the heart of the wicked may be upright in some particular action . . . yet not in the main of their lives. This is proper only to the godly—that they are upright in their way, that is, in the constant tenor of their conversation. Now this deceitfulness here given to the heart is set forth in three ways: first, by the greatness of it . . . ; second, by the cause of it and its evil; and third, by the unsearchableness of it, such that none can know it. That is, no one of themselves, by their own mother's wit, without a higher and clearer light, can know the deceitfulness of one's heart. THE MYSTERY OF SELF-DECEIVING.[4]

15:9-24 Asa Reigns in Judah

PIOUS KING ASA. JOHANNES BUGENHAGEN: Asa was a pious king who tackled idolatry and trusted in God, as his prayer of 2 Chronicles shows. Here you see that the abominable idols were also in Judah, where everything was holy to God and where priests preached God's law. So you should not be amazed at what was happening in Israel at the same time. We are the same, if not outwardly, then certainly in our hearts, whenever we have been without God. All the same, you read that Asa and the others around him were not condemned, except that they did not remove the high places, that is, the shrines and altars in the mountains. For even if the true God was being worshiped and adored there, they were against the law, which forbade people from choosing their own places to worship God unless God had chosen such a place. Therefore the king should have removed them, but he did not. But Scripture says, "Nevertheless, the heart of Asa was wholly true to the Lord all his days." You see how this was not imputed to him. I believe that the one person could not do everything for everyone, because of the weak people who were led into idolatry. And so the king might have been seen as tolerating idols along with worship of the true God. COMMENTARY ON 1 KINGS.[5]

WHY ASA TOLERATED THE HIGH PLACES. KONRAD PELLIKAN: There had been many high places for worship all over the kingdom of Judah, where people could worship no one but the Lord. After the construction of Solomon's temple this was not allowed, even though David and his most holy predecessors had rightly tolerated it. For this reason Asa ignored them and did not tear down these kinds of high places that the people had grown accustomed to having, for they had not yet become places where the worship of idols could be abused. Therefore the text can say that Asa's heart remained "wholly true to the Lord" and that the Lord was pleased with him all his life. COMMENTARY ON 1 KINGS.[6]

---

[3]Bugenhagen, *In Regum duos ultimos libros*, 77; citing 2 Sam 7:18-29. Augustine: *deus coronat in nobis sua dona*; Bugenhagen's citation is a paraphrase that accurately expresses Augustine's words in many places, for example, PL 44:891.
[4]Dyke, *The Mystery of Self-Deceiving*, 4-5*; citing 1 Kings 15:5.
[5]Bugenhagen, *In Regum duos ultimos libros*, 78; citing 2 Chron 14:7, 11.
[6]Pellikan, *Commentaria Bibliorum*, 2:162r.

Becoming Good Despite Bad Background.
John Mayer: It is said here that Maacah was Asa's mother when she was really his grandmother. This can be gathered from other passages, where she is called the daughter of Absalom. . . . Maacah is mentioned to greatly commend Asa who, though coming from such a wicked background, feared God and would not be corrupted by Maacah as his father had been. And for this goodness he was rewarded with rest and quietness for ten years, which was a remarkable blessing in those times since it was not enjoyed either by his father or grandfather. Commentary on 1 Kings.[7]

15:25-32 Nadab Reigns in Israel

The Punishments of Providence in the Present. Konrad Pellikan: In the case of King Nadab we learn how divine providence is arranged so that the ungodly are punished, for no one has an excuse for ungodliness. This is true even when the punishment has been predicted, decreed and understood by God in advance. For God's providence is not based on past or future things that are then applied in this or that present moment. Instead those who break God's law will have been punished and given a worthy retribution for their own disobedience. In their ungodliness they have a clear knowledge of their sins and of knowing they had not been coerced. They are instead compelled to confess that they suffer most justly. Commentary on 1 Kings.[8]

Punishment for the Sins of Another.
Johannes Piscator: In the example of Baasha being stirred up by God to extinguish the posterity of Jeroboam, we are warned that God sometimes punishes sins on account of others' sins. For Baasha planned a conspiracy against Nadab, the son of Jeroboam. And after that the entirety of Jeroboam's family was killed on account of Jeroboam's sins. Commentary on 1 Kings.[9]

Was Baasha Guilty if God Willed This to Happen? John Mayer: Baasha, one of Nadab's ambitious captains of the kingdom, conspired against him near Tirzah and killed him, and reigned in his place. Although there was a divine providence for the punishment of Jeroboam's wicked family in Baasha's act, he still sinned by murder and ambition. . . . In fact he proved to be a worse king than Nadab was. Yet he was made an instrument to execute God's judgment on Jeroboam's house by cutting them all off. . . . But his usurping of the kingdom is not hereby justified. God made Baasha king because he allowed him to come to the kingdom, but God did not approve of the way he did so. This is because God did not give Baasha a calling for kingship, and he straightly condemns murder, especially of kings, to whom everyone should be subject.

If it is demanded that God knew when he threatened Jeroboam that Baasha would be the instrument to cut off his posterity and that he was the one whom God used to shed blood in bringing about God's will, how can sin be laid on Baasha?

I answer that God knew what would happen long before it came to pass. However, God's foreknowledge of the act and his decree of judgment for it to happen is no justification of the act if the performer does it without particular warrant from God against his general laws—seeking not the accomplishment of God's will but his own. Commentary on 1 Kings.[10]

Punishing Evil with Evil. Lucas Osiander: On this occasion, Baasha and his coconspirators stirred up sedition against the king in a castle near Gibbethon. Thus Baasha killed Nadab in the third year of King Asa of Judah's reign and took his place, though he himself was no better than Nadab. Thus God is able to punish evil with evil. Annotations on 1 Kings.[11]

---

[7]Mayer, *Many Commentaries in One*, 85*.
[8]Pellikan, *Commentaria Bibliorum*, 2:162v.
[9]Piscator, *Commentarii in omnes libros Veteris Testamenti*, 2:289.

[10]Mayer, *Many Commentaries in One*, 93*.
[11]Osiander, *Liber Iosue*, 795.

15:33–16:7 *Baasha Reigns in Israel*

DEPRAVED KING BAASHA. JOHANNES BUGEN-HAGEN: We have heard of Baasha's depravity in the previous chapter, seeing the great and grave sin in his hardened heart. Not only did he despise a prophet, but also, when a similar thing was predicted about him, he was not at all deterred by the example of Jeroboam and the destruction of Jeroboam's entire family. Still, the impious consider themselves to be servants of God's judgment, as this Baasha was against Jeroboam, as if their advice and strength had done the work that God had done through them. It is like when the Assyrians gloried in themselves in Isaiah 10. Therefore pride in one's mind is simply the blindness of not being able to see the judgment made against others, so that when that same word is sent to oneself it is hated and persecuted. COMMENTARY ON 1 KINGS.[12]

PROPHETS AGAINST KINGS. KONRAD PEL-LIKAN: The Lord indeed raised up prophets against the impious kings of Israel, even those whom he foreknew would never convert or change. By condemning such great ingratitude from that nation, after so many kindnesses, the Lord more clearly reveals himself to all the people of the world and commends his mercy to all nations. This prophet Jehu the son of Hanani prophesied that King Baasha and his descendants will suffer in the same way that Nadab suffered on account of his depravity by the Lord's will when Baasha conspired against his master Nadab. God had put an impious king in charge of an impious people, so that the one, Baasha, came to be the rod and downfall of the other, Nadab. As much as the people whom God called to be his own people embraced the faithless idolatry that Jeroboam first passed on to all his successors in the kingdom, so much would they be held responsible by the prophets, who unanimously condemned them according to the will of God. COMMENTARY ON 1 KINGS.[13]

JUST PUNISHMENT OF BAASHA. JOHN MAYER: If it is objected that it was the will of God that Baasha should be destroyed, it has already been sufficiently answered, namely, that the fulfilling of God's will unwittingly no more justified Baasha than the Jews' fulfilling of what was before determined by God of their bloody crucifixion of our Lord Jesus. So, then, here is a brief response to this question. It is not idly made, but rather shows once more of God's severity against Baasha and his house. Baasha was to be judged in proportion to what he meted out to others. And the Hebrews say that God was most offended with Baasha for killing Nadab so treacherously at that time when he was besieging Gibbethon, because the taking of it from the Philistines was hereby hindered. . . . Whereas Baasha is said to have slept with his fathers and to have been buried in Tirzah, it is to be understood that the judgment threatened on him of being devoured with dogs and birds is to be applied only to his posterity and not to his own person. COMMENTARY ON 1 KINGS.[14]

GOD GIVES AUTHORITY. JOHANNES BUGENHA-GEN: Through the prophet Jehu, God said to Baasha, "I exalted you." We heard about this in an earlier chapter, when the prophet Ahijah said, "Moreover the Lord will raise up for himself a king over Israel who shall cut off the house of Jeroboam today." Here you see Paul's point in Romans 13 that all power is from God. You also see Christ's words to Pilate, "You would have no authority over me at all unless it had been given you from above." For this reason the apostles commanded us to obey even impious magistrates, unless they ask us to go against God. COMMENTARY ON 1 KINGS.[15]

16:8-14 *Elah Reigns in Israel*

PUNISHING IDOLATRY. JOHANNES PISCATOR: In Baasha and Elah an example of punishing idolatry

---

[12]Bugenhagen, *In Regum duos ultimos libros*, 79-80.
[13]Pellikan, *Commentaria Bibliorum*, 2:162v.
[14]Mayer, *Many Commentaries in One*, 94*.
[15]Bugenhagen, *In Regum duos ultimos libros*, 80; citing 1 Kings 14:14; Rom 13:1; Jn 19:11; Acts 5:29.

is set forth, and thus God's truthfulness too, for, as he foretold Baasha's punishment, so he inflicted it. This is another example that God punishes sins with sins, for God punished Elah and his family on account of their idolatry through Zimri's butchery. COMMENTARY ON 1 KINGS.[16]

ELAH, ANOTHER FOOL. JOHANNES BUGENHAGEN: It says that Elah was "drinking himself drunk." Death comes for the impious when they are feeling secure. This is just as we discussed about Nabal the fool. COMMENTARY ON 1 KINGS.[17]

IMPIOUS FATHERS AND SONS. KONRAD PELLIKAN: Elah was killed by his servant Zimri, who commanded half the army of Israel. This was a righteous judgment on the son of Baasha, matching that which Baasha had done to Nadab the son of Jeroboam. All of this had been predicted by the prophets: that impious descendants would be condemned for their own great impiety. For the punishment of sin can be that one remains in sin. Thus the holy will of God is fulfilled in all things, including through a hostile soul, which is then punished by God. COMMENTARY ON 1 KINGS.[18]

WARNING AGAINST DRUNKENNESS. JOHN MAYER: There is nothing commendable said about Elah, but only that he was killed by Zimri, a captain of half of his chariots, when he was drunk in the second year of his reign. And Zimri reigned in his place. From this all people should learn from Elah's example to beware of drunkenness, which has been the overthrow of many kings and great men. COMMENTARY ON 1 KINGS.[19]

16:15-20 Zimri Reigns in Israel

ZIMRI'S TREACHERY. JOHANNES BUGENHAGEN: Zimri fell on the same judgment of God as his predecessors, except that he did not even get to reign for a time. For his treachery, which God used for God's purposes, he immediately received his reward. In a time of trial, Zimri did what people who are without God so often do, that is, he died in the worst despair, and can be counted along with Cain, Saul and Judas. COMMENTARY ON 1 KINGS.[20]

ANOTHER BAD EXAMPLE. JOHANNES PISCATOR: Zimri is set forth as an example of being avenged from heaven for committing murder and idolatry. For the same example of murder he inflicted on others was perpetrated against him. COMMENTARY ON 1 KINGS.[21]

FITTING END TO A SHORT REIGN. JOHN MAYER: Regarding the manner of that usurper Zimri's death, after the army heard of his murder they immediately proclaimed Omri their captain as their king. Omri then marched with his army to Tirzah, where Zimri had usurped the throne, which was about thirty-six miles from Gibbethon, where Omri had been. After seeing that Omri had taken the city, Zimri entered the king's palace and set it on fire, killing himself in the act. This is set forth as a judgment befalling him for his sins. In this way he was like Baasha, not so much for the sins he committed while king (since he was only king for seven days) but for the sins he committed when he was a private man. COMMENTARY ON 1 KINGS.[22]

16:21-28 Omri Reigns in Israel

PRAY FOR PEACE. JOHANNES BUGENHAGEN: How can a people survive and who can work when there is perpetual idolatry, from which comes perpetual discord and the murder of kings? This is necessarily what happens wherever the God who had previously been known as the liberator is rejected. Once someone has seen this God, it is truly better that a people never knew God and such a very frightening

---

[16]Piscator, *Commentarii in omnes libros Veteris Testamenti*, 2:293; citing 1 Kings 16:11.
[17]Bugenhagen, *In Regum duos ultimos libros*, 81; citing 1 Kings 16:9.
[18]Pellikan, *Commentaria Bibliorum*, 2:163r.
[19]Mayer, *Many Commentaries in One*, 95*.
[20]Bugenhagen, *In Samuelem prophetam*, 81.
[21]Piscator, *Commentarii in omnes libros Veteris Testamenti*, 2:293.
[22]Mayer, *Many Commentaries in One*, 95*.

judgment. So, as Paul teaches, we ought to pray that we might lead a peaceful life even under impious rulers. For even on account of a few good people God gives blessings to many. Otherwise why would God have shown consideration for Sodom if a few righteous ones had been found there? COMMENTARY ON 1 KINGS.[23]

WORSE THAN ALL BEFORE HIM. JOHANNES PISCATOR: Omri is set forth as an example of a worthless rank of kingship. Indeed, he did nothing but toil in discord "and did more evil than all who were before him." COMMENTARY ON 1 KINGS.[24]

MORE GUILTY WHERE PRECEDENTS ARE SET. JOHN MAYER: Concerning Omri, it is said that he did worse before the Lord than all those who were before him. The reason for this is . . . because he followed in the footsteps of those who committed abominations before him even though he had seen God's judgments fall on them. In this way those of us who live in these times—because we have seen so many made examples by God's judgment for their sins—will be judged more strictly than others if we commit similar sins. COMMENTARY ON 1 KINGS.[25]

16:29-34 Ahab Reigns in Israel

AHAB AND JEZEBEL. JOHANNES BUGENHAGEN: King Ahab of Israel was more impious than all the kings before him. Just as true piety grows, impiety cannot become smaller, until (as Paul says of the ungodly) they "fill up the measure of their sins." To complement his impiety, Ahab added a fitting consort, Jezebel. According to the law, he should not have married her, for the Sidonians belonged to the land of Canaan that had been promised to Israel, people with whom the law forbade entering into contracts or marrying their daughters, as we discussed earlier concerning Solomon's wives. These two not only followed the impious hypocrisy

of Jeroboam, who had convinced Israel to worship the calves as God, but they also very openly erected Gentile idolatries. This truly went beyond the history of their impious forefathers, who had perished by following foreign gods in the wilderness and by worshiping Baal in the time of the judges. But neither an effective word nor the appearance of miracles nor even the persistent prophet Elijah could do anything to bring the king to his senses, an obstinacy we have certainly discussed elsewhere. COMMENTARY ON 1 KINGS.[26]

AHAB THE CHIEF OF WICKED KINGS. JOHN MAYER: After Omri died Ahab his son ruled in his place. Ahab is said to have done worse than all who were before him. This may be expounded as that said before touching Omri, but Ahab did worse. Ahab took Jezebel, a Sidonian, as a wife, which was contrary to God's law. He also set up her gods. Ahab then killed the prophets of God, as is afterward stated, which none of his predecessor dared do. Now Jezebel is said to be the daughter of Ethbaal, king of the Sidonians. These two's very names . . . being taken from Bel and Baal, showed how greatly they were addicted to idolatry. And this is why Ahab was to be condemned more than Jeroboam: While Ahab performed all these abominations while he quietly enjoyed his kingdom and did not need to introduce strange gods and build strange temples, Jeroboam felt that he needed to introduce the worship of the golden calves in order to keep the people from going to Jerusalem. Last, Ahab proceeded most unjustly against Naboth by murdering him to get his vineyard. COMMENTARY ON 1 KINGS.[27]

SINNER AND CASTAWAY. ROBERT SANDERSON: Ahab was king of Israel, that is, king over those ten tribes that revolted from Rehoboam the son of Solomon and cleaved to Jeroboam the son of Nebat. Search the whole sacred story in the books of Kings

[23]Bugenhagen, *In Regum duos ultimos libros*, 81.
[24]Piscator, *Commentarii in omnes libros Veteris Testamenti*, 2:293.
[25]Mayer, *Many Commentaries in One*, 96*.

[26]Bugenhagen, *In Regum duos ultimos libros*, 82; citing 1 Thess 2:16. See Bugenhagen's discussion concerning foreign wives in 2 Kings 4, p. 416.
[27]Mayer, *Many Commentaries in One*, 96*.

and Chronicles; and unless we will be so very charitable as notwithstanding many strong presumptions of his hypocrisy to exempt Jehu the son of Nimshi, and that is but one of twenty, we shall not find in the whole list and catalog of the kings of Israel one good one who cleaved to the Lord with an upright heart. There were twenty kings of Israel, and not one (or only one) who was good; and yet, of the twenty, there was scarcely one who was worse than Ahab. It is said that Ahab the son of Omri did evil in the sight of the Lord above all who were before him. . . . He was an oppressor, a murderer, an idolater and a persecutor of that holy truth that God had plentifully revealed by his prophets, powerfully confirmed by miracles and mercifully declared by many gracious deliverances, even to him, in such manner that he could not but know it to be the truth. And therefore Ahab was a hypocrite, and, in all likelihood, an obstinate sinner against the Holy Spirit, and a castaway. To the People.[28]

---

[28]Sanderson, *Works*, 3:6-7*.

17:1-24 ELIJAH AND THE DROUGHT

[1]Now Elijah the Tishbite, of Tishbe[a] in Gilead, said to Ahab, "As the LORD, the God of Israel, lives, before whom I stand, there shall be neither dew nor rain these years, except by my word." [2]And the word of the LORD came to him: [3]"Depart from here and turn eastward and hide yourself by the brook Cherith, which is east of the Jordan. [4]You shall drink from the brook, and I have commanded the ravens to feed you there." [5]So he went and did according to the word of the LORD. He went and lived by the brook Cherith that is east of the Jordan. [6]And the ravens brought him bread and meat in the morning, and bread and meat in the evening, and he drank from the brook. [7]And after a while the brook dried up, because there was no rain in the land.

[8]Then the word of the LORD came to him, [9]"Arise, go to Zarephath, which belongs to Sidon, and dwell there. Behold, I have commanded a widow there to feed you." [10]So he arose and went to Zarephath. And when he came to the gate of the city, behold, a widow was there gathering sticks. And he called to her and said, "Bring me a little water in a vessel, that I may drink." [11]And as she was going to bring it, he called to her and said, "Bring me a morsel of bread in your hand." [12]And she said, "As the LORD your God lives, I have nothing baked, only a handful of flour in a jar and a little oil in a jug. And now I am gathering a couple of sticks that I may go in and prepare it for myself and my son, that we may eat it and die." [13]And Elijah said to her, "Do not fear; go and do as you have said. But first make me a little cake of it and bring it

to me, and afterward make something for yourself and your son. [14]For thus says the LORD, the God of Israel, 'The jar of flour shall not be spent, and the jug of oil shall not be empty, until the day that the LORD sends rain upon the earth.'" [15]And she went and did as Elijah said. And she and he and her household ate for many days. [16]The jar of flour was not spent, neither did the jug of oil become empty, according to the word of the LORD that he spoke by Elijah.

[17]After this the son of the woman, the mistress of the house, became ill. And his illness was so severe that there was no breath left in him. [18]And she said to Elijah, "What have you against me, O man of God? You have come to me to bring my sin to remembrance and to cause the death of my son!" [19]And he said to her, "Give me your son." And he took him from her arms and carried him up into the upper chamber where he lodged, and laid him on his own bed. [20]And he cried to the LORD, "O LORD my God, have you brought calamity even upon the widow with whom I sojourn, by killing her son?" [21]Then he stretched himself upon the child three times and cried to the LORD, "O LORD my God, let this child's life[b] come into him again." [22]And the LORD listened to the voice of Elijah. And the life of the child came into him again, and he revived. [23]And Elijah took the child and brought him down from the upper chamber into the house and delivered him to his mother. And Elijah said, "See, your son lives." [24]And the woman said to Elijah, "Now I know that you are a man of God, and that the word of the LORD in your mouth is truth."

a Septuagint; Hebrew *of the settlers*   b Or *soul*; also verse 22

OVERVIEW: These commentators deeply respect Elijah, connecting him with John the Baptist. Some draw an example from the miraculous sustenance of Elijah and imply that God will sustain all those who remain faithful to him. God tests Elijah by commanding him to live alone by the brook. They acknowledge Christ's retelling of the story about the widow in Sidon in Luke 4, and they laud God's willingness to perform a miracle in Gentile lands for an insignificant woman and her son. Like Elijah himself, the widow is tested during Elijah's stay and has to appeal to the prophet for assistance in resuscitating her son. The commentators recognize Elijah's act here as a genuine miracle that takes place through faith in Christ.

17:1 Elijah the Prophet

THE GREAT PROPHET AND HIS AFFLICTIONS.

JOHANNES BUGENHAGEN: Elijah was truly great in spirit. He can even be called the foremost of the prophets, the promised Elijah whom Malachi said would come before the Messiah in the person of the John the Baptist, which is how Christ interpreted him in Matthew and how the angel described him in Luke. James made his argument about the prayer of faith from this history of Elijah, saying, "The prayer of a righteous person has great power as it is working. Elijah was a man with a nature like ours, and he prayed fervently," etc. No doubt he had been moved by the king's shamelessness to pray against the king and the kingdom, as God denies those who despise his gifts. But this prophet who could make the heavens stop raining, who could open the heavens to make it rain and who could awaken the dead was in the meantime afflicted by nearly dying of hunger, so that you see how God brings such affliction on his holy ones. For God the Father always wants to be acknowledged as the one who blessedly supplies what is necessary for growth, so that we might depend on him and commit all our needs in life to him alone. As Jacob said, this is "the God who has been my shepherd all my life long to this day," and in the Psalms this is the "Shepherd of Israel," who leads Joseph like a flock, and—as Paul said in Acts—this is the living God, who in past generations "allowed all the nations to walk in their own ways. Yet he did not leave himself without witness, for he did good by giving you rains from heaven and fruitful seasons." You truly see how God provided for Elijah, so that where human help was nothing there the ravens fed him, just as he fed the widow who had no food, so that she and her entire household were fed by a miracle from God on account of this one man Elijah. COMMENTARY ON 1 KINGS.[1]

EXAMPLE OF DIVINE SUSTENANCE. JOHANNES

PISCATOR: We have set before us Elijah, whom God wonderfully sustained during a time of famine, first, by ravens and then by the widow at Zarephath. In the same way we have an example from the woman whom God wonderfully sustained through Elijah, so that she had a daily increase in flour and oil. We are taught here that God provides food for those who obey those whom he has sent and who believe his promises. Indeed Elijah obeyed the commandment of God first by remaining at the Cherith brook and then by departing to the home of the widow at Zarephath, believing the promise of God, that in both places God wanted to sustain him. In the same way the widow at Zarephath obeyed the command of God by Elijah concerning his announcement about the food. COMMENTARY ON 1 KINGS.[2]

ELIJAH THE CHASTE. JOHN MAYER: Elijah was the

first of men who lived always in chastity, while the Virgin Mary was the first among women. It is most probable that when Elijah came to Ahab, he came out of some desert place, where he had retired himself from the society of the common sort so that he could converse with God. Elijah had detested the wickedness of those times just as John the Baptist, his antitype, would later do. The sudden entrance of Elijah into this history suggests that he was formerly unknown to the world. But now his zeal for God would not allow him to lie hidden any longer. Rather he must now come forth to declare that the judgment that he had prayed might come would appear. He wanted to show how greatly incensed the Lord was at those wicked times so that he might move Ahab to repentance. COMMENTARY ON 1 KINGS.[3]

17:2-7 Elijah Goes into Hiding at the Brook

ONE DOES NOT LIVE BY BREAD ALONE.

JOHANNES BUGENHAGEN: God told Elijah to go into hiding. Here you see how he was fed by the

---

[1]Bugenhagen, *In Regum duos ultimos libros*, 83-84; citing Mal 4:5;

Mt 17:12; Lk 1:17; Jas 5:16-18; Gen 48:15; Ps 80:1; Acts 14:16-17.
[2]Piscator, *Commentarii in omnes libros Veteris Testamenti*, 2:295.
[3]Mayer, *Many Commentaries in One*, 98*.

Word of God and had enough, for he believed this word of God even when he did not see any food. For one "does not live by bread alone," etc. Commentary on 1 Kings.[4]

FAITH RUN DRY. KONRAD PELLIKAN: Elijah's faith was tested when the brook dried up, as he was sent from place to place to preserve his life. Yet he did not despair but simply and willingly obeyed the Word of God. He who had already been fed by ravens (unclean birds) and existed by the grace of God would soon be sent to a foreign widow in Zarephath in the land of Sidon to labor in extreme poverty, where he would again be nourished through faith in God. Commentary on 1 Kings.[5]

FED BY UNCLEAN BIRDS. JOHN MAYER: The word of the Lord spoke to Elijah about the ravens feeding him to let him know that he would not be without food when he went into such a deserted place. This was a strange way of feeding a person. But it served to set forth the power of God, in the sense that God can make any of his creatures serve his own good, although it may be against their nature.... The ravens especially owed this service to the Lord for the benefit they singularly, above all other birds, enjoyed by his providence when they are young.... For being newly hatched, the mother forsakes the babies until they are feathered; and in all that time they are extraordinarily sustained.... And as the Lord promised, it was performed for his prophet: The ravens brought him bread, flesh each morning and evening. In fact the rabbis are so bold as to say that these ravens took the food out of Ahab's kitchen. But certainly no person knew where the food came from; it is only certain that the one who ordered the ravens to transport the food could have received it from anywhere God pleased, whether by angels, etc....

But seeing that the raven is an unclean bird, why would the Lord have meat brought to Elijah by ravens, or how could Elijah eat the food without being defiled? Peter Martyr Vermigli answers that the same Lord who would have the raven generally counted unclean by appointing the ravens now to bring him meat dispensed with that law. Indeed, in cases of necessity Christ himself teaches that a ceremonial law need not be kept but that a person's necessity for the preservation of his life is always a dispensation to it. Such is how Christ justified his disciples for plucking the ears of corn on the sabbath when they were hungry.... But it is to be noted that although the raven was unclean and therefore those who ate of it or touched its carcass were unclean for a specific period of time, no uncleanness was contracted by it while it lived. Therefore there was no dispensation needed. Allegorically the *Glossa ordinaria* understands the ravens to symbolize the blackness of the Gentiles' sin and idolatry, and that the food they carried symbolized the faith they brought to Christ. Commentary on 1 Kings.[6]

17:8-16 *The Widow at Zarephath*

LACKING NO GOOD THING. JOHANNES BUGEN-HAGEN: When the widow said that she had no bread, this might have tempted the prophet. But he clung to the word. For he knew, "God has sent me here where there is no bread, just as the Israelites began to despair in the wilderness." The widow had only "a couple of sticks," which signifies her extreme poverty. Those who have interpreted these two sticks to represent the holy cross are fools. Then Elijah said, "Do not fear," for the woman no longer had faith in the Word of God. Instead she was seriously tested when he commanded her to first bring the bread to him, because then there may have been little or nothing left. As the Psalm says, "Oh fear the Lord, you his saints, for those who fear him have no lack! The young lions suffer want and hunger; but those who seek the Lord lack no good thing." Commentary on 1 Kings.[7]

---

[4]Bugenhagen, *In Regum duos ultimos libros*, 85; citing Deut 8:3; Lk 4:4.
[5]Pellikan, *Commentaria Bibliorum*, 2:164r.

[6]Mayer, *Many Commentaries in One*, 99*.
[7]Bugenhagen, *In Regum duos ultimos libros*, 85; citing Ps 34:9-10.

Faith Yields Abundantly. Konrad
Pellikan: By faith, the saints are pleasing to
God, through whom they can do all things and
in whom they trust. They command others to
believe as well, and in this case the prophet
Elijah commands not only the chosen people to
listen. Therefore, he first does that which will
testify to faith, showing charity and gracious
hospitality to the foreign woman and her son.
This will yield tenfold because the woman
receives the prophet of the Lord. Thus Elijah
ceased his journey so that he could first be
driven to them and then at the city gate produce
what was needed for such destitute people. For
in this way God tests and trains his prophets, so
that he may always provide for them in faith.
Commentary on 1 Kings.[8]

Protector of Widows. Charles Drelincourt: Our great God and merciful Lord has not
only said in general that he is the judge, protector
and comforter of the widow, but he has vouchsafed to some his most signal favors and extraordinary blessings. In the reign of Ahab while a
cruel famine overspread the land, God sent the
prophet Elijah to a poor widow of Zarephath
who was preparing herself and her son for death
as soon as they had eaten a little remnant of meal
and oil that was left. But the holy prophet
comforted her in this way, "The jar of flour shall
not be spent, and the jug of oil shall not be empty,
until the day that the Lord sends rain upon the
earth." Many poor widows have met with similar
miraculous supplies. For by a secret benediction
God has caused their provisions not to fail them.
Though perhaps they have not enjoyed any
extraordinary plenty, this all-wise benefactor has
furnished them with things necessary for them.
Not only did both they and their children subsist
in the greatest calamities, but they also had the
honor of assisting God's prophets. Christian
Defense Against the Fears of Death.[9]

The Widow as a Figure of the Gentiles.
John Mayer: The drought had now grown very
great, so much so that it dried up the water springs.
God could have, of course, caused the water to
have continued to be of use for his servant Elijah,
but it seemed good to him rather to work another
miracle by providing for a poor faithful widow who
otherwise would have perished with her son
through the famine. She did not live in the land of
Israel, but rather in Zarephath of Sidon, which was
a city of the Gentiles. As Christ said in Luke 4,
this action was done to serve as a figure of the
rejection of the Jews and the calling of the Gentiles.
Commentary on 1 Kings.[10]

17:17-20 The Death of the Widow's Son

**Deliverance amid Despair and Tempta-
tion.** Johannes Bugenhagen: The woman had
overcome the temptation about the food, but she
despaired at the death of her son because of sin. For
in a time of anguish like this, everyone thinks their
sins have come back as punishment. Therefore she
believed that this death came from God, because a
sinner like her had unworthily hosted a holy man.
Such people are then afflicted in their conscience
and perceive the horrors of hell against them. Then
even all the best things are interpreted as being
against them, as if God not only had deserted them
but also was fighting against them. We should be
instructed by this woman's real temptations, so that
we trust in God, who "brings down to Sheol and
raises up," for all of our bodily and spiritual needs.
Who does not see the widow's house to be full of
the kingdom of heaven? What can we do other
than give thanks to God for such greatness, when
we acknowledge God as Father and Savior in all
things? Commentary on 1 Kings.[11]

Receiving More Than a Miracle. Konrad
Pellikan: The woman not only accepted the
miracle, but she was also drawn to faith and the

---

[8]Pellikan, *Commentaria Bibliorum*, 2:164r.
[9]Drelincourt, *Christian's Defense Against the Fears of Death*, 208*.

[10]Mayer, *Many Commentaries in One*, 100*.
[11]Bugenhagen, *In Regum duos ultimos libros*, 85-86; citing 1 Sam 2:6.

favor of God, so that she became pleasing to God and was made holy. Miracles do not in themselves make people better, turning the ungodly from their ungodliness, but the favor of divine election does this. She called Elijah a man of God, devoted to the Lord, and she honored him who called out to the Lord in all things and was heard, who preached the word of the Lord without deception, who said that God was faithful and who judged and punished the faithless. COMMENTARY ON 1 KINGS.[12]

TRIAL BY FAITH. JOHANNES PISCATOR: God exercises the woman's faith in various tests, so that in this passage he has exercised her faith: First, from the fear of death from the famine, and, then, after liberating her from this test, he exercises her faith upon the death of her son. But soon God the Father shows his heart by bringing the boy back from the dead by Elijah. COMMENTARY ON 1 KINGS.[13]

17:21-24 Elijah Stretches Himself over the Boy and Raises Him

DON'T BOTHER IMITATING THE DEEDS OF THE SAINTS. JOHANNES BUGENHAGEN: Elijah "stretched himself upon the child three times." The prophet did many things that were not immediately heard. He who labored with God had been given this work to do, which otherwise would have had nothing to do with reawakening the dead. For if others were to try this, what would it accomplish? Therefore those who want to imitate the deeds of the saints are fools, because everything the saints have done they did through faith, as Hebrews 11 says, "Women received back their dead by resurrection." Then the woman said, "Now I know." She knew not only through the word but also through experience. This is faith tested by trials. COMMENTARY ON 1 KINGS.[14]

THE FIRST TO BE RAISED UP FROM THE DEAD SINCE CREATION. JOHN MAYER: Elijah's strange gesture of stretching himself on the body of the child three times—which the Hebrew version renders "he straightened himself" while the Septuagint renders it as "he breathed on him"—as an instrument of God. Elisha did the same thing in imitation of him, thus helping by the power of the spirit that was strong in him to make the body of the child become warm. Elijah did this so that the child's body would be more fit to be again enlivened by the soul's return, as God initially breathed into Adam the breath of life and he became a living soul. Elijah did thus and prayed three times, to imitate his praying to the blessed Trinity. It's not that God could not have raised the child without such means; rather, it's that God directed Elijah to do so, in a mystery. . . .

Elijah's covering himself on a human body prefigures when Christ took flesh on himself in the womb of the Virgin Mary and again when he lay in the manger. It also prefigured when Christ hung on the cross, whereby humankind—dead in their sins and trespasses—were quickened and came to be united to him by faith. And such means were also used by Elijah to show the imperfection of the law in comparison to the gospel, when, with less ado, Christ and his apostles raised some from the dead. . . . This is the first among those who were raised up from the dead since the creation of the world. Afterward two were raised from the dead by Elisha, three by Christ, one by Peter and one by Paul—to say nothing of those who rose out of their graves at the time of Christ's resurrection, which is the greatest miracle of all. COMMENTARY ON 1 KINGS.[15]

MIRACLES AND GOD'S EXISTENCE. JACOBUS ARMINIUS: An illustrious evidence of God's existence is afforded in the miracles, which God has performed by the stewards of his Word, his prophets and apostles, and by Christ himself, for the confirmation of his doctrine and for the establishment of their authority. For these miracles

---

[12]Pellikan, *Commentaria Bibliorum*, 2:164v.
[13]Piscator, *Commentarii in omnes libros Veteris Testamenti*, 2:295.
[14]Bugenhagen, *In Regum duos ultimos libros*, 86; citing Heb 11:35; 1 Pet 1:6-7.

[15]Mayer, *Many Commentaries in One*, 102*.

are of such a description as infinitely to exceed the united powers of all the creatures and all the powers of nature itself, when their energies are combined. But the God of truth, burning with zeal for his own glory, could never have afforded such strong testimonies as these to false prophets and their false doctrine: nor could he have borne such witness to any doctrine even when it was true, provided it was not his, that is, provided it was not divine. The same reason also . . . induced the widow of Zarephath to say, on receiving from the hands of Elijah her son, who, after his death, had been raised to life by the prophet: "Now by this, I know that you are a man of God, and that the word of the Lord in your mouth is truth." ORATION 4: THE CERTAINTY OF SACRED THEOLOGY.[16]

---

[16]Arminius, *Works*, 1:129-30*.

18:1-46 ELIJAH AND THE PROPHETS OF BAAL

[1]After many days the word of the LORD came to Elijah, in the third year, saying, "Go, show yourself to Ahab, and I will send rain upon the earth." [2]So Elijah went to show himself to Ahab. Now the famine was severe in Samaria. [3]And Ahab called Obadiah, who was over the household. (Now Obadiah feared the LORD greatly, [4]and when Jezebel cut off the prophets of the LORD, Obadiah took a hundred prophets and hid them by fifties in a cave and fed them with bread and water.) [5]And Ahab said to Obadiah, "Go through the land to all the springs of water and to all the valleys. Perhaps we may find grass and save the horses and mules alive, and not lose some of the animals." [6]So they divided the land between them to pass through it. Ahab went in one direction by himself, and Obadiah went in another direction by himself.

[7]And as Obadiah was on the way, behold, Elijah met him. And Obadiah recognized him and fell on his face and said, "Is it you, my lord Elijah?" [8]And he answered him, "It is I. Go, tell your lord, 'Behold, Elijah is here.'" [9]And he said, "How have I sinned, that you would give your servant into the hand of Ahab, to kill me? [10]As the LORD your God lives, there is no nation or kingdom where my lord has not sent to seek you. And when they would say, 'He is not here,' he would take an oath of the kingdom or nation, that they had not found you. [11]And now you say, 'Go, tell your lord, "Behold, Elijah is here."' [12]And as soon as I have gone from you, the Spirit of the LORD will carry you I know not where. And so, when I come and tell Ahab and he cannot find you, he will kill me, although I your servant have feared the LORD from my youth. [13]Has it not been told my lord what I did when Jezebel killed the prophets of the LORD, how I hid a hundred men of the LORD's prophets by fifties in a cave and fed them with bread and water? [14]And now you say, 'Go, tell your lord, "Behold, Elijah is here"'; and he will kill me." [15]And Elijah said, "As the LORD of hosts lives, before whom I stand, I will surely show myself to him today." [16]So Obadiah went to meet Ahab, and told him. And Ahab went to meet Elijah.

[17]When Ahab saw Elijah, Ahab said to him, "Is it you, you troubler of Israel?" [18]And he answered, "I have not troubled Israel, but you have, and your father's house, because you have abandoned the commandments of the LORD and followed the Baals. [19]Now therefore send and gather all Israel to me at Mount Carmel, and the 450 prophets of Baal and the 400 prophets of Asherah, who eat at Jezebel's table."

[20]So Ahab sent to all the people of Israel and gathered the prophets together at Mount Carmel. [21]And Elijah came near to all the people and said, "How long will you go limping between two different opinions? If the LORD is God, follow him; but if Baal, then follow him." And the people did not answer him a word. [22]Then Elijah said to the people, "I, even I only, am left a prophet of the LORD, but Baal's prophets are 450 men. [23]Let two bulls be given to us, and let them choose one bull for themselves and cut it in pieces and lay it on the wood, but put no fire to it. And I will prepare the other bull and lay it on the wood and put no fire to it. [24]And you call upon the name of your god, and I will call upon the name of the LORD, and the God who answers by fire, he is God." And all the people answered, "It is well spoken." [25]Then Elijah said to the prophets of Baal, "Choose for yourselves one bull and prepare it first, for you are many, and call upon the name of your god, but put no fire to it." [26]And they took the bull that was given them, and they prepared it and called upon the name of Baal from morning until noon, saying, "O Baal, answer us!" But there was no voice, and no one answered. And they limped around the altar that they had made. [27]And at noon Elijah mocked them, saying, "Cry aloud, for he is a god. Either he is musing, or he is relieving himself, or he is on a journey, or perhaps he is asleep and must be awakened." [28]And they cried aloud and cut themselves after their custom with swords and lances, until the blood gushed out upon them. [29]And as midday passed, they raved on until the time of the offering of the oblation, but there was no voice. No one answered; no one paid attention.

³⁰Then Elijah said to all the people, "Come near to me." And all the people came near to him. And he repaired the altar of the LORD that had been thrown down. ³¹Elijah took twelve stones, according to the number of the tribes of the sons of Jacob, to whom the word of the LORD came, saying, "Israel shall be your name," ³²and with the stones he built an altar in the name of the LORD. And he made a trench about the altar, as great as would contain two seahs^a of seed. ³³And he put the wood in order and cut the bull in pieces and laid it on the wood. And he said, "Fill four jars with water and pour it on the burnt offering and on the wood." ³⁴And he said, "Do it a second time." And they did it a second time. And he said, "Do it a third time." And they did it a third time. ³⁵And the water ran around the altar and filled the trench also with water.

³⁶And at the time of the offering of the oblation, Elijah the prophet came near and said, "O LORD, God of Abraham, Isaac, and Israel, let it be known this day that you are God in Israel, and that I am your servant, and that I have done all these things at your word. ³⁷Answer me, O LORD, answer me, that this people may know that you, O LORD, are God, and that you have turned their hearts back." ³⁸Then the fire of the LORD

fell and consumed the burnt offering and the wood and the stones and the dust, and licked up the water that was in the trench. ³⁹And when all the people saw it, they fell on their faces and said, "The LORD, he is God; the LORD, he is God." ⁴⁰And Elijah said to them, "Seize the prophets of Baal; let not one of them escape." And they seized them. And Elijah brought them down to the brook Kishon and slaughtered them there.

⁴¹And Elijah said to Ahab, "Go up, eat and drink, for there is a sound of the rushing of rain." ⁴²So Ahab went up to eat and to drink. And Elijah went up to the top of Mount Carmel. And he bowed himself down on the earth and put his face between his knees. ⁴³And he said to his servant, "Go up now, look toward the sea." And he went up and looked and said, "There is nothing." And he said, "Go again," seven times. ⁴⁴And at the seventh time he said, "Behold, a little cloud like a man's hand is rising from the sea." And he said, "Go up, say to Ahab, 'Prepare your chariot and go down, lest the rain stop you.'" ⁴⁵And in a little while the heavens grew black with clouds and wind, and there was a great rain. And Ahab rode and went to Jezreel. ⁴⁶And the hand of the LORD was on Elijah, and he gathered up his garment and ran before Ahab to the entrance of Jezreel.

a A *seah* was about 7 quarts or 7.3 liters

OVERVIEW: These commentators generally commend the steward of Ahab's household, Obadiah. They find many points of application between Obadiah's life and their own. For example, some see Obadiah's provision of the godly prophets as an example of God's provision of all righteous people. Concerning the interaction between Ahab and Elijah, the reformers interpret them as types of Herod the Great and John the Baptist respectively. The contest between Elijah, the prophet of Yahweh, and the 450 prophets of Baal loyal to Ahab and Jezebel elicits denunciation of the worship of false gods and acknowledgment of the jealousy of God, who does not tolerate worship of any other object. Some wonder why Elijah resorts to performing miracles (which are only reserved for unbelievers) instead of appealing to the Scriptures, the written

Word of God, to settle the dispute. Finally, what do our commentators say about Elijah's command to kill all the prophets of Baal? Our interpreters— here all magisterial reformers—are united in their approval of Elijah's order, under the assumption that God directed him to give the command.

18:1-16 Obadiah

THE PROPHET OBADIAH. JOHANNES BUGENHAGEN: Obadiah, who served the king, was a great prophet whose book still remains. He had hidden a hundred prophets of the Lord whom Ahab wanted to kill, for the true prophets were being denied bread and water and even their lives while 850 diabolical prophets were nourished with the king's food. This impious generosity to the ungodly will always remain among those who are against God; it often happens among people who are connected with the worship of God. But God keeps the true and precious prophets, so that they might be honored by the world. For God acknowledges and provides for those who honor him alone. COMMENTARY ON 1 KINGS.[1]

WEAK BUT OBEDIENT. JOHANNES PISCATOR: In Obadiah an example is set forth of both weakness and obedience. His weakness of faith is indicated by his initial protest to obey the command of Elijah to send for Ahab. But Obadiah was also obedient to God to the extent that he accepted Elijah's proposition when he was commanded by the prophet a second time. COMMENTARY ON 1 KINGS.[2]

GOD'S PEOPLE ARE EVERYWHERE. HENRY AIRAY: Let no one think any place is so profane that the Lord does not have his church there. The wealthy members of society, including the politicians, work in places that are full of pride, pleasure, ease and abundance of all things. These type of people commonly choke the Word in them so that it is unfruitful. . . . In great cities, likewise, sins rage and reign in all places. In these places lewdness and wickedness are so grievous and abominable that sin overflows. Yet in all these places the Lord has his people; the Lord has those who know him and believe in his holy name. Even in Jezebel's court he had an Obadiah to hide and feed his prophets. . . . Far be it from us, therefore, to condemn where the Lord has not condemned. Only God knows who are his, but there are people loyal to him in every place of the world. LECTURES ON PHILIPPIANS.[3]

OBADIAH'S TRICKY SITUATION. JOHN MAYER: The Lord directed Elijah not to Ahab at first, who was unworthy for his wickedness, but to Obadiah, who was a godly man and a servant to the Lord's prophets. . . . Obadiah showed this by his speech,

calling him "my lord Elijah." And by this gesture and in bowing down to Elijah to the ground, Obadiah serves as an example to others of giving double honor to elders who rule well and labor in the word. When Elijah heard him ask whether he was not Elijah, he both said that he was and he immediately bade him go tell his lord that Elijah was there. But because Obadiah feared that this might be dangerous to him if the spirit of God should carry Elijah away to another place before Ahab returned to him unless Elijah was resolved to stay, Obadiah tried to win his favor. He told Elijah that he had greatly feared God from his youth and how he was such a friend to the Lord's prophets that he hid and fed one hundred of them in time of danger. Knowing that Ahab had long and anxiously awaited Elijah's capture, Obadiah feared coming with the bad news that he had been deceived by Elijah or that Elijah had escaped since Obadiah did not bring him in person to Ahab. And doubting whether Elijah would then show himself to Ahab if he fetched him—and also knowing that he might also be in danger from the hand of God if he disobeyed— Obadiah sought to win Elijah's favor. Now in setting forth his own goodness in this necessity Obadiah did not sin, although out of such a case in vainglory—to do so that a person may be praised— is not without sin. COMMENTARY ON 1 KINGS.[4]

18:17-19 Elijah Confronts Ahab

GOD'S CARE FOR THE RIGHTEOUS AND UNRIGHTEOUS. JOHANNES BUGENHAGEN: Here you see that God's providential care extends to the pious and the impious. If God cares for the ungodly, how much more will he not care for the faithful? Nevertheless, God wanted to give this clear sign through Elijah, so that people might see that Elijah (God's virtuous one) was not the cause of the present drought but that other causes, namely, the people's habitual impiety, was its source. COMMENTARY ON 1 KINGS.[5]

[1]Bugenhagen, *In Regum duos ultimos libros*, 87. In many traditional interpretations, this is the same Obadiah who wrote the prophetic book of Obadiah.
[2]Piscator, *Commentarii in omnes libros Veteris Testamenti*, 2:298.
[3]Airay, *Lectures on Philippians*, 62*.
[4]Mayer, *Many Commentaries in One*, 104*.
[5]Bugenhagen, *In Regum duos ultimos libros*, 87.

On Reproving Kings. John Mayer: Being undaunted by the king's angry speech, Elijah laid the fault altogether on Ahab and his idolatrous father, by whom God was provoked to this judgment. That's because he and his people had left God's commandments to serve Baals, that is, the planets of heaven, chiefly the sun. As Judges says, "They abandoned the Lord and served the Baals and the Ashtaroth." I have already shown that all the male gods of the heathen were called Baals, of which Jupiter was the chief god. Elijah reprimanded King Ahab in the same way John the Baptist, his antitype, justly reprimanded King Herod. For although the ruler of the people may not be railed on, he may be reproved for his sins. Commentary on 1 Kings.[6]

Trusting God Despite Danger. Johannes Piscator: In the example of Elijah we see obedience to God inasmuch as God imposed peril on him. For it was dangerous for Elijah to show himself to Ahab, because Ahab was offended at the drought imposed on the land. Nevertheless Elijah went in obedience to the command of God and showed himself to Ahab. Commentary on 1 Kings.[7]

18:20-21 *Choosing Between the Lord and Baal*

On Worshiping God Alone. Heinrich Bullinger: All people certainly confess that it is proper to worship God, but not all acknowledge and confess that God alone should be worshiped. It therefore remains to be shown that God alone should be worshiped by people. . . . Accordingly this expression is very often repeated and set forth in the Law and Prophets: "You shall worship the Lord your God, but you shall not worship a strange god." Now a strange god is whatever you delight in worshiping that is outside of or beyond the only living, true and eternal God. . . . As such, only the true, living and eternal God should be worshiped.

In the story of the Gospel we read that the devil tempted Christ our Lord and, having led him on a high mountain, showed him from there all the kingdoms of the world and their glory. He said, "I will give you all this if you will bow down and worship me." The Lord responded, "Go away, Satan, for it is written, 'You shall worship the Lord your God, and him only shall you serve.'" Now certainly worship and serving are linked mutually together so that they cannot be separated. It follows from this that God alone wills to be worshiped. Elijah, the great prophet of God, taught that God rejects being worshiped alongside another god. The prophet therefore proclaimed to those people who were worshiping the true God with the god Baal: "How long will you waiver between two opinions? If the Lord is God, follow him; but if Baal is God, follow him." It is almost as if he had said, "You cannot worship Baal along with God. No one is able to serve two masters." For the Lord our God requires our entire heart, mind and soul. As such, he leaves nothing for us to give to another. Decades 4.5.[8]

Limping on Both Sides. Martin Luther: Elijah accuses the people of limping in two directions and doing one thing in their hearts and feigning something else in their work. This is true of everyone who is outside Christ. Lectures on Hebrews.[9]

A Zealous God and a Silent People. Konrad Pellikan: The Lord is zealous and does not cede honor to another. God wants to be the only one loved with the whole heart, who lives in human hearts without equal. God alone is sufficient for all things and delights in doing good for those who trust in him alone. God alone knows all that his creatures need. In God alone they live, move and have their being. Therefore those who devote themselves to another source of good alone or in addition to God cannot be found pleasing to the true God. Instead their faithlessness and hatred of God is invoked

---

[6]Mayer, *Many Commentaries in One*, 105*; citing Judg 2:13.
[7]Piscator, *Commentarii in omnes libros Veteris Testamenti*, 2:298.
[8]Bullinger, *Sermonum decades quinque*, 284; citing Mt 4:9-10; 1 Sam 18:21.
[9]LW 29:123.

against them, which is exactly what the people of Israel did in this instance. They could not deny the true God entirely, but neither could they dare to believe in this God alone, for they did not believe that law against consenting to the errors of the Gentiles. Therefore they were divided in two opinions and sects, which kept them in great filth and iniquity. For this reason Elijah cried out to the people, "If the Lord is God, follow him; but if Baal, then follow him." But the people of Israel did not respond at all to the prophet's words; after all, there had already been calamitous hunger, uprisings across the country and floods, all of which were sent by the true God alone but none of which had been able to remove the idols. And yet, because of all this they could still not dare to deny their God. And so, placed between the 450 prophets of Baal who were leading the people into the worship of foreign gods and the one Elijah, whom they could not dare to believe, they held their tongues. COMMENTARY ON 1 KINGS.[10]

18:22-39 *Showdown Between the Lord and Baal*

TRIAL BY FIRE. JOHN MAYER: Elijah entered this fight alone, which tended to the magnifying of God's power all the more when, by one, a greater work was wrought than by many hundreds. But why did Elijah turn to miracles and not to the holy Scriptures for the deciding of this controversy? Some think Elijah did so because he was dealing with many who did not regard the Scriptures. Therefore nothing could convince them but miracles, which are expressly for unbelievers. And the coming down of fire first, and then of water, was not without this allegory: The spirit to believe is first given and then baptism follows. By fire sent down on sacrifices God had many times before approved his divine power in this way in Solomon and David's time, in the time of Moses and Aaron ... and in the time of many others including Abel. Therefore Elijah, by a divine instinct, was moved to propound the same at this time. However, he did

not intend to give an example for people at all times to seek to try the truth by miracles, lest we tempt God. COMMENTARY ON 1 KINGS.[11]

COMPETING ALTARS. JOHANNES BUGENHAGEN: The Latin text says that the priests of Baal leapt over the altar they had made. It is better to say that they jumped around the altar according to their custom. The priests of Baal shed much blood until it flowed profusely. Elijah, alone with his faith in God, kept quiet. Here you see an example of those who believe in God and depend on God, in contrast to those who do not believe such righteousness but who trust in their own works and pains and who torment themselves in vain. As the apostle says, "These have indeed an appearance of wisdom in promoting self-made religion and asceticism and severity to the body, but they are of no value in stopping the indulgence of the flesh." Then Elijah "repaired the altar of the Lord that had been thrown down." It is thought that this might have been the altar made by Saul in 1 Samuel 14. And he set the twelve stones back up, just like the twelve tribes of Israel, so that this altar might be acknowledged as belonging to the God who gave the name of Israel, as you read in Genesis. Then Elijah made a trench, which was as wide as two seed troughs. In Hebrew this amount indicates a satisfactory measure, like the "three measures of flour" in Matthew 13. He commanded water to be poured so that the fire would be respected as a miracle that revealed God to the people, as Elijah's words indicate. Then truly the fire from heaven "fell and consumed the burnt offering," showing that this was as acceptable to God as the burnt offerings of Abraham, Aaron, Solomon and others. COMMENTARY ON 1 KINGS.[12]

THE DEVIL'S WORK AT PLAY THROUGH THE FALSE PROPHETS. JOHN MAYER: If any shall wonder at the worshipers of Baal accepting this

---

[10]Pellikan, *Commentaria Bibliorum*, 2:165v.

[11]Mayer, *Many Commentaries in One*, 106-7*.
[12]Bugenhagen, *In Regum duos ultimos libros*, 88-89; citing Col 2:23; 1 Sam 14:35; Gen 32:28; Mt 13:33.

offer, seeing that they could have no hope to have fire sent on their sacrifices by a dumb and dead idol, it is to be understood that the devil can sometimes send down fire from heaven, as on Job's cattle, and as is said of the antichrist working by him in Revelation 13. But against God, Elijah knew that now he should not be permitted so to do. . . . The prophets of Baal . . . also cut themselves until their blood ran over, which they pitifully did to move their idols. But the hand of the devil was doubtless in this act to stir them up to this madness, out of that delight which he takes in the shedding of human blood, as he was a murderer from the beginning. COMMENTARY ON 1 KINGS.[13]

BIG IDOLS EQUAL A SMALL GOD. ANDREAS BODENSTEIN VON KARLSTADT: God is as small in me as my reverence of idols is great. For God desires to indwell my whole and total heart and cannot in any way tolerate my having an image in my mind's eye. And when I trust God with all my heart, I need never fear his enemies. ON THE REMOVAL OF IMAGES.[14]

18:40 Elijah Commands the Execution of the Prophets of Baal

NO WAITING FOR THE KING'S SENTENCE. JOHN MAYER: Elijah's execution of the prophets of Baal was just. Nor could the people consider these prophets as true converts, seeing that they were most notorious for seducing everyone to idolatry. And whoever did so was required by the law of God to be put to death. It was important to do this immediately, because Jezebel the queen would have doubtlessly saved them. If it is asked why Elijah is justified in giving this sentence without waiting for the king's response—who was present there and by his office was the supreme judge—I answer that at this time Elijah had a power above the king, just as Samuel also had over Saul when he gave sentence against Agag and hewed him into pieces. The king

was an idolater, and therefore it was not to be expected that he should now condemn them. Nor was Elijah to wait for the king's sentence. It sufficed that there was one who was extraordinarily stirred up by the Spirit to give this sentence. For God, who is the King of kings, spoke through Elijah. COMMENTARY ON 1 KINGS.[15]

IMPELLED BY GOD'S SPIRIT. MARTIN LUTHER: The Holy Spirit does not always impel godly people; he lets them do some things in accordance with their own will and wish. When Elijah killed the prophets of Baal, he was impelled by the Spirit of God. LECTURES ON GENESIS.[16]

AHAB LEARNS THE TRUTH. VIKTORIN STRIGEL: God adorned the prophet Elijah with such authority that King Ahab was eventually compelled to acknowledge all that Elijah had done. For although Ahab doubtlessly raged and became indignant that his impious sacrifices had been proved wrong, he nevertheless obeyed the voice of Elijah, which God had presented with so many illustrious testimonies, without any objections. BOOK OF KINGS.[17]

NOT GIVEN AS A PATTERN TO FOLLOW. JOHN MAYER: Elijah's act of killing these prophets is not given so that we—whether prophets or private persons—should imitate it. Rather we are to leave the sword of justice to be drawn against evildoers by the public magistrate who, by commission of God, bears the sword. COMMENTARY ON 1 KINGS.[18]

18:41-46 Rain by Prayer

RAIN OF PROVIDENCE. HULDRYCH ZWINGLI: When at the prayer of Elijah rain was given after so long a course of years, a little cloud not bigger than a person's hand appeared, then grew as clouds do, and poured out such generous showers that all

---

[13]Mayer, *Many Commentaries in One*, 107*.
[14]CRR 8:117.

[15]Mayer, *Many Commentaries in One*, 109*.
[16]LW 3:320.
[17]Strigel, *Libri Samuelis, Regum et Paralipomenon*, 278.
[18]Mayer, *Many Commentaries in One*, 109*.

things were restored. If this rain was accidental or given by the power of nature, not by Providence, who could have made Elijah sure of its coming, when he promised rain so persistently, especially in so weighty a matter in which he had brought forward the rain as witness that his Lord who had given the promise was God? Since, then, the rain fell by the providence and arrangement of God, it is immaterial to us whether it was poured out by a combination of natural forces adapted to do this at the time or by a new miracle, provided we understand that before the foundation of the world Providence so foresaw all things and had all things so clearly before it that Providence knew that the conjunction of the natural forces that should produce all that abundance of water would coincide with the wickedness of the world, which it wiped out by the waters at the time of Noah.

So also with the plentiful showers that were brought on after the long drought. For whether these things occurred in regular course or out of course, the warning and prophecy about them show that they were done by Providence. For if they happened in regular course, if a flood in natural course coincided with the wickedness of humankind, divine wisdom and providence are reflected from them. If the waters were poured forth out of course, again we see both these, righteousness as well as power. For God does miracles out of the ordinary course of things, that the astronomers and those who, like them, wage war against the sovereignty of the Deity like the giants may not be able forever to attribute everything to some force of nature, but may be compelled to recognize a greater force. ON THE PROVIDENCE OF GOD.[19]

EFFECTIVE PRAYER. VIKTORIN STRIGEL: In Elijah's prayer, which successfully brought a great rain, we ought to consider first the place of the prayer, second the posture of prayer and third the favorable divine response. For Elijah prayed from the top of Mount Carmel, according to the

command of Christ in Matthew 6: "But when you pray, go into your room and shut the door and prayer to your Father who is in secret. And your Father who sees in secret with reward you." Second, Elijah's posture signifies a remarkable and momentous movement of the heart and the soul. And even though nothing happened immediately, Elijah kept hope, for he obeyed the rule that Christ gave in Luke 18: "They ought always to pray and not lose heart." Finally, he was heard and thereby summoned a great rain. In the letter of James, this example is set forth for the imitation of the entire church: "The prayer of a righteous person has great power as it is working. Elijah was a man with a nature like ours, and he prayed fervently that it might not rain, and for three years and six months it did not rain on the earth. Then he prayed again, and heaven gave rain, and the earth bore its fruit." BOOK OF KINGS.[20]

EARNEST PRAYER TO BE IMITATED. JOHN MAYER: Elijah fell down to the ground in such a way that he neither lay nor kneeled with his body erected, but his head was bowed down toward the earth as he kneeled between his knees. He used this gesture in the greatest humility, as unworthy to look up to heaven, just like the publican commended by our Lord for his humility in Luke 18. In the same way, the cherubim covered their faces with two of their wings. From these examples we should learn to use the most humble gestures in prayer.

And it is to be noted that Elijah was so intent on praying that he did not even look up himself. Rather, he sent his servant to see whether any cloud appeared out of the sea—since this location . . . was close to the sea. And when Elijah's servant brought him word that no cloud appeared, he persevered in prayer even when the servant returned a second, third and even a seventh time before any cloud could be seen. And Elijah did all this, although he knew for certain that God would send rain. Elijah did this because he knew that it was God's will that

[19]Zwingli, *Latin Works*, 2:209 (ZSW 6,3:194-95).

[20]Strigel, *Libri Samuelis, Regum et Paralipomenon*, 279; citing Mt 6:6; Lk 18:1; Jas 5:16-18.

he should earnestly seek him so that rain fell not by natural means but by God's power, so that he would be manifested as the only true God. From this we are to learn that we are to seek all the good things we need by prayer. We are also to learn that we must come to God for prayer for deliverance from evils, even though God's decree would stand without our prayer. Finally, we are to persevere in prayer until we prevail, even though we may see no signs of accomplishment at the moment. COMMENTARY ON 1 KINGS.[21]

SIN AS A MOUNTING STORM. DANIEL DYKE: Our wisdom must take heed . . . of the deceitfulness of sin, lest we be hardened and become accustomed to it. For a habit and hardness in sin does not come at first, but by degrees. It comes, for instance, when by receiving the seed of evil and enticing thoughts, we come to conceive it. As James says: "But each person is tempted when he is lured and enticed by his own desire. Then desire when it has conceived gives birth to sin, and sin when it is fully grown brings forth death." This type of enticement is perfected by daily practice, which turns into a custom and habit. It then becomes a necessity so that we are miserably enthralled to sin. And finally, it leads to death.

Since, therefore, we cannot be totally rid of this unwelcomed guest once entertained, let us be wary how we enter into the most innocent manner of communication with him. . . . The deceitfulness of sin is like Elijah's cloud. At first the cloud seemed very little, no bigger than one's hand. Yet gradually it overspread the whole sky and caused a dashing shower. Therefore, just as the prophet bid the king go to his chariot to avoid the storm when the cloud was barely visible in the sky, so we must fly to shelter once we foresee the danger of a great storm of sin approaching us even when small. THE MYSTERY OF SELF-DECEIVING.[22]

---

[21]Mayer, *Many Commentaries in One*, 110*.

[22]Dyke, *The Mystery of Self-Deceiving*, 197-98*; citing Jas 1:14-15.

19:1-21 ELIJAH AND THE LORD

[1]Ahab told Jezebel all that Elijah had done, and how he had killed all the prophets with the sword. [2]Then Jezebel sent a messenger to Elijah, saying, "So may the gods do to me and more also, if I do not make your life as the life of one of them by this time tomorrow." [3]Then he was afraid, and he arose and ran for his life and came to Beersheba, which belongs to Judah, and left his servant there.

[4]But he himself went a day's journey into the wilderness and came and sat down under a broom tree. And he asked that he might die, saying, "It is enough; now, O Lord, take away my life, for I am no better than my fathers." [5]And he lay down and slept under a broom tree. And behold, an angel touched him and said to him, "Arise and eat." [6]And he looked, and behold, there was at his head a cake baked on hot stones and a jar of water. And he ate and drank and lay down again. [7]And the angel of the Lord came again a second time and touched him and said, "Arise and eat, for the journey is too great for you." [8]And he arose and ate and drank, and went in the strength of that food forty days and forty nights to Horeb, the mount of God.

[9]There he came to a cave and lodged in it. And behold, the word of the Lord came to him, and he said to him, "What are you doing here, Elijah?" [10]He said, "I have been very jealous for the Lord, the God of hosts. For the people of Israel have forsaken your covenant, thrown down your altars, and killed your prophets with the sword, and I, even I only, am left, and they seek my life, to take it away." [11]And he said, "Go out and stand on the mount before the Lord." And behold, the Lord passed by, and a great and strong wind tore the mountains and broke in pieces the rocks before the Lord, but the Lord was not in the wind. And after the wind an earthquake, but the Lord was not in the earthquake. [12]And after the earthquake a fire, but the Lord was not in the fire. And after the fire the sound of a low whisper.[a] [13]And when Elijah heard it, he wrapped his face in his cloak and went out and stood at the entrance of the cave. And behold, there came a voice to him and said, "What are you doing here, Elijah?" [14]He said, "I have been very jealous for the Lord, the God of hosts. For the people of Israel have forsaken your covenant, thrown down your altars, and killed your prophets with the sword, and I, even I only, am left, and they seek my life, to take it away." [15]And the Lord said to him, "Go, return on your way to the wilderness of Damascus. And when you arrive, you shall anoint Hazael to be king over Syria. [16]And Jehu the son of Nimshi you shall anoint to be king over Israel, and Elisha the son of Shaphat of Abel-meholah you shall anoint to be prophet in your place. [17]And the one who escapes from the sword of Hazael shall Jehu put to death, and the one who escapes from the sword of Jehu shall Elisha put to death. [18]Yet I will leave seven thousand in Israel, all the knees that have not bowed to Baal, and every mouth that has not kissed him."

[19]So he departed from there and found Elisha the son of Shaphat, who was plowing with twelve yoke of oxen in front of him, and he was with the twelfth. Elijah passed by him and cast his cloak upon him. [20]And he left the oxen and ran after Elijah and said, "Let me kiss my father and my mother, and then I will follow you." And he said to him, "Go back again, for what have I done to you?" [21]And he returned from following him and took the yoke of oxen and sacrificed them and boiled their flesh with the yokes of the oxen and gave it to the people, and they ate. Then he arose and went after Elijah and assisted him.

a Or a sound, a thin silence

OVERVIEW: Elijah's despair after his great victory against the prophets of Baal captures the attention of these commentators. Luther urges readers to consider the saints of the Bible as no more or less holy than contemporary Christians. Elijah, though a mighty man of God, is still a man who suffers and despairs like all others. Rather than an innate godliness, it is his faith in God that allows him to do such mighty deeds. Some interpret Elijah's despair to die not as fear but as terror to have God's honor besmirched if God's prophet, Elijah, should be killed by blasphemers. Others use the example of Elijah's despair to admonish readers not to be idle since idleness is one of the greatest tools Satan uses to tempt believers. The commentators interpret Elijah's provision of food and water in various ways: some emphasize God's mercy; others find symbolism in the modesty of the food and drink; others identify God's astounding sustenance for his followers in a multitude of creative ways. Elijah's conversation with God's whispering voice prompts the commentators to discuss ecclesiology: Hubmaier, Calvin and Luther cite this incident as a precedent for their views of the true church existing without definable structure.

19:1-3 Jezebel Threatens Elijah's Life

SINS OF OLD TESTAMENT SAINTS. MARTIN LUTHER: I have often stated that I do not free the saints from all sins. For we know that the greatest and most saintly people often fell in a horrible fashion and became contaminated not only with error and common weakness but also with the greatest sins contrary to faith, hope, love, patience, namely, with unbelief, doubt, disrespect and murmuring against God. In this we are willing to have them as allies and examples to comfort us. Let us not think that they were statues, stones or trunks of trees, but they were like ourselves. Elijah received an answer from God to his prayer that it should not rain for three years, but later he felt his flesh trembling and begging that he should be allowed to die. LECTURES ON GENESIS.[1]

A SIN AND AN ACT. JACOBUS ARMINIUS: The murder Ahab and Ahaziah intended against Elijah the Prophet was an act that, if perpetrated, would

have deprived Elijah of life, and it was a sin against God's sixth commandment. God prevented that murder, not as it was a sin, but as an act. AN EXAMINATION OF THE TREATISE OF WILLIAM PERKINS CONCERNING PREDESTINATION.[2]

CONSOLING THE FAITHFUL. JOHANNES PISCATOR: God consoles the faithful by his servants when they are constituted by trials, and he stimulates good hope. Here Elijah is consoled after fleeing from wicked Jezebel by the angel twice and in two ways, by words and by acts. For the angel feeds Elijah on two separate occasions and sends him food and drink, for this was to sustain him for his long trip coming up. And then God consoles Elijah himself as he appeared in the cave at Mount Horeb. He commanded him to return and also that he would make more firm the multitude of the godly in the kingdom of Israel who supported the worship of God. COMMENTARY ON 1 KINGS.[3]

19:4 Elijah Despairs of His Life

ELIJAH DESPAIRS WHILE GOD DELIVERS. HEINRICH BULLINGER: Elijah, that great and excellent prophet of God, as a result of the detestable falling away from God as well as the weariness of that miserable people at that time—in whom there appeared to be no true external sign of God—fled into the wilderness and hid himself in a cave. And after being led by the Lord to answer what he was doing there, he responded, "I have been very zealous for the Lord God Almighty. The Israelites have rejected your covenant, broken your altars, and put your prophets to death with the sword. I am the only one left, and now they are trying to kill me too." However, he was immediately sent back to the land of Israel from where he had fled, and the Lord also added these words: "Yet I reserve seven thousand in Israel—all whose knees have not bowed down to Baal and all whose mouths have not kissed him." This great prophet

---

[1]LW 6:177.

[2]Arminius, *Works*, 3:432*.
[3]Piscator, *Commentarii in omnes libros Veteris Testamenti*, 2:301.

had assumed that he alone had been left of the faithful number of people in Israel; but he heard that seven thousand holy men had been preserved by God, none of whom had not bowed their knees before Baal, that is, served a false god in outward rituals. But who does not realize that the prophet had not assumed that by the number seven was meant a very large number of true worshipers of God who had not been circumcised into the covenant of Baal but rather the covenant of the eternal God? DECADES 5.2.[4]

COMFORT AND FEAR. MARTIN LUTHER: Such errors and sins of the saints are set forth in order that those who are troubled and desperate may find comfort and that those who are proud may be afraid. No one has ever fallen so grievously that they could not have stood up again. On the other hand, no one has such a sure footing that they cannot fall. LECTURES ON GALATIANS.[5]

AHAB LOVED JEZEBEL MORE THAN GOD. JOHANNES BUGENHAGEN: Ahab loved Jezebel more than God, whose work he had just seen. But he did not have enough constancy in his soul to handle the slaughter of the prophets of Baal. While he had not dared to hinder the prophet or the people who supported him, he promptly commanded a sentence of death against Elijah, which God himself declared to be clear impiety. When Jezebel said, "So may the gods do to me and more. . . ." This was a typical Gentile vow. Elijah then left his servant at Beersheba, a place described in Genesis 21. Then you see how completely the prophet had been forsaken. He wanted to be killed by God rather than by the queen. I can rightly say that no one could have seen more impiety than Elijah had, just as it says about Lot in 2 Peter 2. COMMENTARY ON 1 KINGS.[6]

PROOF OF THE LIFE TO COME. JOHN MAYER: Growing weary of this life due to his manifold

troubles, Elijah now desired to die. It may seem strange that Elijah fled for fear of being put to death, only to desire to die at present. But it is to be understood that Elijah feared only the manner of dying at the hands of persecutors, lest the ones who stood for Baal should seem to have won the day in the end. That is, Elijah feared it would appear that the servants of Baal would have overcome the Lord as his champion if Elijah would have died at their hands. It was Elijah's zeal for the Lord, then, that moved him to want to die at the Lord's hands rather than at the hands of idolaters. . . . But in desiring that he might die, Elijah showed that he believed a better life to come after the bodily death. Otherwise he never would have desired to have his life ended. COMMENTARY ON 1 KINGS.[7]

SATAN NEVER RESTS. THOMAS ADAMS: Since Satan is so . . . busy a spirit, this should teach us not to be idle. As a general rule, do not be too busy in other people's affairs nor too lazy in your own. We know that the enemy walks, waits and watches to destroy us, so we have to keep guard. Satan sows tares in the field of our hearts when we sleep. Let us wake up and pluck up the tares, so that they do not choke up the good seed of our graces. It is not allowed for us to sit still. We must be walking—using our eyes for seeing, our ears for hearing, our hands for working and our feet for walking. "Get up and eat, for the journey is too much for you." Arise, O Christian, you have been sitting too long, and you still have a great journey to go. The one who considers the way and distance between mortality and immortality and between corruption and glory must conclude that it is high time to be walking. THE BARREN TREE.[8]

19:5-8 Elijah Eats and Drinks

AN ANGEL FEEDS ELIJAH. JOHANNES BUGENHA-GEN: "And behold, an angel touched Elijah and said,

[4]Bullinger, *Sermonum decades quinque*, 366; citing 1 Sam 19:10, 18.
[5]LW 26:109.
[6]Bugenhagen, *In Regum duos ultimos libros*, 90-91; citing Gen 21:31; 2 Pet 2:7.

[7]Mayer, *Many Commentaries in One*, 112*.
[8]Adams, *Barren Tree*, 29*.

to him, 'Arise and eat.'" This is God the Father's providing for him who had earlier been fed by crows and by the widow. These were fellow creatures, but now, forsaken, Elijah is fed by an angel. Believers can never be without God's provision when they are weak. They cannot perish of hunger, either, as this physical gift of God is a sure sign of the fact of salvation. Neither did God feed him with natural food from the angel, for Elijah did not then hunger for forty days. He did not think of eating, when he certainly ought to have needed it as he fled through the desert where there were no people. Just as God cared for his weakness, so God gladly produced all that Elijah desired at the time. The angel said, "The journey is too great for you." For he knew the prophet wanted to flee and to escape the entire kingdom of Israel, which was a desire he could not otherwise obtain. Commentary on 1 Kings.[9]

Contentment. Thomas Becon: When the prophet Elijah fled from the face of wicked Jezebel ... and was hungry in the wilderness, God did not send through his angel great plenty of dainty dishes or costly wines, but only bread and a cup of water. This happened to illustrate that we should not hunt after superfluous things, but be content with things present; and if we have the necessities ... we should desire no more. A New Catechism.[10]

More Ways Than One. John Mayer: The same God that provided for Elijah miraculously in the time of drought by the ministry of ravens now fed him by the ministry of an angel. And the one who made the meal and oil—which was enough only for one meal—to last many days to feed him and the widow's entire family, gave a new kind of miracle that would strengthen Elijah for more than forty days. How this could be we ought not to question. Rather, we ought to recognize that the Almighty caused it to be so that we might know that the Lord has more ways

than one to sustain those who trust in him. Commentary on 1 Kings.[11]

No Law About Fasting. Johannes Bugenhagen: Why have some established a forty-day fast for us from eating and drinking because of the fasts of Elijah, Moses and Christ? Why do they want to do every single year what those people did once? Fools turn such moments into a holy law; then the fools try in vain to do something that had been a miracle from God. Commentary on 1 Kings.[12]

19:9-17 The Lord Comes in a Whisper

A Whisper to Inspire Destructive Hazael and Jehu. Johannes Piscator: God could have acted in many ways. For instance, God could have destroyed the idolatrous Israelites and the persecutors of godly prophets in an instant. Or he could have overthrown their homes by wind, as happened to Job's children. Or he could have sent an earthquake. Or he could have sent down fire from heaven, as happened to the soldiers later sent to take Elijah. However, God did not do things this way. Rather God brought calamity by means of a calm whisper, by the inspiration of the hearts of Hazael and Jehu. Commentary on 1 Kings.[13]

Thunderous and Gentle. Martin Luther: The law should be revealed with thunderbolts to those who are foolish and stiff-necked, but the gospel should be presented gently to those who are terrified and humbled. Lectures on Hebrews.[14]

Tempted by God's Storms, Comforted by God's Gentleness. Johannes Bugenhagen: See how this prophet had the word of God but God delayed its coming with these grave temptations. Still, Elijah clung to the word when the Lord prepared a terrible storm through the mountains

---

[11]Mayer, *Many Commentaries in One*, 113*.
[12]Bugenhagen, *In Regum duos ultimos libros*, 92.
[13]Piscator, *Commentarii in omnes libros Veteris Testamenti*, 2:301; citing Job 1:18-19; 2 Kings 1:9-14.
[14]LW 29:143.

[9]Bugenhagen, *In Regum duos ultimos libros*, 91.
[10]Becon, *Catechism*, 164.

that shattered the rocks. Then the earth shook and there was fire, but God was not in any of that. Christians might be tempted by these terrors, in which God appears to be fighting against himself, as when God will lay waste, destroy and reduce all things to rubble. And yet, at the same time, where things appear most hopeless with him, God remains friendly through the most hidden Spirit, which says, "My God is otherwise; my God is not in this. Help me, God, so that the weakness of these eyes and senses, which are temptations to faith, may pass right by." After this came the "whistling of a gentle air," which made his soul rise up to God, according to God's Word. Thus the spirit is consoled after temptation. See how God does this, so that the prophet received his soul back through God. God could have strengthened Elijah without this, except that God knows this is necessary to bring him to us, that is, to flesh and blood. Turn against those turbulent spirits who have been urged on by a spirit that has been raised to an uproar. For God was not in the storm, the earthquake or the fire, rather the prophet was approached by God in the "whispering of a gentle air," which is indeed how God approaches us. COMMENTARY ON 1 KINGS.[15]

PARABLE ON THE HISTORY OF ENGLAND. THOMAS ADAMS: God has dealt with us as he did with Elijah. The Lord passed by and a great strong wind tore the mountains and broke in pieces the rocks before the Lord. But the Lord was not in the wind. After the wind came an earthquake, but the Lord was not in the earthquake. After the earthquake, a fire came, but the Lord was not in the fire. And after the fire, a still voice. And the Lord came with that voice.

God has done the same thing to England. In the time of King Henry VIII, there came a great and mighty wind that tore down churches, overthrew altarages[16] and expropriated from ministers their livings. This made laymen substantial parsons and

clergymen their vicar-shadows. It blew away the rights of law into the lap of Issachar. It was a violent wind, but God was not in the wind. In the days of King Edward there first came a terrible earthquake, hideous vapors of treasons and conspiracies, rumbling from Rome, to shake the foundations of that church, which had now left off loving the whore and turned antichrist quite out of his saddle. There were excommunications of prince and people, execrations and curses in their theatricals with bell, book and candle. There were indulgences, bulls, pardons and promises of heaven to all traitors that would extirpate such a king and kingdom. It was a monstrous earthquake, but God was not in the earthquake. In the days of Queen Mary came the fire—an unmerciful fire. It was such a one as was never before kindled in England, and (we trust in Jesus Christ) never shall be again. It raged against all that professed the gospel of Christ. It made bonfires of silly women for not understanding the ineffable mystery of transubstantiation. It burned the mother with the child. . . . It was a raging and insatiable fire, but God was not in that fire. In the days of Queen Elizabeth of blessed memory came the still voice, saluting us with the songs of Zion. And God came with this voice. This sweet and blessed voice is still continued by our gracious Sovereign: God long preserved him with it, and it with him, and us all with them both. THE HAPPINESS OF THE CHURCH.[17]

LIFE LESSONS FOR ELIJAH. JOHN MAYER: In referring to Elijah, these different signs taught Elijah that his earnest seeking of the destruction of the idolatrous Israelites was not pleasing to the Lord. Rather, after the judgment of drought, which Elijah had frequently prayed for, he should now by gentle means seek the conversion and salvation of the idolaters. For it appeared by experience that rigid means would do no good for them, seeing that they were not turned by the long-continued drought. However, when they saw a sign of the Lord's power above Baal's, they cried out, "The Lord, he is God; the Lord, he is God." Some other lessons can also be

---

[15]Bugenhagen, *In Regum duos ultimos libros*, 92-93.
[16]Priests received these stipends for special ecclesial services (e.g., weddings, funerals, baptisms).

[17]Adams, *Happines of the Church*, 340-41*.

added. First, by these signs the Lord showed his power for the comfort of his servant, who was now full of fear. But it is said that the Lord was not in these things; that is, the full knowledge of God is not in seeing such dreadful effects of his power attained, but when in silence we give our minds to divine contemplation. Second, it was here showed that when the Lord executes judgments against the wicked, it is not his ultimate goal to destroy them. Rather, his ultimate goal is the conversion of their souls and in the bringing of the state of the church to peace and tranquility. COMMENTARY ON 1 KINGS.[18]

19:18 The Faithful, Though Few, Shall Prevail

ON THE UNIVERSAL CHURCH AND IDOLS. BALTHASAR HUBMAIER: What is the church? . . . The church is sometimes taken to be all people who are gathered and united in one God, one Lord, one faith and one baptism, and who confess this faith with the mouth, wherever they may be on earth. Now, this is the universal bodily Christian church and fellowship of the saints assembled in the Spirit of God alone. . . . Sometimes the church is understood to mean each particular and outward assembly or parish membership that is under one shepherd or bishop, and which comes together bodily for instruction, baptism and the Lord's Supper. The church as daughter has the same power to bind and to loose on earth as the universal church, her mother, when she uses the keys according to the command of Christ, her spouse and husband. . . . What is the difference between these two churches? . . . The particular church may err, as the papist church has erred in many respects. But the universal church cannot err. She is without spot, without wrinkle, is controlled by the Holy Spirit, and Christ is with her until the end of the world. And God will always preserve for himself seven thousand who will not bend their knee to the idol Baal. A CHRISTIAN CATECHISM.[19]

EXISTENCE WITHOUT APPARENT FORM. JOHN CALVIN: We affirm that the church can exist without any visible appearance, and that its appearance is not contained within that outward magnificence that they foolishly admire. Rather, it has quite another mark: namely, the pure preaching of God's Word and the lawful administration of the sacraments. They rage if the church cannot always be pointed to with the finger. But among the Jewish people how often was it so deformed that no semblance of it remained? What form do we think it displayed when Elijah complained that he alone was left? INSTITUTES: DEDICATION TO KING FRANCIS I.[20]

TWO THINGS TO REMEMBER. MARTIN LUTHER: Therefore we must take careful and conscientious note of the following. First, there always have been, always are and always will be those who glorify God and teach rightly about God, even though their number may be extremely small. Second, the church is not a perfectly holy society or completely free of flagrant faults and blemishes. COMMENTS ON PSALM 90.[21]

GOD PRESERVES THE CHURCH. JEREMIAS BASTINGIUS: For as we see that in one person there is one soul and one body but many . . . members that are quickened by one soul, so the universal and catholic church is one body and has many members. But the soul that quickens this body is the Holy Spirit, by whom the Son of God . . . knits together all the members of the same body, regardless of distance from another. He has done this from the beginning of the world and will continue maintaining and preserving his church always and unto the end of the world, not only in general but also even to every member of his church. . . . For instance, in the time of Elijah did he not miraculously preserve the church as it was in caves? God said to Elijah: "Yet I reserve seven thousand in Israel." AN EXPOSITION ON THE CATECHISM OF THE LOW COUNTRIES.[22]

---

[18]Mayer, Many Commentaries in One, 115*; citing 1 Kings 18:39.
[19]CRR 5:351-52*; citing Mt 28:19.

[20]LCC 20:24-25 (CO 2:22-23); citing 1 Kings 19:10 or 1 Kings 19:14.
[21]LW 13:89.
[22]Bastingius, An Exposition upon the Catechism, 72*.

19:19-21 *Elijah Calls Elisha*

ELISHA'S CALL. JOHANNES BUGENHAGEN: Elijah said to Elisha, "Go back again," that is, "I permit you this physical affection of bidding farewell to your parents. But this is so that you will not go back later, that is, you should not forsake your call on account of this physical affection," for "no one who puts his hand to the plow and looks back is fit for the kingdom of God," and "leave the dead to bury their own dead." Then Elisha killed the oxen; that is, he sacrificed them and shared the sacrifice with his guests. And knowing that he had been called by God, he gave thanks to God for the call. He did not look back to those whom he had left, which would certainly have been understandable, but he had been called by the will of God. COMMENTARY ON 1 KINGS.[23]

WHETHER ELIJAH ACTED RIGHTLY IN ALLOWING ELISHA TO SAY GOODBYE. JOHANNES PISCATOR: A question may be asked whether Elijah acted rightly by giving allowance for Elisha to bid farewell to his parents before departing. The reason for doubting Elijah's action here is because a similar example occurs with Christ, but Christ did not give allowance for a person. I respond that there is no reason to think that Elijah did not act properly. For Elijah perceived that Elisha's request was perfectly just. And Elisha intended to fulfill his vocation. But Christ did not give an allowance for the man in the Gospel because the man longed to first bury his father. He did not have a just cause for excusing himself, but was wicked. The two cases do not correspond. COMMENTARY ON 1 KINGS.[24]

NO MIRACULOUS CLOAK. KONRAD PELLIKAN: While leading twelve yoke of oxen in the fields, Elisha, the son of a wealthy farmer, was called to the highest prophetic office. The Holy Spirit, who easily gives divine gifts to whomever God will, recognized his potential to receive the Spirit's gifts easily, while the mercy of the God whom no one can despise strengthened his humble station. At the same time, all people and ages know that honest agriculture is necessary and useful. Elijah consecrated him, covering him with his cloak as if it were a kind of customary sacrament for ordaining prophets of the Lord. From out of many people, God chooses, designates and calls the best, so that Elisha was immediately filled with the Holy Spirit. This did not happen by some virtue of the cloak but by the influence of divine action, which alone gives the gifts of prophecy and miraculous works. COMMENTARY ON 1 KINGS.[25]

ELIJAH'S RESPONSE IN COMPARISON WITH CHRIST'S. JOHN MAYER: Whereas Elijah bid him to go and say goodbye to his family, the one who asked Jesus if he could first bury his father was refused. But Elijah did not go contrary to Christ's teaching here. For the man who asked permission of Christ sought a longer delay, that is, to remain with his father until he died. Only afterward did he intend to follow Jesus. But Elisha only sought to say goodbye to his family, and then he would come. This of course contrasted with the man who asked Jesus, who did not desire to come. Last, Christ was Lord, and so above father and mother. But Elijah was a fellow servant, and therefore he would not be able to dispense with God's laws. COMMENTARY ON 1 KINGS.[26]

---

[23]Bugenhagen, *In Regum duos ultimos libros*, 94-95; citing Lk 9:62, 60.
[24]Piscator, *Commentarii in omnes libros Veteris Testamenti*, 2:301.

[25]Pellikan, *Commentaria Bibliorum*, 2:167v.
[26]Mayer, *Many Commentaries in One*, 117*.

20:1-43 WAR BETWEEN ISRAEL AND SYRIA

Ben-hadad the king of Syria gathered all his army together. Thirty-two kings were with him, and horses and chariots. And he went up and closed in on Samaria and fought against it. ²And he sent messengers into the city to Ahab king of Israel and said to him, "Thus says Ben-hadad: ³'Your silver and your gold are mine; your best wives and children also are mine.'" ⁴And the king of Israel answered, "As you say, my lord, O king, I am yours, and all that I have." ⁵The messengers came again and said, "Thus says Ben-hadad: 'I sent to you, saying, "Deliver to me your silver and your gold, your wives and your children." ⁶Nevertheless I will send my servants to you tomorrow about this time, and they shall search your house and the houses of your servants and lay hands on whatever pleases you and take it away.'"

⁷Then the king of Israel called all the elders of the land and said, "Mark, now, and see how this man is seeking trouble, for he sent to me for my wives and my children, and for my silver and my gold, and I did not refuse him." ⁸And all the elders and all the people said to him, "Do not listen or consent." ⁹So he said to the messengers of Ben-hadad, "Tell my lord the king, 'All that you first demanded of your servant I will do, but this thing I cannot do.'" And the messengers departed and brought him word again. ¹⁰Ben-hadad sent to him and said, "The gods do so to me and more also, if the dust of Samaria shall suffice for handfuls for all the people who follow me." ¹¹And the king of Israel answered, "Tell him, 'Let not him who straps on his armor boast himself as he who takes it off.'" ¹²When Ben-hadad heard this message as he was drinking with the kings in the booths, he said to his men, "Take your positions." And they took their positions against the city.

¹³And behold, a prophet came near to Ahab king of Israel and said, "Thus says the LORD, Have you seen all this great multitude? Behold, I will give it into your hand this day, and you shall know that I am the LORD." ¹⁴And Ahab said, "By whom?" He said, "Thus says the LORD, By the servants of the governors of the districts." Then he said, "Who shall begin the battle?" He answered, "You." ¹⁵Then he mustered the servants of the governors of the districts, and they were 232. And after them he mustered all the people of Israel, seven thousand.

¹⁶And they went out at noon, while Ben-hadad was drinking himself drunk in the booths, he and the thirty-two kings who helped him. ¹⁷The servants of the governors of the districts went out first. And Ben-hadad sent out scouts, and they reported to him, "Men are coming out from Samaria." ¹⁸He said, "If they have come out for peace, take them alive. Or if they have come out for war, take them alive."

¹⁹So these went out of the city, the servants of the governors of the districts and the army that followed them. ²⁰And each struck down his man. The Syrians fled, and Israel pursued them, but Ben-hadad king of Syria escaped on a horse with horsemen. ²¹And the king of Israel went out and struck the horses and chariots, and struck the Syrians with a great blow.

²²Then the prophet came near to the king of Israel and said to him, "Come, strengthen yourself, and consider well what you have to do, for in the spring the king of Syria will come up against you."

²³And the servants of the king of Syria said to him, "Their gods are gods of the hills, and so they were stronger than we. But let us fight against them in the plain, and surely we shall be stronger than they. ²⁴And do this: remove the kings, each from his post, and put commanders in their places, ²⁵and muster an army like the army that you have lost, horse for horse, and chariot for chariot. Then we will fight against them in the plain, and surely we shall be stronger than they." And he listened to their voice and did so.

²⁶In the spring, Ben-hadad mustered the Syrians and went up to Aphek to fight against Israel. ²⁷And the people of Israel were mustered and were provisioned and went against them. The people of Israel encamped before them like two little flocks of goats, but the Syrians filled the country. ²⁸And a man of God came near and said to the king of Israel, "Thus says the LORD, 'Because the Syrians have said, "The

LORD is a god of the hills but he is not a god of the valleys," therefore I will give all this great multitude into your hand, and you shall know that I am the LORD.'" [29] And they encamped opposite one another seven days. Then on the seventh day the battle was joined. And the people of Israel struck down of the Syrians 100,000 foot soldiers in one day. [30] And the rest fled into the city of Aphek, and the wall fell upon 27,000 men who were left.

Ben-hadad also fled and entered an inner chamber in the city. [31] And his servants said to him, "Behold now, we have heard that the kings of the house of Israel are merciful kings. Let us put sackcloth around our waists and ropes on our heads and go out to the king of Israel. Perhaps he will spare your life." [32] So they tied sackcloth around their waists and put ropes on their heads and went to the king of Israel and said, "Your servant Ben-hadad says, 'Please, let me live.'" And he said, "Does he still live? He is my brother." [33] Now the men were watching for a sign, and they quickly took it up from him and said, "Yes, your brother Ben-hadad." Then he said, "Go and bring him." Then Ben-hadad came out to him, and he caused him to come up into the chariot. [34] And Ben-hadad said to him, "The cities that my father took from your father I will restore, and you may establish bazaars for yourself in Damascus, as my father did in Samaria." And Ahab said, "I will let you go on these terms." So he made a covenant with him and let him go.

[35] And a certain man of the sons of the prophets said to his fellow at the command of the LORD, "Strike me, please." But the man refused to strike him. [36] Then he said to him, "Because you have not obeyed the voice of the LORD, behold, as soon as you have gone from me, a lion shall strike you down." And as soon as he had departed from him, a lion met him and struck him down. [37] Then he found another man and said, "Strike me, please." And the man struck him—struck him and wounded him. [38] So the prophet departed and waited for the king by the way, disguising himself with a bandage over his eyes. [39] And as the king passed, he cried to the king and said, "Your servant went out into the midst of the battle, and behold, a soldier turned and brought a man to me and said, 'Guard this man; if by any means he is missing, your life shall be for his life, or else you shall pay a talent[a] of silver.' [40] And as your servant was busy here and there, he was gone." The king of Israel said to him, "So shall your judgment be; you yourself have decided it." [41] Then he hurried to take the bandage away from his eyes, and the king of Israel recognized him as one of the prophets. [42] And he said to him, "Thus says the LORD, 'Because you have let go out of your hand the man whom I had devoted to destruction,[b] therefore your life shall be for his life, and your people for his people.'" [43] And the king of Israel went to his house vexed and sullen and came to Samaria.

---

a A *talent* was about 75 pounds or 34 kilograms   b That is, set apart (devoted) as an offering to the Lord (for destruction)

OVERVIEW: The commentators here, convinced of Ahab's evil, marvel at God's goodness to him. Like the king of Syria,[1] Ahab is proud and boastful, but because God wants to honor his own name against the pagan world, Ahab is used to bring about Syria's defeat. The prophet who speaks the word of the Lord to Ahab is not explicitly named in the biblical text, though many of our commentators assume that it is Micaiah (who will prophesy to Ahab in 1 Kings 22). Despite the divine favor shown to Ahab, which several of the commentators argue is shown to bring Ahab to repentance, he ultimately does not follow the Lord's instructions. By showing mercy to King Ben-hadad, he violates the command of God. His punishment for violating God's command comes through the mouth of the same prophet who had already spoken to him. Some compare this prophet's confrontation with King Ahab to Nathan's admonition of King David by means of a parable in 2 Samuel 7.

---

[1] That is, Aram.

20:1-12 The Beginning of War Between Ahab and Ben-hadad

INCURABLE AHAB. VIKTORIN STRIGEL: This chapter describes two important and glorious victories with which God honored Ahab. Not that the impious king was worthy of such blessings but rather because God wanted to vindicate his glorious name against the blasphemies of the Syrians, punish the most arrogant king of Syria and—through these blessings as through parental sweetness—to invite Ahab into repentance. But where impious roots have grown deep, change does not come either through punishments or blessings. For after these victories Ahab threw the prophet Micaiah into prison and brought forth other fruits of impiety, which revealed his mind to be utterly incurable. For this reason he was later killed in battle by the Syrians and his descendants completely removed from the kingship. BOOK OF KINGS.[2]

WORKING WITH AHAB. KONRAD PELLIKAN: It was God's providence that Ahab responded with humility, while the king of Syria—relying on physical power—responded with a boastful amount of indignation, as if seeking an occasion to go to war or incite a battle with his ready army. Against the laws of nations, he was not merely content to receive tribute but wanted to usurp the best and most desirable possessions in Israel, taking even wives and children. Amid such calamity, the Lord raised an alarm for Ahab, even though the king did not acknowledge him. And so the Lord did not desert him yet. Instead, as if moving rocks, God dragged away all obstacles from those whom he had called. COMMENTARY ON 1 KINGS.[3]

PREFERRING BLOODY WAR. JOHN MAYER: The Syrian king was proud of his huge army, which he thought the king of Israel was unable to resist. Therefore he sent Ahab a message to which he thought Ahab would by no means consent. He sent this message so that he could more justly enter into battle so that he could get all that Ahab had. But Ahab, being filled with base fear, yielded to Ben-hadad, saying, "I am yours, and all that I have." By this, Ahab did not mean that he was ready to yield everything—his wives and children, and all his goods, to Ben-hadad. Rather, by giving these words Ahab sought to pacify him and thought that he would pay the tribute that was laid on him. But then Ben-hadad sent another letter to Ahab, explaining that on the following day he would send for all the things Ahab had—his treasures, positions, families and even that of his subjects. . . . But rather than allow this Syrian army to come and attack the Israelite's houses, ravish their wives and carry away as many of them as they pleased, they preferred to endure the brunt of the most bloody war than allow that to happen. COMMENTARY ON 1 KINGS.[4]

20:13-25 Ahab Defeats Ben-hadad

GOD'S MERCY TO SAVE. KONRAD PELLIKAN: Seeing the tremendous mercy of the Creator, who—no matter the depth of the depravity—still will not abandon an ungodly multitude for the sake of a good few—Ahab considered this kind humility and recognized his infirmities. But his pride resisted it, as much as he might have fought against it. Therefore the impious king of Israel was comforted but was not humbled enough. So a sign a victory over this great army was promised to him by a prophet of the Lord, whom the Hebrews consider to have been Micaiah son of Imlah. The king of Israel alone would lead, so that he might acknowledge the Lord God of Israel, whose prophet has just promised the victory. COMMENTARY ON 1 KINGS.[5]

---

[2]Strigel, *Libri Samuelis, Regum et Paralipomenon*, 283-84.
[3]Pellikan, *Commentaria Bibliorum*, 2:168r.

[4]Mayer, *Many Commentaries in One*, 120*.
[5]Pellikan, *Commentaria Bibliorum*, 2:168r, with Pellikan giving the name of the prophet as *Semaiah* son of Imlah.

DIVINE GOVERNANCE. JOHANNES PISCATOR: We have here an example of the divine governance of God. For God confounded the boasting of those who were making war against the people of God, since they confided in their own power. However, God gave a victory by means of the few who obeyed God's commands and believed in his promises. And in this way God gave Ahab victory over Ben-hadad, king of Syria. COMMENTARY ON 1 KINGS.[6]

THE PROPHET TELLS AHAB THE NEWS BEFOREHAND. JOHN MAYER: The Lord, having shown himself to Ahab to be the only true God—who by fire and rain through the mediation of Elijah before had done miracles—now promised further to show the same by making an innumerable company of enemies to fall before his people of Israel, being few in number. This was communicated by another prophet who is not named. Many suppose this prophet to be Micaiah, but Peter Martyr Vermigli opposed this opinion because this prophet is said to have never prophesied good to Ahab later on. The reason why this prophecy was given to so unworthy a person as Ahab was so that he would know the Lord to be the only true God. It was also given to destroy the pride of Ben-hadad. This prophet, though we don't know his name, as mentioned above, may have been one of those hidden in caves from the fury of Jezebel. . . . And it is to be noted that God would not give this great victory without telling Ahab of it first, so that he might not ascribe it to Baal or to fortune, but to the Lord only. And therefore the prophet set down the time and the manner in which the war was to be fought. COMMENTARY ON 1 KINGS.[7]

THE EXAMPLE OF JONATHAN. VIKTORIN STRIGEL: Ahab's faith here is worthy of great praise, for in the face of contradictory evidence he did not doubt the victory but accepted the word of the prophet. The followers of such a leader are also worthy of praise when they are small in number and neverthe-less go against a great multitude of enemies, daring to fight hand to hand in battle together with their leader. Such people doubtlessly had in their mouths and souls the example of the holy man Jonathan, who said, "Nothing can hinder the Lord from saving by many or by few." BOOK OF KINGS.[8]

ALWAYS PREPARED FOR THE NEXT BATTLE. JOHN MAYER: Ahab returned in victory and was laden with spoils, for he pursued the Syrians very far. And after returning, he took their tents, which were rich with gold and silver. God prosecuted the wicked king Ben-hadad with evidences of his power and omniscience, so that he might be without excuse. And so God sent now the prophet for a second time to reveal a secret to Ahab, which none but the true God would know for certain, namely, that the king of Syria would come again in the next year to renew the war. Wanting Ahab to consider this, the prophet left Ahab to make use of the premonition accordingly. His intention in doing so was, as with the former miracle, to have Ahab turn from idols and serve the Lord, conceiving that he could never be secure from his enemies if he did not do so. And hereby all kings and commanders should learn some military wisdom about never growing secure. For, after the enemy is once overcome, we must prepare for another encounter because otherwise a battle initially obtained may turn into a loss in the war. COMMENTARY ON 1 KINGS.[9]

20:26-34 Ahab Defeats Ben-hadad Again

IGNORING THE GIFT OF VICTORY. VIKTORIN STRIGEL: Three main things are considered in this and the following narrative: first, the mercy of God invites Ahab to repentance; second, the blindness and extreme folly of the impious king; and third, an example of how blasphemy is punished. God has just honored Ahab with two decisive victories,

---

[6]Piscator, *Commentarii in omnes libros Veteris Testamenti*, 2:304.
[7]Mayer, *Many Commentaries in One*, 121-22*.

[8]Strigel, *Libri Samuelis, Regum et Paralipomenon*, 285; citing 1 Sam 14:6.
[9]Mayer, *Many Commentaries in One*, 122-23*.

which were rich in mighty miracles. In a manner that Ahab could not have possibly imagined concerning his situation, God predicts through the prophet that he would continue to keep his kingdom. Thus he says, "I will give all this great multitude into your hand and you shall know that I am the Lord." As if to say, "I will show you that Baal does not exist, but in giving you the victory, you owe it to me to come back to your senses, turn away from worship of Baal and recognize and honor me alone as the true God." But Ahab, whose impiety was a kind of insanity, was not changed by this miracle and gift. BOOK OF KINGS.[10]

GOD'S POWER IN HILLS AND VALLEYS. KONRAD PELLIKAN: This is now the third time in this chapter that King Ahab has been comforted by a prophet and told that the God of Israel had been offended by the blasphemies of the Syrians, as if God's power did not extend to the valleys. And so no matter how big an army it was, it would be handed over into the hands of Ahab, one to whom God clearly did not need to give a victory any more than God needed to show consideration for the blasphemies and impieties of the Gentiles, who were already familiar with the great power of the God of Israel as the only one worth relying on and worshiping. But all of these people were sinners who consciously persevered in their sin and all the impieties they had committed before. Thus they had no excuse for their ruin. By this, God's justice—with mercy—is commended to godly people. COMMENTARY ON 1 KINGS.[11]

LARGER IS NOT BETTER. JOHN MAYER: It is said that the Israelites looked like "two little flocks of goats." This is here set down to show the great disparity appearing between the armies. It was done so that the power of God might be more magnified. For, in the following part of this history, it would be declared that the much smaller army, which clung to the Lord, greatly overcame the

greater army, which clung to idols. COMMENTARY ON 1 KINGS.[12]

20:35-43 A Prophet Condemns Ahab

VEXED AND SULLEN. KONRAD PELLIKAN: When the king heard these words from the same prophet who had previously told him something that truly came to pass, he did not doubt the future judgment that was predicted against him. But because he was an impious man, he was not moved by guilt to pray, to ask for intercessions or to humble himself now as a victor as before when he was about to be defeated. Instead he was vexed, disturbed, angry and went back to Samaria without the respect of God or people. For this one whom God rejected could not be corrected. COMMENTARY ON 1 KINGS.[13]

SENTENCE AGAINST ONESELF. JOHN MAYER: If any person asks why the prophet lied first before threatening the king and not plainly and directly revealing himself, it is answered that he followed the use of parables that Nathan had used. For if he had been plain and direct first, Ahab would have been conscious that he did not come for a good reason, and he therefore would have refused to hear him. But now Ahab was brought to give sentence against himself before he knew it. And therefore when the prophet spoke plainly to him, he was filled with confusion instead of rage. COMMENTARY ON 1 KINGS.[14]

EMPTY VICTORIES OVER SYRIA. JOHANNES BUGENHAGEN: God often lifted up Israel against its enemies, promising and offering salvation through the prophets in the most desperate moments. At such times they even knew that this was the Lord himself, but they knew it in vain. For no one called out to the Lord in times of danger, and no one gave thanks for God's salvation, so that the people came out worse than before and with greater impiety, as

[10]Strigel, *Libri Samuelis, Regum et Paralipomenon*, 287.
[11]Pellikan, *Commentaria Bibliorum*, 2:169r.
[12]Mayer, *Many Commentaries in One*, 123*.
[13]Pellikan, *Commentaria Bibliorum*, 2:169v.
[14]Mayer, *Many Commentaries in One*, 126*.

the stories of war against Syria indicate. Therefore these miracles did not result in God being acknowledged but in the grave judgment of guilt against the king and the people. As Christ said, "If I had not done among them the works that no one else did, they would not be guilty of sin, but now they have seen and hated both me and my Father." Here, however, the most impious king is seen to obey the word of God well. When the holy prophets spoke to him, he gladly listened and then enjoyed success in all things, as when Saul listened to Samuel. But the victorious Ahab did not truly acknowledge God's word. Instead, he preserved Ben-hadad, just as Saul saved Agag. Ahab added to that sin from the history of Saul, when with fury and indignation he despised the word of the reproachful prophet, as we will see below in chapter 22 concerning Micaiah. For Ahab said, "I hate him, for he never prophesies good concerning me, but evil." COMMENTARY ON 1 KINGS.[15]

ON THE TRANSITORY NATURE OF WORLDLY POWER. JOHN MAYER: It appears that although Ahab was greatly corrupted with idolatry, his religion did sway him to practice clemency. . . . But mercy in this case was not commended in a king of Israel any more than Saul's mercy was to be extended to Agag. For God had made so plain a demonstration that he was for the cutting off of Ben-hadad by his miraculous fighting against him both in the hills and in the plain. Indeed Joshua, when he fought against and prevailed over the five Amorite kings, did not spare any of them since he knew that God's hand was in his victory. But the servants of Ben-hadad, presuming on Ahab's mercy, came to him with ropes on their heads . . . in token of their subjection to be hanged by him if he so pleased. . . . They wore sackcloth about their loins and looked like they were in great pity. And, not to their surprise, Ahab showed them mercy. But note here the mutability of worldly things. Just a year ago Ben-hadad had greatly insulted Ahab, who

seemed to be without any power to resist him. And now Ben-hadad was brought down before Ahab so that he might humbly plea for his life. This is to show that all people of power must beware how they use their power. They are to be taught to "serve the Lord with fear, and rejoice with trembling," as they are admonished. They are not to be lifted up on account of their worldly greatness, since it is so vain and transitory. COMMENTARY ON 1 KINGS.[16]

OBEYING BY GOING AGAINST THE LAW.
JOHANNES PISCATOR: Every command of God must be obeyed. In fact, even those commands that go against common law must be obeyed. COMMENTARY ON 1 KINGS.[17]

CLEVER DELIVERY. THOMAS JACKSON: Had that prophet of whom we read delivered his message from the Lord to King Ahab plainly without saying, as he did: "Because you have let go out of your hand the man whom I had devoted to destruction, therefore your life shall be for his life, and your people for his people," Ahab would have left him inexcusable for meddling in affairs of state. But the same Spirit of God that gave him knowledge of Ahab's transgression and resolution to tax or censure him for it likewise taught him the art of discretion in the manner of delivering his message—and for the clearer conviction of this unruly king. He first disguised himself with ashes on his face, lest the king discern him to be a prophet by the way he was dressed. . . .

Had the prophet told the king the same truth directly and bluntly, it might perhaps have displeased him more. But it could not have made him as heavy as he was now. For his displeasure would have found a vent and ended in rage and fury against the prophet. But being thus left without apology or excuse (by condemning another for a lesser fault than he himself had really committed), his displeasure or rage was swallowed up in silent heaviness of heart.

[15]Bugenhagen, *In Regum duos ultimos libros*, 95-96; citing Jn 15:24; 1 Sam 15:9; 1 Kings 22:8.
[16]Mayer, *Many Commentaries in One*, 125*; citing Ps 2:11.
[17]Piscator, *Commentarii in omnes libros Veteris Testamenti*, 2:30.

If Ahab, upon this conviction, had been as ready to judge himself by humble confession as he was to condemn the disguised prophet for far less, he might have escaped the judgment of the Lord that was here threatened, and that afterward befell him. Commentaries on the Creed.[18]

Ahab's Bad Governance. Johannes Piscator: The office of a magistrate is to destroy blasphemy at the source. Therefore, on account of Ahab's neglect of destroying Ben-hadad, ruin is declared against him. Commentary on 1 Kings.[19]

---

[18]Jackson, *Works*, 675*; citing 1 Kings 20:42.

[19]Piscator, *Commentarii in omnes libros Veteris Testamenti*, 2:30.

21:1-29 AHAB COVETS NABOTH'S VINEYARD AND REPENTS

¹Now Naboth the Jezreelite had a vineyard in Jezreel, beside the palace of Ahab king of Samaria. ²And after this Ahab said to Naboth, "Give me your vineyard, that I may have it for a vegetable garden, because it is near my house, and I will give you a better vineyard for it; or, if it seems good to you, I will give you its value in money." ³But Naboth said to Ahab, "The LORD forbid that I should give you the inheritance of my fathers." ⁴And Ahab went into his house vexed and sullen because of what Naboth the Jezreelite had said to him, for he had said, "I will not give you the inheritance of my fathers." And he lay down on his bed and turned away his face and would eat no food.

⁵But Jezebel his wife came to him and said to him, "Why is your spirit so vexed that you eat no food?" ⁶And he said to her, "Because I spoke to Naboth the Jezreelite and said to him, 'Give me your vineyard for money, or else, if it please you, I will give you another vineyard for it.' And he answered, 'I will not give you my vineyard.'" ⁷And Jezebel his wife said to him, "Do you now govern Israel? Arise and eat bread and let your heart be cheerful; I will give you the vineyard of Naboth the Jezreelite."

⁸So she wrote letters in Ahab's name and sealed them with his seal, and she sent the letters to the elders and the leaders who lived with Naboth in his city. ⁹And she wrote in the letters, "Proclaim a fast, and set Naboth at the head of the people. ¹⁰And set two worthless men opposite him, and let them bring a charge against him, saying, 'You have cursed[a] God and the king.' Then take him out and stone him to death." ¹¹And the men of his city, the elders and the leaders who lived in his city, did as Jezebel had sent word to them. As it was written in the letters that she had sent to them, ¹²they proclaimed a fast and set Naboth at the head of the people. ¹³And the two worthless men came in and sat opposite him. And the worthless men brought a charge against Naboth in the presence of the people, saying, "Naboth cursed God and the king." So they took him outside the city and stoned him to death with stones. ¹⁴Then they sent to Jezebel, saying, "Naboth has been stoned; he is dead."

¹⁵As soon as Jezebel heard that Naboth had been stoned and was dead, Jezebel said to Ahab, "Arise, take possession of the vineyard of Naboth the Jezreelite, which he refused to give you for money, for Naboth is not alive, but dead." ¹⁶And as soon as Ahab heard that Naboth was dead, Ahab arose to go down to the vineyard of Naboth the Jezreelite, to take possession of it.

¹⁷Then the word of the LORD came to Elijah the Tishbite, saying, ¹⁸"Arise, go down to meet Ahab king of Israel, who is in Samaria; behold, he is in the vineyard of Naboth, where he has gone to take possession. ¹⁹And you shall say to him, 'Thus says the LORD, "Have you killed and also taken possession?"' And you shall say to him, 'Thus says the LORD: "In the place where dogs licked up the blood of Naboth shall dogs lick your own blood."'"

²⁰Ahab said to Elijah, "Have you found me, O my enemy?" He answered, "I have found you, because you have sold yourself to do what is evil in the sight of the LORD. ²¹Behold, I will bring disaster upon you. I will utterly burn you up, and will cut off from Ahab every male, bond or free, in Israel. ²²And I will make your house like the house of Jeroboam the son of Nebat, and like the house of Baasha the son of Ahijah, for the anger to which you have provoked me, and because you have made Israel to sin. ²³And of Jezebel the LORD also said, 'The dogs shall eat Jezebel within the walls of Jezreel.' ²⁴Anyone belonging to Ahab who dies in the city the dogs shall eat, and anyone of his who dies in the open country the birds of the heavens shall eat."

²⁵(There was none who sold himself to do what was evil in the sight of the LORD like Ahab, whom Jezebel his wife incited. ²⁶He acted very abominably in going after idols, as the Amorites had done, whom the LORD cast out before the people of Israel.)

²⁷And when Ahab heard those words, he tore his clothes and put sackcloth on his flesh and fasted and

lay in sackcloth and went about dejectedly. ²⁸*And the word of the LORD came to Elijah the Tishbite, saying,* ²⁹*"Have you seen how Ahab has humbled himself*

before me? Because he has humbled himself before me, I will not bring the disaster in his days; but in his son's days I will bring the disaster upon his house."

a Hebrew *blessed*; also verse 13

OVERVIEW: The sheer evil rampant in the story of Naboth's vineyard is apparent to these commentators. Some see the incident as a parable that is played out throughout history: evil reigns, and the just are mistreated. Citing the Decalogue and the demand to lead a holy life, the reformers condemn Ahab's evil acts, endorsing Elijah's reproof of Ahab. They laud Elijah's courage since it could have been very difficult for Elijah to escape from Ahab and Jezebel's wrath while offering the rebuke. The biblical text does not explicitly state that Ahab was privy to Jezebel's machinations, but our commentators assume as much on account of the remorse he felt after Elijah's condemnation. Although many of these interpreters accept the repentance of Ahab as sincere and genuine, some think his regret was based on fear of punishment (attrition) rather than actual remorse for his evil crimes (contrition).

21:1-16 *Naboth's Vineyard*

SOCIAL SIN. JOHANNES BUGENHAGEN: Showing that he had unworthily received the word of the rebuking prophet, the insane Ahab disregarded the words of the righteous Naboth, who—in accordance with God's law—denied the king's desire for his vineyard. What becomes of tranquility where the impious rule in rejection of God? I have nothing to say against otherwise discerning and good kings who rule and judge people for an appointed season according to the flesh. Greatly troubling, however, are those who judge according to their ungodliness, which back then was according to the Baals and now is according to the antichrist. They have closed heaven, brought war, offered kingdoms for sale and done evil. For there is no Word of God in those places where ungodly rulers force the people to believe as they do, until eventually they do not know

what they believe before God. Then they follow human dreams and their own desires, while the will of God—which is known through God's own Word—is persecuted. Alas for their ungodliness! Here we have a description of Ahab's trick: under the appearance of righteousness such people want to be declared innocent before they see that they are judged by God because of this. Further, the most ungodly Jezebel comforted this insane king with an even greater sin, which could not have been worse. The king followed along with her criminal desire. In his conscience, though, he knew that he was very guilty as soon as his sin had been revealed to him. The judges and elders of Jezreel went along with this great ungodliness too, complying with the impiety of the supposedly knowledgeable and wise ones, giving no respect to God or the innocent. We see such savagery wherever advisers, judges, nobility, authorities and elders who have seen great unrighteousness have been asked by their rulers to yield and not to say anything that would ruin their majesties. They are told, "How can you go against your prince? You ought to obey your prince, just as Joab obeyed David against the innocent Uriah." We do need to obey even impious magistrates, but not when they go against God. Similar ugliness is being called Christian today. See how much impiety and blasphemy against God is conducted under the hypocrisy of great religion and righteousness, as when they burned Jan Hus and now are doing to witnesses to Christ in the Rhineland. This is seen in the fasts that deceive the common people, as if to do otherwise in the city would be a great crime that God could not bear, as if such presumptuous people had been made as holy as the children of Israel when they killed Achan for his sin in Joshua 7. To settle this matter, Ahab and Jezebel set Naboth among leaders who were not there and who in their weakness stood with the king.

So that this indignity might be carried by the common people, it was said that he had spoken against the king and that before others he believed the king to be guilty. Two false witnesses proceeded as if according to the law: "Only on the evidence of two witnesses or of three witnesses shall a charge be established." And so Naboth was found guilty of blasphemy against God and the king, for like all rulers (even the ungodly ones) the king had been ordained by God. According to the law, blasphemy was punished by death. It had also been commanded that "you shall not curse a ruler of your people." Moreover, note how Jezebel, who detested God's law, abused this law for her own desires, just like all those people today who gladly establish their impieties on sacred Scripture whenever they possibly can. COMMENTARY ON 1 KINGS.[1]

EXAMPLE OF COVETOUSNESS AND IMPIETY.
JOHANNES PISCATOR: Ahab is set forth as an example of both the evils of covetousness and of impiety. First, Ahab coveted the vineyard of Naboth, which is contrary to the tenth commandment: "You shall not covet your neighbor's house . . . or anything that is your neighbor's." Then we see Ahab's impiety, for he also neglected another portion of the law: "The land shall not be sold in perpetuity, for the land is mine. For you are strangers and sojourners with me." In opposition to this law, Ahab dared to beseech Naboth for his family's inheritance, so that Ahab could then legally buy the property for himself. But he became pitifully sick when Naboth refused to sell the land. Then Ahab's impiety joined with injustice inasmuch as he approved of his wife's way of procuring the vineyard by murder and then he occupied the vineyard of blood. COMMENTARY ON 1 KINGS.[2]

MORE THAN ENVY. ROBERT SANDERSON: Ahab's sin was this: When his mouth first began to water after Naboth's vineyard, he went afterward a great deal further. He broke the eighth commandment, "You shall not steal"; and he broke the sixth commandment also, "You shall not murder," when he took both Naboth's life and vineyard from him by a most unjust and cruel oppression. All this came afterward. But his first sin was merely against the last commandment [about not coveting], in that he could not rest himself satisfied with all his own abundance, but his mind was set on Naboth's plot. And unless he would have that too, lying so conveniently for him to take to his land, he could not be at peace. He had not as yet, so far as anything appears in the story, any settled purpose or any resolved design to wrest it from the owner by violence, or to weary him out of it with unjust deceit, so he might but have it on any fair terms. . . . Naboth should but speak his own conditions, and they should be performed. Many a petty lord of a property with us would think himself disparaged in a treaty of enclosure, to descend to such low actions with one of his poor neighbors, as the great king of Israel then did with one of his subjects, and to sin only as modestly as Ahab did. Here was neither fraud nor violence. There was nothing more than threatening used; rather the whole offer seemed fair enough, and the proposals were not unreasonable. The entire fault, as yet, was within. The thing that made Ahab guilty in the sight of God was the inordinacy of his desire after that vineyard, because it was not his own. Ahab further betrayed this inordinacy on Naboth's refusal of the offered conditions by many signs, which are the effects of a discontented mind. For in the king comes, heavy and displeased; he lies in his bed like an infirmed animal; looks at nobody, and out of sullenness forsakes his supper. Had he well learned this piece of the lesson in the text, to have contented himself with his own, both his body would have been in better temper, his mind at better ease and his conscience at better peace than they presently were. SEVENTEEN SERMONS.[3]

---

[1]Bugenhagen, *In Regum duos ultimos libros*, 97-99; citing 2 Sam 11:14-27; Acts 5:29; Deut 19:15; Ex 22:28. Bugenhagen writes of then-contemporary persecutions in *Germania inferior*, the name for the German regions on the west bank of the Rhine River, often a politically and religiously volatile area during the Reformation.
[2]Piscator, *Commentarii in omnes libros Veteris Testamenti*, 2:306; citing Ex 20:17; Lev 25:23.
[3]Sanderson, *Works*, 1:123*; citing Ex 20:5, 11.

Sick with Sorrow. John Mayer: After being denied the vineyard, which he so earnestly desired—and on so equal of terms, for he offered either to give the full price or trade Naboth for a better one—Ahab was so stricken that he fell sick. But here Ahab exceeded many other kings, who would have simply taken from their subjects what they desired without offering a price. Or, if they had been denied, they would have immediately commanded them to be killed. Ahab was not so tyrannical. But Ahab, thinking that he was not at all able to attain this vineyard that he longed for so desperately and also thinking it to be a great indignity for the king to be denied something from his subject, he fell even more sick in sorrow. Commentary on 1 Kings.[4]

Relief Through Wickedness. Thomas Adams: The wicked cannot be quiet until their vicious desires are accomplished.... Their food and drink is to do their father's will, that is, Satan's: restrain them from wickedness, and they complain of hunger. Either they call for poison, or no food. Ahab is sick, because he is denied Naboth's vineyard. Whether his spleen or his gall is causing more problems, it is hard to say; whether more of anger, or of grief, it is hard to know. But he keeps to his bed and refuses his food, as if he should die no other death. Because he cannot have his will on Naboth, he will take it on himself. Commentary on 2 Peter.[5]

Naboth the Martyr. John Mayer: According to Jezebel's devilish proposition, there were both elders and false witnesses who were ready in Jezreel to execute her will. This shows the miserable estate of those times, for this is what happens whenever the highest authority is corrupted. That's because, then, only those who are wicked rise to be promoted to leadership. And only those who are willing to observe and obey the king and queen are able to receive favor. Concerning

Naboth speaking for himself, we read nothing, nor of any for him. For it was vain when the witnesses had spoken for any to speak. And Naboth's silence showed his patience in suffering to his greater glory. Ambrose, to honor Naboth the more, says that he was a martyr. And this is not unlikely, because Naboth suffered for the law of God. Commentary on 1 Kings.[6]

God's Will. Jacobus Arminius: God permitted Ahab to kill Naboth, not as that foul deed was *an act*, but as it was a *sin*: For God could have translated Naboth, or taken him to himself, by some other method; but it was the divine will that Ahab should fill up the measure of his iniquities, and should accelerate his own destruction and that of his family. Disputation 10: On God's Providence Concerning Evil.[7]

The Sulking King. Thomas Adams: Facility and liberty merely takes off the edge of lust; and what God restrains, people will not refrain from. The adulterer does not care about innocence or a fair and loving spouse. Instead the only sweet thing in his opinion is lusting and stealing from another's bed. In a similar way Ahab's whole kingdom is despised in his thoughts while he lusts after Naboth's vineyard. The Breaking Up of the Feast.[8]

God Punishes Theft. Philipp Melanchthon: A frightful example of theft is depicted in 1 Kings 21, the story of Naboth, from whom King Ahab wished to buy a vineyard; and since Naboth wanted to keep his inheritance and did not wish to sell, Jezebel had him put to death. Then Ahab took possession of the vineyard. God punished this tyranny first through Elijah, so we might know that God is angered over such robbery, and then through the plague that followed on account of the sin. Later God had the robber Ahab and the murderess Jezebel slain. Theological Commonplaces (1555).[9]

[6]Mayer, *Many Commentaries in One*, 129*.
[7]Arminius, *Works*, 1:515-16*.
[8]Adams, *Devil's Banquet*, 101*.
[9]*Melanchthon on Christian Doctrine*, 338.

[4]Mayer, *Many Commentaries in One*, 128*.
[5]Adams, *Commentary upon 2 Peter*, 907*.

21:17-24 *The Lord Condemns Ahab and Jezebel*

Elijah's Heavy Task. Konrad Pellikan: The Lord used the zealous prophet to rebuke the king into penitence. God prepares his ministers at suitable times to condemn sin and admonish the ungodly, even if it yields nothing and is fruitless. Indeed Elijah reluctantly and gravely endured this task, going according to the word of the Lord to reproach and denounce the king and queen in the king's own city, where he would have little hope of fleeing the wrath of the king he was rebuking. Commentary on 1 Kings.[10]

No More Mercy for Ahab. Viktorin Strigel: Sorrow overtakes the outward joy of impious people. Conversely the pious people's sadness turns into a fullness of joy, which can never be taken from them. The impious king went down to Naboth's vineyard in order to possess it. But he was reproached almost immediately by these words of the prophet: "Not only did you kill but you also took possession." As if to say, "Was it not enough to murder a fellow citizen and do it under the pretense of virtue, depriving the man's wife and children of their rightful inheritance? Do you want to add affliction to affliction by snatching away their vineyard and the rest of their resources and reducing them to poverty? When the new crime is added to this unjust murder, therefore, I know that God will apply the law of retribution against you: the one who sinned is the one who will be punished." Book of Kings.[11]

Ahab Breaks the Great Law. Johannes Brenz: We always sin against this law: "You shall love your neighbor as yourself," because we always act according to the natural enmity in our hearts against our neighbors. . . . People do not always see this evil, but God always sees it. . . . We are not able to completely eradicate or eliminate this natural enmity on this earth. Commentary on Galatians.[12]

A Courageous Prophet for a Wicked King. John Mayer: After Ahab committed such a crying sin—which was worthy of the sharpest censure by the most thundering and courageous prophet—Elijah, who was indeed the most zealous father of the prophets, was sent again to threaten Ahab with death. He threatened the licking of his blood by dogs in the place where Naboth was licked. This makes it manifest that Ahab was initially ignorant of Jezebel's ploy, but he liked it so much that he became just as guilty as she. Commentary on 1 Kings.[13]

The Surprise of Death. Charles Drelincourt: Death surprises us at home and abroad, in our homes and in the streets, in our beds and in our vehicles and in the midst of parties and all our pomp. Death offers violence to the sacred person of the greatest kings in their most sumptuous palaces, in their most flourishing cities, in their strongest fortifications, in the midst of their most faithful subjects, in their most victorious armies, in their thrones and in their triumphant chariots. Death will occur just like when King Ahab went to take possession of Naboth's vineyard and he told the prophet Elijah in a rage, "Have you found me, O my enemy?" When profane people dream of nothing but the pleasant enjoyment of their unjust possessions, they will meet unexpected death as they are swimming in the blood and sweat of their unjust actions. Christian Defense Against the Fears of Death.[14]

21:25-29 *Ahab Repents*

Even Ahab Can Repent. Johannes Bugenhagen: Ahab's response to these words shows you that he had approved all that had happened to

---

[10]Pellikan, *Commentaria Bibliorum*, 2:170r.
[11]Strigel, *Libri Samuelis, Regum et Paralipomenon*, 292-93.

[12]Brenz, *Opera*, 7:888; citing Mt 22:39.
[13]Mayer, *Many Commentaries in One*, 129-30*.
[14]Drelincourt, *Christian's Defense Against the Fears of Death*, 65*; citing 1 Kings 21:20.

Naboth. From 2 Kings 9 it also appears that Naboth's sons had been murdered too. If God could be moved by a temporal repentance based on present judgment, as Ahab sensed, so that for a time God removed the punishment of the one whom he knew would not withdraw from impiety, how much more will he pleased in eternity with those who truly and from their soul come to their senses and never return to their unfaithfulness. COMMENTARY ON 1 KINGS.[15]

A FRIGHTENED FOX. KONRAD PELLIKAN: Having been so greatly threatened and jolted, King Ahab felt remorse in his soul and mind, for he could not doubt that what the prophet Elijah said was incorrect or not to be believed. He feared imminent evil, but not due to love of righteousness or of God. He tore his clothing as a sign of sadness and anguish, wearing sackcloth or a coat of hair. He fasted, slept in a coat of hair, walked in lowliness and dejection like a fox who is trembling and afraid. He was made to be an example of hypocrisy to all who were there at the gate. Such people pretend to be holy, but on the inside they are truly destitute of faith and charity, to God and people whom God directs and receives. If a person comes to piety from their heart, then these kinds of penitential ceremonies are not rejected. But without faith they make people doubly impious, for then they know themselves to be impious but want to minimize it before the sight of others. COMMENTARY ON 1 KINGS.[16]

SWINE AND SORROW. DANIEL DYKE: Godly sorrow produces repentance, that is, a change and alteration of heart. This causes us to hate sin and love righteousness. Here's the reason: In godly sorrow, one's molten heart is wholly liquefied and dissolved; and being made soft and tender it receives the stamp and impress of God's Spirit. But in temporary actions like these, no such things

matter. These kinds of people may otherwise shed a few hoarse tears and hang down their heads like a reed for a day. However, filthy swine that they are, after they have washed themselves they soon return to their wallowing in the mire of their former filthiness. Ahab fasts and pinches his body with sackcloth and goes creeping and crouching about. But if he had ever truly repented for oppressing poor Naboth, he would not have so soon fallen into the same sin of oppression. THE MYSTERY OF SELF-DECEIVING.[17]

PARTIAL REPENTANCE. JOHN MAYER: Elijah's prophecy struck Ahab more to hear of the cruel destruction of his wife and family than of the loss of his own life beforehand. It also struck him more than to feel the hand of God in the long-continued drought or to see the miracle of fire sent down on Elijah's sacrifice, or anything else the Lord did miraculously for Ahab. For he was now overcome with terrors. Ahab could not but believe that this prophecy would come to pass. . . . At the same time, his wicked heart could not be moved to true repentance. He only humbled himself out of fear of these judgments. . . . Indeed his malice against Micaiah, a prophet of the Lord, showed that his sorrow was not godly repentance. . . . Rather, it was a worldly repentance. It did not arise out of the love and fear of God and hatred of his sins. Otherwise he would not have later imprisoned God's prophet Micaiah for telling him the truth. COMMENTARY ON 1 KINGS.[18]

LESSONS FROM A KING. ROBERT SANDERSON: Ahab's response offers three notable things to our consideration. See, first, how far a hypocrite, a castaway, may go in the outward performance of holy duties, and particularly in the practice of repentance. Here is Ahab humbled—such a man, and yet so penitent. See again, second, how deep God's word, though in the mouth but of weak instruments, when he is pleased to give strength to

---

[15]Bugenhagen, *In Regum duos ultimos libros*, 100; citing 2 Kings 9:26.
[16]Pellikan, *Commentaria Bibliorum*, 2:170v.

[17]Dyke, *The Mystery of Self-Deceiving*, 94-95*; citing Is 58:5.
[18]Mayer, *Many Commentaries in One*, 131*; citing 1 Kings 22:8.

it, pierces into the consciences of obstinate sinners, and brings the proudest of them to their knees despite their wicked hearts. Here is Ahab quelled by Elijah—such a great one by such a weak one. See yet again, third, how prone God is to mercy, and how ready to take any advantage, as it were, and any occasion to show compassion. Here is Ahab humbled, and his judgment adjourned— such a real substantial favor, and yet on such an empty shadow of repentance. To the People.[19]

Shooting with a Deceitful Bow. Daniel Dyke: When a man shoots with a deceitful bow—even though he levels his arrow and his eye directly to the mark and aims to hit it—the arrow goes in the wrong direction because the bow is deceitful. Our heart is like this bow. It is full of sorrows, desires, purposes and promises, which we conceive and make in our afflictions. The mark at which we aim is repentance, to which we then look with so accurate and attentive an eye as though we would certainly hit it. And this indeed is our purpose and meaning. But our own hearts deceive us. That's because they are not truly renewed. Hence it comes to pass that these arrows of repentance never hit the mark. They never come to any good effect, but vanish in the air as smoke. Ahab did not grossly lie in the humiliation brought about by the prophet's rebuke. Indeed he was sincerely repentant when he clothed himself in sackcloth. However, his heart still remained unregenerate, and so it continued to deceive him. The Mystery of Self-Deceiving.[20]

---

[19]Sanderson, *Works*, 3:7*.

[20]Dyke, *The Mystery of Self-Deceiving*, 262-63*.

22:1-53 ISRAEL AND JUDAH JOIN FORCES

¹For three years Syria and Israel continued without war. ²But in the third year Jehoshaphat the king of Judah came down to the king of Israel. ³And the king of Israel said to his servants, "Do you know that Ramoth-gilead belongs to us, and we keep quiet and do not take it out of the hand of the king of Syria?" ⁴And he said to Jehoshaphat, "Will you go with me to battle at Ramoth-gilead?" And Jehoshaphat said to the king of Israel, "I am as you are, my people as your people, my horses as your horses."

⁵And Jehoshaphat said to the king of Israel, "Inquire first for the word of the LORD." ⁶Then the king of Israel gathered the prophets together, about four hundred men, and said to them, "Shall I go to battle against Ramoth-gilead, or shall I refrain?" And they said, "Go up, for the LORD will give it into the hand of the king." ⁷But Jehoshaphat said, "Is there not here another prophet of the LORD of whom we may inquire?" ⁸And the king of Israel said to Jehoshaphat, "There is yet one man by whom we may inquire of the LORD, Micaiah the son of Imlah, but I hate him, for he never prophesies good concerning me, but evil." And Jehoshaphat said, "Let not the king say so." ⁹Then the king of Israel summoned an officer and said, "Bring quickly Micaiah the son of Imlah." ¹⁰Now the king of Israel and Jehoshaphat the king of Judah were sitting on their thrones, arrayed in their robes, at the threshing floor at the entrance of the gate of Samaria, and all the prophets were prophesying before them. ¹¹And Zedekiah the son of Chenaanah made for himself horns of iron and said, "Thus says the LORD, 'With these you shall push the Syrians until they are destroyed.'" ¹²And all the prophets prophesied so and said, "Go up to Ramoth-gilead and triumph; the LORD will give it into the hand of the king."

¹³And the messenger who went to summon Micaiah said to him, "Behold, the words of the prophets with one accord are favorable to the king. Let your word be like the word of one of them, and speak favorably." ¹⁴But Micaiah said, "As the LORD lives, what the LORD says to me, that I will speak." ¹⁵And when he had come to the king, the king said to him,

"Micaiah, shall we go to Ramoth-gilead to battle, or shall we refrain?" And he answered him, "Go up and triumph; the LORD will give it into the hand of the king." ¹⁶But the king said to him, "How many times shall I make you swear that you speak to me nothing but the truth in the name of the LORD?" ¹⁷And he said, "I saw all Israel scattered on the mountains, as sheep that have no shepherd. And the LORD said, 'These have no master; let each return to his home in peace.'" ¹⁸And the king of Israel said to Jehoshaphat, "Did I not tell you that he would not prophesy good concerning me, but evil?" ¹⁹And Micaiah said, "Therefore hear the word of the LORD: I saw the LORD sitting on his throne, and all the host of heaven standing beside him on his right hand and on his left; ²⁰and the LORD said, 'Who will entice Ahab, that he may go up and fall at Ramoth-gilead?' And one said one thing, and another said another. ²¹Then a spirit came forward and stood before the LORD, saying, 'I will entice him.' ²²And the LORD said to him, 'By what means?' And he said, 'I will go out, and will be a lying spirit in the mouth of all his prophets.' And he said, 'You are to entice him, and you shall succeed; go out and do so.' ²³Now therefore behold, the LORD has put a lying spirit in the mouth of all these your prophets; the LORD has declared disaster for you."

²⁴Then Zedekiah the son of Chenaanah came near and struck Micaiah on the cheek and said, "How did the Spirit of the LORD go from me to speak to you?" ²⁵And Micaiah said, "Behold, you shall see on that day when you go into an inner chamber to hide yourself." ²⁶And the king of Israel said, "Seize Micaiah, and take him back to Amon the governor of the city and to Joash the king's son, ²⁷and say, 'Thus says the king, "Put this fellow in prison and feed him meager rations of bread and water, until I come in peace."'" ²⁸And Micaiah said, "If you return in peace, the LORD has not spoken by me." And he said, "Hear, all you peoples!"

²⁹So the king of Israel and Jehoshaphat the king of Judah went up to Ramoth-gilead. ³⁰And the king of Israel said to Jehoshaphat, "I will disguise myself and

go into battle, but you wear your robes." And the king of Israel disguised himself and went into battle. [31]*Now the king of Syria had commanded the thirty-two captains of his chariots, "Fight with neither small nor great, but only with the king of Israel."* [32]*And when the captains of the chariots saw Jehoshaphat, they said, "It is surely the king of Israel." So they turned to fight against him. And Jehoshaphat cried out.* [33]*And when the captains of the chariots saw that it was not the king of Israel, they turned back from pursuing him.* [34]*But a certain man drew his bow at random[a] and struck the king of Israel between the scale armor and the breastplate. Therefore he said to the driver of his chariot, "Turn around and carry me out of the battle, for I am wounded."* [35]*And the battle continued that day, and the king was propped up in his chariot facing the Syrians, until at evening he died. And the blood of the wound flowed into the bottom of the chariot.* [36]*And about sunset a cry went through the army, "Every man to his city, and every man to his country!"*

[37]*So the king died, and was brought to Samaria. And they buried the king in Samaria.* [38]*And they washed the chariot by the pool of Samaria, and the dogs licked up his blood, and the prostitutes washed themselves in it, according to the word of the* LORD *that he had spoken.* [39]*Now the rest of the acts of Ahab and all that he did, and the ivory house that he built and all the cities that he built, are they not written in the Book of the Chronicles of the Kings of Israel?* [40]*So Ahab slept with his fathers, and Ahaziah his son reigned in his place.*

[41]*Jehoshaphat the son of Asa began to reign over Judah in the fourth year of Ahab king of Israel.*

[42]*Jehoshaphat was thirty-five years old when he began to reign, and he reigned twenty-five years in Jerusalem. His mother's name was Azubah the daughter of Shilhi.* [43]*He walked in all the way of Asa his father. He did not turn aside from it, doing what was right in the sight of the* LORD. *Yet the high places were not taken away, and the people still sacrificed and made offerings on the high places.* [44]*Jehoshaphat also made peace with the king of Israel.*

[45]*Now the rest of the acts of Jehoshaphat, and his might that he showed, and how he warred, are they not written in the Book of the Chronicles of the Kings of Judah?* [46]*And from the land he exterminated the remnant of the male cult prostitutes who remained in the days of his father Asa.*

[47]*There was no king in Edom; a deputy was king.* [48]*Jehoshaphat made ships of Tarshish to go to Ophir for gold, but they did not go, for the ships were wrecked at Ezion-geber.* [49]*Then Ahaziah the son of Ahab said to Jehoshaphat, "Let my servants go with your servants in the ships," but Jehoshaphat was not willing.* [50]*And Jehoshaphat slept with his fathers and was buried with his fathers in the city of David his father, and Jehoram his son reigned in his place.*

[51]*Ahaziah the son of Ahab began to reign over Israel in Samaria in the seventeenth year of Jehoshaphat king of Judah, and he reigned two years over Israel.* [52]*He did what was evil in the sight of the* LORD *and walked in the way of his father and in the way of his mother and in the way of Jeroboam the son of Nebat, who made Israel to sin.* [53]*He served Baal and worshiped him and provoked the* LORD, *the God of Israel, to anger in every way that his father had done.*

a Hebrew *in his innocence*

OVERVIEW: Among several points of interest in this final chapter of 1 Kings, the commentators focus on the lying spirit God reportedly puts into the mouths of false prophets to lead astray King Ahab so that he will be killed in battle against the king of Syria.[1] Many of the reformers acknowledge the difficulty of this passage, asking how God can be said to deceive in light of recurring biblical passages stating that God is holy and free from sin. In the end some decide to cut this theological knot by citing the difference between divine will and divine permission. Lavater, however, identifies Satan as the source of the lying spirit, thereby dodging the attack that God incites evil. Whatever the exact interpretation, the

[1] That is, Aram.

intended result of the prophecy is to urge Ahab to fight against Syria so that he will be killed in battle. Most commentators agree that the "random" arrow that struck Ahab was not random at all, but directed by God to punish Ahab for his many sins and in accordance with the prophecies delivered earlier concerning him (and then later his wife Jezebel).

22:1-12 Jehoshaphat and Ahab

TRUE AND FALSE PROPHETS. JOHANNES BUGEN-HAGEN: Here the words of the Lord spoken through Elijah—that dogs would lick the blood of Ahab—are seen to be fulfilled. Moreover, this chapter also clearly shows how Ahab was led astray, according to the judgments of God, by those false prophets, who in their contempt for the word of God only want to hear that which pleases themselves. As Isaiah 30 says, they hate real instruction. Paul similarly speaks of the seduction of false Christians: God sends them a strong delusion, so that they may believe what is false, they who refused to love the truth and so be saved. The prophets of Baal invented things from their own hearts; prophets of God declare things from the word of God. Those who seek to please and who preach according to our human nature and reason do not speak the word of God. Even so, they are listened to, while true prophets (that is, preach-ers of the gospel) are derided as liars and made to suffer persecution. The world wants to be deceived, especially those who see themselves as great and powerful. Therefore in the judgment of God they perish through their own errors. COMMENTARY ON 1 KINGS.[2]

AHAB DECEIVES HIMSELF. JOHANN ARNDT: If we live in Christ alone and walk in love and humility and direct our total energy and theology to this, we are to mortify the flesh and live in Christ, Adam is to die in us and Christ to live in us, we are to conquer ourselves and are able to overcome the flesh, the devil and the world. [If this

were the case] there would not be so much disputation in doctrine and all heretics would fall by themselves. Why is it that four hundred false prophets led Ahab astray and counseled him to go to war? . . . The answer is his godless, tyrannical life. Out of such a life follows such a false light that he had to believe lies that led him to his own destruc-tion. The true prophet Micaiah told him the truth, that he would be overcome in the way, but he would not believe him. TRUE CHRISTIANITY.[3]

22:13-28 A Lying Spirit Sent by the Lord

SATAN IS UNDER THE AUTHORITY OF GOD. JOHN CALVIN: From other passages where God is said to bend or draw Satan himself and all the wicked to his will there emerges a more difficult question. For carnal sense can hardly comprehend how in acting through them he does not contract some defilement from their transgression, and even in a common undertaking can be free of all blame and indeed can justly condemn his ministers. Hence the distinction was devised between doing and permitting, because to many this difficulty seemed inexplicable, that Satan and all the impious are so under God's hand and power that he directs their malice to whatever end seems good to him, and uses their wicked deeds to carry out his judgments. And perhaps the moderation of those whom the appearance of absurdity alarms would be excusable, except that they wrongly try to clear God's justice of every sinister mark by upholding a falsehood. It seems absurd to them for humans, who will soon be punished for their blindness, to be blinded by God's will and command. Therefore they escape by the shift that this is done only with God's permission, not also by his will; but he, openly declaring that he is the doer, repudiates that evasion. However, that humans can accomplish nothing except by God's secret command, that they cannot by deliberating accomplish anything except what he has already decreed with himself and determines by his secret direction, is proved by

---

[2]Bugenhagen, *In Regum duos ultimos libros*, 100-101; citing Is 30:9; 2 Thess 2:10-12.

[3]Arndt, *True Christianity*, 171-72.

innumerable and clear testimonies. What we have cited before from the Psalm, that God does whatever he wills, certainly pertains to all the actions of humankind. If, as is here said, God is the true arbiter of wars and of peace, and this without any exception, who then will dare say that humans are borne headlong by blind motion unknown to God or with his acquiescence?

But particular examples will shed more light. From the first chapter of Job, no less than the angels who willingly obey, Satan presents himself before God to receive his commands. He does so, indeed, in a different way and with a different end; but he still cannot undertake anything unless God so wills. However, even though a bare permission to afflict the holy man seems then to be added, yet we gather that God was the author of that trial of which Satan and his wicked thieves were the ministers, because this statement is true: "The Lord gave, the Lord has taken away; as it has pleased God, so it is done." Satan desperately tries to drive the holy man insane; the Sabaeans cruelly and impiously pillage and make off with another's possessions. Job recognizes that he was divinely stripped of all his property and made a poor man because it so pleased God. Therefore whatever humans or Satan himself may instigate, God nevertheless holds the key, so that he turns their efforts to carry out his judgments. God wills that the false king Ahab be deceived; the devil offers his services to this end; he is sent with a definite command, to be a lying spirit in the mouth of all the prophets. If the blinding and insanity of Ahab be God's judgment, the figment of bare permission vanishes: because it would be ridiculous for the Judge only to permit what he wills to be done, and not also to decree it and command its execution by his ministers. INSTITUTES 1.18.1.[4]

SATAN THE ANGEL. LUDWIG LAVATER: Satan exists by nature as a spirit. Therefore he is called an angel, because God sent him to accomplish something. In this passage an evil angel was sent to Ahab as a lying spirit in the false prophet. This angel was one of darkness and error, who nevertheless possessed the ability to appear like a good angel, so that he could guide the council of the worshipers of Baal, who doubtlessly prided themselves in being assembled under the guise of the Holy Spirit. If Satan changed himself here, can he not make himself into a holy man by imitating his words, voice, acts and other such things? ON GHOSTS.[5]

SATAN AS THE LYING SPIRIT. JOHN MAYER: The lying spirit, which is said to have come forth and stood before the Lord, is none other than Satan, who appears sometimes among the holy angels as a jailor or a hangman. He sometimes appears at the court to execute the king's will. For although he is not here called an evil spirit, yet because he said he would be a lying spirit in the mouth of Ahab's prophets, we may certainly gather that he was none of the heavenly host, who did not lie. Instead it was the devil, who also came and stood among the good angels in Job 1. And in John 8 he is said to have been "a murderer from the beginning and has nothing to do with truth." COMMENTARY ON 1 KINGS.[6]

TELLING THE TRUTH IN LOVE. CHARLES DRELINCOURT: King Ahab desired to hear a prophecy conveying his happy victory over the Syrian army. Nevertheless, he continued in his impieties and tyranny. At the same time, the prophet Micaiah was not afraid of what he would do to him for speaking the truth. Indeed, Micah told him boldly of the approaching judgment of God that hung over his guilty head. Likewise some sinners desire to be flattered and soothed in their extravagances; despite their great crimes, they expect promises of joy and prosperity. But we should be false prophets possessed with a lying spirit if we did not convey to such people that a most lamentable and miserable death hastens fast toward them. Our love for them would be cruel if we did not labor to save them by fear as out of a

---

[4]LCC 20:228-30 (CO 2:167-68); citing Ps 115:3; Job 1:6, 21; 2:1.

[5]Lavater, *De Spectris*, 154.
[6]Mayer, *Many Commentaries in One*, 135-36*; citing Jn 8:44.

fire, that is, if we did not show them hell with its jaws open ready to swallow them up as well as the eternal torments by which God will punish all impenitent and hardened sinners. Knowing what God's vengeance is, we must persuade people to embrace faith and righteousness. And if we fail in this responsibility, their blood will be required at our hands. CHRISTIAN DEFENSE AGAINST THE FEARS OF DEATH.[7]

RUNNING TO THE THICKET. DANIEL DYKE: This is natural to all the sons of Adam, after the example he gave us. Namely, when we have done evil, we soon run into the thicket to seek out coverings to hide our nakedness. Sometimes we do so by gross and palpable lying, otherwise by a neater and finer kind of lying. I am referring here to that sophisticated equivocation, which is a trick the devil, their master, has taught them by his own example. But so much the worse in them than in him, for the devil equivocated to hide his ignorance of that which he could not reveal. These false prophets equivocate to hide their knowledge of that which they can and ought to reveal. For the devil, being sometimes posed with some questions concerning future events and not knowing well what to answer—and yet not willing to lose his credit with his blind worshipers, either by silence or plain speech—shapes his answers in such an ambiguous manner that he would appear to be right no matter what the outcome. That's because, being upheld with this prop of equivocation, it would stand true even in contrary events. Thus when Ahab demanded of one of his prophets whether he should go to war against Ramoth-gilead and whether it would be successful, the devil's prophet answered: "Go up, for the Lord will give it into the hand of the king."

True, but of what king, you lying, equivocating Spirit? Whether into the hands of the adversary to be subdued or to the one to be rescued and delivered? The false prophet did not determine this, but spoke in suspense and in uncertainty, to egg on Ahab and make him run headlong into his own destruction. And yet here once again, mark how the devil's equivocating is not all so bad. . . . For he confesses his equivocating to be plain lying: "I will go out, and will be a lying spirit in the mouth of all his prophets." He was only an equivocating spirit in their mouths. For the words in some sense, and as the devil might interpret them, might be true. And yet he grants that his words, though they are never so qualified with equivocating quirks, were no better than lies. THE MYSTERY OF SELF-DECEIVING.[8]

GOD'S PERMITTING WILL. JOHN MAYER: God's bidding here is to be understood as nothing else but his permitting the lying spirit to do what he offered to do and what he always longed to practice. If it shall seem that God's bidding and promising success seems to imply more than permission—for no judge commits a malefactor to his executioner without charging and commanding it to be done—it is answered that this circumlocution is made only to set forth the certainty of Ahab's destruction, as well as the means of effecting it. It is as surely as if God, who has all power and cannot be frustrated in any design of his, had commanded it to be done this way. COMMENTARY ON 1 KINGS.[9]

22:29-40 Ahab Disguises Himself Yet Still Dies in Battle

RANDOMLY SHOT DESPITE CONCEALMENT. JOHANNES PISCATOR: Human cunning never aids in escaping God's decrees and pronouncements. Ahab cunningly disguised himself in battle, so that he would not be recognized and captured or shot on command since he was the king. But this was all in vain. He was pierced by an arrow that had been randomly shot. COMMENTARY ON 1 KINGS.[10]

THE DIVINE ARROW. THOMAS ADAMS: The man shot at random, or as the Hebrew puts it, "in his

---

[7]Drelincourt, *Christian's Defense Against the Fears of Death*, 135-36*.

[8]Dyke, *The Mystery of Self-Deceiving*, 21-22*; citing 1 Kings 22:6.
[9]Mayer, *Many Commentaries in One*, 136*.
[10]Piscator, *Commentarii in omnes libros Veteris Testamenti*, 2:310.

simplicity." But God directed the arrow to strike Ahab. The Garden.[11]

Trickery Will Not Thwart God. John Mayer: To ascribe everything to God's providence is to attribute more to God and to make his working in people's hearts all the more admirable than to give a reason whereby Ben-hadad was moved to give this charge. Yet besides the divine providence working secretly, Ben-hadad certainly had his reasons for targeting Ahab, namely, for avenging the shame Ahab had put on him of beating him three times before and especially when Ben-hadad had to beg Ahab for life. . . . That's because disgraces work more on a natural heart to stir up revenge than the very saving of one's life and being thankful. While God's providence worked to save Jehoshaphat, who was the most exposed to danger on account of his attire, it also worked to thwart Ahab, who thought himself the most protected on account of changing his attire. Yet he was randomly wounded to death by the arrow of a Syrian bow to show that no policy can save the one from death whom God has judged on account of his sin. Commentary on 1 Kings.[12]

Just Retribution. Charles Drelincourt: King Ahab of Israel was disguised with a design to fight with the Syrians. . . . However, an unknown soldier let an arrow fly out of his bow by chance, which struck him in the weakest part of his armor and gave him a mortal blow. Then the dogs licked the blood that issued out of his wounds. At this sight a carnal and earthly mind may say that this was but an accident of war. But the Spirit of God informs us better—that this happened to fulfill the prophecy of Elijah and the dreadful words that he had pronounced against this wicked prince who labored by tyrannical and devilish means to invade other people's possessions. Therefore, just as the Lord said, "In the place where dogs licked up the blood of Naboth shall dogs lick your own blood." Christian Defense Against the Fears of Death.[13]

22:41-50 Jehoshaphat Reigns in Judah

Godly Example. Johannes Brenz: Among the kings of Judah is Jehoshaphat, whose history is not unimportant but is ready to be grasped. Because holy Scripture always gives his godly ways and governance a royal commendation, and because the holy Evangelist Matthew counts him among the ancestors of our Lord Jesus Christ, and because—as Paul says—all Scripture is given "for teaching, for reproof, for correction and for training in righteousness," in the same way this history of a Christian, God-fearing prince should not be overlooked as an example of godly government. History of Jehoshaphat.[14]

A King Both Good and Bad. Johannes Piscator: Jehoshaphat is set forth as an example of both some things to be scorned and some things to be praised. Concerning those things that are to be scorned, Jehoshaphat cultivated a friendship with Ahab, a most ungodly man. For this action, Jehoshaphat was reprimanded by a prophet in 2 Chronicles: "But Jehu the son of Hanani the seer went out to meet him and said to King Jehoshaphat, 'Should you help the wicked and love those who hate the Lord? Because of this, wrath has gone out against you from the Lord.'" However, there are some things to praise in Jehoshaphat. For instance, he did demand for Ahab to consult a word from the Lord. In the same way, he suspected that the oracles from the false prophets were false, and he requested for a true prophet to be consulted. And, finally, Jehoshaphat reproved Ahab's for his hatred of Micaiah. Commentary on 1 Kings.[15]

Partially Upright Kings. John Mayer: Jehoshaphat was a good son of a good father. At the same time, neither he nor his father (Asa) was without his faults. It is true that the hearts of both

[11]Adams, *Divine Herbal*, 72*.
[12]Mayer, *Many Commentaries in One*, 137-38*.
[13]Drelincourt, *Christian's Defense Against the Fears of Death*, 74*;

citing 1 Kings 21:19.
[14]Brenz, *Werke: Frühschriften*, 2:133; citing 2 Sam 3:16.
[15]Piscator, *Commentarii in omnes libros Veteris Testamenti*, 2:310; citing 2 Chron 19:2.

of them were upright and that they did that which was right in the sight of the Lord, and that both took away the male prostitutes in the land. But the son exceeded the father in that he allowed none to remain. Yet some . . . think that Asa did not take them all away only because he was prevented by death. But their faults were that they allowed the people to sacrifice in the high places and that Asa entered into a league with the king of Syria, an idolater, so that he might help him against the king of Israel. In the same way, Jehoshaphat made a league with the idolatrous king of Israel, Ahab, and helped him against the king of Syria. COMMENTARY ON 1 KINGS.[16]

CONTRASTING JEHOSHAPHAT AND AHAB.
JOHANNES BRENZ: What's the use of a Christian reading and knowing this history? It appears as if there is not much behind this. Nevertheless, just as no creature—be they as bad as they will—was created by God without some usefulness, similarly not one letter of holy Scripture was written unfruitfully. One may, for instance, pluck this fruit: that the Scriptures want to give examples from one certain highborn nobleman, how he received his kingdom and ruled for a long time without disgrace because he was adorned and crowned with godly virtue. But what good is it to learn about King Ahab, who also came from kingly origins and who himself ruled for twenty-two years in Israel, even though he led a godless and sinful life and died in his sins? Did not his kingdom come to great shame and his soul to eternal condemnation? By contrast, behold how Jehoshaphat, his nobility and his long reign came to great praise and majesty, for he adorned himself with a pious way of life and put his gifts to good use. This shows that our Lord God does not judge by noble birth and a long reign, rather by high divine virtue and Christian governance. He will not ask at the final judgment how long, but rather how well and piously a prince had governed. This verse shows us the high physical nobility that Jehoshaphat had been born into and

how long he reigned, so that we see even better how high his virtue had been and how well and piously he had ruled, which is set as the highest thing. HISTORY OF JEHOSHAPHAT.[17]

22:51-53 *Ahaziah Reigns in Israel*

LOVING THE BAALS. KONRAD PELLIKAN: Ahaziah was just as impious as his father and mother, keeping the kingdom in the impiety that Jeroboam had started. He followed his father's transgressions by being devoted to the Baals, the gods of his mother Jezebel, against the law of the Lord. These Baals could heal nothing but only provoked the wrath of the Lord, which is often what happened. COMMENTARY ON 1 KINGS.[18]

FOLLOWING THE ANCESTORS. JOHANNES BRENZ: How does it come that Jehoshaphat received praise for following his fathers and elders? Do I then hear that it is right and praiseworthy to follow the faith of the fathers and ancestors? Answer: sometimes it is right and pleasing; sometimes it is wrong and evil to do so. If the parents have had a true faith, then why should it be impious to follow them in the same? That is why it is written of Asa that he did what was pleasing to the Lord, like his father David. . . . By contrast, King Abijam is described as dishonorable and scandalous, because "his heart was not wholly true to the Lord his God as the heart of David his father." And of Ahab: "He did not do what was right in the eyes of the Lord his God, as his father David had done." Therefore it is godly to follow the true faith of our parents and ungodly to fall and accept wrongs because of them. Conversely, if the parents have had a false faith, then it is wrong to follow them but right and proper to leave the false faith and accept the right one. For this reason holy Scripture gives King Abijam as an example of shame and error when it says, "He walked in all the sins that his father did before him." The same with King Ahaziah. . . . Do these kings who were given

---

[16]Mayer, *Many Commentaries in One*, 138*.

[17]Brenz, *Werke: Frühschriften*, 2:135.
[18]Pellikan, *Commentaria Bibliorum*, 2:172v.

the shameful and sinful examples of their wrong-believing fathers have an excuse? Even more, do they have a good point if they ask why it is wrong that their fathers were not wise men, since all *their* ancestors were contemptible too? But holy Scripture does not bend to the logic of humans. Such people rightly leave their parents' wisdom and appear to be pious and honorable people before the world, but they cannot justify their own false faith. They rightly leave foolish people to worry unnecessarily about their ancestors, but they pester the godly ones who have left the dead to bury their own dead.... In the meantime, because King Jehoshaphat's ancestors and fathers David and Asa had had true faith, it was godly and good that Jehoshaphat followed them. As mentioned before, from this one should not think that there is justification for following elders in every case. Instead follow their truth and abandon their errors. HISTORY OF JEHOSHAPHAT.[19]

CONCLUSION OF PROSECUTION. JOHN MAYER: Here the writer of the Kings concludes the history of Jehoshaphat, who did not die before Ahaziah, the king of Israel. Rather, he lived and reigned long afterward, as appears in verse 52, where Ahaziah is said to have begun his reign in the seventeenth year of Jehoshaphat and to have reigned but two years; whereas Jehoshaphat made up the time of his reign twenty-five years and therefore died not until six years after him. Moreover, Jehoshaphat is found again joining with Jehoram, king of Israel, in 2 Kings 3 against Moab. His death, then, is here spoken of so that the history of the kings of Israel may be again taken and prosecuted, which the writer of the Kings chiefly intended. COMMENTARY ON 1 KINGS.[20]

---

[19]Brenz, *Werke: Frühschriften*, 2:137-38; citing 1 Kings 15:3; 2 Kings 16:2; Mt 8:22.
[20]Mayer, *Many Commentaries in One*, 144*.

COMMENTARY ON 2 KINGS

OVERVIEW: The commentators introduce 2 Kings as a valuable source of biblical history and as a precious witness to faith for the church across the ages. Although God often punished the Israelite people for their unfaithfulness, the Lord's mercy and love also remain prominent in these books.

Prologomena: What This Book Is About

THREE HUNDRED AND TWENTY YEARS OF STORIES OF KINGS. JOHANNES PISCATOR: This book describes the remaining acts of the kings of Judah, which were sixteen in number. It also talks about the acts of the kings of Israel, which were twelve in number. This does not include those who held interregnums. In Israel the ten tribes were deported to Assyria by Shalmaneser. Also in Judah, the one tribe was deported to Babylon by Nebuchadnezzar. The total years of this story were 320. COMMENTARY ON 2 KINGS.[1]

A STORY OF PEOPLE'S FAITHLESSNESS AND GOD'S FAITHFULNESS. GIOVANNI DIODATI: The sacred history continues the narration of things that happened to the people of God in this book. Specifically it contains the narration of the people of God into the two kingdoms of Israel and Judah. The first kingdom was desolated by the Assyrians, and the other kingdom was taken captive by the Babylonians.

The book carefully points out the true causes of these horrible disasters, and the church in all ages can learn from these examples.

As for the kingdom of the ten tribes, the history sets down how the corruption of God's service was never amended by the successors of Jeroboam, who was the first in that line to follow idolatry and pagan abominations. This refusal to mend its ways caused God to punish the kingdom. There were frequent murders of kings, treasons, changes of royal lines, wars and other accidents that happened on account of God's express command and calling and sometimes through the ambitious and evil motions of people's attempts.

As for the kingdom of Judah, the history declares that idolatry was rampant even though the church—and, consequently, God's Word, sacraments, grace, presence and spirit—were preserved. Indeed, the kingdom of Judah was infected by the idolatry and sin of the kingdom of Israel, for they violated both tables of the law. At the same time, the kingdom was not able to completely root out God's presence and his words of prophecy. And there were occasionally kings who excelled in piety and virtue, whom God raised up from time to time to repair the breaches and hold up the coming ruin. Nevertheless the holy endeavors of these righteous kings and their works were almost always overthrown by their successors' boundless impiety.

All throughout God's rigorous punishment of their sin, a small remnant remained in the

---

[1]Piscator, *Commentarii in omnes libros Veteris Testamenti*, 2:311.

country and was carried to Egypt in a state no less lamentable but far more accursed than those living in Babylon. Indeed this was the most terrible eclipse and interruption that the ancient church ever experienced. Despite these things, David's progeny—and the holy seed of the people of God—were preserved. And at the appointed time it brought forth Christ according to the flesh. And it also brought about the church, which was to be gathered and engrafted into Christ's everlasting spiritual kingdom by the power of God's promises. ANNOTATIONS ON 2 KINGS.[2]

EXAMPLES OF GOOD AND BAD. GENEVA BIBLE: This second book contains the acts of the kings of Judah and Israel. Namely, it narrates the story of Israel from the death of Ahab to the last one, King Hoshea, who was imprisoned by the king of Assyria. His city of Samaria was taken along with the ten tribes by the just plague of God. For their idolatry and disobedience, God led them into captivity. The book also narrates the history of Judah from the reign of Jehoram son of Jehoshaphat to Zedekiah, who despised the Lord's commandment by his prophets and who neglected his many admonitions. By famine and other means, he was taken by his enemies, saw his sons most cruelly killed before his face and his own eyes were put out, just as the Lord had declared to him before by the prophet Jeremiah. What's more, the just judgment of God condemned Jerusalem and destroyed it. God allowed the temple to be burned, and all the people were led away as captives to Babylon. At the same time in this book, there are notable examples of God's favor toward rulers and people, who obeyed his prophets and embraced his words. ARGUMENT OF 2 KINGS.[3]

---

[2]Diodati, *Pious Annotations*, 16-17*.

[3]*Geneva Bible* (1560), 164r-v*.

1:1-18 ELIJAH REPROVES AHAZIAH

¹*After the death of Ahab, Moab rebelled against Israel.*
²*Now Ahaziah fell through the lattice in his upper chamber in Samaria, and lay sick; so he sent messengers, telling them, "Go, inquire of Baal-zebub, the god of Ekron, whether I shall recover from this sickness."* ³*But the angel of the LORD said to Elijah the Tishbite, "Arise, go up to meet the messengers of the king of Samaria, and say to them, 'Is it because there is no God in Israel that you are going to inquire of Baal-zebub, the god of Ekron?* ⁴*Now therefore thus says the LORD, You shall not come down from the bed to which you have gone up, but you shall surely die.'" So Elijah went.*

⁵*The messengers returned to the king, and he said to them, "Why have you returned?"* ⁶*And they said to him, "There came a man to meet us, and said to us, 'Go back to the king who sent you, and say to him, Thus says the LORD, Is it because there is no God in Israel that you are sending to inquire of Baal-zebub, the god of Ekron? Therefore you shall not come down from the bed to which you have gone up, but you shall surely die.'"* ⁷*He said to them, "What kind of man was he who came to meet you and told you these things?"* ⁸*They answered him, "He wore a garment of hair, with a belt of leather about his waist." And he said, "It is Elijah the Tishbite."*

⁹*Then the king sent to him a captain of fifty men with his fifty. He went up to Elijah, who was sitting on the top of a hill, and said to him, "O man of God, the king says, 'Come down.'"* ¹⁰*But Elijah answered the captain of fifty, "If I am a man of God, let fire come down from heaven and consume you and your*
fifty." Then fire came down from heaven and consumed him and his fifty.

¹¹*Again the king sent to him another captain of fifty men with his fifty. And he answered and said to him, "O man of God, this is the king's order, 'Come down quickly!'"* ¹²*But Elijah answered them, "If I am a man of God, let fire come down from heaven and consume you and your fifty." Then the fire of God came down from heaven and consumed him and his fifty.*

¹³*Again the king sent the captain of a third fifty with his fifty. And the third captain of fifty went up and came and fell on his knees before Elijah and entreated him, "O man of God, please let my life, and the life of these fifty servants of yours, be precious in your sight.* ¹⁴*Behold, fire came down from heaven and consumed the two former captains of fifty men with their fifties, but now let my life be precious in your sight."* ¹⁵*Then the angel of the LORD said to Elijah, "Go down with him; do not be afraid of him." So he arose and went down with him to the king* ¹⁶*and said to him, "Thus says the LORD, 'Because you have sent messengers to inquire of Baal-zebub, the god of Ekron—is it because there is no God in Israel to inquire of his word?—therefore you shall not come down from the bed to which you have gone up, but you shall surely die.'"*

¹⁷*So he died according to the word of the LORD that Elijah had spoken. Jehoram became king in his place in the second year of Jehoram the son of Jehoshaphat, king of Judah, because Ahaziah had no son.* ¹⁸*Now the rest of the acts of Ahaziah that he did, are they not written in the Book of the Chronicles of the Kings of Israel?*

OVERVIEW: Through the themes of Moab's rebellion, King Aphasia's decision to consult a foreign god, and Elijah's calling down fire on his enemies, the reformers consider what it means to serve righteously, to worship God faithfully and to administer judgment fairly. Commentators also discuss the practical and
moral aspects of Elijah's garments made of hair.

1:1 *Moab Rebels*

HOW MOAB VIOLATED ITS OATH TO ISRAEL.
ALONSO TOSTADO: It may be asked in what way

Moab rebelled against Israel. I respond that Moab violated the covenant they had made with Israel as a tributary. For the king of Israel had formerly imposed a covenant on the king of Moab in which the king of Moab was to annually pay a tribute to the king of Israel. And after the death of Moab, Mesha, king of Moab, refused to acknowledge his covenant status as a tributary to Ahab's son, Ahaziah. And in this way Mesha went against the covenant and pact he had sworn. Now the tribute was in the amount of 100,000 lambs and the wool of 100,000 rams, as we read about in 2 Kings 3. Mesha's rebellion against Israel was the cause of a war between the two nations. COMMENTARY ON 2 KINGS.[1]

MOAB'S REBELLION REVEALS ISRAEL'S REBELLION. JOHANNES BUGENHAGEN: Moab rebelled against Israel and would no longer pay tribute after Ahab's death. Ahab had gained the world and had been feared as a tyrannical ruler, but it had been God who was preserving the kingdom, otherwise no counsel, wisdom or military would have prevailed. God truly arranged it so that Israel's subordinates would slip away, as long as Israel would not recognize that it was subordinate to God. They should have submitted to God and paid attention to God's rule through faith, as they had during almost the entire time described in the book of Judges. He perceived this correctly who wrote in the psalm that God "subdues peoples under me." For when we submit ourselves to God, all things have been given over to us: heaven, earth, angels, Paul, Cephas, Apollos, rulers, the elements, nourishment, time, Satan, sin, death and hell. For trusting him above all others, even evil will "work together for our good," Romans 8 says. This is little wonder, for when we have God the Father, we are children of God and children of his daylight. The children of Israel had reigned through God. By abandoning God, they would not only serve humans but also be made to be sin. For Satan wants to steal the heart of anyone who does not have God through faith, so

that they can no longer do anything but ungodly things. COMMENTARY ON 2 KINGS.[2]

1:2-6 Inquiring of the God of the Flies

WHETHER AHAZIAH SINNED. ALONSO TOSTADO: It may be asked whether Ahaziah sinned in sending messengers to consult Baal-zebub. I respond that he did sin, for God clearly scolded Ahaziah here, and God would not have scolded him unless he had done something evil. The way Ahaziah sinned was by giving honor to an idol and trying to get a response from it by ascribing to it the status of divinity. But if Ahaziah had truly believed in God, he would not have needed a response from an idol. In a similar way, Ahaziah sinned because he greatly contemned the God of Israel for refusing to seek his counsel and instead preferring an idol. COMMENTARY ON 2 KINGS.[3]

CONSULTING THE LORD OF THE FLIES. JOHANNES BUGENHAGEN: The ungodly accept another righteousness as their god, which is what it means to have a foreign god. Therefore in this righteousness they are blind, so that they do not seek the righteousness of God when they are confronted with despair. Thus Ahaziah sent some people to inquire of Baal-zebub, that is, Baal, or the lord of the flies, who was worshiped in Ekron. This thing about flies is said because of the filth created by the blood sacrifices. But Ahaziah did not have faith that he would be protected by Baal-zebub, which is why he did not ask for such a thing. Having been rightly admonished by Elijah to consult the God of Israel, who is the true God and the Lord of life and death, who hears the faraway ones and even tries to caution them with admonitions about death. This is our righteousness, even though others see only God's judgment and are not satisfied with God's works. Then they cannot help but judge the one who condemned their faith in

---

[2]Bugenhagen, *In Regum duos ultimos libros*, 106-7; citing Ps 144:2; Rom 8:28.
[3]TO 15:4.

[1]TO 15:1-2.

themselves and preached putting faith in God
alone. For they do not care to think about God
through Christ but instead consider the good
works they do or promise to do in the future. And
when they see that they cannot stand firm in these
works, they know of nothing else but to despair.
COMMENTARY ON 2 KINGS.[4]

Not Joining in Ungodliness by Extension.

JOHANNES PISCATOR: We must not provide
assistance to ministers of ungodliness and injustice.
For the messengers or legates of Ahaziah were
denounced here (at least indirectly) for going out
and consulting the idol of Ekron on behalf of the
king. COMMENTARY ON 2 KINGS.[5]

Worshiping Only the True God. LAMBERT

DANEAU: It is clear that we ought to have no
fellowship with Satan, whether it be directly and
mediately, or else indirectly and immediately, as
some term it. Neither ought we to seek any relief by
his help, aide or counsel. For we must make
recourse in all our afflictions unto our only true
God. For why would we seek help and assistance
from Beelzebub, since there is a God in Israel, as
the prophet Elijah worthily grieved and retorted.…
Therefore we ought to cleave to God, to depend
only on him, and by no means should we allow,
condone or seek out Satan himself, or his ministers
(as sorcerers certainly are).… For we cannot serve
two masters, namely, God and the devil. We must
utterly forsake the devil so that we may entirely
cleave to God. DIALOGUE OF WITCHES.[6]

Death on Account of Consulting Idols.

JOHANNES PISCATOR: When sick, we must not
consult idols, that is, the devil. Nor should we
consult with ministers of the devil. Instead we are
only to consult with the true God. Indeed we are to
inquire of God's will from the Word. Ahaziah, in
fact, was denounced by God through his prophet
because he wished to consult the idol of Ekron in

his sickness. And on account of this he was
condemned to death. COMMENTARY ON 2 KINGS.[7]

1:7-8 Elijah's Hair and Garment

Religious Clothing. ALONSO TOSTADO: It

may be asked why Elijah wore this habit of
clothing. I respond that Elijah did not wear this
poor habit out of poverty, in the sense that he did
not have another form of clothing. Instead he wore
this habit out of religious reasons. For we know
that Elijah was a very holy man, and even more
holy than other prophets. By wearing this habit he
wanted to scorn the glory of the world and to
demonstrate that there was something better in the
world above. COMMENTARY ON 2 KINGS.[8]

Clothes Do Not Make the Prophet.

JOHANNES BUGENHAGEN: The Latin describes
Elijah as a hairy man. It is better to say that he was
a man wearing a garment of hair. This was also
what John the Baptist wore. There is not holiness
in such things, but the saints do prefer such things
more than the fancy things of the world. They
content themselves with having what is necessary
and do not seek greatness. On this point, however,
hypocrites imitate the holiness and righteousness
of people like Elijah and John, as if Christ, who ate
and drank with sinners, could not have been holy
because he did not wear similar things. COMMEN-
TARY ON 2 KINGS.[9]

Covered in Faith and Obedience. KONRAD

PELLIKAN: Ahaziah inquired about the habit and
disposition of the prophet who spoke to his
messengers, and he resolved that it was Elijah since
the prophet was covered in hair and wore a leather
belt. Indeed holy men did not choose to wear
delicate or soft clothing. Instead they chose clothes
that were hard to procure and that did not give off
any ostentation. Their provision was not in what

---

[4]Bugenhagen, *In Regum duos ultimos libros*, 107-8.
[5]Piscator, *Commentarii in omnes libros Veteris Testamenti*, 2:312.
[6]Daneau, *Dialogue of Witches*, K6r-v*.

[7]Piscator, *Commentarii in omnes libros Veteris Testamenti*, 2:312.
[8]TO 15:7.
[9]Bugenhagen, *In Regum duos ultimos libros*, 108; citing Mt 3:4; 9:11.

they wore, but they were commended by their faith and obedience. COMMENTARY ON 2 KINGS.[10]

DRESSED TO TEACH HUMILITY. JOHN MAYER: Elijah is said to be hairy according to some because his body, hands and face were hairy. According to others, he was called this because his garments were hairy and coarse just like John the Baptist's. The most probable explanation is that Elijah was both hairy and he wore a hairy garment. The prophets were clothed in this way . . . because they preached repentance, which in those days was made outwardly in sackcloth as well as in word. This is contrary to the way preachers are dressed today . . . whose apparel and ornaments are most costly. Nevertheless preachers should learn to flee from such worldly pomp from the example of the prophets. Preachers should not even wear so much as a gold chain or a ring, but only those things that teach others about humility. COMMENTARY ON 2 KINGS.[11]

1:9-18 Fire from Heaven

GOD'S ANSWERING OF OUR PRAYERS. MARTIN LUTHER: God must answer our prayers . . . just as much as Elijah's, for we are members of his church, which is the bride of his beloved Son. He cannot ignore the church when it earnestly beseeches him. For that reason it is not impossible for God to accomplish deeds as great or greater through us. APPEAL FOR PRAYER AGAINST THE TURKS.[12]

WHETHER ELIJAH VIOLATED THE SIXTH COMMANDMENT. JOHANNES PISCATOR: It may be asked whether Elijah acted rightly when he cursed these military units by asking fire from heaven to consume them. The reason to question his action is because it appears to go against the sixth commandment, "You shall not murder." I respond that he acted rightly because it appears

that this was the curse he heard from God to put on them, and God approved it. From this we may gather that this curse proceeded from a right heart, namely, that this act arose out of zeal for God's glory. For on account of the word of God Elijah had indicated to Ahaziah that his messengers had come to him asking about Ahaziah's illness as if he were a false prophet. But if Elijah had cast down a curse out of his own desire to provide a private punishment, he would have sinned. And God would not have supported it. For such an example appears in the disciples of Christ when they desired to imitate Elijah by sending down fire from heaven out of their wrongful desires. And in response to their request, "Christ turned and rebuked them." COMMENTARY ON 2 KINGS.[13]

FIRE FROM HEAVEN COMING ON THE UNGODLY. JOHN MAYER: It may be asked why Christ did not send down fire from heaven as Elijah did to those living in Samaria who rejected him when his two disciples requested so and instead rebuked his disciples. . . . It is not simply that Jesus did not call forth fire from heaven to show the leniency of the gospel in comparison to the rigor and severity of the law. On the contrary, Peter killed Ananias and Sapphira in Acts 5 and Paul made Elymas blind in Acts 13. The answer for all these is that each person was moved by the Spirit of God to act accordingly. And Elijah was moved by God's Spirit to bring execution on these gross idolaters and rejecters of the true God and of his servants. A similar example of revenge by fire from heaven appeared against Korah, Dathan and Abiram when they envied Moses and Aaron in Numbers 16. The avenging of wrongs done to God's prophets should be a warning to all people not to touch his anointed, nor to do harm to his prophets. For this type of judgment is suggested as the last revenge on all the wicked by fire at the Day of Judgment according to 2 Thessalonians: "in

---

[10]Pellikan, *Commentaria Bibliorum*, 2:173r.
[11]Mayer, *Many Commentaries in One*, 146-47*.
[12]LW 43:227.

[13]Piscator, *Commentarii in omnes libros Veteris Testamenti*, 2:312; citing Ex 20:13; Lk 9:55.

flaming fire, inflicting vengeance on those who do not know God and on those who do not obey the gospel of our Lord Jesus." For as fire now came down from heaven and consumed some, so on the Day of Judgment it will come down for the destruction of all God's enemies and the enemies of his servants. For at that time none will remain incredulous. Rather, they will be assured that the one who sent down fire in one part of the world in previous times both can and will send it down in all places of the world at a later time. COMMENTARY ON 2 KINGS.[14]

FIRE FROM HEAVEN. GIOVANNI DIODATI: Elijah effectively said this to the captain: "Seeing that after so many proofs of my being a prophet and despite my faithfulness, you will yield me no faith or obedience but by a profane scorn you call me 'man of God': I therefore beseech that great Lord whom I serve to confirm and make good my ministry by your exemplary punishment." Such was the zealous motion of the Spirit of God in return for a just punishment. Jesus' disciples later asked their Lord whether they should likewise call fire down from heaven in Luke 9:54. ANNOTATIONS ON 2 KINGS.[15]

---

[14]Mayer, *Many Commentaries in One*, 148*; citing 2 Thess 1:8.

[15]Diodati, *Pious Annotations*, 17*.

2:1-12 ELIJAH TAKEN TO HEAVEN

Now when the Lord was about to take Elijah up to heaven by a whirlwind, Elijah and Elisha were on their way from Gilgal. ²And Elijah said to Elisha, "Please stay here, for the Lord has sent me as far as Bethel." But Elisha said, "As the Lord lives, and as you yourself live, I will not leave you." So they went down to Bethel. ³And the sons of the prophets who were in Bethel came out to Elisha and said to him, "Do you know that today the Lord will take away your master from over you?" And he said, "Yes, I know it; keep quiet."

⁴Elijah said to him, "Elisha, please stay here, for the Lord has sent me to Jericho." But he said, "As the Lord lives, and as you yourself live, I will not leave you." So they came to Jericho. ⁵The sons of the prophets who were at Jericho drew near to Elisha and said to him, "Do you know that today the Lord will take away your master from over you?" And he answered, "Yes, I know it; keep quiet."

⁶Then Elijah said to him, "Please stay here, for the Lord has sent me to the Jordan." But he said, "As the Lord lives, and as you yourself live, I will not leave you." So the two of them went on. ⁷Fifty men of the sons of the prophets also went and stood at some distance from them, as they both were standing by the Jordan. ⁸Then Elijah took his cloak and rolled it up and struck the water, and the water was parted to the one side and to the other, till the two of them could go over on dry ground.

⁹When they had crossed, Elijah said to Elisha, "Ask what I shall do for you, before I am taken from you." And Elisha said, "Please let there be a double portion of your spirit on me." ¹⁰And he said, "You have asked a hard thing; yet, if you see me as I am being taken from you, it shall be so for you, but if you do not see me, it shall not be so." ¹¹And as they still went on and talked, behold, chariots of fire and horses of fire separated the two of them. And Elijah went up by a whirlwind into heaven. ¹²And Elisha saw it and he cried, "My father, my father! The chariots of Israel and its horsemen!" And he saw him no more.

Then he took hold of his own clothes and tore them in two pieces.

OVERVIEW: Regarding the famous story of Elijah's ascent into heaven, these commentators consider the public nature of this departure (especially the role of the college of prophets), Elisha's bold request for a double portion of Elijah's spirit and the nature of eternal life with God. In a compact way, the comments in this section reveal a variety of approaches to Scripture, with methods of interpretation including clarification of the text's plain meaning, lessons about moral application and Protestant uses of allegory and typology.

2:1-6 Elijah Visits the School of Prophets

Elijah the Circuit Prophet. John Mayer: Elijah traveled with Elisha to Gilgal, who minis-

tered to him, after God revealed to him that he would take him away into heaven, and on what day. Gilgal was a famous place for the circumcision of all the males among the children of Israel when they crossed over the Jordan River into the land of Canaan. And near that river, many expositors hold, was a school or college of prophets. Their chief instructor was Elijah. The location of this school was a fit one for men of holy orders, given that it was famous for the children of Israel first pitching their tents there when they came to take possession of that land. From Gilgal, where Elijah must have spent much of his time as a teacher of students, he went to Bethel. There Elijah had more disciples, called the sons of the prophets, whom he instructed and confirmed in their faith. Bethel was also a place of note on account of Jacob's vision and his sacrificing there. For it was, as Jacob professed it to be, a city rightly called "house of God." From Bethel Elijah traveled to Jericho, where even more sons of the prophets resided. Jericho, of course, was also a place of note on account of the great miracle wrought there in Joshua 6. From there he returned to Jordan to go over the place where God would take him up. And he might well have traveled through all of these places in one day, seeing that Gilgal to Bethel was but six miles, and from there to Jericho was four, and from Jericho to Jordan it was only six miles. But Gilgal was far from the place where he dwelled, that is, in Carmel, about fifty-two miles. Therefore Elijah could not usually be there with his students, but only occasionally as their chief master. He would have substituted in each location another teacher over them, as the father of the sons of that place. COMMENTARY ON 2 KINGS.[1]

THE COMPANY OF PROPHETS. JOHANNES BUGENHAGEN: From Gilgal, Elijah went to where many of his followers and children were; that is, these were the followers of the prophets from the time of Samuel (1 Sam 10). He then proceeded to Bethel and Jericho, where there were similarly the sons of the prophets, who were also his own disciples, doubtlessly striking a note of comfort for their faith in God's Word. They knew through a sure revelation of the Spirit that Elijah would be taken by God, and they told this to others. Thus you should not think this being taken was a secret thing, since God wanted the world to take note of it, for the sake of the message about another life that we mentioned above. COMMENTARY ON 2 KINGS.[2]

DISCIPLES OF PROPHETS. ALONSO TOSTADO: It may be asked who the sons of the prophets were. The Hebrews and Nicholas of Lyra respond that they were not sons of the prophets according to the flesh but that they were disciples of the

prophets. They were merely called sons because they were the disciples of their teachers. And there were many men at that time who pursued a religious life, who wished to offer religious instruction to the people. They gathered where the prophets resided, and there they learned their teachings. COMMENTARY ON 2 KINGS.[3]

2:7-8 Dividing the Waters

ELIJAH'S CLOAK. JOHANNES BUGENHAGEN: Elijah used his cloak to part the Jordan, just as Moses used his staff to part the sea in Exodus 14. Neither this cloak nor that staff are anything but the Spirit and Word of God. After this Elisha has Elijah's cloak because he had been called as a prophet, as we discussed above in 1 Kings 19. Then he also used the cloak to part the Jordan, which is not something the cloak could do by itself unless the spirit of Elijah rested on him. These external signs were added for our sake. For these signs happen through people and for people so that God and God's messengers may be acknowledged through things and signs that we could not do ourselves. In the same way below, salt is put in the water. God could have made the water sweet without the salt, but there may still have been doubts about whether Elisha had done it, and God wanted this sign to confirm Elisha's preaching. COMMENTARY ON 2 KINGS.[4]

NO OBSTACLES FOR THE GODLY. JOHANNES PISCATOR: Elijah divided the waters of the Jordan with his cloak and traversed the river on dry ground with Elisha so that Elijah could go to the place where he would be translated to heaven. Likewise, Elisha did the same thing that Elijah did so that he could more quickly and easily return. This documents that there is no insurmountable path for the godly as long as they seek the glory of God. COMMENTARY ON 2 KINGS.[5]

---

[1]Mayer, *Many Commentaries in One*, 150-51*.
[2]Bugenhagen, *In Regum duos ultimos libros*, 111-12; citing 1 Sam 10:5, 10.
[3]TO 15:13.
[4]Bugenhagen, *In Regum duos ultimos libros*, 113-14; citing Ex 14:16; 1 Kings 19:19; 2 Kings 2:19-22.
[5]Piscator, *Commentarii in omnes libros Veteris Testamenti*, 2:314.

2:9-10 *Elisha Seeks a Double Portion*

DOUBLE SPIRIT OR ELIJAH'S SPIRIT? ALONSO TOSTADO: It may be asked whether Elisha asked for a spirit twice as great as Elijah's or whether he simply asked for the spirit of Elijah, which consisted of two parts. Some say that Elisha did not ask for a spirit twice as great as his master, for Elisha would have blushed at asking for a spirit that was greater than what Elijah had. He would have been satisfied with being made equal with his master. For as Jesus said, "A disciple is not above his teacher, nor a servant above his master." On the other hand, others say that Elisha asked for a spirit that was double that of Elijah's. For Elijah knew that Elisha would be his successor by prophecy, since God had spoken to him of this earlier: "And . . . Elisha the son of Shaphat of Abel-meholah you shall anoint to be prophet in your place." And when Elijah asked Elisha what he desired, Elisha informed him of his desire to have a double spirit. This explains why Elijah responded "You have asked a hard thing," namely, because Elisha sought a spirit twice as great as his. COMMENTARY ON 2 KINGS.[6]

ELISHA AS ELIJAH'S SPIRITUAL FIRSTBORN. CARDINAL CAJETAN: I am aware, dear reader, that this term of twofold spirit is also called in Scripture a double portion, which was given to the firstborn son. Therefore the portion of the firstborn was called the double portion because he succeeded with a double inheritance. And this is what Elisha requested in asking for a double spirit, namely, that he would succeed Elijah not in the fields or in his physical body but in the spirit of Elijah in the sense that he would receive a double portion of Elijah's spirit according to the custom of being the firstborn. Therefore he asked for more than a portion of prophecy but also that of the miraculous because he asked to succeed Elijah according to the custom of being the firstborn, in which he received preference among the spiritual sons of Elijah. COMMENTARY ON 2 KINGS.[7]

A DOUBLE EFFECT OF THE SPIRIT. JOHANNES BUGENHAGEN: The Latin calls this a "double spirit." That is, "the Spirit will lead twice as many people through my preaching as it led through your preaching, in order that I might further confound the impious idolatries of those who forsake God's Word and I will complete what you left unfinished." Otherwise there is only one Spirit in each of them, who distributes spiritual gifts differently, as in 1 Corinthians 12. COMMENTARY ON 2 KINGS.[8]

A GREAT REQUEST. JOHN MAYER: As they were traveling, Elijah bid Elisha to ask what he desired, and Elisha asked that his spirit might be doubled on him. This was a great request, and such as one would think that it surpassed the power of any person to grant. But it is to be understood that Elijah did not ask this question without God's suggesting it to him, nor did Elisha respond without the same instinct of the Spirit. By the double portion of Elijah's spirit . . . there are different interpretations. Some understand it to mean twice as much as Elijah's spirit. They base this on the understanding that Elisha performed twice as many miracles as Elijah. For instance, whereas Elijah performed eight miracles, Elisha performed sixteen. Some interpret this as a double portion in respect of other prophets, in the same way that the firstborn had a double portion of the rest of his brothers so that he might be the more fit to succeed him in the prophetic office, who was the father and chief of all the rest. Finally, others interpret this as two parts of Elijah's spirit, first, knowledge to understand and the ability to foresee secret and hidden things and, second, the power to do miracles for the confirmation of the truth and the beating down of idolatry. . . . As for me, I rest on the first interpretation, namely, that Elisha desired and received a double portion of Elijah's spirit. COMMENTARY ON 2 KINGS.[9]

[6]TO 15:16; citing Mt 10:24.
[7]Cajetan, *Opera Omnia in Sacrae Scripturae Expositionem*, 2:229.
[8]Bugenhagen, *In Regum duos ultimos libros*, 114; citing 1 Cor 12:4.
[9]Mayer, *Many Commentaries in One*, 153*.

DESIRING THINGS THAT PROMOTE GOD'S GLORY. JOHANNES PISCATOR: In Elijah giving Elisha the opportunity to ask for what he wanted, an example is set forth of extraordinary faith. For Elijah had convinced himself by means of prayer from God that he was about to grant that for which Elisha was about to ask. And this establishes the hypothesis that . . . nothing is to be asked for unless it comes to promote the glory of God. COMMENTARY ON 2 KINGS.[10]

A RARE THING. GIOVANNI DIODATI: Elisha asked for a rare and singular thing, which is not ordinarily promised. It cannot be obtained but by very fervent and instant prayer. Such is the type of prayer needed, for instance, for the rich person to enter God's kingdom and for even the righteous being saved by God. ANNOTATIONS ON 2 KINGS.[11]

ALLEGORY OF ELISHA'S REQUEST. JOHN MAYER: Concerning Elisha's desire for the spirit to be doubled on him, he is understood in the *Glossa ordinaria* to be a figure of the church. For the church, being emboldened to ask by the Lord's invitation, desires also a double portion of the Spirit to that which Christ had, namely, the gift of miraculous operations and remission of sins. And as Elisha had his request granted on condition that he see Elijah at his ascension, so the faithful who see, that is, believe not only the incarnation and passion but also the resurrection and ascension of Christ into heaven, obtain their request to do greater things in the Spirit than Christ did, as he promised they would. Finally, as Elisha used the name of Elijah to work that miracle at the Jordan, so in the name of Christ the apostles did miracles. COMMENTARY ON 2 KINGS.[12]

2:11-12 Elijah's Heavenly Ascent

THE LIFE TO COME. JOHANNES BUGENHAGEN: Here Elijah was visibly taken up out of this world in the same way, I believe, that Enoch was visibly taken up in Genesis. But how they were taken up to heaven or paradise God sees and knows best and we do not need to know. Indeed it is ignorance when some say that these men who have been taken up keep watch with us in the resurrection to come. Then these ones whom God took up can help preserve us beyond this world. For without a doubt Enoch was a herald of truth, just as Peter wrote of Noah. The same was true of Elijah. But Scripture does not say one clear letter about whether Enoch and Elijah are to return before the final day. Therefore I do not believe in such a future appearance. For in Matthew 17, Christ testified that what Malachi wrote about Elijah had been fulfilled in John the Baptist, as did the angel in Luke 1. Furthermore, this being taken up is primarily a confirmation of the word of God, which these men preached, so that those whom the world despised would be seen as receiving care from God. It reveals that they had been teaching the true God, so that believers might be strengthened and despisers might be confounded. For believers endured no less scandal amid the impious kingdom of Elijah's time than had occurred earlier in the time of Enoch. Therefore it was necessary for God to strengthen his people. Thus this was not only declared to them but also to us that there is another life after this one. For these two men are not dead even though they are not to be found among the living. From this is born the most certain arguments of the godly. If these men who were born in the flesh like us were taken out of this world by God, then we may also be taken if we adhere to God like they did. This is an example of that Christian argument for most certain faith. Christ has been taken from this mortal life to the glory of the resurrection and eternal life, so shall it be for us who are in Christ. But this final glory did not yet belong to these two glorified men, from which I am certain that Christ is the firstborn of the resurrected dead and the "firstfruits of those who have fallen asleep," so that no one could have been glorified with this glory before Christ. COMMENTARY ON 2 KINGS.[13]

---

[10]Piscator, *Commentarii in omnes libros Veteris Testamenti*, 2:314.
[11]Diodati, *Pious Annotations*, 18*.
[12]Mayer, *Many Commentaries in One*, 158*.

[13]Bugenhagen, *In Regum duos ultimos libros*, 110-11; citing Gen 5:24; 2 Pet 2:5; Mt 17:12; Mal 4:5; Lk 1:17; Col 1:18; Rev 1:5; 1 Cor 15:20.

Elijah's Witness to Eternal Life. Philipp Melanchthon: While still living, Enoch and Elijah were taken from this life to God, because God wanted to give visible evidence of the eternal life. For if they were nothing after this life, then they would not be with God; to be with God means to dwell in a new, divine, eternal life. Theological Commonplaces (1555).[14]

Elisha Gazes into Heaven Like Jesus' Disciples Did. Johannes Piscator: Elisha was encouraged by Elijah to desire from God this blessing of being allowed to see Elijah's assumption to heaven. And when the opportunity was given to him of seeing it, he enjoyed it as long as he could. It appears, from what we can gather, that the assumption of Elijah into heaven was a type of the ascension of Christ into heaven. In fact Jesus' disciples also gazed into heaven with the same desire and eager perseverance as Elisha did, as appears from the book of Acts: "And while they were gazing into heaven as he went, behold, two men stood by them in white robes, and said, 'Men of Galilee, why do you stand looking into heaven? This Jesus, who was taken up from you into heaven, will come in the same way as you saw him go into heaven.'" Commentary on 2 Kings.[15]

Two Questions About Elijah's Entrance into Heaven. John Mayer: Two questions here offer themselves. First, why must Elijah be taken into heaven so extraordinarily? Second, to what place did he go—the highest heaven, where Christ now is along with the souls of the faithful departed, or some other place called heaven? In response to the first question, Peter Martyr Vermigli said that it was done to honor the prophet for showing so great and extraordinary zeal against idolatry in the time of such a king and queen. For this king and queen had persecuted to death all the prophets of God that they could find. For whomever before,

being only a private man and an individual, dared to do what Elijah did? Elijah twice threatened King Ahab: first with a drought of three years and six months and then with destruction both of him and his family. Elijah also sharply rebuked the king as a troubler of Israel, and he also put to death four hundred prophets of Baal. To King Ahaziah he threatened death for his idolatry and killed one hundred of Ahaziah's men with fire. And just as King Ahasuerus honored Mordecai for special service done to him by making him ride on his own horse, so God would now honor Elijah by making him ride in a chariot up to heaven. God did this so that Elijah's doctrine might be more regarded in the turning of people away from idols to serve the true God. Elijah was here a figure of Christ also, who ascended visibly into heaven. And he will also meet with all the faithful in the last day in the sky according to 1 Thessalonians 4:17.

In response to the second question, it is generally held that Enoch and Elijah were both taken away into one place. But to what place they were taken is not agreed. . . . [I answer that] it pleased God to take away two to himself before the coming of Christ. That is, he took one under the law of nature or of the world before the flood, and one under the law. And under the Gospel Christ ascended visibly into heaven so that no age might lack some testimony of the faithful being taken up into heaven at the last day. Commentary on 2 Kings.[16]

Elijah's Ascension into Heaven as a Type of Christ's. Johannes Piscator: Elijah ascended into heaven by chariots of fire pulled by horses of fire, which were really holy angels. In this we see a type of the ascension of Christ. For although there is not an express testimony from Scripture that Christ ascended into heaven in exactly the same way, he was accompanied by holy angels. We can partly gather this notion from the words of Paul, which say: "Great indeed, we confess, is the mystery of godliness: He was . . . seen by

---

[14]*Melanchthon on Christian Doctrine*, 285.

[15]Piscator, *Commentarii in omnes libros Veteris Testamenti*, 2:315; citing Acts 1:10-11.

[16]Mayer, *Many Commentaries in One*, 151*; citing Esther 6:1-11.

angels." We can also partly and particularly gather this from the collection of distinguished acts of Christ in which the angels ministered to him. We see this, for instance, at Jesus' nativity: "And suddenly there was with the angel a multitude of the heavenly host praising God." And we see it at his resurrection: "While they were perplexed about this, behold, two angels stood by them in dazzling apparel." And finally, we will see angels accompany Jesus when he returns as judge: "When the Son of Man comes in his glory, and all the angels with him, then he will sit on his glorious throne." COMMENTARY ON 2 KINGS.[17]

DONNING A NEW GARMENT. CHARLES DRELINCOURT: God holds out in his hand a garment of light and glory, which he will bestow on you. For it shall happen to you as to the prophet Elijah, who, having let fall his mantle, found himself all encompassed about with flames of fire and an extraordinary light. As soon as you cast off this miserable body, you will be surrounded with celestial flames in which you will mount up to heaven into the dwelling of immortality, where you shall be like God, who clothes himself with light as with a garment. To this purpose the words of the prophet Zechariah concerning the high priest Joshua are very proper: He was arrayed with filthy garments, but an angel from heaven calls to them who waited before him: "And the angel said to those who were standing before him, 'Remove the filthy garments from him.' And to him he said, 'Behold, I have taken your iniquity away from you, and I will clothe you with pure vestments.' And I said, 'Let them put a clean turban on his head.'" This, O Christian soul, is the true image of your condition at your departure from this life and the lively portrait of your future happiness. At present you are clothed with a body undermined by sickness and weakness. You bear about yourself the relics of the old person. But behold, God calls to you from his holy sanctuary. "Take away from him this old garment. Take off all

remains of this old clothing that is stained with sin, where the devil's image is still seen. Give him the sacred ornaments of a royal priesthood. Clothe this soul with a long garment whitened in the blood of the Lamb and gird it about with the ephod of righteousness. Put on its head an incorruptible crown, and in his hand give him a golden vial that may forever offer up the heavenly perfume in company of the glorified saints." CHRISTIAN DEFENSE AGAINST THE FEARS OF DEATH.[18]

THE CHARIOTS OF ISRAEL. JOHANNES BUGENHAGEN: Elisha did not speak to the chariot of fire that he saw, but he appealed to Elijah. The chariots and riders (or in Hebrew the soldiers and army) were the ones who had carried the people and led them, defended pure doctrine and counsel, and brought rain in unfruitful times. Therefore they were called on by those who dealt with the highest matters of caring for the people. King Joash similarly cried out at the death of Elisha in chapter 13. It is as if Elisha here said, "After you leave, I wonder who will be entrusted with the people's health and care? Whom has God called for the people?" I will likewise not dread him through whom the gospel has again been revealed today, who has been called on for the care, defense and governing of Israel, and on whom our case has been thrust to this entire world. COMMENTARY ON 2 KINGS.[19]

SEVEN WAYS ELIJAH WAS A TYPE OF CHRIST. JOHN MAYER: Elijah departed from this world and entered heaven. He was not only an eminent type of Christ in his ascension but in many other ways as well. First, he entered the biblical history like Melchizedek, without father or mother. Indeed, no mention is made, unlike other prophets, of his father. Second, he lived obscurely for a long time

---

[17]Piscator, *Commentarii in omnes libros Veteris Testamenti*, 2:315; citing 1 Tim 3:16; Lk 2:13; 24:4; Mt 25:31.

[18]Drelincourt, *Christian's Defense Against the Fears of Death*, 373-74*; citing Zech 3:4-5.
[19]Bugenhagen, *In Regum duos ultimos libros*, 114-15; citing 2 Kings 13:14. It is not clear if the quotation should extend to the last sentence. Either way, it appears as if Bugenhagen refers to Luther as a modern Elijah. Melanchthon invoked this passage when he heard the news of Luther's death in 1546.

and then suddenly began to show himself to the king of Israel, just as Christ did himself at the age of thirty. Third, he was fed by a widow, whose son died; but later he raised him to life again. In the same way Christ was shown hospitality by Mary and Martha, and he later raised their brother Lazarus from the dead, just as the widow's son by Elijah. Fourth, Elijah brought fire from heaven to destroy sinners just as Christ sent down the Holy Spirit as fire that would destroy sin. Fifth, Elijah, when full of heaviness and alone in the wilderness, was comforted by an angel, just as Christ was comforted in the garden before his death. Sixth, Elijah fasted forty days, just as Christ did. Finally, the spirit of Elijah rested on Elisha after his ascent, just as the Holy Spirit did on the apostles. COMMENTARY ON 2 KINGS.[20]

---

[20]Mayer, *Many Commentaries in One*, 154*.

2:13-25 ELISHA SUCCEEDS ELIJAH

¹³And he took up the cloak of Elijah that had fallen from him and went back and stood on the bank of the Jordan. ¹⁴Then he took the cloak of Elijah that had fallen from him and struck the water, saying, "Where is the LORD, the God of Elijah?" And when he had struck the water, the water was parted to the one side and to the other, and Elisha went over.

¹⁵Now when the sons of the prophets who were at Jericho saw him opposite them, they said, "The spirit of Elijah rests on Elisha." And they came to meet him and bowed to the ground before him. ¹⁶And they said to him, "Behold now, there are with your servants fifty strong men. Please let them go and seek your master. It may be that the Spirit of the LORD has caught him up and cast him upon some mountain or into some valley." And he said, "You shall not send." ¹⁷But when they urged him till he was ashamed, he said, "Send." They sent therefore fifty men. And for three days they sought him but did not find him. ¹⁸And they came back to him while he was staying at Jericho, and he said to them, "Did I not say to you, 'Do not go'?"

¹⁹Now the men of the city said to Elisha, "Behold, the situation of this city is pleasant, as my lord sees, but the water is bad, and the land is unfruitful." ²⁰He said, "Bring me a new bowl, and put salt in it." So they brought it to him. ²¹Then he went to the spring of water and threw salt in it and said, "Thus says the LORD, I have healed this water; from now on neither death nor miscarriage shall come from it." ²²So the water has been healed to this day, according to the word that Elisha spoke.

²³He went up from there to Bethel, and while he was going up on the way, some small boys came out of the city and jeered at him, saying, "Go up, you baldhead! Go up, you baldhead!" ²⁴And he turned around, and when he saw them, he cursed them in the name of the LORD. And two she-bears came out of the woods and tore forty-two of the boys. ²⁵From there he went on to Mount Carmel, and from there he returned to Samaria.

OVERVIEW: The reformers comment on the meaning of Elisha's first miracles, including an allegorical interpretation of what it means for us to be sweet and savory. They read the story of the boys who are killed after mocking Elisha as an example of what happens when God's Word and God's prophets are despised. Positive conclusions drawn from that passage include the importance of good education and God's mercy in not always punishing sins so harshly.

2:13-22 Elijah's Spirit Rests on Elisha

WHY SOMEONE ELSE PUT SALT IN THE BOWL.
ALONSO TOSTADO: It may be asked why Elisha was unwilling to put salt in the bowl himself but that he wanted someone else to put it in.... I respond that Elisha wished to take occasion to investigate this occurrence himself, and he did not want to diminish the authority of this miracle. Also, if he had put salt in the bowl, he could have been accused of performing some demonic trick. He himself was unwilling to put it in so that whoever put it in could recognize that no demonic trick took place but that it was the work of God. And this is also why he requested a new bowl. He did not want anyone to claim that there was something in the old bowl that could possibly explain away the miracle he performed. Indeed, there are many examples like this of prophets performing elaborate ceremonies so that they may not be charged with demonic activity. For this is how Elijah performed his miracle against the prophets of Baal. He requested that large amounts of water be placed over his sacrifice so that the fire that came

from heaven could rightly be regarded as a miracle from God. COMMENTARY ON 2 KINGS.[1]

NO SWEET SALT. JOHANNES BUGENHAGEN: This sign showed the people that Elijah was a prophet of the Lord, whose word should be believed. You can give as much credit to the salt for the water's sweetness as you give power to the cloak that divided the waters in the story above. For it is against the nature of salt to make water sweet, so that you might see this as a pure miracle of God through the spirit of the prophet, not ascribing it to any physical thing. Likewise the barren land that was irrigated by this water was cleansed, for it is also against nature that salt do this to unfruitful land. And so you see clearly that this happened not because of the salt but because of the word of God that Elisha spoke, "Thus says the LORD, I have healed this water," etc. Our hypocrites think they do a similar thing in the blessing of salt and water, but that is entirely ridiculous. COMMENTARY ON 2 KINGS.[2]

CURSED WATER OF JERICHO. MARTIN BOR-RHAUS: It may be asked here at what time the water of Jericho became defective and when the land became sterile. Older interpreters think that this happened during the time of Joshua when Israel entered into Jericho. Specifically they think it happened when Joshua put a curse on the city: "Joshua laid an oath on them at that time, saying, 'Cursed before the LORD be the man who rises up and rebuilds this city, Jericho. At the cost of his firstborn shall he lay its foundation, and at the cost of his youngest son shall he set up its gate.'" COMMENTARY ON 2 KINGS.[3]

AN ALLEGORY ON SALT AND SWEET. JOHANNES BUGENHAGEN: The Word of God in the Scriptures is water for drinking and crops for eating. Without the Spirit's judgment (that is, the salt), it tastes unpleasant and barren. Truly, a sure word of

God does not appear to you unless you are in the firm judgment of the Spirit and have the Spirit's knowledge. For the Savior says, "Have salt in yourselves." And in Leviticus, "You shall season all your grain offerings with salt." This is how the water and the barren land become sweet. COMMENTARY ON 2 KINGS.[4]

2:23-25 Bear Attack!

BLAME THE PARENTS. JOHANNES BUGENHAGEN: Elisha's zeal here against the children is the same Elijah had for the captains of the fifty men. For he was certainly angered when the word of God, of which he was a prophet, was blasphemed. Through the loss of their children, the impious parents paid the penalty for not instructing them better in the commands of the law, which demands that parents teach the law to their children, as in Deuteronomy 6. As the proverb says, "Bad eggs from bad crows." Thus this external penalty reveals that the impiety of godless children is not a harmless thing, even if people can pretend in front of others not to know that the children have not been taught by their parents. For the children perish along with their parents. COMMENTARY ON 2 KINGS.[5]

TYPICAL CHILDREN. MARTIN LUTHER: They are typical children of the world, these hypocrites. When they hear terrifying sermons on God's wrath, they felt called on to make fun of it secretly, to mock it and to deride us to our face and say: "Yes, yes!" They suppose that they have avenged themselves when they betray us and ridicule us. SERMONS ON THE GOSPEL OF ST. JOHN.[6]

ELISHA DID NOT SIN IN CURSING THE BOYS. JOHANNES PISCATOR: It may be asked here whether Elisha sinned against the sixth commandment—"You shall not murder"—when he cursed and

---

[1]TO 15:26.
[2]Bugenhagen, *In Regum duos ultimos libros*, 115-16. Salt is a traditional element in the preparation of holy water.
[3]Borrhaus, *Mystica Messiae*, 813; citing Josh 6:26.

[4]Bugenhagen, *In Regum duos ultimos libros*, 116; citing Mk 9:50; Lev 2:13.
[5]Bugenhagen, *In Regum duos ultimos libros*, 116-17; citing Deut 6:7 and a Latin proverb: *mali corvi malum ovum.*
[6]LW 23:265.

imprecated these boys of Bethel. I respond that he did not sin. That's because it appears God heeded his prayer. And the reason why God heeded this prayer is because the curse was not the result of an eager and private punishment, but rather one that proceeded from the zeal of God's glory. For Elijah was commanded in his prophetic role, which these boys on account of being brought up in idolatry were mocking. COMMENTARY ON 2 KINGS.[7]

ALLEGORY OF BEAR ATTACK. JOHN MAYER: Concerning the children mocking Elisha and bidding him "Go up, you baldhead!," Augustine understands this as the Jews, who are compared to children sitting in the marketplace. For the place where they crucified Christ was Calvary, and in mocking him they said, "Come down from the cross." In the same way, two bears, that is, Titus and Vespasian, destroyed them about forty-two years after Christ's passion. The *Glossa ordinaria* understands it similarly. Just as Elisha was mocked as he ascended Bethel, so Christ was mocked as he ascended to heaven, that is, the "house of God." COMMENTARY ON 2 KINGS.[8]

JUST PUNISHMENT FOR CALLING A MAN BALD. JOHN MAYER: Here the prophet may seem to have been too impatient, but it is to be understood that Bethel was a place tainted with idolatry. For even though there was a college of prophets there, there was also a golden calf set up by Jeroboam. This was doubtlessly still worshiped by most people, and therefore the prophets of God were not acceptable to them. Instead, when the prophets came there, they were derided and scorned. And just as the elders did, so also the younger children did so to Elisha. Therefore it was just for Elisha to curse them in response to their idolatrous parents. . . . Elisha was not stirred up by impatience, but by the Spirit of God. And it was just for God to take this miraculous revenge on them. Indeed God's revenge here could have happily taken occasion to draw some of them from idolatry. COMMENTARY ON 2 KINGS.[9]

PRAYERS STILL EFFECTIVE. MARTIN BUCER: Even today the prayers of holy people are not ineffective against wicked enemies of the reign of Christ. The curse of Elisha the prophet was not without effect against the boys who were laughing at him, for bears quickly tore them apart. REIGN OF CHRIST.[10]

THE SMALLER THINGS IN LIFE. CHARLES DRELINCOURT: God does not always command the lions and bears of the forest to come out and devour us—as he did when the rebellious prophet was killed and when the ill-tutored children of Bethel mocked Elisha. In short God does not always make use of plagues, judgments or pestilences of war and famine. The unpleasant smell of massacred bodies—a fume that comes from fire and smoke—is able to choke us or kill us in a moment. A fly, the core of an apple, the hair on a person's head, the seed of a grape, ashes, dirt or some other thing may just as easily stop the breath of our life. Therefore God advises us by the prophet Isaiah, "Stop regarding man in whose nostrils is breath, for of what account is he?" CHRISTIAN DEFENSE AGAINST THE FEARS OF DEATH.[11]

---

[7]Piscator, *Commentarii in omnes libros Veteris Testamenti*, 2:315; citing Ex 20:13.
[8]Mayer, *Many Commentaries in One*, 158*; citing Mt 27:40.
[9]Mayer, *Many Commentaries in One*, 157*.
[10]Bucer, *De Regno Christi*, 9.
[11]Drelincourt, *Christian's Defense Against the Fears of Death*, 64*; citing 1 Kings 13:11-24; Is 2:22.

3:1-27 MOAB REBELS AGAINST ISRAEL

¹In the eighteenth year of Jehoshaphat king of Judah, Jehoram the son of Ahab became king over Israel in Samaria, and he reigned twelve years. ²He did what was evil in the sight of the LORD, though not like his father and mother, for he put away the pillar of Baal that his father had made. ³Nevertheless, he clung to the sin of Jeroboam the son of Nebat, which he made Israel to sin; he did not depart from it.

⁴Now Mesha king of Moab was a sheep breeder, and he had to deliver to the king of Israel 100,000 lambs and the wool of 100,000 rams. ⁵But when Ahab died, the king of Moab rebelled against the king of Israel. ⁶So King Jehoram marched out of Samaria at that time and mustered all Israel. ⁷And he went and sent word to Jehoshaphat king of Judah, "The king of Moab has rebelled against me. Will you go with me to battle against Moab?" And he said, "I will go. I am as you are, my people as your people, my horses as your horses." ⁸Then he said, "By which way shall we march?" Jehoram answered, "By the way of the wilderness of Edom."

⁹So the king of Israel went with the king of Judah and the king of Edom. And when they had made a circuitous march of seven days, there was no water for the army or for the animals that followed them. ¹⁰Then the king of Israel said, "Alas! The LORD has called these three kings to give them into the hand of Moab." ¹¹And Jehoshaphat said, "Is there no prophet of the LORD here, through whom we may inquire of the LORD?" Then one of the king of Israel's servants answered, "Elisha the son of Shaphat is here, who poured water on the hands of Elijah." ¹²And Jehoshaphat said, "The word of the LORD is with him." So the king of Israel and Jehoshaphat and the king of Edom went down to him.

¹³And Elisha said to the king of Israel, "What have I to do with you? Go to the prophets of your father and to the prophets of your mother." But the king of Israel said to him, "No; it is the LORD who has called these three kings to give them into the hand of Moab." ¹⁴And Elisha said, "As the LORD of hosts lives, before whom I stand, were it not that I have regard for Jehoshaphat the king of Judah, I would neither look at you nor see you. ¹⁵But now bring me a musician." And when the musician played, the hand of the LORD came upon him. ¹⁶And he said, "Thus says the LORD, 'I will make this dry streambed full of pools.' ¹⁷For thus says the LORD, 'You shall not see wind or rain, but that streambed shall be filled with water, so that you shall drink, you, your livestock, and your animals.' ¹⁸This is a light thing in the sight of the LORD. He will also give the Moabites into your hand, ¹⁹and you shall attack every fortified city and every choice city, and shall fell every good tree and stop up all springs of water and ruin every good piece of land with stones." ²⁰The next morning, about the time of offering the sacrifice, behold, water came from the direction of Edom, till the country was filled with water.

²¹When all the Moabites heard that the kings had come up to fight against them, all who were able to put on armor, from the youngest to the oldest, were called out and were drawn up at the border. ²²And when they rose early in the morning and the sun shone on the water, the Moabites saw the water opposite them as red as blood. ²³And they said, "This is blood; the kings have surely fought together and struck one another down. Now then, Moab, to the spoil!" ²⁴But when they came to the camp of Israel, the Israelites rose and struck the Moabites, till they fled before them. And they went forward, striking the Moabites as they went.ᵃ ²⁵And they overthrew the cities, and on every good piece of land every man threw a stone until it was covered. They stopped every spring of water and felled all the good trees, till only its stones were left in Kir-hareseth, and the slingers surrounded and attacked it. ²⁶When the king of Moab saw that the battle was going against him, he took with him 700 swordsmen to break through, opposite the king of Edom, but they could not. ²⁷Then he took his oldest son who was to reign in his place and offered him for a burnt offering on the wall. And there came great wrath against Israel. And they withdrew from him and returned to their own land.

a Septuagint; the meaning of the Hebrew is uncertain

OVERVIEW: As Elisha asked for a musician before advising the kings, a musical interlude provides a break in this chapter's report of the war against Moab; the reformers laud music's many spiritual blessings. Other important themes of this chapter include the unlikely partnership between evil King Jehoram and righteous King Jehoshaphat, and God's blessing of victory to imperfect parties. Finally, the reformers denounce the king of Moab's sacrifice of his son as an act of idolatry and despair.

3:1-8 Jehoram and Jehoshaphat Join Forces

TWO AND A HALF KINGS. JOHANNES BUGENHAGEN: The pious Jehoshaphat had peace with the king of Israel, despite the latter's impiety, and he fought with him against the people whom God had made subject to Israel. Jehoshaphat probably also persuaded the king of Edom to come with them, because that king was also a subject to him and paid tribute to him. He was called a king, for he was the prince of the Edomites and their leader. But he was not a king, for the Edomites had not had their own king since the time of David, as it says in 2 Samuel 8. COMMENTARY ON 2 KINGS.[1]

CHOOSING BAD FRIENDS. JOHANNES PISCATOR: Jehoshaphat was an otherwise good king, except for the fact that he held a friendship with Jehoram, who was an ungodly and idolatrous king. From this we are given an example of the imperfection of his reform. Jehoshaphat's act was a great sin, on account of which he was formerly denounced by Jehu the prophet for giving aid to Ahab, as we read in 2 Chronicles: "But Jehu the son of Hanani the seer went out to meet him and said to King Jehoshaphat, 'Should you help the wicked and love those who hate the LORD? Because of this, wrath has gone out against you from the LORD.'" COMMENTARY ON 2 KINGS.[2]

3:9-14 Jehoram and Jehoshaphat Inquire of the Lord

FITTING SALUTATION. JOHN MAYER: Upon seeing King Jehoram of Israel, Elisha upbraided him by the prophets of his father and mother, bidding him to go to them. He was not to seek God's prophets, whom he hated, since he preferred to serve lifeless idols rather than the living God. For it is not to be expected that those who hate the servants of God—and will not hearken to them to amend their lives—should have comfort from them in time of necessity. Rather, they are to be left to perish without comfort in their distress. If necessity had not forced Jehoram to it, he would have never deigned to come to such a poor man as Elisha whom, he knew well enough, greeted him fittingly. Elisha did not seek to insult Jehoram; rather, he saw it as a fit time to reprove him in such a way that he might be ashamed of his former idolatry and his seeking of false prophets, which could offer him no help in time of need. COMMENTARY ON 2 KINGS.[3]

ELISHA'S QUESTION AND JEHORAM'S ANSWER. KONRAD PELLIKAN: Elisha asked this pointed question to Jehoram not out of contempt for the king but for the sake of God's glory and to reveal the wickedness the false prophets had spoken and done. For the prophets of the Lord had been killed, in hatred of the truth. Jehoram's mother had persecuted them with a deadly hatred, but now they were asking Elisha for help. The king of Israel responded in humility, as if to say: "Now, O prophet of God, is not the time to quarrel. Many things happened against my will, and now is not the time to repay the wrongs, whether mine or those of my dead parents. Instead please cry out to the Lord right now and, with God's help, come to the aid of the king's threatened armies so we do not succumb to hunger or get carried off by force into the hands of the Moabites." COMMENTARY ON 2 KINGS.[4]

---

[1]Bugenhagen, *In Regum duos ultimos libros*, 118; citing 2 Sam 8:14.
[2]Piscator, *Commentarii in omnes libros Veteris Testamenti*, 2:318; citing 2 Chron 19:2.

[3]Mayer, *Many Commentaries in One*, 159*.
[4]Pellikan, *Commentaria Bibliorum*, 2:175v-176r.

3:15 Elisha Requests a Musician

MUSIC COMBINED WITH GOD'S WORD. MAR-
TIN LUTHER: Next to the Word of God, music
deserves the highest praise. She is a mistress and
governess of those human emotions—to pass over
the animals—which as masters govern people or
more often overwhelm them. No greater commendation than this can be found—at least not by us.
For whether you wish to comfort the sad, to terrify
the happy, to encourage the despairing, to humble
the proud, to calm the passionate or to appease
those full of hate—and who could number all these
masters of the human heart, namely, the emotions,
inclinations and affections that impel men to evil or
good?—what more effective means than music
could you find? The Holy Ghost himself honors
her as an instrument for his proper work when in
his holy Scriptures he asserts that through her his
gifts were instilled in the holy prophets . . . as can be
seen in Elisha. . . . Thus it was not without reason
that the fathers and prophets wanted nothing else
to be associated as closely with the Word of God as
music. PREFACE TO THE GEORGE RHAU'S SYM-
PHONIAE IUCUNDAE.[5]

THE MINISTRY OF SONG. JOHANNES BUGENHA-
GEN: Elisha said to the king of Israel, "What have I
to do with you?" He condemned the king but still
displayed the benefits of God on account of
Jehoshaphat. Just as it has been commanded to us,
"Do not throw your pearls before pigs," still—for
the sake of those who do not despise the word—
we may prophesy even to the ungodly as a good
occasion for turning some of them eventually to
God. The Psalms, for example, say that some
ungodly yet attentive souls have been persuaded to
God. Indeed, they have been moved by the Psalms'
praise of God. Such prayers and songs of faith have
given them a desire for God's benefits and salvation.
For they may not have previously had reason to
consider what it says in God's Word and what the
Psalms often sing, namely, that God is a liberator,

savior, etc. For I marvel at how the various ways of
singing the divine Psalms changes their affect, so
that the ungodly are seen to get better, as we
discussed when David played his harp to improve
Saul's spirit in 1 Samuel. For the various ways of
singing these Psalms is what changes the message.
In this case the prophet wanted his spirit to be
lifted up through the psalm in invocation to God
to help Israel. Through the psalm he began to
prophesy. The godly people who were there were
doubtlessly restored in the word of God, just as it
says in the Acts of the Apostles, "While Peter was
still saying these things, the Holy Spirit fell on all
who heard the word." For the word or songs or
preaching of God cannot be heard in vain, except
by its despisers. The hand of God is said to come
on the prophets because—with the illuminated
and comforting Spirit—they preach, declare and
present the power of God and God himself.
COMMENTARY ON 2 KINGS.[6]

WHY ELISHA REQUESTED A MUSICIAN. JOHN
MAYER: Then Elisha said, "Now bring me a
musician." . . . As for why the prophet would request
music in preparation for his prophesying, there are
many interpretations. . . . Some think that Elisha's
mind, irritated by Jehoram's wickedness, might have
been pacified by the music. Therefore, so that he
might be more fit for divine revelations, which were
not immediately revealed when one's affections were
troubled, he requested the music. Some think he
requested it so that the people present would be
lifted up in their languishing minds, and so be made
more fit to receive comfort. . . . Some think that the
Spirit of God would not enter into a sad mind but
only a cheerful one, for which cause at times of
sacrificing they were bidden to cheer up themselves
by eating and drinking. For instance, before Isaac
gave a blessing, he requested venison. But Peter
Martyr Vermigli, who does not necessarily reject
the interpretations above, adds another. He thinks
that Elisha used music to invite the Spirit of God

---

[5]LW 53:323.

[6]Bugenhagen, *In Regum duos ultimos libros,* 119-20; citing Mt 6:6;
1 Sam 16:23; Acts 10:44.

to speak comfort to him by reciting in some sweet and heavenly tune the most memorable doings of the Lord for his people. That is, he used the music to praise God and to pray for the people. And this seems to me to be the main reason why Elisha called for a musician, the other reasons not being excluded. Elisha had been somewhat stirred in his mind against Jehoram's wickedness, and therefore partly to bring his mind into a calmer temper and partly to receive direction from the Spirit on how to provide against this present evil while hearing the praises of God sung, he called for one skilled in playing an instrument. Most likely, this was not just any musician, but a Levite or a godly man trained in this way. Thus also Theodoret and Procopius conjecture that the musician was a Levite and played some psalms of David. And in imitation of this, it is now happily a custom in our churches to sing a psalm before a sermon. We do this to invite the Spirit to come among us and to inspire us to speak to his glory and our mutual comfort. For this is the way we are to be filled with the Spirit. As Ephesians says, "And do not get drunk with wine, for that is debauchery, but be filled with the Spirit, addressing one another in psalms and hymns and spiritual songs, singing and making melody to the Lord with all your heart." Therefore this way is not only to be followed at church, but it is also to be followed at all times, so that we would be made partakers of divine and spiritual light and comfort. COMMENTARY ON 2 KINGS.[7]

MUSICAL PROPHECY. GIOVANNI DIODATI: Prophesying by music was the custom of prophets at that time. This practice elevated and purified the spirits and organs of the body by sounds and tunes of music. It was meant to prepare the soul to ask and receive prophetic inspirations by some holy subject, lively imprinted and vivified in the mind by the melody of the voice or musical instruments. Elisha was taken by a motion of the Holy Spirit, both to receive the divine revelation and to declare it with actions, motions and other prophetic fashions. ANNOTATIONS ON 2 KINGS.[8]

THE WONDER OF MUSIC. MARTIN LUTHER:

> For truth divine and God's own rede
> The heart of humble faith shall lead.
> Such did Elisha once propound
> When harping he the Spirit found.
> The best time of the year is mine
> When all the birds are singing fine.
> Heaven and earth their voices fill
> With right good song and tuneful trill.
> And, queen of all, the nightingale
> Men's hearts will merrily regale
> With music so charmingly gay;
> For which be thanks to her for aye.
> But thanks be first to God, our LORD,
> Who created her by his Word
> To be his own beloved songstress
> And of musica a mistress.
> For our dear LORD she sings her song
> In praise of him the whole day long;
> To him I give my melody
> And thanks in all eternity.

A PREFACE FOR ALL GOOD HYMNALS.[9]

3:16-20 God Promises Provision and Victory

MORE THAN WE ASK FOR. JOHANNES PISCATOR: God promised victory against Moab to Jehoram and his regal friends even though they had not asked for that. In fact they had only asked for water. But here we have an argument for the remarkable goodness of God, who acts on account of the greatness of his name rather than on account of our unworthiness. COMMENTARY ON 2 KINGS.[10]

WHENEVER GOD WANTS. JOHANNES PISCATOR: In the example of the present miracle whereupon the prayer of Elisha rain suddenly fills the valley

---

[7]Mayer, *Many Commentaries in One*, 160-61*; citing 2 Kings 3:15; Eph 5:18-19.

[8]Diodati, *Pious Annotations*, 18-19*.
[9]LW 53:320.
[10]Piscator, *Commentarii in omnes libros Veteris Testamenti*, 2:318.

with water, we are warned that God is not relegated to perform only second causes. On the contrary, God can demonstrate his power and goodness whenever he wants. COMMENTARY ON 2 KINGS.[11]

3:21-27 The King of Moab Sacrifices His Son

HOW NOT TO PLEASE GOD. JOHANNES BUGEN-HAGEN: The king of Moab burned his oldest son as a sacrifice to his gods, so that they would help him after they had been appeased. He did this "on the wall" in order that, having seen this humiliating thing, his enemies might be moved to pity and stop the battle. Amid the anguishing presence of sin and death, the ungodly despair. Sensing the judgment of God, they flee to their own works and to those who will give better judgments. The same is true today among those numberless sectarians and among those who do works of merit. In the true judgment of God, these works that are done to earn the best judgment are in God's sight the greatest abominations. So it was when this king of Moab had nothing better or more worthy to offer than his oldest son who was to reign in his place, as if it were a work that God Almighty could not possibly condemn. He did this despite the fact that murder is an abomination to God and humans, which God commanded the Israelites not to do in Deuteronomy 12. Perhaps the Gentiles had learned an example of this from the story of Isaac's sacrifice, which they were also aware of. Then some of the Israelites had impiously reaccepted this practice from the Gentiles, as it says in the Psalms, "They sacrificed their sons and their daughters to the demons." But imitating the saints is ungodliness unless you have the Word of God in your hearts, through which you know for certain what it means to please God. COMMENTARY ON 2 KINGS.[12]

BEWITCHED RELIGION. JOHANNES PISCATOR: In the example of the king of Moab offering his son as a sacrifice, we are warned that idolaters are bewitched by the devil. For when they are in dire straits, they do not hesitate to commit a horrible and wicked crime (which is a belief supported in their divine worship). COMMENTARY ON 2 KINGS.[13]

ON THE DISBANDING OF THE ARMIES AFTER THE HUMAN SACRIFICE. JOHN MAYER: The king of Moab, after hearing about his danger, immediately sacrificed his son. Then the angel that was set over Moab put in the mind of the Lord the great wickedness that the Israelites had done, as is complained about in Psalms 105 and 106, for which cause the Lord sent a plague into the camp of Israel. Many were destroyed and forced to depart. . . . Junius said that once the king of Moab's son was sacrificed, the Edomites were moved with indignation against Israel as the cause. And therefore they fell out with Israel and departed. This made the forces of the Israelites weak, which compelled them to depart. . . . There was great indignation in Israel. That is, because they were superstitious, they refused to proceed any more in the siege. They thought that if they did so, it would cost them dearly since so great a sacrifice was made. Others were not moved to fear this sacrifice, but still departed because the army had been greatly disbanded and it was therefore unable to proceed. In this way, by their own fault, the Israelites lost their opportunity to do all to the Moabites what had been prophesied, namely, reducing them to their former tributary status. And it is certainly not improbable that they were moved to disband at the sight of such a sacrifice. This was a gross error of many nations, which thought that the gods must be pacified, and that favor was obtained with these gods by offering human sacrifice. COMMENTARY ON 2 KINGS.[14]

---

[11]Piscator, *Commentarii in omnes libros Veteris Testamenti*, 2:318.
[12]Bugenhagen, *In Regum duos ultimos libros*, 121-22; citing Deut 12:31.

[13]Piscator, *Commentarii in omnes libros Veteris Testamenti*, 2:318.
[14]Mayer, *Many Commentaries in One*, 162-63*.

4:1–6:7 ELISHA'S MIRACLES

¹Now the wife of one of the sons of the prophets cried to Elisha, "Your servant my husband is dead, and you know that your servant feared the Lord, but the creditor has come to take my two children to be his slaves." ²And Elisha said to her, "What shall I do for you? Tell me; what have you in the house?" And she said, "Your servant has nothing in the house except a jar of oil." ³Then he said, "Go outside, borrow vessels from all your neighbors, empty vessels and not too few. ⁴Then go in and shut the door behind yourself and your sons and pour into all these vessels. And when one is full, set it aside." ⁵So she went from him and shut the door behind herself and her sons. And as she poured they brought the vessels to her. ⁶When the vessels were full, she said to her son, "Bring me another vessel." And he said to her, "There is not another." Then the oil stopped flowing. ⁷She came and told the man of God, and he said, "Go, sell the oil and pay your debts, and you and your sons can live on the rest."

⁸One day Elisha went on to Shunem, where a wealthy woman lived, who urged him to eat some food. So whenever he passed that way, he would turn in there to eat food. ⁹And she said to her husband, "Behold now, I know that this is a holy man of God who is continually passing our way. ¹⁰Let us make a small room on the roof with walls and put there for him a bed, a table, a chair, and a lamp, so that whenever he comes to us, he can go in there."

¹¹One day he came there, and he turned into the chamber and rested there. ¹²And he said to Gehazi his servant, "Call this Shunammite." When he had called her, she stood before him. ¹³And he said to him, "Say now to her, 'See, you have taken all this trouble for us; what is to be done for you? Would you have a word spoken on your behalf to the king or to the commander of the army?'" She answered, "I dwell among my own people." ¹⁴And he said, "What then is to be done for her?" Gehazi answered, "Well, she has no son, and her husband is old." ¹⁵He said, "Call her." And when he had called her, she stood in the doorway. ¹⁶And he said, "At this season, about this time next year, you shall embrace a son." And she said, "No, my lord, O man of God; do not lie to your servant." ¹⁷But the woman conceived, and she bore a son about that time the following spring, as Elisha had said to her.

¹⁸When the child had grown, he went out one day to his father among the reapers. ¹⁹And he said to his father, "Oh, my head, my head!" The father said to his servant, "Carry him to his mother." ²⁰And when he had lifted him and brought him to his mother, the child sat on her lap till noon, and then he died. ²¹And she went up and laid him on the bed of the man of God and shut the door behind him and went out. ²²Then she called to her husband and said, "Send me one of the servants and one of the donkeys, that I may quickly go to the man of God and come back again." ²³And he said, "Why will you go to him today? It is neither new moon nor Sabbath." She said, "All is well." ²⁴Then she saddled the donkey, and she said to her servant, "Urge the animal on; do not slacken the pace for me unless I tell you." ²⁵So she set out and came to the man of God at Mount Carmel.

When the man of God saw her coming, he said to Gehazi his servant, "Look, there is the Shunammite. ²⁶Run at once to meet her and say to her, 'Is all well with you? Is all well with your husband? Is all well with the child?'" And she answered, "All is well." ²⁷And when she came to the mountain to the man of God, she caught hold of his feet. And Gehazi came to push her away. But the man of God said, "Leave her alone, for she is in bitter distress, and the Lord has hidden it from me and has not told me." ²⁸Then she said, "Did I ask my lord for a son? Did I not say, 'Do not deceive me?'" ²⁹He said to Gehazi, "Tie up your garment and take my staff in your hand and go. If you meet anyone, do not greet him, and if anyone greets you, do not reply. And lay my staff on the face of the child." ³⁰Then the mother of the child said, "As the Lord lives and as you yourself live, I will not leave you." So he arose and followed her. ³¹Gehazi went on ahead and laid the staff on the face of the child, but there was no sound or sign of life. Therefore he returned to meet him and told him, "The child has not awakened."

³²When Elisha came into the house, he saw the child lying dead on his bed. ³³So he went in and shut the door behind the two of them and prayed to the Lord. ³⁴Then he went up and lay on the child, putting his mouth on his mouth, his eyes on his eyes, and his hands on his hands. And as he stretched himself upon him, the flesh of the child became warm. ³⁵Then he got up again and walked once back and forth in the house, and went up and stretched himself upon him. The child sneezed seven times, and the child opened his eyes. ³⁶Then he summoned Gehazi and said, "Call this Shunammite." So he called her. And when she came to him, he said, "Pick up your son." ³⁷She came and fell at his feet, bowing to the ground. Then she picked up her son and went out.

³⁸And Elisha came again to Gilgal when there was a famine in the land. And as the sons of the prophets were sitting before him, he said to his servant, "Set on the large pot, and boil stew for the sons of the prophets." ³⁹One of them went out into the field to gather herbs, and found a wild vine and gathered from it his lap full of wild gourds, and came and cut them up into the pot of stew, not knowing what they were. ⁴⁰And they poured out some for the men to eat. But while they were eating of the stew, they cried out, "O man of God, there is death in the pot!" And they could not eat it. ⁴¹He said, "Then bring flour." And he threw it into the pot and said, "Pour some out for the men, that they may eat." And there was no harm in the pot.

⁴²A man came from Baal-shalishah, bringing the man of God bread of the firstfruits, twenty loaves of barley and fresh ears of grain in his sack. And Elisha said, "Give to the men, that they may eat." ⁴³But his servant said, "How can I set this before a hundred men?" So he repeated, "Give them to the men, that they may eat, for thus says the Lord, 'They shall eat and have some left.'" ⁴⁴So he set it before them. And they ate and had some left, according to the word of the Lord.

5 Naaman, commander of the army of the king of Syria, was a great man with his master and in high favor, because by him the Lord had given victory to Syria. He was a mighty man of valor, but he was a leper.ᵃ ²Now the Syrians on one of their raids had carried off a little girl from the land of Israel, and she worked in the service of Naaman's wife. ³She said to her mistress, "Would that my lord were with the prophet who is in Samaria! He would cure him of his leprosy." ⁴So Naaman went in and told his lord, "Thus and so spoke the girl from the land of Israel." ⁵And the king of Syria said, "Go now, and I will send a letter to the king of Israel."

So he went, taking with him ten talents of silver, six thousand shekelsᵇ of gold, and ten changes of clothing. ⁶And he brought the letter to the king of Israel, which read, "When this letter reaches you, know that I have sent to you Naaman my servant, that you may cure him of his leprosy." ⁷And when the king of Israel read the letter, he tore his clothes and said, "Am I God, to kill and to make alive, that this man sends word to me to cure a man of his leprosy? Only consider, and see how he is seeking a quarrel with me."

⁸But when Elisha the man of God heard that the king of Israel had torn his clothes, he sent to the king, saying, "Why have you torn your clothes? Let him come now to me, that he may know that there is a prophet in Israel." ⁹So Naaman came with his horses and chariots and stood at the door of Elisha's house. ¹⁰And Elisha sent a messenger to him, saying, "Go and wash in the Jordan seven times, and your flesh shall be restored, and you shall be clean." ¹¹But Naaman was angry and went away, saying, "Behold, I thought that he would surely come out to me and stand and call upon the name of the Lord his God, and wave his hand over the place and cure the leper. ¹²Are not Abanaᶜ and Pharpar, the rivers of Damascus, better than all the waters of Israel? Could I not wash in them and be clean?" So he turned and went away in a rage. ¹³But his servants came near and said to him, "My father, it is a great word the prophet has spoken to you; will you not do it? Has he actually said to you, 'Wash, and be clean'?" ¹⁴So he went down and dipped himself seven times in the Jordan, according to the word of the man of God, and his flesh was restored like the flesh of a little child, and he was clean.

¹⁵Then he returned to the man of God, he and all his company, and he came and stood before him. And he said, "Behold, I know that there is no God in all the earth but in Israel; so accept now a present from your servant." ¹⁶But he said, "As the Lord lives, before whom I stand, I will receive none." And he urged him

to take it, but he refused. [17] Then Naaman said, "If not, please let there be given to your servant two mule loads of earth, for from now on your servant will not offer burnt offering or sacrifice to any god but the Lord. [18] In this matter may the Lord pardon your servant: when my master goes into the house of Rimmon to worship there, leaning on my arm, and I bow myself in the house of Rimmon, when I bow myself in the house of Rimmon, the Lord pardon your servant in this matter." [19] He said to him, "Go in peace."

But when Naaman had gone from him a short distance, [20] Gehazi, the servant of Elisha the man of God, said, "See, my master has spared this Naaman the Syrian, in not accepting from his hand what he brought. As the Lord lives, I will run after him and get something from him." [21] So Gehazi followed Naaman. And when Naaman saw someone running after him, he got down from the chariot to meet him and said, "Is all well?" [22] And he said, "All is well. My master has sent me to say, 'There have just now come to me from the hill country of Ephraim two young men of the sons of the prophets. Please give them a talent of silver and two changes of clothing.'" [23] And Naaman said, "Be pleased to accept two talents." And he urged him and tied up two talents of silver in two bags, with two changes of clothing, and laid them on two of his servants. And they carried them before

Gehazi. [24] And when he came to the hill, he took them from their hand and put them in the house, and he sent the men away, and they departed. [25] He went in and stood before his master, and Elisha said to him, "Where have you been, Gehazi?" And he said, "Your servant went nowhere." [26] But he said to him, "Did not my heart go when the man turned from his chariot to meet you? Was it a time to accept money and garments, olive orchards and vineyards, sheep and oxen, male servants and female servants? [27] Therefore the leprosy of Naaman shall cling to you and to your descendants forever." So he went out from his presence a leper, like snow.

6 Now the sons of the prophets said to Elisha, "See, the place where we dwell under your charge is too small for us. [2] Let us go to the Jordan and each of us get there a log, and let us make a place for us to dwell there." And he answered, "Go." [3] Then one of them said, "Be pleased to go with your servants." And he answered, "I will go." [4] So he went with them. And when they came to the Jordan, they cut down trees. [5] But as one was felling a log, his axe head fell into the water, and he cried out, "Alas, my master! It was borrowed." [6] Then the man of God said, "Where did it fall?" When he showed him the place, he cut off a stick and threw it in there and made the iron float. [7] And he said, "Take it up." So he reached out his hand and took it.

---

a *Leprosy* was a term for several skin diseases; see Leviticus 13   **b** A *talent* was about 75 pounds or 34 kilograms; a *shekel* was about 2/5 ounce or 11 grams   **c** Or *Amana*

Overview: Through the relationship between Elisha and the Shunammite woman, the reformers point to the blessings that come through calling on God and trusting in God's Word in times of trouble. Several commentators also make a contemporary connection between this story of Elisha caring for a prophet's widow and how communities of faith ought to care for ministers' families. The commentators flesh out similarities between Elisha and Christ, which arise with respect to the raising of the widow's son and the multiplication of loaves used to feed a large crowd. The reformers applaud the faith and wisdom of the Israelite serving girl, in contrast

to Naaman's suspicions about the value of bathing in the Jordan. On this point one theologian presents an Arminian interpretation, stating that Naaman's free will had a role in his being healed; others emphasize that Naaman passively received the promise of healing and the healing itself. Commentators differ widely over their interpretation of Naaman and Elisha's final conversation: some view this as an example of Christian freedom, in which those who live in faith are truly free with respect to the law; others do not interpret Elisha's "Go in peace" permissively but rather as a way of saying farewell without endorsing Naaman's future deeds or worship. More harmoniously, all the commentators have strong words of condemnation for Gehazi's greed and hypocrisy.

4:1-7 *The Widow's Oil*

MIRACLES PREACH THE WORD. JOHANNES BUGENHAGEN: The miracles God does through his prophets or preachers create faith in the Word that is preached or compassionately assist the poor in their need, just as you read of all these here in this chapter. Such miracles are certainly not done for show. An exception is when God permits them to be performed by false prophets who are against his Word in order to test whether people can remain in the true Word, as you read in Deuteronomy 13. Again, these miracles described here reveal that nothing is lacking for those who cling to the Word. For here the prophet is consulted; he is no prophet unless he has the Word of God. Thus God helps people through the prophets, that is, through preachers of God's Word. For such people have been afflicted in their hearts and oppressed with anguish in their consciences. For how unfortunate was the woman whose husband had died and who was about to lose her two children to permanent slavery? Or how nicely did Elisha speak to the woman who was suffering because her son, whom she had received through a heavenly blessing, was being carried off by death? Or consider the sons of the prophets, who were continuously fed by the Word of God and were not tempted in the least during a time of famine, even when they went out into the fields collecting herbs for the pot and if they ate it they would die, that is, the bitterness in the pot came to them. Christ truly came back to these miracles, so that the people said, "A great prophet has arisen among us!" and "God has visited his people!" He is the one who said, "I came not to call the righteous, but sinners" and "Blessed are those who hunger and thirst for righteousness, for they shall be satisfied." COMMENTARY ON 2 KINGS.[1]

GOD PROVIDES FOR THE FAITHFUL. JOHANNES PISCATOR: This miracle in which the oil of the widow was enlarged was not only so that the woman could sell the oil to pay back her creditors and become free from debt but also for her and her son to have reinforcement of food in order to live. We are warned from this that God will not desert the godly when in times of trouble as long as they implore his power. Indeed, God is able to abundantly provide all that is needed. COMMENTARY ON 2 KINGS.[2]

LESSON ON TAKING CARE OF A DECEASED MINISTER'S FAMILY. JOHN MAYER: Once the widow's oil had been miraculously increased, the prophet bid her to sell as much of it as would pay the creditors. Then she was to live on the rest. This teaches us that debts must be paid even though the creditor is rich and the debtor is poor, and even though we will have little after paying a lot. Now it is by God's providence that some are rich and others are poor. And the poor may not take or withhold anything from the rich that is theirs. Rather they are to deal justly with everyone. And if this means a person will be destitute for doing so, they must remember that they have a Father in heaven to provide for them. This heavenly Father will not allow those who fear him to lack what is needed. Therefore we are to trust in God and cry to him—he who feeds the very ravens that cry to him. In this instance we see that the widow and children of a prophet had enough on which to live. This shows us that the widows and children of faithful ministers of God's Word are not to be destitute. Rather they are to be provided for by those who have the power to provide for them in their communities. COMMENTARY ON 2 KINGS.[3]

THE WIDOW'S CHOICE. THOMAS JACKSON: It was the poor widow's choice to give or not to give Elisha a cake of her small store of oil and meal. But if she had refused to do as the prophet advised

---

[1]Bugenhagen, *In Regum duos ultimos libros*, 122-23; citing Deut 13:1-5; Lk 7:16; Mt 9:13; Mt 5:6.

[2]Piscator, *Commentarii in omnes libros Veteris Testamenti*, 2:322. [3]Mayer, *Many Commentaries in One*, 164-65*.

her, God would not have miraculously multiplied the oil and meal in her jar. So, then, in the working of this miracle God had no partner. It was merely his doing. But in bestowing these alms to the prophet, the poor widow partly did contribute. This was an act or exercise of her free will and lovingkindness. It was no fruit of her sanctifying grace. In like manner, to humble ourselves or to cast ourselves down before God that we may be partakers of sanctifying grace is partly our work. It is strictly required at every person's hand who hopes to be a partaker of this grace. But the lifting of us up—that is, our conversion to God—is merely, solely and totally God's work. In this work of conversion, we are merely passive. That is, we are as . . . the poor widow's oil and meal in the miracle God wrought in it. But we are not passive to the extent that we played no part in humbling or casting ourselves down. CHRIST'S ANSWER TO JOHN'S QUESTION.[4]

GOD'S PROVISION OF WIDOWS. CHARLES DRELINCOURT: I must . . . take notice here of an admirable story to comfort every faithful servant of God. The widow of a deceased prophet made this bitter complaint to Elisha, "Your servant my husband is dead, and you know that your servant feared the LORD, but the creditor has come to take my two children to be his slaves." God, who hears the cry of the afflicted, had compassion on that poor, distressed widow. Therefore he gave to her by Elisha's means, in a wonderful manner, sufficient payment of her debts and enough nourishment for her family. By this glorious example God declares the care that he will have of his prophets' widows as long as they walk in fear of the LORD and continue in his holy covenant. CHRISTIAN DEFENSE AGAINST THE FEARS OF DEATH.[5]

PROPHETS' WIVES. JOHANNES BUGENHAGEN: The Latin reads, "a woman from the wives of the prophets." The Hebrew says, "from the wives of

the sons of the prophets." Today the "sons of the prophets" would mean those who study sacred Scripture. They are greatly blessed and it is only because of "the teachings of demons" that they have been forbidden to have wives, etc. COMMENTARY ON 2 KINGS.[6]

4:8-17 *The Shunammite Woman*

WEALTH AND HOSPITALITY. VIKTORIN STRIGEL: In the beginning of this chapter, Scripture gives an example of how the widowed woman bore her poverty without being crushed by it. . . . Now it gives an example of how another holy woman rightly used her great wealth. For both women are exemplary: the one in how to bear poverty and the other in how to use riches. These resources and blessings have been given by God not for the sake of luxury or inane ornamentation but to care for one's needs, assist the ministry of the gospel, serve the state and redress the suffering of the poor. Thus the law commands the first tenth of the harvest be brought to the tabernacle and given to the priests for the preservation of the ministry. It also requires giving one-fifth to the king and leaving the gleanings for the poor. This shows, then, that this wealthy Shunammite woman is offering much kindness to the prophet Elisha. For she was not content with just the basic tasks of hospitality but also troubled herself to build him a room with a bed, in which he could sleep, eat or sit and think. She overlooked nothing in how to care for this man of God. To further show how much we ought to imitate this pious example of how to use wealth, remember the promise of Christ: whoever gives a cup of water in the name of God will not lose their reward. Therefore pious wanderers are imitators of Elisha, who conducted himself in such a way that true and holy acts of hospitality might increase. BOOK OF KINGS.[7]

---

[4]Jackson, *Works*, 558*.
[5]Drelincourt, *Christian's Defense Against the Fears of Death*, 208-9*.

[6]Bugenhagen, *In Regum duos ultimos libros*, 123-24; citing 1 Tim 4:1-4.
[7]Strigel, *Libri Samuelis, Regum et Paralipomenon*, 317-18; citing Mt 10:42.

HOSPITALITY TO GOD'S MINISTERS. JO-HANNES PISCATOR: This Shunammite woman sets forth a wonderful example of hospitality and benevolence toward the words of God's ministers. And as a result of her actions she is blessed by God. COMMENTARY ON 2 KINGS.[8]

GENEROUS AND BOUNTIFUL GOD. EDWARD REYNOLDS: God deals with his servants as the prophet did with the woman of Shunem. When Elisha asked her what she needed for the kindness she had done to him, she did not request anything at his hands. He then sent for her again and made her a free promise of that which she most wanted and desired: that she could have son. In a similar way, God is often pleased to give his servants such things as they forget to ask—or gives them the things they ask in a fuller measure than their own desires propose to them. SEVEN SERMONS ON FOURTEENTH CHAPTER OF HOSEA.[9]

4:18-31 The Shunammite's Faith

DISCIPLINE FROM MOTHER CHURCH. THOMAS ADAMS: The best remedy for a headache is discipline, just as the father said to the servant when he heard his son complaining, "My head! My head." "Carry him to his mother," the man said. We should do likewise when people complain of headaches: Take them to their mother, the church, and let her discipline them. DISEASES OF THE SOUL.[10]

EXAMPLE OF FAITH. JOHANNES PISCATOR: A wonderful example of the Shunammite's faith and charity is set forth in this passage. For she was mindful that her son was given by the power of Elisha beyond the means of nature, that is, miraculously and supernaturally. She believed, in a similar way, that Elisha could give life back to her son. . . . Therefore she implored the prophet's power. We see a similar example of David's faith in his fight against Goliath: "David said, 'The LORD who delivered me from the paw of the lion and from the paw of the bear will deliver me from the hand of this Philistine.'" COMMENTARY ON 2 KINGS.[11]

THE WOMAN'S FAITH. JOHANNES BUGENHAGEN: The child whom God gave through the word of the prophet was being taken away as a great affliction. But see the faith of this little woman! She did not despair that God, through Elisha, could bring back the one who had earlier been given as a sign of blessing. But she hastened to Elisha in great fear that her son was in danger of death, that infirmity which is related to faith and of which you have many examples in the Gospels. This is also relevant, that she wanted the prophet to come with his staff and not the servant. The servant could do nothing, because the woman did not believe it would be effective. If she could have believed it, the servant also could have raised the dead boy with the staff through Elisha, for "all things are possible for one who believes." And, as you read, sometimes Jesus did not do any miracles because of the people's unbelief. COMMENTARY ON 2 KINGS.[12]

4:32-37 Elisha Raises the Shunammite's Boy from the Dead

BECOMING ALL THINGS TO ALL PEOPLE. JOHANNES PISCATOR: Ministers of the Word are given an example through Elisha's satisfying the wish of the Shunammite in bringing her son back to life. That is, ministers are advised that it is their ministerial office to accommodate to the weaknesses of the faithful. We see a similar example in Paul: "To the weak I became weak, that I might win the weak. I have become all things to all people, that by all means I might save some." COMMENTARY ON 2 KINGS.[13]

---

[8]Piscator, *Commentarii in omnes libros Veteris Testamenti*, 2:322.
[9]Reynolds, *Works*, 3:321*.
[10]Adams, *Diseases of the Soul*, 7.

[11]Piscator, *Commentarii in omnes libros Veteris Testamenti*, 2:322; citing 1 Sam 17:37.
[12]Bugenhagen, *In Regum duos ultimos libros*, 124-25; citing Mk 9:23; Mt 13:58.
[13]Piscator, *Commentarii in omnes libros Veteris Testamenti*, 2:323; citing 1 Cor 9:22.

Elisha's Prayer. Johannes Bugenhagen: This prayer, which was a prayer of faith, raised the dead. To the temptation of the prophet, it was not heard immediately. The prophet worked anxiously that his cause might be heard by God. But God was affected, for God favored this woman who had already been helped. She urged the prophet through God to do this work for her that you see. Otherwise nothing would prevail for the resurrection of the dead. So God greatly favored the cause and raised the one on whom Elisha laid himself. Commentary on 2 Kings.[14]

Performing Miracles as God Pleases. Johannes Piscator: The example of Elisha's bringing the Shunammite's boy back to life demonstrates how God works miracles in various ways. For instance, sometimes God performs miracles instantly. Such is how Christ brought back to life the daughter of Jairus, the son of the widow in the town of Nain and Lazarus in Bethany. At other times, miracles take time, as if they are completed in degrees. Such is how Elisha raised to life this boy of the Shunammite; and it's also similar to the way Elijah brought back to life the son of the widow at Zarephath. In fact it's also the way Christ restored the sight of the blind man in Mark 8. From this it appears that God is free to act as he chooses, and that he is not at all hindered by second causes. Commentary on 2 Kings.[15]

The Law and the Spirit. John Mayer: Elisha lay on the dead body, his face to the face of the child. First the body began to be warmed, and then Elisha stretched out himself on the child until he sneezed. The child then opened his eyes as if awakened out of sleep. A similar procedure was done before by Elijah in 1 Kings 17. . . . But whereas Elijah stretched himself on the child three times, Elisha did it but twice. By this it may be understood to confirm the promise before saying that the spirit of Elijah should be doubled on Elisha. . . .

And whereas Elisha did one thing that Elijah did not do, namely, cause his staff to be used first—which came to no effect—this teaches us allegorically that the law was used before the coming of Christ to revive people dead in sin by doing it in vain. But afterward Christ came with the Spirit and gave life to all who believe. And the law . . . was aptly set forth by a staff, which supported and struck. But just as Elisha revived this child by applying his own mouth and eyes to the child's, so Christ gives life to the faithful by condescending to be made like us in his incarnation. Commentary on 2 Kings.[16]

4:38-44 Multiplying Bread

Abundance Today. Lucas Osiander: Though such miracles as this one of abundant bread or Christ's miracle of feeding thousands of people with a few loaves and fishes do not happen today, nevertheless Christ—in the name of our heavenly Father—has promised us food and clothing. We should therefore learn from this and similar miracles to trust in our Lord God, not doubting in the slightest that such things are at hand for us. For God is able and willing to create abundance in order that we might be fed and kept safe. And just as Elisha shared with others and still lacked nothing himself but rather had an abundance, so those who by faith assist their neighbors through charity shall never be in want (Proverbs 11, 19 and 28). Annotations on 2 Kings.[17]

Elisha's Servant as Incredulous as Jesus' Disciples. Johannes Piscator: Elisha's act of providing for one hundred people out of twenty loaves of bread sets forth an incredible example of a miracle. A similar miracle takes place in the ministry of Jesus, where his disciples doubt his ability to feed so many people in relation to so little food in John 6. Commentary on 2 Kings.[18]

---

[14]Bugenhagen, *In Regum duos ultimos libros*, 125.
[15]Piscator, *Commentarii in omnes libros Veteris Testamenti*, 2:323.
[16]Mayer, *Many Commentaries in One*, 166, 169*.
[17]Osiander, *Liber Iosue*, 888-89.
[18]Piscator, *Commentarii in omnes libros Veteris Testamenti*, 2:323.

FORETASTE OF JESUS' FEEDING MIRACLES. JOHN MAYER: When Elisha, the man of God, ordered these few loaves of bread to be set before the hundred men, his servant spoke against him since there was too little to satisfy everyone. But Elisha urged him on, saying, "Thus says the LORD, 'They shall eat and have some left.'" God, at this instant, most probably revealed to Elisha that he would work this miracle as Elisha desired. For although no mention is made here of Elisha's blessing the bread by prayer, Theodoret speaks of it as done immediately before the distributing of the bread among them. Therefore it is to be understood that he first prayed for this blessing and then distributed the bread among them. And here Elisha noticeably served as a figure of our Savior Christ, who later fed five thousand with a few loaves of bread and fish, as Christ was far more full of the Spirit than Elisha was. COMMENTARY ON 2 KINGS.[19]

5:1-7 Naaman and the Faith of a Young Captive Girl

OUR GOD REAPS SALVATION FROM THE SEED OF MISFORTUNES. HIERONYMUS WELLER VON MOLSDORF: This example of the captured girl shows why God now and then thrusts the saints into misfortunes: without a doubt so that they would become the occasion and cause of salvation, both for themselves and others, as it is said elsewhere. And so we are not troubled in spirit, nor do we abandon hope in salvation when some astounding misfortune falls on us. By this captured girl's example we should strengthen ourselves. Her captivity was the occasion and cause of both Naaman's cleansing and conversion. We should submit to our spirit; "for those who love God all things work together for good." And this from Augustine: "God is so good that he lets no evil thing happen, unless he knows that from it some good will result," etc.[20] Here we should gather the examples of saints whose misfortunes yielded salva-

tion—like the example of the patriarch Joseph. Why should we not also say this here, that surely God's plan will happen when good and pious people now and then are forced to serve the impious and criminal? Again, pious and peaceful husbands have finicky and impious wives, and holy women are married to rough, churlish and impious husbands, without a doubt, so that by their holy conduct and pious example they should lead them to the true knowledge of God—as the example of St. Augustine's mother Monica shows. ANNOTATIONS ON 2 KINGS.[21]

NAAMAN'S SERVING GIRL. LUCAS OSIANDER: Roused by the Holy Spirit, the Israelite serving girl believed that the prophet could and would heal Naaman, if Naaman would go to him. Naaman's wife reported to him what she had heard from the girl and persuaded him not to reject the girl's suggestion, even though she was a captive, for sometimes such women give salutary advice, providing indispensible aid to sick people. ANNOTATIONS ON 2 KINGS.[22]

THE GOODNESS OF NAAMAN'S SERVANT AND MASTER. JOHANNES PISCATOR: In this servant's longing for the good health of her master an example is set forth of honoring one's superiors, which is demanded in the fifth commandment: "Honor your father and your mother." Similarly, that the king of Syria[23] allowed one of his subjects to go to Israel in order to recuperate his health sets forth an example of a merciful and benign master. COMMENTARY ON 2 KINGS.[24]

5:8-14a Immersion in the Jordan River

HOW NAAMAN'S WASHING DIFFERED FROM BAPTISM. PETER MARTYR VERMIGLI: In the Gospel the man who was blind was sent to the

---

[19]Mayer, *Many Commentaries in One*, 171*.
[20]See, for example, *Enchiridion* 27; NPNF 3:246.

[21]Weller, *Liber secundus Regum*, 15v.
[22]Osiander, *Liber Iosue*, 890.
[23]That is, the king of Aram.
[24]Piscator, *Commentarii in omnes libros Veteris Testamenti*, 2:326; citing Ex 20:12.

pool in Siloam so that he would be healed. And it is not to be doubted that this was a prelude to baptism, seeing that many similar cases on both sides existed. And although they are given here in likeness, there are clear differences. One of these differences is that baptism is not to be repeated, while Naaman's washing in the Jordan River seven times was repeated. It is enough for us Christians to be dipped once. Commentary on 2 Kings.[25]

Water and God's Word. Johannes Bugenhagen: Naaman's bathing in water and the Word is a sign of what Paul said about Christ cleansing the church through the cleansing water of the Word of life. Without the Word and promise of God, the water is nothing, just as others had bathed countless times in the Jordan and were not cleansed. But Naaman was cleansed because he had the promise: "Wash and you shall be clean." If he had had no regard for this promise but had gone into only the water, he would have erred and the leprosy would have remained, just as reason judges our righteousness. This and other great works only condemn those who are given them if they do not have faith in the word God sends. This is so that they may be saved by faith. Thus Naaman mocked the Jordan while he gave greater respect to his native rivers and spoke well of them. That he was washed not once but seven times indicates that he needed to be baptized continuously with a pious bath in the Word through the Spirit. The one who was washed once did not enter into it without the fear of God. Commentary on 2 Kings.[26]

Humble Means of Grace. Lucas Osiander: When Naaman spurned Elisha's instructions about bathing in the Jordan, his servants pleaded with their master, saying, "Why do you have difficulty doing such a small thing? Do you really think that the Lord God is not able to make great and beneficial things happen through the most common means?" For it is wrong when people use human reasoning to make judgments about means of divine healing (like baptism, the Word of God and the Lord's Supper) because those things seem common or useless and not like great things to us. So you see that the servants judged better than their lord; in turn, their master was not too proud to obey the good advice of his servants. Annotations on 2 Kings.[27]

Illustration of Free Will. Thomas Jackson: At this time I will only acquaint you with that which I have elsewhere delivered. It has to do with the true mean between the opposite opinions of the Lutherans and the Calvinists, between the Jesuits and the Dominicans and between the Stoics and the Pelagians. I am referring, of course, to the power of a person to work or to not work out their own salvation. The mean is that, although a person has no freedom of will or ability to do that which is good or to dispose their heart for the better receiving of grace, they have a true possibility or freedom of will to do or not to do something required by God. If this thing is done by a person, God will dispose their heart and make it fit for his grace. If the same thing is not done or is neglected, the person's heart who shows neglect shall be more indisposed and more incapable of grace than beforehand.

For illustration of this point, I have given as an example . . . Naaman the Syrian. . . . Naaman had no power or free will to cleanse himself of his leprosy either in whole or in part. At the same time, he did have a true freedom of will to wash or not to wash himself in the Jordan River. Now, if he had decided to leave in such a sullen fit—as he initially thought upon hearing the prophet's advice—and not at all to have washed himself in the Jordan, he would have returned home a fouler leper than he came. So, then, although the cure of his leprosy was altogether God's work and Naaman had no hand in it, Naaman did have a hand in deciding to

[25]Vermigli, *Regnum Libri Duo*, 238.
[26]Bugenhagen, *In Regum duos ultimos libros*, 128; citing Eph 5:26.
[27]Osiander, *Liber Iosue*, 893.

dip himself in the Jordan. It was an exercise of his free will, which God has taken from no person—even after Adam's fall. CHRIST'S ANSWER UNTO JOHN'S QUESTION.[28]

5:14b-15 A Weak Body Turns into a Strong Faith

RECIPIENT OF THE HOLY SPIRIT. MARTIN LUTHER: Naaman the Syrian was no doubt a good and devout man and had a correct idea of God. And although he was a Gentile and did not belong to the kingdom of Moses . . . still his flesh was purified, the God of Israel was revealed to him and he received the Holy Spirit. LECTURES ON GALATIANS.[29]

BODILY INFLICTIONS CAN BE A GOOD THING. JOHANNES PISCATOR: Naaman was cured miraculously from leprosy, and he also took this occasion to embrace the true religion. From this we are warned that God sometimes allows his elect to experience bodily inflictions so that they may recognize the truth and be led to everlasting salvation. In this way, bodily inflictions are not clear signs of God's disfavor. COMMENTARY ON 2 KINGS.[30]

SICKNESS THEN FAITH. THOMAS ADAMS: Miseries often lead a person to mercies. . . . A weak body is an occasion for a strong faith. . . . It was good for Naaman that he was a leper because this brought him to Elisha, which in turn brought Elisha to God. THE SINNER'S PASSING-BELL.[31]

ELISHA AS A TYPE OF CHRIST. BENEDICT ARETIUS: Naaman the Syrian was cured from his leprosy by Elisha the prophet, just as our leprosy is cured by Christ. COMMON PLACES OF THE CHRISTIAN RELIGION.[32]

BEING CONFORMED TO GOD'S WAYS. JOHN MAYER: Naaman was healed for simply doing what Elisha sent word for him to do. Otherwise Naaman might happily have thought that he was healed by some virtue coming from Elisha and therefore not attributing enough to God's power. But now that God's power was apparent, he could deter the Syrians from advancing on Israel, since Israel had such a mighty God to protect them.

. . . It was not pride but great humility that led Elisha to act the way he did. He wanted to do nothing but attribute God's power to this miracle, by whom he was directed to perform this feat. Also, Naaman's pride was to be pulled down, and by humility and obedience he was to do what was commanded, although it seemed too weak to produce the desired effect. And Naaman initially became angry, thinking himself mocked. . . . The problem was that Naaman had already imagined how the miracle would be performed. He thought Elisha would meet him, pray for him and lay his hand on the leprosy, and by such means healing would take place. He did not imagine there would be any virtue in washing himself in the Jordan River. In this way people sometimes prescribe to God the way in which he should help them. And if God does not act as we demand, we despair. Instead we must allow God to act as he chooses, even though it might seem foolish to us. COMMENTARY ON 2 KINGS.[33]

5:16-19 "Go in Peace"

BOWING IN THE HOUSE OF RIMMON. JOHANNES BUGENHAGEN: It is seen as a truly difficult question when Elisha permits Naaman a certain dissimilation when Naaman wants to worship with his king in the temple of Rimmon though his heart will be turned to God. Could he not instruct the king, so that he might worship and confess God without dissimilation and fear of a person? Here you certainly read what Naaman sensed and feared, but you do not read what

[28]Jackson, *Works*, 558*.
[29]LW 26:211.
[30]Piscator, *Commentarii in omnes libros Veteris Testamenti*, 2:326.
[31]Adams, *Devil's Banquet*, 257*.
[32]Aretius, *Loci communes*, 121.

[33]Mayer, *Many Commentaries in One*, 173-74*.

happened later. Indeed the prophet did not make any recommendation about what he should do or not do. But he simply said, "Go in peace," as if to say, "I do not now require anything of you, whom God has created. You have begun to be justified, you acknowledge the God of Israel, you have a sense of guilt and you know that this dissimilation is not worthy of the worship of God. Go in peace.' He who began a good work in you will bring it to completion,' so that you may do the things that are pleasing to God." COMMENTARY ON 2 KINGS.[34]

NAAMAN ONLY GIVEN PERMISSION TO PERFORM HIS OFFICE. JOHN MAYER: In saying, "Go in peace," Elisha secures Naaman from all danger of sinning in the performance of his office to his master, either outside of the house of Rimmon or inside it. And yet he gives no dispensation to him, or any other, to pretend to give any outward reverence to an idol. For all worship in this way of religion, both outward and inward, is to be given to God alone. For the argument brought forward to prove that Naaman intended to seek pardon for sinning, I give two responses. First, it was Naaman's ignorance that made him fear being in the house of Rimmon to be a sin. And it is no good for us simply to conclude something is a sin based on ignorance. Second, Naaman's public profession made by bringing earth out of Israel to make an altar to sacrifice to the true God alone freed him sufficiently from all appearances of evil before others. It gave the appearance that what Naaman did in the temple of Rimmon was without any respect to the idol and only out of respect to his master. And simply to be present at idolatry for some other end, without in any way supporting that sacrilegious act, is not to be censured as a sin. For instance, the prophet Elijah was present when the worshipers of Baal sacrificed to their god, but he derided them as they did so. Also, the three children in Daniel were present when the golden image was set up by Nebuchadnezzar. But although Naaman did not sin in his service done for his master while in a false temple, those who are present at idolatrous worship services only out of curiosity or because they attend such services out of fear that they may not be seen there, this is tantamount to deceit, which God does not endure. COMMENTARY ON 2 KINGS.[35]

NEITHER APPROVAL NOR REJECTION. GIOVANNI DIODATI: Naaman thought the earth of this country was consecrated to the Lord and that it would be fit for making sacrifices. He therefore wanted to keep it as pledge of his communion with God's people. This demand had a show of good zeal, but it was without knowledge. For the holiness of this washing service was not attached to the material earth but rather to the observing of God's commandment. God alone was to be worshiped in that place.

Naaman's request to bow down was without any intent of committing idolatry. It was only done for a ceremony of honor to the king. But he acknowledges that he did sin by bowing down to Rimmon, an idol of the Syrians, by means of his remorse and doubt. The prophet's reply to "go in peace" does not indicate his approval of this lying or division of the heart from the act of the body. For to do something in one's body contrary to one's heart is condemned everywhere in Scripture. The meaning of this statement, therefore, is that the Lord gave no commission to Naaman. Nor did the Lord reveal to Elisha how he should instruct Naaman any further in true religion or how to incorporate him into the body of God's people. Instead Elisha only takes his leave of Naaman without otherwise answering his question. It is as if Elisha had said: "Content yourself with the benefit that you have already received at God's hands." ANNOTATIONS ON 2 KINGS.[36]

DISMISSED WITHOUT APPROVAL. BENEDICT ARETIUS: Some say that Naaman the Syrian received from Elisha an allowance to worship in the temple of Rimmon without punishment. . . .

---

[34]Bugenhagen, *In Regum duos ultimos libros*, 129-30; citing Phil 1:6.

[35]Mayer, *Many Commentaries in One*, 178*; citing 2 Kings 5:19.
[36]Diodati, *Pious Annotations*, 20*.

But I respond that this is a false notion. For Elisha did not grant Naaman what he asked. He simply sent him out peacefully: "Go in peace," he said. These words did not allow him to do that which was forbidden. They simply allowed him to be dismissed without giving approval. COMMON PLACES OF THE CHRISTIAN RELIGION.[37]

PARDON FOR PAST OFFENSES. DANIEL DYKE: Naaman petitions the prophet, "In this matter may the LORD pardon your servant: when my master goes into the house of Rimmon to worship there...." And the prophet replies, "Go in peace." Here is my response to this passage. The words in the original Hebrew, as some learned scholars have observed, may be read thus: "May the LORD pardon your servant, for I have gone into the house of Rimmon...." This shows that Naaman now desires wholly to cleave to the true God. He craves pardon for that which he had done, not for that which he was to do. The terminology is used in the same manner in the inscription of two psalms together. THE MYSTERY OF SELF-DECEIVING.[38]

PRACTICAL APPLICATION IN WITTENBERG. JOHANNES BUGENHAGEN: On the basis of Elisha's words "Go in peace" to Naaman about bowing to Rimmon, when people write to Wittenberg and ask us what they should do about impiety in this or that case, we do not need to prescribe many laws. Instead, in such matters we commend the magistrate to the Spirit of God, who is already at work in them, which ought to make impious people shudder. For there will never be an occasion in which those whom we have commanded to do one thing may not do something else than what we recommended, just as this washing teaches. For it is those people who cannot go without choosing sides between the impious or our opinions who drive themselves away from the Spirit of God later anyway. Therefore, when we give such advice to people, we say, "Go in peace. We commit you to

God, who will himself care for you." We say this against those who immediately condemn imperfection, ignoring this word of Paul, "Who are you to pass judgment on the servant of another? It is before his own master that he stands or falls. And he will be upheld, for the Lord is able to make him stand." COMMENTARY ON 2 KINGS.[39]

5:20-27 Gehazi's Punishment

GEHAZI LIKE ANANIAS AND SAPPHIRA. JOHANNES PISCATOR: In the example of Gehazi being convicted by Elisha of lying, we have a warning of how not to act. For God shames hypocrites who seek their own glory by lying and by cheating. We have a similar example of this in Ananias and Sapphira in Acts 5. COMMENTARY ON 2 KINGS.[40]

NOTHING UNSEEN. HENRY AIRAY: Beloved, our God whom we serve is not a person who has limited vision. No, God sees all things. He is present everywhere, he searches everyone's heart and mind, and he understands all our thoughts long before they are conceived. There is no fooling God. Whatever we do in the darkness, it is to God as if it were done in the light; for the darkness and light to him are both alike. Gehazi tried to deceive Elisha when he was not watching. But if Elisha could discover (and, in fact, see) his fault, how much more can our God see all our ways, however hidden we think they may be. LECTURES ON PHILIPPIANS.[41]

POWER OF THE SPIRIT. JOHN DAVENANT: "For though I am absent from you in the body, I am present with you in spirit." Here Paul shows that he was never so far absent from the Colossians but that in mind, in care and in thought he was present with them, because he never put the recollection of them out of his mind. For it is the peculiarity of the lover not to be severed in mind

[37]Aretius, *Loci communes*, 728-29.
[38]Dyke, *The Mystery of Self-Deceiving*, 221-22*.
[39]Bugenhagen, *In Regum duos ultimos libros*, 130; citing Rom 14:4.
[40]Piscator, *Commentarii in omnes libros Veteris Testamenti*, 2:327.
[41]Airay, *Lectures on Philippians*, 140*.

from those whom he loves, although separated by distance of place. But Ambrose of Milan, and some modern interpreters also, explain these words, "I am present with you in spirit," not only of that thought and remembrance of them but of some extraordinary presence of the Spirit granted to the apostle by divine power. This is the presence of the Spirit that Elisha had, who perceived in his mind those things that were done by his servant equally as though he had stood before him: "Was not my spirit with you when the man got down from his chariot to meet you?" The prophet remained in his house and yet he says that his heart went with his servant, because he saw as clearly his act as those who were present when he met them. . . . We do not therefore deny that what was granted to the prophets like Elisha could have been granted to an apostle also: since the care of all the churches was laid on the apostle Paul, it is very likely that the state of all the churches was also known to him, not only from the vague report of humans but also from the revelation of the divine Spirit—to the intent that he might better consult and provide for the necessities of the churches. We therefore admit and unite both interpretations, stating that the apostle was with the Colossians as well in the meditation of his mind, as in the revelation of the Spirit—although absent in body. EXPOSITION OF COLOSSIANS 2:5.[42]

GEHAZI'S SACRILEGE AS AN ABOMINATION.

JOHN MAYER: Gehazi's punishment was most just, that having Naaman's money he should together with it have his leprosy. This is in just response to his grasping after filthy money—which is a disease—and for his secretly selling the grace of God. . . . Mystically this teaches us that those who provide for their children by unjust means and seek to get riches for them in this way provide ill for their children. They will justly receive God's judgment. This is most often seen in that the children are either tied with the same servile bands of covetousness or they break out with the leprosy

of riotousness, which can never be healed. . . . God made Gehazi and his seed a lasting monument of the odiousness of sacrilege, so that in the ages to come their kind might be pointed at and said, "Behold, the fruit of sacrilege is to contaminate others," which is an abomination. COMMENTARY ON 2 KINGS.[43]

BAD BARGAIN.

EDWARD REYNOLDS: Gehazi's presumptions were many. He thought he was getting a good bargain: He could now buy garments, olive yards, vineyards, sheep and oxen and male and female servants at the price a soldier's gift. He thought he had provided well for his posterity by the reward of Naaman, but the event proves quite the contrary: What he received in the end was a deformed posterity not only for himself by also for his seed forever. THE VANITY OF THE CREATURE.[44]

6:1-4 The Company of the Prophets Ask Elisha for a Favor

MANY HUMBLE PREACHERS UNDER ELISHA.

JOHANNES BUGENHAGEN: The sons or disciples of the prophet had multiplied so that the area around Elisha could not hold them. This was a great multiplication of the word, a revelation against the ungodly king and for the kingdom of truth, so that no one would have a reason for perishing in error. For, as you see, God does not send the word of prophets and preachers in vain. For many came to the disciples when they condemned the source of people's troubles, especially their riches, powers and wisdom. These disciples were certainly not rich, as the dwelling place was not even large enough for them to live there, while the priests of the golden calves had abundance and were greatly esteemed. If we want to see anything else, then we are fools still today, because the Lord always arranged it thus that the poor are brought the gospel and God makes it the same for the heralds of his word, so that the unworthy ones will judge

---

[42]Davenant, *Exposition of Colossians*, 1:371-72*; citing Col 2:5.

[43]Mayer, *Many Commentaries in One*, 180*.
[44]Reynolds, *Works*, 1:72*.

those who honor themselves and honor those whom the world condemns and neglects. COMMENTARY ON 2 KINGS.[45]

THE LORD OF NATURE. KONRAD PELLIKAN: The sons of the prophets called out to their master not to flatter him but in recognition that the benefits and grace that had been given to their master in such things. He in turn had to ask about the location of the axe head, because prophets do not always know everything but know and act according to the measure of the gifts they have been given in Christ. But this miracle was not performed by Elisha but by the Lord, whose favor was to encourage the students' piety as disciples of the truth. And so the Lord revealed himself as the Lord of nature to the patriarchs and prophets. COMMENTARY ON 2 KINGS.[46]

A GOOD MASTER. JOHANNES PISCATOR: Elisha provides an example of benevolence of a master toward his disciple. For when his disciple was in need, Elisha promptly helped him. In fact Elisha not only helped him but also performed a miracle, which sets forth an illustrious example of faith. COMMENTARY ON 2 KINGS.[47]

6:5-7 Elisha Makes an Axe Head Float

A PROPHET'S HOLINESS. HULDRYCH ZWINGLI: It is plain that the things which are attributed to fortune or chance are the work of God. In approaching this matter, I shall first bring forward illustrations from the realm of inanimate things or things without intelligence, where yet the evident work and care of the Deity are discoverable, and afterward illustrations that have to do with humans. For instance, when the hatchet of the prophet's pupil slipped from its shaft and fell into the river, it was, at first sight, an accident. But when the prophet teacher threw in the piece of wood to

bring back the metal and it obediently floated back from the bottom, we see that the metal fell in for the purpose of making plain the prophet's holiness and his close relationship with God. ON THE PROVIDENCE OF GOD.[48]

MAKING SINNERS FLOAT. JOHANNES BUGENHAGEN: The iron floated against its nature in order that we not disregard the word of God that dwells with the prophet. Nature was changed and made to go against custom to be an effective sign against the natural order through which all things are otherwise preserved. This is also a sign given so that you will not wonder at how those who are born children of wrath are made righteous and become children of God. For the iron was brought up against its nature through an effective word so that it floated on water. The stick is added here, just as salt was used earlier. COMMENTARY ON 2 KINGS.[49]

WHETHER THIS WAS TWO OR THREE MIRACLES. JOHN MAYER: Elisha performed a miracle to comfort and confirm the faith of his disciples all the more, in making iron to float on the water. When one of the men cut down the wood, the head of his hatchet fell into the water, which made him cry out to Elisha. He especially cried out because the hatchet was borrowed, and a just person is troubled more if he cannot restore that which he borrowed than if he had lost his own hatchet. And by the way, see here how plain and poor the sons of the prophets were of old. This shows that they did not seek the world by their profession of faith, but only God's glory.

Elisha, pitying the man's case and being told where the hatchet fell into the water—for God did not reveal everything to him—cut a stick and cast it in the water. Then the iron swam up and was taken up again by the man from whom it fell. Rabbi Solomon said that the cut stick was a new half of the hatchet, for the other was broken; and when this new stick was put into the water, the head

---

[45]Bugenhagen, *In Regum duos ultimos libros*, 131.
[46]Pellikan, *Commentaria Bibliorum*, 2:180r.
[47]Piscator, *Commentarii in omnes libros Veteris Testamenti*, 2:329.

[48]Zwingli, *Latin Works*, 2:214 (ZSW 6,3:203).
[49]Bugenhagen, *In Regum duos ultimos libros*, 133.

connected to it, and they floated together to the bank. Peter Martyr Vermigli follows this line of interpretation, granting a threefold miracle: first, in the floating of the heavy iron; second, the iron's joining with the new half in the water; and third, in supporting the iron with the wood, when it could have easily sunk due to the weight. We could also say that two miracles were performed: first, in the sinking of the half of the stick that was cast in and joined with the iron head that lay at the bottom, as if it had been put into the eye of it by the hand of the man; second, in the halves floating up again, and bringing the head with it, which according to the course of nature would have weighed it down.... To inquire how God did these things as some do, whether by taking away the heavy quality of the iron for a moment or by the ministry of angels, is vain. That's because God is Almighty. He can easily make heavy things float up in the waters, just as he made the body of Christ stand in the Sea of Galilee. COMMENTARY ON 2 KINGS.[50]

---

[50]Mayer, *Many Commentaries in One*, 181*.

6:8–8:29 WAR WITH SYRIA

[8]Once when the king of Syria was warring against Israel, he took counsel with his servants, saying, "At such and such a place shall be my camp." [9]But the man of God sent word to the king of Israel, "Beware that you do not pass this place, for the Syrians are going down there." [10]And the king of Israel sent to the place about which the man of God told him. Thus he used to warn him, so that he saved himself there more than once or twice.

[11]And the mind of the king of Syria was greatly troubled because of this thing, and he called his servants and said to them, "Will you not show me who of us is for the king of Israel?" [12]And one of his servants said, "None, my lord, O king; but Elisha, the prophet who is in Israel, tells the king of Israel the words that you speak in your bedroom." [13]And he said, "Go and see where he is, that I may send and seize him." It was told him, "Behold, he is in Dothan." [14]So he sent there horses and chariots and a great army, and they came by night and surrounded the city.

[15]When the servant of the man of God rose early in the morning and went out, behold, an army with horses and chariots was all around the city. And the servant said, "Alas, my master! What shall we do?" [16]He said, "Do not be afraid, for those who are with us are more than those who are with them." [17]Then Elisha prayed and said, "O LORD, please open his eyes that he may see." So the LORD opened the eyes of the young man, and he saw, and behold, the mountain was full of horses and chariots of fire all around Elisha. [18]And when the Syrians came down against him, Elisha prayed to the LORD and said, "Please strike this people with blindness." So he struck them with blindness in accordance with the prayer of Elisha. [19]And Elisha said to them, "This is not the way, and this is not the city. Follow me, and I will bring you to the man whom you seek." And he led them to Samaria.

[20]As soon as they entered Samaria, Elisha said, "O LORD, open the eyes of these men, that they may see." So the LORD opened their eyes and they saw, and behold, they were in the midst of Samaria. [21]As soon as the king of Israel saw them, he said to Elisha, "My father, shall I strike them down? Shall I strike them down?" [22]He answered, "You shall not strike them down. Would you strike down those whom you have taken captive with your sword and with your bow? Set bread and water before them, that they may eat and drink and go to their master." [23]So he prepared for them a great feast, and when they had eaten and drunk, he sent them away, and they went to their master. And the Syrians did not come again on raids into the land of Israel.

[24]Afterward Ben-hadad king of Syria mustered his entire army and went up and besieged Samaria. [25]And there was a great famine in Samaria, as they besieged it, until a donkey's head was sold for eighty shekels of silver, and the fourth part of a kab[a] of dove's dung for five shekels of silver. [26]Now as the king of Israel was passing by on the wall, a woman cried out to him, saying, "Help, my lord, O king!" [27]And he said, "If the LORD will not help you, how shall I help you? From the threshing floor, or from the winepress?" [28]And the king asked her, "What is your trouble?" She answered, "This woman said to me, 'Give your son, that we may eat him today, and we will eat my son tomorrow.' [29]So we boiled my son and ate him. And on the next day I said to her, 'Give your son, that we may eat him.' But she has hidden her son." [30]When the king heard the words of the woman, he tore his clothes—now he was passing by on the wall—and the people looked, and behold, he had sackcloth beneath on his body— [31]and he said, "May God do so to me and more also, if the head of Elisha the son of Shaphat remains on his shoulders today."

[32]Elisha was sitting in his house, and the elders were sitting with him. Now the king had dispatched a man from his presence, but before the messenger arrived Elisha said to the elders, "Do you see how this murderer has sent to take off my head? Look, when the messenger comes, shut the door and hold the door fast against him. Is not the sound of his master's feet behind him?" [33]And while he was still speaking with

them, the messenger came down to him and said, "This trouble is from the LORD! Why should I wait for the LORD any longer?"

7 But Elisha said, "Hear the word of the LORD: thus says the LORD, Tomorrow about this time a seah[b] of fine flour shall be sold for a shekel,[c] and two seahs of barley for a shekel, at the gate of Samaria." ²Then the captain on whose hand the king leaned said to the man of God, "If the LORD himself should make windows in heaven, could this thing be?" But he said, "You shall see it with your own eyes, but you shall not eat of it."

³Now there were four men who were lepers[d] at the entrance to the gate. And they said to one another, "Why are we sitting here until we die? ⁴If we say, 'Let us enter the city,' the famine is in the city, and we shall die there. And if we sit here, we die also. So now come, let us go over to the camp of the Syrians. If they spare our lives we shall live, and if they kill us we shall but die." ⁵So they arose at twilight to go to the camp of the Syrians. But when they came to the edge of the camp of the Syrians, behold, there was no one there. ⁶For the LORD had made the army of the Syrians hear the sound of chariots and of horses, the sound of a great army, so that they said to one another, "Behold, the king of Israel has hired against us the kings of the Hittites and the kings of Egypt to come against us." ⁷So they fled away in the twilight and abandoned their tents, their horses, and their donkeys, leaving the camp as it was, and fled for their lives. ⁸And when these lepers came to the edge of the camp, they went into a tent and ate and drank, and they carried off silver and gold and clothing and went and hid them. Then they came back and entered another tent and carried off things from it and went and hid them.

⁹Then they said to one another, "We are not doing right. This day is a day of good news. If we are silent and wait until the morning light, punishment will overtake us. Now therefore come; let us go and tell the king's household." ¹⁰So they came and called to the gatekeepers of the city and told them, "We came to the camp of the Syrians, and behold, there was no one to be seen or heard there, nothing but the horses tied and the donkeys tied and the tents as they were." ¹¹Then the gatekeepers called out, and it was told within the king's

household. ¹²And the king rose in the night and said to his servants, "I will tell you what the Syrians have done to us. They know that we are hungry. Therefore they have gone out of the camp to hide themselves in the open country, thinking, 'When they come out of the city, we shall take them alive and get into the city.'" ¹³And one of his servants said, "Let some men take five of the remaining horses, seeing that those who are left here will fare like the whole multitude of Israel who have already perished. Let us send and see." ¹⁴So they took two horsemen, and the king sent them after the army of the Syrians, saying, "Go and see." ¹⁵So they went after them as far as the Jordan, and behold, all the way was littered with garments and equipment that the Syrians had thrown away in their haste. And the messengers returned and told the king.

¹⁶Then the people went out and plundered the camp of the Syrians. So a seah of fine flour was sold for a shekel, and two seahs of barley for a shekel, according to the word of the LORD. ¹⁷Now the king had appointed the captain on whose hand he leaned to have charge of the gate. And the people trampled him in the gate, so that he died, as the man of God had said when the king came down to him. ¹⁸For when the man of God had said to the king, "Two seahs of barley shall be sold for a shekel, and a seah of fine flour for a shekel, about this time tomorrow in the gate of Samaria," ¹⁹the captain had answered the man of God, "If the LORD himself should make windows in heaven, could such a thing be?" And he had said, "You shall see it with your own eyes, but you shall not eat of it." ²⁰And so it happened to him, for the people trampled him in the gate and he died.

8 Now Elisha had said to the woman whose son he had restored to life, "Arise, and depart with your household, and sojourn wherever you can, for the LORD has called for a famine, and it will come upon the land for seven years." ²So the woman arose and did according to the word of the man of God. She went with her household and sojourned in the land of the Philistines seven years. ³And at the end of the seven years, when the woman returned from the land of the Philistines, she went to appeal to the king for her house and her land. ⁴Now the king was talking with Gehazi the servant of the man of God, saying,

"Tell me all the great things that Elisha has done." ⁵And while he was telling the king how Elisha had restored the dead to life, behold, the woman whose son he had restored to life appealed to the king for her house and her land. And Gehazi said, "My lord, O king, here is the woman, and here is her son whom Elisha restored to life." ⁶And when the king asked the woman, she told him. So the king appointed an official for her, saying, "Restore all that was hers, together with all the produce of the fields from the day that she left the land until now."

⁷Now Elisha came to Damascus. Ben-hadad the king of Syria was sick. And when it was told him, "The man of God has come here," ⁸the king said to Hazael, "Take a present with you and go to meet the man of God, and inquire of the LORD through him, saying, 'Shall I recover from this sickness?'" ⁹So Hazael went to meet him, and took a present with him, all kinds of goods of Damascus, forty camels' loads. When he came and stood before him, he said, "Your son Ben-hadad king of Syria has sent me to you, saying, 'Shall I recover from this sickness?'" ¹⁰And Elisha said to him, "Go, say to him, 'You shall certainly recover,' butᵉ the LORD has shown me that he shall certainly die." ¹¹And he fixed his gaze and stared at him, until he was embarrassed. And the man of God wept. ¹²And Hazael said, "Why does my lord weep?" He answered, "Because I know the evil that you will do to the people of Israel. You will set on fire their fortresses, and you will kill their young men with the sword and dash in pieces their little ones and rip open their pregnant women." ¹³And Hazael said, "What is your servant, who is but a dog, that he should do this great thing?" Elisha answered, "The LORD has shown me that you are to be king over Syria." ¹⁴Then he departed from Elisha and came to his master, who said to him, "What did Elisha say to you?" And he answered, "He told me that you would certainly recover." ¹⁵But the next day he took the bed clothᶠ and dipped it in water and spread it over his face, till he died. And Hazael became king in his place.

¹⁶In the fifth year of Joram the son of Ahab, king of Israel, when Jehoshaphat was king of Judah,ᵍ Jehoram the son of Jehoshaphat, king of Judah, began to reign. ¹⁷He was thirty-two years old when he became king, and he reigned eight years in Jerusalem. ¹⁸And he walked in the way of the kings of Israel, as the house of Ahab had done, for the daughter of Ahab was his wife. And he did what was evil in the sight of the LORD. ¹⁹Yet the LORD was not willing to destroy Judah, for the sake of David his servant, since he promised to give a lamp to him and to his sons forever.

²⁰In his days Edom revolted from the rule of Judah and set up a king of their own. ²¹Then Joramʰ passed over to Zair with all his chariots and rose by night, and he and his chariot commanders struck the Edomites who had surrounded him, but his army fled home. ²²So Edom revolted from the rule of Judah to this day. Then Libnah revolted at the same time. ²³Now the rest of the acts of Joram, and all that he did, are they not written in the Book of the Chronicles of the Kings of Judah? ²⁴So Joram slept with his fathers and was buried with his fathers in the city of David, and Ahaziah his son reigned in his place.

²⁵In the twelfth year of Joram the son of Ahab, king of Israel, Ahaziah the son of Jehoram, king of Judah, began to reign. ²⁶Ahaziah was twenty-two years old when he began to reign, and he reigned one year in Jerusalem. His mother's name was Athaliah; she was a granddaughter of Omri king of Israel. ²⁷He also walked in the way of the house of Ahab and did what was evil in the sight of the LORD, as the house of Ahab had done, for he was son-in-law to the house of Ahab.

²⁸He went with Joram the son of Ahab to make war against Hazael king of Syria at Ramoth-gilead, and the Syrians wounded Joram. ²⁹And King Joram returned to be healed in Jezreel of the wounds that the Syrians had given him at Ramah, when he fought against Hazael king of Syria. And Ahaziah the son of Jehoram king of Judah went down to see Joram the son of Ahab in Jezreel, because he was sick.

a A *shekel* was about 2/5 ounce or 11 grams; a *kab* was about 1 quart or 1 liter   b A *seah* was about 7 quarts or 7.3 liters   c A *shekel* was about 2/5 ounce or 11 grams   d *Leprosy* was a term for several skin diseases; see Leviticus 13   e Some manuscripts say, '*You shall certainly not recover*,' for   f The meaning of the Hebrew is uncertain   g Septuagint, Syriac lack *when Jehoshaphat was king of Judah*   h *Joram* is an alternate spelling of *Jehoram* (the son of Jehoshaphat) as in verse 16; also verses 23, 24

OVERVIEW: Reflecting on the war between Israel and Syria,[1] the reformers share various lessons for faith, perseverance and confidence in the hour of death, as well as the important advice that God's ministers provide to political leaders. The siege of Samaria and the resulting famine provokes moral insights about Ben-hadad's foolishness, Israel's ungodliness and God's providence. Some of the commentators understand the lepers who announce good news to the city as a sign of God making good things happen through unlikely people; others craft this same story into an allegory to teach the power of apostolic preaching. As in 2 Kings 4, the Shunammite woman's faith again in 2 Kings 8 provides a striking narrative contrast to the evil and disbelief found among the leaders of Israel and Judah.

6:8-17 "There Are More with Us Than There Are with Them."

ALL EYES ON US. MARTIN LUTHER: In the hour of his death no Christian should doubt that they are not alone. They can be certain, as the sacraments point out, that a great many eyes are on them: first, the eyes of God and of Christi himself, for the Christian believes his words and clings to his sacraments; then also, the eyes of the dear angels, of the saints and of all Christians. There is no doubt, as the sacrament of the altar indicates, that all of these in a body run to him as one of their own, help them overcome sin, death and hell, and bear all things with him. In that hour the word of love and the communion of saints are seriously and mightily active. Christians must see this for themselves and have no doubt regarding it, for then they will be bold in death. The one who doubts this does not believe in the most venerable sacrament of the body of Christ, in which are pointed out, promised and pledged the communion, help, love, comfort and support of all the saints in all times of need. If you believe in the signs and words of God, his eyes rest on you, as he says in Psalm 32, "*Firmabo*, etc., my eyes will constantly be on you lest you perish." If

God looks on you, all the angels, saints and all creatures will fix their eyes on you. And if you remain in that faith, all of them will uphold you with their hands. And when your soul leaves your body, they will be on hand to receive it, and you cannot perish. This is borne out in the person of Elisha, who according to 2 Kings 6 said to his servant, "Fear not, for those who are with us are more than those who are with them." This he said although enemies had surrounded them and they could see nothing but these. The Lord opened the eyes of the young man, and they were surrounded by a huge mass of horses and chariots of fire. The same is true of everyone who trusts God. A SERMON ON PREPARING TO DIE.[2]

MORE ANGELS THAN DEVILS. MARTIN LUTHER: Where there are twenty devils, there are a hundred angels, and if that were not so, we should long since have perished. We are on the battle front whenever we teach the Word, whenever we preach and glorify Christ, and then live, as far as possible, according to the gospel and the Word of God. COMMENTS ON PSALM 2.[3]

GOD IS GREATER. HENRY AIRAY: Although [our adversaries] are many and we are but few, how could we fear them, seeing our great Captain, Christ Jesus, has said to us, "Fear not, little flock"? So, shall we go on fearing something even though Jesus has commanded not to fear? Elisha, we read, did not fear the king of Syria. Nor did he fear all his horses and chariots or his mighty host because he knew that "those who are with us are more than those who are with them."

... But even when we are few and our adversary is many, we are to take to us that weapon of faith ... and to believe that God is with us. Then we shall not fear but with good courage and comfort we can say, "If God is with us, who can be against us"! For surely if God is with us, nothing shall prevail against us. It's true that our adversaries are mighty,

---

[1]That is, Aram.

[2]LW 42:112; citing Ps 32:8.
[3]LW 12:27.

powerful and strong. But it's also true that God, who dwells on high, is more powerful and stronger! Lectures on Philippians.[4]

Difficult Lesson. Martin Luther: But here faith is needed, because God keeps his walls of fire concealed in such a way that not only can a person not see them, but he even lets his own be pursued and killed, as though he had not drawn even a blade of straw or a spider's web, let alone a wall of fire, about them. Therefore the flesh is too weak to comprehend or believe these sayings or comforting promises. The Holy Spirit must grant grace and teach. Lectures on Zechariah.[5]

6:18-19 Elisha Strikes the Syrians with Blindness

Allegory of Syria's Ploy to Destroy Elisha. John Mayer: Mystically, the king of Syria warring treacherously against Israel represents the devil closely seeking the destruction of the faithful. By Elisha we are to understand the godly preachers giving the church warning against his treacheries. And just as the Syrian army, which sought to take Elisha away, was confounded and made to go home without getting what they wanted, so are all the attempts of the devil in taking away godly preachers frustrated. For those who are stirred up to persecute end up like Paul: First they are struck with blindness, and then, after receiving their sight again, they are no longer enemies but rather friends of the church and evangelists of God's wonderful works among them. Commentary on 2 Kings.[6]

The Delusions of the Ungodly. Johannes Bugenhagen: This blindness was not a blindness of the eyes, though Scripture calls it a true blindness, for those who endure this affliction are seen in other places as able to see. Instead they have been exposed through their eyes. The enemies of God's people are always possessed of such delusions when they come very near to the prophet, that is, the Word of God. Against all kinds of prophetic craft, they struggle, perish and are confounded, just as Isaiah says, "Make the heart of this people dull, and their ears heavy, and blind their eyes." Ungodly despisers of God's law are threatened with such delusions in Deuteronomy 28: "The Lord will strike you with madness and blindness and confusion of mind." Commentary on 2 Kings.[7]

Loss of Function, Not Faculty. Martin Luther: This is not a natural blindness; it is a miraculous blindness. It involves the mind and is . . . the loss of function, not of a faculty. . . . God often employs a miracle like this to rescue his own whom he wants to protect even while enemies are looking on. Lectures on Genesis.[8]

6:20-23 Elisha Does Not Allow Jehoram to Kill the Syrians

Mercy to the Captives. Johannes Bugenhagen: Elisha said, "You shall not strike them down." It is as if he said, "I find it better to preach the glory of God—which is our vindication—in this matter, so that our adversaries who think they ought to reign over us can see what we can do through God. This will also show them how different we are from them, for if they were in our position, none of us would be alive. In contrast, we not only send them out in freedom but even give them gifts." Here you see an example of Christian doctrine that is commended sometimes to the Gentiles, which says that it is most noble to win by conquering through graciousness. Then an adversary can be made to blush and cease from fighting, just as you read here that the Syrian army did not return after this. Commentary on 2 Kings.[9]

---

[4]Airay, *Lectures on Philippians*, 93*; citing Lk 12:32; Rom 8:31.
[5]LW 20:188.
[6]Mayer, *Many Commentaries in One*, 185*.

[7]Bugenhagen, *In Regum duos ultimos libros*, 135; citing Is 6:10; Deut 28:28.
[8]LW 3:262.
[9]Bugenhagen, *In Regum duos ultimos libros*, 135-36; citing Prov 25:21-22; Rom 12:20-21.

Honoring God's Ministers. Johannes Piscator: Jehoram provides a good example to kings and leaders on how to fulfill their vocational offices when in doubt. For Jehoram consulted with Elisha on how to treat the Syrians. In the same way, leaders should consult with ministers of the Word when in doubt on how to proceed. Jehoram also provides another example by calling Elisha his "father." Kings and leaders are thereby admonished to show their respect to faithful ministers of the Word of God. Commentary on 2 Kings.[10]

6:24 Ben-hadad's Siege

The Ungrateful Fool. Johannes Piscator: King Ben-hadad of Syria's besieging of Samaria sets forth an example of both ingratitude and insane impiety. He sets forth an example of ingratitude because his army was just shown great kindness in the city of Samaria when it could have been easily destroyed. Ben-hadad sets forth an example of insanity inasmuch as he had not recognized that the God of Israel was leading him and his army into present danger. Nor did he recognize that he was going against Elisha, who had earlier protected him. Commentary on 2 Kings.[11]

Sacred Scripture Agrees with Itself. Johannes Bugenhagen: I want to know who came with Ben-hadad. Why does it say that the entire army of Syria besieged Samaria, even though it had said that the Syrian soldiers immediately before did not return to the land of Israel? First, do not think that the writers of sacred Scripture were stupid, as if from the Spirit one mouth said various things, setting it in conflict with itself. Therefore I realize that those who had experienced the mighty works of God through the prophet did not return. The people were then greatly oppressed by the siege, so that they even ate dove's dung and meat forbidden in the law. Moreover a woman was discovered

to have boiled her son, which is one of the curses of the law against ungodliness, as is written in Deuteronomy 28. Commentary on 2 Kings.[12]

6:25-33 Famine

The Un-Manna. Konrad Pellikan: A famine is described that neither the word of the Lord nor the prophet could address unless the people cried out for the Lord's blessings in this time of great calamity. But the glorious prophet Elisha had been rejected by those who knew him, so that they did not send for him to implore God's grace on their behalf. Neither did they request his counsel, because they hated the Lord and blamed his servant for these problems. In their ignorance they would not suffer his presence. And so, where the prophets of the Lord are not received, there they can give no prosperity. The head of a large donkey is desired as if it were the Word of God and the face of the prophet. They desperately sought out dove's dung, disregarding the manna from above, the food of angels. Commentary on 2 Kings.[13]

Why the King of Israel Raged Against Elisha. John Mayer: To show the greatness of the famine, there follows another example more horrendous. This time there is a woman who cried to the king of Israel for salvation as he went on the wall. After he understood her meaning to be giving her some relief, he asked her to explain herself.... The king soon understood her request to be that he should give her justice to the story she recounted about her child and the other woman's child. But he replied nothing, for he could only express a great rage at the situation. This led him to immediately request the head of Elisha. Now whereas the king had only ascended the wall to see whether he was defended or not, he was surprised at the woman's request; but he found the case too difficult to adjudicate. But why did he react so strongly to the innocent prophet as soon as he heard this? Peter

---

[10]Piscator, *Commentarii in omnes libros Veteris Testamenti*, 2:329.
[11]Piscator, *Commentarii in omnes libros Veteris Testamenti*, 2:329-30.
[12]Bugenhagen, *In Regum duos ultimos libros*, 136; citing Deut 28:53.
[13]Pellikan, *Commentaria Bibliorum*, 2:181r.

Martyr Vermigli gives several explanations of the king's rage. First, the king thought Elisha was to blame for the famine, just as the drought in previous times had been caused by Elijah. Second, the king thought he could have saved the city had he known about the situation sooner. Third, idolatrous prophets were the real cause of the king's rage against Elisha, as they made the king think that Elisha's God was the cause of their extreme situation. A fourth reason could also be given, though it is not as probable: It's the view that Elisha had commanded the king of Israel to hold out and defend the city, and that he promised deliverance for the faithful who were there out of the enemy's hands. . . . I think that the king, remembering how Elisha brought the Syrian army to him earlier, thought that none of this would have ever happened to Samaria if Elisha would have simply allowed him to kill the Syrian army when he had a chance. COMMENTARY ON 2 KINGS.[14]

HORRIBLE FAMINE AND RESULTS IN ACCORDANCE WITH SCRIPTURE. JOHANNES PISCATOR: This is an example of an extraordinary and horrible famine. It teaches us how greatly God is enraged by sins. For this famine was sent down on account of Israel's sin of idolatry, in accordance with the Mosaic law: "When I break your supply of bread, ten women shall bake your bread in a single oven and shall dole out your bread again by weight, and you shall eat and not be satisfied. . . . You shall then eat the flesh of your sons, and you shall eat the flesh of your daughters." COMMENTARY ON 2 KINGS.[15]

7:1-2 Elisha Promises Food

GOD USES BAD TO MAKE GOOD. JOHANNES PISCATOR: An illustrious example of God's providence and governance is set forth in this passage. For God governed that the cheap price of grain would come about in effectively two ways.

The first way was by governing the minds of these lepers, who reprehensively fled to the side of the Syrians once they were certain that the king had left. And the second way was in laying waste to the Syrian army so that the prophecy about the price could come about. In God's governance over these actions we may especially learn two things. First, God sometimes makes use of vile and contemptible instruments, but, second, God also uses these vile instruments to bring about some good. COMMENTARY ON 2 KINGS.[16]

THE UNBELIEVING CAPTAIN. JOHANNES BUGENHAGEN: The captain said, "If the LORD himself should make windows in heaven, could this thing be?" First, the captain had no respect for the word of God that had promised better things. Instead such things appeared before him only in the light of human reason, so that he did not want to believe what he could not see. This is not what it means to believe. Instead he leaned on his own wisdom rather than on God's. Therefore he blasphemed when he said, "If the LORD himself," etc. That is, "The Lord is not able to do that which you said." For this reason this punishment for his impiety was predicted as an example to others, so that they might learn not to condemn the word of God but to trust God for good and needful things. COMMENTARY ON 2 KINGS.[17]

GRACIOUS GOD. JOHN MAYER: Although the king had sent to behead Elisha, seeing the extremity in which the king was Elisha did not argue with him about it. But accepting the king's recantation, he spoke the greatest comfort to him that he could. From this we learn that the Lord is so merciful that he graciously passes over that which is uttered impatiently in extreme circumstances. And it also showed that God, despite our shortcomings, provides for his people in their needs. COMMENTARY ON 2 KINGS.[18]

---

[14]Mayer, *Many Commentaries in One*, 186*.
[15]Piscator, *Commentarii in omnes libros Veteris Testamenti*, 2:330; citing Lev 26:26, 29.
[16]Piscator, *Commentarii in omnes libros Veteris Testamenti*, 2:331.
[17]Bugenhagen, *In Regum duos ultimos libros*, 137-38.
[18]Mayer, *Many Commentaries in One*, 188*.

7:3-20 *The Lepers and the Arameans*

FREEDOM THROUGH FOUR LEPERS. JOHANNES BUGENHAGEN: In this place, God freed the people from the twin evils of war and famine without using human hands, which human reason had thought to be entirely impossible. God brought this about through desperate lepers, who—in accordance with the law—had gone outside the city walls and who then made this known to the city. So you see here God's judgment and contempt for powers and for enemies and God's benevolence to the people of Israel. Moreover, you see that reason ought to judge blessing and causes through God's ordination. COMMENTARY ON 2 KINGS.[19]

EXAMPLE OF UNBELIEF IN GOD. JOHANNES PISCATOR: In these lepers deserting to the Syrians, an example of unbelief toward God is set forth. For if they were confident in God, they would have implored his aid when in dire straits. And they would rather have hoped for death in the famine. But by deserting to the enemies of God, men of idolatry, they took occasion to mock the people of God and also to blaspheme God. COMMENTARY ON 2 KINGS.[20]

THOUGHTFUL LEPERS. KONRAD PELLIKAN: After their unexpected stroke of luck, the lepers came to their senses just as they were about to get drunk. Getting deeper into their cups, they remembered and could not ignore the miserable state of things in the king's city. And so they rightly came to their senses and knew they would be guilty of great inhumanity if they delayed in announcing such good news to the most wretched city and to the king in particular. COMMENTARY ON 2 KINGS.[21]

AN ALLEGORY OF THE LEPERS, SYRIANS AND THE UNFAITHFUL CAPTAIN. JOHN MAYER: Nicholas of Lyra makes a good moral of this story. By these four lepers are to be understood preachers who teach well but live ill. That is, although the leprosy of sin breaks forth on them, they still tell good tidings. By the tents of the Syrians, the noise of them being heard but not seen and the riches they left for the Samaritans we are to understand the Gentiles coming under the power of the church, which is only to be by the sound of the apostles' preaching. By the unbelieving captain we are to understand those who continue to reject the preaching of God's Word. Their final lot is to be trodden in the winepress of God's wrath forever. COMMENTARY ON 2 KINGS.[22]

8:1-6 *The Shunammite's Land Restored*

SAVED BY FAITH. KONRAD PELLIKAN: The woman was saved by her faith. She believed the prophet's word about the famine and moved her entire family to the land of the Philistines, where they were preserved for seven years. In the meantime her home and fields were taken by others, so that she could not get them back without difficulty. Thus she was forced to drive the squatters out with the help and authority of the king. COMMENTARY ON 2 KINGS.[23]

GOD'S GOOD PROVIDING. JOHANNES BUGENHAGEN: Here you see God's providing for this woman and her house or family in a time of famine, as they fled Israel in their time of need. For she had enough of external provisions and then received everything back entirely from the king, who had just been asking Elisha's servant about the mighty works the prophet had done. In the meantime, Elisha and the people of his household had enough during the famine too. Therefore it does not matter whether you remain in your dwelling place or whether like Abraham, Isaac and Jacob you are brought into another land so that you do not die of hunger, so long as you trust in God. COMMENTARY ON 2 KINGS.[24]

[19]Bugenhagen, *In Regum duos ultimos libros*, 138.
[20]Piscator, *Commentarii in omnes libros Veteris Testamenti*, 2:331.
[21]Pellikan, *Commentaria Bibliorum*, 2:181v.
[22]Mayer, *Many Commentaries in One*, 190*.
[23]Pellikan, *Commentaria Bibliorum*, 2:182r.
[24]Bugenhagen, *In Regum duos ultimos libros*, 140.

SHOWING KINDNESS TO OUR BENEFACTORS.
JOHN MAYER: Here it is commemorated how
Elisha foretold to the Shunammite of the famine
of seven years, warning her to depart from the land
so she and her family would survive. It is not to be
conceived that Elisha foretold this after the siege of
Samaria, seeing that it ended not long after this;
and she returned home again as is shown. The fore-
telling of this story, then, occurred about the time
of Elisha's raising her son to life, seeing that within
a while afterward a famine is said to have been in
those parts. . . . But to what year of Jehoram it
refers, whether the beginning or the end, is not
certain. But most probably because the famine
began before the Syrian army came and infested
the country, it continued and increased as they
remained there. The army must have taken away
and destroyed the land's corn and provision, till at
last it grew most extreme. And here Peter Martyr
Vermigli notes well that whereas the famine
threatened by Elijah was but three and a half years,
this was twice as long. Thus after Elijah's judgment
was removed, the people continued sinning.
Therefore God sent a plight more terrible than the
one before. But notice the thankfulness of Elisha to
the Shunammite, since she had been so hospitable
to him. He not only prayed for a son for her but
also gave her a warning of the coming danger so
that she might provide for her family elsewhere.
And such ought to be our thankfulness to our
benefactors if we claim to be servants of God. Like
Elisha, we must do to them all the good that we
can. COMMENTARY ON 2 KINGS.[25]

8:7-15 Hazael Murders Ben-hadad

WE ARE ALL DOGS. DANIEL DYKE: We deceive
ourselves . . . if we fail to take notice of our
corruption to the degree that we think we are
incapable of falling into the gross and scandalous
sins that we formerly overcame. . . . Such is how
Hazael, when the prophet told him that he would
cruelly kill pregnant women and dash their

children against the stones, thought better of
himself. Thinking himself incapable of such
deplorable actions, he broke forth in outrage and in
indignation: "Is your servant . . . a dog . . . ?"

Yes, Hazael, you are a dog. All of the sons of
Adam are. In fact, in our vicious qualities we are
worse than dogs, bears and tigers. And thus, if our
own hearts do not deceive us, shall we think that
there is no sin so odious that we are not sufficiently
liable to commit it? For original sin, in which we are
all bred and born, contaminates the seeds of all
sins—that fearful sin against the Holy Spirit not
being exempt. And therefore by reason of this
corrupt and rotten nature, we are all disposed—even
the best of us—to the vilest and most loathsome sins
imaginable. THE MYSTERY OF SELF-DECEIVING.[26]

THE WET BLANKET. JOHANNES BUGENHAGEN:
From the Hebrew it is possible for you to think
that Ben-hadad spread the bed cloth over himself,
that is, as a blanket soaked in water for cooling his
fevered body and the fires of an internal infection.
But the Latin interpreter thinks that Hazael
suffocated him, which Josephus also thinks. That is
equally possible in the Hebrew. COMMENTARY ON
2 KINGS.[27]

ELISHA WEPT. KONRAD PELLIKAN: With the
Spirit of God giving him knowledge, Elisha stared
at Hazael, knowing the future cruel damage he
would inflict on the people of Israel. He then had
to bring about Hazael's kingship, just as had been
told to Elijah. In Hazael's presence, he was then
brought to tears and was sobbing so that he
wanted to cover his face but could not. He grieved
this coming kingdom, which he knew in advance
would bring such evil to the people of God.
COMMENTARY ON 2 KINGS.[28]

TWO RESPONSES TO ONE QUESTION. JOHN
MAYER: King Ben-hadad of Syria sends Hazael to

---

[25]Mayer, *Many Commentaries in One*, 190-91*.

[26]Dyke, *The Mystery of Self-Deceiving*, 43-44*.
[27]Bugenhagen, *In Regum duos ultimos libros*, 141; citing Josephus,
    Antiquities, 9.4.
[28]Pellikan, *Commentaria Bibliorum*, 2:182v.

inquire whether he would recover. Elisha essentially responds: "Say to him, 'no.' Although you could recover from your sickness, you will die and not recover by some other means." Rabbi David Kimchi says that the prophet respects two different things in his response, and therefore his words are of two minds. First, concerning the sickness, he said that the king would live since he would not die from it. Second, concerning the evil means that Hazael would use to take him out, he said that he would die. Elisha gave one response to be delivered by way of answer to the king's inquiry, and the other to prevent the calling in question of the truth of Elisha's prophecy, which otherwise might have been questioned when the king died soon thereafter. COMMENTARY ON 2 KINGS.[29]

8:16-24 Jehoram Reigns in Judah

MARRYING INTO THE HOUSE OF AHAB. JOHANNES BUGENHAGEN: Jehoram the son of Jehoshaphat was the wicked son of a great father. He followed in the sins of the king of Israel, because he married the daughter of Ahab. Later in the chapter, she is called the daughter of Omri, in a Hebrew manner of speaking of ancestry, for Omri was her grandfather, her father's father. Thus the king of Judah should have shunned her as a Gentile, for the Lord had forbidden marriage to Gentile women so that they not be dragged away to foreign gods through marriage, as we discussed in 2 Kings 4 and elsewhere. And as Paul said, "Do not be unequally yoked with unbelievers. For what partnership has righteousness with lawlessness? Or what fellowship has light with darkness? What accord has Christ is Belial? Or what portion does a believer share with an unbeliever?" Even so, the Lord preserved the people as we discussed in 1 Kings 11. For these words are about Christ, for whose sake David's descendants were preserved, even in the Babylonian captivity. COMMENTARY ON 2 KINGS.[30]

JEHOSHAPHAT'S SON, AHAB'S SON, DAVID'S SON. KONRAD PELLIKAN: This wicked Jehoram, son of a great father, was corrupted by his impious wife, who was a daughter of Ahab. They devoted themselves to the calves more than God's law, following the ungodliness of the king of Israel. Because of his sins, the king deserved to lose the kingdom of Judah. But he was prevented from doing so by God's covenant with David's descendants and God's mercy to David's line, which had been decided before the world came into being about the true David, who is David's son, the Messiah, who reigns from his throne forever. COMMENTARY ON 2 KINGS.[31]

THE LORD'S HATRED OF IDOLATRY AND MURDER. JOHN MAYER: Despite King Jehoram's sin, "the Lord was not willing destroy Judah, for the sake of David his servant, since he promised to give a lamp to him and his sons forever." Of this promise see 2 Samuel 7. The expression "lamp" here is meant to refer to kingly glory that makes a family shine. This lamp ended about the time of the coming of Shiloh, that is, of Christ. This is in accordance with the prophecy of Genesis: "The scepter shall not depart from Judah, nor the ruler's staff from between his feet, until tribute comes to him." This is speaking in respect of a worldly kingdom, yet the lamp also shines by the light of a spiritual king in Christ, who was of the seed of David and who shall continue to reign forever and ever. And this is added as implying that, on account of the wickedness of Jehoram, he and his seed were worthy to be cut off forever so that none of his race would ever reign again. This is to show how much the Lord abominates idolaters and murderers, for his wrath is greatly stirred up against such things. COMMENTARY ON 2 KINGS.[32]

GOD'S MERCY ON ACCOUNT OF DAVID. JOHANNES PISCATOR: God did not gravely punish the people of Judah even though they merited it.

---

[29]Mayer, *Many Commentaries in One*, 193*.
[30]Bugenhagen, *In Regum duos ultimos libros*, 141; citing 2 Cor 6:14-15; 1 Kings 11:13.
[31]Pellikan, *Commentaria Bibliorum*, 2:183r.
[32]Mayer, *Many Commentaries in One*, 196-97*; citing Gen 49:10.

Rather, God refrained from punishing them on account of the glory of his name. Indeed God did not destroy the Judean tribe as was deserving of idolatry. The fact of the matter is that the kingdom only endured on account of the promise that God had made to David. Nevertheless, God meanwhile made Edom and Libnah desert the king of Judah. COMMENTARY ON 2 KINGS.[33]

8:25-29 Ahaziah Reigns in Judah

STILL FIGHTING AHAB'S WARS. JOHANNES BUGENHAGEN: Ahaziah went with Joram to war at Ramoth-gilead. This war had started under Ahab in 1 Kings 22. Ahaziah went down to visit Joram, as God ordained it, so that they would both perish as you see in the following chapter. Meanwhile, the army was left in Ramoth-gilead, according to the same judgment of God. In this way, aligning with the prophet's anointing, the conspiracy against King Joram could come about, as you will soon see below. COMMENTARY ON 2 KINGS.[34]

BAD COMPANY. KONRAD PELLIKAN: Together with King Joram of Israel, King Ahaziah of Judah fought against Hazael, the new king of Syria, near Ramoth-gilead. In the confusion of the battle, Joram was pierced by the Syrians and went back to Jezreel to be healed of his wounds. King Ahaziah also went down to visit the infirm Joram, so that they would both be overthrown in that place by Jehu in the story

that follows. For the Lord is jealous; he is unwilling for his friends to have intimacy with his enemies. All of this unholy alliance between the kings of Judah and Israel and the following destruction of both had its origin in the friendship between the great King Jehoshaphat and the terrible King Ahab, which had been condemned and impugned by the prophets. But they could not stop it, because the Word of God was held in contempt. COMMENTARY ON 2 KINGS.[35]

TAKING HEED OF UNEQUAL YOKING. JOHN MAYER: King Ahaziah was as wicked as his father in the case of idolatry. He followed Ahab and his mother. And those of the house of Ahab were said to be his counselors, which served nothing but to bring him to destruction. All of this wickedness is compressed in just a few words: "He . . . walked in the way of the house of Ahab and did what was evil in the sight of the LORD, as the house of Ahab had done, for he was son-in-law to the house of Ahab." His mother provided him with a wife from Ahab's house. And thus he was strongly influenced by this evil, as if he had been forced to do evil on account of their wickedness: partly from his mother's command and partly from his wife's ungodliness. Thus the idolatry brought forth by marrying with idolaters was so rooted in this dynasty that it could not be rooted out without destroying the entirety of the corrupted stock. This is a warning to all generations to come: take heed of unequal yoking. COMMENTARY ON 2 KINGS.[36]

---

[33]Piscator, *Commentarii in omnes libros Veteris Testamenti*, 2:335; citing 2 Sam 7.
[34]Bugenhagen, *In Regum duos ultimos libros*, 142.

[35]Pellikan, *Commentaria Bibliorum*, 2:183v.
[36]Mayer, *Many Commentaries in One*, 200*; citing 2 Kings 8:27.

9:1–10:17 THE END OF AHAB'S HOUSE

¹Then Elisha the prophet called one of the sons of the prophets and said to him, "Tie up your garments, and take this flask of oil in your hand, and go to Ramoth-gilead. ²And when you arrive, look there for Jehu the son of Jehoshaphat, son of Nimshi. And go in and have him rise from among his fellows, and lead him to an inner chamber. ³Then take the flask of oil and pour it on his head and say, 'Thus says the LORD, I anoint you king over Israel.' Then open the door and flee; do not linger."

⁴So the young man, the servant of the prophet, went to Ramoth-gilead. ⁵And when he came, behold, the commanders of the army were in council. And he said, "I have a word for you, O commander." And Jehu said, "To which of us all?" And he said, "To you, O commander." ⁶So he arose and went into the house. And the young man poured the oil on his head, saying to him, "Thus says the LORD, the God of Israel, I anoint you king over the people of the LORD, over Israel. ⁷And you shall strike down the house of Ahab your master, so that I may avenge on Jezebel the blood of my servants the prophets, and the blood of all the servants of the LORD. ⁸For the whole house of Ahab shall perish, and I will cut off from Ahab every male, bond or free, in Israel. ⁹And I will make the house of Ahab like the house of Jeroboam the son of Nebat, and like the house of Baasha the son of Ahijah. ¹⁰And the dogs shall eat Jezebel in the territory of Jezreel, and none shall bury her." Then he opened the door and fled.

¹¹When Jehu came out to the servants of his master, they said to him, "Is all well? Why did this mad fellow come to you?" And he said to them, "You know the fellow and his talk." ¹²And they said, "That is not true; tell us now." And he said, "Thus and so he spoke to me, saying, 'Thus says the LORD, I anoint you king over Israel.'" ¹³Then in haste every man of them took his garment and put it under him on the bareᵃ steps, and they blew the trumpet and proclaimed, "Jehu is king."

¹⁴Thus Jehu the son of Jehoshaphat the son of Nimshi conspired against Joram. (Now Joram with all Israel had been on guard at Ramoth-gilead against Hazael king of Syria, ¹⁵but King Joram had returned to be healed in Jezreel of the wounds that the Syrians had given him, when he fought with Hazael king of Syria.) So Jehu said, "If this is your decision, then let no one slip out of the city to go and tell the news in Jezreel." ¹⁶Then Jehu mounted his chariot and went to Jezreel, for Joram lay there. And Ahaziah king of Judah had come down to visit Joram.

¹⁷Now the watchman was standing on the tower in Jezreel, and he saw the company of Jehu as he came and said, "I see a company." And Joram said, "Take a horseman and send to meet them, and let him say, 'Is it peace?'" ¹⁸So a man on horseback went to meet him and said, "Thus says the king, 'Is it peace?'" And Jehu said, "What do you have to do with peace? Turn around and ride behind me." And the watchman reported, saying, "The messenger reached them, but he is not coming back." ¹⁹Then he sent out a second horseman, who came to them and said, "Thus the king has said, 'Is it peace?'" And Jehu answered, "What do you have to do with peace? Turn around and ride behind me." ²⁰Again the watchman reported, "He reached them, but he is not coming back. And the driving is like the driving of Jehu the son of Nimshi, for he drives furiously."

²¹Joram said, "Make ready." And they made ready his chariot. Then Joram king of Israel and Ahaziah king of Judah set out, each in his chariot, and went to meet Jehu, and met him at the property of Naboth the Jezreelite. ²²And when Joram saw Jehu, he said, "Is it peace, Jehu?" He answered, "What peace can there be, so long as the whorings and the sorceries of your mother Jezebel are so many?" ²³Then Joram reined about and fled, saying to Ahaziah, "Treachery, O Ahaziah!" ²⁴And Jehu drew his bow with his full strength, and shot Joram between the shoulders, so that the arrow pierced his heart, and he sank in his chariot. ²⁵Jehu said to Bidkar his aide, "Take him up and throw him on the plot of ground belonging to Naboth the Jezreelite. For remember, when you and I rode side by side behind Ahab his father, how the

438

Lord made this pronouncement against him: [26]'As surely as I saw yesterday the blood of Naboth and the blood of his sons—declares the Lord—I will repay you on this plot of ground.' Now therefore take him up and throw him on the plot of ground, in accordance with the word of the Lord."

[27]When Ahaziah the king of Judah saw this, he fled in the direction of Beth-haggan. And Jehu pursued him and said, "Shoot him also." And they shot him[b] in the chariot at the ascent of Gur, which is by Ibleam. And he fled to Megiddo and died there. [28]His servants carried him in a chariot to Jerusalem, and buried him in his tomb with his fathers in the city of David.

[29]In the eleventh year of Joram the son of Ahab, Ahaziah began to reign over Judah.

[30]When Jehu came to Jezreel, Jezebel heard of it. And she painted her eyes and adorned her head and looked out of the window. [31]And as Jehu entered the gate, she said, "Is it peace, you Zimri, murderer of your master?" [32]And he lifted up his face to the window and said, "Who is on my side? Who?" Two or three eunuchs looked out at him. [33]He said, "Throw her down." So they threw her down. And some of her blood spattered on the wall and on the horses, and they trampled on her. [34]Then he went in and ate and drank. And he said, "See now to this cursed woman and bury her, for she is a king's daughter." [35]But when they went to bury her, they found no more of her than the skull and the feet and the palms of her hands. [36]When they came back and told him, he said, "This is the word of the Lord, which he spoke by his servant Elijah the Tishbite: 'In the territory of Jezreel the dogs shall eat the flesh of Jezebel, [37]and the corpse of Jezebel shall be as dung on the face of the field in the territory of Jezreel, so that no one can say, This is Jezebel.'"

10 Now Ahab had seventy sons in Samaria. So Jehu wrote letters and sent them to Samaria, to the rulers of the city,[c] to the elders, and to the guardians of the sons[d] of Ahab, saying, [2]"Now then, as soon as this letter comes to you, seeing your master's sons are with you, and there are with you chariots and horses, fortified cities also, and weapons, [3]select the best and fittest of your master's sons and set him on his father's throne and fight for your master's house." [4]But they were exceedingly afraid and said, "Behold, the two kings could not stand before him. How then can we stand?" [5]So he who was over the palace, and he who was over the city, together with the elders and the guardians, sent to Jehu, saying, "We are your servants, and we will do all that you tell us. We will not make anyone king. Do whatever is good in your eyes." [6]Then he wrote to them a second letter, saying, "If you are on my side, and if you are ready to obey me, take the heads of your master's sons and come to me at Jezreel tomorrow at this time." Now the king's sons, seventy persons, were with the great men of the city, who were bringing them up. [7]And as soon as the letter came to them, they took the king's sons and slaughtered them, seventy persons, and put their heads in baskets and sent them to him at Jezreel. [8]When the messenger came and told him, "They have brought the heads of the king's sons," he said, "Lay them in two heaps at the entrance of the gate until the morning." [9]Then in the morning, when he went out, he stood and said to all the people, "You are innocent. It was I who conspired against my master and killed him, but who struck down all these? [10]Know then that there shall fall to the earth nothing of the word of the Lord, which the Lord spoke concerning the house of Ahab, for the Lord has done what he said by his servant Elijah." [11]So Jehu struck down all who remained of the house of Ahab in Jezreel, all his great men and his close friends and his priests, until he left him none remaining.

[12]Then he set out and went to Samaria. On the way, when he was at Beth-eked of the Shepherds, [13]Jehu met the relatives of Ahaziah king of Judah, and he said, "Who are you?" And they answered, "We are the relatives of Ahaziah, and we came down to visit the royal princes and the sons of the queen mother." [14]He said, "Take them alive." And they took them alive and slaughtered them at the pit of Beth-eked, forty-two persons, and he spared none of them.

[15]And when he departed from there, he met Jehonadab the son of Rechab coming to meet him. And he greeted him and said to him, "Is your heart true to my heart as mine is to yours?" And Jehonadab answered, "It is." Jehu said,[e] "If it is, give me your hand." So he gave him his hand. And Jehu took him up with him into the chariot. [16]And he said, "Come with me, and see my zeal for the Lord." So he[f] had

him ride in his chariot. [17]*And when he came to Samaria, he struck down all who remained to Ahab* *in Samaria, till he had wiped them out, according to the word of the LORD that he spoke to Elijah.*

a The meaning of the Hebrew word is uncertain   b Syriac, Vulgate (compare Septuagint); Hebrew lacks *and they shot him*   c Septuagint, Vulgate; Hebrew *rulers of Jezreel*   d Hebrew lacks *of the sons*   e Septuagint; Hebrew lacks *Jehu said*   f Septuagint, Syriac, Targum; Hebrew *they*

OVERVIEW: God's providence and justice are major themes of this section. Reformers note the fulfillment of Elijah's prophecy against the house of Ahab, which comes through Elisha's sending of Jehu. They also observe the righteous irony that Joram and Ahaziah's deaths occurred in Naboth's vineyard, which Ahab claimed for himself through murder. One of the few powerful queens of Israel, Jezebel inspires many comments about women in leadership and women's roles in church and society. While some commentators make patriarchal statements about women's adornments and equate female faithlessness with prostitution (both spiritual and physical), several commentators add positive pronouncements—a gender-neutral allegory about the deceptiveness of worldly wisdom in contrast to the hidden beauty of God's wisdom and praise for beautiful adornment of faith.

9:1-4 Elisha Commissions a Prophet to Anoint Jehu

DON'T ADD TO GOD'S WORD. JOHANNES BUGENHAGEN: When Elisha said, "Tie up your garments and go," it was the moment when what was spoken in 1 Kings 19 would come to pass. As Elijah commissioned Elisha, Elisha commissioned this son of the prophets so that the words about Jehu would be carried out for the first time. Whether on account of this messenger's fear or frailty, Elisha advised him to "open the door and flee" and not to try to tarry and create some reason to make a mistake. For the word and commands of God do not need the addition of human words. COMMENTARY ON 2 KINGS.[1]

MYSTICAL SIGNIFICANCE OF AN EARTHEN VESSEL. JOHN MAYER: Elisha did not himself go anoint Jehu, but rather he sent another to do it. Some think he sent another person because he was old and could not travel quickly anymore. Others think he sent an unknown person so that the anointing could be done more discreetly, which such a famous prophet as Elisha would not have been able to do. As for me, I think both of these are reasonable considerations that might move Elisha to send another person to do this errand. And, of course, it is likely that God's Spirit also directed him to send another person rather than himself. For the prophet sent took an earthen vessel of oil with him so that the anointing could be done secretly. Therefore it is generally held that he took common oil and none of the holy oil that was kept in the sanctuary, for neither the haste of his errand nor the diminishing of the oil through the course of the journey permitted him to use holy oil. And he used an earthen vessel rather than a horn, as was used to anoint David and Solomon. This was meant to suggest that the kingdom would not forever remain in his family, as in David's. For a similar vessel was used to anoint Saul, which had the same mystical purpose. COMMENTARY ON 2 KINGS.[2]

9:5-13 Jehu Anointed to Wipe Out the House of Ahab

A DANGEROUS ANOINTING. KONRAD PELLIKAN: With this anointing of the head, which happened according to God's word to consecrate Jehu king of Israel, came a marvelous kind of presumption and a danger to life and reputation. But gifted with a strong faith in God, these holy

---

[1]Bugenhagen, *In Regum duos ultimos libros,* 143; citing 1 Kings 19:16.   [2]Mayer, *Many Commentaries in One,* 201*.

men of God did it according to God's command with great trepidation. For what God sent them to do—depose others—put them in great danger of death among the people and the kingdom. But God gave grace to defeat the kingdom of evil and would testify to the truth of God's word for the sake of God's glory, which would soon be opened wide. Jehu would be bound to this all his life. He and the prophet could not value their life more than by willing to meet their death. And so the prophet immediately fled and did not wait for any response or questions. COMMENTARY ON 2 KINGS.[3]

GOD ESTABLISHES KINGS. JOHANNES PISCATOR: In this section we see that God alone transfers and establishes kings. As Daniel says, "God changes times and seasons; he removes kings and sets up kings; he gives wisdom to the wise and knowledge to those who have understanding." In this way, God transferred the kingdom of Israel from Joram to Jehu. (And just as it is the office of a king to take vengeance on injustice, so God punishes all families for the sins of idolatry and of striking down injustice.) COMMENTARY ON 2 KINGS.[4]

IMPULSIVE CAUSE. ROBERT SANDERSON: There is a kind of cause . . . that the learned, for distinction's sake, call the impulsive cause. It is such a cause as moves and induces the principal agent to do that which it does. For example, a schoolmaster corrects a boy with a rod for neglecting his book. Of this correction here are three distinct causes, all in the rank of his efficient cause: the master, the rod and the boy's neglect. But each has its proper causality in a different kind and manner from the other. The master is the cause, as he is the principal agent who does it; the rod is the cause, as the instrument wherewith he does it; and the boy's neglect the impulsive cause, for which he does it. Similarly, in this judgment that

befell Jehoram, the principal efficient cause and agent was God, as he is in all other punishments and judgments. "Does disaster come to a city, unless the LORD has done it?" And here the Lord attributes the role of bringing destruction to himself: "And I will make the house of Ahab like the house of Jeroboam the son of Nebat, and like the house of Baasha the son of Ahijah." . . . But now, what the true, proper, impulsive cause should be, for which he was so punished, and which moved God at that time and in that sort to punish him, that is the point in which consists the chief difficulty in this matter, and into which therefore we are not to inquire, namely, whether it was his own sin, or his father Ahab's sin?

Regardless of whether we answer this way or that way, we say the truth in both. For both sayings are true: God punished him for his own, and God punished him for his father's sin. There is only one difference. His own sins were the impulsive cause that deserved the punishment, while his father's sin was the impulsive cause that occasioned it; and so indeed, on the point, and respectively to the justice of God, his own sins were the cause of it, rather than his father's. This is because justice especially looks at the desert, and also because that which deserves a punishment is more effectually, primarily and properly the impulsive cause of punishing, than that which only occasions it. TO THE PEOPLE.[5]

LOVE THE ACT BUT HATE THE ACTOR? JOHN ROBINSON: Just as God may hate evil in a person, for example, the adultery of David (and other sins accompanying it), so as to punish it severely in this world, and yet not hate the person themselves; so may God, on the other side, love some good in a person and reward it highly in this life, and nevertheless not love but hate the person in whom it is found, as may be seen in the zeal of Jehu for the Lord, against wicked Ahab and his house. ESSAYS.[6]

[3]Pellikan, *Commentaria Bibliorum*, 2:183v.
[4]Piscator, *Commentarii in omnes libros Veteris Testamenti*, 2:337; citing Dan 2:21.
[5]Sanderson, *Works*, 3:77-78*; citing Amos 3:6.
[6]Robinson, *Works*,1:7*.

Why Jehu Was Anointed While Other Israelite Kings Were Not. John Mayer:

Because no king of Israel, other than David's line in Judah, had been anointed king of Israel after Saul, why was Jehu anointed? It is because God had imposed a harder task on him, namely, to execute his judgments on Ahab's posterity. In order for him to be more encouraged to do it and not be in fear, he was anointed to show that he had received authority and assurance to perform his task. Commentary on 2 Kings.[7]

9:14-29 Jehu Kills Joram and Ahaziah

God's Governance of Jehu's Seamless Succession. Johannes Piscator:

Here is set forth God's wise governance of affairs. For God had wished to punish the sin of idolatry and to remove both of these kings Joram and Ahaziah so that the succession of Israel's kingship could go to Jehu. Therefore God so governed the events so that both kings would be joined in a similar place so that they could both fall. God's counsel led both of them. For while Joram was recovering from his wound in the battle, Ahaziah had been visiting him in his sickness. Commentary on 2 Kings.[8]

God's Unstoppable Justice. Konrad Pellikan:

If the Lord has begun to bring recompense against the ungodly, there is no way it can be stopped: "Unless the Lord watches over the city, the watchman stays awake in vain." Joram went out to see an enemy he could not stop. He saw Jehu's troop advancing in uproar and speed. He noted the moment and quickly sent for his horse. But even though neither could stop the Lord's judgment, he was urged on by some ungodly fate, as if running to meet his ruin. He brought Ahaziah with him, enveloping him in a common damnation brought on by their ungodly alliance. And who does not see the infallible providence of God in the fact that they met on the same field of Ahab, which the tyrannous Jezebel had snatched from the honest Jezreelite Naboth, just as God's prophet Elijah had predicted. Commentary on 2 Kings.[9]

In Naboth's Field. Johannes Bugenhagen:

God wanted Jehu's attacks on Joram and Ahaziah to happen at Naboth's fields, so that the word of God spoken by Elijah might be fulfilled. The "whorings" that Jehu described were the idolatries and the other things that Jezebel did against the worship of God and against the prophets and preachers of God's word. As the Psalms say, "You put an end to everyone who is unfaithful to you." Commentary on 2 Kings.[10]

On Eliminating Idolatry. John Mayer:

It is to be noted how divine providence carried Jehu to the very place where execution was to be done, namely, in the field of Naboth the Jezreelite. In response to Joram's question about peace, Jehu answered, "What peace can there be, so long as the whorings and the sorceries of your mother Jezebel are so many?" Nicholas of Lyra understands Jehu's response to refer to Jezebel's idolatries, for idolatry is spiritual fornication and commonly called whoredom and adultery. That's because the church is to God as his spouse. Therefore, just as when a man's wife goes after another man she is a whore and adulteress, so when any who worship the true God follow after idols they become adulterers and adulteresses. And sorcery or witchcraft is spiritual, because those who practice it are carried headlong into destruction by an evil spirit. Josephus understands Jehu's response as referring properly to physical whoredom, while Peter Martyr Vermigli interprets it as both spiritual and physical whoredom, since they commonly go together. But why is Jehoram's own wickedness not objected to, yet only his mother's? The reason is because she was the head of all this wickedness, for she was the one who first brought the worship of Baal into Israel.

---

[7]Mayer, *Many Commentaries in One*, 201*.
[8]Piscator, *Commentarii in omnes libros Veteris Testamenti*, 2:335.
[9]Pellikan, *Commentaria Bibliorum*, 2:184v; citing Ps 127:1.
[10]Bugenhagen, *In Regum duos ultimos libros*, 144; citing 1 Kings 21:19; Ps 73:27.

And now, by her and her daughter Athaliah's means, Judah was likewise corrupted with this idolatry. Moreover it was Jehoram's part as the king not to have allowed Jezebel to go on committing her idolatry, just as Asa refused to allow his mother Maacah to continue practicing it. But by refusing what he ought to have done, he took her sin on himself and was therefore rightly worthy to be killed along with her. This is what Jehu meant when he responded to Joram's plea about peace. Note well: Where idolatry and whoredoms are common, the state cannot be quiet, but the sword and slaughter must follow. Therefore the way to have peace is to purge the land from these evils, as all good kings do. COMMENTARY ON 2 KINGS.[11]

UNANIMITY OF FAITH. JOHN DAVENANT: Love is . . . the fruit of unanimity in faith, which so binds the minds of the godly, as it were, in covenant that, though some light offenses may intervene, yet, as the boughs of the same tree are driven asunder by the wind, they immediately come together again because they are fixed steadily in one and the same root. So something similar takes place as regards the minds of the faithful, because they are still rooted in the same faith. On this account, therefore, he would have them persevere unanimously in the faith, that they may be united also, being knit together in love. Concord of minds is therefore the fruit of perseverance in the doctrine of the gospel.

Yet it is also a condition without which the above-named spiritual comfort is not obtained. For comfort is not had out of Christ: if any one lives without love, he is without Christ, as John says, "Whoever lives in love lives in God, and God in him." And, vice versa, the one who casts off love is rejected of God. For as no member can be recruited and nourished if its union with the rest of the body be dissolved, so no one can participate in that full influx of comfort from Christ if that unanimity that ought to exist between oneself and the rest of the believers is destroyed. . . . It is folly to hope for any firm union between those who differ on the chief

points of religion and fundamental doctrines of the Christian faith. When Joram inquired of Jehu, "Have you come in peace, Jehu?" He replied, "How can there be peace as long as all the idolatry and witchcraft of your mother Jezebel abound?" So do those of the true religion reply, and justly too, to those who maintain a false religion, "What peace, while the errors and corruptions of the church, which you acknowledge as your mother, are so many?" EXPOSITION OF COLOSSIANS.[12]

9:30-37 The Adornment and Death of Jezebel

WOMEN PRECIOUS IN GOD'S SIGHT. JOHANNES PISCATOR: In Jezebel's painting her eyes and adorning her head and reproving Jehu so freely, we are given an example of a prideful woman. But what ought to truly adorn women who profess godliness is taught by Peter. "Wives, be subject to your own husbands, so that even if some do not obey the word, they may be won without a word by the conduct of their wives when they see your respectful and pure conduct. Do not let your adorning be external—the braiding of hair, the wearing of gold, or the putting on of clothing—but let your adorning be the hidden person of the heart with the imperishable beauty of a gentle and quiet spirit, which in God's sight is very precious." COMMENTARY ON 2 KINGS.[13]

MENACING JEZEBEL. KONRAD PELLIKAN: Jehu had set out and entered Jezreel, fearing no one, and made certain of the kingdom by the prophet Elisha. Jezebel went out for an audience and, knowing already what was happening, adorned her face so as to look calm rather than frightened. She dared even to menace Jehu himself with her words, accusing him of faithlessness and treason in coming to his lord's house for murder. She cast him as a new kind of Zimri, who had killed his lord, King Elah of

---

[11]Mayer, *Many Commentaries in One*, 204*.

[12]Davenant, *Exposition of Colossians*, 1:349*; citing 1 Jn 4:16; 2 Kings 9:22.

[13]Piscator, *Commentarii in omnes libros Veteris Testamenti*, 2:337; citing 1 Pet 3:1-4.

Israel, and who reigned for seven days before he was killed by Omri. And so the impudent Jezebel preferred to cast the impending actions in terms of these words to Jehu: "Is it peace, you Zimri, murderer of you master?" COMMENTARY ON 2 KINGS.[14]

AN ALLEGORY ABOUT JEZEBEL. JOHANNES BUGENHAGEN: Jezebel was a beautiful pagan who ruled in Israel with such force that it behooves the people of God to see her as a most apt sign of human traditions, whose doctrines are not from God but from demons yet are nevertheless beautiful. That is, they appear pleasing to human reason and have a kind of piety to them. Meanwhile, they murder, oppress and condemn the prophets (that is, the Word of God) and anyone who assents to the Word of God as heretics, so that the cruel take control of the land. With such power of riches, honor and righteous opinions and against the Word of God they then reign over the people, who are supposed to consider them to be gods and who alone are supposed to be glorified by God's people, namely, Israel. But when the time of judgment comes, the foolishness of these and all who followed them in worship is revealed to all people. Then they begin to decorate themselves, as Jezebel did when Jehu arrived and as you read of the foolish virgins; but this is in vain. To wit, they are made to look foolish. There is no further use for them except to be thrown down and trampled on by the people, so that before God and the people they end in shame and are destroyed, for they had persecuted and killed the prophets, that is, the preachers of God's word and God's glorious gospel. For "all flesh is grass, and all its beauty is like the flower of the field. The grass withers, the flower fades when the breath of the Lord blows on it. But the word of our God will stand forever." Because this history is described to us in such length, it is proper to speak of such unfaithful ones who rule against the Word of God with the molestation of their makeup. COMMENTARY ON 2 KINGS.[15]

ON PAINTING FACES. JOHN MAYER: Touching the painting of faces, Peter Martyr Vermigli here takes occasion to inveigh against the practice, as being censured by Cyprian, Chrysostom, Augustine and the rest of the Fathers. That is because it comes from pride and fleshly lust. It is practiced to allure men, and it changes their natural face into something artificial. But rather than bettering the face, it actually mars it. It is alleged that Cyprian said the devil taught the daughters of men to make themselves appear fair in this way to allure the sons of God to their destruction. COMMENTARY ON 2 KINGS.[16]

10:1-17 Jehu's Zeal for the Lord

WEIGHING IN THE BALANCE. DANIEL DYKE: Among ourselves, we must not reach forth the right hand of fellowship to everyone who begins to cry, "Lord, Lord." But first we must weigh them in the balance of the sanctuary, to see whether they are current metal or not. Jehu's question is for all good Christians to survey before they admit others into their society, "Is your heart true . . . ?" As Christ would not trust some who seemed to trust him because he knew them well enough, so neither should we since we do not know them at all. THE MYSTERY OF SELF-DECEIVING.[17]

PRETENSE OF ZEAL. JOHN ROBINSON: Some deceive others by the pretense of zeal they put on for their advantage. . . . Also, there are not a few who deceive both others and themselves by pretending to have God's zeal—which they completely lack—or pretending to have more than they actually do. Such was the case with Jehu. He loudly cried to Jehonadab, "Come with me, and see my zeal for the LORD." The truth is, however, that Jehu was more zealous for his own house than for the LORD, even though he did not think so. ESSAYS.[18]

---

[14]Pellikan, *Commentaria Bibliorum*, 2:184v-85r.
[15]Bugenhagen, *In Regum duos ultimos libros*, 145-46; citing Mt 25:1-13; Is 40:6-8.
[16]Mayer, *Many Commentaries in One*, 207*.
[17]Dyke, *The Mystery of Self-Deceiving*, 33*.
[18]Robinson, *Works*, 205*.

JUSTICE OR REVENGE? EDWARD REYNOLDS: Jehu was commanded to destroy the house of Ahab. He did so, and for doing what he was commanded to do, he did well. Yet his heart and God's heart were far apart. God wanted Ahab's house destroyed out of justice, while Jehu wanted it destroyed out of policy. Therefore, although Jehu esteemed his destruction as zeal, God considered it murder and the shedding of blood. And although God rewarded Jehu for what he commanded him to do, he still threatened to avenge himself since his execution of God's com-

mandment was excessive. Essentially Jehu was charged with the following by God's command: "I will avenge the blood of Jezebel by the house of Jehu." What, then, is Jehu to commit murder? God forbid! And yet isn't he commanded to commit murder? Yes, for God requires it. So, therefore, he was to perform God's command, but he was not thereby to work out his own agenda: God commanded him to execute his justice, but not his own revenge. THE SINFULNESS OF SIN.[19]

---

[19]Reynolds, *Works*, 1:221-22*.

10:18-36 JEHU STRIKES DOWN
THE PROPHETS OF BAAL

[18]Then Jehu assembled all the people and said to them, "Ahab served Baal a little, but Jehu will serve him much. [19]Now therefore call to me all the prophets of Baal, all his worshipers and all his priests. Let none be missing, for I have a great sacrifice to offer to Baal. Whoever is missing shall not live." But Jehu did it with cunning in order to destroy the worshipers of Baal. [20]And Jehu ordered, "Sanctify a solemn assembly for Baal." So they proclaimed it. [21]And Jehu sent throughout all Israel, and all the worshipers of Baal came, so that there was not a man left who did not come. And they entered the house of Baal, and the house of Baal was filled from one end to the other. [22]He said to him who was in charge of the wardrobe, "Bring out the vestments for all the worshipers of Baal." So he brought out the vestments for them. [23]Then Jehu went into the house of Baal with Jehonadab the son of Rechab, and he said to the worshipers of Baal, "Search, and see that there is no servant of the LORD here among you, but only the worshipers of Baal." [24]Then they[a] went in to offer sacrifices and burnt offerings.

Now Jehu had stationed eighty men outside and said, "The man who allows any of those whom I give into your hands to escape shall forfeit his life." [25]So as soon as he had made an end of offering the burnt offering, Jehu said to the guard and to the officers, "Go in and strike them down; let not a man escape." So when they put them to the sword, the guard and the officers cast them out and went into the inner room of the house of Baal, [26]and they brought out the pillar that was in the house of Baal and burned it. [27]And they demolished the pillar of Baal, and demolished the house of Baal, and made it a latrine to this day.

[28]Thus Jehu wiped out Baal from Israel. [29]But Jehu did not turn aside from the sins of Jeroboam the son of Nebat, which he made Israel to sin—that is, the golden calves that were in Bethel and in Dan. [30]And the LORD said to Jehu, "Because you have done well in carrying out what is right in my eyes, and have done to the house of Ahab according to all that was in my heart, your sons of the fourth generation shall sit on the throne of Israel." [31]But Jehu was not careful to walk in the law of the LORD, the God of Israel, with all his heart. He did not turn from the sins of Jeroboam, which he made Israel to sin.

[32]In those days the LORD began to cut off parts of Israel. Hazael defeated them throughout the territory of Israel: [33]from the Jordan eastward, all the land of Gilead, the Gadites, and the Reubenites, and the Manassites, from Aroer, which is by the Valley of the Arnon, that is, Gilead and Bashan. [34]Now the rest of the acts of Jehu and all that he did, and all his might, are they not written in the Book of the Chronicles of the Kings of Israel? [35]So Jehu slept with his fathers, and they buried him in Samaria. And Jehoahaz his son reigned in his place. [36]The time that Jehu reigned over Israel in Samaria was twenty-eight years.

a Septuagint he (compare verse 25)

OVERVIEW: The reformers wrestle with the moral ambiguity of the lies and murders that accompanied Jehu's divinely appointed task. They also note that the temporal promises given to Jehu and his descendants stand in contrast to the eternal spiritual promises given to David. Representing proto-Puritan Reformed attitudes toward worship, several commentators chide those like Jehu who leave worship only partially reformed.

10:18-27 Jehu Tricks the Prophets of Baal and Slaughters Them

JEHU'S CAREFUL WORDS. VIKTORIN STRIGEL: Jehu did not sin in this deception when he did not reveal his true face. For he did not promise a safe sacrifice to Baal but only that being absent would constitute a capital offense. He did not say, "I will protect Baal" but only that those who were absent would not live. Rulers may certainly pay attention to who is present and who is absent. Therefore Jehu was acting appropriately whether those who came were condemned of a capital offense in public or whether they had been sought out by subterfuge in their homes. BOOK OF KINGS.[1]

JEHU WAS JUST IN LYING TO THE BAAL WORSHIPERS. JOHN MAYER: When Jehu came to Samaria, he struck all who remained to Ahab, that is, all who were in any way allied with him and whom he had used as instruments to advance idolatry. He thus did in Samaria what he did in Jezreel. And having by these means made the kingdom secure—and having cut off all his enemies that might hinder his enjoying of peace—he called the people together. And by a strategy, he endeavored to gather all the worshipers of Baal together in the house of Baal so that he could kill all of them at once. It may be asked, therefore, whether Jehu sinned in lying in order to gather all the Baal worshipers.

Peter Martyr Vermigli answered that he sinned because his lying allured all of the worshipers of Baal together. If they would have known his plan, many of them would have otherwise happily left their idolatry. This act of dissimulation here, he argues, gave occasion for many good people to think ill of him and to surmise that he had no other cause of killing so many Baal worshipers than to get his hands on the kingdom. And what is said by others in justifying Jehu is taken away. . . .

It is true that to lie or dissemble is a sin, and likewise to kill is a sin. But Jehu was commanded by God to judge to death idolaters, which was a fitting judgment according to the law. And because it was his command to do so, it was also lawful to use any subtle means to circumvent and find them out, which to others was unlawful for them to do. . . . Otherwise Joshua's victory over Ai would not have

prevailed, given that he used dissimulation to give the appearance that he was fleeing; nor would the children of Israel have borrowed jewels of gold and silver from the Egyptians as if they planned to return them at a later time. COMMENTARY ON 2 KINGS.[2]

GOD USES SINS FOR GOOD. JOHANNES PISCATOR: Jehu's fraudulent summoning of the priests of Baal with the intent of deceiving them provides an example of the following: God employs the sins of people to do good. COMMENTARY ON 2 KINGS.[3]

FIGHTING IDOLATRY. KONRAD PELLIKAN: The priests of Baal had remained favorites of their impious patrons. They had served the queen and led the king to persecute the true prophets. Jehu convened them all as if to make a solemn assembly for Baal in order to kill them to the very last man, taking care that no prophets of the Lord or other pious people were mixed in among them. These priests had deceived the kingdom, rulers and people with false religion, using tricks and frauds. In God's dispensation, they would now be massacred through a pious deception, through which Jehu would erase the sacrilegious worship of idols from the entire kingdom of Israel and the shrines, sacred groves and statues with all their sacred decorations would be eradicated. COMMENTARY ON 2 KINGS.[4]

10:28-36 Jehu Rewarded with Ruling Descendants to the Fourth Generation

GENERATIONS OF PUNISHING KINGS. KONRAD PELLIKAN: Jehu's zeal and obedience were commended and praised, because he showed no mercy in how he deplored ungodly idolatry. For this reason, he received the kingdom of Israel to the fourth generation as a reward, even as Nebuchadnezzar's family would later be set over Judah to the

---

[1]Strigel, *Libri Samuelis, Regum et Paralipomenon*, 350.

[2]Mayer, *Many Commentaries in One*, 210*.
[3]Piscator, *Commentarii in omnes libros Veteris Testamenti*, 2:340.
[4]Pellikan, *Commentaria Bibliorum*, 2:186r.

third generation as a punishment. COMMENTARY ON 2 KINGS.[5]

JEHU'S EARTHLY REWARD AND GOD'S FIGURATIVE WEARINESS. JOHANNES BUGENHAGEN: Whoever obeys the temporal commands of God receives temporal rewards, as you see here and below in chapter 15. But eternal rewards will only be received if one is obedient in eternal things. This is no surprise, since even the Babylonians received a reward when their army destroyed Tyre in Ezekiel 29. The Latin text then says that the Lord began to weary of Israel. This is a human way of speaking, as if God began to have feelings of contempt for Israel, whom he had wanted to serve in love up to that point. But for this reason Israel was weakened by Syria as it says here and in chapter 13. From this you see that after the sword of Jehu came the sword of Hazael, king of Syria, just as Elijah had predicted in 1 Kings 19. COMMENTARY ON 2 KINGS.[6]

TEMPORARY REWARD FOR A TEMPORARY GOOD. JOHN MAYER: It is to be noted that whereas David, whose whole heart was upright, was promised the throne for himself and his descendants forever, Jehu, whose heart was not fully upright, was promised a descendant only to the fourth generation. That is, he received a temporary reward for a temporary performance of good. But it may be asked how Jehu's doing of good could please God if it came from an evil heart. This is especially stark in the context of the verse that says, "Without faith it is impossible to please God." For whatever is not of faith is sin. I will not here answer others who argue that the things Jehu did pleased God, but that they came from an evil and unbelieving heart. For if the things had not been pleasing to God, Jehu would never have been approved by God and rewarded with a line of descent. But without faith a person cannot so

please God as to be saved or enjoy his favor to the advancing of God's everlasting kingdom—as those faithful persons there spoken of in Hebrews. But people can please God so far as to be graced with temporary honor and blessings. If it is said, then, that God is in some way pleased with sin, I answer: That which is not of faith is sin. It is not sinful in every way, for it may be morally good, and then the act is in itself not evil or sinful but good. It is only styled sin because corruption is contracted for lack of faith and sincerity in the doer, which shall be punished eternally. Nevertheless, God can and sometimes does give temporal rewards. COMMENTARY ON 2 KINGS.[7]

DIFFERENCE BETWEEN ACTIVE AND PASSIVE OBEDIENCE. DANIEL DYKE: Obedience is twofold. The first kind, active, is doing that which God commands. The second, passive, is allowing that which God inflects. The temporary believer seems to have both of these.

For active obedience, the temporary believer may go far. There is no outward good work that a true believer can do but the temporary believer may also do. In fact, the temporary believer can even appear to do so in outward appearance with as great a spirit and zeal as the true believer. Such was the example we have in Jehu. He not only executed God's judgments on Ahab and his house and destroyed Baal and his priests but even did this (as others and he even himself thought) with great zeal and in the heat of godly indignation. In this way the outward eye would see little difference between the actively obedient spirit of Jehu in his reformation and the passive obedience of Josiah in his. THE MYSTERY OF SELF-DECEIVING.[8]

THE SIN OF PARTIAL ABOLISHMENT OF EVIL. JOHANNES PISCATOR: Although Jehu is praised for wiping out the idolatry of Baal, he still nevertheless is to be denounced for retaining the golden calf that Jeroboam had established. From this example

---

[5]Pellikan, *Commentaria Bibliorum*, 2:186r.
[6]Bugenhagen, *In Regum duos ultimos libros*, 149, following the Latin "began to weary" (*taedere*) rather than the ESV "began to cut off" at 2 Kings 10:32.

[7]Mayer, *Many Commentaries in One*, 213; citing Heb 11:6*.
[8]Dyke, *The Mystery of Self-Deceiving*, 110-11*.

we are warned of the following: It is not sufficient for a Christian magistrate to allow for divine worship to be partly absolved of falsity. Rather, false worship must be completely abolished. COMMENTARY ON 2 KINGS.[9]

WARNING NOT TO LOSE SPIRITUAL STEAM.
JOHN MAYER: Jehu did nothing of worth after he fell to the worshiping of the golden calves. His valor is said to be written in the book of the Chronicles of the Kings of Israel, not after. For afterward he had no courage to defend his coasts from the Syrians, but lost both Ramoth-gilead, which was lately recovered, and all the rich country beyond Jordan where the Reubenites, Gadites and the half-tribe of Manasseh dwelt. Because of that, not only were the people in those parts now struck, but also Israel was truncated. Part of the kingdom was taken away and brought under Syria. This appears because Jeroboam is said about sixty years later to have recovered the border of Israel from the entering of Hamath, so it seems that all this while it was held by them. Therefore be warned: Let kings keep all idolatry out of their kingdoms so that they do not invite ruin. Let them not be like Jehu, whose former spirit of courage turned into weakness and his glory turned to shame. COMMENTARY ON 2 KINGS.[10]

---

[9]Piscator, *Commentarii in omnes libros Veteris Testamenti*, 2:340.   [10]Mayer, *Many Commentaries in One*, 214*.

11:1–12:21 KING JOASH OF JUDAH

¹Now when Athaliah the mother of Ahaziah saw that her son was dead, she arose and destroyed all the royal family. ²But Jehosheba, the daughter of King Joram, sister of Ahaziah, took Joash the son of Ahaziah and stole him away from among the king's sons who were being put to death, and she put*ᵃ* him and his nurse in a bedroom. Thus they*ᵇ* hid him from Athaliah, so that he was not put to death. ³And he remained with her six years, hidden in the house of the LORD, while Athaliah reigned over the land.

⁴But in the seventh year Jehoiada sent and brought the captains of the Carites and of the guards, and had them come to him in the house of the LORD. And he made a covenant with them and put them under oath in the house of the LORD, and he showed them the king's son. ⁵And he commanded them, "This is the thing that you shall do: one third of you, those who come off duty on the Sabbath and guard the king's house ⁶(another third being at the gate Sur and a third at the gate behind the guards) shall guard the palace.*ᶜ* ⁷And the two divisions of you, which come on duty in force on the Sabbath and guard the house of the LORD on behalf of the king, ⁸shall surround the king, each with his weapons in his hand. And whoever approaches the ranks is to be put to death. Be with the king when he goes out and when he comes in."

⁹The captains did according to all that Jehoiada the priest commanded, and they each brought his men who were to go off duty on the Sabbath, with those who were to come on duty on the Sabbath, and came to Jehoiada the priest. ¹⁰And the priest gave to the captains the spears and shields that had been King David's, which were in the house of the LORD. ¹¹And the guards stood, every man with his weapons in his hand, from the south side of the house to the north side of the house, around the altar and the house on behalf of the king. ¹²Then he brought out the king's son and put the crown on him and gave him the testimony. And they proclaimed him king and anointed him, and they clapped their hands and said, "Long live the king!"

¹³When Athaliah heard the noise of the guard and of the people, she went into the house of the LORD to the people. ¹⁴And when she looked, there was the king standing by the pillar, according to the custom, and the captains and the trumpeters beside the king, and all the people of the land rejoicing and blowing trumpets. And Athaliah tore her clothes and cried, "Treason! Treason!" ¹⁵Then Jehoiada the priest commanded the captains who were set over the army, "Bring her out between the ranks, and put to death with the sword anyone who follows her." For the priest said, "Let her not be put to death in the house of the LORD." ¹⁶So they laid hands on her; and she went through the horses' entrance to the king's house, and there she was put to death.

¹⁷And Jehoiada made a covenant between the LORD and the king and people, that they should be the LORD's people, and also between the king and the people. ¹⁸Then all the people of the land went to the house of Baal and tore it down; his altars and his images they broke in pieces, and they killed Mattan the priest of Baal before the altars. And the priest posted watchmen over the house of the LORD. ¹⁹And he took the captains, the Carites, the guards, and all the people of the land, and they brought the king down from the house of the LORD, marching through the gate of the guards to the king's house. And he took his seat on the throne of the kings. ²⁰So all the people of the land rejoiced, and the city was quiet after Athaliah had been put to death with the sword at the king's house.

²¹ *ᵈ*Jehoash*ᵉ* was seven years old when he began to reign.

12 In the seventh year of Jehu, Jehoash*ᶠ* began to reign, and he reigned forty years in Jerusalem. His mother's name was Zibiah of Beersheba. ²And Jehoash did what was right in the eyes of the LORD all his days, because Jehoiada the priest instructed him. ³Nevertheless, the high places were not taken away; the people continued to sacrifice and make offerings on the high places.

⁴Jehoash said to the priests, "All the money of the holy things that is brought into the house of the LORD, the money for which each man is assessed—the money from the assessment of persons—and the money that a man's heart prompts him to bring into the house of the LORD, ⁵let the priests take, each from his donor, and let them repair the house wherever any need of repairs is discovered." ⁶But by the twenty-third year of King Jehoash, the priests had made no repairs on the house. ⁷Therefore King Jehoash summoned Jehoiada the priest and the other priests and said to them, "Why are you not repairing the house? Now therefore take no more money from your donors, but hand it over for the repair of the house." ⁸So the priests agreed that they should take no more money from the people, and that they should not repair the house.

⁹Then Jehoiada the priest took a chest and bored a hole in the lid of it and set it beside the altar on the right side as one entered the house of the LORD. And the priests who guarded the threshold put in it all the money that was brought into the house of the LORD. ¹⁰And whenever they saw that there was much money in the chest, the king's secretary and the high priest came up and they bagged and counted the money that was found in the house of the LORD. ¹¹Then they would give the money that was weighed out into the hands of the workmen who had the oversight of the house of the LORD. And they paid it out to the carpenters and the builders who worked on the house of the LORD, ¹²and to the masons and the stonecutters, as well as to buy timber and quarried stone for making repairs on the

house of the LORD, and for any outlay for the repairs of the house. ¹³But there were not made for the house of the LORD basins of silver, snuffers, bowls, trumpets, or any vessels of gold, or of silver, from the money that was brought into the house of the LORD, ¹⁴for that was given to the workmen who were repairing the house of the LORD with it. ¹⁵And they did not ask for an accounting from the men into whose hand they delivered the money to pay out to the workmen, for they dealt honestly. ¹⁶The money from the guilt offerings and the money from the sin offerings was not brought into the house of the LORD; it belonged to the priests.

¹⁷At that time Hazael king of Syria went up and fought against Gath and took it. But when Hazael set his face to go up against Jerusalem, ¹⁸Jehoash king of Judah took all the sacred gifts that Jehoshaphat and Jehoram and Ahaziah his fathers, the kings of Judah, had dedicated, and his own sacred gifts, and all the gold that was found in the treasuries of the house of the LORD and of the king's house, and sent these to Hazael king of Syria. Then Hazael went away from Jerusalem.

¹⁹Now the rest of the acts of Joash and all that he did, are they not written in the Book of the Chronicles of the Kings of Judah? ²⁰His servants arose and made a conspiracy and struck down Joash in the house of Millo, on the way that goes down to Silla. ²¹It was Jozacar the son of Shimeath and Jehozabad the son of Shomer, his servants, who struck him down, so that he died. And they buried him with his fathers in the city of David, and Amaziah his son reigned in his place.

a Compare 2 Chronicles 22:11; Hebrew lacks *and she put*   b Septuagint, Syriac, Vulgate (compare 2 Chronicles 22:11) *she*   c The meaning of the Hebrew word is uncertain   d Ch 12:1 in Hebrew   e *Jehoash* is an alternate spelling of *Joash* (son of Ahaziah) as in verse 2   f *Jehoash* is an alternate spelling of *Joash* (son of Ahaziah) as in 11:2; also verses 2, 4, 6, 7, 18

OVERVIEW: Queen Athaliah's reign in Judah provides the reformers ample opportunity to reprove tyranny, greed and idolatry. They focus much less on her gender than on her behavior as a ruler. While most of the commentators see her death as a just punishment, Strigel pauses to consider her death in light of Jesus' words to love

one's enemies. In contrast to his murderous grandmother, Joash (also called Jehoash in the biblical text) restores right worship, rebuilds the temple and follows the spiritual guidance of the righteous priest Jehoiada. For Protestant commentators, these reforms in Judah provide useful models for their own reforming projects.

11:1-3 *Athaliah Versus Jehosheba*

Satan's Hatred of Christ. Martin Borrhaus: Where did Jehosheba's impulse to save the seed of kingship come from? It came from a divine impulse, so that the following promise would stand: "I will not extinguish the light of David." In this act we see how faithful the Lord is in keeping his promises, and it is demonstrated how he makes a way. God especially keeps his promises when they appear to be forgotten. That is, when hope is very little, the promise will be kept so that more may believe by faith that the light will shine and manifest itself in the darkness. And hope will reveal God's greater strength in the suffering of these adverse things. It unites the increase of divine power with maximum goodness, until the light is distinguished from the darkness and life is brought forth from death.

Among the wise school of the godly, where the wisdom of the cross dwells, Satan incited Athaliah to destroy all the offspring of the kingdom, lest any hope of Christ, whom Satan knew would come from the family of David, would survive. But Satan was disappointed, just as he was disappointed before when he tried to destroy every male in Egypt on account of his hatred of Christ, since Satan understood that Christ would be born from the Israelites in this world. Indeed, Satan carries much hate against Christ, along with his demonic ministers and ungodly ones in this land. We can see this hate originally in Genesis 3. And in this present example of hate, Athaliah and her mother Jezebel, who will be sufficiently recognized as a notorious figure, attempted to shed the blood of the godly on account of their confession in Christ. Commentary on 2 Kings.[1]

Reformation in Israel, Corruption in Judah. Konrad Pellikan: For a while there was a reformation in the kingdom of Israel after Jehu killed the ungodly as God commanded him to do and tore down the sacred groves and shrines where idolatrous sacrifices had been made. But now the same situation is described in the kingdom of Judah in the seven years that followed, as the impious Athaliah reigned there. Athaliah was the wife of Jehoram and the mother of the Judean king Ahaziah, who drank deeply of the impiety of Ahab and Jezebel, for she was their daughter. She then resolved to kill all of Ahaziah's children, desiring to reign herself, so that there would be no descendants from Jehoshaphat or Jehoram remaining in Judah. But Joash was taken into hiding by Ahaziah's sister. This woman named Jehosheba was wife of the priest Jehoiada and a daughter of King Jehoram, who made sure that Joash was not killed with the rest of his siblings. Because Joash was only a nursing baby, he needed a nurse who would also be hidden with him in a secret place with him in a room near the Lord's temple until the infant reached the age of seven. In the meantime the ungodly Athaliah ruled. Commentary on 2 Kings.[2]

Athaliah's Plan and God's Providence. Johannes Bugenhagen: Athaliah wanted to rule alone, therefore she killed all the royal offspring, that is, all the males who might otherwise have ruled, including her own son's children. For what ungodliness would this child of Ahab not dare to commit? But Jehosheba stole Jehoash away, so that not all of her brother's offspring perished. Then the priest sought a time when they might be liberated from this ungodly reign. In the meanwhile, all of this happened according to the judgment and providence of God and the glory of God's Word. For the Lord had preached against the house of Ahab that all who joined themselves to this impiety would perish with him, even in the kingdom of Judah. But through this occasion or theft, one king from the branch of David was preserved, according to the promise made to David. For this history looks to Christ, the promised king descended from David, which is also according to the promise made to Jacob: "The scepter shall not depart from Judah," etc. What are the afflictions of these six years and

---

[1]Borrhaus, *Mystica Messiae*, 873; citing 2 Sam 21:17.

[2]Pellikan, *Commentaria Bibliorum*, 2:186r-v.

the blasphemies of the impious when compared to the promise made to David and the faith of the godly, which sees nothing other than the true future reign of David, and even of Christ, whose coming was promised? COMMENTARY ON 2 KINGS.[3]

A FOREIGN AND IDOLATROUS WOMAN ON DAVID'S THRONE. JOHN MAYER: Athaliah was most earnest in promoting the worship of Baal and of promoting her domineering spirit, killing her own grandchildren and thus extinguishing in herself all sparks of natural affections by means of her ambitious desire of being queen. She was carried on to this tragic act . . . by means of her submission to Baal, and so that the worship of Baal might be upheld in Judah, although it had been exterminated out of her father Ahab's kingdom of Israel by Jehu. For such is the fury of idolaters: they are quick to shed the blood of those who are not supportive of their idolatry. Fearing that the people would take one of her royal seed and make him king—who might easily be opposed to her superstition—she hastened to cut off all those she could find. And it is not doubted that she made this destruction of the royal blood hoping to exterminate the one coming of David and Jehoshaphat, of whom she would not want to leave one alive. Just as Jehu had tried to wipe out her father Ahab's house, so she tried to wipe out David's house.

But how is it that she was able to rule over Israel, given that she descended from the daughter of a Sidonian king, she was not fully an Israelite and she was a woman? For it went against the law for a foreigner to rule God's people. But most probably, having the administration of her son's kingdom in his absence, she now had the power to establish herself. What's more, the just judgment of God was working within her design as punishment of Judah for their idolatry, through which they were drawn by her means. But while she tyrannized in this way, behold the providence of God. According to his

word to David, God continued to preserve a light of David's seed, one suckling child called Joash. COMMENTARY ON 2 KINGS.[4]

TWO DESTRUCTIVE VICES. MARTIN BORRHAUS: Athaliah sets forth a horrible example of ambition for us to consider. And from her example we may recognize what wrongful desire and avarice brings forth. For these two vices of ambition and avarice are always destructive and ruinous to the good of the public. COMMENTARY ON 2 KINGS.[5]

11:4-16 *Jehoiada Puts Athaliah to Death*

LIKE MOTHER, LIKE DAUGHTER. JOHN MAYER: And upon hearing the noise coming forth, Athaliah went into the temple, saw what was done— the king was standing by his pillar—and she tore his clothes crying out "Treason, Treason!" And if Josephus may be believed, she bid the people to take the new king and kill him. However, the people cried out instead, "God save King Joash," and "Let Athaliah die!" Whatever the case, Jehoiada ordered the guards to have her thrown out of the house of the Lord so that she might be killed. This was immediately done. And in the way of the horses' entrance into the king's house, she was killed. We do not read of any person trying to save her. This shows us the miserable condition of tyrants: they may have the bodies of those whom they rule subject to them, but they will never have their hearts. In this way, all those with regal dignity must be fearful of every tyrannizing or unjustly usurping power. Just as the mother Jezebel came to a base end for her tyranny before being trodden underfoot by horses' feet, so most probably did her daughter Athaliah die a similar fate. COMMENTARY ON 2 KINGS.[6]

WASHING HANDS OF ATHALIAH. VIKTORIN STRIGEL: Enemies can be loved in such a way that

[3]Bugenhagen, *In Regum duos ultimos libros*, 149-50; citing Gen 49:10.

[4]Mayer, *Many Commentaries in One*, 214-15*.
[5]Borrhaus, *Mystica Messiae*, 872.
[6]Mayer, *Many Commentaries in One*, 218*.

does not dishonor the righteousness of God through punishment. Thus righteousness is honored in a punishment that does not come from an evil judge but from a good judge. So it was in this case. We may rejoice about the destruction of this tyrannical Athaliah for two reasons. First, this death conforms to the rule "Whoever sheds the blood of man, by man shall his blood be shed." Second, there is the admonishment to repentance, as the Lord said in Luke 13: "Unless you repent, you will all likewise perish." Therefore let us wash our hands of Athaliah's blood. That is, we ought first to give praise to God's righteousness for punishing tyranny and second to exclaim with the Psalm: "Surely there is a reward for the righteous; surely there is a God who judges on earth." Then—having been thus admonished—we should learn righteousness and not despise the things of God. Book of Kings.[7]

Death of a Heinous Woman and Line.

Martin Borrhaus: This heinous woman Athaliah was killed according to the divine *lex talionis* since she had destroyed the offspring of the kingdom and wickedly attempted to rob the kingdom of its legitimate heirs. Therefore this just sentence was sanctioned: The disloyal fall into the pit they have made for themselves. And just as Jehu had destroyed all the family of Ahab in the kingdom of Israel, Jehoiada, the priest of Athaliah the daughter of Ahab, extinguished it in the kingdom of Judah, lest Ahab's ungodly seed prevail. Commentary on 2 Kings.[8]

Allegory of Athaliah. John Mayer:

Rabanus Maurus gives the following allegory based on the life of Athaliah. She, seeking to destroy all the seed of David, symbolizes the synagogue of the Jews seeking to destroy Christ and the church, for Athaliah reigned while the temple and ceremonies of the law stood. But

Jehoiada, symbolizing the church, kept Joash close and so preserved him in an inward place of the temple. In like manner, the church preserves the faith and love of Christ in the hearts of the elect by preaching. Commentary on 2 Kings.[9]

11:17-20 *Making a Covenant with the Lord*

A Renewed Covenant. Konrad Pellikan:

After the death of Athaliah, who brought the idols to the land of Judah, the holy priest Jehoiada renewed the covenant to preserve the law of the Lord and serve the Lord alone, tightening the vows and compact among the king and the people. Like his neighbor Jehu in Israel, he succeeded in eliminating all the idolatry in the kingdom of Judah. To this end the people of the land promptly tore down the temples of the idols, the sacred groves, statues and images, along with the priests of Baal, including the high priest Mattan. Nor would they return to superstitious sacrileges, following and renewing instead the law in the temple that David and Solomon had established and turning from the false and impious snares of idolatry that would catch the people. And so they strengthened places and people in order to show true worship of the Lord in the temple. Commentary on 2 Kings.[10]

Beating Down Idolatry for the Lord.

John Mayer: Things being so much out of order, the wise priest thought it necessary—now that he had made Joash king—to direct him and the people to make a covenant with the Lord to root idolatry out of the land and to restore and maintain the worship of God pure according to God's Word. The priest also thought it time to join the people and king together again. This was accomplished by directing him to make a covenant to rule the people in justice and equity, and for the people to make a covenant to obey and serve Joash as their king and Lord. And this was not done without

---

[7]Strigel, *Libri Samuelis, Regum et Paralipomenon*, 355; citing Gen 9:6; Lk 13:3; Ps 58:11.
[8]Borrhaus, *Mystica Messiae*, 878.
[9]Mayer, *Many Commentaries in One*, 219*.
[10]Pellikan, *Commentaria Bibliorum*, 2:187r.

effect, for immediately the people went about that which their covenant tied them to perform, namely, to destroy the temple of Baal and the idols in it, and to kill Mattan the priest before his altars. And in doing this they had godly Asa going before them who, coming after idolatrous Abijam and Rehoboam together with the people, made a covenant with the Lord and mightily beat down idolatry. COMMENTARY ON 2 KINGS.[11]

11:21–12:21 Jehoash Reigns in Judah

INSTRUCTED IN RIGHTEOUSNESS. JOHANNES BUGENHAGEN: Because Jehoash knew himself to have been rescued by God and was instructed by the priest Jehoiada in the holy ways of Deuteronomy, he provided for the things of God. At first this especially meant having the temple restored by God's chosen one, so that the people could be called out of idolatry according to the dictates of the law. That is, so that they might serve God and call on God in the place of the promise. COMMENTARY ON 2 KINGS.[12]

PRESERVING RIGHTFUL WORSHIP OF GOD. JOHANNES PISCATOR: We are given a good example in the life of Joash. For after he was forced to pay tribute to the king of Syria, he was later taken by force at the hands of two of his servants. All of this occurred because after being subdued he returned to idolatry, as we read about in 2 Chronicles: "Now after the death of Jehoiada the princes of Judah came and paid homage to Joash. Then the king listened to them. And they abandoned the house of the LORD, the God of their fathers, and served the Asherim and the idols. And wrath came upon Judah and Jerusalem for this guilt of theirs." This should serve as a warning to all princes and leaders: If they do not constantly preserve the pure worship of God, they will often be punished by God. COMMENTARY ON 2 KINGS.[13]

CAREFUL STEWARDSHIP. KONRAD PELLIKAN: The monetary offerings given solely for the renovation of the temple were taken out, only when the ministers had collected enough and were to pay for necessary work. It is seen that those of average and below-average means also showed their devotion through liberal offerings, so that they barely had enough to carry out the restoration of the buildings. If the money needed to be spent for other purposes and various temple uses, then there was just enough for that too. COMMENTARY ON 2 KINGS.[14]

WEAK MEANS TO PERFORM GREAT DEEDS. JOHN MAYER: The kingdom of Judah, having been much disordered by Athaliah, now came by divine providence to be under the reins of a child. From these unlikely means it was difficult to imagine what could be expected for the amending of the people's condition. But it pleases God to often work by weak means so that he can magnify his power and mercy. Such is how he worked in this circumstance. Joash, by the good instructions of Jehoiada the high priest, did well and was accordingly rewarded with a long reign. His father and grandfather, by contrast, were wicked and therefore only reigned a short amount of time. COMMENTARY ON 2 KINGS.[15]

REBUILDING THE TEMPLE. JOHANNES BUGENHAGEN: The first work of God under Jehoash was to rebuild the temple. Today that means being built up by God's Word alone. For, as the apostle says, "God's temple is holy, and you are that temple." It is similar now to things back then that the priests and Levites who had been given care of instructing the people were often idlers. Therefore it is necessary that other people be called, or else the house of God would never get rebuilt. But the same was true of Jehoash as was true of King Asa in 1 Kings 15, that the high places were not taken away. COMMENTARY ON 2 KINGS.[16]

---

[11]Mayer, *Many Commentaries in One*, 218*.
[12]Bugenhagen, *In Regum duos ultimos libros*, 151-52.
[13]Piscator, *Commentarii in omnes libros Veteris Testamenti*, 2:344.
[14]Pellikan, *Commentaria Bibliorum*, 2:187v.
[15]Mayer, *Many Commentaries in One*, 219*.
[16]Bugenhagen, *In Regum duos ultimos libros*, 152; citing 1 Cor 3:17.

13:1-25 KINGS JEHOAHAZ AND JEHOASH

[1]In the twenty-third year of Joash the son of Ahaziah, king of Judah, Jehoahaz the son of Jehu began to reign over Israel in Samaria, and he reigned seventeen years. [2]He did what was evil in the sight of the LORD and followed the sins of Jeroboam the son of Nebat, which he made Israel to sin; he did not depart from them. [3]And the anger of the LORD was kindled against Israel, and he gave them continually into the hand of Hazael king of Syria and into the hand of Ben-hadad the son of Hazael. [4]Then Jehoahaz sought the favor of the LORD, and the LORD listened to him, for he saw the oppression of Israel, how the king of Syria oppressed them. [5](Therefore the LORD gave Israel a savior, so that they escaped from the hand of the Syrians, and the people of Israel lived in their homes as formerly. [6]Nevertheless, they did not depart from the sins of the house of Jeroboam, which he made Israel to sin, but walked[a] in them; and the Asherah also remained in Samaria.) [7]For there was not left to Jehoahaz an army of more than fifty horsemen and ten chariots and ten thousand footmen, for the king of Syria had destroyed them and made them like the dust at threshing. [8]Now the rest of the acts of Jehoahaz and all that he did, and his might, are they not written in the Book of the Chronicles of the Kings of Israel? [9]So Jehoahaz slept with his fathers, and they buried him in Samaria, and Joash his son reigned in his place.

[10]In the thirty-seventh year of Joash king of Judah, Jehoash[b] the son of Jehoahaz began to reign over Israel in Samaria, and he reigned sixteen years. [11]He also did what was evil in the sight of the LORD. He did not depart from all the sins of Jeroboam the son of Nebat, which he made Israel to sin, but he walked in them. [12]Now the rest of the acts of Joash and all that he did, and the might with which he fought against Amaziah king of Judah, are they not written in the Book of the Chronicles of the Kings of Israel? [13]So Joash slept with his fathers, and Jeroboam sat on his throne. And Joash was buried in Samaria with the kings of Israel.

[14]Now when Elisha had fallen sick with the illness of which he was to die, Joash king of Israel went down to him and wept before him, crying, "My father, my father! The chariots of Israel and its horsemen!" [15]And Elisha said to him, "Take a bow and arrows." So he took a bow and arrows. [16]Then he said to the king of Israel, "Draw the bow," and he drew it. And Elisha laid his hands on the king's hands. [17]And he said, "Open the window eastward," and he opened it. Then Elisha said, "Shoot," and he shot. And he said, "The LORD's arrow of victory, the arrow of victory over Syria! For you shall fight the Syrians in Aphek until you have made an end of them." [18]And he said, "Take the arrows," and he took them. And he said to the king of Israel, "Strike the ground with them." And he struck three times and stopped. [19]Then the man of God was angry with him and said, "You should have struck five or six times; then you would have struck down Syria until you had made an end of it, but now you will strike down Syria only three times."

[20]So Elisha died, and they buried him. Now bands of Moabites used to invade the land in the spring of the year. [21]And as a man was being buried, behold, a marauding band was seen and the man was thrown into the grave of Elisha, and as soon as the man touched the bones of Elisha, he revived and stood on his feet.

[22]Now Hazael king of Syria oppressed Israel all the days of Jehoahaz. [23]But the LORD was gracious to them and had compassion on them, and he turned toward them, because of his covenant with Abraham, Isaac, and Jacob, and would not destroy them, nor has he cast them from his presence until now.

[24]When Hazael king of Syria died, Ben-hadad his son became king in his place. [25]Then Jehoash the son of Jehoahaz took again from Ben-hadad the son of Hazael the cities that he had taken from Jehoahaz his father in war. Three times Joash defeated him and recovered the cities of Israel.

a Septuagint, Syriac, Targum, Vulgate; Hebrew *he walked*   b *Jehoash* is an alternate spelling of *Joash* (son of Jehoahaz) as in verses 9, 12–14; also verse 25

OVERVIEW: Despite Israel's unfaithfulness, the reformers observe that God delivers the people from many trials because of his own faithfulness. For the reformers, God's faithfulness to his promises is not a function of our worthiness. God's mercy is an invitation for all people to repent and trust in God, though some commentators express little hope that the wicked will ever truly turn. Comments on Elisha's death highlight the contrast between this godly prophet and the continued unfaithfulness of Israel's leaders. With the medieval practice of venerating relics likely in the background, the reformers are quick to deny intrinsic healing power to the bones of the saints. At the same time, they observe many strong testimonies to God's power here, including how Elisha dies confident in the Lord and how God can give life even in the midst of death, as in the revival of the dead man whose body touched Elisha's bones.

13:1-9 Jehoahaz Reigns in Israel

CONCERNING PRAYERS OF HYPOCRITES. JOHANNES PISCATOR: We are warned by the example of Jehoahaz and his being subdued that God also hears the prayers of hypocrites concerning external things. But those given thereafter are to be given to naught. We have an example of this in the case of Ahab: "Have you seen how Ahab has humbled himself before me? Because he has humbled himself before me, I will not bring the disaster in his days; but in his son's days I will bring the disaster on his house." COMMENTARY ON 2 KINGS.[1]

GOD'S MERCY AND AN UNNAMED SAVIOR. JOHANNES BUGENHAGEN: Israel was handed over to the sword of Hazael, king of Syria, as it says above in chapter 10. Still, the mercy of God is truly commended, as God heard the poor people, no matter how impious they had been before, so that they might be well aware of their sin and idolatry

and not go back to such things. So God helped them on account of his name when they called to him, so that it may be glorified by us, even to the coming end of the world as an invocation and record of God's mercy and covenant that he had made with Abraham, Isaac and Jacob, as it says later in this chapter. This story does not tell the name of this savior (that is, this leader and champion) whom God gave to the people. COMMENTARY ON 2 KINGS.[2]

HAZAEL THE WHIP. KONRAD PELLIKAN: The chosen people of God multiplied their sins and even added to their own afflictions. But this led to a change, even though they really did not want to know on whom their salvation depended. They did not want to know that they had a kind father, because they were so impious and despised God. Therefore, even after the idolatrous worship of Baal had been abolished, they still had not fully turned to the Lord. Parts of the kingdom were then given by the king into the hands of Hazael, king of Syria. He acted as a kind of divine whip, for it had been predicted that he would serve such a purpose for the Lord God. COMMENTARY ON 2 KINGS.[3]

GOD'S MOST JUST WAYS. JOHN MAYER: Although in the past a great multitude would have been raised to go to war out of Israel, now there were left only fifty horsemen, ten chariots and ten thousand soldiers. This is set down to show how deeply grounded wickedness was in them by a continual accustoming themselves to sin, so that we may beware of sinful customs. We are to so magnify the goodness of God that he would be entreated to help us and use his power . . . to give great victories to Israel. But God did not merely help the people because they sought him with their lips while their hearts were far away from him. Rather God acted to maintain his covenant with Abraham, Isaac and Jacob. . . . Moreover, God had already predetermined a longer time for them

---

[1]Piscator, *Commentarii in omnes libros Veteris Testamenti*, 2:347; citing 1 Kings 21:29.

[2]Bugenhagen, *In Regum duos ultimos libros*, 156.
[3]Pellikan, *Commentaria Bibliorum*, 2:188r.

before he would destroy them. This is so that his exceedingly great patience would be admired by all people who still upheld their state when they were so near to utter ruin. God also helped them so that when they would later abuse the help he gave them and were eventually destroyed by the Assyrians, they might acknowledge his judgments to be most just. COMMENTARY ON 2 KINGS.[4]

13:10-13 Jehoash Reigns in Israel

DIVINE PROMISES. VIKTORIN STRIGEL: This chapter tells a narrative in which God keeps his promises even to those who are unworthy, simply because God is true and good. For although Jehu's descendants deserved to lose the kingdom, God still remembered the promise to keep Jehu's descendants in power to the fourth generation. This is the firm word of Paul: "God is true." But a distinction about divine promises should be considered between those promises that are absolute and those that are conditional. Absolute promises do not require faith or real obedience, as in Genesis 9, regarding the preservation of the natural order. Conditional promises may then either belong to the law or the gospel. Conditions of the law require the addition of real obedience; conditions of the gospel do not demand our merit or worthiness but only faith, because once the commands have been made, faith is needed to receive the promise. No tool is needed to receive the benefits of the gospel except for faith. BOOK OF KINGS.[5]

THE REASON FOR A BRIEF SUMMARY OF JOASH'S LIFE. JOHN MAYER: The wicked life and death of Joash is spoken of here by anticipation, and Jeroboam's succeeding him in the kingdom, as appears in later verses. . . . The reason for this brief running over the history of Joash at first was . . . because all he did that was worthy of remembrance was to be brought in under the histories of Elisha

and Amaziah, which here follow by the prophesying of the one being encouraged and made successful in his wars against the Syrians, and by the provocation of the other being drawn out to that victory against him. The sacred historian, therefore, did not want to write anything more of Joash other than his wicked life and death. This was also done to hasten to Elisha's last sickness and death, where there is occasion again to speak of that great prophet. And then the history goes to Amaziah, in the time of whose reign what happened between him and Joash is recorded. COMMENTARY ON 2 KINGS.[6]

LIKE PARENTS, LIKE CHILDREN. JOHANNES PISCATOR: In the example of Joash, king of Israel, we are warned: The children of kings and leaders, when they succeed their parents after their parent's death, become attached to their parents' idolatry and sin. COMMENTARY ON 2 KINGS.[7]

13:14-19 Joash Seeks Out Elisha and Receives a Sign

SEEKING COUNSEL OF GODLY MINISTERS. JOHANNES PISCATOR: We are warned by the example of Joash that when kings and leaders are in danger, they should implore the aid of godly ministers of the Word. They should do this so that they may seek counsel from the Word for them and so that they may requests prayers on their behalf. COMMENTARY ON 2 KINGS.[8]

SEALING GOD'S PROMISES. JOHANNES PISCATOR: God often illustrates and seals his promises by employing signs. God did this in this passage to illustrate and seal Joash's victory against the Syrians. It was done by Joash but through Elisha. After first shooting one arrow, Joash was then commanded to beat the arrows on the ground. COMMENTARY ON 2 KINGS.[9]

[4]Mayer, *Many Commentaries in One*, 228*.
[5]Strigel, *Libri Samuelis, Regum et Paralipomenon*, 361; citing Rom 3:4 (Vg).
[6]Mayer, *Many Commentaries in One*, 229*.
[7]Piscator, *Commentarii in omnes libros Veteris Testamenti*, 2:347.
[8]Piscator, *Commentarii in omnes libros Veteris Testamenti*, 2:347.
[9]Piscator, *Commentarii in omnes libros Veteris Testamenti*, 2:347.

LITTLE VIGOR EQUALS PARTIAL VICTORY.
GIOVANNI DIODATI: God had made known to the
prophet Elisha by his Spirit that as many times as
Joash beat on the ground of his own accord was
how often he would overcome the Syrians. But in
foreseeing Joash's laxity and negligence in the
performance of beating forth on the ground and in
freeing his people by not pursuing a full victory,
God allowed Elisha to give this evident sign to the
king. And the prophet Elisha was angry for that
future neglect Joash would commit, that is, for not
beating on the ground more vigorously but only
three times. ANNOTATIONS ON 2 KINGS.[10]

13:20a Elisha Dies

FATHER ELISHA. KONRAD PELLIKAN: Here in
the death of Elisha is the testimony that King
Jehoash visited the sick man in humility, entrusting
him with the salvation of the people, for he did not
want the benefits of the dying prophet to perish
from the king or the people. The fear and worship
of the Almighty God might still be cherished if
some hope of salvation could be found. The king
wept over the face of Elisha, and he mourned his
death, since the prophet was quite old. He had
started accompanying Elijah in the nineteenth year
of King Jehoshaphat's reign, since which time over
fifty or sixty years had passed until the present
moment when Israel would again be saved under
King Jehoash, who now called on his father the
prophet and the chariots and horsemen of Israel.
For the kings had truly owed him reverence as a
father and honor as the apple of their eye, through
whom they were admonished, taught, convicted
and led into the way of salvation through the word
of the Lord. COMMENTARY ON 2 KINGS.[11]

DEATH COMES TO ALL. JOHANNES BUGENHA-
GEN: Elisha became mortally ill. He had healed the
sick and raised the dead. Even in illness, he
promised help against the king of Syria, so that the

dead could be raised. Death comes to the pious
and the impious, but it bewilders the impious
through desperation, while the pious receive peace
and joy in their consciences. Therefore the world
cannot ridicule or condemn a kingdom of such
faith, for while it may appear that those who
preach the Word or boast in faith are separated for
a while, in fact, they are glorified. COMMENTARY
ON 2 KINGS.[12]

13:20b-25 Elisha's Bones Resuscitate a Man

**JESUS' BODY BETTER THAN THE LIFE-GIVING
BONES OF ELISHA.** JOHANN GERHARD: "Whoever
feeds on my flesh," Christ says, "and drinks my
blood has eternal life, and I will raise him up on the
last day." Based on this, I conclude that it cannot
come to pass that your body should abide in the
grave since it is nourished with the body and blood
of our Lord. That is to say, it is nourished with that
food which is the medicine of immortality. It is the
antidote that keeps us from dying. It allows us to
live in God through Christ, and it drives away all
evil. By this food your weakness shall be comforted,
so that you may come through with Elisha to the
hill of the Lord. The bones of Elisha—in fact, even
when he was dead—gave life. How much more so
will the living and quickening flesh of Christ give
you everlasting life if you receive him by faith! THE
CONQUEST OF TEMPTATIONS.[13]

NO ENDORSEMENT OF RELIC VENERATION.
JOHANNES BUGENHAGEN: Here is a case in which
a corpse was thrown into Elisha's grave out of fear
of a coming army. But who does not see that the
Lord here made a great miracle out of this?
Through the raising of this dead man, the Lord
surely confirmed the preaching of Elisha, so that
they might see how much they had despised him
and then how much they were brought back to
their senses whenever they heeded this beloved one
of God who fought against the ungodly. You will

---

[10]Diodati, *Pious Annotations*, 24*.
[11]Pellikan, *Commentaria Bibliorum*, 2:188v.
[12]Bugenhagen, *In Regum duos ultimos libros*, 157.
[13]Gerhard, *Conquest of Temptations*, 40-41; citing Jn 6:54.

not see another miracle like this in all of Scripture. It happened so that they might believe this one whom God sent to prophesy, as we have said elsewhere. But this surely does not mean that some kind of honors should be devoted or an altar erected to Elisha's bones. I should not mention that it would be ungodly to want to make such a thing. But the righteous monks and greedy bishops canonize such things on account of false and deceptive signs, which do not have the smallest warrant in the Word of God or the holy gospel. COMMENTARY ON 2 KINGS.[14]

DEAD MAN'S BONES GIVE LIVING PROPHECY. JOHN MAYER: By their casting of the dead man so speedily into the sepulcher of Elisha it appears that he was not laid into a grave and covered with earth, as the manner now is. Rather he was put in a sepulcher of stone, having either a cover of stone to it or standing open in some vault or cave. For this

is how they buried Lazarus of old, and our Lord. And in the same way, we may well conceive how the dead man's corpse, being cast in, came soon to touch the corpse of Elisha if the stone covering him were but only removed first. What became of this man Scripture does not say. But the rabbis boldly suggest that he eventually fell down dead again. But he was also raised again, since he was not worthy to lie so near the holy prophet. But if this had been so, it might well have been suspected whether he was indeed raised up or not. It is therefore more probable that he lived and went to the king with his bearers, as witnesses, so that both he and all the people might reverence Elisha more and give credence to Elisha's last prophecy for the people to immediately prepare and go to war against the Syrians. This was to show that by a dead man's bones God was able to bring to life a state that seemed dead. COMMENTARY ON 2 KINGS.[15]

---

[14]Bugenhagen, *In Regum duos ultimos libros*, 158.

[15]Mayer, *Many Commentaries in One*, 232*.

14:1–16:20 FROM THE REIGN OF AMAZIAH TO AHAZ

[1] In the second year of Joash the son of Joahaz, king of Israel, Amaziah the son of Joash, king of Judah, began to reign. [2] He was twenty-five years old when he began to reign, and he reigned twenty-nine years in Jerusalem. His mother's name was Jehoaddin of Jerusalem. [3] And he did what was right in the eyes of the LORD, yet not like David his father. He did in all things as Joash his father had done. [4] But the high places were not removed; the people still sacrificed and made offerings on the high places. [5] And as soon as the royal power was firmly in his hand, he struck down his servants who had struck down the king his father. [6] But he did not put to death the children of the murderers, according to what is written in the Book of the Law of Moses, where the LORD commanded, "Fathers shall not be put to death because of their children, nor shall children be put to death because of their fathers. But each one shall die for his own sin."

[7] He struck down ten thousand Edomites in the Valley of Salt and took Sela by storm, and called it Joktheel, which is its name to this day.

[8] Then Amaziah sent messengers to Jehoash[a] the son of Jehoahaz, son of Jehu, king of Israel, saying, "Come, let us look one another in the face." [9] And Jehoash king of Israel sent word to Amaziah king of Judah, "A thistle on Lebanon sent to a cedar on Lebanon, saying, 'Give your daughter to my son for a wife,' and a wild beast of Lebanon passed by and trampled down the thistle. [10] You have indeed struck down Edom, and your heart has lifted you up. Be content with your glory, and stay at home, for why should you provoke trouble so that you fall, you and Judah with you?"

[11] But Amaziah would not listen. So Jehoash king of Israel went up, and he and Amaziah king of Judah faced one another in battle at Beth-shemesh, which belongs to Judah. [12] And Judah was defeated by Israel, and every man fled to his home. [13] And Jehoash king of Israel captured Amaziah king of Judah, the son of Jehoash, son of Ahaziah, at Beth-shemesh, and came to Jerusalem and broke down the wall of Jerusalem for four hundred cubits,[b] from the Ephraim Gate to the Corner Gate. [14] And he seized all the gold and silver, and all the vessels that were found in the house of the LORD and in the treasuries of the king's house, also hostages, and he returned to Samaria.

[15] Now the rest of the acts of Jehoash that he did, and his might, and how he fought with Amaziah king of Judah, are they not written in the Book of the Chronicles of the Kings of Israel? [16] And Jehoash slept with his fathers and was buried in Samaria with the kings of Israel, and Jeroboam his son reigned in his place.

[17] Amaziah the son of Joash, king of Judah, lived fifteen years after the death of Jehoash son of Jehoahaz, king of Israel. [18] Now the rest of the deeds of Amaziah, are they not written in the Book of the Chronicles of the Kings of Judah? [19] And they made a conspiracy against him in Jerusalem, and he fled to Lachish. But they sent after him to Lachish and put him to death there. [20] And they brought him on horses; and he was buried in Jerusalem with his fathers in the city of David. [21] And all the people of Judah took Azariah, who was sixteen years old, and made him king instead of his father Amaziah. [22] He built Elath and restored it to Judah, after the king slept with his fathers.

[23] In the fifteenth year of Amaziah the son of Joash, king of Judah, Jeroboam the son of Joash, king of Israel, began to reign in Samaria, and he reigned forty-one years. [24] And he did what was evil in the sight of the LORD. He did not depart from all the sins of Jeroboam the son of Nebat, which he made Israel to sin. [25] He restored the border of Israel from Lebo-hamath as far as the Sea of the Arabah, according to the word of the LORD, the God of Israel, which he spoke by his servant Jonah the son of Amittai, the prophet, who was from Gath-hepher. [26] For the LORD saw that the affliction of Israel was very bitter, for there was none left, bond or free, and there was none to help Israel. [27] But the LORD had not said that he would blot out the name of Israel from under heaven, so he saved them by the hand of Jeroboam the son of Joash.

[28] Now the rest of the acts of Jeroboam and all that he did, and his might, how he fought, and how he

restored Damascus and Hamath to Judah in Israel, are they not written in the Book of the Chronicles of the Kings of Israel? ²⁹And Jeroboam slept with his fathers, the kings of Israel, and Zechariah his son reigned in his place.

15 In the twenty-seventh year of Jeroboam king of Israel, Azariah the son of Amaziah, king of Judah, began to reign. ²He was sixteen years old when he began to reign, and he reigned fifty-two years in Jerusalem. His mother's name was Jecoliah of Jerusalem. ³And he did what was right in the eyes of the Lord, according to all that his father Amaziah had done. ⁴Nevertheless, the high places were not taken away. The people still sacrificed and made offerings on the high places. ⁵And the Lord touched the king, so that he was a leper^c to the day of his death, and he lived in a separate house.^d And Jotham the king's son was over the household, governing the people of the land. ⁶Now the rest of the acts of Azariah, and all that he did, are they not written in the Book of the Chronicles of the Kings of Judah? ⁷And Azariah slept with his fathers, and they buried him with his fathers in the city of David, and Jotham his son reigned in his place.

⁸In the thirty-eighth year of Azariah king of Judah, Zechariah the son of Jeroboam reigned over Israel in Samaria six months. ⁹And he did what was evil in the sight of the Lord, as his fathers had done. He did not depart from the sins of Jeroboam the son of Nebat, which he made Israel to sin. ¹⁰Shallum the son of Jabesh conspired against him and struck him down at Ibleam and put him to death and reigned in his place. ¹¹Now the rest of the deeds of Zechariah, behold, they are written in the Book of the Chronicles of the Kings of Israel. ¹²(This was the promise of the Lord that he gave to Jehu, "Your sons shall sit on the throne of Israel to the fourth generation." And so it came to pass.)

¹³Shallum the son of Jabesh began to reign in the thirty-ninth year of Uzziah^e king of Judah, and he reigned one month in Samaria. ¹⁴Then Menahem the son of Gadi came up from Tirzah and came to Samaria, and he struck down Shallum the son of Jabesh in Samaria and put him to death and reigned in his place. ¹⁵Now the rest of the deeds of Shallum, and the conspiracy that he made, behold, they are written in the Book of the Chronicles of the Kings of Israel. ¹⁶At that time Menahem sacked Tiphsah and all who were in it and its territory from Tirzah on, because they did not open it to him. Therefore he sacked it, and he ripped open all the women in it who were pregnant.

¹⁷In the thirty-ninth year of Azariah king of Judah, Menahem the son of Gadi began to reign over Israel, and he reigned ten years in Samaria. ¹⁸And he did what was evil in the sight of the Lord. He did not depart all his days from all the sins of Jeroboam the son of Nebat, which he made Israel to sin. ¹⁹Pul^f the king of Assyria came against the land, and Menahem gave Pul a thousand talents^g of silver, that he might help him to confirm his hold on the royal power. ²⁰Menahem exacted the money from Israel, that is, from all the wealthy men, fifty shekels^h of silver from every man, to give to the king of Assyria. So the king of Assyria turned back and did not stay there in the land. ²¹Now the rest of the deeds of Menahem and all that he did, are they not written in the Book of the Chronicles of the Kings of Israel? ²²And Menahem slept with his fathers, and Pekahiah his son reigned in his place.

²³In the fiftieth year of Azariah king of Judah, Pekahiah the son of Menahem began to reign over Israel in Samaria, and he reigned two years. ²⁴And he did what was evil in the sight of the Lord. He did not turn away from the sins of Jeroboam the son of Nebat, which he made Israel to sin. ²⁵And Pekah the son of Remaliah, his captain, conspired against him with fifty men of the people of Gilead, and struck him down in Samaria, in the citadel of the king's house with Argob and Arieh; he put him to death and reigned in his place. ²⁶Now the rest of the deeds of Pekahiah and all that he did, behold, they are written in the Book of the Chronicles of the Kings of Israel.

²⁷In the fifty-second year of Azariah king of Judah, Pekah the son of Remaliah began to reign over Israel in Samaria, and he reigned twenty years. ²⁸And he did what was evil in the sight of the Lord. He did not depart from the sins of Jeroboam the son of Nebat, which he made Israel to sin.

²⁹In the days of Pekah king of Israel, Tiglath-pileser king of Assyria came and captured Ijon,

Abel-beth-maacah, Janoah, Kedesh, Hazor, Gilead, and Galilee, all the land of Naphtali, and he carried the people captive to Assyria. ³⁰Then Hoshea the son of Elah made a conspiracy against Pekah the son of Remaliah and struck him down and put him to death and reigned in his place, in the twentieth year of Jotham the son of Uzziah. ³¹Now the rest of the acts of Pekah and all that he did, behold, they are written in the Book of the Chronicles of the Kings of Israel.

³²In the second year of Pekah the son of Remaliah, king of Israel, Jotham the son of Uzziah, king of Judah, began to reign. ³³He was twenty-five years old when he began to reign, and he reigned sixteen years in Jerusalem. His mother's name was Jerusha the daughter of Zadok. ³⁴And he did what was right in the eyes of the LORD, according to all that his father Uzziah had done. ³⁵Nevertheless, the high places were not removed. The people still sacrificed and made offerings on the high places. He built the upper gate of the house of the LORD. ³⁶Now the rest of the acts of Jotham and all that he did, are they not written in the Book of the Chronicles of the Kings of Judah? ³⁷In those days the LORD began to send Rezin the king of Syria and Pekah the son of Remaliah against Judah. ³⁸Jotham slept with his fathers and was buried with his fathers in the city of David his father, and Ahaz his son reigned in his place.

16 In the seventeenth year of Pekah the son of Remaliah, Ahaz the son of Jotham, king of Judah, began to reign. ²Ahaz was twenty years old when he began to reign, and he reigned sixteen years in Jerusalem. And he did not do what was right in the eyes of the LORD his God, as his father David had done, ³but he walked in the way of the kings of Israel. He even burned his son as an offering,ⁱ according to the despicable practices of the nations whom the LORD drove out before the people of Israel. ⁴And he sacrificed and made offerings on the high places and on the hills and under every green tree.

⁵Then Rezin king of Syria and Pekah the son of Remaliah, king of Israel, came up to wage war on Jerusalem, and they besieged Ahaz but could not conquer him. ⁶At that time Rezin the king of Syria recovered Elath for Syria and drove the men of Judah from Elath, and the Edomites came to Elath, where

they dwell to this day. ⁷So Ahaz sent messengers to Tiglath-pileser king of Assyria, saying, "I am your servant and your son. Come up and rescue me from the hand of the king of Syria and from the hand of the king of Israel, who are attacking me." ⁸Ahaz also took the silver and gold that was found in the house of the LORD and in the treasures of the king's house and sent a present to the king of Assyria. ⁹And the king of Assyria listened to him. The king of Assyria marched up against Damascus and took it, carrying its people captive to Kir, and he killed Rezin.

¹⁰When King Ahaz went to Damascus to meet Tiglath-pileser king of Assyria, he saw the altar that was at Damascus. And King Ahaz sent to Uriah the priest a model of the altar, and its pattern, exact in all its details. ¹¹And Uriah the priest built the altar; in accordance with all that King Ahaz had sent from Damascus, so Uriah the priest made it, before King Ahaz arrived from Damascus. ¹²And when the king came from Damascus, the king viewed the altar. Then the king drew near to the altar and went up on it ¹³and burned his burnt offering and his grain offering and poured his drink offering and threw the blood of his peace offerings on the altar. ¹⁴And the bronze altar that was before the LORD he removed from the front of the house, from the place between his altar and the house of the LORD, and put it on the north side of his altar. ¹⁵And King Ahaz commanded Uriah the priest, saying, "On the great altar burn the morning burnt offering and the evening grain offering and the king's burnt offering and his grain offering, with the burnt offering of all the people of the land, and their grain offering and their drink offering. And throw on it all the blood of the burnt offering and all the blood of the sacrifice, but the bronze altar shall be for me to inquire by." ¹⁶Uriah the priest did all this, as King Ahaz commanded.

¹⁷And King Ahaz cut off the frames of the stands and removed the basin from them, and he took down the seaʲ from off the bronze oxen that were under it and put it on a stone pedestal. ¹⁸And the covered way for the Sabbath that had been built inside the house and the outer entrance for the king he caused to go around the house of the LORD, because of the king of Assyria. ¹⁹Now the rest of the acts of Ahaz that he did,

are they not written in the Book of the Chronicles of the Kings of Judah? ²⁰*And Ahaz slept with his fathers* *and was buried with his fathers in the city of David, and Hezekiah his son reigned in his place.*

a *Jehoash* is an alternate spelling of *Joash* (son of Jehoahaz) as in 13:9, 12–14; also verses 9, 11–16   b A *cubit* was about 18 inches or 45 centimeters   c *Leprosy* was a term for several skin diseases; see Leviticus 13   d The meaning of the Hebrew word is uncertain   e Another name for *Azariah*   f Another name for *Tiglath-pileser III* (compare verse 29)   g A *talent* was about 75 pounds or 34 kilograms   h A *shekel* was about 2/5 ounce or 11 grams   i Or *made his son pass through the fire*   j Compare 1 Kings 7:23

OVERVIEW: Because more details about kings like Amaziah and Azariah (also called Uzziah) can be found in 2 Chronicles, these writers supplement their comments here with information from those passages. The commentators consider how pride infected the otherwise righteous kings of Judah and how God mercifully continued to send prophets and blessings to the idolatrous rulers of Israel. Though these chapters provide no direct prophetic speech, the reformers note that these years include the activity of prophets like Isaiah, Hosea and Jonah, and the beginning of the end of the northern kingdom. Finally, the commentators contrast God's judgment against idolatrous Israel with God's protection of Judah under Jotham.

14:1-22 *Amaziah Reigns in Judah*

THE PRIDE OF AMAZIAH. JOHANNES BUGENHA-GEN: The history of Amaziah is entirely similar to that of his father Jehoash. For at first he was seen as doing that which was right and he listened to the prophet, as you see in Chronicles. The Lord gave him a sign of victory against the Edomites, but that only resulted in showing him to be a hypocrite. For where he had a chance to give thanks to God for the victory, he blasphemously worshiped the gods of the Edomites instead. They, of course, were not able to free his people. Therefore the judgment of God was raised up against him, so that in his pride he provoked Jehoash the king of Israel. The saying goes, "the thrush soils its own nest." Unlike his father David but like his own father Jehoash, he did not remove the high places, which reveals his hypocrisy. For though his works may have been similar to David's, his faith was not.

As Chronicles says, "He did what was right in the eyes of the LORD, yet not with a whole heart." COMMENTARY ON 2 KINGS.[1]

HOW ONE CAN BE PARTLY RIGHT IN GOD'S SIGHT. JOHN MAYER: Amaziah began well, as Joash, but he ended poorly. This is clear from 2 Chronicles 25. Whereas David's heart was upright toward God all the days of his life, so were the hearts of very few kings after him. Their histories show this clearly. And in 2 Chronicles it is said of Amaziah in particular: "And he did what was right in the eyes of the LORD, yet not with a whole heart." But how, then, did Amaziah do that which was right in the Lord's sight? I answer that Amaziah refrained from worshiping idols and restrained the people also from them. He caused both himself and the people to come and worship the Lord only, and this was right in the sight not only of godly people but also of God. He did not do this out of piety and conscience, but rather he was moved to act thus by some other means. This is how Joash's father had done by the instructions and authority of Jehoiada. For Joash, seeing the ruinous estate of the kingdom when he came to it, thought by this he should obtain mercy and be saved from his enemies, by whom his father had suffered griev-ously. But returning to Amaziah, he is said to have done right, but not with a perfect heart as David had done. That's because David bent all the forces of his heart toward the promotion of worship and service solely out of piety without ever looking at any worldly advantage. For whoever does not act in this way does not do good with a perfect heart.

---

[1]Bugenhagen, *In Regum duos ultimos libros*, 159-60; citing 2 Chron 25 and a Latin proverb: *turdus ipse cacat malum sibi.*

That person is always unstable in the true religion, as Amaziah was, who fell therefore into great miseries, as the following history shows. COMMENTARY ON 2 KINGS.[2]

A SHEPHERD TURNED WOLF. KONRAD PELLIKAN: Kings easily grow proud in times of prosperity, forget the fear of God and modesty in times of victory, and think nothing of leading the common people into great harm. They long to satisfy their desire for war, so that those who are supposed to be shepherds of the people become wolves, shedding the blood of their friends in battles with enemies. Amaziah's war against the king of Israel had no cause. His hostile invasion ought to be used for consideration, taught endlessly and remembered often as a terrible thing. COMMENTARY ON 2 KINGS.[3]

FOOLISH COUNSEL INVITES AN ALLEGORY. JOHN MAYER: Now, although Amaziah had a just cause to go against the king of Israel for the wrong he had done him in his absence, it was temerity and not advised wisdom (though, to his credit, he did take counsel) to challenge him in this way. His counselors were probably such as those young men from whom Rehoboam had taken counsel previously when he lost the greatest part of his kingdom. A wise king would have sent to require satisfaction for the wrongs done him, or at least have taken the advantage of suddenly coming on him to salve his losses. But when God intends to bring the wicked to destruction for their wickedness, he helps them run toward their own ruin. And so he did to Amaziah at this time. He let him be lifted up with pride, so he would think his forces were now invincible simply because he had overcome the Edomites. He also pondered what the prophet Elisha had said to him when he went against Edom, namely, that the Lord was not with Israel. Nevertheless Amaziah was not aware of his recent idolatry, although the prophet had warned him

about the success of the wars he would undertak. Thus Jehoash responded to Amaziah through an allegory. . . . In the allegory, Jehoash compared their fighting to a marriage in which the over-matched spouse was always the object of harm. The beast trampling down the thistle, Jehoash compared to his own soldiers, who would easily subdue Amaziah's forces. COMMENTARY ON 2 KINGS.[4]

14:23-29 Jeroboam II Reigns in Israel

SENDING MORE PROPHETS. JOHANNES BUGENHAGEN: Under Amaziah's son Azariah until the time of Manasseh came eminent prophets like Isaiah and Hosea. Amos and Jonah prophesied under this same Azariah and King Jeroboam II of Israel. Thus you see how the grace of God's word abounded even after Elisha to call back those who despised them and blasphemed. Yet God might finally be compelled to thrown them down, so that the judgment might be feared where the word abounded, if—as today—there was contempt and blasphemy for God's preachers. COMMENTARY ON 2 KINGS.[5]

HEARING THE PROPHETS, HONORING THE PROMISES. KONRAD PELLIKAN: Jeroboam increased his ruined kingdom, because he listened to the prophet of the Lord and honored Jonah and Amos, who prophesied at the same time as Isaiah and Hosea. Therefore the former inheritance was restored to Israel, not because of the merit of its people, but because of the mercy of God. For God made promises to the fathers that he did not want to take away from their lame children unless compelled by their crimes. COMMENTARY ON 2 KINGS.[6]

THE PROPHET JONAH. JOHANNES BUGENHAGEN: Through Jeroboam II, who allowed the impious worship of the calves to continue, God freed Israel from Syrian oppression on account of the promises

---

[2]Mayer, *Many Commentaries in One*, 233*; citing 2 Chron 25:2.
[3]Pellikan, *Commentaria Bibliorum*, 2:189r.
[4]Mayer, *Many Commentaries in One*, 237*.
[5]Bugenhagen, *In Regum duos ultimos libros*, 161-62.
[6]Pellikan, *Commentaria Bibliorum*, 2:190r.

made to his fathers (as we have said above) and on account of the word of the prophet Jonah, who promised improvement though his words here are not recorded in his other book. But he spoke the truth and mercy of God, saying that the impious had not earned such things nor were these only the signs of the prophets. Rather, this was a present gift of admonishment to return to the God of their fathers. COMMENTARY ON 2 KINGS.[7]

15:1-7 Azariah Reigns in Israel

AZARIAH THE LEPER. JOHANNES BUGENHA-GEN: The story of Azariah (called Uzziah elsewhere) is similar to his father Amaziah and his grandfather Jehoash. He did things that were seen to be right, for he was instructed by the prophet Zechariah, son of Jehoiada, but no book of that prophet remains, as you see in Chronicles. But Azariah was cut off from the people on account of their defection to idols. For against God's law, he claimed for himself the office of priest and was stricken with leprosy by God, which is what God does when people claim for themselves the seat of priesthood and presume to teach the things of God without having been sent. COMMENTARY ON 2 KINGS.[8]

THE LORD HUMBLES THE PROUD. JOHN MAYER: The Lord miraculously showed the greatness of Uzziah's sin and how highly he was displeased at it, so that all people might learn by this example to keep their hearts humble and not be puffed up by their great wealth, honor and prosperity. For the earthquake happening now . . . see Zechariah, who says: "And you shall flee as you fled from the earthquake in the days of Uzziah king of Judah." . . . For he who was now superior to all people of those times in all things, when his heart was hereby lifted up, in an instant was brought to such an estate that he was sequestered

from the society of people as unfit for his loathsome disease to live among them. Uzziah had no liberty anymore to dwell in his own royal place or to reign as king or to come to the house of the Lord on account of carrying himself so proudly. . . .

Chrysostom also shows many other sins that coincided with Uzziah's pride. The first was ambition, in that Uzziah could not be content to enjoy the kingly dignity; rather, he had to usurp that of the high priest as well. The second was arrogance, in that he thought himself fit to execute both of these high offices. The third was impertinence, in that he was not quelled by the admonition of the high priest, but rather that he went madly on—determined to do what he wanted to do. The fourth was human folly, in that he sought to ascend to higher dignity than became him. The fifth was human viciousness and proneness to sin, in that, having before acted so worthily, he now fell foully. The sixth was impiety, in that he dared to break into that holy place that to come into was prohibited to all others save the high priest. . . .

Hugo well notes that the punishment Uzziah received for his sin was most suitable, in that as the high priest wore a plate of gold on his forehead to adorn himself when he offered incense, this proud king was made to wear the filthy mark of leprosy on his forehead forever as a perpetual ignominy. . . . This example shows that when a person does well—so much so that they come into great grace with God and the devil cannot prevail against them—they are not out of all danger of failing. And judgment will come, if despite the grace conferred on them they are lifted up in their heart. For "God opposes the proud, but gives grace to the humble." God will not tolerate pride in any way, especially in those called to ministry. Finally, whosoever seeks to make himself glorious shall have shame for glory. And instead of rising, this person shall fall from the glory they already had. And they will become the vilest among people, as leprous persons were. COMMENTARY ON 2 KINGS.[9]

---

[7]Bugenhagen, *In Regum duos ultimos libros*, 162.
[8]Bugenhagen, *In Regum duos ultimos libros*, 162-63; citing 2 Chron 24:20-22; 26:1-23.

[9]Mayer, *Many Commentaries in One*, 242*; citing Zech 14:5; Jas 4:6.

AZARIAH'S LEPROSY AND THE PRIESTLY OFFICE. KONRAD PELLIKAN: King Azariah was afflicted with leprosy because he had dared to enter the temple of God and take the priestly office for himself. According to custom, his condition meant that he had to live outside the city, as it says in 2 Chronicles 26. He then appointed his son Jotham over the people in the meantime. The Lord wants to be honored according the rule of the law that if someone tempts another to do what is an abomination and impure, they ought to be cast out of the church. For if God allowed that he could be honored by the ceremonies of everyone everywhere, there would be no end to ceremonies, which God wants to lead to devotion in faith, hope and love. COMMENTARY ON 2 KINGS.[10]

15:8-16 *Zechariah and Shallum Reign in Israel*

THE LAST RULER. KONRAD PELLIKAN: Zechariah was the last ruler from Jehu's line. He only ruled for six months, because he did what was evil in God's sight like the others. Thus God's promise to Jehu was proven true, that his descendants would rule to the fourth generation. He was killed in the presence of the people by Shallum the son of Jabesh, who had plotted how to take the kingdom. COMMENTARY ON 2 KINGS.[11]

GOD'S WORD TO JEHU FULFILLED. JOHANNES BUGENHAGEN: The word of God was fulfilled in this reign of Zechariah, king of Israel, who ruled for half a year. For the Lord had told Jehu in chapter 10 above that his sons would sit on the throne of Israel to the fourth generation. After that, however, there would be no end to impiety, including the overthrow of kings. No king of Israel could hand over the kingdom to his posterity, except for Menahem, whose son reigned for two years after him. All the others perished, even as the entire kingdom come to ruin, according to the saying, "Every kingdom divided against itself is laid waste." This certainly happened according to the judgment of God. COMMENTARY ON 2 KINGS.[12]

WHEN GREAT JUDGMENT FOLLOWS GREAT MERCY. JOHN MAYER: The end of Jehu's line has now come, of which the Lord had spoken of before in favor of Jehu's jealous proceedings. His children would sit on the throne for four generations. Jehoahaz was the first, Joash the second, Jeroboam II the third and Zechariah the fourth. For the Lord had hitherto vowed not to execute judgment on these idolatrous kings, since they were the race of Jehu and God had promised four generations to Jehu. In fact God had made Jeroboam and Joash prosperous so that this line of kings would persist until the kingship of Zechariah, the fourth in the line of Jehu's regal descendants. Yet God would not tolerate the wickedness of these kings now that his promise had been fulfilled. Indeed God broke out in his fierce wrath in judgment after judgment till they were destroyed. Note, then, that . . . God leaves no way unattempted to make sinful people turn to him. First, God acts through mercy, as he did with Jehu in raising him up to kingly dignity and making a great promise to him. Then, once mercy did not work, he sought to terrify his people by judgments. Afterward he returned in much mercy and compassion again, and gave them victory over their enemies. Finally, because God's mercy did not take any effect, he cast the people off, leaving them for a time to stain their hands in the blood of one another. Then God gave them into their enemy's hands, the Assyrians. Note that the greatest prosperity was followed with the greatest misery when no reformation was made. The reason for this is so that none may trust in present circumstances or continued prosperity if they are sinning without fear of judgment. COMMENTARY ON 2 KINGS.[13]

---

[10]Pellikan, *Commentaria Bibliorum*, 2:190r.
[11]Pellikan, *Commentaria Bibliorum*, 2:190v.
[12]Bugenhagen, *In Regum duos ultimos libros*, 164; citing Mt 12:25.
[13]Mayer, *Many Commentaries in One*, 246-47*.

15:17-22 Menahem Reigns in Israel

WASTING BORROWED TIME. KONRAD PEL-
LIKAN: King Menahem would have been unable
to reign if he had not provided aid to Pul the
king of Assyria. He was a beggar to King Pul
and made up for all this money he owed by
draining all the wealth from the kingdom.
Through this and other raids into the territory,
the king of Assyria extorted as much as he
wanted. Israel lacked faith in God and relied on
physical strength, going against the preaching of
all the prophets of the period. For this they
justly suffered oppression, for they despised the
Lord in whom they had previously hoped for
salvation. So it is with all the ungodly. COM-
MENTARY ON 2 KINGS.[14]

GOD WILL JUDGE USURPERS. JOHN MAYER:
After getting the kingdom, Shallum only enjoyed
it for a month. Then he was killed by Menahem,
the son of Gadi, who came from Tirzah and took
the kingship on himself. For, although Zechariah
was worthy to die for his idolatry, and the
appointed time by God had arrived to transfer
the kingdom from the family of Jehu to another,
Shallum was a wicked conspirator against his
lawful king and a murderer. As such, vengeance
from God soon cut him off, as it does to all those
who attain to royal dignity by bloodshed.
COMMENTARY ON 2 KINGS.[15]

**MENAHEM'S CRUELTY AND THE BEGINNING
OF THE BIRTH PANGS.** JOHANNES BUGENHA-
GEN: Menahem cruelly punished the city of
Tiphsah, which did not want to accept him as
king. I wonder how the Israelites could be
crueler than Hazael of Syria himself, of whom
such things had been predicted in chapter 8
above? But these things were only the beginning
of the birth pangs. For this Menahem brought
stability to Israel by making it a vassal of Assyria

and also started to send Israel's wealth to
Assyria. After the death of his son, all the
Israelite lands across the Jordan and some of the
lands not across the Jordan were taken away by
Syria. Thus those who had tried to find stability
through something other than God perished.
Under the penultimate king, Pekah, the Lord
began the transportation and abandonment of
Israel. After Pekah came the total destruction of
Israel, as you will see in chapter 17. COMMEN-
TARY ON 2 KINGS.[16]

BASE LIVING DUE TO IDOLATRY. JOHN MAYER:
Although Menahem was a most cruel tyrant, God
allowed him to continue for ten years to aggravate
his own misery and the misery of this wicked
people. For Menahem continued on just like
Jeroboam had done. And he was therefore forced to
make peace with Pul, the king of Assyria, by paying
great tribute to him. Not only did he exact a very
high amount of money from his subjects, but
Menahem was forced to pay Pul the exorbitant
amount of one thousand talents of silver. This
forced Menahem to live basely for the rest of his
life. COMMENTARY ON 2 KINGS.[17]

15:23-31 Pekahiah and Pekah Reign in Israel

HEAD OF THE MOST VALIANT TROOPS. JOHN
MAYER: Of Pekahiah, nothing is said but that he
went on in the sin of Jeroboam and reigned only
two years before being killed by Pekah the son of
Remaliah. This Pekah is said to have been
Pekahiah's captain. In Hebrew the word used
means "three." This is because either Pekah was
the third man of the kingdom or he had command over the third part of the army, which is
called the rereward. These were the most valiant
soldiers, who were the rear-guard of the army.
COMMENTARY ON 2 KINGS.[18]

---

[14]Pellikan, *Commentaria Bibliorum*, 2:190v.
[15]Mayer, *Many Commentaries in One*, 247*.
[16]Bugenhagen, *In Regum duos ultimos libros*, 164.
[17]Mayer, *Many Commentaries in One*, 247*.
[18]Mayer, *Many Commentaries in One*, 248*.

THE BEGINNING OF ISRAEL'S END. KONRAD PELLIKAN: The exile of the kingdom of Israel began in a large part under King Pekah, the son of Remaliah, when some members of the tribes were taken across the Jordan into Assyria. Not content with such calamities, people conspired against him and he was killed by Hoshea the son of Elah. COMMENTARY ON 2 KINGS.[19]

JUST PUNISHMENT FOR EVIL. JOHN MAYER: Pekah was allowed to reign for twenty years in the kingdom, which he came to by blood. He was also a wicked idolater. And because he was a man of blood, his blood was later required as well. There was a conspiracy against him led by Hoshea, who later killed Pekah. But God avenged him for his treachery, and Hoshea was imprisoned later by the king of Assyria. COMMENTARY ON 2 KINGS.[20]

15:32-38 Jotham Reigns in Judah

JOTHAM HIS OWN MAN. KONRAD PELLIKAN: King Jotham of Judah is commended as sharing the virtues of his father Uzziah, without being equal with respect to his father's evil. He was, however, similarly guilty of negligence with all the kings, in that people not only sacrificed to the Lord in Jerusalem but everywhere made sacrifices to the Lord using the high places. COMMENTARY ON 2 KINGS.[21]

KING JOTHAM. JOHANNES BUGENHAGEN: The stories about Jotham that appear different can be harmonized. For whatever else is considered about this time, it is clear that Jotham ruled while his father was still living. He then continued to rule in the time after his father's death, as the text says. COMMENTARY ON 2 KINGS.[22]

MERCY FOR A GOOD KING. JOHN MAYER: Josephus praises Jotham as a just, godly and excellent prince. Nor does the Scripture speak otherwise of him, but only very well. And his deeds for the good of the church and kingdom, and of God's blessing, are also evident. This, then, makes the people guilty, since they had such a godly king. . . . Yet however good he was, there was a corruption in the service of God, which greatly offended God, seeing that all sacrifices were now supposed to be offered in the temple only, which was built by Solomon. And therefore the Lord showed his dislike of this by raising up adversaries against Judah, Rezin king of Syria and Pekah, who were most likely raised up toward the latter end of Jotham's reign. As such, Jotham may not have lived to see their coming, but was taken away in mercy. But in the days of his wicked son Ahaz, these adversaries fully came against Judah. COMMENTARY ON 2 KINGS.[23]

GOD DEFENDS JUDAH. JOHANNES BUGENHAGEN: This Jotham conducted himself in the way of the Lord God. Therefore God made him strong against his adversaries. He was protected by the Lord, because in his day the king of Syria and the king of Israel began to come together against Judah but they did not prevail, purely on account of God's love for Jotham. COMMENTARY ON 2 KINGS.[24]

16:1-20 Ahaz Reigns in Judah

THE KINGDOM OF DESPAIR. JOHANNES BUGENHAGEN: Chapter 16 shows how titles mean nothing, as Ahaz was the most impious son of a pious father and, in return, he himself had the most pious son Hezekiah. He in turn somehow became the father of the most impious Manasseh. The prerogatives of the flesh are nothing before God, who only looks on the faith of the heart (John 8). This is how the impious today speak of the gospel. They say, "If this doctrine is true, then

---

[19]Pellikan, Commentaria Bibliorum, 2:191r.
[20]Mayer, Many Commentaries in One, 248*.
[21]Pellikan, Commentaria Bibliorum, 2:191r.
[22]Bugenhagen, In Regum duos ultimos libros, 163; referring to the fact that Jotham's father is named as being Azariah and Uzziah in this chapter.

[23]Mayer, Many Commentaries in One, 250*; citing 2 Chron 27:2.
[24]Bugenhagen, In Regum duos ultimos libros, 163.

my fathers are condemned. It condemns our elders and our ancestors, which is something we cannot bear." Ahaz used this mode of impiety, so that the kingdom was always very unwell during his reign, as you see more clearly in Chronicles. He not only followed the sins of the kings of Israel but also erected all the idols of the Gentiles who had previously lived in the land of Canaan, which was prohibited in Deuteronomy 18. Moreover, he turned all the worship of God into sacrifices and oblations to the gods of Syria in all of his cities. Thus he is accused in Chronicles not only of impiety but also of even increasing impiety during times of anguish. By this Scripture is signifying that God handed him over to all of his iniquity so that he might return to the Lord through his afflictions. Manasseh experienced this same example, as we will hear later. Here the distinguished voices of the prophets, who prophesied at that time, were of no benefit. For how much contempt did Ahaz show the brilliant Isaiah, who in a time of great need promised to give a sign of God's protection against the kings of Syria and Israel, as you can see in Isaiah 7. Ahaz then did what is customary under human nature; he decided that trusting himself to the word of God was vain and foolish. So he said, "I will not ask, and I will not put the Lord to the test." In his contempt of the God through whom Isaiah had promised deliverance, he submitted himself to the Assyrians for protection. The Assyrians then laid waste to Damascus and carried the people to Kir. Syria deserved this punishment because of the evil it brought on Israel under Hazael. This happened as the prophet Amos had prophesied shortly beforehand, as you read in Amos 1. Thus runs the hidden judgment of God, which we see as nothing but human activity. Shortly after this came devastation on Judah from Assyria, which had been a protector, as you read in Chronicles. So why did Ahaz submit? For he had to give gold and silver as restitution and placation, because he had also been seen casting away the holy things of God. Who will not gaze on this kingdom that is so lamentable according to God and the world,

where there is only contempt for God and consideration of human things? Is this kingdom anything other than a kingdom of pure despair? COMMENTARY ON 2 KINGS.[25]

SAVED BY THE PROPHETS. KONRAD PELLIKAN: The impious King Ahaz was chastened by God, who sent the enemy armies of two kings against him. The capital city was under siege. But God's mercy and the merit and prayers of the pious prophets Hosea and Isaiah saved the city of Jerusalem. After the death of Jotham, these truly pious fathers did what was commanded, even though they worked under Ahaz. COMMENTARY ON 2 KINGS.[26]

A KING SEEKING AID FROM THE WRONG SOURCE. JOHANNES PISCATOR: In Ahaz is set forth an example of an ungodly king. He first surrendered himself to idolatry, and did so immensely. Then, when he was in danger, he did not seek the help of God at all. On the contrary, he fled to a foreign and idolatrous king. What's more, he changed the divine worship and instead instituted a new form of worship of God that was according to his own evil pleasure. COMMENTARY ON 2 KINGS.[27]

GOD PRESERVES THE TRUE CHURCH. HEINRICH BULLINGER: Despite calamities in the church in which the leaders fall away from the Word and true worship of God and instead embrace and bring in new laws and new rituals—which thereby obscure or cast off the true external marks of the church for a time—God Almighty nevertheless preserves the church on earth for his own sake. God also supports and repairs the church with true teachers, even though they are not acknowledged as true teachers and ministers of the church of God by those who appear to be the true and regular leaders of the church; in fact they are condemned as seditious disturbers and detestable

[25]Bugenhagen, *In Regum duos ultimos libros*, 166-68; citing Is 7:12.
[26]Pellikan, *Commentaria Bibliorum*, 2:191r.
[27]Piscator, *Commentarii in omnes libros Veteris Testamenti*, 2:353.

heretics of the church. I can illustrate my point by an example taken from Scripture. In the time of Ahaz King of Judah, with Uriah the high priest winking at the situation and the princes of the kingdom and the priests not resisting at all, the king closed down the temple of the Lord and removed the holy seat—about which Scripture freely discusses. As a result of this action, the ministry of the word and the lawful and regular sacrifices ceased. Nevertheless there was still a holy church in the kingdom of Judah. DECADES 5.2.[28]

SUBTLE IDOLATRY. KONRAD PELLIKAN: Even though Ahaz sacrificed as king and priest to the idols of Damascus and Assyria according to their customs, not very much appeared to be different from the holy and true Mosaic sacrifice. For he made peace offerings, threw the blood on the altar, offered firstfruits and allowed people to ascend to the altar. Meanwhile he wanted to appear very religious, as if able to serve both the king of Assyria and the Lord. COMMENTARY ON 2 KINGS.[29]

LIKE KING, LIKE PRIESTS, LIKE PEOPLE. JOHN MAYER: Ahaz sinned foully in several ways. First, he sinned by idolatry after the manner of the Israelite kings. In fact he made his son go through the fire to Molech. . . . Second, Ahaz sinned by infidelity. He rejected all confidence in God and put his trust rather in the king of Assyria. Third, he set up a strange altar in the courts of the Lord's house, making the altar built by Solomon give way

to it. Fourth, Ahaz robbed the Lord's house of its ornaments, and he did not allow the people to worship the Lord in the real sanctuary. Fifth, Ahaz sacrificed to the gods of Damascus, which had struck him. And seeking to draw the people to the same idolatry, he set up altars for these gods in many places. Last, Ahaz was incorrigible. Despite being severely punished by the Syrians, Israelites, Assyrians, Edomites and the Philistines, he was completely unwilling to repent. He thus exercised the anger of the Lord in all the ways devisable. The result of his influence was like king, like priests, so that the entire state was intolerably corrupted. COMMENTARY ON 2 KINGS.[30]

NO WARRANT TO SACRIFICE. MARTIN LUTHER: The Jews were not Abraham; that is, they did not have a command, as Abraham did, about immolating their children. Indeed, the fifth commandment forbade in general all kinds of homicide. Yet Ahaz thought he was rendering God a splendid service if he made his children pass through fire. The antecedent was as follows: even a son must be killed on God's account, as the example of Abraham teaches. "Therefore," he said, "I, too, shall kill my son." But this is a false conclusion because of the dissimilarity. It was by a special and new command that Abraham was ordered to immolate his son; this command Ahaz did not have. Therefore he should have undertaken nothing contrary to the clear commandment of the Decalogue. LECTURES ON GENESIS.[31]

[28]Bullinger, *Sermonum decades quinque*, 365-66.
[29]Pellikan, *Commentaria Bibliorum*, 2:191v.
[30]Mayer, *Many Commentaries in One*, 256-57*.
[31]LW 4:102.

17:1-41 THE END OF ISRAEL

¹In the twelfth year of Ahaz king of Judah, Hoshea the son of Elah began to reign in Samaria over Israel, and he reigned nine years. ²And he did what was evil in the sight of the Lord, yet not as the kings of Israel who were before him. ³Against him came up Shalmaneser king of Assyria. And Hoshea became his vassal and paid him tribute. ⁴But the king of Assyria found treachery in Hoshea, for he had sent messengers to So, king of Egypt, and offered no tribute to the king of Assyria, as he had done year by year. Therefore the king of Assyria shut him up and bound him in prison. ⁵Then the king of Assyria invaded all the land and came to Samaria, and for three years he besieged it.

⁶In the ninth year of Hoshea, the king of Assyria captured Samaria, and he carried the Israelites away to Assyria and placed them in Halah, and on the Habor, the river of Gozan, and in the cities of the Medes.

⁷And this occurred because the people of Israel had sinned against the Lord their God, who had brought them up out of the land of Egypt from under the hand of Pharaoh king of Egypt, and had feared other gods ⁸and walked in the customs of the nations whom the Lord drove out before the people of Israel, and in the customs that the kings of Israel had practiced. ⁹And the people of Israel did secretly against the Lord their God things that were not right. They built for themselves high places in all their towns, from watchtower to fortified city. ¹⁰They set up for themselves pillars and Asherim on every high hill and under every green tree, ¹¹and there they made offerings on all the high places, as the nations did whom the Lord carried away before them. And they did wicked things, provoking the Lord to anger, ¹²and they served idols, of which the Lord had said to them, "You shall not do this." ¹³Yet the Lord warned Israel and Judah by every prophet and every seer, saying, "Turn from your evil ways and keep my commandments and my statutes, in accordance with all the Law that I commanded your fathers, and that I sent to you by my servants the prophets."

¹⁴But they would not listen, but were stubborn, as their fathers had been, who did not believe in the Lord their God. ¹⁵They despised his statutes and his covenant that he made with their fathers and the warnings that he gave them. They went after false idols and became false, and they followed the nations that were around them, concerning whom the Lord had commanded them that they should not do like them. ¹⁶And they abandoned all the commandments of the Lord their God, and made for themselves metal images of two calves; and they made an Asherah and worshiped all the host of heaven and served Baal. ¹⁷And they burned their sons and their daughters as offerings[a] and used divination and omens and sold themselves to do evil in the sight of the Lord, provoking him to anger. ¹⁸Therefore the Lord was very angry with Israel and removed them out of his sight. None was left but the tribe of Judah only.

¹⁹Judah also did not keep the commandments of the Lord their God, but walked in the customs that Israel had introduced. ²⁰And the Lord rejected all the descendants of Israel and afflicted them and gave them into the hand of plunderers, until he had cast them out of his sight.

²¹When he had torn Israel from the house of David, they made Jeroboam the son of Nebat king. And Jeroboam drove Israel from following the Lord and made them commit great sin. ²²The people of Israel walked in all the sins that Jeroboam did. They did not depart from them, ²³until the Lord removed Israel out of his sight, as he had spoken by all his servants the prophets. So Israel was exiled from their own land to Assyria until this day.

²⁴And the king of Assyria brought people from Babylon, Cuthah, Avva, Hamath, and Sepharvaim, and placed them in the cities of Samaria instead of the people of Israel. And they took possession of Samaria and lived in its cities. ²⁵And at the beginning of their dwelling there, they did not fear the Lord. Therefore the Lord sent lions among them, which killed some of them. ²⁶So the king of Assyria was told, "The nations that you have carried away and placed in the cities of Samaria do not know the law of the god of the land. Therefore he has sent lions among them, and behold, they are killing them,

because they do not know the law of the god of the land." ²⁷Then the king of Assyria commanded, "Send there one of the priests whom you carried away from there, and let him^b go and dwell there and teach them the law of the god of the land." ²⁸So one of the priests whom they had carried away from Samaria came and lived in Bethel and taught them how they should fear the LORD.

²⁹But every nation still made gods of its own and put them in the shrines of the high places that the Samaritans had made, every nation in the cities in which they lived. ³⁰The men of Babylon made Succoth-benoth, the men of Cuth made Nergal, the men of Hamath made Ashima, ³¹and the Avvites made Nibhaz and Tartak; and the Sepharvites burned their children in the fire to Adrammelech and Anammelech, the gods of Sepharvaim. ³²They also feared the LORD and appointed from among themselves all sorts of people as priests of the high places, who sacrificed for them in the shrines of the high places. ³³So they feared the LORD but also served their own gods, after the manner of the nations from among whom they had been carried away.

³⁴To this day they do according to the former manner. They do not fear the LORD, and they do not follow the statutes or the rules or the law or the commandment that the LORD commanded the children of Jacob, whom he named Israel. ³⁵The LORD made a covenant with them and commanded them, "You shall not fear other gods or bow yourselves to them or serve them or sacrifice to them, ³⁶but you shall fear the LORD, who brought you out of the land of Egypt with great power and with an outstretched arm. You shall bow yourselves to him, and to him you shall sacrifice. ³⁷And the statutes and the rules and the law and the commandment that he wrote for you, you shall always be careful to do. You shall not fear other gods, ³⁸and you shall not forget the covenant that I have made with you. You shall not fear other gods, ³⁹but you shall fear the LORD your God, and he will deliver you out of the hand of all your enemies." ⁴⁰However, they would not listen, but they did according to their former manner.

⁴¹So these nations feared the LORD and also served their carved images. Their children did likewise, and their children's children—as their fathers did, so they do to this day.

a Or made their sons and their daughters pass through the fire   b Syriac, Vulgate; Hebrew them

---

OVERVIEW: The reformers recognize that the fall of the northern kingdom to the Assyrians not only stands as a key moment in the history of Israel but also casts a long shadow into the New Testament, especially because it provides the origin story for the Samaritans of Jesus' time. While commentators offer several explanations for Israel's demise, the most precise explanation is that they lacked faith in their loving, fatherly God. Even so, the reformers note that God does not leave the people entirely but establishes some traditions of faithful preaching and worship in the midst of other practices.

17:1-23 The Kingdom of Israel Overtaken

ISRAEL'S CAPTIVITY. KONRAD PELLIKAN: This calamity that Hoshea provoked from King Shalmaneser of Assyria was worse than others because Hoshea was supposed to serve Assyria and pay tribute, as he had done every other year. But he had also foolishly sought out an alliance with the king of Egypt, through whom he might be rescued from his servitude to Assyria. When the king of Assyria discovered this, he seized Hoshea by force and shut him in prison. In the ninth year of his reign, Samaria was besieged for three years, until all Israel was taken into exile in Assyria. According to the Hebrew people, this exile still endures, except among the tribe of Judah, which was preserved by King Hezekiah. COMMENTARY ON 2 KINGS.[1]

THE FALL OF ISRAEL. JOHANNES BUGENHAGEN: Here at last is the end of the kingdom of Israel, which came because they did not stop the sin they had been accused of. Therefore God withdrew and stripped away all that had been given to their

---

[1]Pellikan, Commentaria Bibliorum, 2:192r.

ancestors. For no blessings, no rebukes and preaching or even miracles of the prophets could win this people over to that which God sought, which was a certain faith, that is, that God be acknowledged as Father. COMMENTARY ON 2 KINGS.[2]

PARTIAL GOODNESS DOES NOT MERIT GOD'S MERCY. JOHN MAYER: God had now been greatly provoked in that kingdom. And even though Hoshea was not as bad as his predecessors, his kingdom was completely tainted with idolatry and he was as guilty as the rest of them. For he did not seek to reform the kingdom as he should have done. God would now spare them no longer. He would first bring them into servitude and thereafter into miserable captivity. Just because we are not as wicked as another, this does not merit God's mercy, which spares us from his most severe judgments. Whoever does evil, despite how small and seemingly inconsequential, is in danger of God's wrath. And certainly those who sin greatly are much more likely in danger. We must learn not to abhor our evil in relation to someone's worse evil, but to hate any evil at all. COMMENTARY ON 2 KINGS.[3]

WHY GOD SWEPT ISRAEL AWAY. JOHN MAYER: Now follow the causes of why God was so severe against his people by means of his sweeping Israel away. Although God had brought them in singular mercy out of the land of Egypt, they continued to serve other gods and forsook the Lord. They became just like the Gentiles, who lived all around them. And when the Lord sent his prophets to admonish the people, they still persisted in their idolatry. They therefore showed themselves contemptuous of his statutes. And from this they proceeded to the casting aside of all the Lord's commandments. Particularly, the people's horrible sins were laid bare. They made golden calves and worshiped them, including the whole host of heaven and Baal. They made their children go

through the fire and gave themselves over to witchcraft. Therefore the Lord removed them in his wrath, leaving behind only the tribe of Judah. Nor did he let this tribe fully escape. For the present they were given over into the hands of robbers, as has been seen in the history of Ahaz. That's because Judah had sinned just like Israel. . . . In short, the incredible length of time the people of Israel sinned—even from the very beginning with Jeroboam until their captivity to Assyria—made them guilty of destruction. There were 262 years from Jeroboam's idolatry till their captivity. . . . Such is a very long time for the Lord to be provoked before he finally judged them in his severity. From this perspective, we see the incredible patience of the Lord, as he endured the people's wickedness for such a long time. But although the Lord is patient, his wrath will at long last break out on any nation for continued disobedience. COMMENTARY ON 2 KINGS.[4]

EXAMPLE OF DIVINE JUDGMENT. JOHANNES PISCATOR: In the ten tribes of Israel's deportation into Assyria is set forth an example of God's judgment on idolatry and on contemning the warnings of the teachers of his Word. Indeed the Israelites set forth a remarkable example of contumacy. For they spurned the warnings of the prophets and did not cease from committing idolatry. COMMENTARY ON 2 KINGS.[5]

REJECTING GOD, MOSES AND THE PROPHETS. KONRAD PELLIKAN: This disaster had its earliest origin when the kingdom of Israel separated from the tribe of Judah. This happened with divine permission on account of the sins of Solomon and David. It was carried out by Jeroboam the son of Nebat, who persuaded the ten tribes to go outside the divine law by saying that it would be better to adhere to human traditions and feelings of the flesh than to the word of the Lord and the worship of God according to God's institution. Their

---

[2]Bugenhagen, *In Regum duos ultimos libros*, 170.
[3]Mayer, *Many Commentaries in One*, 258*.
[4]Mayer, *Many Commentaries in One*, 259-60*.
[5]Piscator, *Commentarii in omnes libros Veteris Testamenti*, 2:356.

unbelief was the most serious of all sins. But that is what King Jeroboam of Israel did, to the death and ruin of faith, and the prophets could not redress such great evil, even when using the best remedies. For how could people who had dared to reject Moses be able to believe the prophets? COMMENTARY ON 2 KINGS.[6]

17:24-41 Assyria Resettles Samaria

RESETTLING SAMARIA. JOHANNES BUGENHAGEN: Because Israel would not be brought back to its land, foreigners were brought into Samaria itself. This did not happen until later in Judah's captivity, so that you see without a doubt that God was protecting them. Thus you see who the Samaritans of the Gospels were. At first Samaria was the capital city for the kingdom of Israel, receiving its name from Shemer (1 Kings 16). The Israelites were not yet called Samaritans. It was then the Gentiles who were brought into the land that the Judeans started to call Samaritans. Therefore, when Judah was restored to its land after the captivity, receiving also Gilead and Galilee, these Samaritans came to live in their midst. Note how Josephus says that the king of Assyria transported the Israelites to Media and Persia and how in the following chapter here it is said that the Israelites were taken to the cities of the Medes. COMMENTARY ON 2 KINGS.[7]

SAMARITANS NOT COMMITTED TO THE LORD. JOHN MAYER: It seems that the Lord did not send lions among the people in Samaria for their idolatry, in which they were bred and born. That's because the people now living in this land were not chosen by God and had no fear of him. They believed that the Lord was a weak god that had no power, since it was believed that he could not keep his people from being carried away captive by the Assyrians. . . . To show, therefore, that the Lord was the God of all power and to make the people fear him, and speak and think reverently of him, God judged them in

this way. But the Lord agreed not to send lions on them when they gave a reverent regard to him, as the priest taught them, leaving their idolatries to be reckoned for and judged at the last day. Yet I do not doubt that the priest who was sent to instruct them taught them that the Lord is the only true God and the other idols were full of vanity and emptiness. The priest surely taught them that the Lord created heaven and earth. . . . Nevertheless the people apparently applied none of the priest's teachings, but only those that were concerned with showing the Lord some reverence. For they could not be taught how to make sacrifices given that the Lord ordered sacrifices to be made only in Jerusalem at the temple.

This shows us that if any of the people of God do abominably, as the heathen do, God will not endure it at their hands even if they seem to also worship the Lord. For inside of them is spiritual adultery, since they are regarded as God's spouse. But ethnically the Samaritans were never part of God's covenant and they are otherwise looked on as wicked adulterers who are committed to another man's wife. And because they were not covenanted with God, the Lord was not as stirred up against them as he was against Israel. COMMENTARY ON 2 KINGS.[8]

NEW PEOPLE, SAME MIXED-UP FAITH. KONRAD PELLIKAN: One priest of Israel was sent back to live in Bethel, teaching the new inhabitants faith in the one true God by means of the Decalogue and the law and mighty deeds of God that are in the books of Moses. They believed, and they devoted themselves to God in faith, hope and love. They sacrificed according to their own native customs and fashions, also devoting themselves to their gods in the high places of the former kingdom of Samaria. And so they wavered just as Israel had, believing in the highest and greatest Lord God who created heaven and earth and (in the Gentile custom) invoking their individual gods for individual needs. COMMENTARY ON 2 KINGS.[9]

[6]Pellikan, *Commentaria Bibliorum*, 2:193r.
[7]Bugenhagen, *In Regum duos ultimos libros*, 171.
[8]Mayer, *Many Commentaries in One*, 260-61*.
[9]Pellikan, *Commentaria Bibliorum*, 2:193r.

Punished by Lions. Johannes Bugenhagen: This was the land of promise, that is, the land of faith, which had been promised to their ancestors; for this reason it could not have been seized by unbelievers without divine retribution. It is therefore no wonder that God sent lions to the foreign Gentiles, just as God sent these children of sinners to Assyria. For God had chosen them for this place so that they might live in it and not worship the idols of the people who had lived there before the children of Israel expelled them. But now God gave the people this plague of lions so that they might recognize their sin. God arranged it so that a priest was sent who heard the word of God. Commentary on 2 Kings.[10]

Modern-Day Samaritans. Johannes Bugenhagen: The Samaritans of today are clerics and their adherents who want to occupy the holy place (that is, to reign in the church of God) without having the word of faith. They see lions rising up against them as a true revelation that they should hate all they have. They are sent the Word of God so that they might not perish, but instead they persist in their errors. They permit the gospel to be preached (for they cannot prohibit it), but they want to mix it together with their impious worship of God, which is where they put their trust, just as the Samaritans trusted in the worship of their gods. Even though they might not be condemned by the world, they will be most seriously judged by God for having disregarded his truth. They will not be Christian, for as Christ said, "Whoever loves their own more than me is not worthy of me." And we see further that it happened as Paul said, "Where sin increased, grace abounded all the more." For when those clergy and monks become preachers of the gospel and are not feigning it like those who hawk the gospel everywhere, then for Christ's sake they might dare to risk and pay with their very souls. For it is not all that different from what happened to the Samaritans. They had unworthily occupied the holy land and, having been instructed by God's law of God's severe judgment, did not cease from their errors. For this reason their name became a great abomination among the Jews. But look how they became the first among the Gentiles to receive the gospel of God's glory because they lived around Judea, just as is written in the Acts of the Apostles. I will also only mention in passing that they heard the preaching of Christ himself, who was sent in the flesh to the Israelites, as it says in John 4 and other places. Commentary on 2 Kings.[11]

---

[10]Bugenhagen, *In Regum duos ultimos libros*, 172.

[11]Bugenhagen, *In Regum duos ultimos libros*, 173-74; citing Mt 10:37; Rom 5:20.

18:1–20:21 KING HEZEKIAH OF JUDAH

¹In the third year of Hoshea son of Elah, king of Israel, Hezekiah the son of Ahaz, king of Judah, began to reign. ²He was twenty-five years old when he began to reign, and he reigned twenty-nine years in Jerusalem. His mother's name was Abi the daughter of Zechariah. ³And he did what was right in the eyes of the Lord, according to all that David his father had done. ⁴He removed the high places and broke the pillars and cut down the Asherah. And he broke in pieces the bronze serpent that Moses had made, for until those days the people of Israel had made offerings to it (it was called Nehushtan).ᵃ ⁵He trusted in the Lord, the God of Israel, so that there was none like him among all the kings of Judah after him, nor among those who were before him. ⁶For he held fast to the Lord. He did not depart from following him, but kept the commandments that the Lord commanded Moses. ⁷And the Lord was with him; wherever he went out, he prospered. He rebelled against the king of Assyria and would not serve him. ⁸He struck down the Philistines as far as Gaza and its territory, from watchtower to fortified city.

⁹In the fourth year of King Hezekiah, which was the seventh year of Hoshea son of Elah, king of Israel, Shalmaneser king of Assyria came up against Samaria and besieged it, ¹⁰and at the end of three years he took it. In the sixth year of Hezekiah, which was the ninth year of Hoshea king of Israel, Samaria was taken. ¹¹The king of Assyria carried the Israelites away to Assyria and put them in Halah, and on the Habor, the river of Gozan, and in the cities of the Medes, ¹²because they did not obey the voice of the Lord their God but transgressed his covenant, even all that Moses the servant of the Lord commanded. They neither listened nor obeyed.

¹³In the fourteenth year of King Hezekiah, Sennacherib king of Assyria came up against all the fortified cities of Judah and took them. ¹⁴And Hezekiah king of Judah sent to the king of Assyria at Lachish, saying, "I have done wrong; withdraw from me. Whatever you impose on me I will bear." And the king of Assyria required of Hezekiah king of Judah three hundred talentsᵇ of silver and thirty talents of gold. ¹⁵And Hezekiah gave him all the silver that was found in the house of the Lord and in the treasuries of the king's house. ¹⁶At that time Hezekiah stripped the gold from the doors of the temple of the Lord and from the doorposts that Hezekiah king of Judah had overlaid and gave it to the king of Assyria. ¹⁷And the king of Assyria sent the Tartan, the Rab-saris, and the Rabshakeh with a great army from Lachish to King Hezekiah at Jerusalem. And they went up and came to Jerusalem. When they arrived, they came and stood by the conduit of the upper pool, which is on the highway to the Washer's Field. ¹⁸And when they called for the king, there came out to them Eliakim the son of Hilkiah, who was over the household, and Shebnah the secretary, and Joah the son of Asaph, the recorder.

¹⁹And the Rabshakeh said to them, "Say to Hezekiah, 'Thus says the great king, the king of Assyria: On what do you rest this trust of yours? ²⁰Do you think that mere words are strategy and power for war? In whom do you now trust, that you have rebelled against me? ²¹Behold, you are trusting now in Egypt, that broken reed of a staff, which will pierce the hand of any man who leans on it. Such is Pharaoh king of Egypt to all who trust in him. ²²But if you say to me, "We trust in the Lord our God," is it not he whose high places and altars Hezekiah has removed, saying to Judah and to Jerusalem, "You shall worship before this altar in Jerusalem"? ²³Come now, make a wager with my master the king of Assyria: I will give you two thousand horses, if you are able on your part to set riders on them. ²⁴How then can you repulse a single captain among the least of my master's servants, when you trust in Egypt for chariots and for horsemen? ²⁵Moreover, is it without the Lord that I have come up against this place to destroy it? The Lord said to me, Go up against this land, and destroy it.'"

²⁶Then Eliakim the son of Hilkiah, and Shebnah, and Joah, said to the Rabshakeh, "Please speak to your

servants in Aramaic, for we understand it. Do not speak to us in the language of Judah within the hearing of the people who are on the wall." ²⁷But the Rabshakeh said to them, "Has my master sent me to speak these words to your master and to you, and not to the men sitting on the wall, who are doomed with you to eat their own dung and to drink their own urine?"

²⁸Then the Rabshakeh stood and called out in a loud voice in the language of Judah: "Hear the word of the great king, the king of Assyria! ²⁹Thus says the king: 'Do not let Hezekiah deceive you, for he will not be able to deliver you out of my^c hand. ³⁰Do not let Hezekiah make you trust in the LORD by saying, The LORD will surely deliver us, and this city will not be given into the hand of the king of Assyria.' ³¹Do not listen to Hezekiah, for thus says the king of Assyria: 'Make your peace with me^d and come out to me. Then each one of you will eat of his own vine, and each one of his own fig tree, and each one of you will drink the water of his own cistern, ³²until I come and take you away to a land like your own land, a land of grain and wine, a land of bread and vineyards, a land of olive trees and honey, that you may live, and not die. And do not listen to Hezekiah when he misleads you by saying, "The LORD will deliver us." ³³Has any of the gods of the nations ever delivered his land out of the hand of the king of Assyria? ³⁴Where are the gods of Hamath and Arpad? Where are the gods of Sepharvaim, Hena, and Ivvah? Have they delivered Samaria out of my hand? ³⁵Who among all the gods of the lands have delivered their lands out of my hand, that the LORD should deliver Jerusalem out of my hand?'"

³⁶But the people were silent and answered him not a word, for the king's command was, "Do not answer him." ³⁷Then Eliakim the son of Hilkiah, who was over the household, and Shebna the secretary, and Joah the son of Asaph, the recorder, came to Hezekiah with their clothes torn and told him the words of the Rabshakeh.

19 As soon as King Hezekiah heard it, he tore his clothes and covered himself with sackcloth and went into the house of the LORD. ²And he sent Eliakim, who was over the household, and Shebna the secretary, and the senior priests, covered with sackcloth, to the prophet Isaiah the son of Amoz. ³They said to

him, "Thus says Hezekiah, This day is a day of distress, of rebuke, and of disgrace; children have come to the point of birth, and there is no strength to bring them forth. ⁴It may be that the LORD your God heard all the words of the Rabshakeh, whom his master the king of Assyria has sent to mock the living God, and will rebuke the words that the LORD your God has heard; therefore lift up your prayer for the remnant that is left." ⁵When the servants of King Hezekiah came to Isaiah, ⁶Isaiah said to them, "Say to your master, 'Thus says the LORD: Do not be afraid because of the words that you have heard, with which the servants of the king of Assyria have reviled me. ⁷Behold, I will put a spirit in him, so that he shall hear a rumor and return to his own land, and I will make him fall by the sword in his own land.'"

⁸The Rabshakeh returned, and found the king of Assyria fighting against Libnah, for he heard that the king had left Lachish. ⁹Now the king heard concerning Tirhakah king of Cush, "Behold, he has set out to fight against you." So he sent messengers again to Hezekiah, saying, ¹⁰"Thus shall you speak to Hezekiah king of Judah: 'Do not let your God in whom you trust deceive you by promising that Jerusalem will not be given into the hand of the king of Assyria. ¹¹Behold, you have heard what the kings of Assyria have done to all lands, devoting them to destruction. And shall you be delivered? ¹²Have the gods of the nations delivered them, the nations that my fathers destroyed, Gozan, Haran, Rezeph, and the people of Eden who were in Telassar? ¹³Where is the king of Hamath, the king of Arpad, the king of the city of Sepharvaim, the king of Hena, or the king of Ivvah?'"

¹⁴Hezekiah received the letter from the hand of the messengers and read it; and Hezekiah went up to the house of the LORD and spread it before the LORD. ¹⁵And Hezekiah prayed before the LORD and said: "O LORD, the God of Israel, enthroned above the cherubim, you are the God, you alone, of all the kingdoms of the earth; you have made heaven and earth. ¹⁶Incline your ear, O LORD, and hear; open your eyes, O LORD, and see; and hear the words of Sennacherib, which he has sent to mock the living God. ¹⁷Truly, O LORD, the kings of Assyria have laid waste the nations and their lands ¹⁸and have cast

their gods into the fire, for they were not gods, but the work of men's hands, wood and stone. Therefore they were destroyed. ¹⁹So now, O Lord our God, save us, please, from his hand, that all the kingdoms of the earth may know that you, O Lord, are God alone."

²⁰Then Isaiah the son of Amoz sent to Hezekiah, saying, "Thus says the Lord, the God of Israel: Your prayer to me about Sennacherib king of Assyria I have heard. ²¹This is the word that the Lord has spoken concerning him:

"She despises you, she scorns you—
    the virgin daughter of Zion;
she wags her head behind you—
    the daughter of Jerusalem.

²²"Whom have you mocked and reviled?
    Against whom have you raised your voice
and lifted your eyes to the heights?
    Against the Holy One of Israel!
²³By your messengers you have mocked the
    Lord,
    and you have said, 'With my many chariots
I have gone up the heights of the mountains,
    to the far recesses of Lebanon;
I felled its tallest cedars,
    its choicest cypresses;
I entered its farthest lodging place,
    its most fruitful forest.
²⁴I dug wells
    and drank foreign waters,
and I dried up with the sole of my foot
    all the streams of Egypt.'

²⁵"Have you not heard
    that I determined it long ago?
I planned from days of old
    what now I bring to pass,
that you should turn fortified cities
    into heaps of ruins,
²⁶while their inhabitants, shorn of strength,
    are dismayed and confounded,
and have become like plants of the field
    and like tender grass,
like grass on the housetops,
    blighted before it is grown.

²⁷"But I know your sitting down
    and your going out and coming in,
    and your raging against me.
²⁸Because you have raged against me
    and your complacency has come into my
        ears,
I will put my hook in your nose
    and my bit in your mouth,
and I will turn you back on the way
    by which you came.

²⁹"And this shall be the sign for you: this year eat what grows of itself, and in the second year what springs of the same. Then in the third year sow and reap and plant vineyards, and eat their fruit. ³⁰And the surviving remnant of the house of Judah shall again take root downward and bear fruit upward. ³¹For out of Jerusalem shall go a remnant, and out of Mount Zion a band of survivors. The zeal of the Lord will do this.

³²"Therefore thus says the Lord concerning the king of Assyria: He shall not come into this city or shoot an arrow there, or come before it with a shield or cast up a siege mound against it. ³³By the way that he came, by the same he shall return, and he shall not come into this city, declares the Lord. ³⁴For I will defend this city to save it, for my own sake and for the sake of my servant David."

³⁵And that night the angel of the Lord went out and struck down 185,000 in the camp of the Assyrians. And when people arose early in the morning, behold, these were all dead bodies. ³⁶Then Sennacherib king of Assyria departed and went home and lived at Nineveh. ³⁷And as he was worshiping in the house of Nisroch his god, Adrammelech and Sharezer, his sons, struck him down with the sword and escaped into the land of Ararat. And Esarhaddon his son reigned in his place.

20 In those days Hezekiah became sick and was at the point of death. And Isaiah the prophet the son of Amoz came to him and said to him, "Thus says the Lord, 'Set your house in order, for you shall die; you shall not recover.'" ²Then Hezekiah turned his face to the wall and prayed to the Lord, saying, ³"Now, O Lord, please remember how I have walked before you in faithfulness and with a whole heart, and have done what is good in your sight." And Hezekiah wept bitterly. ⁴And before Isaiah had gone out of the middle court, the word of the Lord came to him: ⁵"Turn back, and say to Hezekiah the leader of my people, Thus says the Lord, the God of David your father: I have heard your prayer; I have seen your tears. Behold, I will heal you. On the third day you shall go up to the house of the Lord, ⁶and I will add fifteen years to your life. I will deliver you and this city out of the hand of the king of Assyria, and I will defend this city for my own sake and for my servant David's sake." ⁷And Isaiah said, "Bring a cake of figs. And let them take and lay it on the boil, that he may recover."

⁸And Hezekiah said to Isaiah, "What shall be the sign that the Lord will heal me, and that I shall go up to the house of the Lord on the third day?" ⁹And Isaiah said, "This shall be the sign to you from the Lord, that the Lord will do the thing that he has promised: shall the shadow go forward ten steps, or go back ten steps?" ¹⁰And Hezekiah answered, "It is an easy thing for the shadow to lengthen ten steps. Rather let the shadow go back ten steps." ¹¹And Isaiah the prophet called to the Lord, and he brought the shadow back ten steps, by which it had gone down on the steps of Ahaz.

¹²At that time Merodach-baladan the son of Baladan, king of Babylon, sent envoys with letters and a present to Hezekiah, for he heard that Hezekiah had been sick. ¹³And Hezekiah welcomed them, and he showed them all his treasure house, the silver, the gold, the spices, the precious oil, his armory, all that was found in his storehouses. There was nothing in his house or in all his realm that Hezekiah did not show them. ¹⁴Then Isaiah the prophet came to King Hezekiah, and said to him, "What did these men say? And from where did they come to you?" And Hezekiah said, "They have come from a far country, from Babylon." ¹⁵He said, "What have they seen in your house?" And Hezekiah answered, "They have seen all that is in my house; there is nothing in my storehouses that I did not show them."

¹⁶Then Isaiah said to Hezekiah, "Hear the word of the Lord: ¹⁷Behold, the days are coming, when all that is in your house, and that which your fathers have stored up till this day, shall be carried to Babylon. Nothing shall be left, says the Lord. ¹⁸And some of your own sons, who shall be born to you, shall be taken away, and they shall be eunuchs in the palace of the king of Babylon." ¹⁹Then Hezekiah said to Isaiah, "The word of the Lord that you have spoken is good." For he thought, "Why not, if there will be peace and security in my days?"

²⁰The rest of the deeds of Hezekiah and all his might and how he made the pool and the conduit and brought water into the city, are they not written in the Book of the Chronicles of the Kings of Judah? ²¹And Hezekiah slept with his fathers, and Manasseh his son reigned in his place.

a *Nehushtan* sounds like the Hebrew for both *bronze* and *serpent*   b A *talent* was about 75 pounds or 34 kilograms   c Hebrew *his*   d Hebrew *Make a blessing with me*

Overview: Commentators unanimously laud Hezekiah, though they differ on why. Some emphasize the faith of his heart, which gives him courage, allows him to ask for and receive prophetic wisdom, and inspires his reforms of worship. Others emphasize his purification of worship and the religious order he brought to the people. Finally, they reflect on God's providence and power with respect to the miracle of the sun moving backward and the poor decision Hezekiah made regarding the Babylonian envoys.

18:1-3 A Good King

Hezekiah Without Equal. Konrad Pellikan: All of Hezekiah's reforming works came from faith, for he depended entirely on the Lord, desiring that everything be done in observation of divine law. No one before or after him conducted themselves with similar sanctity in all things. Therefore the Lord assisted him so that all he did prospered. He was also freed from his enemies, including the king of Assyria. He dared to stop paying tribute and to end the alliance that his impious father Ahaz had arranged, for he did not want to serve him. COMMENTARY ON 2 KINGS.[1]

A KING LIKE DAVID. JOHANNES BUGENHAGEN: After the fall of the kingdom of Israel, what could the kingdom of Judah do but be consumed by despair? Up to this point they had not wanted the prophets who predicted devastation and they despised them, but now they saw the true fact of what happened to their kin in Israel. But see how suddenly the great Hezekiah was raised up in place of his most ungodly father. Even though the people had become so expert in evil, under him they saw that they were valued and things could be better through God. Those who go back to living holy and humane lives flourish, and it would be seen that everything ancient is restored in godliness and glory. This is an example of divine compassion. For God does not want us to perish, instead he is gladly present with us after we sin and call on him. He pities those in despair—only if they do not scorn the grace offered to them.

Like David, Hezekiah threw down all the recently renewed impieties, and he restored everything that he knew pleased God, according to the Word of God or the law of Moses. This is what David had done, just so you don't think he did otherwise. Here the mind and heart of David who himself gave thanks to God is shown. For God speaks elsewhere of him, "I have found in David the son of Jesse a man after my heart, who will do all my will." To have a similar heart means that Hezekiah really and faithfully gave thanks to God through his works. Otherwise it is ungodly hypocrisy and not faith to imitate the works of the saints. The faithful do not act according to the outward appearance of what David did, but they do their works with the same faith David had. This is what this Scripture means by saying, "He did what was right in the eyes of the Lord, according to all that David his father had done." COMMENTARY ON 2 KINGS.[2]

A LESSON FOR LEADERS. JOHANNES PISCATOR: From the example of Hezekiah kings and leaders are taught the following three things. First, they must abolish all idolatry. Second, they must have faith in God. And finally, they must establish the worship of God in accordance with God's Word. COMMENTARY ON 2 KINGS.[3]

A GREAT KING. JOHN MAYER: It may be asked how Hezekiah's uprightness in relation to previous and future kings can be regarded as completely truthful, seeing that Josiah exceeded him in destroying the high places that Hezekiah allowed to remain, in keeping a Passover feast as no king did before him, in rooting out all sorcery and in removing all abominations from the land. Josiah is highly commended in 2 Kings. "Before him there was no king like him, who turned to the LORD with all his heart and with all his soul and with all his might, according to all the Law of Moses, nor did any like him arise after him." . . . But we must take it according to the meaning and not stand strictly on the words. This verse is not meant to deprive other godly kings of their due commendations. Rather, it is to commend the king being spoken of. And this means that Hezekiah and Josiah were two of the most excellent of kings. As for Hezekiah, he began making reforms during the first month of his reign. He was not deterred by the awful state in which he found the kingdom, namely, one that was completely corrupted by idolatry, influenced by his father. Hezekiah also held an eminent confidence in God. Indeed his breaking in pieces of the brazen serpent, which was in such high estimation at that time among the people, showed this. As such, God's favor was constantly on him, which revealed itself in miraculously delivering Jerusalem from the proud king of Assyria upon his prayer to the Lord and in many other ways as well. COMMENTARY ON 2 KINGS.[4]

[1]Pellikan, *Commentaria Bibliorum*, 2:194r.
[2]Bugenhagen, *In Regum duos ultimos libros*, 174-75; citing Acts 13:22; 2 Chron 29:2.
[3]Piscator, *Commentarii in omnes libros Veteris Testamenti*, 2:358.
[4]Mayer, *Many Commentaries in One*, 262-63*; citing 2 Kings 23:25.

18:4-12 *Moses' Bronze Serpent Destroyed*

PROHIBITING WHAT GOD INSTITUTED.
ANDREAS BODENSTEIN VON KARLSTADT: God
understands all things better than we, no matter
how clever we are or may become. For this reason
he has often suspended the use of external things or
fully prohibited it, even though he himself instituted these things, for he could see how the simple
were offended by them because of their ignorance.
Thus God rejected sacrifice, fire, smoke, temples, the
serpent and the ark . . . saying, "What do I care for
your sacrifice and your incense?" DIALOGUE ON
THE SACRAMENT OF JESUS CHRIST.[5]

WHEN ORDER BECOMES DISORDER. MARTIN
LUTHER: Lent, Palm Sunday and Holy Week shall
be retained, not to force anyone to fast, but to
preserve the passion history and the Gospels
appointed for that season. This, however, does not
include the Lenten veil, the throwing of palms, the
veiling of pictures and whatever else there is of
such tomfoolery—nor chanting the four passions,
nor preaching on the passion for eight hours on
Good Friday. Holy Week shall be like any other
week save that the passion history be explained
every day for an hour throughout the week or on
as many days as may be desirable, and that the
sacrament be given to everyone who desires it. For
among Christians the whole service should center
on the Word and sacrament.

In short, this or any other order shall be so used
that whenever it becomes an abuse, it shall be
straightway abolished and replaced by another,
even as King Hezekiah put away and destroyed the
brazen serpent, though God himself had commanded it be made, because the children of Israel
made an abuse of it. For the orders must serve for
the promotion of faith and love and not be to the
detriment of faith. As soon as they fail to do this,
they are invalid, dead and gone; just as a good coin,
when counterfeited, is canceled and changed
because of the abuse, or as new shoes when they
become old and uncomfortable are no longer worn,
but thrown away, and new ones bought. An order
is an external thing. No matter how good it is, it
can be abused. Then it is no longer an order, but a
disorder. No order is, therefore, valid in itself. . . .
But the validity, value, power and virtue of any
order is in its proper use. Otherwise it is utterly
worthless and good for nothing. THE GERMAN
MASS AND ORDER OF SERVICE.[6]

BURNING NEHUSHTAN. GIOVANNI DIODATI:
King Hezekiah burned the serpent because it was
doubly abused. First, because this serpent was
preserved, the people imagined that some divinity
resided in this figure. They failed to recognize that
it was only a sign of God's grace appointed by
himself for a season. That is, it was only given by
God for people to look on by faith in his promise
at a certain point in time. Second, it was to be
destroyed because the people yielded a divine
honor to the sign beyond the true use of all
sacraments and against God's express command.
The word *Nehushtan* refers to a piece of brass. It
was not to be valued any more than normal brass
was, for none of its sacramental features of the past
remained in it since they existed only for a time.
Rather, this serpent was to be annihilated due to
the irreverent and scornful properties attributed to
it. ANNOTATIONS ON 2 KINGS.[7]

DESTROYING THE BRONZE SERPENT. JO-
HANNES BUGENHAGEN: Because the people had
used it to practice idolatry, Hezekiah broke into
pieces the bronze serpent that God had provided.
Who would not have thought this to be a symbol
that needed to be protected as a sign of God's
preservation in the desert, when all who were
bitten by the fiery serpents were saved from death?
Or, if it were set up among us, which of us today
would not marvel at the mystery of our redemption, as Christ spoke of it in John 3? But here

---

[5]CRR 8:271; citing Is 1:11.

[6]LW 53:90. The Lenten veil refers to a curtain that hides the altar
during Lent.
[7]Diodati, *Pious Annotations*, 26*.

Hezekiah is praised for breaking the serpent, even though it could have been displayed piously. Hezekiah certainly would have been acting impiously if he had used this as a kind of test. But he acted rightly when he cast down that serpent through which the people had been cured of God's wrath, for God had not commanded them to keep it. This is certainly an excellent example of all those ceremonies and institutions that we are free to keep or not keep, since that righteousness of God that comes through faith alone does not depend on such things. COMMENTARY ON 2 KINGS.[8]

LESSON ON DESTROYING THAT WHICH OFFENDS. JOHN MAYER: For the bronze serpent was set up by God's own command. That is, by God's own command this was set up. And it had been preserved to this time as a monument of the cures it performed. But the serpent was superstitiously believed to be of virtue in the days of Ahaz when he offered incense to it. However, Hezekiah broke it and called it *Nehushtan*. By this time it was without all virtue and completely unworthy of adoration. The people foolishly believed that the serpent was powerful instead of recognizing that its curative power came only from God. And here we are taught that whatever is an occasion of offense, it must be destroyed, even if it is the cross of Christ. COMMENTARY ON 2 KINGS.[9]

18:13-16 Hezekiah's Hardships

GOVERNANCE AS UNSTABLE AS THE WEATHER. PHILIPP MELANCHTHON: On account of previous sin, governments experience periods of unrest and, like the weather, are unstable. Hezekiah had no such victories as David, and even though God manifested his wonderful help, Hezekiah's enemies wrought great devastation in the land. But true rulers can with good conscience hold office. To the degree that they have true faith in God, and acknowledge and invoke the Lord Jesus Christ,

they please God and are heirs of eternal salvation. Such were David, Jehoshaphat, Hezekiah, Josiah, Constantine and Theodosius. For the good of the church God occasionally gives such pious sovereigns, who are particularly gracious tools, through whom God again quickens the land, relieves it of the burdens of robbery and extortion, and again establishes discipline, justice, fear of punishments, virtue, the church and true doctrine. THEOLOGICAL COMMONPLACES (1555).[10]

HEZEKIAH'S TEMPTATION. JOHANNES BUGENHAGEN: How could Hezekiah possibly have faith in God at that time? God truly leads all the elect in this way, so that they have seen during times of the worst despair how much God wants to liberate and glorify them, as it happened when the sons of Israel were led to Egypt, including Joseph, who would become a leader in Egypt. Without a doubt, Hezekiah began to think this way himself: "Evil has often been predicted by the prophets and by the law of Moses against this people, because my fathers often led them in grave sin. Therefore the Lord does not want to liberate us from Assyria, who has already taken the strongholds of our cities. Therefore I should not bear to be seen resisting God's judgment and the divine will." How do you think Hezekiah's faith could have endured, when he saw the Lord standing with his enemies against him? This is definitely the very worst temptation anyone would ever have to experience, to have to think that the will of the Lord in judgment was to be yoked to the Assyrians, whom he had previously evaded, and to submit to them. Truly, where he hears such a horrendous blasphemy against God, he then perceives the need to implore for divine mercy and be liberated by God. It is ungodly therefore to submit ourselves to our fates, because we should want God himself to bear us away, and by no means should we resign ourselves to anything else. COMMENTARY ON 2 KINGS.[11]

---

[8]Bugenhagen, *In Regum duos ultimos libros*, 175-76.
[9]Mayer, *Many Commentaries in One*, 263*; citing Num 21:9.
[10]*Melanchthon on Christian Doctrine*, 105.
[11]Bugenhagen, *In Regum duos ultimos libros*, 179-80.

Why Hezekiah Experienced Adversity.
John Mayer: After the prosperity of Hezekiah
has been set forth, now follows his adversity by the
invasions of the Assyrians. He had revolted from
their obedience, in which his father lived. Therefore the Assyrians came now to be avenged on him
and prevail over him. Then Hezekiah sent to
Sennacherib at Lachish, one of the strong cities of
Judah, with a note acknowledging his defeat and
desire to pay tribute to him in exchange for not
being completely destroyed. Nicholas of Lyra
thinks the sins of Hezekiah's father, Ahaz, and of
all the people at this time were the cause of
Hezekiah's adversity. And that when Hezekiah
confessed to the king of Assyria that he had sinned,
he meant only that he had taken on himself the sin
of the people now that he was king. Others think
that the hearts of the people were intent on
idolatry even in the time of this godly king, which
soon appeared in that, immediately after his death
in the time of Manasseh, the people fell headlong
into idolatry. And for this cause God now brought
the Assyrians against them, sparing the king. . . .
Others count it as a sin of Hezekiah's to refuse to
serve the king of Assyria because he was bound to
do so on account of his father's oath to Assyria.
Commentary on 2 Kings.[12]

18:17-37 An Exchange with Rabshakeh

Not Surprised by Evil. John Calvin: We
see . . . how Sennacherib talked when he came to
besiege Jerusalem. . . . For at least his lieutenant
Rabshakeh stated, "Do not think that God must
help you, for he has sent me here." Well, it is
possible that he was definitely aware that God
wanted to chastise his own, and that he and his
master were like rods to correct this people. But
who is it that incited them to wage war? Did they
not manifestly despise God when the enemy said,
"I shall put my camp on the side of the north" (see
Is 14:13), as if God were reproaching Sennacherib
for his audacity in imagining that God had no

remedy with which to help his people? Well then,
here is Sennacherib, who is notoriously fighting
against God, and still his lieutenant does not fail to
boast that God has sent him there. That is how the
wicked always falsify the name of God, and harden
themselves, in order to give themselves license to
do all the more evil—as if God must excuse them,
or as though he were constrained to take part of
their guilt on himself. When we see that, let us not
be surprised, seeing that it has always been this way.
Sermons on 2 Samuel.[13]

A Shameful Man. Johannes Piscator:
Rabshakeh, the legate of the king of Assyria, is set
forth as an example of a proud, ungodly and
blasphemous man. He proudly relied on the
magnitude of his army and denied that the Lord
could preserve the city of Jerusalem. Commentary
on 2 Kings.[14]

Not Casting Pearls Before Swine. John
Mayer: The allegory of a broken reed was very apt
both for the location of Egypt being in a low, reedy
ground and because a reed leaned on gave a person a
fall, and it hurt his hand by piercing it. Rabshakeh
proceeded to show that if Hezekiah trusted in God,
this was vain. That's because Hezekiah had broken
down the high places and altars in other locations,
reserving all his worship for only one place at
Jerusalem. And this he spoke after the manner of the
heathen. Indeed this showed that Rabshakeh was no
Jew, for the heathen thought it tended greatly to the
honor and glory of their gods to set up altars and
temples in various places, and that to break down
any of them was dishonorable and would greatly
anger the gods. But here Rabshakeh was greatly
deceived, for God had commanded Solomon to
build only one altar for the true God to show that
he was one, and that he forbade sacrificing in any
other place. Rabshakeh then asked Hezekiah to
consider how greatly overmatched he was. . . . The
leaders ordered silence in response. This was

---

[12]Mayer, *Many Commentaries in One*, 272*.

[13]Calvin, *Sermons on Second Samuel*, 1:155.
[14]Piscator, *Commentarii in omnes libros Veteris Testamenti*, 2:358.

Hezekiah's way of showing contempt to the Assyrian king, and to show how much he slighted him for the vile speech of his messenger. For Rabshakeh was a dog or swine, before whom pearls and holy things are not to be cast. This request for silence on behalf of the Judean people also teaches us not to respond to the calumnies of those who have no aspirations of mending their ways. And the strict obedience of the people to their king in this case is worthy of imitation of all subjects. It is the safest way in times of great danger. For the king was wise and godly and was careful to preserve the kingdom. COMMENTARY ON 2 KINGS.[15]

A BRUISED REED. THE ENGLISH ANNOTATIONS: Egypt is here likened to a staff, because of the pretense it makes of help and support; to a reed, because of its impotency; and to a bruised or broken reed because of the damage it does, as a broken reed is sharp and full of teeth, and it pierces a person's flesh. ANNOTATIONS ON 2 KINGS.[16]

19:1-7 The Prophet Isaiah Reassures Hezekiah

KEEPING HOLY SILENCE. KONRAD PELLIKAN: If they were to be pious, the people did the right thing by keeping silence at this sacrilegious and blasphemous speech by Rabshakeh. No less pious was that they were written down by Shebnah the secretary, who stood firm in faith, knowing that such vacuous arguments against his God would fall on deaf ears. For it is easy for the unfaithful to be persuaded into pessimism by the pessimistic, so that God's word of salvation is not believed but instead human fabrications and lies are believed, leading people to ruin. It was therefore far better that they obey the king's wise command to respond to such frivolous words with silence and to refrain from paying back in kind. COMMENTARY ON 2 KINGS.[17]

PROPHETIC PROMISE. VIKTORIN STRIGEL: The example of Hezekiah testifies to the fact that God is near to those whose hearts are troubled and saves those of humble spirit. God consoles those who are caught up in the highest anguish, so that the voice of the prophet not only promises freedom to the church but also denounces the destruction of blasphemous tyrants. It is as if the prophet then says, "Do not fear the foolish and baseless words of the tyrant. For because his speech is foolish, I will prove his results to also be foolish. I will strike such fear in him that he will not attack anyone. Thus I will restrain him from being able to make any more trouble for you." BOOK OF KINGS.[18]

HOW LEADERS SHOULD ACT. JOHANNES PISCATOR: Hezekiah gives a great example of how kings and leaders are to act when they are in dire circumstances. First, they are to invoke God for help. Then they are to inquire godly ministers of the Word. Finally, they are to solicit God by prayers for themselves and for the people. COMMENTARY ON 2 KINGS.[19]

KINGLY COMFORT. KONRAD PELLIKAN: Princes who listen to, call on and consult the prophets are given comfort from God in difficult matters and are visited with the consolation of the word of God in times of extreme desperation, if they will believe it. In receiving the prophet of the Lord, faithful King Hezekiah received the prophet and the prophet's gift. He who had lived by God's will now put God's mercy to the test. He was commanded not to fear that the people would suffer great wickedness, for he had governed according to God's Word, reinstated the divine law and had been found well-pleasing to the God of gods through his great devotion. Such foolish abuses do not hurt the pious; instead the pious greet them and glory in them. COMMENTARY ON 2 KINGS.[20]

[15]Mayer, *Many Commentaries in One*, 276*.
[16]Downame, ed., *Annotations* (1645), MM4v*; citing Is 36:6; Ezek 29:6,7.
[17]Pellikan, *Commentaria Bibliorum*, 2:195r.
[18]Strigel, *Libri Samuelis, Regum et Paralipomenon*, 387.
[19]Piscator, *Commentarii in omnes libros Veteris Testamenti*, 2:361.
[20]Pellikan, *Commentaria Bibliorum*, 2:195v.

HUMBLE SEEKING OF ISAIAH. JOHN MAYER: It is said that the servants of Sennacherib spoke more against God and the king. Therefore Hezekiah presently humbled himself in prayer. And while he was doing this, he sent for the prophet Isaiah. Hezekiah considered, says the *Glossa ordinaria*, that the sins of the land might be the cause of his misery, and that's why he mourned. And although it is not expressed what he prayed, Nicholas of Lyra conjectures that it was for pardon, help and mercy toward the people. It was also for justice toward the blasphemers. And because Hezekiah thought that there was more merit in Isaiah's prayers than his own, he sent for him to come pray as well . . . seeing that Isaiah was a prophet of the Lord and so God was most gracious with him, as he was with Elijah, Samuel, Moses, etc. For what can the poor merit at the hands of the rich by begging? Therefore another of the same religion says it better: Hezekiah sent to Isaiah as to one who had most inward familiarity with the Lord, and Hezekiah sent to Isaiah the same messengers who had torn their clothing as a sign of mourning and humility, together with other priests who were in sackcloth. COMMENTARY ON 2 KINGS.[21]

NOW IS THE TIME. THE ENGLISH ANNOTATIONS: This is a parable that likens Jerusalem to a woman in travail; the inhabitants to infants in the womb; the directness of the siege and the threatening of the powerful army enemy to the pains of travail; and the weakness of the Jews to the inability of the woman in travail to help herself. This is the meaning: we are brought to the extremity of danger and are utterly unable to help ourselves. In other words, now is the time for the Lord to show himself. ANNOTATIONS ON 2 KINGS.[22]

19:8-13 Sennacherib Defies the Lord

PUTTING BLASPHEMY IN WRITING. VIKTORIN STRIGEL: Through a letter, Sennacherib now repeats his earlier blasphemies and adds some new attacks, accusing God of emptiness and lies. He said, "Do not let your God in whom you trust deceive you." What a terrible thing to say and think, to cast such false accusations against the God who is not only the truth but also the fount of truth! Thus you see from this example how the fury of the ungodly grows. Not content to merely speak blasphemies, they even put their blasphemies in writing, so that it can be preserved for all posterity. As the common saying puts it: "A heard voice perishes but the written letter remains." BOOK OF KINGS.[23]

GOING AHEAD WITH EVIL PLANS. KONRAD PELLIKAN: The impious king of Assyria wanted to fulfill the evil that he had left undone in blasphemously advancing against the army of the Almighty God. He already knew this army to belong to the God of Israel but acted as if the faithful people and their city could not free the city by themselves, having no strength against the idols of the nation. This was the meaning of Rabshakeh's words and now the letter sent from Libnah. Herodotus tells the story of what happened at the battle and siege that Sennacherib led against Egypt and the coastal city of Pelusium. COMMENTARY ON 2 KINGS.[24]

19:14-19 Hezekiah's Prayer

THE POWER OF PRAYER. VIKTORIN STRIGEL: Hezekiah set forth the subject of his prayer and explained the reason why he was praying for the liberation of his city and himself: "May you, O LORD, bring us aid and salvation, so that this liberation might be a witness to your presence among your church, which is fighting blasphemous enemies. By this, may many nations be invited into the fellowship of your church." We ought to consider such things, praying to God for the liberation or mitigation of public and private punishments. BOOK OF KINGS.[25]

[21]Mayer, *Many Commentaries in One*, 278*.
[22]Downame, ed., *Annotations* (1645), MM4v*.

[23]Strigel, *Libri Samuelis, Regum et Paralipomenon*, 387.
[24]Pellikan, *Commentaria Bibliorum*, 2:195v-96r. In the eighth century BC, the Egyptians defeated Sennacherib, king of Assyria, outside of Pelusium. They attributed this victory to an Egyptian god.
[25]Strigel, *Libri Samuelis, Regum et Paralipomenon*, 388.

CONFIDENCE IN PRAYER. KONRAD PELLIKAN: Hezekiah put his faith in no one but the Lord God himself, spreading out the blasphemous letter from Assyria before the ark of the Lord of hosts. He had a full faith and trusted in an answer to his prayer that the Lord would not allow this thing to happen. He imparted this prayer full of faith and devotion, so that those in a similar situation can pray with pious hearts and not doubt that they will be heard. COMMENTARY ON 2 KINGS.[26]

PREFIGURING CHRIST. JOHANNES PISCATOR: Concerning the words "O LORD, the God of Israel, enthroned above the cherubim. . . ." Just as the invoking of faith used to be directed toward the cherubim in the ark of the covenant since God resided there, in the same way today the invoking of faith is now directed toward Christ, about whom the ark of the covenant prefigured and in whom "all the fullness of God was pleased to dwell." COMMENTARY ON 2 KINGS.[27]

19:20-37 Isaiah Prophesies Sennacherib's Fall

THE MERITS OF THE HOLY DEPARTED. CARDINAL CAJETAN: God says that he will save the city not on account of the people's merits but he will save the city only on account of David's merits and on account of the glory of God's name. And here you see how much credit God puts into the merits of the holy departed in relation to those who remain after them. For David constructed the foremost portions of the city of Jerusalem, both the divine temple and the royal palace. And then God promised to protect the work of David and to save it. COMMENTARY ON 2 KINGS.[28]

HELD IN GOD'S HANDS. VIKTORIN STRIGEL: The words of Isaiah's prophecy contain many doctrines. First, the words testify to the fact that the destruction of kingdoms and republics is not a matter of chance but of destiny. For power has been given a natural duration, or as Paul said, "All power is from God." Thus kingdoms and republics are moved by God. As Plato said, the periods for republics belong to fate. Second, these words agree with the meaning of Psalm 139: "O LORD, you have searched me and known me!" For God clearly says, "I know your sitting down and your going out and your coming in." . . . Third, these words also teach that the fury of tyrants is not only directed against the church but even against God. For he says, "I know your fury against me." It was similarly said to Saul in Acts 9, "Saul, Saul, why are you persecuting me?" and in Zechariah 2, "He who touches you touches the apple of my eye." Therefore, when they stubbornly kick against the goads and rush ahead with the spear, tyrants know what they are doing and against whom they are making war. For the one who dwells in heaven mocks them and the Lord ridicules them. Then he speaks to their wrath and confounds them in their fury. Finally, this text offers the great and essential consolation that God has established boundaries, of which Augustine wrote on Psalm 89: "The world can rage, but it cannot exceed the limits set by the Creator who made all things." Therefore let us give thanks to God, in whom we always hope, fearing neither humans nor devils. For neither of those powers can do anything except what has been permitted for them to do. . . . Thus the violence of tyrants is held in check by the boundaries God has established. BOOK OF KINGS.[29]

GOD WILL HIMSELF VINDICATE HEZEKIAH. JOHN MAYER: The Lord here promises Hezekiah that not only will the king of Assyria not overcome the city, but he will not even be allowed to come and besiege it. But if even an Assyrian should dare shoot an arrow into the city, he shall be completely overthrown and forced away shamefully. And God promised to do this for his sake only, that is, for his

---

[26]Pellikan, *Commentaria Bibliorum*, 2:196r.

[27]Piscator, *Commentarii in omnes libros Veteris Testamenti*, 2:361; citing 2 Kings 19:15; Col 1:19.

[28]Cajetan, *Opera Omnia in Sacrae Scripturae Expositionem*, 2:265.

[29]Strigel, *Libri Samuelis, Regum et Paralipomenon*, 389-90; citing Rom 13:1; Ps 139:1; Acts 9:4; Zech 2:8; Augustine's commentary on Ps 89:12 (PL 37:1127; cf. NPNF 8:432).

glory. In other words, God promised this so that all people would hear it and extol his power, and that they would give thanks to the Lord for honoring his covenant with David. . . . And God's way of removing the proud king of Assyria was not to act indirectly. On the contrary, God would execute the Assyrian army by no other agent than his angel. The Lord did this so that he might vindicate his power against these blasphemers and to show contempt for all their false gods. COMMENTARY ON 2 KINGS.[30]

HEAVEN PERMANENTLY OPEN. MARTIN LUTHER: If this happened in the days of the Old Testament, when heaven was still closed, how much greater are the events that take place in the New Testament, when heaven is permanently open and the angels descend and ascend to protect us against all evil! SERMONS ON THE GOSPEL OF ST. JOHN.[31]

20:1-2 Hezekiah's Sickness and Isaiah's First Prophecy

FERVENT AND FAITHFUL PRAYER WHEN SICK AND IN DANGER. JOHN MAYER: Concerning the cause of Hezekiah's sickness, some say that it was due to unthankfulness and pride, by which his heart was lifted up from his great victory. This interpretation contrasts with Josephus, who said that Hezekiah offered many sacrifices and that he was very pious, which was always known to be in him. But Jerome criticizes Hezekiah, just as 2 Chronicles did when it refers to "the pride of his heart." However, this accusation was after his sickness. But what makes this case difficult is the allegation of Rabbi Solomon, who said that Hezekiah's sickness preceded his pride. . . . Therefore this sickness must have befallen about the time of the Assyrians' first coming into his land, and not after Sennacherib's departure, from which to the death of Hezekiah could not be fifteen but only thirteen or fourteen years. It must

be conjectured, then, that Hezekiah's sickness and danger by Sennacherib's coming against him was about the same time, for the army of that blasphemer had not yet been destroyed. And this agrees with the promises made here in verse 6. But what, then, was the cause of Hezekiah's sickness? We cannot know for sure, but as in the case of the man who was born blind in John 9, it was so that God might be glorified. Hezekiah's faith was made more illustrious by God's miracle, which was performed due to his faithful praying. And this served as an encouragement to all others, namely, that we should fervently and faithfully pray in our sicknesses and dangers. COMMENTARY ON 2 KINGS.[32]

THE THEOLOGICAL USE OF LAW SHOWS SIN. PHILIPP MELANCHTHON: The other use of the law is more important, namely, to preach the wrath of God. Through the preaching of the law God accuses the heart, causes it to be alarmed and drives it to such anguish that, as Hezekiah notes, people say, "Like a lion he has smashed all my bones." People feel God's wrath against sin, and if they do not receive comfort through Christ, they sink into eternal anguish and flight, as did Saul and Judas. THEOLOGICAL COMMONPLACES (1555).[33]

CONDITIONAL PROPHECY. JOHANNES PISCATOR: Sometimes God denounces someone matter-of-factly. But, nevertheless, that person understands the denunciation to be conditional. For instance, in this passage Hezekiah is denounced very matter-of-factly that he is about to die and that he should set things in order before his death. But he understood this denunciation as a conditional statement. That is, as long as he would earnestly seek an extension of his life in prayer, it would be granted. We have a similar example in Nineveh in the book of Jonah when destruction was averted by means of real repentance. COMMENTARY ON 2 KINGS.[34]

---

[30]Mayer, *Many Commentaries in One*, 284*.
[31]LW 22:210.
[32]Mayer, *Many Commentaries in One*, 287*.
[33]*Melanchthon on Christian Doctrine*, 123; citing Is 38:13.
[34]Piscator, *Commentarii in omnes libros Veteris Testamenti*, 2:364.

20:3-7 Hezekiah Prays and Isaiah Delivers a Prophecy Extending Hezekiah's Life

FOREORDINATION AND FATE. HULDRYCH ZWINGLI: Death and the cutting of the thread of life are just as much ordained as creation and the course of life are. For this is properly one's fate. Hence it is to be inferred that no one dies in infancy whose fate has not been determined from eternity, and that no power can cause someone to elude the end, whenever it might be, that has been assigned to him. The fifteen years that the Lord granted to Hezekiah as an addition to his life had been put down as an addition *before* the establishment of the world. For what has once been arranged remains fixed forever. Hezekiah's fate, therefore, had been so arranged that the years should be added in this way, and only after them should Atropos really cut the thread she had only threatened to cut before. ON THE PROVIDENCE OF GOD.[35]

PROVIDENCE AND PRAYER. KONRAD PELLIKAN: Divine providence is not changed. Instead the prophet has become aware of something different that was commanded by the Lord, who does not lie. The Lord can reveal his will to whom he wants and however he wants, for he cannot fail or be failed. As he walked across the city, the prophet could give no holy assurances, but later he could tell the king the Lord's decision, for the Spirit of the Lord furnished the news of God's richness in consoling the king for the sake of his people. God remembered the most worthy David, Hezekiah's holy and gentle father, who was remembered as living with God in eternity. The Lord hears prayers and sees the tears not of those who trust in works or human righteousness but of those who trust in divine mercy. God immediately promised healing and that on the third day Hezekiah would go up to the temple to pray and give thanks. COMMENTARY ON 2 KINGS.[36]

GOD'S PREDETERMINED PLAN WAS NOT THWARTED. JOHN MAYER: This promise that God would add fifteen years to Hezekiah's life should not be understood to mean that Hezekiah lived longer than God had originally decreed.... For as Augustine said, God determined from the beginning that Hezekiah should be struck with this mortal sickness and recover again and live another fifteen years. Therefore God did not do anything against what he originally foreknew and determined. And when Isaiah spoke initially by revelation from God that Hezekiah should now die, there was no contradiction in the Lord in his later prophecy that Hezekiah should not die but live another fifteen years. Rather, having tested Hezekiah with the first prophecy and finding him submissive and unmoving in faith which is apparent by his faithful and fervent prayer—God allowed Hezekiah to live an additional fifteen years, as he had already predetermined.... Concerning the time set by God long before Hezekiah was born, it is true not only of him but also of every person in history: God has already determined the years of our lives, so that we do not live any more or less than what God has foreknown. COMMENTARY ON 2 KINGS.[37]

EXTENSION OF LIFE FOR THE PROCREATION OF A SUCCESSOR. JOHANNES PISCATOR: God hears prayers that arise out of faith. For in this passage God hears the prayer of Hezekiah, receiving an extension of his life. God heeded this prayer so that before his death Hezekiah could beget a son to whom he could relinquish succession of the kingdom. And in this way Hezekiah leaned on the lingering divine promise to David that a male successor would not be extinguished from God's presence, who would sit on the throne of Israel. And all that was necessary was for a son to observe God's laws and to walk before God in the same way David had done, as we see in Solomon's prayer: "Now therefore, O LORD, God of Israel, keep for your servant David my father what you have promised him, saying, 'You shall not

---

[35]Zwingli, *Latin Works*, 2:206* (ZSW 6,3:190). According to Greek mythology, Atropos, Clotho and Lachesis are the three goddesses of fate.
[36]Pellikan, *Commentaria Bibliorum*, 2:198v.
[37]Mayer, *Many Commentaries in One*, 289-90*

lack a man to sit before me on the throne of Israel, if only your sons pay close attention to their way, to walk before me as you have walked before me.'" COMMENTARY ON 2 KINGS.[38]

A PRAYER IN SICKNESS BASED ON HEZEKI-AH'S. JOHANN GERHARD: Hear me, O God, giver and restorer of life, in whose hands is life and death, health and sickness. Do not hear me according to the desire of my will but according to the good pleasure of your will. If you will make whole, say but one word only, and I shall be whole. You are the length of my days, and in your hands are my lots. But if you now call me by the way of death to the heavenly country, rid me first of all excessive love of this life. Give me the strength of the Spirit that I may overcome the sorrows of death and in the midst of the darkness of my eyes—when they wax dim—kindle and increase in me the light of a heart which with you is the fountain of true life, and in your light I shall see light.

Your death, O good Jesus, is the medicine of my death and the merit of eternal life. I embrace your word with a faithful heart. Therefore I am sure that you dwell by faith in my heart. I will not let you depart out of my heart before you bless me and lift me up with quickening consolation.

Lord, you have said, "Everyone who lives and believes in me shall never die." My heart sets this word before you, and in faith I draw near to the throne of grace. By faith I know that you will not turn away the one who comes to you in faith. Let your precious blood wash me from my sins. Let your wounds hide me from the wrath of God and the rigor of judgment. I will die in you, but you will live in me; I will abide in you, and you will abide in me. You will not leave me in death and dust, but will raise me up to the resurrection of life.

You have sought and overcome *for* me, now fight and overcome *in* me. Let your strength be performed in my infirmity. My soul cleaves to you. I will not allow myself to be plucked away from you.

Let your peace, which surpasses all understanding, keep my heart and my senses. Into your hands I commend my spirit. You have redeemed me, O God of truth. Take up the poor soul that you have created; which you have redeemed; which you have washed from sin with your blood; which you have sealed with the earnestness of the Holy Spirit; and which you have fed with your body and blood. It is yours. You have given it to me. Take up that which is yours, and remit the guilt of my sins.

Do not let the fruit of your passion perish in me. Do not let your precious blood produce fruitlessness in me. To you, O Lord, I have prayed and to you I hope. Amen. THE CONQUEST OF TEMPTATIONS.[39]

20:8-11 *Hezekiah's Sign*

HOLY SIGNS AND MIRACLES. VIKTORIN STRIGEL: Hezekiah asked, "What shall be the sign?" God always adds an external sign to the promise, as when God set the rainbow in the arc of the heavens with the promise to preserve creation's natural order. In this instance of promising to heal Hezekiah, God added a new sign: the unusual and unheard-of sign of allowing him to see the sun go backward. Such a great and stupendous miracle seems unthinkable, for the sun runs its course with great enthusiasm and speed. . . . By this sign let us recall the difference between the miracles of the church and the miracles of the pagans. They differ partly in the degree of impossibility and partly in their goals. For the church has those miracles that the devil cannot imitate, no matter how hard he tries, because they are of the kind like the setting and reversal of the sun or the raising of the dead. Such works belong to God alone and not to any creaturely power. Next, the goal of diabolical illusions is to the confirmation of what is clearly indecent, either in the worship of idols or in the confusion of desires. But the goals of the church's miracles are the invocation of the true God, the celebration of the return of those who belong to

---

[38]Piscator, *Commentarii in omnes libros Veteris Testamenti*, 2:364; citing 1 Kings 8:25.

[39]Gerhard, *Conquest of Temptations*, 122-24,* citing Jn 11:26.

God and the confirmation of the doctrine that has been handed down from God. Book of Kings.[40]

More Prominent Miracle. Giovanni Diodati: This passage is referring to that shadow which showed the parts of the day, not by whole hours but by other, lesser spaces of time. This is clear from verse 11, which speaks of the going down of the shadow. In other words, it shows it was the declining of the day after midday. If these degrees that descended had been whole hours, that day must have been (even before this miraculous lengthening) twenty hours at least. Hezekiah remarks that it would be "an easy thing" for the dial to move forward. That's because it is natural for the day to go forward; therefore the miracle would have been less prominent. However, in having the dial move backward, the miraculous motion was more slow and apparent, and it redoubled by the going up again and going down again. Annotations on 2 Kings.[41]

20:12-21 The Babylonian Envoys and Hezekiah's Death

Hezekiah's Pride. Viktorin Strigel: The Babylonian delegation was sent to Hezekiah to ask him about the great portent of the sun going backward that had happened over the earth. When they searched for the reason behind this miracle, they learned what happened because news of this had spread quickly to all nations. They learned it happened on account of the king of Judah's illness, as a clear sign that his health had turned back. In a twist, Hezekiah has become an example of human infirmity by falling into the trap of pride. For he showed off the gifts of God, of which the apostle says, "What do you have that you did not receive? If then you received it, why do you boast as if you did not receive it?" That is, the gifts of God are not given for ostentation but for use in the church and the republic. Again, "we have this treasure in jars of

clay, to show that the surpassing power belongs to God and not to us." "You are a reverent and faithful servant if you do not take for yourself the rich glory of God; for it does not come from you but only passes through your hands." Book of Kings.[42]

Fair Punishment. Johannes Piscator: The one who sins is the one who deserves punishment. That used to be said as a fair penalty. And here Hezekiah sinned by showing off his treasures because he sought to be regarded as a rich and magnificent king. Therefore that guilt of his was denounced. His treasure was to be plundered by those to whom he had shown off his splendor. Furthermore, his posterity would serve that nation to whom he showed off since he wished to be regarded as a magnificent king. Commentary on 2 Kings.[43]

Accepting God's Will. Konrad Pellikan: Faithful and devoted to God in everything, Hezekiah humbly submitted to divine providence and God's will, which is over all things and is invincible. In the meantime he was content to give great thanks to God for the gifts of peace and happiness that God was giving for the rest of his days. Peace, righteousness and truth would not depart from his kingdom until he would join his fathers. He commended the future to the favor and mercy of God, who is holy in all his works and never injurious. Commentary on 2 Kings.[44]

Foolish and Unfaithful Hezekiah. John Mayer: Hezekiah's welcoming of the Babylonian envoys was enough to stir up the wrath of God to abuse the favors of God done to him above all other people. It was the result of pride and vainglory that led Hezekiah to act this way, and to comply so effortlessly with heathen idolaters. For the covenants and leagues he made with the Babylonians never resulted in any good for the

---

[40]Strigel, *Libri Samuelis, Regum et Paralipomenon*, 395.
[41]Diodati, *Pious Annotations*, 27*.

[42]Strigel, *Libri Samuelis, Regum et Paralipomenon*, 394-95; citing 1 Cor 4:7; 2 Cor 4:7; Bernard of Clairvaux, *Sermones in Cantica canticorum*, PL 183:835.
[43]Piscator, *Commentarii in omnes libros Veteris Testamenti*, 2:364.
[44]Pellikan, *Commentaria Bibliorum*, 2:198r.

people of Israel, but instead it only brought hurt. Hezekiah surely showed his distrust in God, who had done so mightily for him, while showing trust in foreign forces, of which God had so lately shown him that he did not need to fear. And if there had been no other fault in Hezekiah but the abusing of God's singular blessings to puff himself up, it would have been intolerable. For Hezekiah's actions were no less than a sacrilegious robbing of God, who does all things for himself and for his own glory. And God protested against giving his things to others. It is as if a steward should rob his lord of his best goods, which had been entrusted to the steward for the master's own use. Therefore the prophet Isaiah came to him in the name of the Lord, and threatened him with the carrying away of all his treasures into Babylon, of which Hezekiah naively had said before that it was a far-off country. COMMENTARY ON 2 KINGS.[45]

---

[45]Mayer, *Many Commentaries in One*, 295*.

21:1-26 KINGS MANASSEH AND AMON OF JUDAH

[1]Manasseh was twelve years old when he began to reign, and he reigned fifty-five years in Jerusalem. His mother's name was Hephzibah. [2]And he did what was evil in the sight of the LORD, according to the despicable practices of the nations whom the LORD drove out before the people of Israel. [3]For he rebuilt the high places that Hezekiah his father had destroyed, and he erected altars for Baal and made an Asherah, as Ahab king of Israel had done, and worshiped all the host of heaven and served them. [4]And he built altars in the house of the LORD, of which the LORD had said, "In Jerusalem will I put my name." [5]And he built altars for all the host of heaven in the two courts of the house of the LORD. [6]And he burned his son as an offering[a] and used fortune-telling and omens and dealt with mediums and with necromancers. He did much evil in the sight of the LORD, provoking him to anger. [7]And the carved image of Asherah that he had made he set in the house of which the LORD said to David and to Solomon his son, "In this house, and in Jerusalem, which I have chosen out of all the tribes of Israel, I will put my name forever. [8]And I will not cause the feet of Israel to wander anymore out of the land that I gave to their fathers, if only they will be careful to do according to all that I have commanded them, and according to all the Law that my servant Moses commanded them." [9]But they did not listen, and Manasseh led them astray to do more evil than the nations had done whom the LORD destroyed before the people of Israel.

[10]And the LORD said by his servants the prophets, [11]"Because Manasseh king of Judah has committed these abominations and has done things more evil than all that the Amorites did, who were before him, and has made Judah also to sin with his idols, [12]therefore thus says the LORD, the God of Israel: Behold, I am bringing upon Jerusalem and Judah such disaster[b] that the ears of everyone who hears of it

will tingle. [13]And I will stretch over Jerusalem the measuring line of Samaria, and the plumb line of the house of Ahab, and I will wipe Jerusalem as one wipes a dish, wiping it and turning it upside down. [14]And I will forsake the remnant of my heritage and give them into the hand of their enemies, and they shall become a prey and a spoil to all their enemies, [15]because they have done what is evil in my sight and have provoked me to anger, since the day their fathers came out of Egypt, even to this day."

[16]Moreover, Manasseh shed very much innocent blood, till he had filled Jerusalem from one end to another, besides the sin that he made Judah to sin so that they did what was evil in the sight of the LORD.

[17]Now the rest of the acts of Manasseh and all that he did, and the sin that he committed, are they not written in the Book of the Chronicles of the Kings of Judah? [18]And Manasseh slept with his fathers and was buried in the garden of his house, in the garden of Uzza, and Amon his son reigned in his place.

[19]Amon was twenty-two years old when he began to reign, and he reigned two years in Jerusalem. His mother's name was Meshullemeth the daughter of Haruz of Jotbah. [20]And he did what was evil in the sight of the LORD, as Manasseh his father had done. [21]He walked in all the way in which his father walked and served the idols that his father served and worshiped them. [22]He abandoned the LORD, the God of his fathers, and did not walk in the way of the LORD. [23]And the servants of Amon conspired against him and put the king to death in his house. [24]But the people of the land struck down all those who had conspired against King Amon, and the people of the land made Josiah his son king in his place. [25]Now the rest of the acts of Amon that he did, are they not written in the Book of the Chronicles of the Kings of Judah? [26]And he was buried in his tomb in the garden of Uzza, and Josiah his son reigned in his place.

a Hebrew *made his son pass through the fire*   b Or *evil*

OVERVIEW: As they have frequently observed elsewhere in these biblical histories, the reformers emphasize that faith and virtue are not hereditary, an example made abundantly clear in the difference between Hezekiah and Manasseh. Our commentators note how easy it is for wickedness and idolatry to go underground until a more opportune time. Amon's murder at the hands of his servants further highlights for them the evil effects that come from evil behavior.

21:1-18 Manasseh Reigns in Judah

EVIL LEADERS CANNOT DESTROY THE CHURCH. HEINRICH BULLINGER: Under Manasseh, the grandson of King Ahaz, the celebration of true doctrine and the rightful administration of the sacraments departed, although circumcision remained. This defection endured until the church was reformed by the godly King Josiah. Meanwhile, prophets were truly sent and the church of God remained in Judah despite the fact that the majority of the population followed the leaders and were led by the ungodly defection of Manasseh. DECADES 5.2.[1]

IDOLATRY GOES UNDERGROUND. KONRAD PELLIKAN: It is the worst condition of humankind that an extremely great father is followed by a great son. For in this case the most godly Hezekiah was followed by his sacrilegious and most ungodly son. When he was twelve years old, the young Manasseh came to the throne. False prophets and the priests of Baal had seized his soul. They had learned to sacrifice from the time of Ahab yet had reluctantly gone underground, afraid of being punished by the pious Hezekiah for false religion. In their hypocrisy, they obeyed the king in restoring reverence for the law of the Lord, watching the high places and idols get destroyed and painfully enduring the worship of the true God. But in their souls they remained truly impious and sacrilegious. They corrupted the young and earnest king by persuading him that the law of the Lord had been a new religion invented by Hezekiah, which he would be wise to revoke entirely. In its place, he should restore the supposedly more ancient (though truly superstitious) rites of the Gentiles that his venerable predecessor Ahab had wisely introduced according to the customs of foreign nations. COMMENTARY ON 2 KINGS.[2]

MANASSEH'S UNSURPASSED WICKEDNESS. JOHANNES BUGENHAGEN: It was a great, effective and immense blessing of God that the ungodliness of Ahaz was followed by the light of divine truth restored by Hezekiah, who called the people back to true worship of God, and prophets like Isaiah, full of the Spirit, preached the word. For who does not see that King Hezekiah and many others had been preserved through the word to eternal life in the midst of corrupt nations? But the rest of the multitude was truly ungrateful to God, which is what we need to discuss now as it is clearly revealed in this history. For immediately upon the death of Hezekiah, God sent an operation of delusion through Manasseh so that with debased minds the people and the king sinned in all the ways that had been handed down to them. In this they even surpassed the impiety of the Canaanites and the idolatry of the Israelites, not frightened by the judgment that they saw carried out on each of those peoples. No one was affected by or feared the law of God; they omitted no impieties. The holy city that God had chosen and the holy temple that had been consecrated for worship became nothing. The promises of God were despised. The prophets were not listened to; rather they were killed with other officials who were doubtless confessors of the truth, a remnant of those who had been consecrated to God under Hezekiah. For this reason we believe what the letter to the Hebrews says about Isaiah being murdered by Manasseh. COMMENTARY ON 2 KINGS.[3]

---

[1]Bullinger, *Sermonum decades quinque*, 366.

[2]Pellikan, *Commentaria Bibliorum*, 2:198v.
[3]Bugenhagen, *In Regum duos ultimos libros*, 181-82; citing Heb 11:37 and the talmudic traditions of Isaiah's death.

VIRTUE IS NOT HEREDITARY. JOHN MAYER: Most probably, since Manasseh came from a good father, so likewise he came of a good mother. Yet he degenerated to show that virtue is not hereditary. Nevertheless, Manasseh lived long and reigned longer than any of the kings of Judah before. . . . But he spent a great part of his time in much misery for his abominable wickedness, where he equaled the most idolatrous heathens. And in that which is said concerning this, it is to be noted that he was most contrary to his godly father. . . . This is seen in many ways. For instance, while his father in the very beginning of his reign endeavored by all means to set up the true worship of God, Manasseh put this true worship down. While his father set the priests and Levites in their order to do the rightful work of the temple, Manasseh drove them from the temple and set up false priests in their stead. While his father converted heathens by his piety to the true faith, Manasseh, by his impiety, corrupted many of the faithful. While his father greatly honored the prophet Isaiah, the history says that Manasseh sawed Isaiah in half, having first dishonored the great prophet in his old age by scourges—even though he was his near kinsman. While his father consulted with God by his prophets, Manasseh consulted with the devil by witchcraft. While his father had the sun and stars obedient to him, Manasseh worshiped most basely the sun, the moon and the stars. While his father's prayers and piety kept away the judgments from his people, Manasseh's impiety brought judgment against himself and his people. Therefore his father obtained a glorious victory over his enemies to the increase of his honor, while Manasseh—to his great infamy—was overcome by his enemy and was bound and carried away like a slave in chains to Babylon. COMMENTARY ON 2 KINGS.[4]

JUST PUNISHMENTS TO COME. KONRAD PELLIKAN: In the end, all the world would know that the people of Judah would suffer justly as the fitting punishment for all their evil. In their wantonness they had mocked and cursed the blessings and care of the Lord God, though they would have otherwise received only goodness and righteousness from the Lord. These are examples of all such ungodly exertions across all ages of people, kings and kingdoms. For they had not erred only once or twice in this way, but had continuously rebelled against God and God's words ever since their ancestors' exodus from Egypt, remaining stubbornly unfaithful despite so many miraculous signs and holy prophets. COMMENTARY ON 2 KINGS.[5]

21:19-26 Amon Reigns in Judah

AMON'S DAYS CUT SHORT. JOHANNES BUGENHAGEN: We have spoken above about God's immense fury against an ungrateful people, which certainly only increased during the long reign of Manasseh. For the sake of the elect, God truly cut short the wicked days of his son Amon, as we will see in the following history and just as Christ said of the devastation facing the people of Judea in his day: "If those days had not been cut short, no human being would be saved." For in the midst of fury, God remembers mercy (as Habakkuk says), so that God might bring salvation. Therefore Amon perished in his hereditary iniquity. He was killed by his servants, who themselves then deserved to die according to the judgment of God, as we have sometimes spoken of such laws above. COMMENTARY ON 2 KINGS.[6]

PRONE TO PERFIDY. KONRAD PELLIKAN: Amon, the iniquitous son of Manasseh, was more prone to perfidy than to piety. He chose the evil he had seen from his father: idolatry and contempt for the divine law. He renewed his father's impieties and disdained the memory of those who had called Manasseh to repent of his foolishness. As is seen in 2 Chronicles 21, he tried to reinstate the evil things

[4]Mayer, *Many Commentaries in One*, 298*.

[5]Pellikan, *Commentaria Bibliorum*, 2:199r.
[6]Bugenhagen, *In Regum duos ultimos libros*, 183-84; citing Mt 24:22.

that Manasseh had changed after his repentance. Therefore it was the just judgment of God that his servants conspired against him and killed him, putting in his place the most pious Josiah, his son. Commentary on 2 Kings.[7]

Corrupted King Who Does Not Repent. Johannes Piscator: In Amon an example is set forth of a corrupted man. For Amon imitated the idolatry of his father. But he was not at all moved by the captivity of his father, which Manasseh on account of his idolatry had fallen on. Nor did Amon later repent like his father and thereby be led to abolish idolatry and truly seek to restore the worship of God, as we read about in 2 Chronicles: "And when [Manasseh] was in distress, he entreated the favor of the Lord his God and humbled himself greatly before the God of his fathers. . . . And he took away the foreign gods and the idols from the house of the Lord, and all the altars that he had built on the mountain of the house of the Lord and in Jerusalem, and he threw them outside of the city. He also restored the altar of the Lord and offered on it sacrifices of peace offerings and of thanksgiving, and he commanded Judah to serve the Lord, the God of Israel." Commentary on 2 Kings.[8]

Admonition to Be More Like Jehu Than Manasseh. John Mayer: Amon was another Joash. That is, despite his good upbringing under Jehoiada, he turned into a wicked idolater. Therefore this king came to have the same end; namely, he was killed by his servants because he had happily been drawn to idolatry through them, as Joash had also been by his, who came down and fell down before him and thus inclined his unsettled mind to their impious desires. And it was a judgment of God singularly to be marked, justly coming on him, that the fame should be the instruments of his destruction, who were the instruments of his seduction. And although his father Manasseh repented and rejected his idols, he was not altogether blameless of this wickedness of his son because he did not burn his idols but only cast them out of the city where they remained to be a snare to Amon. Nor is he said to have done anything for the reforming of other parts of his kingdom but only of Jerusalem—so that from that country, where his corruption still remained, it might easily be derived to the city. Let this be a warning to all reformers to not do as Manasseh. Rather, we are to be like Jehu, who broke down the false images and burned the house of Baal with fire, and so rooted out idolatry from Israel forever. Commentary on 2 Kings.[9]

---

[7]Pellikan, *Commentaria Bibliorum*, 2:199v.
[8]Piscator, *Commentarii in omnes libros Veteris Testamenti*, 2:366; citing 2 Chron 33:12, 15-16.

---

[9]Mayer, *Many Commentaries in One*, 303*.

22:1–23:30 KING JOSIAH OF JUDAH

[1]*Josiah was eight years old when he began to reign, and he reigned thirty-one years in Jerusalem. His mother's name was Jedidah the daughter of Adaiah of Bozkath.* [2]*And he did what was right in the eyes of the LORD and walked in all the way of David his father, and he did not turn aside to the right or to the left.*

[3]*In the eighteenth year of King Josiah, the king sent Shaphan the son of Azaliah, son of Meshullam, the secretary, to the house of the LORD, saying,* [4]*"Go up to Hilkiah the high priest, that he may count the money that has been brought into the house of the LORD, which the keepers of the threshold have collected from the people.* [5]*And let it be given into the hand of the workmen who have the oversight of the house of the LORD, and let them give it to the workmen who are at the house of the LORD, repairing the house* [6]*(that is, to the carpenters, and to the builders, and to the masons), and let them use it for buying timber and quarried stone to repair the house.* [7]*But no accounting shall be asked from them for the money that is delivered into their hand, for they deal honestly."*

[8]*And Hilkiah the high priest said to Shaphan the secretary, "I have found the Book of the Law in the house of the LORD." And Hilkiah gave the book to Shaphan, and he read it.* [9]*And Shaphan the secretary came to the king, and reported to the king, "Your servants have emptied out the money that was found in the house and have delivered it into the hand of the workmen who have the oversight of the house of the LORD."* [10]*Then Shaphan the secretary told the king, "Hilkiah the priest has given me a book." And Shaphan read it before the king.*

[11]*When the king heard the words of the Book of the Law, he tore his clothes.* [12]*And the king commanded Hilkiah the priest, and Ahikam the son of Shaphan, and Achbor the son of Micaiah, and Shaphan the secretary, and Asaiah the king's servant, saying,* [13]*"Go, inquire of the LORD for me, and for the people, and for all Judah, concerning the words of this book that has been found. For great is the wrath of the LORD that is kindled against us, because our fathers have not obeyed the words of this book, to do according to all that is written concerning us."*

[14]*So Hilkiah the priest, and Ahikam, and Achbor, and Shaphan, and Asaiah went to Huldah the prophetess, the wife of Shallum the son of Tikvah, son of Harhas, keeper of the wardrobe (now she lived in Jerusalem in the Second Quarter), and they talked with her.* [15]*And she said to them, "Thus says the LORD, the God of Israel: 'Tell the man who sent you to me,* [16]*Thus says the LORD, Behold, I will bring disaster upon this place and upon its inhabitants, all the words of the book that the king of Judah has read.* [17]*Because they have forsaken me and have made offerings to other gods, that they might provoke me to anger with all the work of their hands, therefore my wrath will be kindled against this place, and it will not be quenched.* [18]*But to the king of Judah, who sent you to inquire of the LORD, thus shall you say to him, Thus says the LORD, the God of Israel: Regarding the words that you have heard,* [19]*because your heart was penitent, and you humbled yourself before the LORD, when you heard how I spoke against this place and against its inhabitants, that they should become a desolation and a curse, and you have torn your clothes and wept before me, I also have heard you, declares the LORD.* [20]*Therefore, behold, I will gather you to your fathers, and you shall be gathered to your grave in peace, and your eyes shall not see all the disaster that I will bring upon this place.'" And they brought back word to the king.*

23 *Then the king sent, and all the elders of Judah and Jerusalem were gathered to him.* [2]*And the king went up to the house of the LORD, and with him all the men of Judah and all the inhabitants of Jerusalem and the priests and the prophets, all the people, both small and great. And he read in their hearing all the words of the Book of the Covenant that had been found in the house of the LORD.* [3]*And the king stood by the pillar and made a covenant before the LORD, to walk after the LORD and to keep his commandments and his testimonies and his statutes with all his heart and all his soul, to perform* the words of this covenant that were written in this book. And all the people joined in the covenant.

⁴And the king commanded Hilkiah the high priest and the priests of the second order and the keepers of the threshold to bring out of the temple of the Lord all the vessels made for Baal, for Asherah, and for all the host of heaven. He burned them outside Jerusalem in the fields of the Kidron and carried their ashes to Bethel. ⁵And he deposed the priests whom the kings of Judah had ordained to make offerings in the high places at the cities of Judah and around Jerusalem; those also who burned incense to Baal, to the sun and the moon and the constellations and all the host of the heavens. ⁶And he brought out the Asherah from the house of the Lord, outside Jerusalem, to the brook Kidron, and burned it at the brook Kidron and beat it to dust and cast the dust of it upon the graves of the common people. ⁷And he broke down the houses of the male cult prostitutes who were in the house of the Lord, where the women wove hangings for the Asherah. ⁸And he brought all the priests out of the cities of Judah, and defiled the high places where the priests had made offerings, from Geba to Beersheba. And he broke down the high places of the gates that were at the entrance of the gate of Joshua the governor of the city, which were on one's left at the gate of the city. ⁹However, the priests of the high places did not come up to the altar of the Lord in Jerusalem, but they ate unleavened bread among their brothers. ¹⁰And he defiled Topheth, which is in the Valley of the Son of Hinnom, that no one might burn his son or his daughter as an offering to Molech.ᵃ ¹¹And he removed the horses that the kings of Judah had dedicated to the sun, at the entrance to the house of the Lord, by the chamber of Nathan-melech the chamberlain, which was in the precincts.ᵇ And he burned the chariots of the sun with fire. ¹²And the altars on the roof of the upper chamber of Ahaz, which the kings of Judah had made, and the altars that Manasseh had made in the two courts of the house of the Lord, he pulled down and broke in piecesᶜ and cast the dust of them into the brook Kidron. ¹³And the king defiled the high places that were east of Jerusalem, to the south of the mount of corruption, which Solomon the king of Israel had built for Ashtoreth the abomination of the

Sidonians, and for Chemosh the abomination of Moab, and for Milcom the abomination of the Ammonites. ¹⁴And he broke in pieces the pillars and cut down the Asherim and filled their places with the bones of men.

¹⁵Moreover, the altar at Bethel, the high place erected by Jeroboam the son of Nebat, who made Israel to sin, that altar with the high place he pulled down and burned,ᵈ reducing it to dust. He also burned the Asherah. ¹⁶And as Josiah turned, he saw the tombs there on the mount. And he sent and took the bones out of the tombs and burned them on the altar and defiled it, according to the word of the Lord that the man of God proclaimed, who had predicted these things. ¹⁷Then he said, "What is that monument that I see?" And the men of the city told him, "It is the tomb of the man of God who came from Judah and predictedᵉ these things that you have done against the altar at Bethel." ¹⁸And he said, "Let him be; let no man move his bones." So they let his bones alone, with the bones of the prophet who came out of Samaria. ¹⁹And Josiah removed all the shrines also of the high places that were in the cities of Samaria, which kings of Israel had made, provoking the Lord to anger. He did to them according to all that he had done at Bethel. ²⁰And he sacrificed all the priests of the high places who were there, on the altars, and burned human bones on them. Then he returned to Jerusalem.

²¹And the king commanded all the people, "Keep the Passover to the Lord your God, as it is written in this Book of the Covenant." ²²For no such Passover had been kept since the days of the judges who judged Israel, or during all the days of the kings of Israel or of the kings of Judah. ²³But in the eighteenth year of King Josiah this Passover was kept to the Lord in Jerusalem.

²⁴Moreover, Josiah put away the mediums and the necromancers and the household gods and the idols and all the abominations that were seen in the land of Judah and in Jerusalem, that he might establish the words of the law that were written in the book that Hilkiah the priest found in the house of the Lord. ²⁵Before him there was no king like him, who turned to the Lord with all his heart and with all his soul and with all his might, according to all the Law of Moses, nor did any like him arise after him.

²⁶Still the LORD did not turn from the burning of his great wrath, by which his anger was kindled against Judah, because of all the provocations with which Manasseh had provoked him. ²⁷And the LORD said, "I will remove Judah also out of my sight, as I have removed Israel, and I will cast off this city that I have chosen, Jerusalem, and the house of which I said, My name shall be there."

²⁸Now the rest of the acts of Josiah and all that he did, are they not written in the Book of the Chroni-cles of the Kings of Judah? ²⁹In his days Pharaoh Neco king of Egypt went up to the king of Assyria to the river Euphrates. King Josiah went to meet him, and Pharaoh Neco killed him at Megiddo, as soon as he saw him. ³⁰And his servants carried him dead in a chariot from Megiddo and brought him to Jerusalem and buried him in his own tomb. And the people of the land took Jehoahaz the son of Josiah, and anointed him, and made him king in his father's place.

a Hebrew *might cause his son or daughter to pass through the fire for Molech*   b The meaning of the Hebrew word is uncertain   c Hebrew *pieces from there*
d Septuagint *broke in pieces its stones*   e Hebrew *called*

OVERVIEW: The reformers highly praise King Josiah after the tyrannies of his predecessors. They observe that Josiah gave religious instructions to his high priest Hilkiah, and not the other way around. With respect to Josiah's consultation of the prophet-ess Huldah, the reformers unreservedly support this passage's example of a woman giving advice to men; they even supplement Huldah's work by mentioning other female leaders from both the Old and New Testaments. Reflecting on Josiah as a faithful leader, some commentators appeal to all Christian leaders to examine themselves according to Josiah's example. The righteous king is also universally applauded for the recovery of the Book of the Law (probably Deuteronomy), his restoration of the Passover and his destruction of the idolatrous high places and the site of human sacrifice called Topheth, which the reformers identified with the New Testament Gehenna. The commentators differ somewhat on the nature and meaning of Josiah's death: some affirm that he died at peace—as Huldah had prophesied; others interpret Josiah's death in battle as a sign that God was displeased with him. Finally, these interpreters note that despite Josiah's righteous reign, the people of Judah return to impiety almost as soon as he dies; Jerusalem's fall is near.

ON ASTROLOGY AND THE FIRST COMMAND-MENT. HIERONYMUS WELLER VON MOLSDORF: Here it may be asked: Is it really not permitted for one to ask astrologers what sort of life one will live, and what good and bad will happen to one in life? I respond: Astrologers must absolutely not be consulted. For the predictions, if they are good and favorable, render the impious even more self-assured, more defiant and more confident, so that, by neglecting the Word of God and omitting prayer, they fling themselves into danger, and they make the predictions of the astrologers greater than divine threats. But if those predictions are gloomy and wicked, they summon anxiety and misery on the pious.

But someone might say why become familiar with the predictions of the theologians? For profane people, when they know that the stars threaten some gloomy events, they are stirred up to repen-tance, so that they direct their behavior more carefully. And the pious, when they hear that such savage wickedness is threatened, will fortify themselves even more so with the word of God and prayer against these wicked acts. I respond: This curiosity, that we be able to foresee and to avoid future dangers, opposes the first commandment: "I am the LORD your God." By these words God prohibits all anxiety and concern about foreseeing future dangers, and he commands that we commit ourselves entirely to him. And as he teaches that we should cast all our anxieties on him. We should let him care for us; whoever wants to know what will happen to him, good or bad, wants to be God himself. For this curiosity about what good or bad will happen to us seizes God's honor from him. He himself is the LORD our God, who provides for us, cares for us, loves us and protects us against all the devil's fury. What graver sin is there than to seize God's honor as one's own? It testifies to that horrible fall of our first parents. Their own curiosity or ambition to be divine flung them, along with their entire posterity, into destruction, from which we have been saved through the Son of God. ANNOTATIONS ON 2 KINGS 23:24.[1]

22:1-7 Praises for Josiah

SPIRITUAL AND BODILY SALVATION BROUGHT BY JOSIAH'S REIGN. JOHN MAYER: Josiah was set forth by his mother's name and parentage, which was Jedidiah, signifying the "beloved of the LORD." And it seems that she did not have this name by chance, but divine providence appointed it. This is seen in her bearing an excellent son, Josiah, whose name signifies the "salvation of the LORD," as he was named before in the time of Jeroboam and prophesied 344 years before he was born. And, indeed, through Josiah all Israel was saved in his time. This salvation came about spiritually by being delivered from the bondage of idolatry and bodily by being protected from the invasion of foreign enemies. COMMENTARY ON 2 KINGS.[2]

THE WAY OF DAVID. KONRAD PELLIKAN: Walking in the way of David means to strive with one's whole heart to the loving God, depending on the Lord through times of prosperity and adversity and carefully dwelling in God's commandments at all times. If some temptation should arise and a sin be committed out of some great weakness, walking in the way of David means not despairing, not turning to a foreign god and not preferring superstitions but clinging to the true and great God alone. COMMENTARY ON 2 KINGS.[3]

NOT TURNING TO THE RIGHT OR THE LEFT. JOHANNES BUGENHAGEN: Not turning to the right would mean not to add to the Word of God and create things about the worship of God that God did not command. Not turning to the left means not removing or casting the Word of God away in derision. In the former, the great impiety comes in seeking another source of holiness; in the latter, God is plainly and truly despised. These things were prohibited in Deuteronomy 12, which says, "Everything that I command you, you shall be careful to do. You shall not add to it or take from it." COMMENTARY ON 2 KINGS.[4]

ADVICE FOR LEADERS. JOHANNES PISCATOR: From the example of Josiah, a pious king, other kings and leaders should learn that they must rightly establish the worship of God. And they must not break the commandments of the divine word, turning aside to the right or to the left. Similarly, when doubt comes, they must consult God through ministers of the Word, who are acquainted with the will of God through the Word, and they will bring God's will to light. In the same way they must command that the buildings for the worship of God be established and that they are watched over and maintained. COMMENTARY ON 2 KINGS.[5]

MORAL TRANSPARENCY. KONRAD PELLIKAN: Josiah is here commended not for spending for spending's sake, for that is easily corrupted by prudent and evil people alike through fraud. But he is commended for spending on all things that were required for doing a good job, which would be believed without needing an accounting, for they would be clearly seen as being honest and faithful. Such a thing is fitting also for bishops of souls as they build up the church of the elect. COMMENTARY ON 2 KINGS.[6]

CONSTANT EVALUATION OF OUR HEARTS. DANIEL DYKE: Let us chastise ourselves every

[1]Weller, *Liber secundus Regum*, 70v; citing Ex 20:2; 1 Pet 5:7.
[2]Mayer, *Many Commentaries in One*, 303-4*.
[3]Pellikan, *Commentaria Bibliorum*, 2:199v.
[4]Bugenhagen, *In Regum duos ultimos libros*, 185; citing Deut 12:32.
[5]Piscator, *Commentarii in omnes libros Veteris Testamenti*, 2:367.
[6]Pellikan, *Commentaria Bibliorum*, 2:199v-200r.

morning and examine ourselves every evening—
even in the still silence of the night—as we lay
awake in our beds. In the matter of disbursement of
money—for the repaying of them—Josiah gave
charge that no reckoning should be made with
them into whose hands the money was delivered,
for, he said, "they deal honestly." Indeed, if our hearts
dealt faithfully with ourselves, we also might spare
this labor of daily count-casting. But because both
the Word of God and our own experience has
sufficiently discovered our unfaithfulness, we must
say, "Let there be daily, indeed, hourly reckonings
kept within our hearts, for they are exceedingly
unfaithful." The Mystery of Self-Deceiving.[7]

22:8-10 *A Book Found*

The Clergy Must Obey the Ruler.
Alexander Alesius: In the eighteenth year of
King Josiah of Judah's reign, the king sent
Shaphan, the scribe of the temple, to Hilkiah the
high priest to explain that all the money gathered
from the people for the temple should be melted
and delivered to smiths to be bestowed on the
temple. And Hilkiah did as the king commanded.
He also sent him through Shaphan a book of the
law that he had found in the house of God. And
when Shaphan had read it to the king, he cut his
clothes and commanded Hilkiah the high priest
to give council to the king from the words of that
book, for he said that the wrath of God was
kindled against them. And Hilkiah did as the
king commanded him. And so it appears that the
king commanded the high priest in regard to the
book, and he obeyed. King Josiah also commanded Hilkiah the bishop, the priests of the
second order and the porters to cast out of the
house of God all vessels that were made for Baal.
They obeyed. These texts prove that kings have
their power directly from God. And it proves
that they judge the world. Everyone within their
dominions is their subjects, and they must obey
the king. In fact, neither bishop nor priest is

exempt in any of these texts. A Treatise
Concerning General Councils.[8]

Finding Deuteronomy. Johannes Bugenha-
gen: Finding the Book of the Law means finding
Deuteronomy, which in Deuteronomy 17 commands that the king read it all of his days. In it is
written the horrible curses that await those who
transgress its laws and many other things. Commentary on 2 Kings.[9]

A Tender Heart Finds the Law. John
Mayer: The book found by the high priest was
delivered to Shaphan, who carried it to the king.
And after restitution was made of the money taken
and delivered for the building, he told the king of
this book. And he read it before him. And when
Josiah the king heard it, he tore his garments and
mourned. The book in which he read and which
troubled the good king so much has been conjectured to be Deuteronomy. For there are many
chapters in this book containing terrible threatening pronouncements against transgressors of the
law. A tender heart could not but be struck when
considering any one of these numerous judgments
as coming on the land. For both Josiah's fathers and
the people had foully sinned by gross idolatries.
And because these never go unpunished, Josiah was
concerned about the grievous judgments that hung
over the land. Therefore he sent immediately to
inquire of the Lord by Huldah, a prophetess, by
what means judgment might be prevented.
Commentary on 2 Kings.[10]

22:11-20 *A Woman Prophet*

Holiness and Authority. Konrad Pel-
likan: The prophetess Huldah lived in Jerusalem,
in the part of the city where the priests lived. She
was of great age and had been recognized for her
holiness and authority, so that the men went to

---

[7]Dyke, *The Mystery of Self-Deceiving*, 367-68*; citing 2 Kings 22:7.

[8]Alesius, *Treatise Concernynge Generall Councilles*, 5-7*.
[9]Bugenhagen, *In Regum duos ultimos libros*, 186.
[10]Mayer, *Many Commentaries in One*, 310*.

her first to discern the will of the Lord and make intercessory prayer to the Lord. COMMENTARY ON 2 KINGS.[11]

ANOTHER EXAMPLE OF A WOMAN IN A TEACHING OFFICE. JOHANNES PISCATOR: Although the public office of teaching ordinarily and regularly pertains to men, God sometimes extends this office to women, though outside of their normal rank, on behalf of his unrestricted power. Indeed there are many more examples of God extending this office to woman besides Huldah. For instance, we see examples in Anna, the daughter of Phanuel and in the four daughters of Philip the deacon. COMMENTARY ON 2 KINGS.[12]

HULDAH THE PROPHETESS. JOHANNES BUGENHAGEN: When King Josiah said, "Go, inquire of the LORD for me," it shows how they consulted the Lord at that time (as you often read in the Scriptures) by seeking out a particular man or woman. Here they consulted Huldah the prophetess. For we do not deny the Lord's counsel when it comes from anyone. COMMENTARY ON 2 KINGS.[13]

WHY DOES HEZEKIAH CONSULT A WOMAN? JOHN MAYER: The reason why Hezekiah sent for Huldah rather than for Jeremiah was because she dwelt nearer to the king, likely in some part of Jerusalem. . . . Jeremiah, meanwhile, was living at this time in Anatoth in Benjamin, about two miles from Jerusalem. For at this time Jeremiah was further off reproaching and threatening sin in another part of the land of Israel, to which he was sent. And it was not without a special providence that Hilkiah's ministers went to Huldah, so that this weaker sex might not be despised. For God has sometimes vowed to make women instruments of revealing his will concerning things to come—including, for instance, Deborah, Miriam and Hannah—so that they may have their due honor and so that marriage might not be vilified

by bad teachers, seeing that it has pleased God to inspire by his Spirit even married women and men. Indeed some of the prophets were married men, including the high priest who oftentimes prophesied. Johannes Wolf seeks a proof of prophetesses under the New Testament based on 1 Corinthians—"every wife who prays or prophesies with her head uncovered . . ."—arguing that although other women in the congregation were to be silent, those women who had the spirit of prophecy were left at liberty to speak there. But this interpretation is contrary to what other expositors say, namely, that those women who are spoken of as prophesying were present at the prophesying of the word. And although women have prophesied even under the new covenant, it has not been publicly endorsed in the congregation but only privately. COMMENTARY ON 2 KINGS.[14]

FEMALE RULE A VIOLATION OF GOD'S LAW. JOHN KNOX: It is true that that there are biblical examples of female leadership, as in the case of Deborah and Huldah. However, these particular examples do not establish common law. The reason God took the spirit of wisdom and force from the men of those ages in order to assist women—something that is both against nature and against his ordinary case of action—is known to God alone. . . . I concede that God worked mightily and miraculously in Deborah and Huldah, and that he gave them a most singular grace and privilege. However, who actually commanded that a public, nay, a tyrannical and most wicked precedent, should be established based upon these examples? It does not matter how many examples are provided. When these examples go against God's law, they cannot set precedents.

If I should ask, for example, what kind of marriage is lawful, it could be answered from biblical examples that it is lawful for a man to have many wives at the same time or to marry sisters simultaneously since we find such examples in the figures of David, Jacob or Solomon,

---

[11]Pellikan, *Commentaria Bibliorum*, 2:200r.
[12]Piscator, *Commentarii in omnes libros Veteris Testamenti*, 2:367.
[13]Bugenhagen, *In Regum duos ultimos libros*, 186.

[14]Mayer, *Many Commentaries in One*, 311*; citing 1 Cor 11:5.

who truly were servants of God. I trust that no one would justify the vanity of such reasoning. Here's another example: Should a Christian be allowed to defraud, steal or deceive since the Israelites did so when God commanded them to plunder the Egyptians by taking their clothes, gold and silver? I think such reasoning should be mocked. This type of argument does not hold up to scrutiny. Are we really supposed to believe that just because Deborah ruled in Israel and Huldah spoke prophecy in Judah that it is therefore lawful for women to govern realms and nations, or to teach in the presence of men? Such reasoning is vain and of no effect. We cannot establish laws based on biblical examples. On the contrary, God himself has written and pronounced what is truly lawful. And God's law forbids any woman from reigning over a man, just as this same law forbids a man to take several wives simultaneously, to marry two sisters at the same time, to steal, to rob, to murder and to lie. Just because one of these laws was transgressed and we did not see that God punished the offense, we cannot build law from these examples of silence. God, who is free to do what he chooses, may allow what is contrary to law according to his indisputable wisdom. Indeed, he may dispense with the rigor of his law and may make use of his creatures as he pleases. But the same luxury is not afforded to people, for God has made them subject to his law and not subject to examples. THE FIRST BLAST.[15]

WHY JOHN KNOX IS WRONG ABOUT WOMEN IN LEADERSHIP. JOHN CALVIN: Two years ago, in a private discussion, John Knox wanted to know how I felt about the right of women to rule. I quite candidly responded that, since female rule was a defect from the actual order of nature from the beginning of time, we should regard it as a judgment upon humankind that was inflicted because of neglect—just as slavery had been. Still, certain women had occasionally been so gifted

that the unique blessing of God was evident in them. They were plainly lifted up by the auspices of God. Such was done either because God wished to condemn the idleness of men or to more radiantly illuminate his own glory. I brought forth the examples of Huldah and Deborah. I similarly added that God promised, through the mouth of Isaiah, that queens would be the "nursing mothers" of the church. Such women were distinguished from private women. Finally, I gave this as a conclusion: Since it had been accepted that women might inherit kingdoms and principalities by custom, public consent and longstanding practice, this question about female rule did not appear to move me to think it troublesome. In my judgment, it's not permitted to overthrow governments that have been ordained by the personal providence of God. LETTER TO WILLIAM CECIL (1559).[16]

A NEW PROMISE. KONRAD PELLIKAN: This prophecy of the demise of the kingdom, the city and the temple was not new but had come from the grievous ungodliness of the kings and the people. But the consolation that the holy Josiah would receive in the meantime was a new promise that came from his religious repairs that he had begun in his youth with reverential and attentive obedience to God's law, even in his heart. He longed to turn the Lord to gentleness, fearing the righteous fury and judgment of God and not doubting that everything that the law of God threatens against its despisers would come to pass. And so the king tore his clothes as a sign of faith and repentance, crying bitterly, pressing himself on the mercy that the holiest God gives to his friends. COMMENTARY ON 2 KINGS.[17]

---

[15]Knox, *The First Blast of the Trumpet*, 37-39*.

[16]CO 17:490-91; citing Gen 3:16; Is 49:23. William Cecil (1520–1598) was a baron and a longstanding advisor to Queen Elizabeth I. Through this letter to Cecil, and thus the Queen of England, Calvin intended to distance himself from John Knox's bombastic treatise *The First Blast of the Trumpet Against the Monstrous Regiment and Empire of Women*, which so greatly offended female rulers like Elizabeth.

[17]Pellikan, *Commentaria Bibliorum*, 2:200r.

23:1-3 A Covenant Made

JOSIAH'S EXAMPLE FOR RULERS. MENNO
SIMONS: Observe, dear reader, what kind of faith
Josiah had, and what the fruits of it were. He heard
the word of the Lord and believed it. He rent his
clothes, inquired of the Lord and renewed the
covenant. For he heard what God had commanded
in the same book: that they should not do according
to their own thoughts, that they should not follow
after strange gods, nor the abominations of the
Canaanite and the other heathen that were dispersed
before them, but that they should serve the Lord
alone and cleave to him and keep his commandments,
statutes and ordinances as he directed them. He was
strong in the Lord, with manly courage, and acted
valiantly in all his doings. For he believed and trusted
God with all his strength, and with earnest zeal he
tore down all that his forefathers and the former
kings out of their own imaginations and choice had
introduced and established as holy service. He
burned all the vessels of Baal and tore down all the
groves, high places and altars in the land of Judea and
Samaria. He defiled Topheth in the valley of the
children of Hinnom. He destroyed the horses sacred
to the sun, and burned the chariots of fire. He broke
down the altar of Bethel after he had sacrificed the
idol priests and dead bones on it, as the man of God
had proclaimed against his altar in earlier times. He
destroyed all that was opposed to and contrary to the
law of God. He kept the Passover of the Lord as it
was written in the book of the covenant in such a
glorious manner as no judge or king had kept it
before. He also swept away all soothsayers and
necromancers, all images and idols, and all the abominations that were seen in the land of Judah and
Jerusalem, in order that they might perform the
words of the Lord that were written in the book that
Hilkiah, the high priest, had found in the house of
the Lord. There was no king like . . . him that turned
to the Lord with all his heart. . . . Hearken now, O
mighty princes and kings, and all those who let themselves think that they are believing rulers and
Christian princes. To you is my admonition. If you
have any fear of God, any love to Christ or his

blessed Word, or any reasonable nature—you who
have understanding—then acknowledge that you are
not gods from heaven, but poor mortal men of the
impure, mortal seed of Adam. Humble yourselves
under the almighty hand of God, and compare this
Josiah and his faith and works with yours. TRUE
CHRISTIAN FAITH.[18]

GATHERING THE ELDERS. KONRAD PELLIKAN:
At the king's call, all the elders of Judah and Jerusalem gathered to the king. With their advice and
assent, the true worship of God that had until then
been neglected would be established and defended
and then received by the general populace. For no
king of Israel reigned without the support of the
tribes of their fathers. COMMENTARY ON 2 KINGS.[19]

SEEKING AVERSION FROM JUDGMENT. JOHN
MAYER: Now Josiah is said to have made this
covenant with all his heart, and the people did
outwardly all bind themselves also. But they did so
insincerely, as appears in Jeremiah's complaint. That
is, they did not turn completely with all their heart
to the Lord, but falsely or deceitfully. As a result
Jeremiah said that rebellious Israel was justified
before Judah because Judah added hypocrisy to all
her abominations, and therefore in Jeremiah 4 he
bids them to break up the fallow ground of their
hearts and not to sow thorns among themselves.
That is, still having an impious and perfidious heart.
It may be asked why Josiah did this now, given that
he was secured by the promise of God, and
afterward the threatening was so peremptory, that
there was no hope of preventing the judgments. I
answer that when any promise is made, the faithful
know that it is tacitly implied that they should
diligently obtain them by all good means. And when
judgments are threatened, as against Nineveh, these
promises may be truly averted by means of repentance. Therefore Josiah did not lack in doing his best
to make sure the promise, if at all possible, could be
averted. And for this judgment to be averted and to

---

[18]Simons, *Complete Writings*, 358-59.
[19]Pellikan, *Commentaria Bibliorum*, 2:200v.

stay faithful to the covenant, Josiah called for the keeping of the Passover in a most solemn and religious manner. COMMENTARY ON 2 KINGS.[20]

23:4-20 *Josiah Cleans House*

STOPPING IDOLATRY NOW. ANDREAS BODEN-STEIN VON KARLSTADT: We see from this that priests are subject to kings by divine right. On this account our magistrates should not wait until priests begin to carry out false idols and their wooden vessels and obstructions. For they may never begin. The supreme temporal power must order and undertake action. ON THE REMOVAL OF IMAGES.[21]

AN ORDERLY REFORMATION. KONRAD PELLIKAN: Hilkiah was the high priest, and after him came a second order of priests. Then there were others who were guardians of the treasures and gatekeepers, caring for the vessels in the temple. The king received all these things and cast out of the temple everything that was against God's law or that pertained to the idols of Baal, the sacred groves and anything else having to do with foreign worship. These things would be burned together in the Kidron Valley and ground to dust. For these were the things that had remained intact after Manasseh had his conversion or that his ungodly son Amon had reintroduced. The king then commanded the collection of the ashes of all that had been burned at Bethel, where the worship of the golden calves had taken place, just as had been prophesied concerning that place. COMMENTARY ON 2 KINGS.[22]

JOSIAH PREFIGURING REFORMATION THEN RELAPSE. JOHN MAYER: It seems strange that these abominations were not done away with sooner, in the days of godly kings like Asa, Jehoshaphat or Hezekiah, who reigned before Josiah. It is to be held that although they were godly and zealous kings, God had previously determined in his mind that Josiah would

be coming into the world to purge the church more than all of them. This was so that, if after this they should fall into idolatry again, they might more justly be given over into the hands of their enemies as desperate, as indeed they were. And here was happily prefigured what should be done in the latter days of the gospel, in which a greater reformation of the religion is now being made. But it shall come to more perfection yet, when the Jews come to convert. And when after this a relapse shall be made again, destruction by the Lord's last coming to judgment shall soon follow. COMMENTARY ON 2 KINGS.[23]

DUST AND BONES. JOHANNES BUGENHAGEN: Josiah burned the Asherah and beat it to dust, casting the dust on the graves of the common people. Here is clearly shown the contamination and filth that had made their way into holy dwelling places through idolatry. According to the law, people became unclean because of contact with the dead. And so you read here and below how Josiah defiled the idols in the high places. That is, he declared them to be filthy by refilling the bones of the dead with their dust. He defiled the altar in Bethel in a similar manner by burning human bones on it. COMMENTARY ON 2 KINGS.[24]

DEFILING THE HIGH PLACES. GIOVANNI DIODATI: King Josiah assembled all the priests who worshiped the true God, even if they did it in the high places rather than in the temple of Jerusalem, which was the only place approved by God. Indeed he had all the high places "defiled"; that is, by his authority he proclaimed them to be unclean and took away all signs of holiness from them. He did this by bringing them to sordid uses, which included filling the land with unclean things according to law such as dead bodies, bones and the like. From Geba to Beersheba was a way of referring to the two bounds of the land of Judah in length. ANNOTATIONS ON 2 KINGS.[25]

---

[20]Mayer, *Many Commentaries in One*, 313*.
[21]CRR 8:118.
[22]Pellikan, *Commentaria Bibliorum*, 2:200v; citing 1 Kings 13:32.

[23]Mayer, *Many Commentaries in One*, 307*.
[24]Bugenhagen, *In Regum duos ultimos libros*, 188.
[25]Diodati, *Pious Annotations*, 28*.

False Motive. Defense of the Augsburg Confession: The people had heard that Abraham had sacrificed his son. Therefore they also put their sons to death in order to appease the wrath of God by this most cruel and severe act. But Abraham did not offer his son with the idea that this work was the payment and atoning sacrifice on account of which he would be regarded as righteous. Thus in the church the Lord's Supper was instituted that our faith might be strengthened by the remembrance of the promises of Christ—of which this sign reminds us—and that we might publicly confess our faith and proclaim the benefits of Christ. Article 4: Justification.[26]

Ending Sacrifice. Johannes Bugenhagen. Topheth, a place of which you often read, was a place in suburban Jerusalem where people sacrificed their children to Molech by burning them, as Ahaz had done. Isaiah had prepared a fire and a judgment of God for this place. "For [Topheth] has long been prepared; indeed, for the king it is made ready, its pyre made deep and wide, with fire and wood in abundance; the breath of the Lord, like a stream of sulfur, kindles it." You decided to burn your religiosity and holiness in a fire at Topheth that God did not command. See, God burns your Topheth, sending a fire that cannot be extinguished. You who had a fire for your worship of God will now perish by fire. It is called here the Valley of the Son of Hinnom, because in that place was the posterity of a man named Hinnom. From this we get the "fires of Gehenna" in the Gospels, which is the name for the fire of eternal punishment. Commentary on 2 Kings.[27]

Like Hell in Three Ways. Thomas Adams: Topheth resembles hell in three ways. First, it resembles hell because it is a low valley, similar to hell's location under the earth. Second, because of the fire, where children were burned in the valley, similar to the way the wicked are tormented in hell. Third,

because the place was unclean and detestable, being the place where all the trash and vile things were cast out from Jerusalem, similar to hell's site as the place where defiled and wicked souls are cast, since they are unworthy of the holy and heavenly city. The Shot.[28]

East Side of Jerusalem. Giovanni Diodati: Topheth was a place on the east side of Jerusalem in the pleasant Valley of the Son of Hinnom. It was so called from the Hebrew word *tof*, that is to say, "a drum." It was called this either by reason of the music, dances and other pastimes that were used there; or by reason of the noise of drums, which was used there in the abominable sacrifices of their children. The noise was made to deafen the ears and dull the senses of the spectators. Annotations on 2 Kings.[29]

The Bones of the Prophets. Johannes Bugenhagen: Josiah wanted to leave the bones of the prophet who had declared such miraculous things. Among us, those who canonize bones are certifiably insane. In former times, honoring tombs was a way for people to honor the bodies of holy people, as you read of Sarah, Joseph, Christ, Stephen and others. It is also read that Christians visited the tombs of the martyrs. There they adored God, sang songs, preached, worshiped and scattered roses. They did this to proclaim faith in the resurrection against the Gentiles who mocked us for letting ourselves be killed for the sake of life. This alone should therefore be the reason for gathering together at tombs. Following this other example of all the ancients, we permit the bones of the saints to rest quietly until they rise again from death. Commentary on 2 Kings.[30]

23:21-27 The Passover

A Public Festival. Konrad Pellikan: During the time of holy kings, prophets and judges,

---

[26]BoC 152; citing Gen 22.
[27]Bugenhagen, *In Regum duos ultimos libros*, 188-89; citing Is 30:33.
[28]Adams, *Devil's Banquet*, 183-84*.
[29]Diodati, *Pious Annotations*, 28*.
[30]Bugenhagen, *In Regum duos ultimos libros*, 189-90.

the Passover had not been omitted. But it had not been kept by all the people together and been praised by a devoted and pious king. Popular piety is such that people easily acquiesce in doing whatever ceremonies seem most pleasing. Still, there were doubtlessly many people in that crowd who grieved that their old holy things had been taken away and come to an end. They had enjoyed those solemn superstitions of theirs. Yet King Josiah gladdened them again with his coming of age in his eighteenth year, adorning it with this most splendid celebration of the Passover. COMMENTARY ON 2 KINGS.[31]

23:28-30 *Josiah Dies*

REASON FOR JOSIAH'S DEATH. HEINRICH BULLINGER: The great prince Josiah fell and was killed by the Chaldeans, because the Lord had intended to punish and bring evil on the whole nation of Israel.[32] The Lord was unwilling to look on him as a holy prince. In this way we must learn that true religion is not to be esteemed by the victory or conquering of any people—so much so that that religion whose worshipers conquer should be seen as true and orthodox, while that religion whose worshipers fall should be false. For we must distinguish between persons or people who hold to that religion who for various reasons suffer the Lord's visitation. DECADES 2.9.[33]

A PEACEFUL DEATH? JOHANNES BUGENHAGEN: This story of Josiah's death is described in more detail in Chronicles. But where now is that promise of God that came through the prophetess Huldah: "You shall be gathered to your grave in peace"? I reply: you see the manner of death as a great matter, but it was a blessing of God that he who had governed so well in the eyes of people and God died when he did. You are seeing this death according to the judgment of the mortal flesh and according to

the ungodly. When Josiah was assailed by the king of Egypt, he was not able to hear him speaking the word of God, yet God still wanted to care for his holy one not only with a quiet rest but also with eternal salvation. As Huldah predicted, this was a quiet rest in which his eyes would not see all the evil done by those whom the Lord would bring on the land of Judah in three months (as you will soon see and read). COMMENTARY ON 2 KINGS.[34]

PROPHETIC FULFILLMENT. CHARLES DRELIN-COURT: When we cast our eyes on the tragic death of Josiah, king of Judah, at first sight it appears merely as the effect of the boiling heat of youth that obstinately carried him against reason to fight with Pharaoh Neco, king of Egypt. . . . But to understand the truth, we must enter further into the sanctuary and adore the wisdom of God's decree. For this decree had resolved to take a way this good and religious prince into eternal rest and bestow on him a nobler and richer crown, before he took in hand the sword of vengeance to punish the people of Israel for the many idolatries and crimes of which they had been guilty. By this God fulfilled the prophecy of Huldah, "Therefore, behold, I will gather you to your fathers, and you shall be gathered to your grave in peace, and your eyes shall not see all the disaster that I will bring on this place." CHRISTIAN DEFENSE AGAINST THE FEARS OF DEATH.[35]

GOD'S JUST VERDICT AGAINST JUDAH. JO-HANNES BUGENHAGEN: Here you have this clear verdict against Judah. Its king and priesthood, which had been established and glorified in holiness, would be carried away. This declares to the world that all external matters, even those things instituted by God, are filthy and abominable when faith in God is forsaken. You will see that this downfall occurs immediately after the death of Josiah, coming to completion in the Babylonian

---

[31]Pellikan, *Commentaria Bibliorum*, 2:201v.
[32]In both scriptural accounts, Josiah dies in battle with the Egyptians (2 Kings 23:29-30; 2 Chron 35:20-24).
[33]Bullinger, *Sermonum decades quinque*, 186.

[34]Bugenhagen, *In Regum duos ultimos libros*, 190-91.
[35]Drelincourt, *Christian's Defense Against the Fears of Death*, 74-75*; citing 2 Kings 22:20.

Captivity or even in this most recent captivity. Commentary on 2 Kings.[36]

Converted for a Day. Konrad Pellikan: The entire people of Israel had been converted to God for a day, content to have a strong king and giving Pharisaical devotion, as happens to almost all who follow another god. The following history will show this. Their hearts had not totally embraced the Word of God. Instead, at the ceremonies they pretended a piety they did not have. For it appears as if they relapsed into faithlessness very quickly and, having grieved the rejection of their beautiful

idols and the sensual pleasures that came with the worship of idols, a certain number of the people had remained ungodly. The prophet Jeremiah revealed this impious conversion, so that he was hated by the people as much as by the prince. Commentary on 2 Kings.[37]

Context for Jeremiah's Lamentations. John Mayer: The place where Josiah died was Jerusalem, about forty-four miles from Megiddo. Josiah was greatly lamented by Judah and Jerusalem. In fact Jeremiah wrote his lamentations upon the king's death and the miseries that ensued. These lamentations were put to song and taught to the people as a daily remembrance. Commentary on 2 Kings.[38]

---

[36]Bugenhagen, *In Regum duos ultimos libros*, 190. "In this most recent captivity" likely refers to the corruption of the late medieval church against which Luther protested in his *Babylonian Captivity of the Church* (1520); see LW 36:11-126 (WA 6:497-573).

[37]Pellikan, *Commentaria Bibliorum*, 2:202r.
[38]Mayer, *Many Commentaries in One*, 318*.

23:31–25:30 THE END OF JUDAH

³¹Jehoahaz was twenty-three years old when he began to reign, and he reigned three months in Jerusalem. His mother's name was Hamutal the daughter of Jeremiah of Libnah. ³²And he did what was evil in the sight of the LORD, according to all that his fathers had done. ³³And Pharaoh Neco put him in bonds at Riblah in the land of Hamath, that he might not reign in Jerusalem, and laid on the land a tribute of a hundred talentsᵃ of silver and a talent of gold. ³⁴And Pharaoh Neco made Eliakim the son of Josiah king in the place of Josiah his father, and changed his name to Jehoiakim. But he took Jehoahaz away, and he came to Egypt and died there. ³⁵And Jehoiakim gave the silver and the gold to Pharaoh, but he taxed the land to give the money according to the command of Pharaoh. He exacted the silver and the gold of the people of the land, from everyone according to his assessment, to give it to Pharaoh Neco.

³⁶Jehoiakim was twenty-five years old when he began to reign, and he reigned eleven years in Jerusalem. His mother's name was Zebidah the daughter of Pedaiah of Rumah. ³⁷And he did what was evil in the sight of the LORD, according to all that his fathers had done.

24 In his days, Nebuchadnezzar king of Babylon came up, and Jehoiakim became his servant for three years. Then he turned and rebelled against him. ²And the LORD sent against him bands of the Chaldeans and bands of the Syrians and bands of the Moabites and bands of the Ammonites, and sent them against Judah to destroy it, according to the word of the LORD that he spoke by his servants the prophets. ³Surely this came upon Judah at the command of the LORD, to remove them out of his sight, for the sins of Manasseh, according to all that he had done, ⁴and also for the innocent blood that he had shed. For he filled Jerusalem with innocent blood, and the LORD would not pardon. ⁵Now the rest of the deeds of Jehoiakim and all that he did, are they not written in the Book of the Chronicles of the Kings of Judah? ⁶So Jehoiakim slept with his fathers, and Jehoiachin his son reigned

in his place. ⁷And the king of Egypt did not come again out of his land, for the king of Babylon had taken all that belonged to the king of Egypt from the Brook of Egypt to the river Euphrates.

⁸Jehoiachin was eighteen years old when he became king, and he reigned three months in Jerusalem. His mother's name was Nehushta the daughter of Elnathan of Jerusalem. ⁹And he did what was evil in the sight of the LORD, according to all that his father had done.

¹⁰At that time the servants of Nebuchadnezzar king of Babylon came up to Jerusalem, and the city was besieged. ¹¹And Nebuchadnezzar king of Babylon came to the city while his servants were besieging it, ¹²and Jehoiachin the king of Judah gave himself up to the king of Babylon, himself and his mother and his servants and his officials and his palace officials. The king of Babylon took him prisoner in the eighth year of his reign ¹³and carried off all the treasures of the house of the LORD and the treasures of the king's house, and cut in pieces all the vessels of gold in the temple of the LORD, which Solomon king of Israel had made, as the LORD had foretold. ¹⁴He carried away all Jerusalem and all the officials and all the mighty men of valor, 10,000 captives, and all the craftsmen and the smiths. None remained, except the poorest people of the land. ¹⁵And he carried away Jehoiachin to Babylon. The king's mother, the king's wives, his officials, and the chief men of the land he took into captivity from Jerusalem to Babylon. ¹⁶And the king of Babylon brought captive to Babylon all the men of valor, 7,000, and the craftsmen and the metal workers, 1,000, all of them strong and fit for war. ¹⁷And the king of Babylon made Mattaniah, Jehoiachin's uncle, king in his place, and changed his name to Zedekiah.

¹⁸Zedekiah was twenty-one years old when he became king, and he reigned eleven years in Jerusalem. His mother's name was Hamutal the daughter of Jeremiah of Libnah. ¹⁹And he did what was evil in the sight of the LORD, according to all that Jehoiakim had done. ²⁰For because of the anger of the LORD it

came to the point in Jerusalem and Judah that he cast them out from his presence.

And Zedekiah rebelled against the king of Babylon.

25 And in the ninth year of his reign, in the tenth month, on the tenth day of the month, Nebuchadnezzar king of Babylon came with all his army against Jerusalem and laid siege to it. And they built siege works all around it. ²So the city was besieged till the eleventh year of King Zedekiah. ³On the ninth day of the fourth month the famine was so severe in the city that there was no food for the people of the land. ⁴Then a breach was made in the city, and all the men of war fled by night by the way of the gate between the two walls, by the king's garden, and the Chaldeans were around the city. And they went in the direction of the Arabah. ⁵But the army of the Chaldeans pursued the king and overtook him in the plains of Jericho, and all his army was scattered from him. ⁶Then they captured the king and brought him up to the king of Babylon at Riblah, and they passed sentence on him. ⁷They slaughtered the sons of Zedekiah before his eyes, and put out the eyes of Zedekiah and bound him in chains and took him to Babylon.

⁸In the fifth month, on the seventh day of the month—that was the nineteenth year of King Nebuchadnezzar, king of Babylon—Nebuzaradan, the captain of the bodyguard, a servant of the king of Babylon, came to Jerusalem. ⁹And he burned the house of the LORD and the king's house and all the houses of Jerusalem; every great house he burned down. ¹⁰And all the army of the Chaldeans, who were with the captain of the guard, broke down the walls around Jerusalem. ¹¹And the rest of the people who were left in the city and the deserters who had deserted to the king of Babylon, together with the rest of the multitude, Nebuzaradan the captain of the guard carried into exile. ¹²But the captain of the guard left some of the poorest of the land to be vinedressers and plowmen.

¹³And the pillars of bronze that were in the house of the LORD, and the stands and the bronze sea that were in the house of the LORD, the Chaldeans broke in pieces and carried the bronze to Babylon. ¹⁴And they took away the pots and the shovels and the snuffers and the dishes for incense and all the vessels of bronze

used in the temple service, ¹⁵the fire pans also and the bowls. What was of gold the captain of the guard took away as gold, and what was of silver, as silver. ¹⁶As for the two pillars, the one sea, and the stands that Solomon had made for the house of the LORD, the bronze of all these vessels was beyond weight. ¹⁷The height of the one pillar was eighteen cubits,ᵇ and on it was a capital of bronze. The height of the capital was three cubits. A latticework and pomegranates, all of bronze, were all around the capital. And the second pillar had the same, with the latticework.

¹⁸And the captain of the guard took Seraiah the chief priest and Zephaniah the second priest and the three keepers of the threshold; ¹⁹and from the city he took an officer who had been in command of the men of war, and five men of the king's council who were found in the city; and the secretary of the commander of the army, who mustered the people of the land; and sixty men of the people of the land, who were found in the city. ²⁰And Nebuzaradan the captain of the guard took them and brought them to the king of Babylon at Riblah. ²¹And the king of Babylon struck them down and put them to death at Riblah in the land of Hamath. So Judah was taken into exile out of its land.

²²And over the people who remained in the land of Judah, whom Nebuchadnezzar king of Babylon had left, he appointed Gedaliah the son of Ahikam, son of Shaphan, governor. ²³Now when all the captains and their men heard that the king of Babylon had appointed Gedaliah governor, they came with their men to Gedaliah at Mizpah, namely, Ishmael the son of Nethaniah, and Johanan the son of Kareah, and Seraiah the son of Tanhumeth the Netophathite, and Jaazaniah the son of the Maacathite. ²⁴And Gedaliah swore to them and their men, saying, "Do not be afraid because of the Chaldean officials. Live in the land and serve the king of Babylon, and it shall be well with you." ²⁵But in the seventh month, Ishmael the son of Nethaniah, son of Elishama, of the royal family, came with ten men and struck down Gedaliah and put him to death along with the Jews and the Chaldeans who were with him at Mizpah. ²⁶Then all the people, both small and great, and the captains of the forces arose and went to Egypt, for they were afraid of the Chaldeans.

²⁷And in the thirty-seventh year of the exile of Jehoiachin king of Judah, in the twelfth month, on the twenty-seventh day of the month, Evil-merodach king of Babylon, in the year that he began to reign, graciously freed^c Jehoiachin king of Judah from prison. ²⁸And he spoke kindly to him and gave him a seat above the seats of the kings who were with him in Babylon. ²⁹So Jehoiachin put off his prison garments. And every day of his life he dined regularly at the king's table, ³⁰and for his allowance, a regular allowance was given him by the king, according to his daily needs, as long as he lived.

a A *talent* was about 75 pounds or 34 kilograms   b A *cubit* was about 18 inches or 45 centimeters   c Hebrew *reign, lifted up the head of*

OVERVIEW: The commentators identify Judah's captivity by the Babylonians as just and thorough punishments for sins against God; they also add observations about the meaning and effects of spiritual captivity for their contemporary contexts. At the same time, some writers also see grace at work amid the destruction of Jerusalem: even if the Holy City, people and land itself are no longer able to receive God's promises, the Lord mercifully preserves a remnant for himself through this exile. In a similar vein, one commentator considers how the Scriptures were preserved through the years of captivity. As 1–2 Kings comes to a close, the commentators give thanks that God's promises to David were remembered during the exile, preparing the way for the Messiah to come from the house of David in the person of Jesus Christ.

23:31-35 Jehoahaz Reigns in Judah

GOD'S VERDICT FULFILLED. JOHANNES BUGENHAGEN: After the fall of the righteous Josiah, who did not deserve to see the evil that was coming, the divine verdict that had been pronounced above immediately took effect. The ungodly continued to work against God, for which reason the kings' powers were stripped. Now they not only had to give tribute to Egypt but the kings also had no power over their people except through the pharaoh (which is the name sacred Scripture gives to all the kings of Egypt). COMMENTARY ON 2 KINGS.¹

KING JEHOAHAZ. KONRAD PELLIKAN: Even in his brief reign, it is clear that Jehoahaz began without pursuing the fear of God. His father's reforms fell flat, and he adopted more of his grandfather's superstitions than his father's pieties. False prophets, hypocritical priests and fickle people of a depraved sort had already worked their way back to him, tempting people to resume their former impieties. They succeeded in large measure, against the prophets of the Lord who continuously resisted them. Therefore the prophets accomplished nothing, because all were going to ruin, exchanging the inheritance of the father for the iniquity of the son. COMMENTARY ON 2 KINGS.²

HASTY ANOINTING. JOHN MAYER: Now that Josiah was dead, Jehoahaz his son was anointed king in his place. He was twenty-three years old. This anointing of a king, who was heir apparent to the crown, was not typical and needed not to have been done. . . . It was only done because the kingdom had been troubled by Pharaoh Neco of Egypt. The anointing, therefore, was used as a signal that the kingdom was now in his hands, as the king-to-be defended the people against the Egyptians and the other enemies. . . . But the people of Judah did not act wisely by neglecting Neco. The people should have fought for peace and liberty, and they should have requested Neco to appoint their new king. For the people's act could not but have greatly provoked Neco, as the rest of the story shows. For, returning from his wars against Assyria, he came and took Jehoahaz and

---

¹Bugenhagen, *In Regum duos ultimos libros*, 192.

²Pellikan, *Commentaria Bibliorum*, 2:202r.

carried him away bound in chains to Egypt, where he died. In fact before his captivity he had only reigned for three months. Pharaoh Neco then made Eliakim his brother the king in Jehoahaz's place, turning his name to Zedekiah. Consequently Zedekiah, who was the younger brother of Jehoahaz, was the rightful heir to the crown. COMMENTARY ON 2 KINGS.[3]

23:36–24:7 Jehoiakim Reigns in Judah

JEHOIAKIM'S BLINDNESS. JOHANNES BUGENHAGEN: According to Josephus, Jehoiakim rebelled against Babylon because he hoped for help from Egypt, which was then the authority behind the king. He saw Egypt as offering great resistance against the king of Babylon. But this misplaced faith came from a blindness that the Lord put in Jehoiakim's heart, so that he and his people would fall into evil. COMMENTARY ON 2 KINGS.[4]

JEHOIAKIM'S DEATH. KONRAD PELLIKAN: This Jehoiakim is said to have "slept with his fathers"; that is, he died. But he did not die in his bed or of natural causes. For according to the prophet Jeremiah, "With the burial of a donkey he shall be buried, dragged and dumped beyond the gates of Jerusalem." Such a burial without the customary pomp and ceremony happened because the city was under siege and there was confusion and havoc all around. Thus it says that Jehoiakim slept with his fathers, but he was not buried with them in any royal tomb. COMMENTARY ON 2 KINGS.[5]

CONJECTURAL HYPOTHESIS FOR TROUBLESOME TIMES. JOHN MAYER: Now that Jehoiakim is dead, Jehoiachin his son was made king. He was eighteen years old when he became king and only reigned for three months. However, in some translations of 2 Chronicles 36:9, Jehoiachin is said to have been eight years old when he became king.

This is commonly resolved by saying that Chronicles mentions the time when he began to reign with his father, which was in the second year of Jehoiakim's reign. And so, if Jehoiachin were but then eight, he was eighteen when his father died and then he began to reign alone. And this is supposedly more probable because the times were troublesome. In this line of thought, Jehoiakim would have thought it necessary to establish his son in the kingdom before his death so that there might be less danger in setting up another after him, which was a thing recently done with his younger brother Jehoahaz. But because no such thing is spoken of in Scripture, that is, as Jehoiachin co-reigning with his father, all this is but conjectural. COMMENTARY ON 2 KINGS.[6]

24:8-9 Jehoiachin Reigns in Judah

JEHOIACHIN'S THREE MONTHS; JUDEA'S SEVENTY YEARS. VIKTORIN STRIGEL: Jehoiachin—also called Coniah—reigned for three months in Judah. And when Nebuchadnezzar surrounded the city of Jerusalem with a siege, Jeremiah, unlike the previous prophets, urged him to surrender it. For both Jeremiah and the other prophets predicted that Jerusalem would be destroyed and that the Judeans would be taken into exile under God's care, so that after seventy years they would return and rebuild their homeland. BOOK OF KINGS.[7]

KING JEHOIACHIN. KONRAD PELLIKAN: It appears as if Jehoiachin's counsel was to rebel against the king of Babylon, trusting instead in the Egyptians who had installed him as king. But this was a foolish faith, because the king of Egypt had already been humbled and defeated by the king of Babylon, who then held all the land of Syria and the other nations from the Euphrates River to nearly the Nile. COMMENTARY ON 2 KINGS.[8]

---

[3]Mayer, *Many Commentaries in One*, 318*.
[4]Bugenhagen, *In Regum duos ultimos libros*, 193.
[5]Pellikan, *Commentaria Bibliorum*, 2:202v; citing Jer 22:19.
[6]Mayer, *Many Commentaries in One*, 320-21*.
[7]Strigel, *Libri Samuelis, Regum et Paralipomenon*, 408.
[8]Pellikan, *Commentaria Bibliorum*, 2:202v.

A Rebellious and Foolish King. John Mayer: The reason why Mattaniah's name was changed to Zedekiah was, according to Nicholas of Lyra, to signify the justice of God. And when Nebuchadnezzar made Mattaniah king, he caused him to be just and true to him by paying him tribute and having nothing to do with the Egyptians. However, it is clear from 2 Chronicles that Mattaniah did not honor this oath: "Zedekiah also rebelled against King Nebuchadnezzar, who had made him swear by God. He stiffened his neck and hardened his heart against turning to the Lord, the God of Israel." But by giving Mattaniah his name, Nebuchadnezzar tried to demonstrate his authority over him. Thus when he did rebel contrary to his oath, Nebuchadnezzar would show himself to be more odious and worthy to come and destroy him, as would be expected for his other abominations. Mattaniah had the same mother as Jehoiakim, and he sinned just like him. But their father Josiah is not once here mentioned, because he was unworthy of that honor, namely, to be styled the father of so ungodly a pair kings. . . . And although the prophet Jeremiah warned Mattaniah not to rebel, he did so. But through his rebellion and obstinacy the judgments of God were hastened against him and his people of Judah and Jerusalem by means of the Babylonians. Commentary on 2 Kings.[9]

24:10-17 Jerusalem Captured

Preserved in Exile. Viktorin Strigel: The church was preserved in a new way, namely, through exile, though the impious ones argued that the promise should be the defense of the Judean line in that place. But the pious ones discerned the eternal kingdom and city. They knew that God had promised even more wonderful things and understood that—with some exceptions—the promises of physical good come through punishment and the cross. They became acquainted with this teaching through this destruction of the city, receiving the strength of true consolation from God, which did not run out, as they looked forward to the return of the Lord. Book of Kings.[10]

Carried into Exile. Konrad Pellikan: The king and his court were not the only ones taken away. So were all the precious materials of the land, as well as the noble people, those who were somehow great or important, including craftsmen, smiths and the mighty warriors among the Jewish people. The precious vessels of the temple of the Lord and the king's palace that Solomon had made were also taken away with the king. Everything was carried off to Babylon, according to the word of the Lord that the prophet Isaiah had told to King Hezekiah. Commentary on 2 Kings.[11]

24:18-20 Zedekiah Reigns in Judah

Divine Punishment. Lucas Osiander: The Lord was angered against Jerusalem and the tribe of Judah because of the great sins of the people. For this reason God did not give them a pious king who could have slowed the punishment like Josiah had done. Instead a king was put in charge who would have no ability to do anything to avert the wrath of God. And so the Lord cast them out from his face; that is, the Lord handed them over to the power of the enemy, no different than if he had cast them all away from his care. Annotations on 2 Kings.[12]

Exile at Hand. Konrad Pellikan: Zedekiah was no less impious than the others. For the people were corrupt and the princes and advisers were ungodly. No one but they could advise the king, so that all would perish under the judgment of God together. On account of the sins and the sins of those who went before committed against God and his saints, the exile of the king and people was at hand. Zedekiah gave the occasion for this when he sinfully vowed to rebel against the king of

[9]Mayer, *Many Commentaries in One*, 323*; citing 2 Chron 36:13.

[10]Strigel, *Libri Samuelis, Regum et Paralipomenon*, 409.
[11]Pellikan, *Commentaria Bibliorum*, 2:203r.
[12]Osiander, *Liber Iosue*, 1046.

Babylon and thereby disobeyed the exhortations of the most faithful prophet Jeremiah. COMMENTARY ON 2 KINGS.[13]

25:1-12 *The Fall and Captivity of Judah*

THE GODLY SEE MERCY. VIKTORIN STRIGEL: The entire history of the fall of Jerusalem is full of many lessons. For the wrath of God is seen in the punishment of the ungodly. On the other hand mercy is also revealed, because amid such calamity God wonderfully preserves a remnant of the church. For King Zedekiah commanded that Jeremiah be spared and permitted him to stay in the land with a remnant of the people. He also promised safety to Jeremiah and his friends Ebed-melech and Baruch the scribe. These examples agree with the saying, "Because of the steadfast love of the LORD, we are not cut off." But we ourselves see this time of the ruin of the empire and other calamities. Therefore we should recognize God's wrath and pray that we be turned back to God. And we should hope that punishment might be alleviated and the church be preserved. BOOK OF KINGS.[14]

THE FALL. JOHANNES BUGENHAGEN: Up to this point, there had been the hope that the kingdom would be restored and that the city of Jerusalem—which God had chosen—would remain standing whole, along with its priests and holy things. But this time the people, kingdom and priesthood were carried off, just as the Lord had preached through Moses and other prophets (as we have discussed above). In the end the ungodly were rounded up to discover the verdict of the word of God that condemned them. The prophets had not only rightly described all of the misery of this captivity, but they also often sketched out the captivity of sin and death, in which a people in whom God is glorified becomes plagued by human traditions to such an extent that they can no longer return to

God. This is an elegant figure or type of Babylonian captivity for us, as we sometimes confess ourselves in the Psalms, especially in the psalm that begins, "O God, why do you cast us off forever? Why does your anger smoke against the sheep of your pasture?" But there is no doubt that we are handed over in this way because of contempt for the truth in our vexed consciences. When the word of faith perishes from among us, our glorification of ourselves as being people of God on account of external sacraments means nothing. For in the time of anguish, we will perish just as they who trusted in themselves as being the holy ones of God did back then. Natural blindness wants to rejoice in itself as being a gift of God, even though anyone who is seized by it is really in contempt of God. Therefore it was revealed that they had trusted in vanities. They were cast out of the land that God had promised to their ancestors, which God had acquired for his people with miracles and with great force and favor by casting out the Canaanites. God had promised this and was believed. After forty years he gave the land, so that his promise may be seen as having been true, even as he threatened to cast away unbelievers and despisers. COMMENTARY ON 2 KINGS.[15]

NO PROTECTION FROM IDOLATRY. JOHANNES PISCATOR: In the destruction of the city of Jerusalem by Nebuchadnezzar we are warned that God greatly abominates idolatrous religion. And God will frustrate those who confide in protection in the city. COMMENTARY ON 2 KINGS.[16]

TEMPORAL PHYSICAL PUNISHMENT BETTER THAN EVERLASTING TORMENT. JOHN MAYER: Judah's fall demonstrates that sin was now grown to the full not only in the court but also in the country. It was also in the clergy, and we see both the universality of sin and the contempt the people had for righteousness.... The people scorned the

---

[13]Pellikan, *Commentaria Bibliorum*, 2:203r.
[14]Strigel, *Libri Samuelis, Regum et Paralipomenon*, 410; citing Jer 38:16; Lam 3:22 Vg.
[15]Bugenhagen, *In Regum duos ultimos libros*, 194-96; citing Ps 74:1, 2 Thess 2.
[16]Piscator, *Commentarii in omnes libros Veteris Testamenti*, 2:374.

prophets as deceivers, false prophets, and thus they went on in their sin until the wrath of God burned against them. So now there could be no healing in this land, which was sick of sin. It had to be utterly destroyed and laid waste. This was also done to make the souls of these wicked people penitent on account of the grievous punishments they experienced so that they might be saved everlastingly. COMMENTARY ON 2 KINGS.[17]

25:13-21 Sacred Things Destroyed or Taken Away

SACRED THINGS IN EXILE. KONRAD PELLIKAN: Although already mentioned in general, the two pillars are also named in particular, along with their parts and ornamentation, as if forcing Jewish readers to recall the memory of all these wonderful and admirable things. For us, the pillars are the Old and New Testaments or the two tables of the Decalogue. The bronze sea is baptism, the sacrament of rebirth and renewal, while the foundations are the articles of the catholic faith. COMMENTARY ON 2 KINGS.[18]

DESTRUCTION OF THE PILLARS. JOHANNES BUGENHAGEN: The pillars that were destroyed are those mentioned in the history of Solomon above. But the Lord had told Solomon that he would cast them down if he abandoned the Lord. Isaiah had said the same thing to Hezekiah. COMMENTARY ON 2 KINGS.[19]

SOLOMON'S VESSELS DESTROYED TO TEACH US A LESSON. JOHN MAYER: It may seem that there could be none of the golden vessels made by Solomon remaining at this time to be carried away, for all the treasures of the Lord's house were taken away a long time before in the time of Rehoboam the son of Solomon. And if under the name of such treasures the vessels were not taken, they are

expressly said to have been carried away in the time of Amaziah. This is to say nothing of these treasures which were again exhausted in the time of Hezekiah.

But it is answered that they are called the vessels of Solomon because they were made *like* Solomon's vessels, in the same sense that they followed the same pattern that Solomon had under the direction of God. This act of having the vessels taken was prophesied to Hezekiah by Isaiah a hundred years before, and now it was fulfilled after so long a time to show the truth of God, so that we may believe. And it is to be noted that Jerusalem was now punished in that which they were proud and vainglorious. This is to teach us that our precious things should not puff us up, lest God be provoked to strip us of them in the same way and bring us misery. COMMENTARY ON 2 KINGS.[20]

EZRA THE RESTORER OF SCRIPTURE. JOHN MAYER: It is a received opinion among many ancient fathers that now also the holy Scriptures were burned, and that God inspired Ezra to write and set them forth perfectly again. This is grounded on 4 Esdras: "For your law has been burned, and so no one knows the things that have been done or will be done by you. If then I have found favor with you, send the Holy Spirit into me, and I will write everything that has happened in the world from the beginning, the things that were written in your law, so that people may be able to find the path, and that those who want to live in the last days may do so." But Athanasius says: "When the sacred books perished by the carelessness of the people and the long captivity, Ezra, who was a very industrious and diligent reader and lover of the truth, kept them all and afterward brought them forth for the common good. And in such a manner, he preserved them from being delivered from destruction." It is said also that Daniel, by reading Jeremiah, found the time of the captivity to be at end, when seventy years had expired. And Josephus said that the book of Isaiah was, by Daniel, showed to Cyrus, where it

---

[17]Mayer, *Many Commentaries in One*, 324-25*.
[18]Pellikan, *Commentaria Bibliorum*, 2:204r.
[19]Bugenhagen, *In Regum duos ultimos libros*, 197.

[20]Mayer, *Many Commentaries in One*, 322*; citing 2 Chron 12:9; 25:24; 2 Kings 18:15-16.

was prophesied of him by name two hundred years before, by which he was the more moved to let the people go. According to Theodoret, on account of the familiarity with which Daniel had with Cyrus, he allowed him to see the prophecy of Isaiah, and was to him the author of returning the captivity. Nor is there any mention in canonical Scripture made anywhere of the burning of all the holy Scriptures, which without a doubt would not have been omitted or passed over unlamented by Jeremiah if it had happened. Last, Ezra himself is said to have read the Scriptures to the people, and other Levites also read to them. But it is not said that Ezra rewrote the Scriptures, but only read them to them and gave them the interpretation. Therefore it is not probable that all the books of holy Scripture were now allowed to perish, but some copy was still preserved by a singular providence, and this was done by Ezra. He was therefore called the restorer of the Scriptures. COMMENTARY ON 2 KINGS.[21]

25:22-26 Gedaliah Reigns in Judah

LEADER OF THE POOR. LUCAS OSIANDER: Because the land still held good vineyards and fields, not everyone was driven into exile. Therefore Nebuchadnezzar did not withdraw from there, but established someone to serve as magistrate there. For people without a leader are like tree trunks without tops. And so, to help harvest the vineyards and fields, Nebuchadnezzar appointed Gedaliah the son of Ahikam, son of Shaphan. He was a Judean and a good man, as is evident from the history given in Jeremiah. The prophet Jeremiah was entrusted to the care of this Gedaliah by the chief officers of the king of Babylon. ANNOTATIONS ON 2 KINGS.[22]

LEAVING THE POOR BEHIND. JOHANNES BUGENHAGEN: The poor were left behind, because they were always easy for a king to come back and assert control over, which is also why the king of Babylon left King Zedekiah's house in ruins. And even of the poor, only so many were left as were needed to be vinedressers and farmers, just as Isaiah had predicted in chapter 7. On the decimation of the people, see Isaiah 6, considering how a remnant would be saved in the last days through Christ. COMMENTARY ON 2 KINGS.[23]

GEDALIAH AS A GOOD MAN. JOHN MAYER: Because the poor people who remained needed someone to govern them or else confusion would follow, Gedaliah, the son of Ahikam, was set over them. Moreover, some of the Babylonians were left to see that all things might be ordered for the best for the king. Of this Gedaliah nothing is recorded among writers, but only that he was a good and loving man. For this cause the captains of the army, who fled out of Jerusalem when it was taken, resorted to Mizpah, the city the king kept in the borders of Judah and Benjamin—which was famous of old, as Gilgal—where Samuel is said to have judged the people. The captains that came to Gedaliah were Ishmael, Johanan, Seraiah and Jaazaniah. He swore to them their security. The captains were probably fearful because they saw some Babylonian soldiers still there, whom they supposed were left to deport or kill those Jews who came out of their hiding places after the departure of Nebuchadnezzar. But as Jeremiah says, Gedaliah gave them his word. . . . Why Ishmael later killed Gedaliah is not said, but it may well be conjectured that he did it out of envy upon seeing Gedaliah preferred before himself, who was not of royal blood. And this was done in the seventh month to the extreme grief and terror of all the Jews who remained, before two months of his government were fully expired. That's because they feared that the Chaldeans would come again and destroy them all for this act. And it is thought by some of great judgment that in this month all the Jews kept a fast during the desolation of their land, and also the fourth month, because in the fourth

---

[21]Mayer, *Many Commentaries in One*, 326*; citing 4 Esdr 14:21-22.
[22]Osiander, *Liber Iosue*, 1049; citing Jer 39–40.
[23]Bugenhagen, *In Regum duos ultimos libros*, 197.

month the city was broken up. And in the fifth month the temple and city were burned, while in the tenth month Nebuchadnezzar first besieged Jerusalem. For all of these events, there is mention made in Zechariah of a promise that the people would soon experience times of rejoicing at their return from captivity: "Thus says the LORD of hosts: The fast of the fourth month and the fast of the fifth and the fast of the seventh and the fast of the tenth shall be to the house of Judah seasons of joy and gladness and cheerful feasts. Therefore love truth and peace." COMMENTARY ON 2 KINGS.[24]

A FINAL SIN. KONRAD PELLIKAN: Here is briefly told what is longer in Jeremiah; namely, how the good Gedaliah was murdered by the ungodly Ishmael, who preferred all to perish in misery than to be governed by a good person. Against the word of Jeremiah, he carried everyone away to Egypt—including Jeremiah—where all who feared the Babylonian Empire gathered, to be slaughtered one and all with the Egyptians. COMMENTARY ON 2 KINGS.[25]

25:27-29 Evil-merodach Releases Jehoiachin from Prison

GIVING BACK HONOR. VIKTORIN STRIGEL: Evil-merodach, whose name means either "Foolish Marduk" or "Son of Marduk," reigned for thirty years. In the first year that he succeeded his father Nebuchadnezzar, he released Jehoiachin from prison, giving him the honor and way of life befitting a king. This is consistent with and amplifies the teaching about the true God that is found in Daniel. For his father Nebuchadnezzar had publicly professed God, so that because of God's mercy then, the son cared for King Jehoiachin. That is why the other ungodly princes may have given him the name "Foolish Marduk." BOOK OF KINGS.[26]

MERCY TO THE CAPTIVES. LUCAS OSIANDER: God wanted to bend the soul of Evil-merodach to such mercy so that the captive people of God in Babylon would see this as an example of divine benevolence. God had not yet forgotten his people, and there would even come a time when they would be liberated. For God does not abandon his people in times of trial: even in God's wrath, God's mercy is remembered. And if we become truly humble under the cross, repenting and believing in the Son of God (who, according to Matthew 1, was descended from this Jehoiachin when he took on human flesh), the Lord will lighten our sorrows and at length carry us from the squalor of the grave and set us in eternal heavenly joy. Amen. ANNOTATIONS ON 2 KINGS.[27]

FAVOR SHOWN TO THE GOOD FIGS OF JUDAH. JOHN MAYER: Evil-merodach lifted up the head of Jehoiachin from his prison house, suggesting two degrees of favor done to him. The first was in freeing Jehoiachin from prison, by which the Babylonian king lifted up the king of Judah. And the second was in raising him from being a prisoner to being one who dined at the royal palace for the rest of his life and was supported by the Babylonian king. What moved Evil-merodach to show this great favor to Jehoiachin is not said. But if it is true, as the rabbis say, that Evil-merodach had been put in the same prison by his father Nebuchadnezzar where Jehoiachin was imprisoned, a friendship may have grown between them during that time.... Whatever the case, we know that the true efficient cause was God's singular providence, by which this event was brought to pass for the verifying of his word. It was also designed to encourage all kings and for the people to obey God's prophets.... As Jeremiah says, "Thus says the LORD, the God of Israel: Like these good figs, so I will regard as good the exiles from Judah, whom I have sent away from this place to the land of the Chaldeans." Jehoiachin and the Jews, who were carried away with him, are said to have been sent away by the Lord and to have

---

[24]Mayer, *Many Commentaries in One*, 327*; citing Jer 40:9-10; Zech 8:19.

[25]Pellikan, *Commentaria Bibliorum*, 2:204v; citing Jer 44.

[26]Strigel, *Libri Samuelis, Regum et Paralipomenon*, 412.

[27]Osiander, *Liber Iosue*, 1052.

been beloved as good figs. They were chosen to have good done to them, whereas those that were carried away afterward under Zedekiah were evil figs that could not be eaten. Therefore they were condemned to dispersion and destruction. It was long indeed before this good was fulfilled to Jehoiachin, and his captive subjects; but now at the end of thirty-seven years it was performed. For although nothing is said of his subjects here, but only of him, it cannot be thought but that Jehoiachin fared well, and that the Judean people also shared with him in the comfort. COMMENTARY ON 2 KINGS.[28]

KINDNESS TO AN ENEMY. JOHANNES PISCATOR: In Jehoiachin's being released from prison by Evil-merodach and given honors and a daily ration of food, an example is set forth on the goodness and mercy of God. For God does what he wants. That is, God may bend the hearts of his enemies to bring about some good. COMMENTARY ON 2 KINGS.[29]

JEHOIACHIN'S COMPENSATION. KONRAD PELLIKAN: King Jehoiachin was once again exalted, this time in the palace of the king of Babylon. Before then he had lived in lowliness, bound in captivity and poverty. But now he was set again in the company of other princes and kings, eating at the king's table and treated like a member of the royal circle as long as he lived. This appears to be a worthy compensation, for Jehoiachin was the only one who submitted to the word of the Lord that Jeremiah spoke, saying that he should surrender himself, his mother and his princes into the hands of the king of Babylon. In contrast, the pitiful

Zedekiah later suffered a most severe career and death. COMMENTARY ON 2 KINGS.[30]

25:30 *Not the End of the Story*

GOD PRESERVES DAVID'S SEED. JOHANNES BUGENHAGEN: It was through neither fortune nor human favor but only by the counsel of God that the seed of King David was preserved all the way to Christ. For it then came to pass that the people of Judah were brought back after seventy years, according to the word of the prophet Jeremiah. In the time and place predicted by God through the prophets would come the fulfillment of all that the people had expected about the Messiah who came from the seed of David. Therefore God, who is known as always remembering mercy, himself gave his prophets the sign of this captivity and, in the end, this release from captivity. No matter how much we have sinned, we would be forsaken without the Word of God, which is truly infinite mercy for us. COMMENTARY ON 2 KINGS.[31]

DAVID'S POSTERITY FULFILLED IN CHRIST. JOHN MAYER: And here is an end of the history of the kings of Judah, who came of David. But this history is not an end of David's posterity, for it continued until Christ, who was the promised seed of David. For such is it declared in the Gospel: "The book of the genealogy of Jesus Christ, the son of David." And between David and the deportation there were fourteen generations, just as there were fourteen generations between the deportation and Christ. COMMENTARY ON 2 KINGS.[32]

---

[28]Mayer, *Many Commentaries in One*, 328-29*; citing Jer 24:5.
[29]Piscator, *Commentarii in omnes libros Veteris Testamenti*, 2:374.

[30]Pellikan, *Commentaria Bibliorum*, 2:204v.
[31]Bugenhagen, *In Regum duos ultimos libros*, 198.
[32]Mayer, *Many Commentaries in One*, 329*; citing Mt 1:1.

COMMENTARY ON 1 CHRONICLES

OVERVIEW: The commentators know that Chronicles was originally written as one book in Hebrew and was only later divided into two when translated into Greek and Latin. They are also fully aware of the slight treatment of Chronicles in the interpretive tradition in comparison with Samuel and Kings, two books that overlap with Chronicles. Despite the long genealogies and similar coverage with the former books of Samuel and Kings, one reformer argues that 1–2 Chronicles are equal in importance to these other ones because they provide useful doctrines and because Christ cites the book during his ministry. These interpreters, following the rabbinic tradition, think that Ezra is the best candidate for authorship of Chronicles.

Prolegomena: What This Book Is About

INTRODUCTION TO CHRONICLES. SEBASTIAN MÜNSTER: They call this book of ours after the Greeks *Paralipomenōn* ("omitted things"), because it narrates histories that are omitted in the books of Kings. But we have preferred to record that title and the one that the Hebrew has in our version, lest there be any disagreement between the Latin and Hebrew titles. Now the Hebrew title is *dibrê hayāmmîm*, that is, "words or deeds of the days," for in this book the deeds and acts of the kings of Judah and Israel are described individually. This title we have translated, not unfittingly, as "annals."

It is uncertain whether this book is that book which the book of Kings mentions whenever it is said "Are these things not written in the book of words of the days of the kings of Judah and Israel?" The Hebrews place it after the book of Ezra, because they think it was written by Ezra at that time when the people of Judah returned to Jerusalem, after the Babylonian captivity, under the governor Zerubbabel and the priest Jeshua—which they gather from the end of this book. And indeed they cannot say that this book is cited in the books of Kings, because at that time it had not yet been written, unless you prefer that the two books of Kings describe matters after the captivity. Still, Moses Kimchi denies this; he asserts they were composed by the prophet Jeremiah.

Moreover, Rashi writes below concerning chapter 7 that Ezra discovered the three books of genealogies out of which he concocted this book. Where he found missing things, he built a bridge. He thought that it happened in this way, for in what follows certain passages are so obscure in the enumeration of genealogies that no one is able to explain them. And genealogies are enumerated until chapter 10. THE TEMPLE OF THE LORD: 1 CHRONICLES 1.[1]

THE PRECIOUS CONTENT OF CHRONICLES. LUCAS OSIANDER: I believe that Ezra was compelled and led by the Spirit of God to collect all the old books that contained the acts of the people of God to attest to the writings that were in the books of Kings and comment briefly on them. And because the Babylonian captivity had caused so much confusion, the author made as

---

[1]Münster, *Miqdaš YHWH*, 1450-51; citing 2 Chron 36:22-23.

great a study as was possible, beginning with a search of the most ancient books, including tribes, families, genealogies and the marriages of Israelites to Gentiles, so that they could trace the lines and know how to describe their people for sure. Whoever preserved these genealogies and family lines did a useful thing for the church of God's people, so that the family of Christ our Savior would not end up in obscurity. That these books (which are one book in Hebrew) deserve equal authority with other books of chronicles is clear from this one place (in Mt 23) in which Christ himself cited from Chronicles the story of Zechariah, who was stoned under King Joash for catching him in idolatry. In both of these volumes one can find many things that shed helpful light on the stories of Kings, along with many useful doctrines and the sweetest consolations for the church of God. ANNOTATIONS ON 1 CHRONICLES.[2]

GENEALOGY TO TEMPLE. GIOVANNI DIODATI: It is plain that these two books of the Chronicles were written after the return from the captivity of Babylon. They must have been gathered by some prophet, perhaps Ezra himself, out of the ancient public records. These records must have contained the people's genealogies and the king's acts, especially of the kings of Judah. These records were kept in Babylon by the priests with faithful care, though not without appearance of some breach and mutilation in some parts of the history. This happened through the injury of the times.

First Chronicles summarily numbers the generation of the holy stock of God's people in which the church was preserved from the creation of the world, from father to son, until the return from the captivity. The book also contains a brief narration of David's acts; in some places, it contains an addition to the history of the books of Samuel. But principally this narration sets down the excellent order that David established in his kingdom. This includes David's political, military and religious services and government. David desired to establish the kingship of his son Solo-

mon, who was nominated by God and later acknowledged by the people and consecrated by the leadership as David's successor while David was living. David made all these preparations so that Solomon would be able to construct the great work of the temple, which God had destined Solomon to build him. Therefore God gave Solomon the model for the construction, and he collected all kinds of materials of great value and quantity. And before long Solomon consecrated the temple to the Lord. Indeed, Solomon added much to the temple by means of his own generosity and that of the people. ANNOTATIONS ON 1 CHRONICLES.[3]

HISTORIES FROM ADAM TO THE CAPTIVITY. GENEVA BIBLE: The Jews combine both 1–2 Chronicles into one book. However, because of the great length, the Greek-speakers divided it into two books and called it Chronicles because they recognized the histories from Adam to the return from their captivity in Babylon. But these are not those books of chronicles that are so mentioned in the books of the kings of Judah and Israel, which more extensively set forth the history of both the kingdoms, which afterward perished in captivity. However, according to the Jews an abridgement of the same history was gathered by Ezra after their return from Babylon. This first book contains a brief rehearsal of the children of Adam to Abraham, Isaac, Jacob and the twelve patriarchs, chiefly of Judah and of the reign of David. That's because Christ came of David according to the flesh. And therefore this first book more amply sets forth David's acts, both concerning civil government and the administration and care of things relating to religion. For the good success of these things David rejoiced and gave thanks to the Lord. ARGUMENT OF 1 CHRONICLES.[4]

JUST LIKE A GREEK CLASSIC. VIKTORIN STRIGEL: Just as Xenophon wrote the events that were left over from the Peloponnesian War

---

[2]Osiander, *Liber Iosue*, 1053-54.

[3]Diodati, *Pious Annotations*, 30*.
[4]*Geneva Bible* (1560), 178r*.

originally set forth by Thucydides, so Ezra compiled these two books of Chronicles from what was left over and lacking in the history of the kings of Judah and of Israel. This first book of Chronicles contains a genealogy of Christ from Adam to David, and it chiefly touches on the things that David did in his old age in the ordering of the priests, Levites, musicians and in preparing everything that was needed for the operation of the temple. This book also repeats the extraordinary promise of a Messiah bound to the seed of David. Book of 1 Chronicles.[5]

---

[5]Strigel, *Libri Samuelis, Regum et Paralipomenon*, 413.

1:1–9:44 GENEALOGY OF THE TRIBES OF ISRAEL

[1] [a]Adam, Seth, Enosh; [2]Kenan, Mahalalel, Jared; [3]Enoch, Methuselah, Lamech; [4]Noah, Shem, Ham, and Japheth.

[5]The sons of Japheth: Gomer, Magog, Madai, Javan, Tubal, Meshech, and Tiras. [6]The sons of Gomer: Ashkenaz, Riphath,[b] and Togarmah. [7]The sons of Javan: Elishah, Tarshish, Kittim, and Rodanim.

[8]The sons of Ham: Cush, Egypt, Put, and Canaan. [9]The sons of Cush: Seba, Havilah, Sabta, Raama, and Sabteca. The sons of Raamah: Sheba and Dedan.[10]Cush fathered Nimrod. He was the first on earth to be a mighty man.[c]

[11]Egypt fathered Ludim, Anamim, Lehabim, Naphtuhim, [12]Pathrusim, Casluhim (from whom the Philistines came), and Caphtorim.

[13]Canaan fathered Sidon his firstborn and Heth, [14]and the Jebusites, the Amorites, the Girgashites, [15]the Hivites, the Arkites, the Sinites, [16]the Arvadites, the Zemarites, and the Hamathites.

[17]The sons of Shem: Elam, Asshur, Arpachshad, Lud, and Aram. And the sons of Aram:[d] Uz, Hul, Gether, and Meshech. [18]Arpachshad fathered Shelah, and Shelah fathered Eber. [19]To Eber were born two sons: the name of the one was Peleg[e] (for in his days the earth was divided), and his brother's name was Joktan. [20]Joktan fathered Almodad, Sheleph, Hazarmaveth, Jerah, [21]Hadoram, Uzal, Diklah, [22]Obal,[f] Abimael, Sheba, [23]Ophir, Havilah, and Jobab; all these were the sons of Joktan.

[24]Shem, Arpachshad, Shelah; [25]Eber, Peleg, Reu; [26]Serug, Nahor, Terah; [27]Abram, that is, Abraham.

[28]The sons of Abraham: Isaac and Ishmael. [29]These are their genealogies: the firstborn of Ishmael, Nebaioth, and Kedar, Adbeel, Mibsam, [30]Mishma, Dumah, Massa, Hadad, Tema, [31]Jetur, Naphish, and Kedemah. These are the sons of Ishmael. [32]The sons of Keturah, Abraham's concubine: she bore Zimran, Jokshan, Medan, Midian, Ishbak, and Shuah. The sons of Jokshan: Sheba and Dedan. [33]The sons of Midian: Ephah, Epher, Hanoch, Abida, and Eldaah. All these were the descendants of Keturah.

[34]Abraham fathered Isaac. The sons of Isaac: Esau and Israel. [35]The sons of Esau: Eliphaz, Reuel, Jeush, Jalam, and Korah. [36]The sons of Eliphaz: Teman, Omar, Zepho, Gatam, Kenaz, and of Timna,[g] Amalek. [37]The sons of Reuel: Nahath, Zerah, Shammah, and Mizzah.

[38]The sons of Seir: Lotan, Shobal, Zibeon, Anah, Dishon, Ezer, and Dishan. [39]The sons of Lotan: Hori and Hemam;[h] and Lotan's sister was Timna. [40]The sons of Shobal: Alvan,[i] Manahath, Ebal, Shepho,[j] and Onam. The sons of Zibeon: Aiah and Anah. [41]The son[k] of Anah: Dishon. The sons of Dishon: Hemdan,[l] Eshban, Ithran, and Cheran. [42]The sons of Ezer: Bilhan, Zaavan, and Akan.[m] The sons of Dishan: Uz and Aran.

[43]These are the kings who reigned in the land of Edom before any king reigned over the people of Israel: Bela the son of Beor, the name of his city being Dinhabah. [44]Bela died, and Jobab the son of Zerah of Bozrah reigned in his place. [45]Jobab died, and Husham of the land of the Temanites reigned in his place. [46]Husham died, and Hadad the son of Bedad, who defeated Midian in the country of Moab, reigned in his place, the name of his city being Avith. [47]Hadad died, and Samlah of Masrekah reigned in his place. [48]Samlah died, and Shaul of Rehoboth on the Euphrates[n] reigned in his place. [49]Shaul died, and Baal-hanan, the son of Achbor, reigned in his place. [50]Baal-hanan died, and Hadad reigned in his place, the name of his city being Pai; and his wife's name was Mehetabel, the daughter of Matred, the daughter of Mezahab. [51]And Hadad died.

The chiefs of Edom were: chiefs Timna, Alvah, Jetheth, [52]Oholibamah, Elah, Pinon, [53]Kenaz, Teman, Mibzar, [54]Magdiel, and Iram; these are the chiefs of Edom.

2 These are the sons of Israel: Reuben, Simeon, Levi, Judah, Issachar, Zebulun, [2]Dan, Joseph, Benjamin, Naphtali, Gad, and Asher. [3]The sons of Judah: Er, Onan and Shelah; these three Bath-shua the Canaanite bore to him. Now Er, Judah's firstborn, was evil in the sight of the LORD, and he put him to death. [4]His daughter-in-law Tamar also bore him Perez and Zerah. Judah had five sons in all.

[5]The sons of Perez: Hezron and Hamul. [6]The sons of Zerah: Zimri, Ethan, Heman, Calcol, and Dara, five in all. [7]The son[o] of Carmi: Achan, the troubler of Israel, who broke faith in the matter of the devoted thing; [8]and Ethan's son was Azariah.

[9]The sons of Hezron that were born to him: Jerahmeel, Ram, and Chelubai. [10]Ram fathered Amminadab, and Amminadab fathered Nahshon, prince of the sons of Judah. [11]Nahshon fathered Salmon,[p] Salmon fathered Boaz, [12]Boaz fathered Obed, Obed fathered Jesse. [13]Jesse fathered Eliab his firstborn, Abinadab the second, Shimea the third, [14]Nethanel the fourth, Raddai the fifth, [15]Ozem the sixth, David the seventh [16]And their sisters were Zeruiah and Abigail. The sons of Zeruiah: Abishai, Joab, and Asahel, three. [17]Abigail bore Amasa, and the father of Amasa was Jether the Ishmaelite.

[18]Caleb the son of Hezron fathered children by his wife Azubah, and by Jerioth; and these were her sons: Jesher, Shobab, and Ardon. [19]When Azubah died, Caleb married Ephrath, who bore him Hur. [20]Hur fathered Uri, and Uri fathered Bezalel.

[21]Afterward Hezron went in to the daughter of Machir the father of Gilead, whom he married when he was sixty years old, and she bore him Segub. [22]And Segub fathered Jair, who had twenty-three cities in the land of Gilead. [23]But Geshur and Aram took from them Havvoth-jair, Kenath, and its villages, sixty towns. All these were descendants of Machir, the father of Gilead. [24]After the death of Hezron, Caleb went in to Ephrathah,[q] the wife of Hezron his father, and she bore him Ashhur, the father of Tekoa.

[25]The sons of Jerahmeel, the firstborn of Hezron: Ram, his firstborn, Bunah, Oren, Ozem, and Ahijah. [26]Jerahmeel also had another wife, whose name was Atarah; she was the mother of Onam. [27]The sons of Ram, the firstborn of Jerahmeel: Maaz, Jamin, and Eker. [28]The sons of Onam: Shammai and Jada. The sons of Shammai: Nadab and Abishur. [29]The name of Abishur's wife was Abihail, and she bore him Ahban and Molid. [30]The sons of Nadab: Seled and Appaim; and Seled died childless. [31]The son[r] of Appaim: Ishi. The son of Ishi: Sheshan. The son of Sheshan: Ahlai. [32]The sons of Jada, Shammai's brother: Jether and Jonathan; and Jether died childless. [33]The sons of Jonathan: Peleth and Zaza. These were the descendants of Jerahmeel. [34]Now Sheshan had no sons, only daughters, but Sheshan had an Egyptian slave whose name was Jarha. [35]So Sheshan gave his daughter in marriage to Jarha his slave, and she bore him Attai. [36]Attai fathered Nathan, and Nathan fathered Zabad. [37]Zabad fathered Ephlal, and Ephlal fathered Obed. [38]Obed fathered Jehu, and Jehu fathered Azariah. [39]Azariah fathered Helez, and Helez fathered Eleasah. [40]Eleasah fathered Sismai, and Sismai fathered Shallum. [41]Shallum fathered Jekamiah, and Jekamiah fathered Elishama.

[42]The sons of Caleb the brother of Jerahmeel: Mareshah[s] his firstborn, who fathered Ziph. The son[t] of Mareshah: Hebron.[u] [43]The sons of Hebron: Korah, Tappuah, Rekem and Shema. [44]Shema fathered Raham, the father of Jorkeam; and Rekem fathered Shammai. [45]The son of Shammai: Maon; and Maon fathered Beth-zur. [46]Ephah also, Caleb's concubine, bore Haran, Moza, and Gazez; and Haran fathered Gazez. [47]The sons of Jahdai: Regem, Jotham, Geshan, Pelet, Ephah, and Shaaph. [48]Maacah, Caleb's concubine, bore Sheber and Tirhanah. [49]She also bore Shaaph the father of Madmannah, Sheva the father of Machbenah and the father of Gibea; and the daughter of Caleb was Achsah. [50]These were the descendants of Caleb.

The sons[v] of Hur the firstborn of Ephrathah: Shobal the father of Kiriath-jearim, [51]Salma, the father of Bethlehem, and Hareph the father of Beth-gader. [52]Shobal the father of Kiriath-jearim had other sons: Haroeh, half of the Menuhoth. [53]And the clans of Kiriath-jearim: the Ithrites, the Puthites, the Shumathites, and the Mishraites; from these came the Zorathites and the Eshtaolites. [54]The sons of Salma: Bethlehem, the Netophathites, Atroth-beth-joab and half of the Manahathites, the Zorites. [55]The clans also of the scribes who lived at Jabez: the Tirathites, the Shimeathites and the Sucathites. These are the Kenites who came from Hammath, the father of the house of Rechab.

3 These are the sons of David who were born to him in Hebron: the firstborn, Amnon, by Ahinoam the Jezreelite; the second, Daniel, by Abigail the Carmelite, ²the third, Absalom, whose mother was Maacah, the daughter of Talmai, king of Geshur; the fourth, Adonijah, whose mother was Haggith; ³the fifth, Shephatiah, by Abital; the sixth, Ithream, by his wife Eglah; ⁴six were born to him in Hebron, where he reigned for seven years and six months. And he reigned thirty-three years in Jerusalem. ⁵These were born to him in Jerusalem: Shimea, Shobab, Nathan and Solomon, four by Bath-shua, the daughter of Ammiel; ⁶then Ibhar, Elishama, Eliphelet, ⁷Nogah, Nepheg, Japhia, ⁸Elishama, Eliada, and Eliphelet, nine. ⁹All these were David's sons, besides the sons of the concubines, and Tamar was their sister.

¹⁰The son of Solomon was Rehoboam, Abijah his son, Asa his son, Jehoshaphat his son, ¹¹Joram his son, Ahaziah his son, Joash his son, ¹²Amaziah his son, Azariah his son, Jotham his son, ¹³Ahaz his son, Hezekiah his son, Manasseh his son, ¹⁴Amon his son, Josiah his son. ¹⁵The sons of Josiah: Johanan the firstborn, the second Jehoiakim, the third Zedekiah, the fourth Shallum. ¹⁶The descendants of Jehoiakim: Jeconiah his son, Zedekiah his son; ¹⁷and the sons of Jeconiah, the captive: Shealtiel his son, ¹⁸Malchiram, Pedaiah, Shenazzar, Jekamiah, Hoshama and Nedabiah; ¹⁹and the sons of Pedaiah: Zerubbabel and Shimei; and the sons of Zerubbabel: Meshullam and Hananiah, and Shelomith was their sister; ²⁰and Hashubah, Ohel, Berechiah, Hasadiah, and Jushab-hesed, five. ²¹The sons of Hananiah: Pelatiah and Jeshaiah, his son[w] Rephaiah, his son Arnan, his son Obadiah, his son Shecaniah. ²²The son[x] of Shecaniah: Shemaiah. And the sons of Shemaiah: Hattush, Igal, Bariah, Neariah, and Shaphat, six. ²³The sons of Neariah: Elioenai, Hizkiah, and Azrikam, three. ²⁴The sons of Elioenai: Hodaviah, Eliashib, Pelaiah, Akkub, Johanan, Delaiah, and Anani, seven.

4 The sons of Judah: Perez, Hezron, Carmi, Hur, and Shobal. ²Reaiah the son of Shobal fathered Jahath, and Jahath fathered Ahumai and Lahad. These were the clans of the Zorathites. ³These were the sons[y] of Etam: Jezreel, Ishma, and Idbash; and the name of their sister was Hazzelelponi, ⁴and Penuel fathered Gedor, and Ezer fathered Hushah. These were the sons of Hur, the firstborn of Ephrathah, the father of Bethlehem. ⁵Ashhur, the father of Tekoa, had two wives, Helah and Naarah; ⁶Naarah bore him Ahuzzam, Hepher, Temeni, and Haahashtari. These were the sons of Naarah. ⁷The sons of Helah: Zereth, Izhar, and Ethnan. ⁸Koz fathered Anub, Zobebah, and the clans of Aharhel, the son of Harum. ⁹Jabez was more honorable than his brothers; and his mother called his name Jabez, saying, "Because I bore him in pain."[z] ¹⁰Jabez called upon the God of Israel, saying, "Oh that you would bless me and enlarge my border, and that your hand might be with me, and that you would keep me from harm[aa] so that it might not bring me pain!" And God granted what he asked. ¹¹Chelub, the brother of Shuhah, fathered Mehir, who fathered Eshton. ¹²Eshton fathered Beth-rapha, Paseah, and Tehinnah, the father of Ir-nahash. These are the men of Recah. ¹³The sons of Kenaz: Othniel and Seraiah; and the sons of Othniel: Hathath and Meonothai.[ab] ¹⁴Meonothai fathered Ophrah; and Seraiah fathered Joab, the father of Ge-harashim,[ac] so-called because they were craftsmen. ¹⁵The sons of Caleb the son of Jephunneh: Iru, Elah, and Naam; and the son[ad] of Elah: Kenaz. ¹⁶The sons of Jehallelel: Ziph, Ziphah, Tiria, and Asarel. ¹⁷The sons of Ezrah: Jether, Mered, Epher, and Jalon. These are the sons of Bithiah, the daughter of Pharaoh, whom Mered married;[ae] and she conceived and bore[af] Miriam, Shammai, and Ishbah, the father of Eshtemoa. ¹⁸And his Judahite wife bore Jered the father of Gedor, Heber the father of Soco, and Jekuthiel the father of Zanoah. ¹⁹The sons of the wife of Hodiah, the sister of Naham, were the fathers of Keilah the Garmite and Eshtemoa the Maacathite. ²⁰The sons of Shimon: Amnon, Rinnah, Ben-hanan, and Tilon. The sons of Ishi: Zoheth and Ben-zoheth. ²¹The sons of Shelah the son of Judah: Er the father of Lecah, Laadah the father of Mareshah, and the clans of the house of linen workers at Beth-ashbea; ²²and Jokim, and the men of Cozeba, and Joash, and Saraph, who ruled in Moab and returned to Lehem[ag] (now the records[ah] are ancient). ²³These were the potters who were inhabitants of Netaim and Gederah. They lived there in the king's service.

²⁴The sons of Simeon: Nemuel, Jamin, Jarib, Zerah, Shaul; ²⁵Shallum was his son, Mibsam his son, Mishma his son. ²⁶The sons of Mishma: Hammuel his son, Zaccur his son, Shimei his son. ²⁷Shimei had sixteen sons and six daughters; but his brothers did not have many children, nor did all their clan multiply like the men of Judah. ²⁸They lived in Beersheba, Moladah, Hazar-shual, ²⁹Bilhah, Ezem, Tolad, ³⁰Bethuel, Hormah, Ziklag, ³¹Beth-marcaboth, Hazar-susim, Beth-biri, and Shaaraim. These were their cities until David reigned. ³²And their villages were Etam, Ain, Rimmon, Tochen, and Ashan, five cities, ³³along with all their villages that were around these cities as far as Baal. These were their settlements, and they kept a genealogical record.

³⁴Meshobab, Jamlech, Joshah the son of Amaziah, ³⁵Joel, Jehu the son of Joshibiah, son of Seraiah, son of Asiel, ³⁶Elioenai, Jaakobah, Jeshohaiah, Asaiah, Adiel, Jesimiel, Benaiah, ³⁷Ziza the son of Shiphi, son of Allon, son of Jedaiah, son of Shimri, son of Shemaiah— ³⁸these mentioned by name were princes in their clans, and their fathers' houses increased greatly. ³⁹They journeyed to the entrance of Gedor, to the east side of the valley, to seek pasture for their flocks, ⁴⁰where they found rich, good pasture, and the land was very broad, quiet, and peaceful, for the former inhabitants there belonged to Ham. ⁴¹These, registered by name, came in the days of Hezekiah, king of Judah, and destroyed their tents and the Meunites who were found there, and marked them for destruction to this day, and settled in their place, because there was pasture there for their flocks. ⁴²And some of them, five hundred men of the Simeonites, went to Mount Seir, having as their leaders Pelatiah, Neariah, Rephaiah, and Uzziel, the sons of Ishi. ⁴³And they defeated the remnant of the Amalekites who had escaped, and they have lived there to this day.

5 The sons of Reuben the firstborn of Israel (for he was the firstborn, but because he defiled his father's couch, his birthright was given to the sons of Joseph the son of Israel, so that he could not be enrolled as the oldest son; ²though Judah became strong among his brothers and a chief came from him, yet the birthright belonged to Joseph), ³the sons of Reuben, the firstborn of Israel: Hanoch, Pallu, Hezron, and Carmi. ⁴The sons of Joel: Shemaiah his son, Gog his son, Shimei his son, ⁵Micah his son, Reaiah his son, Baal his son, ⁶Beerah his son, whom Tiglath-pileser^ai king of Assyria carried away into exile; he was a chief of the Reubenites. ⁷And his kinsmen by their clans, when the genealogy of their generations was recorded: the chief, Jeiel, and Zechariah, ⁸and Bela the son of Azaz, son of Shema, son of Joel, who lived in Aroer, as far as Nebo and Baal-meon. ⁹He also lived to the east as far as the entrance of the desert this side of the Euphrates, because their livestock had multiplied in the land of Gilead. ¹⁰And in the days of Saul they waged war against the Hagrites, who fell into their hand. And they lived in their tents throughout all the region east of Gilead.

¹¹The sons of Gad lived over against them in the land of Bashan as far as Salecah: ¹²Joel the chief, Shapham the second, Janai, and Shaphat in Bashan. ¹³And their kinsmen according to their fathers' houses: Michael, Meshullam, Sheba, Jorai, Jacan, Zia and Eber, seven. ¹⁴These were the sons of Abihail the son of Huri, son of Jaroah, son of Gilead, son of Michael, son of Jeshishai, son of Jahdo, son of Buz. ¹⁵Ahi the son of Abdiel, son of Guni, was chief in their fathers' houses, ¹⁶and they lived in Gilead, in Bashan and in its towns, and in all the pasturelands of Sharon to their limits. ¹⁷All of these were recorded in genealogies in the days of Jotham king of Judah, and in the days of Jeroboam king of Israel.

¹⁸The Reubenites, the Gadites, and the half-tribe of Manasseh had valiant men who carried shield and sword, and drew the bow, expert in war, 44,760, able to go to war. ¹⁹They waged war against the Hagrites, Jetur, Naphish, and Nodab. ²⁰And when they prevailed^aj over them, the Hagrites and all who were with them were given into their hands, for they cried out to God in the battle, and he granted their urgent plea because they trusted in him. ²¹They carried off their livestock: 50,000 of their camels, 250,000 sheep, 2,000 donkeys, and 100,000 men alive. ²²For many fell, because the war was of God. And they lived in their place until the exile.

²³The members of the half-tribe of Manasseh lived in the land. They were very numerous from Bashan to Baal-hermon, Senir, and Mount Hermon. ²⁴These were the heads of their fathers' houses: Epher,^ak Ishi,

Eliel, Azriel, Jeremiah, Hodaviah, and Jahdiel, mighty warriors, famous men, heads of their fathers' houses. [25]But they broke faith with the God of their fathers, and whored after the gods of the peoples of the land, whom God had destroyed before them. [26]So the God of Israel stirred up the spirit of Pul king of Assyria, the spirit of Tiglath-pileser king of Assyria, and he took them into exile, namely, the Reubenites, the Gadites, and the half-tribe of Manasseh, and brought them to Halah, Habor, Hara, and the river Gozan, to this day.

6 [al]The sons of Levi: Gershon, Kohath, and Merari. [2]The sons of Kohath: Amram, Izhar, Hebron, and Uzziel. [3]The children of Amram: Aaron, Moses, and Miriam. The sons of Aaron: Nadab, Abihu, Eleazar, and Ithamar. [4]Eleazar fathered Phinehas, Phinehas fathered Abishua, [5]Abishua fathered Bukki, Bukki fathered Uzzi, [6]Uzzi fathered Zerahiah, Zerahiah fathered Meraioth, [7]Meraioth fathered Amariah, Amariah fathered Ahitub, [8]Ahitub fathered Zadok, Zadok fathered Ahimaaz, [9]Ahimaaz fathered Azariah, Azariah fathered Johanan, [10]and Johanan fathered Azariah (it was he who served as priest in the house that Solomon built in Jerusalem). [11]Azariah fathered Amariah, Amariah fathered Ahitub, [12]Ahitub fathered Zadok, Zadok fathered Shallum, [13]Shallum fathered Hilkiah, Hilkiah fathered Azariah, [14]Azariah fathered Seraiah, Seraiah fathered Jehozadak; [15]and Jehozadak went into exile when the LORD sent Judah and Jerusalem into exile by the hand of Nebuchadnezzar.

[16 am]The sons of Levi: Gershom, Kohath, and Merari. [17]And these are the names of the sons of Gershom: Libni and Shimei. [18]The sons of Kohath: Amram, Izhar, Hebron and Uzziel. [19]The sons of Merari: Mahli and Mushi. These are the clans of the Levites according to their fathers. [20]Of Gershom: Libni his son, Jahath his son, Zimmah his son, [21]Joah his son, Iddo his son, Zerah his son, Jeatherai his son. [22]The sons of Kohath: Amminadab his son, Korah his son, Assir his son, [23]Elkanah his son, Ebiasaph his son, Assir his son, [24]Tahath his son, Uriel his son, Uzziah his son, and Shaul his son. [25]The sons of Elkanah: Amasai and Ahimoth, [26]Elkanah his son, Zophai his son, Nahath his son, [27]Eliab his son, Jeroham his son,

Elkanah his son. [28]The sons of Samuel: Joel[an] his firstborn, the second Abijah.[ao] [29]The sons of Merari: Mahli, Libni his son, Shimei his son, Uzzah his son, [30]Shimea his son, Haggiah his son, and Asaiah his son.

[31]These are the men whom David put in charge of the service of song in the house of the LORD after the ark rested there. [32]They ministered with song before the tabernacle of the tent of meeting until Solomon built the house of the LORD in Jerusalem, and they performed their service according to their order. [33]These are the men who served and their sons. Of the sons of the Kohathites: Heman the singer the son of Joel, son of Samuel, [34]son of Elkanah, son of Jeroham, son of Eliel, son of Toah, [35]son of Zuph, son of Elkanah, son of Mahath, son of Amasai, [36]son of Elkanah, son of Joel, son of Azariah, son of Zephaniah, [37]son of Tahath, son of Assir, son of Ebiasaph, son of Korah, [38]son of Izhar, son of Kohath, son of Levi, son of Israel; [39]and his brother Asaph, who stood on his right hand, namely, Asaph the son of Berechiah, son of Shimea, [40]son of Michael, son of Baaseiah, son of Malchijah, [41]son of Ethni, son of Zerah, son of Adaiah, [42]son of Ethan, son of Zimmah, son of Shimei, [43]son of Jahath, son of Gershom, son of Levi. [44]On the left hand were their brothers, the sons of Merari: Ethan the son of Kishi, son of Abdi, son of Malluch, [45]son of Hashabiah, son of Amaziah, son of Hilkiah, [46]son of Amzi, son of Bani, son of Shemer, [47]son of Mahli, son of Mushi, son of Merari, son of Levi. [48]And their brothers the Levites were appointed for all the service of the tabernacle of the house of God.

[49]But Aaron and his sons made offerings on the altar of burnt offering and on the altar of incense for all the work of the Most Holy Place, and to make atonement for Israel, according to all that Moses the servant of God had commanded. [50]These are the sons of Aaron: Eleazar his son, Phinehas his son, Abishua his son, [51]Bukki his son, Uzzi his son, Zerahiah his son, [52]Meraioth his son, Amariah his son, Ahitub his son, [53]Zadok his son, Ahimaaz his son.

[54]These are their dwelling places according to their settlements within their borders: to the sons of Aaron of the clans of Kohathites, for theirs was the first lot, [55]to them they gave Hebron in the land of Judah and its surrounding pasturelands, [56]but the fields of the

city and its villages they gave to Caleb the son of Jephunneh. ⁵⁷To the sons of Aaron they gave the cities of refuge: Hebron, Libnah with its pasturelands, Jattir, Eshtemoa with its pasturelands, ⁵⁸Hilen with its pasturelands, Debir with its pasturelands, ⁵⁹Ashan with its pasturelands, and Beth-shemesh with its pasturelands; ⁶⁰and from the tribe of Benjamin, Gibeon,ᵃᵖ Geba with its pasturelands, Alemeth with its pasturelands, and Anathoth with its pasturelands. All their cities throughout their clans were thirteen.

⁶¹To the rest of the Kohathites were given by lot out of the clan of the tribe, out of the half-tribe, the half of Manasseh, ten cities. ⁶²To the Gershomites according to their clans were allotted thirteen cities out of the tribes of Issachar, Asher, Naphtali and Manasseh in Bashan. ⁶³To the Merarites according to their clans were allotted twelve cities out of the tribes of Reuben, Gad, and Zebulun. ⁶⁴So the people of Israel gave the Levites the cities with their pasturelands. ⁶⁵They gave by lot out of the tribes of Judah, Simeon, and Benjamin these cities that are mentioned by name.

⁶⁶And some of the clans of the sons of Kohath had cities of their territory out of the tribe of Ephraim. ⁶⁷They were given the cities of refuge: Shechem with its pasturelands in the hill country of Ephraim, Gezer with its pasturelands, ⁶⁸Jokmeam with its pasturelands, Beth-horon with its pasturelands, ⁶⁹Aijalon with its pasturelands, Gath-rimmon with its pasturelands, ⁷⁰and out of the half-tribe of Manasseh, Aner with its pasturelands, and Bileam with its pasturelands, for the rest of the clans of the Kohathites.

⁷¹To the Gershomites were given out of the clan of the half-tribe of Manasseh: Golan in Bashan with its pasturelands and Ashtaroth with its pasturelands; ⁷²and out of the tribe of Issachar: Kedesh with its pasturelands, Daberath with its pasturelands, ⁷³Ramoth with its pasturelands, and Anem with its pasturelands; ⁷⁴out of the tribe of Asher: Mashal with its pasturelands, Abdon with its pasturelands, ⁷⁵Hukok with its pasturelands, and Rehob with its pasturelands; ⁷⁶and out of the tribe of Naphtali: Kedesh in Galilee with its pasturelands, Hammon with its pasturelands, and Kiriathaim with its pasturelands. ⁷⁷To the rest of the Merarites were allotted out of the tribe of Zebulun: Rimmono with its

pasturelands, Tabor with its pasturelands, ⁷⁸and beyond the Jordan at Jericho, on the east side of the Jordan, out of the tribe of Reuben: Bezer in the wilderness with its pasturelands, Jahzah with its pasturelands, ⁷⁹Kedemoth with its pasturelands, and Mephaath with its pasturelands; ⁸⁰and out of the tribe of Gad: Ramoth in Gilead with its pasturelands, Mahanaim with its pasturelands, ⁸¹Heshbon with its pasturelands, and Jazer with its pasturelands.

7 The sonsᵃᑫ of Issachar: Tola, Puah, Jashub, and Shimron, four. ²The sons of Tola: Uzzi, Rephaiah, Jeriel, Jahmai, Ibsam, and Shemuel, heads of their fathers' houses, namely of Tola, mighty warriors of their generations, their number in the days of David being 22,600. ³The sonᵃʳ of Uzzi: Izrahiah. And the sons of Izrahiah: Michael, Obadiah, Joel, and Isshiah, all five of them were chief men. ⁴And along with them, by their generations, according to their fathers' houses, were units of the army for war, 36,000, for they had many wives and sons. ⁵Their kinsmen belonging to all the clans of Issachar were in all 87,000 mighty warriors, enrolled by genealogy.

⁶The sons of Benjamin: Bela, Becher, and Jediael, three. ⁷The sons of Bela: Ezbon, Uzzi, Uzziel, Jerimoth, and Iri, five, heads of fathers' houses, mighty warriors. And their enrollment by genealogies was 22,034. ⁸The sons of Becher: Zemirah, Joash, Eliezer, Elioenai, Omri, Jeremoth, Abijah, Anathoth, and Alemeth. All these were the sons of Becher. ⁹And their enrollment by genealogies, according to their generations, as heads of their fathers' houses, mighty warriors, was 20,200. ¹⁰The son of Jediael: Bilhan. And the sons of Bilhan: Jeush, Benjamin, Ehud, Chenaanah, Zethan, Tarshish, and Ahishahar. ¹¹All these were the sons of Jediael according to the heads of their fathers' houses, mighty warriors, 17,200, able to go to war. ¹²And Shuppim and Huppim were the sons of Ir, Hushim the son of Aher.

¹³The sons of Naphtali: Jahziel, Guni, Jezer and Shallum, the descendants of Bilhah.

¹⁴The sons of Manasseh: Asriel, whom his Aramean concubine bore; she bore Machir the father of Gilead. ¹⁵And Machir took a wife for Huppim and for Shuppim. The name of his sister was Maacah. And the name of the second was Zelophehad, and Zelophehad had daughters. ¹⁶And Maacah the wife of

Machir bore a son, and she called his name Peresh; and the name of his brother was Sheresh; and his sons were Ulam and Rakem. [17]The son of Ulam: Bedan. These were the sons of Gilead the son of Machir, son of Manasseh. [18]And his sister Hammolecheth bore Ishhod, Abiezer and Mahlah. [19]The sons of Shemida were Ahian, Shechem, Likhi, and Aniam.

[20]The sons of Ephraim: Shuthelah, and Bered his son, Tahath his son, Eleadah his son, Tahath his son, [21]Zabad his son, Shuthelah his son, and Ezer and Elead, whom the men of Gath who were born in the land killed, because they came down to raid their livestock. [22]And Ephraim their father mourned many days, and his brothers came to comfort him. [23]And Ephraim went in to his wife, and she conceived and bore a son. And he called his name Beriah, because disaster had befallen his house.[as] [24]His daughter was Sheerah, who built both Lower and Upper Beth-horon, and Uzzen-sheerah. [25]Rephah was his son, Resheph his son, Telah his son, Tahan his son, [26]Ladan his son, Ammihud his son, Elishama his son, [27]Nun[at] his son, Joshua his son. [28]Their possessions and settlements were Bethel and its towns, and to the east Naaran, and to the west Gezer and its towns, Shechem and its towns, and Ayyah and its towns; [29]also in possession of the Manassites, Beth-shean and its towns, Taanach and its towns, Megiddo and its towns, Dor and its towns. In these lived the sons of Joseph the son of Israel.

[30]The sons of Asher: Imnah, Ishvah, Ishvi, Beriah, and their sister Serah. [31]The sons of Beriah: Heber, and Malchiel, who fathered Birzaith. [32]Heber fathered Japhlet, Shomer, Hotham, and their sister Shua. [33]The sons of Japhlet: Pasach, Bimhal, and Ashvath. These are the sons of Japhlet. [34]The sons of Shemer his brother: Rohgah, Jehubbah, and Aram. [35]The sons of Helem his brother: Zophah, Imna, Shelesh, and Amal. [36]The sons of Zophah: Suah, Harnepher, Shual, Beri, Imrah. [37]Bezer, Hod, Shamma, Shilshah, Ithran, and Beera. [38]The sons of Jether: Jephunneh, Pispa, and Ara. [39]The sons of Ulla: Arah, Hanniel, and Rizia. [40]All of these were men of Asher, heads of fathers' houses, approved, mighty warriors, chiefs of the princes. Their number enrolled by genealogies, for service in war, was 26,000 men.

8[1]Benjamin fathered Bela his firstborn, Ashbel the second, Aharah the third, [2]Nohah the fourth, and Rapha the fifth. [3]And Bela had sons: Addar, Gera, Abihud, [4]Abishua, Naaman, Ahoah, [5]Gera, Shephuphan, and Huram. [6]These are the sons of Ehud (they were heads of fathers' houses of the inhabitants of Geba, and they were carried into exile to Manahath): [7]Naaman,[au] Ahijah, and Gera, that is, Heglam,[av] who fathered Uzza and Ahihud. [8]And Shaharaim fathered sons in the country of Moab after he had sent away Hushim and Baara his wives. [9]He fathered sons by Hodesh his wife: Jobab, Zibia, Mesha, Malcam, [10]Jeuz, Sachia, and Mirmah. These were his sons, heads of fathers' houses. [11]He also fathered sons by Hushim: Abitub and Elpaal. [12]The sons of Elpaal: Eber, Misham, and Shemed, who built Ono and Lod with its towns, [13]and Beriah and Shema (they were heads of fathers' houses of the inhabitants of Aijalon, who caused the inhabitants of Gath to flee); [14]and Ahio, Shashak, and Jeremoth. [15]Zebadiah, Arad, Eder, [16]Michael, Ishpah, and Joha were sons of Beriah. [17]Zebadiah, Meshullam, Hizki, Heber, [18]Ishmerai, Izliah, and Jobab were the sons of Elpaal. [19]Jakim, Zichri, Zabdi, [20]Elienai, Zillethai, Eliel, [21]Adaiah, Beraiah, and Shimrath were the sons of Shimei. [22]Ishpan, Eber, Eliel, [23]Abdon, Zichri, Hanan, [24]Hananiah, Elam, Anthothijah, [25]Iphdeiah, and Penuel were the sons of Shashak. [26]Shamsherai, Shehariah, Athaliah, [27]Jaareshiah, Elijah, and Zichri were the sons of Jeroham. [28]These were the heads of fathers' houses, according to their generations, chief men. These lived in Jerusalem.

[29]Jeiel[aw] the father of Gibeon lived in Gibeon, and the name of his wife was Maacah. [30]His firstborn son: Abdon, then Zur, Kish, Baal, Nadab, [31]Gedor, Ahio, Zecher, [32]and Mikloth (he fathered Shimeah). Now these also lived opposite their kinsmen in Jerusalem, with their kinsmen. [33]Ner was the father of Kish, Kish of Saul, Saul of Jonathan, Malchi-shua, Abinadab and Eshbaal; [34]and the son of Jonathan was Merib-baal; and Merib-baal was the father of Micah. [35]The sons of Micah: Pithon, Melech, Tarea, and Ahaz. [36]Ahaz fathered Jehoaddah, and Jehoaddah fathered Alemeth, Azmaveth, and Zimri. Zimri fathered Moza. [37]Moza fathered Binea; Raphah was his son, Eleasah his son, Azel his son. [38]Azel had six sons, and these are their names: Azrikam,

Bocheru, Ishmael, Sheariah, Obadiah, and Hanan. All these were the sons of Azel. ³⁹The sons of Eshek his brother: Ulam his firstborn, Jeush the second, and Eliphelet the third. ⁴⁰The sons of Ulam were men who were mighty warriors, bowmen, having many sons and grandsons, 150. All these were Benjaminites.

9 So all Israel was recorded in genealogies, and these are written in the Book of the Kings of Israel. And Judah was taken into exile in Babylon because of their breach of faith. ²Now the first to dwell again in their possessions in their cities were Israel, the priests, the Levites, and the temple servants. ³And some of the people of Judah, Benjamin, Ephraim, and Manasseh lived in Jerusalem: ⁴Uthai the son of Ammihud, son of Omri, son of Imri, son of Bani, from the sons of Perez the son of Judah. ⁵And of the Shilonites: Asaiah the firstborn, and his sons. ⁶Of the sons of Zerah: Jeuel and their kinsmen, 690. ⁷Of the Benjaminites: Sallu the son of Meshullam, son of Hodaviah, son of Hassenuah, ⁸Ibneiah the son of Jeroham, Elah the son of Uzzi, son of Michri, and Meshullam the son of Shephatiah, son of Reuel, son of Ibnijah; ⁹and their kinsmen according to their generations, 956. All these were heads of fathers' houses according to their fathers' houses.

¹⁰Of the priests: Jedaiah, Jehoiarib, Jachin, ¹¹and Azariah the son of Hilkiah, son of Meshullam, son of Zadok, son of Meraioth, son of Ahitub, the chief officer of the house of God; ¹²and Adaiah the son of Jeroham, son of Pashhur, son of Malchijah, and Maasai the son of Adiel, son of Jahzerah, son of Meshullam, son of Meshillemith, son of Immer; ¹³besides their kinsmen, heads of their fathers' houses, 1,760, mighty men for the work of the service of the house of God.

¹⁴Of the Levites: Shemaiah the son of Hasshub, son of Azrikam, son of Hashabiah, of the sons of Merari; ¹⁵and Bakbakkar, Heresh, Galal and Mattaniah the son of Mica, son of Zichri, son of Asaph; ¹⁶and Obadiah the son of Shemaiah, son of Galal, son of Jeduthun, and Berechiah the son of Asa, son of Elkanah, who lived in the villages of the Netophathites.

¹⁷The gatekeepers were Shallum, Akkub, Talmon, Ahiman, and their kinsmen (Shallum was the chief); ¹⁸until then they were in the king's gate on the east side as the gatekeepers of the camps of the Levites. ¹⁹Shallum the son of Kore, son of Ebiasaph, son of Korah, and his kinsmen of his fathers' house, theKorahites, were in charge of the work of the service, keepers of the thresholds of the tent, as their fathers had been in charge of the camp of the Lord, keepers of the entrance. ²⁰And Phinehas the son of Eleazar was the chief officer over them in time past; the Lord was with him. ²¹Zechariah the son of Meshelemiah was gatekeeper at the entrance of the tent of meeting. ²²All these, who were chosen as gatekeepers at the thresholds, were 212. They were enrolled by genealogies in their villages. David and Samuel the seer established them in their office of trust. ²³So they and their sons were in charge of the gates of the house of the Lord, that is, the house of the tent, as guards. ²⁴The gatekeepers were on the four sides, east, west, north, and south. ²⁵And their kinsmen who were in their villages were obligated to comein every seven days, in turn, to be with these, ²⁶for the four chief gatekeepers, who were Levites, were entrusted to be over the chambers and the treasures of the house of God. ²⁷And they lodged around the house of God, for on them lay the duty of watching, and they had charge of opening it every morning.

²⁸Some of them had charge of the utensils of service, for they were required to count them when they were brought in and taken out. ²⁹Others of them were appointed over the furniture and over all the holy utensils, also over the fine flour, the wine, the oil, the incense, and the spices. ³⁰Others, of the sons of the priests, prepared the mixing of the spices, ³¹and Mattithiah, one of the Levites, the firstborn of Shallum the Korahite, was entrusted with making the flat cakes. ³²Also some of their kinsmen of the Kohathites had charge of the showbread, to prepare it every Sabbath.

³³Now these, the singers, the heads of fathers' houses of the Levites, were in the chambers of the temple free from other service, for they were on duty day and night. ³⁴These were heads of fathers' houses of the Levites, according to their generations, leaders. These lived in Jerusalem.

³⁵In Gibeon lived the father of Gibeon, Jeiel, and the name of his wife was Maacah, ³⁶and his firstborn son Abdon, then Zur, Kish, Baal, Ner, Nadab, ³⁷Gedor, Ahio, Zechariah, and Mikloth; ³⁸and Mikloth was the father of Shimeam; and these also lived opposite their

kinsmen in Jerusalem, with their kinsmen. [39]Ner fathered Kish, Kish fathered Saul, Saul fathered Jonathan, Malchi-shua, Abinadab, and Eshbaal. [40]And the son of Jonathan was Merib-baal, and Merib-baal fathered Micah. [41]The sons of Micah: Pithon, Melech, Tahrea, and Ahaz.[ax] [42]And Ahaz fathered Jarah, and Jarah fathered Alemeth, Azmaveth, and Zimri. And Zimri fathered Moza. [43]Moza fathered Binea, and Rephaiah was his son, Eleasah his son, Azel his son. [44]Azel had six sons and these are their names: Azrikam, Bocheru, Ishmael, Sheariah, Obadiah, and Hanan; these were the sons of Azel.

a Many names in these genealogies are spelled differently in other biblical books   b Septuagint; Hebrew *Diphath*   c Or *He began to be a mighty man on the earth*   d Septuagint; Hebrew lacks *And the sons of Aram*   e *Peleg* means *division*   f Septuagint, Syriac (compare Genesis 10:28); Hebrew *Ebal*   g Septuagint (compare Genesis 36:12); Hebrew lacks *and of*   h Septuagint (compare Genesis 36:22); Hebrew *Homam*   i Septuagint (compare Genesis 36:23); Hebrew *Alian*   j Septuagint (compare Genesis 36:23); Hebrew *Shephi*   k Hebrew *sons*   l Septuagint (compare Genesis 36:26); Hebrew *Hamran*   m Septuagint (compare Genesis 36:27); Hebrew *Jaakan*   n Hebrew *the River*   o Hebrew *sons*   p Septuagint (compare Ruth 4:21); Hebrew *Salma*   q Septuagint, Vulgate; Hebrew *in Caleb Ephrathah*   r Hebrew *sons*; three times in this verse   s Septuagint; Hebrew *Mesha*   t Hebrew *sons*   u Hebrew *the father of Hebron*   v Septuagint, Vulgate; Hebrew *son*   w Septuagint (compare Syriac, Vulgate); Hebrew *sons of*; four times in this verse   x Hebrew *sons*   y Septuagint (compare Vulgate); Hebrew *father*   z *Jabez* sounds like the Hebrew for *pain*   aa Or *evil*   ab Septuagint, Vulgate; Hebrew lacks *Meonothai*   ac *Ge-harashim* means *valley of craftsmen*   ad Hebrew *sons*   ae The clause *These are… married* is transposed from verse 18   af Hebrew lacks *and bore*   ag Vulgate (compare Septuagint); Hebrew *and Jashubi-lahem*   ah Or *matters*   ai Hebrew *Tilgath-pilneser*; also verse 26   aj Or *they were helped to prevail*   ak Septuagint, Vulgate; Hebrew *and Epher*   al Ch 5:27 in Hebrew   am Ch 6:1 in Hebrew   an Septuagint, Syriac (compare verse 33 and 1 Samuel 8:2); Hebrew lacks *Joel*   ao Hebrew *and Abijah*   ap Septuagint, Syriac (compare Joshua 21:17); Hebrew lacks *Gibeon*   aq Syriac (compare Vulgate); Hebrew *And to the sons*   ar Hebrew *sons*; also verses 10, 12, 17   as *Beriah* sounds like the Hebrew for *disaster*   at Hebrew *Non*   au Hebrew *and Naaman*   av Or *he carried them into exile*   aw Compare 9:35; Hebrew lacks *Jeiel*   ax Compare 8:35; Hebrew lacks *and Ahaz*

OVERVIEW: This section contains the genealogies of important biblical patriarchs, the sons and tribes of Israel, and of David and Saul. Although the long genealogies in 1 Chronicles are daunting to many modern readers, the reformers see their importance in preserving the ancestors of Christ and also of illustrating how God has fulfilled his promises since the beginning of Genesis. Working patiently through these genealogies, the commentators recognize how they point to Christ and highlight different features from them. Acknowledging a discrepancy between the genealogies of Christ in 1 Chronicles 3 and in Matthew 1, one commentator encourages readers to follow the one given in the Gospel of Matthew since it has been better preserved. The reformers also use these different genealogies to remind readers of biblical stories connected to the persons mentioned and to draw personal applications from their lives.

The Purpose of Genealogies

CHRIST'S GENEALOGY. LUCAS OSIANDER: On account of Christ, God wanted to preserve the genealogies of the Old Testament, along with the promises that were first given to our ancestors by Moses. For this reason the author gives the genealogy of Christ, beginning with Adam through Noah. . . . Of Shem, Ham and Japheth the first relates to Christ's ancestry, the second was cursed for uncovering his father's nakedness and the third became the father of the Gentiles, who would be brought to Christ. The author begins with this genealogy of Christ so we learn that this is the entire scope of all the teaching in sacred Scripture: to seek Christ and to acknowledge him. ANNOTATIONS ON 1 CHRONICLES.[1]

THE FULFILLING OF GOD'S PROMISES TO THE FIRST FAMILY. JOHANNES PISCATOR: From these genealogies, which are contained in these opening chapters, are noticed the excellence of the sacred history in comparison to secular history. For in this sacred history is indicated the first parents of the human race and from them the propagation of humankind. And we especially see the truthfulness

---

[1]Osiander, *Liber Iosue*, 1055.

of God in implementing his promise to the first family, which was that the first family would be strengthened, grow and fill the earth and subdue it in accordance with Genesis 1:28. COMMENTARY ON 1 CHRONICLES.[2]

1:1–2:55 From Adam to the Sons of Israel

THE TRIBES OF ISRAEL. LUCAS OSIANDER: Having given the origins of all other peoples who did not belong to the Israelites, Scripture now takes us back to a review of the genealogy of the people of God who were descended from the patriarch Jacob. The sons of Jacob (also called Israel) were Reuben, Simeon, Levi, Judah, Issachar, Zebulun, Dan, Joseph, Benjamin, Naphtali, Gad and Asher. These became the twelve patriarchs from whom came the twelve tribes of the Israelites. The tribe of Judah was already set apart from the others as the one from which the Christ would come, as Jacob had predicted in Genesis 49 of the family of Shelah, that one would be born who would be the savior of the nations. That promise of a messiah was renewed in the time of David. ANNOTATIONS ON 1 CHRONICLES.[3]

JUDAH'S PRIVILEGE. KONRAD PELLIKAN: The whole family and progeny of Israel and the inheritance of the Lord and of the peculiar people of God are elected. But from the twelve tribes of Israel, Judah alone is given the prerogative of kingship and of the Messiah from the house of David on account of the description here given and of the genealogy of the fathers written down. COMMENTARY ON 1 CHRONICLES.[4]

NAME UNDER THE LAW AND UNDER THE GOSPEL. THE ENGLISH ANNOTATIONS: Jacob was his first name. The name Israel was given him as evidence of his fervency and faith in prayer. Not only Jacob himself was called Israel, but also the church under the law and under the gospel. All the genealogies following from this man are of such as were of the church. For though Jacob had twelve sons, they were all true believers and heads of the church, and therefore are called the twelve Patriarchs. ANNOTATIONS ON 1 CHRONICLES.[5]

A MOST PLEASING SUCCESSION. VIKTORIN STRIGEL: Just as the succession from Adam to Jacob, who is also called Israel, is recounted in the first chapter, so this chapter is concerned with that succession from Jacob to David. God wished that from this succession we would know that God willed for the Messiah to be born out of this stock, from which we would hope and expect. To see this succession is most pleasing, since the church after the flood was governed and survived. For the mystery of all the Scriptures is Christ and the church. BOOK OF 1 CHRONICLES.[6]

POLYGAMY TOLERATED BUT NOT APPROVED. JOHANNES PISCATOR: We are reminded from the example of Caleb, who had a wife and a concubine, that polygamy was tolerated by God among the people of Israel. God tolerated it temporarily, but he did not approve it. This is especially the case since polygamy struggled with the institution of marriage as outlined in Genesis 1–2. In fact Christ upholds the rule of marriage to the Jews in the Gospel. COMMENTARY ON 1 CHRONICLES.[7]

DIFFERENCE BETWEEN WIFE AND CONCUBINE. GENEVA BIBLE: There was a difference between a wife and a concubine. The wife was taken with certain solemnities of marriage and her children received an inheritance; the concubine had no solemnities in marriage and her children did not receive an inheritance; however, they were given a portion of goods or money. ANNOTATIONS ON 1 CHRONICLES.[8]

---

[2]Piscator, Commentarii in omnes libros Veteris Testamenti, 2:379.
[3]Osiander, Liber Iosue, 1061.
[4]Pellikan, Commentaria Bibliorum, 2:206v.

[5]Downame, ed., Annotations (1657), Rrr3r*; citing Gen 25:26; 32:24; Hos 12:4; Gen 32:28; Ex 4:22; Gal 6:16; Acts 17:8-9.
[6]Strigel, Libri Samuelis, Regum et Paralipomenon, 418.
[7]Piscator, Commentarii in omnes libros Veteris Testamenti, 2:382.
[8]Geneva Bible (1560), 179r*.

3:1-24 The Descendants of David

DAVID'S FIRST WIFE? MARTIN LUTHER: Eglah alone is called David's wife, perhaps because she was the first and only wife while he still tended sheep. MARGINAL GLOSS ON 1 CHRONICLES 3:3 (1545).[9]

THREE TYPES OF LEADERS. VIKTORIN STRIGEL: There are three types of princes or leaders. The first are good leaders, who do what is right according to their office and achieve necessary and beneficial things. David, Solomon, Jehoshaphat, Hezekiah, Josiah, Shealtial and Zerubbabel were such leaders. The second type did some good things in the beginning of their reigns but eventually changed. Asa and Uzziah serve as examples. The third types are tyrants who do not even attempt to act rightly, but are evil. This includes Ahaz and Manasseh. BOOK OF 1 CHRONICLES.[10]

CHRIST'S ANCESTRY THROUGH SOLOMON. JOHANNES PISCATOR: Christ originated from David through Solomon. This was in accordance with the promise given to David in 2 Samuel 7. And we are able to recognize the line of descent from Solomon to Zerubbabel, which was the one ancestry of Christ according to Matthew 1. COMMENTARY ON 1 CHRONICLES.[11]

INTENTIONAL ERROR. THE ENGLISH ANNOTATIONS: These four sons of David in Jerusalem are set down in an intentionally contrary order. For Solomon was the oldest and Nathan was next, as is implied in Luke 3:31. But the author's purpose was to prosecute Solomon's race, and therefore he sets Solomon down in the last place. ANNOTATIONS ON 1 CHRONICLES.[12]

THE GOOD, THE BAD AND THE MEDIOCRE. LUDWIG LAVATER: Here we have enumerated those kings who ruled in Judah from David to the exile of

Babylon according to the promise of God. . . . Among these kings there were some who were good, such as David, Jehoshaphat, Jotham, Hezekiah and Josiah. There were some whose reigns began well but ended poorly, such as Solomon, Rehoboam, Asa, Joash, Amaziah and Azariah. Then there were some whose reigns began poorly but ended well, such as Manasseh and Jeconiah. Finally, there were others who were always evil and tyrannical, such as Joram, Ahaziah, Ahaz, Amon and the sons of Josiah who did not grieve over their evil conditions. We see from these kings all the vicissitudes of humanity, for today we have leaders who also have good, mediocre and bad reigns. COMMENTARY ON 1 CHRONICLES.[13]

DIFFERENCE BETWEEN THE GOSPEL OF MATTHEW AND 1 CHRONICLES. LUCAS OSIANDER: The genealogy now goes from Solomon to Zerubbabel, who was born after the Babylonian captivity. This genealogy does not agree in every place with that given in Matthew 1, especially when considering the names of those who came after Zerubbabel. I think it best to follow Matthew, because it is clear that the genealogies of Chronicles came from ancient and various records that were not very carefully transcribed by the copyists, as there are a great many differences in proper names in the texts. In this place we ought to recall the teaching of Paul that forbids us to dispute genealogies (1 Timothy 1 and Titus 3). For it is certain that the Evangelist Matthew was led by the Holy Spirit to record the best authorities for the genealogy of Christ, so that no one might vainly protest the good work he had done. ANNOTATIONS ON 1 CHRONICLES.[14]

4:1-23 The Descendants of Judah

ATTESTATION OF GOD'S PROMISES. VIKTORIN STRIGEL: After the writing is given concerning the succession of the teachers and kings from Adam, the first man, and the prophets to the return of the

---

[9]WADB 9,2:103.
[10]Strigel, *Libri Samuelis, Regum et Paralipomenon*, 421.
[11]Piscator, *Commentarii in omnes libros Veteris Testamenti*, 2:383.
[12]Downame, ed., *Annotations* (1645), NN4r*; citing 2 Sam 5:14.

[13]Lavater, *In Libros Paralipomenon*, 9.
[14]Osiander, *Liber Iosue*, 1068; citing 1 Tim 1:4; Tit 3:9.

people of Israel from Babylon, remembrance is established concerning the posterity of the sons of Jacob; and in the first part of this chapter is enumerated the seed of Judah. It therefore begins with Judah, the fourth son of Jacob, from whom Christ was born according to the flesh. The succession of Judah is set forth in this chapter as an example that attests to God's promises. BOOK OF 1 CHRONICLES.[15]

APPRECIATING THE COMMON PEOPLE. LUCAS OSIANDER: These things are written of linen workers, potters and other laborers by the Holy Spirit so that we know that there are many offices and works to be fulfilled in a republic. For this reason members of the local nobility should not despise the common people, for they cannot do without the lesser members. ANNOTATIONS ON 1 CHRONICLES.[16]

4:24-43 *The Descendants of Simeon*

THE LAND OF HAM. LUCAS OSIANDER: The descendants of Simeon entered the land that had belonged to Ham, the impious son of Noah. Because his descendants were no better than he had been, they were cast out by the Israelites according to the judgment of God. For in the secular world God punishes and expels impious descendants by means of other impious people. ANNOTATIONS ON 1 CHRONICLES.[17]

5:1-10 *The Descendants of Reuben*

REUBEN'S LOST PORTION. LUCAS OSIANDER: Reuben and his descendants should have had a double portion of everything as his paternal inheritance, and he also should have ruled the republic. But he lost his privileges. In his place were substituted Ephraim and Manasseh, the sons of Joseph. For in Genesis 38, Jacob—going out of order—assigned a double portion of territory to

the tribes of Joseph. At the same time, authority remained with the tribe of Judah. Thus the tribe of Ephraim (descended from Joseph) reigned as kings in Israel, as is told in the history of the kings. But God punished Reuben's incest in his time and for his descendants. We should therefore temper our liberty if we do not want to be passed over and avoid offending the Lord our God with wickedness. ANNOTATIONS ON 1 CHRONICLES.[18]

WHETHER PRIMOGENITURE APPLIES TO CHRISTIANS. JOHANNES PISCATOR: Based on this verse we may ask whether primogeniture[19] should endure to this day, or whether a Christian is obligated to observe and keep it. I respond that, although the law of primogeniture was instituted from God in places like Genesis 4.7 and Deuteronomy 21:15-17, Christians are no longer obligated to observe this practice. Rather, it represents a number of types that adumbrate and prefigure Christ. This is clear from the words of Paul. For instance, Romans says: "For those whom he foreknew he also predestined to be conformed to the image of his Son, in order that he might be the firstborn among many brothers." And Colossians says: "And he is the head of the body, the church. He is the beginning, the firstborn from the dead, that in everything he might be preeminent." So, because Christ is the firstborn, we are now freed from observing this law of primogeniture. COMMENTARY ON 1 CHRONICLES.[20]

JUDAH'S PREEMINENCE. THE ENGLISH ANNOTATIONS: Judah had preeminence in honor even in the wilderness. This is seen in Numbers. . . . Indeed, they had a royal dignity from David's time to the captivity. And after the captivity, some of Israel's chief governors and great leaders descended from

---

[15]Strigel, *Libri Samuel, Regum et Paralipomenon*, 423; citing 1 Cor 12.
[16]Osiander, *Liber Iosue*, 1073; 1 Cor 12.
[17]Osiander, *Liber Iosue*, 1075.
[18]Osiander, *Liber Iosue*, 1076.
[19]Primogeniture was a common practice in the ancient world in which the father selected the firstborn son to receive the majority, all or a high percentage of his father's inheritance in relation to the firstborn's other siblings.
[20]Piscator, *Commentarii in omnes libros Veteris Testamenti*, 2:386; citing Rom 8:29; Col 1:18.

Judah till Christ the everlasting king sprang out of that tribe. Annotations on 1 Chronicles.[21]

5:11-22 The Descendants of Gad

Victory Through Faith. Lucas Osiander: God granted the Gadites victory in battle "because they trusted in him." Victory is therefore not gained through blasphemies or curses but through pious prayers. And faith in God will not give us cause to be ashamed. Annotations on 1 Chronicles.[22]

5:23-26 Protection from Idolatry

Adulterous Idolatry. Lucas Osiander: Because they had forsaken true worship of the eternal God and followed the worship of idols, God had expelled the Canaanites through the Israelites, to whom he then gave possession of the land. Scripture calls idolatrous worship fornication, for God detests idolatry in his people no less than when an upright husband commits adultery against his wife. Is it not a monstrous thing that the Israelites, who had accepted the worship of their own God, did not have the power to remove the worship of the gods of the Canaanites? But where the Lord, governing by the Holy Spirit, removes human things, there is no blindness and no satanic impulses and they cannot be lost. Therefore we pray and are vigilant that we are not led into temptation. Annotations on 1 Chronicles.[23]

6:1-81 The Descendants of Levi

The Levitical Priesthood. Lucas Osiander: The genealogy of the tribe of Levi is described here. Through this tribe came the priests of Israel, from Aaron to Jehozadak, who was taken to Babylon in captivity. The line goes through the family of Zadok, not through Abiathar, so that not all of them recounted here were high priests. . . .

For Solomon cast down Abiathar from being high priest, just as God had threatened the priest Eli. And so, after the rejection of Abiathar from the high priesthood, the line goes through Zadok, an honor handed down all the way to the Babylonian captivity. Annotations on 1 Chronicles.[24]

Christ, the Real and True High Priest. Johannes Piscator: Aaron, and the high priests who succeeded him, were types of Christ to the extent that they made sacrifices of expiation on behalf of the people of God. For they made atonement of death in a ceremonial way, but the true and real atonement was made by the sacrifice of Christ on the altar of the cross when he was executed. As Hebrews says: "For it was indeed fitting that we should have such a high priest, holy, innocent, unstained, separated from sinners, and exalted above the heavens. He has no need, like those high priests, to offer sacrifices daily, first for his own sins and then for those of the people, since he did this once for all when he offered up himself." Commentary on 1 Chronicles.[25]

7:1-40 The Descendants of Issachar, Benjamin, Naphtali, Manasseh, Ephraim and Asher

The Sweet Apostle Paul. Viktorin Strigel: The tribe of Benjamin is a gift to us on account of the apostle Paul, who was born from this tribe. For no one is as famous, sweet and familiar to us as he is, who was esteemed more than any of his co-apostles. For the others did not write Scripture, but are only mentioned in the church. And those who wrote did not write as much or as gracefully as he did. Book of 1 Chronicles.[26]

Deborah and Barak. Viktorin Strigel: Deborah and Barak came from the tribe of Naphtali. They ruled over the people for forty years. They defeated Sisera, the commander for King

---

[21]Downame, ed., *Annotations* (1645), NN4v*; citing Num 2:3.
[22]Osiander, *Liber Iosue*, 1078.
[23]Osiander, *Liber Iosue*, 1079.

[24]Osiander, *Liber Iosue*, 1080; citing 1 Kings 2; 1 Sam 2.
[25]Piscator, *Commentarii in omnes libros Veteris Testamenti*, 2:389; citing Heb 7:26-27.
[26]Strigel, *Libri Samuelis, Regum et Paralipomenon*, 432.

Jabin, who ruled over Hazor. The area of Hazor was then part of the region of Canaan in the allotment of Naphtali. BOOK OF 1 CHRONICLES.[27]

FRUITFUL ASHER. VIKTORIN STRIGEL: Asher was a very beautiful tribe, abounding in wine, oil, fruit and many other things necessary for food. That's because their allotment was in fertile and fecund land by the coast of the sea, becoming the best part of Galilee. Indeed, as Jacob said in Genesis: "Asher's food shall be rich, and he shall yield rich delicacies." That is, the delicacies and fruits coming from Asher were so good and precious that they would be put on the table of kings and princes. What's more, out of this tribe came the prophetess Anna who, together with Simeon, testified of the Messiah in Luke 2. BOOK OF 1 CHRONICLES.[28]

8:1-40 *A Genealogy of Saul*

RESPECT FOR THE TRIBE OF THE FIRST KING. THE ENGLISH ANNOTATIONS: Benjamin's genealogy was set down before in the previous two chapters. But here the author returns to Benjamin again. The reason is because the first king came out of Benjamin: "Then Samuel brought all the tribes of Israel near, and the tribe of Benjamin was taken by lot." And this tribe was later united to Judah in 2 Chronicles 11:12. There is some difference between some of the names in this genealogy and the other ones of Benjamin because many persons had two or three names. ANNOTATIONS ON 1 CHRONICLES.[29]

CONTRAST BETWEEN SAUL AND JONATHAN. VIKTORIN STRIGEL: In this chapter is recounted the genealogy of the tribe of Benjamin and especially that of Saul, the first king of the people of God, and of his son Jonathan. The image of Saul is very sad. After his army was lost, he approved of killing

himself, and fell into eternal punishment. This should often be considered, so that we may recognize the magnitude of the wrath of God against sin. However, in Saul's son Jonathan we are given a meek example of one who had a mild and modest spirit. He is set forth as an example for all generations of people to imitate. BOOK OF 1 CHRONICLES.[30]

SAUL GONE BAD. VIKTORIN STRIGEL: Saul was given the Holy Spirit and decorated with special virtues and distinguished victories, but he was eventually stirred to cruelty and tyranny. For he attempted to kill David and, in a rage, killed the priests in the city of Nob, which is situated between Arimathea and Joppa. Therefore God, his army and his own son Jonathan, a holy man, opposed the slaughter of these as enemies. BOOK OF 1 CHRONICLES.[31]

THREE VIRTUES OF JONATHAN. VIKTORIN STRIGEL: Truly Jonathan had a spirit of courage, love and modesty. We see his courage in that he made an attack with only his armor-bearer against an enemy army and he made a great slaughter. This serves as an immediate and memorable symbol, which is that it is not at all difficult for the Lord to save with little means. Next we see Jonathan's love in that he watched over and defended David against the will of his father. Jonathan had known David's innocence, and he also knew that David was the best person of merit for the church and for the kingdom of Israel. Finally we see Jonathan's modesty in that he did not struggle with jealousy against David. On the contrary, he fully supported him. BOOK OF 1 CHRONICLES.[32]

JONATHAN'S DESCENDANTS. KONRAD PELLIKAN: Jonathan was killed with his father and his two brothers Abinadab and Malkishua. But Jonathan's son survived who was called Meribbaal, who is called Mephibosheth in the book of

---

[27]Strigel, *Libri Samuelis, Regum et Paralipomenon*, 432; citing Judg 4–5.

[28]Strigel, *Libri Samuelis, Regum et Paralipomenon*, 434; citing Gen 49:20.

[29]Downame, ed., *Annotations* (1645), OO1r*.

[30]Strigel, *Libri Samuelis, Regum et Paralipomenon*, 434.

[31]Strigel, *Libri Samuelis, Regum et Paralipomenon*, 435.

[32]Strigel, *Libri Samuelis, Regum et Paralipomenon*, 434.

Samuel. This Meribbaal then had a son named Micah, and from him came four sons: Pithon, Melech, Tahrea and Ahaz. Commentary on 1 Chronicles.[33]

9:1-9 Exile and Persecution

Difference Between Church and Empire. Viktorin Strigel: The glory of the people of Israel was great, with a flourishing kingdom in the land of Canaan. But in many ways the people fared better elsewhere, spending forty years in the desert and seventy years in Babylon. As for when the people were in the desert, manna and even quail was given to them; Moses struck the rock with his rod, and water poured forth abundantly; and the people were sheltered by the cloud in the daytime and by the flaming fire in the nighttime. What's more, the presence of God was exhibited as a wonderful testimony when in battle. The same is true of God's presence in Babylon. When the people were commanded to worship a false statue, God demonstrated his presence to those who, on account of their faith, were thrown into a flaming furnace, where one like the Son of God appeared in the midst of the three men. The people also experienced another miracle in the interpretation of the king's dream and of the punishment of Nebuchadnezzar and of his restitution. The prophet Daniel was also saved when thrown in the lions' den. Each of these things gives ample testimony to the presence of God in the church, and we must consider these things so that we can learn the difference between church and empire. For empires flourish when they are decorated with victories by means of magnitude, resources, laws, judicial power and defenses. However, the church never flourishes more than when it is under the cross. As Paul says, "My power is made perfect in weakness." . . . The church grows and flourishes best in persecution. Book of 1 Chronicles.[34]

Just Punishment but Also Divine Faithfulness. Johannes Piscator: In the deportation of the Judeans to Babylon an example of the just punishment of God and the castigation of the people is set forth. But we also see the example of the fulfilling of divine promises, for those living in Jerusalem after the Babylonian captivity were given homes. For God had promised this in accordance with biblical passages such as the following: "For thus says the Lord: When seventy years are completed for Babylon, I will visit you, and I will fulfill to you my promise and bring you back to this place." Commentary on 1 Chronicles.[35]

9:10-34 Difference Between Levites and Priests

Differences of Ministry Offices. Viktorin Strigel: The offices of the Levites and priests were different. The Levites slaughtered animals just like butchers did, and they also prepared the sacrifices. However, the priests actually offered the sacrifices. In the same way, schools teach the arts, which are instruments of teaching about God. But the ministry itself expounds the law and the gospel by the spoken word. Book of 1 Chronicles.[36]

9:35-44 King Saul's Family Tree

Not Speaking Evil of Families. Lucas Osiander: These are the descendants of that impious man King Saul. It is well known, however, that some members of the family were good and pious people, especially Jonathan and Mephibosheth. For there are hardly any families among the people of God that are so dissolute that there are not also pious people among them. For that reason we ought to take care not to speak evil against entire families. Annotations on 1 Chronicles.[37]

---

[33]Pellikan, *Commentaria Bibliorum*, 2:213v-214r.
[34]Strigel, *Libri Samuelis, Regum et Paralipomenon*, 438; citing 2 Cor 12:9.
[35]Piscator, *Commentarii in omnes libros Veteris Testamenti*, 2:394; citing Jer 29:10.
[36]Strigel, *Libri Samuelis, Regum et Paralipomenon*, 439.
[37]Osiander, *Liber Iosue*, 1101.

10:1–12:40 DAVID'S RISE TO POWER OVER ISRAEL

¹Now the Philistines fought against Israel, and the men of Israel fled before the Philistines and fell slain on Mount Gilboa. ²And the Philistines overtook Saul and his sons, and the Philistines struck down Jonathan and Abinadab and Malchi-shua, the sons of Saul. ³The battle pressed hard against Saul, and the archers found him, and he was wounded by the archers. ⁴Then Saul said to his armor-bearer, "Draw your sword and thrust me through with it, lest these uncircumcised come and mistreat me." But his armor-bearer would not, for he feared greatly. Therefore Saul took his own sword and fell upon it. ⁵And when his armor-bearer saw that Saul was dead, he also fell upon his sword and died. ⁶Thus Saul died; he and his three sons and all his house died together. ⁷And when all the men of Israel who were in the valley saw that the armyᵃ had fled and that Saul and his sons were dead, they abandoned their cities and fled, and the Philistines came and lived in them.

⁸The next day, when the Philistines came to strip the slain, they found Saul and his sons fallen on Mount Gilboa. ⁹And they stripped him and took his head and his armor, and sent messengers throughout the land of the Philistines to carry the good news to their idols and to the people. ¹⁰And they put his armor in the temple of their gods and fastened his head in the temple of Dagon. ¹¹But when all Jabesh-gilead heard all that the Philistines had done to Saul, ¹²all the valiant men arose and took away the body of Saul and the bodies of his sons, and brought them to Jabesh. And they buried their bones under the oak in Jabesh and fasted seven days.

¹³So Saul died for his breach of faith. He broke faith with the Lord in that he did not keep the command of the Lord, and also consulted a medium, seeking guidance. ¹⁴He did not seek guidance from the Lord. Therefore the Lord put him to death and turned the kingdom over to David the son of Jesse.

11 Then all Israel gathered together to David at Hebron and said, "Behold, we are your bone and flesh. ²In times past, even when Saul was king, it was you who led out and brought in Israel. And the Lord your God said to you, 'You shall be shepherd of my people Israel, and you shall be prince over my people Israel.'" ³So all the elders of Israel came to the king at Hebron, and David made a covenant with them at Hebron before the Lord. And they anointed David king over Israel, according to the word of the Lord by Samuel.

⁴And David and all Israel went to Jerusalem, that is, Jebus, where the Jebusites were, the inhabitants of the land. ⁵The inhabitants of Jebus said to David, "You will not come in here." Nevertheless, David took the stronghold of Zion, that is, the city of David. ⁶David said, "Whoever strikes the Jebusites first shall be chief and commander." And Joab the son of Zeruiah went up first, so he became chief. ⁷And David lived in the stronghold; therefore it was called the city of David. ⁸And he built the city all around from the Millo in complete circuit, and Joab repaired the rest of the city. ⁹And David became greater and greater, for the Lord of hosts was with him.

¹⁰Now these are the chiefs of David's mighty men, who gave him strong support in his kingdom, together with all Israel, to make him king, according to the word of the Lord concerning Israel. ¹¹This is an account of David's mighty men: Jashobeam, a Hachmonite, was chief of the three.ᵇ He wielded his spear against 300 whom he killed at one time.

¹²And next to him among the three mighty men was Eleazar the son of Dodo, the Ahohite. ¹³He was with David at Pas-dammim when the Philistines were gathered there for battle. There was a plot of ground full of barley, and the men fled from the Philistines. ¹⁴But he took hisᶜ stand in the midst of the plot and defended it and killed the Philistines. And the Lord saved them by a great victory.

¹⁵Three of the thirty chief men went down to the rock to David at the cave of Adullam, when the army of Philistines was encamped in the Valley of Rephaim. ¹⁶David was then in the stronghold, and the garrison of the Philistines was then at Bethlehem. ¹⁷And

David said longingly, "Oh that someone would give me water to drink from the well of Bethlehem that is by the gate!" ¹⁸Then the three mighty men broke through the camp of the Philistines and drew water out of the well of Bethlehem that was by the gate and took it and brought it to David. But David would not drink it. He poured it out to the LORD ¹⁹and said, "Far be it from me before my God that I should do this. Shall I drink the lifeblood of these men? For at the risk of their lives they brought it." Therefore he would not drink it. These things did the three mighty men.

²⁰Now Abishai, the brother of Joab, was chief of the thirty.^d And he wielded his spear against 300 men and killed them and won a name beside the three. ²¹He was the most renowned^e of the thirty^f and became their commander, but he did not attain to the three.

²²And Benaiah the son of Jehoiada was a valiant man^g of Kabzeel, a doer of great deeds. He struck down two heroes of Moab. He also went down and struck down a lion in a pit on a day when snow had fallen. ²³And he struck down an Egyptian, a man of great stature, five cubits^h tall. The Egyptian had in his hand a spear like a weaver's beam, but Benaiah went down to him with a staff and snatched the spear out of the Egyptian's hand and killed him with his own spear. ²⁴These things did Benaiah the son of Jehoiada and won a name beside the three mighty men. ²⁵He was renowned among the thirty, but he did not attain to the three. And David set him over his bodyguard.

²⁶The mighty men were Asahel the brother of Joab, Elhanan the son of Dodo of Bethlehem, ²⁷Shammoth of Harod,ⁱ Helez the Pelonite, ²⁸Ira the son of Ikkesh of Tekoa, Abiezer of Anathoth, ²⁹Sibbecai the Hushathite, Ilai the Ahohite, ³⁰Maharai of Netophah, Heled the son of Baanah of Netophah, ³¹Ithai the son of Ribai of Gibeah of the people of Benjamin, Benaiah of Pirathon, ³²Hurai of the brooks of Gaash, Abiel the Arbathite, ³³Azmaveth of Baharum, Eliahba the Shaalbonite, ³⁴Hashem^j the Gizonite, Jonathan the son of Shagee the Hararite, ³⁵Ahiam the son of Sachar the Hararite, Eliphal the son of Ur, ³⁶Hepher the Mecherathite, Ahijah the Pelonite, ³⁷Hezro of Carmel, Naarai the son of Ezbai, ³⁸Joel the brother of Nathan, Mibhar the son of Hagri, ³⁹Zelek the Ammonite, Naharai of Beeroth, the armor-bearer of Joab the son of Zeruiah, ⁴⁰Ira the Ithrite, Gareb the Ithrite, ⁴¹Uriah the Hittite, Zabad the son of Ahlai, ⁴²Adina the son of Shiza the Reubenite, a leader of the Reubenites, and thirty with him, ⁴³Hanan the son of Maacah, and Joshaphat the Mithnite, ⁴⁴Uzzia the Ashterathite, Shama and Jeiel the sons of Hotham the Aroerite, ⁴⁵Jediael the son of Shimri, and Joha his brother, the Tizite, ⁴⁶Eliel the Mahavite, and Jeribai, and Joshaviah, the sons of Elnaam, and Ithmah the Moabite, ⁴⁷Eliel, and Obed, and Jaasiel the Mezobaite.

12 Now these are the men who came to David at Ziklag, while he could not move about freely because of Saul the son of Kish. And they were among the mighty men who helped him in war. ²They were bowmen and could shoot arrows and sling stones with either the right or the left hand; they were Benjaminites, Saul's kinsmen. ³The chief was Ahiezer, then Joash, both sons of Shemaah of Gibeah; also Jeziel and Pelet, the sons of Azmaveth; Beracah, Jehu of Anathoth, ⁴Ishmaiah of Gibeon, a mighty man among the thirty and a leader over the thirty; Jeremiah,^k Jahaziel, Johanan, Jozabad of Gederah, ⁵Eluzai,^l Jerimoth, Bealiah, Shemariah, Shephatiah the Haruphite; ⁶Elkanah, Isshiah, Azarel, Joezer, and Jashobeam, the Korahites; ⁷And Joelah and Zebadiah, the sons of Jeroham of Gedor.

⁸From the Gadites there went over to David at the stronghold in the wilderness mighty and experienced warriors, expert with shield and spear, whose faces were like the faces of lions and who were swift as gazelles upon the mountains: ⁹Ezer the chief, Obadiah second, Eliab third, ¹⁰Mishmannah fourth, Jeremiah fifth, ¹¹Attai sixth, Eliel seventh, ¹²Johanan eighth, Elzabad ninth, ¹³Jeremiah tenth, Machbannai eleventh. ¹⁴These Gadites were officers of the army; the least was a match for a hundred men and the greatest for a thousand. ¹⁵These are the men who crossed the Jordan in the first month, when it was overflowing all its banks, and put to flight all those in the valleys, to the east and to the west.

¹⁶And some of the men of Benjamin and Judah came to the stronghold to David. ¹⁷David went out to meet them and said to them, "If you have come to me

in friendship to help me, my heart will be joined to you; but if to betray me to my adversaries, although there is no wrong in my hands, then may the God of our fathers see and rebuke you." [18]Then the Spirit clothed Amasai, chief of the thirty, and he said,

"We are yours, O David,
    and with you, O son of Jesse!
Peace, peace to you,
    and peace to your helpers!
For your God helps you."

Then David received them and made them officers of his troops.

[19]Some of the men of Manasseh deserted to David when he came with the Philistines for the battle against Saul. (Yet he did not help them, for the rulers of the Philistines took counsel and sent him away, saying, "At peril to our heads he will desert to his master Saul.") [20]As he went to Ziklag, these men of Manasseh deserted to him: Adnah, Jozabad, Jediael, Michael, Jozabad, Elihu, and Zillethai, chiefs of thousands in Manasseh. [21]They helped David against the band of raiders, for they were all mighty men of valor and were commanders in the army. [22]For from day to day men came to David to help him, until there was a great army, like an army of God.

[23]These are the numbers of the divisions of the armed troops who came to David in Hebron to turn the kingdom of Saul over to him, according to the word of the Lord. [24]The men of Judah bearing shield and spear were 6,800 armed troops. [25]Of the Simeonites, mighty men of valor for war, 7,100. [26]Of the Levites 4,600. [27]The prince Jehoiada, of the house of Aaron, and with him 3,700. [28]Zadok, a young man mighty in valor, and twenty-two commanders from his own fathers' house. [29]Of the Benjaminites, the kinsmen of Saul, 3,000, of whom the majority had to that point kept their allegiance to the house of Saul. [30]Of the Ephraimites 20,800, mighty men of valor, famous men in their fathers' houses. [31]Of the half-tribe of Manasseh 18,000, who were expressly named to come and make David king. [32]Of Issachar, men who had understanding of the times, to know what Israel ought to do, 200 chiefs, and all their kinsmen under their command. [33]Of Zebulun 50,000 seasoned troops, equipped for battle with all the weapons of war, to help David[m] with singleness of purpose. [34]Of Naphtali 1,000 commanders with whom were 37,000 men armed with shield and spear [35]Of the Danites 28,600 men equipped for battle. [36]Of Asher 40,000 seasoned troops ready for battle. [37]Of the Reubenites and Gadites and the half-tribe of Manasseh from beyond the Jordan, 120,000 men armed with all the weapons of war.

[38]All these, men of war, arrayed in battle order, came to Hebron with a whole heart to make David king over all Israel. Likewise, all the rest of Israel were of a single mind to make David king. [39]And they were there with David for three days, eating and drinking, for their brothers had made preparation for them. [40]And also their relatives, from as far as Issachar and Zebulun and Naphtali, came bringing food on donkeys and on camels and on mules and on oxen, abundant provisions of flour, cakes of figs, clusters of raisins, and wine and oil, oxen and sheep, for there was joy in Israel.

a Hebrew *they*   b Compare 2 Samuel 23:8; Hebrew *thirty*, or *captains*   c Compare 2 Samuel 23:12; Hebrew *they... their*   d Syriac; Hebrew *three*   e Compare 2 Samuel 23:19; Hebrew *more renowned among the two*   f Syriac; Hebrew *three*   g Syriac; Hebrew *the son of a valiant man*   h A *cubit* was about 18 inches or 45 centimeters   i Compare 2 Samuel 23:25; Hebrew *the Harorite*   j Compare Septuagint and 2 Samuel 23:32; Hebrew *the sons of Hashem*   k Hebrew verse 5   l Hebrew verse 6   m Septuagint; Hebrew lacks *David*

Overview: The defeat of the Israelites by the Philistines, for the reformers, reveals the notion that appearances can deceive. The death of Saul prompts these commentators to discuss the nature of his death and the shortcomings of his life. By contrast, David's anointing in Hebron, his conquest of Jerusalem, his gathering of certain Benjaminites and his leadership over his mighty men leads our commentators to see God's favor resting on him.[1]

[1]See commentary on 1 Sam 31:1-13; 2 Sam 5:1-10; 23:8-39.

10:1-12 *The Philistines Defeat the Israelites, Saul Kills Himself and His Body Is Mutilated*

Appearances Can Be Deceiving. Johannes Piscator: We are warned from the example of Israel's defeat by the Philistines under the kingship of Saul that external appearance is not an argument either for or against true religion. For the Israelites had the true religion, while the Philistines had a false religion. Commentary on 1 Chronicles.[2]

True Fortitude Perseveres. Johannes Piscator: It may be asked whether Saul's act of killing himself deserves praise inasmuch as it was an act of fortitude. By no means! For killing oneself goes against the precept of God, "You shall not murder." True fortitude would cause someone to fight against the enemies of God as long as they were at hand. Commentary on 1 Chronicles.[3]

Saul's Line Continues. Konrad Pellikan: All of the house or family of Saul is said to have died. That's because all of his family had gone out with him to the battle against the Philistines, and with him they were killed. But this was not really the end of Saul's family. For it continued to increase more over the years through Jonathan's seed, as was stated earlier. And a son of Saul succeeded him as king. Commentary on 1 Chronicles.[4]

10:13-14 *Saul's Unfaithfulness*

Caution When Speaking About Saul. Konrad Pellikan: Saul died by God's decree on account of his transgression against the Lord, whose word he did not observe in the matter of the Amalekites. He also consulted a witch rather than consulting the Lord, and he was not completely devoted to God's commands. But as regards his salvation or damnation, it is not advantageous to debate. For it is not written here that Saul was damned. Rather it is only said that his kingdom was transferred to David on account of God's previous election of David and of his anointing by the Lord. For the tribe of Judah had been promised kingship on the word of Jacob at his death. And because Saul did not seek out the Lord, the Lord killed him and transferred his kingdom to David, the son of Jesse. Commentary on 1 Chronicles.[5]

Saul's Sins. Lucas Osiander: Saul broke faith with the Lord, for he did not await the sacrifice of the prophet Samuel as he had been commanded (1 Sam 13), he did not completely obliterate the Amalekites with the due severity that the Lord had commanded (1 Sam 15), he persecuted the innocent David with a most bitter hatred (1 Sam 19) and he massacred the priests of the Lord (1 Sam 22). Above all that (as if that were not wicked enough), he rushed into a terrible sin, which led to his miserable death when he consulted the witch—the magical and vile sorceress—about the outcome of the war because he did not hope in the Lord (1 Sam 28). . . . Therefore we ought to seriously learn the fear of God, trusting in him to prosper us even in times of adversity. In this way we will have a helper and protector in God and not ever be cast away from God's face as happened to Saul. Annotations on 1 Chronicles.[6]

False Inquiry. The English Annotations: Saul did not inquire of the Lord in truth, in faith or by those means that God had warranted and sanctified in his Word. For Saul had destroyed the Lord's priests, by whom he should have inquired. This provoked the Lord to take away his Spirit within Saul. Therefore Saul's inquiring of the Lord before seeking the aid of the witch of Endor was a forced, fearful, faithless and hypocritical wish that God would some way or other foretell him how to prepare for the battle of the Philistines against him. But this was in truth no inquiry of the Lord

---

[2]Piscator, *Commentarii in omnes libros Veteris Testamenti*, 2:395.
[3]Piscator, *Commentarii in omnes libros Veteris Testamenti*, 2:395; citing Ex 20:13.
[4]Pellikan, *Commentaria Bibliorum*, 2:215v.
[5]Pellikan, *Commentaria Bibliorum*, 2:216r.
[6]Osiander, *Liber Iosue*, 1103-4.

at all. Rather it was like Balaam's false prayers. ANNOTATIONS ON 1 CHRONICLES.[7]

11:1-3 David Proclaimed King

FOLLOWING DAVID'S EXAMPLE. VIKTORIN STRIGEL: The example of David admonishes us not to snatch away former promises based on our own counsel but rather that we are to await a divine calling. For even though David had been promised the kingdom of Israel by the words of Samuel, he did not seek to occupy the throne either when Saul was living or right after he died. But after the death of Saul David remained in Hebron, and only the tribe of Judah came to him. Then later the remaining eleven tribes of Israel came freely and joined together with David by divine instinct. Afterward all of Israel offered him the crown of the kingdom without any deceit or compulsion. BOOK OF 1 CHRONICLES.[8]

OATHS AND PUBLIC SERVICE. LUCAS OSIANDER: David made a solemn oath binding him to the people that he would want to administer the government piously and justly. The people in turn bound themselves by an oath to the king that they would obey him willingly and remain faithful to him at all times. For God never condemns such oaths. ANNOTATIONS ON 1 CHRONICLES.[9]

11:4-9 David Captures Jerusalem

OBEDIENCE TO GOD'S COMMANDS. JOHANNES PISCATOR: David's going out with the people of Jerusalem to occupy the stronghold of Zion is set forth as an example of the works of obedience to the commands of God. For God had commanded the people of Israel to occupy that land and to throw out the inhabitants. And it expressly refers to Jerusalem of Judah, from which tribe David was. As Numbers says: "You shall drive out all the inhabitants of the land from before you and destroy all their figured stones and destroy all their metal images and demolish all their high places. And you shall take possession of the land and settle in it, for I have given the land to you to possess it." It is also spoken of in Joshua: "Then the boundary goes up by the Valley of the Son of Hinnom at the southern shoulder of the Jebusite (that is, Jerusalem)." COMMENTARY ON 1 CHRONICLES.[10]

DON'T TEASE. LUCAS OSIANDER: David let the people be scorned by the Jebusites, for the stronghold of Mount Zion would soon be taken through strenuous fighting. Because of this, the stronghold was later called the city of David. How foolishly people act when they insolently scorn their enemies! Taking such chances rarely works out well. But through his ministers, Christ overcomes all the difficulties with which people try to oppose the gospel. ANNOTATIONS ON 1 CHRONICLES.[11]

11:10-47 David and His Mighty Men

JUDGED BY DEEDS. KONRAD PELLIKAN: The catalog of mighty men is described according to the rank of their excellence, but they were not esteemed by the nobility or lineage of their blood. Rather they were esteemed on account of the faithful works and the great deeds that they did. COMMENTARY ON 1 CHRONICLES.[12]

WATER OF BLOOD. THOMAS ADAMS: Flee from the devil's wine cellar, beloved . . . where the sweet waters of delight tempt us to drink. Take David as an example. Though he longed for it, he would not drink the water that three of his mighty warriors brought to him since it was the water of blood, for his mighty warriors risked their lives to fetch it. In a similar way, should we put our souls at risk by drinking the waters at the devil's banquet? No, we have to go to the heavenly waters, whether we are poor or rich,

---

[7]Downame, ed., *Annotations* (1645), OO1v*.
[8]Strigel, *Libri Samuelis, Regum et Paralipomenon*, 441.
[9]Osiander, *Liber Iosue*, 1105.
[10]Piscator, *Commentarii in omnes libros Veteris Testamenti*, 2:398; citing Num 33:52-53; Josh 15:8.
[11]Osiander, *Liber Iosue*, 1105.
[12]Pellikan, *Commentaria Bibliorum*, 2:216r.

whether we have money or none. All who come here are welcome. The Devil's Banquet.[13]

Blessed Leaders and Subjects. Lucas Osiander: If David had drunk the water that the three mighty men obtained at the risk of great danger to their lives, he might have appeared to be crassly imbibing of their blood and lives. How blessed is the republic that willingly submits itself to devoted magistrates. And in turn, how blessed are the magistrates who take such obvious care of their subjects' blood and life, so that the people do not come to ruin because of their willing obedience. Annotations on 1 Chronicles.[14]

Second Class of Valiant Men. The English Annotations: The sixteen persons following to the end of this chapter are added to the catalog in 2 Samuel 23 because they also were valiant men. However, they were either not to be compared to the former mighty men or they had no command in the great cities or forts in the land but rather lived in the border towns. Annotations on 1 Chronicles.[15]

12:1-40 *David Gathers Support*

Fatherly Provision. Johannes Piscator: In the coming together of these Israelites to David, first at the time of their exile and then at the beginning of David's reign, an example is set forth of the illustrious example of the governance of Father God. For God protected his faithful servants from danger and finally carried them froth from freedom to honor. Commentary on 1 Chronicles.[16]

When Our Ways Please God. Viktorin Strigel: The proverb spoken by Solomon is true indeed: "When a person's ways please the Lord, he makes even his enemy to be at peace with him." Even though the Benjaminites were the sons of

Saul, they nevertheless bound themselves by David, whom Saul had separated from as a mortal enemy out of hate. Book of 1 Chronicles.[17]

Reckless or Brave? Lucas Osiander: Some mighty men crossed the Jordan when it was flooded, overflowing its banks. It is not recklessness but courage that is praised in these heroes. For it is a dangerous recklessness to attack when there is no compelling reason. But to overcome and disregard danger when circumstances require is truly a sign of the noblest courage. Annotations on 1 Chronicles.[18]

Singing to David. Lucas Osiander: The Spirit of the Lord led the outstanding man Amasai, chief of the thirty heroes, to be a source of comfort to David's heart and soul and—in the name of all his comrades—to bind his faith to David. He said, "We are yours, O David, and with you, O son of Jesse! We do not come only to praise you but to entrust ourselves to you and to help you as the Spirit gives us ability. Peace, peace to you and peace to your helpers!" That is to say, "We pray and promise all happiness to you and all your comrades, for your God helps you. We acknowledge you as the divine king to be defended and assisted. We are willing to learn how to live and die with you." And if faith is not to be found in men, then God led this good man who was so pious in afflictions to speak words of consolation to the others, as it says, "David received them and made them officers of his troops." Seeing that he had been given unique gifts above all others, he nevertheless promoted others up rather than cast them down under him. For it is unwise for eagles to crawl on the ground or for donkeys to fly. Annotations on 1 Chronicles.[19]

Imperial Prudence. Johannes Piscator: In David receiving the Benjaminites we have set forth both an example of imperial prudence and of piety.

---

[13] Adams, *Devil's Banquet*, 32-33*.
[14] Osiander, *Liber Iosue*, 1108.
[15] Downame, ed., *Annotations* (1645), OO2r*.
[16] Piscator, *Commentarii in omnes libros Veteris Testamenti*, 2:401.
[17] Strigel, *Libri Samuelis, Regum et Paralipomenon*, 445; citing Prov 16:7.
[18] Osiander, *Liber Iosue*, 1112.
[19] Osiander, *Liber Iosue*, 1112-13.

For David prudently inquired of their hearts and promised them friendship if they were discovered to be faithful. And in true piety David called on God's power to help if they should be discovered to be faithless; he threatens them with punishment for treachery from God. COMMENTARY ON 1 CHRONICLES.[20]

WHETHER THE WISDOM OF ISSACHAR WAS NATURAL OR CELESTIAL. GIOVANNI DIODATI: Some interpret the knowledge of the people of Issachar to be referring to astrology, by which they could foresee the natural dispositions of the air and seasons as well as occurrences of inferior bodies depending on the influence and government of the celestial bodies. In other words, they were searching for things that are oftentimes of great importance in human enterprises. Nevertheless astrology has always gone beyond its lawful bounds according to Scripture. Other interpreters, however, understand the knowledge of the people of Issachar to refer only the kind of wisdom and sagacity that is either received naturally or by long experience. Such knowledge is very important, as good success of affairs usually depends on it. ANNOTATIONS ON 1 CHRONICLES.[21]

---

[20]Piscator, *Commentarii in omnes libros Veteris Testamenti*, 2:402. [21]Diodati, *Pious Annotations*, 35*.

13:1–16:43 DAVID'S TRANSFER OF THE ARK OF THE COVENANT TO JERUSALEM

¹David consulted with the commanders of thousands and of hundreds, with every leader. ²And David said to all the assembly of Israel, "If it seems good to you and from the LORD our God, let us send abroad to our brothers who remain in all the lands of Israel, as well as to the priests and Levites in the cities that have pasturelands, that they may be gathered to us. ³Then let us bring again the ark of our God to us, for we did not seek it[a] in the days of Saul." ⁴All the assembly agreed to do so, for the thing was right in the eyes of all the people.

⁵So David assembled all Israel from the Nile[b] of Egypt to Lebo-hamath, to bring the ark of God from Kiriath-jearim. ⁶And David and all Israel went up to Baalah, that is, to Kiriath-jearim that belongs to Judah, to bring up from there the ark of God, which is called by the name of the LORD who sits enthroned above the cherubim. ⁷And they carried the ark of God on a new cart, from the house of Abinadab, and Uzzah and Ahio[c] were driving the cart. ⁸And David and all Israel were celebrating before God with all their might, with song and lyres and harps and tambourines and cymbals and trumpets.

⁹And when they came to the threshing floor of Chidon, Uzzah put out his hand to take hold of the ark, for the oxen stumbled. ¹⁰And the anger of the LORD was kindled against Uzzah, and he struck him down because he put out his hand to the ark, and he died there before God. ¹¹And David was angry because the LORD had broken out against Uzzah. And that place is called Perez-uzza[d] to this day. ¹²And David was afraid of God that day, and he said, "How can I bring the ark of God home to me?" ¹³So David did not take the ark home into the city of David, but took it aside to the house of Obed-edom the Gittite. ¹⁴And the ark of God remained with the household of Obed-edom in his house three months. And the LORD blessed the household of Obed-edom and all that he had.

14 And Hiram king of Tyre sent messengers to David, and cedar trees, also masons and carpenters to build a house for him. ²And David knew that the LORD had established him as king over Israel, and that his kingdom was highly exalted for the sake of his people Israel.

³And David took more wives in Jerusalem, and David fathered more sons and daughters. ⁴These are the names of the children born to him in Jerusalem: Shammua, Shobab, Nathan, Solomon, ⁵Ibhar, Elishua, Elpelet, ⁶Nogah, Nepheg, Japhia, ⁷Elishama, Beeliada and Eliphelet.

⁸When the Philistines heard that David had been anointed king over all Israel, all the Philistines went up to search for David. But David heard of it and went out against them. ⁹Now the Philistines had come and made a raid in the Valley of Rephaim. ¹⁰And David inquired of God, "Shall I go up against the Philistines? Will you give them into my hand?" And the LORD said to him, "Go up, and I will give them into your hand." ¹¹And he went up to Baal-perazim, and David struck them down there. And David said, "God has broken through[e] my enemies by my hand, like a bursting flood." Therefore the name of that place is called Baal-perazim. ¹²And they left their gods there, and David gave command, and they were burned.

¹³And the Philistines yet again made a raid in the valley. ¹⁴And when David again inquired of God, God said to him, "You shall not go up after them; go around and come against them opposite the balsam trees. ¹⁵And when you hear the sound of marching in the tops of the balsam trees, then go out to battle, for God has gone out before you to strike down the army of the Philistines." ¹⁶And David did as God commanded him, and they struck down the Philistine army from Gibeon to Gezer. ¹⁷And the fame of David went out into all lands, and the LORD brought the fear of him upon all nations.

15 David[f] built houses for himself in the city of David. And he prepared a place for the ark of God and pitched a tent for it. ²Then David said that no one but the Levites may carry the ark of God, for the LORD had chosen them to carry the ark of the LORD and to minister to him forever. ³And David assembled all Israel at Jerusalem to bring up the ark of the LORD to its place, which he had prepared for it. ⁴And David gathered together the sons of Aaron and the Levites: ⁵of the sons of Kohath, Uriel the chief, with 120 of his brothers; ⁶of the sons of Merari, Asaiah the chief, with 220 of his brothers; ⁷of the sons of Gershom, Joel the chief, with 130 of his brothers; ⁸of the sons of Elizaphan, Shemaiah the chief, with 200 of his brothers; ⁹of the sons of Hebron, Eliel the chief, with 80 of his brothers; ¹⁰of the sons of Uzziel, Amminadab the chief, with 112 of his brothers. ¹¹Then David summoned the priests Zadok and Abiathar, and the Levites Uriel, Asaiah, Joel, Shemaiah, Eliel, and Amminadab, ¹²and said to them, "You are the heads of the fathers' houses of the Levites. Consecrate yourselves, you and your brothers, so that you may bring up the ark of the LORD, the God of Israel, to the place that I have prepared for it. ¹³Because you did not carry it the first time, the LORD our God broke out against us, because we did not seek him according to the rule." ¹⁴So the priests and the Levites consecrated themselves to bring up the ark of the LORD, the God of Israel. ¹⁵And the Levites carried the ark of God on their shoulders with the poles, as Moses had commanded according to the word of the LORD.

¹⁶David also commanded the chiefs of the Levites to appoint their brothers as the singers who should play loudly on musical instruments, on harps and lyres and cymbals, to raise sounds of joy. ¹⁷So the Levites appointed Heman the son of Joel; and of his brothers Asaph the son of Berechiah; and of the sons of Merari, their brothers, Ethan the son of Kushaiah; ¹⁸and with them their brothers of the second order, Zechariah, Jaaziel, Shemiramoth, Jehiel, Unni, Eliab, Benaiah, Maaseiah, Mattithiah, Eliphelehu, and Mikneiah, and the gatekeepers Obed-edom and Jeiel. ¹⁹The singers, Heman, Asaph, and Ethan, were to sound bronze cymbals; ²⁰Zechariah, Aziel, Shemiramoth, Jehiel, Unni, Eliab, Maaseiah, and Benaiah were to play harps according to Alamoth; ²¹but Mattithiah, Eliphelehu, Mikneiah, Obed-edom, Jeiel, and Azaziah were to lead with lyres according to the Sheminith. ²²Chena-

niah, leader of the Levites in music, should direct the music, for he understood it. ²³Berechiah and Elkanah were to be gatekeepers for the ark. ²⁴Shebaniah, Joshaphat, Nethanel, Amasai, Zechariah, Benaiah, and Eliezer, the priests, should blow the trumpets before the ark of God. Obed-edom and Jehiah were to be gatekeepers for the ark.

²⁵So David and the elders of Israel and the commanders of thousands went to bring up the ark of the covenant of the LORD from the house of Obed-edom with rejoicing. ²⁶And because God helped the Levites who were carrying the ark of the covenant of the LORD, they sacrificed seven bulls and seven rams. ²⁷David was clothed with a robe of fine linen, as also were all the Levites who were carrying the ark, and the singers and Chenaniah the leader of the music of the singers. And David wore a linen ephod. ²⁸So all Israel brought up the ark of the covenant of the LORD with shouting, to the sound of the horn, trumpets, and cymbals, and made loud music on harps and lyres.

²⁹And as the ark of the covenant of the LORD came to the city of David, Michal the daughter of Saul looked out of the window and saw King David dancing and celebrating, and she despised him in her heart.

16 And they brought in the ark of God and set it inside the tent that David had pitched for it, and they offered burnt offerings and peace offerings before God. ²And when David had finished offering the burnt offerings and the peace offerings, he blessed the people in the name of the LORD ³and distributed to all Israel, both men and women, to each a loaf of bread, a portion of meat,ᵍ and a cake of raisins.

⁴Then he appointed some of the Levites as ministers before the ark of the LORD, to invoke, to thank, and to praise the LORD, the God of Israel. ⁵Asaph was the chief, and second to him were Zechariah, Jeiel, Shemiramoth, Jehiel, Mattithiah, Eliab, Benaiah, Obed-edom, and Jeiel, who were to play harps and lyres; Asaph was to sound the cymbals, ⁶and Benaiah and Jahaziel the priests were to blow trumpets regularly before the ark of the covenant of God. ⁷Then on that day David first appointed that thanksgiving be sung to the LORD by Asaph and his brothers.

⁸Oh give thanks to the LORD; call upon his
name;
make known his deeds among the peoples!
⁹Sing to him, sing praises to him;
tell of all his wondrous works!
¹⁰Glory in his holy name;
let the hearts of those who seek the LORD
rejoice!
¹¹Seek the LORD and his strength;
seek his presence continually!
¹²Remember the wondrous works that he has done,
his miracles and the judgments he uttered,
¹³O offspring of Israel his servant,
children of Jacob, his chosen ones!

¹⁴He is the LORD our God;
his judgments are in all the earth.
¹⁵Remember his covenant forever,
the word that he commanded, for a
thousand generations,
¹⁶the covenant that he made with Abraham,
his sworn promise to Isaac,
¹⁷which he confirmed to Jacob as a statute,
to Israel as an everlasting covenant,
¹⁸saying, "To you I will give the land of Canaan,
as your portion for an inheritance."

¹⁹When you were few in number,
of little account, and sojourners in it,
²⁰wandering from nation to nation,
from one kingdom to another people,
²¹he allowed no one to oppress them;
he rebuked kings on their account,
²²saying, "Touch not my anointed ones,
do my prophets no harm!"

²³Sing to the LORD, all the earth!
Tell of his salvation from day to day.
²⁴Declare his glory among the nations,
his marvelous works among all the peoples!
²⁵For great is the LORD, and greatly to be praised,
and he is to be feared above all gods.
²⁶For all the gods of the peoples are worthless idols,
but the LORD made the heavens.
²⁷Splendor and majesty are before him;
strength and joy are in his place.

²⁸Ascribe to the LORD, O families of the peoples,
ascribe to the LORD glory and strength!
²⁹Ascribe to the LORD the glory due his name;
bring an offering and come before him!
Worship the LORD in the splendor of holiness;ᵇ
³⁰tremble before him, all the earth;
yes, the world is established; it shall never be
moved.
³¹Let the heavens be glad, and let the earth rejoice,
and let them say among the nations, "The
LORD reigns!"
³²Let the sea roar, and all that fills it;
let the field exult, and everything in it!
³³Then shall the trees of the forest sing for joy
before the LORD, for he comes to judge the
earth.
³⁴Oh give thanks to the LORD, for he is good;
for his steadfast love endures forever!

³⁵Say also:

"Save us, O God of our salvation,
and gather and deliver us from among the
nations,
that we may give thanks to your holy name
and glory in your praise.
³⁶Blessed be the LORD, the God of Israel,
from everlasting to everlasting!"

Then all the people said, "Amen!" and praised the
LORD.

³⁷So David left Asaph and his brothers there
before the ark of the covenant of the LORD to minister
regularly before the ark as each day required, ³⁸and
also Obed-edom and hisⁱ sixty-eight brothers, while
Obed-edom, the son of Jeduthun, and Hosah were to
be gatekeepers. ³⁹And he left Zadok the priest and his
brothers the priests before the tabernacle of the LORD
in the high place that was at Gibeon ⁴⁰to offer burnt
offerings to the LORD on the altar of burnt offering
regularly morning and evening, to do all that is
written in the Law of the LORD that he commanded
Israel. ⁴¹With them were Heman and Jeduthun and
the rest of those chosen and expressly named to give
thanks to the LORD, for his steadfast love endures
forever. ⁴²Heman and Jeduthun had trumpets and

cymbals for the music and instruments for sacred song. *The sons of Jeduthun were appointed to the gate.*

⁴³Then all the people departed each to his house, and David went home to bless his household.

a Or *him* b Hebrew *Shihor* c Or *and his brother* d *Perez-uzza* means *the breaking out against Uzzah* e *Baal-perazim* means LORD *of breaking through* f Hebrew *He* g Compare Septuagint, Syriac, Vulgate; the meaning of the Hebrew is uncertain h Or *in holy attire* i Hebrew *their*

OVERVIEW: These interpreters note that the transference of the ark of the covenant to Jerusalem from Kiriath-jearim was not directed by divine precept but was a matter of personal discretion. Since the text cites God as the one who takes Uzzah's life, the interpreters must explain what he did to warrant such swift divine punishment. Some attribute Uzzah's immediate death to zeal lacking scriptural warrant. After his first attempt failed, David decides again to transport the ark into Jerusalem, this time being very careful to follow all God's precepts. David's command to bring along Levites who sing prompts consideration of whether it is biblically permissible for Christians to use musical instruments in worship. The interpreters laud David's second attempt to transfer the ark and his actions during and after the ceremony, currying favor with both the people of Israel and God.[1]

13:1-5 David Consults the Community

ASKING FOR ADVICE. LUCAS OSIANDER: David said about moving the ark, "if it seems good to you and from the Lord our God." It is as if he asked, "Does it appear to be a godly and useful thing that I am suggesting we undertake?" For the matter of deciding to move the ark to Jerusalem was a matter of freedom, because it had no express command from God. Therefore David wanted his subjects to agree on it. This leader was not ashamed to consult with his best people even on great matters, for more eyes see better than one. ANNOTATIONS ON 1 CHRONICLES.[2]

PIOUS HEART. THE ENGLISH ANNOTATIONS: After David was settled in his kingdom, that is, after he had

taken Zion and built his city, he was resolved to bring the ark to Jerusalem. This reveals David's piety to God and his desire for God's presence and blessing to accompany him. And because this was a great and solemn work to be performed, David consulted with others to ensure that it could be solemnly performed. ANNOTATIONS ON 1 CHRONICLES.[3]

13:6 The Significance of the Ark

FROM THE ARK TO CHRIST. JOHANNES PISCATOR: Formerly in the Old Testament invocation was directed to the ark of the covenant. But today in the New Testament invocation is directed to heaven, where Christ is interceding for us. COMMENTARY ON 1 CHRONICLES.[4]

13:7-11 The Death of Uzzah

NOT BY ZEAL ALONE. BALTHASAR HUBMAIER: The greatest deception of the people is the kind of zeal for God that is unscripturally applied, in the interest of the salvation of souls, the honor of the church, love for the truth, good intentions, use or custom, episcopal decrees and the teaching of reason—all of which come from the light of nature. These are lethal errors, when they are not led and directed according to Scripture. . . . A person should not presume, misled by the masks of his own purpose, to do anything better or surer than God has spoken by his own mouth. . . . Those who rely on their good intentions and believe to do better are like Uzzah and Peter. Jesus called the latter Satan; the former was destroyed miserably. ON HERETICS AND THOSE WHO BURN THEM.[5]

---

[1]See commentary on 2 Sam 6:1-11; 5:11-25; 6:12-23.
[2]Osiander, *Liber Iosue*, 1116.
[3]Downame, ed., *Annotations* (1645), OO2v*.
[4]Piscator, *Commentarii in omnes libros Veteris Testamenti*, 2:403.
[5]CRR 5:64-65; citing Mt 16:23.

Inconsiderate Zeal. John Calvin: Now you might consider this hastiness to be commendable zeal, but in the eyes of God it was inconsiderate zeal, and merited punishment. Let us therefore carefully remember that the death of Uzzah was not cruelty on the part of God, but a just chastisement, for it was a duty of the Levites—and specifically the Kohathites—to be in charge of carrying the ark. Indeed the Kohathites themselves were not to dare to open it (Num 4:19), for it could only be opened by the high priest. Well, if those whom God had dedicated to his obedience and service were not supposed to look in it ... and in fact those who acted so presumptuously were grievously punished (1 Sam 6:19), then what should happen when a private person thrusts himself forward and recklessly touches it, as though to say: "By my help I shall prevent the ark from falling"? In fact both he and his party may have been ambitious ... in that they may have wanted to glorify themselves— since their house had been the lodging place of the ark of God. Well, be that as it may, still his hastiness was displeasing to God. When it says that "his wrath was stirred up" ... let us understand that God was justly angry. For God is not like mortal men, who become angry and whose passions are disordered. Rather, whenever God is annoyed, let us tremble, knowing that his justice is fair, and not like that of sinners. Thus this single word should suffice to condemn Uzzah and to hold us captive so that we do not come to argue with God, or pose questions, or quarrel against him. That, in sum, is what we have to remember from this example. Sermons on 2 Samuel.[6]

Uzziah Out of Order. Geneva Bible: Uzzah provoked God's wrath for usurping that which did not belong to his position, for this charge of carrying the ark was given only to the priests according to Numbers 4:15. All good intentions are condoned unless they go against that which is commanded by the Word of God. Annotations on 1 Chronicles.[7]

13:12-14 *The Ark's Temporary Residence at the House of Obed-edom*

God's Sense of Humor. John Calvin: God made fun of the foolish fear of David, for "David lodged the ark in the house of Obed-edom, and this man prospered and all his family." ... This prosperity gave evident testimony that God accepted the worship of Obed-edom for having lent him his house in which to lodge his ark. In the first place, David's motive was a bad one, for if he feared to bring back the ark of God for himself, why did he charge Obed-edom with it? Was that either right or charitable? He thought that death would draw near if God entered Zion. Well, if the ark of God would cause such trouble, did David not deserve to be paid the same wages as the person with whom he deposited the ark in hopes of avoiding the very evil he feared would ruin the one who kept it? This shows us how one evil brings another, and how the fear that we previously discussed made him forget how to be humane and level-headed. For he should rather have said: "Let us build a place for the ark: let the Levites carry out their duty, that each one may be employed in the service of God, and pure religion be maintained." But he did nothing of the sort! On the contrary, not content with refusing the ark, he actually charged someone else with it, hoping, of course, that he could avoid evil by putting it on someone else. Sermons on 2 Samuel.[8]

Blessings for Those Who Uphold Right Worship. Johannes Piscator: We are admonished by the example of the divine blessing of Obed-edom in watching over and guarding the ark of the covenant that God's blessing remains with those who promote the true worship of God. Commentary on 1 Chronicles.[9]

---

[6]Calvin, *Sermons on Second Samuel*, 1:249-50.
[7]*Geneva Bible* (1560), 184v*.

[8]Calvin, *Sermons on Second Samuel*, 1:257.
[9]Piscator, *Commentarii in omnes libros Veteris Testamenti*, 2:403.

14:1-2 *Hiram and David Join Together*

Unholy Alliance. John Calvin: Now a confirmation is added as an example, namely, that Hiram, "king of Tyre, sent messengers to David" with presents ("cedar wood," to build) and craftsmen ("as many masons as carpenters to build his palace"). Well, when the text adds that God was with David, there is no doubt that this was a testimony of the goodness of God—for King Hiram, who was a miserable pagan, was led to seek friendship, and to act in such a liberal way toward David. But yet, we see that David could not resist abusing this grace. This should serve as very useful instruction for us, to make us accept all the favors of God that he offers us by the hand of pagans, without becoming corrupted, as happened to David. Although they gave him a present of many cedars, it was not right for him to acquiesce to the will of a pagan to make an alliance. He should have been content with the fact that God had granted him his favor and immutable goodness, and should always have hoped for the same, insofar as he behaved faithfully in his vocation. Well, he obeyed (the pagan), and joined with King Hiram in order to advance himself. Yes, but he should have considered using this inestimable gift God gave him, and not have usurped what was not permitted him. Sermons on 2 Samuel.[10]

14:3-7 *David's Many Wives and Children*

Wings to Fly. John Calvin: It is likely that David sought to have children so that the crown would not be taken away. But there is no doubt, also, that he was motivated by his evil lusts and by pride and pomp. Beyond the fact that he committed adultery for its own sake, there was the customary attitude of princes that they ought to be privileged to do wrong above everyone else. They want to be as far above the rank of human beings as is possible for them, and then to show their importance and have allies on every side. Thus it is likely that David

was motivated by all of these considerations. Well, although one can always come up with plenty of excuses, nevertheless one must not do evil that good may come (Rom 3:8). David is to be totally condemned in every way, but especially because he relaxed control over his wicked and perverse pleasures. Then he is condemned on account of vanity and presumption, because of which he extended his wings too far and took off in the air, not knowing his limits. So God . . . tolerated him, in that he did give him offspring, but that is not to say that he approved him. Sermons on 2 Samuel.[11]

14:8-17 *David Defeats the Philistines*

Seeking the Counsel of God. Johannes Piscator: The example of David is a warning to godly kings and leaders and high officials. For here they learn that it is their occupation to consult God when they face difficult and even perilous situations. Today this is to be accomplished by turning to the written Word of God. Commentary on 1 Chronicles.[12]

God Goes Before. Lucas Osiander: David was told, "God has gone out before you to strike down the army of the Philistines." That is, there God will make your enemies scatter. The truth of the matter is that our works are not our own but come from God, even if they happen through us. Neither do our greatest efforts achieve anything unless God has gone before us. Annotations on 1 Chronicles.[13]

God on Behalf of Israel. Johannes Piscator: Even after being defeated by the Israelites the first time, the Philistines once more advanced against Israel for battle. This is an example of foolish and ungodly persistence. For the Philistines were guilty of scorning the judgment of God. Indeed God was fighting on behalf of the Israelites

---

[10]Calvin, *Sermons on Second Samuel*, 1:196.

[11]Calvin, *Sermons on Second Samuel*, 1:207.
[12]Piscator, *Commentarii in omnes libros Veteris Testamenti*, 2:404.
[13]Osiander, *Liber Iosue*, 1122.

by means of his holy angels, just as we see in 2 Kings: "And that night the angel of the Lord went out and struck down 185,000 in the camp of the Assyrians. And when people arose early in the morning, behold, these were all dead bodies." Commentary on 1 Chronicles.[14]

15:1-29 The Ark Comes to Jerusalem with Musical Accompaniment

Establishing Rightful Worship. Johannes Piscator: David's desire to procure and then transport the ark of the covenant serves as an example to kings and leaders as well as Christian officials. The example that David gives is that these officeholders must diligently seek out and establish the right worship of God. Commentary on 1 Chronicles.[15]

Sanctification Before the Lord's Supper. Johannes Piscator: The priests and Levites sanctified their bodies before they transported the ark of the covenant. In the same way, Christians must sanctify themselves when they administer and partake of the sacraments such as the Lord's Supper. Indeed Christians must not only prepare themselves bodily by temperance but they must also prepare themselves spiritually by examining their hearts. Commentary on 1 Chronicles.[16]

Sacred Music. Lucas Osiander: David chose some Levites to be in charge of certain musical instruments, which became the origin of pleasantly played sacred music in order to "raise sounds of joy." It is right to joyfully raise our voices in exaltation, so that they are clearly heard by means of musical instruments and voices clearly singing together. Thus musical instruments belong to holiness as a gift of God for rendering praise and glory to God. And the Psalms are chanted with pleasant melodies so that their words have been known to affect

many of their hearers and help kindle devotion with them. They certainly worked this way for King David. Annotations on 1 Chronicles.[17]

Duties of Levites. Henry Ainsworth: In music there were Levites appointed for several duties . . . some of which excelled in the art of singing and playing on instruments, to whom many psalms are dedicated, that by their care and direction they might be sung excellently to the end. Annotations on Psalms.[18]

Important Leader. The English Annotations: Chenaniah, leader of the Levites in music, taught the people how to begin, how to rise, how to fall and how to rest in music. He taught them, in every way, how to keep tune as skillful singers. And, as one skilful in ordering the ark, he directed others about the manner of carrying the ark, that is, what pace to go, when to stand and when to change bearers. Annotations on 1 Chronicles.[19]

Musical Instruments Allowed in Christian Churches? Johannes Piscator: It may be asked whether the New Testament allows for musical instruments to be used and for vocal accompaniment to be sung in the public worship of God. I respond that although there is nothing explicit in the New Testament that commands musical instruments, there is nothing that prohibits them. That is, there is nothing to be said for employing music in itself, but neither is there anything about it to be rejected as illicit. In the meantime, it is right for Christians to sing in congregations, inasmuch as sacred hymns are sung according to Ephesians, where it speaks about Christians "addressing one another in psalms and hymns and spiritual songs, singing and making melody to the Lord with your heart." Commentary on 1 Chronicles.[20]

---

[14]Piscator, *Commentarii in omnes libros Veteris Testamenti*, 2:404; citing 2 Kings 19:35.
[15]Piscator, *Commentarii in omnes libros Veteris Testamenti*, 2:406.
[16]Piscator, *Commentarii in omnes libros Veteris Testamenti*, 2:406.
[17]Ainsworth, *Annotations on the Psalms*, 9*.
[18]Downame, ed., *Annotations* (1645), OO2v*.
[19]Downame, ed., *Annotations* (1645), np*.
[20]Piscator, *Commentarii in omnes libros Veteris Testamenti*, 2:406; citing Eph 5:19.

Seven, the Perfect Number. The English Annotations: Seven was reckoned as the number of perfection. It made up a week, many feasts, the year of rest and Jubilee, the time of cleansing, consecrating, preparing and keeping the Lord's watch, the stint of sprinkling blood and oil, of washing and fasting, feasting and of making sacrifices.... Thus, in order to make a perfect atonement here, David offered seven bulls. Annotations on 1 Chronicles.[21]

Prideful Woman Punished. Johannes Piscator: David's wife Michal spurned David when she saw him jumping and dancing before the ark of the covenant. Because of this she serves as an example of a prideful woman. And God did not forgive her assault on David. For as we read in 2 Samuel 6, God punished her condemnation of David by means of sterility: "And Michal the daughter of Saul had no child to the day of her death." Commentary on 1 Chronicles.[22]

Christ Is Our Ark. King James VI: What is the ark of Christians under grace but the Lord Jesus Christ? With joy we bring him among us when with sincerity and gladness we receive the new covenant in the blood of Christ our Savior, in our heart we believe his promises, and in word and deed we witness to them before all the world and walk in the light as it becomes the sons of the same. This is the worthiest triumph of our victory that we can make. And although there will doubtlessly be many Michals among us, let us rejoice and praise God for the discovery of them, assuring ourselves that they were never of us. We should consider all those to be against us who either rejoice at the prosperity of our enemies, or do not rejoice with us on account of our miraculous deliverance. "For all who do not gather with us, will be scattered."...

Let us now conclude by bringing in the ark among us in two respects. Since we have already received the gospel, first, be constant, remaining in the purity of the truth, which is our most certain covenant of salvation in the merits of our Savior alone. And second, let us so reform our daily lives as becomes regenerate Christians: the great glory of our God. A Meditation on 1 Chronicles 15.[23]

16:1-7 The Ceremony Continues

Fed Spiritually and Physically. The English Annotations: David distributed this food so that the spirits of everyone might be more quickened to praise God with him. He also did this so that none would repent of their journeys by returning home with empty stomachs. Annotations on 1 Chronicles.[24]

Christian Officials Establishing Rightful Worship. Johannes Piscator: David provides an example that is pertinent to Christian officials today. For David established the sacred ministers. And he teaches Christian officials that it is their occupation to also establish and support ministers of the Word of God and the sacraments. Commentary on 1 Chronicles.[25]

16:8-43 David's Song of Thanks

Praising God in the People's Language. Lucas Osiander: On the occasion of the ark's entry, David first established that God be praised through the hand of Asaph and his brothers. That is, after this time it was usual for God to be celebrated through psalms and sacred music, led by people who were appointed to do it. This is the same as when our Lord God is celebrated for his immense goodness to us either individually in

[21]Downame, ed., *Annotations* (1645), OO2v*; citing Gen 2:2; Lev 23:3, 6, 15, 34; 25:4, 8; 12:3; 14:8, 9; Ex 29:35, 37; Lev 22:27; 8:35; 16:14; 8:11; 2 Kings 5:10; 1 Sam 31:13; 2 Chron 7:9; Job 42:8; 2 Chron 29:21.
[22]Piscator, *Commentarii in omnes libros Veteris Testamenti*, 2:406; citing 2 Sam 6:23.
[23]King James VI, *Ane Meditatiovn vpon the XV chapter of the First Buke of the Chronicles of the Kingis*, B3v-B4r*; citing Mt 12:30.
[24]Downame, ed., *Annotations* (1645), OO2v*; citing Neh 8:10; Mt 14:16.
[25]Piscator, *Commentarii in omnes libros Veteris Testamenti*, 2:409.

private or publicly in the church, especially in the language of the people. In this way God's glory is spread widely and remembrance of God's righteousness and goodness might inspire in many more people the fear of God and faith in God. The Psalms are sung in the common language among us for precisely this reason. Annotations on 1 Chronicles.[26]

Seek God's Presence in Worship and Prayer. Lucas Osiander: In the Scriptures, seeking God's face often directs us to ministers of the Word and sacrament, for there God shows himself, as if showing his own face. In case of some urgent necessity, we can speak our anguish and explore the furthest reaches of God through our ardent prayers in the chamber of our hearts before God's face. We have such opportunities to come together with other Christians in prayer every day, asking for consolation and the confirmation of faith through the Word of God and the sacraments, which is also certainly what it means to seek the face of God. Annotations on 1 Chronicles.[27]

David's First Public Psalm. The English Annotations: This was David's first psalm that

he appointed to be sung publicly in the service of God. Afterward he appointed others to do this. In this respect he is styled "the sweet psalmist of Israel." From this it appears that these psalms were written by David, although his name is not expressed in the titles. Annotations on 1 Chronicles.[28]

Teaching of the Psalm. Johannes Piscator: This psalm teaches that it is the vocation of the Christian faithful to give public thanks for God's goodness, to celebrate his name and to pray for his protection. Commentary on 1 Chronicles.[29]

The People's Amen. Lucas Osiander: The people said, "Amen," meaning "may it be done." That is, the people totally and enthusiastically approved this praise of God and applied themselves to the celebration of God's name. And whenever the church's ministers recite a psalm in praise of God, the people show their approval of this prayer and praise through this word of agreement. Therefore the Psalms (among other things) should be sung in the language of the people, so that whenever the people hear the sacred songs they can say from their souls: Amen! Annotations on 1 Chronicles.[30]

---

[26]Osiander, *Liber Iosue*, 1128-29.
[27]Osiander, *Liber Iosue*, 1130.
[28]Downame, ed., *Annotations* (1645), OO2v-OO3r*; citing 2 Sam 23:1.
[29]Piscator, *Commentarii in omnes libros Veteris Testamenti*, 2:409.
[30]Osiander, *Liber Iosue*, 1136.

17:1-27 THE PROPHECY OF NATHAN

[1]Now when David lived in his house, David said to Nathan the prophet, "Behold, I dwell in a house of cedar, but the ark of the covenant of the LORD is under a tent." [2]And Nathan said to David, "Do all that is in your heart, for God is with you."

[3]But that same night the word of the LORD came to Nathan, [4]"Go and tell my servant David, 'Thus says the LORD: It is not you who will build me a house to dwell in. [5]For I have not lived in a house since the day I brought up Israel to this day, but I have gone from tent to tent and from dwelling to dwelling. [6]In all places where I have moved with all Israel, did I speak a word with any of the judges of Israel, whom I commanded to shepherd my people, saying, "Why have you not built me a house of cedar?"' [7]Now, therefore, thus shall you say to my servant David, 'Thus says the LORD of hosts, I took you from the pasture, from following the sheep, to be prince over my people Israel, [8]and I have been with you wherever you have gone and have cut off all your enemies from before you. And I will make for you a name, like the name of the great ones of the earth. [9]And I will appoint a place for my people Israel and will plant them, that they may dwell in their own place and be disturbed no more. And violent men shall waste them no more, as formerly, [10]from the time that I appointed judges over my people Israel. And I will subdue all your enemies. Moreover, I declare to you that the LORD will build you a house. [11]When your days are fulfilled to walk with your fathers, I will raise up your offspring after you, one of your own sons, and I will establish his kingdom. [12]He shall build a house for me, and I will establish his throne forever. [13]I will be to him a father, and he shall be to me a son. I will not take my steadfast love from him, as I took it from him who was before you, [14]but I will confirm him in my house and in my kingdom forever, and his throne shall be established forever.'" [15]In accordance with all these words, and in accordance with all this vision, Nathan spoke to David.

[16]Then King David went in and sat before the LORD and said, "Who am I, O LORD God, and what is my house, that you have brought me thus far? [17]And this was a small thing in your eyes, O God. You have also spoken of your servant's house for a great while to come, and have shown me future generations,[a] O LORD God! [18]And what more can David say to you for honoring your servant? For you know your servant. [19]For your servant's sake, O LORD, and according to your own heart, you have done all this greatness, in making known all these great things. [20]There is none like you, O LORD, and there is no God besides you, according to all that we have heard with our ears. [21]And who is like your people Israel, the one[b] nation on earth whom God went to redeem to be his people, making for yourself a name for great and awesome things, in driving out nations before your people whom you redeemed from Egypt? [22]And you made your people Israel to be your people forever, and you, O LORD, became their God. [23]And now, O LORD, let the word that you have spoken concerning your servant and concerning his house be established forever, and do as you have spoken, [24]and your name will be established and magnified forever, saying, 'The LORD of hosts, the God of Israel, is Israel's God,' and the house of your servant David will be established before you. [25]For you, my God, have revealed to your servant that you will build a house for him. Therefore your servant has found courage to pray before you. [26]And now, O LORD, you are God, and you have promised this good thing to your servant. [27]Now you have been pleased to bless the house of your servant, that it may continue forever before you, for it is you, O LORD, who have blessed, and it is blessed forever."

a The meaning of the Hebrew is uncertain   b Septuagint, Vulgate *other*

OVERVIEW: David's motives to build a house for the Lord notwithstanding, the reformers acknowledge that when it comes to the worship of God, divine command is essential. Some muse that the setting of the location of the public worship of God has changed from Old Testament to New Testament times but that it only has done so by fiat of God. The divine promise given to David about his ancestors ruling from the throne draws the attention of these commentators because of the long-standing interpretive tradition that it refers to Jesus Christ.[1]

17:1-9 David's Plans and God's Response

READINESS TO OBEY. JOHN DOD: Although David thought he had a purpose to build the temple, this work was afterward laid on Solomon and performed by him. Yet the Lord gave David a good testimony and a large reward for his readiness to obey. He was content to spare him because he had been at great pains before in shedding the blood of many enemies of the church, and some remained yet still to be subdued by him. Yet God tells him for his comfort: "Whereas it was in your heart to build a house for my name, you did well that it was in your heart." And besides this, God bid Nathan to carry him this message: The Lord would build him a house and would raise up his seed after him, and employ his son in that honorable service of building a house to the name of the Lord, and that would establish his throne forever. THE THIRD SERMON OF THE LORD'S SUPPER.[2]

GOOD INTENTIONS NOT ENOUGH. JOHANNES PISCATOR: We see an example of godliness toward the works of God in King David's desire to build a temple in honor of the true God and in the prophet Nathan's support of it. But God later prohibited David from building of the temple. The reason is that, in the worship of God, a person's good intention is not sufficient. In addition, there must be a command from God. COMMENTARY ON 1 CHRONICLES.[3]

NATHAN SPEAKS PREMATURELY. GENEVA BIBLE: As of yet God had not revealed to Nathan the prophet what he purposed concerning David; as such, knowing that God favored David, Nathan spoke what he thought right at the time. ANNOTATIONS ON 1 CHRONICLES.[4]

PUBLIC WORSHIP IS NOW OUTSIDE OF JERUSALEM. JOHANNES PISCATOR: The public worship of God is to be in conformity to however God wishes his worship to be instituted at any particular time. For instance, in former times the public worship was centered on adoring the sacred tabernacle. However, now public worship is beyond the ark of the covenant and beyond the temple of Solomon. That is, today the public worship of God is not attached to any location at all. COMMENTARY ON 1 CHRONICLES.[5]

FROM DWELLING TO DWELLING. THE ENGLISH ANNOTATIONS: The reference to God's moving from tent to tent and dwelling to dwelling refers to the many places to which the tabernacle, in which the ark was set, was moved. This includes not only the wilderness but other places afterward where it may have been moved. Or it may be taken of the tent that Moses first made for the ark and that which David had pitched. In fact it may be referring to another tent besides those two, which was made for the ark at Kiriath-jearim, where it stayed for twenty years. ANNOTATIONS ON 1 CHRONICLES.[6]

17:10-15 God's Promises of David's House and "Son"

THE TRINITY. MARTIN LUTHER: We find here the three persons of the Godhead: first the Holy

---

[1]See commentary on 2 Sam 7.
[2]Dod, *Ten Sermons*, 97*; citing 1 Kings 8:18.

[3]Piscator, *Commentarii in omnes libros Veteris Testamenti*, 2:412.
[4]*Geneva Bible* (1560), 186r*.
[5]Piscator, *Commentarii in omnes libros Veteris Testamenti*, 2:412; citing Jn 4:21.
[6]Downame, ed., *Annotations* (1645), OO3r*; citing Ex 26:33; 2 Sam 6:17; 7:1, 2.

Spirit, who speaks by the prophet Nathan. . . . And immediately after that he presents the person of the Son, saying "that the Lord will build you a house." And yet it is but one God and Lord who speaks through Nathan, makes an announcement to David and builds his house. All three are but one speaker, one announcer, one builder. TREATISE ON THE LAST WORDS OF DAVID.[7]

REFERRING TO CHRIST AND HIS KINGDOM. JOHANNES PISCATOR: It is to be noted that this is testimony referring to both Christ and to his kingdom. For the person to whom this prophecy relates is a true man. As the passage states, he is the son of David and true God. And such is how Christ is interpreted by the apostle Paul: "For to which of the angels did God ever say, 'You are my Son, today I have begotten you'? Or again, 'I will be to him a father, and he shall be to me a son'"? And as for the kingdom that Christ achieves, it is an everlasting one. COMMENTARY ON 1 CHRONICLES.[8]

EVERLASTING HOUSE. MARTIN LUTHER: Therefore this house, to be built by Messiah, the Son of David and of God . . . is the holy Christian church, which extends to the ends of the earth. Furthermore it is an everlasting house, a house that will endure and live forever, a house in which God remains and lives and keeps house forever. TREATISE ON THE LAST WORDS OF DAVID.[9]

GOD'S CHOICE OF HIS SON. JOHN CALVIN: This shows us that our Lord Jesus Christ was chosen to be the Son of God in order to reconcile humankind with God. For that dignity did not pertain to him in his human nature, since the Son of God was higher than the angelic estate. Hence we must come to the first source, which is that God by his infinite goodness chose to honor him whom he had ordained mediator, and to exalt him to the position of calling him Son. And this also explains why our

Lord Jesus Christ has less power than his Father, that is, in regard to his human nature. Well now, let us note that we are not children of God except insofar as it pleases him to draw us to himself. For we cannot say that any of us by his industry or by his virtue has earned such an excellent right. Therefore it comes only because God has blessed us with his infinite goodness. Hence it is his to initiate. SERMONS ON 2 SAMUEL.[10]

THE OLD TESTAMENT AND CHRIST. MARTIN LUTHER: You may feel tempted to ask here: "If the words of David and Nathan reveal the doctrine of Christ's deity so clearly, how do you explain that neither the holy fathers nor any other teacher discovered or ever mentioned this, and that you recent and young Hebraists just became aware of this now? Why do the Jewish rabbis not discern this?" We reply. . . . To be sure, we too would not be able to see it if we could not look the Old Testament straight in the eye because we are illumined by the New Testament. For the Old Testament is veiled without the New Testament. TREATISE ON THE LAST WORDS OF DAVID.[11]

SOLOMON AS A TYPE OF CHRIST. JOHANNES PISCATOR: When the kingdom of Solomon was diminished after his death and the succession was passed on to Rehoboam, ten of the tribes deserted the kingdom. And in the end even the remaining two tribes were extinguished by King Nebuchadnezzar. The firmness of this kingdom was not able to be recognized at the time, but it was recognized in the kingdom of Christ, of whom Solomon was a type. Indeed, as was said in the Gospel of Luke, "Christ will be great and will be called the Son of the Most High, and the Lord God will give to him the throne of his ancestor David. He will reign over the house of Jacob forever, and of his kingdom there will be no end." COMMENTARY ON 1 CHRONICLES.[12]

---

[7]LW 15:280.
[8]Piscator, *Commentarii in omnes libros Veteris Testamenti*, 2:412; citing Heb 1:5.
[9]LW 15:282.
[10]Calvin, *Sermons on Second Samuel*, 1:333.
[11]LW15:287; citing 2 Cor 4:3-4.
[12]Piscator, *Commentarii in omnes libros Veteris Testamenti*, 2:430; citing Lk 1:32-33.

17:16-27 *David's Prayer*

Following David's Gratitude to God.
Johannes Piscator: David serves as a great
example of giving thanks to God and in accepting
his goodness. David also serves as an example by
praying for God's promises to be accomplished. . . .
And David finally teaches us that we are to rely on
God's promises in strong faith. Commentary on
1 Chronicles.[13]

---

[13]Piscator, *Commentarii in omnes libros Veteris Testamenti*, 2:412.

18:1–20:8 DAVID'S WARS

[1]After this David defeated the Philistines and subdued them, and he took Gath and its villages out of the hand of the Philistines.

[2]And he defeated Moab, and the Moabites became servants to David and brought tribute.

[3]David also defeated Hadadezer king of Zobah-Hamath, as he went to set up his monument[a] at the river Euphrates. [4]And David took from him 1,000 chariots, 7,000 horsemen, and 20,000 foot soldiers. And David hamstrung all the chariot horses, but left enough for 100 chariots. [5]And when the Syrians of Damascus came to help Hadadezer king of Zobah, David struck down 22,000 men of the Syrians. [6]Then David put garrisons[b] in Syria of Damascus, and the Syrians became servants to David and brought tribute. And the LORD gave victory to David[c] wherever he went. [7]And David took the shields of gold that were carried by the servants of Hadadezer and brought them to Jerusalem. [8]And from Tibhath and from Cun, cities of Hadadezer, David took a large amount of bronze. With it Solomon made the bronze sea and the pillars and the vessels of bronze.

[9]When Tou king of Hamath heard that David had defeated the whole army of Hadadezer, king of Zobah, [10]he sent his son Hadoram to King David, to ask about his health and to bless him because he had fought against Hadadezer and defeated him; for Hadadezer had often been at war with Tou. And he sent all sorts of articles of gold, of silver, and of bronze. [11]These also King David dedicated to the LORD, together with the silver and gold that he had carried off from all the nations, from Edom, Moab, the Ammonites, the Philistines, and Amalek.

[12]And Abishai, the son of Zeruiah, killed 18,000 Edomites in the Valley of Salt. [13]Then he put garrisons in Edom, and all the Edomites became David's servants. And the LORD gave victory to David wherever he went.

[14]So David reigned over all Israel, and he administered justice and equity to all his people. [15]And Joab the son of Zeruiah was over the army; and Jehoshaphat the son of Ahilud was recorder; [16]and Zadok the son of Ahitub and Ahimelech the son of Abiathar were priests; and Shavsha was secretary; [17]and Benaiah the son of Jehoiada was over the Cherethites and the Pelethites; and David's sons were the chief officials in the service of the king.

19 Now after this Nahash the king of the Ammonites died, and his son reigned in his place. [2]And David said, "I will deal kindly with Hanun the son of Nahash, for his father dealt kindly with me." So David sent messengers to console him concerning his father. And David's servants came to the land of the Ammonites to Hanun to console him. [3]But the princes of the Ammonites said to Hanun, "Do you think, because David has sent comforters to you, that he is honoring your father? Have not his servants come to you to search and to overthrow and to spy out the land?" [4]So Hanun took David's servants and shaved them and cut off their garments in the middle, at their hips, and sent them away; [5]and they departed. When David was told concerning the men, he sent messengers to meet them, for the men were greatly ashamed. And the king said, "Remain at Jericho until your beards have grown and then return."

[6]When the Ammonites saw that they had become a stench to David, Hanun and the Ammonites sent 1,000 talents[d] of silver to hire chariots and horsemen from Mesopotamia, from Aram-maacah, and from Zobah. [7]They hired 32,000 chariots and the king of Maacah with his army, who came and encamped before Medeba. And the Ammonites were mustered from their cities and came to battle. [8]When David heard of it, he sent Joab and all the army of the mighty men. [9]And the Ammonites came out and drew up in battle array at the entrance of the city, and the kings who had come were by themselves in the open country.

[10]When Joab saw that the battle was set against him both in front and in the rear, he chose some of the best men of Israel and arrayed them against the Syrians. [11]The rest of his men he put in the charge of Abishai his brother, and they were arrayed against the Ammonites. [12]And he said, "If the Syrians are too

strong for me, then you shall help me, but if the Ammonites are too strong for you, then I will help you. ¹³Be strong, and let us use our strength for our people and for the cities of our God, and may the LORD do what seems good to him." ¹⁴So Joab and the people who were with him drew near before the Syrians for battle, and they fled before him. ¹⁵And when the Ammonites saw that the Syrians fled, they likewise fled before Abishai, Joab's brother, and entered the city. Then Joab came to Jerusalem.

¹⁶But when the Syrians saw that they had been defeated by Israel, they sent messengers and brought out the Syrians who were beyond the Euphrates,ᵉ with Shophach the commander of the army of Hadadezer at their head. ¹⁷And when it was told to David, he gathered all Israel together and crossed the Jordan and came to them and drew up his forces against them. And when David set the battle in array against the Syrians, they fought with him. ¹⁸And the Syrians fled before Israel, and David killed of the Syrians the men of 7,000 chariots and 40,000 foot soldiers, and put to death also Shophach the commander of their army. ¹⁹And when the servants of Hadadezer saw that they had been defeated by Israel, they made peace with David and became subject to him. So the Syrians were not willing to save the Ammonites anymore.

20 In the spring of the year, the time when kings go out to battle, Joab led out the army and ravaged the country of the Ammonites and came and besieged Rabbah. But David remained at Jerusalem. And Joab struck down Rabbah and overthrew it. ²And David took the crown of their king from his head. He found that it weighed a talentᶠ of gold, and in it was a precious stone. And it was placed on David's head. And he brought out the spoil of the city, a very great amount. ³And he brought out the people who were in it and set them to laborᵍ with saws and iron picks and axes.ʰ And thus David did to all the cities of the Ammonites. Then David and all the people returned to Jerusalem.

⁴And after this there arose war with the Philistines at Gezer. Then Sibbecai the Hushathite struck down Sippai, who was one of the descendants of the giants, and the Philistines were subdued. ⁵And there was again war with the Philistines, and Elhanan the son of Jair struck down Lahmi the brother of Goliath the Gittite, the shaft of whose spear was like a weaver's beam. ⁶And there was again war at Gath, where there was a man of great stature, who had six fingers on each hand and six toes on each foot, twenty-four in number, and he also was descended from the giants. ⁷And when he taunted Israel, Jonathan the son of Shimea, David's brother, struck him down. ⁸These were descended from the giants in Gath, and they fell by the hand of David and by the hand of his servants.

a Hebrew *hand*   b Septuagint, Vulgate, 2 Samuel 8:6 (compare Syriac); Hebrew lacks *garrisons*   c Hebrew *the LORD saved David*; also verse 13   d A *talent* was about 75 pounds or 34 kilograms   e Hebrew *the River*   f A *talent* was about 75 pounds or 34 kilograms   g Compare 2 Samuel 12:31; Hebrew *he sawed*   h Compare 2 Samuel 12:31; Hebrew *saws*

OVERVIEW: David proves victorious over his foes in this section, prompting the reformers to exhort their audience to remain patient in the presence of suffering. They recognize that evil can prevail over good for long stretches of time, just as was the case in the lifetime of David as he patiently endured trouble at the hands of his enemy. The disgracing of David's messengers among the Ammonites leads these interpreters to applaud David for his bravery and also to admonish us not to jump to conclusions or prejudge situations.[1]

18:1-17 The Victories of David

HIDDEN JUDGMENT. JOHN CALVIN: We must contemplate this story as in a mirror, that if the judgments of God are kept hidden, especially for a long space of time, it is only at the end that they will have their effect. And hence let us learn not to

---

[1]See commentary on 2 Sam 8:1-18; 10:1-19; 12:26-31.

flatter ourselves, but when we have heard a threat from God, to tremble. And on the other hand, if we see that God does not immediately carry out all his judgments on the despisers of his majesty, and that they persecute his poor church, let it not astonish us, as though they had escaped and would remain unpunished. Let us wait (I say) not just for a year or for some short time. And should we not see God punishing them during our lifetime, still at the end their time will come, and they will be called to account. If we did not have these testimonies that are recited here, how agitated we would be with temptation, since we would not perceive that God wants to remedy such great confusions that are in the world today. Much blood has already been poured out and horrible torments have been used against the poor faithful. Fires have been started over and over again. Then when it seemed that God ought to have had pity on his church, all of it has started over again more than ever, and then the devil has been unchained and the rage of the iniquitous more than inflamed. Now things are confused, and no one knows what will be the issue. And humanly speaking, one could only think that there will be infinite miseries. SERMONS ON 2 SAMUEL.[2]

DAVID THE GREAT EXAMPLE. JOHANNES PISCATOR: David is set forth as an example of a victorious, godly, just and wise king. He was an example of a victorious king inasmuch as he achieved four military victories, which were reported in a brief time period from among different enemies. He was an example of godliness inasmuch as he manifested himself as one who was not confident in a multitude of horses for battle and as one who consecrated the precious vessels he confiscated in battle. He was an example of justice inasmuch as his governance was praised as being fair to all. Finally, David was an example of wisdom inasmuch as he had regard for ordering the many different officials in his kingdom. COMMENTARY ON 1 CHRONICLES.[3]

19:1–20:8 *David's Success Continues*

A GOOD ACT FOLLOWED BY AN EVIL ONE. JOHANNES PISCATOR: David's sending off of his legates to the king of Ammonites to console the new king on the death of his father serves as an example of gratitude and humanness. For David remembered the king's father and how good he had been. At the same time, King Hanun's response to David's legates—thinking that David had sent the legates with an evil purpose in mind—sets forth an example of evil suspicion, calumny and foolish incredulity. What's worse, Hanun's action toward David's legates wherein he defiled and ignominiously affronted them serves as an example of petulance, barbarity and harmful injustice, which is to be abhorred according to custom and law. COMMENTARY ON 1 CHRONICLES.[4]

A POISED SPIRIT. JOHN CALVIN: Well, this story should serve as an instructive, exemplary warning against this thoroughly perverse vice of distrust. For the counselors of King Hanun distrusted David, and thereby they were the cause of ruining both their master and the whole country. Hence let us learn not to be influenced by our own malice to put a bad interpretation on what could be taken as good, and if something is done that we could doubt, still let us not do so. When we have to deal with people who are full of disloyalty and treason, it is true that we must stay on our guard and carefully watch so as not to be corrupted. When we conclude out of mere suspicion that "here is someone who only thinks of hurting me, and I do not know what they mean," God will certainly punish us at once for such an attitude. For when our useless manipulation of circumstances inevitably brings us down, God will pay us the wages we deserve. What, therefore, happened to the people of Ammon reminds us to take things in good part, and not to let our spirits be poised with suspicion and distrust when it is not necessary. SERMONS ON 2 SAMUEL.[5]

---

[2]Calvin, *Sermons on Second Samuel*, 1:406-7.
[3]Piscator, *Commentarii in omnes libros Veteris Testamenti*, 2:413.
[4]Piscator, *Commentarii in omnes libros Veteris Testamenti*, 2:415.
[5]Calvin, *Sermons on Second Samuel*, 1:452.

Joab's Example of Religious and Military Firmness. Johannes Piscator: David sets forth an example of prudence and bravery for his action of sending Joab to battle against the Ammonites and the Syrians. And Joab's distribution of his troops into two fronts against his enemies, wherein he and his brother worked together to fight, gives an example of resourcefulness and military experience. Indeed Joab committed the war to God by going into battle himself for the people of God with the best of the troops while leaving the rest with his brother. And he sets forth an example of both bravery and godliness. Commentary on 1 Chronicles.[6]

Not Trusting Material Things. Johannes Piscator: These three giant Philistines who tried to kill the servants of David in battle serve as an example for us. We are warned by these men how vain it is to put faith in the strength of our bodies or in our weapons. Commentary on 1 Chronicles.[7]

---

[6]Piscator, *Commentarii in omnes libros Veteris Testamenti*, 2:415.
[7]Piscator, *Commentarii in omnes libros Veteris Testamenti*, 2:416.

21:1–22:19 DAVID'S CENSUS AND PREPARATION FOR THE TEMPLE

[1]Then Satan stood against Israel and incited David to number Israel. [2]So David said to Joab and the commanders of the army, "Go, number Israel, from Beersheba to Dan, and bring me a report, that I may know their number." [3]But Joab said, "May the LORD add to his people a hundred times as many as they are! Are they not, my lord the king, all of them my lord's servants? Why then should my lord require this? Why should it be a cause of guilt for Israel?" [4]But the king's word prevailed against Joab. So Joab departed and went throughout all Israel and came back to Jerusalem. [5]And Joab gave the sum of the numbering of the people to David. In all Israel there were 1,100,000 men who drew the sword, and in Judah 470,000 who drew the sword. [6]But he did not include Levi and Benjamin in the numbering, for the king's command was abhorrent to Joab.

[7]But God was displeased with this thing, and he struck Israel. [8]And David said to God, "I have sinned greatly in that I have done this thing. But now, please take away the iniquity of your servant, for I have acted very foolishly." [9]And the LORD spoke to Gad, David's seer, saying, [10]"Go and say to David, 'Thus says the LORD, Three things I offer you; choose one of them, that I may do it to you.'" [11]So Gad came to David and said to him, "Thus says the LORD, 'Choose what you will: [12]either three years of famine, or three months of devastation by your foes while the sword of your enemies overtakes you, or else three days of the sword of the LORD, pestilence on the land, with the angel of the LORD destroying throughout all the territory of Israel.' Now decide what answer I shall return to him who sent me." [13]Then David said to Gad, "I am in great distress. Let me fall into the hand of the LORD, for his mercy is very great, but do not let me fall into the hand of man."

[14]So the LORD sent a pestilence on Israel, and 70,000 men of Israel fell. [15]And God sent the angel to Jerusalem to destroy it, but as he was about to destroy it, the LORD saw, and he relented from the calamity.

And he said to the angel who was working destruction, "It is enough; now stay your hand." And the angel of the LORD was standing by the threshing floor of Ornan the Jebusite. [16]And David lifted his eyes and saw the angel of the LORD standing between earth and heaven, and in his hand a drawn sword stretched out over Jerusalem. Then David and the elders, clothed in sackcloth, fell upon their faces. [17]And David said to God, "Was it not I who gave command to number the people? It is I who have sinned and done great evil. But these sheep, what have they done? Please let your hand, O LORD my God, be against me and against my father's house. But do not let the plague be on your people."

[18]Now the angel of the LORD had commanded Gad to say to David that David should go up and raise an altar to the LORD on the threshing floor of Ornan the Jebusite. [19]So David went up at Gad's word, which he had spoken in the name of the LORD. [20]Now Ornan was threshing wheat. He turned and saw the angel, and his four sons who were with him hid themselves. [21]As David came to Ornan, Ornan looked and saw David and went out from the threshing floor and paid homage to David with his face to the ground. [22]And David said to Ornan, "Give me the site of the threshing floor that I may build on it an altar to the LORD—give it to me at its full price—that the plague may be averted from the people." [23]Then Ornan said to David, "Take it, and let my lord the king do what seems good to him. See, I give the oxen for burnt offerings and the threshing sledges for the wood and the wheat for a grain offering; I give it all." [24]But King David said to Ornan, "No, but I will buy them for the full price. I will not take for the LORD what is yours, nor offer burnt offerings that cost me nothing." [25]So David paid Ornan 600 shekels[a] of gold by weight for the site. [26]And David built there an altar to the LORD and presented burnt offerings and peace offerings and called on the LORD, and the LORD[b] answered him

with fire from heaven upon the altar of burnt offering. ²⁷Then the LORD commanded the angel, and he put his sword back into its sheath.

²⁸At that time, when David saw that the LORD had answered him at the threshing floor of Ornan the Jebusite, he sacrificed there. ²⁹For the tabernacle of the LORD, which Moses had made in the wilderness, and the altar of burnt offering were at that time in the high place at Gibeon, ³⁰but David could not go before it to inquire of God, for he was afraid of the sword of the angel of the LORD.

22 Then David said, "Here shall be the house of the LORD God and here the altar of burnt offering for Israel."

²David commanded to gather together the resident aliens who were in the land of Israel, and he set stonecutters to prepare dressed stones for building the house of God. ³David also provided great quantities of iron for nails for the doors of the gates and for clamps, as well as bronze in quantities beyond weighing, ⁴and cedar timbers without number, for the Sidonians and Tyrians brought great quantities of cedar to David. ⁵For David said, "Solomon my son is young and inexperienced, and the house that is to be built for the LORD must be exceedingly magnificent, of fame and glory throughout all lands. I will therefore make preparation for it." So David provided materials in great quantity before his death.

⁶Then he called for Solomon his son and charged him to build a house for the LORD, the God of Israel. ⁷David said to Solomon, "My son, I had it in my heart to build a house to the name of the LORD my God. ⁸But the word of the LORD came to me, saying, 'You have shed much blood and have waged great wars. You shall not build a house to my name, because you have

shed so much blood before me on the earth. ⁹Behold, a son shall be born to you who shall be a man of rest. I will give him rest from all his surrounding enemies. For his name shall be Solomon, and I will give peace and quiet to Israel in his days. ¹⁰He shall build a house for my name. He shall be my son, and I will be his father, and I will establish his royal throne in Israel forever.'

¹¹"Now, my son, the LORD be with you, so that you may succeed in building the house of the LORD your God, as he has spoken concerning you. ¹²Only, may the LORD grant you discretion and understanding, that when he gives you charge over Israel you may keep the law of the LORD your God. ¹³Then you will prosper if you are careful to observe the statutes and the rules that the LORD commanded Moses for Israel. Be strong and courageous. Fear not; do not be dismayed. ¹⁴With great pains I have provided for the house of the LORD 100,000 talentsᶜ of gold, a million talents of silver, and bronze and iron beyond weighing, for there is so much of it; timber and stone, too, I have provided. To these you must add. ¹⁵You have an abundance of workmen: stonecutters, masons, carpenters, and all kinds of craftsmen without number, skilled in working ¹⁶gold, silver, bronze, and iron. Arise and work! The LORD be with you!"

¹⁷David also commanded all the leaders of Israel to help Solomon his son, saying, ¹⁸"Is not the LORD your God with you? And has he not given you peace on every side? For he has delivered the inhabitants of the land into my hand, and the land is subdued before the LORD and his people. ¹⁹Now set your mind and heart to seek the LORD your God. Arise and build the sanctuary of the LORD God, so that the ark of the covenant of the LORD and the holy vessels of God may be brought into a house built for the name of the LORD."

a A *shekel* was about 2/5 ounce or 11 grams   **b** Hebrew *he*   **c** A *talent* was about 75 pounds or 34 kilograms

OVERVIEW: The passage recounting David's census of Israel has long intrigued interpreters. The main point of interest has to do with the opening line in this chapter. These commentators confront the tension between 1 Chronicles 21:1 ("Satan stood against Israel and incited David to number Israel")

and 2 Samuel 24:1 ("the anger of the Lord was kindled against Israel, and he incited David against them, saying, 'Go, number Israel and Judah'"). In short this means clarifying how much influence Satan has in this world and explaining whether God can tempt anyone to sin. David's punishment from God leads these interpreters to contemplate how sin is dealt with or removed in a believer's life. David's decision to build a house for the Lord, though noble and pious, was rejected because he was a man of war. The commentators do not read this as a rebuke. Living in a day and age when church and state often cooperated, many reformers took for granted that God had ordered and approved the blood David had spilled.[1]

21:1-6 David Takes a Census

SATAN'S WORK. LUCAS OSIANDER: "Satan stood against Israel"; that is, Satan went before God to accuse the people of Israel of their many sins. He demanded that God—for the sake of God's righteousness   punish their wickedness. Thus the work of Satan himself was used in the execution of divine righteousness. For the devil always fights against the people of God, as is clearly said of Satan in Revelation 12: "The accuser of our brothers has been thrown down, who accuses them day and night before our God." But because God is stirred up to righteous vengeance against the people's sins, God occasionally allows Satan to devise imposing punishments. And so Satan, using the cunning that belongs to him, then arrives to incite and stir up disaster. ANNOTATIONS ON 1 CHRONICLES.[2]

SATAN WORKS THROUGH PEOPLE. LAMBERT DANEAU: Satan can do nothing but by natural means and causes. For whatsoever he does either by himself or by his magicians and sorcerers, it is altogether either illusion of their minds and eyes or only the true effect of natural causes. As for any other thing or something that is of more force, he cannot do it. DIALOGUE OF WITCHES.[3]

SATAN AND THE CENSUS. HENRY AINSWORTH: Properly speaking, God does not tempt humankind to evil. Rather, temptation comes from either

the devil or humankind's evil desires. . . . At the same time, God does allow people's minds to be moved toward evil through the power of Satan. ANNOTATIONS ON PSALMS.[4]

THE DEVIL WITHIN. ROBERT SANDERSON: David derived his evil from himself. Indeed we might have some plea if God were silent when the devil tempts us. But God exhorts always: Why do we not then listen to him? If we did this, we should not be deceived. We must cleanse our hearts of hypocrisy, and then we shall not be so deceived. This should teach us that we must constantly take heed of our thoughts. So I fight, St. Paul says, not "as one beating the air. But I discipline my body and keep it under control." When, therefore, your heart suggests evil, cry out to your heart, "I command you to be subject to God's commands." If we do this, we shall not fail. NOTES OF SERMONS.[5]

SUGARED HABITS. HENRY AIRAY: Now, the enemies with which we have to fight are the world outside us, the flesh within us and the devil seeking continually like a roaring lion to devour us. None of these lacks will, skill or power to overthrow us—unless we hold fast to the rejoicing of our hope to the end. The flesh has so many sugared habits and deceitful delights to allure people to their enticements that sometimes the Davids of the world . . . cannot endure their snares but are entangled by them. . . . These are the enemies with which we have to fight—and those we shall have to fight with so long as we live in this flesh. LECTURES ON PHILIPPIANS.[6]

21:7-17 Judgment from God

GOD'S GRACE TOWARD THE ELECT. JOHANNES PISCATOR: David recognized his sin and candidly confessed it before God. He also humbly submitted to God's punishment and attempted to avert the disaster he had caused, just as he had done

---

[1] See commentary on 2 Sam 24:1-25.
[2] Osiander, *Liber Iosue*, 1156; citing Rev 12:10.
[3] Daneau, *Dialogue of Witches*, I2v*.

[4] Ainsworth, *Annotations on the Psalms*, 281*.
[5] Sanderson, *Works*, 3:362*; citing 1 Cor 9:26-27.
[6] Airay, *Lectures on Philippians*, 185*.

formerly with his family. David's actions set forth an example of godliness as well as God's grace for the elect. For God surely allows the elect to do as they wish, but God lifts them up again after they fall into sin and God leads them into repentance. Commentary on 1 Chronicles.[7]

On Temporal Punishment. John Davenant: Those who are reconciled to God remain still, after the remission of their guilt, bound to make satisfaction for the remission of the temporal punishment they have deserved; and this we see proved by many convincing examples in the Scriptures. . . . After God had forgiven David the sin of numbering the people, he nevertheless punished him by sending a pestilence to lay waste the kingdom. From this sort of expression the papists conclude that the divine justice exacts satisfaction from us for the ends of punishment, after the forgiveness of the guilt itself; and then they add of themselves that this satisfaction may be fully made, not only by our own sufferings and merits, but also by those that are dealt out at the pope's pleasure, from the common treasury.

In answer to all this: I admit that the faithful do experience much chastisement at the hand of God after he has forgiven their guilt; but I deny that the intention of these chastisements is to satisfy divine justice. Although God absolves all true penitents from all satisfaction by punishment, for the sake of Christ's death, he does not excuse them from all salutary and chastening visitations. Exposition of Colossians.[8]

21:18–22:1 David Buys the Threshing Floor of Ornan

The Site of the Temple. Lucas Osiander: The prophet David saw that God had sent down divine fire to light his sacrifice on the altar that he had built on the field of Ornan, in the same way as God had done at the first holy tabernacle in the

wilderness. He knew from Moses' writings that the Lord himself would choose the place on which to build the temple. He also already had the promise that Solomon would build the temple in Jerusalem. Finally, he had learned through a revelation of the Holy Spirit the place where God commanded sacrifice to be made in order to end the plague that had come. He knew this to be the divine plan for where the temple should be built. Annotations on 1 Chronicles.[9]

Location of the Temple. Heinrich Bullinger: Now the temple of the Lord, to be sure, was prepared by David but built by Solomon. The intended location of the temple was given to David by an angel. It is where David first made a sacrifice and also added these words: "The house of the Lord God is to be here, and also the altar of burnt offering for Israel." It is as if he said, "This area is designated for the temple; in this area the house of God will be built. Indeed it is in this area where the only and eternally efficacious sacrifice, by means of the very Son of God made flesh, will be offered." For all the interpreters of the sacred Scriptures here consent that the place was Jerusalem, on Mount Moriah, where Abraham sacrificed his son Isaac. And in this fateful location the temple was placed, where the hill of Golgotha, or Calvary, was not far away. The holy Gospels testify that on top of Mount Moriah, the place of the holy hill, Christ was sacrificed for the sins of the entire world. Now, in Christ all the sacrifices, both of the temple and of the ancients, were prefigured. The use and purpose of the temple was none other than the use and purpose of the tabernacle beforehand. Decades 3.5.[10]

22:2-7 David Prepares for the Construction of the Temple

David the Master Builder. Viktorin Strigel: David imitates the wisdom of master builders who first ponder what the building material

---

[7]Piscator, *Commentarii in omnes libros Veteris Testamenti*, 2:419.
[8]Davenant, *Exposition of Colossians*, 2:288-89.

[9]Osiander, *Liber Iosue*, 1164.
[10]Bullinger, *Sermonum decades quinque*, 150.

will be, then they depict the concept of the work. The building material is a heap of wood, stones and metals. The form is the order or arrangement and connection of every single part. So here David ponders the building material. And below in chapter 29 he shows the form or concept to his son Solomon. Now David is motivated by this reason: to provide the building material necessary for the building. It should be considered as an analogy of activity and patience. "My son Solomon is still at a tender age, and is not yet fit for such massive projects." For Solomon succeeded his father when he was about twenty years old. "Therefore, to my successor I leave behind not only my concept of the future work but also the proper building materials and enough of them." Book of 1 Chronicles.[11]

Raising the Next Generation. Lucas Osiander: David's eagerness to prepare the way for Solomon is greatly worthy of praise. Here he exemplifies the godly office of being a pious parent, who—when the task [of building the temple] was not given to him—began teaching the gospel for the building up of the church of God. That is what such parents bestow on their children who study theology, for they will become supports and treasures of the church. In any case it is certainly good to educate our children in the knowledge of God, so that they might be "living stones in the temple of God." Annotations on 1 Chronicles.[12]

David's Godly Example. Johannes Piscator: David's desire to build the temple sets forth an example of a godly king, which all leading officials should imitate. David also sets forth an example of a godly father, which all parents and leaders should imitate. For before his death David prepared materials for his young son Solomon to build the temple. David also taught Solomon God's commandments and the promise from God about it. David also exhorted Solomon on the construction of the temple, and he wished Solo-

mon prudence in carrying forth with the work. Commentary on 1 Chronicles.[13]

David Prepares Solomon. John Mayer: This wonderful and great treasure, which David had now gathered together, shows how easily God can enrich those whom he pleases. For those who seek his kingdom and the righteousness of it God adds all other things in this world. . . . David prepared Solomon thoroughly so that he would both have materials and workmen and that, after David's death, Solomon might set up this great work and perfect it without any delay. David wanted, as God had directed him, both materials and workmen who were resourced well so that this building would excel all others. The plan was that, by the outward beauty of the temple alone, ungodly people might be drawn from the temples of idols and the high places to worship there. Commentary on Chronicles.[14]

Words Too Great for Solomon. Viktorin Strigel: Since the building material for the work is ready, David calls his son and successor Solomon, and gives him instructions concerning the building of the temple. And lest he seem to follow human reasoning, he urges the clear word of God that expressly commands that the son of David and indeed Solomon should build the house of the Lord. Now since Solomon would reign only forty years and his son Rehoboam would lose ten tribes, these words, which promise the perpetual stability of the royal throne over Israel, cannot be understood about Solomon. Therefore it is necessary to understand these words about the true Solomon, that is, about Christ, whose reign is not limited by any temporal boundary. This interpretation the angel confirms in Luke 1: "He will be great and will be called the Son of the Most High. And the Lord God will give to him the throne of his father David, and he will reign over the house of Jacob forever, and of his kingdom there will be no end." For all

---

[11]Strigel, *Libri Samuelis, Regum et Paralipomenon,* 473.
[12]Osiander, *Liber Iosue,* 1166; citing Eph 2:21; 1 Pet 2:25.
[13]Piscator, *Commentarii in omnes libros Veteris Testamenti,* 2:421.
[14]Mayer, *Many Commentaries in One,* 7*.

other kingdoms come to an end, as Daniel teaches in chapters 2 and 7. But this kingdom will endure for all eternity, which has now been begun through the gospel and the Holy Spirit, and will be brought to completion when God will be all in all. Book of 1 Chronicles.[15]

22:8-19 David and Solomon Compared

Solomon as a Type of Christ Reigning in Heaven. Giovanni Diodati: This passage is not to mean that God condemned David's just and necessary wars, which God commanded, approved and blessed. Instead this passage about bloodshed merely means that David had been continually employed in war and that his work was meant to get a firm and durable peace for the people. And Solomon was being called to regulate and sanctify that peace with piety and religion. David, in other words, took pains to establish peace abroad, while Solomon did so at home. This passage is also intended to show the singular sanctity that was required in the work of building and consecrating the temple, the type of work that is not suitable for a soldier. Mostly, though, this passage is meant to show that the temple was a sacred figure of the state of glory and peace of the church gathered up into heaven. As such it was meant to be built by Solomon, who was the type of Christ reigning in heaven in perpetual peace. For David was a type of Christ who waged combat in this world. Annotations on 1 Chronicles.[16]

David's Violence, Solomon's Peace. Lucas Osiander: The Lord told David, "It is not fitting for you to build my temple, because your hand has shed much human blood in war. Although you did not do this without a proper call, nevertheless the

one who is to build my temple should be a man of peace and not a hardened warrior." In this matter he should be a figure of Christ, the "Prince of Peace." "For in itself it is inhumane to be a man of violence, even if you could often do it without sin. Still, you are truly a man of violence. Therefore it will not be fitting for you to build my temple." Despite this, David was not condemned as a magistrate before God when such events happened because of a command from the fount of supplication or when many enemies were killed by his hand in a just war. For "he is God's servant," and "he does not bear the sword in vain." "But your son who will be born to you" (whom the Lord calls "my son") "will be a man of rest"; that is, he will not wage war. Annotations on 1 Chronicles.[17]

Person of Peace Making Peace. The English Annotations: It is implied that while a war may be just—and the just execution of a criminal for committing a capital crime is lawful— the shedding of blood indefinitely is, on God's account, a strange work. It is also implied that a person of war who sheds much blood is not, in this respect, a fit type of him who "is our peace." Rather, the one who is the chief builder of the Christian church should be a person of peace making peace. Therefore Solomon, whose name means "peaceable," was a fit type of the "Prince of Peace," who was more fit to build so fair and wonderful a house as the temple was. Annotations on 1 Chronicles.[18]

Divine Architect. Martin Luther: Just as David once left behind all the means with which Solomon was to build the temple, so Christ has left behind the Gospel and other writings, in order that the church might be built by means of them, not by human decrees. Lectures on Galatians.[19]

---

[15]Strigel, *Libri Samuelis, Regum et Paralipomenon*, 473; citing Lk 1:32-33; 1 Cor 15:28.
[16]Diodati, *Pious Annotations*, 37*.
[17]Osiander, *Liber Iosue*, 1166-67; citing Is 9:6; Rom 13:4.
[18]Downame, ed., *Annotations* (1645), OO3v*; citing 2 Sam 7:9; Is 28:21; Eph 2:14.
[19]LW 27:165.

23:1–25:31 DIVISION OF LEVITES, PRIESTS AND MUSICIANS

¹When David was old and full of days, he made Solomon his son king over Israel.

²David^a assembled all the leaders of Israel and the priests and the Levites. ³The Levites, thirty years old and upward, were numbered, and the total was 38,000 men. ⁴"Twenty-four thousand of these," David said,^b "shall have charge of the work in the house of the Lord, 6,000 shall be officers and judges, ⁵4,000 gatekeepers, and 4,000 shall offer praises to the Lord with the instruments that I have made for praise." ⁶And David organized them in divisions corresponding to the sons of Levi: Gershon, Kohath, and Merari.

⁷The sons of Gershon^c were Ladan and Shimei. ⁸The sons of Ladan: Jehiel the chief, and Zetham, and Joel, three. ⁹The sons of Shimei: Shelomoth, Haziel, and Haran, three. These were the heads of the fathers' houses of Ladan. ¹⁰And the sons of Shimei: Jahath, Zina, and Jeush and Beriah. These four were the sons of Shimei. ¹¹Jahath was the chief, and Zizah the second; but Jeush and Beriah did not have many sons, therefore they became counted as a single father's house.

¹²The sons of Kohath: Amram, Izhar, Hebron, and Uzziel, four. ¹³The sons of Amram: Aaron and Moses. Aaron was set apart to dedicate the most holy things, that he and his sons forever should make offerings before the Lord and minister to him and pronounce blessings in his name forever. ¹⁴But the sons of Moses the man of God were named among the tribe of Levi. ¹⁵The sons of Moses: Gershom and Eliezer. ¹⁶The sons of Gershom: Shebuel the chief. ¹⁷The sons of Eliezer: Rehabiah the chief. Eliezer had no other sons, but the sons of Rehabiah were very many. ¹⁸The sons of Izhar: Shelomith the chief. ¹⁹The sons of Hebron: Jeriah the chief, Amariah the second, Jahaziel the third, and Jekameam the fourth. ²⁰The sons of Uzziel: Micah the chief and Isshiah the second.

²¹The sons of Merari: Mahli and Mushi. The sons of Mahli: Eleazar and Kish. ²²Eleazar died having no sons, but only daughters; their kinsmen, the sons of Kish, married them. ²³The sons of Mushi: Mahli, Eder, and Jeremoth, three.

²⁴These were the sons of Levi by their fathers' houses, the heads of fathers' houses as they were listed according to the number of the names of the individuals from twenty years old and upward who were to do the work for the service of the house of the Lord. ²⁵For David said, "The Lord, the God of Israel, has given rest to his people, and he dwells in Jerusalem forever. ²⁶And so the Levites no longer need to carry the tabernacle or any of the things for its service." ²⁷For by the last words of David the sons of Levi were numbered from twenty years old and upward. ²⁸For their duty was to assist the sons of Aaron for the service of the house of the Lord, having the care of the courts and the chambers, the cleansing of all that is holy, and any work for the service of the house of God. ²⁹Their duty was also to assist with the showbread, the flour for the grain offering, the wafers of unleavened bread, the baked offering, the offering mixed with oil, and all measures of quantity or size. ³⁰And they were to stand every morning, thanking and praising the Lord, and likewise at evening, ³¹and whenever burnt offerings were offered to the Lord on Sabbaths, new moons, and feast days, according to the number required of them, regularly before the Lord. ³²Thus they were to keep charge of the tent of meeting and the sanctuary, and to attend the sons of Aaron, their brothers, for the service of the house of the Lord.

24 The divisions of the sons of Aaron were these. The sons of Aaron: Nadab, Abihu, Eleazar, and Ithamar. ²But Nadab and Abihu died before their father and had no children, so Eleazar and Ithamar became the priests. ³With the help of Zadok of the sons of Eleazar, and Ahimelech of the sons of Ithamar, David organized them according to the appointed duties in their service. ⁴Since more chief men were found among the sons of Eleazar than among the sons of Ithamar, they organized them under sixteen heads of fathers' houses of the sons of Eleazar, and eight of the sons of Ithamar. ⁵They divided them by lot, all alike, for there were sacred officers and officers of God among both the sons of Eleazar and the sons of Ithamar. ⁶And the scribe Shemaiah, the son of Nethanel, a Levite, recorded them in the presence of the king and the princes and Zadok the priest and Ahimelech the son of Abiathar and the heads of the fathers' houses of the priests and of the Levites, one father's house being chosen for Eleazar and one chosen for Ithamar.

⁷The first lot fell to Jehoiarib, the second to Jedaiah, ⁸the third to Harim, the fourth to Seorim, ⁹the fifth to Malchijah, the sixth to Mijamin, ¹⁰the seventh to Hakkoz, the eighth to Abijah, ¹¹the ninth to Jeshua, the tenth to Shecaniah, ¹²the eleventh to Eliashib, the twelfth to Jakim, ¹³the thirteenth to Huppah, the fourteenth to Jeshebeab, ¹⁴the fifteenth to Bilgah, the sixteenth to Immer, ¹⁵the seventeenth to Hezir, the eighteenth to Happizzez, ¹⁶the nineteenth to Pethahiah, the twentieth to Jehezkel, ¹⁷the twenty-first to Jachin, the twenty-second to Gamul, ¹⁸the twenty-third to Delaiah, the twenty-fourth to Maaziah. ¹⁹These had as their appointed duty in their service to come into the house of the LORD according to the procedure established for them by Aaron their father, as the LORD God of Israel had commanded him.

²⁰And of the rest of the sons of Levi: of the sons of Amram, Shubael; of the sons of Shubael, Jehdeiah. ²¹Of Rehabiah: of the sons of Rehabiah, Isshiah the chief. ²²Of the Izharites, Shelomoth; of the sons of Shelomoth, Jahath. ²³The sons of Hebron:ᵈ Jeriah the chief,ᶜ Amariah the second, Jahaziel the third, Jekameam the fourth. ²⁴The sons of Uzziel, Micah; of the sons of Micah, Shamir. ²⁵The brother of Micah, Isshiah; of the sons of Isshiah, Zechariah. ²⁶The sons of Merari: Mahli and Mushi. The sons of Jaaziah: Beno.ᶠ ²⁷The sons of Merari: of Jaaziah, Beno, Shoham, Zaccur, and Ibri. ²⁸Of Mahli: Eleazar, who had no sons. ²⁹Of Kish, the sons of Kish: Jerahmeel. ³⁰The sons of Mushi: Mahli, Eder, and Jerimoth. These were the sons of the Levites according to their fathers' houses. ³¹These also, the head of each father's house and his younger brother alike, cast lots, just as their brothers the sons of Aaron, in the presence of King David, Zadok, Ahimelech, and the heads of fathers' houses of the priests and of the Levites.

25 David and the chiefs of the service also set apart for the service the sons of Asaph, and of Heman, and of Jeduthun, who prophesied with lyres, with harps, and with cymbals. The list of those who did the work and of their duties was: ²Of the sons of Asaph: Zaccur, Joseph, Nethaniah, and Asharelah, sons of Asaph, under the direction of Asaph, who prophesied under the direction of the king. ³Of Jeduthun, the sons of Jeduthun: Gedaliah, Zeri, Jeshaiah, Shimei,ᵍ Hashabiah, and Mattithiah, six, under the direction of their father Jeduthun, who prophesied with the lyre in thanksgiving and praise to the LORD. ⁴Of Heman, the sons of Heman: Bukkiah, Mattaniah, Uzziel, Shebuel and Jerimoth, Hananiah, Hanani, Eliathah, Giddalti, and Romamti-ezer, Joshbekashah, Mallothi, Hothir, Mahazioth. ⁵All these were the sons of Heman the king's seer, according to the promise of God to exalt him, for God had given Heman fourteen sons and three daughters. ⁶They were all under the direction of their father in the music in the house of the LORD with cymbals, harps, and lyres for the service of the house of God. Asaph, Jeduthun, and Heman were under the order of the king. ⁷The number of them along with their brothers, who were trained in singing to the LORD, all who were skillful, was 288. ⁸And they cast lots for their duties, small and great, teacher and pupil alike.

⁹The first lot fell for Asaph to Joseph; the second to Gedaliah, to him and his brothers and his sons, twelve; ¹⁰the third to Zaccur, his sons and his brothers, twelve; ¹¹the fourth to Izri, his sons and his brothers, twelve; ¹²the fifth to Nethaniah, his sons and his brothers, twelve; ¹³the sixth to Bukkiah, his sons and his brothers, twelve; ¹⁴the seventh to Jesharelah, his sons and his brothers, twelve; ¹⁵the eighth to Jeshaiah, his sons and his brothers, twelve; ¹⁶the ninth to Mattaniah, his sons and his brothers, twelve; ¹⁷the tenth to Shimei, his sons and his brothers, twelve; ¹⁸the eleventh to Azarel, his sons and his brothers, twelve; ¹⁹the twelfth to Hashabiah, his sons and his brothers, twelve; ²⁰to the thirteenth, Shubael, his sons and his brothers, twelve; ²¹to the fourteenth, Mattithiah, his sons and his brothers, twelve; ²²to the fifteenth, to Jeremoth, his sons and his brothers, twelve; ²³to the sixteenth, to Hananiah, his sons and his brothers, twelve; ²⁴to the seventeenth, to Joshbekashah, his sons and his brothers, twelve; ²⁵to the eighteenth, to Hanani, his sons and his brothers,

twelve; [26]*to the nineteenth, to Mallothi, his sons and his brothers, twelve;* [27]*to the twentieth, to Eliathah, his sons and his brothers, twelve;* [28]*to the twenty-first, to Hothir, his sons and his brothers, twelve;* [29]*to the*

twenty-second, to Giddalti, his sons and his brothers, twelve; [30]*to the twenty-third, to Mahazioth, his sons and his brothers, twelve;* [31]*to the twenty-fourth, to Romamti-ezer, his sons and his brothers, twelve.*

a Hebrew *He*   b Hebrew lacks *David said*   c Vulgate (compare Septuagint, Syriac); Hebrew *to the Gershonite*   d Compare 23:19; Hebrew lacks *Hebron*   e Compare 23:19; Hebrew lacks *the chief*   f Or *his son*; also verse 27   g One Hebrew manuscript, Septuagint; most Hebrew manuscripts lack *Shimei*

OVERVIEW: Unlike most of the previous sections, this one is unique to Chronicles. These commentators disagree about the implications of David's actions for their own context. Some applaud David's effort to bring about an alliance between church and state; others do not find David's involvement in religious matters as binding in matters of the church since David lived before the dispensation of Christ. Nevertheless, our interpreters generally approve of David's organization of the Levites, priests and musicians.

23:1-32 David Establishes the Rules for the Levites

PROVIDING FOR THE FUTURE. LUCAS OSIANDER: David assembled all the leaders of Israel and the priests and the Levites in order to arrange things with certain people before the end of his life and to set up good order for the use of the church and tranquility in the republic. Therefore, before he passed from this life, he called an assembly for the kingdom. That is, he held a kind of congress. For this is how matters of church and state are properly handled. First, he had to arrange all the matters of the church. To that end he provided for how many Levites there should be to serve in or around the temple across the generations, separating them into their families. Then he assigned his officers from members of these groups. The text then lists the heads of each house who were at least twenty years old, before proceeding to describe matters of state. In the same way the assembly was concluded with the handling of ecclesiastical affairs. In an imperial congress still today, religious matters usually come first, before temporal matters are brought up for

the care of the body politic. ANNOTATIONS ON 1 CHRONICLES.[1]

A NEW ORDER OF MINISTERS. JOHANNES PISCATOR: It may be asked whether the way David distributed the holy Levites in this passage can be used to defend the current practice of some churches to order their priests. I respond that it is not. The reason is because the ministry of the Levites pertained to the shadow of the Old Testament to prefigure the sacrifice of Christ. But now that Christ has made his offering, the shadow has been abolished. What's more, in the New Testament Christ has instituted new orders for ministers: "And Christ gave the apostles, the prophets, the evangelists, the pastors and teachers." COMMENTARY ON 1 CHRONICLES.[2]

MUSIC TO DROWN OUT THE BUTCHERING AND DRESSING OF MEAT. JOHN MAYER: Regarding the four thousand singers, it is said later that they would stand morning and evening to sing praises to God at the times of sacrificing, including on the sabbaths and on the new moons. They also were to play instruments of music, and they were divided by their courses, which were twenty-four in number. This singing and use of music while the sacrifices were being offered was to stir up people's minds to praise God and to give grace to this part of God's worship, which otherwise might have seemed to have been a mere butchering and dressing of meats. COMMENTARY ON CHRONICLES.[3]

---

[1]Osiander, *Liber Iosue*, 1170.
[2]Piscator, *Commentarii in omnes libros Veteris Testamenti*, 2:421; citing Eph 4:11.
[3]Mayer, *Many Commentaries in One*, 8*.

Five Sorts of Levites. John Mayer: Here five sorts of Levites are set forth: ministers, judges and rulers, porters, singers and priests who serve around the temple. The church of Rome seeks to imitate these five roles. They order their ranks in these seven ways, according to Nicholas of Lyra: first, priests who offer the bread and wine in the sacrament; second, deacons who carry the sacraments to the people; third, subdeacons who prepare the sacraments by putting them into the holy vessels; fourth, acolytes who make it; fifth, exorcists who cast out evil spirits, as judges do criminals; sixth, doorkeepers who keep out unbelievers and excommunicate persons from the church; and, seventh, readers. However, in the New Testament we read only of priests and deacons. Commentary on Chronicles.[4]

24:1-31 *Division of the Priests*

The Organization of the Priests. John Mayer: Given that the Levites had previously been distinguished into ministers, judges, porters and singers and that those who ministers about the sacrifices, twenty-four thousand in number were discussed, this chapter now turns to showing how the priests were more particularly distinguished. It also discusses some principal Levites who were next in honor to the priests in general and over all the rest. The priests were distinguished by Eleazar and Ithamar, the two sons of Aaron, the eldest of each family being from generation to generation the head of all the priests of that family. And at this present time Zadok was the head of Eleazar just as Abiathar (or Abimelech, for one and the same man was set forth by both of these men) was the head of Ithamar. Now because there were many more in the family of Eleazar than of Ithamar, the former had sixteen courses while the later only had eight. And the names of the head of every one of these courses are set down. It is left to be understood that all the other priests served in their courses under them, a similar number being assigned to each one in his course to assist him in the execution of his priestly office. And the understanding was still that they only were appointed to serve in the courses of those of the family of Eleazar. And the same is true of the courses of the family of Ithamar who were of his family. Regarding the means used to distinguish these courses who should have the first, who the second, etc., it is said to have been done by lots. The names of all the heads of their houses were written in twenty-four pieces of paper and put into one vessel by themselves. And the courses were written on twenty-four papers and put into another vessel; then they were shaken together. One was appointed to put one hand into one vessel and to draw a name without seeing it, and another was to do the same in the other vessel. Whoever's course was drawn was to serve for one week. Commentary on Chronicles.[5]

Extinction by God. Johannes Piscator: The two sons of Aaron, Nadab and Abihu, had their lights extinguished by God. The reason was because they offered a strange fire in the holy tabernacle. For this reason they serve as an example of divine punishment for those who violate the rightful and established worship of God. Commentary on 1 Chronicles.[6]

Casting Lots Acceptable Today. Johannes Piscator: David established the priests and the Levites according to lot. This shows us that it is a legitimate practice to moderately employ the casting of lots concerning important matters. However, the practice of casting lots is abused when it is used for matters concerning leisure or sport. Commentary on 1 Chronicles.[7]

Of the Division of Abijah. Lucas Osiander: The eighth division fell to Abijah. From this division came Zechariah, the father of John the Baptist (Luke 1), for in the seventh month it was

---

[4]Mayer, *Many Commentaries in One*, 8*.

[5]Mayer, *Many Commentaries in One*, 8*.
[6]Piscator, *Commentarii in omnes libros Veteris Testamenti*, 2:424.
[7]Piscator, *Commentarii in omnes libros Veteris Testamenti*, 2:424.

the time for the eighth division to preside over the priesthood. ANNOTATIONS ON 1 CHRONICLES.[8]

25:1-31 *Division of the Musicians*

LEADERS IN THEOLOGY AND SACRED MUSIC. LUCAS OSIANDER: The three men Asaph, Heman and Jeduthun were extremely well instructed in theology and had been given the spirit of prophecy, as is testified by the inscriptions of those psalms they composed. Moreover, because these psalmists were chosen by David and the leaders of the army, we are shown that political magistrates are not excluded from the management of ecclesiastical affairs, in contrast to the papal view. For pious governors are counted among the principal members of the church. ANNOTATIONS ON 1 CHRONICLES.[9]

RELIGIOUS SERVICES UNDER DAVID. GIOVANNI DIODATI: It is likely that here the appointment of men from Asaph's family is meant the holy host of those who ministered in the temple according to the frequent use of this word in the law, the heads of which are set down in 1 Chronicles 24:31. The sons of Asaph were yet alive in the time of David. They had been the heads of the musicians, but here the number of them is increased and the order more exactly set down. To prophesy here is to sing and play holy songs in the temple with zeal and fervor, and with motions of the body like to the prophets did. It also refers to using sacred music, to raise up the soul to God in imitation of the prophets. ANNOTATIONS ON 1 CHRONICLES.[10]

A MARRIED PRIESTHOOD. LUCAS OSIANDER: God gave Heman fourteen sons and three daughters. Therefore it is not unbecoming of a theologian to have a wife and produce children. The children of Asaph, Jeduthun and Heman were also called to

the holy office in the temple. Without a doubt they had been examined, instructed and installed by their parents. They were taught the ministry of the church and how to attend to educating their children (if the children's character warranted such instruction) so that they too might serve the church faithfully and usefully in their time. ANNOTATIONS ON 1 CHRONICLES.[11]

MUSIC AS A SACRIFICE TO GOD. JOHN MAYER: Here follows the distinction of the Levites, who were to serve in the temple by singing and playing instruments of music. The chief fathers of the Levites were Asaph, Jeduthun and Heman, who came of the three sons of Levi: Heman came from Kohath, Asaph from Gershom and Jeduthun from Merari. . . . Of these Levites some were so famous for their wisdom—including Ethan and Heman—that they were spoken of as rivaling even the wisdom of Solomon. The sons of these three were twenty-four, according to which number the courses of the singing Levites were distinguished just as the priests were. And these twenty-four were appointed to be the chief in one course and another in another, etc. This was so that the first course came in and went out with the first course of the priests, and likewise for the others in their orders. The chief of these both directed the rest and, by the Spirit, composed some divine songs to be sung to the praise of God. The chief priests were said to be 288, that is, 12 to every course of the 24, for 24 times 12 makes 288. Now for the use of singing and making music in the temple, it was to stir up people's minds to praise God. And when they sang and played music, a sacrifice of praise was offered to God. COMMENTARY ON CHRONICLES[12]

REGARDING SINGING IN CHRISTIAN CHURCHES. JOHANNES PISCATOR: The use of sacred music was instituted by David for the ceremonial worship of God in the Old Testament. However, for the faithful of the New Testament,

---

[8]Osiander, *Liber Iosue*, 1178.
[9]Osiander, *Liber Iosue*, 1180.
[10]Diodati, *Pious Annotations*, 38*.

[11]Osiander, *Liber Iosue*, 1181.
[12]Mayer, *Many Commentaries in One*, 10*.

there is neither an obligation of nor a restriction against the use of music for public worship. At the same time, though, there are passages in the New Testament that mention singing, which are supported and taught by Paul. Besides passages like Ephesians 5:19 and Colossians 3:16, Paul writes the following: "What am I to do? I will pray with my spirit, but I will pray with my mind also; I will sing praise with my spirit, but I will sing with my mind also." COMMENTARY ON 1 CHRONICLES.[13]

---

[13]Piscator, *Commentarii in omnes libros Veteris Testamenti*, 2:425; citing 1 Cor 14:15.

26:1–27:34 DIVISION OF GATEKEEPERS, OFFICERS AND OFFICIALS

¹As for the divisions of the gatekeepers: of the Korahites, Meshelemiah the son of Kore, of the sons of Asaph. ²And Meshelemiah had sons: Zechariah the firstborn, Jediael the second, Zebadiah the third, Jathniel the fourth, ³Elam the fifth, Jehohanan the sixth, Eliehoenai the seventh. ⁴And Obed-edom had sons: Shemaiah the firstborn, Jehozabad the second, Joah the third, Sachar the fourth, Nethanel the fifth, ⁵Ammiel the sixth, Issachar the seventh, Peullethai the eighth, for God blessed him. ⁶Also to his son Shemaiah were sons born who were rulers in their fathers' houses, for they were men of great ability. ⁷The sons of Shemaiah: Othni, Rephael, Obed and Elzabad, whose brothers were able men, Elihu and Semachiah. ⁸All these were of the sons of Obed-edom with their sons and brothers, able men qualified for the service; sixty-two of Obed-edom. ⁹And Meshelemiah had sons and brothers, able men, eighteen. ¹⁰And Hosah, of the sons of Merari, had sons: Shimri the chief (for though he was not the firstborn, his father made him chief), ¹¹Hilkiah the second, Tebaliah the third, Zechariah the fourth: all the sons and brothers of Hosah were thirteen.

¹²These divisions of the gatekeepers, corresponding to their chief men, had duties, just as their brothers did, ministering in the house of the LORD. ¹³And they cast lots by fathers' houses, small and great alike, for their gates. ¹⁴The lot for the east fell to Shelemiah. They cast lots also for his son Zechariah, a shrewd counselor, and his lot came out for the north. ¹⁵Obed-edom's came out for the south, and to his sons was allotted the gatehouse. ¹⁶For Shuppim and Hosah it came out for the west, at the gate of Shallecheth on the road that goes up. Watch corresponded to watch. ¹⁷On the east there were six each day,ᵃ on the north four each day, on the south four each day, as well as two and two at the gatehouse. ¹⁸And for the colonnadeᵇ on the west there were four at the road and two at the colonnade. ¹⁹These were the divisions of the gatekeepers among the Korahites and the sons of Merari.

²⁰And of the Levites, Ahijah had charge of the treasuries of the house of God and the treasuries of the dedicated gifts. ²¹The sons of Ladan, the sons of the Gershonites belonging to Ladan, the heads of the fathers' houses belonging to Ladan the Gershonite: Jehieli.ᶜ ²²The sons of Jehieli, Zetham, and Joel his brother, were in charge of the treasuries of the house of the LORD. ²³Of the Amramites, the Izharites, the Hebronites, and the Uzzielites— ²⁴and Shebuel the son of Gershom, son of Moses, was chief officer in charge of the treasuries. ²⁵His brothers: from Eliezer were his son Rehabiah, and his son Jeshaiah, and his son Joram, and his son Zichri, and his son Shelomoth. ²⁶This Shelomoth and his brothers were in charge of all the treasuries of the dedicated gifts that David the king and the heads of the fathers' houses and the officers of the thousands and the hundreds and the commanders of the army had dedicated. ²⁷From spoil won in battles they dedicated gifts for the maintenance of the house of the LORD. ²⁸Also all that Samuel the seer and Saul the son of Kish and Abner the son of Ner and Joab the son of Zeruiah had dedicated—all dedicated gifts were in the care of Shelomothᵈ and his brothers.

²⁹Of the Izharites, Chenaniah and his sons were appointed to external duties for Israel, as officers and judges. ³⁰Of the Hebronites, Hashabiah and his brothers, 1,700 men of ability, had the oversight of Israel westward of the Jordan for all the work of the LORD and for the service of the king. ³¹Of the Hebronites, Jerijah was chief of the Hebronites of whatever genealogy or fathers' houses. (In the fortieth year of David's reign search was made and men of great ability among them were found at Jazer in Gilead.) ³²King David appointed him and his brothers, 2,700 men of ability, heads of fathers' houses, to have the oversight of the Reubenites, the Gadites and the half-tribe of the Manassites for everything pertaining to God and for the affairs of the king.

27 This is the number of the people of Israel, the heads of fathers' houses, the commanders of thousands and hundreds, and their officers who served the king in all matters concerning the divisions that came and went, month after month throughout the year, each division numbering 24,000:

²Jashobeam the son of Zabdiel was in charge of the first division in the first month; in his division were 24,000. ³He was a descendant of Perez and was chief of all the commanders. He served for the first month. ⁴Dodai the Ahohite*e* was in charge of the division of the second month; in his division were 24,000. ⁵The third commander, for the third month, was Benaiah, the son of Jehoiada the chief priest; in his division were 24,000. ⁶This is the Benaiah who was a mighty man of the thirty and in command of the thirty; Ammizabad his son was in charge of his division.*f* ⁷Asahel the brother of Joab was fourth, for the fourth month, and his son Zebadiah after him; in his division were 24,000. ⁸The fifth commander, for the fifth month, was Shamhuth the Izrahite; in his division were 24,000. ⁹Sixth, for the sixth month, was Ira, the son of Ikkesh the Tekoite; in his division were 24,000. ¹⁰Seventh, for the seventh month, was Helez the Pelonite, of the sons of Ephraim; in his division were 24,000. ¹¹Eighth, for the eighth month, was Sibbecai the Hushathite, of the Zerahites; in his division were 24,000. ¹²Ninth, for the ninth month, was Abiezer of Anathoth, a Benjaminite; in his division were 24,000. ¹³Tenth, for the tenth month, was Maharai of Netophah, of the Zerahites; in his division were 24,000. ¹⁴Eleventh, for the eleventh month, was Benaiah of Pirathon, of the sons of Ephraim; in his division were 24,000. ¹⁵Twelfth, for the twelfth month, was Heldai the Netophathite, of Othniel; in his division were 24,000.

¹⁶Over the tribes of Israel, for the Reubenites, Eliezer the son of Zichri was chief officer; for the Simeonites, Shephatiah the son of Maacah; ¹⁷for Levi, Hashabiah the son of Kemuel; for Aaron, Zadok; ¹⁸for Judah, Elihu, one of David's brothers; for Issachar, Omri the son of Michael; ¹⁹for Zebulun, Ishmaiah the son of Obadiah; for Naphtali, Jeremoth the son of Azriel; ²⁰for the Ephraimites, Hoshea the son of Azaziah; for the half-tribe of Manasseh, Joel the son of Pedaiah; ²¹for the half-tribe of Manasseh in Gilead, Iddo the son of Zechariah; for Benjamin, Jaasiel the son of Abner; ²²for Dan, Azarel the son of Jeroham. These were the leaders of the tribes of Israel. ²³David did not count those below twenty years of age, for the LORD had promised to make Israel as many as the stars of heaven. ²⁴Joab the son of Zeruiah began to count, but did not finish. Yet wrath came upon Israel for this, and the number was not entered in the chronicles of King David.

²⁵Over the king's treasuries was Azmaveth the son of Adiel; and over the treasuries in the country, in the cities, in the villages, and in the towers, was Jonathan the son of Uzziah; ²⁶and over those who did the work of the field for tilling the soil was Ezri the son of Chelub; ²⁷and over the vineyards was Shimei the Ramathite; and over the produce of the vineyards for the wine cellars was Zabdi the Shiphmite. ²⁸Over the olive and sycamore trees in the Shephelah was Baal-hanan the Gederite; and over the stores of oil was Joash. ²⁹Over the herds that pastured in Sharon was Shitrai the Sharonite; over the herds in the valleys was Shaphat the son of Adlai. ³⁰Over the camels was Obil the Ishmaelite; and over the donkeys was Jehdeiah the Meronothite. Over the flocks was Jaziz the Hagrite. ³¹All these were stewards of King David's property.

³²Jonathan, David's uncle, was a counselor, being a man of understanding and a scribe. He and Jehiel the son of Hachmoni attended the king's sons. ³³Ahithophel was the king's counselor, and Hushai the Archite was the king's friend. ³⁴Ahithophel was succeeded by Jehoiada the son of Benaiah, and Abiathar. Joab was commander of the king's army.

a Septuagint; Hebrew *six Levites*   b Or *court*; Hebrew *parbar* (meaning unknown); twice in this verse   c The Hebrew of verse 21 is uncertain   d Hebrew *Shelomith*   e Septuagint; Hebrew *Ahohite and his division and Mikloth the chief officer*   f Septuagint, Vulgate; Hebrew *was his division*

OVERVIEW: This division of the gatekeepers, the military and the tribal leaders follows David's organization of the priests, Levites and musicians. The reformers define the gatekeepers as those who keep the temple free from any violation, a group whom many regard as types of New Testament ministers. The commentators also view the organization of the leaders of Israel as eminently practical and efficient.

26:1-19 *Division of Gatekeepers*

The Gatekeepers and Treasurers. John Mayer: After the singers, the gatekeepers are distinguished by the four gates of the temple: east, west, north and south. One prince was appointed to be over one gate and one over another—four overall by course. For it is not to be doubted but that the porters—being four thousand in number—were distinguished into twenty-four courses as well as the singers and priests coming and going on every sabbath, as they did according to this book. And therefore here twenty-four are named in the beginning of the chapter, which may well be understood to be the chief of these twenty-four courses. And of Obed-edom, it is noted in particular that there were more of his house than of any other. The reason was because the Lord blessed him. Interpreters generally think that this blessing had to do with when the ark of the covenant dwelled at this house. For then it is said that God blessed Obed-edom and all that he had. Indeed one particularly special way of a blessing was by increasing his house and giving him many children. And the twenty-four named were of the posterity of Kohath and Merari. Now besides these and their brothers of their courses, there were some Levites of Gershom who were set over the treasuries of the temple and over the spoils of the enemies, which were dedicated by David, Samuel, Saul, Abner and Joab. Last, for works outside of the gates, there are those named who were over the six thousand appointed to be rulers and judges of the people in matters concerning God and the king. This particularly included teaching and instructing the people in their synagogues and sitting with the judges in certain cities to judge criminal cases. Commentary on Chronicles.[1]

Spiritual Janitors. Lucas Osiander: The gatekeepers were officials who took care that no human profanity entered the temple or was polluted, violated or otherwise desecrated by disgraceful acts or sacrilege. Ministers today are *janitores* of the spiritual temple, the church, and they take care that the temple of God might not become a place where believers are polluted by disgraceful things, as is written in 1 Corinthians 3 and in Colossians: "See to it that no one takes you captive by philosophy and empty deceit." Instead be kept whole in the wonderful heavenly teaching and sacraments. Annotations on 1 Chronicles.[2]

Prefiguring Christian Ministers. Johannes Piscator: The gatekeepers of the temple should be regarded as prefiguring the ministers of the church in the New Testament. For it is the responsibility of ministers as officeholders to guard the church against false doctrine lest by their carelessness falsity creeps into the church. Commentary on 1 Chronicles.[3]

26:20-32 *Treasurers and Other Officers*

Leaving Things in Good Shape. Lucas Osiander: And so, as the text has clearly said, David gave oversight of things pertaining to God and the kingdom. How praiseworthy is this tireless effort of David, who even at the end of his life and his reign is seen as having omitted nothing for the good establishment of the church and the republic. Therefore to governors is given the task of leaving things to their successors as well-ordered in the church and in the kingdom as possible. Annotations on 1 Chronicles.[4]

Deacons as Treasurers. Johannes Piscator: David ordered that certain men would have charge over the treasuries in the temple. In the same way, deacons were appointed by the apostles

---

[1]Mayer, *Many Commentaries in One*, 10*.

[2]Osiander, *Liber Iosue*, 1185; citing Col 2:8.
[3]Piscator, *Commentarii in omnes libros Veteris Testamenti*, 2:427.
[4]Osiander, *Liber Iosue*, 1187-88.

to assist in the good things of the church. That which was instituted back then is still necessary today. Commentary on 1 Chronicles.[5]

David's Last Year. The English Annotations: David's last year alive was his fortieth year. At this time he designated Solomon to be his successor. And following that he appointed distinct orders among the Levites and others for the well-ordering of the church and the commonwealth. And having assembled them all together, he declared his mind to them about these things. Annotations on 1 Chronicles.[6]

27:1-34 Military and Civil Organization

A Ready Army. Lucas Osiander: These orders about the military were not made to weary all the people with frivolous affairs or wars. Instead, if a disturbance were suddenly to arise, there would already be a rested army ready to suppress such evil immediately. Thus is seen how good it is for a republic to establish such a thing, where—for the sake of temporal peace—a magistrate chooses some of his subjects so that he could lead some thousands of armed men (whose names are noted in this chapter) quickly into battle if necessary. Such a wise magistrate pleases God, for in this way the ruler's hope is not placed in armies. Instead he remains constantly vigilant about his neighbors and other disquiet as part of his office. It helps keep the swords of others in their sheaths. Annotations on 1 Chronicles.[7]

The Key to a Safe Kingdom. John Mayer: After the distinction of the priests and Levites, here follows the distinction of the princes. This includes, first of all, those who were over the men of war, who are distinguished by the twelve months of the year—each one having under him twenty-four thousand valiant men. Of these, one with his twenty-four thousand attended to the king one month, and the other another month. This was so that each prince was at liberty to return with his men and attend to their own domestic affairs eleven months of the year, except during extraordinary occasions of war when their service was required for battle. The goal of this organization seems to be for the safety of the king. It was also for the appeasing of tumults. For, should any disturbance occur, a number of highly trained soldiers were at the disposal of the king each month. And it is by this means that Solomon likely enjoyed his peaceable reign during all his days. For if any disturbance would have arisen, Solomon would have had an army at his immediate disposal to defeat his enemies. And whichever king will take the same course of action today, it is not to be doubted but that with God's help he would have a very safe kingdom indeed. Commentary on Chronicles[8]

Economic Stewardship. Lucas Osiander: The treasurers whom David set up not only knew how much money had been handed over in sum but also how much grain and wine had been deposited here and there in the cities, towns and fields where there were storehouses (that is, cellars and silos) for the sake of future use. This use of riches in order to have food ready at hand is not the same as the sin of financial speculation. But it is sin to trust in wealth and take pride in it, abusing it for the sake of one's own lusts and luxury. Like the head of a household, it is proper for a good magistrate to safely set aside what is needed for all kinds of seasons. Annotations on 1 Chronicles.[9]

All Members Different Yet Equal. Johannes Piscator: Farmers, vinedressers, gardeners and shepherds are by no means to be ill regarded. For the necessary use of them is good for the commonwealth, and they themselves harvest honest things in nature. And just as in the church there are not members that are less important than

---

[5]Piscator, *Commentarii in omnes libros Veteris Testamenti*, 2:427.
[6]Downame, ed., *Annotations* (1645), OO4v*; citing 2 Sam 5:4.
[7]Osiander, *Liber Iosue*, 1188.

[8]Mayer, *Many Commentaries in One*, 10-11*.
[9]Osiander, *Liber Iosue*, 1191-92.

others, in the same way the Holy Spirit bestows different kinds of gifts. As the apostle Paul says, "The members of the body that seem to be weaker are indispensable," and "God has so arranged the body, giving the greater honor to the inferior member." COMMENTARY ON 1 CHRONICLES.[10]

HEEDING ONE OF GOD'S COMMANDS, BREAKING ANOTHER. JOHN MAYER: It was said before that the Levites were numbered from the age of twenty years old and upward. Now in speaking of others that were of the other tribes and of the numbers that were under the twelve princes of David's armies—because nothing had been said beforehand from what age they were numbered—it is, therefore, inserted here according to the law in Numbers: "From twenty years old and upward, all in Israel who are able to go to war, you and Aaron shall list them, company by company." In this way they must have also been numbered from twenty years old and upward, but not under. A general

reason for this was based on Genesis 15, when God promised Abram descendants as the stars, that is, innumerable. Now, if any without exception were to be numbered as Abraham's descendants, the number would be so great that it would exceed any ability to count. Therefore to attempt a numbering of the Israelites under the age of twenty would be seen as a great sin, both because it was against the law in Numbers and because it went against Abraham's promise of having a multitude of descendants as numerous as the stars of the sky. This is why David did not number those under the age of twenty.

At the same time, it is noted that David commanded Joab to number his army of men above the age of twenty. But Joab was not able to finish numbering the men before God's wrath fell on Israel. For even though David had been careful not to violate the law of numbering males under the age of twenty, he had violated the law of trusting in God alone for protection. COMMENTARY ON CHRONICLES.[11]

---

[10]Piscator, *Commentarii in omnes libros Veteris Testamenti*, 2:428; citing 1 Cor 12:22, 24.

[11]Mayer, *Many Commentaries in One*, 11*; citing Num 1:3.

28:1–29:30 DAVID AND SOLOMON SEE TO THE COMPLETION OF THE TEMPLE

¹David assembled at Jerusalem all the officials of Israel, the officials of the tribes, the officers of the divisions that served the king, the commanders of thousands, the commanders of hundreds, the stewards of all the property and livestock of the king and his sons, together with the palace officials, the mighty men and all the seasoned warriors. ²Then King David rose to his feet and said: "Hear me, my brothers and my people. I had it in my heart to build a house of rest for the ark of the covenant of the LORD and for the footstool of our God, and I made preparations for building. ³But God said to me, 'You may not build a house for my name, for you are a man of war and have shed blood.' ⁴Yet the LORD God of Israel chose me from all my father's house to be king over Israel forever. For he chose Judah as leader, and in the house of Judah my father's house, and among my father's sons he took pleasure in me to make me king over all Israel. ⁵And of all my sons (for the LORD has given me many sons) he has chosen Solomon my son to sit on the throne of the kingdom of the LORD over Israel. ⁶He said to me, 'It is Solomon your son who shall build my house and my courts, for I have chosen him to be my son, and I will be his father. ⁷I will establish his kingdom forever if he continues strong in keeping my commandments and my rules, as he is today.' ⁸Now therefore in the sight of all Israel, the assembly of the LORD, and in the hearing of our God, observe and seek out all the commandments of the LORD your God, that you may possess this good land and leave it for an inheritance to your children after you forever.

⁹"And you, Solomon my son, know the God of your father and serve him with a whole heart and with a willing mind, for the LORD searches all hearts and understands every plan and thought. If you seek him, he will be found by you, but if you forsake him, he will cast you off forever. ¹⁰Be careful now, for the LORD has chosen you to build a house for the sanctuary; be strong and do it."

¹¹Then David gave Solomon his son the plan of the vestibule of the temple,ᵃ and of its houses, its treasuries, its upper rooms, and its inner chambers, and of the room for the mercy seat; ¹²and the plan of all that he had in mind for the courts of the house of the LORD, all the surrounding chambers, the treasuries of the house of God, and the treasuries for dedicated gifts; ¹³for the divisions of the priests and of the Levites, and all the work of the service in the house of the LORD; for all the vessels for the service in the house of the LORD, ¹⁴the weight of gold for all golden vessels for each service, the weight of silver vessels for each service, ¹⁵the weight of the golden lampstands and their lamps, the weight of gold for each lampstand and its lamps, the weight of silver for a lampstand and its lamps, according to the use of each lampstand in the service, ¹⁶the weight of gold for each table for the showbread, the silver for the silver tables, ¹⁷and pure gold for the forks, the basins and the cups; for the golden bowls and the weight of each; for the silver bowls and the weight of each; ¹⁸for the altar of incense made of refined gold, and its weight; also his plan for the golden chariot of the cherubim that spread their wings and covered the ark of the covenant of the LORD. ¹⁹"All this he made clear to me in writing from the hand of the LORD, all the work to be done according to the plan."

²⁰Then David said to Solomon his son, "Be strong and courageous and do it. Do not be afraid and do not be dismayed, for the LORD God, even my God, is with you. He will not leave you or forsake you, until all the work for the service of the house of the LORD is finished. ²¹And behold the divisions of the priests and the Levites for all the service of the house of God; and with you in all the work will be every willing man who has skill for any kind of service; also the officers and all the people will be wholly at your command."

29 And David the king said to all the assembly, "Solomon my son, whom alone God has chosen, is young and inexperienced, and the work is great, for the palace will not be for man but for the

Lord God. [2]So I have provided for the house of my God, so far as I was able, the gold for the things of gold, the silver for the things of silver, and the bronze for the things of bronze, the iron for the things of iron, and wood for the things of wood, besides great quantities of onyx and stones for setting, antimony, colored stones, all sorts of precious stones and marble. [3]Moreover, in addition to all that I have provided for the holy house, I have a treasure of my own of gold and silver, and because of my devotion to the house of my God I give it to the house of my God: [4]3,000 talents[b] of gold, of the gold of Ophir, and 7,000 talents of refined silver, for overlaying the walls of the house,[c] [5]and for all the work to be done by craftsmen, gold for the things of gold and silver for the things of silver. Who then will offer willingly, consecrating himself[d] today to the Lord?"

[6]Then the leaders of fathers' houses made their freewill offerings, as did also the leaders of the tribes, the commanders of thousands and of hundreds, and the officers over the king's work. [7]They gave for the service of the house of God 5,000 talents and 10,000 darics[e] of gold, 10,000 talents of silver, 18,000 talents of bronze and 100,000 talents of iron. [8]And whoever had precious stones gave them to the treasury of the house of the Lord, in the care of Jehiel the Gershonite. [9]Then the people rejoiced because they had given willingly, for with a whole heart they had offered freely to the Lord. David the king also rejoiced greatly.

[10]Therefore David blessed the Lord in the presence of all the assembly. And David said: "Blessed are you, O Lord, the God of Israel our father, forever and ever. [11]Yours, O Lord, is the greatness and the power and the glory and the victory and the majesty, for all that is in the heavens and in the earth is yours. Yours is the kingdom, O Lord, and you are exalted as head above all. [12]Both riches and honor come from you, and you rule over all. In your hand are power and might, and in your hand it is to make great and to give strength to all. [13]And now we thank you, our God, and praise your glorious name.

[14]"But who am I, and what is my people, that we should be able thus to offer willingly? For all things come from you, and of your own have we given you. [15]For we are strangers before you and sojourners, as all

our fathers were. Our days on the earth are like a shadow, and there is no abiding.[f] [16]O Lord our God, all this abundance that we have provided for building you a house for your holy name comes from your hand and is all your own. [17]I know, my God, that you test the heart and have pleasure in uprightness. In the uprightness of my heart I have freely offered all these things, and now I have seen your people, who are present here, offering freely and joyously to you. [18]O Lord, the God of Abraham, Isaac, and Israel, our fathers, keep forever such purposes and thoughts in the hearts of your people, and direct their hearts toward you. [19]Grant to Solomon my son a whole heart that he may keep your commandments, your testimonies, and your statutes, performing all, and that he may build the palace for which I have made provision."

[20]Then David said to all the assembly, "Bless the Lord your God." And all the assembly blessed the Lord, the God of their fathers, and bowed their heads and paid homage to the Lord and to the king. [21]And they offered sacrifices to the Lord, and on the next day offered burnt offerings to the Lord, 1,000 bulls, 1,000 rams, and 1,000 lambs, with their drink offerings, and sacrifices in abundance for all Israel. [22]And they ate and drank before the Lord on that day with great gladness.

And they made Solomon the son of David king the second time, and they anointed him as prince for the Lord, and Zadok as priest. [23]Then Solomon sat on the throne of the Lord as king in place of David his father. And he prospered, and all Israel obeyed him. [24]All the leaders and the mighty men, and also all the sons of King David, pledged their allegiance to King Solomon. [25]And the Lord made Solomon very great in the sight of all Israel and bestowed on him such royal majesty as had not been on any king before him in Israel.

[26]Thus David the son of Jesse reigned over all Israel. [27]The time that he reigned over Israel was forty years. He reigned seven years in Hebron and thirty-three years in Jerusalem. [28]Then he died at a good age, full of days, riches, and honor. And Solomon his son reigned in his place. [29]Now the acts of King David, from first to last, are written in the Chronicles of Samuel the seer, and in the Chronicles of Nathan the

prophet, and in the Chronicles of Gad the seer, [30]with accounts of all his rule and his might and of the

circumstances that came upon him and upon Israel and upon all the kingdoms of the countries.

a Hebrew *lacks of the temple*   b A *talent was about 75 pounds or 34 kilograms*   c Septuagint; Hebrew *houses*   d Or *ordaining himself*; Hebrew *filling his hand*   e A *daric was a coin weighing about 1/4 ounce or 8.5 grams*   f Septuagint, Vulgate; Hebrew *hope, or prospect*

OVERVIEW: In this last section of 1 Chronicles, we encounter material not found in 1 Kings that leads our commentators to interpret David's remaining years in a positive way that sets Solomon up for success. Some commentators marvel at David's highly effective and persuasive sermon on divine election. David's exhortation to the leaders to make financial contributions to the temple provokes the commentators to extol the virtues of generous giving. Magisterial reformers interpret Solomon's second anointing as a type of the Christian sacrament of baptism. And commenting on the death of David, they admonish us to take David's sins to heart so that we can receive the remission of sins only available through faith in Jesus Christ.

28:1-10 *David's Speech to the People*

DAVID LIKE MOSES AND SOLOMON LIKE JOSHUA. JOHN MAYER: After numbering the princes, priests and Levites, here follows the speech that David made while standing up (so that he might be better heard). And here he shows what his intent was regarding the building of a house for the Lord, and how he had prepared for this. But God had appointed Solomon his son to do this great work and prohibited David from doing it. For this was just as Moses was denied to enter the land of Canaan, even though Moses desperately tried to do so. But like Solomon, Joshua, rather than Moses, was appointed to lead the people into the Promised Land. COMMENTARY ON CHRONICLES.[1]

WILL AND DEED. HENRY AIRAY: The Holy Spirit puts little difference between the will and the deed, especially as the will is inclined to that which is

good. An example of this is found in David's willingness and desire to build a temple for the Lord. . . . He did not end up building it, yet his purpose and desire to build it was accepted by God. And generally this is true: that God accepts the will and desire as the deed; so that the will, desire and endeavor to walk in the ways of God . . . clearly reveals to us that we are the sons of God and are accepted by God as if we are walking holy and without blame. LECTURES ON PHILIPPIANS.[2]

DAVID TEACHES THE TRUTH AND POWER OF DIVINE ELECTION. VIKTORIN STRIGEL: Lactantius famously said in chapter fourteen of his book *On the Wrath of God*: "God wants all human beings to be righteous, that is, to hold God and human beings as beloved, namely, to honor God as Father, to love human beings as brothers. For all righteousness consists in these two things."[3] Therefore David does not preach from an exalted position, but stands on his feet, so that by this gesture he would conduct himself in modesty before others. Now what could be more charming than that such a king—whom God summoned up to the pinnacle of his kingdom and instructed in wisdom, righteousness, strength and other virtues and happiness in conduct—appeals to his servants and subordinates as brothers? But this king was a type of Christ's gentleness and humility—Christ, who, for us miserable maggots, did not hesitate to adorn himself with the title of brother. "Go," he said, "to my brothers and tell them that I am

---

[1]Mayer, *Many Commentaries in One*, 11-12*.

[2]Airay, *Lectures on Philippians*, 157*.
[3]ANF 7:271-72*. Lactantius (ca. 260–ca. 330), a North African rhetorician who converted to Christianity around 305, advised the emperor Constantine (ca. 272–337) and tutored his son Crispus (d. 326).

ascending to my Father and to your Father." Again, "I will proclaim your name to my brothers." The narrative that follows this most charming address agrees with the word of John the Baptist: "No one is able to receive anything, unless it is given to him from above."

"I had resolved to build a house dedicated to the ministry of the Word," which is signified by appeals to the ark of the covenant and the footstool of the Lord. "But God restrained me from this plan, declaring that such work is not fitting for a soldier. For that reason, I submitted, as is only right, to the Lord's plan, and passed the torch to my son Solomon." Now that he has made an opening for himself with this first proposition, he prudently joined this narrative with the commonplace concerning divine election, which is opposed not only as repulsive but even as wicked and impious. That divine election is more powerful than human prerogative he confirms by three examples. First, God chose the tribe of Judah to be the procreator of the king among the people of God, although the tribe of Ephraim was indeed far more powerful, as Psalm 60 testifies, "Ephraim is the strength of my head." Second, in the tribe of Judah the Lord chose the house of Jesse, which was far more lowly and obscure than any other family in its tribe. Finally, in the house of Jesse he called to the royal throne not the firstborn or the other older brothers by birth, but the least by birth, David—indeed a shepherd of sheep, as it is said in Psalm 78: "He chose David his servant, and lifted him up from the sheepfolds; he led him from tending nursing ewes to feed Jacob his servant." David made use of this preparation to reach what he wants to accomplish and to remove confidence in human prerogative from Solomon's brothers by his fatherly example. As the attempts of Saul and Absalom against David, who was divinely chosen and called, were futile, so also Adonijah and the other princes attacked the decree of God in vain. BOOK OF 1 CHRONICLES.[4]

28:11-19 *David Delivers the Plans to Solomon*

HOW DAVID RECEIVED THE PLANS FOR THE TEMPLE. JOHN MAYER: It is said that "David gave Solomon his son the plan" of several of the furnishings of the temple. This suggests that everything came written to David with the hand of the Lord. According to the Hebrews, this is to be understood by the direction of Samuel. However, others say that it was by the direction of Nathan the prophet. Nicholas of Lyra says that it may be that David had received the plan directly from God by revelation. Cajetan, on the other hand, says that these things were written by God in David's mind and not in a book. But he described them by written to Solomon for his direction. Alonso Tostado, on the contrary, says that David had them delivered to him by God already written, just as Moses had received the Ten Commandments. But of all these conjectures, that of Cajetan seems the most probable. That's because verse 12 says that David had had the plan in his mind. In this way, God's revelation to him was in the form of internal revelation. And David spoke to Solomon that he might not at all turn from this pattern. On the contrary, Solomon was to institute the pattern as coming directly from God and not from a human. Indeed David exhorted Solomon to go about this great work with no fear, for the devising of the plan was set by God himself in every way and did not need any help from human design. COMMENTARY ON CHRONICLES.[5]

GOD'S PEOPLE ARE HIS TREASURY. JOHN DONNE: Things dedicated to God are often called "the treasures of God." The treasures of God and the treasures of the servants of God are in the Scriptures the same thing; and so a man may rob God's treasury in robbing a hospital. Now, though to give a talent or to give a jewel or to give a considerable proportion of plate be an addition to a treasury, yet to give a treasury to a treasury is a more precious and a more acceptable present; as to

---

[4]Strigel, *Libri Samuelis, Regum et Paralipomenon*, 484-85; citing Jn 20:17; Ps 22:23 (Vg); Jn 3:27; Ps 60:7; 78:70.

[5]Mayer, *Many Commentaries in One*, 12*; citing 1 Chron 28:11.

give a library to a library is more than to give the works of any one author. A godly person is a library in oneself, a treasury in oneself, and therefore fittest to be dedicated and appropriated to God. Invest yourself therefore with this treasure of godliness. Sermon 136: A Lent Sermon Preached to the King at Whitehall (1629).[6]

28:20-21 David Assures Solomon of the Work Ahead

Great Discrepancy. Martin Luther: There . . . is a great discrepancy and a difference in words between 2 Samuel 7 and this passage. The former states that God will build David an eternal house, the latter that Solomon shall build a house in God's name. The former passage states without any condition or qualification that it shall stand forever and be hindered by no sin. The latter passage conditions its continuance on Solomon's and his descendants' continued piety. . . . The former is a promise of grace, the latter a promise of law. On the Jews and Their Lies.[7]

Completing God's Work. Lucas Osiander: God said, "With the priests and Levites, you will complete everything that pertains to the temple and the carrying out of divine worship; it will not be a work that is left undone." These consolations also assure pious ministers of God's Word who have been commanded to build up Christ's church (the spiritual temple) in any place where the gospel of Christ has not been preached purely before. And because this is a difficult and arduous task to undertake, God gives faithful laborers a spirit, strength and blessed success. Annotations on 1 Chronicles.[8]

29:1-9 Gifts for the Temple

Leading in Generosity. Lucas Osiander: David asked who would volunteer to present their

full hands to the Lord that very day. It is as if he said, "Who here wants to declare that you are contributing some gifts to the construction of the temple by giving liberally of your own belongings?" For it is easier for servants to be admonished and encouraged to works of piety if their superiors have first presented them with good examples and have joined actions to exhortations, as David had. Annotations on 1 Chronicles.[9]

David's Last Speech. John Mayer: David spoke to the people after he had spoken in the previous chapter since the king's strength would not allow him to say anymore at that time. Upon his return he resumed commending the building of the temple to them, setting forth the greatness of the work. . . . He also spoke about how he himself added three thousand talents of pure gold and seven thousand talents of silver to cover and guild over the walls of the most holy place, and he exhorted the princes to make liberal contributions as well. The reason why David also wanted the princes to contribute, according to some, was that the princes would be much less willing to rebel against Solomon if they had contributed to the furnishings of the temple and so exhausted their wealth. But a better explanation is that, by exhorting the princes to give a liberal contribution, David was commending the people to make a sacrifice that was most pleasing to God. Commentary on Chronicles.[10]

Thanks to God. Geneva Bible: We give God nothing of our own, but only that which we have received from him. For whether the gifts are physical or spiritual, we receive them all of God and therefore we must give him the glory. Annotations on 1 Chronicles.[11]

Example of David's Godliness. Johannes Piscator: David exhorted his chief leaders to give a gift and contribute freely toward the building of the temple. And his leaders likewise did the same

---

[6]Donne, *Works*, 5:448*.
[7]LW 47:198.
[8]Osiander, *Liber Iosue*, 1201; citing 1 Cor 3; Mk 16.

[9]Osiander, *Liber Iosue*, 1203.
[10]Mayer, *Many Commentaries in One*, 12*.
[11]*Geneva Bible* (1560), 191r*.

to those under their charge. In all of this, David is set forth as an example of godliness towards God. COMMENTARY ON 1 CHRONICLES.[12]

29:10-20 David's Prayer of Praise

PRAISING THE KING OF KINGS. LUCAS OSIANDER: The king praised God before the entire multitude, that is, the leaders and the populace who had gathered. For there is no shame to us in glorifying God. In his prayer the king proclaimed the majesty of God, to the decrease of himself and his public office. He prayed that God would keep the souls of the people and of King Solomon in godliness and accomplish this. He said, "Blessed are you, O Lord, the God of Israel our father." That is, "You are praised as the patriarch of Israel, who graciously adopted the people as his heirs. In your infinite goodness, you are worthy to be praised from eternity to eternity, from all days to the end of the ages." ANNOTATIONS ON 1 CHRONICLES.[13]

DAVID'S LAST PUBLIC PRAYER. JOHN MAYER: Then David, seeing the assembly's cheerfulness in offering the contributions, blessed God and acknowledged in front of all the people what they had offered. And David conceded that what they had offered had come from God. David then beseeched the Lord to continue working with the people, knowing the fickleness of humankind's heart. Last, David prayed for his son Solomon, namely, that God would give him a perfect heart so that he might do all the things commanded of him. And after blessing God, all the assembly bowed themselves before the king as a show of thanks for his blessing and the benefits they had received under his governance. COMMENTARY ON CHRONICLES.[14]

GOOD SUBJECTS, GOOD RULERS. JOHN DOD: Let inferiors here be admonished that as governors are to serve the Lord on their behalf (the husband for the wife, parents for their children, masters and mistresses for their servants and people), so they on the other side are to be gentle and humble and tractable, so that their superiors have encouragement and good success in the supplications that they make for them. . . . This was what made David so plentifully pour out his heart before the Lord in prayer and in thanksgiving. For when the princes and the people had offered very largely and very willingly, David rejoiced with great joy and blessed and praised the Lord before all the congregation, saying, "Blessed be you, Lord God, forever and ever." . . . Thus may we observe how the good affections and desires of the people stir up and strengthen the hearts of their rulers to pray for them. Whereas, on the contrary, nothing so kills the heart and discourages the spirits of God's servants from prayer than when they see those who are under them to be willful, headstrong, rebellious and utterly void of any good disposition to piety and religious exercises. They can give no good testimony of them, but instead they have need to cry to God that he would humble them and convert them. THE FOURTH SERMON ON THE LORD'S SUPPER.[15]

BEING A JOYFUL GIVER. JOHANNES PISCATOR: A contribution to the worship of God, and not that just given to support the lowly poor in the church, should arise from a sincere heart and a joyful spirit. That's because God, as the apostle Paul says, "loves a cheerful giver." COMMENTARY ON 1 CHRONICLES.[16]

ALL IS FROM GOD. DAVID CLARKSON: Whatever is good is from God. Take a survey of all you have. Begin at the foundation, at your very being . . . [and you will see that] the ground work and the whole structure, the subject and all the accessories, are wholly from God, for all is his own. How then do you or others come to have anything but merely of his favor and goodwill, who disposes of his own to whom he pleases? None could constrain him, none

---

[12]Piscator, Commentarii in omnes libros Veteris Testamenti, 2:433.
[13]Osiander, Liber Iosue, 1204.
[14]Mayer, Many Commentaries in One, 13*.
[15]Dod, Ten Sermons, 116-17*.
[16]Piscator, Commentarii in omnes libros Veteris Testamenti, 2:433; citing 2 Cor 9:7.

could oblige him to part with anything (for by what could they do it, all being his own?), to dispose of his own any otherwise than he would. So that whatever you have, you have it of him and you have it freely. You do not have—you could not have—anything, but of his good pleasure. To this you owe all, and so owe thankfulness for everything. SERMON ON 1 CHRONICLES 29:11.[17]

29:21-25 *Solomon's Anointing*

A SECOND ANOINTING. LUCAS OSIANDER: They established Solomon for a second time as king because the first anointing had taken place hastily and as an emergency measure because of Adonijah's seditious actions in 1 Kings 1. He was anointed "as prince for the Lord"; that is, he was anointed in order that he might govern the people of Israel as a vicar of God. For the magistrate is God's servant and vicar (Rom 13 and Ps 82). To be anointed anew before the entire assembled kingdom was a way of confirming his reign. Not even the Roman emperors were often crowned like this. But in the same way, we Christians not only have the one sacrament of baptism but also a second one, the Lord's Supper, in

which it is confirmed that we possess the kingdom of heaven. ANNOTATIONS ON 1 CHRONICLES.[18]

29:26-30 *Summary of David's Reign and His Death*

DAVID'S GOOD DEATH. JOHANNES PISCATOR: David sets forth an example of dying well. But this was evidently the reward, to some extent, of his godly life. COMMENTARY ON 1 CHRONICLES.[19]

LEARNING FROM DAVID. LUCAS OSIANDER: Thus this book closes with the death of the great and godly King David, who was called from his flocks to be king. In his true piety, fortitude and endurance, he is a type of Christ our Savior. All kings and princes ought to display the virtue of his reign. His very real lapses remind us of human folly and show us the sweetness of consolation, so that we do not despair when we fall into the atrocious ruin of sin. Instead, with David, we ought to repent and receive the remission of sins and life everlasting through faith in the Messiah. Amen. ANNOTATIONS ON 1 CHRONICLES.[20]

---

[17]Clarkson, *Practical Works*, 1:388*.
[18]Osiander, *Liber Iosue*, 1207.
[19]Piscator, *Commentarii in omnes libros Veteris Testamenti*, 2:433.
[20]Osiander, *Liber Iosue*, 1208.

COMMENTARY ON 2 CHRONICLES

OVERVIEW: Introducing this book, these commentators note that 2 Chronicles covers the same material as 1–2 Kings, with the important distinction that the Chronicler primarily focuses on the history of Judah after the division of the kingdom.

Prolegomena: What This Book Is About

THREE THINGS TO CONSIDER. GENEVA BIBLE: This second book contains briefly that which is included in the two books of 1–2 Kings. That is, it touches on the history from the reign of Solomon to the destruction of Jerusalem and the carrying away of the people captive into Babylon. In this story certain things are declared and set forth more abundantly than in 1–2 Kings. They therefore serve greatly to understanding the prophets. But three things are here chiefly to be considered. First, the people made recourse to the Lord, and by earnest prayer were heard; therefore, the plagues were removed. Second, it is a great offense against God for those who fear him and profess his religion to join into relationship with the wicked. Third, good rulers always loved God's prophets, and they were very zealous to set forth his religion throughout all their dominions. But, on the contrary, evil rulers always hated God's ministers, deposed them and—in exchange for the true religion

and Word of God—set up idolatry and served God according to human fantasy. Thus have we hitherto the chief acts from the beginning of the world to the building again of Jerusalem, which was the thirty-second year of Darius. In whole, it contained 3,488 years and six months. ARGUMENT OF 2 CHRONICLES.[1]

472 YEARS OF HISTORY. THE ENGLISH ANNOTATIONS: Second Chronicles contains a history of 472 years, from the beginning of Solomon's reign to Israel's return from captivity. It registers the state of the kingdom of Judah under nineteen of David's posterity and Athaliah the usurper. Only sometimes some of the affairs of the kingdom of Israel, where the two kingdoms had to do with one another, are intermingled. ANNOTATIONS ON 2 CHRONICLES.[2]

A HISTORY OF JUDAH. GIOVANNI DIODATI: The subject of this book is the same as that of the two books of Kings, save only that after the separation of the ten tribes this foregoes the history of the kings of Israel. Indeed, it focuses only on that of the kings of Judah until the time of the captivity of Babylon. ANNOTATIONS ON 2 CHRONICLES.[3]

---

[1] *Geneva Bible* (1560), 191r-v*.
[2] Downame, ed., *Annotations* (1645), PP1v*.
[3] Diodati, *Pious Annotations*, 42*.

1:1–5:1 SOLOMON'S BUILDING OF THE TEMPLE

¹Solomon the son of David established himself in his kingdom, and the LORD his God was with him and made him exceedingly great.

²Solomon spoke to all Israel, to the commanders of thousands and of hundreds, to the judges, and to all the leaders in all Israel, the heads of fathers' houses. ³And Solomon, and all the assembly with him, went to the high place that was at Gibeon, for the tent of meeting of God, which Moses the servant of the LORD had made in the wilderness, was there. ⁴(But David had brought up the ark of God from Kiriath-jearim to the place that David had prepared for it, for he had pitched a tent for it in Jerusalem.) ⁵Moreover, the bronze altar that Bezalel the son of Uri, son of Hur, had made, was there before the tabernacle of the LORD. And Solomon and the assembly sought it*a* out. ⁶And Solomon went up there to the bronze altar before the LORD, which was at the tent of meeting, and offered a thousand burnt offerings on it.

⁷In that night God appeared to Solomon, and said to him, "Ask what I shall give you." ⁸And Solomon said to God, "You have shown great and steadfast love to David my father, and have made me king in his place. ⁹O LORD God, let your word to David my father be now fulfilled, for you have made me king over a people as numerous as the dust of the earth. ¹⁰Give me now wisdom and knowledge to go out and come in before this people, for who can govern this people of yours, which is so great?" ¹¹God answered Solomon, "Because this was in your heart, and you have not asked for possessions, wealth, honor, or the life of those who hate you, and have not even asked for long life, but have asked for wisdom and knowledge for yourself that you may govern my people over whom I have made you king, ¹²wisdom and knowledge are granted to you. I will also give you riches, possessions, and honor, such as none of the kings had who were before you, and none after you shall have the like." ¹³So Solomon came from*b* the high place at Gibeon, from before the tent of meeting, to Jerusalem. And he reigned over Israel.

¹⁴Solomon gathered together chariots and horsemen. He had 1,400 chariots and 12,000 horsemen, whom he stationed in the chariot cities and with the king in Jerusalem. ¹⁵And the king made silver and gold as common in Jerusalem as stone, and he made cedar as plentiful as the sycamore of the Shephelah. ¹⁶And Solomon's import of horses was from Egypt and Kue, and the king's traders would buy them from Kue for a price. ¹⁷They imported a chariot from Egypt for 600 shekels*c* of silver, and a horse for 150. Likewise through them these were exported to all the kings of the Hittites and the kings of Syria.

2 *d*Now Solomon purposed to build a temple for the name of the LORD, and a royal palace for himself. ² *e*And Solomon assigned 70,000 men to bear burdens and 80,000 to quarry in the hill country, and 3,600 to oversee them. ³And Solomon sent word to Hiram the king of Tyre: "As you dealt with David my father and sent him cedar to build himself a house to dwell in, so deal with me. ⁴Behold, I am about to build a house for the name of the LORD my God and dedicate it to him for the burning of incense of sweet spices before him, and for the regular arrangement of the showbread, and for burnt offerings morning and evening, on the Sabbaths and the new moons and the appointed feasts of the LORD our God, as ordained forever for Israel. ⁵The house that I am to build will be great, for our God is greater than all gods. ⁶But who is able to build him a house, since heaven, even highest heaven, cannot contain him? Who am I to build a house for him, except as a place to make offerings before him? ⁷So now send me a man skilled to work in gold, silver, bronze, and iron, and in purple, crimson, and blue fabrics, trained also in engraving, to be with the skilled workers who are with me in Judah and Jerusalem, whom David my father provided. ⁸Send me also cedar, cypress, and algum timber from Lebanon, for I know that your servants know how to cut timber in Lebanon. And my servants will be with your servants, ⁹to prepare timber for me in abundance, for the house I am to build will be great and wonderful. ¹⁰I will give for your servants, the woodsmen who cut timber, 20,000 cors^f of crushed wheat, 20,000 cors of barley, 20,000 baths^g of wine, and 20,000 baths of oil."

¹¹Then Hiram the king of Tyre answered in a letter that he sent to Solomon, "Because the Lord loves his people, he has made you king over them." ¹²Hiram also said, "Blessed be the Lord God of Israel, who made heaven and earth, who has given King David a wise son, who has discretion and understanding, who will build a temple for the Lord and a royal palace for himself.

¹³"Now I have sent a skilled man, who has understanding, Huram-abi, ¹⁴the son of a woman of the daughters of Dan, and his father was a man of Tyre. He is trained to work in gold, silver, bronze, iron, stone, and wood, and in purple, blue, and crimson fabrics and fine linen, and to do all sorts of engraving and execute any design that may be assigned him, with your craftsmen, the craftsmen of my Lord, David your father. ¹⁵Now therefore the wheat and barley, oil and wine, of which my Lord has spoken, let him send to his servants. ¹⁶And we will cut whatever timber you need from Lebanon and bring it to you in rafts by sea to Joppa, so that you may take it up to Jerusalem."

¹⁷Then Solomon counted all the resident aliens who were in the land of Israel, after the census of them that David his father had taken, and there were found 153,600. ¹⁸Seventy thousand of them he assigned to bear burdens, 80,000 to quarry in the hill country, and 3,600 as overseers to make the people work.

3 Then Solomon began to build the house of the Lord in Jerusalem on Mount Moriah, where the Lord^h had appeared to David his father, at the place that David had appointed, on the threshing floor of Ornan the Jebusite. ²He began to build in the second month of the fourth year of his reign. ³These are Solomon's measurements^i for building the house of God: the length, in cubits^j of the old standard, was sixty cubits, and the breadth twenty cubits. ⁴The vestibule in front of the nave of the house was twenty cubits long, equal to the width of the house,^{k} and its height was 120 cubits. He overlaid it on the inside with pure gold. ⁵The nave he lined with cypress and covered it with fine gold and made palms and chains on it.

⁶He adorned the house with settings of precious stones. The gold was gold of Parvaim. ⁷So he lined the house with gold—its beams, its thresholds, its walls, and its doors—and he carved cherubim on the walls.

⁸And he made the Most Holy Place. Its length, corresponding to the breadth of the house, was twenty cubits, and its breadth was twenty cubits. He overlaid it with 600 talents^l of fine gold. ⁹The weight of gold for the nails was fifty shekels.^{m} And he overlaid the upper chambers with gold.

¹⁰In the Most Holy Place he made two cherubim of wood^n and overlaid^o them with gold. ¹¹The wings of the cherubim together extended twenty cubits: one wing of the one, of five cubits, touched the wall of the house, and its other wing, of five cubits, touched the wing of the other cherub; ¹²and of this cherub, one wing, of five cubits, touched the wall of the house, and the other wing, also of five cubits, was joined to the wing of the first cherub. ¹³The wings of these cherubim extended twenty cubits. The cherubim^p stood on their feet, facing the nave. ¹⁴And he made the veil of blue and purple and crimson fabrics and fine linen, and he worked cherubim on it.

¹⁵In front of the house he made two pillars thirty-five cubits high, with a capital of five cubits on the top of each. ¹⁶He made chains like a necklace^q and put them on the tops of the pillars, and he made a hundred pomegranates and put them on the chains. ¹⁷He set up the pillars in front of the temple, one on the south, the other on the north; that on the south he called Jachin, and that on the north Boaz.

4 He made an altar of bronze, twenty cubits^r long and twenty cubits wide and ten cubits high. ²Then he made the sea of cast metal. It was round, ten cubits from brim to brim, and five cubits high, and a line of thirty cubits measured its circumference. ³Under it were figures of gourds,^{s} for ten cubits, compassing the sea all around. The gourds were in two rows, cast with it when it was cast. ⁴It stood on twelve oxen, three facing north, three facing west, three facing south, and three facing east. The sea was set on them, and all their rear parts were inward. ⁵Its thickness was a handbreadth.^{t} And its brim was made like the brim of a cup, like the flower of a lily. It held 3,000 baths.^{u} ⁶He also made ten basins in which to wash, and set five on the south side, and five on the north side. In these they were to rinse off what was used for the burnt offering, and the sea was for the priests to wash in.

[7]And he made ten golden lampstands as prescribed, and set them in the temple, five on the south side and five on the north. [8]He also made ten tables and placed them in the temple, five on the south side and five on the north. And he made a hundred basins of gold. [9]He made the court of the priests and the great court and doors for the court and overlaid their doors with bronze. [10]And he set the sea at the southeast corner of the house.

[11]Hiram also made the pots, the shovels, and the basins. So Hiram finished the work that he did for King Solomon on the house of God: [12]the two pillars, the bowls, and the two capitals on the top of the pillars; and the two latticeworks to cover the two bowls of the capitals that were on the top of the pillars; [13]and the 400 pomegranates for the two latticeworks, two rows of pomegranates for each latticework, to cover the two bowls of the capitals that were on the pillars. [14]He made the stands also,

and the basins on the stands, [15]and the one sea, and the twelve oxen underneath it. [16]The pots, the shovels, the forks, and all the equipment for these Huram-abi made of burnished bronze for King Solomon for the house of the LORD. [17]In the plain of the Jordan the king cast them, in the clay ground between Succoth and Zeredah.[v] [18]Solomon made all these things in great quantities, for the weight of the bronze was not sought.

[19]So Solomon made all the vessels that were in the house of God: the golden altar, the tables for the bread of the Presence, [20]the lampstands and their lamps of pure gold to burn before the inner sanctuary, as prescribed; [21]the flowers, the lamps, and the tongs, of purest gold; [22]the snuffers, basins, dishes for incense, and fire pans, of pure gold, and the sockets[w] of the temple, for the inner doors to the Most Holy Place and for the doors of the nave of the temple were of gold.

5 Thus all the work that Solomon did for the house of the LORD was finished. And Solomon brought in the things that David his father had dedicated, and stored the silver, the gold, and all the vessels in the treasuries of the house of God.

---

a Or *him*   b Septuagint, Vulgate; Hebrew *to*   c A *shekel* was about 2/5 ounce or 11 grams   d Ch 1:18 in Hebrew   e Ch 2:1 in Hebrew   f A *cor* was about 6 bushels or 220 liters   g A *bath* was about 6 gallons or 22 liters   h Septuagint; Hebrew lacks *the Lord*   i Syriac; Hebrew *foundations*   j A *cubit* was about 18 inches or 45 centimeters   k Compare 1 Kings 6:3; the meaning of the Hebrew is uncertain   l A *talent* was about 75 pounds or 34 kilograms   m A *shekel* was about 2/5 ounce or 11 grams   n Septuagint; the meaning of the Hebrew is uncertain   o Hebrew *they overlaid*   p Hebrew *they*   q Hebrew *chains in the inner sanctuary*   r A *cubit* was about 18 inches or 45 centimeters   s Compare 1 Kings 7:24; Hebrew *oxen*; twice in this verse   t A *handbreadth* was about 3 inches or 7.5 centimeters   u A *bath* was about 6 gallons or 22 liters   v Spelled *Zarethan* in 1 Kings 7:46   w Compare 1 Kings 7:50; Hebrew *the entrance of the house*

OVERVIEW: Commentators lift up Solomon's piety as they study his prayer and his careful construction of the temple. Solomon's prayer for wisdom shows that he believed himself and the people to be truly led by God. He undertakes the construction of the temple in order to demonstrate true worship of and service to the Lord of heaven and earth, who cannot be contained by any building. The building of the temple also provides an occasion for these writers to reflect on what it means for God to live in human hearts and in the church as a holy people.[1]

---

[1]See commentary on 1 Kings 3:3-15; 5:1–7:51.

1:1-13 Solomon Prays to God

A GOOD SHEPHERD. VIKTORIN STRIGEL: Solomon did not pray for wealth, honor or victory but rather for that which would far outlast them all, namely, wisdom. He asked that he might serve God by leading and accompanying the people through his office of king. In the same way, pastors of the church should pray to God that they might be able to lead and govern Christ's flock into all goodness.... It is also worth praising the humble phrase from Solomon's prayer in which he admitted that not he but the Lord was the people's true king. Therefore when he said, "Who can judge your people?" he was marvelously showing himself to be a vicar of God. Book of 2 Chronicles.[2]

Prayer for God's Promise to David. The English Annotations: Solomon here prays for the extent of God's promise which was that David's kingdom would be established not only for his time but forever. The prayer was also that Solomon would build God's house. The beginning of that promise was already accomplished, for Solomon was just made king and settled in the throne. Annotations on 2 Chronicles.[3]

A Generous God Who Gives More Than We Ask. John Mayer: Despite the many promises given to Solomon, God did not promise victories over his enemies and power to destroy them. This was omitted because God foresaw the rebellion of Jeroboam, who would escape Solomon's hands. Some think that Solomon asked for all kinds of wisdom not only to govern but also to understand all divine mysteries and all natural things. That's because his understanding was enlarged in these areas. And yet in the promise God does not express this. Instead other things are mentioned for which Solomon did not ask. From this it is intimated that this was asked. But the text is plain: it says that he asked God only for wisdom to govern and to manage the great affairs committed to him. But God, who is wont to give more to his faithful servants than they ask, gave him a most large understanding in all other things also. Yet it is not to be thought that he had such a complete knowledge of heavenly mysteries. On the contrary, those under the gospel were more enlightened in these areas, for such mysteries were hidden in times past but now have been revealed. Commentary on Chronicles.[4]

1:14-17 Solomon Given Wealth

Whether Solomon Sinned by Excess. John Mayer: Some think that Solomon sinned by excess. But this is not to be thought, for his wealth is spoken to his commendation and for the setting forth of his glory. And God, by his example, sought to teach that the riches of this world are at God's disposal. For when it seems good to God, he can extraordinarily enrich his servants. And natural people will not be taught this but by example. For when in the primitive church Christians were poor, the heathen said foolishly that their God was weak and poor because he would have enriched them if he were able. Commentary on Chronicles.[5]

2:1-18 Solomon's Preparations

Physical and Spiritual Temples. Viktorin Strigel: When people are converted to God, it is rightly said that they are holy temples of God, for God lives in them. A temple made of stones, however, can be truly said to be holy when it is dedicated to the service of God. Stephen differentiated between these things in Acts 7, where he said, "It was Solomon who built a house for him. Yet the Most High does not dwell in houses made by hands, as the prophet says, 'Heaven is my throne and the earth is my footstool. What kind of house will you build for me, says the Lord, or what is the place of my rest? Did not my hand make all these things?'" For if God were to be in any one place, then God would not be God, as Augustine clearly teaches in his exposition of Psalm 75 and which Solomon himself means when we say, "Heaven, even highest heaven cannot contain him." Why then did Solomon, who taught about the spiritual temple, build a temple if God does not live in a temple made of human hands? Solomon posed this question to make clear to the people that they would gather at the temple for preaching, prayer and public ceremonies. Book of 2 Chronicles.[6]

---

[2]Strigel, *Libri Samuelis, Regum et Paralipomenon*, 492.
[3]Downame, ed., *Annotations* (1657), Bbbb1v*; citing 1 Chron 17:11, 12.
[4]Mayer, *Many Commentaries in One*, 20*.

[5]Mayer, *Many Commentaries in One*, 23*.
[6]Strigel, *Libri Samuelis, Regum et Paralipomenon*, 493; citing Acts 7:47-50.

Determined to Build the Temple. The English Annotations: The meaning that Solomon purposed to build the temple signifies that he said it in his heart or to himself. After David informed Solomon and others that it was God's mind that Solomon should build him a house, it came upon the heart of Solomon that he should do so, and he determined in his heart, or within himself, to build it. Annotations on 2 Chronicles.[7]

David's Positive Influence on Hiram. John Mayer: It is most probable that this King Hiram had knowledge of the true God, which he probably attained by means of his friendship with David. And this is the reason why he spoke piously in his letter to Solomon. And concerning Hiram's sending to Solomon, it is to be understood that he, being a neighbor and not wanting to defer long in responding, did it at the beginning of Solomon's reign. Commentary on Chronicles.[8]

Two Good Kings. The English Annotations: The kings of Tyre and of Israel were regularly in different realms of their kingdoms, and they were forced to declare their minds to one another through letters and messengers. This proved every way as effectual as if they had spoken together. Hiram took notice of Solomon's letter, which indicated prudence and piety. And in this respect he judged him to be a good king. Hiram knew that Israel was God's peculiar people, and so he inferred that it was God's love for Israel that moved him to provide such a king for them. Annotations on 2 Chronicles.[9]

3:1-17 *The Building Begins*

Christ and the Temple. Viktorin Strigel: Solomon's building of the temple is a figure for Christ. For just as Solomon did not spare gold or precious stones in building the temple, neither in building the church did Christ spare his own blood, which is the most precious thing of all. He shed not just a drop but let his blood flow abundantly like a wave over all the parts of the Lord's body. What, therefore, is left for you to do or not to do? He brought sight to the blind, released the captives, recovered the lost and reconciled sinners, as Bernard said in sermon 22 on the Song of Solomon. Book of 2 Chronicles.[10]

Location of the Lord's House. The English Annotations: The choice of this location was discussed in 1 Chronicles 21. In this place where the angel destroyed the Israelites as a result of David's numbering the people. And it is where God commanded the angel to cease the killing. So David built an altar and offered offerings on it. And then the Lord answered David from heaven on the altar. On these grounds David appointed this place to be the location for the Lord's house. Annotations on 2 Chronicles.[11]

Mount Moriah. John Mayer: Mount Moriah was on the threshing floor of Araunah, which was shown to David. This mount, according to Andronicus, stood on the east side of Jerusalem near the wall and was rocky. Toward the west side of it was Mount Zion. Northward was Mount Bezetha and southward was Mount Acra. Mount Moriah was the place where the Lord ordered Abraham to go sacrifice his son. But after the Lord's appearance to Abraham there, this mount only carried this name of Moriah, or "vision." And it was within the tribe of Benjamin according to some but in the tribe of Judah according to others. The reason why people understand this differently is because sometimes holy Scripture speaks of it in one tribe and sometimes in the other. Some therefore hold that this mount was divided by a line between these two tribes, and so part of the temple stood in the one tribe and part in the other.

---

[7]Downame, ed., *Annotations* (1657), Bbbb1v*; citing 1 Chron 28:6; 1 Kings 5:5.

[8]Mayer, *Many Commentaries in One*, 27*.

[9]Downame, ed., *Annotations* (1657), Bbbb2r*.

[10]Strigel, *Libri Samuelis, Regum et Paralipomenon*, 495.

[11]Downame, ed., *Annotations* (1657), Bbbb2v*; citing 1 Chron 21.

Sometimes the temple is spoken of as standing on Mount Zion. That's because Mount Moriah was contiguous with it, and it was more known. Therefore under that name Mount Moriah is to be understood as an appurtenance to it. COMMENTARY ON CHRONICLES.[12]

CHERUBIM. JOHN MAYER: The entire house was finally overlaid with gold, and all things in it. And the most holy place was covered with the finest gold. And in the most holy place there were also two cherubim made of olive wood. The height of each cherubim was ten cubits. They had wings extending twenty cubits from one side of the house to the other, that is, the two wings of one ten cubits with one of which it touched the wing of the other, and with the other wall on one side. The faces of the cherubim stood toward the temple, which was different from the cherubim set up by Moses. For in Moses' time they looked with their faces toward one another: "The cherubim shall spread out their wings above, overshadowing the mercy seat with their wings, their faces one to another; toward the mercy seat shall the faces of the cherubim be." What manner of faces they had in Solomon's time is not known. Peter Martyr Vermigli thinks they had faces like young men, but Josephus says that it is uncertain what they looked like. COMMENTARY ON CHRONICLES.[13]

4:1-5:1 *The Sacred Furnishings of the Temple*

PREPARING THE VESSELS. VIKTORIN STRIGEL: Solomon's temple contained vessels of gold and bronze, as well as vessels set aside for other use. In the same way, God has ordained various callings within the church to be individually useful, as it says in Ephesians 2: "For we are his workmanship, created in Christ Jesus for good works, which God prepared beforehand, that we should walk in them." In this instance, such preparation means giving vocations and resources, as God prepared Samuel, David, Isaiah, Jeremiah and similar people for admirable works through whom he called, ruled over and preserved the church. As it says elsewhere, "Confirm in us, O God, that which you have worked in us." Therefore Paul wrote that we have been prepared by God for good works; that is, we have not only been commanded, ordained and set in motion but also assisted and made firm. Although the church has struggled with great difficulties, as seen in the afflictions of Jeremiah, Paul and many others, nevertheless the church manages to do great things and bring salvation to many, even though most of the world does not know it. But we do not owe such things to the knowledge of our vocations but to the fact that these works were prepared by God. BOOK OF 2 CHRONICLES.[14]

THE BRONZE ALTAR. THE ENGLISH ANNOTATIONS: Frequent mention is made of this altar in Solomon's time and of the offerings made on it. However, in the book of Kings there is no mention of making it. This altar of burnt offerings far exceeded that altar in the book of Exodus, for the temple far exceeded the tabernacle. The altar's twenty cubits in length and width was at least ten yards squared. It was so large because the priests offered so many oxen and other great beasts on it. The altar's height was at least fifteen feet high, and there was a plain ascent like a hill to go up and make offerings on it. In this respect the priest is said to "come down" from the altar. . . . The reason that it was so high was so that the people in the courts could all see the offerings laid on the altar and, by the sight of the smoke and the flames ascending up, they could be moved to raise up their hearts to heaven. And by the sight of the burnt offerings they could remember their sins and of the sacrifice of Christ to expiate these sins. ANNOTATIONS ON 2 CHRONICLES.[15]

---

[14]Strigel, *Libri Samuelis, Regum et Paralipomenon*, 497; citing Eph 2:10; Ps 68:29 Vg.

[15]Downame, ed., *Annotations* (1657), Bbbb2v*; citing 1 Kings 8:22, 31, 54, 64; 9:25; Ex 27:1; 1 Chron 22:5; Lev 9:22.

---

[12]Mayer, *Many Commentaries in One*, 29*.

[13]Mayer, *Many Commentaries in One*, 32; citing Ex 25:20*.

Candlesticks Foreshadow the Light of the Gospel. John Mayer: Moses made a candlestick only, to which Solomon added ten more. And, if they were like those of Moses, each candlestick held many lights, and a whole talent of gold went with it. The number of lights and tables for showbread multiplied in this way under Solomon, who was a figure of Christ, figuratively foreshadowing the multiplication of light under the gospel. That is, it foreshadowed that the light should be much brighter under the gospel than under the law. In the same way, the spiritual food of the Word of God in the New Testament superseded that of the Old Testament. Commentary on Chronicles.[16]

---

[16]Mayer, *Many Commentaries in One*, 37*.

5:2–7:22 THE DEDICATION OF THE TEMPLE

[2]Then Solomon assembled the elders of Israel and all the heads of the tribes, the leaders of the fathers' houses of the people of Israel, in Jerusalem, to bring up the ark of the covenant of the LORD out of the city of David, which is Zion. [3]And all the men of Israel assembled before the king at the feast that is in the seventh month. [4]And all the elders of Israel came, and the Levites took up the ark. [5]And they brought up the ark, the tent of meeting, and all the holy vessels that were in the tent; the Levitical priests brought them up. [6]And King Solomon and all the congregation of Israel, who had assembled before him, were before the ark, sacrificing so many sheep and oxen that they could not be counted or numbered. [7]Then the priests brought the ark of the covenant of the LORD to its place, in the inner sanctuary of the house, in the Most Holy Place, underneath the wings of the cherubim. [8]The cherubim spread out their wings over the place of the ark, so that the cherubim made a covering above the ark and its poles. [9]And the poles were so long that the ends of the poles were seen from the Holy Place before the inner sanctuary, but they could not be seen from outside. And they are[a] there to this day. [10]There was nothing in the ark except the two tablets that Moses put there at Horeb, where the LORD made a covenant with the people of Israel, when they came out of Egypt. [11]And when the priests came out of the Holy Place (for all the priests who were present had consecrated themselves, without regard to their divisions, [12]and all the Levitical singers, Asaph, Heman, and Jeduthun, their sons and kinsmen, arrayed in fine linen, with cymbals, harps, and lyres, stood east of the altar with 120 priests who were trumpeters; [13]and it was the duty of the trumpeters and singers to make themselves heard in unison in praise and thanksgiving to the LORD), and when the song was raised, with trumpets and cymbals and other musical instruments, in praise to the LORD,

"For he is good,
    for his steadfast love endures forever,"

the house, the house of the LORD, was filled with a cloud, [14]so that the priests could not stand to minister because of the cloud, for the glory of the LORD filled the house of God.

6 Then Solomon said, "The LORD has said that he would dwell in thick darkness. [2]But I have built you an exalted house, a place for you to dwell in forever."

[3]Then the king turned around and blessed all the assembly of Israel, while all the assembly of Israel stood. [4]And he said, "Blessed be the LORD, the God of Israel, who with his hand has fulfilled what he promised with his mouth to David my father, saying, [5]'Since the day that I brought my people out of the land of Egypt, I chose no city out of all the tribes of Israel in which to build a house, that my name might be there, and I chose no man as prince over my people Israel; [6]but I have chosen Jerusalem that my name may be there, and I have chosen David to be over my people Israel.' [7]Now it was in the heart of David my father to build a house for the name of the LORD, the God of Israel. [8]But the LORD said to David my father, 'Whereas it was in your heart to build a house for my name, you did well that it was in your heart. [9]Nevertheless, it is not you who shall build the house, but your son who shall be born to you shall build the house for my name.' [10]Now the LORD has fulfilled his promise that he made. For I have risen in the place of David my father and sit on the throne of Israel, as the LORD promised, and I have built the house for the name of the LORD, the God of Israel. [11]And there I have set the ark, in which is the covenant of the LORD that he made with the people of Israel."

[12]Then Solomon stood before the altar of the LORD in the presence of all the assembly of Israel and spread out his hands. [13]Solomon had made a bronze platform five cubits[b] long, five cubits wide, and three cubits high, and had set it in the court, and he stood on it. Then he knelt on his knees in the presence of all the assembly of Israel, and spread out his hands toward heaven, [14]and said, "O LORD, God of Israel, there is no God like you, in heaven or on earth, keeping covenant and showing steadfast love to your servants who walk before you with all their heart, [15]who have kept with your servant David my father what you declared to him. You spoke

with your mouth, and with your hand have fulfilled it this day. ¹⁶Now therefore, O LORD, God of Israel, keep for your servant David my father what you have promised him, saying, 'You shall not lack a man to sit before me on the throne of Israel, if only your sons pay close attention to their way, to walk in my law as you have walked before me.' ¹⁷Now therefore, O LORD, God of Israel, let your word be confirmed, which you have spoken to your servant David.

¹⁸"But will God indeed dwell with man on the earth? Behold, heaven and the highest heaven cannot contain you, how much less this house that I have built! ¹⁹Yet have regard to the prayer of your servant and to his plea, O LORD my God, listening to the cry and to the prayer that your servant prays before you, ²⁰that your eyes may be open day and night toward this house, the place where you have promised to set your name, that you may listen to the prayer that your servant offers toward this place. ²¹And listen to the pleas of your servant and of your people Israel, when they pray toward this place. And listen from heaven your dwelling place, and when you hear, forgive.

²²"If a man sins against his neighbor and is made to take an oath and comes and swears his oath before your altar in this house, ²³then hear from heaven and act and judge your servants, repaying the guilty by bringing his conduct on his own head, and vindicating the righteous by rewarding him according to his righteousness.

²⁴"If your people Israel are defeated before the enemy because they have sinned against you, and they turn again and acknowledge your name and pray and plead with you in this house, ²⁵then hear from heaven and forgive the sin of your people Israel and bring them again to the land that you gave to them and to their fathers.

²⁶"When heaven is shut up and there is no rain because they have sinned against you, if they pray toward this place and acknowledge your name and turn from their sin, when you afflict° them, ²⁷then hear in heaven and forgive the sin of your servants, your people Israel, when you teach them the good wayᵈ in which they should walk, and grant rain upon your land, which you have given to your people as an inheritance.

²⁸"If there is famine in the land, if there is pestilence or blight or mildew or locust or caterpillar, if their enemies besiege them in the land at their gates, whatever plague, whatever sickness there is, ²⁹whatever prayer, whatever plea is made by any man or by all your people Israel, each knowing his own affliction and his own sorrow and stretching out his hands toward this house, ³⁰then hear from heaven your dwelling place and forgive and render to each whose heart you know, according to all his ways, for you, you only, know the hearts of the children of mankind, ³¹that they may fear you and walk in your ways all the days that they live in the land that you gave to our fathers.

³²"Likewise, when a foreigner, who is not of your people Israel, comes from a far country for the sake of your great name and your mighty hand and your outstretched arm, when he comes and prays toward this house, ³³hear from heaven your dwelling place and do according to all for which the foreigner calls to you, in order that all the peoples of the earth may know your name and fear you, as do your people Israel, and that they may know that this house that I have built is called by your name.

³⁴"If your people go out to battle against their enemies, by whatever way you shall send them, and they pray to you toward this city that you have chosen and the house that I have built for your name, ³⁵then hear from heaven their prayer and their plea, and maintain their cause.

³⁶"If they sin against you—for there is no one who does not sin—and you are angry with them and give them to an enemy, so that they are carried away captive to a land far or near, ³⁷yet if they turn their heart in the land to which they have been carried captive, and repent and plead with you in the land of their captivity, saying, 'We have sinned and have acted perversely and wickedly,' ³⁸if they repent with all their mind and with all their heart in the land of their captivity to which they were carried captive, and pray toward their land, which you gave to their fathers, the city that you have chosen and the house that I have built for your name, ³⁹then hear from heaven your dwelling place their prayer and their pleas, and maintain their cause and forgive your people who have sinned against you. ⁴⁰Now, O my God, let your eyes be open and your ears attentive to the prayer of this place.

⁴¹"And now arise, O Lord God, and go to your
resting place,
you and the ark of your might.
Let your priests, O Lord God, be clothed with
salvation,
and let your saints rejoice in your goodness.
⁴²O Lord God, do not turn away the face of
your anointed one!
Remember your steadfast love for David
your servant."

7 As soon as Solomon finished his prayer, fire came
down from heaven and consumed the burnt
offering and the sacrifices, and the glory of the Lord
filled the temple. ²And the priests could not enter the
house of the Lord, because the glory of the Lord
filled the Lord's house. ³When all the people of Israel
saw the fire come down and the glory of the Lord on
the temple, they bowed down with their faces to the
ground on the pavement and worshiped and gave
thanks to the Lord, saying, "For he is good, for his
steadfast love endures forever."

⁴Then the king and all the people offered sacrifice
before the Lord. ⁵King Solomon offered as a sacrifice
22,000 oxen and 120,000 sheep. So the king and all the
people dedicated the house of God. ⁶The priests stood at
their posts; the Levites also, with the instruments for
music to the Lord that King David had made for
giving thanks to the Lord—for his steadfast love
endures forever—whenever David offered praises by
their ministry;ᵉ opposite them the priests sounded
trumpets, and all Israel stood.

⁷And Solomon consecrated the middle of the court
that was before the house of the Lord, for there he
offered the burnt offering and the fat of the peace
offerings, because the bronze altar Solomon had made
could not hold the burnt offering and the grain
offering and the fat.

⁸At that time Solomon held the feast for seven days,
and all Israel with him, a very great assembly, from
Lebo-hamath to the Brook of Egypt. ⁹And on the eighth
day they held a solemn assembly, for they had kept the
dedication of the altar seven days and the feast seven

days. ¹⁰On the twenty-third day of the seventh month he
sent the people away to their homes, joyful and glad of
heart for the prosperity that the Lord had granted to
David and to Solomon and to Israel his people.

¹¹Thus Solomon finished the house of the Lord
and the king's house. All that Solomon had planned to
do in the house of the Lord and in his own house he
successfully accomplished. ¹²Then the Lord appeared
to Solomon in the night and said to him: "I have
heard your prayer and have chosen this place for
myself as a house of sacrifice. ¹³When I shut up the
heavens so that there is no rain, or command the
locust to devour the land, or send pestilence among my
people, ¹⁴if my people who are called by my name
humble themselves, and pray and seek my face and
turn from their wicked ways, then I will hear from
heaven and will forgive their sin and heal their land.
¹⁵Now my eyes will be open and my ears attentive to
the prayer that is made in this place. ¹⁶For now I have
chosen and consecrated this house that my name may
be there forever. My eyes and my heart will be there
for all time. ¹⁷And as for you, if you will walk before
me as David your father walked, doing according to
all that I have commanded you and keeping my
statutes and my rules, ¹⁸then I will establish your royal
throne, as I covenanted with David your father, saying,
'You shall not lack a man to rule Israel.'

¹⁹"But if youᶠ turn aside and forsake my statutes
and my commandments that I have set before you,
and go and serve other gods and worship them, ²⁰then
I will pluck youᵍ up from my land that I have given
you, and this house that I have consecrated for my
name, I will cast out of my sight, and I will make it a
proverb and a byword among all peoples. ²¹And at
this house, which was exalted, everyone passing by
will be astonished and say, 'Why has the Lord done
thus to this land and to this house?' ²²Then they will
say, 'Because they abandoned the Lord, the God of
their fathers who brought them out of the land of
Egypt, and laid hold on other gods and worshiped
them and served them. Therefore he has brought all
this disaster on them.'"

---

a Hebrew *it is*   **b** A *cubit* was about 18 inches or 45 centimeters   **c** Septuagint, Vulgate; Hebrew *answer*   **d** Septuagint, Syriac, Vulgate (compare 1 Kings 8:36);
Hebrew *toward the good way*   **e** Hebrew *by their hand*   **f** The Hebrew for *you* is plural here   **g** Hebrew *them*; twice in this verse

OVERVIEW: These chapters present the many blessings that come when God, the king and the people are in harmony: Solomon assembles the people in peace and blesses them; the Lord adds divine blessing with a sign from heaven. At the same time, the commentators wrestle with some difficult passages: some juxtapose Solomon's words that God would "dwell in thick darkness" with the words that "God is light"; others compare the contents of the ark as described here with the description given in Hebrews. Most of all, these writers reflect on the rich examples of piety in terms of what it means to worship purely, pray diligently and live together faithfully as the people of God.

5:2 Solomon Assembles the People

GATHERED IN PEACE. VIKTORIN STRIGEL: Nothing is more beautiful than when all kinds of people—teachers, rulers, magistrates, soldiers and the general population—are gathered together in the greatest peace under one head. They gather under the true God in recognition of the promised Messiah and in the light of the promises that have been made, just as the Lord prayed "that they may be one even as we are one." The people of Israel here provide an example of these sure promises for the church, for the priests and Levites are carrying the ark of the covenant, that is, the true teaching about God. Solomon and the entire congregation assist the ministers with all their hearts. We learn from this example that the church should seek to be an assembly that upholds harmonious teaching, makes common prayer and common confession, offers benevolence and kindness, and—as this prayer shows—should be one in God, not seeking occasions for tearing apart. Such things are themselves sin, hinder prayer, and produce the fiercest hatred, factions, war and devastation of humankind. BOOK OF 2 CHRONICLES.[1]

5:3-9 "To This Day"

THE ARK STILL THERE. JOHN MAYER: The ark, that holy figure of God's presence that had hitherto been carried from place to place many times as it had no settled place to rest, now came to rest. And after this time it was never carried out by the priests anymore. Therefore it is said that it is there "to this day." COMMENTARY ON CHRONICLES.[2]

PROVERBIAL SPEECH. THE ENGLISH ANNOTATIONS: It is said that the poles were still there "to this day." If Ezra was the author of this book, this phrase cannot be taken of the time when he lived. For we find no mention of the ark after the burning of the temple. Therefore it must be here taken as a proverbial speech. ANNOTATIONS ON 2 CHRONICLES.[3]

5:10 Nothing Else in the Ark

RECONCILING CHRONICLES WITH HEBREWS. JOHN MAYER: It says that there was nothing in the ark but only the two tables of Moses. This seems to disagree with Hebrews, where it says: "Having the golden altar of incense and the ark of the covenant covered on all sides with gold, in which was a golden urn holding the manna, and Aaron's staff that budded, and the tablets of the covenant." This of course shows that there were two extra things in the ark. But Junius reconciles these two passages. He says that the manna and the staff were laid up *about* the ark, but not actually *in* it. For in the ark only the tablets remained. . . . Another option is that in Moses' time only the tablets were in the ark but later the prophet Jeremiah added the other two. COMMENTARY ON CHRONICLES.[4]

5:11-14 Filled with a Cloud

GOD APPEARS BY MEANS OF A CLOUD. JOHN MAYER: It is said that a cloud filled the house of the

---

[1]Strigel, *Libri Samuelis, Regum et Paralipomenon*, 498-99; citing Jn 17:22.

[2]Mayer, *Many Commentaries in One*, 38*.
[3]Downame, ed., *Annotations* (1657), Bbbb3r*; citing 1 Kings 8:8.
[4]Mayer, *Many Commentaries in One*, 39-40*; citing Heb 9:4.

Lord. This is more largely related, for all the priests were present and not those four only who carried the ark in, the distributions into courses not being at this time observed, and the Levites were also present with instruments of music. And priests with trumpets 120 in number were praising the Lord. Then the cloud filled the house. In fact the priests could not even stand to minister on account of the cloud. Hereby God manifested his presence and showed his acceptance of this house as his own, just as when the tabernacle was newly set up in Numbers: "On the day that the tabernacle was set up, the cloud covered the tabernacle, the tent of testimony." COMMENTARY ON CHRONICLES.[5]

6:1-2 Solomon's Words

GOD IS LIGHT. VIKTORIN STRIGEL: I do not understand what Solomon meant to say here that God "would dwell in thick darkness." For "God is light, and in him is no darkness at all," as 1 John 1 says. And Paul testified in 1 Timothy 6 of the ark of God's covenant, which no one was allowed to approach: this is the Lord "who dwells in unapproachable light, whom no one has ever seen or can see." Though God's essence may be inaccessible, God's will for our salvation is revealed in the temple, that is, in the Word and in the sacraments. This is the most simple explanation of these words that Solomon prayed from his heart. BOOK OF 2 CHRONICLES.[6]

6:3-11 Solomon Blesses the People

THE TEMPLE AND THE CHURCH. JOHN CALVIN: God was not worshiped except through types in this temple of Solomon. Hence let us conclude that, as God is spirit and truth (John 4:24), there must also be a temple that corresponds to his nature. Thus we are bound to glorify God, because his promise has finally been fulfilled in us, who only deserved to be built into a pigsty, since we were so full of infection and rot! Yet our Lord Jesus

Christ has purified us and willed that we be built into a house set apart for him. Furthermore we see that this promise was not restricted to the Jews, but that it had its extension in all nations of the earth when it pleased God to manifest his mercy everywhere. SERMONS ON SECOND SAMUEL.[7]

WHEN WE WILL WHAT GOD DOES NOT. JOHN MAYER: Solomon blessed God for fulfilling what he had promised to David his father in granting him his son to build a house, which was in David's mind and approved beforehand. Indeed, God had appointed it in his providence. From this Peter Martyr Vermigli gathers that a person may sometimes lawfully will that which God does not will. But then the person must submit to God's will. Such is what David did concerning the building of the temple and also how Christ prayed that the cup might pass from him in the Gospels. COMMENTARY ON CHRONICLES.[8]

SPECIAL TYPE OF CHRIST. THE ENGLISH ANNOTATIONS: It is said that "I have chosen no man as prince over my people Israel." However, this is not to be taken literally. For God also chose Saul as king, and other judges. But it refers specifically to David. God never chose such a ruler as David. Indeed David was a special type of Christ, in whose seed a royal succession was established until Christ. ANNOTATIONS ON 2 CHRONICLES.[9]

6:12-42 Solomon's Prayer of Dedication

CHRIST THE DIVINE TEMPLE. JOHANN GERHARD: Let us pray in humility and not place confidence in personal merit, but only in God's grace. If our prayers depend on our worth, they are damned even if the heart were to sweat out blood in devotion. No one pleases God except in Christ. Therefore no one prays rightly but through Christ and according to Christ. Sacrifices that were

[7]Calvin, *Sermons on Second Samuel*, 1:328-29.
[8]Mayer, *Many Commentaries in One*, 41*.
[9]Downame, ed., *Annotations* (1657), Bbbb3r*; citing 1 Sam 9:16; Judg 2:16, 17; Gen 49:10; 2 Sam 7:16.

[5]Mayer, *Many Commentaries in One*, 40*; citing Num 9:15.
[6]Strigel, *Libri Samuelis, Regum et Paralipomenon*, 500; citing 1 Jn 1:5.

offered on the tabernacle's only altar did not please God. And prayer does not please God, unless it is offered in Christ, the only altar. The Israelites' prayers were promised to be heard if they prayed with their faces toward Jerusalem. In the same way we must convert our prayers to Christ, who is the divine temple. SACRED MEDITATIONS.[10]

PRAISE AND PROMISES. JOHN MAYER: Solomon begins his prayer by ascribing all praise and glory to God for his excellence and sure performing of his promises. This especially applies to God's promises to David. In Solomon's saying that "there is no God like you," he does not refer to any specific person in the Trinity, as the Arians wrongly assume. He means that among those the superstitious world accounted as gods there is none like God—for the Father, Son and Holy Spirit is the only one and true God. Then Solomon prayed for the constant performance of the promise made to David. It's not that Solomon doubted the promise, but—inasmuch as it was on condition of his posterity's perseverance in obedience to his laws—he prayed that this grace might be given this posterity continually. COMMENTARY ON CHRONICLES.[11]

ALWAYS IN GOD'S PRESENCE. THE ENGLISH ANNOTATIONS: The phrase "to walk in my law" is an interpretation of 1 Kings, where the phrase "to walk before me" is used. It means that those who set God before them make God's law their rule. And those who make God's law their rule walk before God. That is, they carry themselves as those who know they are always in God's presence. ANNOTATIONS ON 2 CHRONICLES.[12]

PRAYER CAN OPEN OR SHUT HEAVEN. JOHN MAYER: Solomon says, "When heaven is shut up and there is no rain." By the heavens some understand the middle region of the air, where the clouds are produced. Yet Peter Martyr Vermigli understands this word as referring rather to the higher

heavens, where the stars are, by the inference that it is there from which rain comes. And when rain is stopped, the heavens may be said to have been shut up. I rather think according to the common opinion, namely, that the parts from which the rain comes are referred to. And it is here suggested that the rain is shut up by sin and opened by penitent prayer, whereby we may see the extent of sin's power. For sin can shut the heavens from raining, and it can shut one out of the kingdom. And there is also a judgment sometimes by too much rain, but these dry parts in the Bible were seldom annoyed by too much rain. Solomon therefore directs his petition as necessity required, whose punishment was by drought and not by rain. COMMENTARY ON CHRONICLES.[13]

GOD AND THE ARK. THE ENGLISH ANNOTATIONS: The resting place refers to the temple, where the ark was settled. Solomon here entreats God to take possession of that house which he had built for him and to dwell and abide there forever. And because God was wont to manifest his presence over the ark, God and the ark are joined together. ANNOTATIONS ON 2 CHRONICLES.[14]

7:1-3 Fire from Heaven and God's Glory Shown

SEEING THE GLORY OF GOD. VIKTORIN STRIGEL: Ever since the beginning, God has always revealed himself in two ways: through word and act [testimonium]. Thus Adam was first given the word and then placed above all things in nature, which was the sign from God. After the fall the work from God was the assurance of the remission of sins. For that reason God added another word, namely, the promise of grace and—in this case—added the sign that "fire came down from heaven and consumed the burnt offering." Thus God revealed himself to Solomon in two ways: first,

---

[10]Gerhard, *Gerhardi Meditationes Sacrae*, 109-10.
[11]Mayer, *Many Commentaries in One*, 41*.
[12]Downame, ed., *Annotations* (1657), Bbbb3r*; citing 1 Kings 8:25.

[13]Mayer, *Many Commentaries in One*, 42*.
[14]Downame, ed., *Annotations* (1657), Bbbb3r*; citing 1 Chron 28:2; 2 Kings 19:15.

through the sign of reconciliation and, second, according to a clear word which showed that Solomon's prayer had been heard. But what is the glory of God that would entirely fill God's house? Without a doubt, such an appeal to God's glory would be shown to be the Son of God, whom Moses himself asked to see, saying, "Show me your glory." For the Son of God, as testified in the letter to the Hebrews, is "the radiance of the glory of God and the exact imprint of his nature." For this reason the universal church gives thanks to God with the people of Israel for this immense benefit that God established a mediator, the Son, whose obedience would satisfy wrath, who would be victorious through his death, and himself receive and save humankind. The simple meaning of this verse in repeated in Psalm 118: "Oh give thanks to the Lord, for he is good; for his steadfast love endures forever!" BOOK OF 2 CHRONICLES.[15]

GOD'S ACCEPTANCE THROUGH FIRE. JOHN MAYER: It is said that when Solomon was done praying, fire came down from heaven and consumed the burnt offerings and sacrifices. And the majesty of the Lord filled the house. A cloud is said before to have filled the house, which is called the glory of the Lord. And the sacrifices of oxen and sheep offered are said to be innumerable. In fact we are not to think that all of these sacrifices were offered in one day. Rather they were offered over several days. . . . The fire coming down on the sacrifices was to show God's gracious acceptance. And by reason of the great multitudes of sacrifices, which the brazen altar could not contain, Solomon sanctified the middle of the priests' court; that is, he caused the high priest to sanctify the pavement of that court near the altar so that sacrifices might be offered also. COMMENTARY ON CHRONICLES.[16]

CLOUD TO DISGUISE GOD'S GLORY. THE ENGLISH ANNOTATIONS: The glory of the Lord referred to a thick cloud that set out the incomprehensible glory of God. And this glory, if it had shone forth in its brightness, would have utterly dazzled and confounded the beholders. God's glory, therefore, was covered with a cloud to show that it was present there but could not be discerned by a mortal eye. This is how God dwelt with Moses when the Lord had to cover Moses' face with his hand. ANNOTATIONS ON 2 CHRONICLES.[17]

7:4-10 Dedication of the Temple

ONE AND THE SAME. THE ENGLISH ANNOTATIONS: Because the altar was the principal thing about the temple and in the service of God (since it is where the offerings were laid), it is put forward here by synecdoche for the whole house of God and for all things pertaining to it. Therefore it is said that they "dedicated the house of God." This phrase is also said concerning the second temple. This dedication of the house and of the altar set out one and the same thing, unless it should be imagined that there were two dedications: one of the temple and one of the altar. ANNOTATIONS ON 2 CHRONICLES.[18]

7:11-22 If My People Pray

A SECOND APPEARANCE. THE ENGLISH ANNOTATIONS: God appeared to Solomon a second time. The first time was at the beginning of his reign before he began to build the temple. Now the Lord appears to him after the temple had been built. God did this to give testimony of his acceptance of Solomon's prayer and to return a gracious answer to him. ANNOTATIONS ON 2 CHRONICLES.[19]

---

[15]Strigel, *Libri Samuelis, Regum et Paralipomenon*, 505; citing Ex 33:18; Heb 1:3; Ps 118:29.
[16]Mayer, *Many Commentaries in One*, 43*.
[17]Downame, ed., *Annotations* (1657), Bbbb3v-4r*; citing Ex 33:22; 1 Kings 8:10.
[18]Downame, ed., *Annotations* (1657), Bbbb4r*; citing 1 Kings 8:63; Ezra 6:16, 17.
[19]Downame, ed., *Annotations* (1657), Bbbb4r*.

8:1–9:31 SOLOMON'S
ACCOMPLISHMENTS AND EXPLOITS

¹At the end of twenty years, in which Solomon had built the house of the Lord and his own house, ²Solomon rebuilt the cities that Hiram had given to him, and settled the people of Israel in them.

³And Solomon went to Hamath-zobah and took it. ⁴He built Tadmor in the wilderness and all the store cities that he built in Hamath. ⁵He also built Upper Beth-horon and Lower Beth-horon, fortified cities with walls, gates, and bars, ⁶and Baalath, and all the store cities that Solomon had and all the cities for his chariots and the cities for his horsemen, and whatever Solomon desired to build in Jerusalem, in Lebanon, and in all the land of his dominion. ⁷All the people who were left of the Hittites, the Amorites, the Perizzites, the Hivites, and the Jebusites, who were not of Israel, ⁸from their descendants who were left after them in the land, whom the people of Israel had not destroyed—these Solomon drafted as forced labor, and so they are to this day. ⁹But of the people of Israel Solomon made no slaves for his work; they were soldiers, and his officers, the commanders of his chariots, and his horsemen. ¹⁰And these were the chief officers of King Solomon, 250, who exercised authority over the people.

¹¹Solomon brought Pharaoh's daughter up from the city of David to the house that he had built for her, for he said, "My wife shall not live in the house of David king of Israel, for the places to which the ark of the Lord has come are holy."

¹²Then Solomon offered up burnt offerings to the Lord on the altar of the Lord that he had built before the vestibule, ¹³as the duty of each day required, offering according to the commandment of Moses for the Sabbaths, the new moons, and the three annual feasts—the Feast of Unleavened Bread, the Feast of Weeks, and the Feast of Booths. ¹⁴According to the ruling of David his father, he appointed the divisions of the priests for their service, and the Levites for their offices of praise and ministry before the priests as the duty of each day required, and the gatekeepers in their divisions at each gate, for so David the man of God

had commanded. ¹⁵And they did not turn aside from what the king had commanded the priests and Levites concerning any matter and concerning the treasuries.

¹⁶Thus was accomplished all the work of Solomon from[a] the day the foundation of the house of the Lord was laid until it was finished. So the house of the Lord was completed.

¹⁷Then Solomon went to Ezion-geber and Eloth on the shore of the sea, in the land of Edom. ¹⁸And Hiram sent to him by the hand of his servants ships and servants familiar with the sea, and they went to Ophir together with the servants of Solomon and brought from there 450 talents[b] of gold and brought it to King Solomon.

9 Now when the queen of Sheba heard of the fame of Solomon, she came to Jerusalem to test him with hard questions, having a very great retinue and camels bearing spices and very much gold and precious stones. And when she came to Solomon, she told him all that was on her mind. ²And Solomon answered all her questions. There was nothing hidden from Solomon that he could not explain to her. ³And when the queen of Sheba had seen the wisdom of Solomon, the house that he had built, ⁴the food of his table, the seating of his officials, and the attendance of his servants, and their clothing, his cupbearers, and their clothing, and his burnt offerings that he offered at the house of the Lord, there was no more breath in her.

⁵And she said to the king, "The report was true that I heard in my own land of your words and of your wisdom, ⁶but I did not believe the[c] reports until I came and my own eyes had seen it. And behold, half the greatness of your wisdom was not told me; you surpass the report that I heard. ⁷Happy are your wives![d] Happy are these your servants, who continually stand before you and hear your wisdom! ⁸Blessed be the Lord your God, who has delighted in you and set you on his throne as king for the Lord your God! Because your God loved Israel and would establish them forever, he has made you king over them, that

you may execute justice and righteousness." ⁹Then she gave the king 120 talentsᵉ of gold, and a very great quantity of spices, and precious stones. There were no spices such as those that the queen of Sheba gave to King Solomon.

¹⁰Moreover, the servants of Hiram and the servants of Solomon, who brought gold from Ophir, brought algum wood and precious stones. ¹¹And the king made from the algum wood supports for the house of the Lord and for the king's house, lyres also and harps for the singers. There never was seen the like of them before in the land of Judah.

¹²And King Solomon gave to the queen of Sheba all that she desired, whatever she asked besides what she had brought to the king. So she turned and went back to her own land with her servants.

¹³Now the weight of gold that came to Solomon in one year was 666 talents of gold, ¹⁴besides that which the explorers and merchants brought. And all the kings of Arabia and the governors of the land brought gold and silver to Solomon. ¹⁵King Solomon made 200 large shields of beaten gold; 600 shekelsᶠ of beaten gold went into each shield. ¹⁶And he made 300 shields of beaten gold; 300 shekels of gold went into each shield; and the king put them in the House of the Forest of Lebanon. ¹⁷The king also made a great ivory throne and overlaid it with pure gold. ¹⁸The throne had six steps and a footstool of gold, which were attached to the throne, and on each side of the seat were armrests and two lions standing beside the armrests, ¹⁹while twelve lions stood there, one on each end of a step on the six steps. Nothing like it was ever made for any

kingdom. ²⁰All King Solomon's drinking vessels were of gold, and all the vessels of the House of the Forest of Lebanon were of pure gold. Silver was not considered as anything in the days of Solomon. ²¹For the king's ships went to Tarshish with the servants of Hiram. Once every three years the ships of Tarshish used to come bringing gold, silver, ivory, apes, and peacocks.ᵍ

²²Thus King Solomon excelled all the kings of the earth in riches and in wisdom. ²³And all the kings of the earth sought the presence of Solomon to hear his wisdom, which God had put into his mind. ²⁴Every one of them brought his present, articles of silver and of gold, garments, myrrh, spices, horses, and mules, so much year by year. ²⁵And Solomon had 4,000 stalls for horses and chariots, and 12,000 horsemen, whom he stationed in the chariot cities and with the king in Jerusalem. ²⁶And he ruled over all the kings from the Euphratesʰ to the land of the Philistines and to the border of Egypt. ²⁷And the king made silver as common in Jerusalem as stone, and he made cedar as plentiful as the sycamore of the Shephelah. ²⁸And horses were imported for Solomon from Egypt and from all lands.

²⁹Now the rest of the acts of Solomon, from first to last, are they not written in the history of Nathan the prophet, and in the prophecy of Ahijah the Shilonite, and in the visions of Iddo the seer concerning Jeroboam the son of Nebat? ³⁰Solomon reigned in Jerusalem over all Israel forty years. ³¹And Solomon slept with his fathers and was buried in the city of David his father, and Rehoboam his son reigned in his place.

a Septuagint, Syriac, Vulgate; Hebrew *to*   b A *talent* was about 75 pounds or 34 kilograms   c Hebrew *their*   d Septuagint (compare 1 Kings 10:8); Hebrew *men*   e A *talent* was about 75 pounds or 34 kilograms   f A *shekel* was about 2/5 ounce or 11 grams   g Or *baboons*   h Hebrew *the River*

Overview: Solomon was a builder of dwelling places, cities and ships. The commentators observe and consider both the practical and symbolic significance of these building projects, reminding us that Solomon, justly praised for his wealth and wisdom, also acknowledged his own sinfulness. This section concludes with allegorical interpretations of the temple furnishings.[1]

8:1-10 Solomon's Building Projects

Solomon the Wise Builder. The English Annotations: Solomon, like a pious and prudent prince, first built the Lord's house and then his own. Then he built cities for enlarging his kingdom and then for houses for his people to dwell. Annotations on 2 Chronicles.[2]

---

[1]See commentary on 1 Kings 9:1–10:29; 11:41-43.

[2]Downame, ed., *Annotations* (1645), PP2v*.

Cities Without Inhabitants. John Mayer:
Now, for the cities Hiram gave to Solomon, it is
uncertain how many they were or where they
stood. It is only said that when they were given to
Solomon, he built them and put Israelites into
them. Apparently they were cities decayed for lack
of inhabitants. For the country of the king of Tyre
was not so full of people. Commentary on
Chronicles.[3]

8:11-16 Solomon Marries Pharaoh's Daughter

Sin in Solomon. Viktorin Strigel: As
Solomon said in Ecclesiastes 7, "There is not a
righteous man on earth who does good and
never sins." Solomon bears witness to this saying
by his own example. Against the law of God, he
not only took multiple wives but also foreign
wives like the daughter of Pharaoh and others.
Therefore, as Augustine said in tract 84 on the
Gospel of John, there is only one who had
human flesh and was able not to sin. And
Tertullian wrote in his *Against the Heretics* that
only the son of God was allowed to remain
without sin. Book of 2 Chronicles.[4]

Unfit for a Sanctified House. John
Mayer: Solomon brought the daughter of
Pharaoh up from David's city. It is said that
Solomon removed her, for he did not want this
wife to dwell in his house since it was sanctified,
now that the ark was residing in it. This, says Peter
Martyr Vermigli, was spoken according to the laws
in force at the time, whereby women were unclean
by their monthly periods. They were therefore
unfit to be in the same house as the ark was.
Commentary on Chronicles.[5]

A Place Fit for a Princess. The English
Annotations: Solomon at first placed his wife in
the city of David on necessity since he did not have
another place for such a princess. But after he had
built the Lord's house, he built his wife a fair palace,
thereby removing her from the city of David. This
reason was ceremonial. Hereby it appears that he
reserved the place where the ark formerly stood for
some holy use or he left it void. But if Pharaoh's
daughter had continued there still, Solomon must
have taken it in to make a fair and spacious palace
for his wife. Annotations on 2 Chronicles.[6]

8:17-18 Solomon's Ships

Why Solomon Visited the Ships. John
Mayer: As for Solomon's going to Ebion-geber, it
was most probably to see his ships before their going
out. That's because Solomon would give the crews
instructions according to his wisdom regarding the
preparing and directing of the ships. But it is not to
be thought that Solomon only set forth these ships
out of covetousness. Rather, it was so that he might
better provide a way of defraying his great charges of
lumber and to be less burdensome on his subjects.
Commentary on Chronicles.[7]

Mystical Significance of Solomon's Ships.
John Mayer: Solomon's ships prefigure Christ and
his ministers, who gather together the treasures of
wisdom and knowledge and other virtues. And in
this work the servants of Hiram are employed with
the servants of Solomon when they who are learned
in secular wisdom are joined in the unity of faith
with those who are skilful in the law of Moses. And
the gold is brought to Solomon, when all the glory
is given to Christ alone. And Solomon's building of
many cities and fortifying them prefigured Christ's
building of his church in many places and encom-
passing them about by his providence as with a
strong wind. Commentary on Chronicles.[8]

---

[3]Mayer, *Many Commentaries in One*, 45*.
[4]Strigel, *Libri Samuelis, Regum et Paralipomenon*, 508; citing Eccles
7:20; Augustine, *Tractates on the Gospel According to John* 84.2
(NPNF 7:350; PL 35:1847-48); Tertullian, *Prescription Against
Heretics* 3 (ANF 3:244; PL 2:14-15).
[5]Mayer, *Many Commentaries in One*, 46*.

[6]Downame, ed., *Annotations* (1657), Bbbb4v*.
[7]Mayer, *Many Commentaries in One*, 46*.
[8]Mayer, *Many Commentaries in One*, 46*.

9:1-12 Solomon's Wisdom and the Queen of Sheba

The Queen's Speech. Viktorin Strigel: There are many things in the queen of Sheba's speech to please a pious mind. First, Solomon exceeded the reports that had spread about him, just as Philippians 4 says about the peace of Christ that passes all understanding. Second, the queen of Sheba pronounced a blessing on all who regularly listened to Solomon, just as Christ said in Luke 10, "Blessed are the eyes that see what you see!" Third, the queen affirms that a good and salutary prince is an extraordinary gift of God's providing and care, given to those God loves. Finally, in this she admonishes all magistrates about the duties of their offices. Book of 2 Chronicles.[9]

Attracted to Divine Wisdom. John Mayer: Solomon attained his great wisdom by the singular gift of God and not by human help or study. Indeed Solomon's fame for divine knowledge was extraordinarily conferred on him by the Lord, which he did not acquire on his own. For although he excelled in all manner of knowledge, it was his divine wisdom that moved this godly queen to come from so far away to hear him. She did not come to hear Solomon speak about natural things, for she surely had many philosophers around her who were proficient in that type of knowledge. Commentary on Chronicles.[10]

King for God. The English Annotations: Solomon is said to be "king for the Lord your God." This was spoken in general because God is the high supreme king. It's also because kings on earth bear his image and are his vice regents. But this phrase particularly applies to Solomon since Israel, over which Solomon reigned, was God's peculiar people. Annotations on 2 Chronicles.[11]

9:13-31 Solomon's Wealth

Mystical Meaning of Furnishings. John Mayer: These six stones up to the throne showed that as the king is lifted up above others in dignity, so he should excel them all in virtue. . . . The two armrests stood for his armies, that he—by encouraging the good on the right side and punishing the evil on the left—should uphold the commonwealth. The two lions stood for his strength and courage to execute what he decreed. And the two pairs of six lions on either side of the steps represented his ministers, who were to likewise be courageous in the same execution of strength and courage. And this Rabanus applied to the church, in which Christ sits as one shining by his miracles as with gold and ivory. And he is also chaste and incorruptible. Christ is ascended to by the doctrine of the twelve apostles, set forth by the twelve lions. And because the church here excels all other religions, it is said that there was not a rival in any other nation. There is further supplied a footstool of gold: This is a sign for kings to not covetously oppress their subjects, gather worldly riches or set themselves forth in pomp. Commentary on Chronicles.[12]

---

[9]Strigel, *Libri Samuelis, Regum et Paralipomenon*, 510; citing Phil 4:7; Lk 10:23.
[10]Mayer, *Many Commentaries in One*, 48*.
[11]Downame, ed., *Annotations* (1657), Ccccir*.
[12]Mayer, *Many Commentaries in One*, 50*.

10:1–12:16 KING REHOBOAM OF JUDAH

[1]Rehoboam went to Shechem, for all Israel had come to Shechem to make him king. [2]And as soon as Jeroboam the son of Nebat heard of it (for he was in Egypt, where he had fled from King Solomon), then Jeroboam returned from Egypt. [3]And they sent and called him. And Jeroboam and all Israel came and said to Rehoboam, [4]"Your father made our yoke heavy. Now therefore lighten the hard service of your father and his heavy yoke on us, and we will serve you." [5]He said to them, "Come to me again in three days." So the people went away.

[6]Then King Rehoboam took counsel with the old men,[a] who had stood before Solomon his father while he was yet alive, saying, "How do you advise me to answer this people?" [7]And they said to him, "If you will be good to this people and please them and speak good words to them, then they will be your servants forever." [8]But he abandoned the counsel that the old men gave him, and took counsel with the young men who had grown up with him and stood before him. [9]And he said to them, "What do you advise that we answer this people who have said to me, 'Lighten the yoke that your father put on us'?" [10]And the young men who had grown up with him said to him, "Thus shall you speak to the people who said to you, 'Your father made our yoke heavy, but you lighten it for us'; thus shall you say to them, 'My little finger is thicker than my father's thighs. [11]And now, whereas my father laid on you a heavy yoke, I will add to your yoke. My father disciplined you with whips, but I will discipline you with scorpions.'"

[12]So Jeroboam and all the people came to Rehoboam the third day, as the king said, "Come to me again the third day." [13]And the king answered them harshly; and forsaking the counsel of the old men, [14]King Rehoboam spoke to them according to the counsel of the young men, saying, "My father made your yoke heavy, but I will add to it. My father disciplined you with whips, but I will discipline you with scorpions." [15]So the king did not listen to the people, for it was a turn of affairs brought about by God that the Lord might fulfill his word, which he spoke by Ahijah the Shilonite to Jeroboam the son of Nebat.

[16]And when all Israel saw that the king did not listen to them, the people answered the king, "What portion have we in David? We have no inheritance in the son of Jesse. Each of you to your tents, O Israel! Look now to your own house, David." So all Israel went to their tents. [17]But Rehoboam reigned over the people of Israel who lived in the cities of Judah. [18]Then King Rehoboam sent Hadoram,[b] who was taskmaster over the forced labor, and the people of Israel stoned him to death with stones. And King Rehoboam quickly mounted his chariot to flee to Jerusalem. [19]So Israel has been in rebellion against the house of David to this day.

11 When Rehoboam came to Jerusalem, he assembled the house of Judah and Benjamin, 180,000 chosen warriors, to fight against Israel, to restore the kingdom to Rehoboam. [2]But the word of the Lord came to Shemaiah the man of God: [3]"Say to Rehoboam the son of Solomon, king of Judah, and to all Israel in Judah and Benjamin, [4]'Thus says the Lord, You shall not go up or fight against your relatives. Return every man to his home, for this thing is from me.'" So they listened to the word of the Lord and returned and did not go against Jeroboam.

[5]Rehoboam lived in Jerusalem, and he built cities for defense in Judah. [6]He built Bethlehem, Etam, Tekoa, [7]Beth-zur, Soco, Adullam, [8]Gath, Mareshah, Ziph, [9]Adoraim, Lachish, Azekah, [10]Zorah, Aijalon, and Hebron, fortified cities that are in Judah and in Benjamin. [11]He made the fortresses strong, and put commanders in them, and stores of food, oil, and wine. [12]And he put shields and spears in all the cities and made them very strong. So he held Judah and Benjamin.

[13]And the priests and the Levites who were in all Israel presented themselves to him from all places where they lived. [14]For the Levites left their

common lands and their holdings and came to Judah and Jerusalem, because Jeroboam and his sons cast them out from serving as priests of the LORD, [15]and he appointed his own priests for the high places and for the goat idols and for the calves that he had made. [16]And those who had set their hearts to seek the LORD God of Israel came after them from all the tribes of Israel to Jerusalem to sacrifice to the LORD, the God of their fathers. [17]They strengthened the kingdom of Judah, and for three years they made Rehoboam the son of Solomon secure, for they walked for three years in the way of David and Solomon.

[18]Rehoboam took as wife Mahalath the daughter of Jerimoth the son of David, and of Abihail the daughter of Eliab the son of Jesse, [19]and she bore him sons, Jeush, Shemariah, and Zaham. [20]After her he took Maacah the daughter of Absalom, who bore him Abijah, Attai, Ziza, and Shelomith. [21]Rehoboam loved Maacah the daughter of Absalom above all his wives and concubines (he took eighteen wives and sixty concubines, and fathered twenty-eight sons and sixty daughters). [22]And Rehoboam appointed Abijah the son of Maacah as chief prince among his brothers, for he intended to make him king. [23]And he dealt wisely and distributed some of his sons through all the districts of Judah and Benjamin, in all the fortified cities, and he gave them abundant provisions and procured wives for them.[c]

12 When the rule of Rehoboam was established and he was strong, he abandoned the law of the LORD, and all Israel with him. [2]In the fifth year of King Rehoboam, because they had been unfaithful to the LORD, Shishak king of Egypt came up against Jerusalem [3]with 1,200 chariots and 60,000 horsemen. And the people were without number who came with him from Egypt—Libyans, Sukkiim, and Ethiopians. [4]And he took the fortified cities of Judah and came as far as Jerusalem. [5]Then Shemaiah the prophet came to Rehoboam and to the princes of Judah, who had gathered at Jerusa-

lem because of Shishak, and said to them, "Thus says the LORD, 'You abandoned me, so I have abandoned you to the hand of Shishak.'" [6]Then the princes of Israel and the king humbled themselves and said, "The LORD is righteous." [7]When the LORD saw that they humbled themselves, the word of the LORD came to Shemaiah: "They have humbled themselves. I will not destroy them, but I will grant them some deliverance, and my wrath shall not be poured out on Jerusalem by the hand of Shishak. [8]Nevertheless, they shall be servants to him, that they may know my service and the service of the kingdoms of the countries."

[9]So Shishak king of Egypt came up against Jerusalem. He took away the treasures of the house of the LORD and the treasures of the king's house. He took away everything. He also took away the shields of gold that Solomon had made, [10]and King Rehoboam made in their place shields of bronze and committed them to the hands of the officers of the guard, who kept the door of the king's house. [11]And as often as the king went into the house of the LORD, the guard came and carried them and brought them back to the guardroom. [12]And when he humbled himself the wrath of the LORD turned from him, so as not to make a complete destruction. Moreover, conditions were good[d] in Judah.

[13]So King Rehoboam grew strong in Jerusalem and reigned. Rehoboam was forty-one years old when he began to reign, and he reigned seventeen years in Jerusalem, the city that the LORD had chosen out of all the tribes of Israel to put his name there. His mother's name was Naamah the Ammonite. [14]And he did evil, for he did not set his heart to seek the LORD.

[15]Now the acts of Rehoboam, from first to last, are they not written in the chronicles of Shemaiah the prophet and of Iddo the seer?[e] There were continual wars between Rehoboam and Jeroboam. [16]And Rehoboam slept with his fathers and was buried in the city of David, and Abijah[f] his son reigned in his place.

a Or the elders; also verses 8, 13   b Spelled Adoram in 1 Kings 12:18   c Hebrew and sought a multitude of wives   d Hebrew good things were found   e After seer, Hebrew adds according to genealogy   f Spelled Abijam in 1 Kings 14:31

Overview: The commentators here wrestle with questions of freedom and predestination: on one hand, Solomon had already known the prophecy that Jeroboam would rule over part of the kingdom (1 Kings 11); on the other, Solomon's son and successor Rehoboam earned many adversaries through his own free actions. Regardless of divine or human causation, these writers lift up many lessons for contemporary leaders to learn in order to avoid unnecessarily multiplying hardships. Regarding the ease with which Jeroboam led Israel to worship the golden calves, some suppose that it was made easier due to Solomon's lax faith in his later years and to widespread ignorance of Moses' life and witness. Rehoboam's own lack of faith leads to quick punishment from God through the Egyptians.[1]

10:1-19 *Jeroboam and Rehoboam*

God's Work at Play in Solomon's Oversight. John Mayer: Solomon did not act entirely wise with his son, for he delayed in setting his son on the throne during his lifetime. And this is despite the fact that Solomon otherwise saw that Jeroboam would be a threat to the kingdom of his son. What's more, Solomon himself had been given an example of how a king is supposed to establish his son as his successor, given that David had done this for him. So, it is to be understood that either Solomon saw Rehoboam's foolishness and was therefore careless in establishing him as king or Solomon did not think it proper to establish Rehoboam as king while he lived. As it is said in Sirach: "Solomon rested with his ancestors, and left behind him one of his sons, broad in folly and lacking in sense, Rehoboam, whose policy drove the people to revolt." Yet in all these things we must recognize a higher hand at play, which intervened to bring about the punishment that God had decreed for the punishment of Solomon. Commentary on Chronicles.[2]

Fighting God's Will. Viktorin Strigel: The cause of Jeroboam's flight and return is told in 1 Kings 11. Solomon wanted to kill him because of the divine promise that he would reign. So Jeroboam fled Solomon's wrath and went to Egypt. After Solomon's death, he returned to his homeland, hoping to reign. But he did not give the seditious appearance of desiring to have the kingdom transferred to him, but asked instead with all the people that Solomon's son Rehoboam might lighten the people's burdens. After learning that this would not be granted, he knew that the people would be very inclined to rebel. We should therefore learn from this history not to be carried away by advisers who promise material things but look instead for moments of divine blessing. For people struggle against God's plans in vain; they cannot change what God has already decided. Book of 2 Chronicles.[3]

How Jeroboam Came to Be the Spokesman for the People. John Mayer: Because Jeroboam was a man of great note among the people—having been made a prince over them by Solomon in the past—the people sent for him as the most capable man to speak on their behalf to Rehoboam concerning their grievance. For he made it clear that he and the people would revolt if no redress of errors was promised, and that he would be set up as the king of the people. And it is to be assumed that the people had heard of the prophecy given to Jeroboam by Ahijah, who was of the same tribe. That is, the people were aware of God's purpose in advancing Jeroboam, which is why the people sought his help above others. And that's how Jeroboam came to be the spokesman for the people. Commentary on Chronicles.[4]

A Gentle Response Turns Away Wrath. John Mayer: The book of Proverbs says: "A fool gives vent to his spirit." Yet in this case the people had already become exasperated with the new king.

---

[1]See commentary on 1 Kings 12:1-33; 14:21-31.
[2]Mayer, *Many Commentaries in One*, 64*; citing Sir 47:23.
[3]Strigel, *Libri Samuelis, Regum et Paralipomenon*, 513.
[4]Mayer, *Many Commentaries in One*, 64-65*.

But it certainly would have aided Rehoboam to have been lenient and to have replied gently at this time. For this is a general principle among kings: By no means should they show rigor in the beginning of their reign. Rather they should seek to win the hearts of the subjects of their kingdom. COMMENTARY ON CHRONICLES.[5]

11:1-12 Rehoboam Secures His Kingdom

WISE SECURITY MEASURES. THE ENGLISH ANNOTATIONS: Under captains are comprised their soldiers also. Rehoboam placed strong garrisons in those cities to keep them safe from attempts of enemies. These captains are supposed to be his sons, for it is said that later he "distributed some of his sons through all the districts." Here Rehoboam is said to have acted prudently because he could securely confide in his sons. Rehoboam also gave the men food, so that he could keep together his garrison-soldiers. They would be better encouraged to stand out against their enemies if they were well fed. And he also gave oil and wine. These were not only for necessity, but also for delight. Rehoboam furnished these places with these refreshments because his sons and other great men were there. Wine in particular is known to be a generous drink whereby the heart of a person is greatly refreshed and cheered. ANNOTATIONS ON 2 CHRONICLES.[6]

11:13-17 Priests and Levites Go to Jerusalem

GOD'S MAINTENANCE OF THE CHURCH. HEINRICH BULLINGER: In the kingdom of Israel, King Jeroboam kicked the Levites, the teachers of the Lord's law and the preachers of sound truth, out of their offices, and instead gave the people ignorant and ungodly priests and leaders. Jeroboam also built new temples and cathedrals for them, and he instituted idols or calves, new rituals, new altars and new feasts. In this way he abrogated the true worship of God to such a degree that it would appear that there were no external marks of the church of God. Nevertheless it is without doubt that a mighty church of God truly existed in Israel. And for the conservation and repairing of it prophets would regularly be sent from the Lord, even though they were by no means acknowledged to be the true prophets of God by the false church and false prophets. In fact it was under the reign of Jeroboam that the prophet Amos, the shepherd or herder of Tekoa, passed on the true teaching of God. DECADES 5.2.[7]

AN EARLY UNRAVELING. VIKTORIN STRIGEL: The text here tells of no small number of citizens who left the ungodly King Jeroboam to come to Jerusalem to make true sacrifices to God there. This fact would be more laudable had they all remained firmly on this course. But the weave of the fabric that had such a fine beginning quickly started to unravel, as the text says, "They walked for three years in the way of David and Solomon." As Paul says, "Therefore let anyone who thinks that he stands take heed lest he fall." BOOK OF 2 CHRONICLES.[8]

SOLOMON'S BAD EXAMPLE. JOHN MAYER: If anyone should wonder how Jeroboam could persuade the people to accept the worship of a golden calf since God's wrath had previously been declared to be great by Moses against this custom, it may be conceived that Solomon had already opened the way to idolatry during his later time as king. Accordingly the people were, for the most part, already corrupted. In fact they knew little of the sacred history, and they were now most prone to idolatry. COMMENTARY ON CHRONICLES.[9]

ADDITION OF THE GODLY IN JUDAH. JOHN MAYER: The reign of Rehoboam was strengthened by the addition of the priests and Levites from all

---

[5]Mayer, *Many Commentaries in One*, 65*; citing Prov 29:11.
[6]Downame, ed., *Annotations* (1657), Cccc2r*, citing 1 Kings 17:12; 2 Kings 4:2; Judg 9:13; Ps 104:15; Prov 31:6.
[7]Bullinger, *Sermonum decades quinque*, 366.
[8]Strigel, *Libri Samuelis, Regum et Paralipomenon*, 517; citing 1 Cor 10:12.
[9]Mayer, *Many Commentaries in One*, 69*.

parts of Israel since Jeroboam had cast them off and made others his priests, as was discussed in 1 Kings 12. For the priests and Levites, being dispersed among the tribes from where they were to come at certain times to do their service at the temple and to instruct the people where they lived in the laws of God, were now debarred from both these rights by Jeroboam, who would not permit anyone to go to Jerusalem to worship. Nor did Jeroboam allow the Levites and rightful priests to instruct the people, since he desired that the knowledge of the law be abolished. The zealous ministers of God therefore chose to abandon Jeroboam's kingdom and leave their houses and lands rather than to stay and remain guilty of Jeroboam's wickedness. In fact not only Levites and priests but other godly persons from Israel flocked to Rehoboam to dwell in his kingdom, where they might be free from danger and enjoy the comfort of God's ordinances, which they could not enjoy in their new kingdom. And although it is only said that these people from Israel went up to Jerusalem to sacrifice, it must be understood that they actually left their houses and possessions, as the Levites did, to go and dwell in the kingdom of Judah. Now, by means of some coming in this way from all tribes into the kingdom of Judah, it became much more populous and stronger. COMMENTARY ON CHRONICLES.[10]

11:18-23 Rehoboam's Family

REHOBOAM IN THE STYLE OF DAVID. JOHN MAYER: Rehoboam had eighteen wives and sixty concubines, and he fathered twenty-eight sons and sixty daughters. And it was his intention to be aligned with David's house of descent. For he married Mahalath, who was the daughter of David's son Jerimoth and of Abihail. Then Rehoboam married the daughter of David's son, Maacah, who was the daughter of Absalom.... And just as David preferred his younger son Solomon to succeed him as king because Solomon was the wisest, so

Rehoboam made his younger son Abijah chief among the other princes because he was wisest and strongest of all the rest of Rehoboam's twenty-eight sons. And like David's son Solomon, Rehoboam desired many wives. And it is likely that by this means that Rehoboam was drawn into idolatry. COMMENTARY ON CHRONICLES.[11]

UNWISE LOVE. THE ENGLISH ANNOTATIONS: It may be that Maacah's beauty or some other outward matter moved Rehoboam to dote on her so. Absalom himself was very handsome, and so was his daughter Tamar and his sister, also named Tamar. Certainly it was not piety nor any such spiritual endowment that moved Rehoboam to love her, for she was a detestable idolater. ANNOTATIONS ON 2 CHRONICLES.[12]

12:1 Rehoboam and All Israel Abandon the Lord

DANGEROUS TO FORSAKE THE LORD. THE ENGLISH ANNOTATIONS: Rehoboam and his subjects walked in the way of David for three years. But in the fourth year they revolted against the law of the Lord. By doing so they provoked the Lord's wrath against them. And in the fifth year of Rehoboam's reign the Lord therefore stirred up the spirit of the king of Egypt against them. ... But had God been with Judah, Shishak could no more have prevailed against Rehoboam than Zerah did against Asa. But once the Lord left them, they soon fell into Shishak's power. This shows us how dangerous it is to forsake the Lord. ANNOTATIONS ON 2 CHRONICLES.[13]

REHOBOAM IN COMPARISON WITH JEROBOAM. JOHN MAYER: God had chosen Jerusalem to set up his name there, but Rehoboam, in spite of God, set up idols there. And by this means Judah was now also corrupted more than in the time of Solomon or than in any other preceding time. The reason is

---

[10]Mayer, *Many Commentaries in One*, 79-80*.

[11]Mayer, *Many Commentaries in One*, 80*.
[12]Downame, ed., *Annotations* (1657), Cccc2r*, citing 2 Sam 13:1, 14, 25, 27; 1 Kings 15:13.
[13]Downame, ed., *Annotations* (1657), Cccc2v*.

because now idolatry was more generally followed than at any other time before. The sin of Judah was not aggravated by comparing it with Israel's sin under Jeroboam, but only with the sins of former ages. That's because Israel sinned more than Judah for two reasons. First, Jeroboam began his kingdom with idolatry and, second, Jeroboam prohibited the people from going to Jerusalem to worship in the prescribed way, which Rehoboam did not do. On the contrary, Rehoboam allowed people to worship freely in accordance with the law. . . . Yet Rehoboam was certainly guilty of violating the law himself. And he and his court confessed their sins when the prophet Shemaiah confronted them. They were then told that they should not be completely destroyed, but that they would have to serve the king of Egypt so they might know the difference between the service of God and that of pagan kings. And although the king and his princes humbled themselves at the words of the prophet, their repentance was not genuine. COMMENTARY ON CHRONICLES.[14]

FORSAKING GOD'S LAW. THE ENGLISH ANNO-TATIONS: The Lord declares his will to us through the law. And those who do not order their lives based on God's law, especially their course of piety and divine service, but instead follow either their own inventions or those of others forsake God's law. ANNOTATIONS ON 2 CHRONICLES.[15]

12:2-12 Egypt Plunders Jerusalem

SLOWLY FORGETTING TO PRAY. VIKTORIN STRIGEL: Rehoboam commanded the guards to bring the bronze shields back and forth from the temple every day, not to show off his wealth (which had been greatly diminished by the Egyptians) but to be signs of guilt to admonish the king and the people of their sin and repentance. Such an interpretation of this sign comes from the following words: "When he humbled himself the wrath of the Lord turned from him." There was also the added

sign and remembrance that God did not destroy Judah because there were still some upright people there. Such a reason partly involved objects and partly involved people. As long as pure teaching, right worship and true invocation of God remained in the republic and as long as atrocious sins were not committed with impunity, God would spare the kingdom and its citizens. But doctrine and the worship of God were corrupted daily, discipline grew ever more lax and ardent prayers for the people's own good were rarely uttered, whether or not the threats of destruction and ruin were plain to see or clearly approaching. But that is typical of the history of all ages. BOOK OF 2 CHRONICLES.[16]

REGARDING THE VESSELS TAKEN. THE ENGLISH ANNOTATIONS: We are not to think that Shishak had those vessels of gold and silver that were used in the house of the Lord. Rather, this refers to such gold and silver and other precious things as were laid up for repairing the temple or for other sacred uses. Nor are we to think that Shishak himself came into God's house to take these. Rather, by laying a great sum of money on the king and the people of Judah, the people were forced to take the treasures out of the house of the Lord. ANNOTATIONS ON 2 CHRONICLES.[17]

CONCERNING GOOD CONDITIONS. THE ENGLISH ANNOTATIONS: The passage says that "conditions were good in Judah." Another way to translate it would be to say that "in Judah there were good things." According to the first reading, this may be the sense: Notwithstanding all the evil that Shishak had done, the state of Judah continued as before. They enjoyed their liberty of serving God and the benefit of their laws in peace and prosperity. According to the other reading, this may be the sense: God's ordinances were duly observed, judgment and justice were executed, and there were many of the princes and people in whom good things were found, as is said of

---

[14]Mayer, *Many Commentaries in One*, 80-81*.
[15]Downame, ed., *Annotations* (1657), Cccc2v*.
[16]Strigel, *Libri Samuelis, Regum et Paralipomenon*, 519.
[17]Downame, ed., *Annotations* (1657), Cccc2v*, citing 2 Kings 18:14, 15.

Jeroboam's son in 1 Kings 14:13. Besides, there was in Judah the law of God, the seals of his covenant, the ministry of his prophets, priests and Levites, ordinary and extraordinary sacrifices, and many persons who had not conformed to the sins of the kingdom. These, and many other similar things, are implied in the second and preferred reading of the verse. ANNOTATIONS ON 2 CHRONICLES.[18]

12:13-16 *The Acts of Rehoboam*

END OF A WEAK KING. JOHN MAYER: The conclusion of the history of Rehoboam, including all of his acts and all that he did, are recorded in the records indicated. . . . But it was due to his weakness as a king that he yielded his country to the king of Egypt. . . . This is to serve as a threat to the wicked, for they should have a fearful and trembling heart before God. And although it is said that Rehoboam reigned still in Jerusalem, it is intimated that the Egyptian king only took away treasures and imposed tribute; but otherwise the kingdom of Judah remained under Jeroboam only out of God's regard for his promises made previously to David. COMMENTARY ON CHRONICLES.[19]

---

[18]Downame, ed., *Annotations* (1657), Cccc3r*, citing 1 Kings 14:13.

[19]Mayer, *Many Commentaries in One*, 81-82*.

13:1–16:14 KINGS ABIJAH AND ASA OF JUDAH

[1]In the eighteenth year of King Jeroboam, Abijah began to reign over Judah. [2]He reigned for three years in Jerusalem. His mother's name was Micaiah[a] the daughter of Uriel of Gibeah.

Now there was war between Abijah and Jeroboam. [3]Abijah went out to battle, having an army of valiant men of war, 400,000 chosen men. And Jeroboam drew up his line of battle against him with 800,000 chosen mighty warriors. [4]Then Abijah stood up on Mount Zemaraim that is in the hill country of Ephraim and said, "Hear me, O Jeroboam and all Israel! [5]Ought you not to know that the LORD God of Israel gave the kingship over Israel forever to David and his sons by a covenant of salt? [6]Yet Jeroboam the son of Nebat, a servant of Solomon the son of David, rose up and rebelled against his LORD, [7]and certain worthless scoundrels gathered about him and defied Rehoboam the son of Solomon, when Rehoboam was young and irresolute[b] and could not withstand them.

[8]"And now you think to withstand the kingdom of the LORD in the hand of the sons of David, because you are a great multitude and have with you the golden calves that Jeroboam made you for gods. [9]Have you not driven out the priests of the LORD, the sons of Aaron, and the Levites, and made priests for yourselves like the peoples of other lands? Whoever comes for ordination[c] with a young bull or seven rams becomes a priest of what are no gods. [10]But as for us, the LORD is our God, and we have not forsaken him. We have priests ministering to the LORD who are sons of Aaron, and Levites for their service. [11]They offer to the LORD every morning and every evening burnt offerings and incense of sweet spices, set out the showbread on the table of pure gold, and care for the golden lampstand that its lamps may burn every evening. For we keep the charge of the LORD our God, but you have forsaken him. [12]Behold, God is with us at our head, and his priests with their battle trumpets to sound the call to battle against you. O sons of Israel, do not fight against the LORD, the God of your fathers, for you cannot succeed."

[13]Jeroboam had sent an ambush around to come upon them from behind. Thus his troops[d] were in front of Judah, and the ambush was behind them. [14]And when Judah looked, behold, the battle was in front of and behind them. And they cried to the LORD, and the priests blew the trumpets. [15]Then the men of Judah raised the battle shout. And when the men of Judah shouted, God defeated Jeroboam and all Israel before Abijah and Judah. [16]The men of Israel fled before Judah, and God gave them into their hand. [17]Abijah and his people struck them with great force, so there fell slain of Israel 500,000 chosen men. [18]Thus the men of Israel were subdued at that time, and the men of Judah prevailed, because they relied on the LORD, the God of their fathers. [19]And Abijah pursued Jeroboam and took cities from him, Bethel with its villages and Jeshanah with its villages and Ephron[e] with its villages. [20]Jeroboam did not recover his power in the days of Abijah. And the LORD struck him down, and he died. [21]But Abijah grew mighty. And he took fourteen wives and had twenty-two sons and sixteen daughters. [22]The rest of the acts of Abijah, his ways and his sayings, are written in the story of the prophet Iddo.

14 [f]Abijah slept with his fathers, and they buried him in the city of David. And Asa his son reigned in his place. In his days the land had rest for ten years. [2][g]And Asa did what was good and right in the eyes of the LORD his God. [3]He took away the foreign altars and the high places and broke down the pillars and cut down the Asherim [4]and commanded Judah to seek the LORD, the God of their fathers, and to keep the law and the commandment. [5]He also took out of all the cities of Judah the high places and the incense altars. And the kingdom had rest under him. [6]He built fortified cities in Judah, for the land had rest. He had no war in those years, for the LORD gave him peace. [7]And he said to Judah, "Let us build these cities and surround them with walls and towers, gates and bars. The land is still ours, because we have sought the LORD our God. We have sought him, and he has given us peace on every side." So they built and prospered.

⁸And Asa had an army of 300,000 from Judah, armed with large shields and spears, and 280,000 men from Benjamin that carried shields and drew bows. All these were mighty men of valor.

⁹Zerah the Ethiopian came out against them with an army of a million men and 300 chariots, and came as far as Mareshah. ¹⁰And Asa went out to meet him, and they drew up their lines of battle in the Valley of Zephathah at Mareshah. ¹¹And Asa cried to the Lord his God, "O Lord, there is none like you to help, between the mighty and the weak. Help us, O Lord our God, for we rely on you, and in your name we have come against this multitude. O Lord, you are our God; let not man prevail against you." ¹²So the Lord defeated the Ethiopians before Asa and before Judah, and the Ethiopians fled. ¹³Asa and the people who were with him pursued them as far as Gerar, and the Ethiopians fell until none remained alive, for they were broken before the Lord and his army. The men of Judahʰ carried away very much spoil. ¹⁴And they attacked all the cities around Gerar, for the fear of the Lord was upon them. They plundered all the cities, for there was much plunder in them. ¹⁵And they struck down the tents of those who had livestock and carried away sheep in abundance and camels. Then they returned to Jerusalem.

15 The Spirit of God came upon Azariah the son of Oded, ²and he went out to meet Asa and said to him, "Hear me, Asa, and all Judah and Benjamin: The Lord is with you while you are with him. If you seek him, he will be found by you, but if you forsake him, he will forsake you. ³For a long time Israel was without the true God, and without a teaching priest and without law, ⁴but when in their distress they turned to the Lord, the God of Israel, and sought him, he was found by them. ⁵In those times there was no peace to him who went out or to him who came in, for great disturbances afflicted all the inhabitants of the lands. ⁶They were broken in pieces. Nation was crushed by nation and city by city, for God troubled them with every sort of distress. ⁷But you, take courage! Do not let your hands be weak, for your work shall be rewarded."

⁸As soon as Asa heard these words, the prophecy of Azariah the son of Oded, he took courage and put

away the detestable idols from all the land of Judah and Benjamin and from the cities that he had taken in the hill country of Ephraim, and he repaired the altar of the Lord that was in front of the vestibule of the house of the Lord.ⁱ ⁹And he gathered all Judah and Benjamin, and those from Ephraim, Manasseh, and Simeon who were residing with them, for great numbers had deserted to him from Israel when they saw that the Lord his God was with him. ¹⁰They were gathered at Jerusalem in the third month of the fifteenth year of the reign of Asa. ¹¹They sacrificed to the Lord on that day from the spoil that they had brought 700 oxen and 7,000 sheep. ¹²And they entered into a covenant to seek the Lord, the God of their fathers, with all their heart and with all their soul, ¹³but that whoever would not seek the Lord, the God of Israel, should be put to death, whether young or old, man or woman. ¹⁴They swore an oath to the Lord with a loud voice and with shouting and with trumpets and with horns. ¹⁵And all Judah rejoiced over the oath, for they had sworn with all their heart and had sought him with their whole desire, and he was found by them, and the Lord gave them rest all around.

¹⁶Even Maacah, his mother, King Asa removed from being queen mother because she had made a detestable image for Asherah. Asa cut down her image, crushed it, and burned it at the brook Kidron. ¹⁷But the high places were not taken out of Israel. Nevertheless, the heart of Asa was wholly true all his days. ¹⁸And he brought into the house of God the sacred gifts of his father and his own sacred gifts, silver, and gold, and vessels. ¹⁹And there was no more war until the thirty-fifth year of the reign of Asa.

16 In the thirty-sixth year of the reign of Asa, Baasha king of Israel went up against Judah and built Ramah, that he might permit no one to go out or come in to Asa king of Judah. ²Then Asa took silver and gold from the treasures of the house of the Lord and the king's house and sent them to Ben-hadad king of Syria, who lived in Damascus, saying, ³"There is a covenantʲ between me and you, as there was between my father and your father. Behold, I am sending to you silver and gold. Go, break your covenant with Baasha king of Israel, that he may withdraw from me." ⁴And Ben-hadad listened to

King Asa and sent the commanders of his armies against the cities of Israel, and they conquered Ijon, Dan, Abel-maim, and all the store cities of Naphtali. 5And when Baasha heard of it, he stopped building Ramah and let his work cease. 6Then King Asa took all Judah, and they carried away the stones of Ramah and its timber, with which Baasha had been building, and with them he built Geba and Mizpah.

7At that time Hanani the seer came to Asa king of Judah and said to him, "Because you relied on the king of Syria, and did not rely on the LORD your God, the army of the king of Syria has escaped you. 8Were not the Ethiopians and the Libyans a huge army with very many chariots and horsemen? Yet because you relied on the LORD, he gave them into your hand. 9For the eyes of the LORD run to and fro throughout the whole earth, to give strong support to those whose

heart is blameless^k toward him. You have done foolishly in this, for from now on you will have wars." 10Then Asa was angry with the seer and put him in the stocks in prison, for he was in a rage with him because of this. And Asa inflicted cruelties upon some of the people at the same time.

11The acts of Asa, from first to last, are written in the Book of the Kings of Judah and Israel. 12In the thirty-ninth year of his reign Asa was diseased in his feet, and his disease became severe. Yet even in his disease he did not seek the LORD, but sought help from physicians. 13And Asa slept with his fathers, dying in the forty-first year of his reign. 14They buried him in the tomb that he had cut for himself in the city of David. They laid him on a bier that had been filled with various kinds of spices prepared by the perfumer's art, and they made a very great fire in his honor.

---

a Spelled *Maacah* in 1 Kings 15:2   b Hebrew *soft of heart*   c Hebrew *to fill his hand*   d Hebrew *they*   e Or *Ephrain*   f Ch 13:23 in Hebrew   g Ch 14:1 in Hebrew   h Hebrew *They*   i Hebrew *the vestibule of the Lord*   j Or *treaty*; twice in this verse   k Or *whole*

OVERVIEW: The description of the war between Abijah and Jeroboam, Abijah's rousing speech, and Asa's pious reforms are unique to 2 Chronicles and inspire the commentators to compare Judah's faithfulness with Israel's idolatry. Even more than his father Abijah, Asa provides a positive example of a pious leader, showing and establishing good policies for faith and social concern. Nevertheless, later in life, Asa also fell from faith. His use of physicians near the end of his life provides rich opportunity for Reformation-era writers to discuss their views of the relationship between faith and medicine.[1]

13:1-22 Abijah Reigns in Judah

VICTORY FROM BELOW. VIKTORIN STRIGEL: King Abijah is not praised in 1 Kings 15, which says that "his heart was not wholly true to the Lord his God" and that he followed in the footsteps of his father Rehoboam. That he was granted this victory over Israel ought to be attributed more to the

service and prayers of the pious than to his own personal qualities. For God often blesses impious rulers on account of kind and pious subjects. BOOK OF 2 CHRONICLES.[2]

OFFERING TERMS OF PEACE. THE ENGLISH ANNOTATIONS: It is to be supposed that while the armies were set against one another before the fight, Abijah desired and procured a treaty. He therefore chose a fit place where he might best be heard to offer the treaty. It was the usual practice of prudent commanders to desire a treaty before the battle to show the justness of their cause and to persuade the enemy to cease, if at all possible. This was enjoined by the law. . . . Such is how Jephthah proceeded: "Then Jephthah sent messengers to the king of the Ammonites and said, 'What do you have against me, that you have come to me to fight against my land?'" And such is how Abijah proceeded here as well . . . directing his speech to Jeroboam, who had the chief command of the army

---

[1]See commentary on 1 Kings 15.

[2]Strigel, *Libri Samuelis, Regum et Paralipomenon*, 522; citing 1 Kings 15:3.

of Israel, which was also doubtless assembled together to hear exactly what terms of peace Abijah offered to the army. That's why Abijah also directed his speech to "all Israel," as Rabshakeh had done. Annotations on 2 Chronicles.[3]

A Covenant of Salt. The English Annotations: By this metaphor of salt a perpetuity is set forth. For salt makes things last. In this respect, Lot's wife was turned into a pillar of salt so that she might remain a perpetual spectacle. The covenant, therefore, is here declared to be a perpetual covenant, not to be abrogated or nulled. Accordingly these two phrases "a covenant of salt" and "forever" are joined together in Numbers. . . . By this it is implied that this was a most solemn covenant, not to be violated. Others understand this metaphor as pertaining to the making of a covenant with a sacrifice, on which salt was always sprinkled. And both senses of salt tend to the same purpose. Annotations on 2 Chronicles.[4]

A Tender Plant as King. The English Annotations: Rehoboam was called "young." But this did not refer to his age, for he was forty-one years old when he came to the crown. Rather his youngness refers to his understanding and discretion. He was like a young man who lacked experience. In this respect he was foolish. For such is how this word is used elsewhere in the Old Testament. Another interpretation is that this word referred to Rehoboam's breeding. Because he was trained up in a delicate manner under a prince of peace, he had no experience of war. Nor was he ever under the discipline of the military. And in this respect, he was a "young" tree that might easily be plucked up. He was no bruised and seasoned soldier, but a young and fresh prince. Annotations on 2 Chronicles.[5]

Those Who Go Against the Lord. The English Annotations: Here Abijah is trying to show that those who go against the Lord cannot expect any good success. . . . This oration Abijah made, therefore, is a very pithy one. Every sentence is composed of a strong argument to dissuade Jeroboam and his army from fighting against the army of Judah. All the arguments may be drawn to two heads: first, the dishonor that Jeroboam's party had done to God; and, second, the honor which the people of Judah had done to him. But while Abijah was dealing fairly and friendly with Jeroboam, Jeroboam was dealing treacherously with him. He took advantage of Abijah by attacking him by surprise. The Hebrew word translated as "ambush" is referred to as "hiding places" in Psalm 10:8. Our English word *ambush* implies a lying in wait, or a sudden and unexpected coming on someone. Annotations on 2 Chronicles.[6]

God's Assistance in War. John Mayer: It is certain that God was with Abijah. Indeed God miraculously gave him victory over Jeroboam. For Jeroboam had 800,000 troops while Abijah only had 400,000. And although men going out to war sometimes are allowed to prevail unjustly, they are never miraculously assisted as Abijah was. And the reason why Abijah was assisted by God can be easily conceived; namely, it was a way to curb the incorrigible wickedness of Jeroboam. For Abijah maintained the true worship and service of God. Both he and the men of Judah called on God and put their trust in him alone. To show, therefore, how pleasing this was in God's sight—and, conversely, to show how displeasing it is to serve images rather than the true God— God allowed Abijah to have this victory over Israel. Commentary on Chronicles.[7]

[3]Downame, ed., *Annotations* (1657), Cccc3r*, citing Deut 20:10; Judg 11:12; Gen 10:18; 2 Kings 18:28.
[4]Downame, ed., *Annotations* (1657), Cccc3r*, citing Gen 19:26; Num 18:19; Lev 2:13.
[5]Downame, ed., *Annotations* (1657), Cccc3v*, citing 1 Cor 12:20; Eccles 10:16; Is 3:4; Eccles 4:13.

[6]Downame, ed., *Annotations* (1657), Cccc3v*, citing Job 9:4; Ps 10:8; Josh 8:2; Judg 20:33, 34.
[7]Mayer, *Many Commentaries in One*, 83*.

14:1-15 The Beginning of Asa's Reign

ASA TURNS TO GOD. JOHN MAYER: At the death
of Abijah, his son Asa began to reign in the
twentieth year of Jeroboam. . . . In describing Asa's
righteousness, it is said that he beat down the
altars of strange gods and their high places. It is
also said that he broke their images and cut down
their groves. . . . And when Zerah the Ethiopian
came against him with an army of a million men,
Asa called on the Lord and therefore he overcame
the Egyptians. COMMENTARY ON CHRONICLES.[8]

SALUTARY LEADERSHIP. VIKTORIN STRIGEL:
Asa is an image of a good prince, for he thought not
only of himself but also of the public good. Asa
governed his life and morals in such a way that he
demonstrated his God-pleasing obedience. He also
made proclamations that touched on the first and
second tables of the law, because a magistrate is the
voice of the Decalogue. Finally, because the law
without enforcement is a hollow sound, he strove to
tear down the idols and places of ungodly worship,
such as the high places, the sacred groves and the
foreign altars. This piety was not only salutary to
the king but also to the entire kingdom, for God
granted peace to the kingdom of Judah and
decorated the king and the people with victory. In
considering this most praiseworthy example of a
prince, people might similarly perform such private
and public service and devote themselves to pleasing
God through holy teaching and holy acting.
Without a doubt such people can expect recompense in this life and in the life to come, in which
we shall live without any trouble and abound in all
good things. BOOK OF 2 CHRONICLES.[9]

ONGOING WARS. THE ENGLISH ANNOTATIONS:
From here it may be inferred that after ten years
there were open wars between Asa and his enemies.
It is not expressed what enemies troubled the land
before the Cushites. Yet this limitation of peace to

ten years implies that there was some other enemy
that disquieted them. For it may be gathered from
that which is noted of their offering to the Lord
the spoil they had taken from their enemies in the
fifteenth year of Asa, in the next chapter, that the
Cushites were overthrown in that year. Before that,
there might have been war between Judah and
Israel, or between Judah and other nations. Where
it is said in 1 Kings, "And there was war between
Asa and Baasha king of Israel all their days," we
may take this as referring to the skirmishes on the
borders of the kingdoms of Israel and Judah.
ANNOTATIONS ON 2 CHRONICLES.[10]

15:1-7 Azariah's Prophecy

THE BLESSINGS OF FAITH. VIKTORIN STRIGEL:
Jesus said: "To everyone who has will more be given."
Thus God increased Asa's gifts, immediately adding
new companions and coworkers, and this text
clearly affirms that Asa was impelled to act by the
words of the Spirit of God. The prophet's speech
here comes in three parts. First, he teaches that God
does not forsake those who do not forsake him, and
often finds those who have become forsaken.
Second, he prophesies a coming darkness facing the
people of Israel and, in a later age, the church. . . .
Finally, the church is exhorted to persevere in fear
of God, faith, invocation and other offices given by
God, for God promised to give abundant reward to
those who remained constant in these matters. A
similar exhortation is read in Hebrews 10, "Do not
throw away your confidence, which has a great
reward." And again in Hebrews 12, "Therefore lift
your drooping hands and strengthen your weak
knees, and make straight paths for your feet, so that
what is lame may not be put out of joint but rather
may be healed." BOOK OF 2 CHRONICLES.[11]

PROPHECY TO ASA. JOHN MAYER: Concerning the
prophecy of Azariah, it is a tradition of the Hebrews,

---

[8]Mayer, *Many Commentaries in One*, 85*.
[9]Strigel, *Libri Samuelis, Regum et Paralipomenon*, 523.
[10]Downame, ed., *Annotations* (1657), Cccc4r*, citing 1 Kings 15:16; 14:30.
[11]Strigel, *Libri Samuelis, Regum et Paralipomenon*, 525; citing Mt 25:29; Heb 10:35; 12:12-13.

says Jerome, that this Oded, otherwise called Adon son of Azariah, is said to be the prophet sent formerly to Jeroboam to threaten him for his idolatry at Bethel. . . . And when Asa heard the prophecy of Oded, he took courage to remove the gods in the land. He is said to have done this in the beginning of his reign in Judah. . . . In this way the prophecy gave comfort and encouragement to Asa to put down whatever he knew to be an abomination to God, especially now that all fear of other princes, who favored such idols, were cast away from Asa's sight. COMMENTARY ON CHRONICLES.[12]

DISREGARD FOR GOD'S LAW. THE ENGLISH ANNOTATIONS: Azariah's reference about worship of the true God has reference to the ten tribes' first revolt from the house of David and from the house of God and all God's ordinances, which the Scripture shows to be about thirty years from that division till this time. . . . The Israelites had set up idols instead of the true God. And the sons of Aaron, who were the only true priests, were so trained up in the law of God as they could teach well and instruct the people of the truth. But they were cast off by the ten tribes, and in their place the people chose the most base of the people who were ignorant of God's law. They also cast out the Levites, who could have instructed them in the law, for the people had no regard at all for any of the law's ordinances. ANNOTATIONS ON 2 CHRONICLES.[13]

BASED ON GOD'S GRACE AND MERCY. THE ENGLISH ANNOTATIONS: Judgments on those who forsake the Lord should move us to be courageous in removing corruptions and in renewing our covenant with God. . . . The hands are the chief instruments whereby humans do this or that. And if they are weak, nothing can be done. But this is metaphorically to be taken and applied to the mind. Hereby the prophet exhorts them from being fearful, negligent or too dejected. . . . For it is a great

encouragement to stir up a person's spirit and to make them diligent to know that their labor shall not be lost. . . . The reward here promised is not based on worth or merit but on God's free grace and mercy. ANNOTATIONS ON 2 CHRONICLES.[14]

15:8-19 *Asa Reforms His Ways*

DEFECTORS FOR THE SAKE OF THE LORD. THE ENGLISH ANNOTATIONS: The people of Israel voluntarily left their own habitations and came to Judah, as others before them had done at the first revolt. They saw that the Lord was on Asa's side by the continuation of the kingdom of Judah in David's line by the great victory his father had won over the Israelites before and by that victory that he himself had won over the Ethiopians. It was also evident in the long peace he enjoyed. Hereby they knew that the true God whom he worshiped had prospered and blessed him. On the other side, the people observed how Jeroboam, who had forsaken the Lord, never prospered. Rather he and his whole posterity were at this time completely rooted out. This passage shows that these defectors were not forced to come to Judah. Rather, piety and the fear of God brought them. ANNOTATIONS ON 2 CHRONICLES.[15]

EXECUTING GOD'S JUDGMENTS APPROPRIATELY. THE ENGLISH ANNOTATIONS: This command to put to death whoever would not seek the Lord is not to be taken of every failing in that duty of seeking the Lord. Rather it refers to an obstinate refusal to be subject to the Lord and to seek out other gods. This was in accordance with the law. . . . For, also according to the book of Deuteronomy, there must be no partiality in executing judgment; nor are we to be respecters of those who show no respect to others. ANNOTATIONS ON 2 CHRONICLES.[16]

---

[12]Mayer, *Many Commentaries in One*, 87*.
[13]Downame, ed., *Annotations* (1657), Cccc4v*, citing 1 Kings 12:16, 28; Judg 5:8; 1 Kings 12:31; 13:33.

[14]Downame, ed., *Annotations* (1657), Cccc4v-Ddddr*, citing 1 Chron 22:13; 2 Sam 4:1; Heb 12:12; 1 Cor 15:58.
[15]Downame, ed., *Annotations* (1657), Ddddr*.
[16]Downame, ed., *Annotations* (1657), Ddddr*; citing Deut 13:6,9; 33:9; 10:7.

Keeping the Covenant. The English Annotations: To make the covenant more inviolable on their part they swore to the Lord. For an oath is a curb to conscience. This oath was an imprecation against themselves if they should break the covenant (Neh 5:13). It was the practice of the Jews, when they made a solemn covenant, to cut a beast in half. They would lay one part on one side and one on the other; then the oath-takers would pass through the middle. This implied that they desired to be dealt with as these beasts if they did not keep their end of the covenant (Gen 15:10; Jer 34:18). Annotations on 2 Chronicles.[17]

Explanation of Asa's Delay of Godly Acts. John Mayer: It is not to be understood that Asa did not bring these things into the temple until after fifteen years of his reign. For it cannot be thought that being so godly a king, he would defer so long in rendering to God the things of God. But happily he now brought in the spoils he had taken from the Ethiopians, and dedicated them as a way of thankfulness after the repairing of the house. And then he brought in the things dedicated by his father. But both are spoken of together without regard of the time for the sake of brevity. And, in like manner, it may be thought that although the destruction of Maacah and her idolatry are only mentioned now, Asa certainly removed her and her idolatry a long time before, given that no godly king would permit so great an abomination near him. Commentary on Chronicles.[18]

16:1-10 *Reproving Asa*

Four Sins. Viktorin Strigel: Up to this point, Scripture has praised King Asa as an especially exemplary king and prince worthy of imitation. But now it records four of Asa's sins: his treaty with an impious regime, his inciting the king of Syria[19] to violate Syria's existing treaty with King Baasha of Israel, his impious faith in the medical arts and his rage against the prophet Hanani. These sins are recorded for two reasons: first, so that we recognize the common infirmity of our nature; second, so that we remain vigilant against the snares of the devil, not despairing of our lapses but finding consolation in examples of healings. For no matter how great the wound, we shall be restored back to health. Book of 2 Chronicles.[20]

Asa Sins in Four Ways. John Mayer: King Baasha of Israel took Ramah and fortified it so that none of Asa's subjects could enter Jerusalem or vice versa. Yet in response to this assault, Asa did not put trust in God, as he had formerly done. Nor did he confidently go out with his army against King Baasha, as he should have done. For had he done so, he would have been sure to prosper, as he had done against the Ethiopians formerly. But being afraid, he basely begged help from Ben-hadad of Syria, a known idolater and an enemy to true religion. In fact Asa sent to him all the gold and silver in the Lord's house and in his own to make Ben-hadad break his covenant with Baasha and therefore to come to his aid. . . . In this way Asa sinned in four ways: first, he fell from his faith and from his confidence in God; second, he robbed the Lord's house of its precious things when it was not necessary; third, he sought the help of an idolater; and fourth, he gave occasion for Ben-hadad to break his covenant with the king of Israel, which is a violation of a sacred and inviolable act among all nations. Commentary on Chronicles.[21]

Asa Justly Reproved. The English Annotations: This may have reference to that which might have fallen out. If the king of Syria had come against Judah, being in league with Baasha, God would have delivered both those kings into his hands, as he did Zera the Ethiopian in the fourteenth chapter. But Asa, by making an agreement with Ben-hadad, prevented that occasion, and so

---

[17]Downame, ed., *Annotations* (1657), Dddd1r*; citing Neh 5:13; Gen 15:10; Jer 34:18.
[18]Mayer, *Many Commentaries in One*, 89*.
[19]That is, Aram.

[20]Strigel, *Libri Samuelis, Regum et Paralipomenon*, 527.
[21]Mayer, *Many Commentaries in One*, 90-91*.

allowed Ben-hadad's false play and deceitful dealing with Asa. For howsoever he came to Asa at this time, yet after this, when Baasha annoyed Asa, he offered him no help at all. In this sense, this phrase "the king of Syria has escaped you" implies this: "He is so gone as in future distress that he shall afford you no help." The Syrians were such implacable enemies of Israel and Judah that it would have been far better for Asa to have stood out at a distance than to have sought friendship with them. For this, therefore, Asa is justly reproved. Annotations on 2 Chronicles.[22]

Founded on Truth. Edward Reynolds: The word of the Lord is an abiding word because it is founded on the immutability of God's own truth. The one who makes it his refuge relies on God's omnipotence and has all the strength of the Almighty engaged to help him. Asa was safe while he depended on the Lord's promises against incredibly great odds. But when he turned aside to other aids, he purchased for himself nothing but perpetual wars. And this was that which established the throne of Jehoshaphat and caused "the fear of the Lord to fall upon the kingdoms of the lands that were round about Judah," because he honored the Word of God and caused it to be taught to his people. Explanation of Psalm 110.[23]

16:11-12 Trusting in Physicians Rather Than in God

Seeking Help in Vain. Geneva Bible: It is vain to seek help from physicians unless we first seek God to purge our sins, which are the chief cause of all our diseases. And then afterward we may use the help of the physician as a means by whom God works. Annotations on 2 Chronicles.[24]

Seeking God First When Sick. John Mayer: Most likely in the thirty-eighth year of his reign,

Asa developed a foot disease. And to show that this was not a random sickness but one caused by sin, it is added that Asa did not seek the Lord. Rather he trusted only in physicians. His poor example should teach us that we must flee from all sin. For if we commit a sin, like a link of a chain, it draws in more after it. Thus when we become sick we must first and foremost seek out God. And then we may resort to physicians only as a means afterward of recovering our health. But Asa was foolish for seeking only the aid of physicians, because this disease was sent by God as a punishment. As a result Asa should have sought out God alone and not natural means, which were unable to do him any good. Commentary on Chronicles.[25]

Not by Medicine Alone. Charles Drelincourt: The Spirit of God does not blame this prince because he desired the assistance of physicians. He blames him because he neglected to seek the help of God or to implore his aid in the day of his distress. The one who is sick may as freely take medicine as the one who is well may eat and drink; yet we must not altogether relax our confidence and trust in the remedies. Rather we must put our confidence in the God who sends both sickness and health. Just as a person does not live by bread alone but by every word that proceeds from the mouth of God, so it is not by medicine alone that a patient is cured of his sickness. Rather it is by the blessing and power of him who both gives the sickness and cures it, that is, of him who strikes and heals as he pleases. Christian Defense Against the Fears of Death.[26]

A Better Type of Medicine. Thomas Adams: When people are sick, they put their trust in doctors—as Asa did—or they put their trust in medicine, fastening their eyes and hopes on that. However, medicine, without God's blessing on it, does as much harm as it does good. Even nature itself cannot do what it is designed to do if God is

---

[22]Downame, ed., *Annotations* (1657), Ddddiv*.
[23]Reynolds, *Works*, 2:145*; citing 2 Chron 17:10.
[24]*Geneva Bible* (1560), 197v*.
[25]Mayer, *Many Commentaries in One*, 92*.
[26]Drelincourt, *Christian's Defense Against the Fears of Death*, 84*.

against it. God can cure without medicine, but not even the best medicine can cure without God. THE SINNER'S PASSING-BELL.[27]

16:13-14 *Asa's Death and Burial*

ON ASA'S BURIAL. THE ENGLISH ANNOTATIONS: The people made a very great fire for Asa with sweet, fragrant things. This was counted an honorable funeral solemnity. It was denied Jehoram, but afforded to Zedekiah, though he died in a foreign land, for he was their last king. It may be that this burial was done by those who survived Asa, in memory of his former acts and of the things he had done for Judah. Or it may be that at length he repented, and therefore out of respect to him they honored him in this way. Or it is possible that special friends of his arranged this, or that he appointed his own burial for his death. ANNOTATIONS ON 2 CHRONICLES.[28]

---

[27]Adams, *Devil's Banquet*, 307*.

[28]Downame, ed., *Annotations* (1657), Ddddɪr*; citing 2 Chron 21:19; Jer 34:5.

17:1–20:37 KING JEHOSHAPHAT OF JUDAH

¹Jehoshaphat his son reigned in his place and strengthened himself against Israel. ²He placed forces in all the fortified cities of Judah and set garrisons in the land of Judah, and in the cities of Ephraim that Asa his father had captured. ³The LORD was with Jehoshaphat, because he walked in the earlier ways of his father David. He did not seek the Baals, ⁴but sought the God of his father and walked in his commandments, and not according to the practices of Israel. ⁵Therefore the LORD established the kingdom in his hand. And all Judah brought tribute to Jehoshaphat, and he had great riches and honor. ⁶His heart was courageous in the ways of the LORD. And furthermore, he took the high places and the Asherim out of Judah.

⁷In the third year of his reign he sent his officials, Ben-hail, Obadiah, Zechariah, Nethanel, and Micaiah, to teach in the cities of Judah; ⁸and with them the Levites, Shemaiah, Nethaniah, Zebadiah, Asahel, Shemiramoth, Jehonathan, Adonijah, Tobijah, and Tobadonijah; and with these Levites, the priests Elishama and Jehoram. ⁹And they taught in Judah, having the Book of the Law of the LORD with them. They went about through all the cities of Judah and taught among the people.

¹⁰And the fear of the LORD fell upon all the kingdoms of the lands that were around Judah, and they made no war against Jehoshaphat. ¹¹Some of the Philistines brought Jehoshaphat presents and silver for tribute, and the Arabians also brought him 7,700 rams and 7,700 goats. ¹²And Jehoshaphat grew steadily greater. He built in Judah fortresses and store cities, ¹³and he had large supplies in the cities of Judah. He had soldiers, mighty men of valor, in Jerusalem. ¹⁴This was the muster of them by fathers' houses: Of Judah, the commanders of thousands: Adnah the commander, with 300,000 mighty men of valor; ¹⁵and next to him Jehohanan the commander, with 280,000; ¹⁶and next to him Amasiah the son of Zichri, a volunteer for the service of the LORD, with 200,000 mighty men of valor. ¹⁷Of Benjamin: Eliada, a mighty man of valor, with 200,000 men armed with bow and

shield; ¹⁸and next to him Jehozabad with 180,000 armed for war. ¹⁹These were in the service of the king, besides those whom the king had placed in the fortified cities throughout all Judah.

18 Now Jehoshaphat had great riches and honor, and he made a marriage alliance with Ahab. ²After some years he went down to Ahab in Samaria. And Ahab killed an abundance of sheep and oxen for him and for the people who were with him, and induced him to go up against Ramoth-gilead. ³Ahab king of Israel said to Jehoshaphat king of Judah, "Will you go with me to Ramoth-gilead?" He answered him, "I am as you are, my people as your people. We will be with you in the war."

⁴And Jehoshaphat said to the king of Israel, "Inquire first for the word of the LORD." ⁵Then the king of Israel gathered the prophets together, four hundred men, and said to them, "Shall we go to battle against Ramoth-gilead, or shall I refrain?" And they said, "Go up, for God will give it into the hand of the king." ⁶But Jehoshaphat said, "Is there not here another prophet of the LORD of whom we may inquire?" ⁷And the king of Israel said to Jehoshaphat, "There is yet one man by whom we may inquire of the LORD, Micaiah the son of Imlah; but I hate him, for he never prophesies good concerning me, but always evil." And Jehoshaphat said, "Let not the king say so." ⁸Then the king of Israel summoned an officer and said, "Bring quickly Micaiah the son of Imlah." ⁹Now the king of Israel and Jehoshaphat the king of Judah were sitting on their thrones, arrayed in their robes. And they were sitting at the threshing floor at the entrance of the gate of Samaria, and all the prophets were prophesying before them. ¹⁰And Zedekiah the son of Chenaanah made for himself horns of iron and said, "Thus says the LORD, 'With these you shall push the Syrians until they are destroyed.'" ¹¹And all the prophets prophesied so and said, "Go up to Ramoth-gilead and triumph. The LORD will give it into the hand of the king."

¹²And the messenger who went to summon Micaiah said to him, "Behold, the words of the prophets with one

accord are favorable to the king. Let your word be like the word of one of them, and speak favorably." [13]But Micaiah said, "As the Lord lives, what my God says, that I will speak." [14]And when he had come to the king, the king said to him, "Micaiah, shall we go to Ramoth-gilead to battle, or shall I refrain?" And he answered, "Go up and triumph; they will be given into your hand." [15]But the king said to him, "How many times shall I make you swear that you speak to me nothing but the truth in the name of the Lord?" [16]And he said, "I saw all Israel scattered on the mountains, as sheep that have no shepherd. And the Lord said, 'These have no master; let each return to his home in peace.'" [17]And the king of Israel said to Jehoshaphat, "Did I not tell you that he would not prophesy good concerning me, but evil?" [18]And Micaiah said, "Therefore hear the word of the Lord: I saw the Lord sitting on his throne, and all the host of heaven standing on his right hand and on his left. [19]And the Lord said, 'Who will entice Ahab the king of Israel, that he may go up and fall at Ramoth-gilead?' And one said one thing, and another said another. [20]Then a spirit came forward and stood before the Lord, saying, 'I will entice him.' And the Lord said to him, 'By what means?' [21]And he said, 'I will go out, and will be a lying spirit in the mouth of all his prophets.' And he said, 'You are to entice him, and you shall succeed; go out and do so.' [22]Now therefore behold, the Lord has put a lying spirit in the mouth of these your prophets. The Lord has declared disaster concerning you."

[23]Then Zedekiah the son of Chenaanah came near and struck Micaiah on the cheek and said, "Which way did the Spirit of the Lord go from me to speak to you?" [24]And Micaiah said, "Behold, you shall see on that day when you go into an inner chamber to hide yourself." [25]And the king of Israel said, "Seize Micaiah and take him back to Amon the governor of the city and to Joash the king's son, [26]and say, 'Thus says the king, Put this fellow in prison and feed him with meager rations of bread and water until I return in peace.'" [27]And Micaiah said, "If you return in peace, the Lord has not spoken by me." And he said, "Hear, all you peoples!"

[28]So the king of Israel and Jehoshaphat the king of Judah went up to Ramoth-gilead. [29]And the king of Israel said to Jehoshaphat, "I will disguise myself and go into battle, but you wear your robes." And the king of Israel disguised himself, and they went into battle. [30]Now the king of Syria had commanded the captains of his chariots, "Fight with neither small nor great, but only with the king of Israel." [31]As soon as the captains of the chariots saw Jehoshaphat, they said, "It is the king of Israel." So they turned to fight against him. And Jehoshaphat cried out, and the Lord helped him; God drew them away from him. [32]For as soon as the captains of the chariots saw that it was not the king of Israel, they turned back from pursuing him. [33]But a certain man drew his bow at random[a] and struck the king of Israel between the scale armor and the breastplate. Therefore he said to the driver of his chariot, "Turn around and carry me out of the battle, for I am wounded." [34]And the battle continued that day, and the king of Israel was propped up in his chariot facing the Syrians until evening. Then at sunset he died.

19 Jehoshaphat the king of Judah returned in safety to his house in Jerusalem. [2]But Jehu the son of Hanani the seer went out to meet him and said to King Jehoshaphat, "Should you help the wicked and love those who hate the Lord? Because of this, wrath has gone out against you from the Lord. [3]Nevertheless, some good is found in you, for you destroyed the Asheroth out of the land, and have set your heart to seek God."

[4]Jehoshaphat lived at Jerusalem. And he went out again among the people, from Beersheba to the hill country of Ephraim, and brought them back to the Lord, the God of their fathers. [5]He appointed judges in the land in all the fortified cities of Judah, city by city, [6]and said to the judges, "Consider what you do, for you judge not for man but for the Lord. He is with you in giving judgment. [7]Now then, let the fear of the Lord be upon you. Be careful what you do, for there is no injustice with the Lord our God, or partiality or taking bribes."

[8]Moreover, in Jerusalem Jehoshaphat appointed certain Levites and priests and heads of families of Israel, to give judgment for the Lord and to decide disputed cases. They had their seat at Jerusalem. [9]And he charged them: "Thus you shall do in the fear of the Lord, in faithfulness, and with your whole heart:

¹⁰*whenever a case comes to you from your brothers who live in their cities, concerning bloodshed, law or commandment, statutes or rules, then you shall warn them, that they may not incur guilt before the* Lord *and wrath may not come upon you and your brothers. Thus you shall do, and you will not incur guilt.* ¹¹*And behold, Amariah the chief priest is over you in all matters of the* Lord; *and Zebadiah the son of Ishmael, the governor of the house of Judah, in all the king's matters, and the Levites will serve you as officers. Deal courageously, and may the* Lord *be with the upright!"*ᵇ

20 *After this the Moabites and Ammonites, and with them some of the Meunites,*ᶜ *came against Jehoshaphat for battle.* ²*Some men came and told Jehoshaphat, "A great multitude is coming against you from Edom,*ᵈ *from beyond the sea; and, behold, they are in Hazazon-tamar" (that is, Engedi).* ³*Then Jehoshaphat was afraid and set his face to seek the* Lord, *and proclaimed a fast throughout all Judah.* ⁴*And Judah assembled to seek help from the* Lord; *from all the cities of Judah they came to seek the* Lord.

⁵*And Jehoshaphat stood in the assembly of Judah and Jerusalem, in the house of the* Lord, *before the new court,* ⁶*and said, "O* Lord, *God of our fathers, are you not God in heaven? You rule over all the kingdoms of the nations. In your hand are power and might, so that none is able to withstand you.* ⁷*Did you not, our God, drive out the inhabitants of this land before your people Israel, and give it forever to the descendants of Abraham your friend?* ⁸*And they have lived in it and have built for you in it a sanctuary for your name, saying,* ⁹*'If disaster comes upon us, the sword, judgment,*ᵉ *or pestilence, or famine, we will stand before this house and before you—for your name is in this house—and cry out to you in our affliction, and you will hear and save.'* ¹⁰*And now behold, the men of Ammon and Moab and Mount Seir, whom you would not let Israel invade when they came from the land of Egypt, and whom they avoided and did not destroy—* ¹¹*behold, they reward us by coming to drive us out of your possession, which you have given us to inherit.* ¹²*O our God, will you not execute judgment on them? For we are powerless against this great horde that is coming against us. We do not know what to do, but our eyes are on you."*

¹³*Meanwhile all Judah stood before the* Lord, *with their little ones, their wives, and their children.* ¹⁴*And the Spirit of the* Lord *came upon Jahaziel the son of Zechariah, son of Benaiah, son of Jeiel, son of Mattaniah, a Levite of the sons of Asaph, in the midst of the assembly.* ¹⁵*And he said, "Listen, all Judah and inhabitants of Jerusalem and King Jehoshaphat: Thus says the* Lord *to you, 'Do not be afraid and do not be dismayed at this great horde, for the battle is not yours but God's.* ¹⁶*Tomorrow go down against them. Behold, they will come up by the ascent of Ziz. You will find them at the end of the valley, east of the wilderness of Jeruel.* ¹⁷*You will not need to fight in this battle. Stand firm, hold your position, and see the salvation of the* Lord *on your behalf, O Judah and Jerusalem.' Do not be afraid and do not be dismayed. Tomorrow go out against them, and the* Lord *will be with you."*

¹⁸*Then Jehoshaphat bowed his head with his face to the ground, and all Judah and the inhabitants of Jerusalem fell down before the* Lord, *worshiping the* Lord. ¹⁹*And the Levites, of the Kohathites and the Korahites, stood up to praise the* Lord, *the God of Israel, with a very loud voice.*

²⁰*And they rose early in the morning and went out into the wilderness of Tekoa. And when they went out, Jehoshaphat stood and said, "Hear me, Judah and inhabitants of Jerusalem! Believe in the* Lord *your God, and you will be established; believe his prophets, and you will succeed."* ²¹*And when he had taken counsel with the people, he appointed those who were to sing to the* Lord *and praise him in holy attire, as they went before the army, and say,*

> *"Give thanks to the* Lord,
> *for his steadfast love endures forever."*

²²*And when they began to sing and praise, the* Lord *set an ambush against the men of Ammon, Moab, and Mount Seir, who had come against Judah, so that they were routed.* ²³*For the men of Ammon and Moab rose against the inhabitants of Mount Seir, devoting them to destruction, and when they had made an end of the inhabitants of Seir, they all helped to destroy one another.*

²⁴*When Judah came to the watchtower of the wilderness, they looked toward the horde, and behold, there*ᶠ *were dead bodies lying on the ground; none had*

escaped. ²⁵When Jehoshaphat and his people came to take their spoil, they found among them, in great numbers, goods, clothing, and precious things, which they took for themselves until they could carry no more. They were three days in taking the spoil, it was so much. ²⁶On the fourth day they assembled in the Valley of Beracah,ᵍ for there they blessed the LORD. Therefore the name of that place has been called the Valley of Beracah to this day. ²⁷Then they returned, every man of Judah and Jerusalem, and Jehoshaphat at their head, returning to Jerusalem with joy, for the LORD had made them rejoice over their enemies. ²⁸They came to Jerusalem with harps and lyres and trumpets, to the house of the LORD. ²⁹And the fear of God came on all the kingdoms of the countries when they heard that the LORD had fought against the enemies of Israel. ³⁰So the realm of Jehoshaphat was quiet, for his God gave him rest all around.

³¹Thus Jehoshaphat reigned over Judah. He was thirty-five years old when he began to reign, and he reigned twenty-five years in Jerusalem. His mother's name was Azubah the daughter of Shilhi. ³²He walked in the way of Asa his father and did not turn aside from it, doing what was right in the sight of the LORD. ³³The high places, however, were not taken away; the people had not yet set their hearts upon the God of their fathers.

³⁴Now the rest of the acts of Jehoshaphat, from first to last, are written in the chronicles of Jehu the son of Hanani, which are recorded in the Book of the Kings of Israel.

³⁵After this Jehoshaphat king of Judah joined with Ahaziah king of Israel, who acted wickedly. ³⁶He joined him in building ships to go to Tarshish, and they built the ships in Ezion-geber. ³⁷Then Eliezer the son of Dodavahu of Mareshah prophesied against Jehoshaphat, saying, "Because you have joined with Ahaziah, the LORD will destroy what you have made." And the ships were wrecked and were not able to go to Tarshish.

a Hebrew *in his innocence*   b Hebrew *the good*   c Compare 26:7; Hebrew *Ammonites*   d One Hebrew manuscript; most Hebrew manuscripts *Aram* (Syria)   e Or *the sword of judgment*   f Hebrew *they*   g *Beracah* means *blessing*

OVERVIEW: The reformers highly commend Jehoshaphat as a model godly ruler. Here they reflect at length on the good king's virtues and provide detailed comments about the worship of Baal that so often tempted the people of God. They find good practical examples of how to institute and sustain religious reform. Though Jehoshaphat disregarded the message of Micaiah, one commentator holds him as a positive example of trusting in God, since he later heeded the admonition and promises of the prophet Jehu.[1]

17:1-6 Godly Jehoshaphat

JEHOSHAPHAT KNEW GOD'S WILL. JOHANNES BRENZ: "The LORD," says Scripture, "was with Jehoshaphat." Is that supposed to be rare? Isn't the Lord with all people? As Paul says, "In him we live and move and have our being." When one considers and reflects on God's being and omnipotence, then God surely fills heaven and earth. He holds all creatures, all people, he has counted even the worst pagans, and without his ordering and establishment nothing could breathe, but would be silent in the attempt to accomplish anything. But when one considers God's grace, benefits and mercy, then God is not with the pagans and unbelievers but only with the pious and God-fearing, whom he protects from the common natural flow of life by his grace, by his blessings and by his overwhelming mercy. According to this view the Lord was especially with Jehoshaphat. Why? "Because he did what was right in the sight of the Lord." But what is pleasing to the Lord? The Lord does not like what people devise through their cleverness and desires, but rather likes what he has conceived in his divine will and wisdom. But who can know what the Lord thinks and wants? John writes that

---

[1]See commentary on 1 Kings 22.

"no one has seen God," so how then can a person perceive God's mind and heart? Answer: Just as a person's own true mind may remain hidden inside until the mouth acts like a mirror to show and reveal one's own thoughts, so God dwells in a light that no one can approach and his mind and heart is hidden, except that it is revealed and recognized through the Word of God. Therefore, when you want to see into God's heart and discover God's good will, then you must keep his word, commands and prohibitions under your eyes. For what God commands pleases him and what he forbids displeases him. HISTORY OF JEHOSHAPHAT.[2]

SEEK FIRST THE KINGDOM OF GOD. VIKTORIN STRIGEL: The history of the pious and blessed Jehoshaphat confirms the rule given in Matthew 6: "Seek first the kingdom of God and his righteousness, and all these things will be added to you." For when this king had worshiped God in true piety and removed ungodly teaching and worship from their midst, not only spiritual gifts abounded but also a profusion of external gifts like splendor, honor, power and stability in the kingdom. BOOK OF 2 CHRONICLES.[3]

THE BAALS. JOHANNES BRENZ: Because the Bible speaks so frequently of Baal and the Baals, it is important to discern what Baal really is. Some write that Baal had been a god of Tyre. But in Numbers 22 it is written that the king of Moab led Balaam up to the high places of Baal. From this you can gather that Baal was also a god of the Moabites. If you want to translate Baal into our language, it would mean "husband," "lord" and "patron." The Jews generally turned to their neighbors' gods and saw that the idol Baal was esteemed the highest god as a father and patron in Syria (and in Canaan, the land where Judah lay), just as Jupiter (which means "a helping father") was held as the highest and greatest among other pagans around the Mediterranean Sea. So the Syrians named their greatest god Baal and offered him his own sacrifices and worship in the fanciest and finest ways that their wise men could imagine. When the Jews entered Canaan, they observed the worship of Baal from their pagan neighbors. On account of its beauty, blessed images and order of worship they were overcome with desire. This is typical: people love what is devised by reason and made by their own hands more than what the one true God creates and does. After this the Jews left the one true worship, which had been written for them as the true Word of God in the five books of Moses. They took the form and image of Baal worship from their pagan neighbors, as if it were the same as serving the one true God of Israel. Yet they thought they had not exchanged their one true God for an idol, as our Lord God shows through the prophet Hosea 2: "In that day, declares the Lord, you will call me 'My Husband,' and no longer will you call me 'My Baal.' For I will remove the names of the Baals from her mouth, and they shall be remembered by name no more." These words from the Lord our God show that the Jews had named him Baal just like the pagans, sacrificing and worshiping in Baalistic forms and ways. These words show that the same worship of the one true God that holy Scripture describes with praise and honor among the Jews can also become a Baal. Regardless of good intentions to honor the true God of Israel, the holy prophets can nonetheless call it an idolatry and fall from the true God. Certainly the true God is one and fills all in all, so that no one can fall away from God's presence. Still, this does not allow anyone to make and choose another god. Thus it is written how the godless move away from God and take foreign gods. HISTORY OF JEHOSHAPHAT.[4]

17:7-19 Instructional Reform

CHURCH VISITATIONS. VIKTORIN STRIGEL: Jehoshaphat's sending out of officials describes the

---

[2]Brenz, *Werke: Frühschriften*, 2:1; citing Acts 17:28; Jn 1:18.
[3]Strigel, *Libri Samuelis, Regum et Paralipomenon*, 529; citing Mt 6:33.

[4]Brenz, *Werke: Frühschriften*, 2:1; citing Num 22:41; Hos 2:16-17. In the Vulgate and the Luther Bible, Num 22:41 reads: "He brought him to the high places of Baal." Compare the ESV, which says, "and brought him up to Bamoth-baal."

best form of visiting or inspecting the churches.
For when the common people scorn their priests
and scholars, the king's wise advisers supplemented them with political leaders in order to
increase the authority of the teaching. Teachers
should always have the law of the Lord in their
mouth and in their soul, but not in order to invent
new kinds of teaching like the heretics are always
impudently doing. Instead the church always
needs to be led by the Word of God and not
human traditions, as it says in Deuteronomy 12,
"Everything that I command you, you shall be
careful to do. You shall not add to it or take from
it." And in Psalm 68, "Bless God in the great
congregation, the Lord, O you who are of Israel's
fountain." BOOK OF 2 CHRONICLES.[5]

KINGLY ATTEMPT AT REFORM. JOHN MAYER:
The words about the officials of Jehoshaphat going
out to teach in the cities suggest that not only
Levites and priests were sent to teach the people
but also princes were. However, it is conceived by
interpreters to refer generally to the authority of
princes being leveraged to move the people in the
cities to obey the teaching of the Levites and
priests and to go to hear them. . . . The reason why
the king sent these princes out to teach the people
is because the people were addicted to worshiping
in the high places. So the princes were sent out to
encourage people to listen to the true teaching of
doctrine from the Levites and the priests. For God
had appointed only one rightful place of sacrifice.
And although Jehoshaphat was partially successful
in beating down the idolatrous superstitions of the
people, some of them still sacrificed in the high
places. COMMENTARY ON CHRONICLES.[6]

BLUEPRINT FOR REGAL SUCCESS. MARTIN
BUCER: In this story it must first be noted how
properly King Jehoshaphat in the third year of his
reign dedicated himself to restoring a pure and

holy administration of religion and government
for his people, and what great happiness this effort
had for himself and his whole kingdom. It must
then be observed what an excellent delegation of
princes, Levites and priests this king presented for
the first inspection of his kingdom. Then, because
he did not wish to undertake the reformation
either of religion or of public government by
edicts alone and by the removal of the implements
of impiety, he first offered a careful teaching that
came from the book of the law, which he had
faithfully administered to his people through his
delegates who were outstanding men of every
estate of the kingdom. He did this not only
throughout all the provinces and districts of his
kingdom but also in each of the cities. And to
exhibit the certainty and sincerity of this teaching,
he made them carry the book of the law around
with them. REIGN OF CHRIST.[7]

18:1-3 *False Friend*

FEASTING WITH A FRIEND OR FOE? THE
ENGLISH ANNOTATIONS: Jehoshaphat went to pay
his respects and testify to his commitment to Ahab
by covenant and friendship. And upon this meeting,
Ahab took occasion to require Jehoshaphat's
assistance in war. Ahab killed many sheep and oxen
to show his welcome of Jehoshaphat and to endear
himself to him. For friends testified of their mutual
good respect of each other in those days by feasting
with one another. At the same time, Jehoshaphat
had come to Ahab as a king in royal estate and great
pomp, just as the queen of Sheba had done. And by
that which follows, it appears that he came accompanied with bands of soldiers. Therefore, so that all his
train might be liberally entertained, it was necessary
for Ahab to kill an abundance of sheep and oxen.
And Ahab, by his royal entertaining of Jehoshaphat
and his fair speech, worked on Jehoshaphat and
eventually prevailed on him to do what he desired.
ANNOTATIONS ON 2 CHRONICLES.[8]

---

[5]Strigel, *Libri Samuelis, Regum et Paralipomenon*, 529; citing Deut
12:32; Ps 68:26.
[6]Mayer, *Many Commentaries in One*, 140*.

[7]Bucer, *De Regno Christi*, 228.
[8]Downame, ed., *Annotations* (1657), Dddd2v*; citing 1 Kings 10:2.

18:4-34 *Concerning True and False Prophets*

ALLOWING FALSE PROPHETS. VIKTORIN
STRIGEL: There are two reasons why God allows
false prophets to do their work among the people.
The first reason is to give an occasion for searching
out the faith and constancy of the pious. The second
reason is to punish the sins of the impious. The
following words apply to the first reason: The Lord
your God will test you through false prophets, and
"there must be factions among you in order that
those who are genuine among you may be recognized." And here are words that address the second
reason: "My people did not listen to my voice; Israel
would not submit to me. So I gave them over to
their stubborn hearts, to follow their own counsels."
"He loved to curse; let curses come upon him! He
did not delight in blessing; may it be far from him!"
And "God sends them a strong delusion, so that they
may believe what is false, in order that all may be
condemned who did not believe the truth but had
pleasure in unrighteousness." Therefore, when Ahab
did not want to listen to the Lord's prophet Micaiah,
he was punished for his ingratitude, deceived by
false prophets who taught deceits and invented lies.
The false prophets would not have had any authority
with the king unless they preached something other
than what would actually happen. Therefore such
preachers were instruments of Satan, not preaching
any future revealed by the Spirit of God, but instead
they were advised by the devil, who covers his
ministers with a veneer of truth, getting them used
to hiding under such curtains. Relying not on the
Word of God alone but on the whims of King Ahab,
the false prophets promised victory and joined in
making proud and arrogant insults against the
prophet Micaiah. BOOK OF 2 CHRONICLES.[9]

INSINCERE INQUIRY. JOHN MAYER: Ahaz was
ready to proceed to war in Ramoth-gilead without
seeking the Lord. However, Jehoshaphat desired
that they inquire by a prophet before they went

forth, to see if they would be successful. Yet
Josephus says that this was not done until their
armies were already gathered at Samaria, by the
time the troops of the two kings would have
already been paid for their services and were ready
to march on to battle. And if this interpretation is
correct, which it probably is, there was really no
point in seeking out godly counsel, for they
disregarded the words of the prophet Micaiah.
Indeed Jehoshaphat was here to blame just as
much as Ahab was, for they inquired of the Lord
as a pointless ritual, but they proceeded to do what
they originally intended. COMMENTARY ON
CHRONICLES.[10]

A PROPHET OF THE LORD. THE ENGLISH
ANNOTATIONS: Although there were many
prophets, Jehoshaphat asked if there were any
more. It's not that Jehoshaphat thought four
hundred were not enough, but rather that he
discerned that all of these prophets were idolatrous
prophets. Therefore Jehoshaphat was skeptical of
their responses, and so he wanted to be informed
of a prophet of the true God, that is, of the Lord.
ANNOTATIONS ON 2 CHRONICLES.[11]

19:1-11 *Peace in the Reign of Jehoshaphat*

TURNING TO GOD IN TIMES OF TROUBLE. JOHN
MAYER: The story of Jehoshaphat's joining in
league at Ramoth-gilead against the Syrians was
set forth in the previous chapter. And before Ahab
was killed in that war, Jehoshaphat was in great
peril for his life. However, he was preserved by
God, whom he served, so that he could return to
Jerusalem in safety and in peace; the Syrians,
whom he had justly provoked through war, were
restrained from even trying to harm him. But Jehu,
the son of Hanani, a prophet, was sent to Jehoshaphat from God to reprove him upon his
return from battle for helping the wicked. And on
account of his support of Ahab, he was worthy to

---

[9]Strigel, *Libri Samuelis, Regum et Paralipomenon*, 531; citing 1 Cor
11:19; Ps 81:11-12; 109:17; 2 Thess 2:11-12.

[10]Mayer, *Many Commentaries in One*, 133*.
[11]Downame, ed., *Annotations* (1657), Dddd2v*.

receive the heavy wrath of God. But because there were good things found in him and he did seek out the Lord, his judgment was withheld and his sin was pardoned. Therefore, in his uprightness of heart to seek to glorify God and to beat down that which was against his glory, God passed over and pardoned that which was amiss in his actions. In this way we may recognize that God protects his servants in time of greatest dangers so that we may be stirred up to zealously seek out God's glory. COMMENTARY ON CHRONICLES.[12]

FRIENDSHIP WITH THE UNGODLY IS HATRED OF THE LORD. THE ENGLISH ANNOTATIONS: When Jehoshaphat returned from the war in which Ahab was killed, this prophet came to him. And though his message was very sad, and he had to deliver it to a king of all people, he boldly declared the mind of the Lord to Jehoshaphat. Now Ahab, and the rest of the Israelites, were idolaters. And in this respect they were very ungodly. Such ungodliness was even more unlawful because the Israelites were apostates and revolters from the true religion. In fact Ahab himself was one of the worst kings, if not simply the worst, of all the kings of Israel. . . . But by the help Jehoshaphat afforded Ahab, he seemed to give tolerance to his idolatry. Now, although it is not quite unlawful to afford aid to idolaters of other nations in external politics and mutual defense against enemies, revolters are to be detested. And in this respect two circumstances plainly demonstrate that Jehoshaphat had sinned and even aggravated his sin. First, Jehoshaphat loved the ungodly. He did this not only with a political respect, but with an inward entity of affection. Second, the ungodly are so detestable to the Lord that it is as if those who love the ungodly actually profess a hatred of the Lord. ANNOTATIONS ON 2 CHRONICLES.[13]

WORSHIP THAT PLEASES GOD. JOHANNES BRENZ: It says in Leviticus 1 that people should bring burnt offerings of oxen, lambs or birds to the altar as an offering that will be a pleasing aroma to the Lord. But then in 1 Kings 14 it says, "They committed all the abominations—that is worship—of the heathens whom the Lord drove out before the children of Israel." Now how can it be that burnt offerings of oxen, lambs or birds described in Leviticus are a pleasing aroma while the same worship copied from the pagans was an abomination before God, even though they were both given by the people of Israel to praise and honor the Lord God? A burnt ox probably stank more than it gave a pleasing aroma. And the worship borrowed from the pagans probably smelled much better because of its perfumes. Better to leave the stink behind! But I reply: The Word of God is the best spice and the best perfume. For in the burnt offering was found the command and promise of God, and so it certainly was a pleasing aroma before God. But the other worship had no command or law, rather a prohibition. And so it was more an atrocity than a pleasing odor. From this it is good to consider why the worship of Baal, even if done to praise the Lord, was nevertheless called an abomination and idolatry. When done without any basis in the Word of God, an action arises only out of well-intentioned human reason and the customs of paganism. HISTORY OF JEHOSHAPHAT.[14]

LEADING WELL. THE ENGLISH ANNOTATIONS: If those who have a charge over others are concerned with directing them to the right path and warning them of their sins, they do well. They shall neither trespass against God, whose charge they keep, nor against their brothers and sisters, whose good they seek. ANNOTATIONS ON 2 CHRONICLES.[15]

JEHOSHAPHAT'S JUDGES. VIKTORIN STRIGEL: Jehoshaphat had previously instituted judges to rule over certain smaller or individual towns. Here, though, he established two supreme judges in the city of Jerusalem: one for ecclesiastical

---

[12]Mayer, *Many Commentaries in One*, 140-41*.
[13]Downame, ed., *Annotations* (1657), Dddd2v*.
[14]Brenz, *Frühschriften*, 2:140; citing 1 Kings 14:24.
[15]Downame, ed., *Annotations* (1657), Dddd3r*.

matters and one for political matters. The priest Amariah was put in charge of the former, and Zebadiah the son of Ishmael was put in charge of the latter. This is a great use of higher courts of judgment, so that the judges' wisdom and authority might correct errors in the lower courts and render a final decision in individual lawsuits. For it can often be the case that a lower-court judge makes a mistake because of an error or a wrong impression. In contrast, the wise judges of the higher court are less likely to be influenced by errors or false impressions. The higher judges also have the higher authority, because their decisions cannot be appealed, thereby putting an end to the long disputations in which people are divided because of protracted legal battles. Therefore the wisdom of King Jehoshaphat should be praised, for he established judges not only for individual towns but also higher courts for considering and judging ecclesiastical and civil controversies. BOOK OF 2 CHRONICLES.[16]

20:1-30 *Depending on God in a Time of Trouble*

BELIEVING IN THE PROMISE. VIKTORIN STRIGEL: The example set and passed on from Jehoshaphat needs to be remembered: "Believe in the Lord your God, and you will be established; believe his prophets, and you will succeed." For in all things human reason naturally wants to have the experience first. We all know that we would gladly make invocation to God if we were to see the results of the prayer beforehand. But God first requires belief before the effects and the experience come. Moses first believed that God wanted him to lead the people, and then he put the help of God and miraculous defenses into practice. For when faith believes the Word of God, things happen and the certainty of it is recognized. BOOK OF 2 CHRONICLES.[17]

JEHOSHAPHAT TURNS TO THE LORD. JOHN MAYER: After Jehoshaphat's worthy acts done in the chapter before, it is again shown of what high account he was before God. For many enemies were allowed to come against him, uniting all their forces together so that they could destroy him and his kingdom. . . . These armies had come as a form of revenge for his support of Ahab. . . . Upon hearing of these approaching armies, Jehoshaphat first feared but then fled to the Lord in prayer, fasting and in the assembly of all Judah to seek the Lord together. Meanwhile the enemies were remaining at En-gedi, which is a place near to the Dead Sea. Jehoshaphat grounded his prayer on the power of God and in his mercy toward his people, his former acts on behalf of them and his promises to preserve the people when the temple of Solomon was built. All Judah is said to have been gathered along with wives and children. This was done to move the Lord to have more compassion, for if he did not offer protection not only men but also their wives and children would be in danger of destruction. The Lord, being sought in this way, did not delay in giving a comforting answer. The Spirit of the Lord came on Jahaziel son of Zechariah. He prophesied of the victory coming to them without even fighting. . . . When Jehoshaphat and the men of Judah heard this, they all worshiped the Lord and the Levites sang praises to God as if the victory had already been obtained. COMMENTARY ON CHRONICLES.[18]

THE NEW COURT. THE ENGLISH ANNOTATIONS: This was the new court of the priests, which was before in the house of the Lord. It is styled "new" because it was newly repaired and beautified. We read in the fifteenth chapter that Asa renewed the altar of the Lord, which stood in this court. He might also have repaired the whole court, and thereupon this title "new" was given it. Or it may be that Jehoshaphat himself did it. Now, the king stood before this court, namely, before the entrance into it, both because the great altar stood

---

[16]Strigel, *Libri Samuelis, Regum et Paralipomenon*, 536.
[17]Strigel, *Libri Samuelis, Regum et Paralipomenon*, 539.

---

[18]Mayer, *Many Commentaries in One*, 142*.

there and also because through it he might see into the holy place and, in fact, into the most holy place where the ark resided. Annotations on 2 Chronicles.[19]

God's Three Arrows. The English Annotations: These three—war, pestilence and famine—are arrows of God's wrath. God uses them to shoot at those against whom he is offended. Annotations on 2 Chronicles.[20]

---

[19]Downame, ed., *Annotations* (1657), Dddd3v*; citing 1 Kings 8:22, 64.
[20]Downame, ed., *Annotations* (1657), Dddd3v*.

20:31-37 *The High Places Not Taken Away*

The People's Fault. Giovanni Diodati: Even though it was an abuse, this must refer to those high places that were consecrated to the service of the true God, for Jehoshaphat had destroyed those that belonged to the idols according to 2 Chronicles 17:6. It was not Jehoshaphat's fault that this licentiousness of arbitrary places for God's service was not quite abolished, but the people could not be diverted from it. Annotations on 2 Chronicles.[21]

---

[21]Diodati, *Pious Annotations*, 46*.

21:1–22:12 KINGS JEHORAM AND AHAZIAH OF JUDAH

¹Jehoshaphat slept with his fathers and was buried with his fathers in the city of David, and Jehoram his son reigned in his place. ²He had brothers, the sons of Jehoshaphat: Azariah, Jehiel, Zechariah, Azariah, Michael, and Shephatiah; all these were the sons of Jehoshaphat king of Israel.ᵃ ³Their father gave them great gifts of silver, gold, and valuable possessions, together with fortified cities in Judah, but he gave the kingdom to Jehoram, because he was the firstborn. ⁴When Jehoram had ascended the throne of his father and was established, he killed all his brothers with the sword, and also some of the princes of Israel. ⁵Jehoram was thirty-two years old when he became king, and he reigned eight years in Jerusalem. ⁶And he walked in the way of the kings of Israel, as the house of Ahab had done, for the daughter of Ahab was his wife. And he did what was evil in the sight of the Lord. ⁷Yet the Lord was not willing to destroy the house of David, because of the covenant that he had made with David, and since he had promised to give a lamp to him and to his sons forever.

⁸In his days Edom revolted from the rule of Judah and set up a king of their own. ⁹Then Jehoram passed over with his commanders and all his chariots, and he rose by night and struck the Edomites who had surrounded him and his chariot commanders. ¹⁰So Edom revolted from the rule of Judah to this day. At that time Libnah also revolted from his rule, because he had forsaken the Lord, the God of his fathers.

¹¹Moreover, he made high places in the hill country of Judah and led the inhabitants of Jerusalem into whoredom and made Judah go astray. ¹²And a letter came to him from Elijah the prophet, saying, "Thus says the Lord, the God of David your father, 'Because you have not walked in the ways of Jehoshaphat your father, or in the ways of Asa king of Judah, ¹³but have walked in the way of the kings of Israel and have enticed Judah and the inhabitants of Jerusalem into whoredom, as the house of Ahab led Israel into whoredom, and also you have killed your brothers, of your father's house, who were better than

you, ¹⁴behold, the Lord will bring a great plague on your people, your children, your wives, and all your possessions, ¹⁵and you yourself will have a severe sickness with a disease of your bowels, until your bowels come out because of the disease, day by day.'"

¹⁶And the Lord stirred up against Jehoram the angerᵇ of the Philistines and of the Arabians who are near the Ethiopians. ¹⁷And they came up against Judah and invaded it and carried away all the possessions they found that belonged to the king's house, and also his sons and his wives, so that no son was left to him except Jehoahaz, his youngest son.

¹⁸And after all this the Lord struck him in his bowels with an incurable disease. ¹⁹In the course of time, at the end of two years, his bowels came out because of the disease, and he died in great agony. His people made no fire in his honor, like the fires made for his fathers. ²⁰He was thirty-two years old when he began to reign, and he reigned eight years in Jerusalem. And he departed with no one's regret. They buried him in the city of David, but not in the tombs of the kings.

22 And the inhabitants of Jerusalem made Ahaziah, his youngest son, king in his place, for the band of men that came with the Arabians to the camp had killed all the older sons. So Ahaziah the son of Jehoram king of Judah reigned. ²Ahaziah was twenty-twoᶜ years old when he began to reign, and he reigned one year in Jerusalem. His mother's name was Athaliah, the granddaughter of Omri. ³He also walked in the ways of the house of Ahab, for his mother was his counselor in doing wickedly. ⁴He did what was evil in the sight of the Lord, as the house of Ahab had done. For after the death of his father they were his counselors, to his undoing. ⁵He even followed their counsel and went with Jehoram the son of Ahab king of Israel to make war against Hazael king of Syria at Ramoth-gilead. And the Syrians wounded Joram, ⁶and he returned to be healed in Jezreel of the wounds that he had received at Ramah, when he fought against Hazael king of Syria. And Ahaziah the son of

Jehoram king of Judah went down to see Joram the son of Ahab in Jezreel, because he was wounded.

⁷But it was ordained by God that the downfall of Ahaziah should come about through his going to visit Joram. For when he came there, he went out with Jehoram to meet Jehu the son of Nimshi, whom the LORD had anointed to destroy the house of Ahab. ⁸And when Jehu was executing judgment on the house of Ahab, he met the princes of Judah and the sons of Ahaziah's brothers, who attended Ahaziah, and he killed them. ⁹He searched for Ahaziah, and he was captured while hiding in Samaria, and he was brought to Jehu and put to death. They buried him, for they said, "He is the grandson of Jehoshaphat, who sought

the LORD with all his heart." And the house of Ahaziah had no one able to rule the kingdom.

¹⁰Now when Athaliah the mother of Ahaziah saw that her son was dead, she arose and destroyed all the royal family of the house of Judah. ¹¹But Jehoshabeath,ᵈ the daughter of the king, took Joash the son of Ahaziah and stole him away from among the king's sons who were about to be put to death, and she put him and his nurse in a bedroom. Thus Jehoshabeath, the daughter of King Jehoram and wife of Jehoiada the priest, because she was a sister of Ahaziah, hid himᵉ from Athaliah, so that she did not put him to death. ¹²And he remained with them six years, hidden in the house of God, while Athaliah reigned over the land.

a That is, Judah b Hebrew *spirit* c See 2 Kings 8:26; Hebrew *forty-two*; Septuagint *twenty* d Spelled *Jehosheba* in 2 Kings 11:2 e That is, Joash

---

OVERVIEW: Some reformers connect Edom's successful revolt against Judah with a prophecy concerning these two peoples' ancestors, Esau and Jacob, in Genesis 27. They also puzzle over Elijah's words against King Jehoram arriving by letter and provide possible answers—it is especially vexing that Elijah had likely already been taken up to heaven by the time of Jehoram's reign. The violence committed by Jehu against Ahab's house is interpreted as just punishment for idolatry and wickedness, even when committed against Jehoshaphat's grandson Ahaziah.[1]

21:1-10 The Reign of Jehoram and the Revolt of Edom

FULFILLED PROPHECY. JOHN MAYER: The army of Edom rising in the night destroyed the princes of the chariots in Jehoram's army, and the people of Judah with King Jehoram fled to their tents, leaving the work undone. And it was never attempted again because Libnah, a noble city of Judah and close to Edom, joined with them also. . . . And such is how the prophecy of Isaac given to Esau in Genesis was fulfilled: "By your sword you shall live, and you shall

serve your brother; but when you grow restless you shall break his yoke from your neck." That is, Esau, by means of Edom, had not broken off the yoke of his brother Jacob and so the prophecy was fulfilled. COMMENTARY ON CHRONICLES.[2]

EDOM, GOD'S SCOURGE FOR JUDAH. THE ENGLISH ANNOTATIONS: This is added to show that the Lord stirred up those Edomites as his scourge to punish this idolatrous king. This was not the reason that moved the Edomites to revolt: it was their own desire of freedom from being subject to a foreign prince that moved them to do so. Yet by his idolatrous and wicked courses and by his cruelty to his brothers and princes, they might gather that the Lord would forsake him and so take advantage and occasion of revolting. ANNOTATIONS ON 2 CHRONICLES.[3]

21:11-20 A Heavenly Letter

ELIJAH'S LETTER TO JEHORAM. VIKTORIN STRIGEL: The prophet Elijah would doubtlessly have scolded King Jehoram in person if he had

---

[1]See commentary on 2 Kings 8:16-29; 11:1-3.

[2]Mayer, *Many Commentaries in One*, 197*; citing Gen 27:40.
[3]Downame, ed., *Annotations* (1657), Dddd4v*.

been allowed access to the palace. But when this first course of action was not available to him, he used the secondary option of using a letter to warn the king of God's judgment. For the words of a letter make up for the fact that he could not use the better teaching method due to several impediments. There were two great and serious reasons why Elijah sent this letter to the king of Judah. First, he wanted the king to know that the punishments he would undergo would not be by chance but that such calamities were works of divine providence and justice. If the prophet had not predicted these punishments, the opinion of the ungodly king might have been that they had come from some human or natural cause. Second, Elijah wanted these calamities to serve as admonishments and warnings that might lead to repentance. But the ungodly king spurned the letter of Elijah, who taught not in Judah but in the kingdom of Israel, deciding that this was a vain admonition. It therefore happened to him as Romans 2 says: "Because of your hard and impenitent heart you are storing up wrath for yourself on the day of wrath when God's righteous judgment will be revealed." BOOK OF 2 CHRONICLES.[4]

PROPHETIC LETTER FROM ELIJAH. JOHN MAYER: In this letter Jehoram is upbraided for his behavior like the kings of Israel and his refusal to follow the ways of Jehoshaphat and Asa. And Jehoram is threatened for killing his brothers, who were better than himself. And now God intended to strike him with a high hand, including doing so to his family and subjects. Jehoram was to be stricken with a loathsome disease in his belly, causing his guts to come out. This threatening of him for killing his brothers seems to be a good argument, according to Nicholas of Lyra that this letter was written after the ascension of Elijah, because the brothers were killed after Elijah was taken up and not before. Nevertheless it must be remembered, as I said before, that Elijah most likely wrote this letter before his death by the spirit

of prophecy. . . . And this event proved the letter to be a truly prophetic letter. COMMENTARY ON CHRONICLES.[5]

LETTER FROM THE HEAVENS. THE ENGLISH ANNOTATIONS: Without all question, Elijah was translated to heaven before this time. For while Jehoshaphat was living, inquiry was made about a prophet of the Lord in Israel, and the answer that came was: "Elisha the son of Shaphat is here, who poured water on the hands of Elijah." By this it appears that Elisha was then famous as a prophet. But we know that Elisha was not famous as a prophet until after Elijah was taken away. Here, therefore, a great doubt arises. How could a letter from Elijah, who was now in heaven, come to Jehoram, who was on earth? Some prefer to cut the knot rather than untie it. They deny that this was that Elijah whose story is recorded in 1 Kings 17 and following. They say that another man bore this name. Others say that Elisha might be called Elijah just as John the Baptist was called in the Gospel of Matthew. And in the same way, it is mentioned of John that "the spirit and power of Elijah" remained on him in the Gospel of Luke. But a more ready and probable resolution of the doubt is this: The true and famous Elijah had written that which is here set down before his rapture, that is, while he was on earth. He then left behind the letter to be delivered to Jehoram after he would commit the aforementioned abominations. We read in 1 Kings 13:2, for instance, of the man of God prophesying of Josiah by name long before Josiah was born. And Isaiah also prophesied in the same way about Cyrus in Isaiah 45:1. And so Elijah spoke about Jehoram. This might easily be done because this impious king would not endure a living prophet to declare the truth to him. So he might be more easily convinced and convicted of his wickedness if he should see a writing brought to him from one who was then in heaven! ANNOTATIONS ON 2 CHRONICLES.[6]

---

[4]Strigel, *Libri Samuelis, Regum et Paralipomenon*, 542; citing Rom 2:5.

[5]Mayer, *Many Commentaries in One*, 198*.
[6]Downame, ed., *Annotations* (1657), Dddd4v*; citing 2 Kings 3:11; 1 Kings 17; Mt 17:12, 13; Lk 1:17; 1 Kings 13:2; Is 45:1.

22:1-9 Ahaziah Reigns in Judah

CHOOSING THEIR KING. THE ENGLISH ANNO-TATIONS: It seems that Jehoram, given that he was miserably perplexed with a tormenting disease for more than two years, took little care for his successor. Therefore the inhabitants of Jerusalem took that care on themselves. For they recognized that Jerusalem was the chief city and strongest hold of the kingdom. Because the rest of the land had been spoiled by the enemy, they sought to act quickly. ANNOTATIONS ON 2 CHRONICLES.[7]

RIGHTEOUS JEHU. JOHN MAYER: It may be asked whether Jehu went beyond his commission—which was only to strike down the house of Ahab—when he killed Ahaziah, who was not of Ahab's lineage. It is generally answered by expositors that Jehu did no more than what God willed. For it says as much in 2 Chronicles: "But it was ordained by God that the downfall of Ahaziah should come through his going to visit Joram. For when he came there, he went out with Jehoram to meet Jehu the son of Nimshi, whom the Lord had anointed to destroy the house of Ahab." It was the will of God that Ahaziah went to visit Joram, and went out with him against Jehu. For this enabled Jehu to destroy the house of Ahab. God brought them both together into Jehu's hands, the one as a natural member of Ahab's house and the other being made one by marriage through Athaliah's side. Therefore in killing Ahaziah Jehu did no more than was commanded him, that is, to destroy Ahab's house. COMMENTARY ON 2 CHRONICLES.[8]

PIETY, SINCERITY AND INTEGRITY. THE ENGLISH ANNOTATIONS: Piety, sincerity and integrity, which are here noted to have been in Jehoshaphat, are reverenced. Indeed they are held in esteem even among those who do not possess such qualities. But this is also to be taken as a special motion of the Spirit in Jehu and his

ministers, that they are willing to testify to God's respect for his servant Jehoshaphat that they would properly bury his wicked grandson. ANNOTATIONS ON 2 CHRONICLES.[9]

UNWISE COUNSELORS. JOHN MAYER: Ahaziah was made king, and he ended up being as wicked as his father had been on account of his idolatry. For he followed Ahab, as his mother enforced on him. And they of the house of Ahab are said to have been his counselors, thus bringing Ahaziah to destruction. . . . His mother provided him a wife from Ahab's house, and thus he was so strongly carried on as if he had been enforced to that wickedness. This was partly by his mother's command and partly by his wife's importunity. Thus idolatry brought in by marrying idolaters was so rooted that it could not be rooted out without rooting up the corrupted stock. COMMENTARY ON CHRONICLES.[10]

22:10-12 Evil Athaliah

ATHALIAH'S DEMONIC PLAN. VIKTORIN STRIGEL: See what a monstrous and ungodly person the king's mother Athaliah was, for she did not think of sparing her own flesh and blood but cruelly murdered her son's children. Such fury did not only arise from a human infirmity but was also encouraged by the devil, who extinguishes any natural light or feeling in the hearts of the ungodly. Through his instrument Athaliah, the devil wanted even more to destroy all of David's seed, insulting the God who promised that the Messiah would be born from the seed of David according to the flesh. But the power of the devil and of tyrants is not stronger than God's resolve. And so, even though Athaliah thought she had eradicated all of David's descendants, Jehoshabeath stole Joash away from the tyrannical woman. That such a cruel woman could rage against her own offspring meant that it was easy to see that she would rage against all the

---

[7]Downame, ed., *Annotations* (1657), Eeee1r*.
[8]Mayer, *Many Commentaries in One*, 205-6*.
[9]Downame, ed., *Annotations* (1657), Eeee1r*.
[10]Mayer, *Many Commentaries in One*, 200*.

pious for these six years. But God allowed this omen of her six-year reign in order to exercise the faith of the pious, who—looking at the promise— did not doubt the promise that God could raise up a king from the blood of David even from stones, just as the Baptist said, "God is able from these stones to raise up children for Abraham." BOOK OF 2 CHRONICLES.[11]

---

[11]Strigel, *Libri Samuelis, Regum et Paralipomenon*, 544-45; citing Lk 3:8.

23:1–24:27 KING JOASH OF JUDAH

[1]But in the seventh year Jehoiada took courage and entered into a covenant with the commanders of hundreds, Azariah the son of Jeroham, Ishmael the son of Jehohanan, Azariah the son of Obed, Maaseiah the son of Adaiah, and Elishaphat the son of Zichri. [2]And they went about through Judah and gathered the Levites from all the cities of Judah, and the heads of fathers' houses of Israel, and they came to Jerusalem. [3]And all the assembly made a covenant with the king in the house of God. And Jehoiada[a] said to them, "Behold, the king's son! Let him reign, as the Lord spoke concerning the sons of David. [4]This is the thing that you shall do: of you priests and Levites who come off duty on the Sabbath, one third shall be gatekeepers, [5]and one third shall be at the king's house and one third at the Gate of the Foundation. And all the people shall be in the courts of the house of the Lord. [6]Let no one enter the house of the Lord except the priests and ministering Levites. They may enter, for they are holy, but all the people shall keep the charge of the Lord. [7]The Levites shall surround the king, each with his weapons in his hand. And whoever enters the house shall be put to death. Be with the king when he comes in and when he goes out."

[8]The Levites and all Judah did according to all that Jehoiada the priest commanded, and they each brought his men, who were to go off duty on the Sabbath, with those who were to come on duty on the Sabbath, for Jehoiada the priest did not dismiss the divisions. [9]And Jehoiada the priest gave to the captains the spears and the large and small shields that had been King David's, which were in the house of God. [10]And he set all the people as a guard for the king, every man with his weapon in his hand, from the south side of the house to the north side of the house, around the altar and the house. [11]Then they brought out the king's son and put the crown on him and gave him the testimony. And they proclaimed him king, and Jehoiada and his sons anointed him, and they said, "Long live the king." [12]When Athaliah heard the noise of the people running and praising the king, she went into the house of the Lord to the people. [13]And when she looked, there was the king standing by his pillar at the entrance, and the captains and the trumpeters beside the king, and all the people of the land rejoicing and blowing trumpets, and the singers with their musical instruments leading in the celebration. And Athaliah tore her clothes and cried, "Treason! Treason!" [14]Then Jehoiada the priest brought out the captains who were set over the army, saying to them, "Bring her out between the ranks, and anyone who follows her is to be put to death with the sword." For the priest said, "Do not put her to death in the house of the Lord." [15]So they laid hands on her,[b] and she went into the entrance of the horse gate of the king's house, and they put her to death there.

[16]And Jehoiada made a covenant between himself and all the people and the king that they should be the Lord's people. [17]Then all the people went to the house of Baal and tore it down; his altars and his images they broke in pieces, and they killed Mattan the priest of Baal before the altars. [18]And Jehoiada posted watchmen for the house of the Lord under the direction of the Levitical priests and the Levites whom David had organized to be in charge of the house of the Lord, to offer burnt offerings to the Lord, as it is written in the Law of Moses, with rejoicing and with singing, according to the order of David. [19]He stationed the gatekeepers at the gates of the house of the Lord so that no one should enter who was in any way unclean. [20]And he took the captains, the nobles, the governors of the people, and all the people of the land, and they brought the king down from the house of the Lord, marching through the upper gate to the king's house. And they set the king on the royal throne. [21]So all the people of the land rejoiced, and the city was quiet after Athaliah had been put to death with the sword.

24 Joash[c] was seven years old when he began to reign, and he reigned forty years in Jerusalem. His mother's name was Zibiah of Beersheba. [2]And Joash did what was right in the eyes of the Lord all the days of Jehoiada the priest. [3]Jehoiada got for him two wives, and he had sons and daughters.

⁴After this Joash decided to restore the house of the Lord. ⁵And he gathered the priests and the Levites and said to them, "Go out to the cities of Judah and gather from all Israel money to repair the house of your God from year to year, and see that you act quickly." But the Levites did not act quickly. ⁶So the king summoned Jehoiada the chief and said to him, "Why have you not required the Levites to bring in from Judah and Jerusalem the tax levied by Moses, the servant of the Lord, and the congregation of Israel for the tent of testimony?" ⁷For the sons of Athaliah, that wicked woman, had broken into the house of God, and had also used all the dedicated things of the house of the Lord for the Baals.

⁸So the king commanded, and they made a chest and set it outside the gate of the house of the Lord. ⁹And proclamation was made throughout Judah and Jerusalem to bring in for the Lord the tax that Moses the servant of God laid on Israel in the wilderness. ¹⁰And all the princes and all the people rejoiced and brought their tax and dropped it into the chest until they had finished.ᵈ ¹¹And whenever the chest was brought to the king's officers by the Levites, when they saw that there was much money in it, the king's secretary and the officer of the chief priest would come and empty the chest and take it and return it to its place. Thus they did day after day, and collected money in abundance. ¹²And the king and Jehoiada gave it to those who had charge of the work of the house of the Lord, and they hired masons and carpenters to restore the house of the Lord, and also workers in iron and bronze to repair the house of the Lord. ¹³So those who were engaged in the work labored, and the repairing went forward in their hands, and they restored the house of God to its proper condition and strengthened it. ¹⁴And when they had finished, they brought the rest of the money before the king and Jehoiada, and with it were made utensils for the house of the Lord, both for the service and for the burnt offerings, and dishes for incense and vessels of gold and silver. And they offered burnt offerings in the house of the Lord regularly all the days of Jehoiada.

¹⁵But Jehoiada grew old and full of days, and died. He was 130 years old at his death. ¹⁶And they buried him in the city of David among the kings, because he had done good in Israel, and toward God and his house.

¹⁷Now after the death of Jehoiada the princes of Judah came and paid homage to the king. Then the king listened to them. ¹⁸And they abandoned the house of the Lord, the God of their fathers, and served the Asherim and the idols. And wrath came upon Judah and Jerusalem for this guilt of theirs. ¹⁹Yet he sent prophets among them to bring them back to the Lord. These testified against them, but they would not pay attention.

²⁰Then the Spirit of God clothed Zechariah the son of Jehoiada the priest, and he stood above the people, and said to them, "Thus says God, 'Why do you break the commandments of the Lord, so that you cannot prosper? Because you have forsaken the Lord, he has forsaken you.'" ²¹But they conspired against him, and by command of the king they stoned him with stones in the court of the house of the Lord. ²²Thus Joash the king did not remember the kindness that Jehoiada, Zechariah's father, had shown him, but killed his son. And when he was dying, he said, "May the Lord see and avenge!"ᵉ

²³At the end of the year the army of the Syrians came up against Joash. They came to Judah and Jerusalem and destroyed all the princes of the people from among the people and sent all their spoil to the king of Damascus. ²⁴Though the army of the Syrians had come with few men, the Lord delivered into their hand a very great army, because Judahᶠ had forsaken the Lord, the God of their fathers. Thus they executed judgment on Joash.

²⁵When they had departed from him, leaving him severely wounded, his servants conspired against him because of the blood of the sonᵍ of Jehoiada the priest, and killed him on his bed. So he died, and they buried him in the city of David, but they did not bury him in the tombs of the kings. ²⁶Those who conspired against him were Zabad the son of Shimeath the Ammonite, and Jehozabad the son of Shimrith the Moabite. ²⁷Accounts of his sons and of the many oracles against him and of the rebuildingʰ of the house of God are written in the Story of the Book of the Kings. And Amaziah his son reigned in his place.

a Hebrew *he*   b Or *they made a passage for her*   c Spelled *Jehoash* in 2 Kings 12:1   d Or *until it was full*   e Hebrew *and seek*   f Hebrew *they*   g Septuagint, Vulgate; Hebrew *sons*   h Hebrew *founding*

Overview: The righteous priest Jehoiada stands in direct contrast to Queen Athaliah and her priest Mattan; these writers note the blessing that his 130 years of life signifies. Nevertheless, after Jehoiada's death, King Joash defected from righteousness and killed Jehoiada's son Zechariah, which stands not only as an act of brutality but also a warning to readers who—like Joash— might put their trust in the faith and righteousness they had in the past.[1]

23:1-11 *Jehoiada Prepares for the Anointing of the Young King*

Taking Courage Against Athaliah. The English Annotations: Athaliah usurped the crown and attracted many to her side. She therefore destroyed and weakened those who stood for the house of David. As a result Jehoiada dared not oppose her openly and publicly. But from time to time he would get as many collaborators as possible to take part with him. And he secretly set aside weapons and ammunition in the courts and chambers of the house of God, and by this he took courage. Annotations on 2 Chronicles.[2]

Levites Conspire to End Tyranny. John Mayer: The gathering together of the Levites indicates that they were obediently observing the ordinances of God above others, even despite the corrupt times in which they lived. And because the chief strength of the kingdom lay in the heads of the Levitical families, they were called together to go about this great work to set up a new king. For he alone had right to the kingdom, while the bloody queen had none. Commentary on Chronicles.[3]

Ungrateful and Ironic Anointing. The English Annotations: Jehoiada himself probably poured oil on the head of Joash. His sons likely stood close by and assisted him. They would have given their father the vessel in which the oil was contained and also would have taken it back after it was used for the anointing.... It is very probable that Zechariah, the son of Jehoiada, was one of those who helped assist his father in the anointing of Joash. If so, this shows how ungrateful Joash was since he would later have Zechariah stoned to death. Annotations on 2 Chronicles.[4]

23:12-21 *Athaliah Executed and Jehoiada's Reforms*

Undoing Idolatry. Viktorin Strigel: In the righteous judgment of God, not only was Athaliah killed but Mattan—the sacrificing priest of Baal—was also slaughtered. Because Mattan had made sacrifices and turned the temple to idolatry through his impious office, God wanted the location of his punishment to serve as a sign of his wrath. Magistrates often select the place where a terrible crime happened to be the place where a criminal is tried. In the same way, God wanted the place, time and mode of punishment to fit the circumstances of the crime, so that the fitting nature of the punishment would warn and announce God's providence. Thus the bones of the ungodly were burned at the destroyed remains of the altar at Bethel, as it says in 2 Kings 23. Book of 2 Chronicles.[5]

Joined as One. John Mayer: Things being so much out of order, the wise priest thought it necessary, now that he had made Joash the king, to direct him and the people to make a covenant with the Lord to root out idolatry from the land and to restore and maintain the pure worship of God according to his Word. The priest also wanted to join the people and the king again together as one. Commentary on Chronicles.[6]

---

[1]See commentary on 2 Kings 11:4-20; 11:21–12:21.
[2]Downame, ed., *Annotations* (1657), Eeee1v*; citing 2 Kings 11:4.
[3]Mayer, *Many Commentaries in One*, 216*.

[4]Downame, ed., *Annotations* (1657), Eeee1v*; citing 1 Kings 1:34.
[5]Strigel, *Libri Samuelis, Regum et Paralipomenon*, 547.
[6]Mayer, *Many Commentaries in One*, 218*.

24:1-14 Joash Repairs the Temple

Repairs of the Temple. The English Annotations: The Lord was in special manner the God of the priests and Levites by reason of their special attendance in his house and on his service. . . . And from time to time, as need was required, they were to go out to collect money for temple repairs. This detail was added for four reasons. First, the work was great and could hardly be perfected in a year. Second, the manner of collecting the money and providing materials would be long. Third, the collectors were somewhat negligent. And fourth, as one thing was repaired, another thing would need repaired, which would happen year after year. Annotations on 2 Chronicles.[7]

24:15-16 Jehoiada Dies at the Age of 130

Jehoiada's Long Life. Viktorin Strigel: There is no doubt that Athaliah often attempted to oppress the most holy old man Jehoiada. But God granted this faithful minister a long span of life and a royal burial, while Athaliah was murdered and cast away without an honorable burial. Therefore the one who trusts in God alone is more secure than the one who believes in the power of a thousand of the prince's men. Book of 2 Chronicles.[8]

Good for Nothing. John Mayer: All things being prepared about the temple, sacrifices were there constantly offered to God all the days of Jehoiada. But then after living to the advanced age of 130, he died and was honorably buried for his good life in the sepulchers of the kings of Judah. Afterward the princes of Judah came to Joash with comely flattery and lowly reverence to draw him into idolatry even though he had formerly been a good king. These princes drew Joash into worshiping idols in groves and leaving the house of the Lord. This therefore provoked God's fierce wrath

against Judah and Jerusalem. Commentary on Chronicles.[9]

24:17-19 Princes of Judah Undo Jehoiada's Reforms

Allured by His Counselors. The English Annotations: The death of a wise, godly and zealous governor is a great loss to a kingdom. But these princes of Joash's were hollow-hearted, and they concealed themselves while Jehoiada lived. And as soon as he was dead, their impious minds manifested themselves. They made pretense of doing honor to the king, so that they might persuade him into idolatry. Flatterers greatly prevail with kings. Though Joash had been well instructed and was therefore addicted to worshiping the Lord in the temple as was prescribed, yet the princes, by their flattery, allured him to use his regal authority according to his own mind and lust, even in matters of religion. Annotations on 2 Chronicles.[10]

From Saint to Sinner. John Mayer: The words in this passage are too brief to indicate for sure whether the princes fully moved Joash to turn into an idolater like them or whether he merely gave them leave to pursue idolatry but that he did not do so himself. For not much else is said other than that the princes came and bowed to him and he hearkened to them, and then that they abandoned the house of the Lord. But what they requested is not expressed, if they made any request at all to him. . . . Nevertheless, because Joash degenerated so far that he commanded Zechariah, a most godly priest and son of Jehoiada, to be killed when he reproved him, it is most probable that Joash had turned into an idolater together with the princes, seeing that this is peculiar to idolaters to be cruel and bloody toward truth, which occurs by the instigation of that murderer the devil whom they serve. We may note

---

[7]Downame, ed., *Annotations* (1657), Eeee2r*.
[8]Strigel, *Libri Samuelis, Regum et Paralipomenon*, 549.
[9]Mayer, *Many Commentaries in One*, 222*.
[10]Downame, ed., *Annotations* (1657), Eeee2v*.

the following things. First, we have great need always to pray so that we may be upheld in the truth, seeing that Joash was godly for so long yet, now destitute of his tutor, he quickly fell into sin. Second, it is of great avail to commit youth to good tutors and overseers. Third, there is not a more pestilent way of corrupting princes or leaders than by flattery. By showing ourselves hateful of flattery at all times, we may keep out of danger. Finally, to tolerate a false religion is the very way for kings to overthrow themselves and their kingdoms. For even if leaders do not embrace false religion themselves, they will fall into ruin. Commentary on Chronicles.[11]

24:20-22 Joash Kills Zechariah

The Punishment Fits the Crime. Viktorin Strigel: The tragic end of a tyrant signifies the wrath of God and is also a symptom of the tyrant's wrath. For in this case the punishment fit the crime, according to the rule: "The one through whom sin has come will be punished." God makes an example of such a person, so that others are reminded of divine providence. Joash had murdered the most holy and humble Zechariah, the son of the priest Jehoiada. Thus he was in turn murdered by his servants, a form of punishment that fit the form of his crime. Truly, none of this was written for the sake of Joash but rather for our sake, so that such a great example would inspire us to return to the commandments. For since God did not spare King Joash, who was pious at the beginning and did well for the church, how much less will he spare other kings and people who commit similar crimes. Book of Kings.[12]

Zechariah Foreshadows Christ. The English Annotations: Jehoiada had preserved Joash from death, nourished him in the Lord's house until he set him up on the throne, instructed him and blessed him in the ways of the Lord. And yet Joash unjustly and cruelly killed Jehoiada's son

Zechariah only for giving him good counsel. What's more, he dared to kill Zechariah in the house of the Lord. Now, that which Zechariah said at the time of his death was by special instinct. For we must not think that so holy a man would end his days with a revengeful imprecation in his mouth. On the contrary, he spoke like Christ would: "Father, forgive them, for they know not what they do." We see this not only in Christ, but in Stephen too. Annotations on 2 Chronicles.[13]

Unparalleled Tyranny. John Mayer: Jehoiada saved a venomous serpent from destruction only for it to kill his most dear and godly son. Joash's action here was the highest degree of ingratitude, for Zechariah was a child of the family and he had been tenderly brought up in the court. And this was further unnatural, since Zechariah's parents had risked their lives to save Joash from death. The fact that Joash gave this order is an example of unparalleled tyranny. Commentary on Chronicles.[14]

Themes in Joash's Demise. Viktorin Strigel: This history of Joash's slide into ungodliness is brief, but it commends four very important things to readers: first, the difference between good and bad advisers; second, the inconstancy of virtue among those who forsake God; third, the slippery slope between true and false doctrine; and fourth, the forbearance of God. . . . Similarly, the murder of Zechariah teaches three things: the fury of the ungodly, the ingratitude of both royal and common people, and divine vengeance. Book of 2 Chronicles.[15]

24:23-27 Joash Assassinated

Joash's Death. Giovanni Diodati: Joash's servants took an occasion to conspire against him, seeing that he was utterly unable to govern by

---

[11]Mayer, *Many Commentaries in One*, 223*.
[12]Strigel, *Libri Samuelis, Regum et Paralipomenon*, 359.

[13]Downame, ed., *Annotations* (1657), Eeee2v*; citing Lk 23:34; Acts 7:60.
[14]Mayer, *Many Commentaries in One*, 223*.
[15]Strigel, *Libri Samuelis, Regum et Paralipomenon*, 549, 551.

reason of some languishing disease, where God had afflicted him. It is not certain whether these murderers had intended to revenge his cruelty or whether it was only a pretense. There is no mention made of the murder of any other but Zechariah; but the plural number is here set down for the singular unless there were more of the sons of Jehoiada included within that persecution. Annotations on 2 Chronicles.[16]

God Stirs Up Syria to Punish Joash. John Mayer: After so horrible a sin, judgment was not long deterred. The king of Syria[17] at this time was no longer Hazael, since he was now dead. In his place a new king had been established in Syria who did not regard the king of Judah as his predecessor had done. And this king entered Judah with great forces to spoil and destroy those whom the Syrians commonly counted as their deadly enemies, and vice versa. And it seems that the king of Syria was extraordinarily stirred up by God, who hated the abominable wickedness of Joash. Commentary on Chronicles.[18]

---

[16]Diodati, *Pious Annotations*, 47*.

[17]That is, Aram.
[18]Mayer, *Many Commentaries in One*, 225-27*.

25:1–28:27 FROM THE REIGN OF AMAZIAH TO AHAZ

[1]Amaziah was twenty-five years old when he began to reign, and he reigned twenty-nine years in Jerusalem. His mother's name was Jehoaddan of Jerusalem. [2]And he did what was right in the eyes of the Lord, yet not with a whole heart. [3]And as soon as the royal power was firmly his, he killed his servants who had struck down the king his father. [4]But he did not put their children to death, according to what is written in the Law, in the Book of Moses, where the Lord commanded, "Fathers shall not die because of their children, nor children die because of their fathers, but each one shall die for his own sin."

[5]Then Amaziah assembled the men of Judah and set them by fathers' houses under commanders of thousands and of hundreds for all Judah and Benjamin. He mustered those twenty years old and upward, and found that they were 300,000 choice men, fit for war, able to handle spear and shield. [6]He hired also 100,000 mighty men of valor from Israel for 100 talents[a] of silver. [7]But a man of God came to him and said, "O king, do not let the army of Israel go with you, for the Lord is not with Israel, with all these Ephraimites. [8]But go, act, be strong for the battle. Why should you suppose that God will cast you down before the enemy? For God has power to help or to cast down." [9]And Amaziah said to the man of God, "But what shall we do about the hundred talents that I have given to the army of Israel?" The man of God answered, "The Lord is able to give you much more than this." [10]Then Amaziah discharged the army that had come to him from Ephraim to go home again. And they became very angry with Judah and returned home in fierce anger. [11]But Amaziah took courage and led out his people and went to the Valley of Salt and struck down 10,000 men of Seir. [12]The men of Judah captured another 10,000 alive and took them to the top of a rock and threw them down from the top of the rock, and they were all dashed to pieces. [13]But the men of the army whom Amaziah sent back, not letting them go with him to battle, raided the cities of Judah, from Samaria to Beth-horon, and struck down 3,000 people in them and took much spoil.

[14]After Amaziah came from striking down the Edomites, he brought the gods of the men of Seir and set them up as his gods and worshiped them, making offerings to them. [15]Therefore the Lord was angry with Amaziah and sent to him a prophet, who said to him, "Why have you sought the gods of a people who did not deliver their own people from your hand?" [16]But as he was speaking, the king said to him, "Have we made you a royal counselor? Stop! Why should you be struck down?" So the prophet stopped, but said, "I know that God has determined to destroy you, because you have done this and have not listened to my counsel."

[17]Then Amaziah king of Judah took counsel and sent to Joash the son of Jehoahaz, son of Jehu, king of Israel, saying, "Come, let us look one another in the face." [18]And Joash the king of Israel sent word to Amaziah king of Judah, "A thistle on Lebanon sent to a cedar on Lebanon, saying, 'Give your daughter to my son for a wife,' and a wild beast of Lebanon passed by and trampled down the thistle. [19]You say, 'See, I[b] have struck down Edom,' and your heart has lifted you up in boastfulness. But now stay at home. Why should you provoke trouble so that you fall, you and Judah with you?"

[20]But Amaziah would not listen, for it was of God, in order that he might give them into the hand of their enemies, because they had sought the gods of Edom. [21]So Joash king of Israel went up, and he and Amaziah king of Judah faced one another in battle at Beth-shemesh, which belongs to Judah. [22]And Judah was defeated by Israel, and every man fled to his home. [23]And Joash king of Israel captured Amaziah king of Judah, the son of Joash, son of Ahaziah, at Beth-shemesh, and brought him to Jerusalem and broke down the wall of Jerusalem for 400 cubits,[c] from the Ephraim Gate to the Corner Gate. [24]And he seized all the gold and silver, and all the vessels that were found in the house of God, in the care of Obed-edom. He seized also the treasuries of the king's house, also hostages, and he returned to Samaria.

²⁵Amaziah the son of Joash, king of Judah, lived fifteen years after the death of Joash the son of Jehoahaz, king of Israel. ²⁶Now the rest of the deeds of Amaziah, from first to last, are they not written in the Book of the Kings of Judah and Israel? ²⁷From the time when he turned away from the LORD they made a conspiracy against him in Jerusalem, and he fled to Lachish. But they sent after him to Lachish and put him to death there. ²⁸And they brought him upon horses, and he was buried with his fathers in the city of David.ᵈ

26 And all the people of Judah took Uzziah, who was sixteen years old, and made him king instead of his father Amaziah. ²He built Eloth and restored it to Judah, after the king slept with his fathers. ³Uzziah was sixteen years old when he began to reign, and he reigned fifty-two years in Jerusalem. His mother's name was Jecoliah of Jerusalem. ⁴And he did what was right in the eyes of the LORD, according to all that his father Amaziah had done. ⁵He set himself to seek God in the days of Zechariah, who instructed him in the fear of God, and as long as he sought the LORD, God made him prosper.

⁶He went out and made war against the Philistines and broke through the wall of Gath and the wall of Jabneh and the wall of Ashdod, and he built cities in the territory of Ashdod and elsewhere among the Philistines. ⁷God helped him against the Philistines and against the Arabians who lived in Gurbaal and against the Meunites. ⁸The Ammonites paid tribute to Uzziah, and his fame spread even to the border of Egypt, for he became very strong. ⁹Moreover, Uzziah built towers in Jerusalem at the Corner Gate and at the Valley Gate and at the Angle, and fortified them. ¹⁰And he built towers in the wilderness and cut out many cisterns, for he had large herds, both in the Shephelah and in the plain, and he had farmers and vinedressers in the hills and in the fertile lands, for he loved the soil. ¹¹Moreover, Uzziah had an army of soldiers, fit for war, in divisions according to the numbers in the muster made by Jeiel the secretary and Maaseiah the officer, under the direction of Hananiah, one of the king's commanders. ¹²The whole number of the heads of fathers' houses of mighty men of valor was 2,600. ¹³Under their command was an army of 307,500, who could make war with mighty power, to help the king against the enemy. ¹⁴And Uzziah prepared for all the army shields, spears, helmets, coats of mail, bows, and stones for slinging. ¹⁵In Jerusalem he made machines, invented by skillful men, to be on the towers and the corners, to shoot arrows and great stones. And his fame spread far, for he was marvelously helped, till he was strong.

¹⁶But when he was strong, he grew proud, to his destruction. For he was unfaithful to the LORD his God and entered the temple of the LORD to burn incense on the altar of incense. ¹⁷But Azariah the priest went in after him, with eighty priests of the LORD who were men of valor, ¹⁸and they withstood King Uzziah and said to him, "It is not for you, Uzziah, to burn incense to the LORD, but for the priests, the sons of Aaron, who are consecrated to burn incense. Go out of the sanctuary, for you have done wrong, and it will bring you no honor from the LORD God." ¹⁹Then Uzziah was angry. Now he had a censer in his hand to burn incense, and when he became angry with the priests, leprosyᵉ broke out on his forehead in the presence of the priests in the house of the LORD, by the altar of incense. ²⁰And Azariah the chief priest and all the priests looked at him, and behold, he was leprous in his forehead! And they rushed him out quickly, and he himself hurried to go out, because the LORD had struck him. ²¹And King Uzziah was a leper to the day of his death, and being a leper lived in a separate house, for he was excluded from the house of the LORD. And Jotham his son was over the king's household, governing the people of the land.

²²Now the rest of the acts of Uzziah, from first to last, Isaiah the prophet the son of Amoz wrote. ²³And Uzziah slept with his fathers, and they buried him with his fathers in the burial field that belonged to the kings, for they said, "He is a leper." And Jotham his son reigned in his place.

27 Jotham was twenty-five years old when he began to reign, and he reigned sixteen years in Jerusalem. His mother's name was Jerushah the daughter of Zadok. ²And he did what was right in the eyes of the LORD according to all that his father Uzziah had done, except he did not enter the temple of the LORD. But the people still followed corrupt practices. ³He built the upper gate of the house of the

LORD and did much building on the wall of Ophel. ⁴Moreover, he built cities in the hill country of Judah, and forts and towers on the wooded hills. ⁵He fought with the king of the Ammonites and prevailed against them. And the Ammonites gave him that year 100 talentsᶠ of silver, and 10,000 corsᵍ of wheat and 10,000 of barley. The Ammonites paid him the same amount in the second and the third years. ⁶So Jotham became mighty, because he ordered his ways before the LORD his God. ⁷Now the rest of the acts of Jotham, and all his wars and his ways, behold, they are written in the Book of the Kings of Israel and Judah. ⁸He was twenty-five years old when he began to reign, and he reigned sixteen years in Jerusalem. ⁹And Jotham slept with his fathers, and they buried him in the city of David, and Ahaz his son reigned in his place.

28 Ahaz was twenty years old when he began to reign, and he reigned sixteen years in Jerusalem. And he did not do what was right in the eyes of the LORD, as his father David had done, ²but he walked in the ways of the kings of Israel. He even made metal images for the Baals, ³and he made offerings in the Valley of the Son of Hinnom and burned his sons as an offering,ʰ according to the abominations of the nations whom the LORD drove out before the people of Israel. ⁴And he sacrificed and made offerings on the high places and on the hills and under every green tree.

⁵Therefore the LORD his God gave him into the hand of the king of Syria, who defeated him and took captive a great number of his people and brought them to Damascus. He was also given into the hand of the king of Israel, who struck him with great force. ⁶For Pekah the son of Remaliah killed 120,000 from Judah in one day, all of them men of valor, because they had forsaken the LORD, the God of their fathers. ⁷And Zichri, a mighty man of Ephraim, killed Maaseiah the king's son and Azrikam the commander of the palace and Elkanah the next in authority to the king.

⁸The men of Israel took captive 200,000 of their relatives, women, sons, and daughters. They also took much spoil from them and brought the spoil to Samaria. ⁹But a prophet of the LORD was there, whose name was Oded, and he went out to meet the army that came to Samaria and said to them,

"Behold, because the LORD, the God of your fathers, was angry with Judah, he gave them into your hand, but you have killed them in a rage that has reached up to heaven. ¹⁰And now you intend to subjugate the people of Judah and Jerusalem, male and female, as your slaves. Have you not sins of your own against the LORD your God? ¹¹Now hear me, and send back the captives from your relatives whom you have taken, for the fierce wrath of the LORD is upon you."

¹²Certain chiefs also of the men of Ephraim, Azariah the son of Johanan, Berechiah the son of Meshillemoth, Jehizkiah the son of Shallum, and Amasa the son of Hadlai, stood up against those who were coming from the war ¹³and said to them, "You shall not bring the captives in here, for you propose to bring upon us guilt against the LORD in addition to our present sins and guilt. For our guilt is already great, and there is fierce wrath against Israel." ¹⁴So the armed men left the captives and the spoil before the princes and all the assembly. ¹⁵And the men who have been mentioned by name rose and took the captives, and with the spoil they clothed all who were naked among them. They clothed them, gave them sandals, provided them with food and drink, and anointed them, and carrying all the feeble among them on donkeys, they brought them to their kinsfolk at Jericho, the city of palm trees. Then they returned to Samaria.

¹⁶At that time King Ahaz sent to the kingⁱ of Assyria for help. ¹⁷For the Edomites had again invaded and defeated Judah and carried away captives. ¹⁸And the Philistines had made raids on the cities in the Shephelah and the Negeb of Judah, and had taken Beth-shemesh, Aijalon, Gederoth, Soco with its villages, Timnah with its villages, and Gimzo with its villages. And they settled there. ¹⁹For the LORD humbled Judah because of Ahaz king of Israel, for he had made Judah act sinfullyʲ and had been very unfaithful to the LORD. ²⁰So Tiglath-pileserᵏ king of Assyria came against him and afflicted him instead of strengthening him. ²¹For Ahaz took a portion from the house of the LORD and the house of the king and of the princes, and gave tribute to the king of Assyria, but it did not help him.

²²In the time of his distress he became yet more faithless to the LORD—this same King Ahaz. ²³For

he sacrificed to the gods of Damascus that had defeated him and said, "Because the gods of the kings of Syria helped them, I will sacrifice to them that they may help me." But they were the ruin of him and of all Israel. ²⁴And Ahaz gathered together the vessels of the house of God and cut in pieces the vessels of the house of God, and he shut up the doors of the house of the LORD, and he made himself altars in every corner of Jerusalem. ²⁵In every city of

Judah he made high places to make offerings to other gods, provoking to anger the LORD, the God of his fathers. ²⁶Now the rest of his acts and all his ways, from first to last, behold, they are written in the Book of the Kings of Judah and Israel. ²⁷And Ahaz slept with his fathers, and they buried him in the city, in Jerusalem, for they did not bring him into the tombs of the kings of Israel. And Hezekiah his son reigned in his place.

a *A talent was about 75 pounds or 34 kilograms* b *Hebrew you* c *A cubit was about 18 inches or 45 centimeters* d *Hebrew of Judah* e *Leprosy was a term for several skin diseases; see Leviticus 13* f *A talent was about 75 pounds or 34 kilograms* g *A cor was about 6 bushels or 220 liters* h *Hebrew made his sons pass through the fire* i *Septuagint, Syriac, Vulgate (compare 2 Kings 16:7); Hebrew kings* j *Or wildly* k *Hebrew Tilgath-pilneser*

OVERVIEW: The reformers here reflect on the importance of faithfulness to and humility before God. Amaziah's violence and pride come before his fall; even so, these commentators note that this king of Judah still had further opportunities to repent before he came to ruin. Uzziah (called Azariah in 2 Kings) also performed many commendable deeds before being undone by his pride. In contrast, Uzziah's son Jotham humbled himself to such an extent that he never entered the temple, as his father had boastfully done. Surpassing others in wickedness, however, King Ahaz not only removes true worship but also commands false worship. The commentators continue to highlight God's mercy even in such impious times by sending prophets like Oded and Isaiah.[1]

25:1-13 Amaziah Reigns in Judah

PLAIN HYPOCRITE. THE ENGLISH ANNOTATIONS: This Amaziah made show of some good thing. But in the end he was a plain hypocrite. For although there are some good things recorded of him, afterward he was guilty of great sins and was judged accordingly. ANNOTATIONS ON 2 CHRONICLES.[2]

WHY EPHRAIM IS MENTIONED. THE ENGLISH ANNOTATIONS: Ephraim is here put down as representing the ten tribes, just as Judah stood for the two tribes of Judah and Benjamin. This is apparent throughout Scripture. For Ephraim had the privilege of the firstborn in Genesis 48:19. What's more, it was the greatest tribe of the ten in Joshua 17. And to show that the people's revolt was the cause of God's not being with them, mention is made of Ephraim. ANNOTATIONS ON 2 CHRONICLES.[3]

CRUEL PUNISHMENT AS RETALIATION. THE ENGLISH ANNOTATIONS: Some translate the word "rock" as Petra, and take it for the proper name of a place. Some in fact say it is the same place that is called Selah in Scripture, which Amaziah in this expedition took by war. The reason why the children of Judah dealt this way with the Edomites may be because, having been subdued by David and made tributaries, they later rebelled in the day of Joram son of Jehoshaphat and experienced a slaughter. So the Judean army here dashed out the brains of the Edomites, broke their bones and may have violently torn their arms and legs from their bodies. ANNOTATIONS ON 2 CHRONICLES.[4]

---

[1]See commentary on 2 Kings 14:1-22; 15:1-7, 32-38; 16:1-14.
[2]Downame, ed., *Annotations* (1657), Eeee3r*.
[3]Downame, ed., *Annotations* (1657), Eeee3r-v*; citing Hos 6:4; Jer 7:15; Gen 48:19; Josh 17:14, 17; 1 Kings 21:26.
[4]Downame, ed., *Annotations* (1657), Eeee3v*.

25:14-16 *Amaziah's Idolatry*

TURNING FROM A LIVING GOD TO A DUMB IDOL. JOHN MAYER: It is a marvel that Amaziah took to idols, given that he had just obtained victory by God's help over the Edomites, and he knew well enough from Elisha that these idols were worthless. And seeing the helplessness that was in these idols toward the people that served them, it is a marvel that he would be so enamored of their outward appearance that he should fall into this idolatry. But the Hebrew interpreters offer a reason why Amaziah took to these idols. They say that when the one thousand Edomites were cast down from the rock there was a voice heard coming from the idols, saying, "This happened to you because you have been negligent in the worship of us." And as a result of hearing this Amaziah took them home with him. But Nicholas of Lyra confutes this interpretation, since no gloss has ever yielded this as an explanation. What's more, when the prophet sent to Amaziah challenged the king, Amaziah could have responded why he took to these idols. Finally, if such an occurrence would have happened, the holy recorder of Chronicles would have surely written down this act. . . . Yet the reason why Amaziah took to these idols is understandable enough. It was pride arising in his heart after his victory against the Edomites that led him to this act, just as Joash had done. And thus God, who always despises the proud (for he sees into the heart), was angry with Amaziah. COMMENTARY ON CHRONICLES.[5]

MONSTROUS IDOLATRY. THE ENGLISH ANNOTATIONS: This slaughter that Amaziah made after he sent away the one hundred thousand hired soldiers should have raised his heart up to God, whom the man of God put in mind. But instead he made no such use of the word given to him. And rather than burning the gods brought from his enemies, as David did, Amaziah exercised extreme impiety and monstrous idolatry. This was a great

sin since he earlier "did what was right in the eyes of the Lord." ANNOTATIONS ON 2 CHRONICLES.[6]

25:17-28 *Israel Defeats Amaziah*

REPENT OR PERISH. VIKTORIN STRIGEL: Amaziah was humbled by the king of Israel, but he survived because God granted him another chance for conversion. But when Amaziah abused God's forbearance and did not repent, the Lord set before him an extreme sickness with an extreme remedy. We ought to consider what the Son of God said about those who had been killed by Pilate and those who had been crushed by a falling tower in Luke 13: "Unless you repent, you will all likewise perish." For Amaziah is not the only person who ever sinned; rather all people are sinners and lack the glory of God. Therefore we ought to repent so that the wrath of God is not poured out on us. BOOK OF 2 CHRONICLES.[7]

26:1-23 *Uzziah's Pride and Punishment*

FAITH COMES FROM HEARING. VIKTORIN STRIGEL: The prophets are visionaries. Thus the priest Zechariah had been taught well and was versed in Moses, the Prophets, Samuel, David, Gad and the like. The young Uzziah piously cherished listening to this teacher. Although God teaches us internally through the Holy Spirit, "faith comes from hearing." Unfortunately, just as Joash changed after the death of Jehoiada, so did Uzziah start to change after Zechariah's death. For it is not enough to judge merely between what one should do or not do, but to remain firm in the conviction from which one's judgments come. BOOK OF 2 CHRONICLES.[8]

PROSPERITY THEN SIN. JOHN MAYER: From here Uzziah proceeds to set forth the greatness of his forces, namely, 2,600 princes or captains under

---

[5]Mayer, *Many Commentaries in One*, 236-37*.

[6]Downame, ed., *Annotations* (1657), Eeee3v*.
[7]Strigel, *Libri Samuelis, Regum et Paralipomenon*, 555; citing Lk 13:3.
[8]Strigel, *Libri Samuelis, Regum et Paralipomenon*, 555-56; citing Rom 10:17.

whom were 307,500 able warriors all well armed by the king, etc. But it should be recognized that Uzziah prepared these great forces to go forth to war against the Philistines, Arabians and Ammonites beforehand, although it is not mentioned until now. Thus it appears how greatly Uzziah, by God's blessing, increased in wealth and power while he cleaved to the Lord. May other kings learn by his example to do likewise! Moreover Uzziah is said to have made engines by a singular art in Jerusalem, which he placed in the towers and the corners of the wall to shoot arrows and great stones. . . . And hitherto the well-doing and prosperity of Uzziah is followed by his foul sinning and punishment. But his great prosperity made him proud. COMMENTARY ON CHRONICLES.[9]

FORBIDDEN PRESUMPTION. THE ENGLISH ANNOTATIONS: People are prone to abuse God's blessings, giving them a power that eventually leads them to pride and self-confidence. Pride is the forerunner of ruin. It makes people attempt such things as provoke God's wrath on them. For Uzziah's act of entering the temple was expressly forbidden. And this was an aggravation of his sin, given that God had shown himself faithful to Uzziah in so many ways. . . . The golden altar was set close to the entrance into the most holy place. This shows the height of Uzziah's impiety and monstrous presumption. He went through the priest's court, the high porch and the holy place, even to the uppermost part of it, where he was not allowed to be. ANNOTATIONS ON 2 CHRONICLES.[10]

UZZIAH'S PUNISHMENT. VIKTORIN STRIGEL: King Uzziah, during whose reign the prophet Isaiah appeared, is an image of human infirmity and punishment. He started off pious and blessed, doing great and salutary things for the land, but then he later reveled in secondary matters and took a foreign vocation upon himself, so that he was punished with leprosy. Considering his example, we

should pray that God would confirm the works that are in us for the sake of God's own glory and for the salvation of the church and our souls. For no virtue lasts forever without God, but instead they gradually fail without the vigilance and preservation of God's Son. BOOK OF 2 CHRONICLES.[11]

FROM KING TO LEPER. JOHN MAYER: When the king was struck with leprosy, the high priest with his assistants began by force to thrust him out of the temple. That's because no unclean person was to be allowed there. Uzziah did not resist this, but departed and dwelt in a house alone until his dying day. For the Lord had appointed that all leprous persons should do so. COMMENTARY ON CHRONICLES.[12]

WHERE UZZIAH WAS BURIED. THE ENGLISH ANNOTATIONS: This field was within the city of David. . . . It is said to belong to the kings because it was their inheritance. But whether it was that field in which the tombs of David, Solomon and other kings of Judah were honored in their burials is questionable. Some hold that it was the same field, but that Uzziah was buried in a remote place in it, where none of the kings' tombs were. Such was the case also with wicked Jehoram and that notorious apostate Joash. ANNOTATIONS ON 2 CHRONICLES.[13]

27:1-9 Jotham Reigns in Judah

JOTHAM'S CAUTION. VIKTORIN STRIGEL: The text says that Jotham did not enter the temple. This can be understood logically, even if it is not terribly direct. For right after this it says that Jotham "ordered his ways before the Lord his God." From these words it is clear that Jotham's avoidance of the temple was due to a pragmatic concern about what happened to his father, namely, the leprosy inflicted after Uzziah entered the temple. BOOK OF 2 CHRONICLES.[14]

---

[9]Mayer, *Many Commentaries in One*, 242*.
[10]Downame, ed., *Annotations* (1657), Eeee4r*; citing Ex 30:6.
[11]Strigel, *Libri Samuelis, Regum et Paralipomenon*, 555.
[12]Mayer, *Many Commentaries in One*, 244; citing Lev 13:46*.
[13]Downame, ed., *Annotations* (1657), Eeee4r*; citing 1 Kings 2:10.
[14]Strigel, *Libri Samuelis, Regum et Paralipomenon*, 558.

NOTHING BUT GOOD. THE ENGLISH ANNOTA-TIONS: Jotham was the tenth king of Judah after the division. His history is briefly registered in this chapter. Nothing but good is explained in this chapter, with the exception of the people acting corruptly in his time. The great sin of Uzziah, Jotham's father, was to enter the temple of the Lord. And Jotham's restraint of that is here expressed to show that he was not like his father in the evil he did, but in the good only. ANNOTATIONS ON 2 CHRONICLES.[15]

28:1-15 Judah Defeated

THE ISRAELITES' CRUELTY. THE ENGLISH ANNOTATIONS: These sons and daughters taken captive were doubtless young children. This is noted to aggravate the cruelty of the Israelites. For they spared neither sex nor age. Also, it is possible that the phrase "sons and daughters" implies orphans whose fathers were killed in the war. Either way, it was an aggravation of the Israelites' cruelty to take these young people captive. ANNOTATIONS ON 2 CHRONICLES.[16]

NOT TOO QUICK TO JUDGE. JOHN MAYER: The prophet Oded effectively said to Israel: "Do you not have enough sins of your own that you will bring down judgment against yourselves from God for cruelly killing your brothers in Judah?" Oded did not want the Israelites to think that just because they had achieved victory against Judah that they were therefore more accepted by God. For the people of Israel had also greatly sinned against the Lord and were not to insult their Judean brothers lest God should turn the tables on the Israelites and be provoked to destroy them and free the people of Judah. COMMENTARY ON CHRONICLES.[17]

GOD STILL REACHING OUT TO ISRAEL. THE ENGLISH ANNOTATIONS: God afforded prophets to his people in the worst times to try to reclaim

them. This prophet Oded is named after a prophet of the same name in the days of Asa, about two hundred years before this. This prophet met the host of Israel before they entered into Samaria. For though the Israelites had cast off the God of their fathers, God had not cast them off. This is why the prophet uses the title "the God of your fathers" when speaking to the idolatrous Israelites. ANNOTATIONS ON 2 CHRONICLES.[18]

EVIDENT SIN. THE ENGLISH ANNOTATIONS: The idolatry of the whole land and other notorious sins common among the Israelites was so evident that they could not but know and recognize them. This made them afraid. . . . Hereby they imply that they had just cause to fear that some heavy judgment was hanging over their head. For by the word "wrath" here is meant the anger of the Lord, for so great is his wrath as comparatively it alone may be called wrath. ANNOTATIONS ON 2 CHRONICLES.[19]

28:16-21 Appealing to Assyria

FROM FEAR TO WONDER. JOHN MAYER: This sending for help of Assyria is more fully set forth in 2 Kings 16. When King Rezin of Syria and King Pekah of Israel came against Jerusalem and besieged it, Ahaz sent to Tiglath-pileser king of Assyria for help against them. Then Ahaz took the silver and gold in the Lord's house and in the king's treasury and sent a present to him. And thereupon the Assyrian king went against Damascus, the chief city of Syria, and took it and killed the king, who doubtless hearing of his coming hastened from the siege of Jerusalem to defend his own country. This is more amply set forth in Isaiah 7, where it is shown what fear came on Ahaz and the men of Judah when they heard of the coming of these two kings against them. Then the prophet Isaiah was sent to Ahaz to tell him that these

---

[15]Downame, ed., *Annotations* (1657), Eeee4v*.
[16]Downame, ed., *Annotations* (1645), np*.
[17]Mayer, *Many Commentaries in One*, 253*.

[18]Downame, ed., *Annotations* (1657), Ffff1r*.
[19]Downame, ed., *Annotations* (1657), Ffff1v*; citing Num 1:53; 18:5; Josh 22:20.

opposing forces should be able to do nothing against Jerusalem. Therefore Isaiah bid Ahaz not to fear. And then Isaiah gave a sign of a virgin conceiving and bearing a son, extending his prophecy to a far greater comfort to come afterward by the birth of Christ. And to comfort and confirm the people of Judah the more for the present, Isaiah foretold of the destruction of both the Syrian and Israelite kings in a short time, namely, before a child would be born and have knowledge to refuse evil and choose good. And this indeed fell out because Rezin was killed immediately, and Pekah in the twentieth year of his reign was killed by Hoshea, who usurped the kingdom. Commentary on Chronicles.[20]

28:22-27 *Ahaz's Idolatry*

The Heights and Depths of Idolatry. Viktorin Strigel: There are two steps to impiety. The first is to remove true doctrine and true worship from one's midst. The second is to institute false doctrine and vain worship and give honor to these. Ahaz ascended through these steps to the highest heights of impiety. He shut the

temple of the Lord, and—as 2 Kings 16 says—he established new shrines and altars all over Jerusalem and the entire kingdom. The fury of this ungodly king even progressed to the point that he burned his sons as offerings to the idol Moloch in the Valley of Hinnom. This kind of fury or rage has roots not only in human infirmity but even more in the devil. We read this history of Ahaz so that we might consider what it means that he was a vessel of God's wrath and a tool of the devil. We should then pray to God that God does not allow us to be destroyed by Epicurean fury or other fanatical errors. Book of 2 Chronicles.[21]

Foolish Idolater. The English Annotations: Ahaz counted the idols of Syria to be gods and to help those who worshiped them. In this way, he showed himself to be just like the heathen. For idolaters give the same worship to false gods that is due to the true God. Indeed idolatry so blinds people's eyes that it makes them trust in vain help. God had helped Ahaz when two kings came against Jerusalem, yet he was not thereby moved to sacrifice to the Lord. Annotations on 2 Chronicles.[22]

---

[20]Mayer, *Many Commentaries in One*, 253*.

[21]Strigel, *Libri Samuelis, Regum et Paralipomenon*, 559.
[22]Downame, ed., *Annotations* (1657), Ffffiv*; citing Judg 16:23, 24; Hab 1:11; Ex 3:18; 5:3; Is 7:3, 4.

29:1–32:33 KING HEZEKIAH OF JUDAH

[1]Hezekiah began to reign when he was twenty-five years old, and he reigned twenty-nine years in Jerusalem. His mother's name was Abijah[a] the daughter of Zechariah. [2]And he did what was right in the eyes of the LORD, according to all that David his father had done.

[3]In the first year of his reign, in the first month, he opened the doors of the house of the LORD and repaired them. [4]He brought in the priests and the Levites and assembled them in the square on the east [5]and said to them, "Hear me, Levites! Now consecrate yourselves, and consecrate the house of the LORD, the God of your fathers, and carry out the filth from the Holy Place. [6]For our fathers have been unfaithful and have done what was evil in the sight of the LORD our God. They have forsaken him and have turned away their faces from the habitation of the LORD and turned their backs. [7]They also shut the doors of the vestibule and put out the lamps and have not burned incense or offered burnt offerings in the Holy Place to the God of Israel. [8]Therefore the wrath of the LORD came on Judah and Jerusalem, and he has made them an object of horror, of astonishment, and of hissing, as you see with your own eyes. [9]For behold, our fathers have fallen by the sword, and our sons and our daughters and our wives are in captivity for this. [10]Now it is in my heart to make a covenant with the LORD, the God of Israel, in order that his fierce anger may turn away from us. [11]My sons, do not now be negligent, for the LORD has chosen you to stand in his presence, to minister to him and to be his ministers and make offerings to him."

[12]Then the Levites arose, Mahath the son of Amasai, and Joel the son of Azariah, of the sons of the Kohathites; and of the sons of Merari, Kish the son of Abdi, and Azariah the son of Jehallelel; and of the Gershonites, Joah the son of Zimmah, and Eden the son of Joah; [13]and of the sons of Elizaphan, Shimri and Jeuel; and of the sons of Asaph, Zechariah and Mattaniah; [14]and of the sons of Heman, Jehuel and Shimei; and of the sons of Jeduthun, Shemaiah and Uzziel. [15]They gathered their brothers and consecrated themselves and went in as the king had commanded, by the words of the LORD, to cleanse the house of the LORD. [16]The priests went into the inner part of the house of the LORD to cleanse it, and they brought out all the uncleanness that they found in the temple of the LORD into the court of the house of the LORD. And the Levites took it and carried it out to the brook Kidron. [17]They began to consecrate on the first day of the first month, and on the eighth day of the month they came to the vestibule of the LORD. Then for eight days they consecrated the house of the LORD, and on the sixteenth day of the first month they finished. [18]Then they went in to Hezekiah the king and said, "We have cleansed all the house of the LORD, the altar of burnt offering and all its utensils, and the table for the showbread and all its utensils. [19]All the utensils that King Ahaz discarded in his reign when he was faithless, we have made ready and consecrated, and behold, they are before the altar of the LORD."

[20]Then Hezekiah the king rose early and gathered the officials of the city and went up to the house of the LORD. [21]And they brought seven bulls, seven rams, seven lambs, and seven male goats for a sin offering for the kingdom and for the sanctuary and for Judah. And he commanded the priests, the sons of Aaron, to offer them on the altar of the LORD. [22]So they slaughtered the bulls, and the priests received the blood and threw it against the altar. And they slaughtered the rams, and their blood was thrown against the altar. And they slaughtered the lambs, and their blood was thrown against the altar. [23]Then the goats for the sin offering were brought to the king and the assembly, and they laid their hands on them, [24]and the priests slaughtered them and made a sin offering with their blood on the altar, to make atonement for all Israel. For the king commanded that the burnt offering and the sin offering should be made for all Israel.

[25]And he stationed the Levites in the house of the LORD with cymbals, harps, and lyres, according to the

commandment of David and of Gad the king's seer and of Nathan the prophet, for the commandment was from the Lord through his prophets. ²⁶The Levites stood with the instruments of David, and the priests with the trumpets. ²⁷Then Hezekiah commanded that the burnt offering be offered on the altar. And when the burnt offering began, the song to the Lord began also, and the trumpets, accompanied by the instruments of David king of Israel. ²⁸The whole assembly worshiped, and the singers sang, and the trumpeters sounded. All this continued until the burnt offering was finished. ²⁹When the offering was finished, the king and all who were present with him bowed themselves and worshiped. ³⁰And Hezekiah the king and the officials commanded the Levites to sing praises to the Lord with the words of David and of Asaph the seer. And they sang praises with gladness, and they bowed down and worshiped.

³¹Then Hezekiah said, "You have now consecrated yourselves to^b the Lord. Come near; bring sacrifices and thank offerings to the house of the Lord." And the assembly brought sacrifices and thank offerings, and all who were of a willing heart brought burnt offerings. ³²The number of the burnt offerings that the assembly brought was 70 bulls, 100 rams, and 200 lambs; all these were for a burnt offering to the Lord. ³³And the consecrated offerings were 600 bulls and 3,000 sheep. ³⁴But the priests were too few and could not flay all the burnt offerings, so until other priests had consecrated themselves, their brothers the Levites helped them, until the work was finished—for the Levites were more upright in heart than the priests in consecrating themselves. ³⁵Besides the great number of burnt offerings, there was the fat of the peace offerings, and there were the drink offerings for the burnt offerings. Thus the service of the house of the Lord was restored. ³⁶And Hezekiah and all the people rejoiced because God had provided for the people, for the thing came about suddenly.

30 Hezekiah sent to all Israel and Judah, and wrote letters also to Ephraim and Manasseh, that they should come to the house of the Lord at Jerusalem to keep the Passover to the Lord, the God of Israel. ²For the king and his princes and all the assembly in Jerusalem had taken counsel to keep the Passover in the second month— ³for they could not keep it at that time because the priests had not consecrated themselves in sufficient number, nor had the people assembled in Jerusalem— ⁴and the plan seemed right to the king and all the assembly. ⁵So they decreed to make a proclamation throughout all Israel, from Beersheba to Dan, that the people should come and keep the Passover to the Lord, the God of Israel, at Jerusalem, for they had not kept it as often as prescribed. ⁶So couriers went throughout all Israel and Judah with letters from the king and his princes, as the king had commanded, saying, "O people of Israel, return to the Lord, the God of Abraham, Isaac, and Israel, that he may turn again to the remnant of you who have escaped from the hand of the kings of Assyria. ⁷Do not be like your fathers and your brothers, who were faithless to the Lord God of their fathers, so that he made them a desolation, as you see. ⁸Do not now be stiff-necked as your fathers were, but yield yourselves to the Lord and come to his sanctuary, which he has consecrated forever, and serve the Lord your God, that his fierce anger may turn away from you. ⁹For if you return to the Lord, your brothers and your children will find compassion with their captors and return to this land. For the Lord your God is gracious and merciful and will not turn away his face from you, if you return to him."

¹⁰So the couriers went from city to city through the country of Ephraim and Manasseh, and as far as Zebulun, but they laughed them to scorn and mocked them. ¹¹However, some men of Asher, of Manasseh, and of Zebulun humbled themselves and came to Jerusalem. ¹²The hand of God was also on Judah to give them one heart to do what the king and the princes commanded by the word of the Lord.

¹³And many people came together in Jerusalem to keep the Feast of Unleavened Bread in the second month, a very great assembly. ¹⁴They set to work and removed the altars that were in Jerusalem, and all the altars for burning incense they took away and threw into the brook Kidron. ¹⁵And they slaughtered the Passover lamb on the fourteenth day of the second month. And the priests and the Levites were ashamed, so that they consecrated themselves and brought burnt offerings into the house of the Lord. ¹⁶They took their accustomed posts according to the Law of Moses the

man of God. The priests threw the blood that they received from the hand of the Levites. [17]For there were many in the assembly who had not consecrated themselves. Therefore the Levites had to slaughter the Passover lamb for everyone who was not clean, to consecrate it to the Lord. [18]For a majority of the people, many of them from Ephraim, Manasseh, Issachar, and Zebulun, had not cleansed themselves, yet they ate the Passover otherwise than as prescribed. For Hezekiah had prayed for them, saying, "May the good Lord pardon everyone [19]who sets his heart to seek God, the Lord, the God of his fathers, even though not according to the sanctuary's rules of cleanness."[c] [20]And the Lord heard Hezekiah and healed the people. [21]And the people of Israel who were present at Jerusalem kept the Feast of Unleavened Bread seven days with great gladness, and the Levites and the priests praised the Lord day by day, singing with all their might[d] to the Lord. [22]And Hezekiah spoke encouragingly to all the Levites who showed good skill in the service of the Lord. So they ate the food of the festival for seven days, sacrificing peace offerings and giving thanks to the Lord, the God of their fathers.

[23]Then the whole assembly agreed together to keep the feast for another seven days. So they kept it for another seven days with gladness. [24]For Hezekiah king of Judah gave the assembly 1,000 bulls and 7,000 sheep for offerings, and the princes gave the assembly 1,000 bulls and 10,000 sheep. And the priests consecrated themselves in great numbers. [25]The whole assembly of Judah, and the priests and the Levites, and the whole assembly that came out of Israel, and the sojourners who came out of the land of Israel, and the sojourners who lived in Judah, rejoiced. [26]So there was great joy in Jerusalem, for since the time of Solomon the son of David king of Israel there had been nothing like this in Jerusalem. [27]Then the priests and the Levites arose and blessed the people, and their voice was heard, and their prayer came to his holy habitation in heaven.

31 Now when all this was finished, all Israel who were present went out to the cities of Judah and broke in pieces the pillars and cut down the Asherim and broke down the high places and the altars throughout all Judah and Benjamin, and in Ephraim and Manasseh, until they had destroyed them all. Then all the people of Israel returned to their cities, every man to his possession.

[2]And Hezekiah appointed the divisions of the priests and of the Levites, division by division, each according to his service, the priests and the Levites, for burnt offerings and peace offerings, to minister in the gates of the camp of the Lord and to give thanks and praise. [3]The contribution of the king from his own possessions was for the burnt offerings: the burnt offerings of morning and evening, and the burnt offerings for the Sabbaths, the new moons, and the appointed feasts, as it is written in the Law of the Lord. [4]And he commanded the people who lived in Jerusalem to give the portion due to the priests and the Levites, that they might give themselves to the Law of the Lord. [5]As soon as the command was spread abroad, the people of Israel gave in abundance the firstfruits of grain, wine, oil, honey, and of all the produce of the field. And they brought in abundantly the tithe of everything. [6]And the people of Israel and Judah who lived in the cities of Judah also brought in the tithe of cattle and sheep, and the tithe of the dedicated things that had been dedicated to the Lord their God, and laid them in heaps. [7]In the third month they began to pile up the heaps, and finished them in the seventh month. [8]When Hezekiah and the princes came and saw the heaps, they blessed the Lord and his people Israel. [9]And Hezekiah questioned the priests and the Levites about the heaps. [10]Azariah the chief priest, who was of the house of Zadok, answered him, "Since they began to bring the contributions into the house of the Lord, we have eaten and had enough and have plenty left, for the Lord has blessed his people, so that we have this large amount left."

[11]Then Hezekiah commanded them to prepare chambers in the house of the Lord, and they prepared them. [12]And they faithfully brought in the contributions, the tithes, and the dedicated things. The chief officer in charge of them was Conaniah the Levite, with Shimei his brother as second, [13]while Jehiel, Azaziah, Nahath, Asahel, Jerimoth, Jozabad, Eliel, Ismachiah, Mahath, and Benaiah were

overseers assisting Conaniah and Shimei his brother, by the appointment of Hezekiah the king and Azariah the chief officer of the house of God. ¹⁴And Kore the son of Imnah the Levite, keeper of the east gate, was over the freewill offerings to God, to apportion the contribution reserved for the LORD and the most holy offerings. ¹⁵Eden, Miniamin, Jeshua, Shemaiah, Amariah, and Shecaniah were faithfully assisting him in the cities of the priests, to distribute the portions to their brothers, old and young alike, by divisions, ¹⁶except those enrolled by genealogy, males from three years old and upward—all who entered the house of the LORD as the duty of each day required—for their service according to their offices, by their divisions. ¹⁷The enrollment of the priests was according to their fathers' houses; that of the Levites from twenty years old and upward was according to their offices, by their divisions. ¹⁸They were enrolled with all their little children, their wives, their sons, and their daughters, the whole assembly, for they were faithful in keeping themselves holy. ¹⁹And for the sons of Aaron, the priests, who were in the fields of common land belonging to their cities, there were men in the several cities who were designated by name to distribute portions to every male among the priests and to everyone among the Levites who was enrolled.

²⁰Thus Hezekiah did throughout all Judah, and he did what was good and right and faithful before the LORD his God. ²¹And every work that he undertook in the service of the house of God and in accordance with the law and the commandments, seeking his God, he did with all his heart, and prospered.

32 After these things and these acts of faithfulness, Sennacherib king of Assyria came and invaded Judah and encamped against the fortified cities, thinking to win them for himself. ²And when Hezekiah saw that Sennacherib had come and intended to fight against Jerusalem, ³he planned with his officers and his mighty men to stop the water of the springs that were outside the city; and they helped him. ⁴A great many people were gathered, and they stopped all the springs and the brook that flowed through the land, saying, "Why should the kings of Assyria come and find much water?" ⁵He set to work resolutely and built up all the wall that was broken down and raised

towers upon it,ᶜ and outside it he built another wall, and he strengthened the Millo in the city of David. He also made weapons and shields in abundance. ⁶And he set combat commanders over the people and gathered them together to him in the square at the gate of the city and spoke encouragingly to them, saying, ⁷"Be strong and courageous. Do not be afraid or dismayed before the king of Assyria and all the horde that is with him, for there are more with us than with him. ⁸With him is an arm of flesh, but with us is the LORD our God, to help us and to fight our battles." And the people took confidence from the words of Hezekiah king of Judah.

⁹After this, Sennacherib king of Assyria, who was besieging Lachish with all his forces, sent his servants to Jerusalem to Hezekiah king of Judah and to all the people of Judah who were in Jerusalem, saying, ¹⁰"Thus says Sennacherib king of Assyria, 'On what are you trusting, that you endure the siege in Jerusalem? ¹¹Is not Hezekiah misleading you, that he may give you over to die by famine and by thirst, when he tells you, "The LORD our God will deliver us from the hand of the king of Assyria"? ¹²Has not this same Hezekiah taken away his high places and his altars and commanded Judah and Jerusalem, "Before one altar you shall worship, and on it you shall burn your sacrifices"? ¹³Do you not know what I and my fathers have done to all the peoples of other lands? Were the gods of the nations of those lands at all able to deliver their lands out of my hand? ¹⁴Who among all the gods of those nations that my fathers devoted to destruction was able to deliver his people from my hand, that your God should be able to deliver you from my hand? ¹⁵Now, therefore, do not let Hezekiah deceive you or mislead you in this fashion, and do not believe him, for no god of any nation or kingdom has been able to deliver his people from my hand or from the hand of my fathers. How much less will your God deliver you out of my hand!'"

¹⁶And his servants said still more against the LORD God and against his servant Hezekiah. ¹⁷And he wrote letters to cast contempt on the LORD, the God of Israel, and to speak against him, saying, "Like the gods of the nations of the lands who have not delivered their people from my hands, so the God of Hezekiah will

not deliver his people from my hand." [18]And they shouted it with a loud voice in the language of Judah to the people of Jerusalem who were on the wall, to frighten and terrify them, in order that they might take the city. [19]And they spoke of the God of Jerusalem as they spoke of the gods of the peoples of the earth, which are the work of men's hands.

[20]Then Hezekiah the king and Isaiah the prophet, the son of Amoz, prayed because of this and cried to heaven. [21]And the LORD sent an angel, who cut off all the mighty warriors and commanders and officers in the camp of the king of Assyria. So he returned with shame of face to his own land. And when he came into the house of his god, some of his own sons struck him down there with the sword. [22]So the LORD saved Hezekiah and the inhabitants of Jerusalem from the hand of Sennacherib king of Assyria and from the hand of all his enemies, and he provided for them on every side. [23]And many brought gifts to the LORD to Jerusalem and precious things to Hezekiah king of Judah, so that he was exalted in the sight of all nations from that time onward.

[24]In those days Hezekiah became sick and was at the point of death, and he prayed to the LORD, and he answered him and gave him a sign. [25]But Hezekiah did not make return according to the benefit done to him, for his heart was proud. Therefore wrath came upon him and Judah and Jerusalem. [26]But

Hezekiah humbled himself for the pride of his heart, both he and the inhabitants of Jerusalem, so that the wrath of the LORD did not come upon them in the days of Hezekiah.

[27]And Hezekiah had very great riches and honor, and he made for himself treasuries for silver, for gold, for precious stones, for spices, for shields, and for all kinds of costly vessels; [28]storehouses also for the yield of grain, wine, and oil; and stalls for all kinds of cattle, and sheepfolds. [29]He likewise provided cities for himself, and flocks and herds in abundance, for God had given him very great possessions. [30]This same Hezekiah closed the upper outlet of the waters of Gihon and directed them down to the west side of the city of David. And Hezekiah prospered in all his works. [31]And so in the matter of the envoys of the princes of Babylon, who had been sent to him to inquire about the sign that had been done in the land, God left him to himself, in order to test him and to know all that was in his heart.

[32]Now the rest of the acts of Hezekiah and his good deeds, behold, they are written in the vision of Isaiah the prophet the son of Amoz, in the Book of the Kings of Judah and Israel. [33]And Hezekiah slept with his fathers, and they buried him in the upper part of the tombs of the sons of David, and all Judah and the inhabitants of Jerusalem did him honor at his death. And Manasseh his son reigned in his place.

a Spelled *Abi* in 2 Kings 18:2   b Hebrew *filled your hand for*   c Hebrew *not according to the cleanness of holiness*   d Compare 1 Chronicles 13:8; Hebrew *with instruments of might*   e Vulgate; Hebrew *and raised upon the towers*

OVERVIEW: As in the comments on 2 Kings, these writers laud King Hezekiah for his righteous reforms. Here, however, these commentators focus on divinely appointed instruments of reform. They list the virtues of a strong mind, fearless spirit and eloquence of speech as characteristics of these kinds of reforming leaders. Nevertheless Hezekiah's invitation to all the people—including those of the toppled northern kingdom—to join in true worship is met with laughter and scorn by many. This signifies to our commentators the challenges that faithful leaders

will meet, including challenges that come with reform of holy Communion. Finally, the reformers consider Hezekiah's prayers and his establishment of ministers for the sake of the people.[1]

29:1-19 Hezekiah Cleanses the Temple

HEZEKIAH'S EXAMPLE FOR RULERS. HEINRICH BULLINGER: Then King Hezekiah called together the different crowd of priests and Levites according

---

[1]See commentary on 2 Kings 18–20.

to their varied offices and their own ministries. In addition he distributed the priests' different portions and stipends throughout the priesthood. The same king commanded all the people to celebrate Passover and wrote letters plainly to all the people to encourage them in religion and to make true repentance. And there is added after all this, "This is what Hezekiah did throughout Judea, doing what was good and right and faithful before the Lord his God." Therefore with different rulers he ordained religion according to the Word of God, which was pleasing in God's sight. Decades 2.7.[2]

The Pendulum of Reform. Viktorin Strigel: Readers of this history should notice the perpetual swinging between true and false worship. The impious father closed the temple and contaminated the entire kingdom with idols. As a sign of his piety, the son opened the temple, destroyed his father's idols and reinstituted the devotion and positions of the priests and Levites. Hezekiah's zeal was such that he delayed hardly a day to make these religious changes but resolutely started them in the first month of the first year of his reign. This was no small business. Neither was it without danger to make religious changes to practices that carried the confirmation and approval of many years. But the pious and zealous king ardently sought first the kingdom of God, and shortly afterward all good things were added. Thus all pious leaders have nothing more important or more venerable to do than to institute or preserve true doctrine and right worship. To this end, suitable people should be brought in to help, just as Hezekiah called on the priests and Levites as he delegated matters of doctrine and piety. Book of 2 Chronicles.[3]

A Holy Beginning to Hezekiah's Reign. John Mayer: Now, the order of proceeding in cleansing and sanctifying was this: The priests cleansed the house of the Lord, bringing all the filth to the door, and there the Levites took and

carried it away to the Kidron brook. This work began the first day of the first month and was finished in eight days. And in eight more days the courts were cleansed and sanctified with all their appurtenances. From this we may gather that Hezekiah began his reign in the very beginning of the year; and the same day that he began to reign, he spoke to the Levites to begin this work. And it is likely that the Levites began their work that very day. The harmony, consent and diligence pertaining to religion is greatly shown here between Hezekiah and the Levites and priests, which is worthy of imitation by leaders and people of all ages. After this work was finished, they certified the king and cleansed the altar for burnt offerings, including all the utensils that Ahaz had cast aside and removed, setting up an altar like the one he discovered in Damascus. Therefore, without doubt, that altar was broken down by Hezekiah and carried away with the other filth. And then the altar of the Lord was set up again in its proper place.

After good King Hezekiah heard all that the priests had done, he wasted no time. He arose early in the morning and called the princes together. He then ordered seven bullocks, seven lambs, seven rams and seven goats to be brought to the Lord's house. Hezekiah then commanded the priests to offer these sacrifices on the altar for sin, for the kingdom, for the sanctuary and for Judah, which they promptly did. And according to Nicholas of Lyra, the kingdom was for the king and the princes, Judah was for all the people of the land and the sanctuary was for the priests and the Levites who ministered in it. Commentary on Chronicles.[4]

Seasoned with Piety. The English Annotations: When anything is disordered and out of repair, it is weakened. But when it is repaired, it is strengthened. Some interpret the words "doors" as referring only to doors, while others interpret this as synecdoche, meaning that it refers to all of the temple. But some interpret it as referring to the priests and Levites mentioned,

---

[2]Bullinger, *Sermonum decades quinque*, 161-162; citing 2 Chron 31:20.
[3]Strigel, *Libri Samuelis, Regum et Paralipomenon*, 562.

[4]Mayer, *Many Commentaries in One*, 264*.

whom the king strengthened. However the word is to be taken, it implies that Hezekiah's heart was seasoned with piety. And the very first thing he began after being crowned was in reforming religion. He is a worthy pattern to follow. Annotations on 2 Chronicles.[5]

Reforming Doctrine. Viktorin Strigel: This cleansing of the temple is an image for reforming doctrine, just as Dr. Martin Luther, Philipp Melanchthon and others were instruments of reform, whom God in his highest wisdom gave great spirit and eloquence. Such work requires three things: a mind big enough to handle the mysteries of God, a fearless spirit and eloquence of speech. For just as a dirty mirror cannot show a clear image, so a soul that is tangled up in this life and made sluggish by physical cares is not capable of light and spiritual wisdom. Book of 2 Chronicles.[6]

29:20-36 Hezekiah Restores Temple Worship

Bandage Large Enough for the Sore. The English Annotations: The king ordered that a burnt and sin offering be made for all Israel. However, it is not probable that the king himself had yielded to the idolatry committed in his father's days. Yet he well knew that the whole kingdom had yielded to it. Therefore he desired to make reconciliation between God and the people. That is, he desired for the bandage to be as large as the sore was. Annotations on 2 Chronicles.[7]

Extraordinary Work of God. The English Annotations: Hezekiah rejoiced like David and the people did when they brought in the ark to Jerusalem, for Hezekiah had put such grace and zeal into their hearts. And it is God who prepares the heart to good. This thing came about very speedily, sooner than could have expected. The people had long been blinded and led aside into idolatry. Therefore to have their hearts so soon and so thoroughly changed was an extraordinary work of God's Spirit. And the consideration of this work greatly quickened and revived their spirits. Annotations on 2 Chronicles.[8]

30:1-12 Invitations to All People

Few and Far Between. Edward Reynolds: There are few who are wise to salvation and who seriously attend and manage the ministry of the Word to that end. . . . Hezekiah sent messengers to all Israel to invite them to the true worship of God at Jerusalem. However, they were mocked and laughed to scorn. Only a remnant humbled itself and went to Jerusalem. . . . Though a gun is discharged at a whole flight of birds, to state it another way, there are but few that are killed. Though a net is spread over the whole pond, only a few fish are caught. Many thrust their heads into the mud and the net passes over them. In a similar way, most hearers busy themselves with their own sensual or worldly thoughts in order to escape the power of the Word. These people are like mines that are full of dead earth rather than pure metal. Christ's flock in every place is but "a little flock," "few . . . chosen" and "few . . . saved." "For the gate is narrow and the way is hard that leads to life, and those who find it are few." The basest creatures are usually the most numerous, such as flies and vermin. Those that are nobler are rarer. The people of the God of Abraham are, as far as Scripture is concerned, princes and nobles . . . but there are very few compared with the rest of the world. Seven Sermons on Fourteenth Chapter of Hosea.[9]

Letters to Ephraim and Manasseh. The English Annotations: Hezekiah sent letters addressed to the two tribes of Ephraim and Manasseh, that is, of all those who had remained in the land of Israel and not been deported to Assyria.

---

[5]Downame, ed., *Annotations* (1657), Ffff2r*.
[6]Strigel, *Libri Samuelis, Regum et Paralipomenon*, 563.
[7]Downame, ed., *Annotations* (1657), Ffff2v*.

[8]Downame, ed., *Annotations* (1657), Ffff3r*; citing 1 Chron 29:9.
[9]Reynolds, *Works*, 3:399-400*; citing Lk 12:32; Mt 22:14; Lk 13:23; Mt 7:14.

For the king of Assyria had carried many of them away into other lands. The reason why Ephraim and Manasseh were mentioned is because they were the chief tribes of Israel and represented the rest of them. By writing a letter to them Hezekiah thought he might have a better chance of persuading them to accept his invitation. Annotations on 2 Chronicles.[10]

The King's Intercession. John Dod: The early part of this chapter declares how King Hezekiah, in zeal for God's glory and love for his people, made a proclamation throughout all of Israel from Beersheba to Dan, that they should come to keep the Passover to the Lord God of Israel at Jerusalem. For they had not done so for a long time in the manner required by God, because of that idolatry which had overtaken the land of Israel. For this purpose Hezekiah and his princes sent posts with letters throughout all of Israel and Judah, including the ten tribes that were full of sin and misery—in order to admonish them to turn again to the Lord their God that he might return to them. He wanted them to not to be stiff-necked but to humble themselves to serve the Lord, so that his wrath might be turned away from them. But when the messengers came, a great number of the Israelites laughed at, scorned and mocked them. They were so hardened by sin and infected with idolatry that they utterly condemned all the wholesome and holy exhortations of that worthy king and his nobles. Yet some of them whose hearts God touched, including many out of the tribes of Asher, Manasseh and Zebulun, came to Jerusalem. And the hand of God was in Judah, so that he gave them one heart to do the commandment of the king and of the rulers. The Fourth Sermon on the Lord's Supper.[11]

Foreshadowing the Later Pentecost. Viktorin Strigel: Just as in the later Pentecost when the apostles received the gift of languages, some people were positively amazed and others scorned them, saying, "They are filled with new wine." And so some people mocked Hezekiah's announcement, while other pious people obeyed the summons. This is an example of how God's Word is never preached in vain but always brings some to the rebirth of eternal life. Let us, in turn, ridicule those impious and insane people who only criticize. We should then teach and discuss God's Word among ourselves instead, for it is certain that the Lord will not let this labor be in vain. Book of 2 Chronicles.[12]

30:13-27 Pentecost and Passover Celebrated but Not According to the Law

Purpose and Foreshadowing of Passover. The English Annotations: Passover was a solemn feast to be kept every year by the Israelites in memorial of God's delivering their ancestors from bondage in Egypt and of God's passing over the Israelites when he destroyed all the firstborn in Egypt. . . . It was also one of the ordinary sacraments until the coming of Christ, of whose sacrifice the paschal lamb was a special type. . . . The people had not kept the feast according to the prescript of the law. For after their revolt from Judah, the people of Israel had cast off the law of the Lord. And Judah had neglected it all the days of Ahaz. If they did keep the Passover, they did not observe it according to the law. That's because the doors of God's house were shut up. Annotations on 2 Chronicles.[13]

Passover and Reconciliation. John Mayer: After making all the preparations that were necessary to make, the godly king Hezekiah now took into his consideration the great neglect of keeping the Passover. And although the first month of the year was past—at which time it ought to have been kept—he would not allow the feast to be neglected another year. Therefore he

---

[10]Downame, ed., *Annotations* (1657), Ffff3r*; citing 2 Kings 15:29.
[11]Dod, *Ten Sermons*, 110*.

[12]Strigel, *Libri Samuelis, Regum et Paralipomenon*, 566; citing Acts 2:13.
[13]Downame, ed., *Annotations* (1657), Ffff3r*, Ffff3v*; citing Ex 12:12-14; 1 Cor 5:7; Ex 12; 2 Chron 28:24.

proposed to keep the feast on the second month, believing that God would accept his piety although the circumstance of time was not precisely observed. For it was not possible to have the sanctuary cleansed for the first month.

Now Hezekiah's actions were not without warrant, but were allowed (Num 9:10-11). . . . Here are also two other reasons why Hezekiah's actions were warranted. First, there was not a sufficient number of priests sanctified to minister this ceremony; and, second, the people of Israel were not able to be quickly gathered together from all parts of the region. What's more, Hezekiah did not only desire for the people of Judah to be gathered to the feast but also invited those from Israel to come celebrate the Passover in Jerusalem with him. Hezekiah's invitation to Israel was based partly on the fact that the golden calves set up by Jeroboam had now been taken away into Assyria. And although King Hoshea of Israel was an evil king, he did not do all the evil of his predecessors by worshiping idols and keeping his subjects from going to Jerusalem to worship. In Hezekiah's actions toward the Israelites, we see his great charity. For Hezekiah desired to do what he could for the reconciliation of God's favor toward the Israelites and his own kingdom, so that no more of them would be carried away captive into Assyria as some had been before, as recorded in 2 Kings 15. In this example we are taught how we should seek the good of our brothers and sisters in other kingdoms as well as in our own. COMMENTARY ON CHRONICLES.[14]

READINESS OF HEART. JOHN DOD: By reason of the short warning they had, a multitude of the people of Ephraim, Manasseh, Issachar and Zebulun had not cleansed themselves according to the law required by Exodus 12 and Numbers 9. And so, according to Leviticus 7:20, they were in danger of being cut off.

In this regard they were in great distress and in a great bind, yet they thought it better to receive the sacrament even though they delayed in some circumstances of their preparation. Rather than omitting it until next year, because they had wanted it for so long they ventured to eat the Passover. Afterward, because he was in fear of God's displeasure—and in consideration of the people who stood in danger of God's plagues and punishments—Hezekiah rallied to prayer for them and interceded to the Lord on their behalf. He saw their great desire to be made partakers of it as well as the pains that they had taken to come to Jerusalem for that very purpose. Hezekiah perceived a strange hand of God in inclining their hearts to have come so far, and thereby he was encouraged to become an earnest interceder to God for them. And thus he prayed to God for them. "May the good Lord pardon everyone who sets his heart to seek God, the Lord, the God of his fathers." The phrase that is translated "May the good Lord pardon" effectively means the following: "May the good Lord pardon and supply that which is lacking in the one whom prepares their whole heart." For what they had lacked was not so much willingness but readiness. Therefore Hezekiah prayed that the Lord would be favorable to them. THE FOURTH SERMON ON THE LORD'S SUPPER.[15]

RITUAL FLEXIBILITY. VIKTORIN STRIGEL: No one but its author can change the moral law, which is the eternal and unchangeable rule of righteousness. But ceremonial laws can be changed in cases of necessity, as when David and his colleagues were given the bread of preparation, which in the ceremonial law was set aside for the priests alone. Therefore, in this instance, Hezekiah admitted people to the paschal celebration who had not completed the rite of purification. Hezekiah recorded this remarkable truth in his prayer: God considers the state of the heart, so that where he knows it is pure there is no worry about the external cleanliness that would otherwise be required by the ceremonial law. BOOK OF 2 CHRONICLES.[16]

[14]Mayer, *Many Commentaries in One*, 265*; citing Num 9:10-11.
[15]Dod, *Ten Sermons*, 111-12*.
[16]Strigel, *Libri Samuelis, Regum et Paralipomenon*, 567.

Feast Celebrated Without Precise Following of the Law. John Mayer: Regarding Judah, it is said that God gave them one heart to do all they were commanded concerning the Passover and in showing zeal against idolatry by breaking down the altars of the idols, etc. And as the priests and Levites cleansed the temple, so they cleansed both the city and the country from all idolatrous pollution. Then the Passover was kept, and the priests and Levites, who were not yet sanctified, were ashamed and sanctified themselves so that they might be fit to do their duty at this great solemn feast. Therefore they offered the burnt offerings. That which made them ashamed was to see the readiness and zeal of the people to whom they ought to have been leaders. Yet it is said that a multitude of the people were unclean, for which cause the Levites were enforced to kill the paschal lambs for them, so that they might thus be sanctified. They were for the sake of necessity now allowed to eat the Passover although they were unclean by touching something unclean, whether a dead body or something else. However, Hezekiah had prayed for everyone since many were not able to be sanctified as prescribed. Now, the killing of the paschal lamb was of course restricted only to the Levites. For, as Nicholas of Lyra says, it is a great work and more holy to sanctify something than to eat it. This also applies to the holy sacraments in the church. Commentary on Chronicles.[17]

Arguments from God's Nature. John Dod: In order that he might have more assurance that his prayer should be effectual, Hezekiah builds it on strong and sound reasons. First, from the nature of God, implied in the word "good," which goodness of God is never seen so much as in showing mercy to those who are in distress. Hezekiah could have said, "Lord, you are good in yourself, and good to your people, and here are such as stand in great need of your goodness, and therefore be merciful and gracious to them." Second, from the name of God or "Jehovah," which

implies his constancy and unchangeableness in himself; and in his love and the fruits thereof toward his servants. Hezekiah knew that God had been merciful to them in former times—even though they were great sinners—and he knew that he was still the same God. Therefore he entreated God to now manifest himself, in passing by the frailties of these communicants. A third reason is taken from the covenant, that the Lord is "the God of their fathers," for which reason he was bound to them and their children. As such, God could not deny them anything that they should ask in faith. Each of these three arguments are drawn from God himself. The Fourth Sermon on the Lord's Supper.[18]

Inward or Outward Healing. The English Annotations: That "the Lord heard Hezekiah and healed the people" may be taken in one of two ways: inwardly or outwardly. Inwardly, it may be spoken of as inward healing. God forgave their sin and inwardly sanctified and cleansed them by his Spirit, or at least accepted them as cleansed. Outwardly, God removed some judgment that he had inflicted on the people for transgressing his law. Annotations on 2 Chronicles.[19]

How Do We Know God Accepted This Passover? John Mayer: According to Nicholas of Lyra, the rabbis answer that it could be known this way: It was often the case that when people in the Old Testament ate of the holy things of the Lord in their uncleanness, they were stricken with death. As a result, because the people in this present case were not stricken with death, it follows that God's wrath was pacified and not provoked. But Nicholas rejects this interpretation on the grounds that it would have been a case of the people tempting God by celebrating Passover in this way. On the contrary, Nicholas's interpretation is this: The normal legal restrictions were dispensed with for the sake of

---

[17]Mayer, *Many Commentaries in One*, 266*.

[18]Dod, *Ten Sermons*, 112*.
[19]Downame, ed., *Annotations* (1657), Ffff4r*.

necessity and because the people celebrated the ritual in a good and hearty devotion. For regarding the dispensation granted, we have a similar example in the case of David when he and his men ate the showbread of the priests, which was illegal according to the law. And regarding the goodness and heartiness of the people's devotion, it is the faith and righteousness of one's heart that makes the performance of holy things acceptable to God, even if they are not precisely performed according to the rule of the law.

Now, although these reasons are good in regard to the Lord's acceptance of them and his pardon of their error, they do nothing to satisfy the question initially raised, namely, how do we know that God accepted this ceremony? Actually I agree with the rabbis here who say that it is known because God's wrath did not break out against the people. . . . We see an example of the opposite happening in the time of Paul when the Corinthian Christians were being punished with death on account of eating the ritual in uncleanness: "That is why many of you are weak and ill, and some have died." For God has at all times been most severe out of the case of necessity against those who have transgressed the external rites of the law as we may see in the case of Uzzah and in the case of the men of Beth-shemesh. From these cases we may learn that the heart indeed is the principal thing God looks after. But however the heart may be affected, there is danger to any who presume to eat of the holy things of the Lord in the uncleanness of sin. Yet seeing that there is place for repentance for this and for all other sins upon prayer—except that sin against the Holy Spirit—pardon and reconciliation may be attained, as it was at this time by Hezekiah. . . . And the way we know that God approved of this Passover is seen not only in the Lord's not punishing the people but also in the blessing of the people. As the passage concludes: "Then the priests and the Levites arose and blessed the people, and their voice was heard, and their prayer came to the holy habitation in heaven." COMMENTARY ON CHRONICLES.[20]

31:1-21 *Hezekiah Organizes the Priests*

FUNDING THE MINISTRY. VIKTORIN STRIGEL: A collapsed church is reformed in vain, unless its guardians and ministers are set up to give great care for pure teaching and concern for the most important things. The pious king reinstituted the care of priests and Levites, because the church cannot be without pious and learned ministers or without ministers who are devoted to the study of true life-giving doctrine. To this end he gave them wages so that they would not be seen as laboring in poverty with their families, either wasting their time with books while they starved or—on the other hand—needing to neglect the study of the doctrine that leads to life. Therefore Hezekiah allowed ministers of the Word to receive necessary offerings, as Nehemiah and Sirach also instructed. Similar words about providing for teachers stand in 1 Corinthians 9 and Galatians 6. BOOK OF 2 CHRONICLES.[21]

ORGANIZATION OF AND PROVISION FOR GOD'S MINISTERS. JOHN MAYER: Having thus purged both the Lord's house and the whole land, Hezekiah appointed the priests and Levites to offer sacrifices and sing praises to God. And because this could not be done without many helps—which all required due maintenance—he renewed all the divisions of them in their courses as they had been established by David. Hezekiah also stirred up the people to bring in the firstfruits and tithes from where they lived, which they did abundantly. And the king for his part—to free the people from that great charge—undertook at his own costs the maintenance of the morning and evening sacrifices, those of the sabbath and new moon and those of other feasts the Lord had appointed in the books of the law. The firstfruits and tithes were due to the ministers of God as their own share since they did not have any other part or portion in the land. Rather these

---

[20]Mayer, *Many Commentaries in One*, 266-67*; citing 1 Cor 11:30.

[21]Strigel, *Libri Samuelis, Regum et Paralipomenon*, 568.

ministers were commanded to not be distracted by seeking out their maintenance by other means. In other words, says Nicholas of Lyra, they were to focus on reading, studying, teaching and officiating at the temple. And indeed, God's ministers in all times should have maintenance sufficiently provided for them so that they may live without distraction, seeing that even pagan ministers were well provided for by their brothers. COMMENTARY ON CHRONICLES.[22]

MORE SERVICE FOR THE LORD. THE ENGLISH ANNOTATIONS: The maintenance allowed for the priests and Levites was according to the law.... Having their maintenance provided and brought in by the people, the Levites and priests were freed from cares and pains about their livelihood, and so they could more willingly and cheerfully spend their time on such service as the law of the Lord required. ANNOTATIONS ON 2 CHRONICLES.[23]

32:1-23 Sennacherib Invades Judah

FILLING IN THE FOUNDATIONS OF WATER. THE ENGLISH ANNOTATIONS: The city of Jerusalem stood on a hill, and there were many springs outside the walls. This abundance of water was brought into the city for the residents. But with the enemies approaching, the springs could be used by them to refresh themselves. As a result it was agreed that the fountains should be stopped up so that no water would flow forth for the use of the enemies, and yet enough had to be conveyed to the city for the residents by water pipes underground. ANNOTATIONS ON 2 CHRONICLES.[24]

HUMAN AND DIVINE STRENGTH. VIKTORIN STRIGEL: Hezekiah's prayer includes an antithesis between human and divine strength. What can be more pitiful than to speak in praise of human power, which he calls "an arm of flesh"?

For "all flesh is grass and all of its beauty is like the flowers of the field. The grass withers, the flower fades when the breath of the Lord blows on it." But God is true and brings the people to salvation and leads them out of death. These antitheses are often repeated in Scripture, as in Psalm 93, "Mightier than the thunders of many waters, mightier than the waves of the sea, the Lord on high is mighty!" and in 1 John 4, "He who is in you is greater than he who is in the world"; and again in John 10, "my Father . . . is greater than all." Therefore let us not despair, however much the world and the underworld may rage, but believe that God will be our strength, fighting for us so that "the gates of hell shall not prevail." BOOK OF 2 CHRONICLES.[25]

PEOPLE AS THE REAL TREASURES IN GOD'S SIGHT. JOHN MAYER: Hezekiah expressed his true trust and confidence in God, which shows that he did not simply put trust in the Assyrian army. That is, rather than acting out of base fear, he sought the best way to have the Assyrian tyrant to depart and not shed the blood of his people. If it seems that Hezekiah committed sacrilege according to 2 Kings 18—and, if he did so, he certainly should not have done so—in that he took away the treasures and ornaments of the temple, I answer that the present necessity was a dispensation to him. Nor is it sacrilege for any king to do, since it is warrantable by this example to do the same when in a similar situation. For Hezekiah ultimately had in mind the safety and welfare of the people. And accordingly, necessity has no law. Therefore, since people's lives are so precious in God's sight, in order to save them God is not unwilling that his rights should be taken away. That's because God knows that the faithful are his living temples in which he dwells by the Holy Spirit. COMMENTARY ON CHRONICLES.[26]

[22]Mayer, *Many Commentaries in One*, 268*.
[23]Downame, ed., *Annotations* (1657), Ffff4v*; citing Num 18:8.
[24]Downame, ed., *Annotations* (1657), Ggggir*.

[25]Strigel, *Libri Samuelis, Regum et Paralipomenon*, 571; citing Is 40:6-7; Ps 93:4; 1 Jn 4:4; Jn 10:29; Mt 16:18.
[26]Mayer, *Many Commentaries in One*, 274-75*.

32:24-33 Hezekiah's Pride and Achievements

Lack of Return. Edward Reynolds: How many, like swine, trample on the meat that feeds them and tread underfoot the mercies that preserve them! How many are so greedily intent on the things they desire that they cannot see nor value the things they enjoy! . . . It is noted even of good King Hezekiah that he "did not make return according to the benefit done to him." Therefore we should be exhorted in our prayers for pardon and grace. We must . . . make sacrifices of thankfulness and obedience, not as a price to purchase mercy, for our good extends not to God but as a tie and obligation on ourselves to acknowledge and return the praise of mercy to the one who gives it. Seven Sermons on Fourteenth Chapter of Hosea.[27]

Why God Tempts. Geneva Bible: Here we see the reason why the faithful are tempted, namely, to test whether they have faith. Temptation is also given so that they may feel the presence of God, who does not want them to be overcome by temptations, and in their weakness he gives strength. Annotations on 2 Chronicles.[28]

---

[27]Reynolds, *Works*, 3:258*.
[28]*Geneva Bible* (1560), 205r*.

33:1–35:27 FROM THE REIGN OF MANASSEH TO JOSIAH

¹Manasseh was twelve years old when he began to reign, and he reigned fifty-five years in Jerusalem. ²And he did what was evil in the sight of the Lord, according to the abominations of the nations whom the Lord drove out before the people of Israel. ³For he rebuilt the high places that his father Hezekiah had broken down, and he erected altars to the Baals, and made Asheroth, and worshiped all the host of heaven and served them. ⁴And he built altars in the house of the Lord, of which the Lord had said, "In Jerusalem shall my name be forever." ⁵And he built altars for all the host of heaven in the two courts of the house of the Lord. ⁶And he burned his sons as an offering in the Valley of the Son of Hinnom, and used fortune-telling and omens and sorcery, and dealt with mediums and with necromancers. He did much evil in the sight of the Lord, provoking him to anger. ⁷And the carved image of the idol that he had made he set in the house of God, of which God said to David and to Solomon his son, "In this house, and in Jerusalem, which I have chosen out of all the tribes of Israel, I will put my name forever, ⁸and I will no more remove the foot of Israel from the land that I appointed for your fathers, if only they will be careful to do all that I have commanded them, all the law, the statutes, and the rules given through Moses." ⁹Manasseh led Judah and the inhabitants of Jerusalem astray, to do more evil than the nations whom the Lord destroyed before the people of Israel.

¹⁰The Lord spoke to Manasseh and to his people, but they paid no attention. ¹¹Therefore the Lord brought upon them the commanders of the army of the king of Assyria, who captured Manasseh with hooks and bound him with chains of bronze and brought him to Babylon. ¹²And when he was in distress, he entreated the favor of the Lord his God and humbled himself greatly before the God of his fathers. ¹³He prayed to him, and God was moved by his entreaty and heard his plea and brought him again to Jerusalem into his kingdom. Then Manasseh knew that the Lord was God.

¹⁴Afterward he built an outer wall for the city of David west of Gihon, in the valley, and for the entrance into the Fish Gate, and carried it around Ophel, and raised it to a very great height. He also put commanders of the army in all the fortified cities in Judah. ¹⁵And he took away the foreign gods and the idol from the house of the Lord, and all the altars that he had built on the mountain of the house of the Lord and in Jerusalem, and he threw them outside of the city. ¹⁶He also restored the altar of the Lord and offered on it sacrifices of peace offerings and of thanksgiving, and he commanded Judah to serve the Lord, the God of Israel. ¹⁷Nevertheless, the people still sacrificed at the high places, but only to the Lord their God.

¹⁸Now the rest of the acts of Manasseh, and his prayer to his God, and the words of the seers who spoke to him in the name of the Lord, the God of Israel, behold, they are in the Chronicles of the Kings of Israel. ¹⁹And his prayer, and how God was moved by his entreaty, and all his sin and his faithlessness, and the sites on which he built high places and set up the Asherim and the images, before he humbled himself, behold, they are written in the Chronicles of the Seers.ᵃ ²⁰So Manasseh slept with his fathers, and they buried him in his house, and Amon his son reigned in his place.

²¹Amon was twenty-two years old when he began to reign, and he reigned two years in Jerusalem. ²²And he did what was evil in the sight of the Lord, as Manasseh his father had done. Amon sacrificed to all the images that Manasseh his father had made, and served them. ²³And he did not humble himself before the Lord, as Manasseh his father had humbled himself, but this Amon incurred guilt more and more. ²⁴And his servants conspired against him and put him to death in his house. ²⁵But the people of the land struck down all those who had conspired against King Amon. And the people of the land made Josiah his son king in his place.

34

Josiah was eight years old when he began to reign, and he reigned thirty-one years in Jerusalem. ²*And he did what was right in the eyes of the Lord, and walked in the ways of David his father; and he did not turn aside to the right hand or to the left.* ³*For in the eighth year of his reign, while he was yet a boy, he began to seek the God of David his father, and in the twelfth year he began to purge Judah and Jerusalem of the high places, the Asherim, and the carved and the metal images.* ⁴*And they chopped down the altars of the Baals in his presence, and he cut down the incense altars that stood above them. And he broke in pieces the Asherim and the carved and the metal images, and he made dust of them and scattered it over the graves of those who had sacrificed to them.* ⁵*He also burned the bones of the priests on their altars and cleansed Judah and Jerusalem.* ⁶*And in the cities of Manasseh, Ephraim, and Simeon, and as far as Naphtali, in their ruins*[b] *all around,* ⁷*he broke down the altars and beat the Asherim and the images into powder and cut down all the incense altars throughout all the land of Israel. Then he returned to Jerusalem.*

⁸*Now in the eighteenth year of his reign, when he had cleansed the land and the house, he sent Shaphan the son of Azaliah, and Maaseiah the governor of the city, and Joah the son of Joahaz, the recorder, to repair the house of the Lord his God.* ⁹*They came to Hilkiah the high priest and gave him the money that had been brought into the house of God, which the Levites, the keepers of the threshold, had collected from Manasseh and Ephraim and from all the remnant of Israel and from all Judah and Benjamin and from the inhabitants of Jerusalem.* ¹⁰*And they gave it to the workmen who were working in the house of the Lord. And the workmen who were working in the house of the Lord gave it for repairing and restoring the house.* ¹¹*They gave it to the carpenters and the builders to buy quarried stone, and timber for binders and beams for the buildings that the kings of Judah had let go to ruin.* ¹²*And the men did the work faithfully. Over them were set Jahath and Obadiah the Levites, of the sons of Merari, and Zechariah and Meshullam, of the sons of the Kohathites, to have oversight. The Levites, all who were skillful with instruments of music,* ¹³*were*

over the burden-bearers and directed all who did work in every kind of service, and some of the Levites were scribes and officials and gatekeepers.

¹⁴*While they were bringing out the money that had been brought into the house of the Lord, Hilkiah the priest found the Book of the Law of the Lord given through Moses.* ¹⁵*Then Hilkiah answered and said to Shaphan the secretary, "I have found the Book of the Law in the house of the Lord." And Hilkiah gave the book to Shaphan.* ¹⁶*Shaphan brought the book to the king, and further reported to the king, "All that was committed to your servants they are doing.* ¹⁷*They have emptied out the money that was found in the house of the Lord and have given it into the hand of the overseers and the workmen."* ¹⁸*Then Shaphan the secretary told the king, "Hilkiah the priest has given me a book." And Shaphan read from it before the king.*

¹⁹*And when the king heard the words of the Law, he tore his clothes.* ²⁰*And the king commanded Hilkiah, Ahikam the son of Shaphan, Abdon the son of Micah, Shaphan the secretary, and Asaiah the king's servant, saying,* ²¹*"Go, inquire of the Lord for me and for those who are left in Israel and in Judah, concerning the words of the book that has been found. For great is the wrath of the Lord that is poured out on us, because our fathers have not kept the word of the Lord, to do according to all that is written in this book."*

²²*So Hilkiah and those whom the king had sent*[c] *went to Huldah the prophetess, the wife of Shallum the son of Tokhath, son of Hasrah, keeper of the wardrobe (now she lived in Jerusalem in the Second Quarter) and spoke to her to that effect.* ²³*And she said to them, "Thus says the Lord, the God of Israel: 'Tell the man who sent you to me,* ²⁴*Thus says the Lord, Behold, I will bring disaster upon this place and upon its inhabitants, all the curses that are written in the book that was read before the king of Judah.* ²⁵*Because they have forsaken me and have made offerings to other gods, that they might provoke me to anger with all the works of their hands, therefore my wrath will be poured out on this place and will not be quenched.* ²⁶*But to the king of Judah, who sent you to inquire of the Lord, thus shall you say to him, Thus says the Lord, the God of Israel: Regarding the*

words that you have heard, ²⁷because your heart was tender and you humbled yourself before God when you heard his words against this place and its inhabitants, and you have humbled yourself before me and have torn your clothes and wept before me, I also have heard you, declares the Lord. ²⁸Behold, I will gather you to your fathers, and you shall be gathered to your grave in peace, and your eyes shall not see all the disaster that I will bring upon this place and its inhabitants.'" And they brought back word to the king.

²⁹Then the king sent and gathered together all the elders of Judah and Jerusalem. ³⁰And the king went up to the house of the Lord, with all the men of Judah and the inhabitants of Jerusalem and the priests and the Levites, all the people both great and small. And he read in their hearing all the words of the Book of the Covenant that had been found in the house of the Lord. ³¹And the king stood in his place and made a covenant before the Lord, to walk after the Lord and to keep his commandments and his testimonies and his statutes, with all his heart and all his soul, to perform the words of the covenant that were written in this book. ³²Then he made all who were present in Jerusalem and in Benjamin join in it. And the inhabitants of Jerusalem did according to the covenant of God, the God of their fathers. ³³And Josiah took away all the abominations from all the territory that belonged to the people of Israel and made all who were present in Israel serve the Lord their God. All his days they did not turn away from following the Lord, the God of their fathers.

35 Josiah kept a Passover to the Lord in Jerusalem. And they slaughtered the Passover lamb on the fourteenth day of the first month. ²He appointed the priests to their offices and encouraged them in the service of the house of the Lord. ³And he said to the Levites who taught all Israel and who were holy to the Lord, "Put the holy ark in the house that Solomon the son of David, king of Israel, built. You need not carry it on your shoulders. Now serve the Lord your God and his people Israel. ⁴Prepare yourselves according to your fathers' houses by your divisions, as prescribed in the writing of David king of Israel and the document of Solomon his son. ⁵And stand in the Holy Place according to the groupings of the fathers' houses of your brothers the lay people, and according to the division of the Levites by fathers' household. ⁶And slaughter the Passover lamb, and consecrate yourselves, and prepare for your brothers, to do according to the word of the Lord by Moses."

⁷Then Josiah contributed to the lay people, as Passover offerings for all who were present, lambs and young goats from the flock to the number of 30,000, and 3,000 bulls; these were from the king's possessions. ⁸And his officials contributed willingly to the people, to the priests, and to the Levites. Hilkiah, Zechariah, and Jehiel, the chief officers of the house of God, gave to the priests for the Passover offerings 2,600 Passover lambs and 300 bulls. ⁹Conaniah also, and Shemaiah and Nethanel his brothers, and Hashabiah and Jeiel and Jozabad, the chiefs of the Levites, gave to the Levites for the Passover offerings 5,000 lambs and young goats and 500 bulls.

¹⁰When the service had been prepared for, the priests stood in their place, and the Levites in their divisions according to the king's command. ¹¹And they slaughtered the Passover lamb, and the priests threw the blood that they received from them while the Levites flayed the sacrifices. ¹²And they set aside the burnt offerings that they might distribute them according to the groupings of the fathers' houses of the lay people, to offer to the Lord, as it is written in the Book of Moses. And so they did with the bulls. ¹³And they roasted the Passover lamb with fire according to the rule; and they boiled the holy offerings in pots, in cauldrons, and in pans, and carried them quickly to all the lay people. ¹⁴And afterward they prepared for themselves and for the priests, because the priests, the sons of Aaron, were offering the burnt offerings and the fat parts until night; so the Levites prepared for themselves and for the priests, the sons of Aaron. ¹⁵The singers, the sons of Asaph, were in their place according to the command of David, and Asaph, and Heman, and Jeduthun the king's seer; and the gatekeepers were at each gate. They did not need to depart from their service, for their brothers the Levites prepared for them.

¹⁶So all the service of the Lord was prepared that day, to keep the Passover and to offer burnt offerings on the altar of the Lord, according to the command of King Josiah. ¹⁷And the people of Israel who were

present kept the Passover at that time, and the Feast of Unleavened Bread seven days. [18]No Passover like it had been kept in Israel since the days of Samuel the prophet. None of the kings of Israel had kept such a Passover as was kept by Josiah, and the priests and the Levites, and all Judah and Israel who were present, and the inhabitants of Jerusalem. [19]In the eighteenth year of the reign of Josiah this Passover was kept.

[20]After all this, when Josiah had prepared the temple, Neco king of Egypt went up to fight at Carchemish on the Euphrates, and Josiah went out to meet him. [21]But he sent envoys to him, saying, "What have we to do with each other, king of Judah? I am not coming against you this day, but against the house with which I am at war. And God has commanded me to hurry. Cease opposing God, who is with me, lest he destroy you." [22]Nevertheless, Josiah did not turn away from him, but disguised

himself in order to fight with him. He did not listen to the words of Neco from the mouth of God, but came to fight in the plain of Megiddo. [23]And the archers shot King Josiah. And the king said to his servants, "Take me away, for I am badly wounded." [24]So his servants took him out of the chariot and carried him in his second chariot and brought him to Jerusalem. And he died and was buried in the tombs of his fathers. All Judah and Jerusalem mourned for Josiah. [25]Jeremiah also uttered a lament for Josiah; and all the singing men and singing women have spoken of Josiah in their laments to this day. They made these a rule in Israel; behold, they are written in the Laments. [26]Now the rest of the acts of Josiah, and his good deeds according to what is written in the Law of the LORD, [27]and his acts, first and last, behold, they are written in the Book of the Kings of Israel and Judah.

a One Hebrew manuscript, Septuagint; most Hebrew manuscripts *of Hozai*   b The meaning of the Hebrew is uncertain   c Syriac, Vulgate; Hebrew lacks *had sent*

OVERVIEW: In 2 Chronicles, Manasseh's terrible sins are eclipsed only by his true repentance, providing the reformers with an example of God's boundless capacity for mercy. As the reformers point out, however, Manasseh's son Amon managed to imitate him in sinfulness but not in faith or penitence, leading to great ruin. In imitation of his righteous great-grandfather Hezekiah, Josiah started to reform the people as soon as he could in his reign. In Josiah's recovery of the book of the law, the commentators invite their readers to continue to give thanks for the gift of Scripture and its many graces. And as in the parallel passage in 2 Kings 22, Huldah's ability as a woman to preach God's Word to kings and priests is not challenged. The reformers mention the importance of godly ministers and faithful sacramental practices for building up faith. Josiah's death, like in 2 Kings 23, is discussed in terms of both lament for his sin and as a sign of God's compassion that he would not live to see the destruction to come.[1]

33:1-20 Manasseh's Reign and Repentance

DOCTRINE OF FORGIVENESS. VIKTORIN STRIGEL: The example of Manasseh fits with the words of the gospel about taking back those who have fallen, as the Lord says, even seventy seven times. There are such examples of following this rule. The Novatians, however, denied restoration of lapsed believers back into the church but kept them outside. In this they forgot the doctrine of original sin and the doctrine of Christ the eternal mediator and priest. For they believed that he could only save a person once and not in perpetuity. BOOK OF 2 CHRONICLES.[2]

RADICAL CHANGE OF HEART. JOHN MAYER: Verse 13 says that "Manasseh knew that the Lord was God." This refers to a knowledge that is experiential; that is, the knowledge was brought on him by an extraordinary deliverance. Although he was not completely ignorant of it before, as long as he lived in

---

[1]See commentary on 2 Kings 21–23.

[2]Strigel, *Libri Samuelis, Regum et Paralipomenon,* 576.

idolatry he was not reputed as one who knew God. But now that he was reformed, he both knew and acknowledged God indeed. In Manasseh we see the unspeakable mercy of God toward a person who was a most recalcitrant sinner. Indeed he had been a foul sinner, as none who were like him in comparison to his bloody persecution and destruction, yet God extended him mercy and he was greatly humbled. Indeed Manasseh fervently sought the Lord in prayer. COMMENTARY ON CHRONICLES.[3]

GOD HEARS SOLOMON'S PRAYER FOR MANASSEH. THE ENGLISH ANNOTATIONS: When the soul is humbled for sin, the spirit will be quickened to pray for pardon. And God is ready to hearken to the prayers of the penitent, for God granted Manasseh what he desired. It is doubtless that God so wrought on the heart of Manasseh's enemy that he was moved to show mercy to him, to untie his bonds and to allow him to return to his own country. And, in this way, Solomon's prayer in the temple's dedication was fulfilled. ANNOTATIONS ON 2 CHRONICLES.[4]

WORSHIP AND DEFENSE IN TANDEM. JOHN MAYER: After the return of Manasseh from captivity, the sacred historian immediately shows his intention to defend himself and his people against his enemies, out of whose hands he had escaped. Next the history narrates that Manasseh began attending to religion. However, Josephus says that Manasseh first reformed religion and then went about those works of defense. Nor does the sacred history plainly cross this; it only relates the one before the other, and it may be, as in some other things, that the latter may have happened beforehand. For it is most probable that Manasseh, after being brought home a convert, prepared to offer to God eucharistic sacrifices without delay. And he might rightly have done this by, first, taking away the altars set up to idols and, then, by erecting an altar to the Lord in its proper

place. And just as he had originally drawn the people into idolatry, so now he sought by his godly exhortation to draw them back to the Lord. For he recognized that by trusting in the Lord they might be most safe. And this is when he then turned to building another wall for defense. . . . And it is most likely that, while the priests and Levites were busy with workmen about the temple, others were employed in preparing materials for the wall. COMMENTARY ON CHRONICLES.[5]

33:21-25 Amon Reigns in Judah

WRONG IMITATION. VIKTORIN STRIGEL: Many virtues are presented but are not studied as objects for imitation, but instead the imitation of vice produces great ignorance in the theater of people's lives. Thus Amon imitated his father in sin but did not follow his footsteps into a saving conversion. God then allowed him to be murdered by conspirators, who were themselves killed as a punishment for assassination. BOOK OF 2 CHRONICLES.[6]

A WORSE SINNER THAN HIS FATHER. JOHN MAYER: It is said that Amon sinned more than his father Manasseh. But how can this be said given that Amon was not a wizard nor that he shed innocent blood? On the contrary, we only read that he followed in the idolatry of his father. Chrysostom says that Amon sinned more because he said to himself that he would repent of his sins later in life, which was a very presumptuous sin. The Hebrews say that Amon sinned more because he burned the books of the law. This interpretation is more probable. That's because a book of the law was found among the rubbish in the days of Josiah, which was very strange indeed. This would have made Amon's sin greater than his father's because he was taught by his father's example. What's more, whereas his father Manasseh later repented, it is not stated that Amon ever repented of his sins. COMMENTARY ON CHRONICLES.[7]

---

[3]Mayer, *Many Commentaries in One*, 300-301*.
[4]Downame, ed., *Annotations* (1657), Ggggᵥ*; citing 1 Kings 8:28, 30, 46-50.
[5]Mayer, *Many Commentaries in One*, 302*.
[6]Strigel, *Libri Samuelis, Regum et Paralipomenon*, 576-77.
[7]Mayer, *Many Commentaries in One*, 303*.

34:1-7 *Josiah Reigns in Judah*

JOSIAH COMMENDED FOR HIS REFORMATION.
THE ENGLISH ANNOTATIONS: The eighth year of
Josiah's reign was the sixteenth year of his age. This
was the age when kings began to reign without a
successor, and by themselves they governed the state.
In his father's time the whole land was given to
idolatry. And he, coming to the crown when he was
a child, could not reform matters as he would have
liked to have done. But as soon as he now held the
reins of the kingdom in his own hands, he immediately set upon the work. For him, therefore, to begin
reformation for his age was as great a commendation
as for his great-grandfather who began his in the
first year of his reign. For the sixteenth year of one's
age is within the realm of youth. And in relation to
so great a work as reforming religion in a whole
kingdom, a person of sixteen years may well be said
to be young. ANNOTATIONS ON 2 CHRONICLES.[8]

34:8-21 *Book of the Law Found and Josiah Responds Appropriately*

BLESSED PRESERVATION OF THE SCRIPTURES.
VIKTORIN STRIGEL: Even though people would
rather usually write books fit to feed donkeys rather
than discerning ears, nevertheless God—in his
immense goodness—has preserved the books of the
prophets and apostles, which God also preserves
across the rising and falling of all human generations.
For this perpetual conservation of the light that
guides our feet through darkness, we should give
thanks to God with as much of our souls as we
possibly can, remaining highly devoted to remaining
in the Scriptures, doctrine and the consolation of
God so that the Word of God may dwell richly
among us with all wisdom. BOOK OF 2 CHRONICLES.[9]

HIDDEN COPY OF THE LAW FOUND. JOHN
MAYER: Concerning the book of the law said here
to be accidentally found as Hilkiah took the money
out of the chest in the treasury, it may seem strange
that it should be spoken of as so rare. That's
because such a book of the law was appointed to
be kept always in the temple and also by the king,
so that he might constantly read through the law.
Some of the Hebrews say that Amon had burned
as many books of the law as he could find. And
given that one was stored away out of sight so that
it would not be burned up, this would explain why
one was found accidentally. And because this was
the only book left, this also explains why it was
marveled at and why it was taken to the king.
Regardless of the explanation, it is certain that very
few books of the law remained in the land, meaning that they were destroyed at some point. Indeed
neither the high priest nor the great princes of
Judah knew where to find a book of the law at this
time until Hilkiah happened upon it. Based on
these things, I believe that Hilkiah's predecessor
likely hid the book from the wicked King Amon.
And then after Hilkiah's predecessor died, no one
knew that it remained hidden until it was found
accidentally. COMMENTARY ON CHRONICLES.[10]

HUMBLED BY THE LAW. EDWARD REYNOLDS:
The truth is that we preach nothing but salvation.
We come with no other intention but that every
person who hears us might believe and be saved.
We have our power only for edification and not for
destruction, though we do preach salvation *and*
damnation. "Whoever believes and is baptized will
be saved, but whoever does not believe will be
condemned." This is the sum of our commission.
But it is quite observable in this passage that the
preaching of the gospel is one of both salvation and
of damnation. So then, when we preach the law, we
preach salvation to those who fear it, just as the
Lord showed mercy to Josiah when his heart
trembled and humbled itself at his law. When we
preach the gospel, we preach damnation to those
who despise it, for "how shall we escape if we
neglect such a great salvation?" The gospel is
salvation of itself; but the one who neglects

---

[8]Downame, ed., *Annotations* (1657), Gggg2v*.
[9]Strigel, *Libri Samuelis, Regum et Paralipomenon*, 579.

[10]Mayer, *Many Commentaries in One*, 309-10*.

salvation is more certain to perish—and to do so with a double destruction, death unto death. The Sinfulness of Sin.[11]

34:22-33 Huldah the Prophetess

Huldah Preaches Law and Gospel. Viktorin Strigel: The message of Huldah the prophetess is part law and part gospel. First, she repeats the most sorrowful curses, which are the two works of the law. Through them we know God's righteousness to punish sin through such calamities; we should also learn that these calamities are the voice of the law admonishing us to repentance. Then she offers King Josiah the consolation of the remission of sins, the divine willingness to listen to prayer and the mitigation of punishment. We ought to believe that these words are addressed to us as well, for Christ wants repentance and the remission of sins to be preached in his name at all times. Through the law we hear that we ought to fear God's judgment. When we hear the voice of the true gospel, then, we should take refuge in the mercy promised through Christ, not remaining stuck in the hardness and pride of our hearts but recognizing the wrath of God and that we remain subject to punishment. In this we should humble ourselves, just as Josiah humbled himself before God. Book of 2 Chronicles.[12]

Huldah's Word to the King. John Mayer: Huldah's word to Josiah consisted of two parts. The first consisted of a threatening to the city and the inhabitants of all the judgments contained in the book, for these could not be turned away. That's because the people had forsaken the Lord and offered incense to other gods, which was the greatest provocation of all others. This is why this sin alone was mentioned, even though the people were doubtless guilty of other perverse sins. . . . The second part of Huldah's word concerned giving comfort to godly Josiah because his heart melted at

the hearing of the threatening of the law. He humbled himself, rent his garments, wept and prayed. And when the Lord declared to him that "I also have heard you," it is to be understood that God would reduce his judgment and allow Josiah to die in peace. Commentary on Chronicles.[13]

35:1-19 Passover Celebrated

Public Ministry. Viktorin Strigel: To the conservation of public ministry belongs the tasks of gathering the people and using the signs of faith. For the voice of God's doctrines is passed on through upright public gatherings, which give their clear and shared consent through confession and thanksgiving. To strengthen the will of the collective assembly, there are always external signs, which differentiate this assembly from other assemblies and which reveal that this congregation is bound together in one worship, doctrine and invocation. Such was the Passover, which Josiah took care to celebrate regularly so that it might be an external sign of mutual affection and public ministry. He reinstituted the various levels of priests and admonished his people to serve the Lord and the people. There are many hypocrites who seek not Christ but their own power. Under the pretext of religion, they seek to be greater than the Lord's flock whom they shepherd. But whoever rightly observes Josiah's admonition serves God not with an imaginary faith but with a firm hope and sincere love, considering all matters in terms of building up the church. Book of 2 Chronicles.[14]

Only Extraordinary Feasts Recorded. John Mayer: In concluding this history it is said that such a Passover as this had not been kept since the days of Samuel. . . . Nicholas of Lyra notes that no Passover is commemorated to have been kept in the time of the judges but only in the time of Joshua. At the same time, it is not to be doubted that Passovers were kept from year to year

---

[11]Reynolds, *Works*, 1:349*; citing Mk 16:16; Heb 2:3.
[12]Strigel, *Libri Samuelis, Regum et Paralipomenon*, 579.
[13]Mayer, *Many Commentaries in One*, 311*.
[14]Strigel, *Libri Samuelis, Regum et Paralipomenon*, 580-81.

when godly judges and kings presided over the people. For it was not the manner of the sacred historians to commemorate each of the solemn feasts since there were three a year. Rather they only recorded the extraordinary keeping of them, such as in the time of Hezekiah and of Josiah. Commentary on Chronicles.[15]

No Passover Since Samuel's Time. The English Annotations: Samuel was the last judge. So if this passage refers to the end of the government of the judges, this agrees well with the idea that no Passover like this had been kept until his time. Besides, it is probable that no judge kept a more solemn Passover than Samuel did. And in that respect, though the time is reckoned from the beginning of the judges, it may well stand with this of Samuel's days. Annotations on 2 Chronicles.[16]

Passover as a Sign of Christ's Sacrifice. John Mayer: If anyone shall wonder why so great an account was made of the keeping of the Passover since it consisted of nothing but eating and burning fat in fire, it is to be understood that the thankfulness to God for the people's deliverance out of Egypt expressed in this feast by means of faith in Jesus Christ, of whom this was a figure and obedience to God's will. Thus, whereas other nations sacrificed to false gods, the Israelites sacrificed to the true God. And obedience, faith and thanksgiving in a solemn manner are still the duties of the godly. Commentary on Chronicles.[17]

35:20-27 Josiah Killed in Battle

Sin Always Among Us. Martin Luther: Even the greatest kings from the beginning of the world have not governed their realms without great errors and injustices. This is intended to make you realize that it is impossible to govern an earthly commonwealth without sin. Comments on Psalm 45.[18]

Josiah's Error. Viktorin Strigel: Although Josiah's rule had been wise, pious and blessed for thirty years, nevertheless in the end he erred in going to war against Egypt. Many are the sorrows that come from the errors of wise people, as Cicero exclaimed, "O, sad me, never wise!" But where he did not direct his steps correctly, we should take refuge in God, asking for and expecting guidance and help from the Lord. Book of 2 Chronicles.[19]

Enduring Lamentations. The English Annotations: A rule was made for laments to be made for Josiah even well after his death. This came to be a custom, as it were, and a settled ordinance throughout the land that mourners would speak of Josiah in their elegies. It may be that by reason of the great loss of so worthy a king a law was enacted that in all other solemn mournings there should be mourning for Josiah, and that common mourners observed the same. Some also conceive that the lamentations of Jeremiah were recorded as sacred Scripture at this time. But there might be some other public lamentations remaining, which record the loss of Josiah. Annotations on 2 Chronicles.[20]

Divine Providence at Work in Josiah's Death. John Mayer: Whatever the cause of Josiah's going out to battle against Neco and his dying in battle, it was not without divine providence secretly working. For Josiah, being taken out of the way, made room for God's judgments for his sake hitherto withheld to enter among a rebellious and hypocritical people, of whom many secretly practiced abominable idolatry even while Josiah lived. For we may gather as much from the invectives of Jeremiah 5 and 7. Commentary on Chronicles.[21]

---

[15]Mayer, *Many Commentaries in One*, 315-316*.
[16]Downame, ed., *Annotations* (1657), Gggg4r*; citing 1 Sam 3:1.
[17]Mayer, *Many Commentaries in One*, 315-16*.
[18]LW 12:240.
[19]Strigel, *Libri Samuelis, Regum et Paralipomenon*, 582.
[20]Downame, ed., *Annotations* (1657), Gggg4v*.
[21]Mayer, *Many Commentaries in One*, 317*.

36:1-23 THE LAST KINGS AND THE DESTRUCTION OF JERUSALEM

¹The people of the land took Jehoahaz the son of Josiah and made him king in his father's place in Jerusalem. ²Jehoahaz was twenty-three years old when he began to reign, and he reigned three months in Jerusalem. ³Then the king of Egypt deposed him in Jerusalem and laid on the land a tribute of a hundred talents of silver and a talentᵃ of gold. ⁴And the king of Egypt made Eliakim his brother king over Judah and Jerusalem, and changed his name to Jehoiakim. But Neco took Jehoahaz his brother and carried him to Egypt.

⁵Jehoiakim was twenty-five years old when he began to reign, and he reigned eleven years in Jerusalem. He did what was evil in the sight of the LORD his God. ⁶Against him came up Nebuchadnezzar king of Babylon and bound him in chains to take him to Babylon. ⁷Nebuchadnezzar also carried part of the vessels of the house of the LORD to Babylon and put them in his palace in Babylon. ⁸Now the rest of the acts of Jehoiakim, and the abominations that he did, and what was found against him, behold, they are written in the Book of the Kings of Israel and Judah. And Jehoiachin his son reigned in his place.

⁹Jehoiachin was eighteenᵇ years old when he became king, and he reigned three months and ten days in Jerusalem. He did what was evil in the sight of the LORD. ¹⁰In the spring of the year King Nebuchadnezzar sent and brought him to Babylon, with the precious vessels of the house of the LORD, and made his brother Zedekiah king over Judah and Jerusalem.

¹¹Zedekiah was twenty-one years old when he began to reign, and he reigned eleven years in Jerusalem. ¹²He did what was evil in the sight of the LORD his God. He did not humble himself before Jeremiah the prophet, who spoke from the mouth of the LORD. ¹³He also rebelled against King Nebuchadnezzar, who had made him swear by God. He stiffened his neck and hardened his heart against

turning to the LORD, the God of Israel. ¹⁴All the officers of the priests and the people likewise were exceedingly unfaithful, following all the abominations of the nations. And they polluted the house of the LORD that he had made holy in Jerusalem.

¹⁵The LORD, the God of their fathers, sent persistently to them by his messengers, because he had compassion on his people and on his dwelling place. ¹⁶But they kept mocking the messengers of God, despising his words and scoffing at his prophets, until the wrath of the LORD rose against his people, until there was no remedy.

¹⁷Therefore he brought up against them the king of the Chaldeans, who killed their young men with the sword in the house of their sanctuary and had no compassion on young man or virgin, old man or aged. He gave them all into his hand. ¹⁸And all the vessels of the house of God, great and small, and the treasures of the house of the LORD, and the treasures of the king and of his princes, all these he brought to Babylon. ¹⁹And they burned the house of God and broke down the wall of Jerusalem and burned all its palaces with fire and destroyed all its precious vessels. ²⁰He took into exile in Babylon those who had escaped from the sword, and they became servants to him and to his sons until the establishment of the kingdom of Persia, ²¹to fulfill the word of the LORD by the mouth of Jeremiah, until the land had enjoyed its Sabbaths. All the days that it lay desolate it kept Sabbath, to fulfill seventy years.

²²Now in the first year of Cyrus king of Persia, that the word of the LORD by the mouth of Jeremiah might be fulfilled, the LORD stirred up the spirit of Cyrus king of Persia, so that he made a proclamation throughout all his kingdom and also put it in writing: ²³"Thus says Cyrus king of Persia, 'The LORD, the God of heaven, has given me all the kingdoms of the earth, and he has charged me to build him a house at Jerusalem, which is in Judah. Whoever is among you of all his people, may the LORD his God be with him. Let him go up.'"

---

a A *talent* was about 75 pounds or 34 kilograms   b Septuagint (compare 2 Kings 24:8); most Hebrew manuscripts *eight*

Overview: The commentators observe that the destruction of Jerusalem and the beginning of the Babylonian captivity are just punishments for sin from a long-suffering Lord. A kind of restorative justice and blessing, however, appears in the observation that the land itself receives sabbath, after having been the place of so much uncleanliness and ungodliness. The reformers remind us that despite the punishments experienced in this captivity, God preserved the church.[22]

36:1-3 *Jehoahaz Reigns in Judah*

Fearful of Egypt. The English Annotations: Jerusalem, of course, was the royal city where the king's throne and palace resided. It is not likely that Pharaoh Neco of Egypt came into the land of Jerusalem. Rather it is more likely that he sent for Jehoahaz to go to Riblah. And from Riblah he put him in chains and took him off to Babylon. For the men of Judah at this time stood in great fear of the king of Egypt. They dared not deny anything he demanded. Annotations on 2 Chronicles.[23]

36:4-8 *Jehoiakim Reigns in Judah*

Relation Between Chaldea and Babylon. John Mayer: Against Jehoiakim the Lord brought Nebuchadnezzar, king of Babylon. And Jehoiakim became his servant for three years before rebelling against him. Nebuchadnezzar is called the king of the Chaldeans, and it is said that he took Jehoiakim and bound him to be carried into Babylon together with the vessels of the Lord's house. But Chaldea and Babylon were all one. Chaldea was the country and Babylon was the chief city in the country. Commentary on Chronicles.[24]

Brief and Bad Description. The English Annotations: The description of Jehoiakim may have special reference to his breaking covenant

with Nebuchadnezzar and rebelling against him. But the Jews say that idolaters were wont to imprint some marks on their bodies by a stamping device, and that such were found on Jehoiakim. Annotations on 2 Chronicles.[25]

36:9-14 *Jehoiachin Reigns in Judah*

Why Nebuchadnezzar Took Jehoiachin. John Mayer: The cause of Nebuchadnezzar's taking of Jehoiachin is not stated. However, Josephus said that fearing the young king would seek to revenge his father's capture and ignominious casting out of Jerusalem by Nebuchadnezzar, he thought it unsafe to allow Jehoiachin to reign. Therefore he came against him, carried him away to Babylon and set up another king in his stead: Zedekiah. Others think that Nebuchadnezzar, having first made Jehoiachin king, soon repented and returned thus again. . . . But on God's part, the cause of Nebuchadnezzar's being sent against Jehoiachin was due to the latter's wickedness. Commentary on Chronicles.[26]

36:15-21 *Jerusalem Captured and Burned*

Four Causes of God's Wrath. The English Annotations: God's wrath is not easily incensed. Yet here we see four causes: first, there was a conspiracy among the people against the Lord; second, there was a multiplication of transgressions; third, there were monstrous abominations; and fourth, there were great profanities and contempt for God's messengers. By all these and by many other things the people of Judah provoked the wrath of the Lord. And the last means that is ordinarily used to reclaim people is God's messengers, to tell the people of their sins to their faces and to pronounce judgment against them. If this does not prevail, nothing remains but an expectation of God's judgment and wrath. Annotations on 2 Chronicles.[27]

---

[22]See commentary on 2 Kings 23:31–25:30.
[23]Downame, ed., *Annotations* (1657), Gggg4v*; citing 2 Kings 23:33.
[24]Mayer, *Many Commentaries in One*, 319*.

[25]Downame, ed., *Annotations* (1657), Gggg4v*; citing 2 Kings 25:1.
[26]Mayer, *Many Commentaries in One*, 321*.
[27]Downame, ed., *Annotations* (1657), Gggg4v-Hhhh1r*.

God Allows the Temple to Be Destroyed.
The English Annotations: The Babylonians
burned down the temple. This included the
furnishings and glorious ornaments, but the
temple's holy use and what it symbolized was
more important. It was a great loss to the people
of God. But what will enemies not do when they
enter into another kingdom? In fact what will
God allow his enemies to do to his precious things
when they have been profaned? Annotations
on 2 Chronicles.[28]

The Land Observes the Sabbath. The
English Annotations: Sabbath means "rest." And
as long as the people were kept out of the land, the
land observed the sabbath. There was now no one to
plow or dig up the land, or anyone to cause any
tumults or do any work in it. This phrase of "enjoying
the sabbath" is used in an ironic way, for while the
people of Judah lived in the land, they exceedingly
profaned the sabbath. But now that the people were
taken away into captivity, the land finally "enjoyed its
sabbaths." Annotations on 2 Chronicles.[29]

36:22-23 One Chapter Ends, Another Begins

God's Providence at Work. Viktorin
Strigel: After the demise of pious King Josiah, to
whom God had promised peace, we see everything
falling back into evil and ruin. The time of divine
vengeance approached closer every day, and no
remedy was left to the people in that place; instead
the people brought on a destruction that, in turn,
increasingly doomed them. But although Nebuchadnezzar carried the temple vessels away to
Babylon, he did not convert them to profane use but
stored them in his palace so that after seventy years
they could be returned to divine service. Therefore
learn to see God's providence and consider the
marvelous ways that God ordains and manages the
church's affairs. Book of 2 Chronicles.[30]

End of Chronicles, Beginning of Ezra.
The English Annotations: The last two verses
of this book are repeated word for word in the
beginning of the next book, called Ezra. This
proves that the author of both Ezra and Chronicles
share one contained history. It also proves that they
were written by the same author. Annotations
on 2 Chronicles.[31]

**The Chronicles Engraved on Christ's
Flesh.** John Donne: Consider what the Lord
would do! "Jerusalem, Jerusalem, how often would
I have gathered your children together, as the hen
gathers her chicks. And you refused!" Or consider
what he would not do: "As I live, says the Lord, I
do not desire the death of the wicked." If you
consider all this, any of this, dare you, or can you
if you dared, or would you if you could, stand out
in an irreconcilable war against God? Especially if
you consider that that is more to you than what
God is and does and would do and can do for you
or against you. That is, what he has already done.
He who was the offended party has not only
descended so low as to be reconciled first and to
pay so dearly for that as the blood of his own and
his only Son, but also knowing your need better
than you yourself he has reconciled you to
him—even though you did not know it! "God was
in Christ, reconciling the world to himself." . . .
There the work is done. Your reconciliation is
wrought. God is no longer angry, no longer
withholding from you the means. For it follows,
"He has committed to us the word of reconciliation." . . . Even though you were dead in your sin
and enemies to God, and children of wrath (as all
by nature are) when this reconciliation was
wrought, still the Spirit of God may give you this
strength: to dip your pens in the blood of the
Lamb, and so subscribe your names by accepting
this offer of reconciliation. Do but that—subscribe, accept and then all the rest that concerns
your holy history, your justification and sanctification, are they not written in the books of the

---

[28]Downame, ed., *Annotations* (1657), Hhhh1r*.
[29]Downame, ed., *Annotations* (1657), Hhhh1r*.
[30]Strigel, *Libri Samuelis, Regum et Paralipomenon*, 583.

[31]Downame, ed., *Annotations* (1657), Hhhh1r*.

Chronicles of the Kings of Israel, says the Holy Spirit. In another case, are they not written in the books of the chronicles of the God of Israel? Shall you not find an eternal decree and a book of life on your behalf if you look for it by this light and reach out to it with this hand, accepting this reconciliation? They are written in those reverend and sacred records and rolls and parchments, even the skin and flesh of our blessed Savior—written

in his stripes and his wounds, with that blood that can admit . . . no expunction, no satisfaction. But the life of his death lies in your acceptance. And even though he has come to his death, you have not come to your *consummatum est* ["it is finished"] till that be done. SERMON 121.[32]

---

[32]Donne, *Works*, 5:155-56*; citing Mt 23:37 (cf. Lk 13:34); Ezek 33:11; 2 Cor 5:19.

Map of Europe at the Time of the Reformation

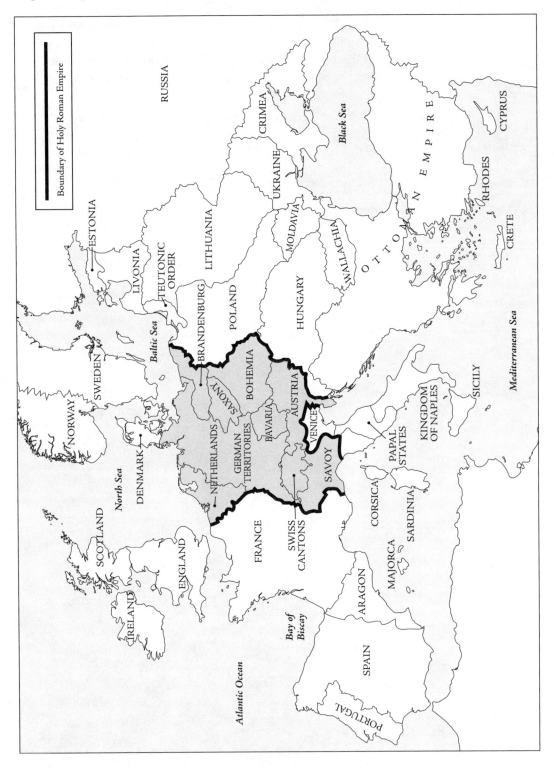

Timeline of the Reformation

	German Territories	France	Spain	Italy	Switzerland	Netherlands	British Isles
1337–1453		d. Nicholas of Lyra Hundred Years' War	b. Paul of Burgos (Solomon ha-Levi)(d. 1435) Alonso Tostado (1400–1455)				Hundred Years' War
1378–1415		Western Schism (Avignon Papacy)		Western Schism			
1384							d. John Wycliffe
1414–1418					Council of Basel (1431–1437)		
1415				Council of Constance; d. Jan Hus; Martin V (r. 1417–1431); Council of Florence (1438–1445)			
1450	Invention of printing press						
1452				b. Leonardo da Vinci (d. 1519)			
1453				Fall of Constantinople			
1455–1485	b. Johann Reuchlin (d. 1522)						War of Roses; rise of House of Tudor
1456	Gutenberg Bible						
1460				*Execrabilis*			
1466		b. Jacques Lefèvres d'Étaples (d. 1536)					
1467						b. Desiderius Erasmus (d. 1536)	b. John Colet (d. 1519)
1469	b. Antoius Broickwy von Königstein (d. 541)						
1470				b. Santes Pagninus (d. 1541)			b. John (Mair) Major (d. 1550)
1475				b. Michelangelo (d. 1564)			
1478	b. Wolfgang Capito (d. 1541)		Ferdinand and Isabella	b. Jacopo Sadoleto (d. 1547)			b. Thomas More (d. 1535)

	German Territories	France	Spain	Italy	Switzerland	Netherlands	British Isles
1480	b. Balthasar Hubmaier (d. 1528); b. Andreas Bodenstein von Karlstadt (d. 1541)						
1481–1530			Spanish Inquisition				
1482					b. Johannes Oecolampadius (d. 1531)		
1483	b. Martin Luther (d. 1546)						
1484	b. Johann Spangenberg (d. 1550)				b. Huldrych Zwingli (d. 1531)		
1485	b. Johannes Bugenhagen (d. 1554)						b. Hugh Latimer (d. 1555)
1486	r. Frederick the Wise, Elector (d. 1525); b. Johann Eck (d. 1543)						
1488	b. Otto Brunfels (d. 1534)						b. Miles Coverdale (d. 1568)
1489	b. Thomas Müntzer (d. 1525); b. Kaspar von Schwenckfeld (d. 1561)						b. Thomas Cranmer (d. 1556)
1491	b. Martin Bucer (d. 1551)		b. Ignatius Loyola (d. 1556)				
1492			Defeat of Moors in Grenada; Columbus discovers America; explusion of Jews from Spain	Alexander VI (r. 1492–1503)			
1493	b. Justus Jonas (d. 1555)						
1494							b. William Tyndale (d. 1536)
1496	b. Andreas Osiander (d. 1552)					b. Menno Simons (d. 1561)	
1497	b. Philipp Melanchthon (d. 1560); b. Wolfgang Musculus (d. 1563) b. Johannes (Ferus) Wild (d. 1554)						
1498				d. Girolamo Savonarola	b. Conrad Grebel (d. 1526)		

	German Territories	France	Spain	Italy	Switzerland	Netherlands	British Isles
1499	b. Johannes Brenz (d. 1570) b. Justus Menius (d. 1558)			b. Peter Martyr Vermigli (d. 1562)			
1500			b. Charles V (–1558)				
1501	b. Erasmus Sarcerius (d. 1559)						
1502	Founding of University of Wittenberg			Julius II (r. 1503–1513)		b. Frans Titelmans (d. 1537)	
1504					b. Heinrich Bullinger (d. 1575)		
1505	Luther joins Augustinian Order			b. Benedict Aretius (d. 1574)			
1506		b. Augustin Marlorat (d. 1562)		Restoration to St. Peter's begins			
1507				Sale of indulgences approved to fund building			
1508	b. Lucas Lossius (d. 1582)						
1509		b. John Calvin (d. 1564)					r. Henry VIII (–1547)
1510	Luther moves to Rome			b. Immanuel Tremellius (d. 1580)			b. Nicholas Ridley (d. 1555)
1511	Luther moves to Wittenberg						
1512				Sistene Chapel completed			
1512–1517				Fifth Lateran Council; rejection of conciliarism			
1513	Luther lectures on Psalms			r. Pope Leo X (–1521)			b. John Knox (d. 1572)
1515	Luther lectures on Romans	r. Francis I (–1547); b. Peter Ramus (d. 1572)					
1516		Est. French National Church (via Concordat of Bologna)		Concordat of Bologna		Publication of Erasmus's Greek New Testament	
1517	Tetzel sells indulgences in Saxony; Luther's Ninety-five Theses						
1518	Heidelberg Disputation; Luther examined by Eck at Diet of Augsburg			Diet of Augsburg			

	German Territories	France	Spain	Italy	Switzerland	Netherlands	British Isles
1519	Leipzig Disputation	b. Theodore Beza (d. 1605)	Cortés conquers Aztecs; Portuguese sailor Magellan circumnavigates the globe		Zwingli appointed pastor of Grossmünster in Zurich; b. Rudolf Gwalther (d. 1586)		
1520	Publication of Luther's "Three Treatises"; burning of papal bull in Wittenberg		Coronation of Charles V	Papal Bull v. Luther: *Exsurge Domine*			
1521	Luther excommunicated; Diet/Edict of Worms—Luther condemned; Luther in hiding; Melanchthon's *Loci communes*	French-Spanish War (–1526)	French-Spanish War; Loyola converts	Papal excommunication of Luther			Henry VIII publishes *Affirmation of the Seven Sacraments* against Luther; awarded title "Defender of the Faith" by Pope
1521–1522	Disorder in Wittenberg; Luther translates New Testament						
1521–1525		First and Second Habsburg–Valois War					
1522	Luther returns to Wittenberg; Luther's NT published; criticizes Zwickau prophets; b. Martin Chemnitz (d. 1586)		Publication of Complutensian Polyglot Bible under Cisneros		Sausage Affair and reform begins in Zurich under Zwingli		
1523	Knight's Revolt	Bucer begins ministry in Strasbourg	Loyola writes Spiritual Exercises	r. Pope Clement VII (–1534)	Iconoclasm in Zurich		
1524	Luther criticizes peasants					Erasmus's disputation on free will	
1524–1526	Peasants' War						
1525	Luther marries; execution of Thomas Müntzer				Abolition of mass in Zurich; disputation on baptism; first believers' baptism performed in Zurich		
1526					Zurich council mandates capital punishment of Anabaptists	Publication of Tyndale's English translation of NT	

	German Territories	France	Spain	Italy	Switzerland	Netherlands	British Isles
1527	d. Hans Denck (b. c. 1500) d. Hans Hut (b. 1490) b. Tilemann Hesshus (d. 1588)			Sack of Rome by mutinous troops of Charles V	First Anabaptist executed in Zurich; drafting of Schleitheim Confession		
1528	Execution of Hubmaier						
1529	Second Diet of Speyer; evangelical "protest"; publication of Luther's catechisms; Marburg Colloquy; siege of Vienna by Turkish forces	Abolition of mass in Strasbourg			d. Georg Blaurock (b. 1492)		Thomas More appointed chancellor to Henry VIII
1530	Diet of Augsburg; Confession of Augsburg	d. Francois Lambert (Lambert of Avignon) (b. 1487)	Charles V crowned Holy Roman Emperor				
1531	Formation of Schmalkaldic League				d. H. Zwingli; succeeded by H. Bullinger		
1532		Publication of Calvin's commentary on Seneca; conversion of Calvin	b. Francisco de Toledo (d. 1596)				
1533	b. Valentein Weigel (d. 1588)	Nicholas Cop addresses University of Paris; Cop and Calvin implicated as "Lutheran" sympathizers	b. Juan de Maldonado (d. 1583)				Thomas Cranmer appointed as Archbishop of Canterbury; Henry VIII divorces
1534	First edition of Luther's Bible published	Affair of the Placards; Calvin flees d. Guillame Briçonnet (b. 1470)		Jesuits founded; d. Cardinal Cajetan (Thomas de Vio) (b. 1469)			Act of Supremacy; English church breaks with Rome
1535	Bohemian Confession of 1535; Anabaptist theocracy at Münster collapses after eighteen months				b. Lambert Daneau (d. 1595)		d. Thomas More; d. John Fisher

	German Territories	France	Spain	Italy	Switzerland	Netherlands	British Isles
1536	Wittenberg Concord; b. Kaspar Olevianus (d. 1587)				First edition of Calvin's *Institutes* published; Calvin arrives in Geneva (–1538); First Helvetic Confession	Publication of Tyndale's translation of NT; d. W. Tyndale	d. A. Boleyn; Henry VIII dissolves monasteries (–1541)
1537					Calvin presents ecclesiastical ordinances to Genevan Council		
1538					Calvin exiled from Geneva; arrives in Strasbourg (–1541)		
1539		Calvin publishes second edition of *Institutes* in Strasbourg		d. Felix Pratensis			Statute of Six Articles; publication of Coverdale's Wheat Bible
1540				Papal approval of Jesuit order			d. Thomas Cromwell
1541	Colloquy of Regensberg	French translation of Calvin's *Institutes* published	d. Juan de Valdés (b. 1500/1510)		d. A. Karlstadt; Calvin returns to Geneva (–1564)		
1542	d. Sebastian Franck (b. 1499)			Institution of Roman Inquisition			War between England and Scotland; James V of Scotland defeated; Ireland declared sovereign kingdom
1543	Copernicus publishes *On the Revolutions of the Heavenly Spheres*; d. Johann Eck (Johann Maier of Eck) (b. 1486)						
1545–1547	Schmalkaldic Wars; d. Martin Luther			First session of Council of Trent			b. Richard Bancroft (d. 1610)
1546	b. Johannes Piscator (d. 1625)						
1547	Defeat of Protestants at Mühlberg	d. Francis I; r. Henri II (–1559)					d. Henry VIII; r. Edward VI (–1553)
1548	Augsburg Interim (–1552) d. Caspar Cruciger (b. 1504)						
1549	d. Paul Fagius (b. 1504)				Consensus Tigurinus between Calvin and Bullinger		First Book of Common Prayer published

	German Territories	France	Spain	Italy	Switzerland	Netherlands	British Isles
1550	b. Aegidius Hunnius (d. 1603)						
1551–1552				Second session of Council of Trent			Cranmer's Forty-Two Articles
1552	d. Sebastian Münster (b. 1488) d. Friedrich Nausea (b. c. 1496)						
1553	d. Johannes Aepinus (b. 1449)						Book of Common Prayer revised; d. Edward VI; r. Mary I (1558)
1554							Richard Hooker (d. 1600)
1555	Diet of Augsburg; Peace of Augsburg establishes legal territorial existence of Lutheranism and Catholicism b. Johann Arndt (d. 1621)	First mission of French pastors trained in Geneva				b. Sibbrandus Lubbertus (d. 1625)	b. Lancelot Andrewes (d. 1626) b. Robert Rollock (d. 1599); d. Hugh Latimer; d. Nicholas Ridley d. John Hooper
1556	d. Pilgram Marpeck (b. 1495) d. Konrad Pellikan (b. 1478) d. Peter Riedemann (b. 1506)		Charles V resigns			d. David Joris (b. c. 1501)	d. Thomas Cranmer
1557					Michael Servetus executed in Geneva		Alliance with Spain in war against France
1558			d. Charles V				b. William Perkins (d. 1602); d. Mary I; r. Elizabeth I (–1603)
1559		d. Henry II; r. Francis II (–1560); first national synod of French reformed churches (1559) in Paris; Gallic Confession		First index of prohibited books issued	Final edition of Calvin's *Institutes*; founding of Genevan Academy	b. Jacobus Arminius (d. 1609)	Elizabethan Settlement
1560	d. P. Melanchthon	d. Francis II; r. Charles IX (1574); Edict of Toleration created peace with Huguenots			Geneva Bible		Kirk of Scotland established; Scottish Confession
1561-1563				Third session of Council of Trent			

	German Territories	France	Spain	Italy	Switzerland	Netherlands	British Isles
1561						Belgic Confession	
1562	d. Katharina Schütz Zell (b. 1497/98)	Massacre of Huguenots begins French Wars of Religion (–1598)					The Articles of Religion—in Elizabethan "final" form (1562/71)
1563	Heidelberg Catechism						
1564				b. Galileo (d. 1642)	d. J. Calvin		b. William Shakespeare (d. 1616)
1566	d. Johann Agricola (b. 1494)			Roman Catechism	Second Helvetic Confession		
1567						Spanish occupation	Abdication of Scottish throne by Mary Stuart; r. James VI (1603–1625)
1568						d. Dirk Phillips (b. 1504) Dutch movement for liberation (–1645)	*Bishop's Bible*
1570		d. Johannes Mercerus (Jean Mercier)		Papal Bull *Regnans in Excelsis* excommunicates Elizabeth I			Elizabeth I excommunicated
1571	b. Johannes Kepler (d. 1630)		Spain defeats Ottoman navy at Battle of Lepanto				b. John Downame (d. 1652)
1572		Massacre of Huguenots on St. Bartholomew's Day		r. Pope Gregory XIII (1583–1585)		William of Orange invades	b. John Donne (d. 1631)
1574		d. Charles IX; r. Henri III (d. 1589)					
1575	d. Georg Major (b. 1502); Bohemian Confession of 1575						
1576		Declaration of Toleration; formation of Catholic League		b. Giovanni Diodati (d. 1649)		Sack of Antwerp; Pacification of Ghent	
1577	Lutheran Formula of Concord						England allies with Netherlands against Spain
1578	Swiss Brethren Confession of Hesse d. Peter Walpot		Truce with Ottomans				Sir Francis Drake circumnavigates the globe

	German Territories	France	Spain	Italy	Switzerland	Netherlands	British Isles
1579			Expeditions to Ireland			Division of Dutch provinces	
1580	Lutheran Book of Concord						
1581			d. Teresa of Avila				Anti-Catholic statutes passed
1582				Gregorian Reform of calendar			
1583							b. David Dickson (d. 1663)
1584		Treaty of Joinville with Spain	Treaty of Joinville; Spain inducted into Catholic League; defeats Dutch at Antwerp			Fall of Antwerp; d. William of Orange	
1585	d. Josua Opitz (b. c. 1542)	Henri of Navarre excommunicated		r. Pope Sixtus V (–1590)			
1586							Sir Francis Drake's expedition to West Indies; Sir Walter Raleigh in Roanoke
1587	d. Johann Wigand (b. 1523)	Henri of Navarre defeats royal army					d. Mary Stuart of Scotland
1588		Henri of Navarre drives Henri III from Paris; assassination of Catholic League Leaders	Armada destroyed				English Mary defeats Spanish Armada
1589		d. Henri III; r. Henri (of Navarre) IV (–1610)	Victory over England at Lisbon				Defeated by Spain in Lisbon
1590		Henri IV's siege of Paris		d. Girolamo Zanchi (b. 1516)			Alliance with Henri IV
1592	d. Nikolaus Selnecker (b. 1530)						
1593		Henri IV converts to Catholicism					
1594		Henri grants toleration to Huguenots					
1595		Henri IV declares war on Spain; received into Catholic Church		Pope Sixtus accepts Henri IV into Church			Alliance with France
1596		b. René Descartes (d. 1650) b. Moïse Amyraut (d. 1664)					

	German Territories	France	Spain	Italy	Switzerland	Netherlands	British Isles
1598		Edict of Nantes; toleration of Huguenots; peace with Spain	Treaty of Vervins; peace with France				
1600	d. David Chytraeus (b. 1531)						
1601							b. John Trapp (d. 1669)
1602					d. Daniel Toussain (b. 1541)		
1603							d. Elizabeth I; r. James I (James VI of Scotland) (–1625)
1604	d. Cyriacus Spangenberg (b. 1528)						d. John Whitgift (b. 1530)
1605						b. Rembrandt (d. 1669)	Guy Fawkes and gunpowder plot
1606							Jamestown Settlement
1607							b. John Milton (d. 1674)
1608							
1610		d. Henri IV; r. Louis XIII (–1643)	d. Benedict Pererius (b. 1535)			The Remonstrance; Short Confession	
1611							Publication of Authorized English Translation of Bible (AV/KJV)
1612							b. Richard Crashaw (d. 1649)
1616							b. John Owen (d. 1683)
1617							b. Ralph Cudworth (d. 1689)
1618–1619						Synod of Dordrecht	
1618–1648	Thirty Years' War						
1620							English Puritans land in Massachusetts
1621							d. Andrew Willet (b. 1562)
1633	d. Christoph Pelargus (b. 1565)						Laud becomes Archbishop of Canterbury
1637	d. Johann Gerhard (b. 1582)					*Statenvertaling*	

	German Territories	France	Spain	Italy	Switzerland	Netherlands	British Isles
1638							d. Joseph Mede (b. 1638)
1640				Diodati's Italian translation of Bible published			
1642–1649							English civil wars; d. Charles I; r. Oliver Cromwell (1660)
1643		d. Louis XIII; r. Louis XIV (–1715)					
1643–1649							Westminster Assembly
1645							d. William Laud (b. 1573)
1648		Treaty of Westphalia ends Thirty Years' War					
1656	d. Georg Calixtus (b. 1586)						
1660							English Restoration; d. Oliver Cromwell; r. Charles II (–1685)
1662							Act of Uniformity
1664						d. Thieleman Jans van Braght (b. 1625)	d. John Mayer (b. 1583)
1671							d. William Greenhill (b. 1591)
1677							d. Thomas Manton (b. 1620)
1678						d. Anna Maria von Schurman (b. 1607)	
1688							Glorious Revolution; r. William and Mary (-1702); d. John Bunyan (b. 1628)
1691							d. Richard Baxter (b. 1615)

BIOGRAPHICAL SKETCHES OF
REFORMATION-ERA FIGURES AND WORKS

For works consulted, see "Sources for Biographical Sketches," p. 726.

Thomas Adams (1583–1653). English Puritan pastor in Buckinghamshire and London. A popular and eloquent Calvinist preacher, many of his sermons were published during his lifetime; his sermons were collected into three volumes after his death.

Johannes Aepinus (1499–1553). German Lutheran preacher and theologian. Aepinus studied under Martin Luther,* Philipp Melanchthon* and Johannes Bugenhagen* in Wittenberg. Because of his Lutheran beliefs, Aepinus lost his first teaching position in Brandenburg. He fled north to Stralsund and became a preacher and superintendent at Saint Peter's Church in Hamburg. In 1534, he made a diplomatic visit to England but could not convince Henry VIII to embrace the Augsburg Confession.* His works include sermons and theological writings. Aepinus became best known as leader of the Infernalists, who believed that Christ underwent torment in hell after his crucifixion.

Johann Agricola (c. 1494–1566). German Lutheran pastor and theologian. An early student of Martin Luther,* Agricola eventually began a controversy over the role of the law, first with Melanchthon* and then with Luther himself. Agricola claimed to defend Luther's true position, asserting that only the gospel of the crucified Christ calls Christians to truly good works, not the fear of the law. After this first controversy, Agricola seems to have radicalized his views to the

point that he eliminated Luther's *simul iustus et peccator* ("at the same time righteous and sinful") paradox of the Christian life, emphasizing instead that believers have no need for the law once they are united with Christ through faith. Luther responded by writing anonymous pamphlets against antinomianism. Agricola later published a recantation of his views, hoping to assuage relations with Luther, although they were never personally reconciled. He published a commentary on Luke, a series of sermons on Colossians, and a massive collection of German proverbs.

Henry Ainsworth (1571–1622/1623). English Puritan Hebraist. In 1593, under threat of persecution, Ainsworth relocated to Amsterdam, where he served as a teacher in an English congregation. He composed a confession of faith for the community and a number of polemical and exegetical works, including annotations on the Pentateuch, the Psalms and Song of Songs.

Henry Airay (c. 1560–1616). English Puritan professor and pastor. He was especially noted for his preaching, a blend of hostility toward Catholicism and articulate exposition of English Calvinism. He was promoted to provost of Queen's College Oxford (1598) and then to vice chancellor of the university in 1606. He disputed with William Laud* concerning Laud's putative Catholicization of the Church of England, particularly over the practice of genuflection, which Airay vehemently opposed. He also opposed fellow Puritans who wished to separate from the Church of England. His lectures on Philippians were his only work published during his lifetime.

Alexander (Ales) Alesius (1500–1565). Scottish Lutheran theologian. Following the martyrdom of his theological adversary Patrick Hamilton (c. 1504–1528), Alesius converted to the Reformation and fled to Germany. In 1535 Martin Luther* and Philip Melanchthon* sent him as an emissary to Henry VIII and Thomas Cranmer.* He taught briefly at Cambridge, but after the Act of Six Articles reasserted Catholic sacramental theology he returned to Germany, where he lectured at Frankfurt an der Oder and Leipzig. Alesius composed many exegetical, theological and polemical works, including commentaries on John, Romans, 1–2 Timothy, Titus and the Psalms.

Moïse Amyraut (1596–1664). French Reformed pastor and professor. Originally intending to be a lawyer, Amyraut turned to theology after an encounter with several Huguenot pastors and having read Calvin's* *Institutes*. After a brief stint as a parish pastor, Amyraut spent the majority of his career at the Saumur Academy. He was well known for his irenicism and ecumenicism (for example, in advocating intercommunion with Lutherans). Certain aspects of his writings on justification, faith, the covenants and especially predestination proved controversial among the Reformed. His doctrine of election is often called hypothetical universalism or Amyraldianism, stating that Christ's atoning work was intended by God for all human beings indiscriminately, although its effectiveness for salvation depends on faith, which is a free gift of God given only to those whom God has chosen from eternity. Amyraut was charged with grave doctrinal error three times before the National Synod but was acquitted each time. Aside from his theological treatises, Amyraut published paraphrases of almost the entire New Testament and the Psalms, as well as many sermons.

Jakob Andreae (1528–1590). German Lutheran theologian. Andreae studied at the University of Tübingen before being called to the diaconate in Stuttgart in 1546. He was appointed ecclesiastical superintendent of Göppingen in 1553 and supported Johannes Brenz's* proposal to place the church under civil administrative control. An ecclesial diplomat for the duke of Württemberg, Andreae debated eucharistic theology, the use of images and predestination with Theodore Beza* at the Colloquy of Montbéliard (1586) to determine whether French Reformed exiles would be required to submit to the Formula of Concord.* Andreae coauthored the Formula of Concord. He and his wife had eighteen children.

Lancelot Andrewes (1555–1626). Anglican bishop. A scholar, pastor and preacher, Andrews prominently shaped a distinctly Anglican identity between the poles of Puritanism and Catholicism. He oversaw the translation of Genesis to 2 Kings for the Authorized Version.* His eight-volume collected works—primarily devotional tracts and sermons—are marked by his fluency in Scripture, the Christian tradition and classical literature.

Benedict Aretius (d. 1574). Swiss Reformed professor. Trained at the universities of Bern, Strasbourg and Marburg, Aretius taught logic and philosophy as well as the biblical languages and theology. He advocated for stronger unity and peace between the Lutheran and Reformed churches. Aretius joined others in denouncing the antitrinitarian Giovanni Valentino Gentile (d. 1566). He published commentaries on the New Testament, as well as various works on astronomy, botany and medicine.

Jacobus Arminius (1559–1609). Dutch Remonstrant pastor and theologian. Arminius was a vocal critic of high Calvinist scholasticism, whose views were repudiated by the Synod of Dordrecht. Arminius was a student of Theodore Beza* at the academy of Geneva. He served as a pastor in Amsterdam and later joined the faculty of theology at the university in Leiden, where his lectures on predestination were popular and controversial. Predestination, as Arminius understood it, was the decree of God determined on the basis of divine foreknowledge of faith or rejection by humans who are the recipients of prevenient, but resistible, grace.

Johann Arndt (1555–1621). German Lutheran pastor and theologian. After a brief time teaching, Arndt pastored in Badeborn (Anhalt) until 1590, when Prince Johann Georg von Anhalt (1567–1618) began introducing Reformed ecclesial policies. Arndt ministered in Quedlinberg, Brunswick, Eisleben and Celle. Heavily influenced by medieval mysticism, Arndt centered his theology on Christ's mystical union with the believer, out of which flows love of God and neighbor. He is best known for his *True Christianity* (1605–1609), which greatly influenced Philipp Jakob Spener (1635–1705) and later Pietists.

John Arrowsmith (1602–1659). English Puritan theologian. Arrowsmith participated in the Westminster Assembly, and later taught at Cambridge. His works, all published posthumously, include three sermons preached to Parliament and an unfinished catechism.

Articles of Religion (1562; revised 1571). The Articles underwent a long editorial process that drew from the influence of Continental confessions in England, resulting in a uniquely Anglican blend of Protestantism and Catholicism. In their final form, they were reduced from Thomas Cranmer's* Forty-two Articles (1539) to the Elizabethan Thirty-Nine Articles (1571), excising polemical articles against the Anabaptists and Millenarians as well as adding articles on the Holy Spirit, good works and Communion. Originating in a 1535 meeting with Lutherans, the Articles retained a minor influence from the Augsburg Confession* and Württemberg Confession (1552), but showed significant revision in accordance with Genevan theology, as well as the Second Helvetic Confession.*

Anne Askew (1521–1546). English Protestant martyr. Askew was forced to marry her deceased sister's intended husband, who later expelled Askew from his house—after the birth of two children—on account of her religious views. After unsuccessfully seeking a divorce in Lincoln, Askew moved to London, where she met other Protestants and began to preach. In 1546, she was arrested, imprisoned and convicted of heresy for denying the doctrine of transubstantiation. Under torture in the Tower of London she refused to name any other Protestants. On July 16, 1546, she was burned at the stake. Askew is best known through her accounts of her arrests and examinations. John Bale (1495–1563), a bishop, historian and playwright, published these manuscripts. Later John Foxe (1516–1587) included them in his *Acts and Monuments*, presenting her as a role model for other pious Protestant women.

Augsburg Confession (1530). In the wake of Luther's* stand against ecclesial authorities at the Diet of Worms (1521), the Holy Roman Empire splintered along theological lines. Emperor Charles V sought to ameliorate this—while also hoping to secure a united European front against Turkish invasion—by calling together another imperial diet in Augsburg in 1530. The Evangelical party was cast in a strongly heretical light at the diet by Johann Eck.* For this reason, Philipp Melanchthon* and Justus Jonas* thought it best to strike a conciliatory tone (Luther, as an official outlaw, did not attend), submitting a confession rather than a defense. The resulting Augsburg Confession was approved by many of the rulers of the northeastern Empire; however, due to differences in eucharistic theology, Martin Bucer* and the representatives of Strasbourg, Constance, Lindau and Memmingen drafted a separate confession (the Tetrapolitan Confession). Charles V accepted neither confession, demanding that the Evangelicals accept the Catholic rebuttal instead. In 1531, along with the publication of the Augsburg Confession itself, Melanchthon released a defense of the confession that responded to the Catholic confutation and expanded on the original articles. Most subsequent Protestant confessions followed the general structure of the Augsburg Confession.

Authorized Version (1611). In 1604 King James I* commissioned this new translation—popularly remembered as the King James Version—for uniform use in the public worship of the Church of England. The Bible and the Apocrypha was divided into six portions and assigned to six companies of nine scholars—both Anglicans and Puritans—centered at Cambridge, Oxford and Westminster.

Richard Bancroft, the general editor of the Authorized Version, composed fifteen rules to guide the translators and to guard against overly partisan decisions. Rather than offer an entirely fresh English translation, the companies were to follow the Bishops' Bible* as closely as possible. "Truly (good Christian Reader)," the preface states, "we neuer thought from the beginning that we should need to make a new Translation, nor yet to make of a bad one a good one . . . but make a good one better, or out of many good ones, one principall good one, not iustly to be excepted against: that hath bene our endeauour, that our mark." Other rules standardized spelling, dictated traditional ecclesial terms (e.g., *church*, *baptize* and *bishop*), and allowed only for linguistic marginal notes and cross-references. Each book of the Bible went through a rigorous revision process: first, each person in a company made an initial draft, then the company put together a composite draft, then a supercommittee composed of representatives from each company reviewed these drafts, and finally two bishops and Bancroft scrutinized the final edits. The text and translation process of the Authorized Version have widely influenced biblical translations ever since.

Robert Bagnall (b. 1559 or 1560). English Protestant minister. Bagnall authored *The Steward's Last Account* (1622), a collection of five sermons on Luke 16.

John Ball (1585–1640). English Puritan theologian. Ball was a respected educator. He briefly held a church office until he was removed on account of his Puritanism. He composed popular catechisms and tracts on faith, the church and the covenant of grace.

Thomas Bastard (c. 1565–1618). English Protestant minister and poet. Educated at Winchester and New College, Oxford, Bastard published numerous works, including collections of poems and sermons; his most famous title is *Chrestoleros* (1598), a collection of epigrams. Bastard was alleged to be the author of an anonymous work, *An Admonition to the City of Oxford*, which revealed the carnal vices of many clergy and scholars in Oxford; despite denying authorship, he was dismissed from

Oxford in 1591. Bastard was recognized as a skilled classical scholar and preacher. He died impoverished in a debtor's prison in Dorchester.

Jeremias Bastingius (1551–1595). Dutch Reformed theologian. Educated in Heidelberg and Geneva, Bastingius pastored the Reformed church in Antwerp for nearly a decade until the Spanish overran the city in 1585; he later settled in Dordrecht. He spent the last few years of his life in Leiden on the university's board of regents. He wrote an influential commentary on the Heidelberg Catechism that was translated into English, Dutch, German and Flemish.

Johann (Pomarius) Baumgart (1514–1578). Lutheran pastor and amateur playwright. Baumgart studied under Georg Major,* Martin Luther* and Philipp Melanchthon* at the University of Wittenberg. Before becoming pastor of the Church of the Holy Spirit in 1540, Baumgart taught secondary school. He authored catechetical and polemical works, a postil for the Gospel readings throughout the church year, numerous hymns and a didactic play (*Juditium Salomonis*).

Richard Baxter (1615–1691). English Puritan minister. Baxter was a leading Puritan pastor, evangelist and theologian, known throughout England for his landmark ministry in Kidderminster and a prodigious literary output, producing 135 books in just over forty years. Baxter came to faith through reading William Perkins,* Richard Sibbes* and other early Puritan writers and was the first cleric to decline the terms of ministry in the national English church imposed by the 1662 Act of Uniformity; Baxter wrote on behalf of the more than 1700 who shared ejection from the national church. He hoped for restoration to national church ministry, or toleration, that would allow lawful preaching and pastoring. Baxter sought unity in theological, ecclesiastical, sociopolitical and personal terms and is regarded as a forerunner of Noncomformist ecumenicity, though he was defeated in his efforts at the 1661 Savoy Conference to take seriously Puritan objections to the revision of the 1604 Prayer Book. Baxter's views on church ministry were considerably hybrid: he was a paedo-baptist, Nonconformist minister who approved of synodical Episcopal government and fixed liturgy. He is most known for his classic writings on the Christian life, such as *The Saints' Everlasting Rest* and *A Christian Directory*, and pastoral ministry, such as *The Reformed Pastor*. He also produced *Catholick Theology*, a large volume squaring current Reformed, Lutheran, Arminian and Roman Catholic systems with each other.

Thomas Becon (1511/1512–1567). English Puritan preacher. Becon was a friend of Hugh Latimer,* and for several years chaplain to Archbishop Thomas Cranmer.* Becon was sent to the Tower of London by Mary I and then exiled for his controversial preaching at the English royal court. He returned to England upon Elizabeth I's accession. Becon was one of the most widely read popular preachers in England during the Reformation. He published many of his sermons, including a postil, or collection of sermon helps for undertrained or inexperienced preachers.

Belgic Confession (1561). Written by Guy de Brès (1523–1567), this statement of Dutch Reformed faith was heavily reliant on the Gallic Confession,* although more detailed, especially in how strongly it distances the Reformed from Roman Catholics and Anabaptists. The Confession first appeared in French in 1561 and was translated to Dutch in 1562. It was presented to Philip II (1527–1598) in the hope that he would grant toleration to the Reformed, to no avail. At the Synod of Dordrecht* the Confession was revised, clarifying and strengthening the article on election as well as sharpening the distinctives of Reformed theology against the Anabaptists, thus situating the Dutch Reformed more closely to the international Calvinist movement. The Belgic Confession in conjunction with the Heidelberg Catechism* and the Canons of Dordrecht were granted official status as the confessional standards (the Three Forms of Unity) of the Dutch Reformed Church.

Theodore Beza (1519–1605). French pastor and professor. Beza was compatriot and successor to John Calvin* as moderator of the Company of Pastors in Geneva during the second half of the sixteenth century. He was a noteworthy New Testament scholar whose *Codex Bezae* formed the basis of the New Testament section of later English translations. A leader in the academy and the church, Beza served as professor of Greek at the Lausanne Academy until 1558, at which time he moved to Geneva to become the rector of the newly founded Genevan Academy. He enjoyed an international reputation through his correspondence with key European leaders. Beza developed and extended Calvin's doctrinal thought on several important themes such as the nature of predestination and the real spiritual presence of Christ in the Eucharist.

Hugh Binning (1627–1653). Scottish Presbyterian theologian. At the age of eighteen, Binning became a professor of philosophy at the University of Glasgow. In his early twenties he left this post for parish ministry, and died of consumption a few years later. His commentary on the Westminster Confession and a selection of his sermons were published after his death.

Bishops' Bible (1568). Anglicans were polarized by the two most recent English translations of the Bible: the Great Bible (1539) relied too heavily on the Vulgate* and was thus perceived as too Catholic, while the Geneva Bible's* marginal notes were too Calvinist for many Anglicans. So Archbishop Matthew Parker (1504–1575) commissioned a new translation of Scripture from the original languages with marginal annotations (many of which, ironically, were from the Geneva Bible). Published under royal warrant, the Bishops' Bible became the official translation for the Church of England. The 1602 edition provided the basis for the King James Bible (1611).

Georg Blaurock (1492–1529). Swiss Anabaptist. Blaurock (a nickname meaning "blue coat," because of his preference for this garment) was one of the first leaders of Switzerland's radical reform movement. In the first public disputations on baptism in Zurich, he argued for believer's baptism and was the first person to receive adult believers' baptism there, having been baptized by Conrad Grebel* in 1525. Blaurock was arrested several times for performing mass adult baptisms and engaging in social disobedience by disrupting worship services. He was eventually expelled from Zurich but continued preaching and baptizing in various Swiss cantons until his execution.

Bohemian Confession (1535). Bohemian Christianity was subdivided between traditional Catholics, Utraquists (who demanded Communion in both kinds) and the *Unitas Fratrum*, who were not Protestants but whose theology bore strong affinities to the Waldensians and the Reformed. The 1535 Latin edition of this confession—an earlier Czech edition had already been drafted—was an attempt to clarify and redefine the beliefs of the *Unitas Fratrum*. This confession purged all earlier openness to rebaptism and inched toward Luther's* eucharistic theology. Jan Augusta (c. 1500–1572) and Jan Roh (also Johannes Horn; c. 1490–1547) presented the confession to King Ferdinand I (1503–1564) in Vienna, but the king would not print it. The *Unitas Fratrum* sought, and with slight amendments eventually obtained, Luther's advocacy of the confession. It generally follows the structure of the Augsburg Confession.*

Bohemian Confession (1575). This confession was an attempt to shield Bohemian Christian minorities—the Utraquists and the *Unitas Fratrum*—from the Counter-Reformation and Habsburg insistence on uniformity. The hope was that this umbrella consensus would ensure peace in the midst of Christian diversity; anyone who affirmed the 1575 Confession, passed by the Bohemian legislature, would be tolerated. This confession was, like the Bohemian Confession of 1535, patterned after the Augsburg Confession.* It emphasizes both justification by faith alone and good works as the fruit of salvation. Baptism and the Eucharist are the focus of the sacramental section, although the five traditional Catholic sacraments are also listed for the Utraquists. Though it was eventually accepted in 1609 by Rudolf II (1552–1612), the Thirty Years' War (1618–1648) rendered the confession moot.

Book of Common Prayer (1549; 1552). After the Church of England's break with Rome, it needed a liturgical manual to distinguish its theology and practice from that of Catholicism. Thomas Cranmer* drafted the Book of Common Prayer based on the medieval Roman Missal, under the dual influence of the revised Lutheran Mass and the reforms of the Spanish Cardinal Quiñones. This manual details the eucharistic service, as well as services for rites such as baptism, confirmation, marriage and funerals. It includes a matrix of the epistle and Gospel readings and the appropriate collect for each Sunday and feast day of the church year. The 1548 Act of Uniformity established the Book of Common Prayer as *the* authoritative liturgical manual for the Church of England, to be implemented everywhere by Pentecost 1549. After its 1552 revision, Queen Mary I banned it; Elizabeth reestablished it in 1559, although it was rejected by Puritans and Catholics alike.

The Book of Homilies (1547; 1563; 1570). This collection of approved sermons, published in three parts during the reigns of Edward VI and Elizabeth I, was intended to inculcate Anglican theological distinctives and mitigate the problems raised by the lack of educated preachers. Addressing doctrinal and practical topics, Thomas Cranmer* likely wrote the majority of the first twelve sermons, published in 1547; John Jewel* added another twenty sermons in 1563. A final sermon, *A Homily Against Disobedience*, was appended to the canon in 1570. Reprinted regularly, the *Book of Homilies* was an important resource in Anglican preaching until at least the end of the seventeenth century.

Martin (Cellarius) Borrhaus (1499–1564). German Reformed theologian. After a dispute with his mentor Johann Eck,* Borrhaus settled in Wittenberg, where he was influenced by the radical Zwickau Prophets. He travelled extensively, and finally settled in Basel to teach philosophy and Old Testament. Despite his objections, many accused Borrhaus of Anabaptism; he argued that baptism was a matter of conscience. On account of his association with Sebastian Castellio (1515–1563) and Michael Servetus (1511–1553), some scholars posit that Borrhaus was an antitrinitarian. His writings include a treatise on the Trinity and commentaries on the Torah, historical books, Ecclesiastes and Isaiah.

John Boys (1571–1625). Anglican priest and theologian. Before doctoral work at Cambridge, Boys pastored several parishes in Kent; after completing his studies he was appointed to more prominent positions, culminating in his 1619 appointment as the Dean of Canterbury by James I. Boys published a popular four-volume postil of the Gospel and epistle readings for the church year, as well as a companion volume for the Psalms.

Thieleman Jans van Braght (1625–1664). Dutch Radical preacher. After demonstrating great ability with languages, this cloth merchant was made preacher in his hometown of Dordrecht in 1648. He served in this office for the next sixteen years, until his death. This celebrated preacher had a reputation for engaging in debate wherever an opportunity presented itself, particularly concerning infant baptism. The publication of his book of martyrs, *Het Bloedigh Tooneel of Martelaersspiegel* (1660; *Martyrs' Mirror*), proved to be his lasting contribution to the Mennonite tradition. *Martyrs' Mirror* is heavily indebted to the earlier martyr book *Offer des Heeren* (1562), to which Braght added many early church martyrs who rejected infant baptism, as well as over 800 contemporary martyrs.

Johannes Brenz (1499–1570). German Lutheran theologian and pastor. Brenz was converted to the reformation cause after hearing Martin Luther* speak; later, Brenz became a student of Johannes Oecolampadius.* His central achievement lay in his talent for organization. As city preacher in Schwäbisch-Hall and afterward in Württemberg and Tübingen, he oversaw the introduction of reform measures and doctrines and new governing structures for ecclesial and educational communities. Brenz also helped establish Lutheran orthodoxy through treatises, commentaries and catechisms. He defended Luther's position on eucharistic presence against Huldrych Zwingli* and opposed the death penalty for religious dissenters.

Guillaume Briçonnet (1470–1534). French Catholic abbot and bishop. Briçonnet created a short-lived circle of reformist-minded humanists in his diocese under the sponsorship of Marguerite d'Angoulême. His desire for ecclesial reform developed throughout his prestigious career (including positions as royal chaplain to the queen, abbot at Saint-Germain-des-Prés and bishop of Meaux), influenced by Jacques Lefèvre d'Étaples.* Briçonnet encouraged reform through ministerial visitation, Scripture and preaching in the vernacular and active study of the Bible. When this triggered the ire of the theology faculty at the Sorbonne in Paris, Briçonnet quelled the activity and departed, envisioning an ecclesial reform that proceeded hierarchically.

Thomas Brightman (1562–1607). English Puritan pastor and exegete. Under alleged divine inspiration, Brightman wrote a well known commentary on Revelation, influenced by Joachim of Fiore (d. 1202). In contrast to the putatively true churches of Geneva and Scotland, he depicted the Church of England as a type of the lukewarm Laodicean church. He believed that the Reformation would result in the defeat of the Vatican and the Ottoman Empire and that all humanity would be regenerated through the spread of the gospel before Christ's final return and judgment.

Otto Brunfels (c. 1488–1534). German Lutheran botanist, teacher and physician. Brunfels joined the Carthusian order, where he developed interests in the natural sciences and became involved with a humanist circle associated with Ulrich von Hutten and Wolfgang Capito.* In 1521, after coming into contact with Luther's* teaching, Brunfels abandoned the monastic life, traveling and spending time in botanical research and pastoral care. He received a medical degree in Basel and was appointed city physician of Bern in 1534. Brunfels penned defenses of Luther and Hutten, devotional biographies of biblical figures, a prayer book, and annotations on the Gospels and the Acts of the Apostles. His most influential contribution, however, is as a Renaissance botanist.

Martin Bucer (1491–1551). German Reformed theologian and pastor. A Dominican friar, Bucer was influenced by Desiderius Erasmus* during his doctoral studies at the University of Heidelberg, where he began corresponding with Martin Luther.* After advocating reform in Alsace, Bucer was excommunicated and fled to Strasbourg, where he became a leader in the city's Reformed ecclesial and educational communities. Bucer sought concord between Lutherans and Zwinglians and Protestants and Catholics. He emigrated to England, becoming a professor at Cambridge. Bucer's greatest theological concern was the centrality of Christ's sacrificial death, which achieved justification and sanctification and orients Christian community.

Johannes Bugenhagen (1485–1558). German Lutheran pastor and professor. Bugenhagen, a priest and lecturer at a Premonstratensian monastery, became a city preacher in Wittenberg during the reform efforts of Martin Luther* and Philipp Melanchthon.* Initially influenced by his reading of Desiderius Erasmus,* Bugenhagen grew in evangelical orientation through Luther's works; later, he studied under Melanchthon at the University of Wittenberg, eventually serving as rector and faculty member there. Bugenhagen was a versatile commentator, exegete and lecturer on Scripture. Through these roles and his development of lectionary and devotional material, Bugenhagen facilitated rapid establishment of church order throughout many German provinces.

Heinrich Bullinger (1504–1575). Swiss Reformed pastor and theologian. Bullinger succeeded Huldrych Zwingli* as minister and leader in Zurich. The primary author of the First and Second Helvetic Confessions,* Bullinger was drawn toward reform through the works of Martin Luther* and Philipp Melanchthon.* After Zwingli died, Bullinger was vital in maintaining adherence to the cause of reform; he oversaw the expansion of the Zurich synodal system while preaching, teaching and writing extensively. One of Bullinger's lasting legacies was the development of a federal view of the divine covenant with humanity, making baptism and the Eucharist covenantal signs.

John Bunyan (1628–1688). English Puritan preacher and writer. His *Pilgrim's Progress* is one of the best-selling English-language titles in history. Born to a working-class family, Bunyan was largely unschooled, gaining literacy (and entering the faith) through reading the Bible and such early Puritan devotional works as *The Plain Man's Pathway to Heaven* and *The Practice of Piety.* Following a short stint in Oliver Cromwell's parliamentary army, in which Bunyan narrowly escaped death in combat, he turned to a preaching ministry, succeeding John Gifford as pastor at the Congregational church in Bedford. A noted preacher, Bunyan drew large crowds in itinerant appearances and it was in the sermonic form that Bunyan developed his theological outlook, which was an Augustinian-inflected Calvinism. Bunyan's opposition to the Book of Common Prayer and refusal of official ecclesiastical licensure led to multiple imprisonments, where he wrote many of his famous allegorical works, including *Pilgrim's Progress, The Holy City, Prison Meditations* and *Holy War.*

Jeremiah Burroughs (c. 1600–1646). English Puritan pastor and delegate to the Westminster Assembly. Burroughs left Cambridge, as well as a rectorate in Norfolk, because of his nonconformity. After returning to England from pastoring an English congregation in Rotterdam for several years (1637–1641), he became one of only a few dissenters from the official presbyterianism of the Assembly in favor of a congregationalist polity. Nevertheless, he was well known and respected by presbyterian colleagues such as Richard Baxter* for his irenic tone and conciliatory manner. The vast majority of Burroughs's corpus was published posthumously, although during his lifetime he published annotations on Hosea and several polemical works.

Cardinal Cajetan (Thomas de Vio) (1469–1534). Italian Catholic cardinal, professor, theologian and biblical exegete. This Dominican monk was the leading Thomist theologian and one of the most important Catholic exegetes of the sixteenth century. Cajetan is best-known for his interview with Martin Luther* at the Diet of Augsburg (1518). Among his many works are polemical treatises, extensive biblical commentaries and most importantly a four-volume commentary (1508–1523) on the *Summa Theologiae* of Thomas Aquinas.

Georg Calixtus (1586–1656). German Lutheran theologian. Calixtus studied at the University of Helmstedt where he developed regard for Philipp Melanchthon.* Between his time as a student and later as a professor at Helmstedt, Calixtus traveled through Europe seeking a way to unite and reconcile Lutherans, Calvinists and Catholics. He attempted to fuse these denominations through use of the Scriptures, the Apostles' Creed, and the first five centuries, interpreted by the Vincentian canon. Calixtus's position was stamped as syncretist and yielded further debate even after his death.

John Calvin (1509–1564). French Reformed pastor and theologian. In his *Institutes of the Christian Religion*, Calvin provided a theological dogmatics for the Reformed churches. Calvin's gradual conversion to the cause of reform occurred through his study with chief humanist scholars in Paris, but he spent most of his career in Geneva (excepting a three-year exile in Strasbourg with Martin Bucer*). In Geneva, Calvin reorganized the structure and governance of the church and established an academy that became an international center for theological education. He was a tireless writer, producing his *Institutes*, theological treatises and Scripture commentaries.

Wolfgang Capito (1478?–1541). German Reformed humanist and theologian. Capito, a Hebrew scholar, produced a Hebrew grammar and published several Latin commentaries on books of the Hebrew Scriptures. He corresponded with Desiderius Erasmus* and fellow humanists. Capito translated Martin Luther's* early works into Latin for the printer Johann Froben. On meeting Luther, Capito was converted to Luther's vision, left Mainz and settled in Strasbourg, where he lectured on Luther's theology to the city clergy. With Martin Bucer,* Capito reformed liturgy, ecclesial life and teachings, education, welfare and government. Capito worked for the theological unification of the Swiss cantons with Strasbourg.

Thomas Cartwright (1535–1606). English Puritan preacher and professor. Cartwright was educated at St. John's College, Cambridge, although as an influential leader of the Presbyterian party in the Church of England he was continually at odds with the Anglican party, especially John Whitgift.* Cartwright spent some time as an exile in Geneva and Heidelberg as well as in Antwerp, where he pastored an English church. In 1585, Cartwright was arrested and eventually jailed for trying to return to England despite Elizabeth I's refusal of his request. Many acknowledged him to be learned but also quite cantankerous. His publications include commentaries on Colossians, Ecclesiastes, Proverbs and the Gospels, as well as a dispute against Whitgift on church discipline.

Mathew Caylie (unknown). English Protestant minister. Caylie authored *The Cleansing of the Ten Lepers* (1623), an exposition of Luke 17:14-18.

John Chardon (d. 1601). Irish Anglican bishop. Chardon was educated at Oxford. He advocated Reformed doctrine in his preaching, yet opposed those Puritans who rejected Anglican church order. He published several sermons.

Martin Chemnitz (1522–1586). German Lutheran theologian. A leading figure in establishing Lutheran orthodoxy, Chemnitz studied theology and patristics at the University of Wittenburg, later becoming a defender of Philipp Melanchthon's* interpretation of the doctrine of justification. Chemnitz drafted a compendium of doctrine and reorganized the structure of the church in Wolfenbüttel; later, he led efforts to reconcile divisions within Lutheranism, culminating in the Formula of Concord*. One of his chief theological accomplishments was a modification of the christological doctrine of the *communicatio idiomatium*, which provided a Lutheran platform for understanding the sacramental presence of Christ's humanity in the Eucharist.

David Chytraeus (1531–1600). German Lutheran professor, theologian and biblical exegete. At the age of eight Chytraeus was admitted to the University of Tübingen. There he studied law, philology, philosophy, and theology, finally receiving his master's degree in 1546. Chytraeus befriended Philipp Melanchthon* while sojourning in Wittenberg, where he taught the *Loci communes*. While teaching exegesis at the University of Rostock Chytraeus became acquainted with Tilemann Heshusius,* who strongly influenced Chytraeus away from Philippist theology. As a defender of Gnesio-Lutheran theology Chytraeus helped organize churches throughout Austria in accordance with the Augsburg Confession.* Chytraeus coauthored the Formula of Concord* with Martin Chemnitz,* Andreas Musculus (1514–1581), Nikolaus Selnecker* and Jakob Andreae.* He wrote commentaries on most of the Bible, as well as a devotional work titled *Regula vitae* (1555) that described the Christian virtues.

David Clarkson (1622–1686). English Puritan theologian. After his dismissal from the pastorate on account of the Act of Uniformity (1662), little is known about Clarkson. At the end of his life he ministered with John Owen* in London.

John Colet (1467–1519). English Catholic priest, preacher and educator. Colet, appointed dean of Saint Paul's Cathedral by Henry VII, was a friend of Desiderius Erasmus,* on whose classical ideals Colet reconstructed the curriculum of Saint Paul's school. Colet was convinced that the foundation of moral reform lay in the education of children. Though an ardent advocate of reform, Colet, like Erasmus, remained loyal to the Catholic Church throughout his life. Colet's agenda of reform was oriented around spiritual and ethical themes, demonstrated in his commentaries on select books of the New Testament and the writings of Pseudo-Dionysius the Areopagite.

Gasparo Contarini (1483–1542). Italian statesman, theologian and reform-minded cardinal. Contarini was an able negotiator and graceful compromiser. Charles V requested Contarini as the papal legate for the Colloquy of Regensburg (1541), where Contarini reached agreement with Melanchthon* on the doctrine of justification (although neither the pope nor Luther* ratified the agreement). He had come to a similar belief in

the priority of faith in the work of Christ rather than works as the basis for Christian life in 1511, though unlike Luther, he never left the papal church over the issue; instead he remainied within it to try to seek gentle reform, and he adhered to papal sacramental teaching. Contarini was an important voice for reform within the Catholic Church, always seeking reconciliation rather than confrontation with Protestant reformers. He wrote many works, including a treatise detailing the ideal bishop, a manual for lay church leaders, a political text on right governance and brief commentaries on the Pauline letters.

John Cosin (1594–1672). Anglican preacher and bishop. Early in his career Cosin was the vice chancellor of Cambridge and canon at the Durham cathedral. But as a friend of William Laud* and an advocate for "Laudian" changes, he was suspected of being a crypto-Catholic. In 1640 during the Long Parliament a Puritan lodged a complaint with the House of Commons concerning Cosin's "popish innovations." Cosin was promptly removed from office. During the turmoil of the English Civil Wars, Cosin sojourned in Paris among English nobility but struggled financially. Cosin returned to England after the Restoration in 1660 to be consecrated as the bishop of Durham. He published annotations on the Book of Common Prayer* and a history of the canon.

Council of Constance (1414–1418). Convened to resolve the Western Schism, root out heresy and reform the church in head and members, the council asserted in *Sacrosancta* (1415) the immediate authority of ecumenical councils assembled in the Holy Spirit under Christ—even over the pope. Martin V was elected pope in 1417 after the three papal claimants were deposed; thus, the council ended the schism. The council condemned Jan Hus,* Jerome of Prague (c. 1365–1416) and, posthumously, John Wycliffe. Hus and Jerome, despite letters of safe conduct, were burned at the stake. Their deaths ignited the Hussite Wars, which ended as a result of the Council of Basel's concessions to the Bohemian church. The council fathers sought to reform the church through the regular convocation of councils (*Frequens*; 1417). Martin V begrudgingly complied by calling the required councils, then immediately disbanding them. Pius II (r. 1458–1464) reasserted papal dominance through *Execrabilis* (1460), which condemned any appeal to a future council apart from the pope's authority.

Miles Coverdale (1488–1568). Anglican bishop. Coverdale is known for his translations of the Bible into English, completing William Tyndale's* efforts and later producing the Great Bible commissioned by Henry VIII (1539). A former friar, Coverdale was among the Cambridge scholars who met at the White Horse Tavern to discuss Martin Luther's* ideas. During Coverdale's three terms of exile in Europe, he undertook various translations, including the Geneva Bible*. He was appointed bishop of Exeter by Thomas Cranmer* and served as chaplain to Edward VI. Coverdale contributed to Cranmer's first edition of the Book of Common Prayer.*

William Cowper (Couper) (1568–1619). Scottish Puritan bishop. After graduating from the University of St. Andrews, Cowper worked in parish ministry for twenty-five years before becoming bishop. As a zealous Puritan and advocate of regular preaching and rigorous discipline, Cowper championed Presbyterian polity and lay participation in church government. Cowper published devotional works, sermon collections and a commentary on Revelation.

Thomas Cranmer (1489–1556). Anglican archbishop and theologian. Cranmer supervised church reform and produced the first two editions of the Book of Common Prayer.* As a doctoral student at Cambridge, he was involved in the discussions at the White Horse Tavern. Cranmer contributed to a religious defense of Henry VIII's divorce; Henry then appointed him Archbishop of Canterbury. Cranmer cautiously steered the course of reform, accelerating under Edward VI. After supporting the attempted coup to prevent Mary's assuming the throne, Cranmer was convicted of treason and burned at the stake. Cranmer's legacy is the splendid English of his liturgy and prayer books.

Richard Crashaw (1612–1649). English Catholic poet. Educated at Cambridge, Crashaw was fluent in Hebrew, Greek and Latin. His first volume of poetry was *Epigrammatum sacrorum liber* (1634). Despite being born into a Puritan family, Crashaw was attracted to Catholicism, finally converting in 1644 after he was forced to resign his fellowship for not signing the Solemn League and Covenant (1643). In 1649, he was made a subcanon of Our Lady of Loretto by Cardinal Palotta.

Herbert Croft (1603–1691). Anglican bishop. As a boy Croft converted to Catholicism; he returned to the Church of England during his studies at Oxford. Before the English Civil Wars, he served as chaplain to Charles I. After the Restoration, Charles II appointed him as bishop. Croft ardently opposed Catholicism in his later years.

John Crompe (d. 1661). Anglican priest. Educated at Cambridge, Crompe published a commentary on the Apostles' Creed, a sermon on Psalm 21:3 and an exposition of Christ's passion.

Caspar Cruciger (1504–1548). German Lutheran theologian. Recognized for his alignment with the theological views of Philipp Melanchthon,* Cruciger was a scholar respected among both Protestants and Catholics. In 1521, Cruciger came Wittenberg to study Hebrew and remained there most of his life. He became a valuable partner for Martin Luther* in translating the Old Testament and served as teacher, delegate to major theological colloquies and rector. Cruciger was an agent of reform in his birthplace of Leipzig, where at the age of fifteen he had observed the disputation between Luther and Johann Eck.*

Jakob Dachser (1486–1567). German Anabaptist theologian and hymnist. Dachser served as a Catholic priest in Vienna until he was imprisoned and then exiled for defending the Lutheran understanding of the Mass and fasting. Hans Hut* rebaptized him in Augsburg, where Dachser was appointed as a leader of the Anabaptist congregation. Lutheran authorities imprisoned him for nearly four years. In 1531 he recanted his Radical beliefs and began to catechize children with the permission of the city council. Dachser was expelled from Augsburg as a possible insurrection-ist in 1552 and relocated to Pfalz-Neuberg. He published a number of poems, hymns and mystical works, and he versified several psalms.

Jean Daillé (1594–1670). French Reformed pastor. Born into a devout Reformed family, Daillé studied theology and philosophy at Saumur under the most influential contemporary lay leader in French Protestantism, Philippe Duplessis-Mornay (1549–1623). Daillé held to Amyraldianism—the belief that Christ died for all humanity inclusively, not particularly for the elect who would inherit salvation (though only the elect are in fact saved). He wrote a controversial treatise on the church fathers that aggravated many Catholic and Anglican scholars because of Daillé's apparent demotion of patristic authority in matters of faith.

Lambert Daneau (1535–1595). French Reformed pastor and theologian. After a decade of pastoring in France, following the St. Bartholomew's Day Massacre, Daneau fled to Geneva to teach theology at the Academy. He later taught in the Low Countries, finishing his career in southern France. Daneau's diverse works include tracts on science, ethics and morality as well as numerous theological and exegetical works.

John Davenant (1576–1641). Anglican bishop and professor. Davenant attended Queen's College, Cambridge, where he received his doctorate and was appointed professor of divinity. During the Remonstrant controversy, James I sent Davenant as one of the four representatives for the Church of England to the Synod of Dordrecht.* Following James's instructions, Davenant advocated a *via media* between the Calvinists and the Remon-strants, although in later years he defended against the rise of Arminianism in England. In 1621, Davenant was promoted to the bishopric of Salisbury, where he was generally receptive to Laudian reforms. Davenant's lectures on Colos-sians are his best-known work.

Defense of the Augsburg Confession (1531). See *Augsburg Confession*.

Hans Denck (c. 1500–1527). German Radical theologian. Denck, a crucial early figure of the German Anabaptist movement, combined medieval German mysticism with the radical sacramental theology of Andreas Bodenstein von Karlstadt* and Thomas Müntzer.* Denck argued that the exterior forms of Scripture and sacrament are symbolic witnesses secondary to the internally revealed truth of the Sprit in the human soul. This view led to his expulsion from Nuremberg in 1525; he spent the next two years in various centers of reform in the German territories. At the time of his death, violent persecution against Anabaptists was on the rise throughout northern Europe.

Stephen Denison (unknown). English Puritan pastor. Denison received the post of curate at St. Katherine Cree in London sometime in the 1610s, where he ministered until his ejection from office in 1635. During his career at St. Katherine Cree, Denison waded into controversy with both Puritans (over the doctrine of predestination) and Anglicans (over concerns about liturgical ceremo-nies). He approached both altercations with rancor and rigidity, although he seems to have been quite popular and beloved by most of his congregation. In 1631, William Laud* consecrated the newly renovated St. Katherine Cree, and as part of the festivities Denison offered a sermon on Luke 19:27 in which he publicly rebuked Laud for fashioning the Lord's house into a "den of robbers." Aside from the record of his quarrels, very little is known about Denison. In addition to *The White Wolf* (a 1627 sermon against another opponent), he published a catechism for children (1621), a treatise on the sacraments (1621) and a commen-tary on 2 Peter 1 (1622).

David Dickson (1583?–1663). Scottish Reformed pastor, preacher, professor and theologian. Dickson defended the Presbyterian form of ecclesial reformation in Scotland and was recog-nized for his iteration of Calvinist federal theology and expository biblical commentaries. Dickson served for over twenty years as professor of philosophy at the University of Glasgow before being appointed professor of divinity. He opposed the imposition of Episcopalian measures on the church in Scotland and was active in political and ecclesial venues to protest and prohibit such influences. Dickson was removed from his academic post following his refusal of the oath of supremacy during the Restoration era.

Veit Dietrich (1506–1549). German Lutheran preacher and theologian. Dietrich intended to study medicine at the University of Wittenberg, but Martin Luther* and Philipp Melanchthon* convinced him to study theology instead. Dietrich developed a strong relationship with Luther, accompanying him to the Marburg Colloquy (1529) and to Coburg Castle during the Diet of Augsburg (1530). After graduating, Dietrich taught on the arts faculty, eventually becoming dean. In 1535 he returned to his hometown, Nuremberg, to pastor. Later in life, Dietrich worked with Melanchthon to reform the church in Regensburg. In 1547, when Charles V arrived in Nuremberg, Dietrich was suspended from the pastorate; he resisted the imposition of the Augsburg Interim to no avail. In addition to transcribing some of Luther's lectures, portions of the Table Talk and the very popular *Hauspostille* (1544), Dietrich published his own sermons for children, a manual for pastors and a summary of the Bible.

Giovanni Diodati (1576–1649). Italian Reformed theologian. Diodati was from an Italian banking family who fled for religious reasons to Geneva. There he trained under Theodore Beza;* on completion of his doctoral degree, Diodati became professor of Hebrew at the academy. He was an ecclesiastical representative of the church in Geneva (for whom he was a delegate at the Synod of Dordrecht*) and an advocate for reform in Venice. Diodati's chief contribution to the Italian reform movement was a translation of the Bible into Italian (1640–1641), which remains the standard translation in Italian Protestantism.

John Dod (c. 1549–1645). English Puritan pastor. Over the course of his lengthy pastoral career (spanning roughly sixty years), Dod was twice suspended for nonconformity and twice reinstated. A popular preacher, he published many sermons as well as commentaries on the Ten Commandments and the Lord's Prayer; collections of his sayings

and anecdotes were compiled after his death.

John Donne (1572–1631). Anglican poet and preacher. Donne was born into a strong Catholic family. However, sometime between his brother's death from the plague while in prison in 1593 and the publication of his *Pseudo-Martyr* in 1610, Donne joined the Church of England. Ordained to the Anglican priesthood in 1615 and already widely recognized for his verse, Donne quickly rose to prominence as a preacher—some have deemed him the best of his era. His textual corpus is an amalgam of erotic *and* divine poetry (e.g., "Batter My Heart"), as well as a great number of sermons.

John Downame (c. 1571–1652). English Puritan pastor and theologian. See *English Annotations*.

Charles Drelincourt (1595–1669). French Reformed pastor, theologian and controversialist. After studying at Saumur Academy, Drelincourt pastored the Reformed Church in Paris for nearly fifty years. He was well known for his ministry to the sick. In addition to polemical works against Catholicism, he published numerous pastoral resources: catechisms, three volumes of sermons and a five-volume series on consolation for the suffering.

The Dutch Annotations (1657). See *Statenvertaling*.

Daniel Dyke (d. 1614). English Puritan preacher. Born of nonconformist stock, Dyke championed a more thorough reformation of church practice in England. After the promulgation of John Whitgift's* articles in 1583, Dyke refused to accept what he saw as remnants of Catholicism, bringing him into conflict with the bishop of London. Despite the petitions of his congregation and some politicians, the bishop of London suspended Dyke from his ministry for refusing priestly ordination and conformity to the Book of Common Prayer.* All of his work was published posthumously; it is mostly focused on biblical interpretation.

Johann Eck (Johann Maier of Eck) (1486–1543). German Catholic theologian. Though Eck was not an antagonist of Martin Luther* until the dispute over indulgences, Luther's Ninety-five Theses (1517) sealed the two as adversaries. After their debate at the Leipzig Disputation (1519), Eck participated in the writing of the papal bull that led to Luther's excommunication. Much of Eck's work was written to oppose Protestantism or to defend Catholic doctrine and the papacy; his *Enchiridion* was a manual written to counter Protestant doctrine. However, Eck was also deeply invested in the status of parish preaching, publishing a five-volume set of postils. He participated in the assemblies at Regensburg and Augsburg and led the Catholics in their rejection of the Augsburg Confession.

English Annotations (1645; 1651; 1657). Under a commission from the Westminster Assembly, the editors of the English Annotations—John Downame* along with unnamed colleagues—translated, collated and digested in a compact and accessible format several significant Continental biblical resources, including Calvin's* commentaries, Beza's* *Annotationes majores* and Diodati's* *Annotations*.

Desiderius Erasmus (1466–1536). Dutch Catholic humanist and pedagogue. Erasmus, a celebrated humanist scholar, was recognized for translations of ancient texts, reform of education according to classical studies, moral and spiritual writings and the first printed edition of the Greek New Testament. A former Augustinian who never left the Catholic Church, Erasmus addressed deficiencies he saw in the church and society, challenging numerous prevailing doctrines but advocating reform. He envisioned a simple, spiritual Christian life shaped by the teachings of Jesus and ancient wisdom. He was often accused of collusion with Martin Luther* on account of some resonance of their ideas but hotly debated Luther on human will.

Paul Fagius (1504–1549). German Reformed Hebraist and pastor. After studying at the University of Heidelberg, Fagius went to Strasbourg where he perfected his Hebrew under Wolfgang Capito.* In Isny im Allgäu (Baden-Württemberg) he met the great Jewish grammarian Elias Levita (1469–1549), with whom he established a Hebrew printing press. In 1544 Fagius returned to Strasbourg, succeeding Capito

as preacher and Old Testament lecturer. During the Augsburg Interim, Fagius (with Martin Bucer*) accepted Thomas Cranmer's* invitation to translate and interpret the Bible at Cambridge. However, Fagius died before he could begin any of the work. Fagius wrote commentaries on the first four chapters of Genesis and the deutero-canonical books of Sirach and Tobit.

John Fary (unknown). English Puritan pastor. Fary authored *God's Severity on Man's Sterility* (1645), a sermon on the fruitless fig tree in Luke 13:6-9.

William Fenner (1600–1640). English Puritan pastor. After studying at Cambridge and Oxford, Fenner ministered at Sedgley and Rochford. Fenner's extant writings, which primarily deal with practical and devotional topics, demonstrate a zealous Puritan piety and a keen interest in Scripture and theology.

First Helvetic Confession (1536). Anticipating the planned church council at Mantua (1537, but delayed until 1545 at Trent), Reformed theologians of the Swiss cantons drafted a confession to distinguish themselves from both Catholics and the churches of the Augsburg Confession.* Heinrich Bullinger* led the discussion and wrote the confession itself; Leo Jud, Oswald Myconius, Simon Grynaeus and others were part of the assembly. Martin Bucer* and Wolfgang Capito* had desired to draw the Lutheran and Reformed communions closer together through this document, but Luther* proved unwilling after Bullinger refused to accept the Wittenberg Concord (1536). This confession was largely eclipsed by Bullinger's Second Helvetic Confession.*

John Fisher (1469–1535). English Catholic bishop and theologian. This reputed preacher defended Catholic orthodoxy and strove to reform abuses in the church. In 1521 Henry VIII honored Fisher with the title *Fidei Defensor* ("defender of the faith"). Nevertheless, Fisher opposed the king's divorce of Catherine of Aragon (1485–1536) and the independent establishment of the Church of England; he was convicted for treason and executed. Most of Fisher's works are polemical and occasional (e.g., on transubstantiation, against Martin Luther*); however, he also published a series of sermons on the seven penitential psalms. In addition to his episcopal duties, Fisher was the chancellor of Cambridge from 1504 until his death.

John Flavel (c. 1630–1691). English Puritan pastor. Trained at Oxford, Flavel ministered in southwest England from 1650 until the Act of Uniformity in 1662, which reaffirmed the compulsory use of the Book of Common Prayer. Flavel preached unofficially for many years, until his congregation was eventually allowed to build a meeting place in 1687. His works were numerous, varied and popular.

Giovanni Battista Folengo (1490–1559). Italian Catholic exegete. In 1528 Folengo left the Benedictine order, questioning the validity of monastic vows; he returned to the monastic life in 1534. During this hiatus Folengo came into contact with the Neapolitan reform-minded circle founded by Juan de Valdés.* Folengo published commentaries on the Psalms, John, 1–2 Peter and James. Augustin Marlorat* included Folengo's comment in his anthology of exegesis on the Psalms. In 1580 Folengo's Psalms commentary was added to the Index of Prohibited Books.

Formula of Concord (1577). After Luther's* death, intra-Lutheran controversies between the Gnesio-Lutherans (partisans of Luther) and the Philippists (partisans of Melanchthon*) threatened to cause a split among those who had subscribed to the Augsburg Confession.* In 1576, Jakob Andreae,* Martin Chemnitz,* Nikolaus Selnecker,* David Chytraeus* and Andreas Musculus (1514–1581) met with the intent of resolving the controversies, which mainly regarded the relationship between good works and salvation, the third use of the law, and the role of the human will in accepting God's grace. In 1580, celebrating the fiftieth anniversary of the presentation of the Augsburg Confession to Charles V (1500–1558), the *Book of Concord* was printed as the authoritative interpretation of the Augsburg Confession; it included the three ancient creeds, the Augsburg Confession, its Apology (1531), the Schmalkald

Articles,* Luther's *Treatise on the Power and Primacy of the Pope* (1537) and both his Small and Large Catechisms (1529).

Sebastian Franck (1499–1542). German Radical theologian. Franck became a Lutheran in 1525, but by 1529 he began to develop ideas that distanced him from Protestants and Catholics. Expelled from Strasbourg and later Ulm due to his controversial writings, Franck spent the end of his life in Basel. Franck emphasized God's word as a divine internal spark that cannot be adequately expressed in outward forms. Thus he criticized religious institutions and dogmas. His work consists mostly of commentaries, compilations and translations. In his sweeping historical *Chronica* (1531), Franck supported numerous heretics condemned by the Catholic Church and criticized political and church authorities.

Leonhard Frick (d. 1528). Austrian Radical martyr. See *Kunstbuch*.

Gallic Confession (1559). This confession was accepted at the first National Synod of the Reformed Churches of France (1559). It was intended to be a touchstone of Reformed faith but also to show to the people of France that the Huguenots—who faced persecution—were not seditious. The French Reformed Church presented this confession to Francis II (1544–1560) in 1560, and to his successor, Charles IX (1550–1574), in 1561. The later Genevan draft, likely written by Calvin,* Beza* and Pierre Viret (1511–1571), was received as the true Reformed confession at the seventh National Synod in La Rochelle (1571).

Geneva Bible (originally printed 1560). During Mary I's reign many English Protestants sought safety abroad in Reformed territories of the Empire and the Swiss Cantons, especially in Calvin's* Geneva. A team of English exiles in Geneva led by William Whittingham (c. 1524–1579) brought this complete translation to press in the course of two years. Notable for several innovations—Roman type, verse numbers, italics indicating English idiom and not literal phrasing of the original languages, even variant readings in the Gospels and Acts—this translation is most well known for its marginal notes, which reflect a strongly Calvinist theology. The notes explained Scripture in an accessible way for the laity, also giving unlearned clergy a new sermon resource. Although controversial because of its implicit critique of royal power, this translation was wildly popular; even after the publication of the Authorized Version (1611) and James I's 1616 ban on its printing, the Geneva Bible continued to be the most popular English translation until after the English Civil Wars.

Johann Gerhard (1582–1637). German Lutheran theologian, professor and superintendent. Gerhard is considered one of the most eminent Lutheran theologians, after Martin Luther* and Martin Chemnitz.* After studying patristics and Hebrew at Wittenberg, Jena and Marburg, Gerhard was appointed superintendent at the age of twenty-four. In 1616 he was appointed to a post at the University of Jena, where he reintroduced Aristotelian metaphysics to theology and gained widespread fame. His most important work was the nine-volume *Loci Theologici* (1610–1625). He also expanded Chemnitz's harmony of the Gospels (*Harmonia Evangelicae*), which was finally published by Polykarp Leyser (1552–1610) in 1593. Gerhard was well-known for an irenic spirit and an ability to communicate clearly.

George Gifford (c. 1548–1600). English Puritan pastor. Gifford was suspended for nonconformity in 1584. With private support, however, he was able to continue his ministry. Through his published works he wanted to help develop lay piety and biblical literacy.

Anthony Gilby (c. 1510–1585). English Puritan translator. During Mary I's reign, Gilby fled to Geneva, where he assisted William Whittingham (c. 1524–1579) with the Geneva Bible.* He returned to England to pastor after Elizabeth I's accession. In addition to translating numerous continental Reformed works into English—especially those of John Calvin* and Theodore Beza*—Gilby also wrote commentaries on Micah and Malachi.

Bernard Gilpin (1517–1583). Anglican theologian and priest. In public disputations, Gilpin defended Roman Catholic theology against John Hooper (c. 1495-1555) and Peter Martyr Vermigli.* These debates caused Gilpin to reexamine his faith. Upon Mary I's accession, Gilpin resigned his benefice. He sojourned in Belgium and France, returning to pastoral ministry in England in 1556. Gilpin dedicated himself to a preaching circuit in northern England, thus earning the moniker "the Apostle to the North." His zealous preaching and almsgiving roused royal opposition and a warrant for his arrest. On his way to the queen's commission, Gilpin fractured his leg, delaying his arrival in London until after Mary's death and thus likely saving his life. His only extant writing is a sermon on Luke 2 confronting clerical abuses.

Glossa ordinaria. This standard collection of biblical commentaries consists of interlinear and marginal notes drawn from patristic and Carolingian exegesis appended to the Vulgate*; later editions also include Nicholas of Lyra's* *Postilla*. The *Glossa ordinaria* and the Sentences of Peter Lombard (c. 1100–1160) were essential resources for all late medieval and early modern commentators.

Conrad Grebel (c. 1498–1526). Swiss Radical theologian. Grebel, considered the father of the Anabaptist movement, was one of the first defenders and performers of believers' baptism, for which he was eventually imprisoned in Zurich. One of Huldrych Zwingli's* early compatriots, Grebel advocated rapid, radical reform, clashing publicly with the civil authorities and Zwingli. Grebel's views, particularly on baptism, were influenced by Andreas Bodenstein von Karlstadt* and Thomas Müntzer.* Grebel advocated elimination of magisterial involvement in governing the church; instead, he envisioned the church as lay Christians determining their own affairs with strict adherence to the biblical text, and unified in volitional baptism.

William Greenhill (1591–1671). English Puritan pastor. Greenhill attended and worked at Magdalen College. He ministered in the diocese of Norwich but soon left for London, where he preached at Stepney. Greenhill was a member of the Westminster Assembly of Divines and was appointed the parliament chaplain by the children of Charles I. Oliver Cromwell included him among the preachers who helped draw up the Savoy Declaration. Greenhill was evicted from his post following the Restoration, after which he pastored independently. Among Greenhill's most significant contributions to church history was his *Exposition of the Prophet of Ezekiel.*

Catharina Regina von Greiffenberg (1633–1694). Austrian Lutheran poet. Upon her adulthood her guardian (and half uncle) sought to marry her; despite her protests of their consanguinity and her desire to remain celibate, she relented in 1664. After the deaths of her mother and husband, Greiffenberg abandoned her home to debtors and joined her friends Susanne Popp (d. 1683) and Sigmund von Birken (1626–1681) in Nuremberg. During her final years she dedicated herself to studying the biblical languages and to writing meditations on Jesus' death and resurrection, which she never completed. One of the most important and learned Austrian poets of the Baroque period, Greiffenberg published a collection of sonnets, songs and poems (1662) as well as three sets of mystical meditations on Jesus' life, suffering and death (1672; 1683; 1693). She participated in a society of poets called the Ister Gesellschaft.

Rudolf Gwalther (1519–1586). Swiss Reformed preacher. Gwalther was a consummate servant of the Reformed church in Zurich, its chief religious officer and preacher, a responsibility fulfilled previously by Huldrych Zwingli* and Heinrich Bullinger.* Gwalther provided sermons and commentaries and translated the works of Zwingli into Latin. He worked for many years alongside Bullinger in structuring and governing the church in Zurich. Gwalther also strove to strengthen the connections to the Reformed churches on the Continent and England: he was a participant in the Colloquy of Regensburg (1541) and an opponent of the Formula of Concord.*

Hans Has von Hallstatt (d. 1527). Austrian Reformed pastor. See *Kunstbuch.*

Henry Hammond (1605–1660). Anglican priest. After completing his studies at Oxford, Ham-mond was ordained in 1629. A Royalist, Hammond helped recruit soldiers for the king; he was chaplain to Charles I. During the king's captivity, Hammond was imprisoned for not submitting to Parliament. Later he was allowed to pastor again, until his death. Hammond published a catechism, numerous polemical sermons and treatises as well as his *Paraphrase and Annotations on the New Testament* (1653).

Peter Hausted (d. 1645). Anglican priest and playwright. Educated at Cambridge and Oxford, Hausted ministered in a number of parishes and preached adamantly and vehemently against Puritanism. He is best known for his play *The Rival Friends,* which is filled with invective against the Puritans; during a performance before the king and queen, a riot nearly broke out. Haustead died during the siege of Banbury Castle.

Heidelberg Catechism (1563). This German Reformed catechism was commissioned by the elector of the Palatinate, Frederick III (1515–1576) for pastors and teachers in his territories to use in instructing children and new believers in the faith. It was written by theologian Zacharias Ursinus (1534–1583) in consultation with Frederick's court preacher Kaspar Olevianus* and the entire theology faculty at the University of Heidelberg. The Heidelberg Catechism was accepted as one of the Dutch Reformed Church's Three Forms of Unity—along with the Belgic Confession* and the Canons of Dordrecht—at the Synod of Dordrecht,* and became widely popular among other Reformed confessional traditions throughout Europe.

Niels Hemmingsen (1513–1600). Danish Lutheran theologian. Hemmingsen studied at the University of Wittenberg, where he befriended Philipp Melanchthon.* In 1542, Hemmingsen returned to Denmark to pastor and to teach Greek, dialectics and theology at the University of Copenhagen. Foremost of the Danish theologians, Hemmingsen oversaw the preparation and publication of the first Danish Bible (1550). Later in his career he became embroiled in controversies because of his Philippist theology, especially regarding the Eucharist. Due to rising tensions with Lutheran nobles outside of Denmark, King Frederick II (1534–1588) dismissed Hemmingsen from his university post in 1579, transferring him to a prominent but less internationally visible Cathedral outside of Copenhagen. Hemmingsen was a prolific author, writing commentaries on the New Testament and Psalms, sermon collections and several methodological, theological and pastoral handbooks.

Tilemann Hesshus (1527–1588). German Lutheran theologian and pastor. Hesshus studied under Philipp Melanchthon* but was a staunch Gnesio-Lutheran. With great hesitation—and later regret—he affirmed the Formula of Concord.* Heshuss ardently advocated for church discipline, considering obedience a mark of the church. Unwilling to compromise his strong convictions, especially regarding matters of discipline, Hesshus was regularly embroiled in controversy. He was expelled or pressed to leave Goslar, Rostock, Heidelberg, Bremen, Magdeburg, Wesel, Königsberg and Samland before settling in Helmstedt, where he remained until his death. He wrote numerous polemical tracts concerning ecclesiology, justification, the sacraments and original sin, as well as commentaries on Psalms, Romans, 1–2 Corinthians, Galatians, Colossians and 1–2 Timothy, and a postil collection.

Christopher Hooke (unknown). English Puritan physician and pastor. Hooke published a treatise promoting the joys and blessings of childbirth (1590) and a sermon on Hebrews 12:11-12. To support the poor, Hooke proposed a bank funded by voluntary investment of wealthy households.

Richard Hooker (c. 1553–1600). Anglican priest. Shortly after graduating from Corpus Christi College Oxford, Hooker took holy orders as a priest in 1581. After his marriage, he struggled to find work and temporarily tended sheep until Archbishop John Whitgift* appointed him to the Temple Church in London. Hooker's primary work is *The Laws of Ecclesiastical Polity* (1593), in which he sought to establish a philosophical and logical foundation for the highly controversial Elizabethan Religious Settlement (1559). The Elizabethan Settlement, through the Act of Supremacy, reasserted the Church of England's independence from the Church of Rome, and, through the Act of Uniformity, constructed a common church structure based on the reinstitution of the Book of Common Prayer.* Hooker's argumentation strongly emphasizes natural law and anticipates the social contract theory of John Locke (1632–1704).

John Hooper (d. 1555). English Protestant bishop and martyr. Impressed by the works of Huldrych Zwingli* and Heinrich Bullinger,* Hooper joined the Protestant movement in England. However, after the Act of Six Articles was passed, he fled to Zurich, where he spent ten years. He returned to England in 1549 and was appointed as a bishop. He stoutly advocated a Zwinglian reform agenda, arguing against the use of vestments and for a less "popish" Book of Common Prayer.* Condemned as a heretic for denying transubstantiation, Hooper was burned at the stake during Mary I's reign.

Rudolf Hospinian (Wirth) (1547–1626). Swiss Reformed theologian and minister. After studying theology at Marburg and Heidelberg, Hospinian pastored in rural parishes around Zurich and taught secondary school. In 1588, he transferred to Zurich, ministering at Grossmünster and Fraumünster. A keen student of church history, Hospinian wanted to show the differences between early church doctrine and contemporary Catholic teaching, particularly with regard to sacramental theology. He also criticized Lutheran dogma and the Formula of Concord*. Most of Hospinian's corpus consists of polemical treatises; he also published a series of sermons on the Magnificat.

Caspar Huberinus (1500–1553). German Lutheran theologian and pastor. After studying theology at Wittenberg, Huberinus moved to Augsburg to serve as Urbanus Rhegius's* assistant. Huberinus represented Augsburg at the Bern Disputation (1528) on the Eucharist and images. In 1551, along with the nobility, Huberinus supported the Augsburg Interim, so long as communion of both kinds and regular preaching were allowed. Nevertheless the people viewed him as a traitor because of his official participation in the Interim, nicknaming him "Buberinus" (i.e., scoundrel). He wrote a number of popular devotional works as well as tracts defending Lutheran eucharistic theology against Zwinglian and Anabaptist detractions.

Balthasar Hubmaier (1480/5–1528). German Radical theologian. Hubmaier, a former priest who studied under Johann Eck,* is identified with his leadership in the peasants' uprising at Waldshut. Hubmaier served as the cathedral preacher in Regensberg, where he became involved in a series of anti-Semitic attacks. He was drawn to reform through the early works of Martin Luther*; his contact with Huldrych Zwingli* made Hubmaier a defender of more radical reform, including believers' baptism and a memorialist account of the Eucharist. His involvement in the Peasants' War led to his extradition and execution by the Austrians.

Aegidius Hunnius (1550–1603). German Lutheran theologian and preacher. Educated at Tübingen by Jakob Andreae (1528–1590) and Johannes Brenz,* Hunnius bolstered and advanced early Lutheran orthodoxy. After his crusade to root out all "crypto-Calvinism" divided Hesse into Lutheran and Reformed regions, Hunnius joined the Wittenberg theological faculty, where with Polykarp Leyser (1552–1610) he helped shape the university into an orthodox stronghold. Passionately confessional, Hunnius developed and nuanced the orthodox doctrines of predestination, Scripture, the church and Christology (more explicitly Chalcedonian), reflecting their codification in the Formula of Concord.* He was unafraid to engage in confessional polemics from the pulpit. In addition to his many treatises (most notably *De persona Christi*, in which he defended Christ's ubiquity), Hunnius published commentaries on Matthew, John, Ephesians and Colossians; his notes on Galatians, Philemon and 1 Corinthians were published posthumously.

Jan Hus (d. 1415). Bohemian reformer and martyr. This popular preacher strove for reform in the church, moral improvement in society, and an end to clerical abuses and popular religious superstition. He was branded a heretic for his alleged affinity for John Wycliffe's writings; however, while he agreed that a priest in mortal sin rendered the sacraments inefficacious, he affirmed the doctrine of transubstantiation. The Council of Constance* convicted Hus of heresy, banned his books and teaching, and, despite a letter of safe conduct, burned him at the stake.

Hans Hut (1490–1527). German Radical leader. Hut was an early leader of a mystical, apocalyptic strand of Anabaptist radical reform. His theological views were shaped by Andreas Bodenstein von Karlstadt,* Thomas Müntzer* and Hans Denck,* by whom Hut had been baptized. Hut rejected society and the established church and heralded the imminent end of days, which he perceived in the Peasants' War. Eventually arrested for practicing believers' baptism and participating in the Peasants' War, Hut was tortured and died accidentally in a fire in the Augsburg prison. The next day, the authorities sentenced his corpse to death and burned him.

George Hutcheson (1615–1674). Scottish Puritan pastor. Hutcheson, a pastor in Edinburgh, published commentaries on Job, John and the Minor Prophets, as well as sermons on Psalm 130.

Roger Hutchinson (d. 1555). English reformer. Little is known about Hutchinson except for his controversies. He disputed against the Mass while at Cambridge and debated with Joan Bocher (d. 1550), who affirmed the doctrine of the celestial flesh. During the Marian Restoration he was deprived of his fellowship at Eton because he was married.

Abraham Ibn Ezra (1089–c. 1167). Spanish Jewish rabbi, exegete and poet. In 1140 Ibn Ezra fled his native Spain to escape persecution by the Almohad Caliphate. He spent the rest of his life as an exile, traveling through Europe, North Africa and the Middle East. His corpus consists of works on poetry, exegesis, grammar, philosophy, mathematics and astrology. In his commentaries on the Old Testament, Ibn Ezra restricts himself to *peshat* (see *quadriga*).

Valentin Ickelshamer (c. 1500–1547). German Radical teacher. After time at Erfurt, he studied under Luther,* Melanchthon,* Bugenhagen* and Karlstadt* in Wittenberg. He sided with Karlstadt against Luther, writing a treatise in Karlstadt's defense. Ickelshamer also represented the Wittenberg guilds in opposition to the city council. This guild committee allied with the peasants in 1525, leading to Ickelshamer's eventual exile. His poem in the Marpeck Circle's *Kunstbuch** is an expansion of a similar poem by Sebastian Franck.*

Thomas Jackson (1579–1640). Anglican theologian and priest. Before serving as the president of Corpus Christi College at Oxford for the final decade of his life, Jackson was a parish priest and chaplain to the king. His best known work is a twelve-volume commentary on the Apostles' Creed.

King James I of England (VI of Scotland) (1566–1625). English monarch. The son of Mary, Queen of Scots, James ascended to the Scottish throne in 1567 following his mother's abdication. In the Union of the Crowns (1603), he took the English and Irish thrones after the death of his cousin, Elizabeth I. James's reign was tumultuous and tense: Parliament and the nobility often opposed him, church factions squabbled over worship forms and ecclesiology, climaxing in the Gunpowder Plot. James wrote treatises on the divine right of kings, law, the evils of smoking tobacco and demonology. His religious writings include a versification of the Psalms, a paraphrase of Revelation and meditations on the Lord's Prayer and passages from Chronicles, Matthew and Revelation. He also sponsored the translation of the Authorized Version*—popularly remembered as the King James Version.

John Jewel (1522–1571). Anglican theologian and bishop. Jewel studied at Oxford where he met Peter Martyr Vermigli.* After graduating in 1552, Jewel was appointed to his first vicarage and became the orator for the university. Upon Mary I's accession, Jewel lost his post as orator because of his Protestant views. After the trials of Thomas Cranmer* and Nicholas Ridley,* Jewel affirmed Catholic teaching to avoid their fate. Still he had to flee to the continent.

Confronted by John Knox,* Jewel publicly repented of his cowardice before the English congregation in Frankfurt, then reunited with Vermigli in Strasbourg. After Mary I's death, Jewel returned to England and was consecrated bishop in 1560. He advocated low-church ecclesiology, but supported the Elizabethan Settlement against Catholics and Puritans. In response to the Council of Trent, he published the *Apoligia ecclesiae Anglicanae* (1562), which established him as the apostle for Anglicanism and incited numerous controversies.

Justus Jonas (1493–1555). German Lutheran theologian, pastor and administrator. Jonas studied law at Erfurt, where he befriended the poet Eobanus Hessus (1488–1540), whom Luther* dubbed "king of the poets"; later, under the influence of the humanist Konrad Muth, Jonas focused on theology. In 1516 he was ordained as a priest, and in 1518 he became a doctor of theology and law. After witnessing the Leipzig Disputation, Jonas was converted to Luther's* cause. While traveling with Luther to the Diet of Worms, Jonas was appointed professor of canon law at Wittenberg. Later he became its dean of theology, lecturing on Romans, Acts and the Psalms. Jonas was also instrumental for reform in Halle. He preached Luther's funeral sermon but had a falling-out with Melanchthon* over the Leipzig Interim. Jonas's most influential contribution was translating Luther's *The Bondage of the Will* and Melanchthon's *Loci communes* into German.

David Joris (c. 1501–1556). Dutch Radical pastor and hymnist. This former glass painter was one of the leading Dutch Anabaptist leaders after the fall of Münster (1535), although due to his increasingly radical ideas his influence waned in the early 1540s. Joris came to see himself as a "third David," a Spirit-anointed prophet ordained to proclaim the coming third kingdom of God, which would be established in the Netherlands with Dutch as its *lingua franca.* Joris's interpretation of Scripture, with his heavy emphasis on personal mystical experience, led to a very public dispute with Menno Simons* whom Joris considered a teacher of the "dead letter." In 1544 Joris and about one hundred followers moved to Basel, conforming outwardly to the teaching of the Reformed church there. Today 240 of Joris's books are extant, the most important of which is his *Twonder Boek* (1542/43).

Andreas Bodenstein von Karlstadt (Carlstadt) (1486–1541). German Radical theologian. Karlstadt, an early associate of Martin Luther* and Philipp Melanchthon* at the University of Wittenberg, participated alongside Luther in the dispute at Leipzig with Johann Eck.* He also influenced the configuration of the Old Testament canon in Protestantism. During Luther's captivity in Wartburg Castle in Eisenach, Karlstadt oversaw reform in Wittenberg. His acceleration of the pace of reform brought conflict with Luther, so Karlstadt left Wittenberg, eventually settling at the University of Basel as professor of Old Testament (after a sojourn in Zurich with Huldrych Zwingli*). During his time in Switzerland, Karlstadt opposed infant baptism and repudiated Luther's doctrine of Christ's real presence in the Eucharist.

Edward Kellett (d. 1641). Anglican theologian and priest. Kellett published a sermon concerning the reconversion of an Englishman from Islam, a tract on the soul and a discourse on the Lord's Supper in connection with Passover.

David Kimchi (**Radak**) (1160–1235). French Jewish rabbi, exegete and philosopher. Kimchi wrote an important Hebrew grammar and dictionary, as well as commentaries on Genesis, 1–2 Chronicles, the Psalms and the Prophets. He focused on *peshat* (see *quadriga*). In his Psalms commentary he attacks Christian interpretation as forced, irrational and inadmissible. While Sebastian Münster* censors and condemns these arguments in his *Miqdaš YHWH* (1534–1535), he and many other Christian commentators valued Kimchi's work as a grammatical resource.

Moses Kimchi (**Remak**) (1127–1190). French Jewish rabbi and exegete. He was David Kimchi's* brother. He wrote commentaries on Proverbs and Ezra-Nehemiah. Sebastian Münster* translated Kimchi's concise Hebrew grammar into Latin; many sixteenth-century Christian exegetes used this resource.

John Knox (1513–1572). Scottish Reformed preacher. Knox, a fiery preacher to monarchs and zealous defender of high Calvinism, was a leading figure of reform in Scotland. Following imprisonment in the French galleys, Knox went to England, where he became a royal chaplain to Edward VI. At the accession of Mary, Knox fled to Geneva, studying under John Calvin* and serving as a pastor. Knox returned to Scotland after Mary's death and became a chief architect of the reform of the Scottish church (Presbyterian), serving as one of the authors of the Book of Discipline and writing many pamphlets and sermons.

Antonius Broickwy von Königstein (1470–1541). German Catholic preacher. Very little is known about this important cathedral preacher in Cologne. Strongly opposed to evangelicals, he sought to develop robust resources for Catholic homilies. His postils were bestsellers, and his biblical concordance helped Catholic preachers to construct doctrinal loci from Scripture itself.

Kunstbuch. In 1956, two German students rediscovered this unique collection of Anabaptist works. Four hundred years earlier, a friend of the recently deceased Pilgram Marpeck*—the painter Jörg Probst—had entrusted this collection of letters, tracts and poetry to a Zurich bindery; today only half of it remains. Probst's redaction arranges various compositions from the Marpeck Circle into a devotional anthology focused on the theme of the church as Christ incarnate (cf. Gal 2:20).

Osmund Lake (c. 1543–1621). English Pastor who ministered at Ringwood in Hampshire.

François Lambert (Lambert of Avignon) (1487–1530). French Reformed theologian. In 1522, after becoming drawn to the writings of Martin Luther* and meeting Huldrych Zwingli,* Lambert left the Franciscan order. He spent time in Wittenberg, Strasbourg, and Hesse, where Lambert took a leading role at the Homberg Synod (1526) and in creating a biblically based plan for church reform. He served as professor of theology at Marburg University from 1527 to his death. After the

Marburg Colloquy (1529), Lambert accepted Zwingli's symbolic view of the Eucharist. Lambert produced nineteen books, mostly biblical commentaries that favored spiritual interpretations; his unfinished work of comprehensive theology was published posthumously.

Hugh Latimer (c. 1485–1555). Anglican bishop and preacher. Latimer was celebrated for his sermons critiquing the idolatrous nature of Catholic practices and the social injustices visited on the underclass by the aristocracy and the individualism of Protestant government. After his support for Henry's petition of divorce he served as a court preacher under Henry VIII and Edward VI. Latimer became a proponent of reform following his education at Cambridge University and received license as a preacher. Following Edward's death, Latimer was tried for heresy, perishing at the stake with Nicholas Ridley* and Thomas Cranmer.*

William Laud (1573–1645). Anglican archbishop, one of the most pivotal and controversial figures in Anglican church history. Early in his career, Laud offended many with his highly traditional, anti-Puritan approach to ecclesial policies. After his election as Archbishop of Canterbury in 1633, Laud continued to strive against the Puritans, demanding the eastward placement of the Communion altar (affirming the religious centrality of the Eucharist), the use of clerical garments, the reintroduction of stained-glass windows, and the uniform use of the Book of Common Prayer.* Laud was accused of being a crypto-Catholic—an ominous accusation during the protracted threat of invasion by the Spanish Armada. In 1640 the Long Parliament met, quickly impeached Laud on charges of treason, and placed him in jail for several years before his execution.

Ludwig Lavater (1527–1586). Swiss Reformed pastor and theologian. Under his father-in-law Heinrich Bullinger,* Lavater became an archdeacon in Zurich. In 1585 he succeeded Rudolf Gwalther* as the city's Antistes. He authored a widely disseminated book on demonology, commentaries on Chronicles, Proverbs, Ecclesiastes, Nehemiah and Ezekiel, theological works, and biographies of Bullinger and Konrad Pellikan.*

John Lawson (unknown). Seventeenth-century English Puritan. Lawson wrote *Gleanings and Expositions of Some of Scripture* (1646) and a treatise on the sabbath in the New Testament.

Jacques Lefèvre d'Étaples (Faber Stapulensis) (1460?–1536). French Catholic humanist, publisher and translator. Lefèvre d'Étaples studied classical literature and philosophy, as well as patristic and medieval mysticism. He advocated the principle of *ad fontes*, issuing a full-scale annotation on the corpus of Aristotle, publishing the writings of key Christian mystics, and contributing to efforts at biblical translation and commentary. Although he never broke with the Catholic Church, his views prefigured those of Martin Luther,* for which he was condemned by the University of Sorbonne in Paris. He then found refuge in the court of Marguerite d'Angoulême, where he met John Calvin* and Martin Bucer.*

Edward Leigh (1602–1671). English Puritan biblical critic, historian and politician. Educated at Oxford, Leigh's public career included appointments as a Justice of the Peace, an officer in the parliamentary army during the English Civil Wars and a member of Parliament. Although never ordained, Leigh devoted himself to the study of theology and Scripture; he participated in the Westminster Assembly. Leigh published a diverse corpus, including lexicons of Greek, Hebrew and juristic terms, and histories of Roman, Greek and English rulers. His most important theological work is *A Systeme or Body of Divinity* (1662).

John Lightfoot (1602–1675). Anglican priest and biblical scholar. After graduating from Cambridge, Lightfoot was ordained and pastored at several small parishes. He continued to study classics under the support of the politician Rowland Cotton (1581–1634). Siding with the Parliamentarians during the English Civil Wars, Lightfoot relocated to London in 1643. He was one of the original members of the Westminster Assembly, where he defended a moderate Presbyterianism.

His best-known work is the six-volume *Horae Hebraicae et Talmudicae* (1658–1677), a verse-by-verse commentary illumined by Hebrew customs, language and the Jewish interpretive tradition.

Lucas Lossius (1508–1582). German Lutheran teacher and musician. While a student at Leipzig and Wittenberg, Lossius was deeply influenced by Melanchthon* and Luther,* who found work for him as Urbanus Rhegius's* secretary. Soon after going to work for Rhegius, Lossius began teaching at a local gymnasium (or secondary school), *Das Johanneum*, eventually becoming its headmaster. Lossius remained at *Das Johanneum* until his death, even turning down appointments to university professorships. A man of varied interests, he wrote on dialectics, music and church history, as well as publishing a postil and a five-volume set of annotations on the New Testament.

Sibrandus Lubbertus (c. 1555–1625). Dutch Reformed theologian. Lubbertis, a key figure in the establishment of orthodox Calvinism in Frisia, studied theology at Wittenburg and Geneva (under Theodore Beza*) before his appointment as professor of theology at the University of Franeker. Throughout his career, Lubbertis advocated for high Calvinist theology, defending it in disputes with representatives of Socinianism, Arminianism and Roman Catholicism. Lubbertis criticized the Catholic theologian Robert Bellarmine and fellow Dutch reformer Jacobus Arminius*; the views of the latter he opposed as a prominent participant in the Synod of Dordrecht.*

Martin Luther (1483–1546). German Lutheran priest, professor and theologian. While a professor in Wittenberg, Luther reinterpreted the doctrine of justification. Convinced that righteousness comes only from God's grace, he disputed the sale of indulgences with the Ninety-five Theses. Luther's positions brought conflict with Rome; his denial of papal authority led to excommunication. He also challenged the Mass, transubstantiation and communion under one kind. Though Luther was condemned by the Diet of Worms, the Elector of Saxony provided him safe haven. Luther returned to Wittenberg with public order collaps-

ing under Andreas Bodenstein von Karlstadt;* Luther steered a more cautious path of reform. His rendering of the Bible and liturgy in the vernacular, as well as his hymns and sermons, proved extensively influential.

Georg Major (1502–1574). German Lutheran theologian. Major was on the theological faculty of the University of Wittenberg, succeeding as dean Johannes Bugenhagen* and Philipp Melanchthon.* One of the chief editors on the Wittenberg edition of Luther's works, Major is most identified with the controversy bearing his name, in which he stated that good works are necessary to salvation. Major qualified his statement, which was in reference to the totality of the Christian life. The Formula of Concord* rejected the statement, ending the controversy. As a theologian, Major further refined Lutheran views of the inspiration of Scripture and the doctrine of the Trinity.

John (Mair) Major (1467–1550). Scottish Catholic philosopher. Major taught logic and theology at the universities of Paris (his alma mater), Glasgow and St Andrews. His broad interests and impressive work drew students from all over Europe. While disapproving of evangelicals (though he did teach John Knox*), Major advocated reform programs for Rome. He supported collegial episcopacy and even challenged the curia's teaching on sexuality. Still he was a nominalist who was critical of humanist approaches to biblical exegesis. His best-known publication is *A History of Greater Britain, Both England and Scotland* (1521), which promoted the union of the kingdoms. He also published a commentary on Peter Lombard's *Sentences* and the Gospel of John.

Juan de Maldonado (1533–1583). Spanish Catholic biblical scholar. A student of Francisco de Toledo,* Maldonado taught philosophy and theology at the universities of Paris and Salamanca. Ordained to the priesthood in Rome, he revised the Septuagint under papal appointment. While Maldonado vehemently criticized Protestants, he asserted that Reformed baptism was valid and that mixed confessional marriages were acceptable. His views on Mary's immaculate conception proved controversial among many Catholics who conflated his statement that it was not an article of faith with its denial. He was intrigued by demonology (blaming demonic influence for the Reformation). All his work was published posthumously; his Gospel commentaries were highly valued and important.

Thomas Manton (1620–1677). English Puritan minister. Manton, educated at Oxford, served for a time as lecturer at Westminster Abbey and rector of St. Paul's, Covent Garden, and was a strong advocate of Presbyterianism. He was known as a rigorous evangelical Calvinist who preached long expository sermons. At different times in his ecclesial career he worked side-by-side with Richard Baxter* and John Owen.* In his later life, Manton's Nonconformist position led to his ejection as a clergyman from the Church of England (1662) and eventual imprisonment (1670). Although a voluminous writer, Manton was best known for his preaching. At his funeral in 1677, he was dubbed "the king of preachers."

Augustin Marlorat (c. 1506–1562). French Reformed pastor. Committed by his family to a monastery at the age of eight, Marlorat was also ordained into the priesthood at an early age in 1524. He fled to Geneva in 1535, where he pastored until the Genevan Company of Pastors sent him to France to shepherd the nascent evangelical congregations. His petition to the young Charles IX (1550–1574) for the right to public evangelical worship was denied. In response to a massacre of evangelicals in Vassy (over sixty dead, many more wounded), Marlorat's congregation planned to overtake Rouen. After the crown captured Rouen, Marlorat was arrested and executed three days later for treason. His principle published work was an anthology of New Testament comment modeled after Thomas Aquinas's *Catena aurea in quatuor Evangelia.* Marlorat harmonized Reformed and Lutheran comment with the church fathers, interspersed with his own brief comments. He also wrote such anthologies for Genesis, Job, the Psalms, Song of Songs and Isaiah.

Pilgram Marpeck (c. 1495–1556). Austrian Radical elder and theologian. During a brief sojourn in Strasbourg, Marpeck debated with Martin Bucer* before the city council; Bucer was declared the winner, and Marpeck was asked to leave Strasbourg for his views concerning paedobaptism (which he compared to a sacrifice to Moloch). After his time in Strasbourg, Marpeck traveled throughout southern Germany and western Austria, planting Anabaptist congregations. Marpeck criticized the strict use of the ban, however, particularly among the Swiss brethren. He also engaged in a christological controversy with Kaspar von Schwenckfeld.*

Johannes Mathesius (1504–1565). German Lutheran theologian and pastor. After reading Martin Luther's* *On Good Works*, Mathesius left his teaching post in Ingolstadt and traveled to Wittenberg to study theology. Mathesius was an important agent of reform in the Bohemian town of Jáchymov, where he pastored, preached and taught. Over one thousand of Mathesius's sermons are extant, including numerous wedding and funeral sermons as well as a series on Luther's life. Mathesius also transcribed portions of Luther's Table Talk.

John Mayer (1583–1664). Anglican priest and biblical exegete. Mayer dedicated much of his life to biblical exegesis, writing a seven-volume commentary on the entire Bible (1627–1653). Styled after Philipp Melanchthon's* *locus* method, Mayer's work avoided running commentary, focusing instead on textual and theological problems. He was a parish priest for fifty-five years. In the office of priest Mayer also wrote a popular catechism, *The English Catechisme, or a Commentarie on the Short Catechisme* (1621), which went through twelve editions in his lifetime.

Joseph Mede (1586–1638). Anglican biblical scholar, Hebraist and Greek lecturer. A man of encyclopedic knowledge, Mede was interested in numerous fields, varying from philology and history to mathematics and physics, although millennial thought and apocalyptic prophesy were clearly his chief interests. Mede's most important work was his *Clavis Apocalyptica* (1627, later translated into English as *The Key of the Revelation*). This work examined the structure of Revelation as the key to its interpretation. Mede saw the visions as a connected and chronological sequence hinging around Revelation 17:18. He is remembered as an important figure in the history of millenarian theology. He was respected as a mild-mannered and generous scholar who avoided controversy and debate, but who had many original thoughts.

Philipp Melanchthon (1497–1560). German Lutheran educator, reformer and theologian. Melanchthon is known as the partner and successor to Martin Luther* in reform in Germany and for his pioneering *Loci communes*, which served as a theological textbook. Melanchthon participated with Luther in the Leipzig disputation, helped implement reform in Wittenberg and was a chief architect of the Augsburg Confession.* Later, Melanchthon and Martin Bucer* worked for union between the reformed and Catholic churches. On account of Melanchthon's more ecumenical disposition and his modification of several of Luther's doctrines, he was held in suspicion by some.

Justus Menius (1499–1558). German Lutheran pastor and theologian. Menius was a prominent reformer in Thuringia. He participated in the Marburg Colloquy and, with others, helped Martin Luther* compose the Schmalkald Articles.* Throughout his career Menius entered into numerous controversies with Anabaptists and even fellow Lutherans. He rejected Andreas Osiander's (d. 1552) doctrine of justification—that the indwelling of Christ's divine nature justifies, rather than the imputed alien righteousness of Christ's person, declared through God's mercy. Against Nikolaus von Amsdorf (1483–1565) and Matthias Flacius (1520–1575), Menius agreed with Georg Major* that good works are necessary to salvation. Osiander's view of justification was censored in Article 3 of the Formula of Concord*; Menius's understanding of the relationship

between good works and salvation was rejected in Article 4. Menius translated many of Luther's Latin works into German. He also composed a handbook for Christian households and an influential commentary on 1 Samuel.

Johannes Mercerus (Jean Mercier) (d. 1570). French Hebraist. Mercerus studied under the first Hebrew chair at the Collège Royal de Paris, François Vatable (d. 1547), whom he succeeded in 1546. John Calvin* tried to recruit Mercerus to the Genevan Academy as professor of Hebrew, once in 1558 and again in 1563; he refused both times. During his lifetime Mercerus published grammatical helps for Hebrew and Chaldean, an aid to the Masoretic symbols in the Hebrew text, and translated the commentaries and grammars of several medieval rabbis. He himself wrote commentaries on Genesis, the wisdom books, and most of the Minor Prophets. These commentaries—most of them only published after his death—were philologically focused and interacted with the work of Jerome, Nicholas of Lyra,* notable rabbis and Johannes Oecolampadius.*

Ambrose Moibanus (1494–1554). German Lutheran bishop and theologian. Moibanus helped reform the church of Breslau (modern Wrocław, Poland). He revised the Mass, bolstered pastoral care and welfare for the poor, and wrote a new evangelical catechism.

Thomas More (1478–1535). English Catholic lawyer, politician, humanist and martyr. More briefly studied at Oxford, but completed his legal studies in London. After contemplating the priesthood for four years, he opted for politics and was elected a member of Parliament in 1504. A devout Catholic, More worked with church leaders in England to root out heresy while he also confronted Lutheran teachings in writing. After four years as Lord Chancellor, More resigned due to heightened tensions with Henry VIII over papal supremacy (which More supported and Henry did not). Tensions did not abate. More's steadfast refusal to accept the Act of Supremacy (1534)—which declared the King of England to be the supreme ecclesial primate not the pope—resulted in his arrest and trial for high treason. He was found guilty and beheaded with John Fisher (1469–1535). Friends with John Colet* and Desiderius Erasmus,* More was a widely respected humanist in England as well as on the continent. Well-known for his novel *Utopia* (1516), More also penned several religious treatises on Christ's passion and suffering during his imprisonment in the Tower of London, which were published posthumously.

Sebastian Münster (1488–1552). German Reformed Hebraist, exegete, printer, and geographer. After converting to the Reformation in 1524, Münster taught Hebrew at the universities of Heidelberg and Basel. During his lengthy tenure in Basel he published more than seventy books, including Hebrew dictionaries and rabbinic commentaries. He also produced an evangelistic work for Jews titled *Vikuach* (1539). Münster's *Torat ha-Maschiach* (1537), the Gospel of Matthew, was the first published Hebrew translation of any portion of the New Testament. Despite his massive contribution to contemporary understanding of the Hebrew language, Münster was criticized by many of the reformers as a Judaizer.

Thomas Müntzer (c. 1489–1525). German Radical preacher. As a preacher in the town of Zwickau, Müntzer was influenced by German mysticism and, growing convinced that Martin Luther* had not carried through reform properly, sought to restore the pure apostolic church of the New Testament. Müntzer's radical ideas led to expulsions from various cities; he developed a highly apocalyptic theology, in which he heralded the last days that would establish the pure community out of suffering, prompting Müntzer's proactive role in the Peasants' War, which he perceived as a crucial apocalyptic event. Six thousand of Müntzer's followers were annihilated by magisterial troops; Müntzer was executed.

John Murcot (1625–1654). English Puritan pastor. After completing his bachelor's at Oxford in 1647, Murcot was ordained as a pastor, transferring to several parishes until in 1651 he moved to Dublin. All his works were published posthumously.

Simon Musaeus (1521–1582). German Lutheran theologian. After studying at the universities of Frankfurt an der Oder and Wittenberg, Musaeus began teaching Greek at the Cathedral school in Nuremberg and was ordained. Having returned to Wittenberg to complete a doctoral degree, Musaeus spent the rest of his career in numerous ecclesial and academic administrative posts. He opposed Matthias Flacius's (1505–1575) view of original sin—that the formal essence of human beings is marred by original sin—even calling the pro-Flacian faculty at Wittenberg "the devil's latrine." Musaeus published a disputation on original sin and a postil.

Wolfgang Musculus (1497–1563). German Reformed pastor and theologian. Musculus produced translations, biblical commentaries and an influential theological text, *Loci communes Sacrae Theologiae* (*Commonplaces of Sacred Theology*), outlining a Zwinglian theology. Musculus began to study theology while at a Benedictine monastery; he departed in 1527 and became secretary to Martin Bucer* in Strasbourg. He was later installed as a pastor in Augsburg, eventually performing the first evangelical liturgy in the city's cathedral. Displaced by the Augsburg Interim, Musculus ended his career as professor of theology at Bern. Though Musculus was active in the pursuit of the reform agenda, he was also concerned for ecumenism, participating in the Wittenberg Concord (1536) and discussions between Lutherans and Catholics.

Friedrich Nausea (c. 1496–1552). German Catholic bishop and preacher. After completing his studies at Leipzig, this famed preacher was appointed priest in Frankfurt but was run out of town by his congregants during his first sermon. He transferred to Mainz as cathedral preacher. Nausea was well connected through the German papal hierarchy and traveled widely to preach to influential ecclesial and secular courts. Court preacher for Ferdinand I (1503–1564), his reform tendencies fit well with royal Austrian theological leanings, and he was enthroned as the bishop of Vienna. Nausea thought that rather than endless colloquies only a council could settle reform. Unfortunately he could not participate in the first session of Trent due to insufficient funding, but he arrived for the second session. Nausea defended the laity's reception of the cup and stressed the importance of promulgating official Catholic teaching in the vernacular.

Melchior Neukirch (1540–1597). German Lutheran pastor and playwright. Neukirch's pastoral career spanned more than thirty years in several northern German parishes. Neukirch published a history of the Braunschweig church since the Reformation and a dramatization of Acts 4–7. He died of the plague.

Nicholas of Lyra (1270–1349). French Catholic biblical exegete. Very little is known about this influential medieval theologian of the Sorbonne aside from the works he published, particularly the *Postilla litteralis super totam Bibliam* (1322–1333). With the advent of the printing press this work was regularly published alongside the Latin Vulgate and the *Glossa ordinaria*. In this running commentary on the Bible Nicholas promoted literal interpretation as the basis for theology. Despite his preference for literal interpretation, Nicholas also published a companion volume, the *Postilla moralis super totam Bibliam* (1339), a commentary on the spiritual meaning of the biblical text. Nicholas was a major conversation partner for many reformers though many of them rejected his exegesis as too literal and too "Jewish" (not concerned enough with the Bible's fulfillment in Jesus Christ).

Johannes Oecolampadius (Johannes Huszgen) (1482–1531). Swiss-German Reformed humanist, reformer and theologian. Oecolampadius (an assumed name meaning "house light") assisted with Desiderius Erasmus's* Greek New Testament, lectured on biblical languages and exegesis and completed an influential Greek grammar. After joining the evangelical cause through studying patristics and the work of Martin Luther,* Oecolampadius went to Basel, where he lectured on biblical exegesis and participated in ecclesial reform. On account of Oecolampadius's

effort, the city council passed legislation restricting preaching to the gospel and releasing the city from compulsory Mass. Oecolampadius was a chief ally of Huldrych Zwingli,* whom he supported at the Marburg Colloquy (1529).

Kaspar Olevianus (1536–1587). German Reformed theologian. Olevianus is celebrated for composing the Heidelberg Catechism and producing a critical edition of Calvin's *Institutes* in German. Olevianus studied theology with many, including John Calvin,* Theodore Beza,* Heinrich Bullinger* and Peter Martyr Vermigli.* As an advocate of Reformed doctrine, Olevianus oversaw the shift from Lutheranism to Calvinism throughout Heidelberg, organizing the city's churches after Calvin's Geneva. The Calvinist ecclesial vision of Olevianus entangled him in a dispute with another Heidelberg reformer over the rights of ecclesiastical discipline, which Olevianus felt belonged to the council of clergy and elders rather than civil magistrates.

Josua Opitz (c. 1542–1585). German Lutheran pastor. After a brief stint as superintendent in Regensburg, Opitz, a longtime preacher, was dismissed for his support of Matthias Flacius's (1520–1575) view of original sin. (Using Aristotelian categories, Flacius argued that the formal essence of human beings is marred by original sin, forming sinners into the image of Satan; his views were officially rejected in Article 1 of the Formula of Concord.*) Hans Wilhelm Roggendorf (1533–1591) invited Opitz to lower Austria as part of his Lutheranizing program. Unfortunately Roggendorf and Opitz never succeed in getting Lutheranism legal recognition, perhaps in large part due to Opitz's staunch criticism of Catholics, which resulted in his exile. He died of plague.

Lucas Osiander (1534–1604). German Lutheran pastor. For three decades, Osiander— son of the controversial Nuremberg reformer Andreas Osiander (d. 1552)—served as pastor and court preacher in Stuttgart, until he fell out of favor with the duke in 1598. Osiander produced numerous theological and exegetical works, as well as an influential hymnal.

John Owen (1616–1683). English Puritan theologian. Owen trained at Oxford University, where he was later appointed dean of Christ Church and vice chancellor of the university, following his service as chaplain to Oliver Cromwell. Although Owen began his career as a Presbyterian minister, he eventually departed to the party of Independents. Owen composed many sermons, biblical commentaries (including seven volumes on the book of Hebrews), theological treatises and controversial monographs (including disputations with Arminians, Anglicans, Catholics and Socinians).

Santes Pagninus (c. 1470–1541). Italian Catholic biblical scholar. Pagninus studied under Girolamo Savonarola* and later taught in Rome, Avignon and Lyons. He translated the Old Testament into Latin according to a tight, almost wooden, adherence to the Hebrew. This translation and his Hebrew lexicon *Thesaurus linguae sanctae* (1529) were important resources for translators and commentators.

Paul of Burgos (**Solomon ha-Levi**) (c. 1351–1435). Spanish Catholic archbishop. In 1391 Solomon ha-Levi, a rabbi and Talmudic scholar, converted to Christianity, receiving baptism with his entire family (except for his wife). He changed his name to Paul de Santa Maria. Some have suggested that he converted to avoid persecution; he himself stated that Thomas Aquinas's (1225–1274) work persuaded him of the truth of Christian faith. After studying theology in Paris, he was ordained bishop in 1403. He actively and ardently persecuted Jews, trying to compel them to convert. In order to convince Jews that Christians correctly interpret the Hebrew Scriptures, Paul wrote *Dialogus Pauli et Sauli contra Judaeos, sive Scrutinium Scripturarum* (1434), a book filled with vile language toward the Jews. He also wrote a series of controversial marginal notes and comments on Nicholas of Lyra's* *Postilla*, many of which criticized Nicholas's use of Jewish scholarship.

Christoph Pelargus (1565–1633). German Lutheran pastor, theologian, professor and superintendent. Pelargus studied philosophy and theology at the University of Frankfurt an der Oder, in Brandenburg. This irenic Philippist was appointed as the superintendent of Brandenburg and later became a pastor in Frankfurt, although the local authorities first required him to condemn Calvinist theology, because several years earlier he had been called before the consistory in Berlin under suspicion of being a crypto-Calvinist. Among his most important works were a four-volume commentary on *De orthodoxa fide* by John of Damascus (d. 749), a treatise defending the breaking of the bread during communion, and a volume of funeral sermons. He also published commentaries on the Pentateuch, the Psalms, Matthew, John and Acts.

Konrad Pellikan (1478–1556). German Reformed Hebraist and theologian. Pellikan attended the University of Heidelberg, where he mastered Hebrew under Johannes Reuchlin. In 1504 Pellikan published one of the first Hebrew grammars that was not merely a translation of the work of medieval rabbis. While living in Basel, Pellikan assisted the printer Johannes Amerbach, with whom he published some of Luther's* early writings. He also worked with Sebastian Münster* and Wolfgang Capito* on a Hebrew Psalter (1516). In 1526, after teaching theology for three years at the University of Basel, Huldrych Zwingli* brought Pellikan to Zurich to chair the faculty of Old Testament. Pellikan's magnum opus is a seven-volume commentary on the entire Bible (except Revelation) and the Apocrypha; it is often heavily dependent upon the work of others (esp. Desiderius Erasmus* and Johannes Oecolampadius*).

Benedict Pererius (1535–1610). Spanish Catholic theologian, philosopher and exegete. Pererius entered the Society of Jesus in 1552. He taught philosophy, theology, and exegesis at the Roman College of the Jesuits. Early in his career he warned against neo-Platonism and astrology in his *De principiis* (1576). Pererius wrote a lengthy commentary on Daniel, and five volumes of exegetical theses on Exodus, Romans, Revelation and part of the Gospel of John (chs. 1–14). His four-volume commentary on Genesis (1591–1599) was lauded by Protestants and Catholics alike.

William Perkins (1558–1602). English Puritan preacher and theologian. Perkins was a highly regarded Puritan Presbyterian preacher and biblical commentator in the Elizabethan era. He studied at Cambridge University and later became a fellow of Christ's Church college as a preacher and professor, receiving acclaim for his sermons and lectures. Even more, Perkins gained an esteemed reputation for his ardent exposition of Calvinist reformed doctrine in the style of Petrus Ramus,* becoming one of the first English reformed theologians to achieve international recognition. Perkins influenced the federal Calvinist shape of Puritan theology and the vision of logical, practical expository preaching.

François Perrault (1577–1657). French Reformed pastor for over fifty years. His book on demonology was prominent, perhaps because of the intrigue at his home in 1612. According to his account, a poltergeist made a commotion and argued points of theology; a few months later Perrault's parishioners slew a large snake slithering out of his house.

Dirk Philips (1504–1568). Dutch Radical elder and theologian. This former Franciscan monk, known for being severe and obstinate, was a leading theologian of the sixteenth-century Anabaptist movement. Despite the fame of Menno Simons* and his own older brother Obbe, Philips wielded great influence over Anabaptists in the Netherlands and northern Germany where he ministered. As a result of Philips's understanding of the apostolic church as radically separated from the children of the world, he advocated a very strict interpretation of the ban, including formal shunning. His writings were collected and published near the end of his life as *Enchiridion oft Hantboecxken van de Christelijcke Leere* (1564).

Johannes Piscator (1546–1625). German Reformed theologian. Educated at Tübingen (though he wanted to study at Wittenberg), Piscator taught at the universities of Strasbourg and Heidelberg, as well as academies in Neustadt and Herborn. His commentaries on both the Old and New Testaments involve a tripartite analysis of a given passage's argument, of scholia on the text and of doctrinal loci. Some consider Piscator's method to be a full flowering of Beza's* "logical" scriptural analysis, focused on the text's meaning and its relationship to the pericopes around it.

Felix Pratensis (d. 1539). Italian Catholic Hebraist. Pratensis, the son of a rabbi, converted to Christianity and entered the Augustinian Hermits around the turn of the sixteenth century. In 1515, with papal permission, Pratensis published a new translation of the Psalms based on the Hebrew text. His *Biblia Rabbinica* (1517–1518), printed in Jewish and Christian editions, included text-critical notes in the margins as well as the Targum and rabbinic commentaries on each book (e.g., Rashi* on the Pentateuch and David Kimchi* on the Prophets). Many of the reformers consulted this valuable resource as they labored on their own translations and expositions of the Old Testament.

Quadriga. The *quadriga*, or four senses of Scripture, grew out of the exegetical legacy of Paul's dichotomy of letter and spirit (2 Cor 3:6), as well as church fathers like Origen (c. 185–254), Jerome (c. 347–420) and Augustine (354–430). Advocates for this method—the primary framework for biblical exegesis during the medieval era—assumed the necessity of the gift of faith under the guidance of the Holy Spirit. The literal-historical meaning of the text served as the foundation for the fuller perception of Scripture's meaning in the three spiritual senses, accessible only through faith: the allegorical sense taught what should be believed, the tropological or moral sense taught what should be done, and the anagogical or eschatological sense taught what should be hoped for. Medieval Jewish exegesis also had a fourfold interpretive method—not necessarily related to the *quadriga*—called *pardes* ("grove"): *peshat*, the simple, literal sense of the text according to grammar; *remez*, the allegorical sense; *derash*, the moral sense; and *sod*, the mystic sense related to Kabbalah. Scholars hotly dispute the precise use and meaning of these terms.

Petrus Ramus (1515–1572). French Reformed humanist philosopher. Ramus was an influential professor of philosophy and logic at the French royal college in Paris; he converted to Protestantism and left France for Germany, where he came under the influence of Calvinist thought. Ramus was a trenchant critic of Aristotle and noted for his method of classification based on a deductive movement from universals to particulars, the latter becoming branching divisions that provided a visual chart of the parts to the whole. His system profoundly influenced Puritan theology and preaching. After returning to Paris, Ramus died in the Saint Bartholomew's Day Massacre.

Rashi (**Shlomo Yitzchaki**) (1040–1105). French Jewish rabbi and exegete. After completing his studies, Rashi founded a yeshiva in Troyes. He composed the first comprehensive commentary on the Talmud, as well as commentaries on the entire Old Testament except for 1–2 Chronicles. These works remain influential within orthodox Judaism. Late medieval and early modern Christian scholars valued his exegesis, characterized by his preference for peshat (see quadriga).

Remonstrance (1610). See *Synod of Dordrecht.*

Johannes Reuchlin (1455–1522). German Catholic lawyer, humanist and Hebraist. Reuchlin held judicial appointments for the dukes of Württemberg, the Supreme Court in Speyer and the imperial court of the Swabian League. He pioneered the study of Hebrew among Christians in Germany, standing against those who, like Johannes Pfefferkorn (1469–1523), wanted to destroy Jewish literature. Among his many works he published a Latin dictionary, an introductory Greek grammar, the most important early modern Hebrew grammar and dictionary (*De rudimentis hebraicis;* 1506), and a commentary on the penitential psalms.

Edward Reynolds (1599–1676). Anglican bishop. Reynolds succeeded John Donne* as the preacher at Lincoln's Inn before entering parish ministry in Northamptonshire. During the English Civil Wars, he supported the Puritans because of his sympathy toward their simplicity and piety—de-spite believing that Scripture demanded no particular form of government; later he refused to support the abolition of the monarchy. Until the Restoration he ministered in London; afterward he became the bishop of Norwich. He wrote the general thanksgiving prayer which is part of the morning office in the *Book of Common Prayer.**

Urbanus Rhegius (1489–1541). German Lutheran pastor. Rhegius, who was likely the son of a priest, studied under the humanists at Freiburg and Ingolstadt. After a brief stint as a foot soldier, he received ordination in 1519 and was made cathedral preacher in Augsburg. During his time in Augsburg he closely read Luther's* works, becoming an enthusiastic follower. Despite his close friendship with Zwingli* and Oecolampadius,* Rhegius supported Luther in the eucharistic debates, later playing a major role in the Wittenberg Concord (1536). He advocated for peace during the Peasants' War and had extended interactions with the Anabaptists in Augsburg. Later in his career he concerned himself with the training of pastors, writing a pastoral guide and two catechisms. About one hundred of his writings were published posthumously.

Lancelot Ridley (d. 1576). Anglican preacher. Ridley was the first cousin of Nicholas Ridley,* the bishop of London who was martyred during the Marian persecutions. By Cranmer's* recommendation, Ridley became one of the six Canterbury Cathedral preachers. Upon Mary I's accession in 1553, Ridley was defrocked (as a married priest). Ridley returned to Canterbury Cathedral after Mary's death. He wrote commentaries on Jude, Ephesians, Philippians and Colossians.

Nicholas Ridley (c. 1502–1555). Anglican bishop. Ridley was a student and fellow at Cambridge University who was appointed chaplain to Archbishop Thomas Cranmer* and is thought to be partially responsible for Cranmer's shift to a symbolic view of the Eucharist. Cranmer promoted Ridley twice: as bishop of Rochester, where he openly advocated Reformed theological views, and, later, as bishop of London. Ridley assisted Cranmer in the revisions of the Book of Common

Prayer.* Ridley's support of Lady Jane Grey against the claims of Mary to the throne led to his arrest; he was tried for heresy and burned at the stake with Hugh Latimer.*

Peter Riedemann (1506–1556). German Radical elder, theologian and hymnist. While traveling as a Silesian cobbler, Riedemann came into contact with Anabaptist teachings and joined a congregation in Linz. In 1529 he was called to be a minister, only to be imprisoned soon after as part of Archduke Ferdinand's efforts to suppress heterodoxy in his realm. Once he was released, he moved to Moravia in 1532 where he was elected as a minister and missionary of the Hutterite community there. His *Account of Our Religion, Doctrine and Faith* (1542), with its more than two thousand biblical references, is Riedemann's most important work and is still used by Hutterites today.

John Robinson (1576–1625). English Puritan pastor. After his suspension for nonconformity, Robinson fled to the Netherlands with his congregation, eventually settling in Leiden in 1609. Robinson entered into controversies over Arminianism, separation and congregationalism. Most of his healthy congregants immigrated to Plymouth in 1620; Robinson remained in Leiden with those unable to travel.

Nehemiah Rogers (1593–1660). Anglican priest. After studying at Cambridge, Rogers ministered at numerous parishes during his more than forty-year career. In 1643, he seems to have been forced out of a parish on account of being a Royalist and friend of William Laud.* Rogers published a number of sermons and tracts, including a series of expositions on Jesus' parables in the Gospels.

Robert Rollock (c. 1555–1599). Scottish Reformed pastor, educator and theologian. Rollock was deeply influenced by Petrus Ramus's* system of logic, which he implemented as a tutor and (later) principal of Edinburgh University and in his expositions of the Bible. Rollock, as a divinity professor and theologian, was instrumental in diffusing a federalist Calvinism in the Scottish church; he lectured on theology using the texts of

Theodore Beza* and articulated a highly covenantal interpretation of the biblical narratives. He was a prolific writer of sermons, expositions, commentaries, lectures and occasional treatises.

Jacopo Sadoleto (1477–1547). Italian Catholic Cardinal. Sadoleto, attaché to Leo X's court, was appointed bishop in 1517, cardinal in 1536. He participated in the reform commission led by Gasparo Contarini.* However, he tried to reconcile with Protestants apart from the commission, sending several letters to Protestant leaders in addition to his famous letter to the city of Geneva, which John Calvin* pointedly answered. Sadoleto published a commentary on Romans that was censored as semi-Pelagian. His insufficient treatment of prevenient grace left him vulnerable to this charge. Sadoleto emphasized grammar as the rule and norm of exegesis.

Heinrich Salmuth (1522–1576). German Lutheran theologian. After earning his doctorate from the University of Leipzig, Salmuth served in several coterminous pastoral and academic positions. He was integral to the reorganization of the University of Jena. Except for a few disputations, all of Salmuth's works—mostly sermons—were published posthumously by his son.

Robert Sanderson (1587–1663). Anglican bishop and philosopher. Before his appointment as professor of divinity at Oxford in 1642, Sanderson pastored in several parishes. Because of his loyalty to the Crown during the English Civil Wars, the Parliamentarians stripped Sanderson of his post at Oxford. After the Restoration he was reinstated at Oxford and consecrated bishop. He wrote an influential textbook on logic.

Edwin Sandys (1519–1588). Anglican bishop. During his doctoral studies at Cambridge, Sandys befriended Martin Bucer.* Having supported the Protestant Lady Jane Grey's claim to the throne, Sandys resigned his post at Cambridge upon Mary I's accession. He was then arrested and imprisoned in the Tower of London. Released in 1554, he sojourned on the continent until Mary's death. On his return to England he was appointed to revise the liturgy and was consecrated bishop.

Many of his sermons were published, but his most significant literary legacy is his work as a translator of the Bishop's Bible (1568), which served as the foundational English text for the translators of the King James Bible (1611).

Erasmus Sarcerius (1501–1559). German Lutheran superintendent, educator and pastor. Sarcerius served as educational superintendent, court preacher and pastor in Nassau and, later, in Leipzig. The hallmark of Sarcerius's reputation was his ethical emphasis as exercised through ecclesial oversight and family structure; he also drafted disciplinary codes for regional churches in Germany. Sarcerius served with Philipp Melanchthon* as Protestant delegates at the Council of Trent, though both withdrew prior to the dismissal of the session; he eventually became an opponent of Melanchthon, contesting the latter's understanding of the Eucharist at a colloquy in Worms in 1557.

Michael Sattler (c. 1490–1527). Swiss Radical leader. Sattler was a Benedictine monk who abandoned the monastic life during the upheavals of the Peasants' War. He took up the trade of weaving under the guidance of an outspoken Anabaptist. It seems that Sattler did not openly join the Anabaptist movement until after the suppression of the Peasants' War in 1526. Sattler interceded with Martin Bucer* and Wolfgang Capito* for imprisoned Anabaptists in Strasbourg. Shortly before he was convicted of heresy and executed, he wrote the definitive expression of Anabaptist theology, the Schleitheim Articles.*

Girolamo Savonarola (1452–1498). Italian Catholic preacher and martyr. Outraged by clerical corruption and the neglect of the poor, Savonarola traveled to preach against these abuses and to prophesy impending judgment—a mighty king would scourge and reform the church. Savonarola thought that the French invasion of Italy in 1494 confirmed his apocalyptic visions. Thus he pressed to purge Florence of vice and institute public welfare, in order to usher in a new age of Christianity. Florence's refusal to join papal resistance against the French enraged Alexander VI (r. 1492–1503). He blamed Savonarola, promptly excommunicating

him and threatening Florence with an interdict. After an ordeal by fire turned into a riot, Savonarola was arrested. Under torture he admitted to charges of conspiracy and false prophecy; he was hanged and burned. In addition to numerous sermons and letters, he wrote meditations on Psalms 31 and 51 as well as *The Triumph of the Cross* (1497).

Leupold Scharnschlager (d. 1563). Austrian Radical elder. See *Kunstbuch.*

Leonhard Schiemer (d. 1528). Austrian Radical martyr. See *Kunstbuch.*

Hans Schlaffer (c. 1490–1528). Austrian Radical martyr. See *Kunstbuch.*

Schleitheim Articles (1527). After the death of Conrad Grebel* in 1526 and the execution of Felix Manz (born c. 1498) in early 1527, the young Swiss Anabaptist movement was in need of unity and direction. A synod convened at Schleitheim under the chairmanship of Michael Sattler,* which passed seven articles of Anabaptist distinctives—likely defined against both magisterial reformers and other Anabaptists with less orthodox and more militant views (e.g., Balthasar Hubmaier*). Unlike most confessions, these articles do not explicitly address traditional creedal interests; they explicate instead the Anabaptist view of the sacraments, church discipline, separatism, the role of ministers, pacifism and oaths. Throughout the document there is a resolute focus on Christ's example. The Schleitheim Articles are considered the definitive statement of Anabaptist theology, particularly regarding separatism.

Schmalkald Articles (1537). In response to Pope Paul III's (1468–1549) 1536 decree ordering a general church council to solve the Protestant crisis, Elector John Frederick (1503–1554) commissioned Martin Luther* to draft the sum of his teaching. Intended by Luther as a last will and testament—and composed with advice from well-known colleagues Justus Jonas,* Johann Bugenhagen,* Caspar Cruciger,* Nikolaus von Amsdorf (1483–1565), Georg Spalatin (1484–1545), Philipp Melanchthon* and Johann Agricola*—these articles provide perhaps the briefest and most systematic summary of Luther's teaching. The document was not adopted formally by the Lutheran Schmalkald League, as was hoped, and the general church council was postponed for several years (until convening at Trent in 1545). Only in 1580 were the articles officially received, by being incorporated into the *Book of Concord* defining orthodox Lutheranism.

Anna Maria van Schurman (1607–1678). Dutch Reformed polymath. Van Schurman cultivated talents in art, poetry, botany, linguistics and theology. She mastered most contemporary European languages, in addition to Latin, Greek, Hebrew, Arabic, Farsi and Ethiopian. With the encouragement of leading Reformed theologian Gisbertus Voetius (1589–1676), van Schurman attended lectures at the University of Utrecht—although she was required to sit behind a wooden screen so that the male students could not see her. In 1638 van Schurman published her famous treatise advocating female scholarship, *Amica dissertatio . . . de capacitate ingenii muliebris ad scientias.* In addition to these more polemical works, van Schurman also wrote hymns and poems, including a paraphrase of Genesis 1–3. Later in life she became a devotee of Jean de Labadie (1610–1674), a former Jesuit who was also expelled from the Reformed church for his separatist leanings. Her *Eucleria* (1673) is the most well known defense of Labadie's theology.

Kaspar von Schwenckfeld (1489–1561). German Radical reformer. Schwenckfeld was a Silesian nobleman who encountered Luther's* works in 1521. He traveled to Wittenberg twice: first to meet Luther and Karlstadt,* and a second time to convince Luther of his doctrine of the "internal word"—emphasizing inner revelation so strongly that he did not see church meetings or the sacraments as necessary—after which Luther considered him heterodox. Schwenckfeld won his native territory to the Reformation in 1524 and later lived in Strasbourg for five years until Bucer* sought to purify the city of less traditional theologies. Schwenckfeld wrote numerous polemical and exegetical tracts.

Scots Confession (1560). In 1560, the Scottish Parliament undertook to reform the Church of Scotland and to commission a Reformed confession of faith. In the course of four days, a committee—which included John Knox*—wrote this confession, largely based on Calvin's* work, the Confession of the English Congregation in Geneva (1556) and the Gallic Confession.* The articles were not ratified until 1567 and were displaced by the Westminster Confession (1646), adopted by the Scottish in 1647.

Second Helvetic Confession (1566). Believing he would soon die, Heinrich Bullinger* penned a personal statement of his Reformed faith in 1561 as a theological will. In 1563, Bullinger sent a copy of this confession, which blended Zwingli's and Calvin's theology, to the elector of the Palatinate, Frederick III (1515–1576), who had asked for a complete explication of the Reformed faith in order to defend himself against aggressive Lutheran attacks after printing the Heidelberg Confession.* Although not published until 1566, the Second Helvetic Confession became the definitive sixteenth-century Reformed statement of faith. Theodore Beza* used it as the organizing confession for his *Harmonia Confessionum* (1581), which sought to emphasize the unity of the Reformed churches. Bullinger's personal confession was adopted by the Reformed churches of Scotland (1566), Hungary (1567), France (1571) and Poland (1571).

Obadiah Sedgwick (c. 1600–1658). English Puritan minister. Educated at Oxford, Sedgwick pastored in London and participated in the Westminster Assembly. An ardent Puritan, Sedgwick was appointed by Oliver Cromwell (1599–1658) to examine clerical candidates. Sedgwick published a catechism, several sermons and a treatise on how to deal with doubt.

Nikolaus Selnecker (1530–1592). German Lutheran theologian, preacher, pastor and hymnist. Selnecker taught in Wittenberg, Jena and Leipzig, preached in Dresden and Wolfenbüttel, and pastored in Leipzig. He was forced out of his post at Jena because of suspicions that he was a

crypto-Calvinist. He sought refuge in Wolfenbüttel, where he met Martin Chemnitz* and Jakob
Andreae.* Under their influence Selnecker was
drawn away from Philippist theology. Selnecker's
shift in theology can be seen in his *Institutio
religionis christianae* (1573). Selnecker coauthored
the Formula of Concord* with Chemnitz, Andreae, Andreas Musculus (1514–1581), and David
Chytraeus.* Selnecker also published lectures on
Genesis, the Psalms, and the New Testament
epistles, as well as composing over a hundred
hymn tunes and texts.

Short Confession (1610). In response to some of
William Laud's* reforms in the Church of
England—particularly a law stating that ministers
who refused to comply with the Book of Common
Prayer* would lose their ordination—a group of
English Puritans immigrated to the Netherlands
in protest, where they eventually embraced the
practice of believer's baptism. The resulting Short
Confession was an attempt at union between
these Puritans and local Dutch Anabaptists
("Waterlanders"). The document highlights the
importance of love in the church and reflects
optimism regarding the freedom of the will while
explicitly rejecting double predestination.

Richard Sibbes (1577–1635). English Puritan
preacher. Sibbes was educated at St. John's College,
Cambridge, where he was converted to reforming
views and became a popular preacher. As a
moderate Puritan emphasizing interior piety and
brotherly love, Sibbes always remained within the
established Church of England, though opposed to
some of its liturgical ceremonies. His collected
sermons constitute his main literary legacy.

Menno Simons (c. 1496–1561). Dutch Radical
leader. Simons led a separatist Anabaptist group
in the Netherlands that would later be called
Mennonites, known for nonviolence and renunciation of the world. A former priest, Simons rejected
Catholicism through the influence of Anabaptist
disciples of Melchior Hoffmann and based on his
study of Scripture, in which he found no support
for transubstantiation or infant baptism. Following the sack of Anabaptists at Münster, Simons

committed to a nonviolent way of life. Simons
proclaimed a message of radical discipleship of
obedience and inner purity, marked by voluntary
adult baptism and communal discipline.

Henry Smith (c. 1550–1591). English Puritan
minister. Smith stridently opposed the Book of
Common Prayer* and refused to subscribe to the
Articles of Religion,* thus limiting his pastoral
opportunities. Nevertheless he gained a reputation
as an eloquent preacher in London. He published
sermon collections as well as several treatises.

Cyriacus Spangenberg (1528–1604). German
Lutheran pastor, preacher and theologian. Spangenberg was a staunch, often acerbic, Gnesio-
Lutheran. He rejected the Formula of Concord*
because of concerns about the princely control of
the church, as well as its rejection of Flacian
language of original sin (as constituting the
"substance" of human nature after the fall). He
published many commentaries and sermons, most
famously seventy wedding sermons (*Ehespiegel*
[1561]), his sermons on Luther* (*Theander Luther*
[1562–1571]) and Luther's hymns (*Cithara Lutheri*
[1569–1570]). He also published an analysis of
the Old Testament (though he only got as far as
Job), based on a methodology that anticipated the
logical bifurcations of Peter Ramus.*

Johann Spangenberg (1484–1550). German
Lutheran pastor and catechist. Spangenberg
studied at the University of Erfurt, where he was
welcomed into a group of humanists associated
with Konrad Muth (1470–1526). There he met
the reformer Justus Jonas,* and Eobanus Hessius
(1488–1540), whom Luther* dubbed "king of the
poets." Spangenberg served at parishes in Stolberg
(1520–1524), Nordhausen (1524–1546) and, by
Luther's recommendation, Eisleben (1546–1550).
Spangenberg published one of the best-selling
postils of the sixteenth century, the *Postilla
Teütsch*, a six-volume work meant to prepare
children to understand the lectionary readings. It
borrowed the question-answer form of Luther's
Small Catechism and was so popular that a monk,
Johannes Craendonch, purged overt anti-Catholic
statements from it and republished it under his

own name. Among Spangenberg's other pastoral works are *ars moriendi* ("the art of dying") booklets, a postil for the Acts of the Apostles and a question-answer version of Luther's *Large Catechism*. In addition to preaching and pastoring, Spangenberg wrote pamphlets on controversial topics such as purgatory, as well as textbooks on music, mathematics and grammar.

Georg Spindler (1525–1605). German Reformed theologian and pastor. After studying theology under Caspar Cruciger* and Philipp Melanchthon,* Spindler accepted a pastorate in Bohemia. A well-respected preacher, Spindler published postils in 1576 which some of his peers viewed as crypto-Calvinist. To investigate this allegation Spindler read John Calvin's* *Institutes*, and subsequently converted to the Reformed faith. After years of travel, he settled in the Palatinate and pastored there until his death. In addition to his Lutheran postils, Spindler also published Reformed postils in 1594 as well as several treatises on the Lord's Supper and predestination.

Statenvertaling (1637). The Synod of Dordrecht* commissioned this new Dutch translation of the Bible ("State's Translation"). The six theologians who undertook this translation also wrote prefaces for each biblical book, annotated obscure words and difficult passages, and provided cross-references; they even explained certain significant translation decisions. At the request of the Westminster Assembly, Theodore Haak (1605–1690) translated the *Statenvertaling* into English as *The Dutch Annotations Upon the Whole Bible* (1657).

Michael Stifel (1486–1567). German Lutheran mathematician, theologian and pastor. An Augustinian monk, Stifel's interest in mysticism, apocalypticism and numerology led him to identify Pope Leo X as the antichrist. Stifel soon joined the reform movement, writing a 1522 pamphlet in support of Martin Luther's* theology. After Luther quelled the fallout of Stifel's failed prediction of the Apocalypse—October 19, 1533 at 8 a.m.—Stifel focused more on mathematics and his pastoral duties. He was the first professor of mathematics at the University of Jena. He published several numerological interpretations of texts from the Gospels, Daniel and Revelation. However, Stifel's most important work is his *Arithmetica Integra* (1544), in which he standardized the approach to quadratic equations. He also developed notations for exponents and radicals.

Viktorin Strigel (1524–1569). German Lutheran theologian. Strigel taught at Wittenberg, Erfurt, Jena, Leipzig and Heidelberg. During his time in Jena he disputed with Matthias Flacius (1520–1575) over the human will's autonomy. Following Philipp Melanchthon,* Strigel asserted that in conversion the human will obediently cooperates with the divine will through the Holy Spirit and the Word of God. In the Weimar Disputation (1560), Strigel elicited Flacius's opinion that sin is a substance that mars the formal essence of human beings. Flacius's views were officially rejected in Article 1 of the Formula of Concord*; Strigel's, in Article 2. In 1567 the University of Leipzig suspended Strigel from teaching on account of suspicions that he affirmed Reformed Eucharistic theology; he acknowledged that he did and joined the Reformed confession on the faculty of the University of Heidelberg. In addition to controversial tracts, Strigel published commentaries on the entire Bible (except Lamentations) and the Apocrypha.

Johann Sutell (1504–1575). German Lutheran pastor. After studying at the University of Wittenberg, Sutell received a call to a pastorate in Göttingen, where he eventually became superintendent. He wrote new church orders for Göttingen (1531) and Schweinfurt (1543), and expanded two sermons for publication, *The Dreadful Destruction of Jerusalem* (1539) and *History of Lazarus* (1543).

Swiss Brethren Confession of Hesse (1578). Anabaptist leader Hans Pauly Kuchenbecker penned this confession after a 1577 interrogation by Lutheran authorities. This confession was unusually amenable to Lutheran views—there is no mention of pacifism or rejection of oath taking.

Synod of Dordrecht (1618–1619). This large

Dutch Reformed Church council—also attended by English, German and Swiss delegates—met to settle the theological issues raised by the followers of Jacobus Arminius.* Arminius's theological disagreements with mainstream Reformed teaching erupted into open conflict with the publication of the *Remonstrance* (1610). This "protest" was based on five points: that election is based on foreseen faith or unbelief; that Christ died indiscriminately for all people (although only believers receive salvation); that people are thoroughly sinful by nature apart from the prevenient grace of God that enables their free will to embrace or reject the gospel; that humans are able to resist the working of God's grace; and that it is possible for true believers to fall away from faith completely. The Synod ruled in favor of the Contra-Remonstrants, its Canons often remembered with a TULIP acrostic—total depravity, unconditional election, limited atonement, irresistible grace, perseverance of the saints—each letter countering one of the five Remonstrant articles. The Synod also officially accepted the Belgic Confession,* Heidelberg Catechism* and the Canons of Dordrecht as standards of the Dutch Reformed Church.

Arcangela Tarabotti (1604–1652). Italian Catholic nun. At the age of eleven, Tarabotti entered a Benedictine convent as a student-boarder; three years later her father forced her to take monastic vows. The dignity of women and their treatment in the male-controlled institutions of early modern Venice concerned Tarabotti deeply. She protested forced cloistering, the denial of education to women, the exclusion of women from public life and the double standards by which men and women were judged. Tarabotti authored numerous polemical works and an extensive correspondence.

Richard Taverner (1505–1575). English Puritan humanist and translator. After graduating from Oxford, Taverner briefly studied abroad. When he returned to England, he joined Thomas Cromwell's (1485–1540) circle. After Cromwell's beheading, Taverner escaped severe punishment and retired from public life during Mary I's reign. Under Elizabeth I, Taverner served as justice of the peace, sheriff and a licensed lay preacher. Taverner translated many important continental Reformation works into English, most notably the Augsburg Confession* and several of Desiderius Erasmus's* works. Some of these translations—John Calvin's* 1536 catechism, Wolfgang Capito's* work on the Psalms and probably Erasmus Sarcerius's* postils—he presented as his own work. Underwritten by Cromwell, Taverner also published an edited version of the Matthew Bible (1537).

Thomas Thorowgood (1595–1669). English Puritan pastor. Thorowgood was a Puritan minister in Norfolk and the chief financier of John Eliot (1604–1690), a Puritan missionary among the Native American tribes in Massachusetts. In 1650, under the title *Jews in America, or, Probabilities that Americans be of that Race*, Thorowgood became one of the first to put forward the thesis that Native Americans were actually the ten lost tribes of Israel.

Frans Titelmans (1502–1537). Belgian Catholic philosopher. Titelmans studied at the University of Leuven, where he was influenced by Petrus Ramus.* After first joining a Franciscan monastery, Titelmans realigned with the stricter Capuchins and moved to Italy. He is best known for his advocacy for the Vulgate and his debates with Desiderius Erasmus* over Pauline theology (1527–1530)—he was deeply suspicious of the fruits of humanism, especially regarding biblical studies. His work was published posthumously by his brother, Pieter Titelmans (1501–1572).

Francisco de Toledo (1532–1596). Spanish Catholic theologian. This important Jesuit taught philosophy at the universities of Salamanca and Rome. He published works on Aristotelian philosophy and a commentary on Thomas Aquinas's work, as well as biblical commentaries on John, Romans and the first half of Luke. He was also the general editor for the Clementine Vulgate (1598).

Alonso Tostado (1400–1455). Spanish Catholic bishop and exegete. Tostado lectured on theology, law and philosophy at the University of Salamanca, in addition to ministering in a local parish. Tostado entered into disputes over papal supremacy and the date of Christ's birth. Tostado's thirteen-volume collected works include commentaries on the historical books of the Old Testament and the Gospel of Matthew.

Daniel Toussain (1541–1602). Swiss Reformed pastor and professor. Toussain became pastor at Orléans after attending college in Basel. After the third War of Religion, Toussain was exiled, eventually returning to Montbéliard, his birthplace. In 1571, he faced opposition there from the strict Lutheran rulers and was eventually exiled due to his influence over the clergy. He returned to Orléans but fled following the Saint Bartholomew's Day Massacre (1572), eventually becoming pastor in Basel. He relocated to Heidelberg in 1583 as pastor to the new regent, becoming professor of theology at the university, and he remained there until his death.

John Trapp (1601–1669). Anglican biblical exegete. After studying at Oxford, Trapp entered the pastorate in 1636. During the English Civil Wars he sided with Parliament, which later made it difficult for him to collect tithes from a congregation whose royalist pastor had been evicted. Trapp published commentaries on all the books of the Bible from 1646 to 1656.

Immanuel Tremellius (1510–1580). Italian Reformed Hebraist. Around 1540, Tremellius received baptism by Cardinal Reginald Pole (1500–1558) and converted from Judaism to Christianity; he affiliated with evangelicals the next year. On account of the political and religious upheaval, Tremellius relocated often, teaching Hebrew in Lucca; Strasbourg, fleeing the Inquisition; Cambridge, displaced by the Schmalkaldic War; Heidelberg, escaping Mary I's persecutions; and Sedan, expelled by the new Lutheran Elector of the Palatine. Many considered Tremellius's translation of the Old Testament as the most accurate available. He also published a Hebrew grammar and translated John Calvin's* catechism into Hebrew.

William Tyndale (Hychyns) (1494–1536).

English reformer, theologian and translator. Tyndale was educated at Oxford University, where he was influenced by the writings of humanist thinkers. Believing that piety is fostered through personal encounter with the Bible, he asked to translate the Bible into English; denied permission, Tyndale left for the Continent to complete the task. His New Testament was the equivalent of a modern-day bestseller in England but was banned and ordered burned. Tyndale's theology was oriented around justification, the authority of Scripture and Christian obedience; Tyndale emphasized the ethical as a concomitant reality of justification. He was martyred in Brussels before completing his English translation of the Old Testament, which Miles Coverdale* finished.

Juan de Valdés (1500/10–1541). Spanish Catholic theologian and writer. Although Valdés adopted an evangelical doctrine, had Erasmian affiliations and published works that were listed on the Index of Prohibited Books, Valdés rebuked the reformers for creating disunity and never left the Catholic Church. His writings included translations of the Hebrew Psalter and various biblical books, a work on the Spanish language and several commentaries. Valdés fled to Rome in 1531 to escape the Spanish Inquisition and worked in the court of Clement VII in Bologna until the pope's death in 1534. Valdés subsequently returned to Naples, where he led the reform- and revival-minded Valdesian circle.

Peter Martyr Vermigli (1499–1562). Italian Reformed humanist and theologian. Vermigli was one of the most influential theologians of the era, held in common regard with such figures as Martin Luther* and John Calvin.* In Italy, Vermigli was a distinguished theologian, preacher and advocate for moral reform; however, during the reinstitution of the Roman Inquisition Vermigli fled to Protestant regions in northern Europe. He was eventually appointed professor of divinity at Oxford University, where Vermigli delivered acclaimed disputations on the Eucharist. Vermigli was widely noted for his deeply integrated biblical commentaries and theological treatises.

Vulgate. In 382 Pope Damasus I (c. 300–384) commissioned Jerome (c. 347–420) to translate the four Gospels into Latin based on Old Latin and Greek manuscripts. Jerome completed the translation of the Gospels and the Old Testament around 405. It is widely debated how much of the rest of the New Testament was translated by Jerome. During the Middle Ages, the Vulgate became the Catholic Church's standard Latin translation. The Council of Trent recognized it as the official text of Scripture.

Peter Walpot (d. 1578). Moravian Radical pastor and bishop. Walpot was a bishop of the Hutterite community after Jakob Hutter, Peter Riedemann* and Leonhard Lanzenstiel. Riedemann's *Confession of Faith* (1545; 1565) became a vital authority for Hutterite exegesis, theology and morals. Walpot added his own *Great Article Book* (1577), which collates primary biblical passages on baptism, communion, the community of goods, the sword and divorce. In keeping with Hutterite theology, Walpot defended the community of goods as a mark of the true church.

Valentin Weigel (1533–1588). German Lutheran pastor. Weigel studied at Leipzig and Wittenberg, entering the pastorate in 1567. Despite a strong anti-institutional bias, he was recognized by the church hierarchy as a talented preacher and compassionate minister of mercy to the poor. Although he signed the Formula of Concord,* Weigel's orthodoxy was questioned so openly that he had to publish a defense. He appears to have tried to synthesize several medieval mystics with the ideas of Sebastian Franck,* Thomas Müntzer* and others. His posthumously published works have led some recent scholars to suggest that Weigel's works may have deeply influenced later Pietism.

Hieronymus Weller von Molsdorf (1499–1572). German Lutheran theologian. Originally intending to study law, Weller devoted himself to theology after hearing one of Martin Luther's* sermons on the catechism. He boarded with Luther and tutored Luther's son. In 1539 he moved to Freiburg, where he lectured on the Bible and held theological disputations at the Latin school. In addition to hymns, works of practical theology and a postil set, Weller published commentaries on Genesis, 1–2 Samuel, 1–2 Kings, Job, the Psalms, Christ's passion, Ephesians, Philippians, 1–2 Thessalonians and 1–2 Peter.

John Whitgift (1530–1604). Anglican archbishop. Though Whitgift shared much theological common ground with Puritans, after his election as Archbishop of Canterbury (1583) he moved decisively to squelch the political and ecclesiastical threat they posed during Elizabeth's reign. Whitgift enforced strict compliance to the Book of Common Prayer,* the Act of Uniformity (1559) and the Articles of Religion.* Whitgift's policies led to a large migration of Puritans to Holland. The bulk of Whitgift's published corpus is the fruit of a lengthy public disputation with Thomas Cartwright,* in which Whitgift defines Anglican doctrine against Cartwright's staunch Puritanism.

Johann Wigand (1523–1587). German Lutheran theologian. Wigand is most noted as one of the compilers of the *Magdeburg Centuries*, a German ecclesiastical history of the first thirteen centuries of the church. He was a student of Philipp Melanchthon* at the University of Wittenburg and became a significant figure in the controversies dividing Lutheranism. Strongly opposed to Roman Catholicism, Wigand lobbied against innovations in Lutheran theology that appeared sympathetic to Catholic thought. In the later debates, Wigand's support for Gnesio-Lutheranism established his role in the development of confessional Lutheranism. Wigand was appointed bishop of Pomerania after serving academic posts at the universities in Jena and Königsburg.

Thomas Wilcox (c. 1549–1608). English Puritan theologian. In 1572, Wilcox objected to Parliament against the episcopacy and the Book of Common Prayer,* advocating for presbyterian church governance. He was imprisoned for sedition. After his release, he preached itinerantly. He was brought before the courts twice more for his continued protest against the Church of England's episcopal structure. He translated some of Theodore Beza* and John Calvin's* sermons into English, and he wrote polemical and occasional works as well as commentaries on the Psalms and Song of Songs.

Johann (Ferus) Wild (1495–1554). German Catholic pastor. After studying at Heidelberg and teaching at Tübingen, this Franciscan was appointed as lector in the Mainz cathedral, eventually being promoted to cathedral preacher—a post for which he became widely popular but also controversial. Wild strongly identified as Catholic but was not unwilling to criticize the curia. Known for an irenic spirit—criticized in fact as *too* kind—he was troubled by the polemics between all parties of the Reformation. He preached with great lucidity, integrating the liturgy, Scripture and doctrine to exposit Catholic worship and teaching for common people. His sermons on John were pirated for publication without his knowledge; the Sorbonne banned them as heretical. Despite his popularity among clergy, the majority of his works were on the Roman Index until 1900.

Andrew Willet (1562–1621). Anglican priest, professor, and biblical expositor. Willet was a gifted biblical expositor and powerful preacher. He walked away from a promising university career in 1588 when he was ordained a priest in the Church of England. For the next thirty-three years he served as a parish priest. Willet's commentaries summarized the present state of discussion while also offering practical applications for preachers. They have been cited as some of the most technical commentaries of the early seventeenth century. His most important publication was *Synopsis Papismi, or a General View of Papistrie* (1594), in which he responded to many of Robert Bellarmine's critiques. After years of royal favor, Willet was imprisoned in 1618 for a month after presenting to King James I his opposition to the "Spanish Match" of Prince Charles to the Infanta Maria. While serving as a parish priest, he wrote forty-two works, most of which were either commentaries on books of the Bible or controversial works against Catholics.

John Woolton (c. 1535–1594). Anglican bishop. After graduating from Oxford, Woolton lived in Germany until the accession of Elizabeth I. He was ordained as a priest in 1560 and as a bishop in 1578. Woolton published many theological, devotional and practical works, including a treatise on the immortality of the soul, a discourse on conscience and a manual for Christian living.

Girolamo Zanchi (1516–1590). Italian Reformed theologian and pastor. Zanchi joined an Augustinian monastery at the age of fifteen, where he studied Greek and Latin, the church fathers and the works of Aristotle and Thomas Aquinas. Under the influence of his prior, Peter Martyr Vermigli,* Zanchi also imbibed the writings of the Swiss and German reformers. To avoid the Inquisition, Zanchi fled to Geneva where he was strongly attracted to the preaching and teaching of John Calvin.* Zanchi taught biblical theology and the *locus* method at academies in Strasbourg, Heidelberg, and Neustadt. He also served as pastor of an Italian refugee congregation. Zanchi's theological works, *De tribus Elohim* (1572) and *De natura Dei* (1577), have received more attention than his commentaries. His commentaries comprise about a quarter of his literary output, however, and display a strong typological and christological interpretation in conversation with the church fathers, medieval exegetes, and other reformers.

Katharina Schütz Zell (1497/98–1562). German Reformed writer. Zell became infamous in Strasbourg and the Empire when in 1523 she married the priest Matthias Zell, and then published an apology defending her husband against charges of impiety and libertinism. Longing for a united church, she called for toleration of Catholics and Anabaptists, famously writing to Martin Luther* after the failed Marburg Colloquy of 1529 to exhort him to check his hostility and to be ruled instead by Christian charity. Much to the chagrin of her contemporaries, Zell published diverse works, ranging from polemical treatises on marriage to letters of consolation, as well as editing a hymnal and penning an exposition of Psalm 51.

Huldrych Zwingli (1484–1531). Swiss Reformed humanist, preacher and theologian. Zwingli, a parish priest, was influenced by the writings of Desiderius Erasmus* and taught himself Greek. While a preacher to the city cathedral in Zurich, Zwingli enacted reform through sermons, public disputations and conciliation with the town council, abolishing the Mass and images in the church. Zwingli broke with the lectionary preaching tradition, instead preaching serial expository biblical sermons. He later was embroiled in controversy with Anabaptists over infant baptism and with Martin Luther* at the Marburg Colloquy (1529) over their differing views of the Eucharist. Zwingli, serving as chaplain to Zurich's military, was killed in battle.

SOURCES FOR
BIOGRAPHICAL SKETCHES

General Reference Works

Allgemeine Deutsche Biographie. 56 vols. Leipzig: Duncker & Humblot, 1875–1912; reprint, 1967–1971. Accessible online via deutsche-biographie.de/index.html.

Baskin, Judith R., ed. *The Cambridge Dictionary of Judaism and Jewish Culture.* New York: Cambridge University Press, 2011.

Bettenson, Henry and Chris Maunder, eds. *Documents of the Christian Church.* 3rd ed. Oxford: Oxford University Press, 1999.

Betz, Hans Dieter, Don Browning, Bernd Janowski and Eberhard Jüngel, eds. *Religion Past & Present: Encyclopedia of Theology and Relgion.* 13 vols. Leiden: Brill, 2007–2013.

Bremer, Francis J. and Tom Webster, eds. *Puritans and Puritanism in Europe and America: A Comprehensive Encyclopedia.* 2 vols. Santa Barbara, CA: ABC-CLIO, 2006.

Haag, Eugene and Émile Haag. *La France protestante ou vies des protestants français.* 2nd ed. 6 vols. Paris: Sandoz & Fischbacher, 1877–1888.

Hillerbrand, Hans J., ed. *Oxford Encyclopedia of the Reformation.* 4 vols. New York: Oxford University Press, 1996.

Kolb, Robert, and Timothy J. Wengert, eds. *The Book of Concord: The Confessions of the Evangelical Lutheran Church.* Translated by Charles Arand et al. Minneapolis: Fortress, 2000.

McKim, Donald K., ed. *Dictionary of Major Biblical Interpreters.* Downers Grove, IL: InterVarsity Press, 2007.

Müller, Gerhard, et al., ed. *Theologische Realenzyklopädie.* Berlin: Walter de Gruyter, 1994.

Neue Deutsche Biographie. 28 vols. projected. Berlin: Duncker & Humblot, 1953–. Accessible online via deutsche-biographie.de/index.html.

New Catholic Encyclopedia. 15 vols. New York: McGraw-Hill, 1967; 2nd ed., Detroit: Thomson-Gale, 2002.

Oxford Dictionary of National Biography. 60 vols.

Oxford: Oxford University Press, 2004.

Pelikan, Jaroslav. *The Christian Tradition.* 5 vols. Chicago: University of Chicago Press, 1971–1989.

Stephen, Leslie, and Sidney Lee, eds. *Dictionary of National Biography.* 63 vols. London: Smith, Elder and Co., 1885–1900.

Terry, Michael, ed. *Reader's Guide to Judaism.* New York: Routledge, 2000.

Wordsworth, Christopher, ed. *Lives of Eminent Men connected with the History of Religion in England.* 4 vols. London: J. G. & F. Rivington, 1839.

Additional Works for Individual Sketches

Akin, Daniel L. "An Expositional Analysis of the Schleitheim Confession." *Criswell Theological Review* 2 (1988): 345-70.

Bald, R. C. *John Donne: A Life.* Oxford: Oxford University Press, 1970.

Burke, David G. "The Enduring Significance of the KJV." *Word and World* 31, no. 3 (2011): 229-44.

Campbell, Gordon. *Bible: The Story of the King James Version, 1611–2011.* Oxford: Oxford University Press, 2010.

Doornkaat Koolman, J ten. "The First Edition of Peter Riedemann's 'Rechenschaft.'" *Mennonite Quarterly Review* 36, no. 2 (1962): 169-70.

Fischlin, Daniel and Mark Fortier, eds. *Royal Subjects: Essays on the Writings of James VI and I.* Detroit: Wayne State University Press, 2002.

Fishbane, Michael A. "Teacher and the Hermeneutical Task: A Reinterpretation of Medieval Exegesis." *Journal of the American Academy of Religion* 43, no. 4 (1975): 709-21.

Friedmann, Robert. "Second Generation Anabaptism as Illustrated by the Walpot Era of the Hutterites." *Mennonite Quarterly* 44, no. 4 (1970): 390-93.

Frymire, John M. *The Primacy of the Postils: Catholics, Protestants, and the Dissemination of Ideas in Early Modern Germany.* Leiden: Brill, 2010.

Furcha, Edward J. "Key Concepts in Caspar von Schwenckfeld's Thought, Regeneration and the

New Life." *Church History* 37, no. 2 (1968): 160-73.

Greaves, Richard L. *Society and Religion in Elizabethan England*. Minneapolis: University of Minnesota, 1981.

Greiffenberg, Catharina Regina von. *Meditations on the Incarnation, Passion and Death of Jesus Christ*. Edited and translated by Lynne Tatlock. The Other Voice in Early Modern Europe. Chicago: University of Chicago Press, 2009.

Grendler, Paul. "Italian biblical humanism and the papacy, 1515-1535." In *Biblical Humanism and Scholasticism in the Age of Erasmus*. Edited by Erika Rummel, 225-76. Leiden: Brill, 2008.

Heiden, Albert van der. "Pardes: Methodological Reflections on the Theory of the Four Senses." *Journal of Jewish Studies* 34, no. 2 (1983): 147-59.

Hendrix, Scott H., ed. and trans. *Early Protestant Spirituality*. New York: Paulist Press, 2009.

Hvolbek, Russell H. "Being and Knowing: Spiritualist Epistelmology and Anthropology from Schwenckfeld to Böhme." *Sixteenth Century Journal* 22, no. 1 (1991): 97-110.

Kahle, Paul. "Felix Pratensis—a Prato, Felix. Der Herausgeber der Ersten Rabbinerbibel, Venedig 1516/7." *Die Welt des Orients* 1, no. 1 (1947): 32-36.

Kelly, Joseph Francis. *The Ecumenical Councils of the Catholic Church: A History*. Collegeville, MN: Liturgical Press, 2009.

Lake, Peter. *The Boxmaker's Revenge: "Orthodoxy", "Heterodox" and the Politics of the Parish in Early Stuart London*. Stanford, CA: Stanford University Press, 2001.

Lockhart, Paul Douglas. *Frederick II and the Protestant Cause: Denmark's Role in the Wars of Religion, 1559–1596*. Leiden: Brill, 2004.

Lubac, Henri de. *Medieval Exegesis: The Four Senses of Scripture*. 3 vols. Translated by Mark Sebanc and E. M. Macierowski. Grand Rapids: Eerdmans, 1998–2009.

Norton, David. *A Textual History of the King James Bible*. New York: Cambridge University Press, 2005

Packull, Werner O. "The Origins of Peter Riedemann's Account of Our Faith." *Sixteenth Century Journal* 30, no. 1 (1999): 61-69.

Papazian, Mary Arshagouni, ed. *John Donne and the Protestant Reformation: New Perspectives*. Detroit: Wayne State University Press, 2003.

Paulicelli, Eugenia. "Sister Arcangela Tarabotti: Hair, Wigs and Other Vices." In *Writing Fashion in Early Modern Italy: From Sprezzatura to Satire*, by idem, 177-204. Farnham, Surrey, UK: Ashgate, 2014.

Pragman, James H. "The Augsburg Confession in the English Reformation: Richard Taverner's Contribution." *Sixteenth Century Journal* 11, no. 3 (1980): 75-85.

Rashi. *Rashi's Commentary on Psalms*. Translated by Mayer I. Gruber. Atlanta: Scholars Press, 1998.

Spinka, Matthew. *John Hus: A Biography*. Princeton, NJ: Princeton University Press, 1968.

———. *John Hus at the Council of Constance*. New York: Columbia University Press, 1968.

———. *John Hus and the Czech Reform*. Hamden, CT: Archon Books, 1966.

Steinmetz, David C. "The Superiority of Pre-Critical Exegesis." *Theology Today* 37, no. 1 (1980): 27-38.

Synder, C. Arnold. "The Confession of the Swiss Brethren in Hesse, 1578." In *Anabaptism Revisited: Essays on Anabaptist/Mennonite Studies in Honor of C. J. Dyck*. Edited by Walter Klaassen, 29-49. Waterloo, ON; Scottdale, PA: Herald Press, 1992.

———. "The Schleitheim Articles in Light of the Revolution of the Common Man: Continuation or Departure?" *Sixteenth Century Journal* 16, no. 4 (1985): 419-30.

Todd, Margo. "Bishops in the Kirk: William Cowper of Galloway and the Puritan Episcopacy of Scotland." *Scottish Journal of Theology*, 57 (2004): 300-312.

Van Liere, Frans. *An Introduction to the Medieval Bible*. New York: Cambridge University Press, 2014.

Voogt, Gerrit. "Remonstrant-Counter-Remonstrant Debates: Crafting a Principled Defense of Toleration after the Synod of Dordrecht (1619–1650)." *Church History and Religious Culture* 89, no. 4 (2009): 489-524.

Wallace, Dewey D. Jr. "George Gifford, Puritan Propaganda and Popular Religion in Elizabethan England." *Sixteenth Century Journal* 9, no. 1 (1978): 27-49.

Wengert, Timothy J. "'Fear and Love' in the Ten Commandments." *Concordia Journal* 21, no. 1 (1995): 14-27.

———. "Philip Melanchthon and John Calvin against Andreas Osiander: Coming to Terms with Forensic Justification." In *Calvin and Luther: The*

Continuing Relationship, edited by R. Ward Holder, 63-87. Göttingen: Vandenhoeck & Ruprecht, 2013.

Wilkinson, Robert J. *Tetragrammaton: Western Christians and the Hebrew Name of God.* Leiden: Brill, 2015.

BIBLIOGRAPHY

Primary Sources and Translations Used in the Volume

Adams, Thomas. *The Barren Tree: A Sermon Preached at Paul's Crosse*. London: August Mathewes, 1623. Digital copy online at EEBO.

———. *The Black Devil: Three Sermons*. London: William Iaggard, 1615. Digital copy online at EEBO.

———. *A Commentary or Exposition upon the Divine Second Epistle General, Written by the Blessed Apostle St. Peter*. London: Jacob Bloome, 1633. Digital copy online at EEBO.

———. *The Devil's Banquet: Described in Four Sermons*. London: Thomas Snodham, 1614. Digital copy online at EEBO.

———. *Diseases of the Soul: A Discourse Divine, Moral, and Physical*. London: George Purslowe, 1616. Digital copy online at EEBO.

———. *A Divine Herbal Together with a Forest of Thorns*. London: George Purslowe, 1616. Digital copy online at EEBO.

———. *Eirenopolis: The City of Peace*. London: August Mathewes, 1622. Digital Copy online at EEBO.

———. *Five Sermons Preached upon Sundry Special Occasions*. London: August Mathewes, 1626. Digital copy online at EEBO.

———. *The Happines of the Church: Or A Description of Those Spirituall Prerogatives Wherewith Christ Hath Endowed Her*. London: John Grismand, 1618. Digital copy online at EEBO.

———. *The Temple*. London: August Mathewes, 1624. Digital copy online at EEBO.

———. *The White Devil, or The Hypocrite Uncased*. London: Thomas Purfoot, 1614. Digital copy online at EEBO.

Aepinus, Johannes. *Liber de Purgatorio*. London: Richard Grafton, 1549. Digital copy online at EEBO.

———. *A Very Fruitful and Godly Exposition upon the 15 Psalm of David*. London: John Daye, 1548. Digital copy online at EEBO.

Ainsworth, Henry. *Annotations on the Psalms*. Amsterdam: Giles Thorpe, 1617. Digital copy online at EEBO.

———. *A Defence of the Holy Scriptures, Worship, and Ministerie Used in the Christian Churches Separated from Antichrist*. Amsterdam: Giles Thorpe, 1609. Digital copy online at EEBO.

Airay, Henry. *Lectures upon the Whole Epistle of St. Paul to the Philippians*. Edinburgh: James Nichol, 1864. Digital copy online at archive.org.

Alesius, Alexander. *A Treatise Concernynge Generall Councilles, the Byshoppes of Rome, and the Clergy*. London: Thomas Bertheleti, 1538. Digital copy online at EEBO.

Andrewes, Lancelot. *Apospasmatia sacra, or, A Collection of Posthumous and Orphan Lectures Delivered at St. Pauls and St. Giles*. London: R. Hodgkinsonne, 1657. Digital copy online at EEBO.

———. *Ninety-Six Sermons*. 6 vols. Oxford: John Henry Parker, 1841. Digital copy online at archive.org.

Aretius, Benedict. *S. S. Theologiae problemata hoc est: loci communes Christianae religionis, methodice explicati*. Bern: Isaiah Le Preux, 1617. Digital copy online at www.e-rara.ch.

Arminius, Jacobus. *The Works of James Arminius.* 3 vols. Translated by James Nichols and W. R. Bagnall. Auburn, NY: Derby, Miller and Orton, 1853. Digital copy online at books.google.com.

Arndt, Johann. *True Christianity.* Translated by Peter Erb. New York: Paulist, 1979.

Arrowsmith, John. *Armilla Catechetica: A Chain of Principles.* Edinburgh: T. Turnbull, 1822. Digital copy online at books.google.com.

Ball, John. *A Treatise of the Covenant of Grace.* London: G. Miller, 1645. Digital copy online at EEBO.

Bastingius, Jeremias. *An Exposition or Commentary upon the Catechism of Christian Religion Which Is Taught in the Schools and Churches Both of the Lowe Countries and of the Dominions of the County Palatine.* Cambridge: John Legatt, 1589. Digital copy online at EEBO.

Becon, Thomas. *The Catechism of Thomas Becon, with Other Pieces Written by Him in the Reign of King Edward the Sixth.* Edited by John Ayre. Cambridge: Cambridge University Press, 1844. Digital copy online at archive.org.

Binning, Hugh. *The Works of the Reverend Hugh Binning, M. A.* Edited by M. Leishman. 3rd ed. Edinburgh, London and Dublin: A. Fullarton, 1851. Digital copy online at archive.org.

Borrhaus, Martin. *In sacram Iosuae, Iudicum, Ruthae, Samuelis et Regum Historiam, mystica Messiae servatoris mundi adumbratione refertam, Martini Borrhai Commentarius.* Basel: Johann Oporinus, 1557. Digital copy online at www.e-rara.ch.

Brenz, Johannes. "Historia Josaphat." In *Werke: Frühschriften,* edited by Martin Brecht, Gerhard Schäfer and Frieda Wolf, 2:132-41. Tübingen: Mohr Siebeck, 1970–1974.

———. *Operum reverendi et clarissimi theologi, D. Ioannis Brentii, praepositi Stutgardiani tomus primus [-octavus].* 8 vols. Tübingen: George Gruppenbach, 1576–1590. Digital copy online at www.gateway-bayern.de.

Brightman, Thomas. *Brightman Redivivus: The Post-Human Offspring in Four Sermons.* London: Thomas Forcet, 1647. Digital copy online at EEBO.

Bucer, Martin. *Instruction in Christian Love.* Translated by Paul Fuhrmann. John Knox Press: Richmond, 1952.

———. *De Regno Christi Iesu servatoris nostri.* Basel: Johann Oporinum, 1557. Digital copy online at www.e-rara.ch.

Bugenhagen, Johannes. *In Regum duos ultimos libros, annotationes Ioannis Bugenhagii Pomerani, post Samuelem iam primum emissae.* Basel: Adam Petri, 1525. Digital copy online at www.e-rara.ch.

———. *Ioannis Bugenhagii Pomerani annotationes ab ipso iam emissae. In Deuteronomium. In Samuelem prophetam, id est duos libros Regum. Ab eodem praeterea conciliata ex Evangelistis historia passi Christi & glorificati, cum annotationibus. Indice adiecto.* Basel: Adam Petri, 1524. Digital copy online at www.e-rara.ch.

Bullinger, Heinrich. *Sermonum decades quinque, de potissimis Christianae religionis capitibus, in tres tomos digestae.* London: Rudolph Newberry and Hugo Jackson, 1587. Digital copy online at EEBO.

Cajetan, Cardinal (Thomas de Vio). *Opera Omnia qvotqvot in Sacrae Scripturae Expositionem Reperiuntur.* 5 vols. Lyon: Jacob and Peter Prost, 1639. Digital copy online at books.google.com.

Calvin, John. *Institutes of the Christian Religion (1559).* Edited by John T. McNeill. Translated by Ford Lewis Battles. LCC 20–21. Philadelphia: Westminster, 1960. Latin text available in CO 2 (1864); digital copy online at archive-ouverte.unige.ch/unige:650.

———. *Sermons on Second Samuel: Chapters 1–13.* Translated by Douglas Kelly. Carlisle, PA: Banner of Truth, 1992.

Clarkson, David. *The Practical Works of David Clarkson.* 3 vols. Edinburgh: James Nichol, 1864–1865. Digital copy online at archive.org.

Daneau, Lambert. *A Dialogue of Witches*. London: T. East, 1575. Digital copy online at EEBO.

———. *True and Christian Friendship*. London: G. Robinson, 1586. Digital copy online at EEBO.

Davenant, John. *Exposition of the Epistle of St. Paul to the Colossians*. 2 vols. London: Hamilton, Adams. 1831–1832. Digital copy online at archive.org.

Denck, Hans. *The Spiritual Legacy of Hans Denck: Interpretation and Translation of Key Texts by Clarence Bauman*. Leiden: Brill, 1991.

Dickson, David. *A Brief Explication of the First Fifty Psalms*. London: Ralph Smith, 1655. Digital copy online at EEBO.

Diodati, Giovanni. *Pious and Learned Annotations upon the Whole Bible*. London: Nicolas Fussell, 1643. Digital copy online at EEBO.

Dod, John. *Ten Sermons: Tending Chiefly to the Tending of Men for the Worthy Receiving of the Lord's Supper*. London: W. Sheffard, 1628. Digital copy online at EEBO.

Donne, John. *The Works of John Donne*. 6 vols. Edited by Henry Alford. London: John Parker, 1839. Digital copy online at books.google.com.

Downame, John, ed. *Annotations upon All the Books of the Old and New Testaments*. London: John Legatt and John Raworth, 1645. The *English Annotations* were expanded in 1651 (London: John Legatt) and 1657 (London: Evan Tyler), when they reached their final form after the general editor's death. Digital copy online at EEBO.

Drelincourt, Charles. *The Christian's Defense Against the Fears of Death: With Seasonable Directions How to Prepare Ourselves to Die Well*. London: D. Midwinter and A. Ward, 1732. Digital copy online at books.google.com.

Dyke, Daniel. *The Mystery of Self-Deceiving: A Discourse and Discovery of the Deceitfulness of Man's Heart*. London: William Stansby, 1633. Digital copy online at EEBO.

Fisher, John. *Commentary on the Seven Penitential Psalms*. London: Manresa, 1914. Digital copy online at archive.org.

[Geneva Bible (1560).] *The Bible and Holy Scriptures Conteyned in the Old and Newe Testament*. Edited by William Whittingham. Geneva: Rouland Hall, 1560. Digital copy online at EEBO.

Gerhard, Johann. *The Conquest of Temptations: Man's Victory over Satan*. London: Roger Jackson, 1614. Digital copy online at EEBO.

———. *Gerhardi Meditationes Sacrae*. Oxford: John Lichfield, 1633. Digital copy online at EEBO.

Gifford, George. *A Dialogue concerning Witches & Witchcrafts*. London: Percy Society, 1842. Digital copy online at books.google.com.

Greef, Wulfert de. *The Writings of John Calvin: An Introductory Guide*. Translated by Lyle D. Bierma. Louisville, KY: Westminster John Knox Press, 2008.

Hubmaier, Balthasar. *Balthasar Hubmaier: Theologian of Anabaptism*. Translated and edited by H. Wayne Pipkin and John H. Yoder. CRR 5. Scottdale, PA: Herald, 1989.

Haak, Theodore, trans. *Dutch Annotations upon the Whole Bible*. London, 1657. Digital copy online at EEBO.

Hutchinson, Roger. *Two Sermons of Oppression, Affliction, and Patience*. Cambridge: Cambridge University Press, 1842. Digital copy online at books.google.com.

Jackson, Thomas. *The Works of the Reverend and Learned Divine*. London: John Martyn and Richard Chiswell, Joseph Clark, 1673. Digital copy online at EEBO.

James VI. *Ane Meditatiovn vopn the xxv, xxvi, xxvii, xxviii and xxix Verses of the XV Chapter of the First Buke of the Chronicles of the Kingis*. Edinburgh: Henrie Charteris, 1589. Digital copy online at EEBO.

Jewell, John. *Writings of John Jewell*. London: Religious Tract Society, 1831. Digital copy online at archive.org.

Karlstadt, Andreas Bodenstein von. *The Essential Carlstadt: Fifteen Tracts by Andreas Bodenstein (Carlstadt) from Karlstadt*. Translated and Edited by E. J. Furcha. CRR 8. Scottsdale, PA: Herald, 1995.

Kellett, Edward. *Miscellanies of Divinity*. Cambridge: Cambridge University Press, 1633. Digital copy online at EEBO.

Knox, John. *The First Blast of the Trumpet against the Monstrous Regiment of Women* (1558). Edited by Edward Arber. Westminster: Archibald Constable & Co., 1895. Digital copy online at babel .hathitrust.org.

———. *Select Practical Works of John Knox*. Glasgow: William Collins, 1845. Digital copy online at archive.org.

Lake, Osmund. *A Probe Theologicall*. London: William Leake, 1612. Digital copy online at EEBO.

Lavater, Ludwig. *De Spectris*. Geneva: Jean Crespin, 1570. Digital copy online at www.e-rara.ch.

———. *In Libros Paralipomenon sive Chronicorum Ludovici Lavateri Tigurini Commentarius*. Zurich: Christoph Froschauer, 1573. Digital copy online at www.e-rara.ch.

Liechty, Daniel, ed. and trans. *Early Anabaptist Spirituality: Selected Writings*. Mahwah, NJ. Paulist, 1994.

Luther, Martin. *Luther's Works [American Edition]*. 82 vols. planned. St. Louis: Concordia; Philadelphia: Fortress, 1955–1986, 2009–.

Mayer, John. *Many Commentaries in One*. London: John Legatt, 1647. Digital copy online at EEBO.

Melanchthon, Philipp. *Loci communes Theologici* (1521). In *Melanchthon and Bucer*, edited by Wilhelm Pauck, 18–152. LCC 19. Philadelphia: Westminster, 1969.

———. *Melanchthon on Christian Doctrine: Loci communes 1555*. Translated by Clyde Manschreck. Oxford: Oxford University Press, 1965.

Menius, Justus. *In Samuelis Librum Priorem enarratio*. Wittenberg: Johannes Lufft, 1532. Digital copy online at www.gateway-bayern.de.

Münster, Sebastian. *Miqdaš YHWH: 'esrîm wĕ'arba' sifrê hammikhtav haqqadôsh 'im 'āthîqathô kol*. Basel: Michael Isinginius and Henricus Petrus, 1546. In English the title is *The Temple of the Lord: The Twenty-Four Books of Holy Scripture with All Its Antiquity*. Digital copy online at www.e-rara.ch.

Osiander, Lucas. *Liber Iosue, Iudicum, Ruth, Primus et Secundus Samuelis, Primus et Secundus Regum, Primus et Secundus Paralipomenon: Iuxta Veterem Seu Vulgatam Translationem*. Tübingen: Georg Gruppenbach 1574. Digital copy online at www.gateway-bayern.de.

Pellikan, Konrad. *Commentaria Bibliorum et illa brevia quidem ac Catholica*. 5 vols. Zurich: Christoph Froschauer, 1532–1535. Digital copy online at www.e-rara.ch.

Perrault, François. *Demonologie: Ou traitte des demons et sorciers*. Geneva: Pierre Aubert, 1653. Digital copy online at books.google.com.

Piscator, Johannes.*Commentarii in omnes libros Veteris Testamenti*. 4 vols. Herborn: Christoph Corvinus, 1643–1645. Digital copy online at books.google.com.

Reynolds, Edward. *The Whole Works of the Right Rev. Edward Reynolds*. 6 vols. London: B. Holdsworth, 1826. Digital copy online at archive.org.

Robinson, John. *The Works of John Robinson*. 3 vols. London: J. Snow, 1851. Digital copy online at archive.org.

Sanderson, Robert. *The Works of Robert Sanderson*. 6 vols. Oxford: Oxford University Press, 1854. Digital copy online at archive.org.

Selnecker, Nikolaus. *Der gantze Psalter des Königlichen Propheten Davids*. 3 vols. Nuremberg: Christoph Heußler, 1565–1566. Digital copy online at www. gateway-bayern.de.

Simons, Menno. *The Complete Writings of Menno Simons*. Translated by Leonard Verduin. Scottdale, PA: Herald, 1956.

Strigel, Viktorin. *Libri Samuelis, Regum et Paralipomenon: Ad Hebraicam Veritatem Recogniti, et Brevibus Commentariis Explicati*. Leipzig: Ernst Vögelin, 1569. Digital copy online at www.gateway-bayern.de.

Tarabotti, Arcangela. *Paternal Tyranny*. Edited and translated by Letizia Panizza. Chicago: University of Chicago Press, 2004.

Tostado, Alonso. *Alphonsi Tostati Opera Omnia*. 27 vols. Venice: Balleoniana, 1728. Digital copy online at babel.hathitrust.org.

———. *Commentaria in libros Paralipomenon*. TO 16–17. Venice: Balleoniana, 1728. Digital copy online at babel.hathitrust.org.

———. *Commentaria in libros Regum*. TO 12–15. Venice: Balleoniana, 1728. Digital copy online at babel.hathitrust.org.

Tyndale, William. *Doctrinal Treatises and Introductions to Other Portions of Holy Scriptures*. London: Parker Society, 1848. Digital copy online at archive.org.

Vermigli, Peter Martyr. *In duos libros Samuelis prophetae qui vulgo priores libri regum appellantur D. Petri Martyris Vermilii Florentini*. Edited by Johann Wolf. Zurich: Christoph Froschauer, 1564. Digital copy online at www.e-rara.ch.

———. *Regum Libri Duo posteriores cum commentariis*. Edited by Johann Wolf. Zurich: Christoph Froschauer, 1571. Digital copy online at www.e-rara.ch.

Weller, Hieronymus von Molsdorf. *Liber secundus Regum, Annotationibus piis simul et eruditis explicatus*. Nuremberg: Johannes Montanus and Ulricus Neuberus, 1560. Digital copy online at www.gateway-bayern.de.

———. *Samuelis liber primus, Annotationibus piis iuxta ac eruditis explicatus*. Frankfurt am Main: Peter Brubach, 1555. Digital copy online at www.gateway-bayern.de.

———. *Samuelis liber secundus, Annotationibus piis iuxta ac eruditis explicatus*. Frankfurt am Main: Peter Brubach, 1555. Digital copy online at www.gateway-bayern.de.

Willet, Andrew. *A Harmony on the First Book of Samuel*. Cambridge: Leonard Greene, 1607. Digital copy online at EEBO.

———. *A Harmony on the Second Book of Samuel*. Cambridge: Cantrell Legge, 1614. Digital copy online at EEBO.

Zwingli, Huldrych. *The Latin Works of Huldrich Zwingli*. 2 vols. Edited by William Hinke. Philadelphia: Heidelberg Press, 1922.

Other Works Consulted

Berry, Lloyd E., ed. *The Geneva Bible: A Facsimile of the 1560 Edition*. Peabody, MA: Hendrickson, 2007.

Biggar, Nigel. *In Defence of War*. Oxford: Oxford University Press, 2013.

Brecht, Martin. *Martin Luther*. 3 vols. Translated by James L. Schaaf. Minneapolis: Fortress, 1985–1993.

Bugenhagen, Johannes. *Ionas Propheta expositus*. Wittenberg: Veit Kreutzer, 1550. Digital copy online at www.gateway-bayern.de.

———. *Johannes Bugenhagen: Selected Writings*. 2 vols. Translated by Kurt K. Hendel. Minneapolis: Fortress, 2015.

Burnett, Stephen G. "The Strange Career of the *Biblia Rabbinica* Among Christian Hebraists, 1517–1620." In *Shaping the Bible in the Reformation: Books, Scholars and Their Readers in the Sixteenth Century*, edited by Bruce Gordon and Matthew McLean, 63-84. Leiden: Brill, 2012.

Charles, J. Daryl. *Between Pacifism and Jihad: Just War and Christian Tradition*. Downers Grove, IL:

IVP Academic, 2005.

Chung-Kim, Esther, and Todd R. Hains, eds. *Acts*. RCS NT 6. Downers Grove, IL, IVP Academic, 2014.

Conti, Marco, ed. *1–2 Kings, 1–2 Chronicles, Ezra, Nehemiah, Esther*. ACCS OT 5. Downers Grove, IL: InterVarsity Press, 2008.

Das Annder teyl des alten Testaments. Translated by Martin Luther et al. Strasbourg: Johann Knoblouch, 1524. Digital copy online at www.gateway-bayern.de.

Eells, Hastings. *The Attitude of Martin Bucer Toward the Bigamy of Philip of Hesse*. New Haven, CT: Yale University Press, 1924. Digital copy online at babel.hathitrust.org.

Franke, John R., ed. *Joshua, Judges, Ruth, 1–2 Samuel*. ACCS OT 4. Downers Grove, IL: InterVarsity Press, 2005.

Greene-McCreight, Kathryn. "Literal Sense." In *Dictionary for Theological Interpretation of the Bible*, edited by Kevin J. Vanhoozer, 455-56. Grand Rapids: Baker Academic, 2005.

———. "Rule of Faith." In *Dictionary for Theological Interpretation of the Bible*, edited by Kevin J. Vanhoozer, 703-4. Grand Rapids: Baker Academic, 2005.

Kolb, Robert. "Luther on the Theology of the Cross." *Lutheran Quarterly* 16, no. 1 (2002): 443-66.

Lohrmann, Martin. *Bugenhagen's Jonah: Biblical Interpretation as Public Theology*. Minneapolis: Lutheran University Press, 2012.

Melanchthon, Philipp. *Melanchthons Werke in Auswahl [Studienausgabe]*. 7 vols. Edited by Robert Stupperich. Gütersloh: C. Bertelsmann, 1951–1975.

Muller, Richard A. *Post-Reformation Reformed Dogmatics: The Rise and Development of Reformed Orthodoxy, ca. 1520 to ca. 1725*. 4 vols. 2nd ed. Grand Rapids: Baker Academic, 2003.

Oberman, Heiko A. *Luther: Man Between God and the Devil*. Translated by Eileen Walliser-Schwarzbart. New Haven, CT: Yale University Press, 2006.

Pak, G. Sujin. *The Judaizing Calvin: Sixteenth-Century Debates over the Messianic Psalms*. Oxford: Oxford University Press, 2010.

Philips, Dirk. *The Writings of Dirk Philips 1504–1568*. Edited by Cornelius J. Dyck, William E. Keeney and Alvin J. Beachy. CRR 6. Scottdale, PA: Herald, 1992.

Plummer, Marjorie Elizabeth. "'The Much Married Michael Kraemer': Evangelical Clergy and Bigamy in Ernestine Saxony, 1522–1542." In *Ideas and Cultural Margins in Early Modern Germany: Essays in Honor of H. C. Erik Midelfort*, edited by Marjorie Elizabeth Plummer and Robin Barnes, 99-115. Farnham, UK: Ashgate, 2009.

Rockwell, William Walker. *Die Doppelehe des Landgrafen Philipp von Hessen*. Marburg: N. G. Elwert'sche Verlagsbuchhandlung, 1904. Digital copy online at babel.hathitrust.org.

Schaff, Philip. *The Creeds of Christendom: With a Critical History and Notes*. 3 vols. New York: Harper & Row, 1877. Reprint, Grand Rapids: Baker, 1977. Digital copy online at ccel.org.

Selderhuis, Herman J., ed. *Psalms 1–72*. RCS OT 7. Downers Grove, IL: IVP Academic, 2015.

Sheridan, Mark. *Language for God in Patristic Tradition: Wrestling with Biblical Anthropomorphism*. Downers Grove, IL: IVP Academic, 2015.

Sophocles. *Antigone, The Women of Trachis, Philocetus, Oedipus at Colonus*. Edited and translated by Hugh Lloyd Jones. Loeb Classical Library 21. Cambridge, MA: Harvard University Press, 1994.

Tomlin, Graham, ed. *Philippians, Colossians*. RCS NT 11. Downers Grove, IL: IVP Academic, 2013.

Weller, Hieronymus von Molsdorf. *Liber primus Regum, Annotationibus piis simuel et eruditis explicatus*. Frankfurt am Main: Peter Brubach, 1557. Digital copy online at www.gateway-bayern.de.

Wengert, Timothy J. "'Peace, Peace . . . Cross, Cross': Reflections on How Martin Luther Relates the Theology of the Cross to Suffering." *Theology Today* 59, no. 2 (2002): 190-205.

Author and Writings Index

Adams, Thomas, *liii*, 12, 18-19, 44, 48, 67, 71, 75-76, 91, 111, 117, 122-23, 127-28, 131, 196-97, 203, 218, 223, 280, 305, 327, 363, 365, 378, 386-87, 417, 421, 506, 541-42, 618-19

Aepinus, Johannes, 50, 208, 320

Ainsworth, Henry, 196, 306, 550, 563

Airay, Henry, 68, 83, 88, 160, 199-200, 205, 209, 237, 269, 355, 423, 430-31, 563, 580

Alesius, Alexander, 501

Ambrose, 82, 116, 378, 423

Andrewes, Lancelot, *liii*, 7-10, 12, 22, 32, 34-36, 57, 66-67, 90-91, 118, 148-49, 171, 179, 206-7, 259-60, 306, 325

Aquinas, Thomas, 183

Aretius, Benedict, 118, 421-23

Arminius, Jacobus, *liii*, 110, 118, 153-54, 177, 225-26, 229-30, 306, 326-28, 351-52, 362, 378

Arndt, Johann, 8, 22, 62, 165, 172, 223, 226, 251-52, 384

Arrowsmith, John, 104, 118

Augsburg Confession, *xlviii*, 34, 506

Augustine, *xlvii*, *liii*, 52, 63, 82, 94-95, 129, 176, 183, 340-41, 406, 419, 444, 487, 489, 589, 602

Ball, John, 178-79

Bastingius, Jeremias, 112, 276, 366

Becon, Thomas, 95, 124, 192, 364

Beza, Theodore, *liii*

Binning, Hugh, 204

Borrhaus, Martin, 162, 187, 210, 405, 452-54

Brenz, Johannes, 21-22, 80, 84, 89-90, 105-6, 111, 194, 224, 326-27, 379, 387-89, 623-24, 627

Brightman, Thomas, 168

Bucer, Martin, *lii*, 4, 17-18, 88-89, 165, 171, 281-82, 406, 625

Bugenhagen, Johannes, *xlvii*, *lii*, 4-9, 11, 17-19, 23, 27-29, 31, 34-35, 37, 41-45, 50-51, 56-59, 61-62, 70, 73-74, 76, 79, 87, 89-90, 94-95, 99-100, 102-7, 109-11, 113, 115-17, 123-25, 127, 129, 135-38, 147, 152-53, 156-57, 159-60, 165-66, 168, 170-71, 174-76, 183-87, 209, 214, 217-19, 223-24, 226, 229, 231-32, 245-47, 251, 259-62, 265-70, 273-76, 278, 281, 283, 285-87, 292-93, 295-301, 304-7, 310-11, 314-16, 318-22, 325-26, 328-29, 332-33, 335-36, 340-41, 343-45, 348-51, 354-55, 357, 363-65, 367, 372-73, 376-77, 379-80, 384, 393-94, 398-400, 402, 405, 408-9, 411, 415-18, 420-25, 431-37, 440, 442, 444, 448, 452-53, 455, 457, 459-60, 464-70, 473-76, 481-83, 494-95, 500-502, 505-8, 511-12, 514-16, 518

Bullinger, Heinrich, *liii*, 16-17, 57, 96, 99, 123, 128-30, 165, 167-68, 177, 203-4, 222-24, 294-95, 327, 329, 356, 362-63, 470-71, 494, 507, 564, 607, 653-54

Cajetan, Cardinal, *liii*, 1, 13, 30, 56, 118-19, 215-16, 244, 399, 487, 581

Calvin, John, *xlvii*, *xlix*, *li-liii*, 13, 58, 62, 66-67, 74, 111-12, 127, 136, 138, 142-44, 146-47, 149, 152-53, 156, 160-62, 165-72, 175, 177-80, 183-89, 191, 193-99, 202, 206-7, 214, 216-17, 224, 229, 293, 307, 362, 366, 384, 484, 503, 548-49, 555, 558-59, 597

Chrysostom, *liii*, 281, 444, 466, 666

Clarkson, David, 13, 245, 583-84

Daneau, Lambert, *liii*, 87-88, 95-96, 98, 100, 111, 130, 144, 186, 225, 228, 245, 394, 563

Davenant, John, 36-37, 51-52, 98-99, 112, 117-18, 187, 195, 209, 423-24, 443, 564

Denck, Hans, *liii*, 12, 74, 104

Dickson, David, 105, 124, 204, 294

Diodati, Giovanni, *lii-liii*, 6, 30-32, 42, 65, 76, 139-40, 275, 279, 298-99, 390-91, 396, 400, 410, 422, 459, 482, 491, 505-6, 520, 543, 566, 571, 585, 629, 639-40

Dod, John, 8-9, 52, 203, 554, 583, 656-58

Donne, John, 581-82, 672-73

Drelincourt, Charles, 30, 58, 75-76, 84, 88, 209-10, 231, 236, 258, 274, 350, 379, 385-87, 402, 406, 416, 507, 618

Dutch Annotations, *lii-liii*, 48, 68

Dyke, Daniel, 6-7, 43-44, 56-58, 62-63, 90-91, 110, 112-13, 131-32, 135-36, 192, 194-95, 198, 215, 218, 222, 235, 258-59, 341, 360, 380-81, 386, 423, 435, 444, 448, 500-501

The English Annotations, *lii-liii*, 59, 202, 279, 305, 319, 485-86, 531-33, 535, 540, 542, 547, 550-52, 554, 566, 576, 585, 589-91, 596-99, 601-3, 607-9, 613-17, 619, 625-29, 631-33, 637-39, 644-48, 654-56, 658, 660, 666-67, 669, 671-72

Erasmus, Desiderius, *lii*

Fisher, John, 71, 85

Geneva Bible, *lii*, 1-2, 73, 262, 391, 520, 531, 548, 554, 582, 585, 618, 661

Gerhard, Johann, 12, 64, 160, 297, 315, 459, 490, 597-98

Gifford, George, 74, 128

Heidelberg Disputation, *xlix*

Hubmaier, Balthasar, *liii*, 235, 362, 366, 547

Hutchinson, Roger, 89, 186

Jackson, Thomas, 23, 70-71, 128, 232, 373-74, 415-16, 420-21

Jerome, *xlvii*, 36, 81, 261, 264,

266-67, 488, 616

Jewel, John, 19

Josephus, *liii*, 29, 32, 56, 68, 71-72, 98, 130, 136, 139, 149, 162, 274, 281, 312, 334, 435, 442, 453, 469, 475, 488, 512, 515, 591, 626, 666, 671

Karlstadt, Andreas Bodenstein von, 256, 333, 358, 482, 505

Kellett, Edward, 154-55

King James VI, 551

Knox, John, 63-64, 94-95, 124, 224, 502-3

Lake, Osmund, 168

Lavater, Ludwig, 383, 385, 532

Luther, Martin, *xlvii*, *li-lii*, *liv*, 4, 9, 12-13, 18, 29-30, 42-43, 46-47, 51, 65-66, 73, 75, 85, 90, 94-96, 128, 176-78, 188, 191, 198, 202, 205, 222, 229-31, 244-46, 248, 251-54, 256-58, 261, 265, 273, 293-94, 318, 356, 358, 361-64, 366, 395, 402, 405, 409-10, 421, 430-31, 471, 482, 488, 508, 532, 554-55, 566, 582, 655, 669

Mayer, John, *liii*, 142-44, 154-55, 157, 162, 191-92, 215-16, 247, 265, 267-70, 273-76, 279-83, 286-88, 294, 296-98, 300, 306-7, 310-12, 319-20, 322, 324-25, 328, 333-37, 342-45, 348-51, 355-60, 363-67, 370-73, 378-80, 385-89, 395-403, 406, 408-11, 415, 418-19, 421-22, 424-26, 431-37, 440, 442-44, 447-49, 453-55, 457-58, 460, 464-69, 471, 474-75, 481, 483-89, 491-92, 495-96, 500-502, 504-5, 508, 511-18, 565, 569-71, 575-77, 580-83, 589-92, 596-99, 602-3, 606-10, 614-18, 625-28, 631-33, 637-40, 645-48, 654, 656-60, 665-69, 671

Melanchthon, Philipp, *xlvii*, *lii*, 4, 16, 18, 37, 45, 89, 99, 106, 127, 202, 206, 234,

236, 256, 378, 401-2, 483, 488, 655

Menius, Justus, *liv*, 97-98, 125

Molsdorf, Hieronymus Weller von, 96, 103, 237, 245-47, 419, 499-500

Münster, Sebastian, *li*, 1, 247, 328, 519

Nicholas of Lyra, *xlvii*, 178, 216, 237, 261, 275, 286, 398, 434, 442, 484, 486, 513, 570, 581, 632, 645, 654, 658, 660, 668

Oecolampadius, Johannes, *lii*

Osiander, Lucas, *xlvii*, *lii*, 1, 6, 21-23, 28-30, 35, 40, 47, 79-80, 224-25, 237, 244, 254, 258-59, 281, 342, 418-20, 513, 516-17, 519-20, 530-34, 536, 540-42, 547, 549-52, 563-66, 569-71, 575-76, 582-84

Pellikan, Konrad, *lii*, 119, 146-47, 191, 216, 282-83, 286-87, 298-99, 304-5, 307-8, 310-11, 314-15, 321, 333-36, 340-44, 349-51, 356-57, 367, 370, 372, 379-80, 388, 394-95, 408, 425, 432, 434-37, 440-44, 447, 452, 454-55, 457, 459, 465,

467-71, 473-75, 480-81, 485-87, 489, 491, 494-96, 500-508, 511-15, 517-18, 531, 535-36, 540-41

Perrault, François, 131

Philips, Dirk, *liii*, 122, 176, 292, 327

Piscator, Johannes, *lii*, 5, 118, 262, 270, 275, 278-81, 286-87, 293-94, 296-97, 311, 314-16, 320-22, 324, 333-35, 342-45, 348, 351, 355-56, 362, 364, 367, 371, 373-74, 377, 386-87, 390, 394-95, 398, 400-402, 405-6, 408, 410-11, 415, 417-19, 421, 423, 425, 432-34, 436-37, 441-43, 447-49, 455, 457-58, 470, 474, 481, 484-85, 487-91, 496, 500, 502, 514, 518, 530-34, 536, 540-43, 547-52, 554-56, 559-60, 563-65, 569-72, 575-77, 582-84

Plato, 286, 487

Ramus, Peter, *lii*

Reynolds, Edward, 7, 62-63, 72, 83-85, 91, 99, 113, 171-72, 199, 219, 222-23, 252, 257, 315, 324-25, 417, 424, 445,

618, 655, 661, 667-68

Robinson, John, 28, 215, 230, 441, 444

Sanderson, Robert, 18, 107, 192, 198-99, 204-5, 219, 311, 328, 345-46, 377, 380-81, 441, 563

Selnecker, Nikolaus, 96

Simons, Menno, *liii*, 61, 99, 177, 194-96, 205-6, 208, 504

Strigel, Viktorin, *lii*, 6, 8, 11-12, 16, 19, 21-22, 28-31, 34-37, 40-41, 45, 47-48, 50-51, 79-80, 234-36, 244, 248, 254, 281, 305, 308, 358-59, 370-72, 379, 416, 446-47, 451, 453-54, 458, 485-87, 490-91, 512-14, 517, 520-21, 531-36, 541-42, 564-66, 580-81, 588-91, 596-99, 602-3, 606-7, 609, 613, 615, 617, 624-28, 631-34, 637-39, 645-46, 648, 654-57, 659-60, 665-69, 672

Tarabotti, Arcangela, 191, 193-94, 203

Theodoret, 52, 410, 419, 516

Thirty-Nine Articles, *xlix*

Tostado, Alonso, *liii*, 156, 161, 165-66, 174, 176, 184, 192-93,

265-69, 273, 392-94, 398-99, 404-5, 581

Tyndale, William, *liii*, 65, 84-85, 105, 111, 123

Vermigli, Peter Martyr, *liii*, 139, 146-48, 152, 159-60, 191, 215, 265, 268, 349, 371, 401, 409, 419-20, 426, 433, 435, 442, 444, 447, 591, 597-98, 602

Walpot, Peter, 137

Willet, Andrew, *liii*, 5, 9, 17, 19, 21-24, 28-32, 35-36, 41-45, 47-48, 50-51, 57-59, 63-68, 70-73, 75, 80-84, 98, 103-4, 106-7, 113, 116-20, 123, 130-31, 136-38, 140, 142-44, 147-49, 153-57, 159, 162-63, 165, 167, 169-70, 172, 174-75, 179, 184-85, 203, 208-10, 214-15, 217-19, 228, 230-31, 235-38, 244-45, 247-49, 252, 254, 257, 259-60

Zwingli, Huldrych, 40-41, 193, 207-9, 258, 321, 358-59, 425, 489

Subject Index

1–2 Chronicles, *li*, 261, 273-
74, 519-21, 585-86, 596,
672-73
  genealogy of, 530-33
1–2 Kings, *li*, 1, 261-62,
390-91
1–2 Samuel, *l-li*, 1, 139-40, 260
Abel, wise woman of, 245-46
Abigail, 116-18
Abijah, 570-71, 613-14
Abijam, 340
Abishag, 265-67, 274-75
Abner, 153-55
Absalom, 216-19, 222-23, 340
  and David's concubines,
  228-30
  death of, 235-37
Adonijah, 267-69, 274-75
affliction. *See* trials and
  tribulations
Agag, 61-62
agriculture, dignity of, 47
Ahab, 345-46, 356, 358, 363,
373-74, 384-85, 388, 625,
627
  death of, 386-87
  and Naboth's vineyard,
  376-81
  at war with Syria, 370-72,
  626
Ahaz, 469-71, 647-48
Ahaziah, 388-89, 393-94, 437,
442, 633
Ahijah, 322, 334
Ahithophel, 229-32
altar
  of David, 260
  horns of, 270
  of the temple, 591, 599
Amaziah, 458, 464-65,
644-45
ambition, 453
amen, meaning of, 552
Amnon, 214-17
Amon, 495-96, 666
Amos, 465, 470
ancestors, godly vs. wicked,
388-89
angels, spiritual protection
of, 430
apathy, 191-92, 356, 363, 444,
464-65, 473, 508
appearance, deceitfulness of
outward, 540
ark of the covenant, 27-32,

165-70, 294-95, 304-5, 487,
547-48, 550-51, 596, 598
arms, right to bear, 144
Asa, 341-42, 388, 615-19
Asahel, 149
Asaph, sons of, 571
Asher, descendants of, 535
astrology, 499-500, 543
Athaliah, 452-54, 633-34, 637
authorities, civil, 186-87, 419,
465, 483, 532, 653-54
  blessing of, 47, 254, 285
  established by God, 441
  as fleeting, 373
  instructions to, 160, 448-
  49, 481, 485, 500, 505,
  542, 551, 575-76
  leniency of, 324
  and religious institutions,
  154, 536, 571
  request for, 35-37, 633
  standing against, 106, 356
  submission to, 83, 111-12,
  123, 222, 324, 501, 583
Azariah (king), 466-67, 469,
645-46
Azariah (prophet), 615-16
Baal, nature of, 624
Baasha, 342-43, 617-18
baptism, 83, 419-20
  of infants, 207, 209
Bathsheba, 268-69
  comfort for, 210
  David's adultery with,
  191-94, 203-4
beauty, vanity of, 218-19, 268
Ben-hadad, 371, 373, 387,
432, 435-36, 617-18
Benjamin
  descendants of, 534-35
  tribe of, 40
Bethshemites, 32
calling, accepting God's, 168-
69, 188, 222
Chenaniah, 550
cherubim, nature of, 591
children
  exasperating one's, 98-99
  praying for, 153
Christ Jesus, 224, 310-11,
459, 487, 534, 555, 597-98,
672-73
  ascension of, 401-2
  baptism of, 70-71
  as fulfillment of prophecy,

13, 176-79
  genealogy of, 518, 532
  as mediator, 6, 36, 218
  obedience of, 80
  as sacrifice, 9, 34-35
  as victor, 79, 84, 88
  church, 209, 237, 249,
  355, 398, 400, 444,
  536, 655
  accountability for, 624-25
  as anointed, 41-42
  discipline of, 417
  division within, 326
  favor of, 517-18
  God's presence with, 160,
  430-31, 598
  as harp of David, 75
  as Israel, 531
  joy of, 171
  and lapsed believers, 665
  love of, 99, 142, 443
  praying for, 51
  preservation of, 160-61,
  262, 366, 470-71, 494,
  514, 518, 607
  protection for, 31, 542,
  549
  role of, 245-46
  as the temple, 555, 589,
  597
  as treasure, 581-82
  unfaithfulness of, 28
  unity of, 596
  universality of, 366
  victory of, 84-85, 534, 613
church leadership, 68, 417,
575, 582, 668
  caring for family of, 415
  importance of, 185
  instructions for, 333, 423,
  485, 500, 627
  integrity of, 16-18
  negligence of, 81-82
  respect for, 187, 432
  seeking counsel from, 458
  as submissive to
  government, 501
  types of, 532
circumcision of the heart, 83
cloud, presence of God as,
596-97, 599
comfort. *See* consolation
confession. *See* repentance
conscience, 225
  guilty, 30, 196, 215, 335

keeping a good, 50, 124
consolation, 8, 362-63, 485
contentment, 364
contrition. *See* repentance
covenant, 252-54, 304-5
  keeping, 617
  renewing, 454-55
  as salt, 614
cross, 224
  foolishness of, 104-5
Dagon, 29-30
  See also Philistines
dancing, guidelines for, 88-89
David, *l-li*, 89-91, 111, 115-
16, 118, 123, 136, 142-44,
154-55, 157, 168-69, 174-75,
179, 185-86, 191, 195-200,
202-4, 207-8, 214-17, 223,
225-26, 229, 237-38, 247,
251, 256-57, 259 268,
340-41, 487, 500, 532, 541,
548-49, 582
  at Achish, 105, 124-25
  anointing of, 72-73,
  147-48
  census of, 256-58, 577
  as chosen one, 13-14
  compared to Saul, 66-67,
  73
  compared to Solomon,
  566, 580
  conscience of, 111, 196
  dancing, 170-72, 551
  death of, 273-74, 576, 584
  example of, 1-2, 80, 98,
  124, 481, 541, 556, 559,
  565, 582-83
  as favored one, 152, 160-61
  as friend of Jonathan, 87-
  88, 98-100, 110-11, 535
  the Holy Spirit and, 73
  joy of, 224
  as merciful, 95, 111-12,
  123, 148, 155-56,
  234-35
  mighty men of, 254,
  541-42
  as musician, 75-76
  as physically cold, 265-67
  piety of, 547
  polygamy of, 152-53,
  161-62
  prayers of, 124, 209, 583
  as prophet, 251
  psalms of, 247-48, 552

repentance of, 205-7
as shepherd, 159-60
and showbread, 102-3
typology of, 73, 79-80, 83-84, 96, 122, 143, 175-76, 178, 232, 235, 248, 274, 580, 597
wisdom of, 218, 542-43
deacons, role of, 575-76
death, 459
and fate, 489
as unexpected, 379, 387
victory over, 84
Deuteronomy. *See* law
devil. *See* Satan
discipline
accepting, 12-13, 202
of God, 205, 208-9 258-59, 564
See also judgment of God
disobedience, warning against, 607-9
doctors. *See* physicians, on visiting
Doeg, 107
drunkenness, 118, 197-98, 344
Ebenezer, 35
Edom, 631, 644-45
Egypt
fear of, 671
metaphors of, 485
Elah, 343-44
elders of Israel, 504
elect. *See* church
election, divine, 179, 209, 580-81
Eli, 6, 8, 18-23, 28, 106
Eliab, 72-73, 82-83
Elijah, 348-51, 355-56, 367, 379, 395-96
ascension of, 400-402
clothing of, 394-95, 398
flight of, 362-66
letter of, 631-32
prayer of, 359-60
and prophetic school, 397-98
and prophets of Baal, 357-58
typology of, 401-3
Elisha, 401, 408-10, 430, 435-36, 440, 458-59
and axe head, 425-26
and bear attack, 405-6
calling of, 367
death of, 459-60
and miracle of bread, 418-19
and prophetic school, 424-25
requesting Elijah's spirit, 399-400

and Shunammite woman, 416-18, 434-35
and siege of Samaria, 432-34
and sweet water, 404-5
and Syrians, 431-32
typology of, 421
and widow's oil, 415-16
Elkanah, 4-5
emotions, human, 137
enemies
love for, 143, 453-54, 518, 541
praying for, 234
value of having, 91
envy, 90
ephods, 17
Ephraim, tribe of, 326, 644, 655-56
error in judgment, 256
evangelism, 385-86
Evil-merodach, 517-18
excommunication, 208
exile
return from, 518
typology of, 514
experiences, remembering past, 104
Ezra (book), 672
Ezra (prophet), 515-16, 519-21
faith, 44-45, 84, 125, 349-50, 394-95, 417, 534
centrality of, 310
and fear, 83
among Gentiles, 136
and works, 42-43, 580
faithfulness of God, 90-91, 390-91, 452, 536
fasting, instructions for, 364
favor, desiring earthly, 142
fear of God, 169
fire, presence of God as, 599
flesh
as corrupt, 307
weakness of, 320
works of, 393-94
food, physical and spiritual nourishment of, 551
fools as wasting God's blessings, 117
forgiveness of God, 205, 665
See also grace of God *and* mercy of God
free will, 230, 415-16, 420-21
friendship
responsibilities in, 186
true, 87-88, 111, 144
Gad, descendants of, 534
gatekeepers, role of, 575
Gedaliah, 516-17
Gehazi, 423-24

generosity, 137, 148, 297, 582-83
Gentiles, 288, 350
faithfulness of, 287
God's plan for, 260
subjugation of, 183-84
Gibeonites, 246-47
gifts, spiritual, 21-22, 42-43, 73
different kinds of, 576-77
removal of, 57, 74
value of, 297
glory
of God, 598-99
seeking human, 259-60
God, 19, 28, 30, 110, 118, 123, 219, 226, 230-31, 237, 340-41, 356-57, 386, 410-11, 441, 447-48, 549-50, 596, 598-99, 658
counsel from, 105, 549
deliverance of, 95
governance of, 371
inscrutability of, 168, 204
kindness of, 71, 321
as Lord of creation, 425
as mother, 162
omnipresence of, 305-6
omniscience of, 230, 423, 489
pleasing, 542, 615, 624
"repentance" of, 63-64, 66-67
reverence for, 67
seeing the heart, 70-71
seeking, 335-36, 552, 624
sovereignty of, 13, 245, 269
submission to, 597, 606
trusting in, 45, 110, 149, 350
voice of, 364-65
godly. *See* church
Goliath
David and, 79-85, 104
sword of, 104
good, evil turned to, 105-6
goodness of God, 322, 410, 417
gospel, 84-85, 206
and law, 12, 364, 668-69
and repentance, 51
gossip, 536
government. *See* authorities, civil
grace of God, 195
for believers, 206
falling from, 199-200
to Gentiles, 29, 31
as temporary, 183
See also mercy of God
gratitude, 117-18, 582-84
greed, 453
half-heartedness. *See* apathy
Hannah, 4-13
Hanun, 186-87, 559
Hazael, 435-36, 457

healing, 658
heart
deceitfulness of the, 110, 112-13, 215, 381, 500-501
guarding one's, 135-36
hell, 506
Hezekiah, 480-92, 502, 653-61
high places, 279-81, 341, 505, 629
See also idolatry
Hiram, 287-88, 602
and David, 549, 590
Solomon's gift to, 311-12
Hophni and Phineas, 16-19, 28-29
Holy Spirit
anointing of, 42-43
guidance of, 47-48, 358
presence of, 423-24
sinning against, 89
as source of faith, 44-45
horn, meaning of, 248-49
Hosea, 465, 470
Hoshea, 469, 473
hospitality, 416-17
Huldah, 501-3, 668
humanity
as fleeting, 262
as treasure, 660
humility, 172, 251, 420-21
Hushai, 228, 230-31
hypocrisy, 56-58, 64, 90
Ichabod, birth of, 28-29
idleness. *See* apathy
idolatry, 29-30, 65, 96, 320, 328-29, 343-44 358, 394, 436, 442-43, 447, 454-55, 471, 494, 514, 534, 616, 629, 638, 645, 648
purging of, 625, 637, 654
See also high places
impatience, 127
infants, death of, 207, 209-10
instruments in worship, 167, 550, 569, 571
interpretation, biblical
caution in, 47
and historical books, *xlvi-l*
of obscure passages, 184-85
and the rule of faith, *xlviii*
Isaiah, 465, 470, 485-87, 494, 647-48
Ish-bosheth, 156-57
Israel (kingdom), 336-37, 390, 393, 468
cruelty of, 647
exile of, 467-70, 473-75
Israel (people), 457, 531
division of, 326-27, 474-75
downfall of, 319-20, 334
expansion of, 183-84

Issachar, tribe of, 543

Jabeshites, 148

Jehoahaz, 457, 511-12, 671

Jehoash. *See* Joash

Jehoiachin, 512, 517-18, 671

Jehoiakim, 512, 671

Jehoida, 453-55, 637-38

Jehoram, 408, 410, 431-32, 436, 631-33

Jehoshaphat, 387-89, 408, 623-29

Jehosheba, 452

Jehu, 343, 440-44, 446-49, 467, 496, 626, 633

Jeremiah, 502, 508, 516, 669

Jericho, curse of, 405

Jeroboam, 321-22, 328-29, 332-33, 336-37, 474-75, 606-10, 614
    as antichrist, 327
    lie of, 335

Jeroboam II, 465

Jesse, sons of, 71-72

Jews, 454

Jezebel, 345, 363, 376-78, 442-44

Joab, 153-54, 198, 217-19, 254, 257
    and Absalom, 236-38
    death of, 275-76
    demotion of, 244-45
    example of, 560

Joash, 452-53, 455, 458-59, 465, 496, 633-34, 637-40

Jonadab, counsel of, 215

Jonah, 465-66

Jonathan, 56, 58, 371, 536
    death of, 137-38
    as friend of David, 87-88, 98-100, 110-11
    godliness of, 99, 535
    the Holy Spirit and, 94
    and Saul's vow, 59

Joram, 437, 442-43

Josiah, 481, 500-507, 667-69

Jotham, 467, 469, 646-47

Judah (kingdom), 336-37, 390, 436-37, 495, 585, 608-10, 656-57
    exile of, 507-8, 511-17

Judah (tribe), 531, 533-34

judges, role of, 627-28

judgment of God, 17-18, 31-32, 183-84, 316, 336, 342-44, 395-96 406, 441-42, 468, 473, 475-76, 504-5, 511, 514-15, 558-59, 570, 616, 639, 647
    causes of, 671
    types of, 629
    See also discipline

justice
    divine, 457-58, 495
    and revenge, 445

kindness, 435, 518

king. *See* authorities, civil

kingdom of God, 281, 298

language
    anthropopathic, 64
    vernacular, 551-52

law, 103-4, 668-69
    ceremonial, 327-28, 657
    discovery of, 501
    freedom from, 102-4
    the Holy Spirit and, 418
    purpose of, 214, 488

leprosy, 434, 466-67, 646

Levi, descendants of, 534

lies, on telling, 95-96, 98, 125, 136, 199, 218, 228, 447

life, eternal, 273, 363, 401-2

lions
    as judgment of God, 475-76
    typology of, 334-35

Lord's Supper, 322, 506, 550

lots, on casting, 44, 570

love, 30, 172
    of God, 45, 219
    and law, 103-4

Manasseh, 494-96, 655-56, 665-66

marriage, 416, 531
    of priests, 571
    unequally yoked in, 436-37, 608

materialism, 249, 560

Mattan, 637

Menahem, 467-68

Mephibosheth, 224-25, 245
    David's kindness to, 185-86
    descendants of, 535-36

mercy of God, 105, 208, 258, 315, 318, 433, 436-37, 457, 467, 469, 473, 517-18, 647, 665
    See also grace of God

Micaiah, 370-71, 385, 626

Michal, 90-91, 95-96, 171-72, 551

ministers. *See* church leadership

miracles, 351-52, 357, 459-60, 490-91
    as aids to faith, 415
    different kinds of, 418

Moab
    human sacrifice of, 411
    rebellion of, 392-93
    subjugation of, 184

Moses
    example of, 50
    rejection of, 474-75

Mount Moriah, 590-91

murder, 436

music, 75-76, 409-10, 550, 571-72

Naaman, 419-23

Nabal, 115-18

Naboth, 378, 442

Nadab and Abihu, 570

Nadab (king), 342

Nahash, 187

Naphtali, descendants of, 534-35

Nathan, 159, 175, 202, 206, 554-55

Nebuchadnezzar, 512-13, 516-17, 671

Neco, 511-12

oaths. *See* vows, on taking

Obadiah, 354-55

obedience to God, 22, 36-37, 43, 61, 168, 224, 311, 333-34, 355-56, 373, 394-95, 500, 541, 554, 582
    different kinds of, 448
    true, 65, 90

Oded, 647

oil of anointing, 42, 440

Old Testament, 555

Omri, 344-45

parents
    comfort for, 209-10
    example of, 458
    honoring one's, 148, 419
    responsibilities of, 18-19, 405, 565

Passover, feast of, 6, 292, 506-7, 656-59, 668-69

pastors. *See* church leadership

patience, 112, 186
    of God, 457-58, 474

Paul, 534

peace
    for believers, 320-21
    from war, 315

Pekah, 468-69

Pekahiah, 468

Pentecost, feast of, 292

persecution, 87, 226

perseverance, 645

Philistines, 29-31
    defeat of, 35, 162-63, 549-50
    wars with, 247
    See also Dagon

physicians, on visiting, 618-19

pleasure, earthly
    consequences of, 6-7
    resisting, 8, 541-42

polygamy, 4-5, 118-20, 152-53, 161-62, 318-21, 531

poor, the, 516

power of God, 258
    for believers, 31

against enemies, 29, 35

praise
    desiring human, 67, 106, 245
    of God, 583

prayer(s), 7-8, 127-28, 320, 486, 488
    answers to, 395
    confidence in, 124, 487
    giving thanks in, 281
    of hypocrites, 457
    instructions for, 305-6, 359-60
    intercessory, 657-58
    for peace, 344-45
    persistence in, 51-52
    power of, 246-47, 406, 598
    purpose of, 180
    for sickness, 488, 490
    types of, 9
    for unbelievers, 306-7

pride, 66, 466, 491, 515, 646

priests and Levites, 184-85, 536, 607-8, 637
    duties of, 51, 550
    organization of, 569-71, 576-77
    provision for, 659-60

primogeniture, 533

promises
    of God, 19, 147, 178-79, 236, 252-54, 458, 465, 532-33, 628
    keeping one's, 88

prophecy
    conditional, 488
    and music, 409-10, 571
    nature of, 96-97

prophets, 43-44, 175, 465, 501-3
    bones of, 459-60, 506
    and Israel's kings, 343
    true and false, 334, 384, 626

providence and will of God, 32, 40-41, 66-67, 74, 96, 231, 321-22, 325, 342, 358-59, 378, 386-87, 433, 442, 447, 452-53, 487, 489, 491, 669, 672

provision of God, 318, 348-49, 355, 364, 415-16, 418, 434, 542, 583-84, 589, 659-60

punishment. *See* discipline *and* judgment of God

Purgatory, 208

Rabshakeh, 484-85

ravens, typology of, 349

rebellion against God, 65-66

rebuke, power of, 203

reform, 625, 637, 654-55

Rehoboam, 324-26, 336, 606-10, 614

religion
    sincerity in, 57-58, 464-65
    true and false, 327-28, 540
repentance, 22-23, 34, 50-51, 72, 198, 205-7, 258-59, 380-81, 563-64, 645
resurrection, 351, 400
Reuben, descendants of, 533
revenge, on taking, 89, 123
rewards, eternal and temporal, 447-48
righteousness, standard of, 198, 207-8
Sabbath, 672
sacraments
    as divine sign, 43
    God's presence in, 166
    and holy water, 405
    and salvation, 27-28
sacrifice
    human, 411, 471, 506
    true, 34-35, 308
saints
    example of, 98
    imitation of, 351
    imperfection of, 362
salvation, 34, 425
    humility in, 420-21
    as spiritual death and resurrection, 12
Samaria
    resettling of, 475-76
    siege of, 432-34
Samuel, 16, 67-68, 71-72, 83-84
    as author, 1
    calling of, 21-24
    death of, 116-17
    "ghost" of, 128-32
    as mediator, 36
    as reformer, 34
    as sinner, 70
    spiritual leadership of, 41, 50-52
    typology of, 9
Satan, 127-29, 131-32, 192, 257, 357-58, 363, 386
    appearances of, 130
    and hatred for Christ, 452
    sent by God, 74-75, 384-85
    works of, 563
Saul, 2, 46, 67-68, 247, 535-36, 540-41
    anger of, 98-100
    as antichrist, 106-7
    calling of, 40-44
    compared to David, 66-67, 73
    cowardice of, 80
    death of, 137-38
    evil spirit of, 74-76, 94
    as farmer, 47

    the Holy Spirit and, 47-48, 73-74
    as king 56, 139
    as peacemaker, 45, 48
    in pursuit of David, 99-100, 111-12, 122-24
    rejection of, 67
    repentance of, 113
    as sinner, 48, 56-57, 61-67, 80-81, 89-91
    vow of, 59
Scripture. See Word of God
self-confidence, 188-89, 247
self-denial, 223, 251-52
Sennacherib, 484, 486-88
serpent, destruction of the bronze, 482-83
seven, symbolism of, 551
Shallum, 467-68
Sheba
    death of, 245-46
    queen of, 314-15, 603
Shiloh, 5-6
Shimei, 225-26, 276
Shishak, 608-9
showbread, nature of, 103
siege of Jerusalem, 660
silence, keeping holy, 485
Simeon, descendants of, 533
sin, 44, 223, 360, 379, 488, 563, 647, 669
    concealing, 196, 198, 386
    different types of, 225, 341
    dying to, 62-63, 72, 195, 235
    fear of, 363, 540
    generational, 447, 453, 458, 469-70, 483-84
    guarding against, 193, 306
    living in, 203, 616
    original, 207, 435
    outcome of, 203-5, 208-9, 223-24, 229, 236
    premeditated, 194, 198-99
    source of, 257
    tempting others to, 328
sola Scriptura, xlviii
Solomon, 159, 261-62, 311-12, 515, 565, 601-3, 606
    anointing of, 584
    as Davidic heir, 268-70
    names of, 210
    palace of, 298-99, 602
    polygamy of, 278-79, 318-21
    prayer of, 305-8, 588-89, 598-99, 666
    proverbs of, 286-87
    sin of, 607
    typology of, 176-78, 270, 274, 286, 315-16, 555, 566, 580

    wealth of, 286, 589, 603
    wisdom of, 270, 280-83, 285-87, 314, 603
soul
    after death, 128-29
    nature of, 235
speech, foolish, 8-9
springtime, metaphor of, 253
stewardship, 455, 500
suspicion, danger of, 186-87, 559
tabernacle, 305, 554
Tabernacles, feast of, 292
talents. See gifts, spiritual
Tamar, rape of, 215-16
Tekoa, woman of, 218
temple, 174-75, 589-91, 599
    construction of, 280, 287, 298, 311, 554-55, 564-66, 581
    destruction and looting of, 609, 672
    location of, 329, 564
    new court of, 628-29
    pillars of, 299-300, 515
    reconstruction of, 455, 638
    typology of, 292-301, 515, 592, 597-98
temptation
    God's role in, 563, 661
    resisting, 541-42
thanksgiving. See gratitude
theft, 378
tithes and offerings, 12
Topheth, 506
treasurers, role of, 575-76
trials and tribulations, 135-37, 192
    as blessing, 89, 421
    fickleness in, 58, 224
    God's presence in, 486
    outcome of, 73, 123, 199
    purpose of, 105, 191, 351, 419, 514-15, 626-27, 661
    rejoicing in, 22
    withstanding, 143, 160, 214, 226
Trinity, 179, 252, 554-55
unbelief, 433-34
ungodly. See wicked
ungratefulness, 311
Uriah, 195-99
Uzzah, 167-69, 547-48
Uzziah. See Azariah (king)
vows, 9-10, 59, 276, 541, 617
war
    God's role in, 614, 629
    mercy in, 431
    nature of, 259
    theory of just, 149, 183, 187-88

weakness, strength in, 455
wealth
    disadvantages of, 89
    proper use of, 416
weather as divine sign, 51
wicked, 484
    assisting, 394
    blindness of, 431
    counsel of, 633, 638
    death of, 137-38
    desires of, 378
    friendship with, 627
    restlessness of, 122-23
widow(s)
    provision for, 318, 416
    of Zarephath, 348-52
wisdom
    asking for, 281-82
    characteristics of, 215
    lack of, 324-25
    learning from, 314-15
witch of En-dor, 127-32
women
    in leadership, 501-3
    and outward adornments, 443-44
Word of God, 135, 293, 325-26, 405
    adding to, 440
    application of, 177, 203
    discrepancies in, 165, 432, 532, 582, 596
    disobedience to, 333
    effectiveness of, 656
    importance of reading, 19, 549
    neglect of, 21, 27-28, 31
    obedience to, 65, 146, 168, 273, 332-33
    preservation of, 667
    revival of, 34, 515-16
    truth of, 618
    See also interpretation, biblical
works, good, 591
worship, 5-6, 88-89
    location of, 554
    peace in, 596
    singing in, 167, 550, 571-72
    true, 299, 356, 394, 455, 464-65, 548, 550, 627, 654
wrath. See discipline and judgment of God
Zechariah, 467, 637-40
Zedekiah, 512-14
Zeruiah, sons of, 155-56
Ziba, 224-25, 245
Zimri, 344

Scripture Index

OLD TESTAMENT

Genesis
1–2, *531*
1:28, *531*
2, *5*
2:2, *551*
2:18, *152*
2:24, *5*
3, *452*
3:16, *503*
4:7, *533*
5:24, *400*
6:3, *74*
9, *458*
9:6, *454*
10, *314*
10:18, *614*
10:26-30, *314*
10:28, *530*
13, *159*
13:18, *159*
15, *577*
15:10, *617*
16:1-6, *5*
17:7, *207*
19:26, *614*
20, *136, 247*
21, *363*
21:8-21, *5*
21:10, *319*
21:31, *363*
22, *506*
22:13, *236*
22:18, *236*
22:24, *319*
25, *318*
25:1, *319*
25:6, *319*
25:23, *5*
25:26, *531*
26:8, *193*
27, *631*
27:40, *631*
30:4, *319*
31:39, *82*
32:24, *531*
32:28, *357, 531*
35:22, *319*
36:12, *530*
36:22, *530*
36:23, *530*
36:26, *530*
36:27, *530*

37:3, *213*
38, *533*
40, *97*
42:1, *144*
48, *326*
48:14-20, *326*
48:15, *348*
48:19, *644*
49, *40, 273, 326, 531*
49:5, *155*
49:8-10, *40*
49:9-12, *326*
49:10, *436, 453, 597*
49:20, *535*
49:22-26, *326*

Exodus
3:18, *648*
4:22, *531*
5:3, *648*
7:1, *246*
7:3, *335*
12, *176, 293, 656, 657*
12:12-14, *656*
12:25, *174, 176*
13:4, *131*
13:21, *299*
14, *398*
14:14, *35*
14:15, *144*
14:16, *398*
17:16, *149*
19, *102*
19:15, *103*
20:2, *500*
20:3, *29*
20:5, *377*
20:11, *377*
20:12, *419*
20:13, *89, 395, 406, 540*
20:16, *95, 276*
20:17, *377*
21, *270*
21:14, *270*
22:1, *202*
22:28, *226, 377*
23:17, *6*
25, *294, 296*
25:8, *296*
25:20, *591*
25:22, *296*
26:33, *554*
27, *270*
27:1, *591*

28, *17*
29, *296*
29:35, *551*
29:37, *551*
29:42-46, *296*
30:6, *646*
33:18, *599*
33:22, *599*
34, *278*
34:7, *148*
34:11-16, *278*
34:16, *120*
36:8, *305*
40:2, *305*

Leviticus
1, *627*
2:13, *405, 614*
7:20, *657*
7:31, *17*
8:11, *551*
8:35, *551*
9:22, *591*
12:3, *551*
13, *414, 429, 464, 644*
13:46, *646*
14:8, *551*
14:9, *551*
15, *193*
15:19-30, *193*
16, *295*
16:14, *551*
17, *329*
17:1-10, *329*
18:18, *5*
20, *127*
20:6, *127*
22:27, *551*
23:3, *551*
23:6, *551*
23:15, *551*
23:34, *551*
24:5-9, *103*
25:4, *551*
25:8, *551*
25:23, *377*
26:26, *433*
26:29, *433*

Numbers
1:3, *577*
1:53, *647*
2:3, *534*
3, *184*

4, *9*
4:15, *548*
4:19, *548*
5:20, *32*
9, *657*
9:10-11, *657*
9:15, *597*
11:25, *43*
12:3, *24*
16, *44, 395*
18, *184*
18:5, *647*
18:8, *660*
18:19, *614*
20:12-13, *333*
21:9, *483*
22, *624*
22:41, *624*
24:1-25, *97*
28:4, *9*
33:52-53, *541*
34, *183*

Deuteronomy
2:21, *79*
5:20, *276*
6, *405*
6:7, *405*
7, *278*
7:1, *279*
7:1-4, *278*
7:3, *279*
7:5, *280*
8:3, *349*
9:2, *79*
10:7, *616*
12, *174, 306, 329, 411, 500, 625*
12:5, *279*
12:10-11, *174*
12:10-12, *174*
12:30, *306*
12:31, *411*
12:32, *500, 625*
13, *129, 333, 415*
13:1-3, *333*
13:1-5, *129, 415*
13:6, *616*
13:9, *616*
16, *5*
17, *34, 37, 41, 161, 273, 286, 318, 319, 501*
17:14, *1*
17:15, *159*

17:16, *286*
17:17, *119, 152, 161, 162, 319*
17:18-20, *273*
17:20, *37*
18, *103, 127, 129, 470*
18:9-14, *128*
18:10-11, *127*
18:11, *129*
18:19, *103*
19:15, *377*
20:6-7, *149*
20:10, *614*
21, *278*
21:10-14, *278*
21:15-17, *533*
22:23-29, *216*
23, *278*
23:2-3, *278*
23:7, *278*
23:20, *95*
25:5-10, *318*
28, *431, 432*
28:28, *431*
28:53, *432*
32:10, *199*
32:30, *258*
33, *40*
33:7, *40*
33:9, *616*

Joshua
1, *273*
1:5, *128*
1:6, *273*
1:7-8, *273*
1:9, *273*
2:11, *279*
4:20, *305*
6, *398*
6:26, *405*
7, *376*
8:2, *614*
9, *246*
9:14, *218*
10:10-11, *35*
11, *79*
11:21-23, *79*
15:8, *541*
15:55, *116*
16–17, *326*
17, *644*
17:14, *644*
17:17, *644*

18:1, 5, *305*
21:17, *530*
22:20, *647*

Judges
2:13, *356*
2:16, *597*
2:17, *597*
4–5, *535*
5, *35*
5:8, *616*
7, *59*
9:13, *607*
11:12, *614*
11:29-40, *59*
13, *21*
14:5, *47*
16:17, *219*
16:23, *648*
16:24, *648*
19:1-2, *319*
20, *41*
20:33, *614*
20:34, *614*
21, *40*

Ruth
4:21, *530*

1 Samuel
1, *1*
2, 2, *18, 534*
2:6, 27, *350*
2:10, *14*
2:17, *16, 17*
2:27, *23*
2:30, *18*
2:35, *14*
3:1, *669*
3:7, *22*
3:10, *22*
3:18, *19*
3:21, *21*
4–5, *295*
4:4, *305*
6:19, *548*
8:1-4, *9*
8:2, *530*
8:7, *37*
8:11, *37*
9:12, *279*
9:16, *597*
10, *398*
10:5, *398*
10:6, *55*
10:7, *43*
10:8, *57*
10:10, *398*
10:26, *48*
11, *187*
12:19, *52*

12:23, *51, 52*
13, *540*
14, *357*
14:6, *371*
14:35, *357*
15, *540*
15–16, *247*
15:9, *373*
15:11, *169*
15:23, *127*
15:29, 63, *67*
16:1-13, *147*
16:2, *116*
16:11, *72*
16:23, *409*
17:13, *72*
17:28, 70, *72*
17:37, *417*
17:45, *84*
18:1, *100*
18:7, *192*
18:21, *356*
19, *540*
19:10, *363*
19:18, *363*
19:24, *172*
20, *98*
20:42, *111*
21:1, *305*
21:13, *105*
22, *540*
22:19, *305*
24:10, *50*
24:16, *113*
25:28, *149*
27, *125*
28, *540*
28:6, *128*
28:16, *131*
28:19, *131, 132*
28:21, *130*
31:1-13, *539*
31:13, *551*

2 Samuel
1:2, *136*
1:9, *138*
1:16, *142*
3, *268*
3:2-5, *161, 266, 267*
3:16, *387*
3:29, *276*
3:39, *155*
4:1, *616*
5, *147, 265*
5:1-10, *539*
5:2, *73*
5:4, *576*
5:11-25, *547*
5:14, *532*
6, *551*

6:1-11, *547*
6:12-23, *547*
6:14, *17, 170*
6:17, *554*
6:20, *171*
6:23, *551*
7, 341, 369, 436, 437,
  532, 554, 582
7:1, *554*
7:2, *554*
7:3, *71*
7:9, *566*
7:11-17, *223*
7:12-13, *177*
7:16, *597*
7:18-29, *341*
7:21, *21*
8, *185, 408*
8:1-18, *558*
8:6, *558*
8:14, *408*
8:16, *244*
8:17, *6*
8:18, *183*
10:1-19, *558*
10:12, *188*
11, *125*
11:14-27, *377*
12:5, *202, 203*
12:7, *203*
12:8, *120, 161*
12:10, *217*
12:11, *214, 223*
12:13, *66, 205*
12:14, *209*
12:23, *209*
12:24-25, *269*
12:26-31, *558*
12:31, *558*
13:1, *608*
13:3, *72*
13:14, *608*
13:21, *216*
13:25, *608*
13:27, *608*
14:33, *219*
15:4, *222*
15:25-26, *224*
15:26, *214*
15:27, *6*
16:2, *265*
16:3, *225*
16:5-13, *276*
16:11, *257*
18:33, *237*
19, *48*
19:23, *276*
19:25, *48*
19:29, *245*
20, *248*
21:17, *452*

22, *247*
23, *542*
23:1, *552*
23:8, *539*
23:8-39, *539*
23:12, *539*
23:19, *539*
23:25, *539*
23:32, *539*
24:1, *562*
24:10, *259*
24:17, *258, 259*

1 Kings
1, *584*
1:29-30, *210*
1:34, *637*
1:39, *42*
2, *153, 534*
2:5, *153*
2:10, *646*
2:15, *268*
2:27, *6*
2:31-32, *153*
2:35, *6*
3:3-15, *588*
3:4, *279*
3:6, *177*
3:7, *281*
5:1-18, *287*
5:1–7:51, *588*
5:5, *590*
6:3, *588*
6:4, *294*
7:23, *464*
7:24, *588*
7:46, *588*
7:50, *588*
8:8, *596*
8:10, *599*
8:18, *554*
8:20, *177*
8:22, *591, 629*
8:25, *490, 598*
8:28, *666*
8:30, *666*
8:31, *591*
8:36, *595*
8:46, *307*
8:46-50, *666*
8:54, *591*
8:63, *599*
8:64, *591, 629*
9:1–10:29, *601*
9:11-13, *311*
9:25, *591*
10:2, *625*
10:4-9, *285*
10:8, *601*
10:26, *285*
11, *436, 606*

11:13, *436*
11:34, *14*
11:39, *14*
11:41-43, *601*
12, *328, 608*
12:10-11, *325*
12:16, *616*
12:18, *605*
12:28, *616*
12:31, *616*
13:2, *632*
13:11-24, *406*
13:32, *505*
13:33, *616*
14, *627*
14:13, *610*
14:14, *343*
14:21-31, *606*
14:24, *627*
14:26-27, *315*
14:30, *615*
14:31, *605*
15, *455, 613*
15:2, *613*
15:3, *389, 613*
15:4, *14*
15:5, *341*
15:13, *608*
15:16, *615*
16, *475*
16:9, *344*
16:11, *344*
17, *418, 632*
17:12, *607*
18:39, *366*
19, *398, 440, 448*
19:10, *366*
19:14, *366*
19:16, *440*
19:19, *398*
20:42, *374*
21, *378*
21:19, *387, 442*
21:20, *379*
21:26, *644*
21:29, *457*
22, *369, 437, 623*
22:6, *386*
22:8, *373, 380*
22:49, *245*

2 Kings
1:9-14, *364*
2:13-25, *404, 405, 406*
2:19-22, *398*
3, *389, 393*
3:11, *632*
3:15, *410*
4, *345, 430, 436*
4:2, *607*
5:10, *551*

5:19, 422
6, 430
8, 430
8:16-29, 631
8:19, 14
8:26, 631
8:27, 437
9, 380
9:22, 443
9:26, 380
10:32, 448
11, 270
11:1-3, 631
11:2, 631
11:4, 637
11:4-20, 637
11:15, 270
11:21–12:21, 637
12:1, 636
13:14, 402
14:1-22, 644
15, 657
15:1-7, 644
15:29, 656
15:32-38, 644
16, 647, 648
16:1-14, 644
16:7, 644
17, 326
18, 660
18–20, 653
18:2, 653
18:14, 609
18:15, 609
18:15-16, 515
18:28, 614
19:15, 487, 598
19:35, 550
21–23, 665
22, 665
22:7, 501
22:20, 507
23, 320, 637, 665
23:24, 500
23:25, 481
23:29-30, 507
23:33, 671
24:8, 670
25:1, 671

1 Chronicles
1, 519
1:32, 319
2:13-15, 71
2:17, 228
3, 530
3:1, 268
3:3, 532
6:16, 9
10:13, 138
10:13-14, 127

11, 244
11:5-6, 244
11:11, 251
11:25, 251
13:1, 165
13:5, 165
13:8, 164, 653
14:3, 162
15, 551
16:39, 305
17:6, 174
17:11, 589
17:12, 589
17:21, 174
18:17, 182, 185
20:5, 243
21, 590
21:1, 257, 562
21:3, 257
21:12, 256
22, 273
22:1, 274
22:5, 591
22:9, 210
22:13, 616
24:3-4, 6
24:31, 571
27:18, 72
28:2, 598
28:6, 590
28:11, 581
29, 1
29:9, 655
29:11, 13, 245, 584
29:29-30, 1

2 Chronicles
6:13, 306
7:9, 551
8, 312
8:2, 311, 312
10:2, 324
11:12, 535
11:17, 336
12:9, 515
13, 340
14:7, 341
14:11, 341
17:6, 629
17:10, 618
19:2, 387, 408
21, 495
21:19, 619
22:11, 451
24:20-22, 466
25, 464
25:2, 465
25:24, 515
26, 467
26:1-23, 466
26:16-17, 185

26:18-21, 184
27:2, 469
28:24, 656
29:2, 481
29:21, 551
31:20, 654
33:12, 496
33:15-16, 496
35:18, 24
35:20-24, 507
36:9, 512
36:13, 513
36:22-23, 519

Ezra
1, 262
6:16, 599
6:17, 599
10:2, 119

Nehemiah
5:13, 617
8:10, 551
13:23-29, 278

Esther
2:14, 319
6:1-11, 401

Job
1, 385
1:6, 385
1:18-19, 364
1:21, 23, 385
2:1, 385
9:4, 614
20:4-5, 138
41, 79
41:27, 80
41:33, 80
42:8, 551

Psalms
2:11, 373
2:12, 14
3:1-2, 5
5, 90
6:2-3, 265
8:6-9, 103
10:8, 614
17:8, 199
18:1, 248
18:49, 248
22:23, 581
27:12, 106
28:7, 199
31:14-15, 96
32:8, 70, 430
33:10, 152, 223
34, 11, 105
34:9-10, 349

34:21, 138
36:2, 310
37:1-5, 124
37:28, 199
39:1, 91
45:6-6, 42
45:8-9, 297
45:13, 297
48:2, 293
51:1, 207
51:4, 28, 168, 276
51:5, 162, 207
52, 107
52:8, 107
58, 90
58:11, 454
60:7, 581
60:11, 35
62:8, 34
68:26, 625
68:29, 591
71:11, 5
72:14, 199
73:27, 442
74:1, 514
75, 246, 248
75:3, 246
75:10, 249
77:5, 104
77:10-11, 104
78:20-22, 159
78:60, 305
78:67-68, 326
78:69, 249
78:70, 581
80:1, 348
81:11-12, 626
82, 584
82:1, 273
89:12, 487
90:10, 265
91:11, 199
93:4, 660
101:8, 316
104:15, 607
105, 411
105:15, 42, 112, 269
108:12-13, 160
109:4, 87
109:13, 155
109:17, 626
110:3, 104
112, 248
112:9, 249
114:2, 249
115:3, 385
116:11, 199, 276
116:15, 138, 237, 334
118:29, 599
119:37, 28
119:74, 87

119:105, 174, 297
127:1, 47, 442
127:5, 254
132:11, 177
139:1, 487
140, 90
143:2, 334
144:1-2, 160
144:2, 393
146:3, 35
147:15, 297

Proverbs
8:15, 36
11, 418
11:19, 418
16:7, 542
16:32, 112
16:33, 44
17:16, 117
18:22, 117
22:15, 18
24:6, 231
25:21-22, 431
27:6, 91
29:11, 607
31, 210
31:6, 607

Ecclesiastes
2:19, 324
4:13, 614
7, 602
7:20, 602
9:8, 17
10:16, 614

Song of Solomon
4, 297
4:8, 297
4:11, 297
4:13, 300
6, 319
6:8-9, 319
8:12, 254

Isaiah
1:11, 482
2, 306, 315
2:4, 315
2:22, 406
3:4, 614
3:8, 34
4, 299
4:5-6, 299
6, 516
6:10, 431
7, 470, 647
7:3, 648
7:4, 648
7:12, 470

8, *127, 129*
8:19, *129*
8:19-21, *127*
9, *311*
9:1, *311*
9:6, *177, 566*
9:7, *210*
10, *343*
10:5, *149*
14:13, *484*
19:14, *257*
28:21, *566*
30, *384*
30:1-7, *325*
30:9, *384*
30:33, *506*
32, *50*
32:1, *50*
33:20, *287*
36:6, *485*
38:13, *12, 488*
40:6-7, *660*
40:6-8, *444*
45:1, *632*
48:22, *321, 336*
49:23, *503*
53, *70, 104*
55, *97*
55:11, *97*
58:5, *380*
59, *90*
60, *297*
60:8, *297*
61:11, *42*
63, *305*
63:12, *305*
63:17, *257*
66, *137*
66:1, *306*
66:7, *73*

Jeremiah
4, *504*
5, *669*
7:4, *310*
7:5-7, *310*
7:12, *305*
7:12-14, *5*
7:15, *644*
7:34, *206*
10:23, *281*
17:5, *45, 110*
22:19, *512*
23, *50*
23:5, *177*
23:6, *50*
24:5, *518*
29:10, *536*
33:15, *177*
34:5, *619*
34:18, *617*

38:16, *514*
39–40, *516*
40:9-10, *517*
44, *517*
50:23, *149*
52:21, *291*

Lamentations
3:22, *514*

Ezekiel
9:1, *103*
18:2, *207*
18:20, *207*
18:22, *209*
29, *448*
29:6, *485*
29:7, *485*
33:8, *82*
33:11, *673*
34:3, *82*

Daniel
2:1-49, *97*
2:21, *441*
3:1-30, *106*
4:1-37, *97*
4:27, *41*

Hosea
2, *624*
2:16-17, *624*
5:15, *204*
6:4, *644*
12:4, *531*

Amos
1, *470*
3:6, *441*
8:11, *21, 34*
8:11-12, *21*

Jonah
3, *209*
3:4, *110*

Habakkuk
1:11, *648*

Zechariah
2, *487*
2:8, *487*
3:4-5, *402*
8:19, *517*
14:5, *466*

Malachi
1:2-3, *5*
2:15, *5*
4:5, *348, 400*

Apocrypha

1 Esdras
1, *44*
1:50-58, *45*

Wisdom of Solomon
4:7, *138*
8:2, *281*

Sirach
3:22, *31*
7, *282*
32:19, *324*
47:23, *606*
51, *282*

Susanna
1:15, *193*

2 Maccabees
2:5, *305*

New Testament

Matthew
1, *517, 530, 532*
1:1, *518*
1:5, *279*
1:25, *266*
3:4, *394*
3:17, *210*
4, *130*
4:1-11, *130*
4:9-10, *356*
5, *315*
5:6, *415*
5:10-12, *224*
5:13-16, *17*
5:40, *315*
5:44, *52, 237*
6, *359, 624*
6:6, *359, 409*
6:10, *94, 100*
6:33, *273, 281, 624*
6:34, *131, 132*
7, *97*
7:14, *655*
7:21-23, *97*
8:22, *389*
9:11, *394*
9:13, *278, 415*
9:38, *34*
10:24, *399*
10:30, *199*
10:37, *476*
10:42, *416*
11:25, *23, 73*
12, *1, 103*
12:1-8, *102, 103, 104*

12:3-4, *1*
12:25, *467*
12:30, *551*
12:42, *315*
13, *357*
13:33, *357*
13:58, *417*
14:16, *551*
16:18, *660*
16:23, *547*
17, *400*
17:12, *348, 400, 632*
17:13, *632*
19:4-6, *5*
19:8, *5*
19:28, *316*
19:30, *5*
22, *252*
22:14, *655*
22:39, *379*
22:45, *252*
23, *520*
23:29-32, *333*
23:35, *106*
23:37, *673*
24:22, *495*
24:24, *129*
25:1-13, *444*
25:29, *615*
25:31, *402*
25:40, *37*
25:45, *37*
27:40, *406*
28, *253*
28:19, *366*
28:20, *254*

Mark
2, *103*
2:23-28, *102, 103*
8, *418*
9:7, *295*
9:23, *417*
9:50, *405*
16, *582*
16:16, *253, 668*

Luke
1, *248, 295, 400, 565, 570*
1:8-10, *296*
1:17, *348, 400, 632*
1:32-33, *555, 566*
1:46-55, *11*
1:47, *12*
1:69, *249*
2, *535*
2:13, *402*
2:41, *6*
2:52, *274*
3:8, *634*

3:14, *37, 149*
3:31, *159, 532*
4, *347, 350*
4:4, *349*
4:24, *43*
5:8, *206*
5:10, *206*
6:1-5, *102*
6:27, *237*
7:16, *415*
7:32, *76*
7:48, *206*
9:54, *396*
9:55, *395*
9:60, *367*
9:62, *367*
10, *603*
10:23, *603*
12:32, *431, 655*
13, *454, 645*
13:3, *454, 645*
13:23, *655*
13:34, *673*
16:8, *218*
16:31, *333*
18, *359*
18:1, *52, 359*
18:9-14, *5*
18:22, *63*
23:34, *639*
23:43, *224*
24, *184*
24:4, *402*
24:44, *251*

John
1:18, *624*
2:19, *294*
2:21, *294*
3, *482*
3:27, *581*
4, *476*
4:21, *554*
4:24, *597*
5:23, *14*
6, *418*
6:54, *459*
7, *97*
7:32-36, *97*
7:45-52, *97*
7:53–8:11, *204*
8, *273, 385, 469*
8:31-32, *273*
8:44, *385*
9, *488*
10, *295, 660*
10:9, *297*
10:23, *296*
10:29, *660*
11:26, *490*
11:49-52, *97*

15:19, *106*
15:24, *373*
16, *253*
16:8-9, *74*
16:21, *28*
16:33, *254*
17:22, *596*
18:28-32, *90*
19:11, *343*
20:17, *581*
21:17, *82*

Acts
1, *44, 184*
1:10-11, *401*
2, *306*
2:13, *656*
4:25, *251, 252*
4:28, *218*
5, *395, 423*
5:29, *106, 343, 377*
5:41, *224*
7, *589*
7:47-50, *589*
7:60, *639*
8, *306*
9, *487*
9:4, *487*
9:15, *103*
10, *149*
10:44, *409*
13, *1, 56, 139, 395*
13:21, *56, 57*
13:22, *481*
14:16-17, *348*
17:8-9, *531*
17:24, *175*
17:28, *624*
20:29, *82*

Romans
1, *337*
1:7, *321*
1:17, *287*
1:26, *320*
2, *632*
2:5, *632*
2:14-15, *113*
2:24, *138, 246*
3:4, *458*
3:8, *228, 549*
3:25, *166*
5, *320*
5:1, *321*
5:11, *34*
5:20, *476*
8, *94, 393*
8:17, *217*

8:28, *214, 393*
8:29, *533*
8:31, *431*
8:38-39, *237*
9:22, *335*
10:14, *34*
10:17, *645*
11:33, *31, 340*
12, *304, 315*
12:1, *304*
12:16, *315*
12:20-21, *431*
13, *37, 41, 111, 343, 584*
13:1, *343, 487*
13:4, *41, 566*
13:6-7, *37*
14:4, *423*
14:8, *237*
14:23, *57, 197*

1 Corinthians
1, *245*
1:26-29, *245*
3, *575, 582*
3:17, *287, 455*
3:21-23, *103*
4:7, *491*
5:7, *656*
6, *315*
6:1-8, *315*
6:19, *294*
7:5, *103*
7:13-15, *279*
7:20, *256*
7:24, *256*
8:5, *179*
9, *659*
9:9, *300*
9:22, *417*
9:26-27, *563*
10:12, *607*
10:22, *74*
11:3, *166*
11:5, *502*
11:19, *626*
11:30, *659*
12, *96, 297, 399, 533*
12:4, *399*
12:4-6, *22*
12:20, *614*
12:22, *577*
12:24, *577*
13:12, *307*
14:15, *572*
15:20, *400*
15:28, *566*
15:58, *616*

2 Corinthians
1, *87*
2:15, *297*
3:6, *267*
4:3-4, *555*
4:7, *293, 301, 491*
5:19, *166, 673*
6:14-15, *436*
7:9-10, *12*
9:7, *583*
10:4, *79*
10:8, *298*
11:14, *129, 130*
12:9, *219, 536*
12:14, *82*

Galatians
2:14, *97*
4:18-20, *82*
4:21-31, *5*
5, *300*
5:22-23, *300*
6, *659*
6:16, *531*

Ephesians
2, *287, 591*
2:3, *207*
2:10, *591*
2:14, *566*
2:14-18, *293*
2:18, *180*
2:19-22, *287*
2:20, *161*
2:21, *565*
3:14-15, *207*
4, *297*
4:4-16, *297*
4:11, *569*
4:13, *287*
5:18-19, *410*
5:19, *167, 550, 572*
5:26, *420*
6, *18, 214*
6:2, *148*
6:4, *18*
6:11, *79*
6:16, *305*

Philippians
1:6, *200, 422*
2:6-7, *80*
4, *603*
4:7, *603*

Colossians
1:9, *52*
1:18, *400, 533*

1:19, *295, 487*
1:24, *217*
2:5, *424*
2:8, *575*
2:23, *357*
3:5, *195*
3:11, *293*
3:15, *118*
3:16, *572*

1 Thessalonians
2:16, *345*
4:3-4, *103*
4:13, *273*
4:16-18, *281*
4:17, *401*
5:17, *52*

2 Thessalonians
1:8, *396*
2, *129, 333, 514*
2:9, *333*
2:9-12, *129*
2:10-12, *384*
2:11-12, *626*

1 Timothy
1, *116, 532*
1:4, *532*
3:16, *402*
4:1, *229*
4:1-4, *416*
4:4, *103*
6, *597*

2 Timothy
1, *116*
1:6, *195*
3:9, *30*

Titus
1:15, *103*
3, *532*
3:9, *532*

Hebrews
1:3, *599*
1:5, *555*
2:3, *668*
7, *184*
7:13-14, *184*
7:26-27, *534*
9:4, *596*
10, *615*
10:31, *258, 259*
10:35, *615*
11, *351*
11:6, *448*

11:35, *351*
11:37, *494*
12, *615*
12:12, *616*
12:12-13, *615*
12:24, *199*
13, *256*
13:10, *260*
13:17, *82*

James
1:5, *282*
1:14-15, *360*
4:6, *466*
5:13, *12*
5:15, *34*
5:16, *52*
5:16-18, *348, 359*

1 Peter
1:6-7, *351*
1:12, *295*
2, *287, 297*
2:2-10, *287*
2:5, *294, 297*
2:25, *565*
3:1-4, *443*
4:4, *107, 300*
5:7, *500*
5:8, *82*

2 Peter
2, *363*
2:5, *400*
2:7, *363*

1 John
1, *597*
1:5, *597*
2, *42*
2:2, *295*
2:15, *30*
2:16, *70*
4, *660*
4:4, *660*
4:16, *443*
5:4, *248, 249*

Revelation
1:5, *400*
2:4, *57*
3:12, *296*
12, *563*
12:10, *563*
13, *358*
21–22, *316*